ENCYCLOPEDIA OF CRIME AND PUNISHMENT

ENCYCLOPEDIA OF CRIME AND PUNISHMENT

VOLUME 2

DAVID LEVINSON, EDITOR

A Sage Reference Publication

SAGE Publications
International Educational and Professional Publisher
Thousand Oaks ▪ London ▪ New Delhi

For information:

Sage Publications, Inc.
2455 Teller Road
Thousand Oaks, California 91320
E-mail: order@sagepub.com

Sage Publications Ltd.
6 Bonhill Street
London EC2A 4PU
United Kingdom

Sage Publications India Pvt. Ltd.
M-32 Market
Greater Kailash I
New Delhi 110 048 India

Printed in the United States of America

Library of Congress Cataloging-in-Publication Data

Main entry under title:

    Encyclopedia of crime and punishment: Volumes I-IV / edited by
David Levinson.
      p. cm.
    Includes bibliographical references and index.
    ISBN 0-7619-2258-X

    1. Criminology—Encyclopedias. 2. Criminal justice, Administration
of—Encyclopedias. I. Title: Crime and punishment. II. Levinson, David, 1947-

HV6017 .E524 2002
346'.03--dc21

                       2002001220

02 03 04 05 06 10 9 8 7 6 5 4 3 2 1

Berkshire Publishing Staff		*Sage Publications Staff*	
Associate Editor:	Marcy Ross	*Acquiring Editor:*	Rolf A. Janke
Project Coordinator:	Robin O'Sullivan	*Editorial Assistant:*	Sara G. Gutierrez
Copy Editors:	Robert L. Cohen	*Production Editor:*	Diana E. Axelsen
	Adam Groff	*Copy Editors:*	Linda Gray
	Elizabeth M. Hayslett		Kate Peterson
	Sharon Lahaye	*Typesetter/Designer:*	Tim Giesen/Straight Line Design
	Laura Anne Lawrie	*Production Artists:*	Michelle Lee
	Stephen V. Lynch		Sandra Ng
	Frank P. Mann	*Indexer:*	Mary Mortensen
	Mike Nichols	*Cover Designer:*	Ravi Balasuriya
	Glenn S. Perkins	*Cover Photographer:*	Scott Hirko
	William Rodarmor	*(Vols. I, II, IV)*	

List of Entries

Reader's Guide

This list is provided to assist readers in locating articles on related topics. It classifies articles into thirteen general topical categories: Crimes and Related Behaviors, Law and Justice, Policing, Forensics, Corrections, Victimology, Punishment, Sociocultural Context and Popular Culture, International, Concepts and Theories, Research Methods and Information, Organizations and Institutions, and Special Populations. Some article titles appear in more than one category.

CRIMES AND RELATED BEHAVIORS

Antisocial Behavior
Armed Robbery
Arson
Art Theft and Fraud
Assassination
Assault
Banditry
Barroom Violence
Blackmail
Bribery
Bullying
Burglary
Campus Crime
Capital Crimes
Carjacking
Career Criminals
Child Homicide
Child Maltreatment
Child Neglect
Child Physical Abuse
Child Sexual Abuse
Civil Disobedience
Civil Order Crime
Collective Violence
Consumer Fraud
Corporate Crime
Crime Classification Systems
Crime Reports and Statistics
Crimes Against Persons With
    Disabilities

Criminal History
Cybercrime
Delinquency
Digital Crime
Driving Under the Influence
Drug Millionaires
Drug Trafficking
Elder Abuse
Environmental Crime
Euthanasia
Family Violence
Fencing
Feuding
Forgery
Fraud
Gambling
Gangs
Genocide
Graffiti
Hate Crimes
Homicide and Murder
Identity Theft
Illicit Antiquities
Infanticide
Juvenile Crime and War
Kidnapping
Mass Murder
Militias
Missing Children
Modus Operandi
Money Laundering
Obscenity and Pornography
Organized Crime—Global

Organized Crime—United States
Piracy, Intellectual Property
Piracy, Sea
Political Corruption
Prostitution
Race and Violence
Rape
Rape, Date and Marital
Recidivism
Religious Deviance
Riots
Road Rage
Robbery
Same-Sex Abuse
School Violence
Scientific Misconduct
Securities Fraud
Sexual Violence
Shoplifting
Sibling Violence
Smuggling
Spectator Violence
Sport Violence
Spree Murder
Stalking
Stranger Violence
Student Threats
Suicide
Terrorism
Vagrancy
War Crimes
Witchcraft
Women as Offenders

Women Who Kill
Workplace Violence

LAW AND JUSTICE

Adversarial Justice
Alternative Dispute Resolution
Appeal/Appellate
Arraignment
Arrestee Drug Abuse Monitoring
   (ADAM) Program
Assembly-Line Justice
Bail and Bond
Cameras in the Courtroom
Charge Attrition
Child Witness
Civil Law Legal Traditions
Clemency
Common Law Legal Traditions
Community Justice Programs
Community Prosecution
Comparative Law and Justice
Competency to Stand Trial
Court Structure, Federal
Court Structure, State
Court Unification
Criminal Defenses
Criminal Insanity
Criminal Justice
Criminal Law
Criminal Trial
Customary Law
Death Sentence Outcomes
Defense Counsel Systems
Determinate Sentences
Differentiated Case Management
Discretionary Justice
Diversion Programs
Domestic Violence Courts
Drug Courts
Drug Legalization
Drug Treatment
Due Process
Entrapment
Exclusionary Rule
Expert Witness
Eyewitness Testimony
Family Court
Family Strengthening Programs
Fines
Get-Tough Initiatives
Grand Jury
Gun Control
Habitual Felony Laws

Harm Reduction
Human Rights
Indeterminate Sentences
Inquisitorial Justice
Intensive Probation Supervision
International Criminal Court
Judicial Selection Process
Jury Nullification
Jury System
Justice
Juvenile Court
Juvenile Justice
Juvenile Offenders in Adult Courts
Mandatory Sentencing
Mercy
Military Justice
Miranda Rights
Online Victimization of Youth
Pardon
Plea Bargaining
Probation
Procedural Justice
Prosecutorial Discretion
Public Defender
Race and Sentencing
Rehabilitation Model
Reintegration Model
Release on Own Recognizance
Restorative Justice
Retributive Justice
Revenge, Retribution, and
   Rehabilitation
Scared Straight Programs
Selective Incapacitation
Sentencing
Sentencing Guidelines
Speedy Trial Legislation
Split Sentence
United States Supreme Court
Whistle-Blowing
Wickersham Commission
Wrongful Convictions
Zero Tolerance Policing

POLICING

Arrest Clearance
Arrest Practices
Alcohol, Tobacco and Firearms,
   Bureau of
Broken Windows Theory
Citizen Review
Community Policing
Comparative Policing

Confession
Counterterrorism
Criminal Investigation
Deadly Force
Detective Work
Federal Bureau of Investigation
Foot Patrol
Geographic Information Systems
Geographic Profiling
Homicide Investigation
Hot Spot Policing
House Arrest
Informants
Interrogation
KGB
Mandatory Arrest
Neighborhood Watch Programs
Net Widening
Police Attitudes and Behavior
Police Corruption
Police Information Systems
Police Organizations
Police Privatization
Police Pursuits
Police Strategies and Operations
Police Technology
Police Training and Selection
Police, Killing of
Private Security
Problem-Oriented Policing
Race and Policing
Racial Profiling
Recreational Law Enforcement
Royal Canadian Mounted Police
Rural Law Enforcement
Scotland Yard
Surveillance Abuse
Women and Policing
Zero Tolerance Policing

FORENSICS

Anthropology, Forensic
Cognitive Interview
Crime Analysis
Crime Laboratory
Crime Scene Assessment
Criminal Profiling
Criminalistics
Detection of Deception
DNA Testing
Firearms Identification
Forensic Behavioral Sciences
Forensic Interrogation

Hinduism
Human Rights
India
Indonesia
International Criminal Court
International Imprisonments
Islam
Italian Mafia
Italy
Japan
Judaism
Latin America, Crime and Violence in
Mexico
Organized Crime—Global
Penal Colonies
Piracy, Intellectual Property
Piracy, Sea
Policing Democracy
Political Corruption
Poverty
Russia
Shinto
Singapore
Smuggling
South Pacific Islands
Sub-Saharan Africa
Terrorism
War Crimes
Witchcraft
Women and Crime in a Global
    Perspective

CONCEPTS AND THEORIES

Attachment Theory
Biocriminology
Broken Windows Theory
Cartographic School of Criminology
Control Theories
Crime as Pathology
Crime Control Model
Critical Criminology
Culture Conflict and Crime
Deterrence Theory
Deviance
Economic Theories of Crime
Education and Employment
Evolutionary Perspectives on Crime
Experimental Criminology
Feminist Theory

Integrative Theories
Life-Course Theories
Nonintervention Model
Peacemaking Criminology
Radical Criminology
Social Control Theory
Social Learning Theories
Sociological Theories
Strain Theory
Trait Theories

RESEARCH METHODS AND INFORMATION

Arrestee Drug Abuse Monitoring
    (ADAM) Program
Crime Classification Systems
Crime Reports and Statistics
Criminal Justice
Criminology
Ethnography of Crime and
    Punishment
Information Systems
National Crime Victimization Survey
Self-Report Surveys
Social Psychology
*Sourcebook of Criminal Justice
    Statistics*
Statistical Methods and Models
Uniform Crime Reports

See also Volume IV, Appendix 1:
    Careers in Criminal Justice;
    Appendix 2: Web Resources for
    Criminal Justice; Appendix 4:
    Selected Bibliography

ORGANIZATIONS AND INSTITUTIONS

Alcatraz
Alcohol, Tobacco, and Firearms
Attica
Auburn State Prison
Devil's Island
Eastern State Penitentiary
Elmira Reformatory
Federal Bureau of Investigation
International Criminal Court
Italian Mafia
Joliet Correctional Center

KGB
Leavenworth Federal Penitentiary
Royal Canadian Mounted Police
San Quentin
Sing Sing
Tucker State Farm
United States Supreme Court

See also Volume IV, Appendix 3:
    Professional and Scholarly
    Associations

SPECIAL POPULATIONS

American Indians and Alaska Natives
Animals in Criminal Justice
Child Homicide
Child Maltreatment
Child Neglect
Child Physical Abuse
Child Sexual Abuse
Child Witness
Ethnicity and Race
Homeless Men and Crime
Homeless Women and Crime
Infanticide
Juvenile Court
Juvenile Crime and War
Juvenile Justice
Juvenile Offenders in Adult Courts
Juvenile Victimization and Offending
Mentally Ill Offenders
Military Justice
Militias
Missing Children
Online Victimization of Youth
Prisoners, Elderly
School Violence
Street Youth
Student Threats
Women and Crime in a Global
    Perspective
Women and Policing
Women as Offenders
Women as Victims
Women in Prison
Women Who Kill
Youth, At-Risk
Youthful Offender

D

▼ DAOISM

Daoism is the indigenous higher religion of traditional China. Daoism sees crime and punishment in a cosmic dimension, understanding "law" to be divine law and placing the individual into the larger context of the universe. The universe is represented by the Dao, the underlying force of creation, and *qi* (vital energy), its material, tangible, and practical aspect. The universe is also represented by a large number of deities, which reside in the human body, society, nature, and the heavens. Crimes in this context are for the most part sins or bad deeds directed toward oneself, the deities, other people, nature, and the social environment. Punishments are meted out by the powers of cosmic balance—*qi* reverberations, karma, and the gods—which bring evil back to the perpetrator. These punishments include misfortune, failing health, a shorter life span, and tortures in a set of underworld prisons (hell). To prevent this fate, believers follow divinely revealed moral guidelines and precepts, calculate their cosmic standing by counting their transgressions and good deeds, and perform rituals of repentance and pardon to atone for their misdeeds.

QI AND KARMA

The fundamental premise of the Daoist view of crime and punishment is the total interconnectedness of everything. Every object, being, act, word, and thought consists of a cosmic life force known as *qi*, which affects everything else that exists. *Qi* moves at different speeds: Thick, slow moving *qi* appears as solid, material objects, and the body; fine, fast-moving *qi* mani-

fests itself as spiritual entities and the mind. But there is only one *qi*; material reality and spiritual beings, the body and mind, are all made up of the same material. *Qi* is in constant motion and transformation, and manifests itself as one of two alternating phases, known as yin and yang. These represent different stages of energy (e.g., quiescent and active, falling and rising, closing and opening, shady and sunny, female and male) that are bound together and that rise and fall in mutual dependence.

Another way of expressing the complete integration of the Daoist world through *qi* is the concept of "impulse and response" (*ganying*): Whenever something happens on one plane of existence, there is an immediate echo on all other planes. Earthquakes, for example, or changes in the course of the planets, have matching events in human society and human bodies, just as political events are mirrored in natural and planetary omens or disasters. Because nothing ever happens without an effect on everything else, all crimes and evil actions—understood as forceful, harsh, or excessive *qi*—will sooner or later return to their originator.

The Daoist notion of cosmic connection was further enhanced by its adoption of the Buddhist doctrine of karma, which was incorporated into native Chinese thinking in the fifth century. Originally part of Hindu religion, this doctrine states that all actions are seeds, the fruits of which inevitably return to their origin. The soul, as carrier of this load, must continue in physical form in order to receive the rewards and punishments necessitated by its former actions. Thus the notion of rebirth, including that in nonhuman and hellish states, became a close correlate to the idea of a personally

The Three Deathbringers

The upper deathbringer is called Peng Ju, also known as Ake (Shouter). He sits in the head and attacks the cinnabar field in the Niwan Palace [center of the head]. He causes people's heads to be heavy, their eyesight blurred, their tears cold. He makes mucus assemble in their noses and their ears go deaf. Because of him, people's teeth fall out, their mouths rot, and their faces shrink in wrinkles. He further deludes people so they desire carriages and horses, crave for fancy sounds and sights, and gloat over evil and filth. . . .

The middle deathbringer is called Peng Zhi, also known as Zuozi (Maker). He enjoys deluding people with the five tastes and makes them greedy for the five colors. He lives in the human heart and stomach and attacks the Scarlet Palace [in the heart, the middle cinnabar field] together with its central heater. He causes people's minds to be confused and forgetful, so that they are full of troubles, dry in saliva and low in energy. Dissipated and melancholy, they follow the false and see things in wrong perspective. . . .

The lower deathbringer is called Peng Qiao, also known as Jixi (Junior). He lives in people's stomachs and legs and attacks the lower parts of the body. He makes energy leak [through the genitals] from the Ocean of Energy [the lower cinnabar field] and thereby invites a multiplicity of ills. Attracting the robbers of human intention, he makes people hanker after women and sex. Courageous and zealous only in the pursuit of passion, people suffering from him are blindly attached to things and waste away. They have no way to control themselves and hold on to life.

Source: *Chu sanshi baosheng jing*, "Scripture on Preserving Life by Removing the Three Deathbringers," a technical manual of exorcism and cultivation (9th century).

created and endured karma that could be neither worsened nor improved by the actions of others.

GODS, SPIRITS, AND ANCESTORS

Another way in which the cosmic interconnectedness of everything is expressed in Daoism is the mythological vision of divine beings. These are divided into three groups: ancestors, body and family spirits, and gods or celestial bureaucrats.

Ancestors are the deceased immediate relatives in the male line and their spouses, usually venerated up to five generations. The early Chinese believed that most events were caused by either the good will or enmity of an ancestor, and their calendars were arranged to allow regular sacrifices to all of them. Nowadays ancestors are believed to reside in an ancestral heaven, where they can be accessed through worship of an ancestral tablet and from whence they follow their descendants' affairs. They require regular supplies of food, wine, incense, and incantations, and will send good fortune and provide protection if properly cared for. A neglected or offended ancestor, however, will visit punishment upon the living through sickness and misfortune.

Body and family spirits include supernatural agents that reside either inside the body or in the home. These report to heaven at regular intervals—usually about once every two months—and then return to mete out the appropriate punishment, again in the form of sickness and misfortune. Inside the body reside the Three Deathbringers (*Sanshi*), also known as the Three Worms or Three Corpses. A cross between demons and souls, these half-human and half-animal figures, called Shouter, Maker, and Junior, reside in the head, torso, and lower body. Representing the baser, instinctual nature, they are responsible for all impulsive and evil deeds, which in turn allows them to make a person sick or unhappy. When their host dies its spirit-soul is sent off to suffer in hell while the Three Worms remain with the corpse, gorging themselves on blood, bone, and muscle.

Having partaken of the human body, they assume its former shape, appearing as ghosts that feast further on the offerings laid out for the dead. They thus have a vested interest in causing people to commit sins, fall ill, and die prematurely. Only impeccable moral conduct, combined with rituals and spells, will keep them at bay.

Among family spirits the most important is the Stove God (*Zaojun*), who has his residence—usually represented in a paper image or poster—at the kitchen hearth. Entirely human in appearance, he too observes people's behavior and reports—on New Year's Eve—to the celestial authorities, who then mete out the proper rewards and punishments. But instead of inciting people to evil, the Stove God is a detached official who keeps a benevolent eye on people's comings and goings. He is the household representative of the celestial administration, which makes all final decisions about life and death, and good and bad fortune.

Numerous deities serve in this administration, which is divided into a number of sections and departments. The agency concerned with crime and punishment is the Department of Destiny, governed by the

Ruler of Fates (*Siming*), Its officials, based on the regular reports of the Deathbringers and the Stove God, keep detailed ledgers of merit and demerit, deciding when a person has to suffer or die. A more recent development is the Celestial Treasury, a branch of the divine administration of Earth, from which everyone receives a loan in order to come to life. This loan must be repaid through good deeds, rituals, and the offering of spirit money. Bad deeds and crime cause the perpetrator to fall further into debt, and bring nothing but unhappiness, sickness, and the tortures of hell.

The divine administration and the various family and body spirits represent the same idea as *qi* and its reverberation. Evil creates a harsh *qi* for perpetrators and their environment. Evildoers will get sick and lose the confidence of their friends, resulting in a further loss of good fortune. They can, of course, attempt to excuse their misfortune by claiming that the Three Deathbringers have been active, or that the celestial officials are meting out punishment, or that a certain kind of karma is being visited upon them. In all cases, however, the idea is that because everything is connected, no deed, whether good or bad, physical or mental, is without repercussion. Although the system is all-inclusive, it leaves a great deal of room to make moral decisions for or against crime.

CRIME AND PUNISHMENT

Within this overall framework, certain activities are evil or criminal. These include killing, sexual misconduct, stealing, lying, cheating, and intoxication, as well as all acts committed in a spirit of anger, aggression, or greed. To ward them off, people are encouraged to follow a set of ten precepts, which prohibit criminal activities and encourage the development of goodwill and care. Following them creates the right kind of *qi* reverberations and gives no offense to gods or ancestors. If, however, a crime or sin is committed, four punishments can ensue: sickness and death, either of oneself or one's relatives; misfortune and poverty, calculated by the exact number of deeds; karmic consequences (e.g., deformity, instability, bad rebirth); and torture in hell.

Punishment by Sickness

In early Daoism all sins and crimes were understood to result in a weakening of the body and its *qi*, which in turn caused sickness—a clear indication of demonic

The Celestial Administration

All living beings of the ten directions in their fate depend on the officials of Heaven; in their bodies they are subject to the administration of Earth. The day anyone receives a human body, he or she is registered with the administration of Earth.

The underworld officials at this time lend him or her a sum for receiving life, a loan from the Celestial Treasury. The more people save on their account in the underworld, the richer and nobler they will be on earth.

Those who are poor and humble are debtors who never repay. They get in worse from eon to eon, since the underworld officials have to borrow more on the account [every time they are reborn]. In the case of those who are impoverished in the world of humanity, the underworld officials have already used up all the yang (positive) credit and are now supplying the account with yin (negative).

Thus it is that in the world there are differences in retribution between noble and humble, rich and poor, happy and miserable.

Source: *Luku shousheng jing*, "Scripture on the Loan of Life From the Celestial Treasury," a popular account of celestial administration (12th century).

The Ten Precepts

1. Don't kill, but be always considerate to all living beings!
2. Don't commit immoral deeds or think depraved thoughts!
3. Don't steal or receive unrighteous goods!
4. Don't lie or misrepresent good and evil!
5. Don't intoxicate yourself, but be always mindful of pure conduct!
6. I will maintain harmony with my ancestors and kin and never do anything that harms my family!
7. When I see someone do good, I will support him in with joy and happiness in my heart!
8. When I see someone unfortunate, I will help him with my strength to recover good fortune!
9. When someone comes to do me harm, I will not harbor thoughts of revenge!
10. As long as all beings have not attained the Dao, I will not expect to do myself!

Source: *Shijie jing*, "Scripture of the Ten Precepts," used in ordination into the lower ranks of the Daoist hierarchy (5th century).

Negative Effects by Numbers of Bad Deeds

1	intention not calm and at peace
10	energy and strength hollow and declining
20	body afflicted by much sickness and disease
30	nothing planned comes to pass
40	constant difficulties, facing decay and destruction
50	never finding equal partner
60	line of descendants dies out
70	harmed by yin demons
80	disasters of water and fire, being burnt and drowned
90	poor and cold, in distress and weak, hungry and going mad
100	harmed by energy of heaven, affairs bad, prison, execution
200	harmed by energy of earth, robbed and stripped by brigands
300	descendants humble and common
400	descendants poor and lowly, destitute and begging
500	descendants cut off family line
600	descendants blind and deaf, mute and mad
700	descendants rebels, unfilial and criminal
800	family has ministers and unfilial sons, cause destruction and beheadings to entire clan
900	family has demonic and evil people, cause destruction to their own and other clans.
1000	descendants malformed and crooked, looking like maimed animals or wild birds

Source: *Chisongzi zhongjie jing*, "The Central Precepts of Master Redpine," a discussion of fate and celestial punishments (4th century).

infestation and moral shortcomings. As a result, healing was undertaken through ritual and magic; acupuncture, herbs, and other medical treatments were expressly prohibited. First the sick person was isolated in a so-called quiet chamber (*jingshi*), where the person attempted to recall all their crimes and sins—from birth—to find an explanation for his or her illness. Once the sins had been identified, a senior priest would write them down—in triplicate—together with a formal petition for their eradication from the divine record. The copies would then be ritually transmitted to Heaven (by burning), Earth (by burying), and Water (by casting into a river), the officials of which were supposed to set the record straight and allow the sinner to recover good health. In some cases, however, the crimes were so heinous that none of this sufficed and the person died. If even this death was not enough to restore the cosmic balance, the evil—in an adaptation of the communal justice commonly practiced at the time—might be visited upon the sinner's relatives, who in turn would get sick and die. As the fourth-century text *Baopuzi* states, "Whenever you interfere with or steal another's goods, the gods may take into account [the life span] of your wife, children, and other members of your household in order to compensate for it, causing them to die, even if not immediately." This concept of inherited evil (*chengfu*) was used to account for the suffering of children and the sicknesses of righteous individuals.

Punishment by Numbers

In the fourth century, Daoists began creating codes that specified what to expect for the number and type of deed committed. On the positive side, one good deed makes the spirit calm, and ten result in a strong physical *qi*. Twenty good deeds free the person from bodily ailments, and thirty result in answered prayers. Hundreds of good deeds ensure that a family brings forth noble, prosperous, and honored progeny for generations to come. On the negative side, one bad deed makes the sinner restless and nervous, ten cause *qi* to decline, twenty cause physical affliction, and thirty result in the failure of one's plans; one hundred bad deeds might result in prison or even execution. Several hundred cause a family to become lowly and destitute, and perhaps even demonic.

Phrased somewhat less esoterically, the effect of increasing numbers of good or bad deeds can be said to expand in concentric circles. By influencing the mind, they cause changes in physical well-being, which in turn leads to a tendency toward success or failure. This leads to a gain or loss in social standing, which in turn influences the prosperity of immediate descendants, and the social standing and excellence of later generations. Looked at from this perspective, the system, although rigid, has a certain psychological and sociological logic that provides a framework for understanding crime and punishment in a cosmically interconnected universe.

Karma and Rebirth

In the fifth century, Daoists adopted major doctrines and rituals from Buddhism, by then firmly established on Chinese soil. They integrated the belief in rebirth and the retribution for sins or good deeds accumulated in former lives, the vision of supernatural torture chambers (known as earth prisons or hells), punishment by being reborn in the body of an animal or hungry ghost, and trust in the efficacy of various rituals, such as rites of repentance and the giving of offerings, to alleviate the karmic burden. All these continue to play an important role in the modern Daoist religion.

Karma in this system is a radical adaptation of the Golden Rule: What you do to another in one lifetime will be done to you the next. People who kill, cutting short the life of another, will themselves be punished with a short life; those who steal, taking away the nourishment of another, will themselves be short of supplies; those who despise others will be short of stature, while those who respect their fellows will be tall and upright. Similarly, typical characteristics of animals are associated with particular types of human behavior: pigs and dogs are linked with lasciviousness and debauchery, foulness and excrement; wild beasts with hunger and cruelty; deer with fear and terror; insects with the darkness of prison and the helplessness of disaster.

With all these potential pitfalls, human life becomes a precious commodity that must not be squandered. All crimes and evil deeds must be avoided, lest they come back to haunt.

Hell

Originally adopted from Buddhism, Hell in Daoism is a series of underworld courts, where sinners undergo punishment before being released for an appropriate rebirth. In the first court, the Terrace of Sins, the sinner faces a judge who looks like a traditional Confucian official, sits behind a high dais, and is assisted by two half-human bailiffs named Horseface and Cowhead. Naked, the sinner must walk before the Mirror of Destiny, which reflects every sin and crime they have ever committed. The judge then decides to which hells the sinner is to be sent, and for how long.

Subsequent hells are arranged in a circle. Each has a judge and bailiffs and specializes in different crimes

---

Bad Situations and Their Karmic Roots

Life as one of the six domestic animals comes from having to atone for killing living beings.

Life as a wild animal or deer comes from having eaten meat and stolen.

Life as a poisonous snake comes from having been jealous and harmed others.

Life as a hungry tiger comes from having cheated, oppressed, or robbed others.

Life as a worm nourishing on excrement comes from having been lascivious, debauched, and unclean.

Life as a skunk comes from having entered the sacred altar [area] in a numinous monastery after eating meat.

Life as a jackal or wolf comes from having been stingy and not giving charity.

Source: *Yinyuan jing*, "Script of Karmic Retribution," a guidebook for both lay and monastic followers (6th century).

---

and punishments. The second hell, for example, is the prison of hunger and thirst, where the dead are thrown into boiling water, dressed in iron clothing, or stretched on racks as punishment for seduction, theft, assault, and marrying for gain. The third hell is a salt desert, where sinners are chained, their faces cut with knives, and their bodies squeezed with pincers. Crimes punished here include treason, ingratitude, and irresponsibility.

After more of the same in the fourth, fifth, and sixth hells comes the Terrace of Repentance, where the sinner is allowed a final opportunity to see the damage done to family, friends, and business associates. Following this they may be consigned to the eighth and ninth hells, where they will be further punished for crimes not yet fully expiated. Eventually they arrive in the last hell, the Palace of Rebirth, where bridges lead to the five forms of rebirth—gods, humans, animals, hungry ghosts, and hell-dwellers—and where all past memories are erased. The dead are equipped with new skins and sent back to Earth to try again—or, if atonement was sufficient, promoted to residence in heaven.

PREVENTION AND REMEDIES

To prevent punishment for sins, either in this life, the afterlife, or the next rebirth, Daoists follow the guidelines of so-called morality books (*shanshu*). These texts, which can be obtained at any Chinese temple, serve to inspire people to act more conscientiously and compassionately. They usually place a heavy emphasis on the hells, describing them in torturous detail, complete with graphic illustrations. They are often linked to another preventative practice, the keeping of so-called ledgers of merit and demerit (*gongguo ge*). These booklets help practitioners record their deeds on a daily basis, assigning plus or minus points to each, so they can see where they stand in the scheme of cosmic retribution, and take remedial actions, such as the offering of goods and money to the gods, or performing rituals. Among the latter are the after-death rites (*gongde*), during which the living present a writ of pardon on behalf of the deceased to the underworld officials, asking them to let the person ascend into heaven. There are also rites of repentance and contrition, in which practitioners undergo make-believe punishments that prevent later misfortune or torture in hell. All these help people to either maintain the right path or recover good standing in the interconnected universe of the Dao.

—*Livia Kohn*

See also CHINA

Further Reading

Brokaw, Cynthia. (1991). *The Ledgers of Merit and Demerit: Social Change and Moral Order in Late Imperial China.* Princeton, NJ: Princeton University Press.

Eberhard, Wolfram. (1967). *Guilt and Sin in Traditional China.* Berkeley: University of California Press.

Hou Ching-lang. (1975). *Monnaies d'offrande et la notion de tresorerie dans la religion chinoise.* Paris: Memoires de l'Institut des Hautes Etudes Chinoises 1.

Kohn, Livia. (forthcoming). *Daoist Precepts.* Cambridge, MA: Three Pines Press.

———. (2001). *Daoism and Chinese Culture.* Cambridge, MA: Three Pines Press.

 DAUBERT

See SCIENTIFIC EVIDENCE

DAY RELEASE

Day release is the short and temporary release of offenders from prisons and jails, usually for a specific purpose. Although day release has been called by different names in different times and places, the underlying idea is that it is neither fair nor safe to release prisoners directly into society without close supervision—supervision greater than that provided by parole or probation. Day release is the intermediate step between total confinement and conditional release. The term has been used interchangeably with work release. The two programs share the same antecedents and some of the same goals. The major difference is that day release offenders may be temporarily released from prison or jail for purposes other than work. These purposes are most often educational (e.g., vocational testing or training), although they may also be rehabilitative (e.g., life skills training, drug and alcohol counseling, workplace orientation), and in some cases are strictly humanitarian (short escorted releases for funerals, family crises, or medical services).

EARLY HISTORY

Temporary release from prison dates from the mid-1800s when British prisoners were sometimes given an opportunity to earn supervised release on tickets-of-leave through display of repentance and good behavior. In the United States, early prison authorities and sheriffs informally allowed day release without any specific legislation or power to do so. Women particularly went out to domestic service during the day and returned to prison at night. The first day release legislation in the United States was the Huber Law. Passed in Wisconsin in 1913, it envisioned work release as providing support for prisoners' dependents. The real impetus for day release, however, came with the Federal Prisoner Rehabilitation Act of 1965, which allowed prisoners to "work at paid employment or participate in a training program in the community on a voluntary basis while continuing as a prisoner" (P.L. 89–176). Much state legislation followed the federal legislation.

LATER HISTORY

Day release programs long preceded halfway houses and other residential community treatment, but the halfway houses also fit the definition as places of partial confinement, especially since offenders perceive release to a halfway house more onerously than does the public. The use of halfway houses in the United States expanded with rehabilitative corrections and the expansion of parole. In 1961, Attorney General Robert Kennedy recommended using federal funds to establish halfway houses, especially grants from the Law Enforcement Assistance Administration and the Office of Economic Opportunity. At first, halfway house programs served to help inmates locate employment; it was only later that they developed into residential programs. By the 1970s, "budget weary legislators often viewed halfway houses as an inexpensive lunch" (Hicks 1987: 7) since costs might run as little as 60 percent of those of incarceration.

When retributive corrections became paramount in the United States in the early 1980s, funding for many day release programs disappeared. The introduction of determinate sentencing at about the same time also had a diminishing effect on day release. Determinate sentencing removed incentives for participation in day release because the offender already had an ensured date for full release. Another disincentive was the increase in prison industries: Prisoners usually preferred to earn money, however little, rather than participate in educational or training programs.

A TYPICAL MODEL

In a typical day release program, offenders remain under the supervision of the prison; they are legally inmates and can be returned to confinement if they fail to meet release conditions. There may be as many as fifteen conditions attendant on day release, the most important of which is "obey all laws." Violent offenders are not eligible for day release programs, in consideration of the safety of the community. Offenders become eligible as they approach the end of their sentences; day release is viewed as a preparole test or preparation.

Inmates are released during the day to work or go to school, and then they return to secure physical restraint at night. One variation is the weekend sentence, more typical of jails than prisons, in which the offender returns to physical confinement only on weekends and maintains family and work responsibilities during the week. Weekend sentences are often called intermittent imprisonment. Another common variation is the work furlough, in which an offender participates in an ongoing project, usually manual labor, and then returns to full-time incarceration after its completion.

Prisoners may come and go in a group to a designated day release site, as they did to classes at the Federal City College program in Washington, D.C. When the day release inmates return to night restraint, it is sometimes to the general prison population, but most often to a separate compound inside or outside prison walls. From an administrative view, separate quarters are desirable since day release prisoners may be asked to carry messages or contraband in and out of prison. A compound outside of prison walls can be supervised either by correctional personnel or by private designees. Sometimes inmates return to a correctional facility closer to their day release site.

CANADA

Is it instructive to examine the Canadian experience since Canada and the United States are among the Western nations with the highest rates of incarceration. Called day parole in Canada, day release has been in use for more than twenty-five years, but its inclusion in Canada's 1992 Corrections and Conditional Release Act sparked renewed interest in its operation and outcome, especially since it redefined the previously diffuse purposes of day parole to be "preparation of offenders for full parole or statutory release."

The Canadian National Parole Board is responsible for determining which offenders can be safely released on day parole. Eligibility begins six months prior to full parole. Instead of the prior automatic review, offenders must apply in writing, which may account for the decreasing numbers in day parole; it previously accounted for 50 percent of all parolees. (Numbers declined by about one-third after the act was put into effect.) Nonviolent, low-risk offenders are typically day paroled; a large percentage have previously completed a work release program.

The 1992 act also changed restraint conditions. Prisoners return every night to a halfway house—either a Community Correctional Center operated by Corrections Canada, or a Community Residential Center operated by a private agency under contract to Corrections Canada. During the day, offenders attend school or treatment centers, or maintain a job. Day parole is for periods of longer than fifteen days. Another program, called Temporary Absence, is for periods of one to three days. Studies indicate that successful completion of day parole in Canada is associated with lower readmission and new offense rates—15 percent recidivism for day parole completers compare to 44 percent for others.

REWORKING THE DAY RELEASE IDEA

In the United States, traditional day release is being reborn all the time under different names, incorporating various program elements. A premise of community corrections, for instance, is the same as day release:

There is a beneficial effect on the offender who has continued interaction with society outside prison walls. An increased reliance on in-community corrections is presently the criminal justice professionals' major hope of returning offenders safely to society and of combating prison overcrowding and spiraling correctional costs.

Day Reporting Centers (DRCs) were "the success story of the 1980s" (Tonry and Hamilton 1995: 131) in England and Wales where they began. These centers reverse the usual paradigm of day release. Offenders spend the day under surveillance at a center, participating in compulsory therapeutic or vocational programs. They spend nights elsewhere, sometimes at home with an electronic monitoring device, or at a residential facility. Employed offenders are required to be in constant contact with their case managers—as many as eighty times per week.

Massachusetts began setting up DRCs in 1986. Their aim was to ease jail and prison crowding. Centers were to serve chronic, less serious offenders who lacked the skills to survive lawfully. As with halfway houses, centers may be run by correctional authorities or contracted out to private organizations. The first centers were aimed at preparolees, as in traditional day release, but later centers mix preparolees, parolees, probationers, pretrial detainees, and the directly sentenced. As developed in the United States, DRCs include the "halfway-out" of incarceration, as well as the "halfway-in." Offenders report at DRCs for periods of two to nine months. Programs can easily be added or subtracted, and DRC unit cost appears to be less than incarceration, $10 a day versus $45 a day in Minnesota for example.

Community Confinement Control (CCC) emerged from the 1996 Wisconsin Governor's Task Force on Sentencing and Corrections recommendation that public safety be the primary corrections measurement, rather than the rate of recidivism or the focus on "too many offenders, not enough cells." In addition to abolishing probation in favor of CCC, the task force recommended that "no felony offender sentenced to prison be granted parole without successfully completing some period in CCC status" (Smith and Dickey 1999: 11). CCC provides intensive surveillance and control, as well as treatment, employment, and other socialization programs. Pilot projects are currently underway.

SUMMARY

Although terminology and program elements vary, the goals of all day release programs are the same: to pre-

pare offenders to live more effective lives after release from supervision and not to recidivate—and to do that at a reasonable cost, in terms of both dollars and community safety. For most of its history day release was a preparation for parole and a test of parole worthiness. Contemporary versions of day release, although still aimed at the less violent offender, mix offenders of varying status. A conclusive positive rehabilitative effect for temporary release programs has never been proven because of a lack of comparable data and controlled research studies.

—Janice K. Dunham

See also PAROLE; REHABILITATION MODEL; WORK RELEASE

Further Reading

Byrne, James M., Arthur J. Lurigio, and Joan Petersilia. (1992). *Smart Sentencing: The Emergence of Intermediate Sanctions.* Newbury Park, CA: Sage.

Clear, Todd R., and Harry R. Dammer. (2000). *The Offender in The Community.* Belmont, CA: Wadsworth/Thompson.

Goldfarb, Ronald L., and Linda Singer. (1973). *After Conviction.* New York: Simon & Schuster.

Grant, Brian A. (1998). *Day Parole: Effects of Corrections and Conditional Release Act of 1992.* Ottawa: Research Branch, Correctional Service of Canada.

Grant, Brian A., and Marlo Gal. (1998). *Case Management Preparation for Release and Day Parole Outcome.* Ottawa: Research Branch, Correctional Service of Canada.

Grant, Brian A., and Christa A. Gillis. (1999). *Day Parole Outcome, Criminal History, and Other Predictors of Sentence Completion.* Ottawa: Research Branch, Correctional Service of Canada.

Hicks, Nancy. (1987). "A New Relationship: Halfway Houses and Corrections." *Corrections Compendium* 12, 10: 1–8.

Junger-Tas, Josine. (1994). *Alternatives to Prison Sentences: Experiences and Developments.* Amsterdam: Kugler.

Lipton, Douglas, Robert Martinson, and Judith Wilks. (1975). *The Effectiveness of Correctional Treatment.* New York: Praeger.

Motiuk, Larry. (1997). "Factors Influencing the Correctional Population in Canada." In *International Seminar on Prison Population in Europe and in North America: Problems and Solutions.* Helsinki: Finnish Ministry of Justice, Department of Prison Administration, 93–103.

Parent, Dale G. (1990). *Day Reporting Centers For Criminal Offenders: A Descriptive Analysis of Existing Programs.* Washington, DC: National Institute of Justice.

Petersilia, Joan. (1999). "Parole and Prisoner Reentry in the United States." In *Crime and Justice: A Review of Research 26*, edited by Michael H. Tonry and Joan Petersilia. Chicago: University of Chicago Press, 479–529.

Smith, Michael E., and Walter J. Dickey. (1999). "Reforming Sentencing and Corrections for Just Punishment and Public Safety." *Sentencing & Corrections: Issues for the Twenty-First Century 4.* Washington, DC: National Institute of Justice, NCJ 175724.

Sullivan, Larry E. (1990). *The Prison Reform Movement: Forlorn Hope.* Boston, MA: Twayne.

Tonry, Michael, ed. (1998). *Handbook of Crime and Punishment.*

New York: Oxford University Press.

———. (1999). "U.S. Sentencing Systems Fragmenting." *Overcrowded Times*. 10, 8: 7–13.

Tonry, Michael H., and Kate Hamilton. (1995). *Intermediate Sanctions In Overcrowded Times*. Boston, MA: Northeastern University Press.

Wilson, George P. (1985). "Halfway House Programs For Offenders." In *Probation, Parole, and Community Corrections*, edited by Lawrence F. Travis. Prospect Heights, IL: Waveland Press, 151–164.

▼ DEADLY FORCE

Police use of deadly force has been a controversial topic since officers were first authorized to control the public and enforce the law. Deadly force is defined as force used with the intent to cause death or serious bodily harm. The use of deadly force has dominated concerns about police actions because the consequences of the use of deadly force in general, and firearms specifically, are serious and irrevocable. In today's world, the prevailing opinion is that police officials and citizens must support and encourage an officer's right to use force to protect lives, control crime, and keep the peace.

Most people learn of police activities from media coverage in newspapers and magazines and on television and in movies. These portrayals often show the police confronting dangerous criminals, with both police officers and criminals firing their weapons. This may make exciting entertainment, but it creates an unrealistic view of police work. In fact, most police officers complete their entire careers without ever discharging a weapon in the line of duty.

LAW AND POLICE POLICY

There are two fundamental authorities that guide the appropriate use of deadly force by the police. The U.S. Supreme Court in *Tennessee v. Garner* (1985) established the minimum legal standard: Deadly force cannot be used against a nondangerous fleeing felon. Of course, police agencies can create policies that are more restrictive than what the Supreme Court requires, limiting officers from using deadly force except under specific conditions. These departmental policies are the second authority that allows police officers to use deadly force.

The *Garner* decision ruled that police shootings must be evaluated as seizures under the Fourth Amendment of the U.S. Constitution. Under this analysis, all purposeful shootings by police that hit their intended target are considered seizures. Reasonable seizures do not violate the Constitution, but seizures that are unreasonable are illegal. Determining the reasonableness of a shooting is a difficult task. The Court acknowledged this in *Graham v. Conner* (1989: 396):

> The test of reasonableness under the Fourth Amendment is not capable of precise definition or mechanical application, however, its proper application requires careful attention to the facts and circumstances of each particular case, including the severity of the crime at issue, whether the suspect poses an immediate threat to the safety of officers or others, and whether he is actively resisting or attempting to evade arrest by flight. . . . The reasonableness of a particular use of force must be judged from the perspective of a reasonable officer on the scene, rather by 20/20 hindsight (citations omitted).

The Court left the understanding of an appropriate use of force to the reasonable officer; stated in a different way, the question is whether a reasonably trained officer would believe the use of deadly force necessary. Unfortunately, "reasonable" and "necessary" were left open to interpretation.

To assist officers in understanding the limits on the application of deadly force, police departments promulgate policies based upon the information presented in *Garner*. A wide range of polices exist: Some agencies adopt language taken directly from *Garner* without any definition or explanation, while others provide specific direction. This range of policies includes what are referred to as *Garner* or forcible felony policies, defense-of-life policies, and protection of life policies. These differ on the type of shooting that is permitted. Under the *Garner* or forcible felony policies, shootings are justified if there is a substantial risk that a person who is escaping will cause death or serious bodily harm if that person's arrest is delayed. This is the policy with the fewest restrictions; thus, departments that adopt it will have the greatest number of shootings. Defense-of-life policies occupy the middle ground. Agencies operating under this policy limit the use of deadly force to situations in which a life is in imminent peril. Protection of life policies require officers to use deadly force only as a last resort; agencies operating under this policy will have the fewest number of shootings. Although more than fifteen years have passed since the *Garner* decision, and many decisions have interpreted its language, it remains the most important court decision concerning police use of deadly force.

FREQUENCY AND ACCURACY

There are approximately 500,000 law enforcement officers in the United States, and it is estimated by the FBI's Supplemental Homicide Reports that police kill between 300 and 350 citizens per year. In 1998, for example, police killed 367 citizens, less than 3 percent of all reported homicides. While this number may appear discouraging, what stands out is how infrequently officers fire their weapons, and how rarely they hit their intended target. Larry Sherman and his associates compiled statistics for U.S. cities with over 250,000 people and concluded: "Police in all cities kill rarely, but at widely varying rates. The average Jacksonville police officer would have to work 139 years before killing anyone. In New York City, the wait would be 694 years. It would be 1,299 in Milwaukee and 7,692 years in Honolulu, all based on 1980–1984 rates of killing" (Sherman et al. 1986: 1).

The study of police use of deadly force is impeded by a lack of good data. Although police agencies compile most of the information on shootings, there is no national repository for the data, and only one state (Minnesota) compiles statewide data. In a study of the Miami-Dade Police Department (Alpert and Dunham 1995), it was discovered that officers rarely use deadly force: There were approximately twenty purposeful shooting incidents per year, and most shots (68 percent) did not hit their intended target. Similar findings have been reported by most agencies that report this information (Geller and Scott 1992).

An ironic aspect of police discharging a weapon is frequently police personnel shoot themselves or other officers. Several studies conducted in New York and Chicago revealed that an alarming proportion of the police officers shot over two decades were shot either by themselves (accidental discharge or suicide) or accidentally by other police officers (Geller and Scott 1992); over a ten-year period, 43 percent of officers were shot by themselves or by other officers. Geller and Scott concluded that "it is the armed robber and, paradoxically, the armed policeman who are the threats to the life of the police" (1992: 453).

SUMMARY

Policing is the only profession that allows the use of force and deadly force. Although the use of deadly force is a rare event, it can result in the most serious consequences. Unfortunately, there is a lack of information on police use of deadly force, and what is known is limited to information from those agencies that are willing to have their data scrutinized. It is hoped that there will be more information generated about police use of deadly force in the future and that alternatives to its use will be developed.

—*Geoffrey P. Alpert*

See also POLICE, KILLING OF

Further Reading
Alpert, Geoffrey, and Roger Dunham. (1995). *Police Use of Deadly Force: A Statistical Analysis of the Metro-Dade Police Department*. Washington, DC: Police Executive Research Forum.

Geller, William A., and Michael S. Scott. (1992). *Deadly Force: What We Know*. Washington, DC: Police Executive Research Forum.

Sherman, Lawrence W. et al. (1986). *Citizens Killed by Big City Police, 1970–1984*. Washington, DC: Crime Control Institute.

Uniform Crime Reports: Supplementary Homicide Reports, 1976–1999. Online database. www.icpsr.umich.edu/NACJD.

Court Cases
Graham v. Conner (1989). 490 U.S. 386.
Tennessee v. Garner (1985). 471 U.S. 1.

▼ DEATH ROW

In the United States 3,527 inmates were under sentence of death at the beginning of the twenty-first century. While awaiting execution, such inmates live in correctional institutions or prisons, usually in areas called "death row." Not every state has a death row, because only thirty-eight states and the federal government authorize the use of the death sentence. The state of Missouri is unique because it authorizes the use of the death sentence but has abandoned the use of death rows and allows its death-sentenced inmates to live among other maximum-security inmates.

Although the majority of death-sentenced inmates are male, at the end of 1999, fifty women in seventeen states were awaiting execution. Therefore, in those states, there are at least two death rows: one or more for the men and one for the women. Awaiting execution is not the same for all death-sentenced inmates because there is great variation in the conditions of confinement among the states. This variation occurs because each state can determine the rules governing the confinement of death-sentenced inmates, as long as the state's rules do not violate the U.S. Constitution.

WHERE ARE DEATH ROWS LOCATED?

According to data collected by the federal Bureau of Justice Statistics, thirty-seven of the thirty-eight states that use the death penalty had death-sentenced inmates in 1999. Ten states (Colorado, Connecticut, Kansas, Montana, Nebraska, New Mexico, New York, South Dakota, Utah, and Wyoming) had 10 or fewer death-sentenced inmates. Ten states (Arkansas, Delaware, Idaho, Indiana, Kentucky, Maryland, New Jersey, Oregon, Virginia, and Washington) had between 13 and 43 death-sentenced inmates. Six states (Mississippi, South Carolina, Missouri, Louisiana, Nevada, and Tennessee) had between 60 and 100 death-sentenced inmates. Six states (Alabama, Arizona, Georgia, Illinois, Ohio, and Oklahoma) had between 116 and 199. The remaining five states (California, Florida, North Carolina, Pennsylvania, and Texas) each had over 200 death-sentenced inmates and accounted for over 51 percent of all death-sentenced inmates in the United States.

The number of death-sentenced inmates that a state has is important because, in many respects, the number of such inmates affects the availability of programs. For states that have as few as one death-sentenced inmate, it is not feasible in terms of economic costs and staff utilization to provide a wide range of programs. Having few death-sentenced inmates adversely affects women inmates more frequently than men inmates. Of the seventeen states that had death-sentenced women as of 1999, nine had only one death-sentenced female inmate.

AVERAGE LENGTH OF TIME ON DEATH ROW

In the United States, because of concerns for fairness, due process, and other constitutional issues, the appeals process for individuals sentenced to death is lengthy. According to the Bureau of Justice Statistics, the average amount of time spent on death row before execution during 1999 was nearly twelve years.

Several factors contribute to this lengthiness. First, states that allow the death sentence usually have mandatory appellate procedures to allow higher courts to review actions of lower courts. Second, issues that are pertinent to capital cases may not be not pertinent to other cases—for example, whether the defendant is mentally retarded. A third factor that can increase the time between sentencing and execution is a change of counsel for the defendant. Often a defendant is unable

to afford private counsel to prepare a defense for his or her first trial, and thus court-appointed counsel handles the case. As the case proceeds to the appellate stages, attorneys who specialize in death penalty cases and who are funded by public interest groups provide counsel to the defendant. These attorneys are sometimes able to pursue avenues of appeal that the previous counsel had not attempted. The final factor that contributes to the lengthy appellate process is the finality of the death penalty: There is no way to bring an individual back to life if he or she is later found to be innocent. Therefore, it is imperative that ample opportunity be given to the defendant to explore all avenues that might result in the reversal of the sentence.

It is difficult to compare the length of death sentence appeals in the United States to that in other industrialized nations because nearly all have abolished the death penalty or have limited its use to exceptional crimes (such as wartime crimes or crimes under military law). For the year 2000, Amnesty International reported that four countries—China, Saudi Arabia, the Congo, and the United States—accounted for 88 percent of all executions worldwide. Information on the length of time between sentencing and execution in China, Iran, and Saudi Arabia is not available. However, in June 2001, Amnesty International reported that in a three-month period in China, nearly 3,000 individuals were sentenced to death, and 1,781 were executed as part of a "Strike Hard Against Crime" campaign.

PHYSICAL CHARACTERISTICS OF DEATH ROWS

The physical layout of a death row is not unlike that of other cell blocks. Death row cells are usually the same as those of other inmates. The length of death row depends on the number of death-sentenced inmates in the state and on the number of cells in the cell block that has been designated to hold them.

When there is only one death-sentenced woman in a state, there may be no area specially designated as death row for her. Many times a lone death-sentenced woman is housed in an area known as administrative segregation or "ad seg," which is reserved for inmates with disciplinary problems.

In nearly all states that have death-sentenced inmates, the area where the inmates are housed is separate from the area where the inmates are executed; many states conduct the executions in a separate building. Inmates are usually transferred from death row to another location in the days immediately preceding the

The controversial Death Row Marv toy based on Frank Miller's comic Sin City *and produced by McFarlane Toys in 2000. When the switch is thrown, "Marv" convulses, his eyes light up, and he says, "That the best you can do, you pansies?"*
Source: © AFP/Corbis; used with permission.

execution, so that they can visit with family, clergy, and members of the correctional staff and the execution can proceed with the least amount of unnecessary emotional stress.

RESEARCH ON DEATH ROWS

Although there has not been comprehensive research on all death rows across the United States, a project completed in 1997 by Patti Salinas, W. Wesley Johnson, and Tana McCoy (1999) examined the conditions for women in twelve of the fourteen states that had death-sentenced women. In a follow-up study in 1999, the death row conditions for men in ten of those fourteen states were examined. From those research projects, a clear picture emerges about the range of conditions. The following examples of each type of death row are drawn from those projects.

INSTITUTIONAL ROUTINES

Personal accounts of men and women who have spent time on death row show that the most important aspects of life are the daily routines and the programs available to these inmates, including opportunities to be with other people in order to engage in conversation and camaraderie. Research on correctional management of inmates shows that busy, occupied inmates are more easily managed than isolated, bored, and angry

inmates—who are more likely to attempt bodily harm or suicide or to engage in acts of aggression directed at correctional staff or other inmates.

UNREFORMED, REFORMED, AND MAINSTREAMED DEATH ROWS

Dr. Robert Johnson, a noted scholar on death rows and the execution process, chronicles the living conditions of death-sentenced inmates in the United States. He notes that in previous centuries, condemned prisoners were held in virtual isolation (but for less time due to nonexistent or much shorter appeals processes) and that despite reforms, in many states little has changed. Johnson (1998: 71) observes that

> death row is the extreme case of the pain and deprivation of imprisonment, the prison's prison. The peculiar silence of death row stems from the empty and ultimately lifeless regimen imposed on the condemned. These offenders, seen as unfit for life in even the prison community, are relegated to this prison within a prison. . . . Deemed beyond correction, they typically are denied access to even the meager privileges, amenities, and services available to regular prisoners.

General prison reforms, brought about by prison riots, the prisoner's rights movement (1960 to 1980), and judicial intervention, did have some impact on the functioning of death rows in the United States. In some states, reforms included increased time out of the cell, increased access to educational programs, increased access to visitors and legal representation, and implementation of work opportunities. Although these reforms were not widespread and might appear to be insignificant, they have great significance to the inmates who are allowed to enjoy them. Therefore, Johnson suggests that death rows in the United States can be categorized as either unreformed or reformed.

Unreformed death rows are those where inmates are held in nearly solitary confinement. Inmates are not allowed contact with other inmates, and when out of their cells, they are shackled and under close scrutiny by prison personnel. Reformed death rows are those that allow inmates greater liberties, including contact with other inmates, time out of their cells in day rooms or communal areas, and in some states, work opportunities. After the introduction of Johnson's typology of death rows, Missouri eliminated its death row. Therefore, today death rows in America can be categorized as unreformed, reformed, or mainstreamed.

The Typical Unreformed Death Row

There is little variation in unreformed death rows from state to state. Life on an unreformed death row for men is one of isolation. The inmates are required to be in their cell for twenty-three hours a day. They are allowed only one hour of recreation a day, and it is only during this hour that they have contact with other individuals. Visitation is noncontact and is allowed twice a week. Showers are allowed three times a week. There are no programs for inmates to work or to continue their education except for correspondence courses, which few have money to pay for. Although they are allowed to meet with their own attorneys, they are not allowed to meet with jailhouse lawyers. They are handcuffed whenever they leave their cells. They are monitored closely, with a staff-to-inmate ratio of 3 to 1.

An even starker image emerges for a lone death-sentenced woman on an unreformed death row. Her cell is located in a special cell block in which no other inmates are housed; therefore, she cannot converse with other inmates. She must remain in her cell for twenty-three hours a day. No TV or radio is allowed in her cell, although she is allowed to watch a TV located outside of her cell. A guard must change the channels for her.

This woman must be handcuffed and anklecuffed whenever she leaves her cell, which means that when she walks to the shower she must be in restraints. The cuffs are removed when she showers, but they are not removed when she engages in her one hour of recreation a day.

Visitors are brought to her cell block, and visits are noncontact. Only immediate family is allowed to visit her, and her visitation is restricted to two visits a month for a total of four hours a month. Only one visitor can be in her cell block at a time unless one is a minor child, in which case an adult is allowed to accompany the child. Two pastoral counselors visit this woman weekly, and a social worker visits two or three times a week.

No work opportunities are available to this woman, although she is able to participate in educational correspondence courses. She may request books from the library and spends most days watching TV, reading, or playing cards. She is virtually isolated from other women inmates with whom she could develop friendships.

Life on a Reformed Death Row

On the typical reformed death row for men, inmates are allowed time out of their cells. Typically, death-sentenced inmates are allowed to congregate in small groups in a common area where they can watch television, talk, or play cards. On some reformed death rows, inmates are allowed to engage in work opportunities and educational or vocational programs that allow their time to pass more quickly. Although these inmates are allowed more freedoms than their counterparts on unreformed death rows, there is not less surveillance.

The typical reformed death row for women is similar to that for men: The women are allowed time out of their cells in communal rooms, and some are allowed to engage in work. But there are fewer women on reformed death rows—sometimes just one woman. This means that, whereas men are allowed to play cards and watch television with other death-sentenced inmates, on death rows with only one woman, the woman must spend time in the communal room by herself. In addition, because there are so few women on reformed death rows, programs such as educational opportunities are not available, because the institution cannot justify providing staff for just one inmate. This is especially true in states that do not allow death-sentenced inmates to mingle with general population inmates. If states do allow a woman to mingle with general population inmates, she may be transferred to another area to engage in the programs. However, transferring her from her cell to another area requires staff members to shut down other areas of the prison as she moves through. If there are insufficient staff members to transfer the prisoner, then she cannot engage in the programs.

Missouri: The Mainstreaming Leader

As of the end of 1999, Missouri had eighty-two death-sentenced men and one death-sentenced woman. These inmates have all the privileges commensurate with their classification. Death-sentenced inmates are classified in the same way that other inmates are classified; factors in classification include institutional behavior and compliance with institutional rules. Therefore, death-sentenced inmates can be classified as minimum security risks. The mainstreaming of death-sentenced inmates was achieved in 1991, following a multiphase and gradual implementation process.

The Missouri policy reflects the belief that mainstreaming death-sentenced inmates benefits inmates and the state. The state benefits because it spends less money. This savings is realized by the reduction in staff formerly required to provide programs to death-sentenced inmates and by a reduction in the legal expenses associated with prisoner litigation. In addition, there is greater flexibility when cells previously designated for use by death-sentenced inmates become available for use by other inmates.

For men and women inmates who are classified as minimum security risks, there are many opportunities to participate in programs, including work. Visitation privileges are earned, and death-sentenced inmates can engage in contact visits with family and friends. They are not handcuffed or shackled when they move about the institution engaging in work or recreation or showering. Meals are taken in the dining hall with the other inmates. If death-sentenced inmates in Missouri experience isolation, it is because they have chosen to disobey the rules.

When the governor of Missouri signs a death warrant, indicating that an inmate will soon be executed unless a court stays the execution, the inmate is withdrawn from the general inmate population. This isolation allows the inmate to engage in spiritual counseling and to meet privately with family and friends.

REASONS FOR VARIATION AMONG THE STATES

During the late 1960s and 1970s, following highly publicized inmate riots, prisoners began to challenge their conditions of confinement in court. During this time, following the lead of the U.S. Supreme Court, many state and federal courts mandated that states change their prison systems to ensure more humane treatment of inmates. Some of the reform litigation affected those on death row and helped to transform some death rows from unreformed to reformed.

Clearly, however, reform litigation did not transform all death rows, and other factors help to determine whether states will have an unreformed, reformed, or mainstreamed death row. The way in which correctional and legislative authorities view death-sentenced inmates is one of the most important factors in establishing rules that govern conditions of confinement on death row. If authorities view death-sentenced inmates as more dangerous than other inmates, death-sentenced inmates will require greater security measures to protect the public from escape and correctional personnel from injury. The death rows in states where authorities have this philosophical view tend to be unreformed. The death rows in states where authorities do not view death-sentenced inmates as greater security risks tend to be reformed.

Research on the Dangers Posed by Death-Sentenced Inmates

Does the research literature show that death-sentenced inmates are more dangerous and thus deserving of the isolation inherent in the unreformed death row model? Because 99 percent of inmates sentenced to death have committed murder at least once, it seems logical to believe that they have no moral or philosophical barriers to murdering again or injuring correctional and therapeutic personnel. How accurate is this belief?

Research conducted in 1989 by James Marquart and Jonathan Sorensen examined the institutional behavior and postrelease behavior of the 558 inmates who had their death sentences commuted to life sentences following the 1972 Supreme Court ruling in *Furman v. Georgia,* wherein the death penalty (as it was being applied by the states and federal government) was held to violate the U.S. Constitution. This research addressed the questions of whether death-sentenced inmates engaged in more serious acts of violence while they were in prison and whether those who were eventually paroled engaged in acts of violence when out of prison. Marquart and Sorensen discovered that as a group, the *Furman* inmates were not a "violent menace" (1989: 169) to the institutional order and did not pose a "disproportionate threat" (1989: 174) to prison personnel, other inmates, or society.

Escape Attempts

Many people believe that because death-sentenced inmates have no hope for being paroled or released, they have "nothing to lose" and are more willing to attempt escape. Although there is no research comparing escape attempts by death-sentenced inmates to attempts by other inmates, a review of records published by the Bureau of Justice Statistics indicates that between 1994 and 1999, there were two escape attempts by death-sentenced inmates, both of them men. In each instance, the escapees died from wounds inflicted by prison personnel.

Variations in Management of Death-Sentenced Men and Women

Many people believe that death-sentenced female inmates are treated more leniently than death-sentenced male inmates. This belief is due to the fact that many think that the criminal justice system in general treats women differently than men. In their research, Salinas, Johnson, and McCoy found that only 20 percent of states treated their death-sentenced women differently than they treated their death-sentenced men. However, in one of the states that treated women differently, the women were treated more harshly than the men. This research, therefore, does not support the idea that death-sentenced female inmates are treated more leniently than death-sentenced male inmates.

Although it is true that some death rows are more "homey" and attractive than others, it is equally true that many operate under the traditional isolation model. Data do not support the suggestion that women on death row are treated in a chivalrous manner.

Data do suggest that there is some differential treatment and that this differential treatment is primarily a function of the small numbers of women on death row. All states routinely allow their death-sentenced men to engage in recreation with other death-sentenced men. This is not true of states with just one death-sentenced woman. These women are allowed to engage in recreation but without companionship. At first glance, this may appear to be a superficial distinction; however, the authors suggest that denial of conversation and companionship, even for the short time that is devoted to recreation, can contribute substantially to the women's feelings of isolation and desperation.

SUMMARY

Historically, offenders sentenced to death in the United States awaited their execution in prison in nearly total isolation in their cells. In the 1960s and 1970s, as a result of highly publicized prison riots and the prisoner's rights movement, courts ordered reforms in the way that prisons treat inmates, including death-sentenced inmates.

Today, there are three types of death rows in the United States: unreformed, reformed, and mainstream. Unreformed death rows are very much like the death rows of days gone by. Inmates are held in their cells in near isolation. They are allowed out of their cells for limited periods of time for recreation or visitation.

On reformed death rows, inmates are allowed more time out of their cells and are allowed to engage in recreation or work with other death-sentenced inmates. They have opportunities to seek counseling from correctional or clerical staff.

Mainstreamed death-sentenced inmates in Missouri have the greatest liberties and least restrictive confinement of any such inmates in the United States. They are allowed all of the rights and privileges that other inmates of similar security classification are allowed, including opportunities to work and to engage in recreation. In addition, these inmates are allowed to have contact visitation with family and friends. The Missouri policy is believed to afford the state maximum cost savings and to reduce the risk of litigation from inmates. In addition, the state believes that inmates suffer fewer medical problems when allowed to mingle with the general inmate population.

Clearly, there is great variation among death rows for men and women across the United States. This variation is most apparent when a comparison is made between the most reformed and the most unreformed death rows. For both men and women, the most reformed death rows are a departure from the traditional isolation model of death row. For both genders, the mainstreaming approach eliminates the classic problems of loneliness, desolation, and dehumanization inherent in the isolation model.

Similarly, for both genders, the most unreformed death rows are classic examples of the traditional isolation model. Inmates on these death rows are not allowed the small comfort of contact with others who are experiencing the emotional trauma that accompanies an uncertain future.

Although there is variation in the way that states treat their death-sentenced men and women inmates, the majority of states are consistent in their death row policy. Therefore, death-sentenced women are not treated more leniently. In addition, because some states have only one death-sentenced woman, that woman may have fewer opportunities to engage in institutional programs due to shortages of staff and the costs associated with providing programs for only one inmate.

—*Patti Ross Salinas*

See also CAPITAL PUNISHMENT; DEATH ROW INMATES; DEATH SENTENCE OUTCOMES; INTERNATIONAL IMPRISONMENTS; RACE AND CORRECTIONS; RACE AND SENTENCING; WRONGFUL CONVICTIONS

Further Reading

Amnesty International. (2001). *China: "Striking Harder" Than Ever Before.* http://www.amnesty.org/ai.nsf/pring/ASA17022 2001?OpenDocument

Dieter, Richard. (1999). "International Perspectives on the Death Penalty: A Costly Isolation for the U.S." http://www.death-penaltyinfo.org/internationalreport.html

Johnson, Robert. (1998). *Deathwork: A Study of the Modern Execution Process*, 2d ed. Belmont, CA: West/Wadsworth.

Lombardi, George, Richard Sluber, and Donald Wallace. (1997). "Mainstreaming Death-Sentenced Inmates: The Missouri Experience and Its Legal Significance." *Federal Probation* 61, 2: 3–11.

Marquart, James, and Jonathan Sorensen. (1997). "A National Study of the *Furman*-Commuted Inmates: Assessing the Threat to Society from Capital Offenders." In *The Death Penalty in America: Current Controversies*, edited by Hugo Adam Bedau. Oxford, UK: Oxford University Press, 162–175.

Salinas, Patti R., Tana McCoy, and W. Wesley Johnson. (1999). "Management Issues Surrounding Women on Death Row." *Corrections Management Quarterly* (Spring): 64–70.

Salinas, Patti R., W. Wesley Johnson, and Tana McCoy. (1999). "Death Rows—What Difference Does Gender Make?" Paper presented at American Society of Criminology, Toronto, Canada.

Snell, Tracy L. (2000). "Capital Punishment 1999." *Bulletin, Bureau of Justice Statistics*. Washington, DC: U.S. Department of Justice.

Court Case

Furman v. Georgia (1972). 408 U.S. 238.

◪ DEATH ROW INMATES

Capital punishment, or the use of death as the sentence to be carried out when someone has been convicted of a crime, is the harshest and most controversial sanction known to humankind. The use of the death penalty dates back to earliest civilizations, with the crucifixion of Christ being but one example. Amnesty International, an organization that opposes the use of capital punishment, reports that by 1999 over half of the countries in the world had abolished the death penalty. It reported that 85 percent of executions in 1999 took place in China, Iran, Saudi Arabia, the Democratic Republic of the Congo, and the United States.

In the United States, the death sentence has been used since the colonial period. Currently, thirty-eight states and the federal government permit execution for capital offenses. As the United States entered the twenty-first century, there were 3,527 death-sentenced individuals housed on death rows in thirty-seven states and the federal prison system.

WHO CAN RECEIVE A DEATH SENTENCE?

The most important U.S. Supreme Court case concerning the use of the death penalty is *Furman v. Georgia* (1972). Prior to the Supreme Court's decision in *Furman*, individuals could be sentenced to death for a variety of offenses, including theft, rape, and murder.

More important, juries and judges had wide discretion and little or no clear statutory guidance in deciding who would be sentenced to death. In *Furman*, the Supreme Court ruled that the arbitrary and capricious application of the death penalty violated the U.S. Constitution. Because all those who had been sentenced to death before 1972 had their constitutional rights violated, their death sentences were commuted to life sentences. It is important to note that the Supreme Court did not rule that the death penalty itself was a violation of the Eighth Amendment, but rather that the way it was being implemented was unconstitutional.

Following the *Furman* decision, many states revised their statutes to give clear guidance on when and how the death sentence could be imposed. The revised death penalty statute of the state of Georgia was challenged in the 1976 case of *Gregg v. Georgia*. The Supreme Court decided that Georgia's revised capital sentencing statute was constitutional. In two other Supreme Court decisions, *Woodson v. North Carolina* (1976) and *Coker v. Georgia* (1977), statutes calling for mandatory death sentences (because they did not allow judges and juries to hear mitigating evidence), and the death sentence for rape were held to be unconstitutional. All states that allow the death sentence provide for its use for murder; however, eleven states also allow the death penalty for other crimes, including treason, train wrecking, perjury causing execution, drug trafficking, kidnapping with bodily injury, aggravated rape of a victim under age twelve, and aircraft piracy. Federal statutes that authorize the use of the death penalty all involve the murder or death of the victim, except for the mailing of injurious articles with intent to kill, espionage, and treason.

Nearly all those who receive the death sentence in the United States are convicted of the crime of capital murder. Each state that allows the death sentence must define by statute those situations or aggravating factors that transform an "ordinary" murder into a capital murder. Examples of aggravating factors are the age of the victim (very young or very old), whether the killer was committing another crime when the murder occurred (usually rape, kidnapping, arson, robbery, or burglary), the occupation or status of the victim (police officer, firefighter, correctional officer, trial witness, judge, or jury member), or facts that made the murder particularly brutal (e.g., the use of torture). Other aggravating factors focus on the status of murderer (e.g., an inmate escaping from prison, or a person with a previous murder conviction).

To pass constitutional muster, a statute must allow the judge and jury to hear mitigating evidence. Mitigating evidence is evidence introduced to show why the defendant should not receive the death sentence. Examples of mitigating evidence include facts showing the defendant is mentally disabled or has significantly impaired reasoning abilities, or was raised or lived in an abusive household.

DEMOGRAPHICS

In 2000, there were 3,527 death-sentenced inmates in the United States. On average, between 1973 and 1999, 291 persons were sentenced to death each year. Of those, on average 26 are executed, 9 die of causes other than execution, 95 have their sentences overturned, 6 have their sentences commuted, and 1 leaves for "other" reasons. Because of the lengthy appeals process that is afforded to death-sentenced defendants, between 1977 and 1999, the average length of time spent on death row before execution was nearly ten years. For the 98 inmates who were executed in 1999, the average amount of time spent on death row was nearly twelve years. Both conservatives and liberals have attacked this lengthy appeals process. Conservatives argue that the process is too long and many of the appeals are frivolous. Liberals attack the narrow focus of the appeals, arguing that inmates should be allowed to introduce new evidence at any point in the process, even if it was evidence that should have been discovered at the time of trial. In support of their position, they point to those who have been found innocent after spending years on death row and who would have been wrongly executed had they not had as much time. Ultimately the conservative position has been more successful. New federal law has placed limits on the number of challenges or appeals that a person can file under habeas corpus proceedings. The writ of habeas corpus is the most common way that prisoners challenge their convictions and confinement in prison.

RACIAL CHARACTERISTICS

Prior to the 1976 reinstatement of the death penalty, the number of African Americans sentenced to death was nearly the same as the number of whites. This was so even though African Americans comprised only 15 percent of the population. In a study of the 558 inmates (excluding those in Illinois) whose sentences were commuted in 1972 following the *Furman* decision,

James Marquart and Jonathan Sorenson reported that 55 percent of the prisoners were black, 43 percent were white, and 1 percent were Hispanic; one inmate was American Indian.

Following the reinstatement of the death penalty, a greater number of whites have been sentenced to death, although the percentage of African Americans remains greater than their percentage of the general population. In 1999, death-sentenced inmates were 55 percent white, 43 percent black, and 2 percent American Indian, Asian, or "other race." Of the 98 who were executed in 1999, 61 were white, 33 were African American, 2 were American Indian, and 2 were Asian.

Many opponents of capital punishment argue that the death penalty is applied in a racially discriminatory manner. This was the argument in the 1987 Supreme Court case *McCleskey v. Kemp*. In this case, the Court considered statistical data indicating that the race of the defendant and the victim were factors influencing the imposition of the death sentence. The statistics indicated that the death sentence was more likely to be given when a nonwhite defendant killed a white victim. However, the Supreme Court refused to rule that this data indicated intent to apply the death sentence in a racially prejudicial manner for this particular defendant. Therefore, the Court ruled, the imposition of the death penalty in this case did not violate the U.S. Constitution.

GENDER

Males commit most crime in the United States, including capital murder, so it is not surprising that in the year 2000 nearly 99 percent of death-sentenced inmates were male: Of 3,527 death-sentenced prisoners, only fifty were women. In addition to the fact that males commit more crime, some argue that even when women commit murder, the criminal justice system is reluctant to execute them. Professor Victor Streib, a noted authority on women and the death sentence, reports that although women account for 13 percent of murder arrests, they account for only .6 percent of those executed in the post-*Furman* era. Since the year 1608, of the 19,200 documented executions in America, only 560 (3 percent) have been women. This reluctance to execute women may be due to the fact that courts are more likely to find mitigating factors that make the death sentence seem less appropriate. Furthermore, women are more likely to kill those with whom they are acquainted, and to kill them without premeditation, which is viewed as less "cold-blooded." Finally, in some instances, the circumstances of the killing are such that the woman is viewed as a victim, as is the case when a woman kills her abusive spouse.

Between 1976 and 1998 only one female was executed in the United States: Velma Barfield was executed in 1984 in the state of North Carolina. But since the 1998 executions of Karla Faye Tucker in Texas and Judy Buenoano in Florida, it appears that the execution of women may become more frequent. There were two executions in 2000: Betty Lou Beets in Texas and Christina Riggs in Arkansas. Three females were executed in 2001, all in Oklahoma: Wanda Jean Allen, Marilyn Plantz, and Lois Nadean Smith.

The execution of Karla Faye Tucker received extensive national and international press coverage. Her execution attracted the media for several reasons. It had been fourteen years since the Barfield execution, making the event unusual. Tucker was a "born again" Christian who garnered the support of various religious leaders because of her work in a Christian prison ministry. Her physical attractiveness made her seem more like "Beauty" than a "Beast" capable of participating in the brutal pick-ax murder of two people in Houston, Texas. The execution of Judy Buenoano less than sixty days later received very limited press coverage, even though she too claimed to have undergone a religious conversion while on death row in Florida.

AGE

One of the most controversial issues regarding the death penalty today is age. In the 1988 case of *Thompson v. Oklahoma,* the U.S. Supreme Court ruled that the execution of an individual who was fifteen or under when he or she committed the offense was a violation of the Eighth Amendment. One year later, in *Stanford v. Kentucky*, the Supreme Court held that the Eighth Amendment was not violated when the death sentence was given to individuals who were sixteen or older when they committed their offense. Currently, twelve states set sixteen as their minimum age, four set seventeen as the minimum age, and fifteen (including the federal government) require that the offender be eighteen in order to receive the death penalty. States that do not specify a minimum age can sentence to death anyone who is sixteen years of age or older.

One of the reasons that age is so controversial is that the U.N. Convention on the Rights of the Child and other international treaties and agreements prohibit the sentencing of those under the age of eighteen to death. Only six countries—Iran, Nigeria, Pakistan, Saudi Arabia, Yemen, and the United States—have executed individuals who were under the age of eighteen when they committed their offense. The United States sentences more juveniles to death than any other nation. As of June 2000, seventy-four juveniles were under sentence of death; twenty were sixteen when they committed their offense, and fifty-four were seventeen. Because the appellate process in death penalty cases is so lengthy, there are currently no death-sentenced inmates younger than eighteen.

The average age of death row inmates in the United States in 1999 was thirty-eight; the youngest inmate was eighteen and the oldest eighty-four. The average age at time of arrest was twenty-eight. The relatively young age of the death-sentenced individuals reflects the fact that young males commit most crime in the United States.

EDUCATION AND MENTAL CAPACITY

The Bureau of Justice Statistics reports that in 2000, over half of all death-sentenced inmates had completed at least the eleventh grade; nearly 40 percent had graduated from high school; and 10 percent had completed some college (U.S. Department of Justice 2000). But the lack of formal education of death-sentenced individuals has not been the focus of controversy in recent years. Rather, it is the mental capacity of individuals sentenced to die that has garnered the attention of the courts and opponents of the death penalty.

Traditionally, mentally ill and mentally retarded individuals (and young children) were held to lack the legal capacity to form the intent necessary to commit a crime (mens rea), and therefore were not legally responsible for their actions. For those who are mentally ill there is the insanity defense, for which each state has clear guidelines. For those who suffer from mental retardation, however, the guidelines are not always clear. People are considered to be mentally retarded when they have an IQ of less than 70 and exhibit deficits in adaptive behavior before the age of eighteen. (The average person has an IQ of about 100.) Eighteen states and the federal government specifically exclude the mentally retarded from capital sentencing.

It is estimated that thirty-seven mentally retarded individuals have been executed in the United States. Their estimated IQs ranged from 55 to 77, and many were convicted without their attorneys presenting any evidence of their mental impairments. It is not known how many of the current 3,527 death-sentenced inmates are suffering from mental impairment, but it is estimated that as many as 10 percent of those sentenced to death have an IQ under 70.

The issue of whether the failure to consider the mitigating nature of mental retardation is a violation of the U.S. Constitution was addressed by the Supreme Court in the 1989 case of *Penry v. Lynaugh*. The defendant, John Penry, had an estimated IQ of 54 and functioned at the level of a six-year-old child. In *Penry,* the Supreme Court declined to hold that the execution of a mentally retarded individual is itself a violation of the Eighth Amendment. However, the Court did hold that evidence of mental retardation must be considered as a mitigating factor when deciding whether to sentence someone to death. Following this decision Penry was retried in Texas and again sentenced to death. The Supreme Court stayed Penry's execution in November 2000 and agreed to hear the appeal of this second death sentence. On June 4, 2001, the Court reversed and remanded (in part) Penry's death sentence because the jury in the second trial had not been properly afforded the opportunity to consider Penry's mental retardation as a factor when deciding whether he should be sentenced to life or death (*Penry v. Johnson*).

In February 2001, the Court agreed to hear *Atkins v. Virginia*, a case that involved a mentally retarded individual sentenced to death. The case is scheduled to come before the Court in 2002, with the Court further addressing the Eighth Amendment issue of whether or not it is cruel and unusual punishment to execute someone who is mentally retarded.

CRIMINAL HISTORY

In a study of inmates whose sentences were commuted to life following the *Furman* decision, Marquart and Sorenson (1989) reported that 55 percent had prior felony convictions. Of these, only 4 percent had prior convictions for murder. The criminal histories of death-sentenced inmates in 1999, as reported by the U.S. Bureau of Justice Statistics (2000), indicated that 64 percent had prior felony convictions and that 8 percent had a previous homicide conviction.

WRONGFULLY CONVICTED INMATES

The most highly publicized issue regarding death-sentenced inmates in the United States today is the ques-

tion of how many innocent individuals have been sentenced to death. In a 1993 report issued by the House Judiciary Committee, forty-eight people were listed as having been released from death row between 1973 and 1993 following findings of significant evidence of their innocence. Subsequent to that report, the Death Penalty Information Center named an additional forty-seven people, bringing to ninety-five the number of individuals who have been released from death row following significant evidence of innocence. Of these, ten were freed when DNA analysis proved their innocence. They had spent between one and thirty-three years on death row; the average length of time between conviction and release was eight years.

Currently there is a growing movement to place a moratorium on the execution of death-sentenced inmates in the United States. The moratorium movement is due in large part to the media attention that has been given to inmates who have been exonerated through the use of DNA evidence, recent reports that cast doubt on the deterrent effect of capital punishment, and the continued decline in the homicide rate. In 1997, the American Bar Association, which takes no stance on the death penalty, called for a temporary halt to executions while states put in place policies to ensure fairness and minimize the risk of executing the innocent. Thus far only one state, Illinois, has issued a halt to executions.

The Illinois moratorium came about as the result of a series of articles that appeared in the *Chicago Tribune*. Noting that Illinois had the dubious distinction of releasing more innocent inmates from death row than it executed, the *Tribune* reported that there were serious problems with the way the death sentence was being used, focusing on the ineptitude of court-appointed counsel, misconduct on the part of criminal justice personnel, and the failure of counsel for the defendant and police officers to fully investigate cases.

In Nebraska, the state legislature called for a moratorium on executions pending a review of the state's administration of capital punishment, but the governor vetoed the bill. Following a legislatively funded comprehensive study of the death penalty that was completed in July 2001, Governor Mike Johanns announced that Nebraska's death sentence was being applied fairly.

In addition to various religious leaders (including the pope) who have called for a moratorium, a bipartisan group of U.S. senators and representatives support the moratorium movement. Citing a survey that was conducted by independent research firms, Senators

Patrick Leahy (Democrat of Vermont), Gordon Smith (Republican of Oregon), and Susan Collins (Republican of Maine) report that 80 percent of Americans support reform or abolition, and 64 percent support a moratorium until issues of fairness are resolved. Other surveys report that more than 50 percent of Americans support the death penalty.

SUMMARY

In the United States, the death penalty has always been used as a means for punishing offenders. In *Furman v. Georgia*, the Supreme Court ruled that the use of the death penalty did not violate the Eighth Amendment prohibition against cruel and unusual punishment unless it was applied in an arbitrary and capricious manner. Following this decision, states that used the death penalty revised their statutes to give more structure and guidance.

At the start of 2001, there were 3,593 people awaiting execution. Only 54 were women. Almost all received the death sentence for the crime of murder. There were more white inmates than blacks or Hispanics, but the proportion of blacks sentenced to death was higher than the proportion of blacks in society. The average age of death-sentenced inmates was thirty-eight; the youngest was eighteen and the oldest eighty-five.

There is considerable controversy surrounding the fairness of the use of the death penalty. Key issues exist regarding the sentencing of minors, the mentally retarded, and the innocent to death. There is growing support for a moratorium on executions while the federal government and states examine the fairness of their systems. The use of DNA testing will play a larger role in determining the guilt or innocence of those already sentenced to death.

—*Patti Ross Salinas*

See also CAPITAL PUNISHMENT; DEATH ROW; DEATH SENTENCE OUTCOMES; INTERNATIONAL IMPRISONMENTS; RACE AND CORRECTIONS; RACE AND SENTENCING; WRONGFUL CONVICTIONS

Further Reading

ACLU Death Penalty Campaign. http://www.aclu.org/death-penalty

Armstrong, Ken, and Steve Mills. (1999). "Death Row Justice Derailed." *Chicago Tribune*, November 14–18.

Bedau, Hugo Adam, ed. (1997). *The Death Penalty in America: Current Controversies*. Oxford, UK: Oxford University Press.

Death Penalty Information Center. www.deathpenaltyinfo.org

Dieter, Richard. (1997). *Innocence and the Death Penalty: The Increasing Danger of Executing the Innocent*. Washington, DC: Death Penalty Information Center.

Henderson, Ky. (1997). "How Many Innocent Inmates Are Executed?" *Human Rights*. 24, 4 (Fall). http://www.abanet.org/irr/hr/deathpen.html

Keyes, William Edward, and Robert Perske. (1997). "People with Mental Retardation Are Dying, Legally." *Journal of Mental Retardation* 35, 1: 59–63.

Marquart, James, and Jonathan Sorensen. (1989). "A National Study of the *Furman*-Commuted Inmates: Assessing the Threat to Society from Capital Offenders." *Loyola of Los Angeles Law Review*. 23, 1: 5–28.

Rueter, Thad. (1996). "Why Women Aren't Executed: Gender Bias and the Death Penalty." *Human Rights* 23, 4 (Fall). www.abanet.org/irr/hr/deathpen.html

Snell, Tracy L. (2000). *Capital Punishment 1999*. Washington, DC: U.S. Department of Justice, Bureau of Justice Statistics.

United States Department of Justice. (2000). *The Federal Death Penalty System: A Statistical Survey (1988–2000)*. Washington, DC: U.S. Department of Justice.

Court Cases

Atkins v. Virginia (2001). No. 009452, cert. Granted Feb. 2001.
Coker v. Georgia (1977). 433 U.S. 584.
Furman v. Georgia (1972). 408 U.S. 238.
Gregg v. Georgia (1976). 428 U.S. 153.
McCleskey v. Kemp (1987). 428 U.S. 262.
Penry v. Johnson (2000). 215 F.3d 504.
Penry v. Lynaugh (1989). 492 U.S. 302.
Stanford v. Kentucky (1989). 492 U.S. 361.
Thompson v. Oklahoma (1988). 487 U.S. 815.
Woodson v. North Carolina (1976). 428 U.S. 280.

DEATH SENTENCE OUTCOMES

Except for a few celebrated cases, the media seldom report about individuals once they have been given the death sentence. There is a notion that these individuals will soon be executed, killed in prison before their execution date, or die of old age while awaiting execution. Data, however, show otherwise. According to the U.S. Department of Justice, Bureau of Justice Statistics (1997), of the 6,228 individuals in the United States who were sentenced to death between 1973 and 1995, only 313 were executed; 141 others died or were killed during this period.

CLEMENCY

Clemency, the act of commuting the sentence of a prisoner under sentence of death, is a discretionary executive power. Reasons for granting clemency vary widely, but they generally fall into one of three categories: to promote justice where the reliability of the conviction is questionable, to promote justice where the reliability of the sentence is questionable, and to promote justice where neither the reliability of the conviction nor the capital sentence is implicated.

Clemency decisions are usually made by either the president or a state governor. The most common situation is a state governor granting clemency, either in the form of a sentence reduction (usually to life imprisonment without possibility of parole) or pardon (which invalidates both guilt and sentence). In most states, the governor has primary authority to grant clemency, a power exercised either directly or in conjunction with an advisory board. A few states allow parole or pardon boards to make clemency decisions. In several states, the governor shares clemency power with a parole or pardon board. Clemency power gives a state governor (and the mayor of the District of Columbia) the final say on whether an inmate will remain in prison or be executed.

Clemency does not mean that an inmate will necessarily be released from prison. Pardons can be either absolute or conditional, and they may either completely forgive the defendant of the offense and all consequences of conviction or impose requirements that the inmate must fulfill either before or after the pardon is granted. In either case, however, the decision to pardon is based upon the belief that public welfare will be better served by imposing a less severe punishment. An executive may grant a pardon for good reasons, for bad reasons, or for any reason at all, but an execution is final and irrevocable.

Between 1973 and 1995, 159 death sentences were commuted, 482 death sentences were declared unconstitutional, 1,348 convictions were affirmed but the death sentence was reduced, and 688 convictions and, therefore, death sentences, were overturned.

COMMUTATION

Executive clemency extended to inmates under sentence of death is usually in the form of a commutation. A commutation, usually granted by a state governor, reduces the original sentence to a lesser degree of punishment. At any stage in the appeals process, a governor has the authority to reduce a death sentence to one of life imprisonment, either with an extended mandatory term or without possibility of parole. Most governors, however, have not welcomed commutation petitions, mostly due to fear of voter reprisal.

Most commutations are granted due to errors committed during the criminal trial. If an error occurs at the sentencing phase of a trial, the case cannot be remanded for a new sentencing proceeding. If the formal sanction was erroneously imposed, the case stands in the same position as if the jury had failed to reach a verdict: The entire case must be retried. A commutation might then be a result of plea bargaining to avoid the time and expense of a retrial.

A commutation, although a more limited form of clemency, shares many attributes of its parent power. But clemency and acquittal are not the same thing. An acquittal means that the defendant did not commit the crime for which he or she was convicted. A commutation is a declaration not that no criminal act occurred but, rather, that the death sentence will be reduced. In the case of a pardon, the conviction ceases to stand.

CAPITAL SENTENCE DECLARED UNCONSTITUTIONAL

A death sentence may be declared unconstitutional for several reasons. The most common is some type of error during the trial process: evidentiary irregularities, inadequate jury instructions, prosecutorial misconduct, defense attorney error, improper exclusion of jurors, and a variety of other reasons. A death sentence may also be declared unconstitutional if a state's death penalty statutes are voided. This does not affect the guilt or innocence of the defendant; instead, the death sentence is reduced to life imprisonment with no opportunity for parole. The most well-known case took place on June 29, 1972, when the U.S. Supreme Court set aside death sentences for the first time in history. In its decisions in *Furman v. Georgia*, *Jackson v. Georgia*, and *Branch v. Texas*, the Supreme Court held that death penalty statutes in Georgia and Texas were unconstitutional. Because all other existing state statutes were very similar, state supreme courts declared their own statutes unconstitutional under the *Furman* reasoning. The practical effect of the *Furman* decision was that all U.S. death row inmates (more than 600) had their sentences reduced to life imprisonment.

CONVICTION AFFIRMED, SENTENCE OVERTURNED BY APPELLATE COURT

The very nature of capital sentencing allows room for error. Trials in capital cases are divided into two parts: a guilt phase and a penalty phase. In the first phase, the jury determines the guilt or innocence of the accused;

in the second, the same jury decides the sentence. When federal judges reverse death sentences that were affirmed by state supreme court justices, it is usually because the defendant had ineffective counsel. According to former U.S. Attorney General Benjamin Civiletti, four in ten death penalty sentences appealed to federal courts on constitutional grounds are ultimately reversed.

CONVICTION AND SENTENCE OVERTURNED BY APPELLATE COURT

Sometimes both the conviction and sentence are overturned by an appellate court. This is partly due to the two-stage process of capital cases. For example, insufficient evidence in the conviction stage might create problems in the sentencing stage and thus may lead to a new trial or resentencing. If either the conviction or the sentence is vacated during appellate review, the case might be remanded to the trial court for additional proceedings or retrial. However, as a result of retrial or resentencing, the death sentence could be reimposed. The following cases are of historical importance not only because they received national attention but because, as Texas judge Bob Perkins once said, they have one significant commonality: "a fundamental miscarriage of justice." The inmate held the longest before exoneration was Mitchell Blazak, convicted of murder in Arizona in 1974 and released in 1995. Another well-known case was that of James Richardson, convicted of murder in 1967 and exonerated in 1989 following a reinvestigation of the case by then Dade County state attorney Janet Reno. More recently, after being in prison for more than eleven years, Christopher Ochoa's murder conviction was overturned by Texas judge Bob Perkins on January 16, 2001. While there are many reasons for reversing a conviction, these convictions were reversed because of doubts about the defendant's guilt, faulty evidence (or lack of evidence), and/or error during the trial.

On a broader scale, Governor George Ryan imposed a moratorium on the Illinois death penalty on January 31, 2000. From 1977 to 2000, "we have now freed more people than we have put to death under our system—thirteen people have been exonerated and twelve have been put to death," Ryan said. The condemned were to remain on death row until the facts (including the thirteen overturned cases) were examined, especially since one of the thirteen exonerated

inmates, Anthony Porter, spent fifteen years on death row and was within two days of execution. The governor's decision makes Illinois the first of the thirty-eight states with capital punishment to suspend all executions while it analyzes its death penalty procedures. (The Nebraska legislature passed a moratorium on executions the previous year but it was vetoed by Governor Mike Johanns.)

SUMMARY

Approximately 3,700 individuals are currently on death row, and several hundred more are given death sentences each year. Some are executed and some are removed from death row, but many remain, awaiting execution. Of the 6,228 individuals sentenced to death between 1973 and 1995, 3,054 were still under a death sentence at the end of 1995. Inmates wait an average of nine years for the judicial review procedures to uncover possible error. Given the nature of the legal process, there is good reason to believe that errors continue to occur. The rate of prejudicial error in capital cases between 1973 and 1995 was 68 percent. Errors may lead to a retrial or new sentencing, or even an acquittal. The most common result, however, is that a death sentence is commuted to life imprisonment, sometimes with the possibility for parole.

—*Martin G. Urbina*

See also CAPITAL CRIMES; CAPITAL PUNISHMENT; CLEMENCY; DEATH ROW; DEATH ROW INMATES; WRONGFUL CONVICTIONS

Further Reading

Ammons, Linda. (1994). "Discretionary Justice: A Legal and Policy Analysis of a Governor's Use of the Clemency Power in the Cases of Incarcerated Battered Women." *Journal of Law and Policy* 3: 1–79.

Anaya, Toney. (1993). "Statement by Toney Anaya on Capital Punishment." *University of Richmond Law Review* 27, 2: 177–183.

Bedau, Hugo Adam, and Michael Radelet. (1987). "Miscarriages of Justice in Potentially Capital Cases." *Stanford Law Review* 40: 21–179.

Palacios, Victoria. (1996). "Faith in Fantasy: The Supreme Court's Reliance on Commutation to Ensure Justice in Death Penalty Cases." *Vanderbilt University Law Review* 49: 311–372.

Radelet, Michael, William Lofquist, and Hugo Bedau. (1996). "Death Penalty Symposium: Prisoners Released from Death Row Since 1970 because of Doubts About Their Guilt." *Thomas and Cooley Law Review* 13: 907–966.

Radelet, Michael, and Glenn Pierce. (1991). "Choosing Those Who Will Die: Race and the Death Penalty in Florida." *Florida Law Review* 43, 1: 1–34.

Radelet, Michael, and Barbara Zsembik. (1993). "Executive Clemency in post-*Furman* Capital Cases." *University of Rich-*

mond Law Review 27: 289–314.

U.S. Department of Justice, Bureau of Justice Statistics. (1997). *Capital Punishment in the United States, 1973–1995* [computer file]. ICPSR version. Ann Arbor, MI: Interuniversity Consortium for Political and Social Research.

Vandiver, Margaret. (1993). "The Quality of Mercy: Race and Clemency in Florida Death Penalty Cases, 1924–1966." *University of Richmond Law Review* 27, 2: 315–343.

Vick, Douglas. (1995). "Poorhouse Justice: Underfunded Indigent Defense Services and Arbitrary Death Sentences." *Buffalo Law Review* 43 2: 329–460.

Court Case

Furman v. Georgia/Jackson v. Georgia/Branch v. Texas (1972). 408 U.S. 238.

◤ DEFENSE COUNSEL SYSTEMS

In the adversary system that has evolved from the English "fighting" trial-by-ordeal of the tenth century and is dominant in the United States and other common law countries, the main task of the defense attorney is the protection of the criminal defendant's legal rights. In this task, a defense attorney has several advantages over the prosecution:

1. The presumption of the defendant's innocence puts the burden of proof on the prosecutor;

2. thus no explanation of the crime other than the one based on the criminal defendant's guilt should be reasonable for there to be a conviction;

3. the prosecution must comply with the defense's formal requests for a summary of the evidence that the state will use against the accused; and

4. the defense attorney goes last in presenting his or her case at trial, thereby making it easier to create doubt in the state's case by attacking its credibility.

The inquisitorial system favored by civil and socialist law countries was developed from the Spanish Inquisition's "search for truth" and is a cooperative continuing investigation orchestrated by an active judge, with the criminal defendant presumed guilty; thus, the task of the defense attorney is to mitigate that guilt.

A criminal defense attorney can be defined as "a person who either specializes in or handles a substantial number of criminal cases" (Holton and Lamar 1991: 123). In the United States, many lawyers are general practitioners who handle whatever criminal or civil cases come their way. Some lawyers take a criminal case only if a special client asks them to or if they feel

it is their ethical obligation to do so. Still other lawyers specialize in criminal law and believe that lawyers who take only an occasional criminal case are not really criminal defense attorneys. The canons of legal ethics in the United States forbid taking a criminal case on a contingency basis as is done with civil cases; thus, there are a variety of fee arrangements made with criminal defendants. Free legal aid for criminal defendants who cannot afford counsel (i.e., indigents) is a matter of due process in most countries, including the United States, regardless of whether they follow an adversary or an inquisitorial system.

More than 80 percent of the defendants in felony cases in the United States are indigent and therefore are represented by court-appointed attorneys, whose fees are paid by the government. American indigent defendants usually obtain legal services by one of three systems. The court-assigned counsel system is the primary system in most jurisdictions in the United States, wherein the defense attorney is usually selected, either randomly or by the trial judge, from a roster of all the practicing attorneys within the court's jurisdiction and is paid at a rate set by that jurisdiction's government. The public defender program differs from the court-assigned counsel system in that the former relies on a full-time salaried staff, including defense attorneys, investigators, and office personnel. Public defender programs serve more indigent defendants than any other system because they are most often located in highly populated urban jurisdictions. The third type of indigent defense system in use and growing in the United States is the contract attorney program, wherein local governments contract with local individual attorneys, multipartner law firms, or local bar associations to provide legal services to indigent defendants.

EDUCATION OF DEFENSE COUNSELS

The training of lawyers in countries of the civil law tradition (i.e., those that rely primarily on codification of laws rather than legal precedent) varies by country and the type of law one wants to pursue. After earning a rather general and interdisciplinary degree in law, the graduate must then choose to pursue a career as a private lawyer, a judge, a government lawyer, or a legal scholar and then pass an entrance exam and complete an apprenticeship before being allowed to practice the type of law chosen, usually for the duration of his or her career.

Lawyers in the socialist legal system (i.e., where socialist economic theory dominates the rule of law)

Famed defense attorney Johnnie Cochran, who led the defense team that won an acquittal for O. J. Simpson on charges of killing his ex-wife and her friend Ronald Goldman on June 12, 1994.
Source: © AFP/Corbis; used with permission.

begin their career in a similar way. The socialist legal system, however, is highly integrated rather than having distinct legal fields, thus allowing socialist lawyers to move from one area to another (e.g., from criminal to civil law or from being a defense attorney to a prosecutor) without additional entrance requirements—as is the case with American lawyers. Although criminal defendants have a right to represent themselves in American courts, this is not the norm, as it is in most Islamic legal systems. In those systems, defendants normally represent themselves or have a family member or character witness without formal legal training act for them. If they do have counsel, it is someone with religious rather than legal training. The practice of law in the United States is a unified legal profession, like most legal systems that follow the common law tradition (i.e., precedent or case law predominates), with the notable exception of Great Britain. Great Britain has a bifurcated legal profession, in which future attorneys must choose to be trained as a barrister, who specializes in arguing legal cases in higher courts, or as a solicitor, who most often prepares cases for barristers.

American lawyers must graduate from law school and pass the bar exam of the state in which they wish to practice, but very few American law schools place any emphasis on the practice of criminal law other than mandatory courses on the fundamentals of criminal law and criminal procedure. Therefore, the vast majority of criminal defense attorneys learn their trade from on-the-job training in civilian law offices or public defender offices. Some public defender offices have in-service training for newly hired attorneys or apprentice them to more experienced defense lawyers. Most put the new public defender into practice quickly because of the lack of resources and funding. Usually new lawyers in private criminal law firms are trained more slowly by helping senior attorneys in the preparation of their cases until the new lawyers are ready to handle cases on their own. However, most private criminal defense attorneys are solo practitioners, who learn on the job from their first cases, which are often as court-appointed counsel for indigent criminal defendants. More formal education is offered through continuing legal education seminars and courses provided by law schools, private educational companies, public defender associations, trial attorney associations, and local, state, and national bar associations. About half the states mandate a certain amount of continuing legal education as a requirement for the renewal of an attorney's license to practice law.

DUTIES OF DEFENSE ATTORNEYS

The criminal defendant had counsel in colonial America, but it was provided by practice rather than by law. Since 1750, it has been the custom in Connecticut to appoint counsel for defendants who requested a lawyer, although the practice was not authorized by statute until 1818. Most other states made such provisions in their constitutions after the revolution. The Sixth Amendment of the U.S. Constitution provides that a criminal defendant "shall enjoy the right . . . to have the assistance of counsel for his defense." However, the U.S. Supreme Court legitimized the right as applying to all indigent defendants in federal criminal felony prosecutions in 1928 and in 1963 to all indigent felony defendants in state courts. The Court broadened the right to counsel to misdemeanor prosecutions punishable by a jail term in 1973. Furthermore, the Court created a "critical stage test" in 1967 in which the criminal defendant has a right to counsel throughout the criminal justice process whenever counsel is necessary to preserve a fair trial. Thus, the right to counsel attaches only after the adversary proceeding against the accused has begun and only to identification procedures where a crime witness confronts the accused. Still, the right to counsel attaches much earlier in the United States than even in other common law countries.

American criminal defense attorneys engage in five activities: fighting, negotiating, drafting, counseling, and administering. Fighting with the prosecution to create a "reasonable doubt" as to the charges against the defendant is at the heart of the adversary system and occurs primarily during trial. In lieu of trial, defense attorneys are responsible for negotiating plea bargains for their clients, in which clients plead guilty for either a reduction in charges or counts or a favorable sentence recommendation from the prosecutor. Defense attorneys are responsible for drafting many court motions, such as those to suppress evidence gained by unconstitutional police actions and those used to discover the prosecution's evidence. Counseling the defendant as to the legal options available to the defendant and their consequences is another important task. Finally, criminal defense attorneys represent many clients at the same time, handling many more cases than prosecutors, and they often appear in several different courtrooms representing cases at various stages in the criminal justice process in the same day; hence, administration of an attorney's schedule is very important.

Holman and Quinn (1996: 245) note that criminal defense attorneys employ many tactics to win at trial, especially when a jury is present, including "confusing the jury; creating doubts among the jurors; appealing to the jury's emotions (provoking sympathy); bringing up secondary arguments that distract the jury; and employing humor so that the crime is taken less seriously." Despite all the preparation for trial by the defense attorney, 90 percent of criminal cases are plea bargained outside the courtroom, thus ensuring that the defendant will not stand trial. Although plea bargaining is often criticized as an unjust process, it has been authorized by the Supreme Court and, although not legitimized in most common law countries, is accepted in practice. Plea bargaining has little importance in civil law countries because a confession of guilt is merely another piece of evidence that does not substitute for trial.

COMPLAINTS ABOUT DEFENSE ATTORNEYS

People in general and criminal defendants in particular cannot understand how attorneys on opposing sides can act impersonally about a court case when court is in session but then are observed socializing with each other in the halls outside that same courtroom. What observers do not understood is that defense attorneys, along with prosecutors, trial judges, clerks of court, bailiffs, and court reporters, are part of a stable work group that meets on a fairly regular basis; thus, group norms are promoted that establish friendly relations among the participants, at least in the United States. Studies of the courtroom work group have shown that cohesive work groups promote cooperation, typified by a high level of plea bargains, rather than the conflict expected of an adversary system.

The defense attorney in the United States has been criticized for promoting the work group's organizational goal of efficiency of resources instead of the defendant's desire for exoneration, because the attorney is an integral part of this courtroom work group. Blumberg (1979: 246) accuses the defense attorney, whether public defender or privately retained, of acting as a "double agent, serving higher organizational rather than professional ends. The lawyer-client confidence game . . . helps to conceal this fact." Casper's (1972) survey of criminal defendants revealed that public defenders were criticized and distrusted more than private attorneys for playing this "game" because they work for the government and lack monetary motivation. Furthermore, Flemming's (1988) survey of defense attorneys found that they believed that clients of public defenders were less willing to accept their authority than were clients of private defense attorneys.

A recent study by the U.S. Department of Justice (Harlow 2000: 1) found that "in both Federal and large state courts, conviction rates were the same for defendants represented by publicly financed and private attorneys . . . However, of those found guilty, higher percentages of defendants with publicly financed counsel were sentenced to incarceration." Champion (1996) concluded from his similar study that private attorneys' cases end in probation more often than public defenders' cases because the attorneys are more willing to engage in plea bargaining with prosecutors and vice versa. He further concluded that, although both public defenders and private defense attorneys are obligated to take care of their clients, the latter are more motivated to work out plea bargain arrangements with prosecutors because they are paid directly by their clients and have a greater attachment to them.

Criminal defendants who have been treated unjustly by their defense attorneys have two primary options against the attorneys. First, every state has an agency responsible for disciplinary actions against attorneys. After a complaint is made, an investigation and hearing may be conducted by the agency. If the agency finds the accused attorney guilty of wrongdoing, then the agency can recommend disciplinary action ranging from private reprimand to permanent disbarment, which means the attorney may no longer practice law. In the end, the Supreme Court of that jurisdiction makes the final decision as to the appropriate disciplinary action. Second, a criminal defendant wronged by a defense attorney can file a malpractice civil suit. If the client can prove with a preponderance of the evidence that his or her attorney was incompetent or was dishonest, then the client may receive monetary compensation from the attorney. Further, a new criminal trial may result from a separate appellate hearing if it is found that the criminal defendant's attorney acted either dishonestly or incompetently in the case.

The U.S. Supreme Court in 1932 interpreted the Sixth Amendment to guarantee a criminal defendant the right to "effective" counsel, but it did not define what that term means. Both state and federal lower courts embraced a "mockery of justice standard," under which "only circumstances so shocking that they reduced the trial to a farce satisfied defendant's claims of ineffective representation" (Samaha 1999: 542). Most jurisdictions have since rejected this standard, applying instead a "reasonably competent attorney standard," wherein a judge compares the lawyer's performance to how a reasonably competent lawyer would act for a client under similar circumstances. If the lawyer is found lacking in the comparison, then the criminal defendant gains a new trial, or the plea bargain is set aside because of ineffective counsel.

The defense attorney is a cornerstone of the adversary system of justice and, unlike the prosecutor, is under no obligation to determine guilt or innocence of the criminal defendant. "The attorney for the accused has a singular purpose: as an advocate, he or she must use every lawful means to exonerate or, failing that, to mitigate punishment" (Abadinsky 1991: 196). On the other hand, defense attorneys in some totalitarian countries are responsible for determining the defendant's guilt and, if so, then seeking the best punishment that will rehabilitate the offender.

Monetary gain is usually not the main motivation for criminal defense attorneys in the United States because criminal law is not very lucrative compared to other fields of law. Rather, motivation may be political because wide publicity often surrounds criminal cases. Or, the motivation may be the meaningful work. As Weston and Wells (1987: 12) surmise, "Or it may be some combination of these motives. In any case, it must be a strong urge because the work is hard, and the demands for excellence are very great."

—Gregory P. Orvis

See also ADVERSARIAL JUSTICE; APPEAL/APPELLATE; COMMON LAW LEGAL TRADITION; CRIMINAL DEFENSES; CRIMINAL INSANITY; CRIMINAL LAW; DUE PROCESS; PLEA BARGAINING; PUBLIC DEFENDER

Further Reading

Abadinsky, Howard. (1991). *Law and Justice: An Introduction to the American Legal System.* Chicago: Nelson-Hall.

Baum, Lawrence. (1990). *American Courts: Process and Policy.* Boston: Houghton Mifflin.

Blumberg, Abraham. (1979). *Criminal Justice: Issues and Ironies.* New York: New Viewpoints.

Calvi, James V., and Susan Coleman. (1989). *American Law and Legal Systems.* Englewood Cliffs, NJ: Prentice Hall.

Casper, Jonathon D. (1972). *American Criminal Justice: The Defendant's Perspective.* Englewood Cliffs, NJ: Prentice Hall.

Champion, Dean J. (1996). "Private Counsels and Public Defenders: A Look at Weak Cases, Prior Records, and Leniency in Plea Bargaining." In *Criminal Justice: Concepts and Issues,* edited by Chris W. Eskridge. Los Angeles: Roxbury, 173–183.

Clynch, Edward J., and David W. Neubauer. (1994). "Trial Courts as Organizations: A Critique and Synthesis." In *The Administration and Management of Criminal Justice Organizations: A Book of Readings,* edited by Stan Stojkovic, John Klofas, and David Kalinich. Prospect Heights, IL: Waveland Press, 51–69.

Flemming, Roy B. (1988). "Client Games: Defense Attorney Perspectives on their Relations with Criminal Clients." In *Criminal Justice: Law and Politics,* edited by George F. Cole. Pacific Grove, CA: Brooks/Cole, 228–252.

Harlow, Caroline W. (2000). *Bureau of Justice Statistics Special Report: Defense Counsel in Criminal Cases.* Washington, DC: U.S. Department of Justice.

Holten, N. Gary, and Lawson L. Lamar. (1991). *The Criminal Courts.* New York: McGraw-Hill.

Holman, John E., and James F. Quinn. (1996). *Criminal Justice: Principles and Perspectives.* St. Paul, MN: West.

Jacob, Herbert. (1978). *Justice in America: Courts, Lawyers, and the Judicial Process.* Boston: Little, Brown.

Neubauer, David W. (1999). *America's Courts and the Criminal Justice System.* Belmont, CA: West/Wadsworth.

Reichel, Philip L. (2002). *Comparative Criminal Justice Systems: A Topical Approach.* Upper Saddle River, NJ: Prentice Hall.

Samaha, Joel. (1999). *Criminal Procedure.* Belmont, CA: West/Wadsworth.

Schmalleger, Frank. (2001). *Criminal Justice Today.* Upper Saddle River, NJ: Prentice Hall.

Terrill, Richard J. (1999). *World Criminal Justice Systems.* Cincinnati, OH: Anderson.

Weston, Paul B., and Kenneth M. Wells. (1987). *The Administration of Justice.* Englewood Cliffs, NJ: Prentice Hall.

Court Cases

Argersinger v. Hamlin (1972). 407 *U.S* 25.
Gideon v. Wainwright (1963). 372 *U.S* 335.
Johnson v. Zerbst (1928). 304 *U.S* 358.
Powell v. Alabama (1932). 287 *U.S* 45.
United States v. Wade (1967). 388 *U.S* 218.

▼ DEFENSIBLE SPACE

See ENVIRONMENTAL DESIGN; GATED
COMMUNITIES; PUBLIC HOUSING

▼ DELINQUENCY

Juvenile justice began in the United States on the last day of the 1899 session of the Illinois legislature, when that body passed the Juvenile Court Act. This comprehensive law created a juvenile court in Illinois and gave it jurisdiction over delinquent, dependent, and neglected children. Although other states had adopted various procedures and regulations to deal with socially deviant and troubled youth, the Illinois Juvenile Statute of 1899 represented the first attempt at establishing a separate system of juvenile justice. Other states quickly followed the Illinois lead, and by 1925 all but two states (Maine and Wyoming) had established juvenile courts. Juvenile courts were officially established in Canada in 1909, the first in Winnipeg, in accordance with the National Juvenile Delinquent Law.

The philosophy underlying the Illinois Juvenile Court Act was that juvenile offenders should not be given the same punitive treatment as adults, but rather be given individual attention for their own protection, as well as that of society. The Illinois juvenile statute had four essential features: It refined the definition of delinquency; removed juveniles from the jurisdiction of the adult criminal courts; authorized the placement of juveniles in separate facilities from adult offenders, for limited periods of time; and provided for a system of probation, allowing the state to supervise the child outside the confinement of an institution.

Since the Juvenile Court Act, the U.S. Supreme Court has further defined the procedural requirements that the judiciary must follow in adjudicating juvenile offenses. *Kent v. U.S.* (1966) was the first case in which the Supreme Court extended limited due process guarantees to juveniles. Perhaps more important, in *Kent* the Court signaled its disenchantment with the operation of juvenile courts as they then existed:

> Juvenile Court history has again demonstrated that unbridled discretion, however benevolently motivated, is frequently a poor substitute for principle and procedure. . . . The absence of substantive standards has not necessarily meant that children receive caring, compassionate, individualized treatment. The absence of procedural rules based upon Constitutional principle has not always produced fair, efficient, and effective procedures.

The second landmark decision was *In re Gault*, in which the Supreme Court ruled that juveniles appearing before a juvenile court have four constitutional rights: to adequate written notice of the charges against them, in order to afford them a reasonable opportunity to prepare a defense; to the assistance of counsel and, if indigent, to the appointment of counsel; to invoke the privilege against self-incrimination; and to confront and cross-examine witnesses. In 1970, the Court in *In re Winship* held that before a juvenile may be adjudicated delinquent there must be proof beyond a reasonable doubt of every fact necessary to constitute the offense with which he or she is charged. Until *Winship*, juvenile courts routinely found delinquency on the basis of less stringent standards. Several other Supreme Court decisions further defined the constitutional rights of juveniles and the inadequacies of juvenile courts.

Juveniles have also been the focus of congressional initiatives. In 1974, following more than a decade of hearings on juvenile crime, courts, and institutions, Congress passed the Juvenile Justice and Delinquency Prevention Act (JJDPA). As the name suggests, its basic philosophy was preventive and it contained a broad mandate for reform. The intent was to deinstitutionalize status offenders (i.e., incorrigibles, truants, runaways), provide alternatives to incarceration for less serious youthful offenders, provide additional funds to localities to improve delinquency prevention programs, establish a federal assistance program to deal with the problems of runaway youth, and ensure that juveniles would not be detained in the same facilities as adults. The JJDPA altered the course of juvenile justice more than any other legislation since the Illinois Juvenile Court Act.

DEFINITIONS

Delinquency is both a legal and social term. Legally, the term is defined as behavior against the criminal code committed by an individual who has not reached adulthood, as defined by state or federal law. In some states, the legal definition includes status offending, which is behavior prohibited only for juveniles, such running away, violating curfew, or truancy. Because status offenses lend themselves to so much subjectivity, it has been argued that they should be removed from the purview of state juvenile courts, and in fact some states have moved in this direction in recent years.

Essentially, a juvenile delinquent is one who commits an act defined by law as illegal and who is adjudicated delinquent by the appropriate court. Although the legal definition is usually restricted to persons under age eighteen, the age varies by state. Under federal law, juveniles may be prosecuted as adults at age fifteen. A handful of states give criminal courts, rather than juvenile courts, automatic jurisdiction over juveniles at age sixteen. However, all states allow juveniles—some as young as seven (New York)—to be tried as adults in criminal courts under certain conditions and for certain offenses.

Social definitions of delinquency include a wide variety of youthful behaviors deemed inappropriate by society but that may not come to the attention of the police. Mental health professionals, for example, have a range of diagnostic labels that qualify as social definitions, running from conduct disorder and antisocial behavior to the more common "troubled youth." The act—delinquency—is the behavior that violates the criminal code, whereas a delinquent is a youngster who deviates from prescribed social norms. However, a youth who commits a delinquent act is not necessarily labeled a delinquent. Usually, the label is reserved for those who commit a series of delinquent or antisocial acts, often serious ones.

THE NATURE AND EXTENT OF DELINQUENCY

During the last quarter of the twentieth century, it was common to read accounts of skyrocketing juvenile crime, young superpredators, declining youth morality, and the woeful state of family life, the latter of which was seen as a major contributor to juvenile vandalism, drug use, crime, and violence. Most of these accounts were overreactions; data demonstrate that the media alarm was largely unjustified. This is especially true for school violence, where the media and the public have largely overreacted to school shootings in recent years. School shootings are traumatic events for those involved, but are relatively rare, especially considering the millions of children who attend schools across the nation every day.

The nature and extent of juvenile delinquency—both reported and unreported—is essentially an unknown area. Although official statistics are collected by law enforcement agencies (including the Department of Justice), the courts, and facilities for delinquents, these official data are often incomplete, and may not reflect the actual number of juvenile offenses. Unofficial crime statistics are data published by private organizations or independent researchers. Self-report data, for example, involve having juveniles in the general population reveal the extent of their own misconduct. Instead of relying on biased or incomplete official records, researchers obtain information from a random sample of youth who report their own norms and law violations. Another type of unofficial data is victimization surveys, in which victims are asked about the nature of the crime they have experienced. Because it is often difficult for victims to provide accurate estimates of the age of offenders, these data are usually not used in estimations of juvenile crime.

The most widely cited official statistics are the FBI's Uniform Crime Reports (UCR), which include law enforcement data on reported crime and juvenile arrests. According to these data, juvenile crime—particularly violent crime—peaked in 1994 and has been decreasing steadily since. After more than a decade of increases, for example, homicide by juveniles dropped by 17 percent in 1995, and has continued to decrease. In 2000, the juvenile arrest rate for violent crime was 36 percent below its 1994 peak, and the juvenile arrest rate for murder its lowest since the 1960s (Snyder 2000).

Gender Differences

It is well established that boys commit far more juvenile crime, particularly violent crime, than girls. Victimization data, self-report data, and official data all support this gender gap in juvenile offending. Boys are so overrepresented in violent crime (approximately an 8 to 1 ratio) that some theorists have suggested that hormonal and biological factors are the most logical explanation for this difference (Wilson and Herrnstein 1985). The most recent data on juvenile arrests suggest, however, that the gender gap is closing. Between 1990 and 1999, arrests of juvenile females generally increased more (or decreased less) than male arrests in most categories (Snyder 2000). In 1999, girls accounted for 17 percent of juvenile arrests for violent crime, which approaches a 6 to 1 male-to-female ratio. Females also accounted for 22 percent of arrests for aggravated assault and 30 percent of arrests for simple assault, a significant increase compared to previous data.

Research is beginning to shed some light on the reasons for gender differences in crime and delinquency, and it is clear that biology is not the primary—or even a significant—factor. Recent research indicates that there are social and cultural differences in the way boys and girls perceive and deal with the world. Social learning theorists have long held that girls are socialized differently than boys, and are usually taught not to be overly aggressive. Anne Campbell (1993: 10), for example, contends that "boys are not simply more aggressive than girls; they are aggressive in a different way." According to Campbell, boys and girls are born with the potential to be equally aggressive, but girls are taught not to be physically aggressive, whereas boys are often encouraged to aggressively defend their rights.

Girls are consistently taken into custody by police for status offending (particularly running away and curfew violations) far more often than boys. The primary explanation for frequent running away by girls is emotional, physical, or sexual abuse in their homes. In one study, for example, 92 percent of juvenile runaways reported that they had been subjected to some form of abuse prior to running away (Acoca and Dedel 1998).

▼

Delinquency and Problems at Home

People who come into contact with delinquent youth have long known that problems at home make children and adolescents especially vulnerable to becoming involved in delinquent behavior. The following extract from a 1924 Pittsfield, Massachusetts, annual police report indicates that this is a problem the police have always had to deal with.

Many times during the past year, the careless parents have been forcibly brought to our attention from a new angle.

Young girls from sixteen to twenty years of age have come into the office for protection and advice. To find any good home that any reasonable person could recommend in order to get away from a jealous mother or petty fault-finding, nagging, disagreeable parents; from a home of discord and quarrelling. In some cases, young girls were nervous wrecks, were attended by physicians or sent to hospitals and taken to the home of a kind hearted relative. In other cases we found children ashamed of their parents. In other cases we found men driven from their homes by their fathers, who thought that the boy should have an old head on young shoulders. They didn't want them to enjoy the decent pleasures of their youth but to turn over to the parent their wages to support young children and to pay for the home. In many cases the Golden Rule could have easily been worked out.

The hardest cases are where the mothers are jealous of their own daughters' good looks and clothes and insisted that the young girls wear old-fashioned clothes; allowed them to go no-where and saw that they, the mothers, received the attention first, from their daughter's boy friends.

It is only fair that the boy and girl of eighteen to twenty-one has a right to live and to make for themselves a place in the civic life of our city; to work out in their own way an honest career, the work that they love and admire, without the unreasonable fault finding of their parents. Some parents, I am sorry to say, do not think, they throw away the love and respect of their own children by slandering them, injuring their character in the eyes of their police officers.

When you try to solve a problem of trouble in the home, between parents and children or vice-versa, it seems sometimes to be beyond human judgment. Such are some of the hardest cases the police as peace officers, have to solve.

Source: *Annual Report of the Police Department of the City of Pittsfield For the Year Ending December 31, 1924.* (1925). Pittsfield, MA: Ben Franklin Press.

The Nature of the Offenses

Both self-report studies and official data indicate that only a small percentage (8 to 12 percent) of the juvenile population engages in serious delinquent behavior, and that frequent offenders do not specialize in any one kind of offense. Instead, they tend to be involved in a wide variety of offenses, ranging from minor property crimes to highly violent ones. Research that focuses on following juveniles across their life span indicates that repeat offenders as a group are unusually troublesome in school, earn poor grades, and have inadequate social skills. Furthermore, their antisocial behavior begins at an early age, and the more serious the offender, the earlier this antisocial behavior appears, sometimes as early as age three.

Juvenile drug offending can be viewed from two perspectives: (1) the use, sale, manufacture, distribution, and possession of an illegal drug and (2) the pharmacological effects of certain drugs on behavior. Research directed at the latter has shown that drugs by themselves rarely cause crime, and consequently does not receive much attention in the literature. The vast majority of drug crimes are of the former variety: Juveniles are especially prone to buy, possess, and use drugs of all types. Over one-third of U.S. citizens aged twelve or older report use of an illicit drug at least once during their lifetime (Office of National Drug Control Policy 1999c). The 1998 Monitoring the Future Study reported that nearly 50 percent of high school seniors had used marijuana at some point in their lives, and 38 percent had used the drug during the past year. In more recent years, "club drugs" or "rape drugs" have become popular among teenagers. Examples include Ecstasy, commonly used at all-night dance parties (raves), and GHB (gamma hydroxybutyrate) and rohypnol, which are taken to produce a rapid state of intoxication. Perhaps the most tragic aspect of drug abuse by juveniles is the number of young persons who die or suffer significant trauma from misuse of illicit drugs each year (e.g., 16,000 in 1999. According to the U.S. Department of Justice, the recent availability of high purity, low cost drugs has led to widespread drug experimentation among middle school and high school students (Federal Bureau of Investigation 1999).

GANGS

No national data are collected on the number of gangs or gang members, nor is there national information on the characteristics of gangs. Although an increasing number of government agencies collect gang-related statistics, there is very little consistency or uniformity. Despite these limitations, the number of gangs in the United States is estimated to be at least 5,000, with a membership well over 250,000 (Snyder and Sickmund 1995).

Classical theories on juvenile gangs suggest that youths form or join gangs in response to being denied opportunities in middle-class society. One the major problems with these theories, however, is that they assume that youth gangs are homogeneous. While these observations have some validity, youth gangs are far more complex and varied then originally supposed. Gangs vary widely by ethnic diversity, age, gender, class, geography, purpose, and a constellation of other variables.

CAUSES OF DELINQUENCY

Many theories and explanations have been offered for the causes of delinquency, but few have been supported by research. One of the major inadequacies of most theories is that they are not broad enough to account for the many factors researchers now realize are involved in the development of delinquency. Researchers can now point with confidence to a large list of risk factors or potential causes associated with juvenile delinquency. More important, not one single variable on the list is the overwhelming favorite as the primary cause of delinquency. Discrimination, racism, family disruption, unsafe living conditions, joblessness, faulty parenting, poverty, social isolation, peer groups, limited social network systems, and many other influences play significant roles in the formation of delinquency.

Perhaps the most useful observations about juvenile offending have been made by Terrie Moffitt and her colleagues (1993a, 1993b). Moffitt views delinquency as proceeding along at least two developmental paths. On one path, a child develops a lifelong trajectory of delinquency and crime at a very early age, probably around three or even younger: "Across the life course, these individuals exhibit changing manifestations of antisocial behavior: biting and hitting at age four, shoplifting and truancy at age ten, selling drugs and stealing cars at age sixteen, robbery and rape at age at age twenty-two, and fraud and child abuse at age thirty" (1993a: 679). These individuals, who Moffitt calls "life-course-persistent" (LCP) offenders, continue their antisocial behavior in all kinds of conditions and situations. Moffitt finds that many LCP offenders exhibit neurological problems during childhood, such as difficult temperaments as infants, attention deficit disorders or hyperactivity as children, and learning problems in their later school years. Because of their strong aggressive and bullying tendencies, LCP offenders often miss opportunities to acquire and practice normal social and interpersonal skills. Judgment and problem-solving deficiencies are often apparent when the children reach adulthood. Also, LCP offenders generally commit a wide range of aggressive and violent crimes over their lifetimes.

According to Moffitt, the great majority of delinquents begin offending during their adolescent years and stop as they approach adulthood. Moffitt calls these individuals "adolescent-limited" (AL) offenders. Their developmental histories do not demonstrate the early and persistent antisocial problems that the LCP group displays. However, the frequency—and in some cases, the level—of offending during the teen years may be as high as that of LCP youth. In effect, the offending patterns of AL and LCP offenders may be highly similar during adolescence, and they may be difficult to distinguish during that time (Moffitt et al. 1996).

The AL delinquent is most likely to be involved in offenses that symbolize adult privilege and demonstrate autonomy from parental control: vandalism, drug and alcohol use, theft, and status offenses such as running away or truancy. However, AL offenders quickly discover they have something to lose if they continue offending into adulthood. In contrast to the LCP, the AL learns to get along with others, and normally has a satisfactory repertoire of academic, social, and interpersonal skills that enable him or her to get along with others in normal ways.

Research shows that the earlier the signs of antisocial or delinquent behavior, the more serious or violent the antisocial behavior will become (Tolan and Thomas 1995). In addition, the LCP offender who enters adolescent fully engaged in serious delinquent behavior is the one most resistant to change. Researchers also find that serious delinquent behavior begins to develop at a much earlier age in children living in economically deprived urban neighborhoods than children living in suburban, middle-class neighborhoods (Tolan and Thomas 1995). The conclusions are clear: Living conditions in poor inner-city neighborhoods are extremely harsh, and the daily onslaught of violence, substance abuse, child abuse, and economic hopelessness are highly disruptive to a child's normal development. For the child with an adverse family life, inadequate living standards, and little opportunity to develop even rudimentary social and interpersonal skills, the risk of delinquency is high.

PREVENTION AND TREATMENT

The number of intervention, prevention, and treatment programs directed at reducing delinquency during the past fifty years runs into the thousands. Some experts have been eager to proclaim that treatment has failed to demonstrate success or significant effectiveness in reducing delinquency. While this conclusion may be valid for the treatment of serious, chronic offenders, some intervention strategies for less serious offenders have been successful.

One of the more useful ways of examining prevention and treatment of juvenile delinquency is the Public Health Model, which divides prevention and treatment strategies into three sometimes overlapping categories: primary, secondary, and tertiary (treatment-based) intervention. Primary prevention programs are designed to prevent delinquent or antisocial behavior before it emerges or before a pattern of behavior occurs. Primary prevention programs are usually aimed at the young, preferably before the age of seven or eight. Primary prevention programs are usually found in schools, where there are large groups of young children, all of whom are exposed to the intervention. Examples include Project Headstart, the Perry Preschool Project, and the many school-based programs directed at first and second graders. Secondary prevention programs are directed at children who show some early signs of aggressive or antisocial behavior, but who have not yet been formally classified or adjudicated as delinquent. The purpose of secondary programs is to quell delinquent behavior before it becomes more serious. A well-known example of this preventive strategy is juvenile diversion, a process that steers juveniles away from official court proceedings, offering them a second chance. Diversion is typically restricted to first-time offenders who commit nonviolent offenses, including those associated with drug abuse. The third program, tertiary intervention, is often described as treatment or counseling for already involved delinquents. The distinction between secondary and tertiary prevention is often blurred, however, because both require the identification of at-risk children, and often provide the same services. However, in most instances, the term *tertiary intervention* is reserved for programs designed to reduce serious delinquent or criminal behavior. Tertiary intervention is usually carried out in residential or institutional settings, but some community-based programs have been implemented as well.

Successful prevention and treatment programs appear to have three things in common. First, they begin early—either before or during the first grade. Second, they work with or within the many environments a child faces each day. Third, they focus on the family. Primary and secondary programs often employ all three features and are frequently successful. The tertiary approach has been less successful, primarily because it deals with the serious delinquent who is already fully involved, and most often in restrictive environments, such as residential treatment or incarceration. There are, however, some success stories. Multisystemic therapy (MST) has demonstrated particular effectiveness in dealing with serious juvenile offenders (Henggeler and Borduin 1990; Henggeler,

Melton, and Smith 1992). MST is a treatment approach that focuses on the family while being responsible to the many other influences surrounding the family, such as the welfare system, the neighborhood, and the school.

SUMMARY

A juvenile delinquent is a youth who commits an act defined by law as illegal and who is adjudicated delinquent by the appropriate court. The nature and extent of delinquent behavior—both what is reported and what is unreported to law enforcement agencies—is essentially an unknown area. There simply is not complete data on the national incidence of juvenile delinquency, broadly defined. Even national data on juvenile gangs are lacking. However, research has found gangs are far more complex than originally supposed, and substantially more research is required before firm conclusions on their characteristics and purpose can be advanced. On the other hand, considerable research has been directed at juvenile use of illegal drugs in recent years. The research on juvenile drug use finds the extent of use and the popularity of specific drugs moves in cycles, with the more recent cycle showing so-called club drugs as the most popular.

Although the causes of delinquency are multiple, the majority of juvenile offending falls into two major categories: (1) the adolescent offending group, in which offending is a response to group and social pressure and (2) the life-course-persistent offending group, members of which engage in criminal actions throughout most of their lifetimes. Fortunately, the data also indicate that only a very small number (less than 1 percent of the juvenile population) engage in serious, violent offending. Current interventions are promising for the first group but are less likely to be successful with second group unless started very early and skillfully in an individual's life course. Successful interventions also deal with the many social systems surrounding the child, particularly the child's family.

—Curt R. Bartol

See also BOOT CAMPS; BULLYING; DEMOGRAPHY; FAMILY COURT; FAMILY STRENGTHENING PROGRAMS; GANGS; GRAFFITI; JUVENILE COURT; JUVENILE CRIME AND WAR; JUVENILE JUSTICE; JUVENILE OFFENDERS IN ADULT COURTS; JUVENILE VICTIMIZATION AND OFFENDING; ONLINE VICTIMIZATIN OF YOUTH; SCARED STRAIGHT PROGRAMS; SCHOOL VIOLENCE; STREET YOUTH; STUDENT THREATS; VIDEO AND COMPUTER GAMES; YOUTH, AT-RISK; YOUTHFUL OFFENDER

Further Reading

Acoca, Leslie, and Katherine Dedel. (1998). *No Place to Hide: Understanding and Meeting the Needs of Girls in the California Juvenile Justice System.* San Francisco: National Council on Crime and Delinquency.

Campbell, Anne. (1993). *Men, Women, and Aggression.* New York: Basic Books.

Federal Bureau of Investigation. (1999). *The FBI's National Drug Strategy.* Washington, DC: U.S. Department of Justice.

Henggeler, Scott W., and Charles M. Borduin. (1990). *Family Therapy and Beyond: A Multisystemic Approach to Treating the Behavior Problems of Children and Adolescents.* Pacific Grove, CA: Brooks/Cole.

Henggeler, Scott W., Gary B. Melton, and Linda A. Smith. (1992). "Family Preservation Using Multisystemic Therapy—An Effective Alternative to Incarcerating Serious Juvenile Offenders." *Journal of Consulting and Clinical Psychology* 60: 953–960.

Moffitt, Terrie E. (1993a). "Adolescence-Limited and Life-Course-Persistent Antisocial Behavior: A Developmental Taxonomy." *Psychological Review* 100: 674–701.

———. (1993b). "The Neuropsychology of Conduct Disorder." *Development and Psychopathology* 5: 135–151.

Moffitt, Terrie E. et al. (1996). "Childhood-Onset Versus Adolescent-Onset Antisocial Conduct Problems in Males: Natural History Form Ages Three to Eighteen." *Development and Psychopathology* 8: 399–424.

"Monitoring the Future Study." (1998) http://monitoringthefuture.org

Office of National Drug Control Policy. (1999) "1998 National Household Survey on Drug Abuse." www.whitehousedrugpolicy.gov

Snyder, Howard N. (2000). *Juvenile Arrests 1999.* Washington, DC: Office of Juvenile Justice and Delinquency Prevention.

Snyder, Howard N., and Melissa Sickmund. (1995). *Juvenile Offenders and Victims: A Focus on Violence.* Pittsburgh, PA: National Center for Juvenile Justice.

Tolan, Patrick H., and Peter Thomas. (1995). "The Implications of Age on Onset for Delinquency II: Longitudinal Data." *Journal of Abnormal Child Psychology* 23: 157–169.

Wilson, James Q., and Richard J. Herrnstein. (1985). *Crime and Human Nature.* New York: Simon & Schuster.

Court Cases

In re Gault (1967). 387 U.S. 1.
In re Winship (1970). 397 U.S. 358.
Kent v. U.S. (1966). 383 U.S. 541.

◤ DEMOGRAPHY

Demography is the study of human population. Demography may be defined narrowly as the "study of the size, territorial distribution, and composition of population, changes therein, and the components of such changes, which may be identified as natality, mortality, territorial movement (migration), and social mobility (change of status)" (Hauser and Duncan 1959: 31). A more inclusive definition of the field—sometimes referred to as population studies—emphasizes the interconnections between demographic phenomena, such as fertility, mortality, and migration, and broader social, economic, biological, and psychological forces. Demography is relevant to the study of crime both because population structure and change influence rates of criminal offending and because criminal behavior and aggregate crime rates affect demographic behavior and events.

CRIMINOLOGY AND DEMOGRAPHY

Criminology and demography share several epistemological and scientific characteristics. Social statisticians and theorists of the eighteenth century drew heavily on both criminological and demographic data. In the United States, the Chicago School of the early twentieth century focused primarily on the linkage between population dynamics and deviant behavior. Both criminology and demography have also emphasized geographical variations and aggregate trends and have grounded their studies within a life-course perspective. From a methodological standpoint, both fields have traditionally favored quantitative over qualitative approaches.

The fields of criminology and demography also intersect in more substantive ways. Individual demographic characteristics and aggregate population processes are central to many theoretical perspectives and empirical models of criminal behavior. At the same time, criminal involvement has been shown to have important consequences for the demography of the life course and macro-level population processes.

INDIVIDUAL DEMOGRAPHIC CHARACTERISTICS AND CRIME

The primary demographic characteristics of age, sex, and race are among the most powerful individual-level risk factors for criminal offending and victimization. Evidence indicates that young people, males, and members of disadvantaged minorities are at comparatively high risk of becoming offenders and victims, at least with respect to the common street crimes. Although the general patterns pertaining to these demographic characteristics and crime are well established, controversies about their interpretation persist.

Age

One noteworthy debate surrounds the relationship between age and crime. Criminologists generally agree that criminal offending increases during adolescence and peaks in early adulthood, declining thereafter as people get older. Some have argued that this pattern is universal or invariant. In other words, the general shape of the age-crime relationship is regarded as the same across social status (e.g., gender and race) and across geographical location (e.g., nations). Proponents of the thesis of "age invariance" conclude that the widely observed "desistance" from crime as people age reflects nothing more than the biological aging of the human organism.

Critics of "age invariance," however, have raised several objections. They observe that the age-crime relationship varies for different offenses. They also claim that this relationship has changed over time. In addition, various scholars have claimed that no single age profile adequately describes the offender population; different types of offenders can be identified based on distinctive trajectories of offending.

Another important debate related to age involves the persistence of antisocial behavior over the life span. A well-established finding is that misbehavior in childhood is a powerful predictor of adult deviance and criminality. Two influential interpretations of this relationship have been advanced. One, the latent trait perspective, maintains that the propensity to commit crime is developed at a young age and that this propensity remains reasonably stable throughout life. Continuity in antisocial behavior reflects the stable differences in criminal propensities across individuals.

The other perspective, the life-course perspective, emphasizes developmental processes. When children misbehave at a young age, they elicit social responses that tend to reinforce and accentuate these early behavioral tendencies. This reinforcement leads misbehaving children to engage in deviant and criminal behaviors later in their lives. In contrast with the latent trait perspective, the life-course perspective views the correlation between childhood and adult behavior as far from perfect. Certain life transitions alter and redirect behavioral trajectories. Studies providing rigorous assessments of these approaches are beginning to appear in the research literature.

Sex

The demographic characteristic of sex has also been at the center of much criminological inquiry. As with age, there is virtually universal agreement concerning the general pattern; males are disproportionately involved in crime as both victims and offenders, especially in the more serious, violent offenses. Once again, however, controversies about the nature and interpretation of gender differences in crime persist.

An ongoing debate concerns change in the gender gap in offending. For decades, criminologists have speculated about the implications of greater gender equality for the relative involvement of males and females in crime. One view links higher female offending with more egalitarian gender roles, the so-called dark side of female liberation (Steffensmeier and Allan 1996: 468). Analyzing arrest rates in the United States, researchers have tried to determine if the gender gap has decreased significantly during the decades when gender roles have been changing. With the exception of those arrested for minor property crimes, the percentage of females among arrestees has remained fairly stable.

Another area of special interest in the study of sex and crime has been the adequacy of "gender-neutral" versus "gender-specific" explanations. Do causal processes operate similarly for males and females? The research suggests that, at least for minor forms of crime and delinquency, the predictors of criminal involvement are reasonably similar for the sexes. At the same time, criminologists have documented that the nature of involvement in crime tends to differ for women in comparison with men. Research indicates that females offend in fewer settings and use different techniques than males do. The more serious the offense, the greater are the differences by gender.

Race

The characteristic of race is the most controversial demographic correlate of crime. Official arrest statistics have long suggested that African Americans are overrepresented as offenders and victims for most types of serious crimes. Although some of the racial differences observed in official statistics can be attributed to differential responses by the criminal justice system, criminologists generally agree that there are real racial differences in patterns of criminal offending as well. Race is thus almost always included in models of crime and delinquency.

Traditionally, explanations for racial differences in crime have juxtaposed cultural arguments with social structural arguments. The cultural approaches have pointed to an alleged "subculture of violence" or a "violent contraculture" among African Americans that reflects the legacy of slavery, discrimination, and racism. The most influential structural approaches, in contrast, have identified contemporary socioeconomic disadvantages as the criminogenic forces underlying racial differences in crime.

Proponents of the structural perspective place strong emphasis on the profound racial differences in the larger community context. Specifically, the evidence reveals that the "ecological niches" occupied by whites and blacks tend to be quite disparate. In particular, blacks commonly confront concentrated disadvantage; they are much more likely to live in neighborhoods characterized by the combination of extreme poverty, widespread unemployment and underemployment, and pervasive family disruption. Exposure to this type of community context increases the likelihood of crime, accounting at least in part for observed racial differentials in offending and victimization.

Another distinguishing feature of recent efforts to explain the race-crime relationship is recognition of the interconnections between cultural and structural factors. Ethnographic studies have described how the distinctive structural contexts encountered by blacks foster cultural adaptations that are conducive to widespread crime and violence. For example, the urban ethnographer Elijah Anderson (1994) explains how the disadvantages and social dislocations in contemporary urban ghettos lead to a "code of the streets," the norms of which are at odds with conventional society. Structural disadvantage and concomitant oppositional cultural values operate in tandem to generate racial differences in crime and victimization.

Finally, researchers have become increasingly sensitive to the need to go beyond the simple black/white dichotomy in the study of crime. Research has documented noteworthy differences in the rates of crime and violence between and within various racial and ethnic groups, and it has found considerable change in racial and ethnic differentials over time.

POPULATION STRUCTURE AND CRIME

In addition to describing and explaining the individual-level demographic correlates of crime, criminologists and demographers consider the implications of population structure for levels and patterns of crime and victimization. Differences in population structure can lead to two general types of processes called "compositional effects" and "contextual effects."

Compositional Effects

Compositional effects are consequences of the individual-level correlates of crime. If persons with different demographic characteristics are at higher or lower risk of criminal involvement, then some of the variation in levels of crime across social aggregates (e.g., communities, nations) will be due to differences in population composition, such as the relative size of the respective demographic groups. Accordingly, demographic factors are routinely controlled in aggregate studies of crime.

One technique to adjust for variation in demographic structure is the computation of standardized crime rates. The general logic is to use information on group-specific criminal involvement (e.g., age- or sex-specific offending or victimization) and to estimate the rates that would be observed if all aggregate units exhibited the same, standard population structure. Research has revealed that some of the observed cross-national variation in crime is reduced when variation in age and sex composition is taken into account.

Researchers have also examined the extent to which crime trends can be attributed to changes in population composition, especially age composition, and they have offered forecasts about future trends in crime based on projected demographic patterns. This research has underscored the contribution of the postwar baby boom in the United States to increasing crime rates in the 1960s and falling rates in the 1980s. At the same time, most studies suggest that trends in crime are at best only partly explained by changes in demographic structure.

Another common procedure to accommodate compositional effects is to include measures of population structure in mathematical models of crime rates. Features of population composition such as the sex ratio (the number of men in a locality per 100 women) and the percent of the population in specified age groups are standard control variables in aggregate studies of crime. Interestingly, indicators of age or sex composition do not always relate to crime rates in the predicted manner, suggesting that individual-level and macro-level relationships are not necessarily analogous.

Contextual Effects

In addition to the compositional effects associated with population distributions, demographic structure has been theorized as an important causal factor for crime. From this perspective, features of population structure alter the criminal motivations, the opportunities for crime, and the controls against crime for the population at large. In other words, these explanations emphasize the implications of population structure for the general context in which people act, and as such, they are often referred to as "contextual" explanations.

Perhaps the best-known causal explanation linking crime and population structure is social disorganization theory. Classical social disorganization theory identifies demographic processes and structures such as population growth, population turnover (migration and residential instability), and racial or ethnic heterogeneity as critical factors affecting a neighborhood's capacity to exert informal social control and to limit criminal activity. Social disorganization theory continues to provide a theoretical linkage between features of population structure and crime in contemporary macro-level research.

Another highly influential illustration of the contextual approach to crime is the work of Richard Easterlin on relative cohort size. A cohort refers to people who experience a demographic event, such as birth, at the same time. Easterlin (1987) hypothesizes that members of relatively large birth cohorts are likely to experience less social control in childhood and adolescence because the size of the cohort strains the capacities of institutions of social control. Later in life, members of these large cohorts confront limited economic opportunities due to greater crowding in the labor market. Given the logic of conventional criminological theories of crime that emphasize economic strain and social control, the prediction follows that relatively large birth cohorts will have high crime rates. A sustained tradition of research assessing the Easterlin thesis has developed, with rather mixed results. Nevertheless, the theory continues to inspire inquiry on the criminogenic consequences of varying age distributions.

Several scholars have expanded this theory to encompass an additional feature of age cohorts: the proportion of a cohort growing up in single-parent homes. This attribute of cohorts is expected to be related to criminogenic propensities through two general mechanisms. First, single-parent households are at high risk of poverty, which hinders their capacity to provide valuable resources to their children. Second, because children often have contacts with parents of friends, all children within cohorts characterized by large numbers of single-parent families (not simply those in single-parent families themselves) are likely to encounter less social control and adult supervision.

Consistent with these theoretical arguments, the evidence indicates that an age cohort's percentage of nonmarital births has a significant positive effect on arrest rates for criminal violence. Moreover, these effects persist throughout the life span of members of the cohort.

A final illustration of an explanation of crime that assigns primary importance to contextual effects is the research by Scott South and Steven Messner (1987) on the sex ratio and women's involvement in crime. They argue that the scarcity or abundance of females affects the cultural valuation of women and the emphasis placed on traditional domestic roles for women. These values and roles are expected, in turn, to affect women's rates of victimization and offending and their protection by the criminal justice system. Consistent with theoretical expectations, the evidence shows that the sex ratio is related to the rate of women's property offenses relative to men's and increases in the percent of rape cases solved by the police (an indicator of protection by the criminal justice system).

HOW CRIME AFFECTS DEMOGRAPHY

Although most studies addressing the linkages between crime and demography examine the impact of individual demographic statuses and aggregate population structure on criminal offending and deviant behavior, an emerging body of research has begun to explore how various dimensions of crime and deviance influence demographic outcomes.

Homicide Mortality

Perhaps the most straightforward way in which crime influences demography is that the crime of homicide is, quite obviously, a cause of death. For some demographic groups, homicide is a particularly prominent cause of death that exerts a significant influence on life expectancy. In 1995, homicide ranked among the most important causes of death for young people in general, and was the leading cause of death among both black males and black females ages fifteen to twenty-four. The homicide death rate for black males in this age group was more than double the death rate from the second leading killer, accidents.

Life table analyses of cause-specific death rates show that not only does homicide mortality exert a substantial influence on life expectancy but also race and sex differences in homicide rates account for a signifi-

cant portion of race and sex differences in overall life expectancy. For example, among males, the higher homicide rates for blacks than for whites accounts for about 20 percent of the racial difference in life expectancy at birth. Among blacks, the higher homicide rate among males than among females accounts for more than 15 percent of the sex difference in life expectancy.

Crime, Deviance, and Family Demography

Just as criminological studies have explored the effects of demographic events and statuses on criminal involvement and deviant behavior, a small but developing literature has begun to examine the impact of criminal and deviant behaviors on the occurrence and timing of key demographic events in the life course. Given demography's traditional concern with the timing of such pivotal events as birth, marriage and divorce, death, and other life transitions, it is not surprising that this field was one of the first to embrace the life-course perspective.

Research has examined the impact of marijuana and other illicit drug use on the timing of family-related events, finding that marijuana use during adolescence delays entry into marriage and parenthood and increases the risk of marital dissolution. Moreover, illicit drug use is associated with an increased probability of premarital cohabitation and increases the likelihood that a premarital cohabitation ends in separation rather than legal marriage. Among women, the use of illicit drugs other than marijuana substantially raises the risk of a premarital pregnancy, and drug use increases the likelihood that a pregnant woman will obtain an abortion rather than having a live birth. Alcohol and drug use during adolescence increases the risk of becoming pregnant (or, for males, impregnating a woman) and becoming a teenage parent. In turn, experiencing these life-course transitions prematurely raises the risk of alcohol and drug use in later life.

Other forms of deviant behavior also appear to influence the timing of important demographic transitions in the life course. Gang membership, chronic drug use, and violent criminal offending, for example, all significantly increase the risk of becoming a teenage father. Having suicidal thoughts and running away from home are associated with early marriage and parenthood, perhaps reflecting a latent desire to exit from the role of adolescent.

Crime, Migration, and Residential Mobility

Much of the research examining the impact of crime on demography focuses on the effects of some aspect of criminal activity or victimization on residential mobility, migration, or overall population redistribution. Using survey data, several studies have examined the effect of a person's or household's perceptions of neighborhood crime on the intention to move and actual residential mobility. The evidence is somewhat mixed. In general, the belief that crime is an important neighborhood problem appears to be related to the intention or motivation to move, but perceptions of neighborhood crime do not appear to be a strong or consistent predictor of actual residential mobility. However, households in which a member has been a victim of a crime are significantly more likely to move than households that are free from victimization.

Consistent with the idea that criminal victimization creates dissatisfaction with the neighborhood of residence and, through this, the desire to move, the impact of victimization on subsequent residential mobility is strongest for victimizations occurring in the respondents' immediate neighborhood. But the effect of criminal victimization on residential mobility is weaker than conventional predictors of moving, such as age of the household head, home ownership, and duration of residence.

A more common strategy for examining the impact of crime on residential mobility is to link official crime rates at the neighborhood or city level to aggregate population flows. Early studies in this area were concerned primarily with examining the effect of central city social problems, including crime, on suburbanization and, in particular, "white flight." Although the evidence here is also not entirely consistent, several studies reveal relatively small effects of city crime rates on city-to-suburb population flows and metropolitan deconcentration. High central city crime rates increase white city-to-suburb mobility largely by increasing the likelihood that movers will select a suburban rather than a central city location, instead of by increasing the overall incidence of mobility.

Some observers suggest that high neighborhood crime rates and residential instability may be mutually reinforcing. High rates of crime and violence drive out relatively affluent households, which leads to a weakened tax base, deteriorating institutional structure, and loss of civic leadership, which in turn lead to a further escalation in crime. Crime and class-selective out-migration may thus intertwine in a downward spiral of neighborhood decay.

SUMMARY

The fields of criminology and demography intersect and inform one another at multiple levels. Demographic variables, including age, sex, and race, are indispensable explanatory factors in many models of criminal and deviant behavior, and demographic methods, particularly standardization, are used frequently in criminological research. A growing body of research recognizes the potential for reciprocal effects of crime on demography, underscoring the importance of criminal and deviant behavior for life course transitions and aggregate population processes.

One of the main contributions demography has made to criminology is to underscore the utility of a structural perspective in the study of crime and deviant behavior. Characteristics such as age, sex, and race locate people in social space; these individual attributes give rise to systematic, patterned social relations with others. At the macro-level, demography directs attention to the important ways in which population distributions yield the distinctive contexts in which people commit—or refrain from committing—criminal acts. The demographic emphasis on social structure constitutes an important counterbalance to the reductionism tendencies that periodically surface in criminology.

Criminologists, for their part, alert demographers to behaviors that on the surface might not seem "demographic" but that are relevant to their inquiry. Homicide is a leading cause of death among certain age and race groups, and engaging in, or being exposed to, criminal and deviant behaviors exerts an important influence on the timing and sequencing of key demographic events, such as marriage, childbearing, and residential mobility. At the macro-level, aggregate crime rates appear to be significant instigators of migration and population redistribution. By focusing on trends of criminal behavior, criminology can help expand the scope of potential explanatory variables in models of demographic behavior.

—Steven F. Messner and Scott J. South

See also ETHNICITY AND RACE; FEAR OF CRIME; JUVENILE VICTIMIZATION AND OFFENDING; LIFE-COURSE THEORIES; RACE AND CORRECTIONS; RACE AND POLICING; RACE AND SENTENCING; RACE AND VIOLENCE; RACIAL PROFILING; WOMEN AS OFFENDERS; WOMEN AS VICTIMS

Further Reading
Anderson, Elijah. (1994). "The Code of the Streets." *Atlantic Monthly* 273: 80–94.
Easterlin, Richard A. (1987). *Birth and Fortune: The Impact of*

Numbers on Personal Welfare, 2d ed. Chicago: University of Chicago Press.

Frey, William H. (1979). "Central City White Flight: Racial and Nonracial Causes." *American Sociological Review* 44: 425–448.

Gottfredson, Michael R., and Travis Hirschi. (1990). *A General Theory of Crime*. Stanford, CA: Stanford University Press.

Hauser, Philip M., and Otis Dudley Duncan. (1959). "The Nature of Demography." In *The Study of Population*, edited by Philip M. Hauser and Otis Dudley Duncan. Chicago: University of Chicago Press, 29–44.

Hawkins, Darnell F. (1999). "What Can We Learn from Data Dis-aggregation? The Case of Homicide and African Americans." In *Homicide: A Sourcebook of Social Research*, edited by M. Dwayne Smith and Margaret A. Zahn. Thousand Oaks, CA: Sage, 195–210.

O'Brien, Robert M., Jean Stockard, and Lynne Isaacson. (1999). "The Enduring Effects of Cohort Characteristics on Age-specific Homicide Rates, 1960-95." *American Journal of Sociology* 104: 1061–1095.

Sampson, Robert J., and Janet L. Lauritsen. (1994). "Violent Victimization and Offending: Individual-, Situational-, and Community-level Risk Factors." In *Understanding and Preventing Violence*, vol. 3, edited by Albert J. Reiss Jr. and Jeffrey A. Roth. Washington, DC: National Academy Press, 1–114.

Short, James F., Jr., ed. (1971). *The Social Fabric of the Metropolis: Contributions of the Chicago School to Urban Sociology*. Chicago: University of Chicago Press.

Skogan, Wesley G. (1990). *Disorder and Decline: Crime and the Spiral of Decay in American Neighborhoods*. Berkeley: University of California Press.

South, Scott J., and Steven F. Messner. (1987). "The Sex Ratio and Women's Involvement in Crime: A Cross-National Analysis." *Sociological Quarterly* 28: 171–188.

Steffensmeier, Darrell, and Emilie A. Allan. (1996). "Gender and Crime: Toward a Gendered Theory of Female Offending." *Annual Review of Sociology* 22: 45–87.

Steffensmeier, Darrell, Emilie A. Allan, Miles D. Harer, and Cathy Streifel. (1989). "Age and the Distribution of Crime." *American Journal of Sociology* 94: 803–831.

Stigler, Stephen M. (1986). *The History of Statistics: The Measurement of Uncertainty Before 1900*. Cambridge, MA: Belknap Press.

Thornberry, Terence P., ed. (1997). *Developmental Theories of Crime and Delinquency*. New Brunswick, NJ: Transaction.

Wilson, William J. (1987). *The Truly Disadvantaged: The Inner City, the Underclass, and Public Policy*. Chicago: University of Chicago Press.

Wolfgang, Marvin E., and Franco Ferracuti. (1967). *The Subculture of Violence: Towards an Integrated Theory in Criminology*. London: Tavistock.

▼ DETECTION OF DECEPTION

Detection of deception is a broad term covering a variety of techniques. Many areas of society have an interest in detecting deception: For example, medical personnel, social workers, and mental health workers all interview clients who, for various reasons, may lie or withhold information from the interviewer to conceal the truth. Not surprisingly, detection of deception is a key issue in criminal investigation, although criminal interrogation is not the same thing as interviewing designed to detect deception. Criminal interrogation normally involves a set of circumstances in which the authorities have decided that a specific suspect is the most likely perpetrator of a crime. Interrogation of this sort uses techniques designed to convince the suspect that a confession is an appropriate response to the encounter. Interviewing for purposes of detecting deception often means that there is a group of possible suspects, and the interviewer is attempting to narrow down the possibilities from a majority of innocent people to one or two suspects who may have actually committed a crime. Techniques for the detection of deception fall into two broad categories: those that are psychophysiologically based and those that are not.

PSYCHOPHYSIOLOGICAL TECHNIQUES

The common element of all approaches to psychophysiological detection of deception is the recognition that external stimuli such as verbal questions may induce physiological reactions in the interviewee. These approaches combine practical applications of psychology with practical applications of biology. Hence, the term *psychophysiology* is used.

Polygraph testing is the most widely known of these techniques. During an interview, polygraph instruments make continuous recordings of physiological reactions from the interviewee's autonomic nervous system. The polygraph examiner reviews a short set of questions (about ten) with the examinee prior to putting the instrument attachments on the person for recording the physiological data. The attachments monitor changes of at least three types: changes in respiration during the question set, changes in blood pressure, and changes in sweat gland activity. There are no physiological reactions that the polygraph examiner can specifically associate with the telling of a lie. The reactions being recorded and evaluated are stress or fear reactions caused by what medical experts call the "fight-or-flight syndrome." The autonomic nervous system responds to a perceived threat by rapidly making changes in the body that are somewhat predictable in their form if not in their magnitude. Questions that directly inquire whether the subject has committed the act under investigation (called relevant questions) pose a serious threat to the subject who is lying. Of course, these questions also provoke reactions for the truthful or innocent subject, because of the threat posed by being falsely accused or fear that the examiner may make an error. So, the question set has comparison questions, as well as irrelevant questions, which allow the examiner to distinguish between liars and truth tellers with a high degree of accuracy.

Of the psychophysiological techniques used for forensic detection of deception, polygraph testing is the only one that has been subjected to large-scale scientific scrutiny. Hundreds of studies on the validity and reliability of polygraph testing have been completed, and U.S. government agencies (as well as those in other nations) continue to conduct and contract out additional research. Other techniques, such as computerized voice stress analysis, kinesic interviewing, or scientific content analysis, have yet to establish a body of supporting research to form a scientific basis necessary for expert witness testimony in a courtroom setting

Still, many courts are hesitant to admit polygraph results, for various reasons. The general public, and many lawyers, misunderstand the reluctance of courts to accept polygraph expert testimony and falsely claim that the reason is inaccuracy of the test. However, modern polygraph techniques and equipment can distinguish truth tellers from liars between 95 and 97 percent of the time, whereas eyewitnesses (highly valued by the court) are mistaken more than 50 percent of the time on the average. What judges really fear is that polygraph results might replace the traditional jury function of distinguishing between truth tellers and liars in the trial setting. That would be entirely inappropriate, because our system of government assigns this role to juries, and sometimes to judges.

A technique that appears to the general public to be

An FBI recruit undergoing a polygraph test at the FBI Academy in Quantico, Virginia, showing that the test is used to detect deception in all aspects of criminal justice work.
Source: © Anna Clopet/Corbis; used with permission.

similar to or the same as polygraph testing is voice stress analysis. Instruments such as Computerized Voice Stress Analysis are being marketed to local law enforcement agencies; these use the psychophysiological approach, but measure stress induced by questions only in the voice. These instruments are highly favored by some law enforcement agencies, because they are relatively cheap and require almost no training for the operator. Failing the voice stress test is fairly common, so the procedure puts additional pressure on the guilty to confess—meanwhile increasing stress on the innocent, who are also pressed to confess. As to accuracy, the manufacturer of Computerized Voice Stress Analysis claims high accuracy based on its own research, but rigorous research conducted by the federal government (the Department of Defense Polygraph Institute, or DoDPI) shows an accuracy rate no better than a coin toss for this procedure.

Kinesic interviewing belongs in this grouping of techniques, and is much more widely practiced than polygraph testing, because it can be done without expensive instrumentation. There probably are no more than 3,000 polygraph examiners in the United States, but many thousands of people have been successfully trained in kinesic interviewing—people in law enforcement, in private policing, and in various other professions that require interviewers to make informed

Oaths and Deception

In trials and other sorts of criminal and other proceedings around the world, the oath is commonly used to ensure that the participants are telling the truth. The oath is believed to ensure the truth because it is backed by divine or supernatural authority, which will guarantee that the truth is told or that an untruth will be exposed. The following is a description of the use of the oath in formal proceedings by the Wolof, the Muslim people of Senegal in West Africa.

> Oath is taken on the Koran, after the rites of purification, while standing, and in the presence of only the opposing party and court assessor. It can be administered only to one of the two parties. It is administered to the defendant when he can bring no proof to support his claims. If the defendant refuses to take the oath, it is administered to the plaintiff. The party who takes the oath is deemed to tell the truth.

Source: Fayet, M. J. C. (1939). *Customs of the Wolof Moslem Ouolof (Circle of Baol)*. New Haven, CT: Human Relations Area Files, p 33.

judgments about the truthfulness of their interviewees. The underlying principles of psychophysiology are here the same as for polygraph testing. People being interviewed, if not truthful, perceive a threat, and their autonomic nervous systems generate the same fight-or-flight reactions recorded by polygraph instruments. The interviewer, who does not have a polygraph instrument, can observe some surface manifestations of these involuntary reactions. Posture, involuntary hand and leg movements, eye movement, changes in the size of eye pupils, and many more manifestations of stress can be observed by a skillful and well-trained observer.

Kinesic interviewing involves making decisions as to truthfulness that are based on careful observation of nonverbal behavior, spontaneous verbal responses induced by stress, and typical verbal behaviors in response to structured questions such as, "What do you think should happen to the person who did this?" Interviewees under pressure often volunteer spontaneous verbal responses: Statements such as "as God is my witness," "may lightening strike me dead," "you have just got to believe me," and so on, can be revealing if other kinesic behaviors associated with deception are also occurring during the interview. The interviewer looks for clusters of behaviors associated with auto-

nomic nervous system responses in people who are under stress because they have to lie to protect themselves in an investigation. Structured questions are questions that are known to produce typical answers from truth tellers and from liars. For example, the interviewer may suddenly ask a burglary suspect if there is any reason why his fingerprints ought to have been found on a stolen cash box that has been recovered, when in reality, no fingerprints were found. An innocent person normally can just say "no," but the thief may begin to manufacture several reasons why his fingerprints might have been there if he does not know that no prints were found.

There are scientific journals that publish academic research on nonverbal behavior, but very little of such research is done for the express purpose of developing criminal investigation techniques. Since investigators primarily use kinesic interviewing to quickly eliminate innocent people who are among those having access and opportunity to commit the crime, the technique does not come up as possible trial evidence the way polygraph testing does, and thus does not generally stir controversy.

A relatively new approach to psychophysiological detection of deception is being investigated as an alternative to polygraph testing, and the Central Intelligence Agency (CIA) is especially active in this area. In this approach, similarly to polygraph testing, the external stimuli generated by raising the possibility of a subject's denied involvement in forbidden events evokes physiological responses that are recorded with instrumentation and analyzed to form an opinion as to truthfulness. Called "brain fingerprinting" by some laypeople, it involves scientists recording electroencephalograms (brain wave activity) that occur in response to words or pictures flashed on computer screens monitored by the subjects. These are known as event-related potentials (ERPs), and experimentation is designed to determine if they can be used to discover if a bit of information is stored in a person's memory when he or she cannot recall it. The methodology records processing in the central nervous system by using biopotential electrodes placed on the scalp to register changes in the electroencephalogram. Momentary changes in voltage are digitally sampled and averaged to give a representation of the activity of the person's different brain areas when processing types of stimuli that are presented.

An example of the brain fingerprinting experimental approach can be found in the CIA's interest in locating and identifying spies from foreign governments that have infiltrated U.S. agencies. Assuming that a spy would have had certain formal training that the average person has not had, images flashed on a computer screen in this process could determine if people have that information stored in their brain, even when they do not consciously remember it. By way of testing this premise, researchers selected 100 people, 50 of whom had FBI training, to see if the FBI agents could be identified and separated from the non-FBI agents by the process. The experiment was able to make this distinction without any errors. Much work remains to be done before this technique can routinely be used in investigations, but it is promising. A possible advantage of this technique is the ability, not only to determine the presence of deception but also to determine a motive for lying (a compassionate lie, for example), since different parts of the brain may be involved with different types of lies.

SCIENTIFIC CONTENT ANALYSIS

One other technique should be noted. It does rely on psychological principles, but it does not try to assess psychological reactions to stimuli as do the techniques already discussed. Avinoam Sapir, a former Israeli polygraph examiner, developed a set of protocols for taking a written statement and then analyzing that statement to determine if the writer is hiding information that may be damaging. For some years, Sapir and a number of his disciples have been offering training in the technique, called SCAN, for "Scientific Content Analysis," to both public and private police. While empirical studies on the validity and reliability of the technique are not in evidence, there is a considerable amount of anecdotal evidence indicating that the technique produces good results. It does not involve handwriting analysis (sometimes used as a vehicle of detection of deception), but rather, as the name indicates, it involves analyzing the form and content of the written statement of a subject.

The techniques discussed represent an overview of the best-known forensic approaches to detection of deception currently in use. It is an ever-evolving field in which new techniques and approaches continue to appear periodically.

—Vergil Williams

See also COGNITIVE INTERVIEW; FORENSIC INTERROGATION; FORENSIC POLYGRAPH; INTERROGATION; QUESTIONED DOCUMENTS/INK DATING

Further Reading

Ansley, Norm. (1990). "The Validity and Reliability of Polygraph Decisions in Real Cases." *Polygraph* 19: 169–181.

Driscoll, Lawrence. (1994). "A Validity Assessment of Written Statements from Suspects in Criminal Investigations Using the SCAN Technique." *Law and Order* 17: 77–88.

Link, Frederick, and Glenn Foster. (1980). *The Kinesic Interview Technique.* Anniston, AL: Interrotec Press.

MacLaren, Vance, and Harald Tauklus. (2000). "Forensic Identification with Event Related Potentials." *Polygraph* 29: 330–343.

Matte, James A. (1996). *Forensic Psychophysiology Using the Polygraph: Scientific Truth Verification—Lie Detection.* Williamsville, NY: J. A. M. Publications.

▼ DETECTIVE WORK

The role of the police detective in the United States is a controversial one and is generally not well understood. In the past, American detectives have been criticized for, among other things, abuse of power, corruption, illegal practices, and resistance to change. On the other hand, they also have been praised as heroes, artists, professionals, and scientists. Although detective work has been highly popularized in the fictional literature and the media, empirical research aimed at providing a more accurate portrayal of that role is both limited and outdated.

The investigation of crime is a critical part of the police crime control function, and as the police continue to evolve in American society, understanding what detectives do and how they do it becomes more important. This entry presents a history of the detective role in the United States and then summarizes recent findings regarding the nature of that role. It concludes with a description of a conceptual model for crime and investigation that examines a scenario of what the future may hold for detective work.

HISTORY

In the early nineteenth century, the powerful economic, political, and social forces unleashed by the Industrial Revolution brought with them burgeoning problems of social disorder in the dynamic and expanding society in the United States. Until that time, the investigation of crimes was done mainly by constables and private detectives. However, their efforts were generally limited and ineffective, and the era of modern policing organizations began to emerge. The first metropolitan police department in the United States was influenced

Detective Work–Truth Versus Fiction

This account by Scotland Yard detective Basil Thomson contrasts his actual experiences with those of Sir Arthur Conan Doyle's fictional Sherlock Holmes.

Real life is quite unlike detective fiction; in fact, in detective work fiction is stranger that truth. Mr. Sherlock Holmes, to whom I take off my hat with a silent prayer that he may never appear in the flesh, worked by induction, but not, so far as I am able to judge, by the only method which gets home, namely, organization and hard work. He consumed vast quantities of drugs and tobacco. I do not know how much his admirable achievements owed to these, but I do know that if we at Scotland Yard had faithfully copied his processes we should have ended by fastening upon a distinguished statesman or high dignitary of the Church the guilt of some revolting crime. . . .

The detection of crime consists in good organization, hard work, and luck, in about equal proportions: when the third ingredient predominates the detective is very successful indeed. Among many hundred examples the Voisin murderer had cut off the head and hands of his victim in the hope that identification would be impossible, and he chose the night of an air raid for his crime because the victim might be expected to have left London in a panic; but he had forgotten a little unobtrusive laundry mark on her clothing, and by this he was found, convicted and executed. That was both luck and organization. Scotland Yard has the enormous advantage over Mr. Sherlock Holmes in that it has an organisation which can scour every pawnshop, every laundry, every public-house, and even every lodging-house in the huge area of London within a couple of hours.

Source: Thomson, Basil. (1923). *My Experiences at Scotland Yard.* Garden City, NY: Doubleday, Page & Company, p. 2.

by the police reforms in England in the 1830s. The force was established in New York City in 1845, and the first detectives were officially assigned to that police department in 1858. By 1880, the local governments of most major American cities had created public police forces and detective units.

The primary function of these new police forces was to reduce the widespread civil disorder and urban unrest generated by growth, industrialization, urbanization, and Western expansion. As part of this order maintenance function, the focus of detectives was essentially offender oriented. Their job was mainly to associate with the criminal underworld, either covertly or overtly, to obtain information about criminals and their activities and also to recover stolen property, generally by negotiation with and payment of money to the thieves. Because police and detectives were organized and funded by city governments, their activities were typically heavily influenced by powerful local politicians, and corruption and abuse of authority were not uncommon. This political era of the police continued into the twentieth century.

In the early twentieth century, the broad-based Progressive reform movement in the United States brought about the reorganization and centralization of the police. The resulting reform period "professionalized" the police by reducing political influence, corruption, and power abuse and by increasing police accountability. The manner in which the reforms were implemented emphasized the police crime control function, and the detective was seen as the primary crime solver. But the centralized case assignment and close supervision reforms of this new police management style fundamentally altered the way detectives did their job. Detectives no longer worked at their own discretion mingling among the underworld community. Instead, they worked in offices and spent their time responding to supervisory and administrative directives to investigate crimes that were reported to the police. In other words, the focus of the detective's tasks evolved from being offender oriented to being case oriented. At the same time, however, the management controls placed on detectives served to restrict their information-collection methods by limiting their contacts with and knowledge of their traditional sources of information in the community.

In the 1960s, amid widespread civil unrest and rising crime rates in urban areas, the police were often viewed by the public as both hostile and repressive, and the "professional" style of police response came under heavy criticism for having isolated the police from the social environment in which they operated. As part of the "Great Society" movement of the 1960s, the U.S. government funded research on this increasing problem of estrangement between the public and the police. This was the first time that extensive empirical research was conducted on policing.

The research found that the public is by far the largest source of crime information for the police; however, the amount of information available about people who commit crimes is mainly a function of the type of crime and the circumstances in which it occurs (i.e., some crimes may involve lots of witnesses and evidence, whereas others may not). For most crimes (i.e., burglaries, larcenies), the amount of information that can be supplied to the police who respond to the scene is very low, and therefore, the capacity of the police to solve these crimes is generally quite limited. As a consequence, the police actually solve only about one-fifth of the serious crimes reported to them, and most of the crimes that are solved are solved because of information provided by victims to the patrol officer who initially responds. Detectives comprise an average of only 17 percent of an agency's sworn officers, and they generally investigate only the more serious crimes. Although their primary investigative task is talking to people, less than one-third of their time is spent actually investigating unsolved cases. One study reported that, on average, 45 percent of a detective's time is spent on noncase activities, 26 percent on postarrest activities, 22 percent on cases that are never solved, and 7 percent on cases that are eventually solved. Overall, the research showed that the case-oriented approach to investigations was relatively ineffective and that the investigative productivity of the police was much more heavily influenced by patrol unit activities and cooperation between citizens and the police than by what detectives do.

In the 1970s, in an effort to decrease public hostility toward the police, some agencies experimented with team policing. Team policing is essentially the assignment of patrol officers and detectives to work together as decentralized teams in neighborhoods to combat crime. However, despite some promising initial results, the approach was virtually abandoned within a few years due to factors ranging from the lack of funding to opposition by middle management. Another approach, called problem-oriented policing, urged officers and detectives to analyze groups of incidents as problems within neighborhoods and to coordinate with public and private community resources to resolve them. Gradually, these and other emerging ideas transitioned into the current community policing (CP) era, in which the police focus on preventing crime by forming close working relationships within the community and by problem solving.

RECENT RESEARCH

Recently, the first nationally representative survey of detective work and the police criminal investigation process was carried out. Its purpose was to collect and describe comprehensive information about police practices, policies, goals, and perspectives regarding the process. The survey included a random sample of general purpose state, county, and municipal police agencies of all sizes in the United States. Of the 3,123 agencies in the sample, 1,746 provided usable responses. These agencies employed more than 50 percent (over 350,000) of the sworn police officers in the United States, and 16 percent (over 50,000) of these were investigators (detectives).

The survey asked about information in six major areas related to investigative work in police agencies: (1) organizational characteristics, (2) the role of patrol officers, (3) the role of investigators, (4) investigation management, (5) investigative support services, and (6) investigative effectiveness. Highlights of the survey findings in each of the six areas are presented next.

Organizational Characteristics

Eighty-four percent of the agencies reported that they employ investigators, and investigators account for 16 percent of the personnel in these agencies. About one-half (56 percent) of the agencies employ female investigators, but very few employ part-time or nonsworn investigators. Centralization, that is, assignment to a headquarters, is the predominant form (83 percent of agencies) of jurisdictional assignment of investigators. In most agencies (67 percent), investigators are generalists (i.e., they investigate all cases) rather than specialists (i.e., they investigate only certain cases). About two-thirds (63 percent) of agencies with investigators assign them to separate organizational units. The three most common types of units are in the person, property, and narcotics crime categories. Most agencies (82 percent) meet regularly with other agencies on investigative matters, and about two-thirds (63 percent) of them are involved in task forces, usually arranged on a multijurisdictional basis. Task forces are targeted primarily against drug-related activities, although they are used for other types of crime problems as well.

The Role of Patrol Officers

Patrol officers typically carry out limited administrative tasks related to investigations, but in more than half of the agencies they also interview victims of and witnesses to crimes. However, interviewing and interrogating of criminal suspects, evidence collecting and processing, coordination with prosecutors, and some proactive techniques are not usually performed by patrol officers. In short, patrol officers generally do not carry out a wide range of investigative tasks.

But there appears to be growing recognition that the patrol officers' role is key to the investigative process because 72 percent of the agencies reported efforts to enhance that role within the past five years. Nevertheless, most agencies do not provide uniformed officers classroom instruction on investigative matters beyond that presented in the basic academy training. In addition, most agencies do not have specific budgets for such training, and most do not specifically evaluate uniformed officers' investigative performance.

The Role of Investigators

Overall, investigators' activities have not been significantly altered by recent changes either in policing or in police organizational developments. The past performance criteria most commonly used to select investigators are those reported to be among the most valid predictors of future performance. However, the selection processes typically used—personal and oral board interviews—are among those reported to be least valid. Only 39 percent of the respondents provide some form of formal training for newly appointed investigators, typically less than two weeks in duration, and 59 percent require at least some refresher or advanced classroom training. This training is usually provided annually, and the types of courses provided are similar whether at the initial stage of appointment or as advanced training.

Although most agencies with investigators (84 percent) rely on funding from their own budgets to support investigative training needs, only 42 percent have a specific budget for such support. Two factors—employee shortage and lack of funding—are seen as significant issues hindering investigative training, and even though training is available from multiple sources, about one-third (32 percent) of police agencies report inadequate access to the training desired.

In about one-half of the agencies, investigators are represented by collective bargaining units; these units most frequently cover salary and promotion. Investigators' positions typically are assigned to either one or two organizational ranks, and upon selection, investigators are automatically entitled to at least one benefit, such as special allowances or a higher pay scale.

Performance evaluation of both investigators and investigative units rests on similar criteria. The top three of these for individual investigators are, in order, investigative success, report writing, and case clearances. When considering unit evaluations, caseload statistics replace report writing in the top three.

Investigation Management

Agencies use similar methods to select both investigators and investigative supervisors. Most agencies follow policies and procedures that allow supervisors to directly influence the investigation process and investigators' activities. Supervisors monitor the status of investigations through regular personal contact, reviews of activity logs, and reviews of investigation reports. In addition, they make decisions regarding what cases to investigate and to whom cases are assigned. Case solvability factors are used to screen cases in about half of the agencies, and typically those factors are applied to all types of cases. In most agencies, investigation reports are prepared and filed on computers, but case management activities are performed manually.

Among the investigations-related problems that agencies identify as significant, the most important ones are the heavy workloads of uniformed officers, investigators, and investigative supervisors. Although most agencies do not assign specific persons to a prosecutor's office, they report having regular meetings and ongoing relationships with prosecutors.

Although most agencies do not have innovative investigative programs, among the 15 percent that do, many cite programs focused on investigation management. Moreover, only a few of the agencies plan major changes in their investigative function in the near future. These changes are related to personnel matters (e.g., employee increases, apparently to address the heavy investigative workload problem) and investigation management. Agencies report that they keep victims apprised of investigative progress; this is especially true with respect to notification of the police disposition of an investigation.

There is broad agreement among agencies that a variety of investigative elements are misrepresented in the popular media. The two elements on which there is the greatest agreement regarding media misrepresentation are the use of excessive force and interrogation.

Investigative Support Services

About one-third of the agencies that employ civilians assign them to investigative support tasks. Most agencies do not employ evidence technicians; however, among those agencies that do, it is typical that such persons are sworn officers who are required to have specialized training.

Most agencies with investigators use state or federal police crime laboratories, but about one-half indicate problems with access to laboratories, and about three-fourths indicate problems with the timeliness of service. Although 33 percent of the agencies said they had cases in which DNA analysis played a critical role, only 9 percent reported a backlog of cases awaiting such analysis. Most (74 percent) agencies receive their automated fingerprint identification service (AFIS) from state agencies. Only about one-half of the agencies with investigators indicate that a number of different types of crime records and investigative support files are available to investigators on computers. Investigators are much more likely than patrol officers to have daily access to various types of modern personal communication devices (pagers, cell phones, e-mail, etc.) for investigative purposes. About one-half of the respondents plan to upgrade their investigative technology resources within the next year.

Investigative Effectiveness

Most agencies consider goals related directly to investigation issues, protecting the public, and recovering and returning property to be slightly more important than those related to keeping victims and the community informed. Twenty-two percent of the respondents experienced a decline in clearance rates for serious crimes in the past ten years. Lack of time, prosecutor reluctance to take action, too many crimes, and lack of witness cooperation were the top four factors said to account for that decline. Across all agencies, increases in employees, technology, and training were the three factors seen as necessary to improve clearance rates. These are the same factors that agencies identified as most in need of additional funding to improve investigative effectiveness overall.

Most agencies did not identify legal issues regarding investigations as important problems. The top two issues—searches and use of informants—were selected by only 7 percent of the agencies. The two research areas identified as those that most directly influence agency policy and/or practice in investigations were computerized databases and forensic science applications. In addition, the two top priorities for future research identified by agencies were technological improvements in investigative techniques and investigator training. These responses are consistent with those given as the primary factors influencing clearance rates and investigative effectiveness.

Overall, the survey findings reveal that in many fundamental respects, the police criminal investigation process, though showing some advances, seems to have been relatively uninfluenced by significant changes in policing, the crime problem, and technological advances made in the past thirty years.

FUTURE DIRECTIONS

Over the past 150 years, three broad social movements in American society have produced massive governmental responses in the form of organizational changes and services, and each of these changes has had profound effects on policing. Social changes brought about by the Industrial Revolution in the nineteenth century led governments to create public police forces to maintain civil order, and detective work in these new organizations was primarily offender oriented. The social reform movement in the early twentieth century redirected the mission emphasis of the police from an order maintenance function to crime control and also reshaped the detective role from an offender orientation to a case orientation. Economic and lifestyle changes, fueled by the civil unrest of the 1960s and the technological and information revolutions of modern society, are pressuring the police function to expand beyond crime control to include community-oriented order maintenance and service-related functions. However, despite its relative ineffectiveness, the police criminal investigation process appears to have not yet been greatly affected by this latest trend.

If the changing social forces in our society prevail as they have in the past, then the predominantly reactive, case-oriented investigative style that the police have practiced since the reform era should eventually evolve into something more closely integrated with the community policing reforms and technological advances that are shaping the police organizations of today. Some insight into the direction in which investigative change may proceed can be obtained by using a model that was developed in the 1980s to describe crime. The model viewed crime as a process consisting of a continuum of five phases. There is first a crime-planning phase and then an action phase wherein the crime is committed. After the action phase, there is an escape phase as the offender escapes from the crime scene. The escaped offender then enters a fugitive phase until he or she is caught or the statute of limitations regarding the crime expires. In addition, in many types of crime there is a disposal phase in which the offender disposes of the fruits of the crime.

Within the framework of this crime continuum model, each phase of an offender's activities can be described in terms of time (the average amount of time an offender may spend in each phase for various types of crimes) and space (spatial areas such as a home, neighborhood, or workplace in which the offender spends time). In addition, the various sources of crime information (people and things) that might be available within the time frames and spatial areas of each crime phase can be inferred.

Using this type of analysis, one can see that for many types of crimes, the typical offender could be expected to spend much more time (months or years) during the fugitive phase in the spatial area of his or her home or neighborhood than in other spatial areas. In addition, although the sources of information regarding a crime (i.e., people who are aware of the criminal's activities or things such as stolen property or other paraphernalia) potentially exist in all five phases, they more likely will exist longer in the criminal's neighborhood than in most other areas. Therefore, an offender's neighborhood can be identified as an important spatial area for crime information. If the offender continues to commit more crimes, then the neighborhood area has the potential to become an increasingly larger repository of crime information (and a more lucrative area for the collection of that information) over time. Importantly, this would be the case for unreported crimes as well as reported crimes.

But by using the crime continuum model to examine the case-oriented approach to solving crime, one can see that the police do not focus on collecting crime information in neighborhoods or other spatial areas associated with an offender's activities in the fugitive phase of the crime. Instead, in most cases the police are notified of a crime while the offender is in the fugitive phase after the action phase and escape phase have passed (the offender has committed the crime, has escaped, and remains a fugitive). The police then respond to the crime scene (the spatial area of the action phase and escape phase) and attempt to collect information about the crime from sources that may still be available there. However, as mentioned, in most cases the amount of information there is quite limited. Nevertheless, unless information regarding the identity of the offender can be obtained from the crime scene area of the action phase and escape phase, the case-oriented investigative approach does not generally extend beyond that point, and the police typically expend minimal effort seeking information that may be available regarding the crime or the offender in other phases.

Community policing, on the other hand, promotes closer working relationships between the police and the community in order to collect and exchange crime information with citizens (the primary source of crime information for police) in an effort to prevent crime, particularly in neighborhoods. As this police-public relationship develops, the opportunity to collect and exchange information with citizens in order to solve crimes could be enhanced as well. To the extent that it occurs in neighborhoods, it may provide the police greater access to information regarding both reported and unreported crimes than may be available in the fugitive phase of offender activities.

Because the police must respond to reports of crime, the case-oriented approach will continue to play a vital role in the investigation process. In addition, the crime continuum model analysis suggests that this traditional approach could be expanded and integrated into the dominant community policing style by enhancing police access to and collection of information in neighborhoods. However, although such a scenario might seem plausible, it is certainly not inevitable.

—Robert T. Meesig,
Yung Hyeock Lee, and Frank Horvath

See also ARREST CLEARANCE; ARREST PRACTICES; CONFESSION; CRIME ANALYSIS; CRIME LABORATORY; CRIME SCENE ASSESSMENT; CRIMINALISTICS; DETECTION OF DECEPTION; FEDERAL BUREAU OF INVESTIGATION; FORENSIC SCIENCE; GEOGRAPHIC PROFILING; HOMICIDE INVESTIGATION; INTERPOL; INTERROGATION; MIRANDA RIGHTS; POLICE STRATEGIES AND OPERATIONS; RACIAL PROFILING; ROYAL CANADIAN MOUNTED POLICE; SCIENTIFIC EVIDENCE; SCOTLAND YARD; SURVEILLANCE ABUSE

Further Reading

Bizzack, John W., ed. (1992). *Issues in Policing: New Perspectives.* Lexington, KY: Autumn House.

Cole, George F. (1995). *The American System of Criminal Justice,* 7th ed. Belmont, CA: Wadsworth.

Eck, John E. (1979). *Managing Case Assignments: The Burglary Investigation Decision Model Replication.* Washington, DC: Police Executive Research Forum.

———. (1983). *Solving Crimes: The Investigation of Burglary and Robbery.* Washington, DC: Police Executive Research Forum.

———. (1992). "Criminal Investigation." In *What Works in Policing? Operations and Administration Examined*, edited by G. W. Cordner and D. C. Hale. Cincinnati, OH: Anderson Publishing, 31–52.

Geller, William A. (1991). "Criminal Investigations." In *Local Government Police Management*, 3d ed., edited by William A. Geller. Washington, DC: International City Management Association, 131–158.

Goldstein, Herman. (1979). "Improving Policing: A Problem-Oriented Approach." *Crime & Delinquency* 25, 2: 237–258.

Greenwood, Peter W., Jan M. Chaiken, and Joan Petersilia. (1977). *The Criminal Investigation Process*. Lexington, MA: D. C. Heath.

Horvath, Frank B. Bucqueroux, and Robert Meesig. (1997). "Community Policing and the Police Criminal Investigation Process." Paper presented at the meeting of the Academy of Criminal Justice Sciences, Louisville, KY.

Horvath, Frank, and Robert Meesig. (1996). "The Criminal Investigation Process and the Role of Forensic Evidence: A Review of Empirical Findings." *Journal of Forensic Science* 41, 6: 963–969.

———. (2001). *A National Survey of Police Policies and Practices Regarding the Criminal Investigation Process: Twenty-Five Years after Rand*. Washington, DC: U.S. Department of Justice, National Institute of Justice.

Kuykendall, Jack. (1982). "The Criminal Investigative Process: Toward a Conceptual Framework." *Journal of Criminal Justice* 10: 131–145.

———. (1986). "The Municipal Police Detective: An Historical Analysis." *Criminology* 24, 1: 175–201.

———. (1989). "The Municipal Police Detective." In *Police and Policing: Contemporary Issues*, edited by D. J. Kenney. New York: Praeger, 88–91.

Langworthy, Robert H., and Lawrence P. Travis III. (1999). *Policing in America: A Balance of Forces*, 2d ed. Upper Saddle River, NJ: Prentice Hall.

Meesig, Robert. (1994). "The Effects of Community Policing on the Processes and Outcomes of Criminal Investigations in Police Agencies in the U.S.: A Literature Review." Unpublished manuscript.

Reppetto, Thomas A. (1978). "The Detective Task: State of the Art, Science, Craft?" *Police Studies* 1, 3: 5–10.

Roberg, Roy, and Jack Kuykendall. (1990). "Police Operations: Patrol and Investigations." In *Police Organization and Management: Behavior, Theory, and Processes*, edited by Roy Roberg and Jack Kuykendall. Pacific Grove, CA: Brooks/Cole, 272–307.

Sherman, Lawrence W., Katherine H. Milton, and Thomas V. Kelly. (1973). *Team Policing: Seven Case Studies*. Washington, DC: Police Foundation.

Skogan, Wesley G., and George E. Antunes. (1979). "Information, Apprehension, and Deterrence: Exploring the Limits of Police Productivity." *Journal of Criminal Justice* 7, 2: 17–241.

Trojanowicz, Robert, and David Carter. (1988). *The Philosophy and Role of Community Policing*. East Lansing: Michigan State University, National Neighborhood Foot Patrol Center.

Walker, Samuel. (1993). "Does Anyone Remember Team Policing? Lessons of the Team Policing Experience for Community Policing." *American Journal of Police* 12, 1: 33–55.

▼ DETERMINATE SENTENCES

The word *determinate* means "with exact and definite limits." Determinate sentencing is defined as a judge sentencing an offender to a fixed prison term, with the sentence closely representing the actual amount of time the offender will serve. Determinate sentencing systems generally provide a provision for early release based on "good time."

The movement toward determinate sentencing arose during the 1960s and 1970s in response to a broad range of concerns about indeterminate sentencing (in which a judge sentences an offender to prison, but the precise amount of time an inmate serves is left to prison officials or a parole board). Chief among these concerns were the potential for discrimination against disadvantaged individuals and the potential for unwarranted leniency in dealing with offenders. Both of these suggest the primary goals of determinate sentencing: to reduce individual discretion in criminal justice decision making and to increase certainty and predictability of punishment. Advocates of determinate sentencing have encouraged both reforms that set specific sentences for specific crimes to sharply reduce judicial discretion, and reforms that eliminate parole boards as a source of discretion. While a majority of states retain predominantly indeterminate sentencing systems, a sizable number have determinate sentencing systems, and most have adopted some elements of determinacy.

ORIGINS

From the late nineteenth century through the early 1970s, all fifty states relied on indeterminate sentencing structures. Under such a structure, judges typically sentenced offenders to either probation or incarceration. For prison sentences, judges did not specify an exact sentence length, leaving the decision about when an offender would be released up to prison officials (thus creating an indeterminate or undetermined sentence). Consistent with the philosophy of the time, this parole decision was based on rehabilitative criteria: whether the offender was reformed and ready to reenter society.

During the 1960s and early 1970s, both conservatives and liberals began to argue for greater determinacy in sentencing. While the latter argued that the unlimited discretion of judges and parole boards led to discrimination against disadvantaged members of society, the former maintained that such discretion allowed judges to be excessively lenient in sentencing offenders. Both sides, though, were in general agreement that the rehabilitative ideal that had led to the development of indeterminate sentencing during the early part of the century was unworkable in practice.

During this time, a series of publications emerged in which academics, legal scholars, and laypeople criticized indeterminate sentencing for allowing biased decision making, violating due process rights, and undermining the deterrent effects of punishment. Among the most important of these were *A Struggle for Justice* (1971), a report written by the American Friends Service Committee (based in part on interviews with convicts), *Criminal Sentences: Law Without Order* (1972), written by Judge Marvin Frankel, and *Doing Justice: A Choice of Punishments* (1976), written by Andrew von Hirsch, a member of the Committee for the Study of Incarceration.

In the Friends' report, the authors argue that the rehabilitative ideal of considering the whole individual in making sentencing decisions encouraged judges and parole board members to consider factors "irrelevant to the purpose of delivering punishment" (1971: 147). The introduction of outside factors—whether race, gender, moral culpability, or family background—introduced the potential for discrimination. Based on this concern, the primary recommendation of the report was that "the law should deal only with a narrow aspect of the individual, that is, his criminal act or acts" (1971: 145). The authors suggested that retribution is a more humane sentencing goal than rehabilitation because it encourages decisions based only on the characteristics of the offense. The hope was to eliminate the abuses that emerge when individuals are free to make decisions based on whatever factors they deem appropriate, without having to justify their decisions.

As the subtitle of his book *Law Without Order* (1976) suggests, Judge Frankel is critical of indeterminate sentencing for its lack of clear guiding principles by which sentencing decisions are made. This lack of guidance, he argues, results in decisions based on personal philosophies regarding the proper goals of sentencing and punishment. Without a clearly understood common goal and consistent standards, there can be no order in sentencing decisions, and without order there can be no justice. Judge Frankel lays out a series of recommendations to lawmakers in the last chapter of his book, including the creation of sentencing guidelines (suggested or mandated penalties for particular offenses) and sentencing commissions to develop and monitor sentencing practices.

Andrew von Hirsch (1976) is also critical of the rehabilitative ideal underlying indeterminacy. He argues that indeterminacy often fails to impose "commensurate deserts" on offenders for any given offense, which he argues should be the guiding principle of sentencing decisions. His premise is that an offender should receive a punishment commensurate with the offense committed, and that any other offender who commits the same offense should receive an identical punishment, regardless of individual characteristics. Von Hirsch suggests that a more equitable and just system will result from basing punishment on past behavior rather than future potential (as in the rehabilitative model), and by ensuring that different offenders committing the same offense receive the same punishments.

USE

Because definitions of determinacy vary, it is impossible to establish with certainty the history and current use of determinate sentencing. Different agencies often quote different numbers when presenting statistics about determinate sentencing. Some states are categorized by some as having determinate sentencing systems, and by others as having indeterminate systems. Determinacy is not an absolute concept; rather, there are varying levels and multiple characteristics of determinacy. Thus a state might be described as more or less determinate, depending on a number of characteristics of its sentencing system.

The two features most commonly used to define determinacy are the abolition of parole and the establishment of sentencing guidelines. By abolishing parole, states can reduce indeterminacy by placing the sentencing decision in the hands of judges. While offenders are generally still eligible for "good time," they go to prison knowing the approximate length of their sentence. Sentencing guidelines reduce indeterminacy by establishing standards for sentencing decisions. While guidelines themselves come in many different forms (e.g., mandatory, presumptive, voluntary), they generally define appropriate sentence lengths based on offense type and an offender's prior criminal history. Because guidelines fix certain punishments to certain offenses, they make punishments more predictable, consistent, and determinate.

In 1975 and 1976, Maine, California, and Indiana became the first states to abolish parole and establish a legislative system for developing sentencing guidelines. These states are generally cited as having the first determinate sentencing structures. In 1978, using the model proposed by Frankel (1972), Minnesota created a determinate sentencing system that relied on a sentencing commission to devise sentencing guidelines and monitor sentencing practices. The federal government also created a sentencing guidelines commission; federal guidelines went into effect in 1987 amid great controversy and have remained controversial to the present day. (For an in-depth history and critique, see *Fear of Judging* by Kate Stith and Jose A. Cabranes, 1998.)

More recently, the "truth in sentencing" movement has emerged in response to pressures for greater determinacy in criminal sentences. Truth in sentencing laws, such as those passed in Arizona in 1980, require that offenders serve a specified amount of the sentence imposed on them by the judge. In Arizona, for example, offenders convicted of homicide, rape, or sexual offenses are legally required to serve 100 percent of their sentences; other offenders must serve at least 85 percent of their sentences.

In a 1996 survey of state sentencing structures, the Bureau of Justice Assistance classified fourteen states as having determinate sentencing structures (based on whether or not the state had abolished parole): Arizona, California, Delaware, Florida, Illinois, Maine, Minnesota, Mississippi, New Mexico, North Carolina, Ohio, Oregon, Virginia, and Washington. Some of these have sentencing guidelines; others do not. The report notes that even in states with indeterminate sentencing structures, sentences are becoming increasingly determinate through the development of truth in sentencing provisions, mandatory minimums, and the increased regulation of parole decisions.

SUCCESSES AND FAILURES

Determinate sentencing directly affects the size and growth of prison populations and a state's ability to control these factors. In considering the impact of determinate sentencing on prison populations, two main themes emerge: (1) the ability to predict and control prison population growth and (2) the widespread increases in prison populations due to long sentences. It is clear that determinate sentencing states gain some control over the growth of their prison populations. Under indeterminate sentencing systems, sentences are by definition unpredictable. With fixed sentences, state legislatures and sentencing commissions can predict and manage prison populations and their growth.

Determinate sentencing, however, can have a huge impact on prison growth, particularly in states where the legislature determines appropriate sentences. If sentences are fixed at a relatively high level—as often happens in politicized situations—determinate sentencing may lead to overcrowding. While many of the original proponents of determinate sentencing had hoped that it would lead to shorter prison sentences and a diminished use of incarceration, this does not appear to have occurred in most jurisdictions.

Two related concerns that are specific not to determinate sentencing, but rather, to sentencing guidelines and mandatory sentencing, are the success of determinate sentencing in reducing racial, ethnic, and gender punishment disparities, and the displacement of discretion from judges and parole boards to prosecutors.

Research on disparities is difficult to summarize, because sentencing systems vary greatly among states, research methodologies vary greatly among studies, and it would be impossible to definitively attribute either an increase or a decrease in disparities to determinate sentencing. A substantial number of studies have concluded either that minimal disparities existed before the change to determinate sentencing, or that the introduction of determinate sentencing has reduced disparities to some degree. However, researchers frequently find that in states that have sentencing guidelines, disparities are most apparent in judicial departures from these guidelines. That is, in cases where judges take exception to guideline recommendations, whites and females are more likely to get reduced sentences, while minorities and males are more likely to get increased sentences.

Finally, there has been some concern that discretion removed from judges may simply shift to prosecutors. Because charging decisions directly affect sentencing decisions, when laws exist that circumvent sentencing decisions, prosecutors can determine sentencing outcomes through initial charging practices and plea bargaining. There is some evidence that this occurs, particularly in states with "three strikes" laws. Where criminal justice personnel view particular sentences as extreme, they may find ways to manipulate charges so that those outcomes are avoided. Discretion is not eliminated, but simply shifts elsewhere.

—Sara Steen

See also GET-TOUGH INITIATIVES; INDETERMINATE SENTENCES; MANDATORY SENTENCING

Further Reading

American Friends Service Committee. (1971). *Struggle for Justice.* New York: Hill & Wang.

Bureau of Justice Assistance. (1996). *National Assessment of Structured Sentencing.* Washington, DC: U.S. Department of Justice.

———. (1998). *1996 National Survey of State Sentencing Structures.* Washington, DC: U.S. Department of Justice.

Frankel, Marvin E. (1972). *Criminal Sentences: Law without Order.* New York: Hill & Wang.

National Institute of Justice. (1984). *Determinate Sentencing and the Correctional Process.* Washington, DC: U.S. Department of Justice.

Stith, Kate, and Jose A. Cabranes. (1998). *Fear of Judging: Sentencing Guidelines and the Federal Court.* Chicago: University of Chicago Press.

Tonry, Michael. (1999). "Reconsidering Indeterminate and Structured Sentencing," Papers from the Executive Sessions on Sentencing and Corrections. Washington, DC: U.S. Department of Justice.

Von Hirsch, Andrew. (1975). *Doing Justice: The Choice of Punishments.* New York: Hill & Wang.

▼ DETERRENCE THEORY

Deterrence is the straightforward, common-sense notion that if you do something wrong, you will be punished, and the punishment itself will prevent you from doing that wrong thing again. According to this notion, fear of a future punishment dictates the actions people choose. This way of thinking is commonplace, and it underpins much—if not most—political discourse and public policy debate. Moreover, it is a mainstay of American foreign military policy, implying to potential enemies that the wrong actions they take will incur the wrath of American military might.

Deterrence also plays a very important role in criminological empirical research. Empirical research in the area of deterrence is well elaborated in modern criminology. That research seeks to determine the accuracy of assumptions about deterrence and its effectiveness. Furthermore, it examines criminal punishment policy to see how adjusting levels and types of punishment practice may alter it to lower crime. Unfortunately, the production of reliable and valid empirical knowledge is a slow and laborious process. While criminology has begun that process in the area of deterrence, it has no final, definitive conclusions for the following core questions: (1) whether, when, and how deterrence "works" on the decision-making processes of individ-

ual human beings and (2) how to implement a public policy that affects individual choices to commit or not commit criminal acts.

BUILDING A FOUNDATION FOR MODERN DETERRENCE THEORY

Three early philosophers have helped develop key ideas that lie at the foundation for modern criminological deterrence theory. They are Thomas Hobbes (1588–1679), Cesare Beccaria (1738–1794), and Jeremy Bentham (1748–1832).

Thomas Hobbes

In 1651, Thomas Hobbes wrote *Leviathan,* an influential book on human nature and its relationship to human organization and government. Like many others, Hobbes assumed that the human being is by nature competitive, distrustful, and engaged in an endless search for his or her own personal glory. This account of the human individual leads to the famous Hobbesian question: How can social order possibly exist? In addition, how, when humans gather together, can war or conflict be avoided? Finally, how can people avoid lives that are "solitary, poor, nasty, brutish, and short?" Somehow, though, citizens in some modern, developed countries do avoid this condition; they do so by establishing a social contract. This contract serves to help constrain those potentially disastrous natural characteristics for the good of all but also for individual good. People sacrifice some of the free reign that they might allow their individual natures in the interest of saving themselves; they do so by voluntarily joining in the social contract. Two important aspects of this social contract are the rules with which each person must abide and the punishments for violating those rules. In Hobbes's view, deterrence is simply the reason why one human being or group of human beings in a social contract punishes another, to save and keep the social contract viable and healthy.

Cesare Beccaria

Beccaria's *Crimes and Punishments,* first published in 1764, helped set in motion a change toward more humane punishment practices. This change was a slow evolution that finally took effect in most civilized societies by roughly the middle of the nineteenth century. Prior to that time, extreme and brutal physical punishments—even for the most minor of crimes—were the standard. Beccaria elaborated two very important aspects of punishment, proportionate punishment and the intended objects of punishment. "The object . . . of punishment is simply to prevent the criminal from injuring anew his fellow-citizens, and to deter others from committing similar injuries; and those punishments and that method of inflicting them should be preferred which, duly proportioned to the offence, will produce a more efficacious and lasting impression on the minds of men and inflict the least torture on the body of the criminal" (Beccaria 1880: 165–166).

The first idea—proportionate punishment—was, at the time Becarria wrote, quite radical and controversial. Becarria emphasized that the type of punishment should be calibrated to the type of offense; stealing a loaf of bread should not warrant capital punishment. Earlier, punishment had been anything but proportionate. By 1760 in England, for instance, there existed 160 capital crimes—those requiring death as the punishment. By 1819, that number had increased to 223 acts punishable by death. The work of Becarria and others helped bring about the humane reform of punishment by encouraging the application of rational criteria in the application of punishment. Foucault labeled this newly emerging period the Age of Sobriety, in which the object of punishment was no longer the body of the accused but, instead, the soul (Foucault 1979: 7–16). The Age of Sobriety replaced the punishment-as-spectacle period, during which the punishment and mutilation of the physical body of the offender, especially in the presence of the general public, was commonplace. (See, for instance, the disturbing account of a 1757 French execution in Foucault 1979: 3–6.)

Beccaria's second idea regarding the intended objects of the punishment is fundamental to modern criminological sciences. In the parlance of modern criminology, the term *specific deterrence* denotes that effect of punishment acting upon the individual who originally committed the offense. If a punishment specifically deters, it prevents that wrongdoer from repeating the offense. The term *general deterrence* designates the punishment's effect upon the general public. If that public sees or hears of the punishment rendered for misbehavior, this knowledge will deter other citizens from committing the similar offenses.

Jeremy Bentham

A third important contributor to modern thinking about deterrence is Jeremy Bentham. Bentham along with his English contemporary John Stuart Mill (1806–1873) founded the commonsense philosophy known as utilitarianism. Utilitarianism is the English response to a general class of normative moral theories known as consequentialism, which suggests that an action is morally right if the consequences of that action are more favorable than not favorable. While consequentialism can provide moral justification for many forms of atrocious behavior, including slavery and torture, Bentham and Mill's utilitarianism fit much better with common moral intuitions about such heinous behavior. Bentham elaborates his utilitarian perspective on punishment in his treatise, Introduction to the *Principle of Morals and Legislation,* which contains many ideas fundamental to the deterrence discourse. In his discussion of the "lot of punishment," Bentham elaborates three aspects of punishment currently thought to have an important impact upon the degree of deterrence from further mischief: severity, celerity (speed), and certainty (Bentham 1970: 189–203). In Bentham's view, those most deterrent punishments are those (a) having a level of severity comparable to—no more, no less—the seriousness of the act and (b) those executed quickly and with certainty.

MODERN CRIMINOLOGICAL DETERRENCE THEORY

In criminology, the commonsense notion of deterrence has been expanded, elaborated, and organized into a theoretical perspective for guiding empirical research. Out of this theoretical perspective arise several questions suitable for empirical research. Does increased punishment lessen the likelihood of misbehavior? Does more speedy punishment prevent misbehavior better than slower punishment? Does certain punishment prevent misbehavior better than erratic, hit-and-miss punishment? These are the kinds of question investigated in modern criminological deterrence research.

The main concepts and assumptions of deterrence theory are those of the classical school of criminology. This influential school bases much of its foundation on the work of Cesare Beccaria and Jeremy Bentham. The classical school in one variant or continues to play a vital role in criminological theory and research. Its adherents conceive of the human being as rational, a free being who is able to review, evaluate, and choose from among his or her behavioral options (Vold, Bernard, and Snipes 1998: 14–26). Among the options facing the rational human being living under a social contract is the possibility of punishment for noncompliance with the laws and rules of that contract. Deterrence theory suggests that a punishment that is sufficiently severe and administered quickly and with certainty will weigh heavily upon the rational person's behavioral decision making. Presumably, behavior choice will be favorable to the continuance of the social contract.

While the reasoning of this theoretical perspective is simple and straightforward, it suffers from a serious problem. The deterrence perspective assumes that the rational mechanism of each human being is the same and that full and accurate information about available punishments is equally available to each and every person in the social contract. In the real world, these assumptions are anything but self-evident. However, adopting them as working or beginning assumptions at least enables a start for empirical research work. As deterrence research evolves, further empirical examination of these assumptions themselves will be in order.

DETERRENCE RESEARCH: THE STATE OF THE ART

An important deterrence researcher and reviewer of empirical research work is Daniel Nagin. At two points in the last thirty years, he has examined the empirical literature in critical review articles (Nagin 1978, 1998). His reviews are important in terms of the in-depth examination of the methodological and statistical difficulties that arise in the conduct of deterrence research. Nagin's most recent review of the state of the art of deterrence research includes two main conclusions. He concludes that the actions of the criminal justice system exert a substantial deterrent effect. Generally speaking, increasing criminal sanctions decreases crime rate. However—and this is an important qualification—the research finding that punishment has a substantial deterrent effect helps little in understanding the formulation of criminal justice policy necessary for systematic control of crime rates. In other words, empirical research has established little as to how to bring the effects of criminal justice punishment policy to bear upon the choices of individual citizens, the ultimate targets of that punishment (1998: 3).

Nagin's review organizes deterrence research into three categories: ecological studies, time series studies, and perceived risk studies. Ecological studies are aimed at isolating how factors such as the level of prison population, police per capita, or arrests per crime influence crime rates. These kinds of deterrence research have

many methodological issues, not the least of which includes the use of data generated by public agencies—including law enforcement agencies and courts—for scientific research. Time series studies investigate the influence of specific criminal justice policy, such as the enactment of drunk driving laws upon the level of drunk driving arrests or the effects of capital punishment upon homicide rates. Again, while the methodological issues associated with this kind of study are substantial, they make up an important component of ongoing deterrence research. The perceived risk studies are premised upon the fact that the real basis of deterrence is the amount of threat of punishment that a person feels as she or he mulls over the possibility of committing a crime. No differently than with the other two categories of deterrence research, methodological issues abound here as well. Researchers attempt to determine the impact of perceived risk of arrest, perceptions of severity, and certainty of sanctions upon intentions to offend. More recently, researchers have also begun examining the interaction effects of certainty and severity upon deterrence (Tittle and Paternoster 2000: 515).

SUMMARY

The idea of deterrence underpins much of common-sense thinking regarding the way to punish. It involves punishment for violations of both informal norms—customs and manners—and formal norms—those codified into law and enforced by the coercive power of the state. Criminological studies of deterrence focus on punishment associated with the violation of formal norms. This area of criminological research is a robust one but yet very much a work in progress. In the last thirty years, the examination of some of the key issues about punishment—how much punishment is enough, who should be punished, when does punishment deter—have occupied many, many researchers. As with other areas of research in the young social science of criminology, only tentative research findings in relation to deterrence questions are available. Deterrence is a difficult area for empirical study, and much attention is being paid to the improvement of the methods of research in the hope of improving the confidence that the general public and policy makers may have in the resultant findings. It seems clear that deterrence research will remain an active and growing area of empirical criminological research well into the twenty-first century.

—*Chris E. Marshall*

See also CAPITAL PUNISHMENT; RETRIBUTIVE JUSTICE; RISK

Further Reading

Beccaria, Cesare. ([1764] 1880). *Crimes and Punishments.* Reprint, trans. by James Anson Farrer. London: Chatto & Windus.

Bentham, Jeremy. ([1789] 1970). *An Introduction to the Principles of Morals and Legislation.* Reprint. Darien, CT: Hafner.

Blumstein, Alfred, Jacqueline Cohen, and Daniel Nagin. (1978). "Deterrence and Incapacitation: Estimating the Effects of Criminal Sanctions on Crime Rates." In *Panel on Research on Deterrent and Incapacitative Effects.* Washington, DC: National Academy of Sciences.

Bouffard, Jeffrey, M. Lyn Exum, and Raymond Paternoster. (2000). "Whither the Beast? The Role of Emotions in a Rational Choice Theory of Crime." In *Of Crime and Criminality,* edited by S. S. Simpson. Thousand Oaks, CA: Pine Forge, 159–178.

Cornish, Derek B., and Ronald V. Clarke. (1986). *The Reasoning Criminal.* New York: Springer-Verlag.

Foucault, Michel. ([1975] 1979). *Discipline and Punish: The Birth of the Prison.* Reprint, trans. by Alan Sheridan. New York: Vintage.

Gibbs, Jack P. (1975). *Crime, Punishment, and Deterrence.* New York: Elsevier.

Hobbes, Thomas. ([1651] 1950). *Leviathan.* Reprint. New York: Dutton.

Nagin, Daniel S. (1978). "General Deterrence: A Review of the Empirical Evidence." In *Deterrence and Incapacitation: Estimating the Effects of Criminal Sanctions on Crime Rates,* edited by Alfred Blumstein, Jacqueline Cohen, and Daniel Nagin. Washington, DC: National Academy of Sciences, 95–139.

———. (1998). "Criminal Deterrence Research at the Outset of the Twenty-First Century." *Crime and Justice: A Review of Research* 23, edited by Michael Tonry. Chicago: University of Chicago Press, 1–42.

Tittle, Charles R., and Raymond Paternoster. (2000). *Social Deviance and Crime: An Organizational and Theoretical Approach.* Los Angeles: Roxbury.

Vold, George B., Thomas J. Bernard, and Jeffrey B. Snipes. (1998). *Theoretical Criminology.* New York: Oxford University Press.

Zimring, Franklin E. (1978). "Policy Experiments in General Deterrence: 1970–1975." In *Deterrence and Incapacitation: Estimating the Effects of Criminal Sanctions on Crime Rates,* edited by Alfred Blumstein, Jacqueline Cohen, and Daniel Nagin. Washington, DC: National Academy of Sciences, 140–186.

Zimring, Franklin E., and Gordon J. Hawkins. (1973). *Deterrence: The Legal Threat in Crime Control.* Chicago: University of Chicago Press.

▼ DEVIANCE

Deviance can be defined as behavior or activities that break generally shared social norms. This simple definition belies a number of complexities: Is behavior still deviant if the norm breaking is not visible to any one else or is not sanctioned by others? Given the plurality of social life, can it be said that there is widespread agreement on social norms? In reality, there is more likely to be disagreement on appropriate behavior, standards, and expectations. Who has or what groups have the power and authority to determine the social rules and enforce them? For example, while there is considerable diversity in dress codes and body presentation, employers have considerable power in enforcing both formal and informal dress codes. Types of norms range from informal, unwritten social rules or etiquette, to mores or ethics, convention, organizational rules, and laws (especially criminal law). Even though there are significant cultural differences in the determination of what constitutes deviance, the existence of activities deemed by others to be deviant is universal; all societies define some behavior as deviant, as offensive to legal or moral norms. This is not to say that certain forms of behavior or activities are regarded as deviant in all societies or historical periods. In Western societies over the course of the twentieth century, there was widespread normative change regarding alcohol use, smoking, sexuality, women in paid work, parenting, the use of violence, and gender relations.

The concept of deviance includes a wide range of behavior. A related concept—social control—usually is defined as all those mechanisms or sanctions aimed at achieving conformity and eradicating or containing deviant behavior. Social control responds to deviance, and the sanctions applied may be informal—a glance, ridicule, gossip, a reprimand, persuasion, or social ostracism—or formal—including fines, probation, and imprisonment, administered by the criminal justice system. Medicine (including psychiatry), welfare, and education also sanction behavior they define as deviant, unacceptable, or abnormal, but their social control functions are less visible than formal legal sanctions and are legitimized by concerns such as treating patients or helping clients and their families.

SOCIOLOGICAL APPROACHES TO DEVIANCE

While some consider the study of deviance to be about deviants—the exotic, marginal, unconventional, criminal, or simply "others," that is, people not like us—deviant behavior and its regulation are aspects of everyday social life. Deviance and social control exist in ordinary social settings in which discussions of appropriate behavior, expectations, and the right thing to do are continuously being articulated.

Three kinds of question can be asked about deviance. Why do some people engage in activities others define and sanction as deviant? Why are some activities/individuals identified or defined as deviant? Who designates some activities and behavior as deviant and enforces social sanctions? Sociological theories address these questions by investigating the social factors that create the opportunities for deviance and the social conditions under which definitions of behavior as deviance emerge. Four broad theoretical approaches to the study of deviance can be identified: normative theories, the labeling perspective, critical theories, and feminist approaches. Postmodern theories also influence the discussion of deviance and normativity, although they do not necessarily engage directly with sociology of deviance framework.

Normative Theories

Normative theories treat deviance and norm violation as synonymous, view social control as responding to deviance, and attempt to identify the social, economic, and environmental factors that create pressure for individuals to engage in deviance. Robert Merton set out to identify the processes through which social structures generate the circumstances in which infringement of social codes constitutes a "normal" response. He sought to explain how "*some social structures exert a definite pressure on certain persons in the society to engage in nonconforming rather than conforming conduct*" (1968: 186, emphasis in original). He proposed that deviant behavior results from a disjunction between culturally defined goals to which most members of society aspire and institutionalized norms, that is, acceptable or legitimate (as defined by the relevant social system) means for achieving the goals. He identified this condition with the term *anomie*, or strain, which individuals must accommodate or manage. Merton identified five possible adaptations: conformity, innovation, ritualism, retreatism, and rebellion.

Conformity prevails when goals are achievable through legitimate means. Innovation results when the individual aspires to such cultural goals as financial success but lacks access to institutional means (e.g., a post-secondary education). Merton suggested that this explained why higher rates of crime occur among working-class and ethnic minorities, who have restricted access to legitimate means for success. Ritualism occurs when the means are followed but the cultural goals lose their relevance, as when the bureaucrat who diligently follows rules loses sight of the purpose of those regulations and the overall goals of the organization. Retreatism involves rejection of both culturally prescribed goals and institutional norms by complete withdrawal from society, as exemplified by psychotics, vagabonds, chronic alcoholics, and drug addicts. Rebellion entails rejection of existing social means and goals along with their replacement by new goals and means.

Merton's theory is atomistic and individualistic, as each person seems to solve problems alone, unaware of others in the same situation. By contrast, Sutherland's differential association theory points to the importance of relationships and the learning process in understanding the emergence of deviance (Sutherland and Cressey 1978: 80–82). Sutherland explained criminal deviance in terms of the learning process, not in terms of personality, poverty, stress, or biological or psychological abnormality. He disagreed that crime is a working-class phenomenon and demonstrated that people in white-collar jobs and powerful positions are not immune from criminological influences and do engage in fraud, embezzlement, and restrictive trade practices. In the process of interaction with others, usually in primary groups, individuals confront various definitions of behavior, some of which are favorable to law violation. An excess of definitions favorable to law violation encourages deviance. Sutherland theorized that associations—not general needs or values—explain criminal behavior. His approach allows us to contemplate deviance among segments of society that are not disadvantaged or marginalized.

Albert K. Cohen combined Sutherland's emphasis on the learning process with Merton's anomie theory in a discussion of subcultures. In *Delinquent Boys*, Cohen argued that individuals engage in criminal and delinquent activities by taking over the criminally oriented subcultures in their environment, but later asked, "Why are such subcultures there to be taken over; what is it about the society that accounts for the distribution of its subcultures?" (1968: 346). He maintained that people confronting strain are often not alone and if several actors in the same situation collectively and simultaneously adopt a solution to their shared problems, including restricted access to achievement, then a deviant or criminal subculture can emerge.

The Labeling Perspective

Labeling theorists question the existence of a consensus on norms and argue that they are continually being contested. They disagree that social control is the automatic and usual response to norm-breaking behavior. Reactions depend not only on the violation of a rule but on who breaks the rules, the time and place, and whether she or he is visible to others motivated and has the authority to invoke sanctions. The definition of behavior as deviant depends on the social audience, not just on the norm-breaking activity. The forms of behavior do not themselves activate the processes of social reaction. Rule violation and the application of deviant labels are distinct. The consequences of a deviant label for an actor's public image, self-identity, and moral career are very different from those of the actor not so labeled, even though both violate the same norms.

Howard Becker offered the most influential and oft-cited formulation of the labeling perspective: "Deviance is *not* a quality of the act the person commits, but rather a consequence of the application by others of rules and sanctions to an 'offender.' The deviant is one to whom the label has successfully been applied; deviant behavior is behavior that people so label" (1963: 9). The persons so labeled, however, may not agree with their designation as deviant, and may seek to resist or ignore that interpretation of them and their behavior (sometimes this will be impossible, given the power and authority of such official labelers as the police and criminal courts); indeed, they may view the labelers as deviant. Becker suggests that the term *deviant* be reserved for those labeled as deviant by some segment of society and concludes that "whether a given act is deviant or not depends in part on the nature of the act (that is, whether or not it violates some rule) and in part what other people do about it" (1963: 33).

Labeling theorists stress that becoming deviant, or acquiring a deviant self-identity, is a process and does not automatically follow rule-breaking behavior: It depends on a social audience's enforcement of a rule, which may entail a degradation ceremony in which an actor's public identity is ritually destroyed and replaced by another of lower status. For example, in a criminal trial, a person's public and personal identity may be transformed from that of ordinary citizen to accused or convicted "criminal," "rapist," "pedophile," "thief," or "prisoner." From then on, others will make new assumptions about the kind of person he or she really is, perhaps affecting that person's access to employment, housing, or insurance, even when the "deviance" does not affect conformity with other social norms. A final stage in the deviant career is participating in a deviant subculture that enables the formation of new identities.

The subculture provides self-justifying rationales and ideologies, often rejecting legal or moral rules and institutions. The labeling perspective has been the subject of a range of criticisms, including proponents' greater attention to the successfully labeled deviants than to social audiences, their neglect of self-labeling processes, the lack of explanations regarding why some individuals are motivated to break rules, the assumption that labeling only escalates deviance (thereby ignoring the deterrent effects of sanctioning), and insufficient attention to questions of power and inequality.

Critical Theories

Critical theorists emphasize power and conflict in the definition, content, and application of criminal laws; here, social norms are not conceptualized as deriving from general consensus, but their substance is linked intimately to the political economy and the interests of dominant segments. They seek to demonstrate how the criminalization of certain types of conduct and the differential enforcement of criminal laws reflect the interests of economically and politically powerful groups. The theories are less concerned with why individuals or groups are motivated to be criminally deviant and more concerned with why the behavior is defined as criminal and thereby subject to state control. Specifically, the activities of lower-class people are disproportionately defined in law as criminal, and they are more likely to be arrested, charged, convicted, and sentenced than are middle- and upper-class people.

Many of these theories commence with the writings of Marx and focus on the influence of an economic elite on the substance of the criminal law. They propose that the causes of crime are bound up with the kind of social arrangement existing at a particular point in time: Thus, for crime to be abolished, the social arrangements also must be transformed. Some maintain that the state, via the legal system, protects its interests and those of the capitalist ruling class. Crime control represents the coercive means of checking threats to the prevailing social and economic order. The contradictions of capitalism produce poverty, inequality, and exploitation, which lead to crime as a means of survival. Burglary and drug dealing, crimes against the person, industrial sabotage, and other predatory crimes are rational responses to the inequities of capitalist society. The irony is that compared with the activities that criminal law prohibits, the capitalist class and the state are engaged in many more serious injurious practices, which are rarely criminalized but affect large numbers of people. Even where price-fixing, discrimination, embezzlement, pollution, and economic exploitation are illegal, enforcement is rare.

Michel Foucault investigated questions of power and knowledge and the ways in which they are used to regulate or control "problem" populations. He was less concerned with the legal system than with the rise of new disciplines in the human sciences—psychology, psychiatry, medicine, education, and demography—that propose conceptions of normality. Practitioners of these disciplines seek to establish conformity through the use of their expert knowledge and via persuasion, advice, and counseling. Moreover, they place their clients under surveillance and control through the maintenance of case files and direct intervention under the guise of therapy, treatment, assistance, and welfare. In *Discipline and Punish* (1979), Foucault describes the increasing subtlety and diffusion of social control, whereby imprisonment replaces the public spectacle of execution, which in turn is currently being replaced by community-based correctional measures. Psychiatrists, psychologists, welfare workers, and educationalists have more input into the administration of the criminal justice system: Judges often rely on expert testimony and knowledge before determining guilt or the sentence to be imposed, and members of these new occupational groups are also involved in the process of punishment.

In later work on governmentality and governance, Foucault described forms of social control that are more regulatory and less repressive than the image of punishment presented in *Discipline and Punish*. The concept of governmentality indicates the dramatic expansion in the scope of government facilitated by the emergence of the human sciences, which provide new mechanisms of calculation, especially statistics, that enable particular kinds of knowledge about populations and, in turn, become the basis for normalization, regulation, intervention, and administration.

Feminist Approaches

Feminists argue that mainstream discussions of deviance are biased because they deal primarily with men and boys. Where research on female deviance exists, it tends to rely heavily on assumptions about women's nature and to centralize marital and reproductive roles, actual and anticipated, as explanations. Such approaches often reflect a deterministic view of women's and girls' behavior by claiming that supposedly essential or natural female qualities—emotionalism, deceit, irrationality, sexuality, and the tendency to promiscuity among single women and girls—constitute key factors in female deviation. Women and girls are depicted as engaging in such sex-specific and gender-related deviance as shoplifting, prostitution, and transgressing motherhood norms.

Moreover, different norms get applied to men and women. Numerous norms regarding the presentation of self, marriage/maternity, sexuality, and occupational choice are applied to women but not to men. Although expectations of men do arise around these issues, arguably the scope for "normal" behavior is much narrower and more restrictive for women. The gender system makes certain kinds of deviance (e.g., mental illness, prostitution, hysteria, obesity, shoplifting) more appropriate to or expected of women than men. Such behaviors often are explained in terms of women's supposed nature—their biology and psychology—whereas men's deviance is explained in terms of social, economic, and political conditions and normal learning processes.

Some contemporary feminist discussions of normativity, social control, and conformity focus on the body and the ways in which women's bodies are subject to greater surveillance as compared with men's bodies. The array of images and expectations regarding women's shape, size, diet, emotions, dress, and adornment tend to be very restrictive and affirm specific feminine models of appearance, attractiveness, and behavior. These models become norms against which many women constantly measure, judge, regulate, discipline, and modify their own bodies, even undergoing elective cosmetic surgery, which is becoming more affordable and accessible. Female bodies evaluated as overweight, aged, or unattractive (to heterosexual men) are often viewed by ordinary citizens and employers as evidence of lack of discipline and control and, therefore, as less morally worthy than others who are judged as exercising restraint or "taking care of themselves" as indicated by their bodies. It is not just the body that is being evaluated; the whole person is labeled as overweight, unattractive, or inappropriately attired, and associated conclusions are drawn regarding the type of person someone is or the nature of his or her personality, reliability, credibility, and perceived authority.

Even though conventional deviance research studied men and boys, neither maleness nor masculinity was addressed as a significant explanatory variables: "The role of men's membership of a *sex* is never investigated as it is for women, by non-feminists and feminists alike" (Allen 1988: 16). The focus should be on the contributions that forms of masculinity make to the construction of criminality as a masculine resort, to the policing or nonpolicing of offenses, and to the criminal justice responses to women offenders. Instead of asking why women do not offend, and what is it about women that results in less criminal deviance or less contact with the criminal justice system, research should investigate how the social construction of maleness explains the fact that most criminals have always been and are men.

Postmodernism

While postmodern theorists examine marginalized groups, alternative perspectives, instances of resistance to "conventional society," and attempt to valorize or affirm multiple or different perspectives and identities, they do not necessarily do this by using deviance theories or concepts. Nonetheless, a postmodern approach would posit that abstract theories or generalized explanations—sometimes termed grand theory or grand narrative—offered by the sociologist in standard deviance topics such as juvenile delinquency, prostitution, homosexuality, drug use, alcohol consumption, graffiti, and even violence cannot capture the lived reality, resistance, perspectives, or subjectivity of those so categorized. Postmodern theorists contest the underlying rationales of classifications such as deviant/nondeviant and conformity/deviance, and emphasize shifting identities that are neither stable nor unitary. They emphasize the importance of social experiences as informed by multiple perspectives, subject positions, and identities with a focus on communities. The social world must be examined from the multiple perspectives of class, race, gender, and sexuality as well as designations of deviance. To assert that certain behavior constitutes juvenile delinquency or a drug problem represents the attempt to impose one interpretation of reality, which may not take account of the young people's view of their own activities, or the subjective awareness of those engaging in the use of certain drugs. Such categories as the "criminal," the "drug addict," or the "prostitute," for example, imply that they are relatively internally homogenous and do not sufficiently account for individuals' own identities and their movement across or between such categories.

Foucault's writings on the body and sexuality and the ways in which discourse creates knowledge and social categories have been particularly influential in the emergence of postmodern theories. Regulation of bodies becomes essential for social control, with the most efficient, effective, invisible, and normal site of enforcement being self-control. With their emphasis on the social construction of everyday life and the assignment of authenticity to a range of perspectives, postmodernist approaches have similarities with the labeling perspective and other microsociological approaches that emphasize the significance of multiple meanings and subjectivities.

FUTURE TRENDS

The most frequent definition of deviance is behavior that violates social norms. Norms, however, are neither static nor completely fluid and ad hoc. As conceptions of deviance are socially constructed, no behavior is inherently deviant; it depends on social definitions and the application of norms. Often conceptions of deviance are not a product of a general agreement among members of a particular community but result from the activities of specific groups that attempt to have their conceptions of right and wrong, of appropriate and inappropriate behavior, translated into law and enforced.

In the last years of the twentieth century, there was much discussion about the continuing relevance of the concept of deviance, especially given greater recognition of issues of difference and identity formation and the demise of generally agreed upon social norms or collective sentiment. Colin Sumner, in *The Sociology of Deviance: An Obituary* (1994), boldly claimed that "the behavioral concept of social deviance had run its course by 1975. . . . In terms of any kind of coherent theoretical development, it had lost its potency. Fatally damaged by waves of successive criticism and undercut by its own logical contradictions it ceased to be a living force. Its time had passed and it did not recover" (309). It is true that the sociology of deviance has undergone numerous changes as new questions of normativity and social control emerge and as various theoretical perspectives are more or less relevant. New concepts and terms have entered into the lexicon—for example, normalization, discipline, compliance, governance, regulation, and censure—and they are not the sole province of the sociologist of deviance, as they are used by theorists and researchers in cultural studies, sociology of the body, discussions of sexuality, and feminist approaches. A significant portion of everyday social life and public policy, however, remains concerned with conformity, control, designations of deviance (or at least attempts to designate some groups or individuals as deviant), and moral evaluations, which affirm the importance of deviance as a site of analysis and research.

—*Sharyn L. Roach Anleu*

See also CONDUCT NORMS AND CRIME; RELIGIOUS DEVIANCE; SOCIOLOGICAL THEORIES

Further Reading

Allen, Judith. (1988). "The 'Masculinity' of Criminality and Criminology: Interrogating Some Impasses." In *Understanding Crime and Criminal Justice,* edited by Mark Findlay and Russell Hogg. Sydney: Law Book Company, 1–23.

———. (1989). "Men, Crime and Criminology: Recasting the Questions." *International Journal of the Sociology of Law* 17: 19–39.

Becker, Howard S. (1963). *Outsiders: Studies in the Sociology of Deviance.* New York: Free Press.

Bordo, Susan. (1993). *Unbearable Weight: Feminism, Western Culture, and the Body.* Berkeley: University of California Press.

Cohen, Albert K. (1955). *Delinquent Boys: The Culture of the Gang.* New York: Free Press.

———. (1965). "The Sociology of the Deviant Act: Anomie Theory and Beyond." *American Sociological Review* 30: 5–15.

———. (1968). "Deviant Behavior." In *International Encyclopedia of the Social Sciences,* edited by David Sills. New York: Macmillan, 148–55.

Foucault, Michel. (1978). "About the Concept of the 'Dangerous Individual' in 19th-Century Legal Psychiatry." Translated by Alain Baudot and Jane Couchman. *International Journal of Law and Psychiatry* 1: 1–18.

———. (1979). *Discipline and Punish: The Birth of the Prison.* Translated by Alan Sheridan. New York: Vintage.

———. (1981). *The History of Sexuality: An Introduction.* Translated by Robert Hurley. Harmondsworth: Penguin.

———. (1984). "Preface to *The History of Sexuality:* Vol. II." In *The Foucault Reader,* edited by Paul Rabinow. London: Penguin.

———. (1991). "Governmentality." In *The Foucault Effect: Studies in Governmentality,* edited by Graham Burchell, Colin Gordon, and Peter Miller. London: Harvester Wheatsheaf.

Garfinkel, Harold. (1956). "Conditions of Successful Degradation Ceremonies." *American Journal of Sociology* 61: 420–424.

Heidensohn, Frances. (1985). *Women and Crime.* London: Macmillan.

Hunt, Alan, and Gary Wickham. (1994). *Foucault and Law: Toward a Sociology of Law as Governance.* London: Pluto Press.

Lyman, Stanford M. (1995). "Without Morals or Mores: Deviance in Postmodern Social Theory." *International Journal of Politics, Culture and Society* 9: 197–236.

Merton, Robert K. (1968). *Social Theory and Social Structure.* New York: Free Press.

Naffine, Ngaire. (1987). *Female Crime: The Construction of Women in Criminology.* Sydney, Australia: Allen &Unwin.

Schur, Edwin M. (1984). *Labeling Women Deviant: Gender, Stigma and Social Control.* New York: Random House.

Smart, Carol. (1976). *Women, Crime and Criminology: A Feminist Critique.* London: Routledge & Kegan Paul.

Sumner, Colin. (1994). *The Sociology of Deviance: An Obituary.* Buckingham, UK: Open University Press.

Sutherland, Edwin H., & Donald R. Cressey. (1978). *Criminology,* 10th ed. Philadelphia: Lippincott.

Taylor, Ian, Paul Walton, and Jock Young. (1973). *The New Criminology: For a Social Theory of Deviance.* London: Routledge & Kegan Paul.

▼ DEVIL'S ISLAND

The Devil's Island prison complex was located in French Guiana off the Atlantic coast. It consisted of a three island cluster, the Iles du Salut (Islands of Salvation), plus some sections of mainland French Guiana. Its reputation as the world's toughest prison was such that it was sometimes called "The Island of No Return."

French Guiana was first used as a penal colony during the French Revolution. Napoleon III (1808–1873) eventually made the settlement permanent and the facility was in operation from 1852 and 1953. Devil's Island itself, known as "Ile du Diable" in French, was the most remote of the islands in the penal colony. Henri Charrière (1906–1973), a former convict, described the island as follows: "After a flat coastal area it rises rapidly to a high plateau where there was the guardhouse and one lone barracks for the *bagnards* [prisoners], who numbered about ten. Officially, Diable was not supposed to receive ordinary criminals, only those condemned and deported for political reasons." (Charrière, 1970).

In addition to political prisoners, violent criminals were sent to the Devil's Island colony. Originally, sentencing rules in France required that all prisoners serve some time at Devil's Island, but this was changed in 1885, when only those with more than eight-year sentences were sent there. Freed prisoners typically continued to work at the prison to earn passage back to France. Administration of Devil's Island, as well as the entire penal colony, was based at St. Laurent du Maroni. One of the best-known residents of Devil's Island was Alfred Dreyfus (1859–1935). Dreyfus was a Jewish captain in the French Army, wrongly accused of writing treasonous documents. He was found guilty by court-martial in 1894 and transported to Devil's Island. In 1899, after new evidence proved his innocence, Dreyfus was pardoned and released.

This 1934 photo shows part of the main detention house and courtyard. The cells have heavy steel doors with small openings above to allow air to circulate.

Source: © Bettmann/Corbis; used with permission.

Devil's Island was known as the "Dry Guillotine" for the numerous convict deaths. Some died violently, but diseases such as malaria were common. Most deadly was working in the timber camps. Here convicts were charged with meeting daily quotas. Failure to do so was punished by withholding food. One estimate is that of the 80,000 prisoners sentenced to Devil's Island, about 50,000 died.

The colony underwent reforms in 1930s, fueled in part by *Dry Guillotine*, written by former prisoner Rene Belbenoit (1899–1959) in 1938. Conditions improved somewhat in the 1930s through assistance from the French Salvation Army. Penal servitude in French Guiana was abolished in 1938. The prison closed in 1953, with Salvation Army personnel attending to those who did not want to be repatriated to France.

Devil's Island assumed an infamous place in popular culture. Its name alone conjured up all sorts of evil associations. Several films have revolved around fictional characters who fled the colony, such as *We're No Angels,* a 1959 film about a trio of convicts who escape. *Papillon*, the book Charrière wrote to chronicle his experiences as a prisoner, was later made into a film starring Steve McQueen and Dustin Hoffman.

Abandoned for years, Ile du Diable is accessible by sea only on days when the swift currents and strong waves surrounding the island are calm. Royale, the largest of the Iles du Salut, is now a tourist attraction.

—*Linda Dailey Paulson*

Further Reading

Bainbridge, J.S. Jr. (1988). "Devil's Island Is Still a Synonym for Hell on Earth." *Smithsonian* 19 (5): 90–103.

Belbenoit, Rene. (1938). *Dry Guillotine: Fifteen Years Among the Living Dead*. New York: Dutton.

Charrière, Henri. (1970). *Papillon*. New York: William Morrow and Company.

Miles, Alexander. (1988). *Devil's Island: Colony of the Damned.* Berkeley, CA: Ten Speed Press.

Zola, Emile. (1998). *The Dreyfus Affair: 'J'Accuse' and Other Writings,* edited by Alain Pages. New Haven, CT: Yale University Press.

DIFFERENTIATED CASE MANAGEMENT

Differentiated case management (DCM) is a method intended to make the processing of court cases more effective. It is based on the notion that all cases are not alike and therefore should not be subject to the same processing events and schedules. Early in the court process, DCM programs sort cases by type of charge, type of offender, and expected disposition. Attempts are made to process less serious cases faster so that more time, resources, and effort can be saved for more serious cases. The goals of DCM are to move cases through the system faster and to make better use of scarce jail space. DCM has the potential to reduce prosecution delays in courts in the United States. These delays can lead to several problems. First, delays can interfere with a defendant's right to a speedy trial. Second, delays can contribute to severe overcrowding in jails and detention centers. Third, delays caused by the vast increase of drug cases leave fewer resources to handle the more serious or violent felony cases. For example, if certain details involving a serious case are overlooked because of insufficient resources, the chances are greater that an innocent person may be incarcerated or that a violent criminal may remain free. Therefore, if DCM is found to be effective, its use could improve the administration of justice, alleviate jail crowding, and better ensure that incarceration is reserved for the most serious offenders.

BACKGROUND AND ISSUES

Since the early 1980s, increased public and political concern in the United States over drug abuse (mainly heroin and cocaine) and its related crime, along with a conservative political movement, has led to a greater emphasis on increased punishment for offenders—especially those who sell and possess illegal drugs. Although this emphasis, along with many other factors, appeared to have contributed to a reduction in violent crime during the mid- to late 1990s, it has led to dramatic increases in the number of court cases and to the numbers of adult prisoners, parolees, and probationers. Because of these circumstances, researchers, policy makers, and judges wanted to develop methods of processing that would move cases through the system quickly while maintaining defendants' legal and constitutional rights.

EFFECTIVENESS OF DCM

The effectiveness of DCM has been evaluated with respect to different types of outcomes. Most studies have compared DCM to standard case processing (in which court cases are not classified by charge type, offender type, or expected disposition) with respect to the average time to disposition. The most common method used in these studies has been to compare DCM processing with standard case processing in a neighboring jurisdiction over the same time period. Results of such comparisons have favored DCM over standard case processing.

Case Processing Studies

An American Bar Association (ABA) study published in 1991 involving Chicago, Milwaukee, and Philadelphia reported that the average time to disposition for drug cases using DCM was about 2 to 3.5 times shorter than the time for drug cases using standard processing. With regard to nondrug cases, DCM processing was found to be 1.3 to 1.5 times faster than standard processing. However, in Philadelphia and Chicago, quicker dispositions were associated with more lenient sentencing. Similarly, in a 1994 study of New Brunswick, New Jersey, drug cases, Joan Jacoby found that DCM cases took an average of 81 days to disposition, whereas cases processed using standard procedures took 191 days. Finally, in the only comparison involving juvenile court cases, Sheldon Zhang's 1996 report described a centralized juvenile justice facility in Los Angeles in which all agencies—the prosecutor, public defender, and social services—were housed under one roof. The average time to disposition under the centralized system was somewhat shorter than that under the conventional system—67 versus 90 days. However, Zhang also noted that use of the centralized system did not reduce reoffending.

Methodological Issues and Other Outcomes

Despite these generally positive findings on disposition time, several issues regarding the effectiveness of

DCM require more precise study. First, as appropriately emphasized by criminologists Faye Taxman and Lori Elis (1999), factors other than the type of case processing (e.g., DCM versus usual) may have a bearing on case outcomes. For example, cases that take place in a given year or in a given jurisdiction may involve more serious offenses, more serious offenders, or fewer resources than those in other years or in other jurisdictions. Therefore, it cannot be clearly identified whether the results are attributable to DCM or to these other factors. Second, studies of DCM have rarely examined outcomes other than case processing time. Other potential benefits—reducing jail crowding, improving the administration of justice, and reducing reoffending—have not been a major focus of most of the studies described earlier.

In one attempt to address these issues, Taxman and Elis studied the effect of DCM versus standard case processing in Baltimore. Cases were randomly assigned to either DCM or conventional processing—a method that minimizes the effects of other factors. Results indicated that, similar to previous studies, cases subject to a modified DCM process had a shorter disposition time compared to cases subject to standard processing and also had shorter detention time for misdemeanants and longer incarceration for felons. However, the modified DCM process was also associated with more guilty dispositions, thus increasing the number of persons processed by the criminal justice system.

Further, researchers affiliated with the New York City Criminal Justice Agency used a statistical technique called "multiple regression" to examine which factors were most important in predicting time to disposition and reoffending. Factors examined included court type (DCM or standard), the borough or district of the city, and the defendant's number of prior felony convictions and release status. Court type was the most important factor in reducing time to disposition for both regular and superior court cases. When controlling for the other factors, DCM procedures reduced disposition time an average of 85 days in regular court and an average of 136 days in superior court. With regard to reoffending, standard court defendants had higher arrest rates, but court type had no bearing on the likelihood of rearrest.

RESEARCH DIRECTIONS

Research suggests that DCM may have several advantages over standard case processing. Compared to tra-

ditional processing, DCM appears to reduce disposition time for court cases and pretrial incarceration time for defendants. Further, although research in other jurisdictions is needed in order to draw more definite conclusions, one study found that DCM is associated with shorter sentences for misdemeanor cases and longer sentences for felony cases.

However, as Taxman and Ellis have emphasized, by increasing the number of guilty dispositions, the use of DCM could indirectly contribute to jail and prison overcrowding through its impact on a defendant's conviction record. These authors further noted that given the current emphasis on harsher punishment, this increase in the number of convictions could increase the probability of future incarceration. Future studies need to examine the extent to which DCM contributes to increasing the number of convictions for all offenders as well as for specific types of offenders. Because a recent article by criminologist William Spelman found that the more effective crime reduction programs increase the conviction rate among the most frequent and dangerous offenders, DCM programs may benefit from adopting that emphasis—another focus for future research.

—Timothy W. Kinlock and Michael S. Gordon

See also ASSEMBLY-LINE JUSTICE; CRIMINAL TRIAL; DRUG COURTS; FAMILY COURT; GRAND JURY; JURY SYSTEM; JUVENILE COURT; PLEA BARGAINING; PROCEDURAL JUSTICE; PROSECUTOR; PUBLIC DEFENDER; WRONGFUL CONVICTIONS

Further Reading

American Bar Association. (1991). *Strategies for Courts to Cope with the Caseload Pressures of Drug Cases*. Chicago: American Bar Association.

Belenko, Steven, and Tamara Dumanowsky. (1993). *Special Drug Courts: Program Brief*. Washington, DC: Bureau of Justice Assistance.

Blumstein, Alfred, and Joel Wallman, eds. (2000). *The Crime Drop in America*. New York: Cambridge University Press.

Jacoby, Joan. (1994). "Expedited Drug Case Management Programs: Some Lessons in Case Management Reform." *The Justice System Journal* 17: 19–40.

Spelman, William. (2000). "The Limited Importance of Prison Expansion." In *The Crime Drop in America,* edited by Alfred Blumstein and Joel Wallman. New York: Cambridge University Press, 97–129.

Taxman, Faye, and Lori Ellis. (1999). "Expediting Court Dispositions: Quick Results, Uncertain Outcomes." *Journal of Research in Crime and Delinquency* 36: 30–55.

Zhang, Sheldon. (1996). "The Efficiency of Working under One Roof: An Evaluation of Los Angeles County Juvenile Justice Centers." *Crime & Delinquency* 42: 257–268.

▼ DIGITAL CRIME

The rapid, global growth of computing and communications technologies (collectively known as "information technologies") has caused an increase in technologically sophisticated criminal activity and international economic espionage. Changes in the world's political, economic, and technological environments are fundamentally altering sophisticated crime. The collapse of communism, the end of the Cold War, the globalization of the economy, and the rapid development of new information technologies have combined to create new vulnerabilities and provide criminals with new capabilities. The reach of criminal sanctions has expanded as lawmakers change criminal codes to establish economic and social policies regarding the use and dissemination of technology and information.

Criminal innovation always accompanies technological advance. The computer and the Internet are radically transforming corporate management and the conduct of commerce. But they also have created new vulnerabilities. With cyberspace comes cybercrime. Malevolent hackers, fraudsters, industrial spies, mafias, terrorists, and other criminals are exploiting the Internet to market scams, steal secrets, sabotage commerce, or conceal illegal activities.

All of these new threats are difficult to assess and nearly impossible to quantify. Many of them, such as terrorism, organized crime, drug trafficking, economic espionage, and cybercrime, have been elevated to the level of national security concerns. Most of these threats transcend national frontiers and combating them effectively will require a level of international cooperation that remains to be achieved.

ATTACK INCIDENTS

According to the most recent annual report from the Department of Defense's Computer Emergency Response Team (CERT), more than 4 million computer hosts were affected by computer security incidents in 1999. Both damaging computer viruses, such as Melissa, Chernobyl, Explorer Zip, and Love Bug, and remote intruders have exploited system vulnerabilities. CERT documented that such incidents grew at a rate of around 50 percent a year, which is greater than the growth rate of the Internet hosts.

A series of well-planned and coordinated attacks on several of the nation's biggest Internet sites began on February 8, 2000 and continued for several days. Within seconds of the first wave of attacks, two popular sites, search engine Yahoo.com and retailer Buy.com, were effectively shut down for several hours. Over the next two days, some of the Internet's flagship sites were similarly disrupted, including news outlets CNN.com and ZDNet.com, retailer Amazon.com, auction house eBay.com, and brokerage house E-Trade. These attacks inconvenienced millions of Internet users and resulted in a loss of revenue for several of the affected sites.

INVESTIGATORY CHALLENGES FOR LAW ENFORCEMENT

The changes the Internet has wrought on our society—to business, education, government, and personal communication—are evident all around us and still very much in flux. The cyberrevolution has permeated virtually every facet of our lives. Unfortunately, that revolution has entered the criminal arena as well. Just as millions of people around the globe have incorporated the Internet and advanced information technology into their daily endeavors, so have criminals, terrorists, and adversarial nations. Cybercrime presents a fundamental challenge for law enforcement in the twenty-first century. By its very nature, the cyberenvironment is borderless, affords easy anonymity and methods of concealment, and provides new tools to engage in criminal activity. Someone on the other side of the planet is now capable of infiltrating a computer network in the United States to steal money, abscond with proprietary information, or shut down e-commerce sites.

Pursuing copyright pirates who operate in cyberspace also presents new challenges for copyright owners and for law enforcement agencies. First, unlike the equipment necessary to make large quantities of physical copies of tapes and discs, computers that can

---

DID YOU KNOW...

In January 2001, the U.S. government and several large corporations announced they were going to work together to prevent and solve digital crimes. The new alliance is called the Information Sharing and Analysis Center for Information Technology (IT-ISAC). The new initiative requires the government and companies such as Microsoft, IBM, and Oracle to share otherwise secret business information to close security gaps and combat security breaches.

copy digital information are relatively inexpensive. Second, there is no deterioration in quality when second or third generation digital copies are made. A copyrighted work can be placed on a Web site and copied by hundreds of people. Those people can then redistribute the copy to others, illegally spreading the material around the world within minutes.

Electronic copyright violations may easily escape detection by law enforcement because, rather than taking place openly in physical space, they take place hidden in cyberspace. Before the advent of inexpensive electronic distribution, international traffickers of pirated copyrighted material had to bring that material physically into or out of the country, giving law enforcement authorities an opportunity to seize it. Now, of course, such materials can enter the United States electronically without passing through any physical location that is subject to government monitoring or inspection. Locating and identifying online copyright pirates can be difficult. Even when law enforcement agents focus on particular computer copyright violations, the lack of a hierarchical distribution scheme makes it difficult for a single case to make a noticeable impact on the amount of copyrighted material available through illegal channels. Software no longer available from one Web site can simply be found elsewhere. Finally, while any law enforcement agent can investigate the offline distribution of copyrighted works, computer violations require technically adept agents. These agents are in short supply, despite the efforts of federal law enforcement agencies to hire and train agents to deal with computer crime. Even when investigative agencies have such resources, they are often needed to investigate other computer crimes, such as attacks on the confidentiality, integrity, and availability of computer systems and data.

Over the past several years, there have been a variety of computer crimes ranging from defacement of Web sites by juveniles to sophisticated intrusions that may be sponsored by foreign powers. Some of these are obviously more significant than others. The theft of national security information from a government agency or the interruption of electrical power to a major metropolitan area would have greater consequences for national security, public safety, and the economy than the defacement of a Web site. But even the less serious categories have real consequences and, ultimately, can undermine confidence in e-commerce and violate privacy or property rights. A Web site hack that shuts down an e-commerce site can have disastrous consequences for a business. An intrusion that results in the theft of credit card numbers from an online vendor can result in significant financial loss and, more broadly, reduce consumers' willingness to engage in e-commerce.

CATEGORIES OF CYBERTHREATS

The following are some of the categories of cyberthreats that law enforcement agencies confront:

1. *Insiders*. The disgruntled insider (a current or former employee of a company) is a principal source of computer crimes for many companies. Insiders' knowledge of the target companies' network often allows them to gain unrestricted access to cause damage to the system or to steal proprietary data. The 1999 Computer Security Institute/FBI report notes that 55 percent of respondents reported malicious activity by insiders.

2. *Hackers*. Hackers (or "crackers") are also a common threat. They sometimes crack into networks simply for the thrill of the challenge or for bragging rights in the hacker community. Recently, however, there have been more cases of hacking for illicit financial gain. While remote cracking once required a fair amount of computer knowledge, hackers can now download attack scripts and protocols from the World Wide Web and launch them against victim sites. While these attack tools have become more sophisticated, they have also become easier to use.

3. *Virus writers*. Virus writers pose a serious threat to networks and systems worldwide. In 1999, several destructive computer viruses or "worms" proliferated, including the Melissa Macro virus, the Explore Zip worm, and the CIH (Chernobyl) virus.

4. *Criminal groups*. Cyberintrusions by criminal groups who attack systems for purposes of monetary gain are also increasing. Unfortunately, cyberspace provides new tools not only for criminals but for national security threats as well. These include terrorists, foreign militaries, and foreign intelligence agencies, which, not surprisingly, have adapted computer tools as part of their espionage tradecraft.

5. *Terrorists*. Terrorist groups use new information technology and the Internet to formulate plans, raise funds, spread propaganda, and communicate securely. The prospect of information warfare by foreign militaries against critical infrastructures is a great threat to national security.

▼

The Internet and Transnational Crime

This e-mail communication shows how easy and quick the Internet makes it to commit crimes across national boundaries. E-mails like this are regularly sent to people around the globe. The purpose is to get the recipient to post money, which is then stolen.

APPEAL FOR URGENT ASSISTANCE

Dear sir,

With due respect and humility I write to you this proposal which I believe will be of great interest to you.

I am Mrs Eryka Kadaba Newman, a sierra- leonean nationality and the wife of late Sir, Arthur K. Newman who was the director of foreign Currency operations with the Central Bank of Sierra Leon..My husband was murdered cold bloodedly by rebels loyal to Foday Sankoh before the powerful community of west African states forces (ECOMOG) intervened. My son Henry and I managed to escape to Abidjan the republic of Côte d'ivoire through the help of my husband's friend who has a fishing trawler . We came to Abidjan with some valuables including a cash with the sum of $24, 500, 000, 00.(twenty four million five hundred thousand Dollars) in two trunk boxes. I deposited the boxes into a private security company here in Abidjan with my son Abubakar as depositor not beneficiary. Due to our political statues and the nature of deposit, we can not serve as beneficiary. The beneficiary must bear the name of a foreigner. The documentary power to appoint a beneficiary is with my son Henry.

For your information, we did not disclosed the real content of the boxes to the security company and we did not wish them to know this under any circumstances rather we deposited the boxes as family valuables. I am therefore soliciting for your assistance hoping that you are honest and trust worthy in transferring this money into your account out of Africa for business investment abroad. I can not do this on my own due to our political statues here in Abidjan. We have it in mind to reward you handsomely for your assistance. We are prepared to compensate you with 25 % of the total sum of money for your assistance in the transaction. If you are interested to help us, you are required to visit Abidjan in three working days for the following reasons.

1. To open a local account in your name here in Abidjan
2. To sign agreement of trust
3. To finalise modalities for a successful transfer
4. To verify and inspect the consignment.

Please help a widow, ensure that no one else knows about this business, it is totally confidential. This business is also 100% risk free. You are required to contact my son Henry through this phone number 00 225 07 99 01 85. Your private phone and fax numbers are also needed for confidential reasons.

I am looking forward to your reply soonest.
God bless you.

Mrs Eryka K. Newman.

PRIVATE SECTOR COOPERATION WITH LAW ENFORCEMENT

The cyberthreats described above, from hacking to foreign espionage and information warfare, require new technologies and skills. The success of law enforcement in battling cybercrime depends on close cooperation with private industry, as most of the victims of cybercrimes are private companies. Therefore, successful investigation and prosecution of these crimes depend on private victims reporting incidents to law enforcement and cooperating with the investigators, and private companies have generally reported incidents and threats to law enforcement officials. In most attacks, the identity, location, and objective of the perpetrator are not immediately apparent. Nor is the scope of the attack, that is, whether an intrusion is isolated or part of a broader pattern affecting numerous targets. It is often impossible to determine at the outset if an intrusion is an act of vandalism, organized crime, domestic or foreign terrorism, economic or traditional espionage, or some form of strategic military attack. The only way to determine the source, nature, and scope of the incident is to gather information from the victim sites and from intermediate sites, such as Internet service providers (ISPs) and telecommunications carriers. Under our constitutional system, such information typically can be gathered only pursuant to criminal investigative authorities.

Private sector computer networks present an attractive target. Computer intruders can penetrate a system without gaining physical access. This increases the difficulty of detecting the theft of information and the origin of the intruder. The growth of information technology makes the emergence of information theft inevitable worldwide. Law enforcement officials in the United States, apparently viewing the U.S. economy as the most likely target, have begun to focus on this new form of crime. New legislative initiatives in the United States may serve as a model that will be followed by other nations. The U.S. initiatives in this area have influenced an international trend to combat digital crime.

—*Hedieh Nasheri*

See also CYBERCRIME; PIRACY, INTELLECTUAL PROPERTY

Further Reading

Jesitus, John. (2000). "Keeping Secrets." *Industry Week* (21 February): 9.

Nasheri, Hedieh, and Timothy J. O'Hearn. (1998). "Crime and Technology: New Rules in a New World." *International Review of Law, Computers and Technology* 7, 2: 145–157. Reprinted in *Criminal Law Bulletin* 134, 6: 520–535.

———. (1999a). "High tech crimes and the American Economic Machine." *International Review of Law, Computers and Technology* 13, 1: 7–19.

———. (1999b). "The Worldwide Search for Techno-thieves: International Competition v. International Co-operation." *International Review of Law, Computers and Technology* 13, 3: 373–382.

Silva, Jeffrey. (2000). "Legislative Relief Sought for Corporate Espionage Cases: High-Tech Companies Must Set Up Defenses." *Radio Communications Report* (25 September): 24.

▼ DISCRETIONARY JUSTICE

In the modern era of criminal justice research, scholars have focused much attention on understanding how the personal choices of criminal justice professionals affect the processing of individuals through the justice system. Police, prosecutors, and judges all make decisions about how cases should be handled, and these decisions can result in different outcomes for individuals who are engaged in similar behavior. Since the mid-1900s, lawmakers and scholars have become increasingly concerned with the disparate treatment of offenders in the criminal justice system because such disparities threaten a principle of modern criminal justice—defendants, regardless of their personal characteristics, should be treated equally under the law. The American Bar Foundation Survey (1953) and the President's Crime Commission (1967) identified the informal and often unchecked discretionary decisions made throughout the criminal justice system as a cause of disparate treatment. During this same period, Kenneth Culp Davis (1969) published the influential book *Discretionary Justice: A Preliminary Inquiry*, which suggested that although discretion is a necessary part of the criminal justice system, it can become problematic when uncontrolled. Over the past four decades, courts and legislators have responded to the critique of discretion by instituting a number of reforms, including formal rules aimed at controlling discretionary decision making and reducing the potential for disparate treatment. These rules include well-known policies such as mandatory arrest procedures, sentencing guidelines, and mandatory minimum sentences.

POLICE DISCRETION

Criminologists, sociologists, and political scientists have devoted a significant amount of energy to the study of police behavior and decision making. As Walker (1993) argues, however, scholarly and political inquiries into the issue of discretionary decision making by the police have historically centered on problems of police misconduct rather than routine police activity. The study of police discretion is complex because police officers must make discretionary decisions at a variety of levels. For example, police officers routinely decide whom to stop, whom to question, whom to detain, and whom to arrest without formal guidance or approval from supervisors.

The majority of research on police discretion has focused on an officer's decision to make an arrest or give a citation. This research has consistently shown that although a number of factors affect an officer's decision to take formal action, the seriousness of the offense is the most significant legal factor found to increase the likelihood of arrest.

The widespread adoption of mandatory arrest policies in domestic violence incidents provides an interesting example of how policymakers have attempted to control police discretion about when an arrest is warranted. Until the 1970s, many police departments nationwide avoided making arrests in domestic violence incidents. Following a high-profile lawsuit in New York City, that city's police department adopted a policy that mandated arrests in domestic felony assault cases. The New York policy specifically stated that the marriage of the assaulting parties would not constitute a legitimate reason to refuse to arrest. As agencies began adopting mandatory arrest policies in response to domestic felony assault cases, the Police Foundation sponsored a study of mandatory arrests in Minneapolis that confirmed that arrest was more successful at deterring future violence than was either requiring mediation or separating the couple (Sherman and Berk 1984). Although the findings of the Minneapolis study have subsequently been challenged, police departments nationwide instituted mandatory arrest policies in cases of domestic violence. While assessment of the success of mandatory arrest policies in reducing future violence continues, little attention focuses on officer compliance with the policies or on evaluation of how the policies have changed police perceptions about the seriousness of domestic violence.

New research suggests that the contexts of the police-citizen encounter may be as important as offense severity for understanding why officers decide to make arrests. Uncooperative suspects are more likely to receive formal sanctions. Consequently, suspect demeanor has been suggested as an explanation of the high arrest rates of blacks. Smith and Visher (1981) found that being black was strongly correlated with antagonism toward the police and the risk of arrest. Further research on discretionary arrest decisions may help explain the relationship between uncooperative demeanor and disparate arrest patterns.

Although the majority of research on police discretion focuses on issues of arrest, police discretion is highest in incidents of police-invoked action, such as traffic enforcement. These incidents are generally minor, are committed by numerous people, and have no direct victim. In addition, patrol officers usually operate under a condition of "low visibility" that limits controls on their discretion. Police, then, are responsible for deciding whom to stop or sanction and whom to ignore, thereby determining who enters the criminal justice system. Although researchers disagree on how much police work is proactive (police initiated) versus reactive (citizen initiated), Ericson (1982) observed that about half of police-citizen encounters are police initiated. Most police-initiated stops are made in reaction to traffic infractions or are based on officer "suspicion." Subsequent sanctions, either formal or informal, are more likely when an officer initiates an encounter than when the encounter is citizen initiated.

Some research has attempted to determine what types of factors influence police officers to stop certain people or cars (in the case of traffic enforcement) from the pool of potential violators. Piliavin and Briar (1964) found that black youths were more likely than white youths to be stopped and questioned by police. In addition, research has shown that low socioeconomic status and youthfulness increase an individual's chance of being stopped and searched by police. Such traffic stops are often used to justify questioning and searching lower-class, younger citizens about other, more serious violations.

The role of race in police stops, citations, and arrests is unclear. Many studies have suggested that the risk of being arrested is higher for blacks than for whites. However, the findings from these studies vary depending on the type of crimes examined, control of other variables, and statistical methods. Recent research on racial disparities in traffic stops suggests that black and Hispanic drivers are stopped in numbers disproportionate to their numbers in the population. Recent changes in police data collection, such as traffic stop studies, incident-based analysis, and early warning systems, have given police administrators new tools to monitor discretionary decisions made by officers.

PROSECUTORIAL DISCRETION

The decisions by prosecutors to bring an individual to court, to charge an individual with a crime, or to offer an individual a plea bargain represent three important forms of discretionary decision making within the criminal justice system. In his landmark work, Frank Miller (1970) identified six factors that affect prosecutorial discretion: (1) attitude of the victim, (2) cost of the prosecution, (3) avoidance of undue harm to the suspect, (4) availability of alternative procedures, (5) potential use of civil sanctions, and (6) willingness of the suspect to cooperate with law enforcement. Prosecutorial screening of potential cases is vital to the smooth functioning of the criminal justice system. Courts would be quickly overwhelmed if all individuals who were arrested were subsequently brought to trial. However, the discretionary decisions made by prosecutors to either drop charges or offer plea bargains have attracted much scholarly attention.

Research has consistently shown that prosecutors dismiss a high percentage of charges before they go to trial. A prosecutor's decision to dismiss a charge is influenced by a number of factors, such as the likelihood of conviction, interests of justice, and political considerations. In addition, some research has shown that characteristics of the victim or defendant may affect a prosecutor's decision to pursue a criminal charge. The "credibility" of victims can be influenced by stereotypes about race, class, and gender. Lisa Frohman's (1991) study of prosecutorial decisions in sexual assault cases illustrates that such decisions about the "credibility" of victims can be affected by the race or social class of the victim. In addition, the relationship between the victim and the defendant influences whether a prosecutor pursues criminal charges. Some research has shown that prosecutors are less likely to pursue criminal charges if the victim is a friend or relative of the defendant, rather than a stranger.

Legislative efforts to limit the discretion of judges through mandatory minimum sentences or sentencing guidelines have increased the discretionary power of prosecutors. Under structured sentencing systems, such as the Federal Sentencing Guidelines, the decisions about which offenses to charge often determine the range of years of imprisonment that a defendant must serve. Therefore, determinate sentencing systems shift much of the control over sentencing outcomes from the judge to the prosecutor. Such legislative changes have raised new concerns about the increasingly unrestrained power of prosecutors. Public debate over prosecutorial discretion has focused on decisions to seek the death penalty and the potential for prosecutors to overcharge individuals due to race, class, or gender biases.

JUDICIAL DISCRETION

Judicial discretion during sentencing has not been static throughout history; rather, paradigm shifts from rehabilitative to retributive penology have strongly influenced the latitude granted to judges. For example, criminal historian Nicole Rafter (1990) argues that at the beginning of the twentieth century, sentencing laws allowed judges to send offenders such as women and children to prison for minor public order offenses for which men were rarely even arrested. Until the 1970s, state sentencing laws allowed judges to sentence women differently than men because women offenders were perceived to be more amenable to rehabilitation and would benefit from longer indeterminate sentences.

In reaction to perceived inequalities in the federal and state sentencing systems, such as gender and race discrimination, social and legal scholars pressed for legislation that would replace indeterminate sentencing with a system that offered greater predictability in determining proper sentence dispositions and lengths of imprisonment. During the 1970s and early 1980s, a number of scholarly studies illustrated a lack of uniformity in judicial sentencing and parole practices in both

federal and state courts. One of the most interesting and illuminating of these studies was conducted in the Second Judicial Circuit in the mid-1970s. In this study, fifty district court judges from the Second Judicial Circuit, which includes the federal districts in New York and Connecticut, were given a set of identical criminal files and instructed to indicate a hypothetical sentence for each case. The sentences imposed by the judges varied dramatically for each case. For example, the sentences for a bank robbery case ranged from five years' imprisonment to eighteen years' imprisonment.

In addition to exposing stark disparities in sentencing practices among judges, a number of studies demonstrated that discretion among judges often led to wide disparity in sentencing based on characteristics of defendants, such as race, gender, education, and income (Kleck 1981; Daly and Bordt 1995). In response to scholarly research and internal governmental pressure to develop standardized models of sentencing, the U.S. Board of Parole was the first agency to experiment with a guidelines model. The parole board guidelines, initially developed in the late 1960s, provided a narrow range within which parole hearing examiners could set the length of incarceration. Deviations from the guideline ranges were granted only by written request. This model was later applied to sentencing in experiments in four local jurisdictions (Essex County, New Jersey; Polk Country, Iowa; Denver, Colorado; and the state of Vermont) from 1974 to 1976. By the late 1970s and early 1980s, nearly all states were experimenting with or adopting variations of these standardized sentencing models.

The Sentencing Reform Act of 1984 was the first significant effort to reform and equalize sentencing in the federal courts, which have jurisdiction for all violations of federal law. The Sentencing Reform Act created the U.S. Sentencing Commission, abolished federal parole, and narrowed judicial discretion in sentencing through the use of standardized sentencing ranges. The Federal Sentencing Guidelines have served as a model for sentencing reform across a number of states. Although states have differed in their approaches to limiting judicial discretion, most have adopted either sentencing guidelines or mandatory minimum penalties that require offenders to serve fixed prison terms without the possibility of parole or probation. Although sentencing guidelines and mandatory minimum penalties provide a level of protection against judicial discretion during sentencing, new research indicates that bias in sentencing has not disappeared; rather, it has shifted, allowing the decisions of other criminal justice officials, such as police or prosecutors, to determine sentencing outcomes.

Allowing individual law enforcement officials to use their own discretion in deciding whom to stop, arrest, prosecute, and sentence has been a critical feature of the modern criminal justice system. Mandatory arrest procedures, mandatory minimum sentences, and sentencing guidelines are just a few examples of policies that have resulted from increased public attention to discretion in the criminal justice system. These policies were designed to prevent the abuse of discretionary power to determine sentence outcomes. However, critics have increasingly argued that such policies are overly rigid and have failed to eliminate race, social class, and gender bias in sentencing outcomes. By targeting the control of discretion of a single agency, such policies subsequently expand the discretion of other actors within the criminal justice system, resulting in a shift of discretion rather than control of discretion. In the end, discretionary decision making is a necessary component of the criminal justice system—one that may be monitored but never completely eliminated.

—*Amy S. Farrell*

See also DETERMINATE SENTENCES; INDETERMINATE SENTENCES; MANDATORY ARREST; MANDATORY SENTENCING; RACE AND POLICING; RACE AND SENTENCING; SENTENCING; SENTENCING GUIDELINES

Further Reading

Black, Donald, and Al Reiss. (1970). "Police Control of Juveniles." *American Sociological Review* 35: 733–748.

Daly, Kathleen, and Rebecca Bordt.(1990). "Sex Effects and Sentencing: An Analysis of the Statistical Literature." *Justice Quarterly* 12: 141–175.

Davis, Kenneth Culp. (1969). *Discretionary Justice: A Preliminary Inquiry*. Baton Rouge: Louisiana State University Press.

Ericson, Richard. (1982). *Reproducing Order: A Study of Police Patrol Work*. Toronto: University of Toronto Press.

Frankel, Michael. (1973). *Criminal Sentences: Law without Order*. New York: Hill & Wang.

Frohman, Lisa. (1991). "Discrediting Victims' Allegations of Sexual Assault: Prosecutorial Accounts of Case Rejections." *Social Problems* 38: 218–224.

Kleck, Gary. (1981). "Racial Discrimination in Criminal Justice Sentencing: A Critical Evaluation of the Evidence with Additional Evidence on the Death Penalty." *American Sociological Review* 46: 783–804.

Miller, Frank. (1970). *The Decision to Charge a Suspect with a Crime*. Boston: Little, Brown.

Piliavin, Irving, and Scott Briar. (1964). "Police Encounters with Juveniles." *American Journal of Sociology* 70: 206–214.

Rafter, Nicole Hahn. (1990). *Partial Justice: Women, Prison, and Social Control*. Boston: Northeastern University Press.

Sherman, Lawrence. (1980). "Causes of Police Behavior: The Current State of Quantitative Research." *Journal of Research in Crime & Delinquency* 17: 69–100.

Sherman, Lawrence, and Richard Berk. (1984). "The Specific Deterrent Effects of Arrest for Domestic Assault." *American Sociological Review* 49: 261–272.

Smith, Douglas, and Christine Visher. (1981). "Street-Level Justice: Situational Determinants of Police Arrest Decisions." *Social Problems* 29: 167–177.

von Hirsch, Andrew. (1976). *Doing Justice: The Choice of Punishment*. New York: Hill & Wang.

Walker, Samuel. (1993). *Taming the System: The Control of Discretion in Criminal Justice 1950–1990*. New York: Oxford University Press.

DISCRIMINATION IN THE CRIMINAL JUSTICE WORKPLACE

At the beginning of the twentieth century, there were virtually no women or minorities employed in the U.S. criminal justice system, as employment discrimination by law and practice kept qualified individuals from pursuing criminal justice careers. Although changes in employment law since the 1960s have reversed the legal bias, some discrimination still exists. By the turn of the twenty-first century, great strides had been taken towards greater representation of women and minorities in criminal justice administration. Still, discriminatory practice can keep qualified candidates from being hired and promoted, and minority and female employees in the criminal justice system may suffer significantly greater job stress than their white male counterparts.

CRIMINAL JUSTICE TODAY

As of June 1998, federal agencies employed over 83,000 full-time nonmilitary personnel authorized to carry firearms and make arrests (i.e., sworn officers); 14.2 percent of these were women, and 29.4 percent were members of a racial or ethnic minority. Percentages varied by agency. For example, 25.2 percent of the sworn officers in the Internal Revenue Service were women, and 32.9 percent in the U.S. Postal Inspection Service were minorities. On the other hand, only 7.9 percent of sworn Drug Enforcement Agency officers were women, and only 8.3 percent of U.S. Fish and Wildlife Service officers were minorities.

Similar percentages exist in the over 18,000 state

and local police agencies nationwide that employ some 660,000 sworn officers. Minority representation among local police officers was 21.5 percent in 1997, compared to 14.5 percent ten years earlier. Minorities accounted for 19 percent of sworn personnel in sheriff departments in 1997, as opposed to 13.4 percent in 1987. Recent studies find that women account for 62 percent of all civilian employees and 24 percent of all police employees—although largely in support positions—in surveyed state and local police agencies. Overall, only about 10 percent of sworn officers are women. Women make up 15.6 percent of full-time sworn officers in sheriff departments in general, although only a little over 11 percent in departments serving communities with populations under 25,000. Women fare less well in local police departments: 10 percent of full-time sworn personnel in local police departments are women; in departments serving communities of less that 25,000, the percentage drops to a little over 5 percent.

In 2000, 12.1 percent of sworn officers in the Federal Bureau of Prisons were women and 37.4 percent minorities. Support and logistical staff were 27.4 percent female and 74.6 percent minority. The numbers are similar at the state and local level. Women make up almost 30 percent of all correctional personnel in state adult correctional facilities and 35 percent in juvenile systems; 30 percent of all jail payroll staff and 24 percent of all jail correctional officers are female.

Statistics are not as forthcoming as to the ethnic and gender composition of court personnel. However, former President Clinton pursued an aggressive plan to appoint more women and minorities to federal judgeships. From 1993 to 1998, 33.3 percent of then President Clinton's forty-eight appointees to the U.S. Courts of Appeals were women, and 22.9 percent minorities; of former President Bush's thirty-seven similar appointees, 18.9 percent were female and 10.8 percent minorities. The record as to U.S. District Court judgeships is similar: 28.2 percent of Clinton's appointees were female and 26.2 percent minorities; 19.6 percent of Bush's appointees were women and 10.8 percent a race other than white. From 1980 to 1991, the representation of women among state judges increased from 4 percent to 9 percent; women accounted for 10 percent of trial court judges, 12 percent of intermediate appellate court judges, and 9.5 percent of top appellate court judges.

Many attribute these increases to affirmative action mandated by several employment laws. Bennett and Hess (1992: 224) define an affirmative action plan as "a written plan to ensure fair recruitment, hiring and promotion practices. Their intent is to undo the damage caused by past discrimination in employment." Recently, some affirmative action plans have successfully been challenged by claims of reverse discrimination: White males have proven that women and minorities were given preferential treatment in hiring and promotion. Still, as Cordner and Sheehan (1999: 82) note, "In numerous instances, the federal courts have found entrance level tests and job qualifications to be discriminatory against blacks, women, and Spanish-speaking Americans. More recently, attention has also focused on older citizens and disabled persons. Patterns of discrimination have also been identified in promotion and transfer practices."

EMPLOYMENT LAW

From 1935 to 1964, the law governing employment in the workplace was dominated by the National Labor Relations Act (NLRA) and centered on the rights of employees to organize into unions and bargain collectively. Its application to the criminal justice workplace, however, was somewhat limited due to public necessity. Furthermore, not all employees were covered by the NLRA, and not all employees wanted to or could bargain collectively. Eventually federal lawmakers decided that all employees should be protected and passed a series of laws designed to provide comprehensive workplace protection. The primary difference between the old and new employment laws was that the latter focused on unjust treatment of the individual employee and not the worker as the member of a group. Some states have enacted laws to fill possible gaps in federal legislation protecting the worker, but federal laws still provide the main remedies to illegal employment discrimination.

The Civil Rights Acts of 1964 and 1970 are still the primary legislation protecting the individual employee from discrimination based on race, sex, religion, and ethnicity. Title VII is of particular importance in that it guarantees equal employment opportunity and charges the Equal Employment Opportunity Commission with enforcing its provisions. The U.S. Supreme Court interpreted Title VII to prohibit "disparate treatment"—discrimination against an employee of a protected class—as well as unintentional "disparate impact"—a pattern of discrimination against a protected group of employees over the course of time.

Title VII was further interpreted by the Supreme Court to forbid sexual harassment as a type of illegal sex discrimination, whether it is in of the form of quid pro quo, where "an employee is subject to unwelcome sexual harassment that affects the worker's term and condition of employment," or the hostile workplace form, where an employer creates " a hostile environment by subjecting workers to offensive remarks, sexual innuendoes of verbal and nonverbal nature, and unwelcome physical contacts" (Wolkinson and Block 1996: 71). Sexual harassment claims against a criminal justice agency may have unique aspects. Paula Rubin notes that "Inmates, suspects, arrestees, crime victims, and others having interaction with the agency can be involved with this unlawful conduct. In these instances, the agency may be liable if the agency, its agents, or supervisory employees knew or should have known of the conduct but failed to take immediate action" (1995: 4).

Some federal discrimination laws focus on employment groups specifically protected by Title VII, but only deal with certain limited issues. The Equal Pay Act (1963), for example, makes wage discrimination based on sex illegal. Title IX of the 1972 Education Amendments prohibits discrimination in education benefits based on race, religion, sex, or ethnicity. The Pregnancy Discrimination Act of 1978 forbids discrimination in employment on the basis of pregnancy, childbirth, and related conditions. And the Civil Service Reform Act of 1978 requires the federal government to have a workforce reflecting the nation's diversity.

Other federal laws and the court cases interpreting them have expanded the categories of employees who cannot be discriminated against in the criminal justice workplace. The Age Discrimination in Employment Act of 1967 prohibits discrimination based on age for people aged forty and above. The Immigration Reform and Control Act of 1986 prohibits discrimination against qualified aliens, as well as discrimination based on national origin. Most recently, the Family and Medical Leave Act of 1993 allows employees of both genders twelve weeks per year of unpaid leave for the birth or placement of a child, the care of an immediate family member with a serious health condition, or the employee's own medical care for a serious health condition.

Perhaps the federal laws with the potentially greatest effect are those forbidding discrimination against qualified persons who are handicapped. The Rehabili-

tation Act of 1973, as amended in 1980, prohibits discrimination against disabled individuals by the federal government, federal contractors, and recipients of federal aid, which covers most state and local agencies. The Americans with Disabilities Act of 1990 broadened this coverage to include all state and local governments. A person with a disability is an individual who has a physical or mental impairment that substantially limits one or more major life activities, has a record of such impairment, or is regarded as having such an impairment. Courts have used an expansive definition of "impairment," including coverage of alcoholism and HIV infection, but excluding drug addiction and gender identity disorders. If such impairment exists, employers must make a reasonable accommodation so that the employee may continue to work. Dilemmas unique to the criminal justice workplace can occur: For example, although an agency cannot bar a qualified employee with a mental impairment from doing a particular job, it may also be liable if its clients are harmed by the employee. Furthermore, as Walter Olson (1997: 114) warns,

> Employers' biggest accommodation challenge may arise less from the gravely disabled, who are relatively few in number and often far from keen on forcing their services on reluctant hirers, than from the general working population—people who manifest or announce less profound disabilities after they've already been on the job for a while.

SUMMARY

State and federal laws have been enacted to eliminate employment discrimination in government, and courts at all levels have enforced those laws during the last four decades. Those groups whose members were historically discriminated against in the employment practices of criminal justice agencies saw their numbers increase dramatically in employment at those same agencies during the 1990s.

Although historically discriminated against groups have made some strides in equal employment in criminal justice agencies, it has usually been at the lower level positions and not in management. Title VII and hostile workplace suits continue to plague managers in criminal justice agencies. Furthermore, new groups, such as the aged and the disabled, are continually being recognized by the law as protected from workplace discrimination. It may be that socialization and time are the factors that finally eliminate discrimination in the criminal justice workplace, as well as in American society itself.

—*Gregory P. Orvis*

See also RACE AND POLICING; WOMEN AND POLICING

Further Reading
American Bar Association. (1997). *Guide to Workplace Law*. New York: Times Books.
Bennett, Wayne W., and Karen M. Hess. (1992). *Management and Supervision in Law Enforcement*. St. Paul, MN: West.
Bureau of Justice Statistics. (2000). *Sourcebook of Criminal Justice Statistics, 1999*. Washington, DC: U.S. Department of Justice.
Cordner, Gary W., and Robert Sheehan. (1999). *Police Administration*. Cincinnati, OH: Anderson.
National Center for Women and Policing. (2001). *Recruiting and Retaining Women: A Self-Assessment Guide for Law Enforcement*. Washington, DC: U.S. Department of Justice.
National Crime Prevention Council. (1995). *Lengthening the Stride: Employing Peace Officers from Newly Arrived Ethic Groups*. Washington, DC: U.S. Department of Justice.
Office of Justice Programs. (1998). *Women in Criminal Justice: A Twenty Year Update*. Washington, DC: U.S. Department of Justice.
Olson, Walter K. (1997). *The Excuse Factory: How Employment Law is Paralyzing the American Workplace*. New York: Martin Kessler Books.
Rubin, Paula N. (1994). *The Americans with Disabilities Act and Criminal Justice: Hiring New Employees*. Washington, DC: U.S. Department of Justice.
———. (1995). *Civil Rights and Criminal Justice: Primer on Sexual Harassment*. Washington, DC: U.S. Department of Justice.
Rubin, Paula N., and Susan W. McCampbell. (1995). *The Americans with Disabilities Act and Criminal Justice: Mental Disabilities and Conditions*. Washington, DC: U.S. Department of Justice.
Stone, Christopher. (1999). "Race, Crime, and the Administration of Justice." *National Institute of Justice Journal* 4: 26–32.
Wolkinson, Benjamin W., and Richard N. Block. (1999). *Employment Law*. Malden, MA: Blackwell.

▼ DISTRICT ATTORNEY

See PROSECUTOR

▼ DIVERSION PROGRAMS

Diversion is a strategy that seeks to avoid formal processing of an offender by the criminal justice system. Diversion occurs when a person has been accused of a crime, but officials decide to halt or suspend the processing of the offender into the system. The case is suspended while the offender is referred to a treatment or care program, or until the offender can prove to the court that he or she will not reoffend. Although diversion generally occurs when it is believed that both the offender and the community will be better off without formal criminal justice processing, it can also occur after conviction.

BACKGROUND

Diversion is probably as old as the justice system itself. Police officers and court officials have always exercised their discretion to prevent the formal processing of offenders. During colonial times, a cobbler from Boston named John Augustus developed an idea to keep offenders out of the criminal justice system: probation. The current practice of diversion as an acceptable activity of the justice system originated in 1965 in Genesee County, Michigan. Soon after, in 1967, the U.S. Department of Labor began to fund pretrial diversion programs, and the Law Enforcement Assistance Administration funded experimental alcohol detoxification programs. With the support of the 1967 President's Commission on Law Enforcement and the Administration of Justice, and the 1973 National Advisory Commission on Criminal Standards and Goals, diversion programs prospered during the 1970s. During the decade, over 1,200 diversion programs were established, at a cost of over $112 million. Although federal funding for diversion programs waned in the 1980s, many still exist. In most cases, state and local governments have assumed the cost. All states and the federal government use some form of diversion.

One critical area for the use of diversion is drug offenses. Because of the large number of drug offenders that are brought into the criminal justice system, local, state, and federal authorities in over one hundred jurisdictions have implemented drug courts as a form of diversion. Drug courts provide nonviolent substance-abusing adults with the sanctions and services necessary to change their behavior and avoid long-term incarceration. Research indicates that such treatment can reduce substance abuse, criminal behavior, and recidivism.

No national statistics are kept on diversion programs, so it is not known exactly how many people are diverted from the justice system each year, but there is good evidence that the number is quite large. It is estimated that in a year when there are 3 million index crime arrests, there will be less than 900,000 felony convictions and less than 500,000 prison sentences. Some of this drop-off reflects cases that are too weak to obtain a conviction, but by far most is due to diversion at each stage of the criminal justice process, including probation. For most offenders, diversion is the first option authorities consider when deciding how to proceed in a particular case.

In a sense, every offender not in jail or prison is living in the community because of some form of diversion. Even if every arrest were prosecuted and punished to the full extent of the law, there would still be large numbers of offenders living in the community. These would be former offenders, however, and, having been punished as fully as the law allows, they would be free citizens. Many of the offenders living in the community today, however, are under some form of diversion authority: pretrial services, probation, parole, or community corrections. The existence of diversion as a correctional strategy is a way of sustaining correctional control over offenders, while at the same time allowing them to live in the community.

FORMS

There are two types of diversion: informal and formal. Informal diversion occurs when an official in the justice system decides, using the appropriate discretion, that a case would be better kept out of the justice system. Such decisions occur every day. For example, police will consider diverting a suspect when the offense is minor (e.g., a traffic violation) and the suspect is calm and deferential. In more formal situations, there is typically a program that the accused must complete as a condition of diversion. The offender is offered some form of treatment or voluntary sanction that, once completed, justifies the closing of the original case. For example, an offender who commits an act of domestic violence may be sent to an anger management program. If the offender successfully completes the program, the case will be dropped or closed in an unofficial capacity.

Diversion occurs at different stages of the system. The most common diversion decision occurs when a police officer decides not to arrest a suspect, even when there is considerable evidence that a crime has been committed. If the officer does make an arrest, a different form of diversion may be used. Arrest gives the criminal justice system control over the accused—control that can be used to force the accused into a social service program. The idea is that many people get in trouble with the law because of personal problems (e.g., substance abuse, uncontrollable anger, or the inability to earn a legitimate living); it is thought that treatment of these behaviors will prevent a reoccurrence of the crime. Therefore, authorities will often forego prosecution if a defendant enrolls in a treatment program, especially if the defendent is a first-time offender.

Jail diversion programs typically have a very simple aim: to allow the offender to avoid confinement while awaiting trial. The benefits of avoiding confinement are considerable. A pretrial jail term, even if only a few weeks long, can mean loss of a job and disruption of family life and other social ties. Being locked up also makes it harder for the defendant to assist in the preparation of his or her defense.

Jail diversion frequently is an option exercised by the arresting officer. In the case of a minor offense, a summons can be given, indicating a date and time for the accused to face the charges in court. A summons operates much like a traffic ticket: The accused is technically arrested but is free to go after agreeing to a court date. Because of fears that a summons may underplay the seriousness of a criminal accusation, its use is restricted to only the least serious misdemeanors. A more frequent jail diversion approach occurs after the suspect has been brought to the station house and booked: release on recognizance (ROR). Under ROR, the accused promises to appear in court at a specified date and time in exchange for release from custody.

Diversion can also occur after formal admittance to the criminal justice system, even after conviction. Once convicted, the offender faces the bench for sentencing. For most felonies, the judge imposes a term of incarceration. But most offenders will not serve the full term. Instead, they will likely be considered for a form of diversion, either probation, or in the case of nonviolent crimes, restitution or community service. Restitution requires the offender to participate in service designed to make reparation for the harm resulting from a criminal offense. Restitution is used most often for economic offenses, such as theft or property damage. Community service requires the offender to work for a community agency. It is unpaid service to the public, which symbolically atones for the harm caused by the crime. Both restitution and community service provide victims and the community with compensation, and provide alternatives for judges that are somewhat less punitive and far less expensive than jail or prison time.

GOALS AND BENEFITS

For the offender, the main goal of diversion is rehabilitation: Diversion programs provide offenders with essential services that can address the underlying causes of criminal behavior, such as alcohol and drug abuse. It is hoped that diversion will allow offenders to establish a normal lifestyle, without the burden of a criminal record. Diversion may also be less costly for the offender. For example, an offender who remains in the community can retain their his or her, and has no need to hire an attorney. Job loss especially can cause further difficulties, especially if wages are needed to pay for counseling, restitution, fines, or court costs.

Diversion also holds important benefits for the system. It is these benefits that ensure the continuation of diversion in the face of detractors. The system needs diversion. The fact that nearly all offenders experiences diversion at some point in their criminal careers is an indication of how central diversion is to the penal system. There are not enough police to arrest every offender, not enough prosecutors to give every offender a trial, and not enough prisons and jails to incarcerate every convict. Diversion makes our current justice system possible, fiscally and strategically.

Diversion can be less costly than other criminal justice processing. In many cases, treatment or counseling is less expensive than prosecution and incarceration. The most obvious benefit of diversion programs is that they avoid the expense and harshness of the full operation of the criminal law. Diversion also influences the balance of power among criminal justice officials, thereby increasing the options of the system, and enabling justice officials to tailor penalties to the unique circumstances of each case. This discretion allows officials to balance the needs of the offender and the demands of justice. This is an example of the principle of exchange relationships: Every actor in the court system has needs that can only be met if other officials cooperate. Judges need to avoid time-consuming jury trials, which means that offenders must be willing to plea bargain. Prosecutors want convictions and defensible penalties, and these are made most likely by guilty pleas. The defense wants to control and limit the severity of the penalty, which requires the cooperation of both the court and the prosecution. The idea is that each actor gives up something in exchange for his or her own needs being met.

LIMITS

Successful diversion programs appear to save tax dollars, improve life circumstances for offenders, satisfy victims, and provide services to the community. Yet these programs are not without controversy. Among the criticisms of diversion are that such programs are lenient, that they neglect victims, that they may be more costly in the long run, that they promote net widening, and that individual rights may be compromised.

Diversion programs are criticized as being unduly lenient because they allow offenders to be sanctioned in an unconventional manner. In the United States, many feel that if an offender is not incarcerated, then the punishment is not severe enough, and justice has not been served; neither do many people want criminals living among them. The average citizen is unfamiliar with the benefits of diversion programs and is unlikely to support them.

Some argue that because diversion often considers the needs of the offender and the savings to the criminal justice system, little concern is shown for victims. This problem can be solved by involving victims in the diversion process. Such involvement may allow victims to better understand the reasons behind crime, which may help them psychologically adjust to their victimization. And those who commit crimes may also benefit from meeting with victims. Offenders who meet victims may better appreciate the harm their illegal behavior causes.

Diversion is also criticized because not all programs are successful. In some cases, programs are poorly designed or implemented. In other cases, the offender fails to abide by the requirements of diversion, or is engaged in behavior that is uncorrectable. When diversion programs fail, individuals suffer, tax dollars are wasted, victimization is increased, and the system loses credibility. And in some of these cases diversion can actually be more expensive than normal processing because offenders later have to be reprocessed and possibly incarcerated.

Some critics argue that diversion contributes to net widening. Net widening occurs when the net of social control is broadened to manage the behavior of individuals who otherwise would not be part of the system. Net widening is a problem because it is in direct conflict with the goal of diversion: to keep people out of the criminal justice system. Through net widening, diversion may actually result in more severe treatment of offenders, as, for example, when an offender's failure to comply with the conditions of a diversion program results in probation or incarceration.

Diversion programs can also create problems related to the legal rights and treatment of those accused of illegal acts. An offender who chooses diversion over formal processing may give up certain due process guarantees that the formally prosecuted offender does not. In some cases, diversion can even be used to force treatment on people who have not committed a crime. For example, given the choice between facing the possibility of incarceration or placement in a diversion program a suspect may choose the latter—even if he or she is in fact not guilty. In other cases, police or prosecutors may coerce treatment when a crime has been committed but evidence is insufficient to obtain a conviction. There is a danger that diversion can be used to cover up inappropriate or careless police procedures that produce evidence that is inadmissible in court.

The controversies surrounding diversion programs often are presented as though diversion reflects some sort of unusual undercutting of the penal system. In fact, at every stage of justice processing, from arrest to imprisonment, policy makers provide alternative routes that allow the offender and the system to avoid the full consequences of the penal law. The criticisms of prison diversion programs may have merit, but to the degree they are based on a claim that every offender should face the full impact of the penal law, they are contrary to history and practice.

SUMMARY

Diversion is a mechanism by which offenders avoid formal processing by the criminal justice system. This can be accomplished either formally by requiring an offender to meet a condition to close a case or informally by keeping an offender from even entering the system. The use of diversion as an alternative strategy is not unusual in the justice system. In fact, the twin rationales of diversion—to minimize the human and financial costs of justice processing and to provide services outside the justice system—are used to justify diversion at every stage of criminal justice. Experts recognize that the justice system is expensive and sometimes ineffectual, and that it should be possible to avoid the full force of the law when circumstances warrant.

Surprisingly, with the proliferation of diversion programs there has as yet been only limited study of their effectiveness. Analysis shows that diversion programs have an uneven history. As sensible as these programs seem at first glance, many are controversial. Successful diversion programs appear to save tax dollars, improve life circumstances for offenders, satisfy victims, and provide services to the community. Yet even these are criticized as being unduly lenient. Unsuccessful pro-

grams cost tax dollars, increase victimization, and lead to a lack of credibility for the system. Through net widening, they may actually result in more severe treatment of offenders. As the costs of incarceration continue to increase, local, state, and federal officials will likely see diversion as a low cost punishment alternative despite the lack of evidence of their effectiveness.

—*Carrie A. Weise-Pengelly and Harry R. Dammer*

See also COMMUNITY SERVICE; HARM REDUCTION; NET WIDENING

Further Reading

Anglin, M. Douglas, and Thomas H. Maugh. (1992). "Ensuring Success in Interventions with Drug-Using Offenders." *Annals of the American Academy of Political and Social Sciences* 521: 66–90.

Austin, James, and Barry Krisberg. (1981). "Wider, Stronger, and Different Nets: The Dialectics of Criminal Justice Reform." *Journal of Research in Crime and Delinquency* 18: 165–196.

Clear, Todd R., and Harry R. Dammer. (1999). *The Offender in the Community*. Belmont, CA: Wadsworth-Thompson.

Falkin, Gregory P., Douglas S. Lipton, and Harry K. Wexler. (1992). "Drug Treatment in State Prisons." In *Treating Drug Problems*, edited by Dean R. Gerstein, Douglas S. Lipton, and Hendrick J. Harwood. Washington, DC: National Academy Press, 89–113.

National Association of Pretrial Services Agencies. (1995). "Performance Standards and Goals for Pretrial Release and Diversion." Washington, DC: National Association of Pretrial Services Agencies.

▼ DNA TESTING

English geneticist Alec Jeffreys first described a method for "typing" human DNA in 1985. Since that time, DNA typing technology has advanced rapidly, and the new DNA tests have been embraced eagerly by the criminal justice system. DNA tests are now routinely used to help identify the source of blood, semen, hair, and other biological materials found at crime scenes and to establish family relationships in cases of disputed parentage. DNA tests have helped prosecutors obtain convictions in thousands of cases, and they have helped establish the innocence of thousands of individuals who might otherwise have become suspects.

HOW DNA TESTS WORK

Deoxyribonucleic acid, or DNA, is a long, double-stranded molecule configured like a twisted ladder or "double helix." The genetic information of all organisms is encoded in the sequence of four organic compounds (bases) that make up the rungs of the DNA ladder. Most DNA is tightly packed into structures called chromosomes in the nuclei of cells. In humans, there are twenty-three pairs of chromosomes; half of each pair is inherited from the individual's mother, half from the father. The total complement of DNA is called the genome.

By some estimates, 99.9 percent of the genetic code is the same in all humans. To identify individuals, DNA tests focus on a few loci (plural of "locus," a specific location on the human genome) where there is variation among individuals. These loci are called polymorphisms because the genetic code can take different forms in different individuals. Each possible form is called an allele.

Forensic DNA tests have examined two types of polymorphisms. Sequence polymorphisms vary only in the sequence of the genetic code. Length polymorphisms contain repeating sequences of genetic code; the number of repetitions may vary from person to person, making the section longer in some people and shorter in others. Analysts begin the testing process by extracting DNA from cells and purifying it. To do this, they use test tubes, chemical reagents, and other standard procedures of laboratory chemistry.

In sexual assault cases, spermatozoa (containing male DNA) may be mixed with epithelial (skin) cells from the victim. Analysts generally try to separate the male and female components into separate extracts (samples) using a process called differential lysis, which employs weak detergents to liberate DNA from the epithelial cells, followed by stronger detergents to liberate DNA from the tougher spermatozoa. After the DNA is extracted, it can be "typed" using several different methods.

RFLP Analysis

When DNA tests were first introduced in the late 1980s, most laboratories employed a method called RFLP analysis (restriction fragment length polymorphism analysis), which uses enzymes to break the long strands of DNA into shorter fragments (restriction fragments) and separates these by length (using a process called electrophoresis). A pattern of dark bands on an X-ray or photographic plate reveals the position (and hence the length) of target fragments that contain length polymorphisms.

Figure 1 shows RFLP analysis of a single locus

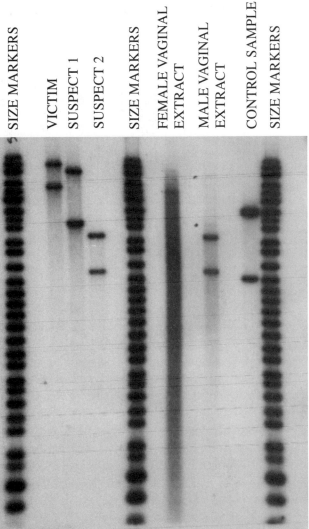

Figure 1. RFLP Test Results in a Rape Case
Source: William C. Thompson.

(containing a length polymorphism) in a case in which a woman was raped by two men. Each "lane" contains DNA from a different sample. The lanes labeled "size markers" contain DNA fragments of known size from bacteria and are used for calibration. Lanes on the left side show the band patterns produced by reference samples from the victim and two suspects. There are two bands in each lane because each individual has two copies of the relevant locus, one from the paternal half of the chromosome, the other from the maternal half.

Lanes on the right side of Figure 1 show the band patterns of evidence samples. The lane labeled "female vaginal extract" contains DNA from the female component (epithelial cells) of a vaginal sample taken from the victim. The DNA in this sample was too degraded to produce a distinct band pattern. The lane labeled "male vaginal extract" shows the band pattern of DNA from the male component (spermatozoa) of the same vaginal sample. This lane contains a band pattern similar to that of Suspect 2, which indicates that the spermatozoa could have come from Suspect 2.

In a typical case, four to six different loci (each containing a different length polymorphism) are examined in this manner. The full set of alleles identified in a sample is called its DNA profile. Because the probability of a matching pattern at any locus is on the order of one in hundreds to one in thousands, and the probabilities of a match at the various loci are assumed to be statistically independent, the probability of a match at four or more loci is generally put at one in many millions or even billions.

Although RFLP analysis is generally reliable, it sometimes entails subjective judgment. Whether the lane labeled "male vaginal extract" also contained bands corresponding to those of Suspect 1 is a matter of judgment on which experts in this case disagreed. Dots to the left of the lane are felt-tip pen marks placed by a forensic analyst to indicate where he thought he saw bands matching those of Suspect 1.

RFLP analysis requires samples that are relatively large (blood or semen stains about the size of a quarter) and well preserved. It is also slow. A typical case takes four to six weeks.

DQ-Alpha and Polymarker Tests

In the early 1990s, newer methods of DNA testing were introduced that are faster (producing results in a day or two) and more sensitive (i.e., capable of typing smaller, more degraded samples). The new methods use a procedure called polymerase chain reaction (PCR), which can produce billions of copies of target fragments of DNA from one or more loci. These

"amplified" DNA fragments (called amplicons), can then be typed using several methods.

In 1991, Perkin-Elmer (PE), a biotechnology firm, developed a test kit for amplifying and typing a sequence polymorphism known as the DQ-alpha gene. Six distinct alleles (variants) of this gene can be identified by exposing the amplified DNA to paper test strips containing allele-specific probes (see Figure 2). The dots on the strip signal the presence of particular alleles. This test has the advantage of great sensitivity (DNA from just a few human cells is sufficient to produce a result) and allows more rapid analysis (one to two days), but it is not as discriminating as RFLP analysis.

In 1993, PE introduced an improved kit that typed DQ-alpha and five additional genes simultaneously, thereby improving the specificity (the ability to discriminate among individuals) of this method (see Figure 2). With this new kit, known as the Polymarker/DQ-alpha test, individual profile frequencies are on the order of one in tens of thousands, however it still is not as discriminating as RFLP analysis. As with RFLP analysis, interpretation of the test strips may require subjective judgments. For example, experts disagreed on whether the dot labeled 1.3 in the lower strip shown in Figure 2 is dark enough to reliably indicate the presence of the allele designated 1.3.

STR Tests

The late 1990s saw the advent of STR (short tandem repeat) DNA testing. STR tests combine the sensitivity of a PCR-based test with great specificity (profile frequencies potentially as low as one in trillions) and therefore have quickly supplanted both RFLP analysis and the Polymarker/DQ-alpha test in forensic laboratories. An STR is a DNA locus that contains a length polymorphism. At each STR locus, people have two alleles (one from each parent) that vary in length depending on the number of repetitions of a short core sequence of genetic code. For example, a person with genotype 14, 15 at an

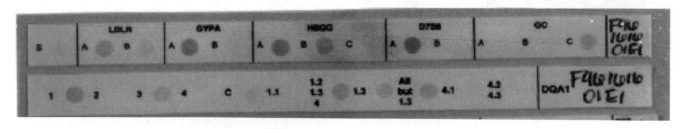

Figure 2: Results of Polymarker Test (top) and DQ-Alpha Test (bottom)
SOURCE: William C. Thompson.

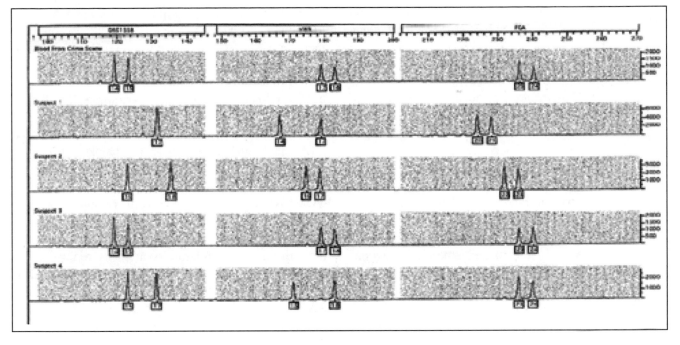

Figure 3. STR Test Results
Source: William C. Thompson.

STR locus has one allele with fourteen repeating units, and another with fifteen repeating units.

Figure 3 shows the results of STR analysis of five samples: blood from a crime scene and reference samples of four suspects. This analysis includes three loci, labeled "D3S1358," "vWA," and "FGA." Each person has two alleles (peaks) at each locus, one from the maternal portion and the other from the paternal portion of the chromosome. The position of the peaks on each graph (known as an electropherogram) indicates the length (and hence the number of core sequence repeats) of each STR. As can be seen, the profile of Suspect 3 corresponds to that of the crime scene sample, indicating he is a possible source. Suspects 1, 2, and 4 are eliminated as possible sources.

In 1997, the FBI identified thirteen STR loci that it deemed appropriate for forensic testing. Commercial firms quickly developed test kits and automated equipment for typing these STRs. The most popular test procedure, developed by Applied Biosciences International (ABI), a PE subsidiary, includes a PCR kit known as ProfilerPlus that simultaneously "amplifies" DNA from up to nine STR loci and labels the loci with colored dyes. An automated test instrument called the ABI 310 Genetic Analyzer then separates the resulting amplicons by length (using electrophoresis) and uses a laser to cause fluorescence of the dye-labeled fragments. A computer-controlled electronic camera detects the size and relative position of the fragments, identifies alleles, and displays the results as shown in Figure 3. STR tests have greatly improved the capabilities of forensic laboratories, allowing highly specific DNA profiles to be derived from tiny quantities of cellular material. Test results generally allow a clear-cut determination of whether a particular individual could be the source of an evidentiary sample, although experts have differed over interpretation of results in some cases.

Mitochondrial DNA Tests

The tests described thus far examine DNA from cell nuclei (nuclear DNA). DNA is also found in cell mitochondria, which are organelles (structures) in which the process of cellular respiration occurs. Mitochondrial DNA (often designated "mtDNA") contains sequence polymorphisms. In the late 1990s, forensic scientists began testing mtDNA by using a procedure known as genetic sequencing to produce a readout of the genetic code from two polymorphic areas of the mitochondrial genome. Forensic scientists describe an mtDNA profile by stating how its sequence differs from that of a reference standard called the Anderson sequence (named after the donor of the first DNA tested with this method).

Mitochondrial DNA tests are highly sensitive and can produce results from samples that are not suitable for other DNA tests, such as hair shafts, bone, and teeth. Because mtDNA is present in hundreds or thousands of copies per cell, it often survives much longer than nuclear DNA in old, degraded cellular samples. DNA tests on very old samples, such as the bones of Czar Nicholas II of Russia, have detected and typed mtDNA.

Mitochondrial DNA tests are far less discriminating than STR tests. The frequency of mtDNA profiles is generally put at one in hundreds. In addition, because mtDNA is inherited maternally, mtDNA tests generally cannot distinguish between individuals in the same maternal line. Hence, sons of the same mother would be expected to have the same mtDNA profile, and this profile would also be found in daughters of the mother's sister and all of their children.

Minor variations are sometimes found in mtDNA profiles of different cells from the same person due to mutations. This phenomenon, known as heteroplasmy, complicates the process of determining whether two mtDNA profiles match. The appropriate standards for declaring an mtDNA match, and for estimating the rarity of matching profiles, are issues that have been debated in the courtroom.

Mitochondrial DNA tests are expensive and require special laboratory facilities and techniques. At this time only a few forensic laboratories perform these tests and they are used only where other types of DNA testing fail or cannot work. However, future technical improvements may lead to wider use of mtDNA tests.

RELIABILITY AND QUALITY ASSURANCE

Although current DNA technology is capable of producing valid and highly reliable results, questions are sometimes raised about the quality of laboratory work. Key issues include the potential for biased or mistaken interpretation of laboratory results and the possibility for error due to mishandling of samples. Acknowledging problems with the quality of early DNA testing procedures, a 1992 report of the National Research Council called for broader scrutiny of forensic DNA testing by a scientific body from outside the law enforcement community.

In response, the U.S. Federal Bureau of Investigation (FBI) created its own advisory body that was initially called the Technical Working Group for DNA Analysis Methods (TWGDAM) and more recently called the Scientific Working Group for DNA Analysis Methods (SWGDAM). The FBI director appoints its members. Although it has not satisfied all critics of forensic laboratory practices, this body has been credited with issuing guidelines that have improved the quality of forensic DNA work. For example, SWGDAM guidelines call for each analyst to take two proficiency tests each year.

Another quality assurance mechanism is laboratory accreditation. The American Society of Crime Laboratory Directors Laboratory Accreditation Board (ASCLAD-LAB) is a nonprofit organization that reviews the protocols and procedures of forensic DNA laboratories and issues a certificate of accreditation to those meeting its standards. To help ensure the competence of laboratory workers, a professional organization called the American Board of Criminology has developed a certification programs for DNA analysts.

Despite these efforts, problems occasionally come to light. Errors have occurred in proficiency tests, although they are infrequent. Occasional errors arising from accidental switching and mislabeling of samples or misinterpretation of results have come to light in court cases. In one case, misinterpretation of a DNA test contributed to the wrongful rape conviction of a man who was later exonerated when more extensive DNA tests, by another laboratory, proved he could not have been the rapist.

A 1996 report of the National Research Council suggested that retesting of samples is the best way to address remaining concerns about the quality of laboratory work. The great sensitivity of PCR-based DNA tests makes it possible, in most cases, to split samples for duplicate analysis.

DATA BANKS AND DRAGNETS

The United Kingdom and all fifty American states now have government-operated data banks containing the DNA profiles of known offenders. Many crimes have been solved when a data bank search revealed a match between the DNA profile of a blood or semen sample left by the perpetrator at a crime scene and the profile of a known individual in the data bank. A data bank match is called a "cold hit."

The FBI maintains a national data bank of DNA profiles known as CODIS (Combined DNA Indexing System), which includes a Convicted Offender Index (containing profiles of offenders submitted by states) and a Forensic Index (containing DNA profiles of

Social, Ethical, and Legal Issues in DNA Testing

The following is an excerpt from a report by the Research and Development Working Group of the National Institute of Justice.

We are aware that a number of issues raised in this report have social, ethical, and legal implications beyond the assignment of the working group. We have no special qualifications for dealing with them. Instead, we identify some of the problems and call them to the attention of the Commission and other groups.

Group and trait identification. We have mentioned that STR allele frequencies differ in different population groups. Thus, a particular profile in a crime scene sample may be more probable in one group that in another. This can be used as a likelihood ratio with appropriate prior probabilities to provide evidence for the group origin of the DNA sample. There are also genes that are common in some groups and rare in others; one Duffy blood group allele is an example. Such information can be of value for crime investigation. Like an eyewitness account it can be helpful in narrowing the search for a suspect. But, also like an eyewitness account, it may be quite unreliable. There are objections on the grounds that classifying possible suspects on ancestral grounds can be interpreted as stigmatizing some groups. There is already much public discussion of "racial profiling." This is not the same, but to some it is too close for comfort.

This is a time of very rapid progress in gene identification, thanks to the Human Genome Project and numerous research laboratories. Genetic markers for eye, hair, and skin color, for color-blindness, for baldness, and for less common traits such as albinism will soon be discovered, if they have not been already. We can expect the number to increase rapidly. We again note that the identification for complex traits will almost always be likelihoods rather than certainties, at least in the near future. But even imprecise information can be useful. We also emphasize that genes used for trait identification are not currently used in ordinary forensic work, with the exception of amelogenin for sex identification. The 13 STR loci, as we have emphasized, are not associated with specific, observable traits. Throughout this report, our emphasis has been on identifying individuals as such and not as members of groups. Consistent with this view, we emphasize for future development the desirability of markers for traits rather than for groups.

Identification of Relatives. With 13 STR loci it is quite likely that a search of a database will identify a person who is relative of the person contributing the evidence sample. We discussed earlier a pair of profiles that almost certainly came from siblings, and parent–child combinations can also often be identified. Other close relatives may also be identified, but with much less certainty. Suppose a crime scene profile shows a partial match with someone in the database. Are law enforcement officers entitled to investigate the relatives? At present, laws in different States are different. In Virginia, for example, this is forbidden.

Broadening the database. The largest database at present is that of convicted felons, usually perpetrators of major crimes. There is considerable interest in increasing the database to include persons convicted of lesser crimes or arrestees. In Britain everyone arrested for offenses that would lead to prison terms if convicted has a DNA sample taken at the time of arrest, but the profile is removed from the database if the person is not convicted. These are issues beyond the responsibilities of this Research and Development Working Group. We note that increasing the database size will increase the number of crimes solved though its use. This benefit will require the inclusion of methods to deal with the changes in the prior odds for a suspect to be found in such a database search.

Source: *The Future of Forensic DNA Testing: Predictions of the Research and Development Working Group.* (2000). Washington, DC: National Institute of Justice.

evidence related to unsolved crimes). CODIS allows government crime laboratories at a state and local level to conduct national searches that might reveal, for example, that semen deposited during an unsolved rape in Florida could have come from a known offender from Virginia.

Government data banks were initially limited to convicted violent or sex offenders. However, there has been serious discussion of expanding data banks to include arrestees, or even to make them universal (perhaps by sampling DNA from all citizens at birth), in the interest of better crime control.

Civil libertarians have expressed concern that government agencies could use the genetic information they collect in an intrusive or inappropriate manner. The information included in CODIS is limited to numerical data that designate RFLP and STR profiles. These profiles are useful for identifying individuals but are linked to no known medical or behavioral characteristics. However, most states have retained blood samples from those included in state data banks. State and federal statutes limit the disclosure of information contained in government data banks and generally specify that it be used solely for law enforcement purposes.

When police have the DNA profile of a perpetrator but cannot establish his or her identity, they sometimes conduct what has become known as a "DNA dragnet," in which large numbers of individuals in the relevant community are asked to voluntarily submit samples for DNA testing. Police generally collect samples by rubbing inside the individual's cheek with a cotton swab. Even if the guilty party does not submit a sample, the DNA dragnet may help police by narrowing the number of possible suspects. The first DNA dragnet, which was chronicled in Joseph Wambaugh's book *The Blooding,* helped police solve two murders in Leicester, England in 1987. The guilty man was identified when, in an effort to avoid suspicion, he asked a friend to submit a sample in his place. DNA dragnets have since been used repeatedly in Britain and are becoming more common in the United States.

Prosecutors in some jurisdictions have developed a procedural innovation called a "DNA warrant" as a means of avoiding the statute of limitations in cases where the authorities have DNA from the perpetrator but have not yet identified a suspect. Before the statute of limitations runs out, charges are formally filed in the case, but the defendant is identified by DNA profile rather than by name. The legality and constitutionality of this practice is still subject to debate at this writing.

DNA EVIDENCE IN THE COURTS

Judges in the United States have traditionally acted as "gatekeepers" for scientific evidence, excluding evidence that is deemed insufficiently reliable to be heard by a jury. Many state courts apply the *Frye* standard (first articulated in a 1923 appellate case, *Frye v. United States)*, which requires that scientific testimony be based on a method or technique that is "generally accepted" by the "relevant scientific community." Since 1993, federal courts (and some state courts) have

applied a standard articulated by the U.S. Supreme Court in a case called *Daubert v. Merrill Dow Pharmaceuticals,* which requires the judge to consider whether scientific testimony is "valid," based on such factors as whether the underlying method has been tested, is subject to error, has been published, has been performed in accordance with appropriate standards, and is generally accepted.

In the early 1990s, a number of state courts ruled DNA evidence inadmissible on grounds that the underlying methods were not yet "generally accepted." The key issue was the assumption of statistical independence of alleles that underlay the methods used for estimating the rarity of RFLP DNA profiles. A number of prominent scientists questioned whether sufficient research had been done to validate the independence assumption. Their major concern was that human populations might be "structured," so that people of Italian ancestry, for example, would be unusually likely to have some profiles, while those of Norwegian ancestry would be likely to have other profiles, and so on. Forensic laboratories generally computed separate statistical estimates for major racial/ethnic groups (i.e., for those of Caucasian, Hispanic, African, and sometimes Asian ancestry), but they had insufficient data to generate reliable estimates for subgroups.

A 1992 report of the National Research Council gave credence to concerns about population structure and suggested that a conservative method called the "ceiling principle" be used for estimating the rarity of DNA profiles. A few appellate courts thereafter overturned convictions in cases in which the ceiling principle calculations had not been used. However, after further research found relatively little evidence of population structure for RFLP profiles, and a 1996 report of the National Research Council declared that the ceiling principle was no longer necessary, the admissibility of RFLP DNA tests was solidly established.

As each new generation of DNA technology reaches the courtroom, its reliability must be established under either the *Frye* or *Daubert* standard. To make this determination, judges sometimes hold pretrial hearings in which the parties can present scientific testimony. Often there is scientific debate about the reliability of new procedures and the adequacy of the underlying validation, and hence there is a period of uncertainty over whether the "general acceptance" test will be met. The issue has been complicated by the tendency of some forensic laboratories to begin using new tests before the underlying validation research has been published, and by the refusal of some commercial vendors to reveal complete scientific details of new methods on the grounds that they are trade secrets.

Once the admissibility of a particular method is established by appellate ruling, courts in *Frye* jurisdictions generally admit the results of that method automatically. However, under the *Daubert* standard and in a few *Frye* states (California is a prominent example), judges may still rule DNA evidence inadmissible if they find that a laboratory failed to follow reliable scientific procedures in the case at hand.

DNA test results that are admitted into evidence can still be challenged in front of the jury. When lawyers attack DNA evidence, they generally try to show that the results were misinterpreted, that the laboratory may have mixed up or cross-contaminated samples, or that an innocent transfer of DNA could have produced the incriminating results. In the O. J. Simpson trial, for example, defense lawyers argued that the crime laboratory either inadvertently transferred Simpson's blood from a reference vial to samples collected at the crime scene, or, alternatively, that Simpson's blood may have been intentionally planted.

POSTCONVICTION DNA TESTING

A number of convicted men in prison have sought to prove their innocence through DNA testing. As of early 2002, ninety-nine men had been released from U.S. prisons after being exonerated by DNA tests. Several of these men had been facing execution. DNA exonerations prompted a number of states to pass laws requiring the government to afford convicted men access to biological evidence and to fund postconviction DNA testing in cases where DNA testing was not done.

How were these innocent men convicted in the first place? Mistaken eyewitnesses were a key factor in the majority of these cases. Other factors that contributed to false convictions (in some but not all cases) include faulty forensic science (such as misleading conclusions from hair and fiber comparisons), fraudulent forensic science testimony (including the fabrication of serological test results in several cases), false confessions, lies told by so-called snitches (government informants), prosecutorial misconduct (such as failure to reveal exculpatory evidence), and incompetent defense lawyers.

The use of DNA testing to reexamine old cases was pioneered by the Innocence Project (www.innocenceproject.org), a legal clinic at Benjamin Cardozo Law School in New York City. Lawyers Peter Neufeld and Barry Scheck, who codirect the Innocence Project, personally represented over forty of the exonerated men and have played a key role in investigating the causes of these miscarriages of justice.

DNA TYPING IN THE FUTURE

Technical advances will continue to reduce the time and expense of DNA testing. Improvements in test kits should soon allow simultaneous PCR amplification of larger numbers of STRs, affording even greater speed and specificity to STR testing. Gene chip technology is already available that will allow typing of DNA within a few minutes on a custom-designed computer chip. In the near future, this technology will make it feasible for police to perform STR typing of suspects and samples in the field using devices small enough to carry by hand.

The range of information that can be extracted from biological samples will also improve. New genetic probes that identify features on the Y-chromosome (which is possessed only by males) should help distinguish male from female DNA in sexual assault cases. Probes are also becoming available that can show what a DNA contributor looks like. The British Forensic Science Service has experimented with a probe that detects genes associated with red hair and a ruddy complexion.

Genetic tests capable of identifying behavioral propensities have been widely discussed due to their potentially profound ethical and social implications. However, because the association between genes and behavior is complex, the use of DNA tests to predict behavior is unlikely to be feasible in the near future.

—*William C. Thompson*

See also WRONGFUL CONVICTIONS

Further Reading

Butler, John. M. (2001). *Forensic DNA Typing: Biology and Technology Behind STR Markers.* San Diego, CA: Academic Press.

Evett, Ian. W., and Bruce S. Weir. (1998). *Interpreting DNA Evidence: Statistical Genetics for Forensic Scientists.* Sunderland, MA: Sinauer.

Inman, Keith, and Norah Rudin. (1997). *An Introduction to Forensic DNA Analysis.* Boca Raton, FL: CRC Press.

Kaye, David. H., and George F. Sensabaugh. (2000). "Reference Guide on DNA Evidence." In *Reference Manual on Scientific Evidence*, edited by Joseph Cecil. Washington, DC: Federal Judicial Center, 485–576.

National Commission on the Future of DNA Evidence. (2000). *DNA Testing: Predictions of the Research and Development Working Group.* Washington, DC: National Institute of Justice.

National Research Council. (1992). *DNA Technology in Forensic*

Science. Washington, DC: National Academy Press.

———. (1996). *The Evaluation of Forensic DNA Evidence.* Washington, DC: National Academy Press.

Scheck, Barry, Peter Neufeld, and Jim Dwyer. (2000). *Actual Innocence.* New York: Doubleday.

Thompson, William C. (1996). "DNA Evidence in the O. J. Simpson Trial." *University of Colorado Law Review* 67, 4: 827–857.

———. (1997). "Forensic DNA Evidence." In *Expert Evidence: A Practitioner's Guide to Law, Science and the FJC Manual,* edited by Bert Black and Patrick Lee. St. Paul, MN: West Group, 195–266.

Thompson, William C., and Simon Ford. (1991). "The Meaning of a Match: Sources of Ambiguity in the Interpretation of DNA Prints." In *Forensic DNA Technology,* edited by Mark Farley and James Harrington. New York: CRC Press, 93–152.

Wambaugh, Joseph. (1989). *The Blooding.* New York: Morrow.

Court Cases

Daubert v. Merrill Dow Pharmaceuticals, Inc. (1993). 509 U.S. 579.

Frye v. United States (1923). 293 F. 1013.

DOMESTIC VIOLENCE COURTS

Domestic violence is one of the most significant issues facing the criminal justice system today. It is estimated that domestic violence is the leading cause of injuries in women aged fifteen to forty-four. In the 1980s, C. Everett Koop, the U.S. surgeon general, called domestic violence the number one health risk for adult women—greater than the risk of muggings, auto accidents, and cancer deaths combined. The passage of the 1994 Violence Against Women Act heightened public awareness of domestic violence and its detrimental effects on society. As awareness of domestic violence has increased, society has been more willing to acknowledge the complexity and prevalence of the problem.

Although law enforcement was the first segment of the criminal justice system to institute major reforms in its response to domestic violence, court systems across the nation are increasingly forming institutional partnerships aimed at improving the prosecution and adjudication of domestic violence cases. Since 1996, the Conference of Chief Justices and the Conference of State Court Administrators have maintained a joint Domestic Violence Task Force to assist state courts in developing effective policies and practices to address domestic violence. The impetus for seeking alternative approaches to how courts handle domestic violence cases has been heightened as court officials become more concerned with managing crowded court dockets. It is estimated that domestic violence filings in state courts increased 178 percent between 1989 and 1998, and today account for the fastest growing proportion of domestic relations caseloads.

A growing trend in court management has been the proliferation of specialized courts that develop calendars and procedures to handle a particular category of crime. For example, it is now common for jurisdictions to have separate courts to adjudicate drug-related offenses. These courts typically incorporate case management techniques that encourage the use of early screening of cases and a classification system that schedules cases according to their complexity and priority. Furthermore, many drug courts incorporate a treatment approach to responding to drug offenders. In these jurisdictions, offenders are diverted into a drug treatment program. A central component of these programs is the development of a team approach, in which court and community professionals work together in monitoring the drug treatment program.

Although specialization has occurred in juvenile and family courts for quite some time, the use of dedicated domestic violence courts is relatively new but rapidly becoming more popular. It is estimated that more than 300 courts now have specialized structures, processes, and practices to address the distinct nature of domestic violence cases. Examinations of these programs indicate a significant diversity in processes. Although many courts are employing specific procedures and coordinated community responses to address domestic violence, there are relatively few discrete domestic violence models. Despite the lack of one particular model of domestic violence courts, several major factors emerge from these various practices that distinguish domestic violence courts from other judicial proceedings. The most common reasons courts cite for implementing specialized domestic violence courts are improved assistance to victims, enhanced victim safety, and increased batterer accountability. The major features of domestic violence courts are case coordination, specialized intake units, specialized calendars, specialized court personnel, service provision, and monitoring.

CASE COORDINATION

A fundamental goal of domestic violence courts is the integration of all issues related to domestic violence. Domestic violence can be an issue in a variety of cases that span different jurisdictions within the court system, including those involving civil protection orders, criminal prosecutions, divorce, child custody and support, dependency, and juvenile delinquency. Although legal issues and remedies intertwine, these cases are typically adjudicated in separate courts before different judges and may involve several criminal justice and community advocacy agencies with little or no coordination. Effective resolution of domestic violence cases necessitates that case information be coordinated among various agencies to ensure that the victims and their children are not placed in dangerous situations, and to minimize confusion about each party's obligations or restrictions. The use of specialized intake units and specialized calendars are some of the mechanisms used to coordinate and track the scheduling of court hearings for related cases.

SPECIALIZED INTAKE UNITS

Courts employ a variety of strategies to link related cases and to screen cases in order to provide services for domestic violence victims and enhance case processing. Specialized intake units orient victims to court procedures, assist victims in seeking referrals to other court divisions or outside service agencies, and encourage early intervention for victims and their children. The goal is to integrate intake for civil, family, and criminal cases, in effect providing a comprehensive multiagency center designed to allow "one-stop shopping" for victims. Because victims are in the most danger immediately after they leave their abusers, multiagency coordinated intake is critical because it functions as the main doorway into the court system. Specialized intake units can also facilitate the coordination of case management by linking the present case to any related case currently pending or subsequently filed.

SPECIALIZED CALENDARS

The assignment of cases to a specialized calendar is a fundamental feature of domestic violence courts because it allows a central location for hearing domestic violence cases. Specialized calendars allow courts to combine civil and criminal cases on one calendar, promote the use of uniform procedures by judges and court staff, and facilitate efficient case processing. The benefits of this assignment system are that court personnel are better able to develop solutions that completely address the domestic violence problem, to impose accountability on the offender, and to assist in the coordination of services. In addition, victims may feel better

understood and more confident in the criminal justice system when they are familiar with court personnel. Perpetrators are also more likely to obey court rules if they know they will be returning to the same judge at a later date.

SPECIALIZED COURT PERSONNEL

Another central component of domestic violence courts is assigning judges who specialize in these types of cases. In some instances, all domestic violence cases are assigned to one judicial officer, while other courts reserve certain days of the docket for hearings on domestic violence cases conducted by judges who handle mixed caseloads. This allows for judges and other court personnel to develop expertise in domestic violence issues. Many jurisdictions require all court personnel working in domestic violence courts to attend training on the dynamics of domestic violence and may even require that they participate in public education on domestic violence and court issues.

SERVICE PROVISION

The needs of domestic violence victims, perpetrators, and children exposed to domestic violence frequently go beyond traditional forms of court intervention. Domestic violence courts work closely with community service agencies to provide services not traditionally available through the court. Domestic violence courts encourage the use of a team perspective whereby court personnel work collaboratively with local civic organizations, battered women shelters, counseling agencies, and other public and private organizations in establishing court orders or services needed by litigants. This component of domestic violence courts uses an integrated systems model to encourage the development of meaningful treatment programs.

MONITORING

Domestic violence courts also aim to establish more meaningful procedures for monitoring compliance with court orders. One way to accomplish this is through the creation of judicial review dockets. These hearings allow the judge who entered an order or accepted a plea to periodically monitor the perpetrator's compliance with the court order. For example, some courts schedule monitoring compliance hearings every thirty, sixty, or ninety days to monitor batterers' compliance with orders. Courts may also institute procedures for increasing sanctions for repeated noncompliance with court orders. In California, monitoring procedures require the participation of court reporters, clerks, bailiffs, victim witness assistance, social service agencies, and judicial officers.

EVALUATION

To date there is little empirical research to assess the effectiveness of domestic violence courts. Only modest progress has been made with regard to the development and testing of models. Anecdotal assessments exist, but clearly there is a need for more extensive empirical study.

In January 1999, the National Center for State Courts conducted a national survey of 160 courts identified as having some type of specialized process, structure, or service. Their survey indicates that the most common reasons courts cite for implementing specialized processes for domestic violence cases are improved assistance to victims, enhanced victim safety, and increased batterer accountability. Yet survey results indicate that a majority of courts have not accomplished these goals. Many courts lacked standard screening and case coordination, available information systems for case screening and tracking, information to effectively guide decisions, systematic mechanisms for monitoring batterer compliance, and sufficient judicial training.

While specialization of domestic case management holds great potential, jurisdictions must be cautious in their implementation. One reality is that it may not be feasible for some jurisdictions to implement a fully integrated domestic violence court. Successful implementation of these programs requires a tremendous investment in the planning phase. Officials need to closely examine existing practices (identifying system strengths and weaknesses), identify funding sources, and develop an implementation plan whereby the court becomes a part of a larger integrated system for reducing domestic violence in the community.

THE FUTURE

Domestic violence courts are a recent and innovative approach to addressing the complexities associated with domestic violence. This strategy holds tremendous promise. Proponents recognize that effective responses to domestic violence require a more integrated systems approach than is available in traditional court structures. To that end, the proliferation of domestic violence courts is encouraging court officials to work more collaboratively with other components of the justice system and the community. Experiences with community policing and community prosecution programs indicate that the criminal justice system is often more effective when it is able to foster more of a problem-solving approach to settling disputes.

Specialized domestic violence courts have the potential to better address victim needs and enhance treatment opportunities for batterers, while simultaneously enhancing the effective management of crowded court dockets. Yet the real success of these programs will be dependent on the courts' ability to foster interagency collaboration and develop integrated information systems that allow for efficient tracking of cases and sharing of information.

—*Anita Neuberger Blowers*

Further Reading

Buzawa, Eve, and Buzawa, Carl. (1996). *Domestic Violence: The Criminal Justice Response*. Thousand Oaks, CA: Sage.

Karan, Amy, Susan Keilitz, and Sharon Denaro. (1999). "Domestic Violence Courts: What Are They and How Should We Manage Them?" *Juvenile and Family Court Journal* 50, 2: 75–86.

Keilitz, Susan. (2000). *Specialization of Domestic Violence Case Management in the Courts: A National Survey*. Williamsburg, VA: National Center for State Courts.

MacLeod, Dag, and Julia Weber. (2000). *Domestic Violence Courts: A Descriptive Study*. San Francisco: Judicial Council of California Administrative Office of the Courts.

Ostrom, B. J., and N. B. Kauer. (1999). *Examining the Work of State Courts, 1998: A National Perspective from the Court Statistics Project*. Williamsburg, VA: National Center for State Courts.

Tsai, B. (2000). "The Trend Toward Specialized Domestic Violence Courts: Improvements on an Effective Innovation." *Fordham University Law Review* 68: 1285–1327.

▼ DRIVING UNDER THE INFLUENCE

One of the most common and tragic of alcohol-related social problems is that of driving under the influence of alcohol (DUI), colloquially known as drunk driving. Given the longstanding social acceptance of alcohol use, it is not surprising that for as long as there have been wheeled vehicles, drivers have consumed alcohol and driven while impaired by its influence. Legislation penalizing driving while intoxicated existed in England even in the early nineteenth century. The clamor for such legislation increased dramatically in the twentieth century as automobiles were invented and as they became more pervasive, powerful, and perilous.

MAGNITUDE OF THE PROBLEM

Alcohol is the single largest identifiable cause of traffic fatalities. Although the use of alcohol can increase mortality rates in a variety of ways, the problem created by alcohol-impaired drivers is that their risk of having a serious accident is significantly elevated. Alcohol-related highway accidents cause a considerable number of deaths annually in countries as diverse as France, Sweden, Australia, the United Kingdom, and the United States.

The rate of these accidents is exceptionally high in the United States, where transportation policy is organized almost exclusively around the automobile and where the culture of recreation frequently features alcohol. The National Highway Traffic Safety Administration estimates that three of every ten Americans will be involved in an alcohol-related accident in their lives. In the United States in the 1980s, there were a quarter of a million traffic fatalities in which alcohol was involved. (The actual figures may be even higher because alcohol testing is not done for every accident.) A large disproportion of these fatalities occurred during nights and on weekends rather than during daytime hours on weekdays. In 1982, 57.3 percent of traffic deaths were estimated to have involved alcohol. These figures describe a public health issue of extraordinary proportions.

Research reveals that there were approximately 1 million alcohol-related crashes in the United States in 1995, killing more than 17,000 people and causing injuries to hundreds of thousands more. Research further reveals that nearly half of the fatal accidents could have been avoided if the drivers had consumed no alcohol. Beyond the human carnage, alcohol-related traffic accidents are estimated to cost the United States tens of billions of dollars each year in property damage, hospital and rehabilitation expenses, and loss of productivity. In 1998 and 1999, nearly 16,000 traffic deaths—38 percent of all the traffic deaths in each of those years—involved alcohol, amounting to one alcohol-related traffic fatality every thirty-three minutes. Although such figures represent a marked decrease from 1982, the first year extensive data were collected, they reveal how devastating the problem of driving under the influence continues to be.

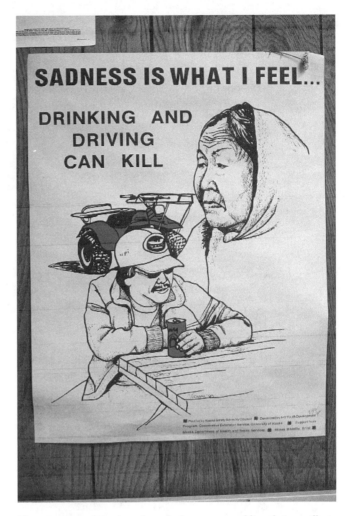

Government agencies have launched numerous public relations efforts to prevent accidents that often result from driving under the influence. This poster from St. Lawrence Island in Alaska seeks to appeal to both whites and Native Americans.

Source: © Nik Wheeler/Corbis; used with permission.

Moreover, the problem is widespread. Researchers estimate that 20 percent of American drivers, approximately 33 million people, drive while impaired beyond legal alcohol limits at least once a year. Approximately one third of college students report that they have driven after drinking. Although nearly 1.5 million drivers are arrested for alcohol-impaired driving each year in the United States, this figure clearly represents a small percentage of the actual number of offenders.

SCIENTIFIC CONTRIBUTIONS

A scientific breakthrough that revolutionized law enforcement in the arena of drinking and driving occurred on the brink of World War II when Scandinavian scientists invented the technology to measure the percentage of alcohol in blood, known as the blood-alcohol concentration, as the index of intoxication. Through analysis of blood or breath samples, the blood-alcohol concentration (BAC) could be determined. A BAC of .05 percent means that alcohol comprises five one-hundredths of one percent of all the blood in a person's system.

Since the invention of this technology, researchers have been studying the effects of drinking alcohol on the skills required to drive an automobile, demonstrating that elevated BAC levels have an adverse effect on coordination, reaction time, judgment, and vision and consequently are causally related to a higher risk of serious traffic accidents. A BAC level, produced by the rate at which alcohol is consumed over a specific period, varies in individuals according to characteristics such as body weight. Food consumption is also an important variable in calculating the degree of alcohol impairment because food slows the absorption of alcohol into the bloodstream.

Recent studies demonstrate that a BAC of .05 percent, reached by some people after two to three drinks in an hour, measurably impairs most drivers' skills and doubles the probability of a fatal traffic accident. For this reason, the American Medical Association recommends .05 percent as the BAC level defining intoxication. Research further indicates that a BAC level of .08 percent, reached by some people after three to four drinks in an hour, multiplies the risk by a factor of ten. A BAC of .10 percent, reached by an average person after five to six drinks in an hour, multiplies the risk by a factor greater than twenty. BACs of .15 percent multiply the risk by hundreds.

In sum, research shows that the higher the driver's blood-alcohol level, the greater the likelihood of the driver being in an accident and being responsible for that accident. Further, the more serious the traffic accident, the greater the likelihood that alcohol was a contributing factor. Alcohol is implicated in approximately 10 percent of minor accidents, 20 percent of accidents causing serious injuries, 50 percent of fatal accidents, and 60 percent of fatal accidents involving only one vehicle. It is also well documented that the vast majority of drivers involved in serious accidents had blood-alcohol levels of .10 percent or higher, although some drivers had blood-alcohol levels ranging from .05 to .10 percent.

For more than forty years, the scientific community has been seeking to understand not only how alcohol affects driving but also how drinking and driving can be best prevented. Researchers have been evaluating the comparative efficacy of various approaches to the problem of intoxicated drivers. One finding that has emerged clearly is that increases in the rate of detection and the certainty of punishment produce decreases in the frequency of drinking and driving behavior, whereas increases solely in the severity of punishment have no such effect. To some extent, scientific findings have informed the legislative activity regarding driving under the influence, although a gap remains between scientific evidence and political outcomes.

POLITICAL RESPONSES

The U.S. government became involved in the states' regulation of drinking and driving when officials of the National Highway Safety Bureau, later known as the National Highway Traffic Safety Administration, met with representatives from every state in 1966 to 1967 to discuss traffic safety. Following these discussions, the first federal standard on driving under the influence of alcohol was issued. Calling on the states to enact laws more reflective of scientific knowledge regarding drinking and driving, the federal standard defined "intoxicated" and "under the influence of alcohol" as having a blood-alcohol concentration no higher than .10 percent. By 1971, every state defined intoxication as a specific blood-alcohol concentration, but not until 1981 had each state set this level at .10 or lower for motor vehicle violations.

Federal efforts to combat drinking and driving continued in the 1970s, but significant policy changes in how society addressed the issue did not begin to occur until powerful nonprofit citizens' lobbies such as Mothers Against Drunk Driving (MADD) were formed. Founded in 1980 by the mother of a young woman killed by a repeat drunk driver who received lenient treatment in the court system, MADD emerged from the victims' rights movement that coalesced in the 1970s and 1980s. Headquartered in Texas, MADD quickly established hundreds of chapters, working in every state and serving more than a million members, many of them the victims or family members of victims of drunk drivers. MADD's visibility in the 1980s led to the creation of other grassroots organizations such as Students Against Drunk Driving (SADD) and Business Against Drunk Driving (BADD). Another large nationwide nonprofit organization actively campaigning against drunk driving is Remove Intoxicated

Drivers (RID), founded in New York in 1978 by the family member of a victim of a drunk driver. The impassioned crusade of citizens' organizations such as these to enhance criminal penalties for intoxicated drivers garnered considerable public attention and support in the 1980s.

When this citizens' movement began, the perception was that DUI was not taken seriously enough as criminal behavior by American courts. Spurred in large part by the advocacy of groups such as MADD, a cultural shift began to occur in the early 1980s when DUI came to be understood widely not as socially acceptable behavior but rather as a serious crime deserving of aggressive criminal justice enforcement and harsh criminal and civil sanctions. Forty-one states created commissions or task forces in 1981 to 1982 to examine the problem of drinking and driving, and the recommendations that they issued led to the legislative enactment of tough laws that dramatically increased criminal and civil penalties for DUI offenses. In some states, this legislation took the form of comprehensive amendments to existing DUI statutes. By 1985, state legislatures had enacted more than 1,000 DUI statutes. In 1987 alone, 216 DUI laws were enacted in forty-five states. Between 1980 and 1990, no area of the law received more attention or more nationwide legislative activity than did laws governing intoxicated drivers.

Political pressure from organizations such as MADD and RID sparked legislative change not only at the state level but also at the federal level. Their efforts were instrumental in the passage of the Federal Uniform Drinking Act of 1984, a law that provided federal highway funds only to states that raised their legal drinking age to twenty-one. Not surprisingly, all states soon complied. In addition, MADD and RID orchestrated the public demand for White House involvement on the subject of drinking and driving, which led President Reagan to make the issue a priority of his administration.

In April 1982, President Reagan appointed a Presidential Commission on Drunk Driving. The commission systematically surveyed state laws and local programs addressing the problem of drinking and driving, held hearings in eight cities, and issued a final report in 1983. The report made a series of recommendations that formed the basis for much of the state legislative activity surrounding DUI offenses in the 1980s and 1990s. The commission's recommendations also led to the creation of the National Commission Against Drunk Driving. The commission is a private nonprofit public service agency that monitors DUI legislation, researches programs to combat drunk driving, disseminates information about the problem of drunk driving, and helps private employers communicate with workers about the problem.

In 1998, President Clinton directed the secretary of transportation to work with other agencies, Congress, the states, and representatives of concerned organizations to set new standards for attacking the problem of drinking and driving. The National Highway Traffic Safety Administration took the lead in formulating a plan to implement the president's directive. Setting a goal to reduce alcohol-related traffic fatalities to 11,000 by the year 2005, the plan called for highly visible law enforcement, public education programs, and legislative changes, including making driving with a BAC of .08 percent or higher a strict liability offense. Congress enacted much of this plan into law in 1998 through the Transportation Equity Act for the 21st Century (TEA-21) and the transportation spending bill of 2000.

DEFINITION

Public awareness that alcohol consumption causes highway collisions was evident even at the advent of the automobile era in the early twentieth century. Driving a motor vehicle while under the influence of alcohol, known in some states as DWI (driving while intoxicated/impaired) or OUI (operating a motor vehicle while under the influence of alcohol), had been codified as a crime in many states, such as New York, California, and Connecticut, since World War I. In these states, potential punishment included jail terms and suspension of drivers' licenses. Although some offenders were prosecuted and punished, enforcement was hindered by the difficulty of proving beyond a reasonable doubt in a court of law that a driver was in fact impaired by alcohol.

This difficulty was eased immensely after Scandinavian scientists invented the technology to measure blood-alcohol concentrations, obtainable through tests of blood or breath. Armed with this technology, Norway and Sweden soon enacted laws that prohibited driving a motor vehicle when the driver could be proven to have a blood-alcohol concentration above a prescribed level. In Norway, this level was set at .05 percent, a level deemed sufficient to have a noticeable effect on driving ability. In Sweden, the legal limit was set at .08 percent.

Other countries soon followed the Scandinavian

approach to the DUI problem. In 1939, Indiana became the first state to follow the Scandinavian model by prohibiting the driving of a motor vehicle with a blood-alcohol level above a specific concentration, although this concentration was set at the extremely high level of .15 percent. By 1963, thirty-nine other states and the District of Columbia had enacted similar laws, most of them adopting .15 percent as the prohibited BAC level. By contrast, in the Road Safety Act of 1967, the United Kingdom prohibited driving with a blood-alcohol level of .08 percent, as did Austria in 1961, Canada in 1969, Germany in 1973, and France in 1978. In the 1990s, Austria, Germany, and France lowered their legal BAC levels to .05 percent, which is now the prevailing standard in most of Europe as well as in Australia. Some countries retain .08 percent as the legal BAC limit, although Sweden has reduced its limit to .02 percent, and the Norwegian government has proposed to follow suit.

In America, after the legislative changes of the 1980s and 1990s, most states set the legal BAC limit at .10 percent. Some states, among them California, Washington, Florida, Illinois, and Virginia, set the BAC limit at .08 percent. Prompted by the federal government, many more states will soon be joining the .08 group. In October 2000, Congress set a .08 percent BAC level as the national standard for alcohol-impaired driving and set up financial incentives, through its transportation spending powers, for states to adopt a BAC level of no more than .08 percent by October 1, 2003. Federal financial incentives had previously been successful in influencing all of the states to adopt a .02 percent alcohol limit for drivers under the age of twenty-one.

Variations on DUI laws exist in a number of jurisdictions. For example, a handful of states define a separate aggravated DUI offense for drivers with high BAC levels of .15 or .20 percent, whereas some states approach the same problem simply by increasing the statutory penalties for drivers with high BAC levels. Maine sets a lower BAC limit of .05 percent for repeat offenders. New York allows evidence of a .05 percent BAC level to support a conviction not for driving under the influence of alcohol but rather for the lesser offense of driving with impaired ability. The Transportation Research Board favors a BAC of .04 percent, and the U.S. Department of Transportation has adopted this level as the legal limit for commercial drivers.

Generally, evidence of blood-alcohol concentration is obtained by a police officer who, after stopping a driver and making observations sufficient to support a DUI arrest, conducts a breath alcohol test at the police station. "Breathalyzer" is the trade name for equipment that performs chemical analysis of breath samples to determine their alcohol content. After the arrested person blows a breath sample into its mouthpiece, the breathalyzer analyzes it and provides a printout of the blood-alcohol concentration. In order to be legally admissible in court, a trained operator on a machine must administer the test according to a strict protocol with records indicating that it was calibrated regularly for accuracy. Occasionally, the BAC level is obtained from equipment housed in a police van or from blood tests administered by medical personnel, as when an unconscious driver is taken from a crash scene to a hospital for treatment.

ENFORCEMENT

Public demand for tougher drunk driving legislation in the 1980s and 1990s led to greater law enforcement efforts to detect alcohol-impaired drivers. DUI arrests rose accordingly. A DUI arrest typically occurs when a police officer observes an act of illegal driving, such as speeding, weaving, or having a missing headlight, that provides reasonable cause to stop a car. Having stopped the car and approached the driver, the officer may make observations indicative of DUI. The driver may have slurred or incoherent speech, bloodshot eyes, or the smell of alcohol on his or her breath, or there may be open alcoholic beverage containers in the car. The driver may fumble when attempting to produce identification or may openly admit to drinking and driving.

After making observations such as these, the officer generally requests that the driver perform field sobriety tests. These are tests of motor coordination administered according to standard instructions that help police obtain evidence of driving under the influence. Common tests include asking a driver to recite the alphabet, pick up coins, stand on one foot while counting to a certain number, walk a straight line by placing heel to toe and then turning around to walk back, and touch his or her nose with the tips of index fingers after extending arms to the side. Indications of intoxication in the performance of field sobriety tests support a DUI arrest. In the typical scenario, the breath test will be administered subsequently at the police station to obtain a precise blood-alcohol concentration. Even if the driver refuses to take any of these tests, the officer may feel that sufficient observational evidence exists to justify a DUI arrest.

Another field sobriety test, known as the horizontal gaze nystagmus test, involves an officer horizontally moving a small object, typically a pen, in front of the driver's face. Instead of following the motion of the pen smoothly, as the eyes of a sober person can, the eyes of an intoxicated person will oscillate noticeably. Although this test has been shown to be scientifically reliable, there are sometimes questions as to an officer's ability to administer it properly. In addition, because few jurors will understand the implications of the test, and few officers will be qualified to explain its scientific underpinnings, expert testimony will likely be required if evidence of the horizontal gaze nystagmus test is to be admitted in court. For these reasons, officers tend to favor the use of other field sobriety tests.

Another law enforcement technique used to detect alcohol-impaired drivers is the sobriety checkpoint. Used extensively in Canada, Australia, a number of European countries, and a number of American jurisdictions, the checkpoint is a roadblock where officers briefly stop all drivers, or a subset selected by neutral criteria, to assess the drivers' sobriety. Whereas apparently sober drivers are permitted to proceed, drivers who appear intoxicated are treated as if they had been stopped for cause and will likely be asked to perform field sobriety tests. In a 1990 case known as *Michigan Department of State Police v. Sitz,* the U.S. Supreme Court upheld the constitutionality of such checkpoints when conducted in a regularized manner according to established guidelines, based on their public importance and limited intrusiveness.

Some police departments use portable devices to assist officers on the street in gauging whether a driver is legally intoxicated. Small handheld breath testers called preliminary breath testing (PBT) machines function much like their stationhouse counterparts. Another device is the passive alcohol sensor (PAS). The PAS appears to be a large flashlight, but when held close to the driver's mouth, it analyzes a breath sample to provide a BAC reading.

Another important technology used in DUI enforcement is the videotape. Some police departments have cameras in patrol cars to videotape roadside encounters and field sobriety tests, documenting evidence relevant to intoxication. Other police departments videotape the suspect's booking at the police station and may ask the suspect to repeat field sobriety tests on tape at the station in order to record the suspect's apparent degree of impairment . If DUI is charged and the case is tried, these videotapes may sometimes be admitted into evidence.

To convict a driver of DUI charges, a prosecutor must prove beyond a reasonable doubt that the driver operated a motor vehicle on a public road or in an area to which the public had access while the driver was under the influence of alcohol or, in some jurisdictions, other impairing substances. The prosecutor need not show that the driver was drunk or even that he or she was driving unsafely. Rather, a prosecutor must offer evidence that the driver's capacity to operate the motor vehicle was diminished by virtue of the consumption of alcohol or perhaps other drugs. Such evidence often consists of the results of a breath test, or a blood test if available, but observations and opinions offered into evidence by police officers or other witnesses constitute evidence as well. In nearly all jurisdictions, a driver's refusal to take a breath test is admissible in court, and jurors may draw inferences from this refusal.

Virtually all states make driving with a blood-alcohol level above the legal limit a per se offense. This means that drivers are strictly liable when there is evidence that their BAC levels were over the legal limit. Defense evidence that they were driving slowly, carefully, and flawlessly or that other factors contributed to their physical condition cannot legally exonerate drivers in a per se jurisdiction because credible evidence of the illegal BAC level alone can constitute prima facie proof beyond a reasonable doubt of the impairment element of the offense. Courts have routinely rejected constitutional challenges to per se statutes. In TEA-21, Congress created financial incentives for states not only to set a BAC limit of .08 percent but also to define it as a per se offense.

PUNISHMENT

Historically, DUI offenders were often treated leniently by the American criminal justice system, presumably because they were seen not as criminals but rather as decent people who happened to drink too much on one occasion or, in the case of repeat offenders, were suffering from an affliction. Leniency no longer characterizes the American criminal justice response to DUI offenses. Whereas European countries tend to tailor penalties to BAC levels on an escalating scale, American states are more likely to escalate penalties according to the number of prior DUI convictions.

Prison sentences and license suspensions are available either on a discretionary or a mandatory basis for a first DUI conviction in many states. These penalties are mandatory in most states upon second and subsequent convictions. Punishment for DUI convictions may also include paying substantial fines, making restitution, and undergoing mandatory alcohol education and treatment. Although stiff criminal penalties are not responsive to the causes of the crime of driving under the influence, the rationale is that they will be sufficiently stigmatizing and onerous to diminish the threat of drinking and driving through deterrence.

License suspensions are a sanction not only after conviction but also after arrest. Arrested persons who fail or refuse a breath test may have their licenses suspended for a specified period. The period of suspension for refusal is typically longer than the period of suspension for failure, in order to discourage drivers from refusing to take the test. The theory under which refusals are punished with license suspension is that of "implied consent." By virtue of obtaining a driver's license, all drivers are considered to have consented to a chemical test of their BAC level when arrested by the police. Accordingly, upon the driver's refusal to take the test or upon the officer's obtaining a reading above the legal BAC limit, the officer can immediately confiscate the license and submit it to the state's licensing authority. The officer may issue a temporary driver's permit to the arrested person pending his or her decision about whether to request an administrative hearing on the issue of breath test refusal or failure. If no hearing is requested, or if the driver does not prevail after a hearing, the suspension is entered.

Some states allow work-related hardship exceptions to license suspensions, allowing violators to continue to drive to and from work. Other states do not grant exceptions, fearing that they will compromise the deterrence gained from a rapid and certain administrative penalty. These administrative penalties have been upheld against constitutional challenges. Studies have found that administrative license revocation laws are the single most effective method of reducing alcohol-related highway crashes. For this reason, Congress built into TEA-21 financial incentives for states to use administrative license revocation programs.

Some offenders who have had their licenses suspended continue to drive, although evidence suggests that many try to drive carefully and for short distances in order to avoid detection. Nevertheless, in order to reduce the threat that these offenders may pose on the highways, a number of states have enacted discretionary or mandatory DUI sanctions that permit an offender's vehicle or license plates to be seized or altered. When an offender is convicted of a DUI offense, some states may withdraw his or her vehicle registration or allow the vehicle to be impounded, immobilized with a boot or a steering wheel club, or confiscated and sold at auction. Other states impound license plates or issue specially marked license plates to DUI offenders. These distinctive plates make it easier for the police to detect offenders and may also function as a shaming sanction, if the general public is able to see that these are the license plates of someone convicted of DUI.

One of the most creative and effective vehicle sanctions available on a discretionary or mandatory basis for repeat DUI offenders in some states is the installation of an ignition interlock device. The device is a portable breathalyzer attached to the vehicle's ignition system. Before the vehicle's engine can be started, the driver must blow a breath sample into the device and obtain a BAC reading below a prescribed level. If the BAC reading exceeds that level, the ignition will lock, and the engine will not start. Because studies have shown that the ignition interlock and other vehicle sanctions have reduced rates of DUI recidivism, Congress provided financial incentives in TEA-21 for states to enact such sanctions for repeat offenders.

Another experiment undertaken in a few jurisdictions is the creation of specialized courts to hear DUI cases exclusively or the inclusion of DUI cases in specialized drug courts. The goal of such courts is to reach chronic offenders through intensive substance abuse treatment and supervision that address the causes of recidivism. Some of these courts make use of victim-witness panels, requiring the offender to attend meetings with the family and friends of victims of drunk drivers. Although the effectiveness of these innovations remains to be seen, they are examples of the creativity that has marked some of the recent approaches to the problem of drinking drivers.

SUMMARY

The dominant global paradigm for combating drinking and driving has become one of deterrence through criminal law. More than many other nations, America encourages both driving and recreational drinking, suggesting that alcohol-impaired drivers will wreak havoc on American roadways for years to come. Nevertheless, significant progress has been made in reducing this hazard, primarily through improved methods of DUI detection, enforcement, punishment, and treatment. It is hoped that such progress will continue.

—*Phyllis Goldfarb*

See also ALCOHOL; BARROOM VIOLENCE

Further Reading

Jacobs, James B. (1989). *Drunk Driving: An American Dilemma.* Chicago: University of Chicago Press.

Laurence, Michael D., John R. Snortum, and Franklin E. Zimring. (1988). *Social Control of the Drinking Driver.* Chicago: University of Chicago Press.

Light, Roy. (1994). *Criminalizing the Drink-Driver.* Brookfield, VT: Dartmouth.

National Highway Traffic Safety Administration. (1998). *Presidential Initiative for Making .08 BAC the National Limit, Recommendations from the Secretary of Transportation.* DOT HS 808 756.

———. (1998). *Traffic Safety Facts 1998: Alcohol.* DOT HS 808 950.

———. (2001). *Alcohol Involvement in Fatal Crashes 1999.* DOT HS 809 104.

Robin, Gerald D. (1991). *Waging the Battle against Drunk Driving: Issues, Countermeasures, and Effectiveness.* New York: Greenwood Press.

Ross, H. Laurence. (1982). *Deterring the Drinking Driver: Legal Policy and Social Control.* Lexington, MA: Lexington Books.

———. (1992). *Confronting Drunk Driving: Social Policy for Saving Lives.* New Haven, CT: Yale University Press.

Sloan, Frank A., Emily M. Stout, Kathryn Whetten-Goldstein, and Lan Liang. (2000). *Drinkers, Drivers, and Bartenders: Balancing Private Choices and Public Accountability.* Chicago: University of Chicago Press.

Stewart, Kathryn. (2000). *On DWI Laws in Other Countries.* DOT HS 809 037.

Court Case

Michigan Department of State Police v. Sitz (1990). 496 U.S. 444.

▼ DRUG COURIER PROFILES

During the 1980s, the drug courier or drug importer, also known as a "mule," rose to prominence as both a symbol and a target of the antidrug policies put into effect after President Ronald Reagan's 1981 inauguration. Drug couriers—low-level players who are merely pawns in the hands of those in control of the drug trade hierarchy—physically transport illegal drugs across international, rather than national, borders. Border patrols comprising U.S. Customs employees and Drug Enforcement Agency (DEA) officers target drug couriers for arrest. If these individuals are then arrested and convicted, they are subject to long terms of imprisonment.

DRUG COURIERS: THE REALITY

The press has characterized drug traffickers as ruthless, violent, corrupt, and wealthy. Recent research on imprisoned couriers from Europe, Latin America, and the United States has challenged the validity of these stereotypes and highlighted the ineffectiveness of the current efforts to stop importation and distribution of illegal drugs. The research showed that the most pronounced difference between high- and low-level drug traffickers is not in the quantity of drugs imported, but rather, in the personal characteristics of the low-level players, who are disproportionately poor, female, and of foreign nationality.

A British study showed that from 1985 through 1994, approximately 20 percent of female prisoners were drug importers, and that from 1995 through 2000, this percentage rose steeply. In contrast to the data regarding female prisoners, drug importers represented 4 percent of the British male prison population during the 1985 through 1994 period. Another British study found that during the 1990s, almost three-quarters of a sample of 900 imprisoned drug couriers were foreign nationals. Research in the United States, Europe, and Australia for the same time period showed that a similar, disproportionately large, percentage of imprisoned drug couriers were foreign nationals. Because of the paucity of repatriation treaties between most drug demand countries and drug supply or transit countries, foreign nationals convicted of being drug couriers tend to serve long prison sentences, thousands of miles from their families and friends, without resolution of the problems that led to the criminal behavior.

Writers of realistic fiction have followed the example of journalists, who have frequently used creative interpretation of facts in order to characterize greed as the motivation for most drug couriers. In fact, drug couriers are consistently shown to be motivated by a generalized experience of economic hardship or deprivation of basic necessities or by a very specific, immediate, personally and morally justifiable economic need, such as medical treatment for a sick child or elderly relative or repayments to loan sharks. There is also evidence that a significant minority of drug couriers engage in this illegal activity only under duress.

Fees paid to couriers are relatively small when

> ### Drug Courier Characteristics Used by Law Enforcement to Develop Drug Courier Profiles
>
> Travel from a source city
> Carries little luggage
> Nervous appearance
> Carries excess luggage
> Cash-paid ticket
> Frequent travel to source cities
> Use of an alias
> Use of public ground transportation
> Made several cell phone calls
> Fast turn-around time
> Left false information with airline
> One-way ticket
> Carries large amount of cash
> Circuitous routes
> Known courier or trafficker
>
> Source: Markowitz, Michael W., and Delores D. Jones-Brown. (2000). *The System in Black and White: Exploring Connections Between Race, Crime, and Justice.* Westport, CT: Praeger, p. 94.

compared to the inherently high-risk nature of this business. Drug couriers commonly use one of these methods to hide drug packets from law enforcement officers: (1) secreting packets of drugs in concealed luggage compartments, (2) strapping drug packets to several different body parts, and (3) swallowing a large numbers of small, drug-filled condoms or packets. In the third situation, the drug courier risks not only personal liberty but also, if one of the swallowed packages ruptures, the release of a severely detrimental and potentially lethal dose of a dangerous drug directly into the bloodstream. Research at various sites throughout the world has reinforced the concept of the drug courier as a generally nonviolent individual, who has had no previous criminal convictions, no evidence of drug use prior to accepting the courier's job, and no general knowledge of the value and nature of the substances he or she has smuggled. For example, many Nigerian couriers, interviewed in British prisons throughout the 1990s, reported that they believed they were not smuggling drugs, but were instead carrying gemstones, foreign currency, or some other form of contraband. Drug couriers are basically unskilled, uneducated, and living at or below the poverty level. Yet because of their visibility, they are the weakest link—the class of employees most likely to be arrested. From the perspective of an individual manag-

ing the illegal drug enterprise, it is vitally important to minimize risk to their operations by giving the courier absolutely minimal information about the organizations and individuals who orchestrate the drug trade. If the courier is then apprehended and detained by law enforcement officers, (1) the courier will be unable to reveal damaging facts about the drug selling business, because the business will not have given the courier this information, and (2) it will be more cost efficient for the traffickers to hire another courier, from the huge pool of impoverished, desperate, and reckless individuals, than to pay for legal defense of the arrested person.

A British study has shown that drug couriers are indeed given minimal information about their employers. The British researchers found that if an apprehended drug courier is offered sentence mitigation in exchange for information on the operation of his or her employer's illegal drug enterprise, the courier will probably not have any information of value to the enforcement authority, H. M. Ministry of Customs and Excise Taxation.

SENTENCING

Drug trafficking is a capital offense in many nations, including Singapore, Thailand, China, and Egypt. Western democracies tend to approach this crime from a completely different perspective, by instead mandating extremely long prison sentences for drug couriers. In the United Kingdom, the 1971 Misuse of Drugs Act distinguished between the possession and trafficking of illegal drugs and established, for the proscribed trafficking of a class A or B drug, a maximum sentence of fourteen years. In 1985, the Controlled Drugs Penalties Act increased the maximum sentence for trafficking from fourteen years to life imprisonment. The Drug Trafficking Offences Act of 1986 and the Drug Trafficking Act of 1994 first empowered and then strengthened the power of the courts to confiscate the proceeds of drug trafficking. The Crime Sentences Act of 1997 significantly increased the punitive face of British drug law enforcement when it introduced, for the first time, mandatory sentences for drug offenses.

During the mid-1990s, British researchers showed that drug importers represented only 9 percent of all drug traffickers who were cautioned, found guilty, or dealt with by compounding. (Compounding is the payment of a penalty in lieu of prosecution of cases involving the importation of small amounts of cannabis.) However, the same group of drug importers represented an enormous 34 percent of all drug traffickers sentenced to immediate custody,

Currently, the average sentence handed down to a convicted drug courier in Britain is six and one-half years. For drug importers, personal circumstances such as good character, age, illness, or pregnancy are not considered as mitigating factors in the sentencing process. Instead, if the defendant agrees to plead guilty, the court may reduce the sentence if the defendant provides information on drug networks.

In the United States, the Controlled Substances Act prohibits possession, trafficking, and manufacture of illegal drugs and provides guideline penalties for these offenses. In the 1990s, the U.S. Congress and many state legislatures established harsh criminal penalties for a wide range of drug offenses, frequently relying on mandatory minimum prison sentences set forth in the federal sentencing guidelines. As a consequence, drug offenders in the United States face sentences that are uniquely severe among those in constitutional democracies.

By the late 1980s, drug enforcement policies overwhelmed the federal courts with drug cases. In an attempt to relieve the burden on the federal judiciary, prosecutors began to reinterpret state laws to give state courts jurisdiction over drug importers. In some states—most notably New York State—while the state courts relieved some of the federal courts' overburden, use of harsh drug laws such as New York's Controlled Substances Offenses Act of 1973 (known as the Rockefeller drug laws) proved inequitable for minor drug offenders.

Under the Rockefeller laws (so named because they were passed with the strong support of Nelson Rockefeller, governor of New York State at the time), individuals who have committed minor drug-related offenses must serve lengthy, mandatory prison terms. The most stringent of these statutes requires that a person convicted of selling two ounces of a narcotic or possessing four ounces of a narcotic receive a minimum prison term of fifteen years to life. In addition, the Second Felony Offender Law (1973) mandates a prison term for all repeat felons regardless of both the nature of the offense and the background or motivation of the offender. These New York laws provide no distinction between a person who on only one occasion delivers a small amount of a drug for a small fee, and a major drug dealer, whose daily profits are thousands of times more than the first offender's single event profits. Mandatory sentencing and the two central sentencing concerns of drug weight and the existence of prior con-

victions means that judges are unable to set fair sentences tailored to the conduct and culpability of each defendant and the danger they pose to society. The majority of drug offenders incarcerated under mandatory sentencing laws are nonviolent men and women convicted of low-level drug offenses. "In New York, murderers, arsonists and kidnappers face the same penalties as 'drug mules,' Rape, the sexual abuse of a child and armed robbery carry lesser sanctions" (The Correctional Association of New York 1999: 1).

DRUG COURIER PROFILING

The issue of drug courier profiling has provoked heated controversy, particularly in New York State, where 94 percent of all incarcerated drug offenders are nonwhite, despite the fact that the majority of drug users and drug sellers are white. At the end of the 1990s, the New York State prison population was 49 percent African American and 46 percent Latino, while less than 5 percent of the prison populace was white.

Drug courier profiling is an attempt by drug enforcement agencies to construct a set of physical and other characteristics to assist in identifying drug smuggling suspects. Federal agencies such as the Drug Enforcement Agency (DEA) and Federal Bureau of Investigation (FBI) began to use profiling in the late 1970s. Profiles included descriptions of typical luggage used by couriers, typical flight arrival and departure times, typical airline used, and the typical behavior and demeanor of possible couriers. Within the past decade, the profiles expanded to include gender and race. The typical drug courier was then identified as a Latina female in her twenties or thirties.

Drug courier profiling has come under heated attack from civil liberties organizations in the United States. In an annual report that summarizes the nation's drug intelligence, the National Narcotics Intelligence Consumers Committee concluded: "Distribution groups were comprised chiefly of African-American street gangs and the Dominican, Cuban, Haitian, Jamaican, Mexican, and Puerto Rican criminal groups that controlled cocaine and crack sales at the retail level" (National Narcotics Intelligence Consumers Committee 1998: 73). By the mid 1990s, the DEA stopped distributing training videos in which all the drug suspects had Spanish surnames. However, the DEA continues to use profiling in its drug enforcement work, despite the fact that it has long been tarnished with claims of racial stereotyping.

According to a 1999 General Accounting Office

report to Congress, the federal government spends nearly $300 million a year and employs 1,400 people in a vast intelligence network that monitors international and domestic drug markets, and then informs state and local police how to spot a trafficker. This information is also used by U.S. policymakers in the formulation of drug control policy and drafting drug control legislation.

SUMMARY

Most drug couriers are vulnerable, impoverished, and desperate individuals, either from low-income neighborhoods in the developed world, or from the developing world. For the unethical entrepreneurs who earn huge amounts of money selling illegal drugs, couriers constitute a cheap and expendable source of labor that maximizes illegal profits. Drug enforcement efforts have focused on this vulnerable population, in hopes of reducing the illegal drug trade. Instead, incarceration of these replaceable individuals has, according to criminologist Tracy Huling (1996: 59), "so far resulted in the re-victimization of many people suffering under grinding poverty and corrupt political regimes."

—Penny Green

See also DRUG MILLIONAIRES; DRUG TRAFFICKING; DRUG TREATMENT; INTERNATIONAL IMPRISONMENTS; ORGANIZED CRIME—GLOBAL; WOMEN IN PRISON

Further Reading

Abernethy, Rosemary, and Nicholas Hammond et al. (1992). *Drug Couriers: A Role for the Probations Service*. London: Middlesex Area Probation Service.

Albrecht, Hans-Jorg. (1996). "Drug Couriers: The Response of the German Criminal Justice System." In *Drug Couriers: A New Perspective*, edited by Penny Green. London: Quartet Books.

Correctional Association of New York. (1999). *Mandatory Sentencing Laws and Drug Offenders in New York State*. New York: Correctional Association of New York.

Del Olmo, Rosa. (1990). "The Economic Crisis and the Criminalization of Latin American Women." *Social Justice* 17, 2: 40–53.

———. (1996). "Drug Couriers: Discourses, Perceptions and Policies." In *Drug Couriers: A New Perspective*, edited by Penny Green. London: Quartet Books.

Green, Penny. (1991). *Drug Couriers*. London: Howard League.

———, ed. (1996). *Drug Couriers: A New Perspective*. London: Quartet Books.

———. (1998). *Drugs, Trafficking and Criminal Policy: The Scapegoat Strategy*. Winchester, UK: Waterside Press.

Huling, Tracy. (1996). " Prisoners of War: Women Drug Couriers in the United States." In *Drug Couriers: A New Perspective*, edited by Penny Green. London: Quartet Books.

National Narcotics Intelligence Consumers Committee. (1998). *The NNICC Report, 1997*. Washington, DC: Drug Enforcement Administration.

▼ DRUG COURTS

From 1974 until 1980, Presidents Gerald Ford and Jimmy Carter adhered to policies that allocated more than half of the federal government's antidrug budget to programs designed to reduce demand for illegal drugs through treatment of drug abusers and prevention of drug use by young people. However, after President Reagan's 1981 inauguration, the treatment and prevention approach was virtually abandoned. His policy appropriated more than 50 percent of the antidrug budget for programs to reduce the supply of illegal drugs through (1) enacting, and then strictly enforcing, stronger antidrug laws and (2) adhering to a policy of zero tolerance for all drug dealers and users.

When President Reagan's antidrug policy was put into effect, the intensified law enforcement effort led to the more arrests, prosecutions, and incarcerations. From 1980 to 1998, the total number of criminal arrests nationwide increased by 40 percent, from 10,441,000 to 14,528,300, while the number of drug arrests rose by 168 percent, from 580,900 to 1,559,100 (FBI 1980: 19, FBI 1999: 210). As the result of the steep escalation in the number of arrests, the number of inmates in U.S. prisons increased by 300 percent, from 501,886 (Brown 1996: 7) to 1,825,000 (Beck and Mumola 1999:1).

The federal, state, and local judiciary systems were not prepared to handle this enormous increase in the number of arrests. Already-crowded court dockets were packed with even more cases, so that the time necessary to process an individual case increased dramatically. As more drug-abusing individuals were sent to short-term drug treatment programs prior to release, it became apparent that President Reagan's strict enforcement policy did not to reduce the demand for illegal drugs. At completion of short-term treatment programs, the vast majority of participants immediately renewed their drug abusing habits. The courts saw these people repeatedly as they completed a cycle of addiction, short-term program, and readdiction.

PREADJUDICATION AND POSTADJUDICATION DRUG COURTS

Dedicated drug treatment courts, or "drug courts" have provided the judiciary system with an equitable method of handling nonviolent drug cases. This court is highly specialized, having jurisdiction over only nonviolent, drug-related cases. In each case, the judge, attorneys, and defendants use a collaborative approach, focused on the defendant's referral to and successful completion of a substance abuse treatment program. Drug courts fall into two major categories, preadjudication and postadjudication courts.

In a preadjudication court, also known as a diversion court, if an alleged drug law violator has had no previous criminal conviction, and then enters into and successfully graduates from a treatment program, no criminal record is generated because the court will not keep a record of the drug offense that set the drug court process in motion. Consequently, in this situation, no criminal record is generated. However, if an alleged drug law violator with no previous convictions enters into, but fails to graduate from, a preadjudication drug treatment program, the court records the criminal charges, and the prosecutor initiates the case, generating a criminal record for the individual.

In postadjudication courts, if a person who has no criminal record is charged with violating a drug law, the case proceeds. If the individual pleads guilty to the drug law violation, when the plea is entered, even if he or she immediately agrees to enter drug court treatment. In this situation, the individual's criminal record has been established prior to entering drug court treatment. If that person remains in and then graduates from the treatment program, the court either will reduce the duration of the previously ordered sentence of incarceration or will change the sentence to require only probation and/or community service. In the postadjudication court, if the individual follows the above procedure but fails to graduate from the treatment program, the original sentence(s) will be fully implemented.

The existence and operation of drug courts is based on the premise that addiction is a treatable disease. Since the drug court is an essential component of the treatment of each of its participants, that court must recognize that in most cases, one or more relapses may well occur prior to recovery, and also that punitive action would be inappropriate if a relapse is an expected occurrence. The drug court maintains both responsibility and flexibility by responding to a patient's relapses with progressive sanctions or more intense treatment of the disease, instead of terminating a participant's treatment.

COLLABORATIVE MODEL OF CRIMINAL JUSTICE

In the United States, the traditional model of criminal justice is adversarial. The prosecution attempts to demonstrate that the defendant committed the offenses for which he or she was charged. The defense disputes the prosecution's claims and provides its own evidence showing that the defendant could not have committed the alleged acts. During the trial, the judge can confer with the prosecutor and defense attorney, but is prohibited from talking to the defendant. If there is a guilty verdict, the judge determines the defendant's sentence, according to rules that establish punishment appropriate for each type of crime.

The judge is the central figure in a trial conducted according to the drug courts' collaborative model of justice. Unlike the judge in the adversarial situation, a drug court judge must personally supervise the defendant and actively participate in the treatment program. Because drug treatment has the greatest chance of success if it begins immediately after arrest, when the defendant is most motivated to recover, the judge meets the each participant as soon as he or she enters the program. If the judge can establish a good rapport with a drug program participant, they can work together toward the drug court's twin goals, which are to provide psychological support to the defendant and to instill individual responsibility for recovery.

At periodic intervals during an addict's participation in a treatment program, the judge must conduct status hearings to assess the participant's program compliance and progress toward recovery. If the hearing judge believes that the participant is putting effort into self-improvement, and is complying with the treatment program, the judge may offer praise or counsel. However, if a participant is not progressing in the program, or is noncompliant, or otherwise demonstrates lack of effort to achieve recovery, the judge has authority to cajole, threaten, or punish the participant. In this context, "punishment" may include a short period of incarceration and/or placing the noncompliant drug abuser in a residential treatment facility that offers more intensive treatment.

GRADUATED SANCTIONS

Many programs employ a system of graduated sanctions, pioneered in by the Oakland, California Drug Court (Bedrick and Skolnick 1999). Under this type of system, if a drug treatment program participant repeatedly violates program rules, each successive violation will trigger a more serious sanction. Whereas punitive action administered for a rule violation tends to drive participants away from drug treatment centers, graduated sanctions help people to control their behavior so that they can remain enrolled in treatment programs.

INCREASING NUMBER OF DRUG COURTS

The first specialized drug courts employing a dedicated treatment modality were created in Miami in 1989. In January 1991, Alameda County, surrounding Oakland, California, opened the next drug treatment court. During the next year, at least five more states took the initiative and established drug courts. Since that time, the number of dedicated drug treatment courts in the United States has increased rapidly, and some jurisdictions have even subdivided these specialized courts into adult, juvenile and family drug courts.

As of June 2000, American University's Drug Court Clearinghouse reported that 508 jurisdictions throughout the United States have operational drug courts, and that approximately 300 drug courts are in various planning stages. Drug courts are functioning or planned in each of the fifty states, the District of Columbia, Puerto Rico, Guam, two federal jurisdictions and forty-four Native American Tribal Courts. Approximately 200,000 drug offenders have entered drug court programs since 1989. Approximately 55,000 participants have successfully graduated, and 69,000 are currently attending drug court programs. In addition, the collaborative, drug court process has been used as a model for specialized courts dealing with other negative behaviors, including abuse and neglect cases, driving while impaired/intoxicated, and domestic violence.

THE FUTURE

Drug court treatment programs have longer average retention rates than other programs based in the criminal justice system or in the community. According to Belenko's two reviews of drug court research (1998 and 1999), these programs have successfully graduated some participants who initially appeared likely to leave their programs prior to completion, including felony offenders who had little or no prior substance abuse treatment.

Participants in drug court treatment are more closely supervised than individuals in other forms of community-based addiction treatment. When compared with individuals enrolled in other addiction treatment programs, drug court treatment program participants are less likely to use drugs or to be incarcerated for another form of criminal behavior.

Drug court treatment programs are successful not only in terms of participants who graduate and recover from addiction but also in dollars and cents. Recidivism rates are significantly lower for drug court graduates than for individuals who have participated in other addiction treatment programs. If the success rate continues during the current, rapid increase in the number of drug courts in the United States, the long-term effect of incarcerating fewer individuals will be a reduction in the overall cost of criminal justice.

—W. Clinton Terry III

See also DRUG TREATMENT; HARM REDUCTION; WOMEN IN PRISON

Further Reading

Beck, Allen J., and Christopher J. Mumola. (1999). *Prisoners in 1998*. Washington, DC: U.S. Department of Justice.

Bedrick, Brooke, and Jerome Skolnick. (1999). "From 'Treatment' to 'Justice' in Oakland, California." In *The Early Drug Courts: Case Studies in Judicial Innovation*, edited by W. Clinton Terry III. Thousand Oaks, CA: Sage, 43–76.

Belenko, Steven. (1998). "Research on Drug Courts: A Critical Review." Alexandria, VA: National Drug Court Institute 1, 1: 1–42.

———. (1999). "Research on Drug Courts: A Critical Review." Alexandria, VA: National Drug Court Institute 2, 2: 1–58.

———. (2000). "The Challenges of Integrating Drug Treatment into the Criminal Justice Process." *Albany Law Review* 63: 833–876.

Brown, Jodi M., et al. (1996). *Correctional Populations in the United States—1994*. Washington, DC: U.S. Department of Justice.

Drug Court Standards Committee of the National Association of Drug Court Professionals. (1997). *Defining Drug Courts: The Key Components*. Washington, DC: U.S. Department of Justice, Office of Justice Programs, Drug Courts Program Office.

Federal Bureau of Investigation (FBI). (1980), *Uniform Crime Reports for the United States*. Washington, DC: U.S. Department of Justice

———. (1999), *Uniform Crime Reports for the United States, 1998*. Washington, DC: U.S. Department of Justice.

Goldkamp, John S. (2000). "The Drug Court Response: Issues and Implications for Justice Change." *Albany Law Review* 63, 3: 923–961.

Office of Justice Programs. (2000). "U.S. Department of Justice, Drug Court Clearinghouse and Technical Assistance Project: Summary of Drug Court Activity by State and County." http://www.american.edu/academic.depts/spa/justice/2kCompos.htm

Terry, W. Clinton, III, ed. (1999). *The Early Drug Courts: Case Studies in Judicial Innovation*. Thousand Oaks, CA: Sage.

———. (1996). "A Collaborative Model of Justice for Local Government." *Spectrum* 69 3: 37–47.

U.S. General Accounting Office. (GAO). (1995). *Drug Courts: Information on a New Approach to Address Drug-Related Crime*. Washington, DC: U.S. General Accounting Office.

▼ DRUG LEGALIZATION

In a series of speeches delivered between June and September 1986, President Ronald Reagan declared a War on Drugs in the United States. Reagan proposed huge increases in federal expenditures, roughly 70 percent of which was earmarked for strict enforcement of newly strengthened drug laws.

According to Gallup and *New York Times*/CBS News polls, between July 1986 and September 1989, the percent of the American public naming drug abuse as the "number one problem facing the country today" skyrocketed from 8 to 64 percent (Goode 1999: 71). Reagan's proclamations were followed by enactment of a series of stringent laws that escalated penalties for possession and sale of controlled substances. Law enforcement was stiffened, resulting in huge increases in the numbers of arrests and incarcerations for drug offenses. Between 1980 and 2000, while the number of inmates in federal prisons quadrupled, the number incarcerated for drug offenses increased more than ten times. During the same time period, the number of new commitments to state prisons tripled, while the number of new commitments specifically for drug offenses increased more than tenfold. Currently, 56 percent of all federal and a quarter of all state inmates are imprisoned for drug offenses. Between 1980 and the beginning of the twenty-first century, the average time served in prison by a convicted drug offender rose by over 100 percent, from thirty-three to seventy months. In the federal system, penalties for drug possession—a victimless crime—seem disproportionately large. For instance, a person convicted of possession of five grams of crack cocaine is subject to a mandatory five-year sentence. Incarceration for this duration seems genuinely egregious when compared to the average criminal homicide sentence of five years and four months.

It has been argued that the concept of a "drug war" is counterproductive, and that enforcement of victimless crimes, such as possession offenses, can harm society. Gathered under a broad rubric of "legalization," numerous critics, scholars, researchers, journalists, and politicians have suggested that the laws governing controlled substances be drastically rewritten, reformed, or even abolished altogether.

The outcome of the drug legalization debate will affect not only the fate of current and future drug users and sellers but also the well being of the nation as a whole, because broad changes in drug policy can generate repercussions that will be perceived throughout society. Drug policy has a direct affect on many facets of daily life, including but not limited to (1) the number of arrests and incarcerations for crimes such as possession and/or sale of illegal drugs; (2) the staff and devices needed by, as well as priorities of, law enforcement agencies; (3) health care costs related to use of illegal drugs; (4) federal and state budgets, which are partially responsible for funding local law enforcement agencies; and (5) the overall crime rate, because users of illegal drugs may commit other crimes to support their habits.

HISTORY OF GOVERNMENT REGULATION OF DRUGS

During the nineteenth century, drug possession and sale were virtually unregulated in the United States. The limited range of available psychoactive substances could be purchased without prescription from physicians, grocers, general stores, pharmacies, and by mail from catalogues. Patent medicines—sold and used indiscriminately as panaceas for every medical and psychiatric ailment known to humanity—frequently contained opium, morphine, or cocaine. In addition, many beverages contained cocaine. Because advertising was totally unregulated, some people made outrageous claims about the effects of their products. Labels on medicines and other products could be similarly creative, because there was no law requiring that labels list ingredients. In short, nineteenth-century America was truly a "dope-fiend's paradise" (Brecher and colleagues 1972: 3). Experts estimate that at the turn of the nineteenth century, there were roughly half a million narcotic addicts in the United States, which converts, on a per-population basis, to four times the current figure (Musto, 1999; Inciardi, 1992). During the first decade of the twentieth century, America's laissez faire approach to drugs began to change. In 1906, Congress passed the Pure Food and Drug Act, which outlawed the interstate sale of substances that were adulterated or whose contents were mislabeled. That same year, China launched an antiopium campaign. To ensure uninterrupted trade with that country, the U. S. government banned the importation of all opium into the United States. In 1912, Congress amended the Pure Food and Drug Act of 1906 by extending its provisions to false and fraudulent advertising claims. Also in that same year, twelve countries, including the United States, signed the Hague Convention, an agreement to restrict opium and cocaine production

In December 1914, Congress passed the Harrison Act, the model for all subsequent drug legislation. This law required producers, sellers, and distributors of (1) cocaine and (2) opium and its derivatives, including morphine and heroin, to register with the Treasury Department and, thereafter, to pay taxes on the transactions. In 1919, the Supreme Court found that the Harrison Act prohibited doctors and pharmacists from supplying addicts with maintenance doses of narcotics. In the decade after the passage of the Harrison Act, approximately 30,000 physicians were arrested for supplying narcotics to addicts. Approximately 10 percent of the arrested physicians were imprisoned for this crime. At the behest of Internal Revenue agents, municipal and state officials set up clinics around the country in fifty cities to treat and/or maintain narcotic addicts. Either because of widespread abuses and the clinics' self-admitted failure to treat addicts, or as a result of pressure from the Treasury Department, by 1923, every one of these clinics had closed its doors. By 1928, approximately one-third of all federal prisoners were incarcerated specifically for drug offenses.

During the 1930s, Congress launched a campaign against marijuana distribution and use, and also consolidated the changes in drug legislation and enforcement that had swept the country during the first two decades of the twentieth century. By 1937, not only had all states prohibited the possession and sale of cannabis, but also the federal government passed the Marihuana Tax Act. It is particularly ironic that the 1933 repeal of the national prohibition against alcohol occurred simultaneously with the crusade to criminalize marijuana. The nation had begun to make sharp legal and cultural distinctions between and among various psychoactive substances. From the 1920s through the 1960s, there were no serious challenges to the prevalent concept that criminal penalties should attach to immoral acts such as recreational drug use and the administration of narcotics to addicts.

During a brief period in the early 1970s, the attitude toward the use of illegal drugs in the United States became more tolerant. However, by the beginning of the 1980s, intolerance prevailed once again. Between 1981 and 1989, drug use declined; the percentage of the population favoring legalization of marijuana fell; the percentage of the populace who believed that drug use was physically and/or psychologically harmful grew; the number of arrests on drug charges increased; the likelihood that a drug offender would be incarcerated increased; and the number of drug offenders who were imprisoned, as well as the ratio of drug offenders to all prisoners, increased dramatically.

Many critics reacted to what they regarded as the excesses of the new prohibitionist era. The late 1980s witnessed publication of a plethora of books and articles in favor of repealing drug prohibition. In spite of their agreement concerning the ills of the current system of drug prohibition, however, advocates of legalization expressed an extremely diverse range of views. Some argued for a complete laissez faire or "hands off" policy, with no government controls whatsoever—a position that should be referred to as complete decriminalization (Szasz 1992)—while most legalizers base their argument on some form of government control over the dispensation of drugs (Nadelmann 1989). Many observers urge legalization for some but not all drugs. A few observers believe all adults should have complete access to all drugs. Still others advocate that only those who are already drug dependent should have complete access. In truth, "legalization" is a coat of many colors. Nonetheless, there are features common to all of the legalizers' arguments, since legalization is as much critique of the current system of prohibition as it is advocacy of an alternate program.

DRUG LEGALIZATION: THE MAIN POINTS

There are two parts to the legalization argument. The first component is moral; the second component is its consequentialist or utilitarian component. The moral component argues that prohibition is unjust and discriminatory, a policy that unfairly and tragically persecutes innocent parties. The consequentialist component argues that, as measured by any conceivable, widely agreed-on, concrete standard, criminalization does more harm than good. In contrast, they state that legalization, would do more good than harm, and would represent a vast improvement over the current policy.

To advocates of legalization, drug prohibition is immoral and unjust and should be abolished. These legalizers argue that it is unfair and discriminatory to prohibit the possession and sale of substances (such as marijuana and cocaine) that cause relatively little harm while legally permitting those that cause a great deal of harm (alcohol and tobacco). More specifically, it is discriminatory to arrest users of the currently illegal substances while permitting drinkers and smokers to go their merry way. The legalizers also contend that drug abuse is a victimless crime, an obsession no different from playing chess or climbing mountains. Since the drug laws and their enforcement are immoral, the legalizers say, these laws must be repealed.

Legalizers frame the drug problem as a human rights issue. This means not arresting people with a medical condition because of their affliction, and adopting a therapeutic approach to drug abuse. What legalization advocates are talking about when they discuss drug reform is "treating drug addiction as a health problem, like depression and alcoholism, and not as a law enforcement problem" (Schillinger 1995: 21). Criminalizing drug users has no moral justification; it is a kind of witch-hunt, it penalizes the unfortunate and the afflicted. "Hundreds of thousands have been ruined by imprisonment for what are essentially victimless crimes," according to Ethan Nadelmann (1995: 39), the legalizers' most prominent spokesperson. It is the suffering of the drug user that is foremost on the legalizers' minds. As Nadelmann (1990: 46) has commented, "My strongest argument for legalization is a moral one. Enforcement of drug laws makes a mockery of an essential principle of a free society—that those who do no harm to others should not be harmed by others, particularly the state."

The consequentialist part of the legalizers' argument can be reduced to one master message: Most drug-related harms are caused by the drug laws and their enforcement, not by the direct or primary effects of the illicit drugs themselves. The legalization argument can be broken down into the following ten points:

1. Criminalization makes illegal drugs expensive and, hence, profitable to sell. In fact, profits are so huge that the arrest of one drug dealer will inevitably result in another stepping in and taking over the business. (This is the "push down/pop up" factor.) It is the illegality of drug sale that makes prohibition impossible—a contradiction in terms. Prohibition equals high drug prices; high prices equal huge profits for dealing; huge profits equal an irresistible lure for the enterprising entrepreneur; and an irresistible lure equals a quite literally endless supply of drug dealers willing to risk arrest. Drugs can never be stamped out through the criminal law. It is the very criminalization of illicit drugs that guarantees "business as usual."

2. Prohibition is futile because criminalization has not deterred, and cannot possibly deter, drug use. Drug use is as high now, under a punitive policy, as it would be under legalization. Legalizing the currently illicit drugs would not produce an increase in use—at least, not a significant increase. Anyone who wants to use drugs now is doing so. Prohibition is a logistical impossibility; there are too many holes in the net of law enforcement. Too many people are willing to do anything and to pay any price to use and continue to use drugs for law enforcement to put a stop to it.

3. The currently illegal drugs are less harmful than is commonly thought. The number of deaths caused by the consumption of the illicit substances is actually quite small. In fact, the legal drugs (mainly alcohol and tobacco) are extremely dangerous, vastly more harmful than the illegal drugs (including cocaine and heroin). The yearly death toll in the United States from the use of alcohol and tobacco is roughly half a million, whereas the annual number of deaths caused by all illegal drugs combined is 3,500 (Nadelmann 1989: 943). Which category of drugs should be prohibited?

4. Prohibition encourages the use of harder, stronger, more dangerous drugs. Because of the problem of concealment and distribution, criminalization places a premium on selling drugs that are less bulky and more concentrated, those that turn over a large profit per transaction. This has been referred to as "The Iron Law of Prohibition": The stricter the law enforcement, the more potent the prohibited substances become (Thornton, 1992: 70). Under legalization, its proponents argue, users will be free to gravitate to natural, safer substances, such as opium (rather than heroin), coca leaves (rather than powdered and crack cocaine), and lower-potency rather than higher-potency marijuana.

5. Under the current system of prohibition, the potency and purity of illicit substances cannot be controlled. As a consequence, users are always consuming contaminated (and dangerous) substances. Additives such as rat poison, strychnine, and Drano find their way into the veins, lungs, or nasal passages of users and addicts, with lethal consequences. In addition, the variability of the potency of street drugs is itself dangerous. An addict who is used to administering heroin that is 10 percent pure will overdose if he or she accidentally takes doses that are 50 percent pure. Legalization would enforce controls on potency and purity, thereby virtually eliminating drug overdoses.

6. Having the government or some other legal, authorized agent distribute the currently illicit drugs would take the profit motive out of the sale of drugs. As a result, organized crime and criminal gangs of all kinds would be weakened because they would lose a major source of revenue. The stranglehold that criminals have

on the neighborhoods in which they are now entrenched would be released, and the residents would be able to reclaim their communities.

7. Most drug-related violence is a product of the illegality of the drug trade. The majority of drug-related murders are the result of disputes over dealing territory or "turf," robberies of drug dealers, assaults to collect a drug debt, the sale of bogus or bad drugs, or a drug theft (Goldstein et al., 1989). Therefore, eliminating prohibition eliminates the profit motive; the elimination of the profit motive eliminates drug-related violence. Under legalization, the overall murder rate will decline, communities will be safer, and society will be vastly better off.

8. The current system of prohibition encourages police corruption, brutality, the widespread violation of civil liberties, rousts, false arrests, and the seizure of property of innocent parties. Under legalization, such violations of human rights would not occur. The police would not be pressured to make questionable arrests or tempted by bribes. Consequently, they will be better able to serve the community.

9. Prohibition is extremely expensive. Currently, the annual federal drug budget is $20 billion, and the combined state, county, and local budgets add up to roughly $30 billion—about 70 percent of which is devoted to law enforcement. Hence, billions of tax dollars are being wasted in a futile, harmful, counterproductive endeavor. Under a program of legalization, law enforcement could be redeployed to focus more attention on violence and other high-impact crimes. Moreover, the sale of drugs could be taxed, and those revenues could be used to finance the treatment of drug addicts. In short, legalization would represent using the tax dollar wisely.

10. Under legalization, useful therapeutic drugs, prematurely banned by the government, could be reclassified so that they can find their rightful place in medicine. Marijuana, defined by the federal law as a drug with no legitimate medical utility, can be used to treat glaucoma and the nausea that follows chemotherapy. (According to the laws of nine states, marijuana as medicine is legal, but it remains illegal according to federal law.) Physicians when necessary could use heroin, an even more effective painkiller than morphine. Moreover, under the present legal system, other illicit drugs such as LSD and MDMA (Ecstasy) virtually cannot be studied—even though research on the workings of these drugs may prove to be scientifically and medically important. Legalization would make such research possible.

THE PROHIBITIONIST RESPONSE

Like the legalization camp, prohibitionists encompass a broad range of views. Some are "hawks" who believe that drug use is immoral, the drug war can be won, and the solution to the drug problem is more arrests, stiffer penalties, and longer sentences. Others are "owls" who believe that drug abuse is a public health issue, not a law enforcement issue (Reuter 1992). Their platform includes needle exchange, condom distribution, an increase in enrollment in methadone maintenance programs, as well as a huge expansion in drug treatment programs, the legalization of marijuana as medicine, and drug education. Despite their differences, all prohibitionists agree that outright legalization is an extremely unwise policy. They base their argument on the following particulars:

1. One would have to be a wide-eyed optimist, the prohibitionists say, to believe that any conceivable form of legalization will not make the currently illicit drugs more readily available to the public, and that greater availability will not result in significantly higher levels of use than is presently the case. The fact is, legalizers ignore the distinction between absolute deterrence and relative deterrence. Criminalization has not—and cannot—eliminate illicit drug use ("absolute" deterrence), but it almost certainly has reduced levels of drug use below what would be the case under legalization ("relative" deterrence). Viewed in this light, prohibition has been at least a partial success. True, as the legalizers say, under legalization, most people would not begin using the formerly illicit substances, and most people who do use them would do so in moderation. But some—a minority, but nonetheless in an absolute sense, many—people who do not now use illegal drugs would begin to do so, and many who now do would do so more frequently. Alcohol and tobacco are extremely widely used drugs in part because they are legal; cocaine and heroin are used far less because they are illegal and there is some likelihood of arrest for the user.

Legalizers use national alcohol prohibition (1920–1933) as a case study in failure (Thornton 1992), but in fact, alcohol consumption actually declined by more than half during Prohibition (as did hospitalizations for alcohol-related dementia and new cases of cirrhosis of the liver); after repeal, the use of alcohol rose to its pre-Prohibition levels (Lender and Martin 1987: 205–207). Focusing on the widespread flouting of a law ignores the fact that even partial compliance results in significant reductions in levels of a given activity.

2. Currently, not only do far more people use the legal than the illegal drugs, they are also more likely to remain loyal to or "stick with" them longer. Legal drugs have vastly higher "continuance" rates than do illegal drugs. Nearly two-thirds of all at least one-time alcohol users (64 percent) drank an alcoholic beverage in the past month, and 40 percent of all one-time smokers consumed tobacco during the past thirty days. For marijuana, the most "legal" of the illegal drugs, the "continuance" figure is 15 percent. For heroin, perhaps the most "illegal" of the illegal drugs, this continuance or loyalty rate is only 5 percent. This same pattern also prevails in the Netherlands (Sandwijk, Cohen, and Musterd 1991: 20–21, 25; Goode 1999: 128–130). Clearly, prohibition dampens continued use: The more illegal a drug is, the less "loyal" its users are, and the less likely they are to continue using it.

3. It is possible that the drug laws are more effective in reducing levels of use among heavy, frequent drug abusers than among potential casual users. Most current heavy users want to take drugs more than they actually do but are deterred from even further, heavier use by the "hassle factor," that is, the difficulty of committing crimes, raising enough money to pay for an expensive drug habit, and purchasing illicit substances (Johnson et al. 1985; McAuliffe and Gordon 1974). It is naive, prohibitionists say, to point to widespread use and abuse of illegal substances to argue that levels are as high as they would be under legalization. This does not take into account that, if currently illicit drugs were legal and freely available, the heaviest users would take them even more frequently than they do today.

4. Although it is entirely possible that, as the legalizers say, under legalization, rates of violence related to the drug trade would decline, other forms of violence are likely to rise. The majority of heavy drug users live in a world in which violence is routine, and the heavier the use of psychoactive substances, the greater the volume of violence. This is as true of cocaine (Goldstein et al. 1991) as it is of alcohol (Parker 1995). Currently, violence caused by the direct effects of psychoactive substances—referred to as "psychopharmacological" violence—is not as common as violence caused by conflicts over the drug trade, or "systemic" violence (Goldstein et al. 1989). Under legalization, while systematic violence is likely to decline, psychopharmacological violence is almost certain to increase, producing an even higher total or overall level of violence than currently prevails (Inciardi 1999).

5. The legalizers devote much attention to the ills of criminalization—and many of their criticisms are entirely valid, say the prohibitionists—but very rarely come up with a viable, workable, concrete program of legalization. Which drugs should be legalized? What should their level of potency be? What age limits should be set on their purchase, sale, and use? Should drugs be legal to anyone who wants to use them? Or only to persons currently dependent on them? Where and how should drugs be sold? In pharmacies? Supermarkets? What about prescriptions; how should they be obtained? Or will drugs be available over the counter, off the shelf without a prescription? What about price? Should that be set by the government or the free market? Should advertising be permitted for drug products? What restrictions should the government set on drug use? Should driving under the influence be a crime? As with alcohol, should some establishments, such as restaurants, be permitted to serve drugs to their customers? What penalties should be set for noncompliance with the new drug laws? What agency should be empowered to sanction offenders (Inciardi and McBride 1991: 47–49)? Drug legalizers have made virtually no effort to address absolutely crucial nuts-and-bolts legalization issues such as these, a fact that weakens their argument.

6. Public opinion does not support any form of legalization of the currently illicit drugs. With the exception of cannabis as medicine, public opinion polls show that only 20 to 25 percent of the American population supports legalized marijuana, and no more than 5 to 10 percent supports the legalization of the "harder" drugs such as cocaine, heroin, and LSD. In fact, the War on Drugs enjoys very nearly universal support for the hard drugs, and moderately strong support for marijuana. However, polls also demonstrate a strong split between adults and teenagers with respect to the possession and use of marijuana. In 1999, only a third of high school seniors (33 percent) believed that the use of marijuana should be a crime. At the other end of the spectrum, over a quarter (27 percent) thought it should be entirely legal, and just under a quarter (23 percent) felt it should be a "minor violation like a parking ticket" (Johnston,

O'Malley, and Bachman 2000: 287). The fact is, legalization advocates simply do not have the force of public opinion behind them to mount an offensive against prohibition and criminalization. It is possible, however, that when this current teenage cohort matures, the political picture may change.

DRUG POLICY OUTSIDE THE UNITED STATES

In many nations, such as Singapore, Iran, and China, thousands of drug dealers are executed every year. However, among the mature industrialized nations, the United States stands alone in the severity of its drug laws and their enforcement. While no country pursues a policy of outright drug legalization, a number have put less punitive and more treatment-oriented programs in place. Legalization advocates point to countries such as the Netherlands, the United Kingdom, and Switzerland, as beacons of enlightenment and models for the reform of U.S. drug policy. For the most part, Western Europe pursues a "harm-reduction" strategy with respect to the illegal drugs, that is, reducing harm is the ultimate goal, not reducing drug use per se.

The Netherlands makes a sharp distinction between "hard" and "soft" drugs and, for the hard drugs, between use and low-volume sale on the one hand and high-level, high-volume dealing on the other. The state does not interfere in the use, possession, and sale of illegal but nondeviant drugs, mainly marijuana, whose use is regarded as a personal choice. "Hash coffee shops" operate in quiet, out-of-the-way streets in Amsterdam and other large cities where cannabis may be sold in small quantities (up to 30 grams, or slightly more than an ounce) to, and used by, persons above the age of sixteen (eighteen in some locales). But if advertising becomes too blatant or lurid, if hard drugs are sold, if drugs are sold to minors, or if large quantities of the drug are sold, the police will close down the establishment. Hence, in the Netherlands, small-quantity cannabis possession and sale is de facto legalized, although still technically against the law (Jansen 1994). Surveys indicate that marijuana use is no higher in the Netherlands than in the United States (Sandwijk, Cohen, and Musterd 1991).

In contrast, the Dutch consider the use of the "hard" drugs to pose an "unacceptable risk." However, as with cannabis, they make a distinction between laws on the books and laws "in action." While the possession and sale of heroin and cocaine are against the law, the police often look the other way in transactions between addicts and abusers and low-volume street sellers. Addiction is considered a medical rather than a police matter. Free drug treatment programs are available on demand for addicts, and there is no waiting period. In contrast, Dutch law enforcement is repressive toward large-scale sellers of the hard drugs. Prosecution demands a year in prison per kilo for heroin and cocaine traffickers (Leuw and Marshall 1994). Roughly a third of Dutch prisoners are drug offenders. Many observers wonder whether the Dutch policy toward drugs will eventually influence that of the other European Union (EU) countries or whether the drug policy of the other EU countries influence that of the Dutch.

SUMMARY

Nineteenth-century America was marked by a more or less complete laissez faire policy toward psychoactive substances: There were virtually no controls on drug distribution, possession, and use. By the last decade of the nineteenth century, however, reform movements began to press for the control of psychoactive substances, and a number of drug laws were passed, and enforced, between 1914 and 1937. The early part of the twentieth century was marked by legal repression and public intolerance of the sale and possession of marijuana, cocaine, and the narcotics, and this repression continued virtually unabated into the 1960s and 1970s.

While the 1970s manifested a brief detour toward a more tolerant legal and cultural climate toward drugs, the 1980s slammed that door shut. Between 1980 and today, legal repression toward drug offenses has been intensified, and the number of inmates incarcerated for the possession and sale of controlled substances increased by over 10 times, and is now at a historically all-time high. This crackdown on drugs has stimulated a call by scholars and a few politicians for a reform of the drug laws and an end to criminalizing drug users and abusers. Some argue in favor of legalization. While legalization represents a diverse and heterogeneous banner, all advocates who march under it criticize the current policy of drug prohibition. They say that the current drug laws are unfair, discriminatory, and harmful; and that, drug law enforcement causes more harm than good; and that, in fact, it is the drug laws that make psychoactive substance abuse harmful, not the effects of the drugs themselves. Legalization, its advocates say, would produce more good for the society than harm.

The opposition to legalization is as diverse an ideological platform as that put forth by its proponents. All, however, agree that drug legalization would do more harm than good. Specifically, any conceivable legalization plan would make psychoactive substances more readily available to the public and, hence, would increase the total volume of use and the total number of users. Today, opponents of legalization say that illegal drug use causes less harm than legal drug use because its volume is low; a higher volume of use of the currently illicit drugs would mean significantly higher levels of drug-related harms, and increases in use are most likely among current high-volume abusers. Moreover, legalizers do not and cannot answer most of the practical, nuts-and-bolts questions that any large-scale policy change entails, and they say that the vast majority of Americans oppose any form of drug legalization (marijuana as medicine excepted). Hence, legalization is not only a bad idea, it is impractical, unworkable, and utopian, opponents of legalization say.

Drug policy is one of the more crucial issues facing the United States. Even if outright legalization is all but impossible during the next decade or two, the legalizers have mounted a serious challenge to the current U.S. drug policy. They raise important questions that demand answers. The present system works badly and is desperately in need of repair. Legalization offers a public forum that permits drug policy issues to be hammered out and proposals to emerge—perhaps to be shaped, at some future date, into a more workable program. In fact, some legalizers have shifted to a more plausible scenario: a strategy of harm reduction, similar to that which prevails in much of Western Europe (Nadelmann 1998). Perhaps the key to the drug problem lies in harm reduction, not legalization.

—Erich Goode

See also DRUG COURTS; DRUG TREATMENT; HARM REDUCTION; WOMEN IN PRISON

Further Reading

Brecher, Edward et al. (1972). *Licit and Illicit Drugs*. Boston: Little, Brown.

Goldstein, Paul J. et al. (1989). "Crack and Homicide in New York City, 1988: A Conceptually-Based Analysis." *Journal of Drug Issues* 16 (Winter): 651–687.

———. (1991). "Volume of Cocaine Use and Violence: A Comparison Between Men and Women." *Journal of Drug Issues* 21 (Spring): 345–367.

Goode, Erich. (1999). *Drugs in American Society,* 5th ed. New York: McGraw-Hill.

Inciardi, James A. (1992). *The War on Drugs II*. Mountain View, CA: Mayfield.

———. (1999). "Legalizing Drugs: Would It Really Reduce Violent Crime?" In *The Drug Legalization Debate*, 2nd ed., edited by James A. Inciardi. Thousand Oaks, CA: Sage, 55–74.

Inciardi, James A., and Duane C. McBride. (1991). "The Case *Against* Legalization." In *The Drug Legalization Debate*, edited by James A. Inciardi. Thousand Oaks, CA: Sage, 45–79.

Jansen, A. C. M. (1994). "The Development of a 'Legal' Consumers' Market for Cannabis: The 'Coffee Shop' Phenomenon." In *Between Prohibition and Legalization: The Dutch Experiment in Drug Policy*, edited by Ed Leuw and I. Haen Marshall. Amsterdam and New York: Kugler, 169–181.

Johnson, Bruce D., et al. (1985). *Taking Care of Business: The Economics of Crime by Heroin Abusers*. Lexington, MA: Lexington Books.

Johnston, Lloyd D., Patrick M. O'Malley, and Jerald G. Bachman. (2000). *Monitoring the Future: National Survey Results on Drug Use, 1975–1999, Vol. I, Secondary School Students*. Bethesda, MD: National Institute on Drug Abuse.

Lender, Mark Edward, and James Kirby Martin. (1987). *Drinking in America: A History*. Rev. and expanded ed. New York: Free Press.

Leuw, Ed, and I. Haen Marshall, eds. (1994). *Between Prohibition and Legalization: The Dutch Experiment in Drug Policy*. Amsterdam and New York: Kugler.

McAuliffe, William E., and Robert A. Gordon. (1974). "A Test of Lindesmith's Theory of Addiction: The Frequency of Euphoria Among Long-Term Addicts." *American Journal of Sociology* 79 (January): 795–840.

Musto, David F. (1999). *The American Disease: Origins of Narcotic Control,* 3rd ed. New York: Oxford University Press.

Nadelmann, Ethan A. (1989). "Drug Prohibition in the United States: Costs, Consequences, and Alternatives." *Science,* 245 (1 September): 939–947.

———. (1990) "Should Some Drugs Be Legalized." *Issues in Science and Technology* 6: 43–46.

———. (1995). "Europe's Drug Prescription." *Rolling Stone* (26 January): 38–39.

———. (1998). "Experimenting with Drugs." *Foreign Affairs* (January/February): 111–126.

Parker, Robert Nash. (1995). *Alcohol and Homicide: A Deadly Combination of Two American Traditions*. Albany: State University of New York Press.

Reuter, Peter. (1992). "Hawks Ascendant: The Punitive Trend of American Drug Policy." *Daedalus* 121, 3: 15–52.

Sandwijk, J. P., P. D. A. Cohen, and S. Musterd. (1991). *Licit and Illicit Drug Use in Amsterdam*. Amsterdam, The Netherlands: Instituut voor Sociale Geografie.

Schillinger, Liesl. (1995). "The Drug Peacenick." *New York* (23 January): 20–21.

Szasz, Thomas. (1992). "Our Right to Drugs: The Case for a Free Market." Westport, CT: Praeger.

Thornton, Mark. (1992). "Prohibition's Failure: Lessons for Today." *Journal of the Society for Advancement of Education* 120, 2562 (March): 70–73.

▼ DRUG MILLIONAIRES

Trading in narcotics on a wholesale level is probably the most profitable illegal occupation there is.

Traffickers who succeed in hauling in just two or three substantial shipments stand a good chance of becoming overnight multimillionaires. When they manage to avoid investigators and steer clear of violent competitors and criminal predators, they often enjoy a rich life—at least for a time. While there is little reliable information on highly successful drug traffickers, case studies of less fortunate mid- to high-level drug traffickers illustrate the vulnerable and often temporary nature of their material wealth.

CRIME IS MONEY

The primary motivation of nearly all narcotics traffickers operating above retail levels are the substantial financial gains. (The term *retail levels* generally means the daily quantities of drugs that a dealer would sell to a narcotics user.) The kicks, the frenzied lifestyle, and peer pressure all provide their own stimuli, but the promise of financial wealth is what seduces most people into becoming involved in smuggling or selling drugs on any scale. For some, drug trafficking is the logical continuation of a criminal career that started in property crime. More alarming is the number of people who enter the drug trade as a career change from a legitimate business. In societies or subcultures generally permissive of certain kinds of drug use, the step to becoming personally involved in the drug trade is apparently not blocked by feelings of guilt or fear of stigmatization, although users of heroine or cocaine who become involved in dealing drugs to finance their own consumption seldom store and distribute more than a few ounces at a time. Their habit makes them a business risk for potential partners, as they are often known to law enforcement agents and are vulnerable to blackmail.

ASCENDANCE OF THE DRUG MILLIONAIRES

Entrepreneurs making huge profits on narcotics deals have been around since at least the 1920s, when American mafiosi such as Charles Luciano and Vito Genovese became involved in importing and peddling heroin into the United States from the Middle East. By the mid-1930s they were making hundreds of thousands of dollars a year. Profits soared by the mid-1950s, when the New York godfather Carmine Galante, together with Luciano and the Montreal crime boss Frank Petrula, organized the "French Connection," which refined Turkish opium into heroin in Marseilles

to be shipped to Canada and the United States (Nash 1992: 171). Then, in the late 1970s, Colombian traffickers such as Jorge Luis Ochoa Vasquez, Pablo Escobar Gaviria, Carlos Lehder Rivas, and others began making many millions of dollars by organizing large imports of cocaine into the United States . Their profit rate has been estimated at 80 percent. Operating from a country where corruption was endemic, they became drug billionaires in the 1980s, with an economic and political influence that has, in all likelihood, never been matched by other traffickers. Until the mid-1980s, they remained virtually untouchable by law enforcement.

PROFITABILITY OF ILLEGAL DRUGS

Estimates of the revenue generated by the illicit drug industry vary considerably, from about $100 billion to more than $1,000 billion a year, but the most reasonable estimate is probably somewhere between $300 and $500 billion a year. (United Nations International Drug Control Programme 1998: 3). In 1999, the United Nations Office for Drug Control estimated the value of the unprocessed coca base and opium produced around the world at $1.1 billion (United Nations International Drug Control Programme 2000: 48). Such relatively low basic production costs leave very substantial profit margins for the middlemen who refine, smuggle, and distribute the narcotics on their way to the end users.

Actual seizures of drug money seldom involve more than about $10 million, with some notable exceptions. One such case was the dismantling of the "Pizza Connection," which replaced the earlier "French Connection." In 1984, a large number of Italian American mafiosi were arrested either for smuggling heroin and cocaine into the United States by using pizza restaurants as fronts or for laundering the profits. During the investigation, it was established that over a three-year period tens of millions of dollars, mostly drug profits, were transferred from traffickers operating in New York and New Jersey to European bank accounts.

Operation Polar Cap, conducted jointly in 1989 by the DEA, FBI, IRS, and U.S. Customs Service, revealed how Armenian jewelers in Los Angeles laundered $1.2 billion within two years for the Medellín cartel (Gugliotta and Leen 1990: 575). In 1992, Operation Green Ice culminated in a wave of arrests, when police forces from eight nations arrested some 200 people involved in the cocaine trade and money laundering, including leading Italian Mafia and Colombian Cali cartel members. Investigators discovered some $54 million in cash, and 750 kilos of cocaine. Six years later, in 1998, the U.S. Customs Service concluded the largest drug money laundering case in the history of U.S. law enforcement. Operation Casablanca, an extensive undercover investigation, resulted in the seizure of over $98 million in U.S. currency, more than four tons of marijuana, and two tons of cocaine. The indictment charged twenty-six Mexican bank officials and three Mexican banks with laundering drug money, and it alleged that officials from twelve of Mexico's nineteen largest banking institutions were involved in money laundering activities.

PERSONAL WEALTH OF DRUG BARONS

In the underground narcotics economy, the individual wealth of drug barons is difficult to assess. Pablo Escobar, the most notorious Colombian cocaine baron of the 1980s, was estimated to be worth over $3 billion when he was killed while being arrested in 1993. This figure may have been exaggerated, but it is certainly much higher than the figures associated with the typical drug millionaire in Europe or the United States. For example, the profits of several world-scale Dutch cannabis traffickers of the 1990s, Johan Verhoek and Charles Zwolsman, were estimated by the court to be in the order of $10 to $20 million over a period of some four years. However, only substantially smaller amounts of cash and property were actually seized in these cases. In January 2001, the Dutch authorities were preparing a deal with Curtis Warren, Britain's most renowned narcotics trafficker of the 1990s, in which he would have to pay some $7 million to avoid five more years in jail. Warren's global drugs trafficking operation is estimated to have earned him between $110 and $250 million before he was jailed in 1997 for attempting to smuggle $175 million worth of narcotics into Britain from his base in Holland. Reportedly, in the mid-1990s Warren owned some two hundred properties in northwestern England, mansions in Liverpool and Holland, a casino in Spain, a discotheque in Turkey, and even a winery in Bulgaria (Barnes et al. 2000; Mendick 2001).

HANDLING DRUG MONEY

Drug trafficking can bring in such large amounts of money that simply handling the bills can become a

▼ Drug Millionaires

Sociologist Patricia Adler had the opportunity to study a group of affluent Californian drug dealers and smugglers in the 1970s through participant observation over a period of six years (Adler 1993). The Californian drug peddlers consistently emphasized the boredom of the straight world, contrasted with the opportunities for thrills, spontaneity, emotionality, and partying offered by their chosen lifestyle. There was an odd tension of "work and play" between the planned rationality and often hard work required by operating in the narcotics business, and the irrational hedonism that one could engage in as a consequence of this work. Adler concluded that "the dealing crowd was strongly driven by the pleasures they derived from their way of life. This lifestyle was one of the strongest forces that attracted and held people to the drug trafficking business" (Adler 1993: 83, 98). The "fast life" in question is described by Adler as emulating "the jet set with all of its travel, spending, and heavy partying."

Members of the "glitter crowd" were known for their irresponsibility and daring, their desire to live recklessly and wildly. They despised the conservatism of the straight world as lowly and mundane. For them, the excitement of life came from a series of challenges where they pitted themselves against the forces that stood in their way. Although they did not create arbitrary risks, dealers and smugglers were gamblers who enjoyed the element of risk in their work, being intoxicated with living on the edge of danger. They relished more than just the money; they reveled in the thrill-seeking associated with their close scrapes, their ever-present danger, and their drug-induced highs. Gone was the quiet, steady home life of soberly raising children and accumulating savings, as they set themselves on a continuous search for new highs.

Source: Adler, Patricia A. (1993). *Wheeling and Dealing: An Ethnography of an Upper-Level Drug Dealing and Smuggling Community.* 2d ed. New York: Columbia University Press, pp. 84–85.

physical problem. Although a luxurious lifestyle can make millions melt like snow, many large-scale drug traffickers sooner or later amass an excessive amount of cash and look for sensible ways to handle it. Money laundering is an obvious option, but not every drug millionaire has the need or the knowledge to adopt this solution.

Organized crime investigators have developed the

Continuum of Money Management Sophistication as a means to classify the various methods of handling profits from illicit activities. It ranges from fairly primitive means of using this money to extremely refined methods of laundering it (Peterson 1998: 11–13). Investigators use the following classification system:

1. Criminal profits used to obtain criminal products for self.
2. Criminal profits spent on luxury items and living expenses.
3. Criminal profits saved in currency, hidden by criminal.
4. Criminal profits moved through nonbanking financial institutions for use off-shore.
5. Criminal profits placed into the traditional banking system through multiple accounts.
6. Criminal profits invested locally in real estate through nominees.
7. Criminal profits used to purchase stocks, financial instruments, and business interests.
8. Criminal profits moved to other geographic locations and used to invest or make purchases of property there.
9. Financial professionals, attorneys, or others used as intermediary facilitators to acquire property with profits.
10. Criminal profits are integrated into "legitimate" investments and businesses and criminal becomes "legitimate."
11. Criminal profits used to invest in financial institutions that can be manipulated to hide or invest other funds.
12. Criminal profits used to manipulate governments.

Recent investigations by the U.S. Financial Crimes Enforcement Network (FinCEN) indicate that transnational organized crime groups such as the Latin American cocaine cartels still opt for relatively simple, but effective methods to launder their profits (Washington Crime News Service 2000).

LIFESTYLES OF DRUG KINGPINS

Although money is obviously a prime motivator to stay in the drugs trafficking trade, judging from their telephone conversations (intercepted and taped by law enforcement authorities), the simple desire for money provides an insufficient explanation for the activities of these millionaires. It is the entire lifestyle, with all its fun, tensions, reputation, and excitement, that makes it attractive to remain in the business even at an opera-

tional (and, therefore, risky) level long after substantive amounts of money have been secured. From evidence gathered by studying the day-to-day activities of members of a major Dutch cannabis-smuggling network for over two years, it is clear that in comparison with people from a similar background and education who are employed in other ways, drug traffickers lead rather interesting lives (Klerks 2000). Naturally, many of them have also spent a good many years in prison, and they run the risk of a violent death at the hands of criminal opponents, but most of them, even when they are middle aged, choose to continue taking risks to maintain their lifestyle. In criminology, this is a fact that too often seems to be ignored: In addition to being highly profitable, crime can be fun. For talented and lucky entrepreneurs operating in a liberal environment, it offers the prospect of the sort of intense life that most people will never have.

Furthermore, the immense wealth of drug millionaires allows them to use their worldly possessions in a very indifferent way, thereby continuing the somewhat crude and uncomplicated lifestyle of their childhood. Their manifest need to show off in a material way is aimed at gaining respect, compensating perhaps the lack of more customary means, such as a title or a formal position.

SUMMARY

Drugs trafficking can be a highly profitable, yet risky business. Drug millionaires have been around since the 1920s, but the 1980s saw the advent of the cocaine billionaires. The average personal wealth of a successful, top-level drug trafficker can be estimated at between $10 and $20 million. Drug millionaires engage in various ways of spending and laundering their profits, but they appear to show a preference for effective, simple ways of doing so. While money obviously is a prime motivator for participation in drug trafficking, research has shown that the pleasure derived from its flashy and adventurous lifestyle also attracts and keeps people in the drug trafficking business.

—*Peter Klerks*

See also DRUG COURIER PROFILES; DRUG TRAFFICKING

Further Reading
Adler, Patricia A. (1993). *Wheeling and Dealing: An Ethnography of an Upper-Level Drug Dealing and Smuggling Community,* 2d ed. New York: Columbia University Press.
Barnes, Tony, Richard Elias, and Peter Walsh. (2000). *Cocky: The*

Rise and Fall of Curtis Warren, Britain's Biggest Drug Baron. Bury, Lancashire, UK: Milo Books.

Bureau for International Narcotics and Law Enforcement Affairs. (2000). *International Narcotics Control Strategy Report, 1999.* Washington, DC: Department of State.

Gugliotta, Guy, and Jeff Leen. (1990). *Kings of Cocaine: An Astonishing True Story of Murder, Money, and Corruption.* New York: Harper.

Klerks, P.P.H.M. (2000). *Groot in de Hasj. Theorie en praktijk van de georganiseerde criminaliteit.* Alphen aan den Rijn, The Netherlands: Samsom Kluwer.

Mendick, Robert. (2001). "How to Get Out of a Dutch Prison: Hand Over £5m." *Independent on Sunday* (14 January): 4.

Peterson, Marilyn B. (1998). *Assessing Criminal Organizations Through Their Management of Profits.* Manuscript.

United Nations International Drug Control Programme. (1998). *Economic and Social Consequences of Drug Abuse and Illicit Trafficking. Technical Series No. 6.* Vienna: United Nations Office for Drug Control and Crime Prevention. http://www.odccp.org/technical_series_1998-01-01_1.html

———. (2000). *Global Illicit Drug Trends 2000.* Vienna: United Nations Office for Drug Control and Crime Prevention.

Washington Crime News Service. (2000). "Cartels Use Simple, Effective Techniques for Laundering." *Organized Crime Digest* 21, 16 (31 August): 1–2.

▼ DRUG TRAFFICKING

Trade in prohibited narcotics and other psychoactive drugs is today the illegal activity with the largest turnover worldwide. According to the United Nations International Drug Control Program (UNDCP), this turnover varies between $300 and $500 billion yearly, corresponding to 8 percent of the international trade volume (UNDCP 1997a: 123–124). Scholars, however, consider this estimate excessive, up to ten times the actual figure. Relying on data on American expenditures on illicit drugs (ONDCP 2001), Peter Reuter convincingly argues that consumers in the United States and Western Europe yearly spend about $120 billion to buy illicit drugs, and he assumes a total of $30 billion for the developing world. Following this down-to-earth calculation, a total world consumer expenditure of $150 billion on illicit drugs seems a reasonable estimate. The international trade component of drug sales is, however, much smaller. For all commodities, in fact, this component is calculated on the basis of the landed price (the amount for which the drug is sold by the importer to the first dealer or trafficker at the beginning of the domestic drug chain), about 15 percent of the final price paid by consumers. Thus, the international trade component of drug sales corresponds to merely about 15 percent of the total expenditures: $20 to $25 billion, a small share of total international trade, currently estimated at $5,000 billion (Reuter 1998).

Though much lower than the U.N. estimate, these figures are quite considerable in absolute terms and sufficient to make the drug market the largest illegal market worldwide and drug smuggling the transnational crime generating the greatest revenues for participants.

DRUGS AND THE SOURCE COUNTRIES

The bulk of international drug trafficking concerns three plant-based drugs, which are among the most commonly consumed illicit psychoactive substances worldwide. The pole position is undoubtedly held by cannabis: Either in the form of cannabis herb (marijuana) or cannabis resin (hashish), it is used in almost all countries across the globe and is almost everywhere the most popular illicit drug. Out of the estimated 14.8 million Americans who used an illicit drug in 1999, 75 percent used only marijuana, and 18 percent used marijuana and another illicit drug (U.S. Department of Health and Human Services, SAMHSA 2000). Marijuana consumers are estimated to represent 6.2 percent of the U.S. population twelve years old and older. In the late 1990s, around 15 million Europeans (about 6 percent of those aged fifteen to sixty-four) had used cannabis in the previous twelve months (EMCDDA 2000: 7). Worldwide there are 144 million consumers of cannabis products (UNODCCP 2001: 69–72).

In much of the developed world, the second most popular plant-based drug is cocaine, an alkaloid obtained from the leaves of the coca bush. Cocaine is a white powder with stimulant effects. According to the *National Household Survey on Drug Abuse* in 1999, an estimated 1.5 million U.S. residents were cocaine users. This represented 0.7 percent of the population aged twelve and older (SAMHSA 2000). In the countries belonging to the European Union (EU), cocaine has

---

DID YOU KNOW...

Most international drug trafficking involves drugs derived from three plants: cannabis (marijuana and hashish) from the Cannabis sativa plant; cocaine from the leaves of the coca bush; and heroin, a semisynthetic derivative of opium, itself an extract of the opium poppy.

been tried at least once by 1 to 6 percent of all those aged sixteen to thirty-four (EMCDDA 2000: 7). Worldwide there are about 14 million users of cocaine (UNODCCP 2001: 74).

About 13.5 million people are estimated to consume opiates; most of these people are heroin users, who total about 9 million. Heroin is a semisynthetic derivative of opium, itself an extract of the opium poppy. Almost two-thirds of all users of opiates and heroin are found in Asia. In the United States, according to the *National Household Survey on Drug Abuse,* there are about 200,000 heroin users, representing 0.1 percent of the population aged twelve and older (SAMHSA 2000). In Europe, too, heroin experience remains low in the general population (1 to 2 percent of young adults have tried it at least once), but in most Western countries there is a largely aging group of heroin addicts with serious health, social, and psychiatric problems (EMCDDA 2000: 8). Moreover, heroin injection is spreading rapidly in all Eastern European countries, including Russia (Paoli 2001). In all, 1.5 million people are thought to regularly consume heroin in Europe (UNODCCP 2001: 78).

In addition to plant-based drugs, drug trafficking involves a variety of synthetic drugs, above all amphetamine-type stimulants, many of which were freely on sale until the late 1960s. In many countries in the Far East (such as Japan, the Republic of Korea, and the Philippines), but also in some northern European countries, the use of amphetamines is more widespread than the use of cocaine and heroin combined (UNDCP 1996: 101). Methamphetamine, according to the U.S. Drug Enforcement Administration (DEA), "represents the fastest growing drug threat in America today," and its consumption is especially widespread in the western and southwestern regions of the country (DEA 2001: 1). Ecstasy, the market name of methylenedioxymethamphetamine (MDMA) and its derivatives, rapidly gained popularity in the 1980s and early 1990s in Europe, Australia, and elsewhere, spreading among middle-class students and other socially integrated young people. This new trend in drug use developed within a mass recreation and music culture. In the European Union, between 1 and 5 percent of those aged sixteen to thirty-four have taken amphetamines and/or Ecstasy. Rates are higher in narrower age groups but rarely exceed 10 percent (EMCDDA 2000: 7). There are an estimated 4.5 million users of Ecstasy worldwide, whereas 24 million are thought to use amphetamine or methamphetamine (UNODCCP 2001: 72–74).

Unlike plant-based drugs, synthetic drugs are rarely trafficked across long distances because they are usually manufactured in, or close to, areas of consumption. Hence, for example, the majority of the Ecstasy pills consumed in Europe are produced in the Netherlands and, to a much lesser extent, in Belgium and some Eastern European countries (Paoli 2000b; DEA 1999). Likewise, the U.S. demand for methamphetamine is traditionally supplied by clandestine laboratories in California and, increasingly, in Mexico. A significant quantity is also produced by independent labs ("mom and pop" laboratories), particularly in the Midwest (NNICC 1998: 61–62; DEA 2000).

Plant-based drugs, on the other hand, are produced in a small number of poor countries, which are often thousands of miles from end users. More than 98 percent of the coca leaf cultivation is concentrated in three Andean countries: Peru, Bolivia, and Colombia. Although Peru and Bolivia were the world's leading producers of coca leaf in the late 1980s and early 1990s, both successfully reduced the areas of cultivation at the end of the twentieth century (UNODCCP 2001: 28–30; see Figures 1 and 2). Coca cultivation has, however, expanded in Colombia, where most of the cocaine hydrochloride has been processed since the 1980s (U.S. State Department 2000). From Colombia, cocaine is exported into the United States by air, sea, and land, usually through one or more Central American countries and, more and more frequently, Mexico. Concealed in maritime or air cargo, but also carried by body packers, cocaine is also continuously smuggled into Western Europe. The Netherlands, because its commercial ports are the largest in the world, and

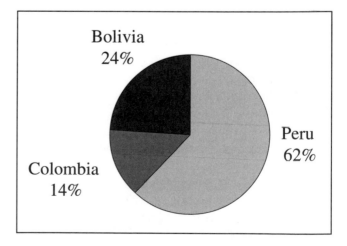

Figure 1. Coca Leaf Production in 1990 (Total: 319,200 Metric Tons)
Source: UNODCCP (2001: 28).

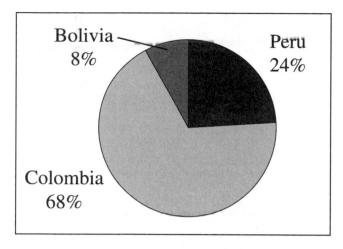

Figure 2. Coca Leaf Production in 1999 (Total: 287,000 Metric Tons)
Source: UNODCCP (2001): 28.

Spain, because of the common language and a relatively large community of Colombian residents, are the two countries most frequently selected by Colombian traffickers to import cocaine into Europe (EMCDDA 1997: 37, 2000: 22).

Four countries account for the bulk of the world nonmedical production of opium, from which heroin is extracted. Afghanistan in southwestern Asia and Myanmar (formerly Burma) in southeastern Asia compete for the unenviable title of the world's largest producer of opium gum (U.S. State Department 2000). Afghan heroin is imported into Europe largely via Iran and Turkey and then moved along the so-called Balkan route through the former Yugoslavia and along its southern and northern variants. A growing portion of Afghan heroin is also smuggled through Tajikistan and other former Soviet states along the old "Silk Road" (Paoli 2001; see Figure 3). Only a small part of the high-quality heroin produced in Myanmar reaches the Western European markets (above all, the Netherlands). Most of it is smuggled into the United States via Thailand, Hong Kong, and China or, increasingly, is consumed in Southeast Asia itself (UNODCCP 2001: 23–42; U.S. State Department 2000; NNICC 1998).

With a poppy crop responsible for less than 4 percent of the world's opium production, Colombia is nonetheless the Western Hemisphere's largest grower of opium poppies. High-purity Colombian heroin now accounts for much of the heroin in the eastern United States. Mexico follows suit, producing a low-purity smokable type of heroin ("black tar"), and it supplies the bulk of the heroin flowing to states west of the Mississippi (U.S. State Department 2000).

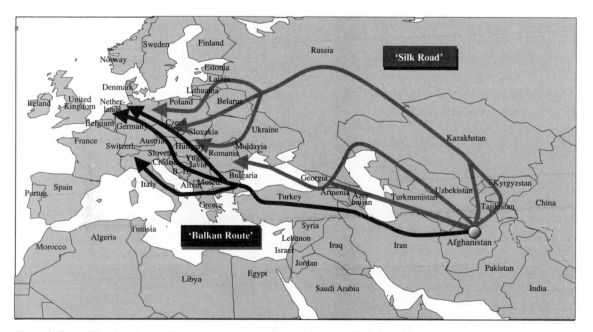

Figure 3. Drug Smuggling Routes From Afghanistan Into Western Europe: The "Balkan Route," the "Silk Road," and Their Variations
Source: Paoli (2001: 85).

Mexico is also the main foreign supplier of marijuana in the United States. A considerable share of U.S. demand is satisfied, however, by domestically grown marijuana. According to reliable estimates, cannabis has already become the no. 1 cash crop in several states, such as Kentucky, Tennessee, and West Virginia (*International Herald Tribune,* March 1, 2001). Whereas in the 1980s Lebanon was also a major supplier to Europe, virtually all hashish consumed in Europe at the beginning of the twenty-first century comes from Morocco. In the late 1990s, unofficial sources estimated that up to 85,000 hectares of land were devoted to cannabis cultivation (NNICC 1998: 70–88). Due to Morocco's geographical proximity, hashish is largely smuggled into Europe via Spain. As in the United States, a growing portion—up to one third—of the cannabis consumed in Western Europe is cultivated domestically (both outdoors and hydroponically) (UNODCCP 2001: 31).

Many of the source countries have become dependent on the cultivation and production of illicit drugs. Opium and heroin are practically the only source of hard currency in Afghanistan and in parts of northern Myanmar, where the fields of opium poppy are largely located. In Afghanistan, narcotic trafficking probably has been the major source of revenue for the country (U.S. State Department 2000). In the early 1990s, coca production represented 10 to 15 percent of the Bolivian GDP, and only because of generous international aid programs has the country succeeded in eradicating most of its cultivation (UNDCP 1997b: 13–14). The Rif Mountains in northern Morocco, where cannabis cultivation is concentrated, have also become economically dependent on this illicit crop, and for this reason, despite the official pledges of the Moroccan government, so far there has been no serious attempt at eradication (NNICC 1998: 88).

DEVELOPMENT OF DRUG MARKETS AND DISTRIBUTION SYSTEMS

Notwithstanding the large number of illegal drug users worldwide and the magnitude of the world drug economy, illicit drug trafficking is a relatively new phenomenon. In fact, only in the last three decades of the twentieth century did it assume mass proportions. Until the beginning of the twentieth century, opium, coca, and their derivatives—including their most powerful ones, heroin and cocaine, respectively—could be freely consumed not only in the countries of production

but also in most Western countries (Berridge 1999). Their consumption, possession, and trade began to be prohibited in Western countries only after the Opium Convention was released in The Hague in 1912 (Lowes [1966] 1981). The new international prohibition regime, whose enforcement was entrusted after World War I to the League of Nations and then to the United Nations, seemed quite successful at first. During the 1920s, 1930s, and 1940s the consumption of all the prohibited substances rapidly declined in the United States as well as in Europe (Musto 1987). Under the pressure of the United States, cannabis consumption and trade were also increasingly restricted and, finally, subjected to the international control regime in the early 1960s (Lindesmith 1966: 222–242; Bruun et al. 1975: 181–203).

In the decades following World War II, the demand for heroin, cocaine, and cannabis again rose, first in the United States and then in Western Europe. At the end of the twentieth century, it also grew in Second (former Communist) and Third World countries. The postwar expansion of illicit drug use was caused by both contingent events—such as the Vietnam War, which brought thousands of young American soldiers into contact with heroin—and macrosocial changes. Among the latter, two are most important: (1) the rise of a youth mass subculture, which resorted to illegal psychoactive substances to distinguish itself from the mainstream culture, and (2) technological progress, which made communication, travel, and trade of both legal and illegal commodities easier and faster.

Emergence of Distribution Systems

From the 1960s onward, the rising demand for illicit drugs fostered the development of drug distribution systems able to transfer drugs from the producers to the consumers. In the beginning, illegal drugs were imported by the consumers themselves, who used some of them and sold the rest within a close circle of friends. It was a sort of "ants trafficking." Soon, however, in both the United States and Western Europe the professional role of the drug dealer began to consolidate. In a few years, the development of a large-scale drug market fostered the progressive conversion of professional crime into the drug business. The microcosm of thieves, robbers, "pimps," gamblers, and "fencers" has largely disappeared: A variety of skilled criminal professionals have moved into the distribution chains of heavy drugs in the anonymous and interchangeable roles of traffickers, dealers, and mediators.

In source countries, where the state authorities are often weak, corrupt, or considered illegitimate by the general population, large organizations have sometimes emerged to coordinate the opium and coca cultivation and to refine heroin and cocaine. In northern Myanmar, for example, the refinement and export of heroin were first organized by the nationalistic Chinese Koumintang Army, which long enjoyed the protection and even the support of the U.S. Central Intelligence Agency (McCoy 1991), and more recently by several armies representing local ethnic minorities. Though the Myanmar government has negotiated cease-fire agreements with most of these groups, many of them, such as the United Wa State Army (UWSA) and the Myanmar National Democratic Alliance Army (MNDAA-Kokang Chinese), remain armed and heavily involved in the heroin trade (U.S. State Department 2000).

Much of the coca cultivation in Colombia also takes place in the inland areas controlled by guerrilla movements—by the FARC (Fuerzas Armadas Revolucionarias de Colombia) in particular. In Colombia, two large-scale "cartels" consolidated during the 1980s to process cocaine and smuggle large shipments into the United States. Composed of dozens of smaller drug-trafficking enterprises, the cartels were thus able to exploit economies of scale and share risks (Thoumi 1995; Lee 1989). In the following decade, however, first the Medellin cartel and then its counterpart in Cali disintegrated under the pressure of law enforcement and their leaders' arrest and/or death. During the second half of the 1990s a move "toward the decentralization of the cocaine trade" became evident (NNICC 1998: 4). Though some of the old shipping agreements have survived on a smaller scale, new independent operations have emerged in different parts of the country. According to the Observatoire Geopolitique des Drogues, as many as 40 medium-sized groups and 3,000 small groups are active (OGD 2000).

In developed countries, where the largest drug markets are located, the constraints deriving from the illegal status of the drugs have so far prevented the consolidation of large-scale, hierarchically organized drug-trafficking enterprises. These constraints arise from two facts: All illegal market actors—particularly drug traffickers and dealers—are obliged to operate (1) without the state and (2) against the state.

The first fact means that, because the goods and services that illegal market suppliers provide are prohibited, they cannot resort to state institutions to enforce contracts and have the violations of contracts prosecuted, nor does the illegal arena host an alternative sovereign power to which a party may appeal for redress of injury (Reuter 1983, 1985). As a result, property rights are poorly protected, employment contracts can hardly be formalized, and the development of large, formally organized, enduring companies is strongly discouraged.

The second fact means that all suppliers of illegal commodities—specifically drugs—are bound to operate under the constant risk of being arrested and having their assets confiscated by law enforcement institutions. In reality, the risk of arrest and interception of assets varies according to the situation and the counterparts involved. Some illegal entrepreneurs are so successful in bribing representatives of state institutions, and the latter are so weak and inefficient, that the risk is, in effect, strongly reduced. In most Western countries, however, the risk of arrest and interception of assets can hardly be disregarded. To varying degrees, all illegal market actors risk imprisonment and the seizure of their properties by law enforcement agencies and must take precautions against such events. All participants in the drug trade will thus try to organize their activities to ensure that the risk of police detection is minimized. Incorporating drug transactions into kinship and friendship networks and reducing the number of customers and employees are two of the strategies that drug entrepreneurs most often employ to reduce their vulnerability to law enforcement efforts (Reuter 1983, 1985; Moore 1974: 15–31).

Factors Limiting the Development of Distribution Bureaucracies

The constraints on illegal drug trafficking have so far prevented the rise of large, hierarchically organized firms to mediate economic transactions in the illegal marketplace. The factors promoting the development of bureaucracies in the legal section of the economy—namely the advantages deriving from economies of scale and the specialization of roles—are outweighed in the illegal section by the very consequences of product illegality. Due to these constraints, within the drug economy there is no tendency toward the consolidation of large-scale, modern bureaucracies.

Especially in Western Europe (Paoli 2000b; Ruggiero and South 1995; Dorn et al. 1992), but to a large extent in North America as well (Reuter and Haaga 1989; Adler 1993), the great majority of drug deals, even those involving large quantities, seem to be carried out by numerous, relatively small, and often ephemeral enterprises. Some of them are family businesses; that is, they are run by the members of a blood family who resort on an ad hoc basis to a net of nonkin to carry out the most dangerous tasks. Some are veritable nonkin groups, which are formed around a charismatic leader and then manage to acquire a certain degree of stability and develop a rudimentary division of labor. Others are "crews": loose associations of people who form, split, and reform as opportunity arises.

Even southern Italian Mafia families, whose members were deeply involved in large drug deals in southern Europe during the 1980s and early 1990s, do not seem to operate like monolithic productive and commercial units. On the contrary, their members frequently set up crews with a few other Mafia affiliates or even with external people to make drug deals. These crews are far from being stable working units that could be compared to the branch office of a legal firm. Their composition frequently changes depending on the moment when deals take place or on the availability of single members. After one or a few drug transactions some crews are disbanded, whereas others continue to operate for a longer time, eventually changing their composition to some extent (Paoli 2000a, 2000b).

Especially at the intermediate and lower levels, many dealers work alone, either to finance their own drug habits or, more rarely, to earn fast money. Most of these drug dealers have no contact whatsoever with the underworld but rather are often inconspicuous people who can hardly be distinguished from "normal" people.

In most European and North American cities, the street drug market is dominated by foreign or ethnic dealers. In Europe, a veritable substitution process has taken place within a few years: The lowest and most dangerous positions, which used to be occupied by the most marginalized local drug users, are increasingly taken over by foreigners, especially those who have immigrated recently, are applicants for political asylum, or do not have a residence permit. As with other forms of crime in the past, immigrants use involvement in the illegal drug market as what Daniel Bell (1965: 127) termed a "queer ladder of social mobility." Moreover, to a greater extent than in the past, immigrants now have a harder time accessing the legal economy and, due to the restrictive policies

adopted by most Western states, are more likely to find survival means only in the informal and illegal economies. Many of these immigrants, finally, are also drug users who have begun to deal drugs in order to finance their drug use.

In hardly any city of the industrialized world has a person or group ever succeeded in controlling the local drug markets. These tend to be open markets, in which anybody can try to earn a living selling, importing, or producing drugs. Even the relationships between drug-dealing enterprises are usually closer to competition than to collusion. Although some suppliers may occasionally enjoy a considerable monopoly over a local (usually small) market, in most cities drug enterprises seem to be price takers rather than price givers. That is, none of them is able to influence the commodity's price appreciably by varying the quantity of the output sold.

IMPLICATIONS

Since the mid-1960s, illegal drug trafficking has become one of the world's most profitable criminal activities. To fight it, a large and growing amount of public resources is invested in both developed and developing countries. In 1980, the U.S. government spent around $1 billion on drug control. In 1999, federal, state, and local spending exceeded $30 billion. Over two-thirds of this sum was invested in supply reduction programs, including domestic law enforcement, crop eradication, border patrols, and sting operations (ONDCP 2000). The effectiveness of these programs may be doubted, however, because even the Drug Enforcement Administration and the Office of National Drug Control Policy (ONDCP) admit that all the most common illegal drugs are readily available in virtually every U.S. city. Indeed, the prices of all the most common illegal drugs have fallen considerably since the illegal drug market began to expand. A kilogram of cocaine, which cost from $40,000 to $50,000 in the early 1980s, now costs as little as $13,000 to $30,000 (NNICC 1991, 1998: 1). A gram of heroin can cost as little as $100 (ONDCP 1998), whereas in the 1990s it cost up to $450 (DEA 1993). Purity has also increased. In the 1980s, street heroin was so adulterated that injecting straight into the blood was the surest way to get a high. In the 1990s, retail doses became commonly more than 50 percent pure, which meant that users who might be deterred by needles could smoke or snort the drug instead (NNICC 1998: 39; GAO 1992). In the last two decades of the twentieth century, prices dropped in Western Europe as well (although this drop was accompanied at the retail level by a comparable drop of purity levels) (Paoli 2000b; see also UNDCP 1994). Finally, at the beginning of the twenty-first century, illegal drugs are increasingly marketed in countries, such as the former Soviet states, Eastern European countries, and Third World states, that had no previous experience of widespread illegal drug consumption.

The only certain effect produced by the repression of drug trafficking has been a phenomenal increase of drug arrests and convictions in most Western nations. At the end of 1999, the number of people in U.S. state or federal prisons or local jails rose to an all-time high of more than 1.86 million, more than doubling since 1985 (see Figure 4).

Over one-third of this growth is due to the increase of drug law violators behind bars. As the Office of National Drug Control Policy recognizes, "the number of prisoners serving time for drug offenses is climbing—up more than 1000 percent since 1980" (ONDCP 2001: 82). The increase has been most phenomenal in federal prisons. In 1980, there were 6,120 inmates convicted for drug offenses, representing 25.1 percent of the prison population. By 2000, their number had escalated to 63,448, representing 58 percent of the prison population (FBP 2000; see Figure 5).

Even in European Union (EU) countries, drug offenders make up from 15 to 50 percent of the prison population. In 75 percent of these cases, the main drug offense committed by prisoners was related to dealing/trafficking. In the United States, over one-third of drug-related prisoners are nonviolent offenders with little or no criminal history (Lindesmith Centre 2001). The possession—not the sale—of an illicit drug is the reason for 80 percent of drug-related arrests (ONDCP 2001). This is why the European incarceration rate is five to ten times lower than that of the United States (EMCDDA 2000).

—*Letizia Paoli*

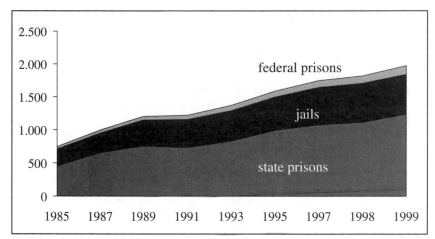

Figure 4. Number of People in U.S. State or Federal Prisons or Local Jails in Millions, 1985–1999
Source: ONDCP (2001: 82).

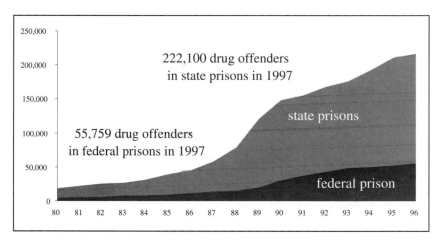

Figure 5. Drug Offenders Imprisoned in U.S. Federal and State Prisons, 1980–1997
Source: ONDCP (2001: 81).

See also CARIBBEAN; DRUG COURIER PROFILES; DRUG MILLIONAIRES; DRUGS; LATIN AMERICA, CRIME AND VIOLENCE IN; MEXICO; ORGANIZED CRIME—GLOBAL

Further Reading
Adler, Patricia A. (1993). *Wheeling and Dealing: An Ethnography of an Upper-Level Drug Dealing and Smuggling Community.* New York: Columbia University Press.
Bell, Daniel. (1965). *The End of Ideology.* New York: Free Press.
Berridge, Virginia. (1999). *Opium and the People: Opiate Use and Drug Control Policy in Nineteenth and Early Twentieth Century England.* London: Free Association.
Bruun, Kettil, Lynn Pan, and Ingemar Rexed. (1975). *The Gentlemen's Club: International Control of Drugs and Alcohol.* Chicago: University of Chicago Press.
Dorn, Nicholas, Karim Murji, and Nigel South. (1992). *Traffickers: Drug Markets and Law Enforcement.* London and New York: Routledge.
Drug Enforcement Administration (DEA). (1993). *Illegal Drug*

Price/Purity Report. January 1990–June 1993 (December). Washington, DC: Drug Enforcement Administration.

———. (1999). "MDMA-Ecstasy." *Drug Intelligence Brief.* http://www.usdoj.gov/dea/pubs/intel.htm

———. (2000). "An Overview of Club Drugs." *Drug Intelligence Brief.* http://www.usdoj.gov/dea/pubs/intel.htm

———. (2001). "Drugs of Concern: Methamphetamine." http://www.usdoj.gov/dea/concern/meth.htm

European Monitoring Centre for Drugs and Drug Addiction (EMCDDA). (1997). *Extended Annual Report on the State of the Drugs Problem in the European Union: 1997.* Lisbon: EMCDDA.

———. (1999). *Extended Annual Report on the State of the Drugs Problem in the European Union: 1999.* Lisbon: EMCDDA. http://www.emcdda.org/publications/publications_annrep.shtml

———. (2000). *Annual Report on the State of the Drugs Problem in the European Union.* Lisbon: EMCDDA. http://www.emcdda.org/publications/publications_annrep.shtml

Federal Bureau of Prisons (FBP). (2000). "Quick Facts." http://www.bop.gov/fact0598.html

General Accounting Office (GAO). (1992). *War on Drugs: Heroin Price, Purity, and Quantities Seized over the Past 10 Years.* Washington, DC: General Accounting Office.

Lee, Rensselaer W., III. (1989). *The White Labyrinth: Cocaine and Political Power.* New Brunswick, NJ: Transaction.

Lindesmith, Alfred R. (1965). *The Addict and the Law.* Bloomington: Indiana University Press.

Lindesmith Centre. (2001). "Research in Brief: Drug Prohibition & the U.S. Prison System." http://www.lindesmith.org/cites_sources/brief3.html

Lowes, Peter D. ([1966] 1981). *The Genesis of International Narcotics Control.* New York: Arno Press.

McCoy, Alfred W. (1991). *The Politics of Heroin: CIA Complicity in the Drug Trade.* Brooklyn, NY: Lawrence Hill Books.

Moore, Mark H. (1974). *The Effective Regulation of an Illicit Market in Heroin.* Lexington, MA: Lexington Books.

Musto, David F. (1987). *The American Disease: Origin of Narcotic Control.* New York and Oxford: Oxford University Press.

Nadelmann, Ethan A. (1990). "Global Prohibition Regimes: The Evolution of Norms in International Society." *International Organization* 44: 479–526.

National Narcotics Intelligence Consumers Committee (NNICC). (1991). *The NNICC Report 1990: The Supply of Illicit Drugs to the United States.* Washington, DC: Drug Enforcement Administration.

———. (1998). *The NNICC Report 1997: The Supply of Illicit Drugs to the United States.* Washington, DC: Drug Enforcement Administration. http://www.usdoj.gov/dea/pubs/intel.html

Observatoire Géopolitique des Drogues (OGD). (2000). *The World Geopolitics of Drugs: 1998–1999.* http://www.ogd.org/2000/en/99en.html

Office of National Drug Control Policy (ONDCP). (1998). *Pulse Check: Trends in Drug Abuse: January–June 1998.* http://www.whitehousedrugpolicy.gov/pubs/fastfind.html

———. (2000). *National Drug Control Strategy: FY 2001 Budget Summary—2000 Annual Report.* http://www.whitehousedrugpolicy.gov/policy/budget.html

———. (2001). "Data Snapshot: Drug Abuse in America." http://www.whitehousedrugpolicy.gov/drugfact/index.html

Paoli, Letizia. (2000a). *Fratelli di Mafia: Cosa Nostra e 'Ndrangheta.* Bologna, Italy: Mulino.

———. (2000b). *Pilot Project to Describe and Analyse Local Drug Markets—First Phase Final Report: Illegal Drug Markets in Frankfurt and Milan.* Lisbon: EMCDDA. http://www.emcdda.org

———. (2001). *Illegal Drug Trade in Russia: A Research Project Commissioned by the United Nations Office for Drug Control and Crime Prevention.* Freiburg, Germany: Edition Iuscrim.

Parker, Howard, Judith Aldridge, and Fiona Measham. (1998). *Illegal Leisure: The Normalization of Adolescent Recreational Drug Use.* London: Routledge.

Reuter, Peter. (1983). *Disorganized Crime: The Economics of the Visible Hand.* Cambridge: MIT Press.

———. (1985). *The Organization of Illegal Markets: An Economic Analysis.* Washington, DC: National Institute of Justice.

———. (1998). "Review: United Nations International Drug Control Program, World Drug Report." *Journal of Policy Analysis and Management* 18: 730–733.

Reuter, Peter, and John Haaga. (1989). *The Organization of High-Level Drug Markets: An Exploratory Study.* Santa Monica, CA: RAND.

Ruggiero, Vincenzo, and Nigel South. (1995). *Eurodrugs: Drug Use, Markets, and Trafficking in Europe.* London: UCL Press.

Thoumi, Francisco E. (1995). *Political Economy and Illegal Drugs in Colombia.* Boulder, CO: Lynne Rienner.

U.N. International Drug Control Programme (UNDCP). (1994). "Cocaine and Heroin Trafficking and Prices in Europe 1983–93." Discussion paper. Vienna: United Nations International Drug Control Programme.

———. (1996). *Amphetamine-Type Stimulants: A Global Review.* UNDCP Technical Series no. 3.

———. (1997a). *World Drug Report.* Oxford, UK: Oxford University Press.

———. (1997b). *Economic and Social Consequences of Drug Abuse and Illicit Trafficking.* UNDCP Technical Series no. 6.

U.N. Office for Drug Control and Crime Prevention (UNODCCP). (2001). *World Drug Report 2000.* Oxford, UK: Oxford University Press.

U.S. Department of Health and Human Services, Substance Abuse and Mental Health Services Administration (SAMHSA). (2000). *1999 National Household Survey on Drug Abuse.* http://www.SAMHSA.gov/ household99.htm

U.S. State Department, Bureau of International Narcotics and Law Enforcement Affairs. (2000). *1999 International Narcotics Control Strategy Report.* http://www.state.gov/www/global/narcotics_law/narc_reports_mainhp.html

 **DRUG TREATMENT**

According to the National Institute on Drug Abuse, more than 1.5 million people entered drug treatment in 1998. Nearly half of these entries were for alcohol treatment, while the majority of the remaining entries were for heroin or other opiates, crack, or

powder cocaine, or marijuana. Two-thirds of the people who enter treatment are men, and about 60 percent are white. While the age at which people enter drug treatment varies considerably, the average age of entry was thirty-three.

To serve the diverse needs of clients, drug treatment takes several forms. It can be intensive, such as a residential program (e.g., Phoenix House), or more limited. It can be a part of a criminal justice sentence, or an individual can enter a drug treatment program independent of judicial intervention.

HISTORY OF DRUG TREATMENT

Opiate use emerged as a significant social problem in the United States during the first half of the nineteenth century. The response by social activists and local and state policymakers included both prohibition and treatment. Early efforts to treat morphine and opium addiction frequently used medical interventions, including both heroin (developed in 1898) and purgative compounds, such as the Towns-Lambert Cure, which was developed in 1908. Such "cures" occasionally proved fatal. The alternative was to punish the addict and, through incarceration, deprive him or her of the drug.

Select states and localities had enacted laws regulating the production, distribution, and use of opiates since the mid-1880s. However, the nation as a whole did not do so until the passage of the Harrison Act in 1914, which effectively criminalized drug possession. That act was the culmination of decades of concern about drug use. While the legislation included efforts to treat addiction, the principal effect of the Harrison Act was to increase the number of drug users incarcerated in federal prisons. Consequently, concern arose that prisons were inappropriate and ineffective in curing addicts, and in 1929, Congress passed legislation creating the first federally funded treatment programs, which were called "narcotic farms." These mandatory residential treatment facilities, the first of which opened in 1935, used a regime of detoxification and mental and physical development.

Drug treatment efforts made a significant advance between 1941 and 1945, when pharmaceutical researchers tested methadone, a synthetic narcotic developed by German researchers during World War II. Methadone prevents the euphoria of opiate use, which makes morphine and heroin less desirable. It also prevents the painful physical effects of withdrawal from those drugs. Methadone has been used since its discovery to maintain abstinence from drug use. Beginning in the 1950s, health professionals recognized the need for services and treatment beyond abstinence, however, funding to provide those services was limited.

Dramatic increases in drug use in the 1960s led to state and federal legislation mandating civil commitment for treatment purposes (Narcotic Addict Rehabilitation Act of 1966). These efforts largely failed. Continued heroin use both in cities and among U.S. soldiers in Vietnam led to renewed efforts to reduce drug use, which were introduced as the War on Drugs by the Nixon administration in 1971. Within eight years, with the help of federal funding (along with funds from state and local governments and private sources), community drug treatment centers increased from six facilities in 1969 to over 3,000 in 1977. Since the late 1970s, the War on Drugs has spent approximately 80 percent of its resources on interdiction (law enforcement); however, funding for treatment has also continued. Despite the fact that drug use remained high in the 1980s and 1990s, and continues to be an issue in the twenty-first century, public funding for treatment and private insurance coverage are limited and insufficient.

In the 1980s, the emergence of cocaine as the primary abused illegal drug forced treatment providers and policymakers to examine treatment programs that were originally designed for heroin users. Today, providers continue to refine the content and structure of programs, adapting to the changing needs and increased numbers of treatment clients.

SUBSTANCE ABUSE TREATMENT MODALITIES

There are several different modalities, or types, of drug treatment; while most programs share broad underlying concepts, they vary widely. The goal of most treatment programs is abstinence. That is pursued with numerous interventions including medication, counseling, self-help groups, skill development, and a combination of these approaches. Program structure also varies depending on such factors as staff credentials (a staff that is clinically trained works very differently from one that is encouraged to rely on personal experiences) and the program environment (a strictly disciplined structure, or one that allows greater client autonomy).

Residential and Outpatient Treatment

Residential treatment may be short-term (one week to three months) or long-term (up to two years). Considered by many to be the most effective form of treatment, residential treatment is also the most expensive and the most demanding of participants. Frequently, residential treatment is provided by "therapeutic communities" (TC), or treatment programs designed to provide a community-like alternative to the social environment from which participants come. The TC philosophy is based on the idea that addicts can only recover if they remove themselves from social contexts in which drug use is normalized. Treatment typically consists of highly structured group classes about drug use, group sessions designed to elicit confrontations between participants about their underlying beliefs and habits, individual counseling, and an elaborate hierarchy of chores and peer support. Participants progress through a series of treatment phases in which lasting sobriety is a prerequisite for job development and independent living. Staff members are primarily recovered addicts themselves, and participants are restricted in their contact with anyone outside of the treatment program, particularly during the early phases of treatment. Research has demonstrated the effectiveness of combining residential treatment with aftercare treatment, however, many programs lack the funding to provide follow-up treatment.

Outpatient treatment, like residential treatment, varies considerably in length and content. While outpatient programs are divided into "intensive outpatient" and "outpatient," the number of treatment hours is inconsistent and varies regionally within these designations from one hour to thirty-five hours each week. Less isolating than residential treatment, participants live at home or in another community-based residence and attend the programs during the week. Typically, treatment involves intensive group and individual counseling, peer support, drug testing, vocational and educational training, and additional skills-building classes. However, some outpatient programs provide little more than drug testing. Some programs anticipate participant resistance and require the most structured activities during the early phases of treatment. As in residential programs, treatment is often structured by phases that correspond to individual development. Again, while aftercare is recommended, it is frequently not funded.

Pharmaceutical Treatments

Methadone and other medical treatments such as levo-alpha-acetylmethadol (LAAM) are some of the most effective, but also controversial, treatments for opiate addiction. Other medical treatments are being developed in clinical trials for other addictive drugs, notably cocaine. Medical treatment involves daily doses that are generally taken orally (although nicotine addiction is treated topically). Methadone can be used for limited time periods in abstinence-based therapy, or prescribed indefinitely, in methadone maintenance therapy. Medical treatment may include counseling, drug testing, and case management, but it may also be used independently of such psychological approaches. In order for medical treatment to be effective, dosage levels must be high enough to prevent the desire to use the illegal drug—generally 60 to 100 milligrams daily—and must be tailored to the individual client. However, some treatment professionals are ambivalent about using high doses of methadone because of concern that the medical treatment is itself an addictive treatment that can be abused. This concern is at the center of debates about methadone maintenance. In addition, drug treatment providers who are licensed to provide drug-free treatment by state regulatory agencies are prohibited from incorporating medical treatment into their protocols. Because of the controversy surrounding methadone maintenance, methadone is one of the most restricted medications available today.

Detoxification, or "detox" as it is commonly referred to, involves short stays in a hospital or another temporary residential facility where the patient agrees to remain for the duration of the process. Patients are given methadone or LAAM in rapidly decreasing doses for a period of time, usually between seven and twenty-eight days. Typically used for opiate addiction, detox facilities may be locked units, however, less expensive facilities that rely on client willingness to remain are increasingly used. Detox is frequently used as a treatment for drug addiction, particularly in states where insurance and public funds for drug treatment are scarce. However, it is more accurately viewed as an introduction to treatment, as there is little evidence that it is effective without follow-up treatment.

Another Alternative

Rather than striving for complete abstinence from the drug of choice, the goal of harm reduction is to foster healthier, more productive lives among drug users who are unwilling or unable to stop using drugs. Better health practices, educational and vocational development, and assistance in attaining public entitlements are all components of harm-reduction programs. Harm reduction was originally associated with the AIDS epidemic and the syringe exchange programs that were started to prevent HIV transmission among intravenous drug users. The approach has been used independently and in combination with other drug treatments. The clearest example of harm reduction in traditional forms of treatment is the increased willingness of treatment programs to retain participants who test positive for drug use. While treatment programs used to expel participants who used drugs during treatment, many programs now address drug use with sanctions and increased counseling, rather than immediately expelling those clients.

DRUG ADDICTION TREATMENT AND THE CRIMINAL JUSTICE SYSTEM

Many defendants arrested for selling drugs and other criminal acts engaged in their crimes in order to support an addiction. As court officials have become frustrated with what has been termed the "revolving door" of criminal activity and drug use, judges, prosecutors, and corrections administrators have used drug treatment to supplement or replace traditional sentences. The criminal justice system uses treatment at the "front end," as part of a sentence, and at the "back end," as part of corrections.

One of the most recent developments in the link between criminal justice system and drug treatment is the drug court movement. Drug courts are special courts for offenders in need of drug treatment. These courts differ from other criminal courts in that they are intended to be nonadversarial, the district attorney and defense work together with the judge and court staff to place and monitor the offender in treatment. The judge in a drug court speaks directly to the defendant, providing regular support, counseling, and supervision that is not possible in general courts. The offender agrees to enter drug treatment in return for reduction or dismissal of charges upon completion. Drug courts accept that participants may relapse and use drugs or violate other court rules in their effort to remain sober; however, if the defendant continually fails to adhere to treatment protocol and fails treatment, the court imposes a custodial sentence. The courts are characterized by a system of graduated sanctions and rewards. In ten years, drug courts have developed from a regional experiment to a national initiative of some 500 courts.

Outpatient and residential treatment are used in other courts across the country as alternative sentences or as conditions of probation sentences. Several large jurisdictions have created specialized drug courts within the criminal courts to handle the large number of drug cases. Frequently, sentences in these courts combine probation supervision with drug treatment. In New York, judges use residential programs for teenagers and adults convicted of second-felony drug offenses. Defendants agree to enter drug treatment for up to two years instead of going to state prison. First-time felony offenders may also be sentenced to intensive outpatient treatment. In both cases, the treatment programs report on participant progress to the sentencing judge every month, and participants who fail to complete treatment are sentenced to custodial sentences that are typically longer than they would have received absent the drug treatment intervention. In 2000, California voters approved drug treatment instead of custodial sentences for most drug offenders. This sweeping initiative will add thousands of criminal defendants to treatment rosters, and its implementation and effects remain to be seen.

Jail and prison administrators may also implement drug treatment within correctional facilities. Due largely to limited resources and political pressure, self-help groups are the most common treatment available in jails and prisons since they cost little. However, a growing number of local corrections administrators and state policymakers allocate resources to provide more structured treatment to inmates. Treatment varies according to each institution's policies; it may include drug and alcohol education, relapse prevention skills, and therapeutic counseling. It generally is available for a few hours each week to those inmates who choose to attend. More intensive treatment may also be made available to inmates on a voluntary basis, typically in therapeutic, community-style programs. These programs may serve inmates from throughout a prison, or they may be isolated to the units where inmates live. Some states, such as Pennsylvania, have entire prisons devoted to drug treatment. Some prisons require that inmates attend treatment, and others use early release as an incentive to enter treatment in prison. Ideally, treatment initiated in prison continues, in the form of parole-monitored aftercare, when inmates are released from prison. However, such services are rarely available due to a lack of resources and coordination. Consequently, of the estimated 450,000 prisoners released each year with substance abuse problems, the majority do not receive treatment.

The tremendous need for drug addiction treatment

among offenders does not translate into shared criminal justice and treatment goals. Therapeutic use of drug treatment focuses on individual well-being, which does not always coincide with the principal concerns of sentencing, which include punishment and security. Judges and prosecutors may reason that defendants who would otherwise be incarcerated should not be permitted to remain at liberty, and therefore sentence offenders to residential drug treatment, rather than outpatient treatment, even if residential treatment is not clinically appropriate. Similarly, corrections officials may revoke drug treatment for disciplinary reasons. This could happen as a sanction for individual behavior, or as part of a facility-wide measure, such as a prison lockdown.

RESEARCH ON DRUG ADDICTION TREATMENT

The federal government has supported three major research efforts in drug treatment that have yielded several key findings. Between 1969 and 1973, the Drug Abuse Reporting Program (DARP) collected information on some 44,000 participants in fifty-two treatment programs. DARP established the effectiveness of community-based treatment, and highlighted the importance of remaining in treatment for at least ninety days. DARP findings also showed that methadone treatment was more effective the longer participants remained in treatment.

In a second study, the Treatment Outcome Prospective Study (TOPS), which began in 1979, researchers analyzed data on 11,000 participants in forty-one programs. TOPS examined both short and long-term outcomes, demonstrating that treatment could reduce drug use and criminal activity both during and after program participation. The TOPS research also showed that legal coercion did not hamper treatment compliance, as had been previously suggested, which paved the way for increases in court and correctional use of treatment. Finally, a cost-benefits analysis within TOPS argued that drug treatment was a cost-effective approach to using public funds to address drug addiction.

The third major study was the Drug Abuse Treatment Outcome Study (DATOS). Conducted between 1989 and 1995, DATOS demonstrated differences between treatment modalities in ninety-nine facilities. Results from DATOS confirm the importance of a client remaining in treatment and receiving ancillary services (such as family and vocational counseling) in addition to drug treatment, but it also indicated that few treatment programs provide these services. DATOS suggested the utility of matching the treatment to individual needs and confirmed the diversity of socioeconomic and drug use profiles among treatment clients. The research indicated the importance of serving distinct populations; it showed that drug addicts frequently enter treatment after initial contact with the criminal justice or mental health systems, and frequently enter treatment repeatedly prior to successful completion.

RESEARCH DIRECTIONS

In spite of the extensive body of research these and other studies have produced, a great deal remains unknown about what makes some treatment effective for some people. Further, the research that has been undertaken generally lacks the strongest possible methodological design—random assignment—so the conclusions that can be drawn from it are limited. Standards in assessment, treatment protocol, staff training, treatment content, and aftercare are necessary to efficiently address drug addiction. Individual factors, such as background characteristics, community and family support, and motivation to enter and remain in treatment may be critical to understand who stays in drug treatment and to respond to client needs. While research is under way examining many of these factors, they are frequently difficult to isolate. Because the content and quality of drug abuse treatment programs vary enormously and are difficult to measure, evaluations of these programs are both complicated and costly. Yet drug treatment that is not rigorously evaluated offers little hope of solving the national problem of addiction.

—Rachel Porter

See also DRUG COURIER PROFILES; DRUG TRAFFICKING; DRUGS; HARM REDUCTION; REHABILITATION MODEL

Further Reading
Anglin, M. Doug, and Yih I. Hser. (1990). "Treatment of Drug Abuse." In *Drugs and Crime,* edited by Michael Tonry and James Q. Wilson. Chicago: University of Chicago Press, 393–460.
Bayer, Ronald, and Gerald M. Oppenheimer, eds. (1993). *Confronting Drug Policy: Illicit Drugs in a Free Society.* Cambridge, UK: Cambridge University Press.
Belenko, Steven, ed. (2000). *Drugs and Drug Policy in America: A Documentary History.* Westport, CT: Greenwood Press.
Boren, John J., Lisa S. Onken, and Kathleen M. Carroll. (2000).

Approaches to Drug Abuse Counseling. Bethesda, MD: U.S. Department of Health and Human Services, National Institute of Drug Abuse.

Gerstein, Dean R., and Henrick J. Harwood, eds. (1990). *A Study of the Evolution, Effectiveness, and Financing of Public and Private Drug Treatment Systems*. Vol. 1 of *Treating Drug Problems*. Washington, DC: National Academy Press.

———, eds. (1992). *Commissioned Papers on Historical, Institutional and Economic Contexts of Drug Treatment*. Vol. 2 of *Treating Drug Problems*. Washington, DC: National Academy Press.

Inciardi, James, A., ed. (1993). *Drug Treatment and Criminal Justice*. Newbury Park, CA: Sage.

Massing, Michael. (1998). *The Fix*. New York: Simon & Schuster.

Musto, David F. (1987). *The American Disease: Origins of Narcotic Control*, expanded ed. New York: Oxford University Press.

Simpson, Dwayne, D., and Susan J. Curry. (1997). "Special Issue: Drug Abuse Treatment Outcome Study (DATOS)." *Psychology of Addictive Behaviors* 11, 4.

U.S. General Accounting Office. (1998). *Drug Abuse: Research Shows Treatment Is Effective but Benefits May Be Overstated*. Washington, DC: U.S. General Accounting Office.

▼ DRUGS

A drug is defined broadly by the World Health Organization, as "Any substance that, when taken into the living organism, may modify one or more of its functions" (WHO 1980: 1–2). The history of drug use dates back to the discovery of psychoactive properties of the poppy plant (Stimmel 1993), whose seeds and pods have been found in the remains of Stone Age settlements. The poppy plant was cultivated between 4000 and 3000 BCE by the Sumerians in Mesopotamia (present-day Iraq) to provide opium, known as *gil*, which meant "happiness and joy." Similarly, *cannabis sativa* (marijuana) has been known almost since the beginning of recorded history. Practically every human malady has been treated with this plant. For centuries, Andean peasants chewed coca leaves for mild stimulus; Africans used snuff, *khat*, and kola nuts for cultural rituals; and indigenous peoples throughout the Americas used plants with psychoactive properties in religious rituals. Caffeine, cocaine, nicotine, and alcohol have been used for centuries, playing integral roles in different cultures. In the colonial United States, coca and opium were common ingredients in popular patent medicines. Today, however, abuse of these long-popular drugs has caused concern not only in the United States but also worldwide. In the twentieth century, scientific advances changed the properties and potencies of long-used drugs such as opium and coca, transforming them into heroin and crack cocaine, and also made possible a variety of new synthetic drugs. Because the new forms of these drugs are more potent, they are more addictive and pose a greater health threat.

A distinction should be made between drugs classified as licit (legal) and illicit (illegal). Licit drugs include stimulants (e.g., amphetamines), sedatives (e.g., barbiturates such as Mandrax), paregoric elixir (a common sedative), alcohol (e.g., beer and wine), tobacco, prescription drugs, and over-the-counter medications. Illicit drugs include cocaine, crack, heroin, LSD, marijuana, and PCP.

The concern over illegal drugs focuses on psychoactive drugs. Psychoactive drugs principally affect the central nervous system—the brain and the spinal cord. Most psychoactive drugs have mood- and mind-altering effects, and nonmedicinal use of these drugs can cause social or physical harm to the user. "Nonmedicinal use" means that a drug is taken for recreational use. "Medicinal use" means that a drug is taken to prevent or cure a disease or disabling condition. There is relative condemnation of mood-altering drugs because of their adverse effects. Penalties for their production, consumption, and distribution are severe. But in spite of the severe penalties, some people use these drugs for various reasons, ranging from reducing pain to producing pleasurable effects. These effects may be mood change, excitement, relaxation, pleasure, analgesia, stimulation, or seduction. Some drugs are taken in the belief that they enhance physical and mental performance. On the other hand, there is a growing feeling in some areas of the world where drugs have become a serious problem that their use reflects despair among users, a symptom of malaise in a society where children no longer respect parents or elders and feel that they have a doubtful future. Drug use provides solace for those hoping to escape life's challenges, but eventually many realize the inverse relationship between taking drugs and escaping life's challenges. This entry discusses illegal drugs, their producing countries, the politics of illegal drugs, problems associated with drug use, and control efforts. Table 1 shows major producers of the highly regulated illegal drugs.

Table 1 shows worldwide potential production of opium, coca leaf, and cannabis from 1991 to 1999. The major countries and quantity of production on an annual basis are shown. The drugs listed in Table 1 are highly regulated by the international community because of their effects when misused. Over the past

Table 1. Worldwide Potential Illicit Drug Production, 1991–1999 (All Figures in Metric Tons)

	1999	1998	1997	1996	1995	1994	1993	1992	1991
Opium Gum									
Afghanistan	1,670	1,350	1,265	1,230	1,250	950	685	640	570
India			30	47	77	90			
Iran									
Pakistan	37	65	85	75	155	160	140	175	180
Total SW Asia	**1,707**	**1,415**	**1,380**	**1,352**	**1,482**	**1,200**	**825**	**815**	**750**
Burma	1,090	1,750	2,365	2,560	2,340	2,030	2,575	2,280	2,350
China					19	25			
Laos	140	140	210	200	180	85	180	230	265
Thailand	6	16	25	30	25	17	42	24	35
Total SE Asia	**1,236**	**1,906**	**2,600**	**2,790**	**2,564**	**2,157**	**2,797**	**2,534**	**2,650**
Colombia	75	61	66	63	65				
Lebanon				1	1		4		34
Guatemala									11
Mexico	43	60	46	54	53	60	49	40	41
Vietnam	11	20	45	25					
Total Other	**129**	**141**	**157**	**143**	**119**	**60**	**53**	**40**	**86**
Total Opium	**3,072**	**3,462**	**4,137**	**4,285**	**4,165**	**3,417**	**3,675**	**3,389**	**3,486**
Coca Leaf									
Bolivia	22,800	52,900	70,100	75,100	85,000	89,800	84,400	80,300	78,000
Colombia	521,400	437,600	347,000	302,900	229,300	35,800	31,700	29,600	30,000
Peru	69,200	95,600	130,200	174,700	183,600	165,300	155,500	223,900	222,700
Ecuador							100	100	40
Total Coca	**613,400**	**586,100**	**547,300**	**552,700**	**497,900**	**290,900**	**271,700**	**333,900**	**330,740**
Cannabis									
Mexico	3,700	8,300	8,600	11,700	12,400	5,540	6,280	7,795	7,775
Colombia	4,000	4,000	4,133	4,133	4,133	4,138	4,125	1,650	1,650
Jamaica			214	356	206	208	502	263	641
Belize									49
Others	3,500	3,500	3,500	3,500	3,500	3,500	3,500	3,500	3,500
Total Cannabis	**11,200**	**15,800**	**16,447**	**19,689**	**20,239**	**13,386**	**14,407**	**13,208**	**13,615**

SOURCE: Bureau for International Narcotics and Law Enforcement Affairs (2000).

thirty years the United Nations has established several international conventions to control illegal production, trafficking, and use of drugs. For example, the 1961 Single Convention on Narcotic Drugs (as amended by a 1972 protocol) established schedules for psychotropic substances and quotas limiting production and export of legal pharmaceuticals. As of 1990, 129 nations were party to the convention in its original or amended form. The signatories committed themselves to cooperate to control these substances (Bureau of Justice Statistics 1992).

The 1971 Convention on Psychotropic Substances dealt with limitations on manufacture and importation, as well as special provisions relating to international trade and actions against illegal traffic. The convention expanded the international control system to prevent trafficking from diverting psychotropic drugs from legal channels. The 1988 Convention Against Illicit Traffic in Narcotic Drugs and Psychotropic Substances included provisions to accomplish the following:

1. share evidence with law enforcement and prosecuting agencies of the signatory nations,

2. legalize seizure of drug-related assets,

3. criminalize money laundering and relax bank secrecy rules,

4. permit extradition of individuals charged with drug law violations,

5. control shipment of precursor and essential chemicals, and

6. reaffirm commitment to crop eradication and reduction.

The 1988 convention came into force on November 11, 1990; by the end of 1990, thirty-one countries, Byelorussia (Belorussia), and the European Economic Community (EEC) had ratified it. Under this convention, the United States plays a major role in structuring the United Nations' institutional capacity to respond to the drug problem.

As shown in Table 1, production of illegal drugs is confined to developing nations, for example, Afghanistan, Pakistan, Burma, Laos, Mexico, and Thailand (opium); Bolivia, Colombia, Peru, and Ecuador (coca leaf—cocaine); and Mexico, Colombia, Jamaica, and Belize (cannabis). The destination for these drugs is the developed countries, for example, the United States and European nations. For example, the amount of cocaine imported into the United States was estimated at 432 to 545 metric tons in 1989 and 287 to 376 metric tons in 1995 (Office of National Drug Control Policy 1997). The major illegal drugs destined for U.S. drug markets are cocaine, heroin, and marijuana. The majority of the cocaine entering the United States comes from South American nations such as Colombia, Bolivia, and Peru. Much of marijuana imported into the United States, along with some of the heroin, comes from Mexico. The majority of heroin, hashish, and opium in the United States comes from Myanmar, Laos, Thailand, Afghanistan, Iran, Pakistan, Lebanon, and Syria (Swisher 1991). In view of this great incursion of illegal drugs, the United States has been the pioneering force on global efforts to control illegal drugs in order to rid itself of the associated social problems (i.e., crime, violence, prostitution, crack kids, etc.).

THE POLITICS OF ILLEGAL DRUGS

In the global community, where goods are produced and distributed according to market forces (i.e., demand and supply), who determines the legality or illegality of these goods? With regard to controlled substances—for example, illegal drugs such as cocaine, heroin, and hashish, and legal ones such as tobacco and alcohol—what parameters are used in determining regulation? The fundamental question is, Who defines exactly what a "drug" is and is not? Who decides which drugs should be controlled? What kinds of controls should be imposed on various types of drugs? Why do other addictive substances, equally if not more dangerous, remain outside the scope of control? Who defines the parameters of licit and illicit use? Answers to these

A 35-year-old dock worker in Thailand injects himself with heroin. In Thailand as elsewhere, many people addicted to heroin also are infected with HIV, which is most often transmitted through the sharing of needles and by involvement in prostitution.
Source: © Reuters NewMedia Inc./Corbis; used with permission.

questions will explain why some drugs are subject to international control and others are not

For instance, dose for dose, alcohol is one of the most toxic and violence-producing drugs, but it has escaped international regulation. International drug control treaties have repeatedly exempted tobacco and alcohol irrespective of the harm caused. These treaties make no attempt to impose a rational system of control over drugs according to the dangers they pose to humans. The worldwide trade in these two highly addictive substances is immune, profitable, and dominated by Europe, North America, and Japan (McAllister 1994). The fact that these two drugs escaped the attention of the international control community is evidence of the power relationship that animates the system.

The evidence (U.N. drug control treaties 1961, 1971, and 1988) indicates that Western industrialized nations, particularly the United States, have had paramount influence in the creation and operation of the international drug control system. The system reflects Western cultural, social, economic, and religious biases about which drugs to control and how stringent those controls should be. To buttress this view, look at the other side of the coin. If South America, Asia, or Muslim states were in a position to impose restrictions according to their cultural, social, economic, and religious biases, an entirely different system of international drug controls would be in place. Cocaine, heroin,

The Life of a Crack Addict

The following are quotes about her life from S., a twenty-eight-year-old woman from the southern United States:

About smoking crack:
"Smoke till you croak!" was my motto, 9 to 10 day binges were common. There was at least one 15-day binge. After that I had the coke bugs. I thought someone had sewn my eyelids shut. I heard the police in the air conditioning vent. I could feel my central nervous system deteriorating.

About withdrawal from crack:
They call it "Jonesing"—you're nervous, jumpy, dry mouth, eyes bothering you. You want no noise. You are pacing back and forth. There is just one thing on your mind. Have to have it! The crash is bad, mental pain. Mentally, I could not just ride it out.

About getting money:
Years ago he was down-and-out alcoholic who shoplifted meat to buy booze. Then he gave up on booze and started selling drugs. Later he would give the meat to the ones in the neighborhood who really needed it. They really liked him for that and so they called him the "Meatman," but it was a good name for him. He was the dope man, I was the "Rock Monster," or they call 'em "rock stars."

Dealers don't use. They are all about money. I saw what the money was one time on the beach at the motel during Spring Break. I saw my husband make $12,000 profit in three hours, and that was not all. After that I stopped counting.

About relationships with men:
He [S's father] came into my bed one time during the night. It was never mentioned. But I knew that it happened . . . fondling. Shortly after that my brothers started experimenting, touching me. They were 4 and 5 years older than me. They knew better. For a long period, 2-3 years, they kept after me. It was bad enough that it led me to leave home at 14 to get away from them.

At 12, I was raped by a neighbor. I went over there to see my friend, but his dad was home alone, and he offered me a cigarette. I was taken in because I thought it was neat that he would let me smoke. Once he got me inside, he used intimidation to penetrate me.

My second husband beat me so much I lost count. He said he beat me to get me to stop using crack. I thought that he just wanted me to stop because of the money. But he said it was for my own good. Afterward he would feel guilty, and then he gave me dope. It was crazy. . . . I saw him for what he really was for the way he treated addicts. He had a power trip over them, like little slaves to him. He would degrade them, treat them really bad, and they would beg him.

About violence:
I know of three women who are dead from robbing tricks. One got cracked in the head with a club, another got her eyes and tongue cut out. . . . About one or two out of five tricks turns into a rape with them taking sex without paying. I was punched, had my throat grabbed, my hair pulled.

About prostitution:
In the beginning, crack stimulates sex. Later, men cannot perform, and women get nothing, not even wet. But they have to do it to get crack. A woman who uses crack must prostitute or steal. She will turn a trick for $20–15 if it comes to it, anything. She can find lots of tricks, no problem to find tricks, unless she's robbing or "got something." Word gets around if she is robbing some guy, she's going to be right back out there. It is just a matter of time and they will find her.

At the bottom level of prostitution you have someone who will be on her knees in a crack house. She is dirty; has no regulars. Up from that you have someone who gets $10 to $20 for a trick, but she will exchange sex for dope, too. She is on the street. Higher you have prostitutes who make $50 to $100 for a trick. They have some regulars, but they are also out on the street picking up dates. Maybe they can sit in the lounge of a hotel somewhere.

Source: Mahan, Sue. (1996). *Crack, Cocaine, Crime, and Women*. Thousand Oaks, CA: Sage Publications, pp. 22–24.

marijuana, opium, and hashish would have been exempt from international control, whereas alcohol and tobacco would have been strictly controlled. Weaker nations have to put up with coercion from stronger industrialized nations who impose strict controls on substances indigenous to their societies.

ILLEGAL DRUG USE AND ASSOCIATED PROBLEMS

Illegal drug use and its consequences, including crime, permeate every corner of the global community. Drug use affects the rich and poor, educated and uneducated, professional and blue-collar workers. Addictive drugs are more likely to precipitate criminal activities and exacerbate social problems than other drugs are. Cocaine and heroin are especially notable for their addictive power. The frequency of drug use is also a major factor because of the fear of creating an addicted population. A frequent drug user is at higher risk of involvement in crime than is a nonuser or an infrequent user. The global community tries to control illegal drugs because of their link with crime and destruction of the social fabric.

The link between drug use and crime is complex. The use or distribution of some drugs is illegal, and violators are subject to criminal sanctions. Some crimes that do not involve drugs directly are a result of illegal drug use or distribution. For example, some users steal to support their drug use habit, prostitution is sometimes engaged in to support drug use, and violence in drug markets is used to gain competitive advantage.

The human cost of illegal drug use is well documented. For example, data from the National Institute on Drug Abuse suggest that many of the 56 million women of childbearing age in the United States use alcohol, cocaine, or marijuana to the detriment of their pregnancies (NIDA 1985). Drug abuse impairs cognitive ability and the potential for a full, productive life (National Drug Control Strategy 1999). According to a Bureau of Justice Statistics national report (1992), illegal drug use can harm family life by causing parents to fail to provide economic support due to large expenditures for drug use and to fail to provide an adequate role model for children. When parents are serious drug users, their ability to care for their children can be diminished. In some situations, grandparents or other relatives must raise these children. The rest are taken in by the social service system. And, of course, the extreme result of drug abuse is death.

Illegal drug use harms the community in several ways. The economy of the community is hurt because businesses leave drug-infested neighborhoods. Violence in the community as a result of rival gangs fighting for neighborhood control further hurts the economy of the community. The community's revenue-generating mechanism is destabilized.

CONTROL EFFORTS

Controlling the production and distribution of illegal drugs requires global efforts. The producers are the developing countries, as shown in Table 1, and the consumers are the developed countries. The Federal Drug Seizure System (FDSS) estimates that in the year 2000 alone, federal authorities seized 2,856,462 pounds of illegal drugs—heroin, cocaine, marijuana, and hashish.

The massive and complex system that supplies illegal drugs to the United States and European countries involves cultivation, manufacture, and distribution. International control efforts began in 1912 when it appeared that an estimated 10 million Chinese had become opium addicts (Bassiouni 1990). The world community (particularly developed nations) sought to keep opium addiction from making its way to the United States and Western Europe. Under the auspices of the United Nations, the three conventions previously mentioned were promulgated but did not stop the worldwide illegal drug trade.

The United States has imported a disproportionate share of illegal drugs and has been in the forefront of the effort to eradicate illegal drugs. The U.S. War on Drugs was officially declared in 1971 during President Nixon's administration. The two primary goals of U.S. drug policy are to reduce the production of illegal drugs in foreign countries and to stop drug traffickers from smuggling drugs into the United States. The control efforts are centered on demand and supply reductions. The demand for drugs in America is what drives supply, and drugs are supplied by traffickers only because a profit can be made.

People's demand for drugs sets the drug abuse cycle in motion. If demand reduction is to be successful, prevention should be the focus. Clearly, preventing drug use in the first place is preferable to waiting to address drug use later with law enforcement and treatment. The strategy of demand reduction focuses on young people, seeking to educate them about the dangers of illegal drugs during their formative years. Along with prevention and treatment, law enforcement is an important component in efforts to reduce drug use in the United States. Such efforts include surveillance, investigation, and prosecution of drug trafficking organizations. Federal spending to counter illegal drug use has steadily increased between 1995 and 2000. In fiscal year 2000, for example, federal agencies had a total budget $18.5 billion for supply reduction (i.e., law enforcement, interdiction, and drug crop reduction) and demand reduction (i.e., prevention, education, and treatment) of illegal drugs.

Illegal drugs destroy old and young, men and women, people from all racial and ethnic groups and every walk of life. The federal government's commitment in preventing drug use in the United States is also reflected in congressional legislation (e.g., the Controlled Substance Act, Title II of the Comprehensive Drug Abuse Prevention and Control Act of 1970, the Violent Crime Control and Law Enforcement Act of 1994) and executive orders (e.g., Executive Order 12880 [1993] and Executive Orders 12992 and 13023 [1996]).

In addition to controlling drugs domestically, strategies are in place to control illegal drug trafficking in the transit zones between source countries and the United States. The strategies support a number of international efforts to curb trafficking within and across international borders. Such efforts are coordinated with the United Nations, the European Union, and the Organization of American States. Successfully addressing the social problems associated with illegal drugs requires a multifaceted, balanced program that attacks both supply and demand. Supply reduction and demand reduction must be applied simultaneously.

Due to their increased toxicity and addictiveness, illegal drugs produce devastating crime and health problems and could constitute a hazard to safety and freedom. Crime, violence, workplace accidents, family misery, drug-exposed children, and addiction are only part of the price that the world pays.

Solving the drug problem requires global cooperation between producing and consuming countries. The U.S. War on Drugs, in spite of its ammunition, has not rid the nation of its drug problem. International and national attempts to control cultivation, production, traffic, and use of drugs have so far failed. Consuming states cannot control consumption, and producing states cannot control production because as long as there is demand, there will be supply, and as long as there is supply, there will be demand. The official drug control apparatus has largely ignored alternative solutions such as preventive education, treatment, rehabilitation, and alleviation of the social conditions that create the demand for drugs in the first place. Demand reduction and supply reduction are plausible solutions, but the international drug control policy has consistently favored supply reduction over demand reduction, notwithstanding abundant evidence that supply reduction is, at best, insufficient.

—*Jonathan C. Odo*

See also HARM REDUCTION; DRUG COURIER PROFILES; DRUG COURTS; DRUG LEGALIZATION; DRUG MILLIONAIRES; DRUG TRAFFICKING; DRUG TREATMENT; ORGANIZED CRIME—GLOBAL; ORGANIZED CRIME—UNITED STATES

Further Reading
Bassiouni, Cherif M. (1990). "Critical Reflections on International and National Control of Drugs." *Denver Journal of International Law and Policy* (Spring): 132–133.
Bureau for International Narcotics and Law Enforcement Affairs. (2000*). International Narcotics Strategy Report, 1999.* Washington, DC: Bureau for International Narcotics and Law Enforcement Affairs, U.S. Department of State. http://www.state.gov/www/global/narcotics_law/1999_narc_report
Bureau of Justice Statistics. (1992). *Drugs, Crime, and the Justice System: A National Report from the Bureau of Justice Statistics.* Washington, DC: U.S. Department of Justice.
McAllister, William B. (1994). *The International Nexus: Where Worlds Collide. Reported: Drug Trafficking in the Americas.* Miami, FL: University of Miami Press.
Office of National Drug Control Policy. (1997). *What America's Users Spend on Illegal Drugs, 1988–1995.* Washington, DC: Office of National Drug Control Policy.
Pinkert, Theodore M. (1985). *Current Research on the Consequences of Maternal Drug Abuse.* Research monograph series 59, DHHS publication (ADM). 85-1400. Rockville, MD: National Institute on Drug Abuse.
Stimmel, Barry. (1993). *The Facts about Drug Use: Coping with Drugs and Alcohol in Your Family, at Work, in Your Community.* Binghamton, NY: Haworth Medical Press.
Swisher, Karim L. (1991). *Drug Trafficking, Current Controversies.* San Diego, CA: Green Heaven Press.
Trebach, Arnold S. (1994). "Thinking through Models of Drug Legalization." *The Drug Policy Letter* (July/August): 10–11.
World Health Organization (WHO). (1980). *Problems Related to Alcohol Consumption.* Geneva, Switzerland: KLHO.

▼ DUE PROCESS

In the United States, the justice system is expected to be fair. But what does "fairness" mean? Because it can mean different things to different people, and that meaning can change over time, it is not easy to come up with a definition of fairness that fits all occasions and will be interpreted the same way by all who are asked to comment on it. The same may be said for the very important words *due process*, which are often heard in reference to the American system of justice. These words affect all Americans in one way or another, and they have had a profound effect on society, particularly in the area of criminal justice.

The words *due process* are found in two important amendments to the U.S. Constitution: the Fifth Amendment and the Fourteenth Amendment. The Fifth

Amendment, which is a part of the Bill of Rights, stipulates that no person shall be deprived of life, liberty, or property without due process. This has been interpreted to mean that U.S. citizens have certain protections against inappropriate actions by their national government. For example, the government cannot arbitrarily execute or imprison a person, or take a person's home away without just cause.

Through the Fourteenth Amendment, these protections have also been extended to the relationship to state governments. The Fourteenth Amendment, which was adopted as a result of the Civil War, stipulates that no state shall deprive any person of life, liberty, or property without due process of law. It is also an amendment through which most other basic guarantees found in the Bill of Rights have been extended to citizens in their relationship with state governments. The extension of these rights has often been referred to as incorporation. Although full incorporation of the Bill of Rights has not yet taken place, an individual now has constitutional protection against unfair, arbitrary, or capricious actions by the government in state as well as federal courts. Considering the fact that most criminal cases involve state courts, it is obvious that incorporation has had a tremendous effect on the American criminal justice system.

TYPES OF DUE PROCESS RIGHTS

There are two types of due process rights. One type is referred to as *substantive due process.* Examples of substantive due process rights are the right of privacy, the right to personal choice in matters of marriage and family life, and the right to refuse unwanted medical treatment. *Procedural due process* rights are different in that they are concerned with the procedures that a government must follow in order to deprive a person of certain rights. For example, when the state attempts to secure information involving an individual who is a suspect in a criminal case, it must follow a particular procedure to obtain this information. Similarly, when the state is trying a person in court for a crime, it must also follow the correct procedure. To do otherwise in either of these situations would constitute a violation of a person's procedural due process rights.

There is disagreement among Americans regarding both substantive and procedural due process rights. For those who are concerned about the U.S. criminal justice system, this is quite apparent in the area of procedural due process. Perhaps this is due to a popular view that many of these rights have made it more difficult for the criminal justice system to convict individuals who are guilty of a crime but for one reason or another have not been brought to justice. This may be evident when the police apprehend a person who has committed a serious crime, but the individual cannot be prosecuted for it because of official misconduct in securing evidence in the case.

Although it is true that some individuals who have committed crimes do escape prosecution, it is also true that these rights protect innocent people as well. No system of justice is perfect, but probably most people would agree that it is better to allow one guilty person to escape punishment than to allow one innocent person to be found guilty. When the government has a mass of power directed toward an individual, especially one who is disadvantaged, it becomes evident that the individual needs some assistance to level the playing field. This is especially evident when the government's advantage can lead to the loss of a valuable right such as the right to life, liberty, or property. Hence, it only seems natural to take precautions to lessen this unfair and unfortunate situation, and the of U.S. system of justice has at times done so.

HISTORY OF DUE PROCESS IN THE U.S. LEGAL SYSTEM

The due process clause has an interesting and controversial history, but that is understandable in view of the fact that its meaning has been interpreted differently by various courts. As with other parts of the U.S. Constitution that affect criminal justice, the due process clause has evolved in meaning over the years. Lawrence M. Friedman (1984: 186–187), a legal scholar, has noted that there was a great expansion of judicial activity during the latter part of the nineteenth century, and that it "pivoted on the due process clause. Doctrines sprang out of these few words like rabbits from a magician's hat."

During the twentieth century, perhaps the most dramatic expansion of due process came as a result of efforts by Earl Warren, who served as chief justice after being appointed by President Dwight Eisenhower. The Warren Court has sometimes been described as a liberal court characterized by judicial activism, which suggests that it took the lead in demonstrating the need for various reforms. Although the Warren Court was instrumental in bringing about momentous changes, it brought controversy to many issues.

The Warren Court's activism was especially evident

in a number of cases concerning individuals who encountered the criminal justice system in an adversarial manner. For example, in *Betts v. Brady* (1942), the Supreme Court had ruled that it was not necessary for a state to supply a poor person who was charged with a state felony court with a court-appointed attorney. Subsequently, however, when Earl Warren was chief justice, a similar case reached the Supreme Court. This time, in the landmark case of *Gideon v. Wainwright* (1963), the Court decided that such a person did indeed have a right to a court appointed-attorney.

Other cases emanating from the Warren Court affected the procedures police use to obtain evidence. For example, in *Mapp v. Ohio* (1961), the court extended the exclusionary rule to the states. Before this decision it had been possible to convict an individual in state court by using evidence that had been obtained from an unreasonable search and seizure, although in federal court a defendant did have this protection. In *Escobedo v. Illinois* (1964), the Warren Court ruled that before a suspect could be interrogated by the police with the intention of obtaining incriminating evidence, he or she must be informed of certain rights. Later, in the famous *Miranda v. Arizona* (1966) case, the court noted the importance of informing arrested individuals of certain rights, including the right to remain silent and the right to have an attorney present during questioning. This case also requires police to inform arrested suspects that any statements they make may be used in a court of law and that if they cannot afford an attorney, one will be appointed for them prior to questioning. Rolando V. del Carmen and Jeffrey T. Walker (2000: 181) note the impact of the Earl Warren's decision in this case in the following way:

> *Miranda v. Arizona* is, arguably, the most widely known case ever to be decided by the U.S. Supreme Court. It also has had the deepest impact on the day-to-day investigation phase of police work and has led to changes that have since become an accepted part of routine procedure. No other law enforcement case has generated more controversy inside and outside police circles.

The actions of the Warren Court relating to criminal justice are important because they show that important decisions, such as the one in the *Betts v. Brady* case, can be changed, and that the court has the power to extend the amount of due process, or fairness, that citizens have. In fact, the right to have a court appointed attorney has now been extended in states to misdemeanor cases as a result of the case of *Argersinger v. Hamlin* (1972).

The extension of due process has also affected the relationship between the federal and state governments relating to power or control over the individual. For example, now the balance of power appears to be with the federal court system, and it will probably continue to be so in the future. This is explained by a number of reasons. The federal government seems to have taken the lead in expanding the rights of the poor, women, the disadvantaged, and especially those facing an adversarial relationship with the criminal justice system. Most indications suggest that as long as our state courts fail to provide important remedies for various inequities in our society, we can expect our federal court system to try to do so.

SUMMARY

Due process does not mean that a government cannot take a person's life, liberty, or property. It does, however, suggest that a particular process, such as a proper trial, must be followed before this occurs. Americans have long been distrustful of their government, and with good reason. American history is full of examples of the government's misconduct and ill-treatment of its citizens, especially the poor and the disadvantaged. Although it is difficult to believe that government misconduct toward citizens can be completely eliminated, it is possible to limit it with certain constitutional protections, such as the Bill of Rights, and especially by expanding the meaning of due process.

The scope of the due process clause is broad. For example, the legal scholars Harold J. Grilliot and Frank A. Schubert (1989: 20) have noted:

> The guarantee of due process of law contained in the U.S. Constitution binds and restrains the federal and state governments in each of their branches. This fundamental principle of justice applies to every governmental proceeding that may interfere with property or personal rights, whether the proceeding is legislative, judicial, executive, or administrative.

It is important to note that the meaning of the words found in the U.S. Constitution will change with the passage of time. This is understandable given that new challenges to the criminal justice system seem to evolve with each new generation. It is also commendable, because it allows society to adapt its words to a new environment. The meaning of due process will doubtless continue to evolve. It is hoped that change will reflect an increased protection for Americans, especially those who are disadvantaged when in an adversarial relationship with our government.

Due process is important because, without it, the government would be able to perpetrate serious harm upon its citizens. It is also important because it requires the government to prove the need for any action depriving people of life, liberty, or property. Without due process, the government would have an easier time convicting an innocent person of a crime. A government needs to be limited in its behavior toward its citizens, or the citizens will have less freedom.

—William E. Kelly

See also ASSEMBLY-LINE JUSTICE; CRIMINAL TRIAL; DIFFERENTIATED CASE MANAGEMENT; DRUG COURTS; FAMILY COURT; GRAND JURY; JUVENILE COURT; JURY SYSTEM; PLEA BARGAINING; PROCEDURAL JUSTICE; PROSECUTOR; PUBIC DEFENDER; RACE AND SENTENCING; WRONGFUL CONVICTIONS

Further Reading

Barron, Jerome A, and C. Thomas Dienes. (1990). *Constitutional Law*. St. Paul, MN: West.

del Carmen, Rolando V., and Jeffery T. Walker. (2000). *Briefs of Leading Cases in Law Enforcement*. Cincinnati, OH: Anderson.

Friedman, Lawrence M. (1984). *American Law*. New York: W. W. Norton.

Grilliot, Harold J., and Frank A. Schubert. (1989). *Introduction to Law and the Legal System*. Boston: Houghton Mifflin.

Court Cases

Argersinger v. Hamlin (1972). 407 U.S. 25.

Betts v. Brady (1942). 316 U.S. 455.

Escobedo v. Illinois (1964). 378 U.S. 478.

Gideon v. Wainwright (1963). 372 U.S. 335.

Mapp v. Ohio (1961). 367 U.S. 643.

Miranda v. Arizona (1966). 384 U.S. 436.

E

▼ EARLY RELEASE PROGRAMS

Sooner or later, almost every incarcerated person is released back into society. Early release is the means by which a convicted offender, serving a sentence in some type of correctional facility, is discharged some time before completing his or her total term, be it days, months, or years. The released prisoner, however, is not completely free and usually must adhere to a considerable number of conditions. Violations of these conditions can lead to the repeal of his or her freedom, and the convict may have to serve out the rest of the original sentence. Over time, a variety of such programs have evolved throughout the United States. Parole, perhaps the most famous of early release programs, is but one of countless local and national policies, from halfway houses to boot camps, responsible for moving inmates out of custody and into a situation of provisional liberty before their time under governmental control is up. The practice is burdened with practical concerns as well as controversy, and its design and implementation are affected by the political, ideological, and philosophical opinions of the day. Early release has changed dramatically over time, as have the justifications, complaints, and methodology shaping and driving this integral component of American corrections.

HISTORY

Early release is not applicable to all forms of punishment; a flogging in the town square, for example, does not lend itself to the possibility of emancipation before completion. Until the birth of the penitentiary at the dawn of the nineteenth century, most sanctions could be modified only by a lessening of severity or total reprieve.

During the same time that prisons were taking shape in America, Governor Philip King began a practice in Australia—then a penal colony of the British Empire—that would prove to be the forerunner of early release. English convicts were transported to New South Wales, on the east coast of the colony, as a form of punishment. They served considerable time and were forced to do hard labor for the duration of their sentence. King, who was governor from 1800 to 1806, granted to convicts who showed the ability to support themselves something called a "ticket-of-leave," essentially an early form of parole. "Gentlemen offenders" who arrived at the colony with means or letters of introduction also received this special dispensation. Men with a ticket-of-leave were free to make their own way in New South Wales before completing their sentence. They were, in effect, released early.

Later in the century, Ralph Darling, governor of New South Wales from 1826 to 1831, sought to reinstate the eroded punitive character of the penal colony; once a feared and awful place, it had developed a reputation as an excellent place for a man to make his way. Under Darling, tickets-of-leave became a reward available only to those who had served at least a minimum sentence and then had been evaluated as deserving. This approach required a method for keeping abreast of convict behavior. Darling assigned numbers to each convict; record-keeping became systematized and integral to running the colony. Good behavior and lots of hard work were now the prerequisites for early release.

By the mid-1800s, transportation, the practice of sending convicts away came under attack. Increasingly, offenders were serving their sentences in Britain's emerging prisons. In the 1850s, Sir Joshua Jebb, chairman of the directors of convict prisons, recommended replacing transportation with early release for good behavior. Confinement was then divided into stages for conduct evaluation. Early release was obtained only by moving through each phase, which was routinely accompanied by a conduct badge. This came to be called the "progressive stage system." A term of isolated confinement characterized the first stage. There was no agreement as to the appropriate time for this stage, and complaints about the impact of prolonged separation led to a term that averaged about nine months. As prisoners moved to the second stage, they worked together at labor-intensive assignments benefiting the public. The third stage was conditional release granted on the basis of good behavior during the previous phases. This was controversial, with disputes over how early release was to be earned. Some argued it should be based on proof of reform rather than a mere following of the regulations. As the dust settled, the administrative benefits of this new process determined that prisoners who played by the rules moved through the various stages.

If a prisoner misbehaved, any gains could be lost, and he or she could be sent back to the previous stage. Constant awareness of where inmates stood with regard to their release was considered vital to the process and served to control prisoners. Early release became another conditional phase of the sentence. Not only did early release depend on success at each phase, but a prisoner's ticket-of-leave could now be revoked. Released inmates were monitored, and if they misbehaved, they were returned to prison to serve their remaining time, frequently suffering additional punishment.

GOOD TIME, THE INDETERMINATE SENTENCE, AND PAROLE

As the penitentiary emerged in America, penal policy and practice dictated fixed sentences. By the latter half of the nineteenth century, enthusiasm about the rise of the penitentiary had waned. Neither intended result—repentance or deterrence—had come about. Incarcerating people proved extremely expensive, and overcrowded and deteriorated conditions were pervasive.

Prisoners showed signs of being worse off at the end of their sentence than when they went in. Concerns about protracted incarceration were on the rise. Therefore, innovations to try to correct these problems were introduced.

"Good time" laws, which allow a prisoner who behaves to receive a reduction in sentence, became popular, and their use continues today. The nation's first good time law was created in 1817 in New York, and similar legislation was implemented widely later in the century. Twenty-three states passed some form of good time legislation by 1869. Today, as in the past, statutes and regulations differ from jurisdiction to jurisdiction and usually include a ratio dictating the relationship between time spent exhibiting good behavior and sentence reductions. Earned good time may be revoked, so that prison officials and corrections officers possess meaningful controls over inmates.

In 1870, the first American Prison Congress convened in Cincinnati, Ohio. The penitentiary became the target of reform, and adjustment and integration of the inmate back into society were the primary goals. In these reform efforts, the ideas and practices of the Englishmen Alexander Maconochie (1787–1860) and Walter Crofton (1815–1897) figured prominently. During the first half of the century, Maconochie, a British penal colony official, proposed a system of marks (for completion of work and good behavior) in lieu of fixed prison terms and the subjugating conditions he had witnessed. His reform efforts had little success in England, but they took root in Ireland as Walter Crofton, in charge of that country's prisons, implemented Maconochie's punishment methodology. The conference and its ideals resulted in a new institution, the reformatory, where the indeterminate sentence was essential and parole figured prominently.

The key component of America's redesigned prison was the indeterminate sentence and its promise of an earlier release for good behavior. In 1877, New York instituted the first indeterminate sentencing law, and other states quickly followed suit. Rather than a set amount of time, the statutes prescribed a minimum sentence, often one year. They rarely calculated a corresponding maximum, however, so that the potential to serve a lifetime was always present, and any release was theoretically early. The intent was to facilitate and encourage rehabilitation with the incentive of a possible lesser sentence. A prisoner was to serve only the time needed for reform, which, it was posited, could be determined by an effective system of classification. The indeterminate sentence shifted the focus from the act to the actor in need of correction. This type of sentencing ultimately superseded fixed terms, as evidenced in New York State, which in 1901 made indeterminate sentencing mandatory for all first-time offenders.

The use of parole, a conditional early release program, spread along with use of the indeterminate sentence; it was similar in requiring an elaborate bureaucracy of classifying professionals, who further inundated the American prison system with specialists employed in the scientific endeavor of curing criminals and controlling their discharge. It was the job of these specialists to assess when an inmate was ready to leave prison. Conditions and terms of release varied, often mandating employment and ongoing contact with an official. By the early twentieth century, this highly discretionary program was ubiquitous.

The first reformatory opened in July of 1876 in Elmira, New York, and by 1913 almost twenty states had built correctional facilities based on this model; existing institutions adopted similar methods. Classification and evaluation of the prisoner were crucial to the new practices. This resulted in extraordinary power and discretion on the part of prison administrators, who were free to develop their own standards and procedures regarding release. Inmates mounted appeals, claiming these new sentencing methodologies violated their constitutional rights, but the courts did not agree.

Pardon, commutation, and clemency are additional forms of sentence mitigation, which, before the nineteenth century, were the exclusive means of early release. Pardons are an exemption from penalty. Commutations are a reduction in the severity of a sanction. Clemency is a merciful release from punishment. All rely on the executive branch, which has the sole power to grant such reprieves, making them highly political in nature. Doled out on a case-by-case basis, without uniform guidelines of any kind, they have required access to governors and presidents. They have never been understood as routine social policies, and their use waned with the rise of the new wave of significant penal reform. Though not commonplace, these practices remain a part of the criminal justice system today, and each year in the United States, a few of these reprieves are granted at both the state and federal levels.

BACKLASH: A SENTENCING SHIFT

Though initially a means of rehabilitation, early release became a management tool as it proved an effective way to control inmate behavior and deal with overcrowding problems. Like so many penal "innovations," the practice did not ultimately match the initial aim. The best of intentions could not combat the problems early release presented with regard to the practical considerations of implementation, cost, and volume. Supervision of those released early drifted from the original rehabilitative intent, and parole officers grew overwhelmed. The indeterminate sentence and early release, penal practices that ushered in the twentieth century, lost credibility over time as they failed to deliver what they promised. Criticisms and dissent were brewing, and by the start of the 1970s, change was in the air.

The penal structure was attacked from every direction. Those on the political left argued that the discretionary nature of parole and the indeterminate sentence allowed for bias, inequality, and abuses of power that were unconstitutional; they attacked sentence uncertainty as cruel and unusual. Those on the right claimed short sentences made a mockery of justice, coddled prisoners, put dangerous people on the street prematurely, and diluted deterrent effects, rendering punishment ineffective and nonretributive. Additionally, the rehabilitative ideal suffered a deadly blow with the publication, in 1973, of the Martinson report. Robert Martinson, a sociologist hired by the federal government, aimed to assess the effectiveness of penal programs by embarking on an empirical scientific investigation. The findings (which the government initially tried to suppress), though complex and inconclusive, were interpreted as determining that "nothing works," thereby discrediting the prospect of rehabilitation. This reductionist and inaccurate appraisal was quickly touted throughout the press and became gospel virtually overnight.

A backlash, shaped by an emerging political conservatism, began in the 1970s, sparking a fiercely retributive response to crime. Policy shifted toward increased prison terms and fewer opportunities for early release. Structured sentencing schemes were established that vastly reduced the discretion of judges and correctional authorities. Voluntary or advisory sentencing guidelines were the first innovations to emerge. Because they were voluntary, however, the effect was limited. Determinate sentences made a comeback in some jurisdictions, and remain in place to this day. In 1973, Governor Nelson Rockefeller of New York ushered in mandatory minimum sentences, presenting them as vital tools in the war against drugs.

Mandatory minimum sentencing statutes specify a certain amount of time, usually of considerable length, that an offender must serve, regardless of the circumstances particular to the offender or offense. Judges have absolutely no room to individuate the sentence or mitigate the specified prison term that is now mandated by law for anyone convicted of that crime. An example might include a mandatory minimum of at least fifteen years for anyone convicted of possessing one ounce or more of cocaine. Within this statutory framework, there is no legal avenue for this person to serve one day less than fifteen years, no early release, no parole, no good time, nothing prior to completing the mandatory minimum of fifteen years. Such sentences continue to be popular at the state and federal level and are most often associated with drug- and handgun-related crimes.

Though struggling to create standardized and increasingly punitive penalties, most jurisdictions retain a sentencing format that continues to allow for a range of possible prison terms. In the 1980s, sentencing commissions and presumptive sentencing guidelines were developed to inform, direct, and control the process. Over a quarter of the states and the federal government make use of this approach, in which legislatures establish commissions that are charged with the task of developing clear-cut and exceedingly structured guidelines to which judges must adhere. There is often a grid or quantitative scoring mechanism in which certain factors, such as previous criminal convictions and whether a weapon was involved in the current offense, are scored and used to produce a presumptive sentence, usually of a limited range. Any deviation from this formula requires substantial procedural measures. This sentencing turnabout has resulted in more offenders actually doing some time and inmates serving much longer terms, and the possibility of early release was dramatically reduced.

Parole was also significantly curtailed during the latter part of the twentieth century. There was a great drive to curb the discretionary nature of the process, as well as a profound interest in reducing the possibility of an inmate's being discharged before serving a sizable prison term. In the mid-1970s, some states began to abolish the use of parole boards completely. Throughout the next two decades, this trend accelerated, and the practice has faded from the corrections repertoire. Deterrence and retribution through stern, unrelenting punishment were the punitive goals fuel-

ing the trend away from early release. The merciful and rehabilitative nature of early release had no place in the landscape of "just deserts." "Truth in sentencing" became a pervasive battle cry, demanding that the actual amount of time a prisoner serves correspond closely to the imposed sentence. In 1984, Washington state enacted the first truth-in-sentencing law, and the federal government passed the Comprehensive Crime Control Act. These types of statutes proliferated and drastically restricted or eliminated parole and good time credits.

The Violent Crime Control and Law Enforcement Act of 1994 set aside $4 billion in federal prison construction funds. To be eligible for these monies, called Truth in Sentencing Incentive Funds, states must guarantee that certain violent offenders will serve at least 85 percent of the length of their sentences. By the end of the 1990s, almost thirty states, including the District of Columbia, met the requirements.

INTERMEDIATE SANCTIONS: EARLY RELEASE TODAY AND TOMORROW

Inmates sentenced prior to these new regulations have access to parole, though their numbers are dwindling. Prisons are filling up with prisoners who are subject to an array of stiff penalties that require them to serve extended terms. The prison population at the end of the 1990s was at an all-time high, and today there are few mechanisms for leaving prison early. Corrections departments confront expenses they cannot meet, and overcrowded facilities are plagued by management and safety problems. Concerns about the effectiveness of prolonged incarceration are resurfacing; rehabilitation is creeping back into the public's consciousness as a goal of corrections. Parole is out of favor, and early release lambasted in the political rhetoric, but practical concerns and remaining rehabilitative programs ensure that there is, in fact, considerable programming resulting in de facto early release.

A popular term for current programs that in effect release inmates early is *intermediate sanctions.* These practices are understood as a form of punishment or sentence unto themselves, less harsh than a long prison term but more severe than probation, and not a merciful reduced penalty. Programming that does not imprison or that reintroduces an offender into society also falls under the rubric of community corrections. Post-detention diversion moves inmates from inside a correctional facility to a treatment program suited to their needs. This, as well as drug and alcohol treatment, which can be residential (either inside or outside of a prison or jail), is believed by many to be among the appropriate channels for dispensation. However, these programs are too few in number and fail to meet the sizable demand for such services.

Though some places retain parole, intensive supervisory parole (ISP), which mandates stricter conditions and far more frequent contact with a parole officer, is more common. Shock, often designed for the first-time offender, uses a boot-camp style militaristic approach to incarceration. Inmates who opt for, or are sentenced to, this incarceration program usually serve a shorter sentence. Day reporting centers emerged in the 1980s, modeled after similar programs in Britain. These facilities provide both surveillance of the conditionally released and a multitude of social services. Often located in jurisdictions without ISP, these centers allow for ongoing contact with and supervision of released inmates.

Advancing technology is making its mark in the sphere of punishment, and electric monitoring is becoming increasingly popular. Individuals are confined to their homes, and to be sure that they do not leave unless they are allowed to do so—for example, to go to work—random phone calls and electronic bracelets indicate their whereabouts. Work release, another transitional program, discharges inmates during the day to go to work and returns them to the correctional institution at night. Halfway houses provide shelter and supervision for released prisoners who are not considered ready to be on their own.

Though unique, these programs share common roots and goals with each other and their predecessors. Early release programs are a way to express rehabilitative ideals and to provide a means to relieve overcrowded correctional departments, which would come to a grinding halt without them. Some of these programs are run by the government, while others are private ventures. Providing an opportunity for conditional and supervised freedom, such programming also helps to avoid delivering offenders back into society with no governmental controls or authority over them. On more than one occasion, the U.S. Supreme Court has upheld due process rights for people on any type of early release, regardless of whether it is termed parole. Freedom cannot be revoked without a hearing; the Fourteenth Amendment protects the right to challenge the grievous loss of liberty in a formal proceeding.

Despite efforts to the contrary, the process of discharging inmates before their time is up is not disappearing. Early release is functionally necessary as a back-door solution to stem the crisis of overcrowding and mounting expenditures. Our collective conscience seems unable to settle on one punitive ideal, and efforts toward reintegration and rehabilitation never vanish for long. A wide variety of programs that conditionally release offenders back into the community continue despite uncertainty about how to assess eligibility and risk. Jurisdictions employ a variety of approaches. Though language has changed and terms and designs have become rather creative, early release programs flourished during the last quarter of the twentieth century; this practice is entrenched and is unlikely to be renounced in the twenty-first century.

—*Dana Greene*

See also HALFWAY HOUSE; INDETERMINATE SENTENCES; INTERMEDIATE SANCTIONS; PARDON; PAROLE; REHABILITATION MODEL

Further Reading

Austin, James. (1986). "Using Early Release to Relieve Prison Crowding: A Dilemma in Public Policy." *Crime & Delinquency* 32, 4 (October): 404–502.

Friedman, Lawrence M. (1993). *Crime and Punishment in American History*. New York: Basic Books.

Hirst, John. (1995). "The Australian Experience: The Convict Colony." In *The Oxford History of the Prison*, edited by Morris Norval and David J Rothman. New York: Oxford University Press, 235–265.

Irwin, John, and James Austin. (1994). *It's about Time: America's Imprisonment Binge*. Belmont, CA: Wadsworth Publishing Company.

O'Brien, Patricia. (1995). "The Prison on the Continent: Europe, 1865–1965." In *The Oxford History of the Prison*, edited by Morris Norval and David J Rothman. New York: Oxford University Press, 178–201.

Rothman, David J. (1971). *The Discovery of the Asylum: Social Order and Disorder in the New Republic*. Boston: Little, Brown.

Rotman, Elgardo. (1995). "The Failure of Reform: United States, 1865–1965." In *The Oxford History of the Prison*, edited by Morris Norval and David J Rothman. New York: Oxford University Press.

Simon, Jonathan. (1993). *Poor Discipline: Parole and the Social Control of the Underclass, 1890-1990*. Chicago: University of Chicago Press.

U.S. Department of Justice, Office of Justice Programs. (1999). *Bureau of Justice Statistics Special Report: Truth in Sentencing in State Prisons*, by Paula M. Ditton and Doris James Wilson. Washington, DC: Government Printing Office.

Walker, Samuel. (1998). *Sense and Nonsense about Crime and Drugs: A Policy Guide*. 4th ed. Belmont, CA: Wadsworth Publishing Company.

EASTERN STATE PENITENTIARY

Eastern State Penitentiary in Pennsylvania holds an important place in the evolution of U.S. penology theory because of its history and its unique architecture. It is also significant because it is associated with the establishment of lengthy incarceration as standard punishment for serious crimes. Eastern State Penitentiary was the first major walled penitentiary in the country, as well as one of the most controversial during the nineteenth century.

As penology systems were being debated and developed in the 1800s, Pennsylvania officials questioned the popular system of penology developed in

An interior hallway in Eastern State Penitentiary in 1996. The prison was built in the 1820s outside Philadelphia as a model prison that corrected the abuses linked with Auburn State Prison in New York State.

Source: © Buddy Mays/Corbis; used by permission.

Auburn, New York. They had a theory based on the Quaker philosophy that solitude brings penitence. Under this theory, inmates were incarcerated in a single cell for the entirety of their sentence, and contact with other prisoners was forbidden.

Architect John Haviland (1792–1852) designed Eastern State Penitentiary. Haviland, a British architect who immigrated to the United States in 1816, gained his commission by winning a design competition. Construction of the facility began in 1823 and lasted more than seven years. The design of Eastern State was unique in that the cellblocks radiated from the center of the prison like a seven-spoked wheel, a scheme partially based on ideas developed by other British architects. The prison was constructed on ten acres. Surrounding the building was a fortress-like wall that was thirty feet high. This building became a model for other penitentiaries.

Located outside Philadelphia, Eastern State Penitentiary opened in 1829. It served to demonstrate the original ideas that state officials had had about the ideal penitentiary system, although the system envisioned by Pennsylvania officials was never fully implemented. In isolation, prisoners typically committed suicide or suffered insanity. Officials initially attributed these events not to isolation but, rather, to "excessive masturbation" or illnesses. The Auburn system was ultimately deemed superior because it allowed inmates to have some contact with people, if only other inmates.

British author Charles Dickens (1812–1870) visited Eastern State in 1842. His observations in *American Notes* (1874: 115) further fueled debate about the humanity of the experiment. "I hold this slow and daily tampering with the mysteries of the brain to be immeasurably worse than any torture of the body," he wrote, "and because its ghastly signs and tokens are not so palpable to the eye and sense of touch as scars upon the flesh . . . I the more denounce it, as a secret punishment." The "separate and solitary" provisions of sentencing were dropped in 1913.

Eastern State slowly continued its legacy of experimentation with innovations in penology. It became a research magnet of sorts. The first Alcoholics Anonymous meeting for inmates was held there in the 1960s. The popular evangelist Billy Graham held a revival at Eastern State. In the mid-1960s, inmates could participate in activities including chess, yoga, and a debate team.

The prison was closed in 1970 after 141 years of

operation. The building was designated as a National Historic Landmark in 1965 but was neglected after its closure. Preservation efforts began in 1991, and by 1995, the building had reopened for tours. In 1996, the Pennsylvania Prison Society was awarded a ten-year license by the city of Philadelphia to develop the landmark site. In addition to tours and art exhibits, education programs on prison history are regularly presented, along with events such as "Terror Behind the Walls," a Halloween adventure within the "crumbling walls" and "rusting cell doors" of the former penitentiary (www.easternstate.org/events/index.html).

—*Linda Dailey Paulson*

Further Reading

Dickens, Charles. (1874). *American Notes*. London: Chapman and Hall. Electronic Text Center, University of Virginia Library. http://etext.lib.virginia.edu.

Johnston, Norman. (1973). *The Human Cage: A Brief History of Prison Architecture*. New York: Walker.

———. (1994). *Eastern State Penitentiary: A Crucible of Good Intentions*. Philadelphia, PA: Philadelphia Museum of Art.

Meranze, Michael. (1996). *Laboratories of Virtue: Punishment, Revolution, and Authority in Philadelphia, 1760–1835*. Chapel Hill, NC: University of North Carolina Press.

Perrott, Mark. (2000). *Hope Abandoned: Eastern State Penitentiary*. Charlottesville, VA: Howell Press.

ECONOMIC THEORIES OF CRIME

Economic theories of crime consider criminal activity as a decision made by rational individuals, based on the perceived costs and benefits of the criminal act. There are individuals who commit crimes under any circumstance without regard to the consequences of their actions, and there are individuals who would not commit crimes under any circumstance. Economic theories of crime, however, postulate that most individuals respond to incentives pertaining to criminal behavior. Accordingly, economic theory asserts that the level of crime in the society can be affected by making changes in the costs and benefits of crime.

THE ECONOMIC APPROACH TO CRIME: THE BASIC MODEL

You go to your bank to deposit a check, and you see a $100 bill on the counter. Will you pick it up and put it in your pocket? Would your answer change if you saw $1 or $1000 instead of $100? Would your answer change if you saw a security guard standing near the end of the counter? Would your answer be different if you currently had a high-paying job? The basic economic theory of crime considers criminal activity a decision made by individuals. It is acknowledged that individuals are intrinsically different in many ways, ranging from morals to attitudes toward risky behavior. Nevertheless, the decision to commit a crime is thought to be not much different from other economic decisions that are based upon the consideration of the benefits and costs associated with such decision. Gary Becker, a Nobel laureate in economics, created the foundation for the economic analysis of crime. He describes its conception as follows:

> I began to think about crime in the 1960s after driving to Columbia University for an oral examination of a student in economic theory. I was late and had to decide quickly whether to put the car in a parking lot or risk getting a ticket for parking illegally on the street. I calculated the likelihood of getting a ticket, the size of the penalty, and the cost of putting the car in a lot. I decided it paid to take the risk and park on the street. (I did not get a ticket.)
>
> As I walked the few blocks to the examination room, it occurred to me that the city authorities had probably gone through a similar analysis. The frequency of their inspection of parked vehicles and the size of the penalty imposed on violators should depend on their estimates of the type of calculations potential violators like me would make. (Becker 1996: 143)

Becker's paper (1968), which provides a mathematical model of how individuals would engage in criminal activity, considers individuals as rational decision makers. The important issue in Becker's model, as well as in others that followed, is that criminal activity is not treated as deviant behavior; rather, it is a reaction of individuals to prices and incentives. In Becker's model, individuals aim to maximize their consumption of market goods that provide satisfaction for them, which depends on the income they can generate from both legal and criminal activities. They can spend time in both the legal market and the illegal sector (by committing income-generating crime). The income in each market depends on the amount of time spent in that market. Individuals have subjective beliefs regarding the probability of apprehension and punishment if they are caught committing crimes. Therefore, individuals also have beliefs about the probability of escaping apprehension. Thus, in this framework, an individual's decision regarding which sector to participate in (legal versus criminal) depends on his or her labor market opportunities, such as the probability of employment and the wage rate that could be earned if employed, as well as the expected payoffs and costs of criminal activity. The expected costs of criminal activity include the probability of being caught, the probability of conviction, and the severity of punishment, such as the length of sentencing. Of course, just as individuals react differently to variations in prices of many goods and services, they also respond differently to variations in the costs and benefits of crime. Some individuals are more risk loving than others; some individuals may be less averse to committing a crime. Economic models explicitly acknowledge this, and they incorporate individuals' risk aversion as a determinant of criminal behavior.

One objection to the basic economic model of crime is that it hinges upon the ability of individuals to gauge the risk associated with criminality. How reasonable is it to assume that people can determine the likelihood of apprehension during a criminal act? Is it meaningful to think that potential criminals can observe and determine the variations in the probability of conviction when arrested, or the increase or decrease in the average length of a sentence for a particular crime? Economists believe that individuals can assess the risks of apprehension and punishment, which does not suggest that every potential criminal makes these calculations based upon police and court records. Economist and Nobel laureate Milton Friedman uses the game of billiards to demonstrate this point. The laws of physics govern the game of billiards—the force applied to a particular ball and the angle with which that ball hits another one determines the speed and direction of the second ball. Billiard players make these calculations before they decide how hard, and at which angle, to hit a ball. This, however, does not mean that they are aware of particular laws of physics, or that they make these calculations using a

physics textbook and a calculator before each move. Economic theory says that an increase in the probability of arrest constitutes an increase in the cost of criminal activity, and therefore, if all else is the same, the increase should lower the propensity for criminality. The probability of arrest can be measured by comparing the number of arrests to the number of crimes. Another indicator of the probability of apprehension is the number of police officers in uniform. Like the billiard player who does not need to know the exact laws of physics to make the calculations before each move, potential criminals need not know the exact number of police officers in uniform, or the exact value of the arrest rate. They can obtain this information from formal and informal sources, and they can read signals by, for example, observing more police officers on the streets than before. Readers who are uncomfortable with this formulation should be reminded that recent economic models of crime allow for more flexible methods through which individuals determine their subjective risks (discussed previously). However, it should be noted that such formulations do not alter the predictions of the model substantively.

Ultimately, the success of any theory in describing a phenomenon hinges on whether the theory is consistent with observation. This means that an investigation of whether individuals' behavior is consistent with economic theory can be accomplished by empirical analysis. For example, as discussed above, economic theory predicts that an increase in the size of the police force should reduce criminal activity. Figure 1 displays the monthly number of robberies in New York City between 1970 and 1999. The average number of rob-

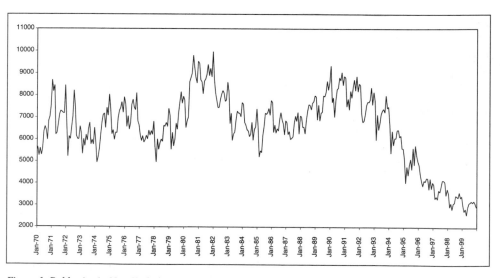

Figure 1. Robberies in New York City, January 1970–December 1999

beries per month was 6,700 in the period of 1970 to 1972. It increased to 8,450 in the period from 1980 to 1982. During the same time period, the number of police officers in New York City decreased from 31,000 to 23,000 (See Figure 2).

Figures 1 and 2 show a correlation between decrease in the police force and an increase in robberies. For example, the size of the police force increased between 1982

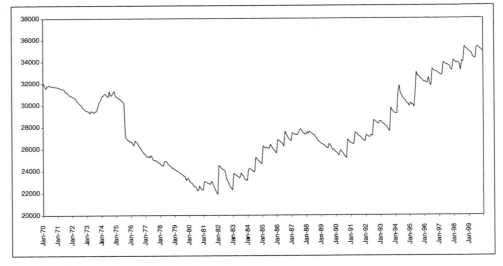

Figure 2. Police Officers in New York City, January 1970–December 1999

and 1988, and the number of robberies declined in the same time period. As the police force got smaller between 1988 and 1991, robberies rose, and the steady expansion of the police force after 1991 coincided with the steady decline in robberies during the same time period. In this particular case, the police force and robberies in New York City are negatively correlated; that is, the more police, the fewer robberies, and vice versa. This correlation between the two variables, however, does not provide information about the cause-effect relationship between them. As the police force is expected to influence crime, crime is expected to have an impact on police as well—for example, an increase in crime prompts the city to hire more police officers. In addition, economic theory suggests the importance of other factors in determining criminal activity, such as legal market opportunities. These can be approximated by local economic conditions, such as the unemployment rate, and/or some average wage in the market (e.g., the minimum wage). The unemployment rate in New York City between 1970 and 1999 is displayed in Figure 3.

The unemployment rate rose between 1988 and 1993 and declined afterwards. The immediate question is, to what extent is the decline in crime depicted in

Figure 1 attributable to the increase in the police force, and to what extent to the decline in the unemployment rate? Econometrics, a branch of economics that combines economic theory with statistics, aims to investigate questions of this type. More specifically, econometric studies of criminal activity investigate whether there is a cause-effect relationship between criminal activity and its determinants as identified by economic theory, as well as the magnitude of such relationships. Statistical challenges in these studies are described in Corman and Mocan (1998).

Econometric models of crime combine economic theory and statistics in a rigorous fashion, in the sense that they consider only those variables that are identified as determinants of crime based on the theory of a cause-effect relationship. This means that such studies

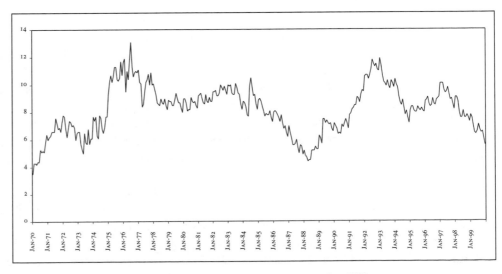

Figure 3. Unemployment Rate in New York City, January 1970–December 1999

do not entertain a variable as a potential determinant of crime simply because it makes sense or is known to be correlated with crime. For example, air pollution is positively correlated with crime in a cross-section of cities. However, econometric studies do not consider air pollution a potential determinant of crime. This is because economic theory does not posit a cause-effect relationship between air pollution and crime, as air pollution is not related to the costs or benefits of committing a crime. The correlation between crime and air pollution may be an indication that more crime is committed in urban areas than rural ones; but attempts to decrease air pollution, say by more stringent emission standards, will not have an impact on crime rates.

Econometric studies have employed a variety of different data sets. For example, micro data sets are based on information obtained from individuals regarding their personal characteristics and self-reported information on criminal involvement. These data are typically merged with information on local area characteristics (e.g., the unemployment rate and measures of deterrence). Aggregate data sets are the ones where the unit of observation is a locality (e.g., cities or states). Time-series data sets record the information about a given location over time, and panel data sets include repeated observations of the units (e.g., individuals, cities) over a period of time. The majority of these econometric studies have verified the predictions of economic theory that increases in criminal justice sanctions deter criminal activity (e.g., Corman and Mocan 2000; Levitt 1997; Levitt 1996; Layson 1985), and that improved labor market conditions lower the incidence of crime (e.g., Gould et al. 1998; Raphael and Winter-Ebmer 2001; Grogger 1998; Tauchen et al. 1994).

It can be argued that the model of crime is sensible for crimes where the gains are monetary, such as property crimes and tax evasion, but it is questionable whether the model can explain the behavior of individuals who commit violent crimes or "crimes of passion." Empirical evidence obtained from economic models of crime demonstrate that violent crime is also responsive to deterrence. For example, Corman and Mocan (2000) find that murders and robberies in New York City declined in response to increases in arrests. Katz, Levitt, and Shustorovich (2001) show that an increase in prison deaths has a negative impact on violent crime rates, and Mocan and Gittings (2001) and Ehrlich (1975) find that the death penalty is a deterrent to murder.

EXTENSIONS OF THE BASIC MODEL

The basic economic model of crime has been extended in a number of ways. For example, drug use is considered a determinant of criminal activity. Following the conceptual framework of Goldstein (1985), drug use can affect criminal activity through three channels. The first is the *pharmacological effect*—the direct impact of drug use on criminal activity (drug use may increase aggression). The second is the *economic effect*—higher expenditures on drugs cause some users to finance these expenditures by committing crime. The third is the *systemic effect*—the violence due to the illegality of the drug market, because the participants cannot rely on contracts and courts to resolve disputes. Corman and Mocan (1998) discuss the conceptual and empirical issues in adding drug use to the economic model of crime, and Corman and Mocan (2000) empirically investigate the relationship between crime, deterrence, and drug use in the framework of an economic model. Benson, Kim, and Rasmussen (1994) provide an in-depth analysis of economic issues of the drug-crime relationship.

Criminologists, sociologists, and psychologists emphasize the role of childhood experiences and family in delinquent behavior. Similarly, individuals' perceptions and evaluations of one another's values and beliefs are theorized to impact criminal behavior (Kahan 1997). The basic economic model of crime has been modified to account for such factors. For example, Sah (1991) extended the basic economic model by making the subjective probability of punishment for a potential offender a function of the information obtained from his past experiences as well as his acquaintances. Similarly, Glaeser, Sacerdote, and Scheinkman (1995) explore the impact of social interactions on criminal activity. They find higher levels of social interactions among criminals in cities with more female-headed households and suggest that social interactions among criminals are higher if the family units are not intact. An empirical study by Glaeser and Sacerdote (1999) finds that between one-third and one-half of the urban effect on crime can be explained by the presence of more female-headed households in cities. Mocan and Rees (2001) show that male juveniles who come from two-parent families are less likely to assault and sell drugs, and juvenile females from two-parent families are less likely to sell drugs, assault, or rob than are those from single-parent families.

Donohue and Levitt (2001) note that abortion reduces the number of unwanted births, and they postulate that unwanted children are at higher risk of criminal involvement. This suggests that legalized abortion would reduce the number of unwanted births and therefore would decrease criminal activity for that particular cohort. Donohue and Levitt's econometric analyses show that legalized abortion reduces crime rates twenty years later. Their results indicate that an increase of 100 abortions per 1,000 live births reduces a cohort's crime by about 10 percent.

RECENT ECONOMIC MODELS OF CRIME

In recent years, the basic economic model of crime has been expanded in many dimensions. One such development is the "general equilibrium" models of crime. Although they differ in their specific compositions, the general framework of these models is one in which the well-being of individuals is thought to depend on consumption and leisure. Individuals have the option of working at a given wage rate or receiving unemployment benefits if they are unemployed. Individuals can allocate their time between legitimate work, crime, and leisure. The government collects taxes, provides subsidies to individuals, and spends money to apprehend criminals. Production of consumption goods takes place using physical capital and the total labor supplied by legal workers. These are called "general equilibrium" models because they consider simultaneous solutions to individuals' decisions (e.g., those regarding work, leisure, and crime), the government's decisions (taxation and spending), and other aspects of the economy (e.g., goods produced being equal to goods purchased). The outcomes of these models allow an analysis of how certain variables that can be manipulated by public policy interact with the rest of the economy, and how mutual interactions between many determinants of crime influence individuals' decisions regarding criminal activity. Two examples of these models are Imrohoroglu, Merlo, and Rupert (2000) and Platania and Schlagenhauf (2000).

Recent positive trends in both the levels of criminal activity and incarceration rates have motivated economists and other social scientists to reexamine the channels through which incentives impact criminal behavior. There has been an increase in criminal activity in the United States in recent decades. The number of violent crimes more than doubled between 1970 and 1998, reaching 1.5 million. Property crimes increased during the same period from 7.4 million to roughly 11 million. The number of people incarcerated in state and federal prisons increased from 290,000 in 1977 to more than 1.2 million in 1998. One reaction to the increased level of criminal behavior over time, despite increased incapacitation, is to question the importance of deterrence (e.g., arrests). Some social scientists have indicated that deterrence may have a limited impact on crime, especially for juvenile criminals, because habits and other social factors may be more significant for them. For example, as cited by DiIulio (1996), Wilson (1994) states that "[we need to understand] that people facing the same incentives often behave in characteristically different ways because they have been habituated to do so," while "changing incentives will not alter the behavior of poorly habituated people as much as we would like, at least in the near term." Along the same lines, DiIulio (1996) indicates that urban ethnographers believe that today's crime-prone youngsters are too oriented towards immediate gratification for any type of conventional criminal deterrence to work.

Recent empirical evidence shows that even juveniles, who may be more present oriented than adults, respond to sanctions and incentives as predicted by economic theory (Levitt 1998; Mocan and Rees 2000). Nevertheless, economists proposed new models of criminal activity to formally incorporate factors such as habit formation, persistence in criminal behavior, and the impact of social factors. For example, Mocan, Billups, and Overland (2000) have constructed a dynamic model of criminal behavior, where individuals are endowed with legal and criminal human capital. Legal human capital includes the skills of an individual that are marketable in the legal sector. It can be measured by the amount of schooling and labor market experience obtained by the person. Similarly, illegal human capital is the criminal know-how accumulated by the person through participation in illegal acts. Potential income in the legal and illegal sectors depends on the level of the relevant human capital, the rate of return (e.g., the wage rate in the legal sector), and unpredictable shocks to the economy.

Both types of human capital can be enhanced by participation in the relevant sector; legal human capital can also be increased through savings. Each type of human capital is subject to depreciation; that is, people lose their skills if they are not employed. Individuals aim to maximize their lifetime well-being, which depends on consumption. In this model, the individual decides in which sector to participate (legal or illegal), gains income in that sector, and makes his or her consumption and saving decisions. A particular decision (e.g., participation in the criminal sector) has implications both for future decisions and for the very choices available to the individual in later periods in life.

This model not only allows for an analysis of the impact of deterrence and legal market opportunities on criminal activity, but also permits analyses of the nature of the incarceration experience; for example, do inmates receive job training and education, or are they left to simply enhance their "criminal human capital"? In traditional crime models, recidivism (repeated criminal behavior) is a rational response to unchanging opportunities faced by the criminal; if it was optimal for the individual to engage in criminal activity given his or her environment (the return to legal and illegal activities, the cost of punishment, and the probability of apprehension) before he or she went to prison, it will still be optimal after the individual leaves the prison (if he or she faces the same environment). In this model, the individual may or may not engage in criminal activity after leaving the prison, because part of the environment that affects behavior depends on whether human capital appreciates or depreciates while the individual is in prison. More specifically, if prisoners enhance their legal human capital in prison through education and training, and if their illegal human capital depreciates in prison, then it may be optimal for them to switch to the legal sector after being released. On the other hand, if the individual's illegal human capital increases more than his or her legal human capital in prison because of interaction with other inmates, then it will be optimal for him or her to stay in the illegal sector after leaving the prison.

Finally, the dynamic structure of this model permits the analysis of the multi-period behavior of the individual, which provides insights in addition to those obtained from static models. For example, basic static crime models predict that an increase in the probability of unemployment in the legal sector, as indicated by an increase in the unemployment rate, increases the likelihood of entry into the illegal sector. These models postulate that the above relationship between unemployment and criminal participation is symmetrical: A decrease in unemployment decreases criminal participation. However, the dynamic model of Mocan, Billups, and Overland (2000) generates a different pre-diction. A recession increases the incentive to participate in the illegal sector, as predicted by standard theory. But contrary to the symmetry implied by the standard model, this model shows that an individual who enters the criminal sector tends to remain there after the recession ends. This is due to the simultaneous depreciation of legal human capital and the appreciation of criminal human capital during the recession; in terms of labor market opportunities, he or she is not the same person post-recession. The model also considers the impact of the individual's degree of risk aversion and the impact of social capital and neighborhood effects on criminal activity. In a similar vein, Lochner (1999) developed an "estimated dynamic" model in which individuals decide on work, education, and crime.

SUMMARY

Economic models of crime consider individuals to be rational decision makers. Committing a criminal act is a decision based on the perceived costs and benefits associated with crime in comparison to those associated with legal work. This suggests that the certainty and severity of punishment and legal labor market opportunities are factors that impact criminal behavior, despite the fact that individuals are heterogeneous in many dimensions, including the degree of their aversion to risk and their moral beliefs. The majority of empirical studies confirm the predictions of the economic model of crime using a variety of data sets.

Recent economic models of crime add new dimensions to the basic model by incorporating noneconomic variables, such as social interactions and neighborhood effects, habits, and the impact of imprisonment and rehabilitation. Still, there needs to be more empirical and theoretical work on crime, as some questions relevant to public policy are not yet fully answered. Among these are whether labor market conditions are a more important influence on criminal activity than is deterrence, and how the theoretical models can be modified further to create empirical formulations capable of explaining the regularities observed in aggregate data, such as the rise in crime during the 1970s and its decline in the 1990s.

—*H. Naci Mocan*

See also EDUCATION AND EMPLOYMENT; POVERTY; PUBLIC HOUSING; RADICAL CRIMINOLOGY; SOCIAL CLASS

Further Reading

Becker, Gary S. (1968). "Crime and Punishment: An Economic Approach." *Journal of Political Economy* 76, 2:169–217.

———. (1996). *Accounting for Tastes*. Cambridge, MA: Harvard University Press.

Benson, Bruce L., Iljoong Kim, and David W. Rasmussen. (1994). "Estimating Deterrent Effects: A Public Choice Perspective on the Economics of Crime Literature." *Southern Economic Journal* 61, 1: 161–168.

Bound, John, and Richard B. Freeman. (1992). "What Went Wrong? The Erosion of Relative Earnings and Employment Among Young Black Men in the 1980s." *Quarterly Journal of Economics* 107, 1: 301–232.

Corman, Hope, and Naci H. Mocan. (1998). "An Economic Analysis of Drug Use and Crime." *Journal of Drug Issues* 28, 3: 613–629.

———. (2000). "A Time Series Analysis of Crime, Deterrence, and Drug Abuse in New York City." *American Economic Review* 90, 3: 584–604.

DiIulio, John. J., Jr. (1996). "Help Wanted: Economists, Crime and Public Policy." *Journal of Economic Perspectives* 10, 1: 3–24.

Donohue, John J., III, and Steven D. Levitt. (2001). "The Impact of Legalized Abortion on Crime." *Quarterly Journal of Economics* 116, 2: 379–420.

Ehrlich, Isaac. (1975). "Deterrent Effect of Capital Punishment: A Question of Life and Death." *American Economic Review* 65, 3: 397–413.

Freeman, Richard B. (1996). "Why Do So Many Young American Men Commit Crimes and What Might We Do About It?" *The Journal of Economic Perspectives* 10, 1: 25–42.

Glaeser, Edward L., and Bruce Sacerdote. (1999). "Why Is There More Crime in Cities?" *Journal of Political Economy* 107, 6: 225–258.

Glaeser, Edward L., Bruce Sacerdote, and Jose A. Scheinkman. (1996). "Crime and Social Interactions." *Quarterly Journal of Economics* 111, 2: 507–548.

Goldstein, P. (1985). "The Drugs/Violence Nexus: A Tripartite Conceptual Framework." *Journal of Drug Issues* 15, 4: 493–506.

Gould, Eric D., David B. Mustard, and Bruce A. Weinberg. (2001). "Crime Rates and Local Labor Market Opportunities in the United States: 1979–1997." University of Georgia Working Paper No. 98-472.

Grogger, Jeff. (1998). "Market Wages and Youth Crime." *Journal of Labor Economics* 16, 4: 756–791.

Imrohoroglu, Ayse, Antonio Merlo, and Peter Rupert. (2000). "On the Political Economy of Income Redistribution and Crime." *International Economic Review* 41, 1: 1–25.

Kahan, Dan M. (1997). "Social Influence, Social Meaning, and Deterrence." *Virginia Law Review* 83, 2: 349–395.

Katz, Lawrence, Steven D. Levitt, and Ellen Shustorovich. (2001). "Prison Conditions, Capital Punishment, and Deterrence." Manuscript. Harvard University, Department of Economics.

Layson, Stephen. (1985). "Homicide and Deterrence: A Reexamination of the United States Evidence." *Southern Economic Journal* 52: 68–89.

Lochner, Lance. (1999). "Education, Work, and Crime: Theory and Evidence." Rochester Center for Economic Research Working Paper No. 465.

Levitt, Steven. (1996). "The Effect of Prison Population Size on Crime Rates: Evidence from Prison Overcrowding Litigation." *Quarterly Journal of Economics* 111: 319–352.

———. (1997). "Using Electoral Cycles in Police Hiring to Estimate the Effect of Police on Crime." *American Economic Review* 87, 3: 270–290.

Mocan, Naci H., Steve Billups, and Jody Overland. (2000). "A Dynamic Model of Differential Human Capital and Criminal Activity." NBER Working Paper No: 7584.

Mocan, Naci H., and R. Kaj Gittings. (2001). "Pardons, Executions and Homicide," Manuscript. University of Colorado at Denver, Department of Economics Working Paper No. 2001-18.

Mocan, Naci H., and Daniel Rees. (2001). "Economic Conditions, Deterrence and Juvenile Crime: Evidence from Micro Data." National Bureau of Economic Research (NBER) Working Paper No: 7405.

Platania, Jennifer, and Don E. Schlagenhauf. (2000). "The Falling Crime Rate in the United States: A Dynamic General Equilibrium Approach." Manuscript, Florida State University, Department of Economics.

Raphael, Steven, and Rudolph Winter-Ebmer. (2001). "Identifying the Effect of Unemployment on Crime." *Journal of Law and Economics* 44 (April): 259–283.

Sah, Raaj K. (1991). "Social Osmosis and Patterns of Crime." *The Journal of Political Economy* 99, 6: 1272–1295.

Tauchen, Helen, Ann Dryden Witte, and Harriet Griesenger. (1994). "Criminal Deterrence: Revisiting the Issue with a Birth Cohort." *Review of Economics and Statistics* 76, 3: 399–412.

Wilson, James Q. (1994). "Culture, Incentives, and the Underclass." In *Values and Public Policy*, edited by Henry J. Arron, Thomas E. Mann, and Timothy Taylor. Washington, DC: Brookings Institution, 57–84.

▼ EDUCATION AND EMPLOYMENT

Employment and education are inextricably intertwined in the history of American society. The American economy is based on employment and levels of employment—from the highest paying professions to the lowest—depend on education. The pleasure of learning has never been a central idea in American education, except for the children of the wealthiest families The link between employment and crime argued in criminological theory proposes that people with gainful employment are not likely to risk criminal behavior, in spite of high profits associated with crimes such as drug distribution. The reasons behind this theory are twofold. First, crime carries a high risk of imprisonment. Second, legal employment creates social and emotional community attachments that control personal behavior. Building on this argument, work training programs have been developed to provide the least skilled wage earners with job training or to enhance their low job skills with more valuable skills. Such job training, it is argued, offers low-skill workers greater opportunities for earning more income and achieving a personally rewarding and legal niche in the community. This criminological argument has overlooked the decision making of people who choose crime, employment, or both. Individual choice is complicated by personal motivation, opportunities to gain an economically valuable education, and addiction.

PUBLIC EDUCATION AND EMPLOYMENT

Public education has always been based on the idea that it should prepare learners for employment. In its simplest form, the mission of American public education was to teach children to read and write. These basic skills were considered to be vocational skills, and those who did not have literacy skills were relegated to forms of employment now called menial labor.

Twentieth-century industrialization brought increased job specialization, and with that specialization, American schools adjusted their curricula to ensure that students were prepared for the workplace. Soldiers who had not finished high school before entering World War II were allowed to acquire a General Education Diploma (GED), which was developed specifically for the returning troops. In the 1960s and 1970s, high school students learned to type on manual typewriters, in preparation for clerical jobs. Today, however, office clerical staff must know how to use computers, word-processing programs, and spreadsheets to qualify for entry-level employment. The stakes of employment have grown and so has the pressure on educators.

Complaints about public education failures expose the link between education and employment. The city of Chicago encountered a serious dilemma involving education and employment in the latter years of the 1990s. Local high schools were graduating students with literacy skills so poor that local employers complained to the mayor's office that high school-educated employees could not write well enough to meet the demands of entry-level jobs. Chicago's mayor pressured public educators, and now a standardized test measures students' abilities in junior high school prior to senior high. Employment pressure curtailed the practice of social promotion.

The notion that a good education is necessary to earn a good income is firmly engrained in American

thinking about employment. But what is a good income? Between the 1960s and 1990s, the federal government increased the minimum wage, in an effort to provide workers who had the lowest levels of education with income sufficient to support a household. In the late nineteenth and early twentieth centuries, labor unions emerged to ensure that workers had sufficient income to support families. Today, supporting a family means being able to buy or rent a residence, purchase groceries and clothes, and have sufficient cash to make initial payments on a car or other expensive item that most workers cannot afford to purchase fully at the time of sale. Credit cards are now a handy way for workers to obtain a short-term loan, in order to buy goods today and pay for them tomorrow.

The credit system depends entirely on workers' ability to pay their short-term loans. We can borrow money for a washing machine or even a college education. Why would a bank finance a college education? College education is an economic investment in American society. College-educated men and women earn millions of dollars more in their lifetimes than do high school graduates. That means these workers will buy more goods and pay more taxes.

State colleges and universities offer majors that lead specifically to employment. College students can choose from among computer science, business, industrial technology, pre-law, and pre-medical programs. Clearly, the eighteenth- and nineteenth-century concept that education is vocational training has persisted, and as higher education has expanded to include more young people, so has the opportunity to acquire specialized job training in institutions of higher education.

The social fabric of American society depends on employment. Achievement in employment as measured by income depends in large part on a worker's level of education. American society rewards a high level of education, if such education supports the most important economic activities at the moment. By the year 2000, men and women—even teenagers—who were accomplished in the highly technical skills required by the age of the World Wide Web could earn high salaries, without a college degree or even a high school diploma.

EDUCATION AS A CURE FOR CRIME

Education is linked to employment; employment is linked to income; income is linked to the purchase of houses, televisions, and dishwashers; and income is also linked to paying taxes to local communities, states, and the federal government. Those taxes enable the delivery of services, such as public education, the armed forces, and the national highway system. Education is also linked to crime. The lack of education is thought to be a primary motivation for profit-oriented crime, such as robbery, burglary, car theft, shoplifting, and drug selling. A review of data provided by state correctional agencies shows that the overwhelming majority of the men and women in state prisons have low levels of education, and hundreds of thousands of adult state prisoners are illiterate or cannot read and write better than elementary school students. Although the association between a low level of education and crime is clear, the link between a poor education and crime is unclear.

The idea that people with the lowest levels of education will be those most likely to commit crime dates back hundreds of years. In American society, education is thought to be an effective "cure" for misbehavior. People convicted of offenses ranging in severity from murder to shoplifting are required to complete some type of education program. In Illinois, if prison inmates have not received a high school diploma or cannot pass a basic literacy examination, they are required to attend at least 90 days of primary education focused on literacy skills. Correctional agencies are expected to provide inmates with basic education, as if such education will be the key in facilitating an inmate's transition from an unlawful to a lawful lifestyle. The curative nature of education is seen as well in the prevention of social misconduct. The Drug Abuse Resistance Education (DARE) program is based on the idea that learning about drug abuse will prevent it. Even though research has shown that DARE does not prevent adolescent drug use, DARE is an everyday component of public education.

EMPLOYMENT, EDUCATION, AND SOCIAL BONDS

Education, whether of school-age children or convicted felons, rests on the subtle idea that education will cement the bond between citizens and their communities. Once students are educated and become workers, they bond to their employers and rely on them for income. Ideally, workers and employers develop a mutual emotional bond as well, as students bond to schools. A mutual economic and emotional bond between workers and employers establishes a mutual need, which theoretically limits lawbreaking behavior. If a person receives a material reward (a paycheck) and also an emotional reward (a feeling of belonging and being personally satisfied on the job), that person will be less likely to violate an employer's rules or a community's rules. Breaking the rules would likely mean that the person's link to an employer would be severed (dismissal). In serious cases, breaking a community's rules might sever a person's tie to the community through imprisonment.

Recent criminology research suggests that the link between education and legal employment is even more complex. The logic linking education and employment presumes that education provides people with the tools necessary to obtain legal employment, which then short-circuits the need for profit-motivated crime. This logic is accurate only under certain assumptions: that people in society are equally motivated to obtain legal jobs; that people would forgo a high level of illegal income in preference for a low level of legal income; that people have an equal opportunity to obtain an education of equal quality; and that such factors as mental and emotional illness, alcoholism and drug abuse, serious family problems such as domestic violence, child neglect and abuse, and extreme poverty have little or no effect on the link between education and opportunities to gain legal employment.

Current research suggests that serious family conflict has permanent negative effects on the bond between children, families, and public education. School failures include children who have been unprepared by their families for the social and emotional rigors of education, have received little social and emotional support from parents or guardians, and have attended school tired, hungry, and ill. Such children do not perform well either in the classroom or in social school life. They fight with peers, disrupt class, argue with teachers, and will likely be suspended or expelled and relegated to less-than-adequate alternative schools, which separate troubled children from the mainstream school and the community as well. Once that separation occurs, it is likely that these children will not receive an education necessary to attend college or even to graduate from high school. These children are the ones most likely to engage in street crime in order to obtain cash for survival.

Recent research with male and female prisoners shows that men and women with a high school and even a college education may commit serious crimes—bank robbery, drug conspiracy, bank fraud, and major drug conspiracies. Life histories of inmates with a high school or a college education show many of them had drug addictions that led to high-profit crime, which they committed to obtain cash to buy illegal drugs for personal use. Many inmates suffered alcoholism, which led to poor job performance, an erosion of family life, and then to crime as a last resort to obtain money. Research conducted in impoverished communities shows that poorly educated earners who depend on minimum-wage employment rarely have enough income to support a household with children, even with government-support programs, such as food stamps, medical aid, and public housing. Profit-oriented crime is a viable option in cases of economic deprivation, especially if viable legal alternatives are not available in the community.

SUMMARY

Employment in America is a critical issue for the world economy. Industrialized societies worldwide have a major interest in ensuring that youth are well educated because well-educated youth support a global economy. These workers continue to be well rewarded for their skills, but there are millions of Americans who are not well educated and face a life of low-wage employment. Many of these citizens face a dilemma, whether to continue forever in low-wage employment or to engage in profitable crime. There are no simple ways to ensure that all children have an equal opportunity to obtain an education sufficient to provide good employment. To be sure, however, the link between employment, education, crime, and family life is extremely complex and requires much more careful study.

—*Mark S. Fleisher*

See also ECONOMIC THEORIES OF CRIME; POVERTY

Further Reading
Bossler, Adam, Mark Fleisher, and Jessie Krienert. (2000). "Employment and Crime: Revisiting the Resiliency Effect of Work on Crime." *Corrections Compendium* 25, 2: 1–3, 16–18.
Fleisher, Mark S. (1989). *Warehousing Violence*. Newbury Park, CA: Sage Publications.
———. (1995). *Beggars and Thieves: Lives of Urban Street Criminals*. Madison, WI: University of Wisconsin Press.
———. (1998). *Dead End Kids: Gang Girls and the Boys They Know*. Madison, WI: University of Wisconsin Press.
Fleisher, Mark S., and Jessie Krienert, with Kelly Hird. (2001). "Employment and Crime: An Overview and Redefinition of Issues." *Corrections Management* 5, 4.
Hagan, John, and Bill McCarthy. (1997). *Mean Streets*. New York: Cambridge University Press.
Hine, Thomas. (1999). *The Rise and Fall of the American Teenager*. New York: Avon Books.
Hirschi, Travis. (1969). *Causes of Delinquency*. Berkeley, CA: University of California Press.
Krienert, Jessie, and Mark S. Fleisher. (2001). "Economic Rehabilitation: An Re-assessment of the Link between Employment and Crime." *Corrections Management Quarterly* 5, 4.
Sherman, Lawrence W., Denise C. Gottfredson, Doris L. Mackenzie, John Eck, Peter Reuter, and Shawn D. Bushway. (1998). *Preventing Crime: What Works, What Doesn't, What's Promising*. National Institute of Justice, Research in Brief Series. Washington, DC: U.S. Department of Justice, Office of Justice Programs.
Singer, Mark I., and Daniel J. Flannery. (2000). "The Relationship between Children's Threats of Violence and Violent Behavior." *Archives of Pediatric and Adolescent Medicine* 154 (August): 785–790.

◤ ELDER ABUSE

Elder abuse is a relatively recent area of concern for legislators, policy makers, protective service employees, social service employees, criminal justice practitioners, and others who come into contact with victims of elder abuse. During the last decades of the twentieth century, concern in this area grew, along with legislative changes and increases in the number of elderly persons throughout the world. In the late 1990s, however, there was a dearth of academic research (a situation that has begun to change in the early twenty-first century). What academic research there was focused on the definition of elder abuse, types of elder abuse, consequences of abuse, and the justice system's response to elder abuse. Legislative changes included the creation of laws mandating the reporting of suspected cases of abuse, increased sanctions for elder abusers, and the development of nursing home ombudsmen programs. In essence, elder abuse has slowly become criminalized, with various actors expected to work together to respond to abuse, despite the fact that very little research has considered whether criminalization should occur.

DEFINING, MEASURING, AND RESPONDING TO ELDER ABUSE

One of the most difficult aspects of elder abuse research is the development of an integrated and acceptable definition of elder abuse. Because the problem is so vast and scholars from so many different disciplines examine various aspects of the problem, it is sometimes difficult to integrate the jargon from the various disciplines into one solid definition. Also, there was a tendency to search for parallels between child abuse and elder abuse in developing definitions of elder abuse. Research shows, however, that elder abuse is often more similar to spousal abuse than child abuse. Yet not all cases of elder abuse directly parallel cases of spousal abuse. Making it even more difficult to define is the fact that practitioners from vastly different areas responding to elder abuse tend to define it differently. In general, police officers tend to define elder abuse from a legal perspective, while social service providers define elder abuse from a moral or ethical perspective. These differences in definitions can have important repercussions for the ways in which individuals respond to elder abuse. Due to the problems arising out of vastly different definitions of elder abuse, researchers have asked social service providers and law enforcement officials to help in developing an integrated definition of elder abuse. Based on input from these groups, the following definition has been developed: "Elder abuse is any criminal, physical, or emotional harm or unethical taking advantage that negatively affects the physical, financial, or general well being of an elderly person" (Payne, Berg, and Byars 1999: 81).

Official estimates suggest that about one million individuals are victims of elder abuse each year in the United States alone. These estimates are believed to underestimate the true extent of elder abuse. Many cases of elder abuse are not reported to authorities because of fear of reprisal, the inability to report abuses, and fear that reporting will do more harm than good. For example, some victims worry that they will be placed in nursing homes or other long-term care settings if they report the abuse.

Statutory definitions governing elder abuse in the United States and other countries were developed in the late 1970s and early 1980s, when concern about elder abuse spread among lawmakers and practitioners in response to articles in British medical journals about what was then called "granny bashing." Legal definitions of elder abuse as established by statutory law vary from jurisdiction to jurisdiction and country to country. Variations include the age at which one is elderly, the types of behaviors included as elder abuse, the existence of penalty enhancement laws for some kinds of abuse, and whether certain groups must legally report suspected cases of abuse. Some nations classify those 60 and over as elderly, while other nations use the age of 65 as the standard. Also, some legal codes include neglect and emotional abuse as examples of elder abuse, while other nations legally define elder abuse in terms of physical behaviors committed against elderly persons. Furthermore, some nations have penalty enhancement laws calling for stricter penalties for cases with elderly victims; others use traditional penalties for elder abusers. Finally, in the United States, forty-two states have mandatory reporting laws requiring certain professionals to report suspected cases of elder abuse. Mandatory reporting laws from state to state with respect to the types of professionals expected to report abuse.

Mandatory reporting laws are a source of contention among some academics, policy makers, and practitioners. Some individuals fully support mandatory reporting laws on the grounds that they offer a way to protect victims in quite vulnerable states. Critics of mandatory reporting laws are less optimistic about the potential for the laws to protect elderly persons and, instead, see the potential for harm to arise out of the application of the laws. They note that the laws (1) threaten the autonomy of older persons; (2) weaken the sanctity of the confidential relationship between the older person and the mandatory reporter (e.g., patient and doctor); (3) assume older persons are in need of help; and (4) are not based on any sound research. One of the biggest problems with mandatory reporting laws is that many mandated reporters do not fully understand their duties to report suspected cases of abuse.

The National Center on Elder Abuse (www.elder-abuse.org) cites seven types of elder abuse:

1. Physical abuse is abuse in which physical force is used to harm an older person.

2. Material abuse/financial exploitation involves instances in which caregivers or other trusted individuals steal money or goods from older adults. Material abuse cases include grandchildren stealing pension checks, children stealing treasured silver, nursing home employees stealing residents' money, or a trusted acquaintance persuading an older person to sign documents effectively giving the acquaintance ownership of property such as a home, an automobile, or some other irreplaceable item.

3. Sexual abuse captures a range of behaviors, including any type of unwanted sexual contact, and more subtle cases in which offenders force older persons to watch pornography or hear offensive sexual language.

4. Psychological/emotional abuse involves inflicting anguish or distress through nonphysical means such as harassment, intimidation, humiliation, and insulting behavior.

5. Neglect involves instances in which individuals fail to provide care or fulfill legal duties to advance or maintain the care of an older adult.

6. Abandonment entails deserting an older person in a particular place such as a hospital, nursing home, or mall.

7. Self-neglect occurs when an older person does things that threaten his or her health, security, and safety.

Each type of abuse reveals problems that are international in scope. Interestingly, there is cultural variation in both definitions and types of elder abuse common in particular cultures. For instance, research shows that in Arab nations, psychological abuse is the most prevalent type of elder abuse, while physical abuse, emotional abuse, and financial abuse are more common in Western nations. Consequently, the response systems vary among these different nations.

Each type of abuse can occur at the hands of family members and acquaintances (e.g., familial elder abuse), or service providers such as nursing home employees, adult day-care workers, or other health-care providers (e.g., institutional elder abuse). Where the abuse occurs and who commits the abuse will determine which government agency gets involved in responding to the abuse. For example, in familial elder abuse cases, adult protective services and the local police may respond to the abuse allegation. In institutional elder abuse cases in the United States, nursing home ombudsmen and Medicaid Fraud Control Units often are the agencies responding to the abuse. Although the location of the abuse influences the agency having jurisdiction over the case, it does not generally influence the consequences of the abuse, which can be devastating.

CONSEQUENCES AND CAUSES OF ELDER ABUSE

The consequences of elder abuse are similar to the consequences of other types of victimization but may be more severe for older persons, who are at a higher risk of injury and generally have a greater fear of crime levels than do younger persons. Official victimization statistics suggest that older adults have the lowest murder rate. The number of deaths occurring from elder abuse is unknown, however, because many of the deaths resulting from elder abuse cases are likely misidentified as deaths from natural causes. In elder abuse cases in which death does not occur, serious physical harm is possible. Moreover, many older victims will experience significant financial losses as the result of various financial abuses. Because they may have limited incomes and little savings to support their losses, financial losses are believed to affect older adults more severely than younger persons, who have a lifetime to recover from financial victimization.

There are multiple causes of elder abuse, and different types of elder abuse are thought to be caused by different factors. For example, it is believed that the causes of familial elder abuse are different from the causes of institutional elder abuse. Physical abuse caused by a family member may be the result of the stress caregivers experience trying to care for elderly persons, while financial abuse is believed to be caused by the offender's financial dependency on the older person. The stress explanation is seen by many to be oversimplified and overutilized. After all, a lot of people get stressed, but only a few become abusive. Early anecdotal research suggested that familial elder abuse could be explained by the intergenerational cycle of violence (e.g., it was believed that adult offspring abused their parents because their parents abused them when they were children). Virtually no empirical research has shown support for this explanation, however. There is limited support for explanations suggesting that the abuser's dependence on the victim makes the abuser feel powerless and subsequently in need of ways to gain control over the victim. Offenders resort to abuse as a means to regain control over the victim. Institutional elder abuse is generally explained by considering the situational characteristics surrounding the abuse. In particular, staff burnout, conflict with residents, lack of training, low salaries, and drug use have been shown to cause institutional elder abuse.

Elder abuse is a multidisciplinary problem that requires a multidisciplinary response system. This means that actors from various agencies need to work together in responding to allegations of abuse. Of the limited research that has considered the response to elder abuse, most has examined cases of elder abuse committed by family members or relatives.

Officials most likely to get involved in elder abuse cases occurring in the United States include adult protective services workers, nursing home ombudsmen, and criminal justice employees. Adult protective service workers receive and handle all types of elder abuse cases but are more likely to respond to cases of familial elder abuse. If these workers find that abuse has occurred, or is likely to occur, they take measures to protect the victim. These measures include educating abusers, developing treatment plans, or, where necessary, notifying the police or the courts.

Nursing home ombudsmen are officials who receive and handle allegations of elder abuse. The term *ombudsman* is a Swedish word meaning "a public official appointed to investigate citizens." The specific responsibilities of nursing home ombudsmen are outlined in Title VII of the Older Americans Act. Investigations are seen as one of the major duties they perform, although they spend a great deal of effort educating consumers about nursing homes, notifying nursing homes about abuse allegations, working with the district attorney and protective service workers to determine if allegations are true, and finding a way to stop the abuse if it has occurred. In the United States in 1997, 880 paid employees and 6,800 certified volunteers handled 191,000 complaints and shared information with 200,000 citizens.

Because elder abuse was not criminalized until the late twentieth century, the police and the courts have had rather limited and sporadic involvement in elder abuse cases. Some police have been involved in developing triad crime prevention programs (cooperative efforts between AARP [the American Association of Retired Persons], and local sheriff's and police departments), along with other services to prevent crimes against seniors. Others have been less active in advocating for the protection of elderly persons. Police determine whether a crime has been committed, enforce the law where applicable, and tell elderly victims about services available in the community. Obstacles that police face include a fear of reporting on the part of victims, a lack of resources to aggressively respond to these cases, inadequate training, communication problems with victims, and a general lack of trust for police among older victims.

The criminal and civil courts also get involved in elder abuse cases. In cases in which the prosecutor chooses to press charges, elder abuse cases can be heard in criminal court. Prosecutors face an array of problems, including the facts that (1) some judges have a limited understanding of elder abuse, (2) it may be difficult to get victims to testify, (3) victims may have problems getting to courts because of transportation difficulties, and (4) juries are reluctant to believe trusted caregivers could bring harm to elderly persons.

Civil courts may get involved in determining whether the elderly victim needs to be appointed a guardian or a conservator. Guardianship involves appointing individuals or government officials to take care of the elderly person's personal affairs, while conservatorship entails having individuals handle the elderly person's estate. Both measures are taken to prevent older persons from being abused.

Some victims and their family members will seek recourse in civil courts by filing lawsuits against nursing homes. Changes in laws making it easier to pursue these kinds of lawsuits have led to an increase in the number of lawsuits filed against nursing homes. In fact, some lawyers actually specialize in handling these cases. Punitive damages in the six-figure range are being awarded to nursing home abuse victims and their families somewhat regularly. The justification for the large awards is that they will deter future misconduct. Very little support has been offered, however, for the deterrent aspects of large awards, because the penalties are random, too severe, and not applied in a timely fashion.

FUTURE TRENDS

Experts expect that elder abuse will only increase as a problem in the future. In 2025, demographers expect that the elderly will make up one-fourth of the U.S. population. In contrast, only 4 percent of the population were elderly in 1900. When there are more elderly persons, there will be more elderly victims. The systems that respond to elder abuse need to be prepared for this increase.

—Brian K. Payne

See also EUTHANASIA; FAMILY VIOLENCE; VICTIMIZATION

Further Reading

Anetzberger, Georgia. (1987). *The Etiology of Elder Abuse by Adult Offspring*. Springfield, IL: Charles C Thomas.

Harris, Diane K., and Michael L. Benson. (1996). "Theft in Nursing Homes: An Overlooked Form of Elder Abuse." In *Advances in Bioethics: Violence, Neglect, and the Elderly*, edited by L. B. Cebik, G. C. Graber, and F. H. Marsh. Greenwich, CT: JAI Press, 171–178.

Korbin, Jill E., Georgia J. Anetzberger, and Craig Austin. (1995). "The Intergenerational Cycle of Violence in Child and Elder Abuse." *Journal of Elder Abuse and Neglect* 7, 1: 1–15.

Payne, Brian K. (2000). *Crime and Elder Abuse: An Integrated Perspective*. Springfield, IL: Charles C Thomas.

Payne, Brian K., Bruce Berg, and Kristin Byars. (1999). "A Qualitative Examination of the Similarities and Differences of Elder Abuse Definitions among Four Groups: Nursing Home Directors, Nursing Home Employees, Police Chiefs and Students." *Journal of Elder Abuse and Neglect* 10, 3/4: 63–86.

Pillemer, Karl. (1986). "Risk Factors in Elder Abuse: Results from a Case-control Study." In *Elder Abuse: Conflict in the Family,* edited by Karl A. Pillemer and Rosalie S. Wolf. Dover, MA: Auburn House, 239–263.

Pillemer, Karl, and Ronet Bachman. (1991). "Helping and Hurting: Predictors of Maltreatment of Patients in Nursing Homes." *Research on Aging* 13, 1: 74–95.

Quinn, Mary J., and Susan Tomita. (1997). *Elder Abuse and Neglect: Causes Diagnosis and Intervention Strategies.* 2d ed. New York: Springer Publishing.

Sharon, Nachman, and Sameer Zoabi. (1997). "Elder Abuse in a Land of Transition: The Case of Israel's Arabs." *Journal of Elder Abuse and Neglect* 8, 4: 43–58.

▼ ELECTRONIC MONITORING

Electronic monitoring (EM) is the use of technological equipment to verify that offenders are at specified locations during particular times. EM is always used in conjunction with house arrest (HA), although HA can be used as a stand-alone sanction. House arrest (sometimes referred to as home confinement or home detention) is simply a sanction to be served within the confines of the offender's home. Strict rules regulate when an offender is allowed to leave the home and for what reasons. This sanction can be enforced through a variety of methods, including, but not limited to, curfew checks by a probation/parole officer, home visits, or the use of technology such as EM. Although many offenders under house arrest are away from their homes regularly, either working or doing other types of specifically authorized tasks (such as undergoing drug and alcohol counseling or completing community service), it is important to note that HA, with or without EM, is always employed as a condition of probation, not a form of probation. Once offenders are finished with the EM component of their sentence, most remain on some type of community supervision.

THE HISTORY OF ELECTRONIC MONITORING

There is nothing new about the use of house arrest and/or home confinement as a form of punishment. What is relatively new, however, is the advent of electronic technology that verifies compliance with the sanction. The development of EM can be traced back to experiments that were conducted at Harvard University in 1964, the results of which were reported in several articles by Ralph Schwitzgebel. These early experiments used a two-pound transceiver that was worn on the belt, a network of repeater stations throughout the Boston and Cambridge areas, and a central monitoring station. From 1964 to 1970, in Boston, Massachusetts, the first EM system was used to monitor the location of mental patients, parolees, and volunteers. Schwitzgebel (1969: 607) discusses several advantages in using such technology to electronically rehabilitate chronic recidivists: It promotes reduction of criminal offenses, (2) facilitates therapy (more frequent contact with a parole officer allows for increased use of positive or negative reinforcement for certain behaviors), and offers a humanitarian alternative to incarceration. He also discusses the potential danger of the tendency to use such "electronic rehabilitation" simply for surveillance rather than for the purposes of rehabilitation. Both the advantages and the potential dangers are still being discussed, debated, and researched today.

The development of the "electronic bracelet" was initiated by Judge Jack Love, a New Mexico district court judge who got the inspiration for it while reading a Spiderman comic strip in 1977. The Spiderman character was being tracked by a transmitter worn on his wrist. Liking the idea, the judge persuaded a computer salesman (Michael Goss) to develop a similar device and, in 1983, the first of these new monitors was developed for the monitoring of five offenders in Albuquerque, New Mexico. Subsequent tests and evaluations deemed the equipment a success and a cost-effective alternative to incarceration.

DIFFERENT TYPES OF ELECTRONIC MONITORING

According to Morris and Tonry (1990), there are three main types of EM systems: (1) active or continuous signaling telecommunications, (2) passive or programmed contact systems, and (3) tracking technology systems.

Active Systems

An active or continuous signaling telecommunication system consists of a small transmitter, strapped to the ankle or wrist of the offender, that emits a signal to a receiver-dialer unit connected via the offender's telephone to a centrally based computer. Provided the offender remains within a 150- to 200-foot radius of the receiver-dialer, no interruption in the signal occurs. If there is an interruption, the receiver-dialer conveys this to the central computer. Such a signal is also transmitted if the strap attaching the transmitter to the offender is interfered with. This system thus provides constant monitoring.

Passive Systems

Passive or programmed contact systems also make use of the telephone and a centrally located computer, but instead of a transmitter and a receiver-dialer they depend on an encoder device and a verifier box. The encoder is strapped to the offender, and the verifier box is connected to his or her telephone. Random or scheduled calls are made to offenders; they must make voice identification and also insert the encoder to verify their presence. If the telephone call does not go through to the offender, possibly because his or her telephone line was engaged, or if verification is not satisfactorily made, the computer reports this fact. The probation officer can then check whether the offender is indeed not where he or she should be and take whatever action seems appropriate. This kind of equipment may also include breath testing for alcohol. Some continuously signaling devices also contain features of programmed contact devices, for example, voice verification technology.

Tracking Technology

Tracking systems are at an earlier stage of development than other devices and are built on technology that has been used to track wild and domestic animals. There are two different types of tracking technology. "Drive-by" units allow a community supervision officer to check whether an offender is at a particular location, such as home, counseling sessions, or work. A transmitter worn by the offender emits a constant radio signal to a portable receiver in the monitoring officer's car when the officer is sufficiently close to pick up the signal. The probation officer can at any time check where an offender is—or, more precisely, where he or she is not, without the offender being aware of the check. This device offers great flexibility for enforcing house arrest orders, which are fashioned to allow the offender to leave his or her place of residence at spe-

cific times for work or training purposes. Global positioning systems (GPSs) allow for an offender's specific location to be tracked and monitored continuously. This relatively new technology uses satellites to triangulate a reference point and transmit the exact location of an object or an offender in "real time," allowing for the tracking or monitoring of an offender's entire day.

According to Pro Tech Monitoring (www.ptm.com), a GPS technology company:

> The Global Positioning System (or GPS) is a collection of satellites owned by the U.S. Government that provides highly accurate, worldwide positioning and navigation information, 24 hours a day. It is made up of twenty-four Navstar GPS satellites that orbit 11 thousand miles above the earth, constantly transmitting the precise time and their position in space. GPS receivers, on (or near) the earth's surface, listen in on the information received from three to twelve satellites and, from that, determine the precise location of the receiver, as well as how fast and in what direction it is moving.

With the GPS, an offender is fitted with an ankle bracelet (as the offender would be with an active or passive EM system), but here the offender is given a portable tracking device (PTD) that he or she must carry at all times. This allows the GPS satellite network to track the offender's location twenty-four hours a day, provided the offender follows program rules and keeps the tracking device within a certain pre-set limit of his or her ankle bracelet. The location and movements of the offender can then be observed by the monitoring center and ultimately by the probation officer supervising the offender. Any area can be declared off-limits to the offender, and probation officers are notified (sometimes immediately) by e-mail, fax, or pager if an offender enters an unauthorized area. Also, unlike previous technology, the GPS has the capability to notify offenders themselves of any problems by sounding an alarm and sending them messages on the PTD. Criminal justice personnel may also send messages to an offender from the convenience of their desktop or laptop computer. Crime victims can be given portable devices that transmit the victim's position to the surveillance center which can warn them if the offender is nearby.

EM can be very cost-efficient. The average cost of active and passive EM is estimated to be between $5 and $25 per day, compared to the $40 to $50 average required to keep an offender behind bars. GPS systems do cost more—about $30 to $40 a day. According to the *St. Petersburg Times* of Florida (December 15, 1997, p.13), "The actual monitoring cost of the SMART [GPS] system is higher than other electronic systems—an average of 62 cents an hour compared with about 40 cents an hour for other systems."

Even though the technology has advanced in recent years, these systems are not foolproof, and they are not to be used on offenders who have escape histories. Likewise, they are unsuitable for use with offenders who pose a serious threat to the community or who require more supervision than EM can provide. As the technology continues to develop and advance in sophistication, more and different types of hybrid systems are likely to develop.

WHERE ELECTRONIC MONITORING IS USED IN THE CRIMINAL JUSTICE SYSTEM

EM offers a versatile sentencing or judicial alternative because it can be used in many different ways in different parts of the criminal justice system for adults and juveniles alike. For instance, it can be used on a pretrial basis (before guilt or innocence has been determined) in lieu of incarceration. In fact, many jurisdictions now offer an EM alternative to suitable offenders who are incarcerated awaiting judicial action on their cases. EM can also be used on recently convicted offenders as a condition of probation to help supervise an offender who requires more control and/or surveillance than ordinary probation would provide. Finally, EM can be used on offenders being released from jail or prison as a condition of their parole for those serving the remainder of their sentences within the community.

EXTENT OF USE

The precise amount of EM use is unknown; however, it seems to have grown within the past decade. There are estimates that, in 1991, approximately 7,000 probationers were on EM and approximately 12,000 to 14,000 offenders were being monitored in the United States by 1991. One researcher reported the population under EM in 1991 at around 20,000. As evidence of EMs increasing presence in the criminal justice community, it was estimated that "as of January 1998, approximately 1,500 programs existed and 95,000 electronic monitoring units were in use, including those being used by individuals on pretrial status, home detention, probation, and parole as well as in juvenile detention" (National Law Enforcement Cor-

rections Technology Center Bulletin, 1999:1). Even though EM usage is growing, some, no doubt particularly manufacturers, are disappointed that EM has not "taken off" as fast as they had hoped or expected.

EFFECTIVENESS

The results of research conducted on the recidivism (failure) rates of EM participants vary widely. Several of the initial reports, called "promotional pieces" by some, presented glowing and uncritical accounts of individual programs. The literature that is available suggests that recidivism rates range anywhere from 1 to 40 percent. The majority of these reports have been plagued by methodological problems, the most serious of which have been the lack of a control group, the lack of a comparable control group, and/or random assignment. Although few methodologically rigorous studies have been conducted to date, EM has often been found to be no less effective than other sanctions like jail and standard probation supervision. Some EM programs boast very high success rates, in large part because, through a process called "creaming," they take the "cream of the crop" offenders—offenders without extensive criminal histories. Although there have been some highly politicized failures of offenders on EM (for example, an offender who cuts his or her bracelet off and goes on a crime spree), these have not been common occurrences. Most studies have found that offenders do remarkably well during their monitoring period, which can last anywhere from 2 to 180 days. As with any other correctional program, success is closely related to the selection process. More, and more methodologically sound, studies continue to be conducted on EM, although it seems clear that EM's biggest advantage lies in its ability to alleviate jail or prison crowding; the potential for cost savings or at least cost avoidance (reducing the need for new incarcerative facilities) is an attractive feature. Because many jurisdictions mandate that offenders pay EM supervision fees, many EM programs have proven cost-effective, particularly if jail-bound offenders are selected for program participation. (See Courtright, Berg, and Mutchnick 1997, for evidence of this.) For a review of EM program descriptions and evaluations in the late 1990s, see Schmidt (1998).

CONCERNS FOR THE FUTURE

Some jurisdictions have widened the net of social control by using EM on offenders who would have received regular probation. (For a discussion of this, see Palumbo, Clifford, and Snyder-Joy 1992.) *Net widening* refers to the expansion of social control, exercised either by social service systems or by the criminal justice system over offenders for whom such services were not originally designed. Thus, when an offender who would typically have received a sentence of regular probation, or perhaps have had his or her case dismissed, receives house arrest with EM, net widening is said to occur. Net widening is both an ethical concern and a cost issue. Because a sentence of house arrest with EM may be more expensive than a regular probation sentence, increased costs may result from net widening. Net widening can be avoided by using EM on jail or prison-bound offenders only.

Some are concerned that the use of such technology in the control and punishment of offenders may cause invasion of privacy problems, either now or in the future. The courts, however, have yet to rule EM unconstitutional or representative of privacy invasion. Others are concerned about the possibility that technology has replaced or may in the future replace the necessary and important human component of offender supervision (see, for instance, Corbett and Marx 1991). Most experts agree that EM should always be used in conjunction with frequent supervision by criminal justice personnel (home and office visits, urine screens, etc.).

As with many other innovations in corrections, some saw EM as a panacea—in this case, as a solution to the overcrowding crisis. Tischler (1998: 3) made this comment: "Ultimately, no matter what astonishing and sophisticated devices are available, the success of a probation or parole program will depend on whether the right tools for the job have been chosen, and whether those tools are being used properly by quality staff." EM has not been a cure-all, but it has given criminal justice personnel another versatile sanction to use for appropriate offenders. Provided that appropriate offenders are selected for participation, the sanction has allowed many jurisdictions to reduce jail and/or prison populations and save money (or at least avoid spending more money) while not unduly jeopardizing the safety of the community.

—*Kevin E. Courtright*

See also HOUSE ARREST

Further Reading

Corbett, Ronald, and Gary T. Marx. (1991). "Critique: No Soul in the New Machine: Technofallacies in the Electronic Monitoring Movement." *Justice Quarterly* 8: 359–414.

Courtright, Kevin E., Bruce L. Berg, and Robert J. Mutchnick. (1997). "The Cost Effectiveness of Using House Arrest with Electronic Monitoring for Drunk Drivers." *Federal Probation* 61, 3: 19–22.

Gable, Ralph K. (1986). "Application of Personal Telemonitoring to Current Problems in Corrections." *Journal of Criminal Justice* 14: 167–176.

Lilly, J. Robert., and Richard A. Ball (1987). "A Brief History of House Arrest and Electronic Monitoring." *Northern Kentucky Law Review* 13: 343–374.

Lilly, J. Robert, Richard A. Ball, G. David Curry, and Richard C. Smith (1992). "The Pride, Inc., Program: An Evaluation of 5 Years of Electronic Monitoring." *Federal Probation* 56, 4: 42–47.

Morris, Norval, and Michael Tonry. (1990). *Between Prison and Probation: Intermediate Punishments in a Rational Sentencing System.* New York: Oxford University Press.

National Law Enforcement and Corrections Technology Center. (1999). *Keeping Track of Electronic Monitoring.* A Program of the National Institute of Justice, October 1999.

Palumbo, Dennis J., Mary Clifford, and Zoann K. Snyder-Joy. (1992). "From Net Widening to Intermediate Sanctions: The Transformation of Alternatives to Incarceration from Benevolence to Malevolence." In *Smart Sentencing: The Emergence of Intermediate Sanctions,* edited by James M. Byrne, Arthur J. Lurigio, and Joan Petersilia. Newbury Park, CA: Sage Publications, 229–244.

Pro Tech Monitoring Inc. http://www.ptm.com

Renzema, Marc. (1992). "Home Confinement Programs: Development, Implementation, and Impact." In *Smart Sentencing: The Emergence of Intermediate Sanctions,* edited by James M. Byrne, Arthur J. Lurigio, and Joan Petersilia. Newbury Park, CA: Sage Publications 41–53.

Schmidt, Annesley K. (1998). "Electronic Monitoring: What Does the Literature Tell Us?" *Federal Probation* 62, 2: 10–19.

Schwitzgebel, Ralph K. (1969). "Issues in the Use of an Electronic Rehabilitation System with Chronic Recidivists." *Law & Society Review* 3: 597–611.

St. Petersburg (FL) *Times.* (1997). "The Unblinking Eye." 15 December 1997: 13.

Tischler, Eric. (1998). "Does Technology Enhance or Hinder Community Supervision?" *On the Line* (American Correctional Association) 21, 2: 1, 3.

ELMIRA REFORMATORY

A new era in corrections was born in Elmira, New York, on July, 24 1876, when thirty inmates were transferred from Auburn Prison to Elmira Reformatory. Elmira, the world's first adult reformatory for offenders ranging in age from sixteen to thirty, was opened by Zebulon Reed Brockway, who served as its superintendent for twenty-four years.

HISTORY

When the Elmira Reformatory opened, it rejected nineteenth-century penology's ideals of silence, obedience, and labor. Elmira's goal would be to reform the convict—its methods would be psychological rather than physical. Instead of coercing with the lash, Elmira would encourage with rewards, and mass regimentation would yield to classification and individualized treatment. Instead of fixed sentences to fit the crime, the indeterminate sentence would be adjustable to fit the criminal.

Judges—convinced of Elmira's merits—sent inmates faster than they could be paroled. Additions to the original 504 cells were made in 1886 and again in 1892, raising the total to 1,296, but by the late 1890s there were nearly 1,500 occupants. In 1970, the reception center was administratively joined to the main facility, and the complex was renamed the Elmira Correctional and Reception Center. Although no longer a reformatory, Elmira's concentration on younger offenders continued into the early 1990s, when the Department of Correctional Services (DOCS) established facilities for those under twenty-one in the Washington, D.C.-New York hub. Elmira's population currently averages around thirty-five years of age. It is now a general confinement facility for adult males and operates a modern correctional program along the lines laid down by Brockway.

PRISONS VERSUS REFORMATORIES

A primary difference between prisons and reformatories was the sentencing structure that was used in each. Prisons during this time set fixed (or "determined") sentences. These sentences were reduced by "good time" that was earned, generally one day served for one day of good time. Reformatories introduced the concept of indeterminate sentences, which inmates could shorten by exhibiting good behavior while in prison. Elmira quietly redefined the term *reform*, which until then had been understood only in purely religious terms. Through teaching rather than preaching, they downplayed religious conversion in favor of the more realistic goal of law-abiding behavior.

TRAINING AND EDUCATION

The main emphasis of the reformatory system was on reforming youths through vocational training and academic education. Reformers believed that an education and job skills that could be used after release would lead to reform of the offenders. Beginning in 1878, several educated inmates taught elementary classes six nights a week, and a professor from Elmira Women's College conducted courses in geography and the natural sciences for advanced students. The next year, six public school teachers and three attorneys were engaged to teach elementary classes, and advanced classes were expanded to include geometry, bookkeeping, and physiology. A professor from the Michigan State Normal School was recruited as "moral director" to begin courses in ethics and psychology. Lectures in history and literature were added in the early 1880s. In 1882, a summer school was started. Throughout the period, Elmira attracted prominent visitors as "Sunday lecturers." In 1888, an entire building was set aside as a trades school and, by 1894, instruction was provided in thirty-four trades.

THE IMPACT OF ELMIRA

The new reformatory generated tremendous excitement and pushed American corrections into the future. Between 1876 and 1913 seventeen states copied the first reformatory that was established at Elmira, which claimed to have a rehabilitation rate of 80 percent (prisons at that time claimed a rehabilitation rate of only 40 percent). Elmira's premises—individual treatment, the indeterminate sentence, and parole—were universally embraced and would not be seriously questioned until the 1970s, when a new concern for individual liberties and due process would begin to chisel away at the rehabilitative ideal.

—*Amy J. Benavides*

Further Reading

Champion, Dean. (2001). *Corrections in the United States: A Contemporary Perspective.* 3d ed. Upper Saddle River, NJ: Prentice Hall.

DOCS Today. (October 1998). "Elmira." http://www.geocities.com/MotorCity/Downs/3548/facility/elmira.html

Jacobs, Nancy R., Mark A. Siegel, and Jacquelyn Quiram, eds. (1995). *Prisons and Jails: A Deterrent to Crime?* Wylie, TX: Information Plus.

University of Louisiana. (2001). "Prison Reform." http://complicity.english.louisville.edu/haymarket/marsh/prison.html

▼ ENTRAPMENT

Governmental inducement of criminal activity is widely regarded as essential for effective law enforcement, especially when the government is seeking to prosecute persons engaged in crimes committed in secret among willing participants (e.g., drug offenses, bribery, receipt of stolen property, and trafficking in pornography). To detect and punish persons engaged in such activities, the police frequently find it necessary to feign participation in a criminal scheme, offering inducements designed to gather evidence of the individual's criminal plans. Common tactics include offering to sell or purchase contraband, promising financial rewards for criminal acts, and agreeing to participate or assist in a criminal enterprise.

Although it is a useful law enforcement technique, the government's encouragement of criminal acts poses serious risks for a society that values individual freedom and autonomy. Our criminal justice system assumes that, in principle, people have the capacity for free choice, and the state should "respect the autonomy and capacity for self-actuation of its citizens" (Fletcher 1978: 431). Punishment should not be imposed on the basis of speculation about a person's "thoughts and emotions . . . , personality patterns and character structures" (Packer 1968: 73). Criminal penalties are appropriate only for individuals who fail to exercise self-restraint, whose antisocial inclinations are revealed in antisocial behavior.

Permitting the government to engage in the solicitation and inducement of crime can violate these basic principles. When the government tests the morality of a citizen by enticing that person to commit a criminal act, the government itself actuates the criminal behavior in some sense and creates a risk that an otherwise innocent and law-abiding person—someone who would normally restrain himself or herself from criminal conduct—will be caught in the government's net. To limit this risk, every jurisdiction in the United States provides that excessive government encouragement of a criminal act may give the perpetrator a defense of "entrapment" to the resulting criminal charges. The precise contours of the entrapment defense have long been the subject of debate and disagreement among American courts and commentators.

DEVELOPMENT OF THE ENTRAPMENT DEFENSE

Prior to 1900, the entrapment defense was rarely asserted and was usually limited to cases in which the use of decoys or tricks to induce a crime had resulted in the allegedly wrongful acts not being criminal at all.

For example, if the purported victim of a burglary had allowed the defendant to enter his or her home, there was no burglary. However, in the early twentieth century, appellate courts decided dozens of cases in which defendants argued that they should not be prosecuted because their admittedly criminal conduct was the result of improper government inducement. This rise in claims of entrapment was probably due to an increase in the government's use of undercover operations to detect those engaged in crime. Such operations were necessitated by new legislation, such as narcotic and liquor laws, criminalizing behavior that is easily hidden and difficult to detect.

Whatever the cause, a true entrapment defense began to emerge in the judicial decisions of this period. The availability of a federal entrapment defense was definitively established by the U.S. Supreme Court's 1932 decision in *Sorrells v. United States*. Reversing a lower court decision denying the defense, the justices held by an 8-1 vote that the government was entitled to use traps and deception to identify and punish those already engaged in crime, but that it abused its authority when it used persuasion, deceit, or inducement for the purpose of creating criminal acts that the accused would not otherwise have committed. The eight justices who supported an entrapment defense in *Sorrells*, however, could not agree on the proper test by which to determine whether entrapment had occurred. Their differing views led to the development of two distinct tests for entrapment—the so-called subjective and objective tests.

The federal courts and a majority of states adhere to the "subjective" or "predisposition" test for entrapment. According to this test, the entrapment defense is designed to ensure that an "otherwise innocent" defendant is not punished for acts that were the product of government instigation. To raise the defense, the defendant has the initial burden of producing evidence that the government induced or encouraged the alleged crime. Some jurisdictions further demand that the defendant prove the fact of inducement by a preponderance—or majority—of evidence. Once the issue of inducement has been properly raised, the critical question is whether the government's actions led to the detection of a criminal or to the seduction into crime of an otherwise innocent citizen. To establish that the defendant is not "otherwise innocent," the government may undertake a "searching inquiry" into the defendant's subjective "predisposition" to commit the offense (*Sorrells v. United States* 1932: 451). This

▼

The U.S. Supreme Court on Entrapment

In Sorrells v. United States (1932), the defendant had been was convicted of the possession and sale of whiskey, in violation of the National Prohibition Act. The United States Supreme Court decided that the lower courts should have permitted the defendant to raise an entrapment defense.

[Chief Justice Hughes, for the five justices in the majority]: "[T]he evidence was sufficient to warrant a finding that the act for which defendant was prosecuted was instigated by the prohibition agent, that it was the creature of his purpose, that defendant had no previous disposition to commit it but was an industrious, law-abiding citizen, and that the agent lured defendant, otherwise innocent, to its commission by repeated and persistent solicitation in which he succeeded by taking advantage of the sentiment aroused by reminiscences of their experiences as companions in arms in the World War. Such a gross abuse of authority given for the purpose of detecting and punishing crime, and not for the making of criminals, deserves the severest condemnation . . . ."

"Artifice and strategem may be employed to catch those engaged in criminal enterprises. . . . [But] the processes of detection and enforcement [are] abused by the instigation by government officials of an act on the part of persons otherwise innocent in order to lure them to its commission and to punish them. . . .

[Justice Roberts, for the three concurring justices]: "Society is at war with the criminal classes, and courts have uniformly held that in waging this warfare the forces of prevention and detection may use traps, decoys, and deception to obtain evidence of the commission of crime. . . . But the defense here asserted involves more than obtaining evidence by artifice or deception. Entrapment is the conception and planning of an offense by an officer, and his procurement of its commission by one who would not have perpetrated it except for the trickery, persuasion, or fraud of the officer."

"There is common agreement that where a law officer envisages a crime, plans it, and activates its commission by one not theretofore intending its perpetration, for the sole purpose of obtaining a victim through indictment, conviction and sentence, the consummation of so revolting a plan ought not to be permitted by any self-respecting tribunal."

Source: *Sorrells v. United States*, 287 U.S. 435 (1932).

From its early use, the subjective approach has been criticized because the type of evidence admitted to prove entrapment is frequently both unreliable—consisting of hearsay, suspicion, and rumor—and unfair, as it seems to put the defendant on trial for his or her past behavior and character. These problems are exacerbated by the fact that the subjective approach can predispose a jury against a defendant, regardless of the merits of the current case against him or her. Because of these problems, a significant minority of states—including Alaska, California, Iowa, Michigan, and Vermont—have adopted the objective approach to entrapment. According to this approach, the critical issue in an entrapment case is the nature of the government's conduct. Police incitement of a criminal act is improper when the police use methods of encouragement that create a significant risk that a person who is normally law-abiding would commit such a crime. In most jurisdictions following the objective approach, the defendant must establish all aspects of the defense by a preponderance of the evidence.

In principle, the objective approach does not require or permit an inquiry into the particular defendant's character or predisposition to commit the crime; rather, the focus of the objective approach is on the probable impact of the government's conduct on a hypothetical law-abiding person. Moreover, the issue is typically decided by a judge rather than a jury. Consequently, the risk that the defendant will be convicted for his or her character, rather than on the basis of the criminal charges, is significantly reduced.

Critics of the objective approach argue that the test is misguided in its exclusion of evidence about the

inquiry may include the consideration of such evidence as the defendant's prior convictions, prior arrests, and general reputation, as well as evidence of the defendant's conduct in connection with the charged offense, including the defendant's ready acquiescence to the proposed criminal scheme, access to contraband, or participation in planning the crime. To successfully rebut the claim of entrapment, the government must prove predisposition (or the absence of any inducement) beyond a reasonable doubt.

defendant's character, past criminal acts, and predisposition to commit the crime. The propriety of police conduct, they contend, cannot be evaluated accurately unless one knows what the police knew about the defendant's character. Inducements that might be objectionable if offered to a hypothetical law-abiding person could be entirely proper when offered to a suspected drug dealer whose past caution and wariness have allowed the dealer to avoid criminal prosecution.

A more fundamental problem is that the objective approach permits, in principle at least, the conviction of an otherwise law-abiding defendant who surrendered to police blandishments in a moment of uncharacteristic weakness. So long as the inducements offered were not so extreme as to create a substantial risk that a hypothetical law-abiding person would be led to crime, it makes no difference (under the objective approach) that the particular defendant was a law-abiding person seduced into crime by the government. To avoid this problem, a few jurisdictions combine the objective and subjective approaches, allowing a defense if the defendant can show that the police conduct was likely to induce criminal action by the innocent or that the particular defendant was not, in fact, predisposed to commit the criminal act.

LIMITATIONS ON THE ENTRAPMENT DEFENSE

The entrapment defense is available only when the alleged inducement was offered by a government official or by someone acting in concert with government agents, such as an informer. A defendant who is encouraged to commit criminal acts by a private party has no defense unless the inducements were sufficiently extreme to permit a claim that the defendant acted under duress.

The entrapment defense is also unavailable for certain crimes. The Model Penal Code and some state statutes expressly exclude the possibility of an entrapment defense when the charged offense involves "causing or threatening bodily injury to a person other than the person perpetrating the entrapment" (American Law Institute 1985: section 2.13[3]). The rationale for this limitation is that the proper remedy for police misconduct in such cases is not to release the dangerous defendant, but to prosecute both the defendant and the government agents who instigated the harmful behavior. Although there is little case history on the subject, it would seem that this limitation on the entrapment defense might properly be extended to any situation where the government induces action that involves causing or threatening serious and particularized social harm, such as arson or killing endangered animals. However, the entrapment defense is generally raised only in cases in which the induced crimes are "victimless" crimes (e.g., drug offenses, bribery, prostitution) and are committed under circumstances in which there is such extensive police involvement and control over the acts that there is little risk that the "criminal" behavior will cause any immediate social harm. It may well be the case that courts would deny the defense entirely if faced with a defendant whose induced actions did cause (or threaten to cause) serious damage to innocent persons or property.

FUTURE OF THE ENTRAPMENT DEFENSE

The entrapment defense is a well-established feature of American criminal law. Despite occasional calls for its abolition, the risks to individual freedom and autonomy posed by overzealous governmental encouragement of criminal acts are substantial enough that the courts are likely to maintain some version of an entrapment defense to protect against the government's abuse of power. Nevertheless, debate continues over whether the defense should focus on the defendant's character or on some objective evaluation of the propriety of police conduct.

One recent suggestion is that the presence of entrapment should be determined by whether the inducements offered by the police were market-level inducements or above-market inducements. According to this standard, if the police offered inducements at or below those that a defendant might encounter in everyday life, then a defendant who succumbed to those inducements should be punished for his or her crime. If, however, the inducements exceeded what one might normally encounter, the defendant is not likely to be a threat under ordinary circumstances and should not be punished. An alternative suggestion is that any level of inducement should prevent prosecution for the instigated crime, because no one can ever know whether, absent government enticement, the defendant would have acted criminally. Under these guidelines, however, if the government's sting operation permitted it to secure evidence that the defendant committed other crimes, entrapment would not be a defense to conviction for those crimes.

Although the entrapment defense is not based on constitutional principles, a few courts have stated that the techniques used by government agents to incite criminal activity for the purpose of punishing it might be so outrageous that due process principles would forbid the prosecution of the defendant. The few cases that address this issue suggest that a violation of due process is most likely to be found when the government's conduct is directed against a defendant who was not suspected of criminal behavior and who would not, or could not, have engaged in the crime without the support or encouragement of the government agent. In other words, even the emerging due process defense seems to turn on the question that has motivated entrapment law from the beginning: Did the government manufacture a crime or did it detect a criminal?

—*Jonathan C. Carlson*

Further Reading

Allen, Ronald J., Melissa Luttrell, and Anne Kreeger. (1999). "Clarifying Entrapment." *Journal of Criminal Law and Criminology* 89: 407–431.

American Law Institute. (1985). *Model Penal Code and Commentaries.* Philadelphia: American Law Institute Publishers.

Carlson, Jonathan C. (1987). "The Act Requirement and the Foundations of the Entrapment Defense." *University of Virginia Law Review* 73: 1011–1108.

Fletcher, George. (1978). *Rethinking Criminal Law.* Boston: Little, Brown and Company.

LaFave, Wayne R., and Austin W. Scott. (1986). *Criminal Law.* 2d ed. St. Paul, MN: West Publishing Company.

Marcus, Paul. (1989). *The Entrapment Defense.* Charlottesville, VA: Michie Company.

Packer, Herbert L. (1968). *The Limits of the Criminal Sanction.* Stanford, CA: Stanford University Press.

Park, Roger. (1976). "The Entrapment Controversy." *University of Minnesota Law Review* 60: 163–274.

Perkins, Rollin M., and Ronald N. Boyce. (1982). *Criminal Law.* 3d ed. Mineola, NY: Foundation Press.

Seidman, Louis Michael. (1981). "The Supreme Court, Entrapment, and Our Criminal Justice Dilemma." In *The Supreme Court Review.* Chicago, IL: University of Chicago Press, 111–155.

Court Cases

Hampton v. United States (1976). 425 U.S. 484.
Jacobson v. United States (1992). 503 U.S. 540.
Sherman v. United States (1958). 356 U.S. 369.
Sorrells v. United States (1932). 287 U.S. 435.
United States v. Russell (1973). 411 U.S. 423.

▼ ENVIRONMENTAL CRIME

Modern society has been forever plagued by the problem of ensuring the proper disposal of refuse. Until recently, most people did not make a distinction between innocuous and dangerous wastes. *Waste* was considered by most people to be a common term describing all types of garbage. The ultimate destination of both innocuous and dangerous waste was the local landfill. Business firms dumping their wastes were considered to be nuisances, rather than criminals. The common images of the dumper and the criminal were worlds apart. In the 1970s, however, the growing threat to public health was underscored by an increasing number of high-profile acts of improper dumping of highly toxic wastes. This led to the enactment of the federal Resource Conservation and Recovery Act of 1976 (RCRA), which made the indiscriminate disposal of wastes that posed significant risks for human health and for the general environment a crime. Since the RCRA was enacted, every state has developed laws modeled after it establishing criminal penalties for environmental crimes.

Grassroots movements have helped elevate the issue of environmental protection to a serious matter of community safety that has increasingly been seen by local public officials as an important obligation. Community leaders and the public they represent have turned to their elected officials for the type of protection they have come to expect from them for more traditional crimes. After years of setbacks in their attempts to raise environmental violations to the level of criminal behavior, environmental crime control officials have witnessed a change in the winds of sentiment on this issue. For example, in a 1991 study conducted by Environmental Opinion Study Inc., U.S. citizens were found to overwhelmingly favor terms of incarceration for corporate or government officials convicted of deliberately violating pollution laws.

The criminalization of human behavior judged to be harmful to the public is typically a slow process in common-law jurisdictions. The momentum for criminalization, gained through problem identification and pressure exerted by special-interest groups, can easily span decades before legislatures classify undesirable actions as crimes. A rare exception to this problem has been the relatively speedy transformation of acts of pollution into official crimes against the environment. National media coverage of toxic tragedies like those occurring at Love Canal, New York, in the late 1970s, and at Times Beach, Missouri, in the early 1980s, altered forever the American public's perception of the dangers of the improper disposal of hazardous waste. These events also sparked the quick passage of crimi-

▼

How Are the Courts Treating Environmental Criminals?

One of the criticisms lodged against the U.S. criminal justice system is that it has been historically "soft" on environmental offenders. Convicted criminal polluters rarely are sentenced to incarceration and, when they are, the penalties may seem unsuitably mild to those who are environmentally conscious. There is some evidence that there may be a toughening stance by federal judges. On April 28, 2000, one day before the thirty-ninth anniversary of Earth Day, Judge Lynn Winmill imposed the longest prison term for an environmental crime. Alan Elias, owner of a chemical reprocessing company named Evergreen Resources, was sentenced to seventeen years of incarceration for endangering the health and safety of his employees. Elias had directed employees at his Soda Springs, Idaho, facility to improperly dispose of cyanide waste collected from the bottom of a 25,000 gallon tank. Elias did not supply the employees with proper safety equipment, and as a result, one of the workers suffered brain damage. In addition to the prison sentence, Elias was ordered to pay $6 million in restitution.

This sentence is one example of how the courts are attempting to make up for lost time in the imposition of environmental crime penalties that reflect the seriousness of the offenses and may have a deterrent effect. The following are summaries of sentences imposed in fiscal year 1999 for environmental crime cases prosecuted by the Environment and Natural Resources Division of the U.S. Department of Justice.

Individuals

Alan Elias, Evergreen Resources, Pocatello, ID: endangering health/safety of employees, ordering hazardous disposal of cyanide waste—7 years in prison, $6 million in restitution.

Robert F. Kelly, Kelly Spraying Services, Memphis, TN: pesticide misuse and distribution; applying methyl parathion, a farming pesticide intended for open field use, to the insides of hundreds of Memphis homes—20 months in prison, $250,000 fine.

Buddy Frazier, Chance Gaines, and *James Brag*, Marshfield, WI: asbestos work practice violations; recruited homeless men in Chattanooga, TN, to improperly handle demolition debris—prison sentences of 30 months, 33 months and 24 months respectively.

Gary Benkovi, Bay Drum and Steel Inc., Tampa, FL: storm sewer discharge of thousands of gallons of wastewater into storm sewers into McKay Bay—13 years in prison.

Companies

Colonial Pipeline Co. (CPC–Oil company consortium of Mobil, Amoco and Texaco), Simpsonville, SC: negligent dumping of 1 million gallons of diesel fuel from a ruptured pipeline into Reedy River—$7 million fine, 5-year probation.

BP Exploration Inc. (BP Amoco parent company), Endicott Island, AK: injection of hazardous waste down the outer rims of oil well—$22 million fine.

Royal Caribbean Cruises Ltd., Miami, New York, Los Angeles, Anchorage, U.S. Virgin Islands, San Juan: intentional routine dumping of oil, plastics, and hazardous waste—$18 million fine.

Mid-South Terminal Company, Memphis, TN: discharge of scrap metal into Mississippi River during barge loading—$200,000 fine.

---

nal laws on both the federal and state levels prohibiting offenses against the environment.

WHAT IS ENVIRONMENTAL CRIME?

Even though national news magazines and newspapers frequently cover incidents of environmental crime and the general public in opinion polls has reported a growing concern with it, a consistent and comprehensive definition of environmental crime has been elusive for years. However, criminologists now tend to agree that an environmental crime is any act committed for economic gain or advantage (whether it be for the individual committing the offense or the organization he or she represents) that in some way harms ecological and/or biological systems and that is punishable by criminal sanctions. To be considered crimes, these acts must be in violation of local or federal criminal statutes. This separates them from less serious acts of pollution that may only be violations of regulatory or civil statutes.

Environmental crimes are most commonly associated with the improper disposal, treatment, and/or storage of hazardous waste. Since the 1970s, the most infamous cases of environmental crime in the United States have involved the improper handling of hazardous waste. Hazardous waste is refuse that, because of its chemical composition, quantity, or concentration, can pose serious harm to human health or the environment when improperly disposed of, treated, or stored. Much of the hazardous waste in the United States is generated as a by-product of legitimate manufacturing and other business processes. The volume of hazardous waste generated in the United States has risen since the beginning of the Industrial Revolution. In the post-World War II era, science has been able to imitate the diverse characteristics of organic chemicals, forming the basis for products like plastics, electronic components, and construction materials. This has led to a dramatic surge in the amount of hazardous waste.

Legitimate hazardous waste disposal methods, including high temperature incineration, biological treatment, and chemical decomposition, are available to generators of waste, but at a high price. It can cost more than $1,000 to properly treat a 55-gallon drum of hazardous waste. Such costs can be problematic for a small business owner, who may feel unable to afford legitimate treatment, and for large business executives bent on increasing their profit margins. The quick solution is often illegal dumping, for which all that is needed is a truck and a lack of regard for public safety. These illegal acts are sometimes referred to as "midnight dumping."

WHO COMMITS THE CRIMES?

Those committing environmental crimes can be separated into three general categories: situational offenders, routine offenders and entrepreneurial offenders. *Situational offenders* are by and large law-abiding individuals who, because of a certain set of circumstances, decide to break the law through illegal disposal. This might be a one-time occurrence. An example of this would be the owner of a failed fish packing business who must physically close his site and decides to release used refrigerant substances into a nearby stream, instead of paying for proper treatment. *Routine offenders* are those who break environmental laws as part of a daily, weekly, or monthly practice that may fit within the parameters of an informal business norm. A cruise line that makes a weekly practice of dumping its wastes into the ocean to save on costs of proper treatment is guilty of being a routine environmental offender. *Entrepreneurial offenders* commit repeated acts of environmental crime as an illegitimate business

designed to generate financial profits. Waste treatment company owners who properly treat only half of the annual volume of wastes they have contracted to treat, illegally dumping the other half, are operating as entrepreneurial offenders.

Environmental offenders range from chief executive officers who order illegal disposal to the line-level truck drivers who do the actual dumping. Offenders often dispose of wastes in the nearest isolated area. These offenses can be directly committed by agents of waste-generating companies, or the companies can criminally conspire with waste transporters or with those who, although ostensibly in the legitimate treatment business, will illegally dump the wastes for a fraction of the legitimate treatment cost. In some cases, hazardous waste generators become victims of fraud committed by midnight dumpers. In these instances, the waste generator unsuspectingly pays the treater for services that are never performed.

HOW ARE THE CRIMES COMMITTED?

The most recent evidence demonstrates that many of the most popular methods of illegal waste disposal have remained unchanged through the years. The most common offenses continue to be waste abandonment or disposal in wooded areas, vacant lots, or abandoned buildings, and discharging into public waters. Many U.S. coastal cities have been faced by the growing problem of vessel pollution—the intentional dumping of oil, plastics, and hazardous wastes. The most serious vessel pollution offenses were by the fleet of Royal Caribbean Cruises Ltd., which routinely dumped off the coasts of Miami, New York, Los Angeles, Anchorage, and the U.S. Virgin Islands. As part of a plea agreement, the company pled guilty to twenty-one felony counts for dumping hazardous chemicals and oil. The company was fined $18 million.

The factor of "opportunity" is central to the commission of environmental crime. The key to success for the skillful environmental offender is his or her awareness and knowledge of opportunities to avoid detection. This often translates into taking advantage of the topography of a given location to hide evidence of the illegal disposal. Features that might seem unsightly to the average citizen may be a boon for the offender searching for just the right setting for his environmental crime. A blighted landscape pockmarked with boreholes descending to abandoned coal mines could represent a criminal bonanza to an enterprising offender wishing to unload a tank truck filled with electroplating wastes. A massive garbage landfill could be viewed as just the right spot to bury a truckload of benzene.

Another key to success for the skillful environmental criminal is obtaining knowledge about the weaknesses of those entrusted with monitoring waste-producing and waste-treating facilities. Research on environmental crime in New Jersey revealed that when operators of hazardous waste treatment/storage and disposal facilities wanted to illegally dispose wastes, they often did so only after carefully assessing the weaknesses of regulatory inspectors. Veteran offenders were able to successfully hide their criminal actions by accurately identifying which inspectors were ill-informed on legitimate treatment applications, and then duping these inspectors into approving mock methods of treatment. Entrepreneurial offenders were also found to be especially adept at accurately predicting regulators' patterns of inspection visits and targeting those regulators most susceptible to being co-opted.

Some investigative journalism in the 1970s and early 1980s claimed that U.S. environmental crime was controlled by traditional criminal syndicate families. Later empirical research demonstrated that, although most environmental crime is organized, it is organized within or between relatively small criminal groups. This research found that entrepreneurial crime organized within businesses tended to involve apprenticeship systems of criminal conversion, isolating new employees seen as being likely to obey criminal directives and indoctrinating them into the ways of illegal disposal. Such businesses cultivate deeply entrenched, covert rewards systems that help ensure that the criminal environment is sustained even as employees who resign are replaced. Most of these operations are responsible for developing "core groups" of veteran criminal disposers responsible for committing the most serious disposals in terms of chemical toxicity, concentration, and volume.

Besides being organized internally within single companies, environmental offenders have been known to form external bonds in concert with individuals in other companies. One industry that has fallen prey to these types of crimes is the waste oil recycling industry. The typical scenario is one in which a waste generator possessing a load of hazardous waste conspires with an owner or employee of a waste oil recycling firm. The objective is to mix the hazardous waste with waste oil and misrepresent the untreated mixture as recycled waste oil suitable for home heating. The payment to the waste oil firm owner or employee is a fraction of full cost, allowing the waste generator to avoid full payment for proper treatment. The waste-oil firm owner or employee profits on two ends: by receiving the payment from the generator and by increasing the volume of "recycled" waste oil for ultimate sale as heating oil. Such polluters have learned to refine their methods of crime commission in an effort to escape quickly evolving enforcement strategies. They have tried to take advantage of perceived loopholes in federal definitions of "recycling" to blend hazardous wastes with innocuous substances and thus create aggregates represented as being legitimate recycling products

HOW ARE THE CRIMES CONTROLLED?

Those conducting research into environmental crime have sometimes disagreed on what characteristics seem to be the most representative of environmental criminals. The work of these researchers, however, has stimulated additional interest in studying both the conditions and circumstances that are determinants of environmental crime and the elements needed to effectively suppress these violations. Through empirical research, it has been suggested that the ideal equation for the reduction of environmental crime is:

> tightened environmental legislation +
> toughened enforcement +
> increases in legitimate disposal alternatives =
> reduced rates of environmental offenses.

Given the early enforcement problems experienced in the 1970s and 1980s and the public's impatience with attainment of effective control, public policy emphasis for the twenty-first century has been on improved and progressive enforcement of environmental laws.

As environmental crime became more prevalent in the 1990s and the crimes themselves attracted greater media attention, the general population showed signs of becoming less tolerant of environmental crime commission and more demanding of strong control programs. The public's frustration with environmental crime came into sharp relief in the form of the Rocky Flats affair, a case that proved to be a catalyst to both intensified criminal prosecution of environmental offenses and the imposition of stronger sentences. In 1992, Rockwell Corporation, a nuclear weapons facility in Rocky Flats, Colorado, pled guilty to federal criminal violations involving the illegal disposal and storage of hazardous wastes. The plea resulted in an $18.5 million penalty for Rockwell, but federal prosecutors chose not to bring individual indictments against Rockwell employees. In an unusual expression of public outrage, grand jury members disregarded the prosecutor's decision to refrain from pursuing individual indictments and attempted on their own to indict Rockwell employees. This incident, in addition to questions regarding the handling of other environmental pollution cases by federal prosecutors, eventually became the target of a House oversight committee chaired by Rep. John Dingell (D-MI). The Dingell panel was assembled to review U.S. Department of Justice policy on environmental crime and to investigate charges of leniency toward polluting corporations. The panel unearthed patterns of a "soft" approach by federal prosecutors toward environmental crime, prompting a reexamination of the roles that law enforcement, on all government levels, can play to control environmental crime.

Broad responsibilities for the control of environmental crime have been assumed by a growing number of individuals specializing in environmental crime investigation and prosecution. Once found exclusively within the Department of Justice, environmental crime investigators and prosecutors now populate many state attorney general offices, as well as the offices of local district attorneys in urban-metropolitan jurisdictions. In response to a groundswell of public demand, local law enforcement officials, particularly in densely populated jurisdictions, have confronted the mammoth task of solving and prosecuting these crimes locally rather than passing them up to federal or state agencies, a common practice in the past. Through this direct involvement, local investigators and prosecutors seize the opportunity to display their level of concern for constituents' well-being, rather than deferring enforcement responsibilities to other government agencies by claiming lack of ability or expertise.

State and federal agencies traditionally responsible for the enforcement of environmental laws were characterized by some observers in the early 1990s as isolated, specialized, and only mildly sensitive to local issues. Investigators and prosecutors at the local level now integrate environmental crime control into the routine functions of law enforcement. Greater investigation and prosecution at the local level has helped to produce an efficient response to environmental crimes, reducing environmental risk and damage. Local investigation and prosecution has also helped to deter criminal behavior within a class of violators too numerous for the Environmental Protection Agency to reach. In addition, enforcement operations are tailored to community conditions to meet community needs, and cooperative relationships have been established among local, state, and federal agents to form task forces necessary to investigate and prosecute environmental crimes effectively.

Research on the growing movement of local environmental crime control by Hammett and Epstein, by Rebovich, and by Situ and Emmons shows that local investigators and prosecutors have broadened the definition of their roles to include protection of the county's public health. In this role, local investigators and prosecutors must become intimately familiar with a variety of areas that require technical expertise, such as environmental science, chemistry, waste-sampling techniques, and regulatory enforcement. Through recent research, local investigators and prosecutors have vividly portrayed the imposing difficulties inherent in the development of a sound expertise in this unique prosecution field, a field that intermingles elements of law, public health, and science. It is a field where local law enforcement officials find themselves nurturing relationships with a broad range of government agencies necessary for successful crime control. It is also a field where it can be a seemingly endless struggle to rally support for the environmental protection mission from a criminal justice system that can, at times, be ambivalent to the environmental protection cause.

Research by Hammett, Epstein, Rebovich, Situ, and Emmons underscores how pivotal the environmental crime task force unit can be as a cohesive force bringing together the diverse entities necessary to help ensure successful environmental crime control. Recent research has provided us with fresh insight into how multi-jurisdictional and multidisciplinary task forces can be most effectively used to stem the illegal disposal, transportation, storage, and treatment of wastes, if concentrated efforts are made to reconcile the divergent interests of the task force participants. The task force director acts as the catalyst in consolidating these interdependent agencies, transforming their members into functional, autonomous units. In this role, the task force director must wear several hats: those of leader, manager, facilitator, and communicator. To make a difference in controlling environmental crime in the localities, the task force director must keep the representatives of these various groups on track and be sure that they complement each other's work and work in concert to routinely capitalize on each other's expertise through a structured means of information exchange. This approach not only builds teamwork and a sense of mission within the task force but also strengthens the quality of environmental crime control and helps to advance more open routes of environmental case referrals.

For a young task force, the culmination of the task force director's efforts at cultivating a competent task force is uncovering and successfully prosecuting a high profile environmental case, one that can draw media attention and have a lasting impact on the general public's impressions of the diligence of the task force's efforts. Environmental task force directors hoping to make their mark in environmental crime control would find this to be a requisite first step toward creating a presence in the local battle against environmental crime, generating additional case referrals in the future and establishing a track record for a tough stance on punishing polluters.

ENVIRONMENTAL CRIME: A RAPIDLY EVOLVING CRIME AREA

Environmental crimes are clearly crimes of opportunity. They are committed by those trying to sidestep onetime costs for an isolated dumping of accumulated chemical wastes, by those hoping to defray continual business costs for the conventional treatment of their manufacturing wastes, and by others who have turned their entire firms into illegal dumping businesses. The offender could be a truck driver, the owner of an auto body shop, or an executive from a Fortune 500 company. What they all have in common is a desire to avoid the cost of proper waste treatment and a total disregard for the effects their actions may have on public health. Historically, these individuals have been able to successfully commit their offenses by taking advantage of opportunities provided them through ineffective enforcement and through their ability to capitalize on the natural environment to shield their crimes from the eyes of the public.

Increasing public concern about the effects that environmental crime can have on human health has prompted federal and state legislatures to enact tougher laws and has helped convince law enforce-

ment agencies to engineer aggressive campaigns to control environmental crime. Federal sentencing guidelines have put teeth into punishment options, and leniency toward corporate polluters is now questioned at the highest levels of government. By raising the level of consciousness of government officials with respect to the criminality of acts of pollution, prosecutors have also raised expectations that may prove difficult to meet in the future. As time goes on, a more aware public will increasingly demand that law enforcement act at all government levels to control environmental crime.

In the future, it can be expected that those responsible for controlling environmental crime will continue to have their hands full. Law enforcement should be on the alert for changes in the makeup of criminal conspiracies as a reaction to advances in environmental crime-control programs. Enforcement method evolution has forced offenders to aggressively search for jurisdictional havens, that is, states and counties with weaker laws and enforcement. As law enforcement has become more proficient in controlling environmental crime in those urban, highly populated areas most likely to be victimized, rising incidents of environmental crime are expected to "spill over" into adjoining suburban and rural districts. Without greater uniformity in the quality of enforcement prowess on the environmental crime front, less populated counties with less experienced enforcement units are destined to become tomorrow's unsuspecting recipients of environmental offenders migrating from areas where environmental enforcement units have perfected their craft.

—Donald J. Rebovich

See also CORPORATE CRIME

Further Reading

Clifford, Mary, and Terry Edwards. (1998). "Defining Environmental Crime." In *Environmental Crime: Enforcement, Policy and Social Responsibility,* edited by Mary Clifford. Gaithersburg, MD: Aspen Publishers.

Environmental Opinion Study Inc. (1991). *Environmental Issues Ranked.* Washington, DC: EDS, Inc.

Hammett, Ted, and Joel Epstein. (1993). *Prosecuting Environmental Crime: Los Angeles County. Program Focus.* Washington, DC: U.S. Department of Justice, National Institute of Justice.

Hammett, Ted, and Joel Epstein. (1994). *Local Prosecution of Environmental Crime: Issues and Practices.* Washington, DC: U.S. Department of Justice, National Institute of Justice.

Hammit, James, and Peter Reuter. (1988). *Measuring and Deterring Illegal Disposal of Hazardous Waste.* Santa Monica, CA: RAND Corporation.

Meehan, Jack. (1992). "Policy Issues in Environmental Crimes for America's Metropolitan Prosecutors." Paper presented at the NDAA Annual Conference for Metropolitan Prosecutors, Washington, DC, April 17, 1992.

Murphy, William. (1991). Presentation to the National Environmental Enforcement Council, Washington, DC, October 22, 1991.

Rebovich, Donald .(1992). *Dangerous Ground: The World of Hazardous Waste Crime.* New Brunswick, NJ: Transaction Publishers.

———. (1996). "Prosecutorial Decision Making and the Environmental Prosecutor: Reaching a Crossroads for Public Protection." In *Environmental Criminality: Definitions, Explanations, Prosecutions,* edited by Sally M. Edwards, Terry D. Edwards, and Charles B. Fields. New York: Garland Publishing.

———. (1998a). "Evolving toward a Specialization of Environmental Crime Prosecution at the County Level: Issues and Concerns of County Prosecutors within Local Environmental Task Forces." In *Environmental Crime: Enforcement, Policy and Social Responsibility,* edited by Mary Clifford. Gaithersburg, MD: Aspen Publishers.

———. (1998b). "Environmental Crime Research: Where We Have Been, Where We Can Go." In *Environmental Crime: Enforcement, Policy and Social Responsibility,* edited by Mary Clifford, Gaithersburg, MD: Aspen Publishers.

Rebovich, Donald, and Richard Nixon. (1994). *Environmental Crime Prosecution: A Comprehensive Analysis of District Attorneys' Efforts in this Emerging Area of Criminal Enforcement.* Washington, DC: U.S. Department of Justice, National Institute of Justice.

Situ, Yi, and David Emmons. (2000). *Environmental Crime: The Criminal Justice System's Role in Protecting the Environment.* Thousand Oaks, CA: Sage Publications.

U.S. Environmental Protection Agency. (1990). *Reducing Risk: Setting Priorities and Strategies for Environmental Protection.* Washington, DC: U. S. Environmental Protection Agency.

———. (1992). *Environmental Equity: Reducing Risk for All Communities.* Washington, DC: U. S. Environmental Protection Agency.

———. (1999). *Fiscal Year Summary of Litigation Accomplishments: Environmental and Natural Resources Division.* Washington, DC: U.S. Environmental Protection Agency.

▼ ENVIRONMENTAL DESIGN

Planners, architects, and criminologists are collaborating to prevent crime though the appropriate design of neighborhoods and buildings. The built environment often inadvertently offers opportunities for criminal behavior. Many of these opportunities can be "designed out."

The rational choice perspective on crime treats the criminal as a rational being who chooses whether to commit a crime. Economists were major contributors to the development of this concept. Behavior is assumed to be rational, and choices are made based on an individual's perception of opportunities, costs, and benefits. Factors encouraging criminal activity include the ease of carrying out the crime, the chances of detection, the presence of an escape route, and the absence of witnesses. The rational offender perspective states that crimes are most likely to occur when a potential offender, faced with a crime target, believes that the chances of detection, identification, and apprehension are low.

Situational crime prevention focuses on removing or minimizing the opportunities available for crime. The environment, rather than the criminal, is the focus of attention. Situational crime prevention is defined by Clarke as comprising "opportunity reducing measures that (1) are directed at highly specific forms of crime, (2) involve the management, design or manipulation of the immediate environment in as systematic and permanent way as possible, (3) make crime more difficult and risky, or less rewarding and excusable" (Clarke 1997: 4). The aim of crime prevention through environmental design (CPTED) programs is to reduce both crime and the fear of crime.

ORIGINS

In response to the shortage of housing following World War II, many housing projects were erected in the United States and Europe. Architect Le Corbusier's (1887–1965) "Radiant City" concept of towers surrounded by park land was a source of inspiration for many of the designs. Unfortunately, the tower blocks proved to be utterly unsuitable for housing families, particularly poor families. Many buildings rapidly degenerated under an onslaught of vandalism, garbage, and crime. Hundreds of these tower blocks have since been torn down, including one of the most infamous complexes, the Pruitt-Igoe housing project in St. Louis, which was demolished a decade after construction.

To make room for these tower blocks, decaying urban neighborhoods had frequently been razed. The old neighborhoods, though physically decaying, had contained vibrant communities and businesses that were destroyed by slum clearance. While many of the inhabitants moved to the new apartments, the communities rarely survived. Although the apartment interiors were usually superior to the inhabitants' previous accommodations, the communal areas deteriorated disastrously, becoming dangerous and unattractive and earning the label of "vertical slums."

In 1961, Jane Jacobs, a writer with no formal experience in planning, published a book, *The Death and Life of Great American Cities*, based on her experiences of living in New York's Greenwich Village. This work contained no empirical research, yet it became one of the most influential books on city planning of the century. Jacobs condemned the urban renewal megaprojects popular during the postwar period. She advocated mixed-use urban neighborhoods, arguing that many eyes watching the street deterred criminal activity.

A decade later, Oscar Newman published his theory of "defensible space." Newman is an architect who specializes in designing and redesigning low-income housing with the aim of reducing criminal and antisocial activities. His concept of defensible space was first published in 1971 and amended in later works. Defensible space "is about the reassignment of areas and of responsibilities—the demarcation of new spheres of influence" (Newman 1996: 3). Instead of being communal, spaces should be clearly demarcated as belonging to an individual dwelling, thus encouraging territorial behavior. Intruders would be less likely to enter the space, and if they did enter, they would be noticed and challenged. Small buildings with a minimum of shared areas and shared entry points are considered by Newman to be more defensible than large anonymous blocks. Newman advocates the use of design to maximize the natural surveillance of public and semipublic areas by residents. Outdoor space, such as gardens and entryways, should be overlooked by windows, and not hidden from the view of passing pedestrians and motorists.

Newman has used his defensible space concept in designing and redesigning a number of federally funded housing projects. For one low-income housing project in Yonkers, New York, Newman scattered small groups of two-story row houses, each with its own front- and backyard, throughout a middle-income community of privately owned, mainly single family houses. The design was similar to that of private housing developments, and it included no public outdoor or indoor spaces and no communal garbage areas.

The phrase "Crime Prevention Through Environmental Design" (CPTED) was coined by behavioral criminologist C. Ray Jeffery. Jeffery was influenced by the work of the physiological psychologist B. F. Skinner, and he applied Skinner's theories to criminology. Jeffery described criminal behavior as involving four elements: reinforcement available from the criminal act, risk, the individual's past conditioning, and opportunity. He stressed that criminal behavior was *the* problem, not just a symptom of other problems, such as poverty.

During the early 1980s in Britain, Alice Coleman surveyed over 4,000 apartment blocks and 4,000 houses, identifying fifteen design variables affecting antisocial behavior. Antisocial behavior was assessed indirectly by measuring the number of children in care and the presence of litter, graffiti, urine, feces, and vandalism. Building height and the number of dwellings per building entrance were positively correlated with antisocial behavior levels. Design features that encouraged passive surveillance were associated with lower levels of antisocial behavior. Outdoor space that was assigned to specific adjacent dwelling units was associated with lower levels of antisocial behavior than communal outdoor space. Coleman criticized the planning profession's attempts at what she called "utopian" housing projects. She argued that the most successful British housing style, the semi-detached house with its own private fenced rear and front gardens, which evolved independently of planners and government programs, was the best prototype for future housing developments. Coleman echoes Jacobs in her condemnation of the massive institutionalized public housing projects common in the post-World War II decades.

CPTED TODAY

The term *CPTED* is now used to describe a broad range of programs that use design as an aid to reducing crime and fear of crime. It involves examining the creation and use of space, land use, and the position and architecture of buildings, including such factors as lighting, access, and landscaping. A widely used definition states that CPTED is "the proper design and effective use of the built environment [that] can lead to a reduction in the fear and incidence of crime, and an improvement in the quality of life" (Crow 1991: 1). There are different interpretations of what exactly constitutes CPTED, with some practitioners relying on design alone, and others including active and organizational security controls such as guards, cameras, locks, and other "target hardening devices." Target hardening devices are anti-theft devices, such as locks on car steering wheels, shutters on windows, and locks on doors.

Crowe (1991) suggests three overlapping strategies for CPTED projects:

1. Natural access control. These are design devices that restrict entry to authorized users. Reducing the number of entrances, particularly those that can serve intruders as shortcuts through the property, is a common natural access control method. Demolishing aboveground walkways connecting apartment buildings in Britain, thus restricting entry to ground-level entrances, has improved access control and reduced vandalism and other criminal activity.

2. Natural surveillance. Design features that allow natural surveillance include windows, unrestricted sight lines, lighting, and non-obstructive landscaping. Glass walls in stairwells, unobstructed views into parks, and windows (rather than blank walls overlooking sidewalks) all enable natural surveillance to take place. On the other hand, "entrapment spots," such as dead end corridors and unlocked storage areas, offer opportunities for criminal activity to take place unobserved. Bathrooms and laundry rooms hidden away in basements are less secure than those located adjacent to well-trafficked areas, such as beside the main entrance to the building.

3. Territorial reinforcement. Territorial reinforcement distinguishes between private, semiprivate, and public areas. Such reinforcement can be accomplished with landscaping, gate posts, changes in ground levels, different-colored walls, fences, or variations in the pavement treatment. Maintenance within the territory, such as removing litter and graffiti, cutting grass, and generally taking care of the appearance of the space, indicates that the area is under the control of the owner. In their influential "Broken Windows" article (1982), Wilson and Kelling discussed the relationship between disorder and crime, observing that removing disorder from public areas reduced fear of crime.

In *Physical Environment and Crime* (1996), Taylor and Harrell outlined a classification scheme for CPTED projects, based on four theoretical perspectives. One perspective addresses housing design and block layout, another looks at land use and circulation patterns, the third utilizes territorial features, and the last is concerned with controlling physical deterioration. The authors concluded that integrating these four perspectives might lead to a more powerful understanding of the relationship between crime and design.

SPECIFIC EXAMPLES OF CPTED

There has been much discussion regarding the relationship between land use mix and crime. Retaliating against postwar urban planners segregation of urban functions, Jane Jacobs advocated mixing residential, commercial, and industrial premises together, thus increasing the activity at all times within the area. Areas that are dedicated to a single use, such as commuter parking lots, offices, or residences, can be attractive locations for criminals, because they are deserted for long periods of time. Research carried out in the 1980s and 1990s has not supported Jacobs's hypothesis. Taylor and Harrell, citing numerous reports, conclude that "residents living on blocks with higher levels of nonresidential land use are more concerned for their personal safety and less likely to intervene if they see something suspicious; they experience higher victimization rates and call the police more often" (Taylor and Harrell 1996: 13). At a local level, providing "activity generators" within former single use areas is quite popular. Activity generators attract legitimate users. Examples include locating recycling collection points in parking lots, cafes in alleys or courtyards, and playgrounds and chess tables in parks.

Street Closures

Allowing vehicular traffic to travel easily through and away from an area encourages crime within the area by providing easy escape routes. Some communities have closed streets in order to reduce through traffic. Newman used this approach to create mini-neighborhoods in the residential area of Five Oaks in Dayton, Ohio (see Figure 1). Gates were erected turning the grid pattern of the streets into a series of deadends. Within a year, through traffic was reduced by 67 percent, traffic accidents by 40 percent; overall crime dropped by 26 percent, and violent crime by 50 percent. In Dayton as a whole, crime dropped 1 percent during the same period. Five Oaks house values increased 15 percent versus 4 percent in the region (Newman 1966: 55).

In Miami Shores, Florida, streets were closed using soil barricades planted with low shrubs and trees. Larceny in Miami Shores decreased after the street closures, and other crime rates did not increase appreciably in the years immediately following the project. Outside the area, crime rates increased at a greater rate, both in Miami as a whole and in a demographically similar Miami neighborhood (Atlas and LeBlanc 1994: 14–15).

In Los Angeles, traffic barriers were used to block automobile access to a ten-block hot spot for gang-on-gang homicide and assault. Violent crime was reduced during the two-year program and was not displaced to adjacent neighborhoods (Lasley 1998: 2, 4).

Street closures alone may not be responsible for crime rate changes. One aim of street closing is to encourage a strong sense of community among the residents. Successful implementation of the projects involves a lot of community involvement. The social and organizational changes involved with implementing a CPTED program may influence the crime rate regardless of the actual design changes. Street closure programs are controversial, and they have been labeled by some racist, elitist, and undemocratic. In their most extreme form, they are essentially gated communities.

Convenience Stores.

Gainesville, Florida, adopted an ordinance in 1986 requiring convenience stores to improve their security in specific ways. These included improving visibility from outside by removing signs and posters from windows, locating the cash register so that it was visible from the street, ensuring bright and even parking lot lighting, installing a security camera, and training employees. A later ordinance required two clerks to be present if the store was open between 8:00 P.M. and 4:00 A.M. Robberies were reduced by 64 percent, and the ordinances served as models for Florida's Convenience Business Security Act (Zahm 1997: 58).

CIVIL LIABILITY

In premises liability cases involving crimes, victims sue the managers and owners of crime locations, arguing that security lapses allowed the crime to occur. Courts are using the "totality of circumstances" test to determine whether deficiencies in security measures were a substantial contributing factor to the occurrence of the crime, and whether the security measures were generally below standards for that particular industry. Design is usually just one of several factors that lead to the crime. Cases that have been decided in the plaintiff's favor have arisen from crimes in apartment buildings, shopping malls, and convenience stores. In one case, brought by the father of a clerk fatally shot during a convenience store robbery, the criminals acknowledged that the store design influenced their target choice (Gordon and Brill 1996: 4).

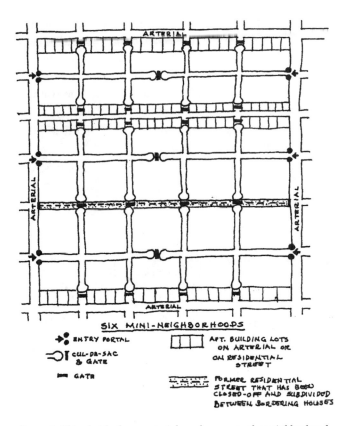

Figure 1. This sketch shows arterials and access to the neighborhood of Five Oaks in Dayton, Ohio. The plan is designed to limit through traffic flow into the neighborhood and thereby to reduce crime.
Source: Newman, Oscar. (1996). *Creating Defensible Space.* Washington, D.C.: U.S. Department of Housing and Urban Development, p. 45.

Some local jurisdictions have included aspects of CPTED in their building codes. Some require the police department to approve plans before building commences. This is similar to the common requirement that prior to building, the fire department approve fire safety features.

CPTED: AN IMPORTANT TOOL

Criticisms of CPTED include charges that CPTED projects reduce crime in the short term but have little or no long-term effect. Some critics object to designs aimed at making people feel safer while not addressing the underlying social and economic causes of crime. Others claim CPTED and defensible space theories are overly deterministic. Another fear is that crime is simply displaced from one community to the next. More empirical research is needed to clarify the role design can play in preventing crime.

The rationale behind CPTED is a belief that given the right environmental cues, people will be more inclined to behave in a civil and socially responsible manner. CPTED is being used increasingly both in new projects and in retrofitting older buildings and spaces. CPTED concepts have been used to design safer car parks, shopping malls, housing projects, schools, and convenience stores. CPTED is not the ultimate solution to crime, but it is an important tool that may be effectively used as part of a comprehensive crime prevention program.

—*Ellen Sexton*

See also BROKEN WINDOWS THEORY; GATED COMMUNITIES; PUBLIC HOUSING

Further Reading

Atlas, Randall, and William G. LeBlanc. (1994). "Environmental Barriers to Crime: Street Closures and Barricades in Miami Shores Did as Much for Community Cohesion as for Crime Reduction." *Ergonomics in Design* (October): 9–16.

Clarke, Ronald V. (1997). *Situational Crime Prevention: Successful Case Studies*. 2d ed. Guilderland, NY: Harrow and Heston.

Coleman, Alice. (1985). *Utopia on Trial: Vision and Reality in Planned Housing*. London: Hilary Shipman.

Crowe, Tim. (1991). *Crime Prevention through Environmental Design: Applications of Architectural Design and Space Management Concepts*. Boston: Butterworth-Heinemann.

Ekblom, Paul. (1995). "Less Crime, by Design." *Annals of the American Academy of Political and Social Science* 539: 114–129.

Gordon, Corey L., and William Brill. (1996). *The Expanding Role of Crime Prevention through Environmental Design in Premises Liability*. Washington, DC: U.S. Department of Justice, Office of Justice Programs, National Institute of Justice.

Jacobs, Jane. (1961). *The Death and Life of Great American Cities*. New York: Random House.

Jeffery, C. Ray. (1971). *Crime Prevention through Environmental Design*. Beverly Hills, CA: Sage Publications.

Lasley, James. (1998). *"Designing Out" Gang Homicides and Street Assaults*. Washington, DC: U.S. Department of Justice, Office of Justice Programs, National Institute of Justice.

Newman, Oscar. (1972). *Defensible Space*. New York: Macmillan.

———. (1996). *Creating Defensible Space*. Washington, DC: U.S. Department of Housing and Urban Development, Office of Policy Development and Research.

Rosenbaum, Dennis P., Arthur J. Lurigio, and Robert C. Davies. (1998). *The Prevention of Crime: Social and Situational Strategies*. Albany, NY: West/Wadsworth.

Taylor, Ralph B., and Adele V. Harrell. (1996). *Physical Environment and Crime*. Washington, DC: U.S. Department of Justice, Office of Justice Programs, National Institute of Justice.

Wekerle, Gerda R., and Carolyn Whitzman, (1995). *Safe Cities: Guidelines for Planning, Design and Management*. New York: Von Nostrand Reinhold.

Wilson, James Q., and George Kelling. (1982). "Broken Windows." *Atlantic Monthly* 249, 3: 29–38. http://www.theatlantic.com/politics/crime/windows.htm

Zahm, Diane (1997). *Designing Safer Communities: A Crime Prevention through Design Handbook*. Washington, DC: National Crime Prevention Council.

▼ ETHICS

Ethics refers to the normative standards by which human beings relate to each other and the world. Ethics is distinguished, on the one hand, from etiquette and protocol, which focus on social expectations, and on the other from law and regulation, which focus on jurisdictionally prescribed behavioral demands usually backed by formal sanction. Although distinguished from these and other normative activities (e.g., politics, religion), ethics is not detached from them. Rather, ethics and morality are generally accorded priority in the structuring and assessment of human conduct; that is, ethical considerations are invoked in the formation and assessment of customary, legal, and political demands, rather than vice versa.

CONCEPTS

There are several categories of basic ethical concepts. For example, there are values (e.g., happiness, enlightenment), which are closely tied to moral significance. Conduct that contributes to or detracts from the realization of these values is characterized as either good or bad. Associated with specific values are virtues (e.g., courage, integrity, justice), as well as types of conduct that are considered morally wrong (e.g., murder, lying). It is impossible to give an account of these without reference to some specific—and perhaps controversial—moral framework (consider, for example, blasphemy). The situation is also complicated by the fact that some concepts apply in more than one setting—that is, what is murder morally may not be murder legally. Morality is also characterized by various principles—broadly speaking, statements of acts that should be done or avoided (e.g., Thou shall not kill). Obligations associated with rules are either social (killing is wrong) or personal (one ought to keep one's promises). Finally, for present purposes, certain values are designated as human rights—fundamental and inviolate privileges that individuals possess by virtue of their humanity (life, liberty, etc.). Linked with these are controversies over the status of duties regarding such things as animals and the environment.

THEORY

Although some ethical theories view morality as relative, most propose universally acceptable standards for the ways in which people should conduct themselves. There is a distinction to be drawn, however, between impersonal and situational ethics—that is, between standards that hold generally and those that are dependent on a particular relationship or association. A central problem for post-Enlightenment ethical theory has been to accommodate both universal and particular demands.

The classic division in moral theory is between deontology and consequentialism. Broadly speaking, deontological theories seek to locate the rightness or wrongness of acts in features that are intrinsic to them, whereas consequentialist theories assess acts by their impact on some core value such as happiness or well-being. Major deontological theories have been propounded by Thomas Aquinas (natural law theory), Immanuel Kant (the categorical imperative), and Bishop Butler (the deliverances of conscience); consequentialist views have been defended by the utilitarians, notably Jeremy Bentham and John Stuart Mill. Contractarian or conventionalist theories, which see ethics as a product of social agreement, and virtue theories (Aristotle), which focus on the development of character, offer alternative approaches.

PRACTICAL AND PROFESSIONAL ETHICS

Ethical decision making does not always occur as an encounter between two strangers. It also occurs in the context of role relationships—parent and child, judge and defendant, doctor and patient, and so forth. There is considerable debate about whether such relationships entitle one party to act in ways that would otherwise be prohibited to an individual. That is, a doctor may invade one's privacy in ways that others may not, and a police officer may use force that would be improper if used by others; the question is whether such distinctions reflect a morality distinct from common morality. Perhaps these professional entitlements are best viewed as ultimately answerable to the demands of ordinary morality; that is, the conduct must be necessary to the fulfillment of a duty imposed by a role essential to a morally justifiable institution. So, for example, to be ethical, a particular use of police force must be necessary to enforce a statute that serves some legitimate government purpose.

CRIMINAL JUSTICE ETHICS

Criminal justice ethics embraces a range of interrelated governmental functions generated by the need to secure the rights of citizens against encroachment by others. Among its foundational concerns are issues in legislative ethics relating to the establishment of criminal justice policies. Although its main foci are police, judicial, and correctional ethics, criminal justice ethics also incorporates legal and prosecutorial ethics, and it extends to ancillary areas such as witness conduct and forensic science.

Legislative issues that have important implications for criminal justice ethics include the allocation of resources (such as those of various criminal justice agencies, which have implications for the incidence of crime), policies regarding vice and other social practices that a legislature might wish to discourage, and sentencing policies (e.g., capital punishment, mandatory sentencing, hate crimes, prison privatization).

Police ethics encompasses questions concerning the ethics *of* policing as well as ethics *within* policing; that is, it may include discussion of the foundations of police authority as well as questions concerning the legitimate exercise of police authority. Within the latter, it may contemplate the shape of the police role as well as constraints that need to be observed in its exercise. In liberal democratic theory, police authority is generally construed as a branch of governmental authority, derived from the consent of the governed to institutional arrangements deemed essential to the preservation and exercise of fundamental human rights. Within that understanding, broader and narrower conceptions of the police role vie for acceptance—narrower understandings focusing on the crime-fighting role, broader understandings favoring a primarily social service or peacekeeping role (within which crime fighting is seen as a partial expression).

Apart from debates about the institutional role of the police, the central problems of police ethics have generally concerned tactics—the legitimate use of deception and force—although more general questions about the limits of discretion, the boundaries of privacy, the limits of solidarity, and the ways in which police organizations manage themselves also fall within its purview. Many of the ethical problems specific to police are addressed (albeit only generally) in the codes of ethics promulgated by many police organizations (Kleinig and Zhang 1993); codes of ethics, however, do not absolve those to whom they apply from exercising the personal judgment that lies at the heart of ethical decision making.

For historical reasons (i.e., the fact that most

criminal justice programs have been directed to the institutional needs of policing and corrections), much that has been written about criminal justice ethics has not specifically addressed the judiciary. Instead, judicial ethics has been addressed within legal ethics, because it is from the ranks of lawyers that judges are generally drawn. Yet the courts are an integral part of the criminal justice system, and ethical questions concerning the various exercises of prosecutorial and judicial discretion are of considerable importance.

Correctional ethics has traditionally been preoccupied with punishment theory—initially by the question "What is the appropriate response to wrongdoing?" but then, usually, with attempts to justify a punitive response by reference to its effect (e.g., deterrence, rehabilitation, incapacitation). A limiting but practically important debate has centered on the use of capital punishment—a debate that has extended beyond the confines of punishment theory to questions about racism, the sanctity of life, and decision making under conditions of uncertainty.

Frequently, discussions in correctional ethics have assumed that punishment will take the form of a fine or imprisonment. Yet a number of writers recently have challenged the view that wrongdoing warrants retribution, arguing instead that the moral rupture constituted by crime is better dealt with in restorative ways, in which the goal is a reconciliation of the victim and society with the offender. Although some form of reparation is not excluded, the goal is healing. At the heart of such debates reside questions about the nature of justice and the shape of a decent society.

To those for whom punishment—particularly imprisonment—is seen as a legitimate moral option, correctional ethics primarily encompasses the relationship between prison officers and inmates, but it may also consider relations among officers, staff, and prison administration, and, even more remotely, relations between prison administrators, legislators, and the communities they serve. Particular prison practices—such as solitary confinement, strip searches, visitation rules—also raise important ethical questions, too rarely addressed because of an overarching and sometimes exaggerated concern with security.

Beyond these questions, additional concerns arise at other points in the criminal justice system—over the use of expert witnesses, the role of jurors and the practice of jury nullification, and the conduct of forensic science laboratories. Indeed, a comprehensive criminal justice ethic will consider relevant any systemic decision that has implications for human well-being—whether it involves the use of deadly force, the institution of boot camps, the setting of entry requirements and promotional polices for personnel, the role of health care professionals within prison settings, or the determination of appeal procedures for staff and offenders. Although all these questions, like any of the other questions in criminal justice ethics, impinge on matters of law, politics, religion, and economics, keeping their ethical dimensions in the foreground is central to the maintenance of a civilized society.

SUMMARY

The centrality of ethics to the way in which individuals relate to one another makes it inherently controversial. In the context of criminal justice, where institutional responses to the breakdown of those relations are considered, the problems are rendered doubly difficult as civilized responses must accommodate natural sentiments of retaliation.

—John Kleinig

See also BUDDHISM; CAPITAL PUNISHMENT; CHRISTIANITY; CIVIL LAW LEGAL TRADITIONS; COMMON LAW LEGAL TRADITIONS; DAOISM; DEVIANCE; HINDUISM; ISLAM; JUDAISM; MERCY; MORAL PANIC; SHINTO; SOCIALIST LEGAL TRADITIONS; VENGEANCE

Further Reading

Aquinas, Thomas. ([1265-1273]1993). *Treatise on Law (Summa Theologica, QQ 90-97)*. Notre Dame, IN: University of Notre Dame Press.

Aristotle. (1962). *Nicomachean Ethics*. Indianapolis, IN: Bobbs-Merrill.

Bentham, Jeremy. (1960). *An Introduction to the Principles of Morals and Legislation*. Oxford: Basil Blackwell.

Butler, Joseph. (1900). *The Works of Bishop Butler*. London: Macmillan.

Institute for Criminal Justice Ethics. http:www.lib.jjay.cuny.edu/cje/html/sitesofinterest.html

Kleinig, John. (1996). *The Ethics of Policing*. Cambridge, UK: Cambridge University Press.

Kleinig, John, and Yurong Zhang. (1993). *Professional Law Enforcement Codes: A Documentary Collection*. Westport, CT: Greenwood Press.

Luban, David. (1988). *Lawyers and Justice: An Ethical Study*. Princeton, NJ: Princeton University Press.

Mill, John Stuart. (1962). *Utilitarianism*. London: Collins/Fontana.

Paton, H. J. (1963). *The Moral Law: Kant's Groundwork of the Metaphysic of Morals*. New York: Barnes and Noble.

Rachels, James. (1999). *The Elements of Moral Philosophy*. New York: McGraw-Hill.

▼ ETHNICITY AND RACE

America is a nation of immigrants, with a population composed of a wide diversity of people with different ethnic, racial, and national backgrounds. Some groups have been in this country for centuries, while others have lived in the United States for only two or three generations, and some groups have just recently arrived. Many came voluntarily; others came by force. Even for those who have lived in the United States for many generations, country of origin and ethnic background remain important sources of identity. In America, crimes of foreign-born and recent immigrants have always been an issue. Historically, the most recent immigrants have tended to be singled out as more criminal than natives. Thus, in the early part of the twentieth century, when immigration into the United States was dominated by Europeans, the criminality of white ethnic immigrants (in particular the Italians and the Irish) was a major concern.

In the middle of the twentieth century, interest in crimes committed by people of color (in particular, blacks) began to overshadow the focus on white ethnic criminality. More recently, the rapid growth in the Hispanic population in the United States has pushed the criminality of Hispanics into the public limelight. Over the last century, virtually any group whose members were visibly different from and less powerful than the dominant white Anglo-Saxon Protestants (WASPs) has been viewed as playing a key role in the American crime picture. This entry focuses on what is currently known about crime and criminal justice among four key minority groups in the United States: (1) blacks, (2) Hispanics, (3) American Indians, and (4) Asian Americans.

RACE, ETHNICITY, AND CRIME IN THE UNITED STATES

"In the social sense, race is a reality; in the scientific sense, it is not," according to anthropologist Kenneth Kennedy (quoted in Wheeler 1995: A15). He made this statement when discussing the growing number of American scholars who reject the concepts of race and racial classifications as senseless and objectionable. The American Anthropological Association has formally decided that differentiation of people into biologically defined races is senseless and unscientific. Yet, although race is no longer viewed as a bona fide scientific concept, race continues to have a crucial social meaning; it is still seen as an important way of differentiating among people. The government thinks in racial categories with regard to registration (driver's licenses, birth certificates, education, welfare, crime statistics), and so does the American public. Indeed, it is not an exaggeration to say that America remains obsessed by race.

In the United States, race influences human behavior and attitudes, family life, income, education, politics, and crime. Racism, ideas about superiority and equality, and the national preoccupation with race divides the United States into two parts, as suggested by the title of a popular book: *Two Nations, Black and White, Separate, Hostile, Unequal* (Hacker 1992). Although blacks are currently America's largest racial minority group, the official and unofficial racial differentiation in the United States goes beyond the simple black/white division. The 2000 U.S. Census used six racial categories: (1) American Indian or Alaska Native; (2) Black (or African American); (3) Asian; (4) Native Hawaiian or Other Pacific Islander; (5) White; and (6) Some Other Race. These six official racial categories are grossly oversimplified: Each of these consists of a large number of subgroups with often widely divergent national, ethnic, or racial backgrounds. Although in popular language, *race* and *ethnicity* are often used interchangeably, they have different meanings; *ethnicity* refers to a shared culture (language, religion, custom), whereas *race* implies a presumed common genetic heritage (based on visible physical characteristics such as skin color). Again oversimplifying for the purposes of registration, the U.S. Census uses two categories for ethnicity: "Hispanic or Latino," and "Not Hispanic or Latino." Hispanics and Latinos may be of any race. Although the scientific validity of official racial and ethnic categories is questionable, most of the research and theorizing on race and ethnicity and crime in the United States does focus on the "big four": blacks, Hispanics, American Indians, and Asian Americans. For lack of a better alternative, the following discussion will do the same.

BLACKS AND CRIME

According to the 2000 U.S. Census, blacks remain the largest minority group in the United States, with a population of about 35 million in 2000, up from 30 million in 1990. In American society, public concerns with crime and fears of personal victimization are primarily directed towards racial minorities, in particular blacks.

Ethnicity and Crime Reporting

It is common in many nations for ethnic minorities to have a higher official crime rate than the majority population. Such reports are always open to criticism, and, as the extract below shows, criminologists have long known that the link between ethnicity and crime is very complex.

The extent to which Mexicans violate our laws appears to be magnified unduly not only by the northeastern Colorado community but even by the officers who handle the Mexican offenders. Examination of the books of one officer who vigorously denounced the criminal quality of Mexicans showed only 40 per cent of the proportion of Mexican arrests which he said emphatically his records would show. In another country the percentage shown by the records was only 16 per cent of the a priori asserted proportion of cases. When this was ascertained the officer insisted that many non-Mexican entries should be deducted before arriving at the true proportion of Mexican cases. Even when this was done and all arrests of traffic law violators, insane persons, runaways, persons held for investigation or arrested for other than county officers were deducted, the proportion of Mexican cases proved to be only 34 per cent of the number originally stated by the officer to be Mexicans.

Both the sugar company and the more stable elements in the Mexican population are sensitive to criticisms of disorderly conduct by the Mexicans. In its labor booklet the company devotes more than a page to a statement of the laws with which Mexicans are most likely to get into difficulty in order that they may be fully informed concerning them. The company advises the laborers to observe these laws not only that they may avoid punishment but also that they may establish for themselves a good reputation in the community.

The Mexicans themselves exhibit concern over the attacks upon them as law violators. Spanish Americans attribute the social pressure of the American community against them to the disorderly conduct of the Mexicans from old Mexico. The more settled old Mexico Mexicans lay the blame for the disturbances which bring them, together with the Spanish Americans, into disrepute on the migratories who come in for the season only. Members of the company colonies pride themselves on their preservation of order and on the fact that it has been very rarely necessary to call the police or sheriff to preserve order among them. In order to overcome the criticism and discrimination based in part upon their reputation for lawlessness, the Mexicans in Longmont staged in 1927 a particularly elaborate celebration of their national holiday, the 16th of September. At the foot of the handbill advertising the program a conspicuous note was appended which, translated, reads as follows:

> "NOTE:–our compatriots are earnestly requested to preserve the best possible order, for they well know that the object of this celebration in Longmont is to alter the opinion which is held of the Mexicans, and for that reason we hope that they will conduct themselves in the best manner possible."

Source: *Report on Crime and the Foreign Born.* (1931). Washington, D.C.: Government Printing Office, National Commission on Law Observance and Enforcement. pp. 216–217.

Perceptions of blacks in the United States have always included an assumption of criminality (Myers 1995: 146). American scholars have engaged in a lengthy history of discussions about the crime rates for blacks versus those for whites. This focus is not without foundation. To a large extent, America's street crime problem is a black problem. In every stage of the criminal justice system—from arrest through incarceration—blacks are present in numbers greatly out of proportion to their presence in the population. In 1999, about one-third of those arrested for aggravated assault (34.8 percent) and forcible rape (36.2 percent) were black. Over half of the arrests for homicide (51.8 percent) and robbery (54.4 percent) in 1999 involved a black suspect. Not only are blacks more likely than whites to be arrested, they are also more likely to become victims of crime. According to the National Crime Victimization Survey, blacks report a higher level of personal victimization than whites (Rennison 2000: 6). It is a well-established fact that street criminals tend to victimize those in their immediate environment. Because the United States remains in many ways a racially segregated society, it is not surprising that—as a general rule—blacks victimize blacks, and whites victimize whites. Crime victim surveys and police homicide reports support the conclusion that street crime tends to be intraracial.

Contrary to common belief, by far the largest proportion of street crime is committed not by blacks but by whites—who, after all, remain numerically the largest population group in the United States. This is not to minimize the crime problem among blacks: Serious violent crime remains a pressing and immediate public health threat for the black community. Compared to other Western societies, America has a high level of criminal violence, but not everybody is affected by this violence in the same manner. Criminal violence is not evenly distributed among racial, ethnic, and social class lines. Violence (e.g., slavery and lynchings) has historically affected blacks disproportionately. In the United States, blacks have always been more likely to be murdered than whites. However, a distinct change has taken place in the nature and extent of lethal violence among blacks over the last few decades. An increasing polarization of America's black population has taken place: a growing, well-to-do black middle class, separated from an expanding number of poor, "underclass" blacks whose homes tend to be clustered in the slum neighborhoods of the larger American cities. It is in America's slum areas that crime has grown to be a tremendous problem, with the odds of being a homicide victim about seven times higher for blacks than for whites.

With the exploding drug-trafficking business in the mid-1980s, gun-related lethal violence started to grow disproportionately among black inner-city youth. The current drop in serious violent crime in the United States is primarily the result of the decline in violence among young, urban male blacks (Blumstein 2000: 34–35).

A variety of explanations compete to account for the recent decline in urban violence among young African Americans: changed policing practices, more use of prison, successful community organization efforts, and/or changes in the drug markets. Recent declines in violence notwithstanding, the level of violent crime among young blacks remains at an unacceptably high level in today's inner cities. Decades ago, discussion of youth gangs focused on white youth organized along ethnic lines (Irish, Polish, Italian). Interest in these white ethnic gangs has diminished, replaced by a preoccupation with black gangs. Currently, about one-third of the membership of the more than 26,000 gangs identified in the National Youth Gang Survey is black, compared to 47 percent Hispanic and 13 percent white (Egley 2000: 1).

In 1997, about 9 percent of black adults in the United States were under correctional supervision, compared to 2 percent of white adults (Beck et al. 2000: 1). When focusing on the most at-risk group of young males, the numbers become even more staggering: "On an average day in America, 1 out of 3 African American men aged 20 to 29 was either in prison or jail, on probation or parole" (Donziger 1996: 105). The United States, a country that already has a high incarceration rate relative to other industrialized nations, locks up black men at a rate nine times that of white men—1,743 blacks versus 198 whites per 100,000 (Beck et al. 2000: 2). On an average day, blacks make up nearly 50 percent of those in prison. In 1999, 1,514 blacks were under sentence of death, as compared to 1,948 whites (Snell 2000: 1). There has historically been an overrepresentation of blacks in prison, but the differences have grown in recent decades. The incarceration rates for blacks rose 63 percent between 1990 and 1997, compared to an increase of 36 percent for whites, and 35 percent for Hispanics (Beck et al. 2000: 2). It is primarily the national War on Drugs that is responsible for the increase in the incarceration of blacks. The skyrocketing of drug-related arrests of blacks is a result of police oversurveillance of the inner-city African American area in the name of the War on Drugs. In 1998, more than half of all sentenced prisoners for drug offenses under state jurisdiction were black—more than four times their proportion in the population.

There is no doubt that African Americans are much more likely to be arrested, prosecuted, convicted, sent to jail, and sentenced to the death penalty than their white counterparts. Is this because of a greater involvement in crime, or because of antiblack bias in the criminal justice system? The answer is both. Researchers have concluded that much of the race difference in arrests for violence is due to greater involvement in offending on the part of blacks (Hawkins et al. 2000: 2). Research no longer supports the allegation of pervasive and systematic discriminatory treatment by police and the courts on the basis of race. The most obvious racial inequalities in the criminal justice system have been eliminated; however, it is not correct to claim that there is no racism in the system. After all, how could one expect a completely bias-free criminal justice system in a society that remains racist in many other areas? The relationship between the police and black citizens has always been wrought with conflict and accusations of racism. "Many minority communities in America feel both overpoliced and underprotected" (Donziger 1996: 160). Things are improving, however. Early studies concluded that police officers were more likely to shoot and use excessive force when dealing with blacks; more recent research indicates that the racial disparity in people shot and killed by police has declined. Police forces now take citizens' complaints about racial discrimination much more seriously than in the past.

While the police have historically ignored or downplayed such complaints, recent actions by the U.S. Department of Justice and several lawsuits filed by aggrieved citizens have led to greater police attention to these complaints. The improper use of race as a criterion for the police to stop people (i.e., "racial profiling") has recently come under close scrutiny by both researchers and the courts. Although most of the public focus tends to be on the police, there is ample evidence that antiblack racism continues to exist at virtually every juncture of the criminal justice system. Racial bias exists in both juvenile and adult courts in some jurisdictions, at least some of the time. Blacks and whites are also treated differently as suspects are processed through the justice system (Office of Juvenile Justice and Delinquency Prevention 1999: 3). Finally, death penalty research has consistently and thoroughly documented that this ultimate punishment is definitely not color-blind. To the contrary, a rather uniform pattern of discrimination based on the race of the victim has been found; offenders killing whites are more likely to be given the death penalty than those killing blacks. The lives of black victims simply have less value in the criminal justice system than do those of whites.

HISPANICS AND CRIME

In 2000, Latinos (or Hispanics) totaled around 34 million, a huge increase from 22.4 million in 1990. Like African Americans, Hispanics (who can be classified as belonging to different races) as a group are relatively powerless (politically, culturally, and economically); they have been (or are) seen as "different," often threatening, problematic, or deviant; they have been subject to discriminatory laws and regulations, prejudice, and negative stereotyping; they have been (or are) the focus of public fear and violence; and they have been (or are) the targets of political campaigns. On average, they are less educated, more likely to be unemployed, poorer, and less healthy than the non-Hispanic population. It should be noted that there are huge differences among the different Latino groups; some are wealthier and better educated than the rest of the United States (Cubans), whereas others rank at the bottom of the scale (Mexicans). People of Mexican

origin are numerically the largest Hispanic group; this is also the group that has attracted much of the public fear (related to the influx of undocumented aliens from Mexico) and allegations of crime.

It is difficult to know the exact amount of criminal involvement of Hispanics in the United States. Victim surveys show some slight differences between Hispanics and non-Hispanics. A large proportion of criminal victimization is intra-ethnic (i.e., Hispanics victimizing other Hispanics). Arrest statistics do not include information on ethnicity. Prison statistics do distinguish between Hispanic and non-Hispanic inmates, but there are large variations in classification procedures, as well as a large percentage of "unknowns," which make these statistics of questionable utility. In 1990, 10.4 percent of all Latino males were either on probation, on parole, or in prison. About 3.1 percent of Hispanic males age twenty-five to twenty-nine were in prison in 1999, compared to 1 percent of white males and 9.4 percent of non-Hispanic black males. Hispanic inmates are incarcerated disproportionately for drug-related offenses. In 1999, 325 Latinos were on death row (10 percent of inmates with a known ethnicity). Although there is not much research in that area, the studies that exist have shown that Hispanics are treated more severely than non-Hispanics by the police and courts, that they feel less safe, and that they do not trust the police. Language barriers handicap many Latino defendants, contributing to misunderstandings and reinforcing prejudice among police (Mann 1993: 103).

Hispanics figure prominently in the youth gang literature; life in the urban barrios has historically been associated with gangs. Since the 1980s, guns, drugs, and violence have become a more central feature of these gangs. According to the 1999 National Youth Gang Survey, almost half of the membership of the 26,000 youth gangs in the United States were identified as Latino. There is disagreement about the degree to which these street gangs are involved in drug trafficking. What is evident, however, is that organized crime has important ties to the Hispanic community in the United States, particularly with regard to drug trafficking. Latin American traffickers make a healthy profit by supplying American drug users with heroin, cocaine, and marijuana. Many Cuban nationals residing in the United States are involved in the illicit drug business (Abadinsky 2000: 241). Mexico produces a significant proportion of the heroin and marijuana consumed in the United States, which creates opportunities for profitable criminal involvement for Mexican

Americans. Next to Cubans and Mexicans, the Justice Department has identified about 3,000 Colombian drug trafficking groups operating in the United States (Lyman and Potter 2000: 310).

ASIAN AMERICANS

The term *Asian* refers to a mixture of racial, national, and cultural identities. The total population of Asians jumped to around 12 million in 2000, a dramatic rise from 7.3 million a decade earlier. This population group has been the subject of legal discrimination, police harassment, and hate crimes, both past and present. Some Asian American groups are doing extremely well, both socially and economically (e.g., the Japanese), whereas others (some Chinese, Filipinos) are barely able to survive economically. Nationally, Asians make up 1.5 percent of those arrested for crimes in 1999 (1.3 percent of those arrested for homicide), which is lower than would be expected given their presence in the general population. These arrest statistics should be approached with caution, because state-level statistics do provide a less favorable picture than national data. Asian Americans are concentrated in a few states (California, Washington, New York, and Nevada). In California, Asians and Pacific Islanders, mostly immigrants from Southeast Asia, China, and the Philippines, constitute 9 percent of the new admissions to the California Youth Authority (Donziger 1996: 104). Arrest data ignore important variations in criminality among the diverse Asian groups. For example, Japanese Americans have lower crime rates than Chinese Americans. Prior to 1965, crime rates within Chinese communities were low, but crime and violence among the Chinese have increased since then, partly because of the influx of young immigrants from Hong Kong (who have formed youth gangs), and partly because of the "extremely high unemployment rates, depressing poverty, and disheartening living and social circumstances" of the people living in Chinatowns (Takagi and Platt, as cited in Mann 1993: 97). Arrest statistics do not fully capture the involvement of Asian groups in organized crime. In the United States, both Chinese and Japanese organized criminals have long been active in drug trafficking, gambling, and prostitution. Since the mid-1980s, Asian organized crime has exerted much criminal influence in drug distribution in the United States, through members residing in the many Asian communities throughout the country (Lyman and Potter 2000: 320).

AMERICAN INDIANS

Although this population rose dramatically during the last decade, reaching a range of 2.5 million to 4.1 million (compared with 2 million in 1990), this remains the smallest racial group identified in the U.S. Census for 2000. Indians tend to be a loose residue of tribes, rather than a racial entity (Hacker 1992: 5). There is the problem of multiple jurisdictions: Tribal members are subject to the tribe, the state, and the federal government jurisdiction, depending on the type of crime, whether it happened on or off the reservation, and whether Indians or non-Indians were involved (Zatz et al. 1991: 101). Thus, multiple jurisdictions are often involved, making it difficult to obtain accurate statistics on criminal victimization and offending among Indians. There are a total of 135 tribal law enforcement agencies; in addition, the U.S. Bureau of Indian Affairs has 339 full-time officers authorized to make arrests and carry firearms (Greenfield and Smith 1999).

American Indians have a low life expectancy, as well as very high rates of illiteracy, unemployment, infant mortality, suicide, and alcoholism—factors that make this group very vulnerable. The most current profile of delinquency, crime, arrest, prosecution, and incarceration among Native Americans "paints an extremely grim picture" (Armstrong et al. 1996: 81). Crime is a major problem for American Indians. On any given day an estimated one in twenty-five American Indians eighteen years old and over is under the jurisdiction of the nation's criminal justice system. This is 2.4 times the per capita rate for whites and 9.3 times the per capita rate for Asians, but about half the rate for blacks. Discrimination and oversurveillance in Indian communities may be one of the reasons for the higher arrest and incarceration rates of American Indians (Mann 1993). Both male and female American Indians experience violent crime at higher rates than people of other races. For the years 1992 through 1996, the average annual rate of self-reported violent victimizations (sexual assault and rape, robberies, aggravated and simple assaults) among Indians was 124 per 1,000 residents ages twelve and older, compared to 61 violent victimizations per 1,000 blacks, 49 per 1,000 whites, and 29 per 1,000 Asians (Greenfield and Smith, 1999). Unlike blacks, whites, and Hispanics, American Indians are more likely to be victimized by someone of another race (seven out of ten violent victimizations are intra-racial according to victimization surveys). The homicide rate for American Indians is much higher on-reservation than off-reservation, which makes the official arrest statistics misleading. Homicide accounts for 3.2 percent of all Native American deaths in comparison to 1.1 percent of the larger American population (Armstrong et al., 1996: 81). Among Native Americans, alcohol use plays a large role in violent victimization, offending, and reasons for arrests. In the past, American Indian youth have had little involvement with street gangs, but recently there have been reports of the emergence of Indian youth gangs (Nielsen and Silverman, 1996).

SUMMARY

There has been a massive surge in immigration during the 1990s. The size of nonwhite racial groupings in the United States and the ethnic mix within them has increased. In the 2000 U.S. Census, almost one-third of the population labeled themselves minorities. The United States still has a white majority, but it is increasingly diverse. Experience shows that surges in immigration increase the likelihood of crimes motivated by racial hatred and xenophobia targeting minorities. Population changes are altering the racial/ethnic profile of violent and serious offenders, many of whom are involved in youth groupings and in gangs of Eastern European, Asian, Latin American, and Caribbean ancestry (Hawkins et al. 2000: 5). The members of these new population groups are visibly different from and less powerful than the dominant white Anglo-Saxon Protestants (WASPs). American history shows that any racial and ethnic group that lags seriously behind more established white Americans in education, income, quality of housing, life expectancy, health, and political power is likely to get involved in crime and criminal justice—as offender, as victim, or both. With the increasing ethnic diversity, organized crime groups operating internationally have growing opportunities to make profitable connections with diverse population groups residing in the United States. As long as economic hardship, inequality, and discrimination are unevenly distributed along ethnic and racial lines, crime will continue to be clustered in particular racial and ethnic groups.

—Ineke Haen Marshall

See also AMERICAN INDIANS AND ALASKA NATIVES; DISCRIMINATION IN THE CRIMINAL JUSTICE WORKPLACE; GANGS; RACE AND CORRECTIONS; RACE AND POLICING; RACE AND SENTENCING; RACE AND VIOLENCE; RACIAL PROFILING

Further Reading

Abadinsky, Howard. (2000). *Organized Crime.* Belmont, CA: Wadsworth.

Armstrong, T. L., M. H. Guilfoyle, and A. P. Melton. (1996). "Native American Delinquency: An Overview of Prevalence, Causes, and Correlates." In *Native Americans, Crime, and Justice,* edited by M. O. Nielsen and R. A. Silverman. Boulder, CO: Westview, 75–88.

Beck, Allen J. (2000). *Prisoners in 1999.* Washington DC: U.S. Government Printing Office, Bureau of Justice Statistics.

Beck, Allen J., Thomas P. Bonczar, Paula M. Ditton, Lauren E. Glaze, Caroline Wolf Harlow, Christopher J. Mumola, Tracy L. Snell, James J. Stephan, and Doris James Wilson. (2000). *Correctional Populations in the United States, 1997: Executive Summary.* Washington DC: U.S. Government Printing Office, Bureau of Justice Statistics.

Blumstein, Alfred. (2000). "Disaggregating the Violence Trends." In *The Crime Drop in America,* edited by Alfred Blumstein and Joel Wallman. Cambridge, UK: Cambridge University Press.

Donziger, Steven R., ed. (1996). *The Real War on Crime: The Report of the National Criminal Justice Commission.* New York: HarperCollins.

Egley, Arlen Jr. (2000). "Highlights of the 1999 National Youth Gang Survey." Fact Sheet (November, No. 20). Washington, DC: U.S. Department of Justice, Office of Juvenile Justice and Delinquency Prevention (OJJDP).

Greenfield, Lawrence A., and Steven K. Smith. (1999). *American Indians and Crime.* Washington, DC: U.S. Department of Justice, Bureau of Justice Statistics.

Hacker, Andrew. (1992). *Two Nations Black and White, Separate, Hostile, Unequal.* New York: Ballantine.

Hawkins, Darnell F. (1994). "Ethnicity: The Forgotten Dimension of American Social Control." In *Inequality, Crime and Social Control*, edited by George S. Bridges and Martha A. Myers. Boulder, CO: Westview, 99–116.

———, ed. (1995). *Ethnicity, Race, and Crime. Perspectives Across Time and Place.* Albany, NY: State University of New York Press.

Hawkins, Darnell F., John H. Laub, Janet L. Lauritsen., and Lynn Cothern. (2000). "Race, Ethnicity, and Serious and Violent Juvenile Offending." *OJJDP Juvenile Justice Bulletin* (June).

Healy, Joseph F. (1998). *Race, Ethnicity, Gender, and Class.* Thousand Oaks, CA: Pine Forge Press.

Lyman, Michael D., and Gary W. Potter. (2000). *Organized Crime.* Upper Saddle River, NJ: Prentice Hall.

Mann, Coramae Richey. (1993). *Unequal Justice: A Question of Color.* Bloomington: Indiana University Press.

Mann, Coramae Richey, and Marjorie S. Zatz. (1998). *Images of Color, Images of Crime.* Los Angeles, CA: Roxbury.

Marshall, Ineke Haen, ed. (1997). *Minorities, Migrants, and Crime. Diversity and Similarity Across Europe and the United States.* Thousand Oaks, CA: Sage Publications.

Mauer, Marc. (1999). *Race to Incarcerate.* New York: The New Press.

Myers, Martha A. (1995). "The New South's 'New' Black Criminal: Rape and Punishment in Georgia, 1870–1940." In *Ethnicity, Race, and Crime, Perspectives Across Time and Place,* edited by Darnell F. Hawkins. Albany, NY: State University of New York Press, 145–168.

Nielsen, Marianne O., and Robert A. Silverman, eds. (1996). *Native Americans, Crime, and Justice.* Boulder, CO: Westview Press.

Office of Juvenile Justice and Delinquency Prevention. (1999). "Minorities in the Juvenile Justice System." *OJJDP Juvenile Justice Bulletin* (December).

Parrillo, Vincent N. (1996). *Diversity in America.* Thousand Oaks, CA: Pine Forge Press.

Rennison, Marie. (2000). *Criminal Victimization 1999. Changes 1998-99 with Trends 1993-99.* Washington, DC: U.S. Government Printing Office, U.S. Department of Justice, Office of Justice Programs.

Short, James F. Jr. (1997). *Poverty, Ethnicity and Violent Crime.* Boulder, CO: Westview Press.

Snell, Tracy L. (2000). *Capital Punishment 1999.* Washington, DC Bureau of Justice Statistics, Office of Justice Programs.

Tonry, Michael. (1995). *Malign Neglect: Race, Crime, and Punishment in America.* New York: Oxford University Press.

———. (1996). "The Effects of American Drug Policy on Black Americans, 1980–1996." European Journal on Criminal Policy and Research 4, 2: 36–62.

———, ed. (1997). *Ethnicity, Crime, and Immigration. Comparative and Cross-National Perspectives.* Chicago: The University of Chicago Press.

Walker, Samuel, Cassia Spohn, and Miriam DeLone. (2000). *The Color of Justice: Race, Ethnicity and Crime in America.* Belmont, CA: Wadsworth.

Wheeler, David L. (1995). "A Growing Number of Scientists Reject the Concept of Race." *The Chronicle of Higher Education* (17 February): A8, A9, A15.

Zatz, Marjorie S., Lugan Chiago, and Z. K. Snyder-Joy. (1991). "American Indians and Criminal Justice: Some Conceptual and Methodological Considerations." In *Race and Criminal Justice*, edited by Michael J. Lynch and E. Britt Patterson. New York: Harrow and Heston, 100–112.

ETHNOGRAPHY OF CRIME AND PUNISHMENT

Ethnography is the process of conducting firsthand research within a community. Researchers who do ethnography are called ethnographers. The process involves learning the local language, participating in daily routines, and becoming sufficiently part of the local social environment that people go about their daily lives in the presence of the ethnographer without playing to an audience. Anthropologists have practiced ethnography for more than a hundred years in foreign venues. Over the past forty years, however, sociologists and anthropologists have used ethnographic techniques to study American inner-city community life, as well as the lifestyles of lawbreakers and the forms of punishment to which lawbreakers are subject.

The ethnography of crime and punishment is the study of crime, criminals, and forms of institutionalized punishment, conducted by gathering data firsthand among criminals on the street and in correctional settings.

ETHNOGRAPHY

The study of crime has been conducted principally in two ways. The first way to study crime is characteristic of sociological and criminological studies whose purpose is to identify crime patterns using cross-sectional and/or longitudinal numeric data. Cross-sectional data describe a behavior as it occurred at a particular time within a population or portion of a population. The homicide rate in the United States in 1998 is an example of a cross-sectional crime pattern. The homicide rate in the United States from 1990 to 1999 is an example of a longitudinal crime pattern, that is, a behavior as it occurred over a span of years. Such longitudinal data may show increases, decreases, or no change in the rate of homicide. Given that pattern of homicide, researchers might gather additional data as well, on the income, race, ethnicity, education, or employment of the perpetrators. Such data would assist researchers in correlating, or matching, increases and decreases in the homicide pattern to patterns in other data. Researchers may also conduct interviews with criminals, asking them for their motives and purposes in committing crime. The research methods for conducting cross-sectional and longitudinal studies of crime are those most commonly used in criminology.

The second way to study crime and punishment is to conduct studies of criminals' activities and forms of punishment, such as daily life inside correctional institutions, by participating in and observing the behavior of criminals and those with whom they interact. To conduct such research requires ethnographers to learn as much as possible about crime, criminals, and punishment by experiencing firsthand the world of criminals. Once a research plan is formulated, a crime ethnographer proceeds to where criminals "hang out." That may mean sharing a street corner with sellers of cocaine, or spending months participating in the daily activities inside a penitentiary, or observing police officers as they interact with suspected offenders on the street. Such a research process requires the ability to blend in with the social setting and from that vantage point, to ask questions, make observations, listen to conversations, and observe the behaviors of criminals. These activities are central to the ethnography of crime and punishment.

The first challenge facing a crime and punishment ethnographer is learning what questions to ask. If a crime ethnographer had personal experiences as a criminal, he or she would have a good idea of what questions to ask and how to ask them; however, most crime ethnographers have not been criminals. Asking the most insightful questions requires learning enough about crime and criminals to generate the best questions—something that takes time, patience, and skill. As an ethnographer learns more about criminals and crime, questioning becomes more insightful and detailed. Improved interviewing allows an ethnographer to write a more insightful narrative analysis portraying a criminal lifestyle, culture, and worldview.

CRIMINAL CULTURE AND WORLDVIEW

Observing and interviewing criminals and participating in a criminal lifestyle is the first step in creating an ethnographic study of crime and punishment. An important outcome of such research is a detailed description of how criminals perceive and conceptualize their world using criminals' own words; however, ethnography requires more than writing summaries of interviews or descriptions of how criminals commit crime. The scholarly burden on an ethnographer is to create a narrative that captures the culture and worldview of criminals.

Culture refers to the plans of action and rules of behavior characteristic of a group of people or an entire society. A cultural narrative must explain the nature of criminal acts as those acts mesh with other facts about criminals' lives, as well as how they mesh with broader social and economic issues affecting criminals' lives. To write effectively about the culture of crime and criminals, an ethnographer must truly understand the world of crime and criminals; he or she must be able to convey to readers the actual patterns of behavior typical of criminals, as well as the ways criminals explain, rationalize, justify, and account for their behavior.

A goal of the ethnography of crime and punishment is to gather sufficient data and learn enough about criminals' lifestyles to be able to characterize the criminal worldview. The conceptualization, perceptions, and descriptions people have of their own lifestyle represent a cultural worldview. Recent findings in the ethnographic study of crime and punishment show that the worldview of noncriminals in America is different from the criminal worldview. That difference in worldviews helps to explain why formal criminal justice sanctions, or punishments—such as probation and imprisonment—have had little effect on the behavior of criminals.

CRIME AND PUNISHMENT: ETHNOGRAPHIC FINDINGS

Sellers of cocaine do not think their behavior is different, in principle, from that of liquor stores that purvey liquor to people who become alcoholics, or who drink and drive drunk and then cause accidents with personal injury to bystanders. Crime ethnographies of youth gangs, street criminals, burglars, hobos of the 1950s and 1960s, and drug dealers of the 1980s and 1990s have shown that the lifestyle of a criminal culture is rational and involves complex decisions and plans of action. In other words, there is a "criminal culture." A careful study of the behavior and speech of "urban nomads" (homeless drug addicts and alcoholics, in the parlance of the 1990s) on Seattle's Skid Row in the 1960s revealed a complex system of labeling people and places. That labeling system was linked to urban nomads' survival strategies. A gang ethnography conducted among members of a coed, multiracial youth gang in Kansas City, Missouri, in the mid-1990s revealed that youthful male and female gang members were often homeless and estranged from their families. As a survival strategy, gang-affiliated adolescents sold drugs and committed economic crimes, in order to provide cash needed for food, shelter, and clothing. A study of adolescent "street families" in Canada yielded results similar to those of the Kansas City youth gang study. The Canadian study showed that adolescents surviving on the street in closely arranged groups often relied on crime, such as prostitution and shoplifting, as survival strategies.

A common finding of the ethnography of punishment is that convicted felons do not generally perceive punishment in the same way that the public and legislators perceive it. The most common type of punishment for serious crime is imprisonment. Studies of the conditions of prison inmate life have shown that, for the most part, modern prison life compares favorably to the often desperate conditions affecting the lives of impoverished citizens. Those poor citizens are, in fact, the most common inmates in American prisons. Ethnographic research on formerly imprisoned street criminals shows that while imprisoned, their general health improved. While imprisoned, these street criminals did not use alcohol and illegal drugs; they received medical care, enjoyed recreation, and had an adequate diet. On the street, however, these same men had no access to medical care, recreation, or proper nutrition. Ethnographic research on prison management and violence has shown that most inmate violence is directly related to breakdowns in prison management or to inadequate planning for large inmate populations. Research has shown, in general, that imprisonment has a central role in the lives of street criminals and has little deterrent or reforming effect on the lives of persistent criminals.

ETHNOGRAPHY AND SOCIAL POLICY

The ethnography of crime and punishment has direct implications for national welfare and criminal justice policies. Crime ethnography has shown that a criminal lifestyle has its roots in early family life, child abuse and neglect, and parental drug and alcohol use. Policies such as imprisonment, probation, and other forms of criminal justice-based behavior control will be unlikely to alter an adult criminal lifestyle. Social policy recommendations predicated on long-term ethnographic studies of crime and punishment suggest that crime prevention and intervention are best accomplished with social programs to strengthen families and provide children, preadolescents, and adolescents with continuous social and emotional support and treatment options for addiction and emotional issues.

—Mark S. Fleisher

Further Reading

Adler, Patricia. (1993). *Wheeling and Dealing: An Ethnography of an Upper-level Drug Dealing and Smuggling Community.* New York: Columbia University Press.

Agar, Michael H. (1973). *Ripping and Running: A Formal Ethnography of Urban Heroin Addicts.* New York: Seminar Press.

———. (1980). *The Professional Stranger.* New York: Academic Press.

———. (1986). *Speaking of Ethnography.* Beverly Hills, CA: Sage Publications.

Anderson, Elijah. (1978). *A Place on the Corner.* Chicago: University of Chicago Press.

Bernard, H.R. (1994). *Research Methods in Cultural Anthropology: Qualitative and Quantitative Methods,* 2d ed. Thousand Oaks, CA: Sage Publications.

Bourgois, Philippe. (1995). *In Search of Respect: Selling Crack in El Barrio.* (Series in Structural Analysis in the Social Sciences.) New York: Cambridge University Press.

Fleisher, Mark S. (1989). *Warehousing Violence.* Newbury Park, CA: Sage Publications.

———. (1995). *Beggars and Thieves: Lives of Urban Street Criminals.* Madison, WI: University of Wisconsin Press.

———. (1998). *Dead End Kids: Gang Girls and The Boys They Know.* Madison, WI: University of Wisconsin Press.

Geertz, Clifford. (1988). *Words and Lives: The Anthropologist as Author.* Stanford, CA: Stanford University Press.

Hagan, John, and Bill McCarthy. (1997). *Mean Streets.* New York: Cambridge University Press.

Keiser, R. Lincoln. (1969). *The Vice Lords: Warriors of the Street.* New York: Holt, Rinehart, and Winston.

Klockars, Carl. (1974). *The Professional Fence.* New York: Free Press.

Liebow, Eliot. (1967). *Tally's Corner.* Boston: Little, Brown and Company.

Malinowski, Bronislaw. (1922). *Argonauts of the Western Pacific.* London: Routledge and Kegan Paul.

Rosenbaum, Marsha. (1981). *Women on Heroin.* New Brunswick, NJ: Rutgers University Press.

Rossi, Peter. (1989). *Down and Out in America.* Chicago: University of Chicago Press.

Spradley, James. (1970). *You Owe Yourself a Drunk: An Ethnography of Urban Nomads.* Boston: Little, Brown.

———, ed. (1972). *Culture and Cognition: Rules, Maps, and Plans.* San Francisco, CA: Chandler Press.

Valentine, Bettylou. (1978). *Hustling and Other Hard Work: Life Styles in the Ghetto.* New York: Free Press.

Whyte, William F. (1943). *Street Corner Society: The Social Structure of an Italian Slum.* Chicago: University of Chicago Press.

◤ EUROPE, CENTRAL EASTERN

The transition to a democratic market society during the 1990s brought major political, economic and social transformations to Central Eastern Europe. One of the many social consequences of the collapse of Soviet-style communism in the nations of this region (Albania, Bulgaria, Croatia, Czech Republic, Hungary, Macedonia, Poland, Romania, Slovakia, Slovenia, and Yugoslavia) is a change in both the type and amount of reported crime. Although information about crime and justice in Central Eastern Europe was scarce prior to 1989, the liberalization of the countries in this region has allowed public access to information about these issues.

CRIME UNDER STATE SOCIALISM

For more than forty years, from the end of World War II until 1989, the countries of Central Eastern Europe were ruled by Soviet-style communism (state socialism), which controlled all aspects of life, including politics, business, religion, education, and civil society. Based on Marxist-Leninist ideology, the goal of state socialism was to create a classless society, thereby eliminating social inequality. To this end, the economy was a command economy with planned production and distribution, the abolition of private property, full employment for all adults, and extensive social welfare benefits to ensure the equal distribution of wealth and property. Under the single-party political structure, the Communist Party dictated economic development and maintained tight control over citizens through limited mobility, censorship, public persecution of dissenters, and the brute force of the militarized police.

Crime does not exist in a utopian communist society; however, it did exist in Central Eastern Europe under state socialism. Such crime was explained as a "remnant of capitalism" that would dissipate when state socialism became true communism (that is, a society without classes or private property). According to communist ideology, "crime and conflict, which are seen as resulting from the demoralizing conditions of the class society based on private property, will vanish, thereby making superfluous any permanent apparatus of coercion in the form of the army, police and corrections" (Los 1988: 1). In reality, communism not only failed to eliminate crime but also created new forms specific to the legal conditions of the existing socialist order, including hooliganism (violating public order or disrespecting society), parasitism (not working or contributing equally to economic life), theft against socialist property (typically, workplace theft), and crimes against the centralized distribution of goods (hoarding). Additionally, state socialist countries were plagued with the more common crimes of juvenile delinquency, alcoholism, drug abuse, and corruption. Conventional street crimes, such as burglary, homicide, rape, and assault also existed in socialist countries, but it is difficult to measure their prevalence because of the lack of reliable data. There is considerable evidence, however, to suggest that rates of conventional crimes were lower in Central Eastern Europe during state socialism than in capitalist countries.

CRIME AND SOCIAL CHANGE IN THE POST-SOCIALIST TRANSITION

In 1989, the era of Soviet-style communism came to an end in Central Eastern Europe, followed shortly thereafter by the breakup of the Soviet Union itself.

Weak economic performance, low standards of living, a growing underground civil society, widespread corruption, and international pressure together undermined the authoritarian regimes of these countries and led to relatively peaceful transitions of power. Within a few months, more than forty years of communist rule gave way to the public will. For the next decade, the countries of Central Eastern Europe became "transition societies," simultaneously overhauling their political, economic, legal, and social structures. Although each nation followed its own reform path, and there was considerable debate as to the direction of reform, the general goal was to replace state socialism with some form of democratic capitalism. The single-party rule of the Communist Party was replaced by open multiparty elections; the command economy was replaced by a market economy based on supply and demand; property was once again privatized; and the social sphere was liberalized through freedom of speech, religion, press, and association. As a result of the opening of national borders, the liberalization of trade, and the privatization of the media, citizens of Central Eastern Europe were exposed to the Western material and cultural life from which they had been shielded for decades.

The initial excitement over the end of socialist rule was short-lived, however, as the problems associated with such a massive societal transformation began to take their toll. Once the euphoria of the 1989 revolutions had passed and the reality of the long and difficult transition process set in, it soon became clear that filling the void left by the communist system would be difficult, error-prone, and costly. Some of the social consequences of the reforms included a drop in real wages, high inflation, unemployment, decreasing social welfare benefits, and growing social inequalities. In addition, crime became a highly visible social problem, and the fear of crime among the public became a serious political problem.

Some Western observers and Central Eastern European reformers treated the growth of crime in this region as a natural consequence of the transition process. For example, a Polish statesman was quoted in *The Atlanta Constitution* as saying, "It's paradoxical, but the growth in crime is the price one has to pay for freedom" (Salome 1993). Both the real and perceived threat of crime affected the quality of life for citizens in Central Eastern Europe. Researchers noted a deterioration of personal and material security in the region. According to Bulgarian survey data, for example, crime and unemployment have consistently ranked high among citizens' perceptions of the risks facing their society (Genov 1998).

Official crime statistics from various sources confirm popular beliefs and media accounts of increasing crime rates in all countries in the region. According to the *United Nations World Surveys on Crime Trends and Criminal Justice Systems* (Burnham and Burnham 1999), reported homicide and total theft rates increased between 1989 and 1994 in all Central Eastern European countries that reported data (Bulgaria, Croatia, Hungary, Poland, Romania, Slovakia, and Slovenia), although the amount of increase varied by country. For example, reported homicide rates in Hungary and Romania, which had decreased more than 20 percent during the socialist period from 1986 to 1989, increased 39 percent during the first four years of the postsocialist transition period in Hungary, and increased 9 percent in Romania. The total reported theft rate in Slovakia had remained fairly stable between 1986 and 1989, but it increased 163 percent during the transition years of 1990 to 1994. Additional support can be found in the *European Sourcebook for Criminal Justice Statistics* (European Committee on Crime Problems 1999), which noted that the reported motor vehicle theft rate increased more than 100 percent in Bulgaria, the Czech Republic, and Hungary, and over 200 percent in Poland between 1990 and 1996. During the same time period, the reported assault rate rose between 18 and 86 percent in Slovenia, Hungary, Romania, and Poland, and more than 600 percent in Bulgaria.

Although official crime statistics confirm that there was a dramatic increase in crime rates across Central Eastern Europe in the early 1990s, this simple statement obscures differences among countries experiencing similar transition processes. An examination of crime rates across countries, years, and types of crime paints a much more complex picture. For example, data from the U.N. survey show that Bulgaria experienced a large jump in the reported homicide rate from 1989 to 1990, which continued to increase steadily through the mid-1990s. In contrast, Romania had a higher pretransition reported homicide rate than most other Central Eastern European countries and showed a fairly stable trend in the early 1990s. With respect to total reported theft, Bulgaria, Romania, and Slovakia showed increases from 1989 to 1994, while reported theft rates in Croatia, Hungary, and Slovenia reached peak levels in 1991 or 1992 and began to decline by the mid-1990s.

One key question is whether crime rates will continue to rise in Central Eastern Europe or whether they will level off as the countries begin to stabilize. Data from the British Home Office (Barclay and Tavares 2000) show considerable fluctuations across countries and types of crime in the late 1990s. For example, from 1997 to 1998, the reported homicide rate increased 8 percent in the Czech Republic, decreased 6 percent in Poland, and did not change in Hungary. During the same period, however, reported motor vehicle theft decreased 5 percent in the Czech Republic, increased 15 percent in Poland, and increased 6 percent in Hungary. However, yearly changes in crime data are not necessarily the best predictors of future trends because of random fluctuations and reporting and recording errors. Data from the International Criminal Police Organization (ICPO) from 1990 to 1997 indicate that crime rates in many Central Eastern European countries may indeed be stabilizing at levels higher than in pre-transition years. Once data are available from the United Nations and ICPO for the complete decade, more accurate estimates can be made about the future direction of crime trends in the region.

CHANGES IN TYPES OF CRIMES AND CRIMINALS

Not only has the amount of crime in Central Eastern Europe increased, but the types of crimes have changed as well. Crimes that were products of communist political and economic organization (hooliganism, parasitism, etc.) have been replaced by crimes reflecting the current system. For example, the privatization of property and the introduction of market reforms without a fully developed legal and contractual framework have led to new forms of economic crime, such as tax evasion, illegal employment, and rent-seeking (economic privileges exploited for money or influence). Additionally, desirable consumer goods that were unobtainable during socialism became available after 1989, but high inflation decreased citizens' legal purchasing power. This resulted in increased theft of popular items such as cars, computers, and audiovisual entertainment and created illegal markets for such products.

The opening of national borders has meant that this region is now a major player in transnational crime, particularly organized crime: "The end of the Cold War, the collapse of state authority in some countries and regions, and the process of globalization—of trade, finance, communications, and information—have all provided an environment in which many criminal organizations find it profitable and preferable to operate across national borders rather than confine their activities to one country" (Newman 1999: 221). Transnational crimes involving Central Eastern Europe include illegal migration, trafficking in women, corruption, motor vehicle theft, and computer crimes. According to data from the United Nations, the number of cases of trafficking in women in Austria increased sixfold from 1990 to 1994, and almost half of the victims were from the Czech Republic and Slovakia. Of all regions in the world reporting crime data to the United Nations, Central Eastern Europe had the highest overall software piracy rate.

Organized crime in Central Eastern Europe, particularly the Russian Mafia, has gained much media attention in the United States and elsewhere. While it is difficult to measure the extent of the problem, the existence of such groups has been documented by journalists and researchers. "Organized crime groups early established links in Hungary, Poland, and the Czech Republic. Lower level personnel would control the highways and the markets in these countries. Upper level figures would be involved in large international movements of money using the countries of Eastern and Central Europe as conduits to the West" (Shelley 1999a: 27). These networks consist of former criminals, businesspeople, and some former Communist Party elite, as well as military and law enforcement personnel. They are not limited to traditional types of organized crime, such as drug trafficking, prostitution, extortion, and racketeering, but also trade in a variety of profitable commodities, including automobiles.

Another change in the type of crime in Central Eastern Europe is the increasing visibility of violent crime. During the period of communist rule, most violence was controlled by the state through public persecution, police brutality, prison camps, and even executions. Private acts of violence, such as homicide, assault, and rape, were often concealed from the public. The post-socialist transition not only brought an increase in violent crimes but also opened media coverage of such events. Increasing violence can be partially attributed to organized crime: "In efforts to seize control of prostitution and drug markets and to establish control over areas already dominated by crime groups from other regions, crime groups from the East have used significant violence" (Shelley 1999a: 28).

Violence committed by juveniles has also increased. While juvenile delinquency was recognized as a problem in Central Eastern Europe under socialism, it continued to grow during the transition. In Poland, the rate of juvenile delinquency among youth aged thirteen to sixteen doubled between 1989 and 1995. According to information from ICPO (1989–1997), youth in Central Eastern Europe were not only more criminally active during the 1990s but also more involved in violent crime. In Poland, 3.6 percent of murder suspects in 1991 were juveniles, which increased to 6 percent by 1997. In Hungary, the proportion of juvenile murder suspects rose from 5.3 percent in 1991 to 7.4 percent in 1994 and then declined to 5.5 percent in 1997. In Slovenia, the proportion of juvenile suspects for serious assault grew from 7.1 percent in 1991 to 11.8 percent in 1994, then dropped to 10.8 percent in 1997.

The post-socialist era has brought new types of criminal activity in the form of economic, transnational, and organized crime. The actors have also changed, as organized criminal networks reach out to different social spheres and juveniles become more involved in crime. Moreover, crime appears to have become more violent, particularly among youth.

EXPLAINING CRIME TRENDS IN POST-SOCIALIST CENTRAL EASTERN EUROPE

The changes that have taken place in Central Eastern Europe since 1989 have affected every aspect of life—political, economic, and social. Given the breadth of these changes, there is no single cause of rising crime rates in this region and the literature on the subject often cites several explanatory factors and theoretical perspectives. Several researchers have pointed to anomie theory and the general "normlessness" of society following a social revolution. Citizens in Central Eastern Europe were frustrated by the social upheaval, economic difficulties, and social inequalities and, therefore, some turned to illegitimate means to achieve their goals. Society was also disorganized in terms of the social institutions providing social control. Family units were disrupted, the education system was in crisis, and many youth organizations and child-care centers were closed, leaving juveniles without constructive activities or supervision. Furthermore, the end of state socialism brought the collapse of authoritarian social control. The state and all its formal control mechanisms—the law, courts, corrections, police, and the military—were in a state of flux that created opportunities for increased criminal behavior. Other social changes, such as migration within and between countries, reduced guardianship, and the greater availability of desirable consumer goods, have also increased opportunities for criminal behavior. While there are several reasonable explanations for these changing crime trends, more research is needed to understand the relationship between social change and crime in Central Eastern Europe, particularly with respect to varying experiences across countries.

CHANGES IN THE CRIMINAL JUSTICE SYSTEM

Along with all other social institutions, the criminal justice systems of Central Eastern Europe were also affected by the reforms initiated after 1989. The countries adopted new constitutions for their young democracies, and the legal systems changed to reflect the new social orders. The transition had an impact on every aspect of the criminal justice system, including definitions of what was considered a crime, policing practices, prosecutions, court processes, and corrections.

Policing

The communist model of policing consisted of a centralized, standardized, and militarized police force, called the militia. As the force behind the Communist Party, the militia was responsible not only for crime control but for political and social control as well: "During 74 years of Soviet rule, the militia was transformed from a militarized body suppressing political opposition to a law enforcement body responsible primarily for social and economic order" (Shelley 1999b: 76). Communist ideology also dictated policing methods. For example, in order to maintain complete authoritarian control, all crimes had to be cleared by the police, which meant that a suspect had to be arrested and convicted for every reported crime. Police officers resorted to coercive investigative methods or falsified reports to ensure that they cleared all of their cases.

In the early 1990s, many Central Eastern European countries expanded their police forces in response to social disorder and rising crime rates. According to data from the United Nations, between 1990 and 1994, police forces increased 65 percent in Slovakia, 45 percent in Croatia, 38 percent in Romania, 25 percent in Hungary, and 17 percent in Slovenia. However, the increasing size of police forces was of little comfort to

citizens of these countries, whose relationship to the militia was one of fear rather than respect. Citizens concerned for their safety in the post-socialist period were reluctant to turn to the police for assistance, and these organizations faced a serious legitimacy crisis. After 1989, the militia changed its name to "police" to disassociate its new image from that of the socialist period, but more than a name change was needed to create police forces based on the rule of law and the rights of citizens.

Some countries quickly recognized the need for progressive change in the police. Hungary, Germany, Poland, the Czech Republic, and Slovakia conducted detailed reviews of policing practices soon after 1989. Personnel who were found to be corrupt or unable to adapt to new methods of policing were fired, and policing techniques were reviewed for their compatibility with the newly emerging democratic market societies. Despite these efforts, it has proven difficult to overcome the communist legacy of "demoralized and corrupted police forces with little or no respect for citizens' rights" (Shelley 1999b: 76). The police must compete with other government branches for scarce financial resources at a time when these countries are in the midst of economic upheaval. Such constraints make it nearly impossible to fulfill basic equipment needs (e.g., cars), much less fund needed technological improvement (computerization, etc.). The low pay of police officers has made it difficult to recruit new talent, as those trained in the field are likely to work for private security agencies that offer a greater financial incentive. Moreover, economic problems encourage corruption within law enforcement and collaboration with organized criminal networks.

Western countries have supplied much of the impetus and financial support for creating police forces consistent with democratic rule. Many Western European countries have bilateral training and financial support agreements with particular Central Eastern European countries. The United States established a training academy in Budapest, Hungary, to teach investigative, management, and forensic skills to law enforcement personnel from the region. In some countries, there has been a tendency to emulate the more specialized components of Western policing systems, such as anti-organized crime units. In 1994, for example, the Slovak Republic established organized crime units in all major cities, and the Hungarian National Police also created specialized central and regional units. The creation of elite units addresses particularly problematic crime areas but also drains financial and personnel resources from more basic police restructuring.

Corrections

Punishment has also changed in Central Eastern Europe as part of the post-socialist transition. In 1989 and 1990, countries such as Bulgaria, the Czech Republic, Slovakia, Hungary, Poland, and Romania significantly reduced their prison populations by granting general amnesties to prisoners held for political reasons by the Communist Party. In countries such as Bulgaria and Slovenia, the prison populations in the mid-1990s remained at about the same level as in 1990.

However, in several other countries, the increases in reported crime rates and ensuing public fear led to more punitive sanctions for criminals and the prisons filled again. For example, according to data reported to the United Nations, the prisoner rate doubled in the Czech Republic between 1990 and 1994; in addition, prison occupancy rates increased substantially in the Hungary, Slovakia, and Croatia. This has led to prison overcrowding in some countries, which, in turn, has strained criminal justice personnel and stretched financial resources.

CHALLENGES FOR THE FUTURE

The transition in Central Eastern Europe from state socialism to democratic capitalism has produced many social problems, including a significant increase in rates of reported crime. Official crime statistics support media accounts and public perceptions of crime as a growing problem. These same sources, however, also show that there is considerable variation in crime trends across time, countries, and types of offense. Just as state socialism produced crimes specific to that social order, the transition societies also experienced new forms of crime as a result of the new political and economic systems. The appearance of organized criminal networks and the increasing violence, particularly among youth, have been the cause for much public concern. Moreover, the criminal justice system has had to respond to public and political pressure regarding rising reported crime rates, while at the same time being restructured to better fit the new social order. Criminal justice institutions such as the police and prisons face many challenges in dealing with the crime situation in a period of fiscal constraint and organiza-

tional upheaval. At the same time, the greater availability of data from Central Eastern Europe and access to other information sources have created new opportunities for researchers to further explore crime and justice issues.

—*Janet P. Stamatel*

See also Organized Crime—Global; Socialist Legal Traditions

Further Reading

Barclay, Gordon C., and Cynthia Tavares. (2000). "International Comparisons of Criminal Justice Statistics 1998" [Research Bulletin]. London: Home Office, Research Development and Statistics Directorate.

Burnham, R. W., and Helen Burnham. (1999). *United Nations World Surveys on Crime Trends and Criminal Justice Systems, 1970–1994: Restructured Five–Wave Data* [Computer file]. ICPSR version. Washington, DC: U.S. Department of Justice, National Institute of Justice [producer], 1997. Ann Arbor, MI: Interuniversity Consortium for Political and Social Research [distributor].

Cebulak, Wojciech. (1997). "Social Turmoil in PostSocialist Eastern Europe—A Revolution Gone Astray?" *East European Quarterly* 31, 1 (March): 111–119.

Connor, Walter D. (1969). *Deviance in Soviet Society: Crime, Delinquency, and Alcoholism*. New York: Columbia University Press.

European Committee on Crime Problems. (1999). *European Sourcebook of Crime and Criminal Justice Statistics*. Strasbourg, France: Council of Europe.

Frank, Gregory. (1998). "Policing Transition in Europe: The Role of Europol and the Problem of Organized Crime." *Innovation* 11, 3: 287–305.

Genov, Nikolai. (1998). "Transformation and Anomie: Problems of Quality of Life in Bulgaria." *Social Indicators Research* 43: 197–209.

Illner, Michal. (1998). "The Changing Quality of Life in a Post-Communist Country: The Case of Czech Republic." *Social Indicators Research* 43: 141–170.

International Criminal Police Organization (ICPO). (1989–1997). *International Crime Statistics*. Lyons, France: ICPO–Interpol General Secretariat.

Kangaspunta, Kristiina, Matti Joutsen, and Natalia Ollus, eds. (1998). *Crime and Criminal Justice in Europe and North America 1990–1994*. Helsinki, Finland: European Institute for Crime Prevention and Control (HEUNI).

King, Mike. (1998). "Policing Change in Eastern and Central Europe: Some Contemporary Concerns." *Innovation* 11, 3: 277–285.

Los, Maria. (1988). *Communist Ideology, Law, and Crime: A Comparative View of the USSR and Poland*. London: Macmillan Press.

Lotspeich, Richard. (1995). "Crime in the Transition Economies." *Europe-Asia Studies* 47, 44: 555–589.

Matutinovic, Igor. (1998). "Quality of Life in Transition Countries: Central East Europe with Special Reference to Croatia." *Social Indicators Research* 43: 97–119.

Neapolitan, Jerome L. (1997). *Cross–National Crime: A Research Review and Sourcebook.* Westport, CT: Greenwood Press.

Newman, Graeme, ed. (1999). *Global Report on Crime and Justice.* New York: Oxford University Press.

Salome, Louis J. (1993). "Crime After Communism." *The Atlanta Constitution* (28 December).

Salvesberg, Joachim J. (1995). "Crime, Inequality, and Justice in Eastern Europe: Anomie, Domination and Revolutionary Change." In *Crime and Inequality*, edited by John Hagan and Ruth D. Peterson. Stanford, CA: Stanford University Press, 206–224.

Shelley, Louise I. (1981). *Crime and Modernization: The Impact of Industrialization and Urbanization on Crime.* Carbondale: Southern Illinois University Press.

———. (1996a). *Policing Soviet Society: The Evolution of State Control.* New York: Routledge.

———. (1996b). "Post-Soviet Organized Crime: A New Form of Authoritarianism." *Transnational Organized Crime* 2, 2/3 (Summer/Autumn): 122–138.

———. (1999a). "Crime of the Former Socialist States: Implications for Western Europe." In *International Police Institue Twente: Public Safety in Europe.* Enschede, The Netherlands: Febodruk, 19–30. http://www.american.edu/traccc/work/shelleyarticles.html.

———. (1999b). "Post-Socialist Policing: Limitations on Institutional Change." In *Policing Across the World*, edited by R. I. Mawby. New York: Garland Publishing, 75–87.

Siemaszko, Andrzej, ed. (2000). *Crime and Law Enforcement in Poland on the Threshold of the 21st Century.* Warsaw, Poland: Instytut Wymiaru Sprawiedliwoœci i Oficyna Naukowa.

▼ EUTHANASIA

Euthanasia (literally, "good death") refers to several distinct forms of mercy killing, all involving action or inaction, undertaken for the sake of someone else and intended to cause that person's death. Active euthanasia involves administering lethal drugs, actively asphyxiating the patient, or killing the patient by other invasive means. Assisted suicide means helping patients end their own lives by supplying instructions, drugs, or other equipment. Passive euthanasia involves withholding or withdrawing medical treatment, respiratory assistance, nutrition, or water. Although there is no crime called "euthanasia," each of these practices constitutes a criminal act under certain conditions. Euthanasia remains controversial among ethicists, medical professionals, and lawmakers, and the law in this area continues to evolve.

HISTORY

The Hippocratic Oath, taken by most Western physicians for over two millennia, states, "Neither will I administer a poison to anybody when asked to do so, nor will I suggest such a course" (Clendening 1960: 14). Nonetheless, some medical historians believe that many Greeks in Hippocrates' day (c. 470–c. 410 BCE) did not view euthanasia as invariably criminal or unethical. By the nineteenth century, however, the medical establishment had come to regard as unethical any action or inaction taken by a caregiver that could be reasonably foreseen to result in death, and Anglo-American common law criminalized such actions as homicide and assisting in a suicide (which itself was a crime at the time).

In the twentieth century, legal developments began to qualify this absolute ban. Suicide itself was decriminalized in the United States, and courts began to recognize a general legal right to refuse medical treatment. Eventually, the latter was found to imply a further right to refuse "extraordinary" treatment, such as life support, even when such an action was certain to end the patient's life. Recognized by state and federal courts, including the U.S. Supreme Court, and by physician's organizations, such as the American Medical Association (AMA), by the end of the twentieth century, this right had expanded to include the right to refuse food and water. A physician who fulfills a patient's request to withdraw life support, nutrition, hydration, or other treatment has not committed a crime. Individuals can make such requests prospectively, via an advance directive; a living will, for example, specifies conditions under which caregivers are to withhold treatment.

THE "EUTHANASIA PROGRAM" IN NAZI GERMANY

For some, the prospect of decriminalizing euthanasia raises the specter of a dark episode in human history. In the first decades of the twentieth century, when the German government became concerned with cutting the costs of operating mental hospitals (known then as asylums), some German psychiatrists began to contemplate "eugenic" measures to deal with acute, chronic, untreatable mental patients. When the Nazi party rose to power, the government instituted what was known as "euthanasia program." Many psychiatrists participated, sterilizing mental patients and authorizing the execution of acute, untreatable individuals. Hundreds of thousands of men, women, and children were gassed, starved to death, or killed by lethal injection.

Opponents of euthanasia, especially Germans, empha-

▼

Selections from Oregon's Death With Dignity Act

Written Request for Medication to End One's Life in a Humane and Dignified Manner

Section 2
127.805

s.2.01. Who may initiate a written request for medication.

(1) An adult who is capable, is a resident of Oregon, and has been determined by the attending physician and consulting physician to be suffering from a terminal disease, and who has voluntarily expressed his or her wish to die, may make a written request for medication for the purpose of ending his or her life in a humane and dignified manner in accordance with ORS 127.800 to 127.897.

(2) No person shall qualify under the provisions of ORS 127.800 to 127.897 solely because of age or disability.

[1995 c.3 s.2.01; 1999 c.423 s.2] 127.810

Safeguards
Section 3
127.815

s301. Attending physician responsibilities.

(1) The attending physician shall:

(a) Make the initial determination of whether a patient has a terminal disease, is capable, and has made the request voluntarily;

(b) Request that the patient demonstrate Oregon residency pursuant to ORS 127.860;

(c) To ensure that the patient is making an informed decision, inform the patient of:
 (A) His or her medical diagnosis;
 (B) His or her prognosis;
 (C) The potential risks associated with taking the medication to be prescribed;
 (D) The probable result of taking the medication to be prescribed; and
 (E) The feasible alternatives, including, but not limited to, comfort care, hospice care and pain control;

(d) Refer the patient to a consulting physician for medical confirmation of the diagnosis, and for a determination that the patient is capable and acting voluntarily;

(e) Refer the patient for counseling if appropriate pursuant to ORS 127.825;

(f) Recommend that the patient notify next of kin;

(g) Counsel the patient about the importance of having another person present when the patient takes the medication prescribed pursuant to ORS 127.800 to 127.897 and of not taking the medication in a public place;

(h) Inform the patient that he or she has an opportunity to rescind the request at any time and in any manner, and offer the patient an opportunity to rescind at the end of the 15 day waiting period pursuant to ORS 127.840;

(i) Verify, immediately prior to writing the prescription for medication under ORS 127.800 to 127.897, that the patient is making an informed decision;

(j) Fulfill the medical record documentation requirements of ORS 127.855;

(k) Ensure that all appropriate steps are carried out in accordance with ORS 127.800 to 127.897 prior to writing a prescription for medication to enable a qualified patient to end his or her life in a humane and dignified manner;

size these horrors. Some find any form of euthanasia reminiscent of the Nazi program. Others fear that legalization would set us on a path that would eventually endanger basic human rights, including the rights of the poor, the disabled, and the socially disfavored.

Proponents argue that the right to determine the circumstances of one's own death is itself a basic human right, and that decriminalizing voluntary euthanasia would give individuals the right to end their own life or have it ended at their behest. This, they insist, differs from the genocide perpetrated by the Nazi government, which occurred against the will of its victims.

THE LEGAL IMPORTANCE OF PURPOSE

The AMA Code of Ethics does not forbid a physician from prescribing treatments that are likely to result in death, so long as the doctor's intention is not to cause death but to achieve some other purpose for the patient, such as pain relief. The criminal law takes a similar position, distinguishing between intention and mere "knowledge" or "foresight." For example, a doctor does not commit murder if he or she administers painkillers, even though death is likely to result, so long as the doctor does so for the purpose of relieving the patient's pain, rather than for the purpose of causing the patient's death. By contrast, when undertaken for the purpose of ending life, this same action constitutes active euthanasia, which the AMA vigorously opposes and which constitutes murder in every state. Consent of the patient is not a defense.

Assisted suicide, by definition, is undertaken for the purpose of bringing about death, and in all but six of the U.S. states, it constitutes the statutory or common law crime of assisting in a suicide or homicide. Again, consent of the patient is no defense. Withdrawing nutrition, hydration, or life support can also constitute a crime under certain conditions. As with active euthanasia, the question is whether the action is taken for the purpose of ending human life, or simply with the knowledge that death may result. If someone withholds or withdraws medical treatment, nutrition or hydration for the purpose of ending life, he or she commits murder, whereas an attending physician is legally permitted (and typically required) to withdraw treatment when the patient has so requested, because the doctor's purpose in doing so is not to kill the patient, but rather to obey the patient's legally binding instructions.

In the United States, a patient has the legal right to terminate life-sustaining treatment but not to receive a lethal injection, which might permit a quicker and less traumatic death. Some critics deplore this as cruel and arbitrary; other commentators, including the AMA, regard the distinction between intending and merely foreseeing death as being both morally and legally important.

COURTS

Euthanasia raises many legal and constitutional issues. In the United States, the first major judicial decision concerning passive euthanasia was the famous 1976 case of Karen Quinlan. Quinlan, a young woman in a persistent vegetative state, had irreversible brain damage and no cognitive or cerebral functioning; nourished and hydrated intravenously, she breathed with the assistance of a respirator. Quinlan's family wanted to disconnect her from the respirator, but hospital officials refused to do so. In a landmark decision, the Supreme Court of New Jersey held that the right to privacy, as developed in U.S. constitutional law, gave Quinlan the legal right to have the respirator disconnected. Moreover, those who disconnected her were immunized from criminal charges and civil liability (i.e., lawsuits for medical malpractice and wrongful death). The ruling in *Quinlan* was followed by many other courts, which began to acknowledge a constitutional right of incompetent patients in persistent vegetative states to have extraordinary means of support withdrawn or withheld.

With a few exceptions, courts have taken a similar approach with respect to the removal of nutrition and hydration. They hold that competent adult patients can refuse any medical treatment for any reason, and they classify artificial nutrition and hydration as "medical treatment." Although the U.S. Supreme Court has never squarely confronted this issue, in 1990 it declared its agreement with lower courts on these points in the case of Nancy Cruzan—although it should be noted that the Court's statement to this effect was not necessary to the holding, and hence does not constitute binding precedent.

The *Cruzan* case is equally significant for its direct holding on the issue of incompetent patients. Cruzan, too, was a young woman in a persistent vegetative state following a car accident in 1983. Her parents sued the hospital to force the removal of the gastronomy tube that provided her nutrition and hydration, and, at trial, presented testimony that Cruzan herself would have chosen this course of action. The court, however, rejected this testimony as insufficient evidence of Cruzan's intent. On appeal, the U.S. Supreme Court held that although Cruzan would have had the absolute right to have the tube removed had she been competent, the state was entitled (although not obligated) to require "clear and convincing evidence" of that fact. Thereafter, Cruzan's parents presented the trial court with persuasive evidence that she would have wanted the tube removed; it was, and Cruzan died shortly thereafter. The case affirmed an incompetent patient's right to have nutrition and hydration removed, but it also permitted states to require "clear and convincing" evidence of the incompetent's presumed intent.

All states criminalize active euthanasia, and virtually all states criminalize assisted suicide as well. Several states have faced constitutional challenges to these bans. On June 26, 1997, the U.S. Supreme Court issued its first opinions on the subject. In two unanimous decisions, the Court, in denying challenges to statutes in New York and Washington, refused to find any constitutional right to assisted suicide, although it left open the door for states to continue experimenting with policies in this area. Some commentators have also highlighted the Court's insistence that states must not impede a patient's right to receive "palliative care" aimed at alleviating pain and physical symptoms.

The first case, *Quill v. Vacco*, concerned a challenge to provisions of the New York Penal Law stating that a person is guilty of second-degree manslaughter when "he intentionally . . . aids another person to commit suicide" and that "a person is guilty of promoting a suicide attempt when he intentionally . . . aids another person to attempt suicide." The plaintiffs—three terminally ill, mentally competent adults and three physicians who maintained that doctors should be allowed to participate in a patient's assisted suicide—challenged the statute under the Equal Protection and Due Process Clauses of the Fourteenth Amendment to the U.S. Constitution. The Second Circuit Court of Appeals held that the ban on assisted suicide did violate equal protection, but the Supreme Court reversed the decision.

The companion case, *Washington v. Glucksberg*, concerned a challenge to a similar statute in Washington State. The plaintiffs here—patients, physicians and a public-interest organization—alleged that terminally ill, competent adults have a constitutional right under the due process clause to receive life-ending medication, and they claimed that Washington law denied them this right by criminalizing assisted suicide. They also argued that the law violated the equal protection clause, because it treated the plaintiff patients differently from terminally ill patients who need life support and are able to refuse or withdraw it. The Supreme Court rejected both of these arguments.

LEGISLATIVE INITIATIVES

In the early 1990s, some western states began to entertain the idea of legalizing euthanasia and physician-assisted suicide. In November 1991, by a margin of 8 percent, voters in Washington defeated a ballot measure called Initiative 119, which would have authorized voluntary active euthanasia by permitting physicians to administer lethal injections to terminally ill patients. It would have required a written request witnessed by two impartial parties, and diagnoses by two doctors that the patient had less than six months to live. A year later, California voters rejected a similar proposal by the same margin.

Then, in 1994, by a margin of 2.6 percent, Oregon voters passed the Oregon Death With Dignity Act, making it the first state to legalize assisted suicide. As did the earlier proposals, Oregon's law—which until 2001 permitted doctors to prescribe, but not administer, lethal medication—requires a second medical opinion and applies only during the last six months of life; it also requires both multiple requests by the patient and two waiting periods. In the first two years after the act

went into effect in November 1997, there were 43 documented cases of physician-assisted suicide in Oregon. However, on November 31, 2001, Attorney General John Ashcroft issued an order stating that physicians are to be punished for participating in assisted suicides. The order was intended to end euthanasia in Oregon.

DR. JACK KEVORKIAN

No one has brought more attention to the issue of physician-assisted suicide than Dr. Jack Kevorkian, a pathologist from Detroit, Michigan. During the 1990s, Kevorkian helped 130 individuals commit suicide with the "Mercitron," a machine of his own invention. Kevorkian had been charged over the years with a variety of crimes, including assisting suicide, first-degree murder, and murder under the common law. Then, in 1998, after the television program "60 Minutes" aired a videotape of Kevorkian injecting a fatal solution into a paralyzed man dying of Lou Gehrig's disease, he was charged with first-degree murder; on March 26, 1999, a jury convicted him of a lesser offense, second-degree murder. This was Kevorkian's first conviction. Under Michigan law, he could have received as much as a life sentence, but the judge sentenced him to the minimum possible: ten to twenty-five years in prison.

Some herald Kevorkian as a hero. Others criticize him harshly, on several grounds: Kevorkian had only brief associations with those he assisted; he had little experience practicing medicine with living patients; he operated without regulation and supervision; and, of course, he worked outside of the law.

THE NETHERLANDS—LEGALIZED EUTHANASIA

Both proponents and opponents of euthanasia point to The Netherlands as a revealing case study on decriminalization. Although the letter of the Dutch penal code still criminalizes euthanasia, since 1973 Dutch courts have permitted physicians (but only physicians) to end a patient's life, under specific conditions: The patient, in the final stages of a terminal illness and in unbearable pain, must make a written request to the attending physician. In 1984, the Dutch Supreme Court narrowed these criteria, specifying that the death must not cause unnecessary suffering to others, that the patient's family must be consulted (unless the patient objects), and that a second physician must agree with the prognosis. In 1993, the Dutch parliament passed a law that protects doctors from prosecution if they follow these

Dr. Jack Kevorkian enters the Oakland County Courthouse in Pontiac, Michigan on March 22, 1999, to stand trial for the murder of Thomas Youk. Seated in the wheelchair is Carol Cleigh of the Not Dead Yet organization, which protests against Kevorkian's euthanasia philosophy.
Source: © AFP/Corbis; used by permission.

procedures. In April 2001, the parliament finalized this policy, enacting legislation that specifically legalizes euthanasia and assisted suicide. The Netherlands is the first nation in history to take this step.

THE FUTURE

In the United States, *Quill* and *Glucksberg* left open more legal issues than they resolved, although many of those issues will now be settled by state legislatures rather than by the courts.

It is too early to tell what ramifications Oregon's law and Attorney General Ashcroft's order will have. This is not surprising. After two decades of study,

commentators still cannot agree on the merits of the Dutch policy. Several things are certain, however. Each year, caregivers, friends, and family members of the terminally ill facilitate thousands of deaths in the United States. In most cases, their motives are beneficent. Unless those who assist others to die make spectacles of themselves, as did Dr. Kevorkian, they are very rarely prosecuted. This is so despite the fact that euthanasia and assisted suicide are de jure criminal acts in almost every jurisdiction. Some have predicted that, in the new century, euthanasia will supplant abortion as our most divisive legal, moral, and political issue.

—*Jeffrey Brand-Ballard*

Further Reading

American Medical Association, Council on Ethical and Judicial Affairs. (2000). *Code of Medical Ethics*. Chicago: American Medical Association.

Burleigh, Michael. (1994). *Death and Deliverance: "Euthanasia" in Germany 1900–1945*. New York: Cambridge University Press.

Burt, Robert A. (1997). "The Supreme Court Speaks: Not Assisted Suicide but a Constitutional Right to Palliative Care." *New England Journal of Medicine* 337: 1234–1236.

Clendening, Logan. (1960). *Source Book of Medical History*. New York: Dover Publications.

Dworkin, Ronald. (1994). *Life's Dominion: An Argument about Abortion, Euthanasia, and Individual Freedom*. New York: Random House.

Emanuel, Linda L., ed. (1998). *Regulating How We Die: The Ethical, Medical, and Legal Issues Surrounding Physician-Assisted Suicide*. Cambridge: Harvard University Press.

Gomez, Charles F. (1991). *Regulating Death: Euthanasia and the Case of the Netherlands*. New York: Free Press.

Humphry, Derek, and Ann Wickett. (1986). *The Right to Die: Understanding Euthanasia*. New York: Harper & Row.

Johnson, Dirk. (1999). "Kevorkian Sentenced to 10 to 25 Years in Prison." *New York Times* (April 14, A1).

Rachels, James. (1975). "Active and Passive Euthanasia." *New England Journal of Medicine* 292: 78–80.

Singer, Peter. (1995). *Rethinking Life and Death*. New York: St. Martin's Press.

Sunstein, Cass. (1997). "The Right to Die." *Yale Law Journal* 106: 1123–1162.

Velleman, J. David. (1992). "Against the Right to Die." *Journal of Medicine and Philosophy* 17: 665–681.

Zucker, Marjorie B., ed. (1999). *The Right to Die Debate: A Documentary History*. Westport, CT: Greenwood Press.

Court Cases

Cruzan v. Director, Missouri Department of Health (1990). 467 U.S. 261.

Quill v. Vacco (1996). 80 F.3d 716 (2nd Cir.).

Quill v. Vacco (1997). 521 U.S. 793.

Quinlan, Karen, an Alleged Incompetent, In the Matter of (1976). 355 A.2d 647 (N.J.).

Washington v. Glucksberg (1997). 521 U.S. 702.

▼ EVIDENCE

See CRIMINAL INVESTIGATION, FIREARMS IDENTIFICATION; SCIENTIFIC EVIDENCE

▼ EVOLUTIONARY PERSPECTIVES ON CRIME

Although evolutionary theory was developed by biologists, social scientists since the last quarter of the twentieth century have been applying its principles to the study of human culture (anthropology) and the human mind (psychology). This fusion has been called sociobiology (Wilson 1975). Recently, criminologists interested in biosocial theory have begun to apply an evolutionary understanding to the study of the causes of crime. This development promises to expand the reach of criminological theory.

THE MODERN SYNTHESIS

Modern evolutionary theory began with the early nineteenth-century effort by theologians to enlist the assistance of naturalists and philosophers in proving the existence of God. In an argument originating with Thomas Aquinas, the perfection of the design of the natural world was said to demonstrate the existence of a divine creator. In 1859, in *The Origin of Species,* Charles Darwin provided a convincing argument that the design of living organisms can be explained by the process of evolution by natural selection. Because individual members of a species encounter slightly different obstacles to survival (one seed lands in fertile soil, another in dry soil), some survive and others do not, particularly as environments change. A species is composed of descendants of ancestors whose traits enabled them to survive long enough to reproduce. Darwin's theory hypothesized that living organisms are subject to physical processes and natural laws, just as the rest of the natural world is. In some cases, Darwin's supporters understood his theory as little as his critics did; the social Darwinists, most prominently the philosopher Herbert Spencer, emphasized phrases such as "the struggle for survival" and "the survival of the fittest" in order to argue that the superiority of British culture justified its rule over its far-flung empire.

Darwin's theory, however, lacked a mechanism whereby living things can inherit traits from their ancestors. In 1866, an Austrian monk named Gregor Mendel published a paper describing his theory of inheritance by genes, but this paper did not become widely known until its rediscovery in 1900 by plant biologists interested in hybridization. Geneticists then proposed that the evolution of species was the result of genetic mutations rather than of natural selection. The dispute was not settled until 1937, when Theodosius Dobzhansky set forth the modern synthesis of Darwinian natural selection and Mendelian genetics in *Genetics and the Origin of Species.* In 1953, James Watson and Francis Crick deduced the structure of the deoxyribonucleic acid (DNA) molecule, which is the building block of the gene.

THE PARADOX OF INDIVIDUAL FITNESS AND ALTRUISTIC BEHAVIOR

The modern synthesis marked the beginning of modern evolutionary thinking. However, a number of major problems remained to be solved. Tennyson called nature "red in tooth and claw," but biologists were aware of examples of apparent altruism, where one animal sacrifices itself for the sake of the group. How could a gene for altruism confer an adaptive advantage such that the gene would spread throughout a population? William Hamilton (1970) developed the concept of inclusive fitness to explain the concepts of altruism and selfishness. Inclusive fitness is the sum of an individual's own fitness plus the sum of the effects it causes to the fitness of all its relatives. The stinging bee dies to save its hive because it shares a high percentage of its genes with the members of the hive. In the human realm, work by economists and game theorists with a simulation known as the Prisoner's Dilemma had also given rise to concerns about explaining altruism. In 1971, Robert Trivers developed the concept of reciprocal altruism, in which one person helps another today in return for future help. Not only humans but also animals such as bottle-nosed dolphins and vampire bats display reciprocal altruism, a trait requiring a relatively large brain to discriminate between cooperators and cheaters.

EVOLUTION AND HUMAN BEHAVIOR

Journalist Robert Wright writes that "The basic evolutionary logic common to people everywhere is opaque to introspection. Natural selection appears to have hidden our true selves from our conscious selves" (1995: 10).

Objections to the study of human evolution are often based on the assumption of human exceptionalism (because of culture, humans are said to be fundamentally different from animals), the charge of determinism or reductionism (the argument that evolutionary theory views people's behavior as determined by or reduced to biological factors alone), and the naturalistic fallacy (the belief that what *is* reflects what *must be* or *should be*). An example of this last objection might be the fear that evolutionarily based differences between men and women could be used to justify calls for weakening laws designed to protect women's equality. Science

The Prisoner's Dilemma

Economists and game theoreticians are interested in a simulation called the Prisoner's Dilemma, which seems to demonstrate that ruthless individualism is the way to survive. Imagine that two individuals, A and B, agree to rob a bank together. They promise each other never to "rat" on the other one, that is, never to tell the police that the other one was involved in the crime. Both are arrested and are held in separate cells, where they can't communicate with one another. The prosecutor offers a deal to A: "Right now I have enough evidence to send each of you away on a charge of carrying an unlicensed gun. That will get you each a year's sentence. However, if you turn state's evidence against B, you'll go free, and B will serve ten years for bank robbery. If, however, you turn down this deal, but B accepts it, B will go free and you'll serve ten years. If you *both* confess, I'll charge you both with a lesser offense and you'll each serve only three years." What should A do? Should A trust that B will remember their mutual promise not to rat on each other? What if A keeps his promise—but B doesn't? Likewise, B must be thinking along the same lines. Most people would agree that, unless there is some way to know that B will keep silent, A's best course of action is to rat on B. Either B will keep silent (in which case A goes free) or B will rat on A (in which case they each serve three years). The most desirable solution (from the perspective of the prisoners themselves) is also the least likel—the one in which they both keep silent. The Prisoner's Dilemma seems to show that self-interest will win out over cooperation, because it is an example of a zero-sum game. Game theoreticians have shown, however, that cooperation does not have to be a zero-sum game, just as Robert Trivers showed that reciprocal altruism ("I'll help you today if you'll help me tomorrow") is a non-zero-sum game (also called a win-win solution). Thus, if A and B are captured military officers, or husband and wife, the chances of their being able to trust one another's promise are greatly increased because of the likelihood of future interactions with one another. Thus, the Prisoner's Dilemma rests on unstated assumptions which, if changed, lead to a different solution.

Source: Randall Grometstein. In *Non-Zero: The Logic of Human Destiny*, by Robert Wright (2000). New York: Pantheon Books.

seeks to describe what *is* and to understand how it came to be—whether something *should be* is in the realm of politics or philosophy. On the subject of whether something *must be*, most scientists strive to be cautious and open-minded.

The mistaken charge that evolutionary theory is determinist, however, may arise from a fundamental difference in the way social and natural scientists view human nature. According to biologist E. O. Wilson (1998: 204), social scientists "turn the intuitively obvious sequence of causation upside down: Human minds do not create culture but are themselves the product of culture." In other words, Wilson argues that the social sciences have ignored the role of human beings as culture-creators and have focused only on the socialization of individuals into their culture. Evolutionary theory considers the interaction of the individual and culture by asking: How do different cultural forms represent solutions to the problems of individual survival in both our ancestral environment and that of our present-day environment? In recognizing this interaction, evolutionary theory avoids the trap of determinism.

EVOLUTIONARY THEORY IN PSYCHOLOGY AND ANTHROPOLOGY

Psychologists and anthropologists are developing evolutionary models of human cognition and social structures. For example, anthropologist John Tooby and psychologist Leda Cosmides (1992) argue that human intelligence, rather than being general or global, is oriented toward the solving of particular problems related to survival in our ancestral environment, such as detecting cheaters in a system of social exchange. Anthropologist Sarah Blaffer Hrdy (1999) explores the evolutionary pressures on maternal behavior, and anthropologists Richard Wrangham and Dale Peterson (1996) propose an evolutionary basis for male violence. Evolutionary analysis has thrown new light on differences in social structures, such as polygyny and monogamy (Ridley 1993), child-rearing practices in which fathers are largely absent and children are raised by peers (Draper and Harpending 1988; Harpending and Draper 1988), bride-price customs (MacDonald 1988), and the socialization of children in extended kinship cultures (MacDonald 1988). An appreciation of the evolutionary roots of human behavior usually results in a greater appreciation of the role played by culture in shaping that behavior.

EVOLUTIONARY THEORY IN CRIMINOLOGY

Theories of crime have generally focused on explaining either particular kinds of crime or crime in the con-text of advanced industrial societies of the late twentieth century. Recently, criminologists interested in developing a more comprehensive theory have begun to explore evolutionary theories concerning crime. Augustine Brannigan (1997) suggests that the theory proposed by Michael Gottfredson and Travis Hirschi in *A General Theory of Crime* (1990) is compatible with an evolutionary perspective. Their theory suggests that criminals are people with a low level of self-control and that low self-control shows up not only as crime but also as a tendency to smoke, drink, get into automobile accidents, have children out of wedlock, and get fired from jobs. Two of the most important pieces of evidence they cite are that low self-control manifests itself by the time a child is six or eight and that the rate at which men commit crimes is highest between the ages of sixteen and twenty-six. Brannigan cites the work of psychologists Martin Daly and Margo Wilson (1988) on homicide to argue that much crime committed by young males is motivated by the need to acquire resources in a competition with other males for status and mates. Brannigan equates the low self-control described by Gottfredson and Hirschi with what he labels impulsiveness, a "vestigial tendency" or "default setting" for young men who have not been effectively socialized and supervised as children.

Lee Ellis and Anthony Walsh (1997) review what they term gene-based evolutionary theories in criminology. Evolutionary theory, they propose, provides an understanding of a category of crimes that includes rape, spousal assault or murder, and child abuse and neglect. It also provides some general models for understanding crime and antisocial behavior, including the cheater and *r/K* selection theories.

Both models begin with the observation that, beginning with pregnancy and nursing, females invest more care and effort in the nurturing of offspring than males do. Males have the option whether to invest a lot of care and resources in their offspring; if not, a male can continue to seek more sexual partners and let the mother raise the offspring. A male with many partners can sire a larger number of offspring than the male who shares in the raising of his offspring; however, the offspring of two parents have a greater chance of survival than the offspring of single parents.

The cheater model proposes that women have evolved to prefer men who will invest in their children. Men who are genetically inclined toward a low parental investment strategy will not be able to find mates unless they can deceive a mate into thinking they will indeed provide for their offspring. Cheaters employ various forms of deception and may therefore commit crimes such as fraud, theft, bigamy, rape, and other violent crimes in order to gain reproductive success.

The *r/K* theory employs terms developed by biologists to describe a spectrum of reproductive behavior. At the *r* end of the spectrum are animals who reproduce in large numbers and invest little or no time in raising their offspring (for example, the sea turtles who come to shore to lay eggs and then return to the sea, leaving the eggs to hatch by themselves). At the *K* end of the spectrum are animals who reproduce in small numbers over great time intervals (for example, gorilla females who have one baby approximately every eight years) and care intensely for their offspring. There are *r/K* differences within a species as well as between species. Applied to human beings, this theory proposes that people employing an *r* strategy will manifest what we call criminal and antisocial behavior, whereas parents who are *K* strategists not only will cooperate with one another to raise children but also will cooperate with other groups within the community.

Evolutionary theory describes a new framework for understanding crime in the context of adaptations to our ancestral environment and also sheds light on the development of cultural institutions designed to deal with crime. Many societies have punished rapists as severely as murderers; evolutionary theory suggests why. Anthony Walsh (2000) argues that "the human sense of justice is an evolved solution to problems faced by our distant ancestors." Because of reciprocal altruism, it is important for people to detect and punish cheaters. As societies have evolved from simple to complex, punishing cheaters has evolved from simple vengeance to reconciliation and reintegration. But the desire to punish cheaters is as basic as the desire to cheat.

THE NATURE OF HUMAN NATURE

Gottfredson and Hirschi (1990) point out the deep division among criminological theories based on unexamined assumptions about human nature. Classical theories (including control theory, deterrence theory, and rational choice theory) rest on the idea that children must be socialized properly in order to become law-abiding; hence, criminals are people who have not been properly socialized. Positivist theories assume that crime occurs in the presence of one or more positive factors (e.g., poverty, social disorganization, anomie,

and strain) and thus the essential nature of human beings is to be law-abiding. Both assumptions are philosophical rather than scientific. Evolutionary theory, by contrast, offers the potential to develop a scientific view of human nature that will allow predictions to be made and tested. As Gottfredson and Hirschi's (1990) theory does, future criminological theories will consider crime in relation to other forms of human behavior, and such theories will be able to mesh well with evolutionary theories from other disciplines. The twenty-first century should see the development of a general theory of human behavior, including crime.

—*Randall Grometstein*

See also BIOCRIMINOLOGY

Further Reading

Brannigan, Augustine. (1997). "Self-Control, Social Control and Evolutionary Psychology: Towards an Integrated Perspective on Crime." *Canadian Journal of Criminology* 39, 4 (October): 403–431.

Daly, Martin, and Margo Wilson. (1988). *Homicide.* Hawthorne, NY: Aldine de Gruyter.

Draper, Patricia, and Henry Harpending. (1988). "A Sociobiological Perspective on the Development of Human Reproductive Strategies." In *Sociobiological Perspectives on Human Development*, edited by Kevin B. MacDonald. New York: Springer-Verlag.

Ellis, Lee, and Anthony Walsh. (1997). "Gene-Based Evolutionary Theories in Criminology." *Criminology* 35, 2: 229–276.

Gottfredson, Michael R., and Travis Hirschi. (1990). *A General Theory of Crime.* Stanford, CA: Stanford University Press.

Hamilton, William D. (1970). "Selfish and Spiteful Behaviour in an Evolutionary Model." *Nature* (London) 228, 5277: 1218–1220.

Harpending, Henry, and Patricia Draper. (1988). "Antisocial Behavior and the Other Side of Cultural Evolution." In *Biological Contributions to Crime Causation*, edited by Terrie E. Moffitt and Sarnoff A. Mednick. The Hague, The Netherlands: Martinus Nijhoff.

Hrdy, Sarah Blaffer. (1999). *Mother Nature: Maternal Instincts and How They Shape the Human Species.* New York: Pantheon.

MacDonald, Kevin B., ed. (1988). *Sociological Perspectives on Human Development.* New York: Springer Verlag.

Ridley, Matt. (1993). *The Red Queen: Sex and the Evolution of Human Nature.* New York: Penguin Books.

———, ed. (1997). *Evolution.* New York: Oxford University Press.

Tooby, John, and Leda Cosmides. (1992). "The Psychological Foundations of Culture." In *The Adapted Mind: Evolutionary Psychology and the Generation of Culture*, edited by Jerome H. Barker, Leda Cosmides, and John Tooby. New York: Oxford University Press.

Trivers, Robert L. (1971). "The Evolution of Reciprocal Altruism." *Quarterly Review of Biology* 46, 4: 35–37.

Walsh, Anthony. (2000). "Evolutionary Psychology and the Origins of Justice." *Justice Quarterly* 17, 4 (December): 841–864.

Wilson, Edward O. (1975). *Sociobiology: The New Synthesis.* Cambridge, MA: Harvard University Press.

———. (1998). *Consilience: The Unity of Knowledge.* New York: Random House.

Wrangham, Richard W., and Dale Peterson. (1996). *Demonic Males: Apes and the Origin of Human Violence.* Boston: Houghton Mifflin.

Wright, Robert. (1995). *The Moral Animal: The New Science of Evolutionary Psychology.* New York: Vintage.

———. (2000). *Non-Zero: The Logic of Human Destiny.* New York: Pantheon.

▼ THE EXCLUSIONARY RULE

The exclusionary rule provides that evidence obtained by law enforcement officers in violation of the Fourth Amendment guarantee against unreasonable search and seizure is not admissible in a criminal trial to prove guilt. The rule was applied by the U.S. Supreme Court to the states in *Mapp v. Ohio* (1961). The primary purpose of the exclusionary rule is to deter police misconduct. Although some proponents argue that the rule emanates from the Constitution, the Supreme Court has indicated it is merely a judicially created remedy for violations of the Fourth Amendment. Because application of the rule may lead to the exclusion of important evidence and the acquittal of persons who are factually (if not legally) guilty, the exclusionary rule is perhaps the most controversial legal issue in criminal justice. Proponents argue that it is the only effective means of protecting individual rights from police misconduct, while critics decry the exclusion from trial of relevant evidence. Despite calls for its abolition and shifts in the composition of the Supreme Court, the exclusionary rule remains entrenched in American jurisprudence. But while the rule has survived, it has not gone unscathed. Supreme Court decisions over the years have limited the scope of the rule and created several exceptions.

HISTORY

The Supreme Court first addressed the issue of the admissibility of illegally obtained evidence in 1886, when it held in *Boyd v. United States* that the forced disclosure of papers amounting to evidence of crimes violated the constitutional right of the defendant against unreasonable search and seizure, and that such items were inadmissible in court proceedings. In 1914 the Supreme Court held in *Weeks v. United States* that evidence illegally obtained by federal law enforcement officers was not admissible in a federal criminal trial. Because the *Weeks* decision applied only to the federal government, however, state law enforcement officers were still free to seize evidence illegally without fear of its exclusion from state criminal proceedings. Moreover, evidence seized illegally by state police could be turned over to federal law enforcement officers for use in federal prosecutions because federal officers were not directly involved in the illegal seizure. In 1960, in *Elkins v. United States*, the Court put an end to this practice, prohibiting the introduction of illegally seized evidence in federal prosecutions regardless of whether the illegality was committed by state or federal agents.

In *Wolf v. Colorado* (1949), the Supreme Court applied the Fourth Amendment to the states, incorporating it into the due process clause of the Fourteenth Amendment. However, the Court refused to mandate the remedy of the exclusionary rule. Just three years later, the Court modified its position somewhat, holding in *Rochin v. California* that evidence seized in a manner which "shocked the conscience" must be excluded as violative of due process. Exactly what type of conduct shocked the conscience was left to be determined on a case-by-case basis. The exclusionary rule thus became applicable to state criminal proceedings, but its application was uneven.

Finally, in 1961, the Court took the step in *Mapp v. Ohio* that it had failed to take in *Wolf:* It explicitly applied the remedy of the exclusionary rule to the states. The Court did so because it acknowledged that the states had failed to provide an adequate alternative remedy for violations of the Fourth Amendment. Although there was language in *Mapp* that suggested the exclusionary rule originated from the Constitution, subsequent decisions indicate that the Court views the rule as a judicial means of enforcing the Fourth Amendment prohibition against unreasonable search and seizure.

EXCEPTIONS

In *Mapp,* the Supreme Court stated that the exclusionary rule serves at least two purposes: the deterrence of police misconduct and the protection of judicial integrity. In recent years, however, the Court has focused almost entirely on the deterrence of police misconduct, creating several exceptions to the rule. In addition, the Court has held that there are a variety of proceedings in which the exclusionary rule is inapplicable.

In 1984, the Court held in *Massachusetts v. Sheppard* that evidence obtained by police acting in good faith on a search warrant issued by a neutral and detached magistrate may be admitted at trial, even if the search warrant is ultimately found to be invalid. The Court stressed that the primary rationale for the exclusionary rule—deterrence of police misconduct—did not warrant exclusion of evidence obtained by police who act reasonably and in good faith reliance upon the actions of a judge. By "good faith," the Court meant the police are unaware that the warrant is invalid.

The Court emphasized that the good faith exception did not apply to errors made by the police, even if the errors were entirely inadvertent. The exception applies only to situations where the police relied on others who, it later turns out, made a mistake. Subsequent cases reiterated this point. In 1987, in *Illinois v. Krull*, the Court extended the good faith exception to instances where the police act in reliance on a statute that is later declared unconstitutional. In 1995, in *Arizona v. Evans*, the Court refused to apply the exclusionary rule to evidence seized by a police officer who acted in reliance on a computer entry made by a court clerk, which was later found to be in error.

The Court has also established the "inevitable discovery" exception to the exclusionary rule. This exception, developed in *Nix v. Williams*, permits the use at trial of evidence illegally obtained by the police they can demonstrate that they would have otherwise discovered the evidence by legal means. The burden is on the police to prove that they would in fact have discovered the evidence lawfully, a burden they have met only infrequently.

LIMITATIONS

The Supreme Court has been reluctant to extend the reach of the exclusionary rule to proceedings other than the criminal trial. Indeed, as recently as 1998, the Court stated, in *Pennsylvania Board of Probation and Parole v. Scott*, that as the primary purpose of the rule is deterrence of police misconduct, extension of the rule should be limited "to those instances where its

---

The U.S. Supreme Court on the Exclusionary Rule in *Mapp v. Ohio*

Since the Fourth Amendment's right of privacy has been declared enforceable against the States through the Due Process Clause of the Fourteenth [Amendment], it is enforceable against them by the same sanction of exclusion as is used against the Federal Government. Were it otherwise, then just as without the *Weeks* rule the assurance against unreasonable searches and seizures would be a 'form of word,' valueless and undeserving of mention in a perpetual charter of inestimable human liberties, so too, without that rule the freedom from state invasions of privacy would be . . . ephemeral.

Source: *Mapp v. Ohio*, 367 U.S. 643 (1961).

---

remedial objectives are thought to be most efficaciously served." The Court has consistently refused to apply the exclusionary rule to evidence seized by private parties, if they are not acting in concert with, or at the behest of, the police. The rule does not apply to evidence presented to the grand jury. An unlawful arrest does not bar prosecution of the arrestee, as the exclusionary rule is an evidentiary rule rather than a rule of jurisdictional limitation. The rule is inapplicable in both civil tax assessment proceedings and civil deportation proceedings. The exclusionary rule does not apply to parole revocation hearings. The Court has also been reluctant to apply the exclusionary rule to aspects of the criminal trial that are not directly related to the determination of guilt. Thus illegally obtained evidence may be used to impeach a defendant's testimony or to determine the appropriate sentence for a convicted defendant.

SUMMARY

The exclusionary rule has aroused much debate since its application to the states some forty years ago. The rule remains in place, although its application has been limited and exceptions have been created. Nonetheless, the rule still has a major and continuing impact on police practices, acting as the primary constraint on unlawful search and seizure. The recent decision in *Scott* neatly summarizes the Court's position on the applicability of the rule and suggests how the rule may be dealt with by law enforcement agencies in the future.

In *Scott*, the Court again refused to apply the exclusionary rule to a proceeding other than a criminal trial, even though the illegally seized evidence could be used to reincarcerate a parolee. By explicitly holding that the exclusionary rule does not apply to parole revocation hearings, the Court opened up a tremendous window of opportunity for police officers seeking to use illegally seized evidence against a suspect. The police may now avoid the prohibition on unreasonable search and seizure by using illegally seized evidence as the basis for parole revocation rather than as evidence of guilt in a criminal trial. This has tremendous implications for future law enforcement practices, as the number of persons under community supervision currently exceeds three million, and this number is predicted to grow steadily in the next decade (Bureau of Justice Statistics 1997).

The exclusionary rule continues, albeit in a limited form. Given the current composition of the Supreme Court, it seems unlikely that the rule will be expanded. The Court has refused numerous opportunities to discard the rule, however. So long as the exclusionary rule exists, it will serve, to some extent, as a limitation on police overreaching. It will also continue to result in the freeing of some "guilty" people. It is both the reward and the price we pay for living under a government of limited powers.

—*Craig Hemmens*

See also ARREST PRACTICES

Further Reading

Amar, Akhil Reed. (1997). *The Constitution and Criminal Procedure.* New Haven, CT: Yale University Press.

Bureau of Justice Statistics. (1997). *Correctional Populations in the United States, 1995.* Washington, DC: U.S. Department of Justice.

Cole, David. (1999). *No Equal Justice.* New York: The New Press.

Decker, John F. (1992). *Revolution to the Right: Criminal Procedure Jurisprudence During the Burger-Rehnquist Court Era.* New York: Garland.

del Carmen, Rolando V. (2000). *Criminal Procedure: Law and Practice.* Belmont, CA: Wadsworth/Thomson.

LaFave, Wayne R., and Jerold H. Israel. (1992). *Criminal Procedure.* Minneapolis, MN: West Publishing.

Court Cases

Arizona v. Evans (1995). 514 U.S. 1.
Boyd v. United States (1886). 116 U.S. 616.
Burdeau v. McDowell (1921). 256 U.S. 465.
Elkins v. United States (1960). 364 U.S. 206.
Illinois v. Krull (1987). 480 U.S. 340.
INS v. Lopez-Mendoza (1984). 468 U.S. 1032.
Mapp v. Ohio (1961). 367 U.S. 643.
Massachusetts v. Sheppard (1984). 468 U.S. 981.
Nix v. Williams (1984). 467 U.S. 431.

Pennsylvania Board of Probation and Parole v. Scott (1998). 118 S. Ct. 2014.
Rochin v. California (1952). 342 U.S. 165.
United States v. Alvarez-Machain (1992). 504 U.S. 655.
United States v. Calandra (1974). 414 U.S. 338.
United States v. Janis (1974). 428 U.S. 433.
United States v. Leon (1984). 468 U.S. 897.
Weeks v. United States (1914). 232 U.S. 383.
Wolf v. Colorado (1949). 338 U.S. 25.

EXPERIMENTAL CRIMINOLOGY

Experimental criminology is the body of criminal justice research that employs experimental designs to test the effectiveness of criminal justice interventions. While experimental designs abound in other disciplines, they tend to be less common in criminal justice research. Several explanations have been offered for the relative underutilization of experimental designs in criminological research. Experimental designs have been described as impractical, time-consuming and cost-prohibitive to implement. In some instances, researchers cannot meet the requirements of an experimental design. In other instances, implementing an experimental design would be considered unethical. Despite these and other obstacles, in recent years numerous influential criminologists have advocated for more frequent and systematic utilization of experimental designs in the evaluation of criminal justice policies and practices.

THE EXPERIMENTAL DESIGN

Virtually every undergraduate textbook on research methods describes experimental designs as the "gold standard" of research methodology. While there are many variations on the experimental design, the classic experimental design involves an independent and a dependent variable, random assignment to experimental and control groups, and pre- and posttesting. In the classic experiment, the independent variable can be thought of as the cause, and the dependent variable as the effect. The researcher believes that the independent variable causes changes in the dependent variable and conducts an experiment to test this belief. To conduct a classic experiment, the researcher selects a target population and randomly assigns subjects to either an experimental or a control group. Random assignment of subjects to the treatment and control groups ensures equivalency of the groups. The researcher then conducts a pretest by measuring both groups on the dependent variable. Following the pretest, the experimental group receives the experimental stimulus while the control group does not. The researcher then remeasures both groups on the dependent variable. Changes in the dependent variable seen in the experimental group (but not in the control group) are presumed to result from exposure to the experimental stimulus.

A criminal justice example might be helpful to demonstrate these points and clarify the definitions. Imagine a researcher interested in the effectiveness of juvenile "boot camps." Specifically, the researcher decides to test the hypothesis that juvenile boot camps increase a juvenile delinquent's respect for authority. The researcher identifies a target population as juvenile delinquents and draws subjects for the experiment from that population. The researcher then randomly assigns juvenile delinquents to the experimental and control groups and pretests each group's respect for authority prior to any intervention. The researcher then exposes only the subjects in the experimental group to the experimental stimulus, in this case boot camp. Following boot camp, both the experimental and control groups are remeasured on the dependent variable (respect for authority). Changes in the dependent variable observed in the experimental group but not the control group are presumed to result from exposure to the experimental stimulus (the boot camp). If the experimental group exhibits a greater respect for authority in the posttest, the researcher has proved his or her hypothesis and demonstrated the positive effect of boot camps on respect for authority.

The advantages of the experimental designs are widely acknowledged. Random assignment in an experimental design reduces conscious (or subconscious) bias in the assignment of subjects and also controls for the possibility of chance affecting the outcome. Control groups, a key element of an experimental design, provide a distinct advantage. The control group allows the researcher to attribute any changes in the dependent variable observed only in the experimental group to the experimental stimulus. Without a control group, it would be almost impossible to know whether the experimental stimulus, or something else, affected the experimental group. Due to the unique features of experimental designs, these research designs more readily allow for "causal inferences" (a statement of the cause-and-effect relationship between the experimental stimulus and outcome). While researchers frequently acknowledge the benefits of experimental designs, they also recognize that there are often significant barriers to conducting such experiments. Some of these barriers are particularly salient in the field of criminal justice.

EXPERIMENTAL DESIGNS IN CRIMINOLOGY

Although experiments provide the most scientifically sound evidence of the effect of an experimental stimulus, experimental studies can be particularly difficult to design in criminology. Criminal justice policy and agency cooperation are two additional obstacles to employing experimental designs in criminological research. As a result of criminal justice policies, criminological researchers are restricted in both the types of interventions they can study and the assignment of subjects to those interventions. Criminal justice policy frequently dictates both the nature of the design of criminal justice interventions and the exposure of individuals to those interventions. For example, current sentencing policy mandates prison for certain crimes. In mandatory sentencing schemes, prison is the only criminal justice intervention permitted. It is difficult for criminological researchers to develop an experimental research design to test the effects of the prison when a control group of similar offenders who are not sentenced to prison cannot be generated because of mandatory sentencing. Even if these sentencing policy requirements could be overcome, securing agency cooperation to conduct the research would present an additional obstacle. Judges and other criminal justice personnel are often reluctant to permit disparity in sentences for the purposes of research. Moreover, this type of experimental design might be widely condemned as unethical. Despite the additional obstacles that often face criminological researchers, experimental designs can be and have been successfully employed in criminological research.

EXPERIMENTAL CRIMINOLOGY: PAST AND PRESENT

In recent years, there has been a resurgence of literature on experimental methods in criminology. While this resurgence might seem to suggest the birth of a burgeoning field, the experimental method actually enjoys a rather extensive history in the social sciences. Within the social sciences, the field of psychology is widely accepted as having pioneered the use of the experimental method. As early as 1880, psychological researchers recognized the need for control groups in order to distinguish experimental effects and began utilizing controlled randomized studies. In the late 1890s, sociologists at the University of Chicago were applying experimental methods to studies of a wide variety of social problems. Not long after, criminologists began employing randomized experimental designs in studies of criminal justice policies and practices.

A delinquency prevention experiment conducted in Cambridge and Somerville, Massachusetts, in the 1930s is recognized as one of the earliest randomized experiments in criminal justice. In the Cambridge-Somerville experiment, a researcher hypothesized that delinquency might be preventable through friendship. Young boys were scored based on their risk for delinquency, matched in pairs on the basis of those scores, and then randomly assigned to either the intervention or control group. The intervention in this study consisted of the friendly counseling of a social worker over a period of several years. The results seemed to indicate that those who received the intervention were actually more likely to engage in delinquent behavior. More important, the research demonstrated that the levels of delinquency among these at-risk boys were actually much lower than was expected. Had there not been a control group, these low levels of delinquency might have been attributed to the intervention. The surprising results of the Cambridge-Somerville experiment demonstrated the potential importance of experimental designs in criminological research.

Early applications of the experimental method in the social sciences eventually led to "the flourishing in America of a golden age of evaluation between the 1960s and the 1980s" (Oakley 2000: 322). During this "golden age," social scientists utilized experimental methods to test the effectiveness of numerous social policy interventions, beginning with further controlled trials of delinquency prevention programs. Following the golden age, experimental designs seemed to largely fade from the criminal justice landscape with only a few diligent researchers continuing to employ these methods. However, toward the end of the 1990s, numerous influential criminologists began once again advocating for the increased use of experimental methods in criminological studies.

Over the past few years, several indicators of the growing popularity of experimental criminology have surfaced. In 1997, the American Society of Criminology (ASC), the largest national membership organization in the field of criminal justice, was prepared to officially endorse the use of experimental methods in criminal justice evaluation research and make a statement in support of the principle "that random assignment to treatment options is the best scientific method for determining the effectiveness of options" (Short et al. 2000: 296). In the year 2000, several important events marked the increasing stature of experimental criminology. Several distinguished scholars founded the Academy of Experimental Criminology (AEC), an academy whose fellows have significantly advanced criminal justice knowledge through conducting experiments within the field. In the same year, the Campbell Collaboration, an international group committed to collecting and evaluating randomized experiments in criminal justice and other social science fields, was also established. Finally, an entire issue of the journal *Crime & Delinquency* was devoted to experimental criminology (July 2000). The articles in the special issue explored the possibilities, limitations, and ethical implications of employing experimental methods in criminal justice research. These recent events demonstrate the growing interest in applying classical experimental research methods to the field of criminology.

SUMMARY

True experiments are the gold standard in social science research. Carefully designed experiments that employ the random assignment of subjects to experimental and control groups provide the best evidence of the effectiveness of interventions. These experiments allow the researcher to measure the effects of the independent variable on the dependent variable while controlling for the operation of bias or chance. While formidable obstacles must sometimes be overcome to conduct an experiment in criminological research, these research designs are once again becoming more common. Advocates of experimental criminology argue that randomized controlled experiments add to the knowledge base and will ultimately lead to more informed criminal justice policy. With the recent coalescence of activity highlighting the importance of utilizing experimental designs in criminological research, enthusiasm for experimental criminology continues to grow.

—*Natasha A. Frost*

Further Reading

Feder, Lynette, and Robert F. Boruch. (2000). "The Need for Experiments in Criminal Justice Settings." *Crime and Delinquency* 46, 3 (July): 291–294.

Maxfield, Michael G., and Earl Babbie. (1998). *Research Methods for Criminal Justice and Criminology.* Belmont, CA: Wadsworth Publishing Company.

Oakley, Ann. (2000). "A Historical Perspective on the Use of Randomized Trial in Social Science Settings." *Crime & Delinquency* 46, 3 (July): 315–329.

Petrosino, Anthony, Carolyn Turpin-Petrosino, and James O. Finckenauer. (2000). "Well Meaning Programs Can Have Harmful Effects! Lessons from Experiments of Programs Such as Scared Straight." *Crime & Delinquency* 46, 3 (July): 354–379.

Sherman, Lawrence. (2000). "Reducing Incarceration Rates: The Promise of Experimental Criminology." *Crime & Delinquency* 46, 3 (July): 299–314.

Sherman, Lawrence and David Weisburd. (1995). "General Deterrent Effects of Police Patrol in Crime 'Hot Spots': A Randomized Controlled Trial." *Justice Quarterly* 12: 625–648.

Short, James F., Margaret Zahn, and David P. Farrington. (2000). "Experimental Research in Criminal Justice Settings: Is There a Role for Scholarly Societies?" *Crime & Delinquency* 46, 3 (July): 295–298.

EXPERT WITNESS

An expert witness testifies to help judges and jurors find the truth and administer justice. To clarify scientific or technical issues, the expert brings special knowledge into court that laypersons are not expected to know. Unlike non-expert witnesses, whose testimony is limited to personal observations directly related to the case, expert witnesses are allowed to express and explain opinions by virtue of their knowledge, training, and experience. Judges must allow expert testimony if an individual's scientific, technical, or other knowledge is helpful and relevant to the case. However, reliance on expert witnesses does not always guarantee that the interests of truth and justice are served.

EARLY EXPERTS

Courts used expert, but nonscientific, knowledge as early as the fourteenth century, when juries composed of craftsmen or tradesmen often heard cases within their specialties. In other cases, jurors were scholars, engineers, and physicians. Ideas from science affected legal practice as early as the 1692 witch trials in Salem, Massachusetts. At least nineteen people were executed and others incarcerated and ruined finan-

cially before questions about the reliability of the evidence ended the trials. Thus, ideas from science heightened concerns about false identifications and executions. In 1782, a civil engineer became the first known expert to testify from the witness stand.

EARLY PHYSICAL SCIENCE

Most early expert witnesses used techniques that identified types of physical evidence. These techniques helped determine whether a crime had been committed and guided the collection of evidence. This work is now known as forensic science. "Forensic science in its broadest definition is the application of science to law" (Saferstein 2001: 1).

Matthieu Orfila (1787–1853) published the first scientific work on the detection and effects of poisons. Alphonse Bertillon (1853–1914) created the first system of personal identification; although fingerprints replaced his body measures, he is known as the father of criminal identification. In 1892, Francis Galton (1822–1911) published *Fingerprints*, a book that is still used today. Leone Lattes (1887–1954) built on Karl Landsteiner's 1901 discovery of the four blood types: A, B, AB, and O. In 1915, Lattes developed an investigative procedure using dried bloodstains. Calvin Goddard's (1891–1955) comparison microscope improved the ability to compare crime scene bullets with ones fired from suspects' guns. Albert S. Osborn's (1858–1946) book *Questioned Documents*, published in 1910, still guides document examinations. In 1893, Hans Gross (1847–1915) described how information from several scientific disciplines can apply to criminal investigations.

Eventually, forensic crime labs became centers of training and technical assistance for police. The first U.S. lab was established in 1923 by August Vollmer in Los Angeles, California. The best-known lab was created in 1932 by the Federal Bureau of Investigation (FBI). Most persons performing lab tests or testifying worked for the prosecution and were law enforcement officers or had law enforcement experience. This link still exists: "About 80 percent of forensic scientists in North America are affiliated with police or prosecution agencies" (Kelly and Wearne 1998: 15).

The first important case relating to the qualifications of expert witnesses was *Frye v. United States* (1923). The defendant, Alphonso Frye, confessed to committing murder, but he later withdrew his confession, saying that he had passed a deception test that measured blood pressure. A federal court ruled that this lie detector did not have "general acceptance" within the scientific community. This judgment became known as the Frye Rule: without general acceptance, techniques and the evidence they produced were excluded from court. For more than fifty years, this rule applied in most federal and state courts.

SOCIAL SCIENCE

Some early social and psychological research focused on biases, false identifications, and human well-being. In 1816, the astronomer Friedrich Bessel discovered that using numbers helped him understand how humans perceive and record data. In 1796, an astronomer's assistant had been fired because his telescope readings of when a star crossed a hairline were almost a second later than the master astronomer's. Bessel referred to these variations in observations as "a personal equation," a human factor affecting behavior and science (Anastasi 1958: 5).

In 1879, German psychologists created a lab to study perception and memory. In 1908, Hugo Münsterberg described how these studies helped explain human bias and false eyewitness identifications. Another German psychologist, Louis William Stern, conducted reality experiments that exposed students to unexpected but staged events. He testified about identification problems in 1903. However, criticisms from legal scholars largely prevented such testimony in the United States until the 1970s.

In *Muller v. Oregon* (1908), Louis Brandeis's legal brief on women's health played a key role in limiting their excessively long workdays. His use of empirical data provided the groundwork for the use of research by several scholars, including psychologist Kenneth Clark and sociologist Gunnar Myrdal, on the effects of school segregation, in *Brown v. Board of Education* (1954). Ruling that segregated schools were unconstitutional, the Supreme Court cited these expert opinions that segregated schools hurt black children's personalities and academic performance.

Some historical research suggests that bias rather than truth-seeking may determine who testifies as an expert witness. Although biblical scholars and evolutionary biologists volunteered testimony in the 1925 Scopes "monkey" trial following an instructor's arrest for teaching evolution, the judge did not allow it. In addition to resistance from the prosecutor, opposition came from "Governor Peay and other prominent Tennesseans" (Larson 1997: 155).

DEVELOPMENTS SINCE THE 1970S

Recent cases show a similar hesitancy by the U.S. Supreme Court to allow expert testimony on evolution and certain criminal justice issues. The decision in *Daubert v. Merrell Dow Pharmaceuticals, Inc.* (1993), however, opened courts to more expert testimony by replacing the Frye Rule with Rule 702 of the Federal Rules of Evidence:

> If scientific, technical, or other specialized knowledge will assist the trier of fact to understand the evidence or to determine a fact in issue, a witness qualified as an expert by knowledge, skill, experience, training, or education, may testify thereto in the form of an opinion or otherwise, if (1) the testimony is based upon sufficient facts or data, (2) the testimony is the product of reliable principles and methods, and (3) the witness has applied the principles and methods reliably to the facts of the case.

Daubert and cases that followed it "placed the matter of science in the law at the top of both federal and state courts' agendas" (Faigman 1999: xiii) and posed two major problems for judges. First, how can judges, who want clear and final answers such as guilty or not guilty, manage the uncertainties of science? This difficulty stems from differences in legal and scientific vocabularies and from the ways that law and science understand causation and problem solving. Second, how can judges identify persons with helpful scientific knowledge and weed out testimony on junk science that uses biased inferences rather than reliable testing procedures? In *Daubert,* "a new phrase—'scientific knowledge'—had replaced 'general acceptance'"; Federal Rule 702 now guided attempts to separate scientific knowledge from junk science (Foster and Huber 1999: 13).

Since the 1970s, advances in criminology, criminal justice, and related fields have complicated the task of managing both of these issues. Judges now face new types of knowledge claims by increasing numbers of persons in increasingly complex cases. Further difficulties have arisen as these developments produce serious disagreements in the scientific community about which data are relevant and even about the meaning of such basic concepts as facts, harm, and justice itself.

Also since the 1970s, many organizations, books, and Web sites have provided resources to help interested parties find experts, review their qualifications, and prepare for courtroom work. Preparation for testimony should begin early so that attorneys and witnesses can learn how to understand each other and blend their legal and expert knowledge. This helps experts use language that a jury of laypersons can understand, in an adversarial arena where opponents attempt to "win" by discrediting witnesses. Experts can let attorneys know what data and supporting documents are necessary for acceptable testimony. Sometimes huge amounts of money or the quest for prestige and power undermine scientific procedures, ethical principles, and reliable testimony.

ETHICS

To manage such threats, experts and attorneys should agree on their ethical responsibilities before any work occurs. In particular, reliable principles and written procedural criteria should guide all data management and tests. These criteria should not allow experts to be pro-prosecution or pro-defense. This issue erupted in 1989 when an FBI forensic expert, Frederic Whitehurst, revealed to defense attorneys his concerns about FBI lab tests and testimony. His actions mirrored principles in Rule 702 and came after numerous memos sent through the FBI chain of command were ignored.

Whitehurst complained about tainted evidence and "juicing testimony," (i.e., of agents "stretching the truth or even lying on the witness stand"; Kelly and Wearne 1998: 312). A report by the Inspector General's Office of the Justice Department confirmed some but not the most serious of Whitehurst's complaints and led to Congressional hearings. These events underscore every expert's ethical and scientific responsibility to wear the moral hat of the knowledge specialist.

REAL-WORLD SCIENCE

Much like Bessel, Whitehurst discovered personal equations that undermined objectivity in the FBI lab. He attributed these human factors to a culture with poor scientific standards, lax supervision, inadequate resources, and prosecutorial biases. Victor Kappeler, an expert witness on police culture, expressed similar concerns. Another expert, James Fyfe, described difficulties jurors have in understanding a police organization's failure to train officers how to use legal force. These opinions indicate two things. First, the quest for truth and justice needs information about organizational culture and individuals. The law assumes that individuals are primarily responsible for behavior. At

least since 1935, however, psychologists such as Kurt Lewin have attributed most responsibility for behavior to cultural and situational forces. Because these forces determine how persons learn to understand reality, the forces themselves guide perception, judgment, and behavior.

Second, any technique loses reliability when data are covered up, tainted, or slanted during testimony. Examples are widespread: Although the Atomic Energy Commission (AEC) knew that radiation threatened public health, this was not public knowledge until 1978. The AEC "had lied in Congressional hearings, destroyed documents, given false testimony, and denied in the media any harm to the public" (Situ and Emmons 2000: 87). For decades corporate executives denied that tobacco is addictive and "kills people—when used as intended" (Kessler 2001: 388). Sexual abuse of incarcerated females in state prisons is frequent but often covered up and followed by further mistreatment of victims who complain. Even DNA typing, an excellent technique for identifying people, can lose reliability by data mismanagement or "juicing" testimony.

HUMAN NATURE

Scientific knowledge about how bias affects behavior and the understanding of human nature rarely influences the majority opinions of the Supreme Court. Yet, such knowledge often appears in professional writings and in dissenting Supreme Court opinions and footnotes. Dissenting opinions in two cases upholding the legality of capital punishment by 5-4 rulings illustrate this fact.

Dissenting justices in *McCleskey v. Kemp* (1987) cited scientific data and historical patterns that suggest racial bias in the practice of capital punishment. Their opinion shows how many experts understand the influence of biased history and racism on law. Frustrations in this area lead some scholars to conclude that the pursuit of justice needs democratic expansion and, in some situations, procedures such as South Africa's Truth and Reconciliation Commission.

In *Stanford v. Kentucky* (1989), the majority assumed that one's reason is free from emotions by age sixteen. Therefore, juveniles are rationally developed persons capable of committing crimes that should be punishable by death; imposing the death penalty on individuals sixteen years or older is not a violation of the Eight Amendment ban on cruel and unusual punishment. The minority, citing expert opinions, opposed juvenile executions because of the offenders' moral immaturity and because of international human rights treaties. These justices understood young offenders in a lifespan context as developing persons whose potential for moral growth frequently suffered developmental harm because of child abuse and neglect. This understanding builds upon scientific evidence that abuse and neglect interfere with neurological brain development and biochemistry. Especially during childhood, research shows that humans need proper care and fairness to "harmonize head and heart" and avoid "emotional hijacking" of self-control (Goleman 1995: 29). This fuller understanding of the nature of juveniles challenges traditional legal beliefs.

Scientific knowledge often challenges traditional beliefs about persons and justice. Although predictions of dangerousness often justify executions or incarceration, predictions rarely follow appropriate mathematical procedures as described by Thomas Bayes and published in 1763. Therapists who believe their patients recall repressed memories during treatment may testify about these in child sexual abuse cases. Other experts believe that therapists teach their patients to imagine images and then accept them as real.

IMPROVING THE PROCESS

After a tradition of legal rules that restricted testimony by expert witnesses, Supreme Court decisions in the last decade of the twentieth century made such information more available. However, debate among scholars shows no agreement on the benefits and risks of the changed rules. The primary risk involves flooding courts with testimony based upon biased opinions rather than scientific knowledge (Foster and Huber, 1999). Evidence shows that biased and unreliable testimony can be found readily among both prosecution and defense experts. Several suggested changes may help control these biases. One alternative is for courts to hire independent experts who have exemplary records of following appropriate scientific procedures and ethical principles.

Two other possible changes are guided by substantial experience. First, laws can be strengthened to protect whistleblowers and encourage them to provide critical information despite pressures to conceal it. Second, laws that require full disclosure of relevant documentation and data to both parties in legal disputes can be strengthened. Without access to these essential building blocks of scientific knowledge, no

party or person in court can have confidence in claims of scientifically reliable evidence. On the positive side, as provided in Federal Rule 702, it is helpful for decision makers in court to hear the opinions of qualified expert witnesses in complex cases or where new scientific knowledge exists.

—*Thomas E. Reed*

See also CRIMINAL INSANITY; MEDICAL EXAMINER; PSYCHIATRY, FORENSIC; PSYCHOLOGY, FORENSIC

Further Reading

Adams, Guy, and Danny Balfour. (1998). *Unmasking Administrative Evil*. Thousand Oaks, CA: Sage Publications.

Anastasi, Anne. (1958). *Differential Psychology*. New York: The Macmillian Company.

Anderson, Patrick, and L. Thomas Winfree, Jr., eds. (1987). *Expert Witnesses: Criminologists in the Courtroom*. Albany: State University of New York Press.

Brodsky, Stanley. (1991). *Testifying in Court: Guidelines and Maxims for the Expert Witness*. Washington, DC: American Psychological Association.

Damasio, Antonio. (1994). *Descartes' Error: Emotion, Reason, and the Human Brain*. New York: Avon Books.

Faigman, David. (1999). *Legal Alchemy: The Use and Misuse of Science in the Law*. New York: W. H. Freeman and Company.

Foster, Kenneth, and Peter Huber. (1999). *Judging Science: Scientific Knowledge and the Federal Courts*. Cambridge, MA: The MIT Press.

Friedrichs, David, ed. (1998). *State Crime*. Brookfield, VT: Ashgate Publishing Company.

Goleman, Daniel. (1995). *Emotional Intelligence: Why It Can Matter More than IQ*. New York: Bantam Books.

Higginbotham, A. Leon, Jr. (1996). *Shades of Freedom: Racial Politics and Presumptions of the American Legal Process*. New York: Oxford University Press.

Kappeler, Victor, Richard Sluder, and Geoffrey Alpert. (1998). *Forces of Deviance: Understanding the Dark Side of Policing*. Prospect Heights, IL: Waveland Press, Inc.

Kelly, John, and Phillip Wearne. (1998). *Tainting Evidence: Inside the Scandals at the FBI Crime Lab*. New York: The Free Press.

Kessler, David. (2001). *A Question of Intent: A Great American Battle with a Deadly Industry*. New York: Public Affairs.

Larson, Edward. (1997). *Summer of the Gods: The Scopes Trial and America's Continuing Debate over Science and Religion*. Cambridge, MA: Harvard University Press.

Lewin, Kurt. (1935). *A Dynamic Theory of Personality: Selected Papers*. New York: McGraw-Hill Book Company.

Loftus, Elizabeth. (1979). *Eyewitness Testimony*. Cambridge, MA: Harvard University Press.

Malone, David, and Paul Zwier. (2000). *Effective Expert Testimony*. Notre Dame, IN: National Institute for Trial Advocacy.

Saferstein, Richard. (2001). *Criminalistics: An Introduction to Forensic Science*. Upper Saddle River, NJ: Prentice Hall.

Situ, Yingyi, and David Emmons. (2000). *Environmental Crime: The Criminal Justice System's Role in Protecting the Environment*. Thousand Oaks, CA: Sage Publications.

Court Cases

Brown v. Board of Education (1954). 348 U.S. 483.
Daubert v. Merrell Dow Pharmaceuticals, Inc. (1993). 509 U.S. 579.
Frye v. United States (1923). 293 F. 1013.
McCleskey v. Kemp (1987). 481 U.S. 279.
Muller v. Oregon (1908). 208 U.S. 412.
Stanford v. Kentucky (1989). 492 U.S. 361.
Scopes v. State (1927). 154 Tenn 105, 289 SW 363.

▼ EYEWITNESS TESTIMONY

Eyewitness testimony refers to verbal statements from people regarding what they observed and can purportedly remember that would be relevant to issues of proof at a criminal or civil trial. Such statements constitute a common form of evidence at trials. Eyewitness identification is a specific type of eyewitness testimony in which an eyewitness claims to recognize a specific person as one who committed a particular action. In cases where the eyewitness knew the suspect before the crime, issues of the reliability of memory are usually not contested. In cases where the perpetrator of the crime was a stranger to the eyewitness, however, the reliability of the identification is often at issue. Researchers in various areas of experimental psychology, especially cognitive and social psychology, have been conducting scientific studies of eyewitness testimony since the early 1900s, but most of the systematic research has occurred only since the mid- to late 1970s. There now exists a large body of published experimental research showing that eyewitness testimony evidence can be highly unreliable under certain conditions. In recent years, wrongful convictions of innocent people have been discovered through post-conviction DNA testing, and these cases show that more than 80 percent of these innocent people were convicted using mistaken eyewitness identification evidence. These DNA exoneration cases, along with previous analyses of wrongful convictions, point to mistaken eyewitness testimony as the primary cause of the conviction of innocent people.

Psychologists commonly partition memory into three distinct phases. The first phase is *acquisition.* The acquisition phase refers to processes involved in the initial encoding of an event and the factors that affect the encoding. Problems in acquisition include the effects of expectations, attention, lighting, distance, arousal, and related factors that control the types, amount, and accuracy of the encoded information. Eyewitnesses to crimes often witness the event under poor conditions because the event happens unexpectedly, rapidly, and/or under conditions of fear. Also, their attention may be focused on elements that are of little use for later recognition of the perpetrator, such as focusing on a weapon. The second phase is *retention.* Information that is acquired must be retained for later use. Memory generally declines rapidly in the initial time periods and more slowly later, in what psychologists describe as a "negatively decelerating curve." Importantly, new information can be acquired during this phase and mixed together with what was previously observed to create confusion regarding what was actually seen by the eyewitness and what was perhaps overheard later. It is now well established through controlled experiments that witnesses will use false information, contained in misleading questions, to create what appear to be new memories that are often dramatically different from what was actually observed. The final phase is the *retrieval* phase. The two primary types of retrieval are recall and recognition. In a recall task, the witness is provided with some context (e.g., the time frame) and asked to provide a verbal report of what was observed. In a recognition task, the witness is shown some objects (or persons) and asked to indicate whether any of them were involved in the crime event. Retrieval failures can be either errors of omission (e.g., failing to recall some detail or failing to recognize the perpetrator) or errors of commission (e.g., recalling things that were not present or picking an innocent person from a lineup). Problems at any of the three phases of memory lead to unreliability in testimony.

EVENT MEMORY

Eyewitnesses often give verbal reports of details of events, such as conversations, actions, and objects, that can have considerable importance to solving crimes. Psychologists have studied this process, and patterns of error in such recollections, in a variety of ways. One of the most informative approaches has been the three-part procedure that shows how recollections can be distorted by events that occur after the person has already witnessed the event in question. In the three-part procedure, experimental witnesses first see a complex event, such as a simulated violent crime or an automobile accident. Subsequently, half of the witnesses receive new misleading information about the event. The other half do not get any misinformation. Finally, all of the witnesses attempt to recall the original event.

In a typical example of a study using this paradigm, witnesses saw a simulated traffic accident. They then received written information about the accident, but some people were misled about what they saw. A stop sign, for instance, was referred to as a yield sign. When asked whether they originally saw a stop sign or a yield sign, those given the phony information tended to adopt it as their memory; they said they saw a yield sign. This change in eyewitness reports arising after receipt of misinformation is often referred to as the "misinformation effect." Researchers have shown that misinformation procedures can make people believe and remember that earlier in their lives they had been hospitalized when they had not, that they had been victims of vicious animal attacks as children even though they had not been, and even that they had witnessed demonic possession when they were very young.

Psychological science has built a strong case over the last twenty-five years that human memory is much more malleable than most people think it is. In addition, false memories of various types can be held with very high certainty, thereby making it difficult or even impossible at times to prove that the testimony of an eyewitness is wrong. The implications of this for criminal and civil trials can be enormous if the critical elements of proof rely on the testimony of eyewitnesses, especially if the eyewitnesses have been exposed to considerable amounts of new information (which might or might not be accurate) after the witnessed event. This situation has spawned considerable legal debate about the role of eyewitness experts in the courtroom. Throughout the 1980s and 1990s, defense attorneys have tended to maintain that such expert testimony is needed to inform jurors about the problems with eyewitness reliability, while prosecutors have tended to maintain that jurors already understand these matters or that such testimony would invade the traditional province of the

jurors as the only ones who should be making judgments about the credibility of eyewitnesses.

EYEWITNESS IDENTIFICATION

One of the most direct ways in which eyewitnesses can affect the outcome of a trial is through testimony stating that a particular person was the perpetrator of the crime. In cases where the eyewitness knows the alleged perpetrator (e.g., a friend or relative), the chances of an honest mistaken identification are not usually considered to be high. However, in cases where the perpetrator was a stranger, the contention of the eyewitness that the identified person is the actual perpetrator can be quite controversial. Considerable research has been directed at the question of how reliable such identifications tend to be.

The methods used in the scientific study of eyewitness identification evidence typically involve staging live crimes or showing video events to people. Because the events are created by the researchers, it is known with certainty who the actual "perpetrator" was and the performance of eyewitnesses in picking him or her from a lineup can be scored systematically. These eyewitnesses can also be asked to indicate their confidence in the identification decision, thereby permitting analysis of the relation between confidence and accuracy. Systematic manipulations of key variables (e.g., the structure of the lineup) allows for a causal analysis of variables that affect identification accuracy, eyewitness confidence, and the relation between the two.

The scientific eyewitness identification literature has tended to rely on a distinction between "estimator variables" and "system variables." Estimator variables are those that affect the accuracy of eyewitness identifications but cannot be controlled by the criminal justice system. System variables also affect the accuracy of eyewitness identifications, but the criminal justice system can control those variables. Estimator variables tend to revolve around factors involved in the acquisition phase, such as lighting conditions, distance, arousal, the presence of weapons, and so on. System variables tend to revolve around factors involved in the retrieval phase, such as the structure of a lineup, instructions given to witnesses prior to viewing a lineup, and so on.

One of the estimator variables that has received considerable attention is the race of the perpetrator relative to the race of the eyewitness. Another estimator variable that is frequently cited is "weapon focus."

DID YOU KNOW...

Mistaken eyewitness testimony is the major reason that innocent people are convicted of crimes. Other reasons include false confessions, false informant testimony, errors in forensic processing of evidence, prosecutorial misconduct, and poor legal representation. Today, DNA evidence is increasingly used to rule out potential suspects, to identify possible offenders, and to exonerate those who have been wrongfully convicted.

Experiments suggest that the presence of a weapon draws attention toward the weapon and away from the weapon holder's face, resulting in less reliable identification performance by eyewitnesses. Stress, fear, and arousal have been less effectively studied because of the problems with studying these variables in an ecologically valid manner. Sex, intelligence, and personality factors appear to be weakly, if at all, related to the tendency to make correct or mistaken identifications.

System variable research has focused primarily on four factors: the instructions to eyewitnesses, the content of a lineup, the presentation procedures used during the lineup, and the behaviors of the lineup administrator. A dominant account of the process of eyewitness identification that has emerged is the "relative judgment process." According to this account, eyewitnesses tend to select the person from the lineup who most closely resembles the perpetrator relative to the other members of the lineup. This process works reasonably well for eyewitnesses as long as the actual perpetrator is in the lineup. When the actual perpetrator is not in the lineup, however, there is still someone who looks more like the perpetrator than the remaining members of the lineup, thereby luring eyewitnesses to pick that person with surprising frequency.

It is critical to instruct eyewitnesses that the actual perpetrator might or might not be present in the lineup before showing the lineup to eyewitnesses. Proper instructions warning the eyewitness that the perpetrator might not be present do not eliminate the relative judgment tendency altogether, but they do reduce the magnitude of the problem.

The relative judgment process also has implications for how investigators should select "lineup fillers." A lineup filler is a known-innocent member of a lineup. Normally, a lineup will have one suspect and several (five or more) fillers whose primary purpose is to prevent the eyewitness from simply guessing. If an eyewitness is merely guessing, then odds against selecting the suspect are N:1 (where N is the number of fillers). However, if the fillers do not fit the general description of the suspect (as provided previously by the eyewitness) whereas the suspect does fit that description, then the lineup is said to be biased against the suspect.

The usual procedure for lineups is one that eyewitness researchers have called the "simultaneous procedure" because all members of the lineup are presented at one time. Simultaneous procedures tend to encourage eyewitnesses to compare one lineup member to another lineup member and home in on

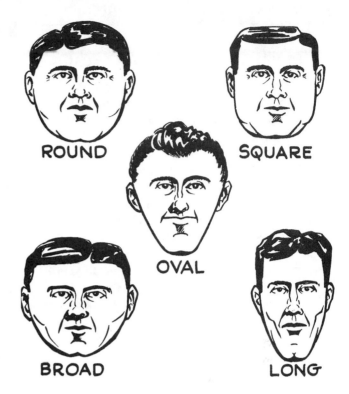

Eyewitness identification of offenders is an important source of evidence in criminal trials. Training provided police officers involves observing and recording facial attributes such as shape (as shown above), slope, width, and patterns of baldness.

Source: U.S. Department of the Army. (1961). *Observation, Description, and Identification.* Department of the Army Technical Bulletin.

the one who looks most like the perpetrator. An alternative procedure, called the "sequential lineup," was originally developed and tested in 1985. The sequential procedure presents the eyewitness with one lineup member at a time, and requires the eyewitness to make a yes/no decision on each lineup member before viewing the next lineup member. The sequential procedure prevents the eyewitness from merely making a decision as to which lineup member looks most like the perpetrator.

A major concern of eyewitness researchers has been the behaviors of the lineup administrator. The case detectives are well aware of which lineup member is the suspect. The "experimenter expectancy effect," well known in psychology, occurs when the person (e.g., an experimenter) is aware of the desired response and unintentionally (even without awareness) influences the subject to give the desired response. In a lineup situation, verbal and nonverbal interactions between the witness and the investigator should be of great concern because the eyewitness is supposed to use only his or her

The Pitfalls of Eyewitness Testimony

Although eyewitness identification can be a potent and effective tool available to police and prosecution, it is unfortunately not always reliable. Even victims who are certain they recognize their attackers are often mistaken. Work by groups such as the Innocence Project and Truth in Justice suggests that mistaken identity is the single most important cause of wrongful convictions.

The Innocence Project is a nonprofit legal clinic founded in 1992 by attorneys Barry C. Scheck and Peter J. Neufeld at the Benjamin N. Cardozo School of Law in New York City. It handles only cases where postconviction DNA testing of evidence can yield conclusive proof of innocence. Cases are first reviewed by volunteer attorneys. Then, law students handle the case work while supervised by a team of attorneys and clinic staff. Since its founding, 101 inmates have been exonerated and released as a result of DNA testing. In 60 of the first 82 cases, mistaken eyewitness identification played a major role in the wrongful conviction.

Truth in Justice is a nonprofit organization working to free innocent men and women convicted of crimes they did not commit and to prevent wrongful convictions by educating the public regarding the vulnerabilities in the U. S. criminal justice system that make these mistakes possible. Like the Innocence Project, Truth in Justice maintains a Web site reporting on cases of wrongful conviction and publicizes research analyzing its causes.

As a result of work by the Innocence Project, Truth in Justice, and other groups, public concern over wrongful conviction has grown. Many states have now enacted laws addressing this issue, and legislation is pending in other states and in both houses of Congress. As of February 2002, the following states had enacted laws aimed at preventing the conviction of innocent persons and compensating victims who have been wrongfully imprisoned:

Legislation recommending, requiring, and/or funding DNA testing:	Laws on preservation of evidence that can be used in DNA testing:	Laws providing compensation for wrongful conviction:
Arizona	Arkansas	California
Arkansas	California	Maryland
California	Delaware	New York
Delaware	Illinois	Texas
Florida	Louisiana	
Idaho	Maine	
Illinois	Maryland	
Indiana	Michigan	
Louisiana	Minnesota	
Maine	Missouri	
Maryland	Nebraska	
Michigan	New Mexico	
Minnesota	New York	
Missouri	Oregon	
Nebraska	Texas	
New Mexico	Virginia	
New York	Washington	
Oklahoma	Wisconsin	
Oregon		
Tennessee		
Texas		
Virginia		
Washington		
Wisconsin		

Sources: The Innocence Project Web site: www.innocenceproject.com; Truth in Justice: www.truthinjustice.org

memory, free from external influences, to make the decision. Recent research indicates that the knowledge of the person administering the lineup can influence the eyewitness to pick the wrong person when the lineup administrator has the wrong person as the suspect. Eyewitness researchers have argued strongly that the person who administers the lineup should not know which person in the lineup is the suspect.

Research has shown the confidence of an eyewitness is the principal determinant of whether jurors will believe that an eyewitness made an accurate identification. Research shows that there is only a modest relation between eyewitness confidence and eyewitness accuracy. Importantly, research also shows that procedures by many law enforcement agencies are probably harming the already modest relation between eyewitness identification confidence and accuracy. Specifically, eyewitnesses are commonly given "confirming feedback" after they identify a suspect. This feedback takes many forms, such as "Good, that's the guy we thought it was," or "You got him!" Research shows that feedback of this sort to eyewitnesses who are in fact mistaken can erase eyewitnesses' recollections of their initial uncertainty. This feedback problem is another factor leading eyewitness researchers to strongly advocate double-blind testing with lineups. (This testing entails having someone administer the lineup who does not know which person in the lineup is the suspect—preventing the person administering the test from influencing the eyewitness.) Repeated questioning of eyewitnesses tends to have similar confidence-inflating properties such that eyewitnesses tend to become more confident in their incorrect reports with repeated questioning.

Since about 1990, when forensic DNA evidence came into accepted usage in the justice system, dozens of cases have come to light in which innocent persons were convicted of serious crimes by juries. In most of these cases, the primary evidence that was used was eyewitness identification evidence. These cases have given research into eyewitness identification a credibility that did not exist before the advent of forensic DNA.

SUMMARY

Scientific studies have uncovered numerous problems that can plague the reliability of eyewitnesses. These problems can occur at the time of acquisition, storage, or retrieval of memories. Witnesses can be led to recall details incorrectly and even to report recalling entire events that never occurred. The certainty of an eyewitness can be misleading. Eyewitness researchers have been used in trials, both civil and criminal, to educate jurors about factors that can lead to mistaken eyewitness memories. Since the discovery in the 1990s of mistaken identifications based on DNA analyses, the justice system in the United States has started to take more seriously the problems with eyewitness evidence and the types of solutions that have been proposed by psychological scientists.

—Gary L. Wells

See also WRONGFUL CONVICTIONS

Further Reading

Cutler, Brian L., and Steven D. Penrod. (1995). *Mistaken Identification: The Eyewitness, Psychology, and the Law.* New York: Cambridge University Press.

Goldstein, Alvin G., June E. Chance, and George R. Schneller. (1989). "Frequency of Eyewitness Identification in Criminal Cases: A Survey of Prosecutors." *Bulletin of the Psychonomic Society* 27, 1: 71–74.

Huff, Ronald, Arye Rattner, and, Edward Sagarin. (1986). "Guilty until Proven Innocent." *Crime & Delinquency* 32: 518–544.

Lindsay, Roderick C. L., and Gary L. Wells. (1985). "Improving Eyewitness Identification from Lineups: Simultaneous versus Sequential Lineup Presentations." *Journal of Applied Psychology* 70: 556–564.

Lindsay, Roderick C. L., Gary L. Wells, and Carolyn Rumpel. (1981). "Can People Detect Eyewitness Identification Accuracy within and between Situations?" *Journal of Applied Psychology* 66: 79–89.

Loftus, Elizabeth F. (1979). *Eyewitness Testimony.* Cambridge, MA: Harvard University Press.

Malpass, Roy S., and Patricia G. Devine. (1981a). "Eyewitness Identification: Lineup Instructions and the Absence of the Offender." *Journal of Applied Psychology* 66: 482–489.

Meisner, Chris, and John C. Brigham. (2001). "Twenty Years of Investigating the Own-Race Bias in Memory for Faces: A Meta-Analytic Review." *Psychology, Public Policy, and Law* 7: 3–35.

Scheck, Barry, Peter Neufeld, and Jim Dwyer. (2000). *Actual Innocence.* New York: Random House.

Shaw, John S., III, and Kevin A. McClure. (1996). "Repeated Postevent Questioning Can Lead to Elevated Levels of Eyewitness Confidence." *Law and Human Behavior* 20: 629–654.

Sporer, Sigfried, Steven Penrod, Don Read, and Brian L. Cutler. (1995). "Choosing, Confidence, and Accuracy: A Meta-Analysis of the Confidence-Accuracy Relation in Eyewitness Identification Studies." *Psychological Bulletin* 118: 315–327.

Steblay, Nancy M. (1992). "A Meta-Analytic Review of the Weapon Focus Effect." *Law and Human Behavior* 16: 413–424.

———. (1997). "Social Influence in Eyewitness Recall: A Meta-Analytic Review of Lineup Instruction Effects." *Law and*

Human Behavior 21: 283–298.

Wells, Gary L. (1978). "Applied Eyewitness Testimony Research: System Variables and Estimator Variables." *Journal of Personality and Social Psychology* 36: 1546–1557.

———. (1993). "What Do We Know about Eyewitness Identification?" *American Psychologist* 48: 553–571.

Wells, Gary L. and Bradfield, Amy L. (1998). " 'Good, You Identified the Suspect': Feedback to Eyewitnesses Distorts their Reports of the Witnessing Experience." *Journal of Applied Psychology* 83: 360–376.

Wells, Gary L., Roy S. Malpass, Roderick C.L. Lindsay, Ron P..Fisher, John W. Turtle, and Solomon Fulero. (2000). "From the Lab to the Police Station: A Successful Application of Eyewitness Research." *American Psychologist* 55: 581–598.

Wells, Gary L., Mark Small, Steven Penrod, Roy S. Malpass, Sol M. Fulero, and Elizabeth Brimacombe. (1998). "Eyewitness Identification Procedures: Recommendations for Lineups and Photospreads." *Law and Human Behavior* 22: 603–647.

▼ FAMILY COURT

Family court is a specialized court created by a state legislature. Family courts exist in a number of states to respond to serious hardships faced by children and families. The family court's purpose is more reformative than punitive. Family courts were formed to allow matters pertinent to the welfare and interest of a family to be heard in one place. Such an approach recognizes that many families will come back to court frequently—with long-term issues, as well as new problems. In addition, family courts exist to aid those who can find no other method of obtaining needed services. Family courts then become service coordinators, matching the needs of the individual to available community services.

JURISDICTION

The jurisdiction of the family court differs somewhat from state to state. Typically, a family court will have jurisdiction over matters such as child abuse and child neglect, termination of parental rights by reason of permanent neglect, determination of paternity, order and enforcement of child support, and the determination of juvenile delinquency and subsequent need of supervision. The court also handles a variety of "family offense" (domestic violence) proceedings. In family court proceedings, the person asking for the court's assistance is referred to as the "petitioner." The person who must answer the petitioner's allegations is referred to as the "respondent."

CHILD ABUSE AND NEGLECT PROCEEDINGS

When a child younger than eighteen years old has been abused or neglected or is in danger of being abused or neglected, a petition is filed by a child protection agency. The petition asks the family court to assist in protecting the child. At the time the petition is filed, the child may already be in foster care due to an emergency removal from the home by the agency or police. The parent or guardian against whom the petition is filed receives written notice that the court will hold a hearing to determine whether the child has been abused or neglected.

If the court decides that the child has been abused or neglected, it will determine appropriate action in the best interest of the child. The court might order one of several dispositions. The court might order that the child be released to the parent or guardian, on the condition that no further neglectful or abusive acts be committed. Alternatively, the court might order that the child be released to the parent or guardian and that supervision and services be provided by child protection agencies. Most typically, the court will order placement of the child into foster care for a period of time during which services will be provided to the parent to allow for possible return of the child at a future date.

TERMINATION OF PARENTAL RIGHTS PROCEEDINGS

Termination of parental rights refers to a court order directing a permanent end to parental rights. This legal process usually begins with the filing of a petition by an authorized child protection agency or by foster parents; it asks the court to permanently terminate a parent's right to a child. Family court notifies the parents about the petition and the date of a hearing on the issue.

At the hearing, the petitioner must present evidence and witnesses to prove that the child has been permanently neglected. If the court finds that the petitioner has not proven the case, the petition will be dismissed, and the child may remain in foster care. If the court finds that the statements or charges in the petition have been proven, it will grant the petition, terminating the parent's rights to the child. The child may then be adopted.

PATERNITY PROCEEDINGS

When a child is born to parents who are not married to one other, the biological father is not considered the child's legal parent unless one of two conditions has been met: the father has signed a document acknowledging paternity, or an order has been entered declaring the person to be the legal father. Each of three parties has a right to request a determination of paternity by court order. These parties are the child's mother, the alleged father, and the child.

After the petition has been filed, the court holds a hearing. If the man admits that he is the child's father, the court enters an order so stating. If the man denies that he is the father, the court will order blood or DNA tests of the child's mother, the alleged father, and the child. After the tests have been completed, the court will explain the test results. The court will then enter a decision based on the test results and other evidence introduced at the hearing.

CHILD SUPPORT PROCEEDINGS

States define how long parents are obligated to support a child. In the state of New York, for example, parents must provide support for a child until the child reaches the age of twenty-one. However, if the child is younger than twenty-one years of age and is married or self-supporting, or in the military, the child is considered "emancipated," and the parents' support obligation ends.

When parents live separately and one parent has custody of the child, the "custodial parent"(i.e., the parent holding custody) may file a petition asking the court to enter an order for the "noncustodial parent" to pay child support. Each party must provide family court with a completed financial disclosure statement to show earnings and expenses. During a subsequent hearing, the court hears testimony concerning the parties' income and expenses, as well as the cost of supporting the child. At the conclusion of the hearing, the court determines the amount of support the noncustodial parent must pay to the custodial parent. Either party has the right to file a petition to modify the order if circumstances change.

JUVENILE DELINQUENCY PROCEEDINGS

Each state defines the age span during which a person may be deemed a juvenile delinquent. In New York, for example, a person older than six years of age, but younger than sixteen years of age who commits an offense deemed a crime by state statute might be designated a juvenile delinquent.

In a juvenile delinquency case, the judge decides whether the child, known as the "respondent," has committed the acts described in the petition. If the prosecutor proves the case beyond a reasonable doubt, the judge makes a legal "finding" that the juvenile committed some or all of the acts described in the petition. The judge also decides what will happen to the juvenile. The court may decide that the juvenile should live at home without court supervision, but with specific conditions set forth by the court. The court may decide that the probation department should supervise the respondent while the juvenile lives at home. The court could also decide to place the respondent in a facility away from home, such as a group home or a secure facility.

PERSONS IN NEED OF SUPERVISION (PINS) PROCEEDINGS

A child who does not attend school, or who behaves in a way that is dangerous or out of control, may be found to be a Person in Need of Supervision, or "PINS." A PINS petition may be filed by one of a number of parties. These include a parent or other person legally responsible for the care of the child, a peace officer or police officer, a person who has been injured by a child, or a school or other authorized agency. The PINS petition contains a description of the child's behavior; it asks the court to find that the child is in need of supervision. If the judge decides that the child committed the acts described in the petition, the judge decides whether the child is a person in need of supervision. If the child does need supervision, the judge can place the child into a foster group home or a social service facility. Alternatively, the court may send the child home under the supervision of a probation officer.

FAMILY OFFENSE PROCEEDINGS

A family offense proceeding is a court case in which a petitioner claims that harassment or physical harm—or the threat of harm—has been committed by one of three parties: a present or former spouse, another family member, or someone with whom the petitioner has had a child. The petitioner files a petition that describes the acts complained of and asks that the court issue an order of protection, also known as a restraining order. When the petition is filed, the judge sets a date for a hearing and may issue a Temporary Order of Protection.

When both parties appear in court, the judge holds a hearing to decide whether the respondent committed the alleged acts. If the judge decides that the alleged incident did occur, then the judge may issue an Order of Protection to set forth conditions for the respondent's future conduct. The order specifies the period of time during which the conditions will be in effect.

CONTROVERSIES

Creation of family court is a major change that necessarily affects the jurisdiction of other courts. Some critics contend that specialized courts are unnecessary because judges in any court can, in a relatively short period of time, obtain the skills required to handle family matters. Other critics of the family court system question whether such courts can attain the coordination needed to serve families. Moreover, many judges prefer not to deal with both the charged emotions inherent in intrafamily disputes and the lack of services available to families. However, advocates of the one-family/one-judge position stress the virtues of continuity and the important role provided by family court in linking families with needed services.

—*Patricia E. Erickson*

See also FAMILY STRENGTHENING PROGRAMS; JUVENILE COURT

Further Reading
Beyer, Margaret. (1986). *An Emerging Judicial Role in Family Court*. Washington, DC: American Bar Association.
Busby, Dean. (1996). *The Impact of Violence on the Family: Treatment Approaches for Therapists and Other Professionals*. Needham Heights, MA: Allyn & Bacon.
Bianchi, Anne. (2000). *Everything You Need to Know About Family Court*. New York: Rosen.
Bianchi, Anne. (2000). *Understanding the Law: A Teen Guide to Family Court and Minors' Rights*. New York: Rosen.
Cardarelli, Albert. (1997). *Violence Between Intimate Partners: Patterns, Causes, and Effects*. Needham Heights, MA: Allyn & Bacon.
Eigenberg, Helen. (2001). *Woman Battering in the United States: Till Death Do Us Part*. Prospect Heights, IL: Waveland Press.
Fabricant, Michael. (1983). *Juveniles in the Family Courts*. Lexington, MA: Lexington Books.
Gelles, Richard. (1996). *The Book of David: How Preserving Families Can Cost Children's Lives*. New York: Basic Books.
Haller, Bruce, Alan Oshrin, and James Pulcrano. (1999). *Family Practice in New York State: A Practical Approach*. Fresh Meadows, NY: Looseleaf Law Publications.
Mariani, Cliff. (1996). *Domestic Violence Survival Guide*. Fresh Meadows, NY: Looseleaf Law Publications.
Ross, Richard. (1997). *A Day in Part 15: Law and Order in Family Court*. New York: Four Walls Eight Windows.
Rubin, H. Ted, and Victor Flango. (1992). *Court Coordination of Family Cases*. Williamsburg, VA: National Center for State Courts.
Sagaturn, Inger, and Leonard Edwards. (1995). *Child Abuse and the Legal System*. Chicago: Nelson-Hall Publishers.
Wallace, Harvey. (1999). *Family Violence: Legal, Medical, and Social Perspectives*. Needham Heights, MA: Allyn & Bacon.

▼ FAMILY STRENGTHENING PROGRAMS

Families face numerous challenges to raising happy and healthy children. Major societal problems such as divorce, drugs, gangs, teen pregnancy, depression, suicide, and juvenile violence contribute to environments that are difficult for young people to navigate successfully. Parents work outside of their homes more now than ever before and have less time to spend with their children and to monitor and supervise activities. Single-parent homes are becoming more common. The proportion of children living in single-parent homes more than doubled between 1970 and 1997, with more than 28 percent of children living with one parent. School, once thought to be a safe haven for youth, has become a place where youth are exposed to increasing levels of violence. In recent studies, 70–80 percent of youth report having witnessed violence at their school within the last year.

In 1997, more than 2.8 million juvenile arrests were made for all types of offenses, an increase of 14 percent from 1993. More problematic is the fact that juveniles were involved in 17 percent of all violent crime index arrests in 1997. Drug use is a major health problem for youth. By twelfth grade, approximately 88 percent of youth have used alcohol, 37 percent have used marijuana, 85 percent have used cocaine, and 63 percent have smoked cigarettes. Girls are committing more juvenile offenses, with drug abuse violations up 132 percent and person offenses up 155 percent in the last ten years. Youth who are in extremely serious jeopardy are those with an incarcerated parent. They are five to six times more likely than their peers to be incarcerated eventually. More than ever before, it is imperative that parents have access to and employ the most effective parenting techniques.

Fortunately, social science has advanced to the point that people know what works for successful parents and families. It was only twenty years ago that people had limited knowledge about family-based prevention programs. Currently, scientists are conducting research to further refine prevention strategies, with funding from major research institutions such as the National Institute on Drug Abuse (NIDA) and the Office of Juvenile Justice and Delinquency Prevention (OJJDP). Research has highlighted controversial effects such as "contagion effects" for youth participating in programs with other high-risk youth. These youths can hone their negative behaviors by establishing new friends and learning undesirable behaviors from their peers. Family programs can also be more expensive than programs in which only youth participate. The costs and benefits of this approach are being compared to other approaches, and preliminary data suggest that family programs are more effective than youth-only programs.

THE STRENGTHENING AMERICA'S FAMILIES PROJECT

In the late 1980s, the Office of Juvenile Justice and Delinquency Prevention (OJJDP) began, a federal government agency, began examining the research on family-focused prevention programs. Calling this innovative initiative the Strengthening America's Families Project, the OJJDP began working with Karol L. Kumpfer, a researcher at the University of Utah, to identify the most effective parent and family programs. National searches were conducted, with nominations for programs being solicited from every state. Program curriculums and evaluation materials were reviewed and rated by experts in family programs, primarily using stringent research and effectiveness criteria. Over

the past thirteen years, the research was updated to stay in line with the most current information. Thirty-five family-based programs have proven effective.

The Strengthening America's Families Project not only has sought to identify these programs but also has worked to disseminate these programs to community service providers across the country via national conferences, program training workshops, the project Web site (www.strengtheningfamilies.org), and a program booklet. The project's goal is to get the programs into the hands of people who touch the lives of families every day with the goal of reducing juvenile delinquency.

PROGRAMS THAT WORK

It is critical that a number of types of programs be available to communities because no one program can best meet the needs of all families. Factors such as the age of the child and the needs of the family (general population, high risk, or in crisis) must be taken into consideration to select the best program. Attributes such as the cultural and language background of the family, immigration status, working status of the parent/caregiver, and age of the parents/caregivers (teen, grandparent) should be examined. Other elements such as whether the parent is single, incarcerated, or substance abusing must be explored. Programs that have been identified as "best practice" approaches include models that address many of these factors. Typically, skills such as effective communication, discipline techniques, problem solving, limit setting, coping skills, stress management, and the ability to understand feelings are taught and practiced as part of most program curriculums. Additional information on all thirty-five model programs can be viewed at the project Web site (www.strengtheningfamilies.org).

Model programs cover such topics as the following:

1. Parenting skills. Preparing for the Drug Free Years is a five-week interactive program, with each session conducted for two hours. The program is for parents of children in grades four through eight and is meant to reach parents before their children begin experimenting with drugs and participating in other negative behaviors. The sessions are skill based, with opportunities for parents to practice new skills and receive feedback from their peers. Family involvement by parents and youth, consequences for undesirable behavior, and communication through the use of family meetings are cornerstones of the program.

2. Home visitation. The Prenatal and Early Childhood Nurse Home Visitation Program, developed by Dr. David Olds of the University of Colorado, is a well-tested program that improves the health and social functioning of low-income, first-time mothers and their babies. The goal is preventing precursors related to juvenile delinquency. Beginning during mothers' pregnancy, nurses visit the homes of the families with whom they work and teach them about the effects of nutrition and substance abuse on the health of their baby. They work with a woman to prevent school dropout and future unintended pregnancies—factors that may lead to poverty. After delivery of the infant, the emphasis is on enhancing the care-giving skills of the parents The nurses work with the family until the child reaches the age of two.

3. Family skills. The Strengthening America's Families Project is designed to increase resilience and reduce risk factors for substance abuse, depression, violence, and aggression in families with children six to ten years of age. The fourteen-week curriculum uses three courses: one for parents, one for children, and one for the entire family. During a session, parents and children meet separately for the first part of the session and then join as a family to practice the skills they learn. This program, which was designed for families with a substance-abusing parent, has been adapted for families with preteens and for Latino, African American, American Indian, and Pacific Island families.

4. Family therapy. The brief strategic family therapy (BSFT) model focuses on adolescents. This short-term, problem-focused model is aimed at preventing and treating child and adolescent behavior problems by improving family interactions. It is preventive because services can be directed at youth who are in the early stages of problem behavior. A trained therapist typically works with a family for three months. BSFT has been tailored to work with inner-city minority families, including Hispanic and African American families.

Other models are disseminated as part of the Strengthening America's Families Project. The NICASA (Northern Illinois Council on Alcoholism and Substance Abuse) Parent Project is designed for working families, with sessions taught at the work site. Parenting Wisely is an interactive program that uses a CD-ROM for instruction. Project SEEK (Services to Enable and Empower Kids) focuses on supporting families in which one of the parents is incarcerated. Treatment Foster Care is designed for foster parents,

A father and son participate in a family strengthening program.
Source: Photo courtesy of the Department of Health Promotion and Education, Salt Lake City, Utah.

and Families and Schools Together (FAST) focuses on helping families work with schools to improve children's functioning.

Children are exposed to numerous environmental elements that increase their risk of delinquent behavior and criminal involvement. Parents need to understand and value their role as their children's first and most important teachers. They must be equipped to address the evolving needs of their children and understand the stresses their children face on a daily basis. If the parenting and family programs of the Strengthening America's Families Project can be implemented across the country, the potential exists to enhance family functioning, decrease delinquency, and improve life for youth in the United States.

—Rose Alvarado

See also FAMILY COURT; FAMILY VIOLENCE; JUVENILE JUSTICE; JUVENILE VICTIMIZATION AND OFFENDING

Further Reading

Alvarado, Rose, Karol L. Kumpfer, Kay Kendall, Sally Beesley, and Christine Lee-Cavaness, eds. (2000). *Strengthening America's Families: Model Family Programs for Substance Abuse and Delinquency Prevention.* Salt Lake City: Office of Juvenile Justice and Delinquency Prevention, Center for Substance Abuse Prevention, and University of Utah.

Johnston, Denise. (1995). "Effects of Parental Incarceration." In *Children of Incarcerated Parents,* edited by Katherine Gabel and Denise Johnston. New York: Lexington Books, 59–88.

Kaufman, Phillip, Xianglei Chen, Susan P. Choy, Kathryn A. Chandler, Christopher D. Chapman, Michael R. Rand, and Cheryl Ringel. (1998). *Indicators of School Crime and Safety.* Washington, DC: U.S. Departments of Education and Justice.

Office of Juvenile Justice and Delinquency Prevention. (1999). *OJJDP Research: Making a Difference for Juveniles.* Washington, DC: U.S. Department of Justice.

Snyder, Howard N., and Melissa Sickmund. (1999). *Juvenile Offenders and Victims: 1999 National Report.* Washington, DC: Office of Juvenile Justice and Delinquency Prevention.

▼ FAMILY VIOLENCE

In the past thirty years, society has recognized family violence as a serious social problem requiring the intervention of professionals. Recent studies have indicated that the incidence of family violence in the United States remains extremely high and shows no indication of significant decrease. Violence has been a part of the family throughout its history not only in the United States but also in England, Western Europe, and many other countries.

The majority of research on family violence has focused on violence toward children and women. However, family violence encompasses many forms of behavior, including child abuse, sexual abuse, violence against women, sibling abuse, and elder abuse. Family violence also encompasses maltreatment between individuals who may not actually be members of a family—for example, violence in dating relationships.

NATURE AND CONSEQUENCES OF FAMILY VIOLENCE

Data on family violence are estimates; the true nature of family violence is difficult to capture. Data about family violence can be gleaned from official data, self-report surveys, victimization surveys, and clinical studies of victims. The most commonly cited source of data is the Uniform Crime Reports, which reports information gathered from law enforcement agencies. Official data are also reported by child protective services agencies. The National Study of Child Neglect and Abuse Reporting estimated that there was a threefold increase in child maltreatment cases from 1976 to 1987. In 1994, forty-seven of one thousand children were estimated to be victims of physical and sexual abuse and neglect. Official data underestimate the extent of violence in that they most often reflect only the most serious incidents of violence.

Self-report data are also used to measure the nature and extent of family violence. The National Family Surveys, two nationally representative surveys, relied on the Conflict Tactics Scale developed by Strauss and colleagues to estimate adolescent violence, dating violence, and elder violence. Survey data indicate that family violence is pervasive and severe, with 16 percent of respondents experiencing an act of violence within the previous year. The data also indicate there may be a pattern of "mutual combat" in many homes characterized by violent interactions.

Violence Against Women

The National Crime Victimization Survey administered by the U.S. Bureau of Justice Statistics collects national data on victimization. The survey was redesigned in 1992 to better capture the extent of violence between intimates. According to the data, approximately one million women per year experience violence at the hands of an intimate partner. Other data estimate that marital rape accounts for approximately 25 percent of all rapes in the United States. Women and girls are sexually harassed, physically abused, and raped by their male partners, former partners, boyfriends, relatives, employers, and teachers, as well as by strangers. Additionally, more than a third of all women who go to emergency rooms in the United States go because of domestic violence, and more than 250,000 women and children used shelters in 1997.

Women who experience violence in their home at the hands of an intimate suffer long-term physical and psychological effects. Such women live in a constant state of fear and develop feelings of helplessness. They may suffer from emotional trauma characterized by depression and anxiety. Evidence suggests that women exposed to long-term violence may have symptoms of posttraumatic stress disorder (PTSD). A subcategory of PTSD, the battered woman's syndrome, has been identified in women who suffer long-term abuse. The term *battered woman's syndrome* refers to a series of characteristics common to women who are victims of psychological and physical abuse.

CHILDREN AS VICTIMS OF VIOLENCE

Children, regardless of race or social class, are victimized at higher rates than adults in both urban and rural

▼

A Woman's Role

Research shows that women who are emotionally and economically dependent on their husbands are more likely to be the victims of spousal violence than are women who are more independent and self-reliant. This article from Housekeeping Monthly *magazine in 1955 suggests that female dependency was at that time thought to be a desirable attribute of American women.*

THE GOOD WIFE'S GUIDE

Have dinner ready. Plan ahead, even the night before, to have a delicious meal ready, on time for his return. This is the way of letting him know that you have been thinking about him and are concerned about his needs. Most men are hungry when they come home and the prospect of a good meal (especially his favorite dish) is part of the warm welcome needed.

Prepare yourself. Take 15 minutes to rest so you'll be refreshed when he arrives. Touch up your make-up, put a ribbon in your hair and be fresh looking. He has just been with a lot of work-weary people.

Be a little gay and a little more interesting for him. His boring day may need a lift and one of your duties is to provide it.

Clear away the clutter. Make one last trip through the main part of the house just before your husband arrives.

Gather up schoolbooks, toys, paper, etc. and then run a dust cloth over all of the tables.

Over the cooler months of the year, you should prepare and light a fire for him to unwind by. Your husband will feel he has reached a haven of rest and order, and it will give you a lift too. After all, catering for his comfort will provide you with immense personal satisfaction.

Prepare the children. Take a few minutes to wash the children's hands and faces (if they are small), comb their hair and, if necessary, change their clothes. They are little treasures and we would like to see them playing the part. Minimize all noise. At the time of his arrival, eliminate all noise of the washer, dryer or vacuum. Try to encourage the children to be quiet.

Be happy to see him.

Greet him with a warm smile and show sincerity in your desire to please him.

Listen to him. You may have a dozen important things to tell him, but the moment of his arrival is not the time. Let him talk firs—remember, his topics of conversation are more important than yours.

Make the evening his. Never complain if he comes home late or goes out to dinner, or other places of entertainment without you. Instead, try to understand his world of strain and pressure and his very real need to be at home and relax.

Your goal: try to make sure your home is a place of peace, order and tranquility where your husband can renew himself, mind, body and spirit.

Don't greet him with complaints and problems

Don't complain if he's late for dinner or stays out all night. Count this as minor compared to what he might have gone through that day.

Make him comfortable. Have him lean back in a comfortable chair or have him lie down in the bedroom. Have a cool or warm drink ready for him.

Arrange his pillow and offer to take his shoes. Speak in a low, soothing and pleasant voice.

Don't ask him questions about his actions or question his judgment or integrity. Remember, he is the master of the house and as such he will always exercise his will with fairness and truthfulness. You have no right to question him

A good wife knows her place.

Source: *Housekeeping Monthly,* May 13, 1955.

---

areas. Children are victimized in multiple ways—sexual and physical assaults, sexual exploitation (such as forcing a child or teenager to engage in prostitution or pose for pornography), neglect, homicide, and abduction. Their assailants are frequently their parents but may be other family members, friends, acquaintances, caretakers, and strangers.

In this country, children witness violent crimes on a daily basis, including homicide, rape, assault, and domestic violence. Even when child witnesses do not suffer physical injury, the emotional consequences of viewing or hearing violent acts are severe and long lasting. In fact, children who witness violence often experience many of the same symptoms and lasting effects (including PTSD) as children who are victims of violence themselves.

Witnessing family violence appears to have both short- and long-term effects on children. Children who are victims of or witnesses to violent crime are at an increased risk for delinquency, adult criminality, and violent behavior. National studies have shown that being abused or neglected as a child increases the likelihood of arrest as a juvenile by 53 percent and of arrest as an adult for a violent crime by 38 percent. It also places children at significant risk for substance abuse, mental illness, and suicide.

Children are substantially more vulnerable to crime victimization in general than are adults. Not just more likely to be offenders, young people are also more likely to be victims. Young people, particularly teens, commit about 18 percent of crime but make up about 25 percent of victims. Annually, an estimated 1 million violent crimes involving child victims are reported to the police, and another 1.1 million cases of child abuse are substantiated by child protection agencies. As many as half a million children may be encountered by police during domestic violence arrests. Of the nation's 22.3 million adolescents aged twelve to seventeen, approximately 1.8 million reported having been victims of a serious sexual assault, 3.9 million reported having been victims of a serious physical assault, and almost 9 million reported having witnessed serious violence during their lifetimes.

Sibling Aggression

Sibling abuse is a form of family violence that has received limited attention, although some have suggested that it is more common than either child or spouse abuse. In fact, children are often the most violent people in American families. More than 36 million acts of sibling aggression are estimated to occur each year in the United States. Sibling abuse ranges from pushing and shoving to extreme forms of violence involving the use of weapons. Emotional abuse such as teasing, name-calling, and isolation is also common. Sibling abuse also includes forced sexual activity between brothers and sisters.

Evidence indicates that long-term serious consequences result from being a victim of sibling abuse. Women and men who suffer abuse as children suffer from depression, anxiety, and low self-esteem as adults. The inability to trust, relationship difficulties, and alcohol and drug abuse have also been linked to childhood sibling abuse.

ABUSE OF THE ELDERLY

Elder abuse is a form of family violence that has received increased attention. Relatives and caregivers physically and emotionally abuse over one million elderly Americans each year. This is especially notewor-

thy in that people over the age of eighty-five represent the fastest-growing elderly population in the United States. Most elderly people who are abused live at home with their families, on whom they are financially dependent. They are often isolated from their communities and depend on caretakers for their physical and emotional needs. Elder abuse can be classified as passive abuse or active abuse and can include physical maltreatment, financial exploitation, neglect, misuse of medication, and psychological abuse. Passive abuse involves omitting an act, such as when relatives are unable or unwilling to provide adequate care. Active abuse involves committing an act, such as when relatives make a conscious attempt to inflict injury or emotional stress on an older person. Abuse can also be deliberate withdrawal of health services, food, or other necessities.

UNDERSTANDING FAMILY VIOLENCE

Family violence cannot be explained by one factor alone. The characteristics of the child, parent, family, social situation, and community are factors in determining the nature and circumstances of abuse. Family structure and family situations influence individual emotional states of caretakers, psychological characteristics, and community factors, such as cultural attitudes regarding violence. In addition, power and control are common features of nearly all forms of family violence, especially violence and abuse of women.

Theoretical Models

Despite the enormous growth of professional and public interest in family violence, there is no single theory or body of knowledge that guides the investigation of efforts to prevent and treat family violence. Family violence has been explained using three general theoretical models: (1) the psychiatric model, (2) the social-psychological model, and (3) the sociological or sociocultural model. The psychiatric model focuses on the offender's personality characteristics as the chief determinants of violence, although some extensions of the model focus on the personality characteristics of the victims. The psychiatric model links personality disorders, character disorders, mental illness, alcohol and substance abuse, and other intra-individual processes to acts of family violence.

The social-psychological model assumes that violence and abuse can best be understood by careful examination of the environmental factors that affect the family, family organization, and structure and the everyday interactions between intimates that precede acts of violence. Theoretical approaches that examine family structure, stress, the transmission of violence from one generation to the next, and family interaction patterns fit the social-psychological model. Such general theories as learning theory, frustration aggression, exchange theory, and attribution theory approach family violence from the social-psychological level.

The sociocultural model examines violence from a macro level of analysis. Violence is examined in light of socially structured variables such as inequality, patriarchy, or cultural norms and attitudes about violence and family relations.

Researchers have developed several additional psychosocial theories to explain family violence. For example, social learning theorists propose that individuals who experience violence are more likely to use violence in the home than are individuals who have experienced little or no violence. Social situation/stress and coping theory explains why violence is used in some situations and not others. The main premise of this theory is that abuse and violence occur because of two main factors. The first is structural stress and the lack of coping resources in a family. For instance, the association between low income and family violence indicates that one important factor in violence is inadequate financial resources. The second factor is the cultural norm concerning the use of force and violence. Thus individuals learn to use violence to express feelings as well as a means of coping when stressful events become overwhelming.

The basic assumption of resource theory is that all social systems (including the family) rest to some degree on force or the threat of force. The more resources—social, personal, and economic—a person can command, the more force he or she can muster. In exchange theory, child abuse and violence against women are explained by the principle of cost and benefits. Violence is used as a strategy when benefits are greater than the costs. The private nature of the family, the reluctance of social institutions and agencies to intervene—in spite of mandatory child abuse reporting laws or mandatory arrest laws for domestic violence—and the low risk of other interventions reduce the costs of abuse or violence. The cultural approval of violence as both expressive and instrumental behavior raises the potential benefits of violence. The most significant benefit is social control or power.

Feminist theorists see violence against women as a unique phenomenon that has been overshadowed by what they refer as a "narrow" focus on domestic violence. The central focus of their theory is that economic and social processes operate directly and indirectly to support a patriarchal social order and family structure. Much of the violence research conducted from the feminist perspective focuses on the ways in which patriarchal social systems support the dynamics of heterosexual relationships. Feminists assert that marriage still institutionalizes the control of wives by husbands through the structure of husband-wife roles. Under such circumstances, wives are subservient and are likely to become victims of males' physical violence and psychological abuse. The use of violence for control in marital relationships is perpetuated not only through norms about men's rights in marriage but also through women's economic dependence on their husbands.

RESPONSES TO FAMILY VIOLENCE

Feminists and women's rights advocates brought attention to family violence in the 1960s and 1970s. Their grassroots movement resulted in the establishment of a number of services for victims of family violence across the nation. Battered women's shelters, crisis hotlines, support groups, and counseling for victims were established in the majority of states. Over the years, additional services became available, such as community-based counseling for parents and children, parenting education classes, lay therapy, and home visitor services. Anger management classes have also been used with perpetrators.

Changes in Criminal Justice

Legal changes have also been implemented. All fifty states have enacted mandatory reporting laws for suspected child abuse cases. State laws permit out-of-home placement for severely abused children. In addition, states have eliminated marital exemption laws for rape. States have also enacted adult protective services legislation to protect the elderly against abuse. States have passed legislation designed to establish domestic violence prosecution units, improve protection for victims of stalking, and develop more effective legal sanctions against domestic violence offenders.

In addition, there have been changes in police responses to family violence. Historically, criminal justice professionals arrested offenders only in cases of extreme violence. In recent years, the predominant criminal justice response has been to mandate arrest and prosecution of domestic violence offenders. However, given the historical reluctance of the criminal justice system to intervene in domestic violence cases, it is still unclear whether mandatory arrest laws and policies actually increase the probability of arrest of criminal domestic abusers. If mandatory arrest laws are not protecting victims of domestic violence, legislatures and public safety officials may have to develop new methods to deal with domestic violence and to ensure that its victims have access to law.

Preferred arrest policies encourage police to arrest offenders in domestic violence cases. The movement toward preferred arrest policies has resulted in greater caseloads for prosecutors and the criminal courts. However, like the police, public prosecutors have not traditionally been overly zealous about pursuing cases against domestic violence offenders. The issues that made police officers reluctant to arrest spouse abusers have made prosecutors reluctant to prosecute. These issues have included the belief that domestic violence is essentially a family matter and that, unless there is serious injury (generally resulting in a felony charge), the criminal courts should not be involved. There are several other reasons why criminal justice professionals are reluctant to get involved in domestic violence cases. Officials are concerned about victim reluctance to follow through with prosecution and believe that there would be little to gain by prosecuting the offender. Furthermore, officials fear that prosecution may make matters worse by depriving the family of its breadwinner.

Federal Legislation

The federal government has taken a strong stance against family violence. In 1994, Congress passed the Violence Against Women Act, which was signed into law by President Clinton on September 13, 1994. This marked the first time the federal government had adopted a comprehensive approach to addressing violence against women. Since then, programs under the act have aided in prosecuting domestic violence, sexual assault, and child abuse cases and have increased services for victims and resources for law enforcement personnel. A major component of the act was the creation of the National Domestic Violence Hotline, which has responded to more than 250,000 calls since it began in 1996.

On October 28, 2000, President Clinton signed legislation reauthorizing the Violence Against Women Act, which set funding for VAWA programs at a landmark $3.33 billion over the next five years. Among many new provisions are expanded coverage that includes dating violence and improved services to—and clarification of immigration status for—battered immigrant women. The legislation also authorized Department of Justice studies on child custody, abuse, and parental kidnapping, and comprehensive research on violence against women. Major funding was allocated for legal services for domestic and sexual violence survivors, education and training for violence reduction on college campuses, and national rape prevention and education. Funds were also allocated for police, prosecutors, and survivor services. Additional funds were allotted for the creation of a national stalker and domestic violence database.

PREVENTIVE MEASURES

Currently, the majority of programs that deal with family violence, such as shelters, crisis day care centers, police intervention programs, and parent support groups, are treatment programs that are implemented after an abusive incident. What are needed—but have not been attempted on any large scale—are services that would prevent abuse before it begins. But such services require sweeping changes in both society and the family. Steps that have been suggested for preventing family violence include eliminating the norms that legitimize and glorify violence in society and the family. The elimination of spanking as a child-rearing technique and corporal punishment in school has been suggested by many in the field of family violence.

Another suggestion has been to reduce violence-provoking stress created by society. Reducing poverty, inequality, and unemployment and providing adequate housing, food, medical and dental care, and educational opportunities are steps that could reduce stress in families. Furthermore, integrating families into networks of community would help reduce violence in families. Reducing social isolation would be a significant step to help reduce stress and increase the abilities of families to manage stress.

Some suggest that the sexist character of society needs to be addressed. Sexual inequality makes violence possible in homes. The elimination of so-called men's work and women's work would be a major step toward equality in and out of the home.

Finally, society needs to support breaking the cycle of violence in the family. Violence cannot be prevented as long as people are taught that it is appropriate to hit the people they love. Physical punishment of children is perhaps the most effective means of teaching violence, and eliminating it would be an important step in violence prevention.

Violence in the family affects the lives of millions of Americans on a daily basis. Although the focus on family violence in the past several years has resulted in changes in policy as well as attitudes toward violence in the home, acceptance of violence endures. The support of federal, state, and local law enforcement agencies may significantly reduce violence in the future. However, eradicating violence in the home will take more than law enforcement strategies. Long-term strategies aimed at both prevention and education must be the goal for the future.

—Karen Casey-Acevedo and Any A. Stern

See also CHILD HOMICIDE; CHILD MALTREATMENT; CHILD NEGLECT; CHILD PHYSICAL ABUSE; CHILD SEXUAL ABUSE; ELDER ABUSE; FAMILY COURT; FAMILY STRENGTHENING PROGRAMS; MISSING CHILDREN; RAPE, DATE AND MARITAL; SAME-SEX ABUSE; SEXUAL VIOLENCE; SIBLING VIOLENCE; STALKING; WOMEN AS VICTIMS; WOMEN WHO KILL

Further Reading

Avakame, Edem F., and James J. Fyfe. (2001). "Differential Police Treatment of Male-on-Female Spousal Violence: Additional Evidence on the Leniency Thesis." In *Violence Against Women*, 22–45. Thousand Oaks, CA: Sage.

Barnett, Ola W., Cindy L. Miller-Perrin, and Robin D. Perrin. (1997*). Family Violence Across the Lifespan: An Introduction.* Thousand Oaks, CA: Sage.

Browne, Angela. (1987). *When Battered Women Kill*. New York: Free Press.

Buzawa, Eve S., and Carl G. Buzawa. (1996). *Domestic Violence: The Criminal Justice Response*, 2d ed. Thousand Oaks, CA: Sage.

Hampton, Robert. L. (1999). *Family Violence: Prevention and Treatment,* 2d ed. Thousand Oaks, CA: Sage.

Hirschel, David, and Ira W. Hutchison. (2001). "The Relative Effects of Offenders and Victim Variables on the Decision to Prosecute Domestic Violence Cases." In *Violence Against Women*, 46–59. Thousand Oaks, CA: Sage.

Iadicola, Peter, and Anson Shupe. (1998). *Violence: Inequality and Human Freedom*. Dix Hills, NY: General Hall.

Meadows, Robert J. (1998). *Understanding Violence and Victimization*. Upper Saddle River, NJ: Prentice Hall.

Merlo, Alida V., and Jocelyn Pollock. (1995). *Women, Law and Social Control*. Boston: Allyn & Bacon.

Muraskin, Roslyn, and Ted Alleman. (1993). *It's a Crime: Women and Justice*. Englewood Cliffs, NJ: Regents/Prentice Hall.

Office of Human Development Services, National Center on Child Abuse and Neglect. (1991). *Family Violence: An Overview*. Washington, DC: Department of Health and Human Services.

Swisher, Karin, and Carol Wekesser. (1994). *Violence Against Women*. San Diego, CA: Greenhaven Press

U. S. Department of Justice. (1999). *Breaking the Cycle of Violence: Recommendations to Improve the Criminal Justice Response to Child Victims and Witnesses*. Washington, DC. Office of Justice Programs. http://www.ojp.usdoj.gov/ovo/factshts/monograph.htm

▼ FEAR OF CRIME

Fear of crime is a complex phenomenon. It is also an important one, because how people feel about and react to crime is a major influence on how they lead their lives and how society deals with crime. Fear of crime involves a variety of emotional and judgmental responses to crime, and it includes one's fear of being a victim; fear that a family member, neighbor, or friend will be a victim; fear of property loss or damage; and one's assessment of the risk faced by oneself, significant others, or one's property. The general topic also includes a range of subjective states, from irrational responses to vague threats and media-driven anxiety to personal evaluations of the level of perceived threat or risk. During the past three decades, social scientists have done extensive research on assessing the fear of crime. Studying such a complex topic and the emotional reactions of people is a difficult task, and social scientists continue to debate the definition and conceptualization of fear of crime and struggle with how best to measure fear of crime in individuals and communities.

MEASUREMENT OF FEAR OF CRIME

The most common measurement of fear of crime used by researchers, especially in the early years of fear of crime research, uses national data sets or regional equivalents. Researchers adopt a single item question from either the National Crime Victimization Survey (NCVS) or the General Social Survey (GSS) to measure fear of crime. The NCVS asks people, "How safe do you feel or would you feel being out alone in your neighborhood at night? During the day?" The GSS asks people, "Is there any area right around here—that is, within a mile or so—where you would be afraid to walk at night?" Both questions are very similar in style and intent and try to capture a generalized fear of crime in the person being interviewed.

Several researchers criticized this reliance on single-question data for its limited scope and its exclusion of a broader range of crimes. Although crimes that take place at night in public places (i.e., street crime) do provoke high levels of fear, many other situations that may occur during the day or at home or outside the neighborhood are overlooked. These limited questions lead to imprecision and potentially inaccurate conclusions, because general measures tend to mask variation in fear of crime across offenses, as well as possibly overestimating the level of fear in the general public.

More sophisticated approaches to measuring fear of crime focus on specific fears and the fear of harm caused by personal violence. This approach has greatly expanded the understanding that fear of crime is not universally distributed in response to different crimes. Further clarification was offered by identifying trust as an underlying factor in fear of crime. The work of Kenneth Ferraro (1995) and others reconceptualized fear of crime by differentiating fear from perceived risk and recognizing that risk is not a sufficient explanation in and of itself, but a necessary factor in the fear of crime equation. Relying primarily on a national sample, Ferraro explores the significance of both objective and perceived risk on fear of crime, suggesting that the fear of crime is mostly mediated through perceived risk of crime. And since people rely on local conditions, such as those in their neighborhood, to make judgments about personal risk, it follows that some social groups will perceive higher risks, and fear of crime will vary according to individual and situational factors.

INDIVIDUAL FACTORS

The intensity and type of crime fears vary based on gender, age, race, and income. Prior victimization experience also plays a role in people's level of fear.

Gender

A wealth of research strongly suggests that women fear crime more than men do, even though women are at less risk overall of becoming crime victims than men. This seeming paradox is explained by fear of rape as a "master offense" that heightens women's fear of all crimes. It is also explained by the fact that women are at greater risk because they have less physical strength than men and may have been raised to be passive and dependent, adding to their feelings of vulnerability. Also, women may report more fear in research studies because, when surveyed, they are more open and revealing in expressing their feelings of fear than are men.

Age

Age is another significant predictor of fear of crime. Some researchers note that the elderly are more fearful than younger people, because they are physically weaker and often more socially isolated. Their higher levels of fear may also reflect an evaluation of risk based on their environment or victimization experiences. Moreover, a disproportionately high number of the elderly are women, and therefore some of the high level of fear among the elderly reflects the higher level of fear among women in general. Other researchers suggest that both older and younger people express high levels of fear. Studies that confirm this pattern often suggest that younger people are fearful because of lifestyle choices and routine activities that place them in dangerous settings, increasing their perception of risk.

Race

According to some social scientists, African Americans in the United States express higher levels of fear than do white people. This pattern is in line with African Americans' experiences as victims of or witnesses to crime. Most researchers ascribe the link between race and fear of crime to crime-related conditions in areas where a high proportion of nonwhites reside. This can be seen in many discussions of crime in ethnographic studies (e.g., Ida Susser's *Norman Street*) that focus on whites and their fears of blacks. This suggests that fear of crime and racial distrust may be intertwined. Some studies report that part of the explanation for high levels of fear by whites toward black men, primarily those who are young and associate in small groups, is related to racial stereotyping and racial prejudice. Likewise, Elijah Anderson (1990: 206) notes, "The public awareness is color-coded: white skin denotes civility, law-abidingness, and trustworthiness, while black skin is strongly associated with poverty, crime, incivility, and distrust." Anderson argues because law-abiding people are taught to fear young male black strangers, perceived risk and fear is higher for whites. The evidence suggests that both whites and blacks exhibit fear in response to crime-related concerns, and that race and ethnicity are important in shaping the way danger is interpreted.

Income

Lower-income individuals experience higher levels of fear of crime than do wealthier people. Income has not been as carefully studied as have other factors, but the relationship to fear of crime is explained as a product of a feeling of social vulnerability, primarily due to limited resources. People living in poverty are more fearful and express higher levels of vulnerability than do better-off respondents. Feelings of vulnerability are an important factor in explaining fear of crime in relation to gender, age, race and income. As with race, some researchers explain the tie between income and fear of crime by citing the reality that low-income people are more likely to be confronted with crime and disorder in their daily lives than are wealthier people.

Victimization Experience

It is not clear whether the experience of being a crime victim is related to one's fear of crime. It may be that fear of crime is related only to specific types of victimization. For example, according to Skogan and Klecka (1977), robbery is the only victimization experience that has a clear attitudinal effect on fear of crime. In fact, victims of other types of crime were found to be less fearful. In addition to direct personal experience with crime, indirect victimization (i.e., in which a family member, close friend or neighbor was victimized recently) or vicarious victimization can also be a powerful predictor of fear of crime. Individuals develop a wide variety of perceptions about crime as a consequence of their ties to neighbors and friends and their exposure to local knowledge, including gossip. Exposure to the mass media and news reports may also inform these perceptions. Research shows that the effect of media coverage on fear of crime depends on the type of media source, the focus of the news report, the crime rate in the neighborhood, sociodemographic characteristics, feelings of vulnerability, personal victimization experiences and resonance, and affinity with victims reported in the media.

SITUATIONAL FACTORS

People perceive certain times and places as safe and others as dangerous—in their perception, risks are concentrated in time and space. For example, fear of personal victimization is stronger at night than during the day. Not surprisingly, during the day residents feel more secure, as activities are under closer watch and are therefore subject to more control. Generally, people are most likely to fear personal attacks by strangers at night and to believe that attacks are more likely to occur on the streets or in other public places. People perceive public spaces as being unsafe or dangerous, according to social scientist Sally Merry (1981), based on seven factors: territory, ethnic hostility, presence of hostile teenagers, familiarity, availability of friends, design of space (e.g., low visibility), and incidence of crime.

The public realm can be divided into interior and exterior public places. As regards interior public space, establishments such as bars, stores, and banks are perceived as less dangerous and intimidating. However, in Oscar Newman's (1972, 1973: 27) detailed discussion of urban design, he highlights the importance of interior spaces that are outside the view and surveillance of residents or people on the street, which opens up the potential for lingering strangers: "But unlike the well-peopled and continuously surveyed public streets, these interior areas are spatially used and impossible to survey; they become a nether world of fear and crime." City streets and squares make up the exterior public places. The streets of a city or neighborhood are crucial to the safety and security felt by its residents. As Jane Jacobs argues in her influential *The Death and Life of Great American Cities*, "If a city's streets are safe from barbarism and fear, the city is thereby tolerably safe from barbarism and fear" (1961: 29–30).

Years of research show clearly that fear of crime is much higher in cities, so much so that fear of crime is sometimes classified as a primarily urban problem. However, the relationship may not be so simple, as some research suggests that it is not the fact of living in the city that causes residents to be fearful, but rather the nature of the neighborhood that leads to higher levels of fear. People living in neighborhoods plagued by high crime rates experience higher levels of fear than do those in low crime areas.

Skogan (1990) and Wilson and Kelling (1982) argue that areas characterized by high levels of disorder will be plagued by high levels of crime. According to Skogan, disorder factors associated with fear of crime are either physical or social. Physical disorder includes visual conditions and signs of neglect such as abandoned cars or buildings, rundown buildings, poor lighting, overgrown shrubs and trees, trash, and empty lots. Social disorder includes behaviors or activities such as public drinking, public drug use, public drug sales, vandalism or graffiti, prostitution, panhandling or begging, loitering, truancy, and transients or homeless people sleeping on the street. Both types of disorder are considered "signs of crime" indicating that the social control mechanisms within the neighborhood have broken down, making residents feel more vulnerable to crime. According to Wilson and Kelling (1982), "broken windows" or incivilities that create disorder also elevate feelings of anxiety and lead to more fear. This "incivility" approach suggests that these conditions have adverse effects on the individuals within the neighborhood, the community as a whole, and the entire city.

Beyond crime and disorder, the racial and ethnic composition and level of integration within the neighborhood are crucial concerns. Some research suggests that as the minority population (i.e., percent black) increases, or people perceive a changing racial composition, they will perceive risk and a corresponding fear of crime. In situations where whites perceive themselves to live in predominantly black neighborhoods, Moeller (1989) finds that they report higher levels of fear. However, according to recent work by Chiricos, Hogan, and Gertz (1997) blacks do not seem to be more fearful in predominantly black or predominantly white neighborhoods. Stinchcombe and associates (1980) found that blacks were more afraid than whites in all neighborhood types except for whites in integrated city neighborhoods, who were more afraid than whites in all-white neighborhoods.

CONSEQUENCES OF FEAR OF CRIME

Research suggests that in an effort to reduce the risk of being a crime victim, people may alter their behavior and attitudes about crime. Toward these ends, people take self-defense classes, restrict their activities (avoid going out at night or alone, avoid certain areas), attend community meetings, get to know the police in their neighborhood, and carry weapons to feel safer and reduce their risk of victimization. Behavioral modifications that are more directly tied to fear of being victimized at home include watching out for others' safety, installing a security system, owning a guard dog, installing extra locks, keeping a weapon at home, and adding outside lighting, among others. Clearly, some social groups, such as women and the elderly, may be more likely than others to take precautionary measures in response to crime concerns. Despite people's efforts to feel and be safer, research suggests that these efforts often actually make people fear being a victim of crime even more.

To alleviate their fears, people have reportedly taken action to reduce perceived risks. Furthermore, fear of crime may influence people's attitudes toward the criminal justice system and its agents. Public safety is an important political issue and one that is a regular component of the political and media discourse. Crime and fear of crime are used as issues in political campaigns in ways that readily shape perceptions of crime. Some research has addressed the link between fear of crime and attitudes about the criminal justice system. Reflecting on increasing public and political support for severe punishments, David Garland asserts, "Fear of crime can thus exhibit irrational roots and often leads to disproportionate (or 'counter-phobic') demands for punishment" (1990: 239). However, this view is questioned by Stinchcombe and his associates (1980), who report that fearful people are only slightly more punitive than less fearful people. However, it may be that those with higher levels of fear express a lack of trust and confidence in the ability of state and legal institutions to combat the problems.

Many urban and criminological studies suggest that perceptions about the police and interactions between the police and community residents differ according to certain demographic variables and neighborhood location. Residents in certain urban neighborhoods, due to class or racial characteristics, may see themselves as being ignored by local authorities. This, in turn, may alter their assessment of perceived risk and thus lead to a higher level of fear or to behavior to reduce their perceived risk of victimization. More research needs to be done to address the relationship between fear of crime and attitudes about punitiveness and the effectiveness of the police.

COLLECTIVE RESPONSES

Fear of crime may have severe consequences for both individuals and the entire community. Neighborhoods whose residents are overwhelmed by fear express ambivalence about the future of the neighborhood and its residents, and they often withdraw emotionally from contact with others. People who see their neighborhoods as having more social problems are more fearful and less committed to their neighbors than those in other neighborhoods. These people are less likely to engage in community life and collective action to combat crime-related problems, because crime has weakened the social fiber of the community. When residents do engage in collective action to strengthen social controls through formal and informal means, such as participating in community meetings with the police or neighborhood watch programs, it may revitalize the neighborhood and reduce the risk of crime. However, fearful residents may reap the same benefits of imposed social control without doing any of the work, and thus may remain fearful despite the actual reduction in risk.

FUTURE RESEARCH

There seems to be a consensus among social scientists that individual and situational factors affect fear of crime. However, there is much debate about how strongly, and in what ways, these variables explain crime fears. The most consistently reported findings in research on fear of crime include the correlation between gender, age, or neighborhood conditions and the fear of crime. Female respondents, older individuals, and residents of high crime neighborhoods are more likely to report higher levels of crime fears. The significance of other sociodemographic factors and other situational contexts are less consistent, thus more research is needed to explore the dynamics of fear of crime. Concerns and anxieties about crime and disorder need to be further linked to broader concerns about social change at the global, national, and local level. Fear of crime has a significant impact on people's lives, as well as on the vitality and safety of urban areas. Consequently, reducing these fears and fostering a greater commitment to safer communities are integral to the future of American cities and the quality of public life.

—*Karen A. Snedker*

See also MEDIA; RISK; SECURITY MANAGEMENT

Further Reading

Anderson, Elijah. (1990). *Streetwise: Race, Class and Change in an Urban Community*. Chicago: University of Chicago Press.

Bankston, William B., Quentin A.L. Jenkins, Cheryl L. Thayer-Doyle, and Carol Y. Thompson. (1987). "Fear of Criminal Victimization and Residential Location: The Influence of Perceived Risk." *Rural Sociology* 52 (Spring): 98–107.

Beckett, Katherine. (1997). *Making Crime Pay: Law and Order in Contemporary American Politics*. New York: Oxford University Press.

Belyea, Michael J., and Matthew T. Zingraff. (1988). "Fear of Crime and Residential Location." *Rural Sociology* 53 (Winter): 473–486.

Chiricos, Ted, Sarah Eschholz, and Marc Gertz. (1997). "Crime, News and Fear of Crime: Toward and Identification of Audience Effects." *Social Problems* 44: 342–357.

Chiricos, Ted, Michael Hogan, and Marc Gertz. (1997). "Racial Composition of Neighborhood and Fear of Crime." *Criminology* 35: 107–129.

Clemente, Frank, and Michael B. Kleiman. (1977). "Fear of Crime in the United States: A Multivariate Analysis." *Social Forces* 56 (December): 519–531.

Covington, Jeanette, and Ralph B. Taylor. (1991). "Fear of Crime in Urban Residential Neighborhoods: Implications of Between- and Within-Neighborhood Sources of Current Models." *Sociological Quarterly* 32: 231–249.

Ferraro, Kenneth F. (1995). *Fear of Crime: Interpreting Victimization Risk*. Albany: State University of New York Press.

———. (1996). "Women's Fear of Victimization: Shadow of Sexual Assault?" *Social Forces* 75: 667–690.

Ferraro, Kenneth F., and Randy LaGrange. (1987). "The Measurement of Fear of Crime." *Sociological Inquiry* 57: 70–101.

Garland, David. (1990). *Punishment and Modern Society: A Study in Social Theory*. Chicago: University of Chicago Press.

Garofalo, James, and John Laub. (1978). "The Fear of Crime: Broadening Our Perspective." *Victimology* 3: 242–253.

Hindelang, Michael J., Michael Gottfredson, and James Garofalo. (1978). *Victims of Personal Crime: An Empirical Foundation for Theory of Personal Victimization*. Cambridge, MA: Ballinger.

Jacobs, Jane. (1961). *The Death and Life of Great American Cities*. New York: Vintage Books.

Killias, Martin, and Christian Clerici. (2000). "Different Measures of Vulnerability in Their Relation to Different Dimensions of Fear of Crime." *British Journal of Criminology* 40: 437–450.

LaGrange, Randy L., and Kenneth Ferraro. (1989). "Assessing Age and Gender Differences in Perceived Risk and Fear of Crime." *Criminology* 27: 697–719.

Lee, Gary R. (1982). "Residential Location and Fear of Crime Among the Elderly." *Rural Sociology* 47 (Winter): 655–669.

Lewis, Dan A., and Greta Salem. (1986). *Fear of Crime: Incivility and the Production of a Social Problem*. New Brunswick, NJ: Transaction Books.

Liska, Allen E., Andrew Sanchirico, and Mark D. Reed. (1988). "Fear of Crime and Constrained Behavior: Specifying and Estimating a Reciprocal Effects Model." *Social Forces* 66: 827–37.

Madriz, Esther. (1997). *Nothing Bad Happens to Good Girls: Fear of Crime in Women's Lives*. Berkeley: University of California Press.

Merry, Sally Engle. (1981). *Urban Danger: Life in a Neighborhood of Strangers*. Philadelphia: Temple University Press.

Moeller, Gertrude L. (1989). "Fear of Criminal Victimization: The Effect of Neighborhood Racial Composition." *Sociological Inquiry* 59: 208–221.

Newman, Oscar. (1972). *Defensible Space: Crime Prevention Through Urban Design*. New York: Macmillan.

Olson, Mancur. (1965). *The Logic of Collective Action*. Cambridge, MA: Harvard University Press.

Pantazis, Christina. (2000). "Fear of Crime, Vulnerability and Poverty: Evidence From a British Crime Survey." *British Journal of Criminology* 40: 414–436.

Riger, Stephanie, Margaret T. Gordon, and Robert Le Bailly. (1978). "Women's Fear of Crime: From Blaming the Victim to Restricting the Victim." *Victimology* 3: 272–284.

Skogan, Wesley G. (1990). *Disorder and Decline: Crime and the Spiral of Decay in American Neighborhoods*. New York: Free Press.

Skogan, Wesley G., and William R. Klecka. (1977). *The Fear of Crime*. Washington DC: American Political Science Association.

Skogan, Wesley G., and Michael G. Maxfield. (1981). *Coping With Crime: Individual and Neighborhood Reactions*. Beverly Hills, CA: Sage Publications.

St. John, Craig, and Tamara Heald-Moore. (1996). "Racial Prejudice and Fear of Criminal Victimization by Strangers in Public Settings." *Sociological Inquiry* 66: 267–284.

Stafford, Mark, and Omer Galle. (1984). "Victimization Rates, Exposure to Risk, and Fear of Crime." *Criminology* 22 (May): 173–185.

Stinchcombe, Arthur L., Rebecca Adams, Carol A. Heimer, Kim Lane Scheppele, Tom W. Smith, and D. Garth Taylor. (1980). *Crime and Punishment: Changing Attitudes in America*. San Francisco: Jossey-Bass.

Susser, Ida. (1982). *Norman Street: Poverty and Politics in an Urban Neighborhood*. New York: Oxford University Press.

U.S. Department of Justice, National Institute of Justice. (1999). *Attitudes Toward Crime, Police, and the Law: Individual and Neighborhood Differences*, by Robert J. Sampson and Dawn Jeglum Bartusch. Washington, DC: U.S. Department of Justice, National Institute of Justice.

———. (1999). *Crime, Grime, Fear, and Decline: A Longitudinal Look*, by Ralph B. Taylor. Washington, DC: U.S. Department of Justice, National Institute of Justice.

Walklate, Sandra. (1998). "Excavating the Fear of Crime: Fear, Anxiety or Trust?" *Theoretical Criminology* 2, 4: 403–418.

Warr, Mark. (1984). "Fear of Victimization: Why Are Women and the Elderly More Afraid? *Social Science Quarterly* 65: 681–702.

Warr, Mark, and Mark Stafford. (1983). "Fear of Victimization: A Look at the Proximate Causes." *Social Forces* 61 (June): 1033–1043.

Wilson, James Q., and George L. Kelling. (1982). "Broken Windows." *Atlantic Monthly* 249: 29–38.

Zimring, Franklin E., and Gordon Hawkins. (1997). *Crime Is Not the Problem: Lethal Violence in America*. New York: Oxford University Press.

FEDERAL BUREAU ▼ OF INVESTIGATION

The Federal Bureau of Investigation (FBI), the primary investigative branch of the U.S. Department of Justice (DOJ), is the nation's largest and most diverse federal police agency. Its primary functions are to investigate and prevent threats to national security and violations of federal criminal law. FBI priorities include cases involving terrorism, espionage, white-collar crime, organized crime, and crimes of bias and violence.

With over 11,000 agents and 16,000 support staff, the FBI maintains fifty-six field offices throughout the United States and Puerto Rico, along with over forty liaison posts in foreign countries. In addition, the Bureau operates a centralized support network of administrative and specialized units, including the Training and Laboratory Divisions. The FBI provides service and aid to local, state, national, and international agencies. Fingerprint and DNA analyses, ballistic and forensic investigations, and police training are among the specialized services offered. The FBI also maintains the Uniform Crime Reports—an annual measure of crime in the United States.

FBI agents are highly trained and skilled investigators. The media often depict agents' activities as perpetually exciting and dangerous. In reality, an agent's average day often consists of long hours of surveillance, research, evidence collection, and report writing.

The FBI traces its origins to 1908, when the DOJ hired former Secret Service agents to investigate several types of federal crime, including antitrust and banking violations. The creation of the Bureau was controversial. In the early twentieth century, the idea of a federal police force conjured up images of an internal spy system and of weakened local and state control over policing. Nevertheless, as interstate crimes increased and threats to national security became a greater concern, the need for a strong federal police force was realized. The FBI grew in size and scope throughout the century. Known as the Bureau of Investigation in 1909, the FBI gained its current title in 1935.

The single most influential figure in FBI history was J. Edgar Hoover (1895–1972). Director of the FBI from 1924 until his death, Hoover inherited an organization that was engulfed in scandal and corruption.

No. 1
THOMAS J. HOLDEN

First Most Wanted Listing:
March 14, 1950
Apprehended:
June 23, 1951

The first man listed as Most Wanted by the FBI. Holden was wanted for train robbery, escape from prison, and three murders. After escaping from prison twice, Holden was captured a final time after being identified by a coworker in Oregon.

Source: Sabljak, Mark, and Martin H. Greenberg (1990). *Most Wanted: A History of the FBI's Ten Most Wanted List*. New York: Bonanza Books, p. 26.

Hoover instituted a series of reforms meant to remove political influence and promote a positive image of the FBI. Unqualified or corrupt Bureau officials were removed, and new standards of education and training were set. Hoover successfully portrayed his agents as professional law enforcers who utilized science and determination to solve serious crime and catch dangerous felons. This crime-fighting "G-man" image was fueled by the creation of the "Public Enemy" list and by successful (and well-publicized) cases against notorious criminals like John Dillinger and Charles "Pretty Boy" Floyd. Although the "crime fighter" image was publicized, the FBI also engaged in covert activities during the Hoover years. These activities included the controversial surveillance of political leaders, social activists, and other private citizens who supposedly posed a threat to national security. Despite these controversies, the successes of the FBI allowed it to grow into one of the most recognized and respected police agencies in the world.

—*William H. Sousa, Jr.*

Further Reading

Federal Bureau of Investigation. http://www.fbi.gov

Powers, Richard Gid. (1987). *Secrecy and Power: The Life of J. Edgar Hoover.* New York: Free Press.

Theoharis, Athan G., Tony G. Poveda, Susan Rosenfeld, and Richard Gid Powers, eds. (1999). *The FBI: A Comprehensive Reference Guide.* Phoenix, AZ: Oryx Press.

Wilson, James Q. (1978). *The Investigators: Managing FBI and Narcotics Agents.* New York: Basic Books.

▼ FEMINIST THEORY

Numerous feminist criminologists have noted the irony that although sex is likely the strongest predictor of criminal behavior, traditional theories of crime rarely included gender. In contrast, feminist theorists have paid more attention to these areas in recent years. Their work has greatly enhanced our understanding of the ways in which gender influences involvement in crime, including both offending and victimization.

FEMINIST SOCIAL THEORY

As Rosemarie Putnam Tong (1998: 280) asserts in her review of feminist theory, the greatest strength of the feminist perspective is its recognition of the complexity of human behavior and its ability to offer a "kalei-doscopic" view of the world, rather than assert a single, all-encompassing view of society. Feminist theories draw upon many different disciplines, including liberalism, Marxism, socialism, psychoanalytic theory, existentialism, postmodernism, and multiculturalism. Although united in their commitment to understanding and fighting the oppression of women in society, feminist thinkers posit different causes to the problem of female subordination, depending on their theoretical feminist perspective. For example, Marxist feminists purport that capitalism is responsible for women's inequality, for they believe that women, like the proletariat (the working class), are exploited by a class system controlled by male bourgeois capitalists. However, radical feminists assert that overthrowing capitalism will not end women's oppression, because sexist injustice is rooted in "patriarchy," the system created by men to control women that influences all political, cultural, and social institutions.

Despite these varied perspectives, there are several underlying principles that unite feminist theorists. Above all, feminists challenge commonly accepted views about the world, and how these views have been constructed. Feminists emphasize that understanding of the social and biological world has been developed and disseminated mainly by men, often using exclusively male samples, and as a result, it often excludes, misrepresents, and further oppresses women.

An important contribution of more recent feminist thought has been the recognition that gender issues are interrelated to other forms of oppression, such as that based on class, race and/or ethnicity, sexuality, age, ability, and so on. As multicultural feminists point out, women do not exist only as "women" in society. Rather, their experiences are shaped by other important characteristics, and they may face oppression on many different levels (e.g., racism, classism, and heterosexism). As a result, feminists stress that systems of domination are interlocking and change must occur in multiple realms if one wants a truly equitable society.

FEMINIST CRIMINOLOGY

Just as feminist social theorists expose the limitations of traditional ways of understanding the social world, feminist criminologists assert that criminology has been too long concerned with explaining males offending against males, and has not considered women's involvement in crime as both victims and perpetrators. Most traditional criminological studies used exclusively male samples, focused primarily on offending (relative to victimization), and then, simply generalized to women and girls, if addressing them at all. In those rare cases where girls and women were specifically addressed beyond generalizing from the all-male studies, it was to reinforce sexist stereotypes. For example, Cesare Lombroso's theory on the "atavistic" female offender, published in the late 1800s, distorted and demonized the female criminal by highlighting the "unnatural" aspects of her biology. Likewise, "strain theory" purported that males' delinquency was typically a result of lower-class status and restricted access to legitimate options of achieving the "American dream." Girls were overlooked by this theory, presumably based on the assumption that their only strain was in finding boyfriends and husbands.

In contrast to these limited conceptualizations of crime, feminist theory significantly enhanced the field by offering more in-depth and realistic portrayals of female offenders and female victims, as well as illuminating the differences between males' and females' lives that might account for the vast gender disparity in criminal offending and victimization. Feminist criminology not only more accurately explains gender differences in the likelihood of offending but is also primarily responsible for identifying the frequency, and indeed epidemic rates, of intimate partner violence, incest and other sexual assaults and abuses, and sexual harassment. In these cases, women and girls are predominantly the victims and males are predominantly the offenders. In addition, these male-perpetrated crimes against females are primarily committed in private settings, by males well-known to the victims (e.g., husbands, fathers, and boyfriends). The sexist nature and discrimination in the perpetration of these offenses are compounded by the criminal processing system's historical focus on and response to public crimes and male victims.

The Link Between Victimization and Offending and Its Gendered Nature

A considerable amount of research suggests that girls are more likely than boys to be sexually abused, and their victimization starts earlier, lasts longer, is more likely to be perpetrated by family members, and has more traumatic consequences than boys' similar victimizations. Moreover, girls are especially vulnerable to abuse based simply on their female status, as they are more likely than boys to be viewed as "sexual prop-

erty," and to be kept at home where they are more accessible to their abusers. Even when they are outside of their homes, they are more likely than boys to be viewed as sexual and public property.

In addition to raising awareness about the offenses for which women and girls are largely the victims and males are largely the perpetrators, feminist scholars have made a significant contribution to the understanding of crime by identifying the link between victimization and subsequent offending. A number of feminist criminologists report that physical and sexual abuses often lead girls to run away from home, which, in turn, increases the odds that they will engage in illegal sex work and other offenses. That is, once they are living on the streets, girls frequently engage in prostitution and other crimes, as they have little access to legitimate resources and few legitimate skills at their disposal. A number of studies indicate extraordinarily high rates of incest, other child sexual abuse, and nonsexual physical abuse reported by female sex workers (prostitutes). These studies consistently identify the common path of abuse in the home leading to running away, which leads to sex work, theft, drug and alcohol use, and other crimes. Additionally, studies indicate that girls and women experience high rates of victimization while they are living on the streets, particularly as sex workers.

In addition to identifying the gendered link between youthful victimization and subsequent offending, feminist criminologists also identify the relationship between intimate partner victimization and subsequent offending. Similar to the extraordinarily high rates of childhood sexual abuse among female offenders, surveys of women in prison demonstrate disproportionately high rates of intimate partner violence victimization. Alternatively stated, incarcerated women are more likely than nonincarcerated women to report histories of being battered. Moreover, much research demonstrates the direct connection between being battered and subsequent offending. For example, some interviews of incarcerated, battered women reveal that they broke the law either because they were forced to do so by their abusive partners, or because they believed such actions would bring them closer to their abusive spouses and/or lower the amount of abuse they endured. The battering relationships may involve co-addiction to drugs, resulting in a gendered division of labor to obtain money for drugs (e.g., women, but not their male abusers, working as prostitutes to support both of their drug addictions). Based on this evidence, some feminist scholarship stresses that much of female offending is intimately related to problems with drug addiction or violent partners and should not be viewed as a commitment to a deviant lifestyle.

Victimization, Drug Use, and Crime

There is a significant amount of evidence to support the relationship between victimization, drug use, and other crimes. Moreover, research indicates that this relationship is gendered. There is some indication that female offenders are more likely than male offenders to report addiction to drugs and/or alcohol, likely due to the gendered nature of childhood victimizations. Given that girls experience more maltreatment than boys, female offenders report more drug and alcohol addiction than do male offenders.

Abuse histories, homelessness, and sex work also increase the likelihood that runaway girls will use and sell drugs for survival. Victims who become users of drugs and alcohol to "self-medicate" (alleviate the trauma and lowered self-esteem brought on by victimization) appear at greater risk for engaging in crime. In addition to using drugs for self-medication, female offenders often resort to selling drugs to support their drug addictions and/or for mere survival. Thus, sex work, drug sales, robbery, theft, and other offenses may all become means of surviving on (and off) the streets.

Race, Class, Gender, and Crime

Feminist criminologists emphasize that women's involvement in crime as both victims and offenders frequently reflects their overall position in society, and is strongly influenced by racism, poverty, single-parent status, and other factors. For example, some African American feminist scholars argue that even the relationship between victimization and offending is highly related to racism and other inequalities. Dislocated from major social institutions (e.g., school, work, family), the only way many racially and economically marginalized girls can survive is to engage in delinquency. Similarly, feminists assert that victimization alone may not lead directly to criminality, but when coupled with other forms of oppression (e.g., racism and poverty) and few legitimate opportunities to make money, female victims often resort to crime. Moreover, a significant body of research documents harsher treatment by the police and courts for women and girls of color and those who are less wealthy, compared to their white and wealthier counterparts.

IMPLICATIONS FOR THE OFFICIAL PROCESSING OF FEMALE OFFENDERS

Feminist scholarship typically includes not only raising awareness about women's and girls' oppression but advocating for change. For example, feminist criminological research advocates not only for increased awareness about child abuse to deter its occurrence but also for improved interventions for maltreated children, so that victims receive treatment before they become involved in the official system. Likewise, advocates for battered women have called for increased recognition of domestic violence issues, including better services for victims and more effective processing by the official system.

In terms of public policies, feminist scholarship also presses for more effective redress against poverty and racism. Specifically, racial profiling and other racist practices seriously affect both males and females of color, as victims and offenders. Additionally, feminist criminologists identify the "war on drugs" as more damaging to female than male offenders. At the same time, they identify the paucity of services available to institutionalized female offenders, relative to their male counterparts. Feminists also stress the importance of offering "gender-specific" programs that address the gendered nature of victimization and drug addiction and provide educational or vocational training to bolster women's and girls' skills. Finally, feminists assert that victimization often occurs within prisons, and they emphasize that this abuse may be especially traumatic for women and girls with histories of victimization. Thus, they have called for the elimination of strip searches conducted by male guards, as well as other policies that reduce the access of male officers to female prisoners.

It is important to note that feminists are not in agreement on policies and their implementation. For example, while some feminists advocate for mandatory or presumptive arrest policies in domestic violence cases, others argue against these practices, claiming they further disempower battered women by taking away their input. Similarly, while some feminists argue the need for "gender-specific" approaches to female offenders, others are concerned that this approach will reinforce stereotypic gender roles and responses (e.g., girls and women as psychologically "sick" relative to boys and men).

THE FUTURE OF FEMINIST CRIMINOLOGY

In general, future research needs to more closely examine the frequency and nature of crimes routinely committed against women and girls by males (e.g., sexual abuse and assault, intimate partner violence, sexual harassment, and stalking). Criminological research must also more carefully address girls' and women's involvement in crime, and how it is and is not gendered. Similarly, further investigations of the link between victimization and subsequent offending, and the complex ways in which gender affects this relationship, is required. Clearly, not all victims of physical and sexual violence become offenders, and further research is needed to illuminate risk and protective factors that influence some victims to break the law and make others more resistant to offending. Moreover, such work must also identify the ways in which gender, as well as other important demographic characteristics (including race and/or ethnicity, socioeconomic status, family structure, etc.) and other life experiences (e.g., school performance, involvement with delinquent peers, attitudes towards crime, etc.) are related to these risk and protective factors.

Furthermore, it is clear that physical or sexual violence against them is only one possible explanation for women's and girls' involvement in crime, and feminists have suggested other important pathways to crime. Importantly, feminist theory allows for divergent views of the causes and consequences of crime and recognizes that women exist in very different social environments that influence their involvement in crime. This inclusiveness is one of the most important contributions feminist theory can make to criminology, for it is increasingly evident that criminal behavior is a complex phenomenon that necessitates multicausal explanations for both females and males.

—*Abigail A. Fagan and Joanne Belknap*

See also RADICAL CRIMINOLOGY; WOMEN AND CRIME IN A GLOBAL PERSPECTIVE; WOMEN AND POLICING; WOMEN AS OFFENDERS; WOMEN AS VICTIMS; WOMEN IN PRISON; WOMEN WHO KILL

Further Reading

Arnold, Regina A. (1990). "Processes of Victimization and Criminalization of Black Women." *Social Justice* 17, 3: 153–166.

Belknap, Joanne. (2001). *The Invisible Woman: Gender, Crime, and Criminal Justice*, 2d ed. Belmont, CA: Wadsworth.

Chesney-Lind, Meda. (1997). *The Female Offender: Girls, Woman and Crime*. Thousand Oaks, CA: Sage.

Chesney-Lind, Meda, and John M. Hagedorn, eds. (1999). *Female Gangs in America: Essays on Girls, Gangs and Gender*. Chicago: Lakeview Press.

Chesney-Lind, Meda and Randall G. Shelden. (1998). *Girls, Delinquency and Juvenile Justice*, 2d ed. Belmont, CA: Wadsworth.

Daly, Kathleen. (1994). *Gender, Crime, and Punishment*. New Haven, CT: Yale University Press.

Daly, Kathleen and Meda Chesney-Lind. (1988). "Feminism and Criminology." *Justice Quarterly* 5: 497–538.

Gilfus, Mary E. (1992). "From Victims to Survivors to Offenders: Women's Routes of Entry and Immersion Into Street Crime." *Women and Criminal Justice* 4: 63–90.

Greene, Peters, & Associates. (1998). *Guiding Principles for Promising Female Programming*. Washington, D.C.: The Office of Juvenile Justice and Delinquency Prevention.

Human Rights Watch Women Rights Project. (1996). *All Too Familiar: Sexual Abuse of Women in U.S. State Prisons*. New York: Human Rights Watch.

Jaggar, Alison M. (1983). *Feminist Politics and Human Nature*. Totowa, NJ: Rowman & Littlefield.

Maher, Lisa. (1997). *Sexed Work: Gender, Race and Resistance in a Brooklyn Drug Market*. Oxford: Clarendon Press.

Naffine, Ngaire. (1987). *Female Crime: The Construction of Women in Criminology*. Sydney, Australia: Allen & Unwin.

———. (1996). *Feminism and Criminology*. Philadelphia: Temple University Press.

Owen, Barbara. (1998). *In the Mix: Struggle and Survival in a Women's Prison*. Albany: State University of New York Press.

Richie, Beth E. (1996). *Compelled to Crime: The Gender Entrapment of Black Battered Women*. New York, NY: Routledge.

Tong, Rosemarie Putnam. (1998). *Feminist Thought: A More Comprehensive Introduction*. Boulder, CO: Westview Press.

Widom, Cathy Spatz. (1989). "The Cycle of Violence." *Science* 244: 160–166.

▼ FENCING

There has been little research to date on the role of thieves, fences, and consumers in the overall redistribution of stolen goods. Given that burglary and theft are considered such important social problems, it is odd that these factors have been so neglected by criminologists. To address the need for further research, the U.K. Home Office Research Development and Statistics Directorate has undertaken pioneering research on stolen goods. Following the publication in the United Kingdom of the first systematic research in this area (Sutton 1998), the Market Reduction Approach (MRA) was recommended as a potentially useful strategy for tackling theft. In essence, the MRA is designed to tackle theft by reducing the number of outlets for stolen goods.

MARKET SUPPLY CREATED BY THEFT

Most crimes require convergence in space and time of likely offenders, suitable targets, and the absence of capable guardians against crime (Cohen and Felson 1979). Stolen goods markets motivate thieves, because most thieves steal to sell goods and thus obtain cash. Market demand for particular items has an essential role in creating two of the three preconditions of theft incidents outlined by Cohen and Felson's model: "likely offenders" and "suitable targets."

Simple linear explanations of demand and supply do not really fit the dynamics of stolen goods markets. Knowingly buying or selling stolen goods (handling) clearly creates a demand for more of the same stuff—therefore fueling theft. In addition to providing motivation for theft, however, handling stolen goods is a crime that is committed as a simple downstream consequence of stealing. This is because the prolific thieves themselves regularly groom business owners in order to open new markets (Sutton 1998).

A sizable section of the public is not particularly capable as guardians of law and order when it comes to the opportunity to resist an illegitimate bargain. Nationally representative research in the United Kingdom (Sutton 1998) found that 11 percent of the population of England and Wales admitted buying stolen goods in the past five years and that a staggering 70 percent thought that some of their neighbors had stolen goods such as VCRs and TVs in their homes. This should not be too surprising, because social commentators, lawyers, and criminologists have been raising this issue since the time of Patrick Colquhoun (1796). Later writers (see Hall 1952; Walsh 1977; Henry 1978; Cromwell et al.) also have classified buyers of stolen goods according to their degree of guilty knowledge or recklessness. In addition to these works, there are two classic ethnographic studies that follow the business of individual professional fences (Klockars 1974; Steffensmeier 1986).

The Handling Study (Sutton 1998) identified five main types of market for stolen goods:

1. *Commercial fence supplies.* Stolen goods are sold by thieves to commercial fences (e.g., jewelers, pawnbrokers, secondhand dealers) operating out of shops.

2. *Residential fence supplies.* Stolen goods (particularly electrical goods) are sold by thieves to fences, usually at the home of a fence.

3. *Network sales.* Stolen goods are passed on and each participant adds a little to the price until a consumer is found; this may involve a residential fence, and the buyer may be the final consumer or may sell the goods on again through friendship networks.

4. *Commercial sales.* Stolen goods are sold by commercial fences for a profit, either directly to the (innocent) consumer or to another distributor who thinks the goods can be sold again for additional profit. More rarely, such sales are made to another distributor.

5. *Hawking.* Thieves sell directly to consumers in places such as bars and clubs, or door-to-door (e.g., shoplifters selling clothes or food).

Probing the dynamics of stolen goods markets, the U.K. Home Office "Handling Study" (Sutton 1998) conducted in-depth interviews with thieves, fences, and consumers of stolen goods. These interviews revealed the key role that stolen goods markets play in motivating people to steal. They also revealed that inexperienced thieves tend to rely on existing markets, usually a single residential fence who is either a relative or neighbor. Experienced and prolific thieves, however—particularly frequent drug users—are more proactive in finding new buyers, and, therefore, sell to a variety of people. They are able to sell quickly and quite closely to where the theft was committed, even if they are not in close proximity to their usual buyers. This minimizes risk of arrest, because thieves need only transport stolen goods short distances and store them for brief periods.

Although the Handling Study found that particularly active fences tend to encourage thieves to increase their offending, it was revealed that stolen goods markets are mainly fueled by thieves offering goods for sale, rather than by proactive demand from dealers. It appears that offers from thieves to sell stolen goods have the greatest influence on the way that the stolen goods markets operate. This is because most dealers and consumers do not actively seek out stolen goods. Therefore, these items need to be offered them in order to be able "knowingly" to buy them. Stealing-to-order does go on, and the practice is quite widespread, but it is not as common as what should, perhaps, be called "stealing-to-offer."

In the United Kingdom, this new knowledge about the importance of stealing-to-offer was first used to create an initial menu of *situational* tactics recommended to reduce theft through an MRA (Sutton 1998). That menu has been further developed to form the core element of a report that provides a strategic and systematic "toolkit" for tackling stolen goods markets (Sutton, Schneider, and Hetherington 2001).

THE MARKET REDUCTION APPROACH

The MRA model utilizes the core principles of situational crime prevention (Clarke 1997, 1999), intelligence-led

Two Thieves Tell How It Is Done

When I broke into houses, I'd always look for money first, then jewellery, any jewellery that was going. In those days, when I was about 16, like, you didn't have to look for it; it was on the mantle piece etc. . . . people were much more trusting than they are today, they would just leave doors open. With jewellery, in them days, I would just go to the old-secondhand shops which were in abundance in those days, or go to a pawnbrokers – there would be no questions asked like . . . just be 'alright mate, how much do you want for it?'

. . . never no questions asked really. It was just too easy in those days.

I've never bought stolen goods—I've sold them, but never bought them myself. If there is something that I wanted, I would just go out and get it for myself. Hardly ever bought my own clothes—just pinched them. If you get into it, it's hard to get out of . . . it's like an addiction. Cos you just keep getting away with it or only getting a caution if you do get caught. I stopped shoplifting when I was fifteen and a half. The stuff I nicked, I sold around the estate.

Source: Sutton, Mike. (1998). *Handling Stolen Goods and Theft: A Market Reduction Approach.* Home Office research Study 178. London: Home Office, p. 107, 111.

policing (ILP), problem-oriented policing (Goldstein 1990), and, in part, zero tolerance policing. With the aim of reducing theft, the MRA model identifies the following steps that should be taken to reduce the number of stolen goods markets within an area: (1) gather information on local stolen goods markets; (2) analyze the information to determine which of the five types of stolen goods market (Sutton 1998) are operating, how those markets are operating, and who is involved; (3) devise a plan to reduce the most significant market(s) in operation; (4) implement the plan; (5) evaluate the outcome; and (6) revise the plan in accordance with any market changes.

The general theory of the MRA—that reducing dealing in stolen goods will reduce motivation to steal—means that all MRA theft reduction strategies will begin with the following two strategic aims: (1) to instill an appreciation among thieves that selling, transporting, and storing stolen goods has become at least as risky as it is to steal the goods in the first place and (2) to make buying, dealing, and consuming stolen goods appreciably more risky for all those involved. To achieve these aims, the MRA sets out to reduce the number of offers made to potential buyers, the number of outlets for stolen goods, and the number of thieves and handlers by encouraging them to explore noncriminal alternatives, rather than just alternative crimes.

The MRA model proposes that these objectives can be achieved by cracking down on stolen goods markets with a program of carefully coordinated tactical operations, and then consolidating any success with longer-term strategies to tackle the things that help stolen goods markets to take hold and thrive. The various markets—thieves, dealers, and consumers—need to be monitored, to determine whether they should be tackled simultaneously or in turn. This will help to maximize crime reduction and also limit any opportunities for displacement of dealing activity from one market type to another.

THE WAY FORWARD: TESTING THE MRA

Research conducted in the 1990s revealed the important role of stolen goods markets in motivating thieves to steal in the first place. There has been great interest in the MRA, and this report describes the latest developments in methods to tackle stolen goods markets. While the thinking behind the MRA is straightforward, logical, and appears to have great crime-reducing potential, it is at this stage an innovative crime-reducing philosophy. The MRA has been adopted in several projects funded under the U.K. government's £250 million Crime Reduction Programme. In the early years of the twenty-first century, this innovative approach will receive an independent evaluation of its costs and benefits.

—*Mike Sutton*

See also ART THEFT AND FRAUD; ILLICIT ANTIQUITIES; PROPERTY CRIME; SMUGGLING

Further Reading

Clarke, Ronald. (1997). "Introduction." In *Situational Crime Prevention: Successful Case Studies*, 2d ed., edited by R. V. Clarke. Guilderland, NY: Harrow & Heston, 2–43.

Clarke, Ronald. (1999). *Hot Products: Understanding, Anticipating, and Reducing Demand for Stolen Goods.* Police Research Series Paper 122, Policing and Reducing Crime Unit, Research Development and Statistics Directorate. London. Home Office.

Cohen, Lawrence, and Marcus Felson. (1979). "Social Change and Crime Rate Trends: A Routine Activity Approach." *American Sociological Review* 44: 580-608.

Colquhoun, P. (1796). *A Treatise on the Police of the Metropolis; Containing a Detail of the Various Crimes and Misdemeanours by Public and Private Security Are, at Present, Injured and Endangered: And Suggesting Remedies for their Prevention*, 3d ed. London: C. Dilly Poultry.

Cromwell, Paul, J. Olson, and D. Avary. (1994). *Breaking and Entering: An Ethnographic Analysis of Burglary.* Thousand Oaks, CA: Sage.

Goldstein, Herman. (1990). *Problem Oriented Policing.* New York: McGraw-Hill.

Hall, Jerome. (1952). *Theft, Law and Society*, 2d ed. Indianapolis, IN: Bobbs-Merrill Co.

Henry, Stuart. (1978). *The Hidden Economy: The Context and Control of Borderline Crime.* London. Martin & Robertson.

Klockars, Carl. (1974). *The Professional Fence.* New York: Free Press.

Steffensmeier, D. J. (1986). *The Fence: In the Shadow of Two Worlds.* Lanham, MD: Rowman & Littlefield.

Sutton, Mike. (1995). "Supply by Theft: Does the Market for Second-hand Goods Play a Role in Keeping Crime Figures High?" *British Journal of Criminology* 35, 3 (Summer): 400–416.

Sutton, Mike. (1998). *Handling Stolen Goods and Theft: A Market Reduction Approach.* Home Office Research Study 178. London: Home Office.

Sutton, Mike, Jacqueline Schneider, and Sarah Hetherington. (2001). *Tackling Theft With the Market Reduction Approach.* Crime Reduction Research Series. London. Home Office

Walsh, Marilyn. (1977). *The Fence: A New Look at the World of Property Theft.* Westport, CT: Greenwood Press.

◤ FEUDING

Feuding is a form of violent crime. It is a series of revenge-based killings that result in the loss of human life and contribute to the disruption of the social order. In contrast to the view of feuding as disruptive, however, there are some theories of feuding that treat revenge-based killings as performing a positive social function. Feuding has been described throughout history and in the ethnographic record, and it continues into modern times.

A review of definitions of feuding revealed several essential elements (Otterbein 1996: 493): (1) kinship groups are involved, (2) homicides take place, (3) the killings occur as revenge for injustice (the terms *duty, honor, righteous,* and *legitimate* appear in discussions of the motivation for the homicides), (4) three or more alternating killings or acts of violence occur, and (5) the acts of violence and killing occur within a political entity, such as a tribe, nation, or country. Together these elements form a comprehensive definition of feuding. This definition can be stretched to include feuds in which an unsuccessful attempt at a counterkilling leads to the killing of one or more of the revenge seekers, as occurred on several occasions in the Turner-Howard feud in nineteenth-century eastern Kentucky. Mortality

in this feud was one-sided, as thirteen Turners died while no Howards were killed (Otterbein 1999: 234).

In many feuding societies, feuds can be ended by the payment of compensation. Indeed, feuding practices can be divided into two main categories:

1. Feuding without compensation, in which there is no institutionalized means by which compensation can be paid

2. Feuding with compensation, in which payment of compensation can prevent a counterkilling, thereby stopping a feud.

Kentucky feuding rarely ever involved the payment of compensation to bring to an end an escalating cycle of violence and killing, whereas Montenegro feuding in the Balkans in the nineteenth century was surrounded with rules, which, if followed, could prevent a counterkilling. In a cross-cultural study of fifty societies, 16 percent fell into the first type and 28 percent into the second type. The majority of cases (56 percent) fell into a third category that included societies in which homicides are rare, or in which, following a homicide, a formal judicial procedure comes into effect, independent of the two feuding parties, leading to settlement through compensation or punishment (Otterbein and Otterbein 1965: 1470–1471).

In addition to whether or not compensation can be paid, two other dimensions of feuding are important. First, feuds can be classified using a range of six categories to describe the degree of legitimacy of kin group vengeance: (1) moral imperative, (2) most appropriate action, (3) circumstantial, (4) last resort, (5) formal adjudication only, and (6) individual self-redress. Second, feuds can be categorized in terms of the possible targets of vengeance: (1) anyone in the wrongdoer's kin group, (2) the wrongdoer if possible, otherwise selected members of his kin group, or (3) the wrongdoer only (Ericksen and Horton 1992).

FEUDING IN COMPARATIVE PERSPECTIVE

Feuding can be differentiated from four other forms of killing, using three criteria. Table 1 lists the criteria that are present or absent for each of five forms of human killing (Otterbein 1985: 11):

Feuding is differentiated from warfare, which occurs between political communities. These two types of violent conflict can be distinguished if a political community can be identified, as by looking for a polit-

Table 1. Feuding and Other Forms of Killing

Elements	Feuding	Homicide	Capital Punishment	Warfare	Human Sacrifice
(1) Occurs within political community	Present	Present	Present	Absent	Present
(2) Is considered appropriate	Absent	Absent	Present	Present	Present
(3) Addresses an injustice	Present	Absent	Present	Present	Absent

ical leader who announces group decisions; the group is often small. Some researchers include feuding under the rubric of "internal war" (war within the same cultural or ethnolinguistic unit). But to most researchers, feuding and warfare appear qualitatively different. Feuding is differentiated from capital punishment because it is not considered appropriate by political leaders or people not directly involved in the feud. Table 1 shows injustice as being present in the case of feuding, because revenge of an injustice is an integral part of the definition of feuding.

It is possible to question whether feuding is a legitimate course of action for a kin group that believes itself to be wronged (Otterbein 1985: 77–80). Although feuding may be carried out according to a large body of culturally defined rules, the political leaders and members of kinship groups not involved in the feud usually wish to see the feud end or be settled. Political leaders by their nature almost always reserve the exclusive right to judge whether a crime has been committed and to do the punishing. For these reasons, feuding can be viewed as being not a legal action but a highly disruptive sequence of antisocial acts. Actions taken by political leaders to prevent feuding are viewed as legal; the revenge killings of kinship groups as extralegal. The feuds of nineteenth-century eastern Kentucky illustrate this well. Wilson Howard, who admitted to killing five Turners, was executed by hanging. In the French-Eversole feud, Tom Smith, a French supporter and killer of six Eversoles, was also hanged. Furthermore, in the Martin-Tolliver and Baker-Howard feuds, the governor of Kentucky sent in troops to prevent further killings (Otterbein 1999: 234–238).

The extent of feuding can be inferred from two cross-cultural studies, one by Otterbein and Otterbein (1965), the other by Ericksen and Horton (1992); each examined ethnographic descriptions of the feuding practices of a sample of societies. The former found

that 44 percent of their sample societies had feuding, and the latter found that 54 percent of their sample also did. A cross-cultural study of homicide conducted by Martin Daly and Margo Wilson found that 95 percent of their sample societies accepted the idea of taking a life for a life (1988: 224–226). The authors achieved near universality by including both feuding and capital punishment as evidence of the desire for blood revenge. The result is not surprising since Otterbein found, using the same sample, that 51 of the 53 societies, or 96 percent, for which there was information had the death penalty (1986: 40). The results of these studies lead to the conclusion that although approximately half of the world's societies practice feuding, the desire for revenge—a life for a life—may be nearly universal.

ORIGIN OF FEUDING

Feuding has deep roots that probably extend back to the time of early man. Once kinship groups had formed and related males continued to live together after reaching adulthood, the social basis for feuding was in place. While not all early hunting-gathering bands had this form of social structure, many probably did. Those bands with localized groups of related males developed what are known as fraternal interest groups. A series of cross-cultural studies show fraternal interest groups to predict violence that occurs within local groups (Thoden van Velzen and van Wetering 1960), and specific forms of violence: rape (Otterbein 1979), feuding (Otterbein and Otterbein 1965), and internal war (Otterbein 1968). The cross-cultural studies provide evidence that early man, if he had fraternal interest groups (as he probably did), engaged in feuding and internal war. If the killings are between rival fraternal interest groups within the band, they are feuding; if between bands, they are warfare. This argument has been taken a step further with the identification of two types of societies both in prehistory (Otterbein n.d.) and in the ethnographic record (Otterbein 1985: 79). One type is societies with fraternal interest groups, which have much conflict, rape, feuding, internal war, and intraclan executions; the other type is societies without fraternal interest groups, which have little conflict, no rape, no feuding, no internal war, and polity-wide executions. The first type of society is exemplified by the Higi of northeastern Nigeria. These patrilineal-patrilocal people, who practiced polygamy, had well-defined fraternal interest groups. The groups played a central role in between-lineage conflict, rape, and feuding and served as the military organizations in warfare between polities (Otterbein 1994b). The Cheyenne of the Great Plains of North America are an example of the second type of society, because they lacked descent groups, practiced matrilocal residence, and were monogamous. The Cheyenne were used as the type case of an internally peaceful society by Thoden van Velzen and van Vetering in their cross-cultural study (1960). Internal conflict and rape were rare, feuding did not occur, and the Northern and Southern Cheyenne did not war with each other. Executions were rare, but when they occurred, kinship did not play a role.

Societies with fraternal interest groups may have arisen in response to a hostile environment—hostile in the sense that food was scarce, other hunting-gathering bands competed for the same resources, or there were large predators present. Localized groups of related males could have formed to provide protection for the band. Furthermore, fraternal interest groups are an efficient way to organize for hunting.

Feuding is found at all levels of sociopolitical complexity, not just among many of the hunting and gathering bands of prehistory. However, some bands in the ethnographic record do not have fraternal interest groups and feuding, or war, for that matter. Raymond Kelly (2000) has described these warless societies as "unsegmented societies." The three warless societies in Kelly's sample were the Mbuti, pygmies of the Congo; the Semang, hunter-gatherers of Malaysia; and the Central Eskimo of the Arctic. Once kinship groups arise, the societies become segmented and warfare arises.

In another study, Otterbein shows how fraternal interest groups, feuding, and capital punishment were interrelated in tribal society (1986: 61–73). Tribes with fraternal interest groups and feuding can be classified based on whether councils of elders are present. In tribes with fraternal interest groups and councils of elders, executions of wrongdoers are carried out by members of the wrongdoer's own clan at the insistence of the political leader and the elders. The homicides that occur between feuding clans, however, are not capital punishment. In tribes without fraternal interest

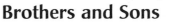

Brothers and Sons

Feuds involve groups of related men who seek revenge against men from other families. Major feuds can involve large numbers of related men and last for generations, as shown by this example from Albania, a region in southern Europe where feuds have been common for centuries.

A murdered man found his most natural avenger in his brother, especially if they had not separated. If his father was not too old, and his son too young, to bear arms, they shared the brother's obligation. In slightly less degree so did his father's brothers and cousins in the male line, and their sons and grandsons, that is to say, all the other males who were in the collective sense his "father," "brother" and "son," through being at the time, or having recently been, members of his household. If his son was in the cradle, the child's mother and the neighbors told him of the crime as he grew up and urged him, failing another avenger, not to rest until he had done his duty . . . . [If one] of these relatives took revenge, his "rifle could be hung up" and "go to sleep," to quote the picturesque phrases of Diber and the North. The lawful representative of his murdered kinsman because he belonged to the same household, he had only made the two sides equal, with one of two results; either peace could be made or the feud continued between the two families.

Source: Hasluck, Margaret. (1967). "The Albanian Blood Feud." In *Law and Warfare: Studies in the Anthropology of Conflict*, edited by Paul Bohannan. Garden City, NY: The Natural History Press, p. 382.

groups but with councils of elders, only political leaders perform executions.

More complex societies, known as centralized political systems (chiefdoms and states) are as likely to have feuding as are uncentralized political systems (bands and tribes) (Otterbein and Otterbein 1965: 1476). Nevertheless, in these societies warfare can have an influence upon feuding. Centralized political systems at war, even if fraternal interest groups are present, do not have feuding. Presumably, political leaders under the circumstance of war have the power to prevent feuds (Otterbein and Otterbein 1965: 1478; Otterbein 1994a: 110–111). While in the ethnographic record, feuding and warfare do not go hand in hand in centralized political systems (as they do in uncentralized political systems), in market-based societies in recent centuries,

Feuding and Justice in Appalachia

Feuding has been described as a type of informal justice, a view supported by this story from Kentucky.

But hardly a county was without its "war," and some had a whole series. The "troubles" in Breathitt won for that county the somber sobriquet of "Bloody Breathitt" and gained for its populace the shocked attention to the world. An eighty-year-old lawyer once related to me the unique manner in which court adjournments were occasionally obtained in its Circuit Court. A murder case was docketed for trial and numerous friends of the defendant appeared at the courthouse heavily armed and in a belligerent mood. When the judge called the case for trial, the defendant's father, a man of about fifty with huge handlebar whiskers and two immense pistols, rose and walked to the judicial bench. Wringing the gavel from the fingers of the startled judge, the feudist rapped the bench and announced, "Court is over and ever' body can go. We ain't agoin' to have any court here this term, folks." The red-faced judge hastily acquiesced in this extraordinary order and promptly left town. When court convened at the next term the court and sheriff were bolstered by sixty militiamen, but by then the defendant was not available for trial. He had been slain from ambush.

Source: Caudill, Harry M. (1963). *Night Comes to the Cumberlands: A Biography of a Depressed Area.* Boston: Little, Brown and Company. p. 49.

feuding and crime do go hand in hand. The two major examples of this are the feuding kinship groups of southern Appalachia and the Sicilian kinship groups that are parts of the Mafia (Otterbein 1999: 241–242). Control of the illegal whiskey market has been a major factor in feuding in both societies. The use of hired killers and the corruption of government officials has as its goal the control of an area in which illegal activities can flourish.

OTHER THEORIES OF FEUDING

Theories of feuding that treat revenge-based killings as performing a positive social role number at least six. The first theory reviewed is not a theory of feuding, but it is appropriately placed in the list because all the elements of feuding are present except for the lack of involvement of kinship groups in attempted counterkillings. The theories range from apologies to justifications for homicide.

1. Southern homicide has been referred to as "folk justice" by William C. Montell (1986). In the area of Tennessee and Kentucky that he describes, homicides frequently resulted from fights between males. Montell does not present a theory of feuding, since in only 3 out of 56 cases did family members of the victims blame the killer (1986: 155). Feuding did not arise, probably because kinship groups were scattered (Otterbein 1999: 242). Presumably, if feuds occurred, Montell would classify them as examples of "folk justice." Folk justice arises from an individual exercising what he believes is his right to get even. Kinsmen of the disputants do not become involved, and they do not cooperate with outside authorities investigating the homicide.

2. World systems theory comes into play in Altima Waller's study of the Hatfield-McCoy feud (1988). She argues that social change brought on by commercial expansion in the period from 1860 to 1900 created this famous feud. Prior to 1860, these mountain peoples lived peacefully; their feud was caused by the disruption that logging and mining brought to Kentucky and West Virginia. According to John Ed Pearce, however, some feuding took place prior to 1860.

3. For some researchers, feuds occupy an intermediate position between law and crime, and thus have been designated "quasi-law" or "self-help." Paul Bohannan presents a schema showing how a killing creates "a breach of norm" and how a revenge killing, a "counteraction," leads to a "correction" (1963: 284–291). Nevertheless, Bohannan states that "a feud occurs when the principle of self-help gets out of hand" (1963: 290).

4. In societies with patrilineages organized into segmentary lineage systems, Max Gluckman (1982) observes that lineages may make peace, through the payment of compensation, thus uniting to form larger kinship groups, which are in opposition to each other. These larger kinship groups remain at peace within, while they feud with each other; Gluckman calls this "peace in the feud."

5. Christopher Boehm argues that feuding with compensation is a means of controlling conflict; in his view, it is an alternative to warfare. Feuding arises, Boehm suggests, because the potential combatants realize that uncontrolled warfare at close quarters

would be disastrous (1984: 202–207).

6. A theory stemming from sociobiology views blood revenge as not only defining groups but preserving them. Vengeance may establish deterrence and in so doing prevent counteraggression. If the victim's kin accept compensation and refrain from homicidal retaliation, both groups survive, and their members continue to procreate. Not to have compensation paid could lead to the massacre of one group and the decimation of the other (Daly and Wilson 1988: 221–238).

7. Retaliatory killing by an individual, kinship group, or a nation-state is sometimes considered self-defense by the party engaged in the counterkilling. The purpose is to prevent one's enemy from killing one, by killing them or by so frightening the enemy that they refrain from attacking. This doctrine of retaliation, based on deterrence theory, is embodied in the national policies of several North African and Middle Eastern states. It is employed against both foreign nations as well as against ethnic groups within the nations.

ASSESSMENT

A feud is a series of revenge-based killings. Each killing in the sequence is a crime. Although numerous theories have been set forth to explain feuding, many theories are apologies or justifications for homicide (1, 2, and 7 above). Even when they are not explicitly apologies or justifications, they may seek to find a positive role for feuding within the society under examination (3 to 6 above). It is the theme of this review, however, that feuding is disruptive of the social order. Revenge-based killings tend to escalate. Even those societies with social mechanisms for paying compensation have great difficulty stopping feuds. An attempt at counterkilling may fail; someone other than the intended victim may be killed. The group seeking vengeance may then feel the need to try again. A study of five Kentucky feuds makes this manifestly clear. In the Turner-Howard feud, 13 Turners died, and no Howards (Otterbein 1999: 234). At no time was the score even in the other four feuds; no tit-for-tat pattern emerged. The side behind, while eager for more deaths, often fell further behind as their attempts at homicidal revenge failed.

SUMMARY

Feuding is a peculiar institution. It arose early in human existence as the natural result of the male offspring of a couple residing together into adulthood. If environmental conditions made it desirable for them to remain together, they so did. The resulting element of social organization, termed a fraternal interest group, played a positive role in the perpetuation of many human populations. However, a downside developed. In defending group members, fraternal interest groups may turn violent and set off a series of revenge-based killings—feuding—that not only result in the loss of life but disrupt the social order. Feuding, therefore, does not perform a positive social role, although the kinship groups that make feuding possible played a positive role in the development of early societies.

—*Keith F. Otterbein*

Further Reading

Boehm, Christopher. (1984). *Blood Revenge: The Anthropology of Feuding in Montenegro and Other Tribal Societies*. Lawrence: University Press of Kansas.

Bohannan, Paul. (1963). *Social Anthropology*. New York: Holt, Rinehart & Winston.

Daly, Martin, and Margo Wilson. (1988). *Homicide*. New York: Aldine de Gruyter.

Ericksen, Karen Paige, and Heather Horton. (1992). "Blood Feuds: Cross-Cultural Variation in Kin Group Vengeance." *Behavior Science Research* 26: 57–85.

Gluckman, Max. (1982). *Custom and Conflict in Africa*. Oxford, UK: Oxford University Press.

Kelly, Raymond. (2000). *Warless Societies and the Origin of War*. Ann Arbor: University of Michigan Press.

Montell, William L. (1986). *Killings: Folk Justice in the Upper South*. Lexington: University Press of Kentucky.

Otterbein, Keith F. (1968). "Internal War: A Cross-Cultural Study." *American Anthropologist* 70: 277–289.

———. (1979). "A Cross-Cultural Study of Rape." *Aggressive Behavior* 5: 425–435.

———. (1986). *The Ultimate Coercive Sanction: A Cross-Cultural Study of Capital Punishment*. New Haven, CT: Human Relations Area Files Press.

———. (1994a). *Feuding and Warfare: Selected Works of Keith F. Otterbein*. Langhorne, PA: Gordon & Breach.

———. (1994b). "Higi Armed Combat." In *Feuding and Warfare: Selected Works of Keith F. Otterbein*. Langhorne, PA: Gordon & Breach.

———. (1996). "Feuding." In *The Encyclopedia of Cultural Anthropology*, vol. 1, edited by David Levinson and Melvin Ember. New York: Henry Holt, 254–257.

———. (1999). "Five Feuds: An Analysis of Homicides in Eastern Kentucky in the Late Nineteenth Century." *American Anthropologist* 102: 231–243.

———. *When War Began*. (forthcoming). Boulder, CO: Westview Press.

Otterbein, Keith F., and Charlotte Swanson Otterbein. (1965). "An Eye for an Eye, a Tooth for a Tooth: A Cross-Cultural Study of Feuding." *American Anthropologist* 67: 1470–1482.

Pearce, John Ed. (1994). *Days of Darkness: The Feuds of Eastern*

Kentucky. Lexington: University Press of Kentucky.

Thoeden van Velzen, H. U. E., and W. van Wetering. (1960). "Residence, Power Groups, and Intrasocietal Aggression." *International Archives of Ethnography* 49: 169–200.

Waller, Altina. (1988). *Feud: Hatfields, McCoys, and Social Change in Appalachia, 1860–1900*. Chapel Hill: University of North Carolina Press.

FINANCIAL COSTS AND BENEFITS OF CRIME PREVENTION

The financial costs and benefits of crime prevention present important issues nationally and internationally, but study of this subject remains a relatively neglected area of research. In recent years in the United States, Canada, the United Kingdom, and other industrialized nations, there has been a growing interest on the part of governments and other stakeholders in identifying the monetary value of crime prevention measures through the use of economic evaluation techniques such as benefit-cost analysis. Many of these nations have begun to reorient their crime prevention (and criminal justice) policies around an evidence- and efficiency-based model, seeking to put in place programs with demonstrated effectiveness and cost savings. This has occurred for many reasons, including rising criminal justice costs (particularly in the area of prisons), evidence of the magnitude of the financial costs of crime and victimization to society, governmental fiscal restraints, and a movement towards general efficiency practices in government.

Evidence of the economic efficiency of crime prevention programs can be quite persuasive. Lawrence J. Schweinhart and his colleagues (1993), for example, have reported that each dollar spent will eventually save seven dollars. Consequently, the potential financial benefits of crime prevention have gained wide appeal in political, policy-making, and more recently, academic settings. In many ways, the interest in attaching dollar values to crime prevention programs can be seen as an outgrowth of the focus on "what works" in preventing crime. However, the comparison of dollars saved and dollars spent is much more understandable to policymakers and the general public than other measures of the effects of intervention programs. "Efficiency," "performance measures," and "targeting resources," among other terms, have become the common currency of discussions about crime prevention. Surprisingly, compared to the number of outcome evaluation studies of crime prevention programs, which themselves are relatively few, there is a dearth of economic analysis studies in the area of financial costs and benefits.

Despite the lack of extensive research, some studies show the financial costs and benefits of crime prevention strategies. This entry discusses studies of the two principal strategies: developmental prevention and correctional intervention. The focus of these studies is on "real-life" programs, that is, programs whose outcomes can be assessed based on more than just statistical modeling techniques or case study data. The studies employed research designs (such as experimental and quasi-experimental) with the capacity to control for threats to internal and external validity. Threats to internal validity (alternative plausible explanations of a program's observed effect on crime) and external validity (generalizing internally valid results) include such things as selection, preexisting trends, and changes in measurement. It is important to disentangle real program effects from these alternative explanations.

ECONOMIC ANALYSIS OF COSTS AND BENEFITS OF CRIME PREVENTION

Economic analysis is a tool for helping to make the best choice among alternative uses of resources or alternative distributions of services. Many criteria can be used in economic analyses. The most common is "efficiency," or achieving maximum outcomes from minimum inputs. A specific focus on economic efficiency, however, is not meant to imply that crime prevention programs should only be continued if benefits outweigh costs. There are many important noneconomic criteria by which these programs can be judged (e.g., their effect on the self-esteem of the subject).

Benefit-cost analysis and cost-effectiveness analysis are the two most widely used techniques of economic analysis. A cost-effectiveness analysis can be described as an incomplete benefit-cost analysis, because no attempt is made to estimate the monetary value of program effects produced (benefits or disbenefits), only resources used (costs). Benefit-cost analysis, on the other hand, monetizes both costs and benefits and compares them. A cost-effectiveness analysis makes it possible to specify, for example, the number of crimes prevented per thousand dollars expended on each program. Another way to think about how benefit-cost and cost-effectiveness analyses differ is that, unlike benefit-cost analysis, "cost-effectiveness analysis may help one decide among competing program models, but it cannot show that the total effect was worth the cost of the program" (Weinrott, Jones, and Howard 1982: 179).

An economic analysis is a step-by-step process that follows a standard set of procedures. Six main steps have been articulated:

1. Define the scope of the analysis.
2. Obtain estimates of program effects.
3. Estimate the monetary value of costs and benefits.
4. Calculate present value and assess profitability.
5. Describe the distribution of costs and benefits (an assessment of who gains and who loses—e.g., program participant, government/taxpayer, crime victim).
6. Conduct sensitivity analyses.

In the case of benefit-cost analysis, all six steps are carried out; for cost-effectiveness analysis, the estimation of the monetary value of benefits in Step 3 is omitted and Step 5 is consequently omitted.

Two other key features of economic analysis require brief mention. First, an economic analysis is an extension of an outcome evaluation, and is only as defensible as the evaluation upon which it is based. Weimer and Friedman (1979) recommended that economic analyses be limited to programs that have been evaluated with an "experimental or strong quasi-experimental design" (264). The most convincing method of evaluating crime prevention programs is the randomized experiment. This is because, providing that a sufficiently large number of people or areas are randomly assigned, those in the experimental group will be equivalent to those in the control group on all possible extraneous variables. Consequently, any subsequent differences between the two groups must be attributable to the intervention. Second, there are many perspectives from which program costs and benefits can be measured. Some benefit-cost analyses adopt a society-wide perspective that includes the major parties who can receive benefits or incur costs, such as government or taxpayer, crime victim, and program participant. Other analyses may take a more narrow view, focusing on only one or two of these parties. For example, for programs paid for by government, cost savings to government may be studied, rather than benefits to crime victims from crimes prevented. The benefit-cost findings of crime prevention programs that follow have taken a middle-of-the-road approach by reporting, as far as possible, from a combined government/taxpayer and

crime victim perspective. However, it is often difficult to compare programs because of their different ways of calculating costs and benefits.

DEVELOPMENTAL CRIME PREVENTION

Developmental prevention aims to influence the scientifically identified risk factors or "root causes" of juvenile delinquency and later criminal offending. Some of the major risk factors include growing up in poverty, living in poor housing, inadequate parental supervision and harsh or inconsistent discipline, parental conflict and separation, low intelligence and poor school performance, and a high level of impulsiveness and hyperactivity. Developmental prevention is generally informed by motivational or human development theories of criminal behavior, and specifically by longitudinal studies that follow samples of young persons from their early childhood experiences to the peak of their involvement with crime in their teens and twenties.

Six developmental crime prevention programs were identified that carried out a benefit-cost analysis. Table 1 shows program effects on delinquency and crime, the benefit-cost findings, and the key features of the six programs. All of the programs were carried out in the United States. Four of the six programs produced a desirable benefit-cost ratio (i.e., the benefits outweighed the costs), one program produced an undesirable benefit-cost ratio, and one program produced mixed results. For the four economically efficient programs, benefit-cost ratios ranged from a low of 1.40 to a high of 7.16, meaning that for each dollar spent on the programs, the government and taxpayers and crime victims received in return $1.40 to $7.16 in various savings.

Started in 1962 in Ypsilanti, Michigan, the Perry Preschool program is perhaps the best-known and most successful longitudinal study to have rigorously charted the effects of an early intervention on delinquency and later offending. For two years, children attended a daily preschool program, supported by weekly home visits involving the mother. At the most recent assessment, 22 years after the program ended, children in the treatment group were better off than their control counterparts according to a wide range of outcomes (see Table 1). A benefit-cost analysis showed that program benefits were substantial, with a benefit-cost ratio of 7.16; over seven dollars were saved for every dollar expended. In contrast, Hawaii Healthy Start, a statewide program offered to all new parents for the purpose of reducing child abuse and neglect, produced an undesirable benefit-cost

Table 1. Summary of Developmental Crime Prevention Programs

Author and Location	Main Type of Intervention	Sample Size	Evaluation Design	Intervention Effects[a]	Benefit-Cost Ratio[b]
Long, Mallar, and Thornton (1981), Job Corps, multiple sites in U.S.	Vocational training, education, health care	5,100 youths: T = n.a., C = n.a.	Before-after, experimental-control, with matching	Police arrests +, substance abuse +, school achievement +, employment +, wages +	1.45
Lipsey (1984), Los Angeles County Delinquency Prevention Program	Family counseling, academic tutoring, employment training	7,637 youths (all in program) youths = n.a. (for T and C)	Before-after and before-after, experimental-control	Police arrests +	1.40
Schweinhart, Barnes, and Weikart (1993), Perry Preschool, Ypsilanti, Michigan	Preschool intellectual enrichment, parent education	123 children: T = 58, C = 65	Randomized experiment (stratified assignment)	Police arrests +, school achievement +, social service use +, educational achievement +	7.16
Hahn (1994, 1999), Quantum Opportunities Program, 5 sites in U.S.	Education, skill development	250 youths: T = 125, C = 125	Randomized experiment	Police arrests +, school achievement +, social service use +	3.68
Earle (1995), Hawaii Healthy Start	Parent education, parent support, family planning, community support	2,706 families: T = 1,353, C = 1,353	Before-after, experimental-control	Child abuse and neglect +	0.38
Olds et al. (1997, 1998), Prenatal/Early Infancy Project, Elmira, New York	T1 = parent education, parent support, community support, family planning, T2 = T1 minus postnatal home visits, C = not receiving home visits	400 mothers: T1 = 116, T2 = 100, C = 184	Randomized experiment	T1 vs C: mothers: child abuse and neglect +; higher risk mothers: arrests and convictions +, social service use + children (of higher risk mothers): arrests +	Higher risk sample = 4.06 Lower risk sample = 0.62

a: + = desirable intervention effects.

b: Expressed as a ratio of benefits to costs in dollars.

Notes: T = treatment group; C = control group; n.a. = not available.

ratio of 0.38. For each dollar spent on the program, only $0.38 was recouped in savings from reduced child abuse and neglect.

The program that showed mixed benefit-cost results—the Elmira, New York, Prenatal/Early Infancy Project (PEIP), a nurse home-visitation intervention for first-time mothers—was found to be economically efficient for the higher-risk sample of disadvantaged, unmarried mothers (and their children), but not for the lower-risk sample of mothers (and their children) thirteen years after the completion of the program. The higher-risk mothers (those in the treatment group), compared to those in the control group (those not receiving home visits), had fewer arrests and convictions, relied less on social services, and had children with fewer arrests. For the lower-risk mothers, few differences were evident between the treatment and control groups. The benefit-cost ratio was a desirable 4.06 for the higher-risk sample and an undesirable 0.62 for the lower-risk sample.

All of the studies used methodologically rigorous research designs, with two employing randomization and the others also utilizing control groups, making it possible to control for threats to internal validity and ensure that the intervention is what produced the observed effects. For the most part, the benefit-cost analyses were methodologically rigorous and, in the case of the Perry Preschool and Job Corps programs, were comprehensive in their coverage of costs and benefits. Overall, developmental crime prevention appears to be a promising strategy for reducing monetary costs associated with delinquency and later offending, and for improving the life-course development of at-risk children and their families.

Table 2. Summary of Correctional Intervention Programs

Author and Location	Main Type of Intervention	Sample Size	Evaluation Design	Intervention Effects[a]	Benefit-Cost Ratio[b]
Holahan (1974), Project Crossroads, Washington, D.C.	Pretrial diversion with counseling, job training, and remedial education	307 adults: T = 200, C = 107	Before-after, experimental-control	Police arrests +	2.36
Friedman (1977), Supported Work Social Experiment, New York City	Employment	229 adults: T = 120, C = 109	Randomized experiment	Police arrests +, social service use +, employment +, health, education-	1.13
Gray and Olson (1989), Maricopa County, Arizona	Multiple services, deterrence, incapacitation, rehabilitation	61 adults	Before-after (no C)	n.a.	Probation = 1.70 Prison = 0.24 Jail = 0.17
Austin (1986), Illinois	Early release from prison	1,557 adults and juveniles: T=1,202, C=355	Before-after, experimental-control	Police arrests +	2.82
Pearson (1988), Pearson and Harper (1990), New Jersey Intensive Supervision Program	Employment, intensive supervision, incapacitation	686 adults: T = 554, C = 132	Before-after, experimental-control	Convictions +, institution time +	1.48
Prentky and Burgess (1990), Massachusetts	Rehabilitation	182: T = 129 (adults), C = 53	Before-after, experimental-control (retrospectively chosen C)	Victim-involved sexual offenses (15 charges) +	1.16
Gerstein et al. (1994), California Drug and Alcohol Treatment Assessment	Substance abuse treatment (4 modalities)	1,859 adults	Before-after (no C)	Criminal activity +, substance abuse +, health +, social service use +, employment -	7.14
Courtright, Berg, and Mutchnick (1997), county in Western Pennsylvania	House arrest with electronic monitoring	57 adults	Before-after (no C)	Police arrests for DUI +	4.02
Robertson, Grimes, and Rogers (in press), Madison, Lowndes, and Forrest Counties, Mississippi	T1 = intensive supervision and monitoring (ISM), T2 = intensive outpatient counseling with cognitive behavioral therapy (CB), C = regular probation or parole (RP)	153 juveniles: T1 = 61, T2 = 47, C = 45	Before-after, experimental, control	T2 vs T1, C: significantly less mean expenditures; T1 vs C: slightly greater mean expenditures	CB = 1.96, ISM = n.a., RP = n.a.

a: + = desirable intervention effects; - = undesirable intervention effects.

b: Expressed as a ratio of benefits to costs in dollars.

Notes: T = treatment group; C = control group; n.a. = not available.

CORRECTIONAL INTERVENTION

Correctional intervention attempts to modify offender behavior through some combination of treatment and external controls. According to Ted Palmer (1992: 3), treatment attempts to "affect the individual's future behavior, attitudes toward self, and interactions with others by focusing on such factors and conditions as the individual's adjustment techniques, interests, skills, personal limitations, and/or life circumstances."

Nine correctional intervention programs were identified that performed a benefit-cost analysis. Table 2 shows program effects on reoffending (recidivism) in the community, the benefit-cost findings, and key features of the nine programs, all of which were carried out in the United States. All nine studies demonstrated a favorable program benefit-cost ratio. The program study by Tara Gray and Kent Olson calculated benefit-cost ratios for each of the three treatments being compared (probation, prison, and jail), but only the analysis of probation is considered, because probation more closely relates to correctional (rehabilitative) intervention than does prison or jail. For the nine studies, the benefit-cost ratios ranged from a low of 1.13 to a high of 7.14, meaning that for each dollar spent on the programs, government, taxpayer, and crime victims received in return $1.13 to $7.14 in various savings.

Project Crossroads was a three-month pretrial diversion program for adult property offenders that was started in the early 1970s. It showed a significant reduction in police arrests twelve months after program completion for those who received the program, compared to those in a control group, who were adjudicated. This effect, along with an improvement in employment, translated into a desirable benefit-cost ratio of 2.36. The New York City Supported Work Social Experiment, the other program that took place in the 1970s, also proved to be (just) economically efficient, showing a benefit-cost ratio of 1.13. Prior to the program, eligible candidates were randomly assigned either to the treatment group that received supported employment or to a control group that did not. Sixteen months after the completion of the program, treatment group members, compared to controls, were less likely to be arrested, were employed for a longer period of time, and relied less on social services, but were more likely than the controls to have poorer health and lower educational attainment. These undesirable noneconomic results somewhat diminished the total financial benefits produced by the program. For the most recent correctional intervention program, which took place in three Mississippi counties, cognitive behavioral therapy was found to reduce juvenile offending at a much lower cost than either intensive supervision with monitoring or regular probation or parole.

Most of the programs had large samples. Five of the programs had a methodically rigorous research design: an experimental-control design with before-and-after measures. For these five programs, the benefit-cost ratio ranged from 1.13 to 2.82. The use of before-after measures without a control group, or a retrospectively chosen control group in the other four programs, limits the reliability of their reported treatment effects and benefit-cost results. Despite the method-

ological limitations of some of the programs reviewed here, the available evidence on the financial costs and benefits of correctional intervention programs suggests that this approach to reducing reoffending in the community is promising.

RESEARCH DIRECTIONS

Based on the existing evidence of benefit-cost studies of these prevention strategies, each one shows promising signs of returning to taxpayers and crime victims a wide range of cost savings and reimbursement of program costs. In addition, the benefit-cost findings from these two crime prevention strategies demonstrate that the financial benefits go beyond reduced crime; they may also include secondary benefits such as increased tax revenues from higher earnings, savings from reduced use of social services, and savings from lower health care costs.

Advancing knowledge about the financial costs and benefits of crime prevention should begin with policymakers and researchers playing a greater role to ensure that programs include, as part of the original research design, provision for an economic analysis, preferably a benefit-cost analysis. Prospective economic analyses have many advantages over retrospective ones—the most important being the ability to establish ahead of time procedures for collecting program costs and data collection. Researchers must also ensure that benefit-cost analyses are not only methodologically rigorous but also comprehensive: All resources used (costs) and all relevant program effects (benefits) need to be valued.

Future economic evaluation research should also be concerned with standardizing the measurement of benefits and costs. The development of a standard list of program benefits and costs would overcome some of the difficulties with which researchers are presently faced in reviewing and conducting benefit-cost analyses, and it would greatly facilitate comparisons of benefit-cost findings of different crime prevention programs. Focusing just on crime at the present time, the Washington State Institute for Public Policy has initiated a program of research to examine the comparative benefit-cost advantages of different crime prevention programs.

Another top priority for advancing knowledge about the financial costs and benefits of crime prevention programs is to increase the use of high-quality research designs in assessing the effectiveness of programs. Because an economic analysis is only as strong as the evaluation upon which it is based, the stronger the research design of the outcome evaluation, the more confidence that can be placed in the findings of the economic analysis.

Lastly, funding bodies must be prepared to finance economic evaluation research. Governmental agencies with responsibility for the prevention of crime should commit a percentage of their research budgets to supporting benefit-cost analyses of a number of new and existing methodologically rigorous programs. The United Kingdom has recently adopted such an approach, offering a model for others to follow.

—Brandon C. Welsh and David P. Farrington

See also DIVERSION PROGRAMS; DRUG TREATMENT; EARLY RELEASE PROGRAMS; ECONOMIC THEORIES OF CRIME; EDUCATION AND EMPLOYMENT; ELECTRONIC MONITORING; FAMILY STRENGTHENING PROGRAMS; HOUSE ARREST; PAROLE; POVERTY; REHABILITATION MODEL; SELECTIVE INCAPACITATION

Further Reading

Aos, Steve, Polly Phipps, Robert Barnoski, and Roxanne Lieb. (1999). *The Comparative Costs and Benefits of Programs to Reduce Crime: A Review of National Research Findings With Implications for Washington State: Version 3.0.* Olympia: Washington State Institute for Public Policy.

Austin, James. (1986). "Using Early Release to Relieve Prison Crowding: A Dilemma in Public Policy." *Crime and Delinquency* 32, 4 (October): 404–502.

Barnett, W. Steven. (1993). "Cost-Benefit Analysis." In *Significant Benefits: The High/Scope Perry Preschool Study Through Age 27*, by Lawrence J. Schweinhart, Helen V. Barnes, and David P. Weikart. Ypsilanti, MI: High/Scope Press, 142–173.

Cohen, Mark A. (2000). "Measuring the Costs and Benefits of Crime and Justice." In *Criminal Justice 2000: Vol. 4. Measurement and Analysis of Crime and Justice*, edited by David Duffee. U.S. Department of Justice, National Institute of Justice. Washington, DC: Government Printing Office, 263–315.

Cook, Philip J., and Jens Ludwig. (2000). *Gun Violence: The Real Costs.* New York: Oxford University Press.

Cook, Thomas D., and Donald T. Campbell. (1979). *Quasi-Experimentation: Design and Analysis Issues for Field Settings.* Chicago: Rand McNally.

Courtright, Kevin E., Bruce L. Berg, and Robert J. Mutchnick. (1997). "The Cost Effectiveness of Using House Arrest With Electronic Monitoring for Drunk Drivers." *Federal Probation* 61, 3 (September): 19–22.

Dhiri, Sanjay, Peter Goldblatt, Sam Brand, and Richard Price. (2001). "Evaluation of the United Kingdom's 'Crime Reduction Programme': Analysis of Costs and Benefits." In *Costs and Benefits of Preventing Crime*, edited by Brandon C. Welsh, David P. Farrington, and Lawrence W. Sherman. Boulder, CO: Westview Press, 179–201.

Earle, Ralph B. (1995). "Helping to Prevent Child Abuse—and Future Consequences: Hawaii Healthy Start." *Program Focus* (October). U.S. Department of Justice, National Institute of Justice. Washington, DC: Government Printing Office.

Farrington, David P. (1983). "Randomized Experiments on Crime and Justice." In *Crime and Justice: A Review of Research*, vol. 4, edited by Michael Tonry and Norval Morris. Chicago: University of Chicago Press, 257–308.

———. (1996). "The Explanation and Prevention of Youthful Offending." In *Delinquency and Crime: Current Theories*, edited by J. David Hawkins. Cambridge, UK: Cambridge University Press, 68–148.

Friedman, Lee S. (1977). "An Interim Evaluation of the Supported Work Experiment." *Policy Analysis* 3, 2: 147–170.

Gerstein, Dean R., Robert A. Johnson, Henrick J. Harwood, Douglas Fountain, Natalie Suter, and Kathryn Malloy. (1994). *Evaluating Recovery Services: The California Drug and Alcohol Treatment Assessment (CALDATA).* Sacramento, CA: Department of Alcohol and Drug Programs.

Gray, Tara, and Kent W. Olson. (1989). "A Cost-Benefit Analysis of the Sentencing Decision for Burglars." *Social Science Quarterly* 70: 708–722.

Hahn, Andrew. (1994). *Evaluation of the Quantum Opportunities Program (QOP): Did the Program Work?* Waltham, MA: Brandeis University.

———. (1999). "Extending the Time of Learning." In *America's Disconnected Youth: Toward a Preventive Strategy*, edited by Douglas J. Besharov. Washington, DC: Child Welfare League of America Press, 233–265.

Holahan, John. (1974). "Measuring Benefits From Prison Reform." In *Benefit-Cost and Policy Analysis 1973: An Aldine Annual on Forecasting, Decision-Making, and Evaluation*, edited by Robert H. Haveman, Arnold C. Harberger, Laurence E. Lynn, William A. Niskanen, Ralph Turvey, and Richard Zeckhauser. Chicago: Aldine, 491–516.

Knapp, Martin. (1997). "Economic Evaluations and Interventions for Children and Adolescents with Mental Health Problems." *Journal of Child Psychology and Psychiatry* 38, 1: 3–25.

Layard, Richard, and Stephen Glaister, eds. (1994). *Cost-Benefit Analysis*, 2d ed. Cambridge, UK: Cambridge University Press.

Lipsey, Mark W. (1984). "Is Delinquency Prevention a Cost-Effective Strategy? A California Perspective." *Journal of Research in Crime and Delinquency* 21, 4 (November): 279–302.

Long, David A., Charles D. Mallar, and Craig V. D. Thornton. (1981). "Evaluating the Benefits and Costs of the Job Corps." *Journal of Policy Analysis and Management* 1, 1: 55–76.

Maguire, Kathleen, and Ann L. Pastore, eds. (1998). *Sourcebook of Criminal Justice Statistics 1997.* U.S. Department of Justice, Bureau of Justice Statistics. Washington, DC: Government Printing Office.

Miller, Ted R., Mark A. Cohen, and Brian Wiersema. (1996). *Victim Costs and Consequences: A New Look.* U.S. Department of Justice, National Institute of Justice. Washington, DC: Government Printing Office.

Olds, David L., John Eckenrode, Charles R. Henderson, Harriet Kitzman, Jane Powers, Robert Cole, Kimberly Sidora, Pamela Morris, Lisa M. Pettitt, and Dennis Luckey. (1997). "Long-Term Effects of Home Visitation on Maternal Life Course and Child Abuse and Neglect: Fifteen-Year Follow-Up of a Randomized Trial." *Journal of the American Medical Association* 278, 8 (August): 637–643.

———. (1998). "Long-Term Effects of Nurse Home Visitation on Children's Criminal and Antisocial Behavior: 15-Year Follow-

Up of a Randomized Controlled Trial." *Journal of the American Medical Association* 280, 14 (October): 1238–1244.

Palmer, Ted. (1992). *The Re-emergence of Correctional Intervention.* Newbury Park, CA: Sage.

Pearson, Frank S. (1988). "Evaluation of New Jersey's Intensive Supervision Program." *Crime and Delinquency* 34: 437–448.

Pearson, Frank S., and Alice G. Harper. (1990). "Contingent Intermediate Sentences: New Jersey's Intensive Supervision Program." *Crime and Delinquency* 36, 4 (October): 75–86.

Prentky, Robert, and Ann W. Burgess. (1990). "Rehabilitation of Child Molesters: A Cost-Benefit Analysis." *American Journal of Orthopsychiatry* 60, 1 (January): 108–117.

Robertson, Angela A., Paul W. Grimes, and Kevin E. Rogers. (2001). "A Short-Run Cost-Benefit Analysis of Community-Based Interventions for Juvenile Offenders. *Crime and Delinquency* 47, 2 (April): 265–284.

Schweinhart, Lawrence J., Helen V. Barnes, and David P. Weikart. (1993). *Significant Benefits: The High/Scope Perry Preschool Study Through Age 27.* Ypsilanti, MI: High/Scope Press.

Sherman, Lawrence W., Denise C. Gottfredson, Doris L. MacKenzie, John E. Eck, Peter Reuter, and Shawn D. Bushway. (1997). *Preventing Crime: What Works, What Doesn't, What's Promising.* U.S. Department of Justice, National Institute of Justice. Washington, DC: Government Printing Office.

Waller, Irvin, and Brandon C. Welsh. (1999). "International Trends in Crime Prevention: Cost-Effective Ways to Reduce Victimization." In *Global Report on Crime and Justice*, edited by G. Newman. New York: Oxford University Press, 191–220.

Weimer, David L., and Lee S. Friedman. (1979). "Efficiency Considerations in Criminal Rehabilitation Research: Costs and Consequences." In *The Rehabilitation of Criminal Offenders: Problems and Prospects*, edited by Lee Sechrest, Susan O. White, and Elizabeth D. Brown. Washington, DC: National Academy of Sciences, 251–272.

Weinrott, Mark R., Richard R. Jones, and James R. Howard. (1982). "Cost-Effectiveness of Teaching Family Programs for Delinquents: Results of a National Evaluation." *Evaluation Review* 6, 2 (April): 173–201.

Welsh, Brandon C., and David P. Farrington. (2000). "Monetary Costs and Benefits of Crime Prevention Programs." In *Crime and Justice: A Review of Research*, vol. 27, edited by Michael Tonry. Chicago: University of Chicago Press, 305–361.

Welsh, Brandon C., David P. Farrington, and Lawrence W. Sherman, eds. (2001). *Costs and Benefits of Preventing Crime.* Boulder, CO: Westview Press.

▼ FINES

The fine is one of the oldest penal sanctions in history. According to Bonneville de Marsangy (1864: 260), "There was even a time where all the sanctions were fines." The first form of human justice was the idea of simple vengeance, an eye for an eye. After this, the idea of compensation and reparation of the "prejudice" (the injury or damage) appeared. In numerous legal systems, money compensation replaced private vengeance. In Rome, the fine was considered the main penal sanction, whereas imprisonment was only a particular kind of torture. During the sixth century, the Germans created a system with two kinds of sanctions: the *wergild* and the *fredum*. The *wergild* represented the compensation given to the victim and/or to the victim's family to avoid their private vengeance. The *fredum* was a certain amount of money to be paid to the authorities to diminish the public trouble caused by the crime and to make sure that the authorities enact the "peace treaty" concluded by the payment of the *wergild*. According to some authors, the *fredum* is the forerunner of the current fine system, the *wergild* having lost its importance through the centuries. However, other historians think that today's fines are the result of a progressive junction of *fredum* and *wergild*.

Wherever the truth may be, today's fine system seems to have many advantages. Contrary to imprisonment, it does not take the condemned person away from his or her family; it does not push him or her to give up working; it does not cost society a lot of money and may even be lucrative. But every coin has a flip side: Fining privileges the rich to the prejudice of the poor, gives the idea that one can buy impunity and the right to commit crimes, and affects not only the offender but also his or her whole family.

INDIVIDUAL OR COLLECTIVE SANCTIONS

One of the main principles of criminal law is that a person who commits a crime has to be punished and, consequently, that a person who did nothing wrong should not be punished. Unfortunately, that "no crime, no sanction" principle is not respected by the fine—fines affect the offender's family by diminishing the family's budget. In other words, the fine is not an individual sanction, but a collective one.

Although the same argument could be made with other sanctions (e.g., incarceration, community service), these penalties touch primarily the offender, and only indirectly his or her family. In the case of a fine, the sanction affects the economic resources of the entire family. Therefore, each family member is directly and equally touched by a fine. Politicians and criminologists around the world are aware of this problem, but no one has yet found an acceptable solution. Because every fine system also affects innocent people, the fine sanction is inherently unfair.

THE GOAL OF THE SANCTION

Sanctions may have several goals, such as punishment, rehabilitation, specific and general deterrence, elimination (death penalty, expulsion, incapacitation), reconciliation, and reparation. Rehabilitation is the main goal of most criminal justice systems around the world. Fines, however, can be imposed only for punishment, deterrence, and eventually, reparation; they cannot serve the goal of rehabilitation. Here again, there is no solution to the problem. One has to accept that fines almost have no educational potential for offenders, except with regard to deterrence.

CONVERSION OF FINES

An important problem is created when people do not pay their fines. Generally, most countries are more tolerant with those who *cannot* pay than with people who *do not want* to pay. The latter often go to prison, where they are put under pressure in order to pay, or where, after a conversion of their fine into a prison sentence, each day in prison diminishes the amount to be paid. Nevertheless, in some countries, a fine cannot be converted into imprisonment, but only into community service, electronic monitoring, and so on.

THE FINE AS AN UNFAIR SANCTION

As already mentioned, fines are an unfair sanction because they affect the rich (who may simply dip into their savings, without endangering their standard of living) much less than the poor (who have to tighten their belts to be able to pay the fine). Although fines are normally set in proportion to the income and wealth of the offender, most fine systems set a maximum amount of fine (which favors the rich), and judges are reluctant to impose a very low fine on a very poor offender.

To improve the situation, some nations introduced the "day-fine" system, in which the final amount of the fine depends on two independent decisions. First, the judge delivers his or her sentence in "day units," and second, he or she decides how much money each of those units represents. To make this second decision, the judge must take into account the income, the expenses, and the wealth of the offender in determining a "global daily income." In other words, the final fine amount is determined by multiplying the number of days by the daily income.

This system partly solves the problems of the fair-

Fines for Minor Offenses in Sixteenth-Century England

1558 Fines of 4d. each for having pigs in the Churchyard; 4d. for a pig straying into a common street.

1557 Robt. Farrer, 16d. for saying words in abuse of his brethren the Governors.

1545 Fine of 2d. for leaving wood in the street.

1520 Richard Trollop, Alderman of Painters, fined 2/- because his Play, of The Three Kings (in the Pageant plays) was badly played in contempt of the community, when strangers were present.

1520 John Peake, 8d. for selling a measly pig in the common market.

1502 Wm. Hewson, cooper, fined 12d. for speaking malicious words in the town and in taverns saying that Charters belonging to the town and community were either absent or stolen.

1494 John Belton, weaver, fined 2d. for abusing the common Sergeant while in the execution of his office. Robt. Smith, walker, for refusing to bury a dead pig, 8d.

Source: Pettifer, Ernest W. (1992). *Punishments of Former Days.* Winchester: Waterside Press, p. 165.

---

ness of the fine sanction and of fine conversion. Indeed, every day-fine unit may be converted into a day in prison if the offender is not willing to pay. But the system also has some disadvantages. The public often has difficulty understanding why two similar offenses, committed under the same conditions, are not punished by the same fine amount, when the only difference is that one offender earns more than another. Therefore, if an offender is very poor and has no income, the judge will hesitate to order a fine of a dollar a day for ninety days and may prefer to order ninety days of imprisonment instead. It is necessary that a solution to this problem be found, because the important legal principle of "individualization of the sentence" holds that two offenders who commit a similar offense in similar conditions should suffer in a similar way. As far as fines are concerned, similar suffering is not realized by imposing on the offenders a similar amount of fine, but by fining them a similar proportion of money with regards to what the offender owns, owes, and earns.

Several nations across the world use such a system.

It was used for the first time in Finland in 1921, followed by Sweden in 1931, Cuba in 1936, and Denmark in 1939. In the United States, the first day-fine experiment was in 1988 at the Richmond County Criminal Court in Staten Island, New York. The Swedish system presents an interesting alternative. In Sweden, public disclosure of the judgment covers only the number of day units. Neither the daily income nor the total amount of the fine is revealed to the public. This system resembles the one used for imprisonment, where the public is only told the length of the sentence. The public does not know what kind of prison the offender is sent to (high, medium, or low security; jail, state, or federal prison, etc.), nor whether the condemned will be released on parole before the end of their sentence, or if he or she will really spend time in a prison, or if the sentence will be converted into community service or another alternative to prison. Therefore, as for prison sentences, the public knowledge of the severity of the day-fine sentence could only cover the number of day units. In this way, public opinion would still be satisfied and fines could really be personalized.

SUMMARY

Taking money from the offender has always been a response to offenses. It was first used as a method of compensation before becoming a real punishment. As long as it was merely a compensation for the harm caused by the offense, it was understandable that, for the same crime, two different offenders had to pay the same amount of money. Later, as fining became a real punishment, it had to be adapted to the offender's financial situation. With prison sentences, equity means that the length of the sentence has to be equal for two similar offenders who commit similar crimes in similar circumstances. Nevertheless, this "equal harm for equal culpability" principle is much harder to apply in the field of fines, because the harm of a fine depends not only on the amount of money the offender has to pay but also on the restrictions the payment of the fine creates in his or her life. These restrictions are closely related to the wealth and the income of the offender. As a result, the day-fine system seems to be the best way to achieve equity in fining.

In order to increase the personalization of the sentence, the ideal day-fine system would only publicize the sentence in days, keeping the amount of money fined a secret. It would also provide for two independent decisions: one concerning the number of day units and the second concerning the daily income. Both decisions should be made by two different authorities.

—André Kuhn

Further Reading

Bonneville de Marsangy. (1864). *De l'amélioration de la loi criminelle en vue d'une justice plus prompte, plus efficace, plus généreuse et plus moralisante*. Vol. 2. Paris: Cosse et Marchal.

Grebing, Gerhardt. (1982). *The Fine in Comparative Law: A Survey of 21 Countries*. Institute of Criminology Occasional Paper No. 9. Cambridge: Institute of Criminology.

Neumaier, Robert. (1947). *Die geschichtliche Entwicklung der Geldstrafe vom 15. Jahrhundert bis zum RStGB*. Tübingen: Eberhard-Karls-Universität.

Petitcuenot, Charles. (1898). *De l'amende: Du rôle à lui attribuer dans un système pénal rationnel; Des réformes à introduire dans son exécution*. Dijon: Imprimerie Barbier Marilier.

Winterfield, Laura A., and Sally T. Hillsman. (1991). *The Effects of Instituting Means-Based Fines in a Criminal Court: The Staten Island Day-Fine Experiment*. New York: Vera Institute of Justice.

◤ FIREARMS IDENTIFICATION

Firearms identification is the objective, scientific examination and analysis of firearms-related evidence. The scientific role of the firearms examiner in forensic laboratory examinations is multifaceted. In many instances, it is limited only by the ingenuity of the firearms examiner and/or by the evidence submitted to them for examination. Through their expertise, firearms examiners can assist an investigator in a homicide and/or shooting investigation.

Examinations will usually include, but not necessarily be limited to, the following:

1. Microscopic examination of fired bullets and cartridge cases to determine if they can be identified or eliminated as having been fired from a suspect firearm

2. Examination of fired "evidence bullets" in an attempt to determine the caliber, make, and type of firearm from which the bullet could have been fired

3. Administration of a firearms distance determination test

4. Conducting a fired cartridge case ejection pattern test

5. Administering a firearms operation performance test

6. Examination and comparison of toolmark evidence

7. Conducting crime scene examinations

8. Execution of shooting scene reconstructions

The principles of firearms and toolmark identification are based upon the theory that it is impossible to manufacture two items that will be exactly alike. Although items may appear similar to the naked eye, when examined under a microscope by a trained examiner, the imperfections and differences are readily visible.

In some cases, only a fired bullet or fired cartridge case is submitted to the crime laboratory for examination, because no firearm has been recovered. The firearms examiner will microscopically examine the "evidence item" in an attempt to determine the caliber, type, and manufacturer of the firearm. If a firearm is being examined, the identification also includes the examination of the firearm to determine whether it operates safely, whether it has been altered, whether the trigger pull has been lightened, whether the safeties operate properly, and whether the firearm has been fired. The examination will reveal the all-around operating condition and functioning of the firearm.

The manufacturing imperfections caused by the various machining processes during the manufacturing of a firearm or tool are what the firearms examiner will look for when conducting a microscopic examination of the evidence. These imperfections will be displayed on the surface of the machined part as machining marks or "striations" (small grooves or scratches). Microscopic identification is made possible by the manufacturing marks that appear on the surface areas of such items as the interior bore (gun barrel) of a firearm, bolt faces, firing pins, extractors, ejectors, or tools. Through each step of the manufacturing process, microscopic imperfections are left on the surfaces of the manufactured part.

HISTORY OF FIREARMS IDENTIFICATION

Firearms identification in the United States dates back to 1897 and the case of *Dean v. Commonwealth*. This was the first case in which an appellate court admitted testimony on the similarities between a "fatal" and a "test-fired" bullet. Testimony in the case did not address the identification of class rifling impressions or individual characteristics; rather, it focused on a process of elimination of all other firearms accounted for in the community. Testimony in the case also involved a toolmark impression left on a garden fence post. The defendant allegedly rested the rifle on a fence and shot the victim, who was working in the garden. Examination of the fence revealed an impression mark, which was characteristic of a small metal

piece attached under the barrel of the firearm near the muzzle.

Photographs of a bullet comparison were used in *Commonwealth v. Best*. The examiner in this case pushed a test bullet through the barrel of the suspect firearm and then photographed the pushed bullet and the fatal bullet. Photographs of the test bullet and the fatal bullet were then compared.

Oliver Wendell Holmes was a member of the Massachusetts Supreme Court at that time. Concerning the identification, Judge Holmes said in *Commonwealth v. Best*:

> We see no other way in which the jury could have learned so intelligently how that gun barrel would have marked a lead bullet fired through it, a question of much importance to the case. Not only was it the best evidence obtainable, but the sources of errors suggested are trifling. The photographs avowedly were arranged to bring out the likeness of the markings in the different bullets and were objected to on this further ground. But the jury could correct them by inspection of the originals, if there were other aspects more favorable to the defense.

In 1916, in upstate New York, a farm laborer named Henry Stielow was convicted of murdering his employer and his maid with a .22-caliber revolver. Questions concerning his guilt resulted in the formation of a New York humanitarian group to raise money for additional investigation into the case. A prominent investigator, C. E. "Judge" Waite, was hired by the defense. The investigation by Waite led him to a microscopist at Bausch and Lomb, in Rochester, New York. A microscopic examination of the fatal and test-fired bullets revealed sufficient differences to rule out the possibility that the revolver fired the fatal evidence bullet. Eventually, Stielow was pardoned and released. C. E. Waite went on to form a partnership with Calvin Goddard. The Waite-Goddard association was instrumental in the development and formation of the modern approach to firearms identification.

FIREARMS RIFLING

Rifled firearms, which include pistols, revolvers, and rifles (and some shotgun barrels used for firing shotgun slugs), contain rifling in the bore of the firearm. Rifling is a series of "lands" and "grooves," which are raised and recessed surfaces in the interior of the barrel of a rifled firearm. This rifling will have a varying number of lands and grooves and will possess either a left- or

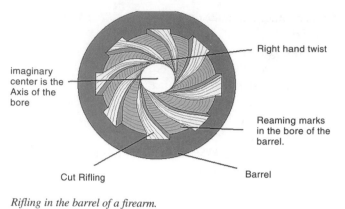

Rifling in the barrel of a firearm.
Source: Illustration by Charles H. A. Bain.

right-hand twist, depending on the manufacturer's rifling specifications. The number of lands and grooves, their direction of twist, and their width are referred to as "class rifling characteristics." The lands and grooves may vary in number; in most cases, rifling will be four to eight lands and grooves, but in some cases there may be sixteen to twenty lands and grooves with a left- or right-hand twist.

The rifling in the bore of the firearm makes contact with the bearing surface of the bullet fired in the firearm. The purpose of the rifling is to cause the fired bullet to rotate on its longitudinal axis and to impart a gyroscopic rotation or spin to the bullet. This spin (to the left or right, depending on the rifling) imparts stability to the fired bullet and provides for accuracy for the bullet. To fire a modern conical-shaped bullet in a firearm that does not contain rifling would be much like shooting an arrow that does not contain fletching from a bow. The flight of the arrow would be unsteady; it would wobble in flight with no accuracy. The same would be true of a conical-shaped bullet fired from a smoothbore firearm.

Manufacturers of firearms use a variety of means to place rifling in the barrel of the firearm that determines the class rifling characteristics. When a bullet is fired from a rifled firearm, the rifling within the bore of the barrel is pressed into the sidewall bearing surfaces of the fired bullet. The bullet travels down the length of the barrel, engaged in the rifling. It is the rifling in the barrel of the firearm that the examiner will use to microscopically identify a fired bullet as having been fired from a specific firearm.

A fired bullet in evidence can be positively eliminated as having been fired from a particular firearm based on the class rifling characteristics exhibited by the fired bullet. For instance, a fired bullet from a ".38

special" is submitted as evidence. Examination of the bullet reveals it to exhibit class-rifling characteristics of five lands and grooves with a right twist. Further examination reveals that the evidence bullet exhibits land and groove impression widths that are the class rifling characteristics for certain models of Smith & Wesson revolvers. When a .38 special revolver made by Colt is submitted for comparison purposes with the evidence bullet, examination of the Colt revolver reveals it to possess class-rifling characteristics of six lands and grooves with a left twist. Based upon the class rifling characteristics alone, the suspect Colt revolver can be eliminated as having fired the .38 special caliber evidence bullet.

However, a fired bullet cannot be positively identified as having been fired from a particular firearm simply because the class rifling characteristics of the evidence bullet and the suspect firearm are the same. In order to make a positive identification, the evidence bullet and the suspect firearm must exhibit not only the same class rifling characteristics but also matching individual characteristics. The identification will be based upon the evidence bullet and the test-fired bullet exhibiting the same class rifling characteristics and matching individual microscopic imperfections present on the evidence and test-fired bullet.

Firearms class rifling characteristics can be thought of as the "facial features" of a firearm. For instance, the normal facial features for a human being include a nose, mouth, lips, teeth, two eyes, and two ears. What allows us to identify and distinguish one person from the other? It is the individual characteristics of the facial features—the shape of the nose, mouth, lips, teeth and ears, the set and color of the eyes. If it were

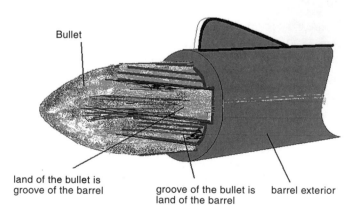

A bullet firing from the barrel of a firearm.
Source: Illustration by Charles H. A. Bain

not for the individual characteristics of a person's facial features, we would all look alike; we would not be able to identify our loved ones, our relatives and friends, or the "good guys and bad guys."

The manufacturing imperfections caused during the rifling and machining of the firearm distinguish fired bullets from one firearm from bullets fired by another firearm. The firearms examiner will microscopically examine these imperfections in making a comparison and an identification of a fired evidence bullet or cartridge case with a suspect firearm.

MICROSCOPIC INSTRUMENTATION

Two instruments of primary importance to the firearms examiner are the "stereoscopic microscope" and the "comparison microscope." The stereoscopic microscope is used by the firearms examiner when conducting the initial examination of an evidence item. A fired bullet can be microscopically examined for trace evidence in its initial state as received from the investigator.

The comparison microscope is basically two compound microscopes having the exact same magnification and optical qualities, connected by an optical bridge. An eyepiece present on the bridge allows the firearms examiner to view two separate objects, one under each stage of the microscope, simultaneously and in a juxtaposed (side-by-side) position. The comparison microscope is used in the microscopic examination, for comparison of fired bullets and cartridge cases and for toolmark examinations. In many instances, the comparison microscope will have a camera mounted on it, for the purpose of taking photomicrographs of trace evidence, or positive firearms and toolmark identifications.

INITIAL MICROSCOPIC BULLET EXAMINATION

When examining a fired bullet, the firearms examiner will first check an evidence bullet for the presence of trace evidence. The examiner then looks at the fired bullet for the presence of blood, hair, bone, fibers, tissue, fabric and fabric impressions, paint, wood, plaster, glass, or soil. The examiner will also conduct a microscopic examination for any material that is foreign to the evidence bullet.

Upon completion of the examination for trace

Microscopic markings on two fired cartridges.
Source: Photo courtesy of David Townshend.

evidence, the firearms examiner tries to determine the class rifling characteristics exhibited by the fired bullet (number of lands and grooves and direction of twist). The evidence bullet will then be checked to determine its weight in grains and its diameter measured in thousandths of an inch. The firearms examiner will then place the evidence bullet under the comparison microscope and measure the width of the land and groove impressions present on the fired bullet. Information obtained from the examination of the evidence bullet will then be compared with information compiled in the "General Rifling Characteristics File" (GRC file) developed by the FBI Laboratory, and/or microscopically compared with known test-fired standards. The GRC file contains classrifling specifications of thousands of various makes, models and types of firearms and is updated annually. The accuracy of the land and groove impression measurements is critical in determining the possible list of firearms from which the evidence bullet may have been fired. Upon completion of the examinations, unless the evidence bullet is severely mutilated, the firearms examiner will be able to provide the investigator with a list of firearms manufacturers having class rifling characteristics similar to those displayed by the evidence bullet.

TRACE EVIDENCE

Microscopic examination for the presence of trace evidence should always be conducted on firearms evidence received in the crime laboratory. In some shooting cases, the question is not so much "Who fired the shot?" or "What firearm fired the shot?" but "How was the shot fired?" The presence of trace evidence on an evidence bullet may assist in answering that question.

Some items of trace evidence that may be microscopically observed on a fired evidence bullet are blood, hair, bone, fibers, tissue, fabric, paint, wood, plaster, glass, sand or soil, fabric impressions, and toolmarks. Basically, any material that may be foreign to the evidence bullet may be observed.

A fired evidence bullet, discovered in a large saturated pool of blood on the shoulder of a gravel roadway, was submitted to the Michigan State Police Scientific Laboratory for examination in a suspected abduction-homicide case. Microscopic examination of the .38 special caliber hollow-point fired bullet revealed the presence of a piece of green Michigan State University sweatshirt fabric, blood, tissue, and several long blonde-colored hairs. The detectives working the case were advised of the results of the initial microscopic examination. The female victim, whose badly decomposed body was found in a shallow grave approximately five months later, had long blonde hair and was wearing a green Michigan State University sweatshirt. At trial, the trace evidence discovered on the submitted evidence bullet was instrumental in linking the bullet to the victim, and subsequently, to a firearm in possession of a suspect, who was later found guilty of first-degree murder.

Trace evidence present on a fired bullet played an important part in a police shooting case. An ex-convict on parole, and in possession of a stolen 9-mm semiautomatic pistol, was shot by a police office as he was pointing the pistol at the officer. The estate of the victim subsequently sued the officer, the police agency, and the city. A witness for the plaintiff testified that damage present on the nose of the fired bullet was caused by the bullet striking a sharp edge of concrete after passing through the victim's body, while the victim was lying on the ground.

Microscopic examination of the evidence bullet revealed that the damage present on the nose of the bullet was not characteristic of having struck a concrete edge. Furthermore, microscopic examination failed to reveal the presence of trace evidence on the damaged nose of the fired bullet that could be associated with concrete. The damage exhibited by the fired bullet was similar to an inverted "V" and was smooth on the edges of the damaged area. Additional micro-

scopic examination revealed the presence of white paint present in the damaged area on the evidence bullet. Examination of the crime scene photographs revealed the presence of sections of white-painted steel porch railings located immediately behind the deceased. Photomicrographs of the trace evidence (the paint on the fired bullet) and the configuration of the damage exhibited by the fired bullet were instrumental in proving that, at the time of the shooting, the assailant was not lying on the ground. Shooting scene reconstruction demonstrating the angles of the fired bullet entrance and exit holes showed that the deceased was in a kneeling position and was pointing the pistol at the officer at the time that he was shot. Based upon the physical evidence and the shooting scene reconstruction, the jury ruled in favor of the police officer.

PHOTOMICROGRAPHS

Photomicrographs are photographs that are taken through a microscope. The photomicrograph may be used to illustrate the presence of trace evidence on an item of evidence such as a fired bullet or toolmark. And photomicrographs may be used to photographically record a positive firearms and/or toolmark identification for demonstrative court exhibits.

Juries like photographs. The old adage "a picture is worth a thousand words" is applicable to a photomicrograph of a firearms and/or toolmarks identification used during trial testimony. With the use of the photomicrograph one is not just telling the jury the results of one's examination, but one is also showing them the results by means of the photographic exhibit.

Digital Photomicrographs

Excellent photomicrographs can be obtained by the use of a digital camera photographing through the microscope eyepiece. The item to be examined is prepared on the microscope. The lens of the digital camera is placed against one of the microscope eyepieces, or against the folded-down rubber eyepiece cover. The examiner will then adjust the focus and check the composition and alignment in the camera's LCD screen. The examiner may have to move the camera around a little to get good alignment before taking the photograph. If the photo on replay is out of focus or not properly aligned, it may be simply be deleted and retaken. Although an examiner may have to practice this technique several times, the results will be very rewarding.

The microscopic imperfections caused during the machining and rifling process are readily visible in the photomicrographs of a cutaway revolver barrel. The cutaway allows for an interior view of a rifled firearms barrel. The photomicrograph allows the viewer to observe the numerous machining marks left on the rifled interior surface of a barrel from the various manufacturing processes.

FIREARMS RESIDUE

An important aspect of firearms identification is examination of evidence items such as clothing and skin sections for the presence of firearms residue. Firearms residue evidence will normally consist of a bullet entrance abrasion ring, no matter what distance the shot was fired from, with the exception of contact and near-contact shots. Also present, depending on the distance, may be, charring, sooting, powder stippling, burned and partially burned powder particles, and particulate and vaporized lead particles.

When a firearm is fired, a rapid burning of the smokeless powder contained within the cartridge case takes place. This rapid burning causes heat, flames, soot, and burned and partially burned powder particles to be discharged from the muzzle of the firearm. It is the size and density of the expulsion pattern of this material from the muzzle that makes firearms distance determination possible.

As would be expected, the materials exiting the muzzle of the firearm are very minute in size and light in weight and are greatly affected by the atmospheric conditions. Subsequently, firearms residue will only travel a very short distance and can be affected by temperature, humidity, wind, and air currents. The residue pattern of a firearm discharged outdoors on a windy, rainy day, or on a hot humid day, will vary greatly from that of the same firearm discharged within the confines of a protected shelter, dwelling, firearms range, or home.

At contact and near-contact shots, heavy sooting, charring, and bullet entrance hole deformation will occur from the burning powder and the tremendous gas

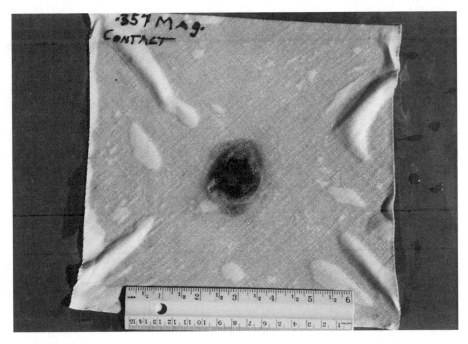

Distance determination test: Chemically treated to show presence of firearms residue pattern.

pressure at the muzzle of the firearm. As the distance between the muzzle of the firearm and the subsequent target increases, the size of the residue pattern will increase, while the density of the residue pattern will decrease. This residue pattern change will occur until the point where the distance between the target and the muzzle of the firearm is too far for the firearms residue to travel.

On some handguns, pistols, and revolvers, the maximum distance where firearms residue will be found on an item is approximately four feet; on others it will be less. Long guns, such as shotguns and rifles, can exceed this distance. It is not unusual, in shotgun discharges, to find shot buffer material, especially from buckshot loads, at a distance greater than ten feet from the muzzle of the firearm.

Examination for Firearms Residue

A careful microscopic examination for firearms residue of the area adjacent to the bullet entrance holes will be the first procedure the firearms examiner will conduct. If sooting, charring, entrance hole deformation, powder particles, or residue is present, detailed notes, sketches, measurements and photographs should be taken of the residue pattern. The residue pattern should be photographed in its original condition, using color film. After these photographs are taken, a scale should be placed at the outer edge of the residue pattern and the pattern should be photographed again. These photographs will be used to demonstrate the original condition of the residue pattern and then the incorporation of the scale will be used to demonstrate the size of the residue pattern. Digital photography is useful for recording firearms residue patterns.

Chemical Firearms Residue Test

If the microscopic examination of an item of evidence reveals a sparse residue pattern, or fails to reveal the visual presence of firearms residue, it does not mean that firearms residue, powder particles, and lead residue may not still be present on the evidence garment. The residue may just not be visible to the naked eye or to microscopic examination. In order to detect the residue, or to enhance a sparse residue pattern, it may be necessary to conduct chemical testing on the evidence item.

The first chemical test to be performed is a "Griess test," which is for the presence of nitrites from burned, smokeless powder. After the Griess test is conducted, a "sodium rhodizonate test" follows. This test is for the presence of vaporized or particulate lead that may be present on the evidence item. The lead can be from the primer residue and also from lead fouling discharged from the barrel of the firearm.

Both chemical tests can result in a discernable firearms residue pattern being established and duplicated by conducting a distance determination test firing with the suspect firearm. Photographing the chemical test pattern results with color film or a digital camera is the best means for recording the results of the test.

Based upon the microscopic examination and chemical test, the firearms examiner should be able to determine if the suspect firearm was fired within the residue-depositing range of the suspect firearm and ammunition. Using the information obtained from the microscopic, visual, and chemical testing, the firearms examiner will fire a series of distance determination tests in an attempt to duplicate the residue pattern (or lack of residue) on the evidence garment.

To perform a firearms distance determination test, the examiner must test-fire the evidence firearm using the same ammunition as the evidence and, as nearly as possible, under the same environmental conditions. A white twill cloth measuring approximately twelve-by-twelve feet will be attached to a heavy cardboard backer. The firearms examiner will fire the first shot

from the evidence firearm at or near contact with the twill cloth. The cloth will be marked with the date, the distance the shot was fired, initials of the examiner, and the make and caliber of firearms and ammunition test fired, for example: 7/04/01; near contact; D.G.T. .357 mag. cal. S&W; mod. 66, R-P. The cloth will be taken down from the cardboard and protected, for the present, by covering it with a clean sheet of white paper.

As the procedure continues, a new cardboard backer and section of test cloth will be put up; the firearms examiner will then, depending on the appearance of the evidence residue pattern, fire the second shot at a distance of six inches or possibly closer. This test cloth will be marked with the information placed on the previous one, except for the distance. The examiner will continue increasing the distance until they reach a point where no residue is deposited upon the test cloth. The matching residue pattern should be somewhere between the contact shot and the point where no firearms residue is deposited.

Once the maximum distance that the suspect firearm deposits residue has been reached, the entrance hole will appear the same, all the way out to the distance the fired bullet is capable of traveling. In other words, the examiner cannot determine from his or her test and examination whether the muzzle of the firearm was ten feet or one hundred yards from the item of evidence at the time the evidence bullet was fired.

Gunshot Residue Testing

Another important aspect of firearms discharge is the "gunshot residue test" (GSR). The GSR is a test performed on the hands of a suspect for the presence of primer residues, such as barium antimony and lead. Time is of the essence in conducting a GSR test. Gun shot residue on the hands of a suspect can be easily destroyed by such things as washing the hands or rubbing them together, by placing the hands in pockets, handcuffing, transporting in a patrol car, and so on.

NATIONAL INTEGRATED BALLISTIC INFORMATION NETWORK (NIBIN)

With the advent of computerization, firearms identification technology has improved greatly in recent years. In May 1997, the FBI and the Bureau of Alcohol, Tobacco, and Firearms (ATF) became partners in the formation of a National Integrated Ballistic Information Network, known as NIBIN. The independent technology and systems previously operated by the FBI, known as Drugfire, and IBIS, operated by the ATF, were incompatible with one another and are being phased out. NIBIN will allow crime laboratories to examine and compare fired bullets and cartridge cases obtained in violent crimes with other laboratories using the NIBIN system throughout the country.

TOOLMARK IDENTIFICATION

Toolmark examination is a forensic science discipline that will often, but not always, fall within the realm of the firearms examiner. A toolmark examination can range from a suspect tool with a pry mark on the side of a safe or file cabinet to the examination of a stab, chop, or cut mark on a skull or bone of a homicide victim from a knife, hatchet, or axe. Toolmark identification is based upon the same scientific principles as firearms identification. Two tools, even those manufactured consecutively, may appear to be the same to the naked eye. However, microscopic imperfections and differences will appear on the surface of the tool, just as they are present in the bore of a firearm.

The toolmark examiner first checks the suspect tool and the evidence toolmark for the presence of trace evidence. Paint or metal shavings from the object containing the evidence toolmark may be on the edges and surface of the suspect tool. Also, segments of the suspect tool may be present in the toolmark. That is why it is imperative that a microscope examination for the presence of trace evidence be conducted as soon as possible.

Suspect tools that are obtained should be protected from the loss of trace evidence. The portion of the tool capable of making the evidence mark should be placed in a paper bag and sealed, to protect the tool and to prevent the loss of trace evidence. The bag containing the tool should then be marked with all pertinent information, such as date and time obtained, from where obtained, initials of investigator, and complaint number.

A toolmark will exhibit class characteristics that the firearms examiner will examine microscopically. The class characteristics will be representative of the type of tool used to make the toolmark—for example, a striated or an impressed toolmark. A striated toolmark could be a pry mark made by the tip of a screwdriver while attempting to pry open a file cabinet, or a cut mark made by a knife while slicing an automobile tire. An example of an impressed toolmark would be the striking of the file cabinet with an object such as a hammer. Some toolmarks can be a combination of a striated and impressed

mark, and in some instances, can cause a problem for the examiner in ascertaining the type of tool used to make the mark, or in replicating the evidence mark while making a test mark with the suspect tool.

Just as firearms have class characteristics, so can a toolmark. Examination of the toolmark will, in many cases, provide the examiner with evidence as to the type of tool that made the mark and its approximate size. For instance, an opposed-jaw tool, such as pliers, channel locks, vise grips, pipe wrenches, and so on, will usually impart toolmarks on the top and bottom of the object with which they come in contact. The size and shape of the toolmark will be examined microscopically and an attempt to determine the width of the tool and type of tool making the mark will be made.

A pry mark from a screwdriver, tire iron, crow bar, and the like will often leave an evidence mark that will allow the examiner to determine the approximate width of the tool. An opposed jaw tool (such as pruning shears) will leave a toolmark that is different from a cut mark made by a pair of scissors.

A toolmark can be made by items other than a standard tool. Any item that is harder than the surface with which it makes contact may leave a toolmark. This should be considered when investigating a hit-and-run accident scene. For instance, a portion of a bicycle pedal making contact with the fender of a hit and run automobile can leave an identifiable toolmark. A taillight license plate bracket from a motorcycle striking the hood of an automobile can leave an identifiable toolmark. Segments of a broken headlight and taillight glass found at the scene of a fatal hit-and-run accident can be positively identified by fracture marks back to a suspect vehicle.

DISTANCE DETERMINATION

Of paramount importance in investigations of homicides and shootings is the distance the muzzle of the firearm was from the victim at the time that the shots were fired. The firearms examiner can only make this determination in the crime laboratory if the investigator properly protects, collects, and submits for examination the clothing or skin sections of the victim for analysis. If the firearm has been fired within the range of firearms residue deposit for that particular firearm, the examiner, in most cases, can make a muzzle-to-target distance determination.

In conducting the distance determination test, it is best if the firearms examiner has the suspect firearm and

Ejection pattern test.

uses the same ammunition. Distance determination tests have been conducted using a firearm of the same make and model as the evidence firearm where the evidence firearm is known, but is not recovered. The test results will specify that they are for an "exemplar" firearm and not the evidence firearm, and that they may produce a similar residue pattern as the evidence firearm.

EJECTION PATTERN TEST

The importance of the location of fired cartridge cases at the shooting scene cannot be overemphasized. The location of the fired cartridge cases in conjunction with test firings of the evidence firearm can assist in providing the approximate location and position of the shooter in the crime scene at the time shots were fired. In conducting ejection pattern tests, using the evidence firearm and the same ammunition as the evidence is of major importance. When conducting an ejection pattern test, the firearms examiner must allow the fired cartridge cases to strike the same type of surface as was present at the crime scene. Whether carpet, lawn, concrete, asphalt, or tile, the same surface must be utilized for testing purposes.

SHOOTING SCENE EXAMINATION AND RECONSTRUCTION

In conducting a homicide or shooting scene investigation, it is essential to ensure that all firearms and toolmark evidence is properly photographed and collected, and proper measurements are taken at the crime scene.

Although this may sound like a basic principle of crime scene investigation and processing, which it is, in many cases it is not adhered to by field investigators. The entire case will be judged on the quality of the crime scene investigation, photographs, notes, sketches, measurements, and the evidence obtained from the scene.

The shooting scene must be photographed using at least 35-mm color film and video, if possible, and recorded in its original uncontaminated condition. Only those individuals actively engaged in the processing of the crime scene should be allowed entry into the crime scene. All high-ranking officials should be kept out of the scene. The only thing that they can do at the crime scene is contaminate the scene and destroy physical evidence—footwear impressions, latent fingerprints, fabric impressions—and step on or alter the position of evidence at the scene. However, high officials like to appear at notorious crime scenes, not necessarily to provide assistance to the investigators, but because they know the news media will be present. A crime scene entry log should be maintained, listing the names and the time of entry and exit of all individuals who enter the crime scene, with their reason for being there clearly stated in the log.

In processing the shooting scene, the exact location and position of the victim must be recorded. Measurements must be taken from different locations of the body, for example, from the head to two different stationary locations, from both feet to two stationary locations, and also from the positions of the hands. The victim must be photographed from all angles, with photos taken from the general to the specific—that is, photographs showing the location of the victim in the crime scene and close up and macro-photographs showing the location of the victim's hands, all bullet entrance and exit holes, firearms residue patterns, any defensive injuries, all wounds, cuts, or abrasions. Particular attention should be paid to the victim's hands for the presence of firearms residue, sooting, and so on. Clothing that is damaged or torn also should be noted. Prior to removing the victim from the scene, an evidence tag should be attached to the victim's body (e.g., the toe, foot, shoe). The tag should not be attached to the victim's hands or fingers, because the victim's hands must be bagged.

Bagging of Victim's Hands

After the victim has been examined and photographed from all angles, and prior to the victim being removed from the scene, the victim's hands should be placed in clean paper bags and sealed on the victim's wrist. The use of a plastic bag can result in condensation occurring. The bagging of the hands will prevent the loss of any trace evidence (in the form of blood, hairs, fibers, fabric, tissue, gun shot residue, etc.) present on the victim's hands or under their fingernails. At the autopsy, the bags should be removed and the hands and fingernails carefully examined for firearms sooting and residue or other trace evidence. Fingernail scrapings of each nail should be taken and packaged separately. The fingernail scrapings and the bags removed from the victim's hands should be properly packaged and submitted to the crime laboratory for analysis.

GUN EXAMINATION

Another duty of the firearms examiner is the examination of evidence firearms, airguns, paintball guns, and in some instances, homemade guns, and projectile firing devices. The procedure will include an examination to determine its operational design, how and if the safety or safeties work properly, and the "trigger pull force"—the amount of pressure applied to the trigger of the firearm to cause the gun to fire. This force is measured in pounds and ounces, and in both the single and double action mode, when applicable. The examiner will try to determine if the gun operates in the manner in which it was designed, if the gun has been altered, if parts are missing from it. He or she will also try to determine if, from the full cocked position, the hammer can be pushed off and if there is firearms residue present in the barrel or cylinder of the gun; whether the firearm has an altered or obliterated serial number; and if the firearm is in a safe operating condition.

The gun will only be test-fired after careful examination and determination that it is safe to fire. During test firing, the examiner will note its operation. He or she will try to determine whether the firing pin, extractor, ejector, and/or cylinder all work properly; if the cylinder timing is proper; whether the cylinder indexes properly; if overtravel of the cylinder is present; whether cartridges properly feed from the magazine to the chamber; and if there is a malfunction or obstruction present. These are some, but not all, of the tests and examinations the firearms examiner will conduct on an evidence firearm.

SERIAL NUMBER RESTORATION

In many laboratories, it is the duty of the firearms examiner to conduct serial number restorations. This involves the use of an acid-etching solution in an attempt to restore the obliterated or altered serial number from a firearm, or any other object that may be stamped with a serial number. Even though an obliterated serial number may not be visible on a firearm, it still may be present in the metal of the firearm, and it may be possible to restore the number. When a serial number is stamped into the metal of a firearm, the molecular structure of the metal comprising the serial number is altered. The metal is compressed or hardened by the number stamping process, thereby changing the molecular structure of the metal comprising the serial number.

A simple example would be to take a piece of wood and strike it with a hammer. The impressed hammer mark in the wood has not removed wood; it has just compressed it. This is what occurs when a serial number is stamped into a firearm. The type of metal used in the manufacturing of the firearm will dictate the type of acid-etching solution that will be used in restoring the serial number of the firearm. The acid reacts to the altered molecular composition of the metal and makes it possible, in many cases, for the obliterated number to be restored.

SUMMARY

The sole purpose of the firearms examiner in the crime laboratory is to provide technical assistance, supports, and information to the field investigators. This short section has attempted to briefly cover some, but not all, of the methods of technical assistance a firearms examiner may provide. The firearms examiner can only work with the evidentiary items that are provided to him by the investigator. Therefore, it is of paramount importance for the investigator to have a thorough understanding of the services and technical assistance a firearms examiner or crime lab personnel can provide. An investigator should visit their crime laboratory and become familiar with laboratory personnel.

An investigator must know his or her limitations and not be reluctant to ask for assistance from crime lab experts when necessary. Crime laboratory examiners would gladly provide technical assistance or information that would assist an investigator on a case, rather than see the investigator make a mistake. The better evidence the investigator provides, the better the assistance he or she will receive from the crime laboratory expert. As stated previously, as a basic rule of thumb, if one is going to err, one should always err on the side of caution and measure and make note of all evidentiary items, as well as collect photographs and sketches, when processing a crime scene.

—*David G. Townshend*

Further Reading

Association of Firearms and Toolmark Examiners (AFTE). (1980). *Glossary of the Association of Firearms and Toolmark Examiners (AFTE)*. Augusta, GA: Fonville Printing Company.

Firearms Toolmark Unit, FBI Laboratory. (1999). *Gunpowder and Gunshot Residue.*1999 ed. Washington, DC: Federal Bureau of Investigation.

———. *General Rifling Characteristic File 2000*. (2000). Washington, DC: Federal Bureau of Investigation.

Florida Department of Law Enforcement (FDLE) Crime Lab. *Gunshot Residue Analysis (GSR) Submission Criteria*. Information factsheet.

Geberth, Vernon J. (1983). *Practical Homicide Investigation*. New York: Elsevier Science.

Hodge, Evan E., and Bobby D. Blackburn. (1979). "The Firearms/Toolmark Examiner in Court." Paper presented at the tenth anniversary meeting of the Association of Firearms and Toolmark Examiners.

Mathews, J. Howard. (1973). *Firearms Identification*. 3 vols. Springfield, IL: Charles C Thomas.

National Integrated Ballistic Information Network (NIBIN). http://www.atf.treas.gov/firearms/nibin

Court Cases

Commonwealth v. Best (1902). 180 Mass. 492, 62 N.E. 748.
Dean v. Commonwealth (1897). 32 Gratt (Va.) 912.

◤ FOOT PATROL

Police patrol is often referred to as the backbone of policing. Patrol activities typically account for more than two-thirds of a department's personnel. While 80 percent of American police departments employ fewer than twenty officers—and more than half employ fewer than ten—the principal activities among these officers is patrol work. Because the patrol unit also tends to be the most visible unit in a police agency, it has a significant effect on the public's perception of that agency.

The police role in society is highly diverse and complex, and this is reflected in the varied goals associated with patrol. The primary goals in patrol are (1) crime prevention and deterrence, (2) apprehension of offenders, (3) establishment of an atmosphere of safety and security throughout the community, (4) traffic control and safety, and (5) provision of an assortment of non-crime-related services (rescuing the fabled cat up a tree or extricating small children from inside of locked bathrooms). In order to accomplish these goals, police agencies rely upon strategies that include visibility of officers on patrol, interdiction of offenders, counseling of victims and community members, and education of the public. These strategies are used either formally, in settings such as news conferences, town meetings, and neighborhood watch meetings, or informally, as when officers speak casually with citizens while on patrol.

HISTORICAL DEVELOPMENT OF FOOT PATROL

During colonial times in America, the two major patrol activities were watching and responding to what was seen. Watching took place as a means for preserving the peace and identifying crime. The colonial night watch was originally the civic responsibility of private citizens (usually members of the mercantile class). This citizen watcher would patrol the local streets at night to detect whether crime had occurred or whether livestock had wandered out of their pens and into the streets. Usually this meant discovering a broken window or open door to a store that had been burgled or observing a cow or horse grazing or moseying around. Occasionally, it might mean discovering an actual crime in progress, although this was not the intention of the watch or the citizen watchman.

Eventually, these citizen watchers became paid watchmen, who were the forerunners of the nineteenth-century patrol officer. Later, patrol officers were dispersed throughout the community in an effort to prevent crime, rather than simply to discover crime after it had occurred. The visibility of these officers allowed them in turn to be watched by potential criminals, who would not commit crimes in the officers' presence. Also during the nineteenth century, police extended their patrols to cover day and night. Because patrol officers were available when other governmental services were not, patrol functions expanded beyond crime discovery and crime prevention. Their activities began to take on a decided social service character, including assisting the aged without heat in winter and securing unsafe conditions in residential homes (for example shutting off water valves when water heaters burst).

FROM WATCHMEN TO CRUISERS

Police patrols that began as walking watches became the first formal police foot patrols, and the cop on the beat continues to be the major image of policing in the minds of most American citizens. However, during the 1930s, even before the automobile had become an integral part of the average American's life, foot patrols had begun to disappear in favor of the more efficient and faster car patrols.

Several rationales encouraged agencies to use police cruisers. First, they could cover larger geographic areas than a man walking and do it faster. Second, they could be fitted with a new device, a radio transceiver (filling most of the vehicle's trunk), which allowed the officers in the car to remain in communication with the station. Third, roadways were developing, and criminals were using cars on these roads to reach crime locations and to flee the scene after committing crimes.

By the 1940s, police administrators emphasized the importance of using motorized patrol as a means of deploying patrol officers and increasing efficiency. The International City Management Association (ICMA) reported that the number of cities using motorized patrols increased from 840 in 1946 to 1,000 in 1954, and to 1,334 in 1964 (President's Commission 1967: 55). The efficiency of foot patrols began to be called into further question. They were geographically limiting, required a greater number of personnel than vehicular patrol, and could not be as easily communicated with (foot patrol officers during the 1960s did not carry portable radios, which became more commonly used in the 1970s).

Many cities had shifted away from foot patrol and toward the more versatile two-person motorized patrol car by the late 1960s, but debates about the benefits of two person patrol cars soon began to arise. In 1964, the International Association of Chiefs of Police (IACP) argued that highly conspicuous patrols conveyed a sense of police omnipresence. The association felt this could be best achieved using a highly mobilized force of one-person marked patrol cars: "The more men and more cars that are visible on the streets, the greater is the potential for preventing a crime. A heavy blanket of conspicuous patrol at all times and in all parts of the city tends to suppress violations of the law. The most economical manner of providing this heavy blanket of patrol is by using one-man cars when and where they are feasible" (IACP 1964: 89).

The shift from foot to motorized patrol revolutionized American policing. In many ways it surpassed early police administrators' expectations for providing fast, efficient, and visible patrols. However, a serious but unforeseen consequence also accompanied this

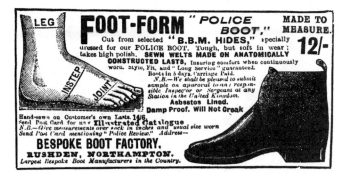

This advertisement for police boots from The Police Review *was published in London in January 1898.*

change, a consequence that continues to pester policing today. As William A. Westly (1970: 35) succinctly stated this problem, "In contrast to the man on the beat, the man in the car is isolated from the community."

Motorized patrols were very efficient, but they minimized relationships that could be forged between the patrol officers and the residents of neighborhoods these officers patrolled. Officers had limited contacts with ordinary citizens during the normal course of their patrols and no longer tended to reside in the communities they patrolled. The Task Force on the Police of the President's Commission on Law Enforcement and Administration of Justice (1967: 54) noted, "The most significant weakness in American motor patrol operations today is the general lack of contact with citizens except when the officer has responded to a call. Forced to stay near the car's radio, awaiting an assignment, most patrol officers have few opportunities to develop closer relationships with persons living in the district." Yet in a police practice survey conducted in 1978 by the Police Foundation, it was reported that only 10 percent of all police patrols in the nation were conducted through foot patrols.

A RETURN TO FOOT PATROL

As a kind of vestige of the early watchman style of patrolling, modern day police foot patrols hearken back to this community-centered orientation. Although there was a considerable drop-off in its use during the 1960s and 1970s, the 1980s witnessed a significant movement back to foot patrol. By the 1990s, it had become almost synonymous with the term "community policing." Trends suggest that police agencies in a growing number of communities are continuing to return officers to walking beats in an attempt to work more closely with their communities to reduce crime and fear

A "Flatfoot's" Plaint

Feet, feet, how they ache and pain,
Feet, feet, they'll never be the same;
Gee, Whiz! You wonder why I complain—
'Cause there's no soft spots on the sidewalk.

Feet, feet, once so trim and small,
Feet, feet, now flatter than the wall;
Bunions, blisters, and still that isn't all—
'Cause there's no soft spots on the sidewalk.

Feet, feet, you try to do your share,
Feet, feet, you don't get anywhere;
The way you sadly shuffle makes everybody stare—
'Cause there's no soft spots on the sidewalk.

Feet, feet, for ten years—tried and true,
Feet, feet, at twenty—black and blue;
Just a few years more—then you'll be all through—
Trying to find soft spots on the sidewalk.

A humorous presentation of the foot patrolman's greatest problem, from the New York City police journal Spring 3100, *August, 1939.*

of crime. Foot patrols are fairly expensive and limit an officer's ability to pursue suspects in vehicles and to get from one area to another rapidly. Used in conjunction with motorized patrol, however, foot patrol programs can be extremely effective.

In the highly regarded article "Broken Windows: The Police and Neighborhood Safety," James Q. Wilson and George Kelling called for the police to leave the shells of their patrol cars and take to the streets. Wilson and Kelling suggested that walking the beat allows officers and citizens to better come to know and support one another. Wilson and Kelling also suggested that the neighborhoods are where police can best instill public confidence and inspire feelings of safety—even if these locations are not in the areas that receive the highest number of calls for police services. Ensuring a sense of community, public safety, and maintaining the order, not crime fighting, should be the mandate for police officers on patrol: "Just as physicians now recognize the importance of fostering health rather than simply treating illness, so the police—and the rest of us—ought to recognize the importance of maintaining intact communities without broken windows" (1982: 37).

Research tends to support that, although it is less efficient in some ways than its motorized counterpart, foot patrol holds a number of benefits for communities. For example, when foot patrols are publicized in a community, fear of crime tends to decrease significantly, and citizen approval and satisfaction tend to increase. At the same time, officers who walk foot patrols have a greater appreciation for the values of the community and residents than they do when isolated in a patrol car. Moreover, officers who walk foot patrols tend to have greater job satisfaction, feel safer, and have higher morale.

When people are left to decide, there is evidence that they prefer foot patrols to motorized efforts. For example, in 1982 and 1985 the citizens of Flint, Michigan voted to raise their taxes in order to support extended foot patrols throughout the entire city. In 1988, Robert Trojanowicz and Dennis Banas reported findings from a four-year study of the Flint foot patrols. Rojanowicz and Banas found that the Neighborhood Foot Patrol program had significantly improved police and community relations. In interviews, community members indicated that they believed the police had become much more responsive the citizens' needs than they had been before the foot program began. Other studies have similarly found that citizens become more actively involved in policing where such programs have been initiated.

THE BENEFITS OF FOOT PATROL

Research consistently suggests that citizens regard foot patrol as desirable and even more effective than motorized patrol. Explanations for this include the fact that unlike car-bound officers driving swiftly by, foot patrol officers tend to pay attention to disorderly behavior and minor offenses. Consequently, they are in a better position to hear from community members about what is of concern to them. In addition, they are able to recognize situations on their beat where something is out of the ordinary, threatening, or inappropriate. These officers are in the unique position to be responsive to the problems confronting community members in their daily lives—derelicts loitering in the park, petty thefts and shoplifting in local stores, rowdy or disorderly behavior by teenagers, and other nuisances—even though these may not constitute serious criminal behaviors.

Clearly, it is not simply the existence of a foot patrol program that improves the police and community relationship. Rather, it is the action of the officer on patrol. If an officer walks his or her beat in a manner similar to driving down the street, he or she is not likely to change either the crime rate in the area or the relationship between the police and the community. But when the officer walking the beat becomes involved with the community residents, gets to know their names, where they work, how their families are doing, and so forth, then there can be a significant impact in the area's crime problem and a reduction in the gap between police and the community. Foot patrol is a proactive strategy rather than a reactive one, allowing officers to address the problems of a community before they become crimes.

Moving Foot Patrol and Fixed-Post Foot Patrol

To a large measure, the discussion of foot patrol presented here has focused chiefly on moving foot patrol, which is commonly associated with an officer walking a designated limited area of space—the beat. It is particularly useful in high-density pedestrian areas such as business and shopping areas, near bars and taverns, in high crime neighborhoods, by theater and restaurant areas, hospitals, and where there are many multiple-family dwellings or apartment complexes.

In addition, there are also fixed-post foot patrols that involve a stationary police presence. Fixed-post foot patrols are ideally suited for such activities as traffic direction, surveillance, and crowd control at special events, such as the Super Bowl, boxing matches, political events, or movie premieres. Fixed-position officers in these situations demonstrate a police presence, and they are well placed in positions where they can assist tourists, monitor traffic, and observe the flow of crowds.

CURRENT SITUATION

Foot patrol strategies and programs have a long history in the United States. During the early periods of watches and municipal policing, walking a beat was the common form of police patrol. By the 1960s, however, most police departments had shifted away from foot patrol strategies in favor of motorized patrols. During the past several decades foot patrol programs have been revived across the country. These programs have not replaced motorized patrols and probably will not. Still, in communities where foot patrol has resurfaced, it has generally been met with enthusiasm and citizen support. It has additionally received high marks from police officers, who often indicate greater job satisfaction and higher morale. Even among those officers who might prefer more "exciting" work such as drug squads or assignments that provide more opportunity for recognition, there is an understanding that one must first gain field experience on patrol.

—*Bruce L. Berg*

See also BROKEN WINDOWS THEORY; COMMUNITY POLICING

Further Reading

Adams, Thomas F. (1994). *Police Field Operations*, 3d ed. Englewood Cliffs, NJ: Prentice Hall Career and Technology.

Berg, Bruce L. (1999). *Policing Modern Society*. Boston: Butterworth/Heinemann.

Cordner, Gary, and Robert Trojanowicz. (1992). "Patrol." In *What Works in Policing? Operations and Administration Examined*, edited by Gary Cordner and Donna C. Hale. Cincinnati, OH: Anderson Publishing Co., 143–158.

Dempsey, John. (1999). *An Introduction to Policing*, 2d ed. Belmont, CA: Wadsworth.

Federal Bureau of Investigation. (2000). *Uniform Crime Reports for the United States, 2001*. Washington, DC: Government Printing Office.

Heaphy, John. (1978). *Police Practices: The General Administration Survey*. Washington, DC: Police Foundation, 11.

Kelling, George. (1987). *Foot Patrol*. Washington, DC: National Institute of Justice.

Napper, George. (1986). "Partnership Against Crime: Sharing Problems and Power." *Police Chief* (February): 43–46.

President's Commission on Law Enforcement and Administration of Justice. (1967). *Task Force Report: The Police.* Washington, DC: Government Printing Office.

Smith, Bruce. (1949). *Police Systems in the United States.* New York: Harper & Brothers.

Trojanowicz, Robert C., and Dennis W. Banas. (1985). *Perceptions of Safety: A Comparison of Foot Patrol Versus Motor Patrol Officers.* East Lansing: Michigan State University, School of Criminal Justice, National Neighborhood Foot Patrol Center.

Trojanowicz, Robert C., and Dennis W. Banas. (1988). *The Impact of Foot Patrol on Black and White Perceptions of Policing.* East Lansing: Michigan State University, School of Criminal Justice, National Neighborhood Foot Patrol Center.

Walker, Samuel. (1992). *The Police in America: An Introduction.* New York: McGraw-Hill.

Wilson, James Q. and George Kelling. (1982). "Broken Windows: The Police and Neighborhood Safety." *Atlantic Monthly* (March): 29–38.

Wrobleski, Henry M., and Karen M. Hess. (2000). *Introduction to Law Enforcement and Criminal Justice,* 6th ed. Belmont, CA: Wadsworth.

FORENSIC BEHAVIORAL SCIENCES

On the night of October 25, 1994, the McCloud family of Union County, South Carolina, answered a loud knocking at their front door. There was Susan Smith, asking for help: "Please call 911 and get the police." When the police arrived, Susan told the responding officer that at about 9 p.m. she had been idling at a red light at the junction of Highway 49 and Highway 215. While she was awaiting a green light, a black male approached her car on the passenger side, showed a small handgun, and got into her car. He told her to drive north on Highway 49. When they got to J. D. Long Lake, he told her to stop, forced her out of the car, and drove off. He refused to let her get her two young children—Michael and Alexander—out of the car. She went to a nearby home, the McClouds', for help.

There was an immediate and intensive search of the area by air and ground. Police agencies in the state were notified by telephone and teletype of the crime. A police artist was called. He composed a drawing of the abductor, whom Susan Smith said she could identify, and this was given to the media and the police. The next day Susan Smith was interviewed. She restated what she had told police already. Her phone was tapped in the event the perpetrator called her home, and her credit card information was taken by police. Immedi-

ately, officers were assigned to record and check on all leads of possible sightings of the missing car and children. Many leads were followed up but to no avail. No trace of the abductor, the car, or the children was found.

This case was atypical in that it immediately received nationwide attention. Television and print media called for help in locating the missing children and the missing car. Susan Smith and her husband appeared on television to beg the abductor to return the children. These efforts produced no new evidence and no solid leads for police. Aside from the nationwide attention, this case was far more typical than is commonly realized. In this case, as in about 70 percent of all cases of serious offenses, there was no physical, scientifically analyzable evidence to enable conventional forensic techniques to be of benefit. That is, neither the alleged perpetrator, the car, the children, nor any other tangible property of interest was available. The police in this case had to rely on techniques that lie in the realm of the behavioral forensic sciences.

Behavioral forensic techniques are typically based on theory and research in the behavioral as opposed to the physical sciences. In many cases these techniques are controversial: Their scientific foundation may be inadequate, the way in which they are typically applied may be at odds with what scientific research supports, and other features of their usage may be problematic. Nevertheless, without the use of these techniques there is little doubt that many more criminal cases would go unsolved and that a great number of criminal investigations would go unprocessed. (On average in the United States, only about 20 percent of all serious criminal cases are "cleared" by the police. That usually means only that an arrest was made; it does not mean a court conviction.) In the Susan Smith case, as in many others of a similar nature, three forensic techniques played a role in arrest and conviction: forensic interrogation, forensic interview, and forensic polygraphy.

FORENSIC INTERROGATION

An interrogation, to those who teach and practice that technique, is viewed as an accusatory questioning of a person whose guilt is either known or reasonably certain. Surprisingly, many persons, including some police officers, perceive it as a somewhat psychologically, if not physically, abusive process in which the interrogator badgers the suspect into making an admission (a statement confirming partial involvement in an offense, such as an admission of being at the scene of a crime) or a confession (a statement in which a person acknowledges responsibility for commission of a crime). It is likely that such perceptions are derived from the misperceptions provided by the popular media in, for instance, television and Hollywood portrayals of policing and criminal investigations. In fact, a forensic interrogation, if done competently, is quite different from the popular image. Although it is true that psychological influence is important to the interrogator (e.g., the interview should be private, the belief in the suspect's involvement is emphasized, etc.), in most properly conducted interrogations, the suspect listens and the interrogator talks; the interrogator's primary task is to get the suspect to listen. What does a suspect hear? Usually appeals to emotion or logic to persuade him or her to reveal his or her involvement in the offense. It is not often that the interrogator finds a need to raise the voice, yell in the suspect's ear, or to do many of the other practices that are dramatized in the media.

It is commonly believed that forensic interrogation techniques are effective because many persons involved in criminal events are not only willing to discuss their involvement but also want to share it. They perhaps find it therapeutic to "confess," even knowing that a confession may lead to legal and other consequences. It is important to note, of course, that there are many legal restrictions on what is proper during a police interrogation. It is well known, for example, that in the United States a suspect must be advised of Miranda rights before police questioning. There is some evidence, though limited, to show that the use of Miranda rights warnings has decreased the number and value of confessions. In addition, there are some things that a police interrogator cannot say or do to a suspect if a confession is to be legally admissible in court proceedings. For example, a threat, a promise, or a beating will invalidate a confession, however accurate. In some instances, especially when dealing with suspects who are mentally deficient or very young, even legal interrogation tactics might produce false confessions. Experts do not know how frequently this occurs, but the evidence shows it to be extremely rare given the number of interrogations that are conducted.

In the United States, forensic interrogation involves constitutional issues (e.g., the Fifth Amendment protects persons from being required to incriminate themselves); therefore, it must be carefully conducted, and those who practice it must be well trained, highly ethical, and subject to close review. Unfortunately, some

police officers "learn" interrogation practices on the job, and often what they learn are not acceptable practices. Surprisingly, given the reliance on forensic interrogation in policing, the amount and quality of training that most police officers receive are inadequate. Moreover, the oversight of many interrogations is minimal.

FORENSIC INTERVIEW

In many police investigations, an interrogation of a person is preceded by an interview, the purpose of which is to help the police determine if the person is, in fact, a likely suspect and warrants closer questioning. This sort of interview, commonly known as a behavioral analysis interview, will be discussed separately. In other cases, the police carry out a forensic interview of persons who are witnesses and victims, that is, persons who are not perceived to be suspects. In such cases, the interview differs from an interrogation. In a forensic interview, the purpose is not to get the interviewee to "listen" but rather to get him or her to talk freely and honestly about the matter at hand. This may sound easy to do, but it is not. Consider, for instance, an interview with someone who falsely reports a burglary (perhaps to fraudulently collect on an insurance claim) or the victim of a rape who is asked to reveal details of a very traumatic, perhaps physically abusive, event. In these as well as other instances, an interviewer must focus on obtaining as much factual information as possible.

COGNITIVE INTERVIEW

It is not uncommon for interviews to lead to inaccurate information, for interviewees to refuse to talk or to be hostile to police, or for interviewees to lie to confound a police investigation. But it is this sort of interpersonal communication that is critical to police success, and so it is important that the police deal with it properly. When dealing with a willing witness, however, different problems arise. Sometimes it may be difficult for a rape victim to reconstruct the crime. Perhaps the victim fears making an error in identifying a suspect or perhaps, as is true for many eyewitnesses, has difficulty recalling the event. A relatively recent technique for dealing with willing witnesses is known as the cognitive interview.

The cognitive interview enhances both the quality and quantity of information given to the police interviewer by willing victims and witnesses. In such an interview, specific techniques designed to enhance the recall of events are used. For example, instead of merely asking a witness for a narrative statement of what happened, the interviewer may give the witness instructions to apply these four conditions:

1. Reconstruct the circumstances of the crime.

2. Give a complete account of the event, not choosing what is believed to be most important.

3. Recall the event in different orders.

4. Change the perspective of the event from that of the interviewee to someone who played a different role in the event.

Each of these four conditions, as well as others that have been shown to enhance memory recall, may be applied during the cognitive interview. Research on this approach has been promising and shows that the approach is preferable to "standard" police interview procedures in some circumstances, at least for those willing to talk to the police.

FORENSIC POLYGRAPHY

Perhaps no forensic technique is more controversial and more misunderstood than forensic polygraphy. The use of a polygraph instrument to determine if a person is "lying" about an event has been incorrectly referred to as "lie detection." The polygraph is not really a "lie detector"; it is just an instrument that records physiological activity when a person is asked particular questions about, for example, involvement in a crime. The person who interprets the polygraph instrument's recordings is actually the "lie detector." It is important to note that polygraphy was used with great effectiveness in the Susan Smith case. (She "failed" three polygraph examinations, whereas others, including her estranged husband, did not. This led the police, of course, to go further in their questioning of her.) Because many cases similar to the Smith case do not yield useful, scientifically analyzable forensic evidence, polygraphy is widely applied because it has such great utility.

Although polygraphy is indeed useful in detecting those who have committed a crime, its value in "clearing" those not involved in a crime is especially useful. When a police investigation involves many suspects, each of whom appears initially to be equally culpable, polygraphy is used to narrow the focus, thereby saving investigative time and resources. And although polygraph testing results are not now typically admitted as evidence in court (over the objection of opposing counsel), they are widely used by judges, prosecutors, defense attorneys, and others in the justice system to help determine what course of action to take in a particular matter.

Although the usefulness of polygraph testing has been established in criminal investigations, as well as in other areas (e.g., intelligence agency processes such as in the CIA and National Security Agency), its accuracy is a matter of great scientific controversy. Proponents claim that it is, overall, about 90 percent accurate; opponents, about 70 percent. And aside from this issue, there are others of almost equal importance in the debate. It is unlikely that any of these issues will be resolved soon. Nevertheless, polygraph testing will continue to play a significant role in almost every major criminal investigation in the United States as well as in the work of intelligence agencies.

BEHAVIORAL ANALYSIS INTERVIEW

The behavioral analysis interview (BAI) differs considerably from the typical information-seeking, narrative-style interview or the cognitive interview. The purpose of the behavioral analysis interview is to evaluate the interviewee's verbal, nonverbal, and paralinguistic behaviors in order to determine the likelihood that the interviewee is concealing information regarding a matter under investigation. The BAI consists of the interviewer asking a structured protocol of demographic questions, a set of questions to establish "baseline" behaviors, and a set of what are termed "behavior provoking" questions. As each of these questions is asked, the interviewer pays special attention to both what the interviewee states in response (i.e., the words and ideas that are expressed) and the accompanying behavioral characteristics. Simply stated, persons who are concealing involvement in the specific matter exhibit behaviors different from those of persons who are not concealing "guilt."

Although research on the BAI is not extensive, what is available is quite supportive. Also, the experiences of those who apply this process correctly document its effectiveness. This, by the way, is in contrast to much more extensive research dealing only with assessments of nonverbal behavior, most of which tends to show that the accuracy of such assessments is only slightly greater than guesswork. And in spite of the popular literature stating that nonverbal behaviors have general applicability to evaluations of "deceptive" behaviors in a wide variety of circumstances, there is little scientific support for such a position.

SCIENTIFIC CONTENT ANALYSIS AND STATEMENT VALIDITY ANALYSIS

Scientific Content Analysis (SCAN) and Criteria-Based Statement Analysis (CBSA) are somewhat related techniques that are said to have investigative value in identifying individuals who are concealing involvement in or information about a crime. In general, the basis for these techniques lies in the analysis of narrative statements given freely by persons who are suspects.

Considering SCAN first, a basic premise is that people will choose, at least in certain circumstances, not to "lie" about involvement in crime. A guilty suspect, asked to prepare a written statement of his or her understanding of what occurred, will, for example, be truthful in the statement but will "lie" by omission—by what is not included rather than by what is. The message, properly analyzed, will reveal the truth. The trained SCAN analyst evaluates the statement with respect to how the suspect uses particular words (e.g., pronouns) and how they are linked to ideas and actions as the suspect describes them. Changes in tense, in word usage, and in other language characteristics yield information about the suspect's status even though he or she is trying not to reveal it. For example, in the case of a report of a stolen automobile, "My car was parked" is not the same as "I parked my car." A SCAN analyst might assume that although both statements are true, the first one represents a suspect who is making a false claim (he or she did not park the car but arranged to have someone else do so); the second more likely represents someone telling the truth.

Although SCAN is used on a regular basis in investigations in the United States, its effectiveness has not yet been validated in scientific research. There are no studies in the peer-reviewed literature to show how well or, for that matter, if it works, in what situations it may be most effective, or if its effectiveness is influenced by language skills, cultural differences, and so forth.

Although few, some studies suggest that criteria-based statement analysis (CBSA) in specified circumstances can be used to distinguish between statements that are "true," based on actual experience, and those that are not true based on direct experiences but are products of invention. In short, CBSA may be used to differentiate between truth tellers and "liars." In this

approach a set of "content" criteria in five categories, each with a number of subcategory features, is applied to the analysis of a written statement. The main categories are the following:

1. Criteria that are general in nature
2. Criteria that relate to specific detailed contents
3. Criteria that deal with peculiarities of the content
4. Criteria that concern motivational characteristics
5. Criteria that relate to offense-specific items

It is possible to judge each of the major categories, and each of the items in the subcategories, in either a gross way (e.g., present or absent) or in a more detailed way, such as with respect to their strength and the degree to which they apply in the statement being analyzed. An analysis by a trained person who judges the presence or absence of the items, as well as their strength, usually produces a probabilistic statement regarding the credibility of the "suspect." In practice there are no accepted, fixed rules for determinations of outcomes.

A basic premise of CBSA is, of course, that a statement that is true differs in discernible ways from one that is not true. Research directed at testing this premise has yielded promising results. Most informed observers agree, however, that the empirical base is inadequate, a problem common to almost all of the techniques discussed here.

CRIME SCENE ASSESSMENT AND CRIMINAL PROFILING

In order to be applied, the techniques discussed to this point require the police to have a suspect available. What can be done when there is no identifiable suspect? One approach is crime scene assessment, also referred to as "criminal profiling"—as in the popular movie *The Silence of the Lambs*. This approach evaluates the scene of an offense, most often a homicide or a serious sexual assault or a series of such crimes, in order to determine personality and other characteristics of someone who might commit such an offense. The evaluation is not meant to identify a particular person as the offender but rather to assist the police in narrowing the scope of their investigation and to speed up the capture of the offender. In some cases, the profile assists the police in focusing their investigative efforts on specific persons who may already be under suspicion.

Crime scene assessment, when done by an experienced, capable profiler, permits the profiler to estimate from the characteristics of a crime scene such things as the offender's age, race, general occupational category, the type of relationship he or she has with others, marital status, and certain other demographic and personality characteristics. The profiler will examine the crime scene to assess whether the offender was organized or disorganized, how much planning the offense required, how brutally the offense was carried out, and what specific actions were necessary to execute the crime, to leave the scene, and to hide or display certain items. The experienced profiler will note not only what is present but also, equally important, what is not. Was the crime scene staged? Was the offender mocking the investigators?

One important part of the work of a profiler is to assist the police in linking offenses. It is not uncommon in serial homicide cases, for example, for victims' bodies to be found in different police jurisdictions. Sometimes multiple police agencies investigate what ostensibly are single homicides when in fact the same offender is responsible for all of them. An experienced profiler is often able to link multiple homicides by the offender's "signature"—a unique offense characteristic. This is extremely valuable to investigators, and in some instances it is the key that leads to resolution.

Crime scene assessment, or profiling, though commonly practiced in law enforcement today, is primarily an experience-based technique and appears to be dependent on the skills of individual profilers. In the Unabomber case, for example, quite different "profiles" were developed, and their value to the investigation was problematic. (The case was eventually solved by a tip from the bomber's brother.) Nevertheless, the technique has demonstrated value, and scientific research on its effectiveness is just now being initiated.

GEOGRAPHIC PROFILING

Geographic profiling is a second approach that police may use to locate an offender when they do not have a particular one identified. The adoption of computers in policing—and their usefulness in analyzing a wide variety of information from large databases concerning crime, criminals, and related sources—has led to the regular use of this approach. In it, special computer software is used to determine the probable location of a repeat offender's home area by plotting incidents of crime along with other information. For example, the

location of a serial killer who dumps victims' bodies at various sites, often in different police jurisdictions, may be determined by the use of geographic profiling systems. In actual use, of course, the offender is not specifically identified. Rather, the area in which the police are directed to search is narrowed. In one well-known case, for instance, this technique is credited with focusing police efforts in a four-square-block area around the home of a person whose eleven victims' bodies were left at sites miles from the offender's residence.

Although this has been only a brief review of forensic behavioral sciences, the techniques included are the primary ones relied upon in the criminal justice system. There is little doubt, however, that in spite of their widespread use, more research remains to be done on all of these techniques. These techniques, many of which are used more frequently and with greater confidence than "standard" forensic procedures, are still not admissible as trial evidence and appear to be more controversial than techniques about which less is known. The validation, development, and enhancement of these techniques are open to those with an interest and motivation to do so.

—Frank Horvath

See also Cognitive Interviewing; Crime Scene Assessment; Criminal Profiling; Forensic Interrogation; Forensic Polygraph; Psychiatry, Forensic; Psychology, Forensic

Further Reading

Cassell, Paul, and Richard Fowles. (1998). "Handcuffing the Cops? A Thirty-Year Perspective on Miranda's Harmful Effects on Law Enforcement." *Stanford Law Review* 50: 1055–1145.

Chaiken, Jan M., Peter W. Greenwood, and Joan Petersilia. (1977). "The Criminal Investigation Process: A Summary Report." *Policy Analysis* 3, 2: 187–217.

Ericson, Richard. (1993). *Making Crime: A Study of Detective Work.* Toronto, Canada: University of Toronto Press.

Fisher, Ronald P., and R. Edward Geiselman. (1992). *Memory-Enhancing Techniques for Investigative Interviewing: The Cognitive Interview.* Springfield, IL: Charles C Thomas.

Greenwood, Peter, Jan Chaiken, and Joan Petersilia. (1977). *The Criminal Investigation Process.* Lexington, MA: D. C. Heath.

Holmes, Ronald M. (1998). "Psychological Profiling Use in Serial Murder Cases." In *Contemporary Perspectives on Serial Murder,* edited by R. Holmes and S. Holmes. Thousand Oaks, CA: Sage, 173–186.

Horvath, Frank, Brian Jayne, and Joseph Buckley. (1994). "Differentiation of Truthful and Deceptive Criminal Suspects in Behavior Analysis Interviews." *Journal of Forensic Sciences* 39, 3: 793–807.

Horvath, Frank, and Robert Meesig. (1996). "The Criminal Investigation Process and the Role of Forensic Evidence: A Review of Empirical Findings." *Journal of Forensic Science* 41, 6: 963–969.

———. (1998). "A Content Analysis of Textbooks on Criminal Investigation: An Evaluative Comparison to Empirical Research Findings on the Investigative Process and the Role of Forensic Evidence." *Journal of Forensic Science* 43, 1: 125–132.

———. (2001). *A National Survey of Police Policies and Practices Regarding the Criminal Investigation Process: Twenty-Five Years after RAND.* Washington, DC: U.S. Department of Justice, National Institute of Justice.

Inbau, Fred, John Reid, Joseph Buckley, and Brian Jayne. (2001). *Criminal Interrogation and Confessions*, 4th ed. Gaithersburg, MD: Aspen.

Keppel, Robert, and William Birnes. (1995). *The Riverman*. New York: Pocket Books.

Nordby, Jon. (2000). *Dead Reckoning: The Art of Forensic Detection*. Boca Raton, FL: CRC Press.

Peterson, Joseph L., Steven Mihajlovic, and Michael Gilliland. (1984). *Forensic Evidence and the Police: The Effects of Scientific Evidence on Criminal Investigations*. Washington, DC: U.S. Department of Justice.

Ressler, Robert K., Ann W. Burgess, and John E. Douglas. (1988). *Sexual Homicide: Patterns and Motives*. Lexington, MA: Lexington Books.

Ressler, Robert K., and Thomas Shachtman. (1992). *Whoever Fights Monsters*. New York: St. Martin's.

———. (1997). *I Have Lived in the Monster*. New York: St. Martin's Press.

Rossmo, Kim D. (1993). "A Methodological Model." *American Journal of Criminal Justice* 17, 2: 1–21.

Simon, David. (1991). *Homicide: A Year on the Killing Streets*. Boston: Houghton Mifflin.

▼ FORENSIC INTERROGATION

The purpose of a forensic interview or interrogation is to obtain information relevant to a particular crime or incident. Investigators are constantly receiving information, both from other people and from their own analysis of evidence. Frequently, investigators must seek information from individuals, who may or may not be directly involved in the matter under investigation.

The process for gathering information from individuals is identified as either an interview or an interrogation. Typically, an interview involves discussions with people who are not suspected of any offense, such as an eyewitness to a crime. The term *interrogation* is often used when an investigator is questioning a person who is or could be a suspect in a crime. The line between an interview and an interrogation is not always clear; as the case proceeds and more information accumulates, what was first an interview may become an interrogation.

The goal for any such data-gathering process is to gain sufficient information to identify the people responsible for the offense and pursue appropriate legal action. Placing the type of inquiry neatly into a category of being either an interview or an interrogation is relatively unimportant, except insofar as there is a need to ensure the legal safeguards of any individual who may become a suspect. In this case, certain legal requirements must be carefully followed to insure that all information is obtained in an appropriate and legal fashion, and that it can later be used in a court of law.

INTERVIEWING

In most cases, law enforcement agents find it important to begin interviewing witnesses, victims, complainants, or others who might have useful information as soon as possible. This allows for the information to be fresh in the minds of the individuals and can help prevent "contamination" that might occur from their hearing each other's version of events. Also for this reason, individual interviews are often conducted separately.

If an investigator is to be successful in obtaining valuable information from either a suspect or a witness, he or she must possess excellent communication skills. A seasoned investigator must not only know what to say and what to avoid saying but must also be able to read an individual's verbal and nonverbal cues. This communications process can be fraught with pitfalls, and depending on the circumstance, the interviewer may want to spend some time preparing for the type of discussion that will occur and develop a plan to best achieve his or her goals.

Although conditions and timing are not always ideal, the interviewer should attempt to create an environment that is conducive to the process. Identifying a private location eliminates distractions, allows focus on the matter at hand, and removes concerns that a person may have about telling his or her story in front of others. A sense of rapport between the interviewer and the person being questioned is crucial; the interviewer should attempt to make the individual as comfortable as possible and be considerate of the person's emotional state, especially if he or she has just been a victim of a crime or has witnessed a disturbing event.

The physical environment can play an important role in the success of the interview or interrogation.

Depending on the circumstance, an interviewer may remove physical barriers, such as tables, desks, countertops, or other things that can separate the interviewer from the subject, psychologically as well as physically. A good interviewer will make the subject as comfortable as possible, for example by sitting rather than standing, and by providing encouraging verbal and physical cues to facilitate continued discussion.

The interviewer needs to ask questions that are easily understood by the subject, questions that are free from police jargon and terminology. The best questions to ask are open-ended and require more than a simple "yes" or "no" response. The interviewer should avoid any leading questions or questions that imply preexisting knowledge. For example, the interviewer may wish to ask, "What type of vehicle did you see leaving the scene?" rather than "Did you see the truck leave the scene?" The first question is open-ended, allowing the person to offer a full description of the vehicle that he or she may have observed; the second is worded in such a way that it could be answered with one word and assumes that the person knew that the vehicle in question was a truck.

The individual should be allowed to respond fully to the question that has been asked; important information may be missed if the interviewer interrupts, moves too quickly, or does not allow the individual to fully answer the question. One of the most important factors in the interview procedure is listening, an active process that can be more difficult than one might expect; it is important because the payoff for a carefully crafted question is the response provided by the subject. Therefore, interrupting or interjecting other issues is usually counterproductive. Furthermore, fully focusing on the person and what he or she is saying also allows the interviewer time to consider what the person is doing. Does the person appear nervous, embarrassed, guilty, or sad? Observing these behavioral and nonverbal cues can be just as important as listening to what the person is saying and can make a more effective interview process.

The interviewer must maintain the proper demeanor and attitude to be successful. Although there are times when certain emotions may work in favor of the interviewer, it is usually best to remain objective, avoiding expressions of anger or disdain. The most effective interviewers are those who can adapt to varying circumstances and individuals, are confident in their approach, have excellent communication skills,

maintain personal self-control, and can remain focused on the goal of the interview process. The interviewer must balance the desire to obtain information with the needs of the individual and the importance of insuring that all information is derived with legal protections intact. Keeping the goal of the investigation in mind and knowing how to prioritize can help keep the investigator on track.

THE COGNITIVE INTERVIEW APPROACH

One interviewing method that has been particularly useful for victims or witnesses who may have difficulty recalling certain events is the "cognitive interview approach" (CIA). In this approach, the subject is asked to recreate the setting of the event in his or her mind's eye, including how he or she may have felt, the weather, surroundings, people present, or other stimuli that might trigger a better recollection of critical details. This process must not involve leading or suggestive information by the interviewer, lest the information obtained become tainted. After the subject has these background details in mind, various techniques may be employed to enhance the recall of central events.

Using the CIA, a subject may be asked to focus and report on every aspect of the incident, including things that he or she may think are unimportant. It is essential that the investigator provide for the free flow of information and descriptions, and not interrupt the person providing the detail. The subject may also be asked to provide details in a reverse chronological order, or take the perspective of another person who was at or near the scene. These techniques can be valuable in eliciting new and useful information. More focused questions may follow, including asking for details of a person's appearance, his or her name, or manner of speech. It is sometimes useful to ask for comparisons of the person the subject saw with another the subject might know. For example, "Did this person remind you of anyone?" or "Was the name similar to another one you may have heard?"

The CIA can be very involved and time-consuming. Building a positive rapport with the subject and creating a quiet, well-suited environment are extremely important parts of the process. Further, this approach can be valuable for victims and witnesses, but is not usually appropriate for suspect interrogation in which constitutional rights regarding self-incrimination become salient.

INTERROGATION

Interrogational techniques involve many of the same elements as interview techniques. However, aside from the constitutional and legal protection issues, there may be other elements that are not always evident in an interview setting: A skilled interrogation involves not only eliciting useful and pertinent information but may involve subtle psychological cues that provide an easier avenue for a person who may wish to confess. Allowing the subject the opportunity for rationalization, ego enhancement, or minimizing of the crime or its effects may be useful. However, threats of violence, use of force, or other physical or psychological tactics are inappropriate, illegal, and do not help achieve the goal of a successful investigation and prosecution of a case.

Interviews and interrogations, like many issues faced by criminal justice professionals in a complex social world, are a mix of art, science, experience, and skill. Those asking the questions must be sensitive to the individual, the environment where the discussion occurs, and the psychology of the communication process. Ethical and legal issues must always be at the forefront of the investigator's mind to ensure that the goal of a successful investigation can be realized.

—R. L. Garner

See also DETECTION OF DECEPTION; FORENSIC POLYGRAPH; INTERROGATION

Further Reading

Garner, R. L. (1996). *Criminal Investigations Interviews.* Huntsville, TX: SHSU Press.

Inbau, Fred E., John E. Reid, Joseph P. Buckley, and Brian C. Jayne. (2001). *Criminal Interrogation and Confessions*, 4th ed. Gaithersburg, MD: Aspen.

Swanson, Charles, Neil Chamelin, and Leonard Territo. (1996). *Criminal Investigation.* New York: McGraw-Hill.

Weston, Paul, and Kenneth Wells. (1997). *Criminal Investigation: Basic Perspectives,* 7th ed. Upper Saddle River, NJ: Prentice Hall.

▼ FORENSIC POLYGRAPH

Since the recording of history, human beings have believed that certain physiological changes occur in individuals when they are lying. In ancient China, individuals accused of being deceptive were required to speak with their mouths full of dry rice. The person was determined to be truthful if the rice could be easily spewed out. If the rice stuck to the inside of the mouth, the person was assumed to be lying. Similarly, Egyptians and other peoples used a red-hot poker to determine an individual's truthfulness: The searing end of the poker was placed on the tongue of the accused, and if it sizzled and did not stick to the tongue, the individual was set free. If, however, the poker stuck to the tongue, the accused was deemed guilty and often promptly executed.

This primitive "lie detector" process does have some physiological basis. A person in a highly emotional state, fearing detection, could have difficulty forming saliva, which could cause the rice to stick to the sides of the mouth, and the poker to stick to the tongue. Unfortunately, the innocent as well as the guilty can be emotionally aroused when facing such a process. People can get a dry mouth from being excited, nervous, or fearful, all while telling the truth.

Although the validity of these techniques for the purpose of lie detection can be seriously questioned, the current state of the art for the psychophysiological detection of deception is somewhat more promising. Current polygraph instruments ("polygraph" meaning literally, "many writings or recordings") record tracings on paper or in computers of several different physiological measures. Most instruments used by licensed polygraph examiners have a minimum of three recording channels: the cardiosphygmograph, which measures relative changes in cardiovascular activity such as blood pressure and heart rate; the pneumograph, which measures changes in the thoracic area of the body (mostly due to respiration); and the galvanic skin response (GSR), which measures skin resistance or conductance. There are many other physiological measures that may be recorded, including cardiac activity monitors, plethysmographs (for measuring variations in the size of an organ or limb), and other instruments, to assess if the individual is attempting to employ countermeasures during the examination. Also, the use of computer programs for assessment of the physiological data has become commonplace.

POLYGRAPH TECHNIQUE

The term "lie detector" is misleading and is not used by most examiners or researchers: No instrument can determine if a person is telling the truth or telling a lie. The polygraph technique is a complicated mix of science, skill, and interrogational art that nonetheless makes the assessment of veracity difficult. Traditionally, many polygraph examiners arrive at an opinion based on a variety of factors in addition to interpreting the polygrams (recordings of the psychophysiological measures.)

In addition, there are numerous polygraph techniques and testing procedures available to the polygraphist. Depending on the examiner's training, the approach employed for the purpose of determining indications of deception can vary. Further, because different techniques may require special information or circumstances, the data available to the examiner may dictate the technique that is employed.

The Relevant-Irrelevant Technique

Polygraph examinations may involve several standardized methods, including the Relevant-Irrelevant (R-I) technique, the Control Question Technique (CQT) or the Guilty-Knowledge (G-K) test. In the R-I approach, the polygraph examiner asks the subject a series of questions, some relevant to the issue under investigation and some irrelevant. In this case the physiological recordings made during the irrelevant questions are compared with those made during the relevant items. The theory is that there will be little concern on the part of the subject about answering the irrelevant items, but if trying to be deceptive, the subject will exhibit physiological arousal from the relevant questions.

The Control Question Technique

The CQT technique involves a comparison of various zones in which the relevant questions are compared with noncritical "control" questions. Unlike the R-I technique, the control questions are designed in such a way that most subjects would not be completely truthful in their response to them, or not feel comfortable in answering them (e.g., "Have you ever stolen anything of value?"). The CQT theory assumes that a guilty subject would be less concerned with control questions, as they are of little significance in relation to the relevant questions. Conversely, the theory asserts that subjects who did not commit the offense under investigation would be more concerned with their lack of complete honesty on the control questions and less concerned with the relevant questions, which would be unrelated to their actual experience.

The CQT polygrams are usually scored using a method in which the control questions are compared to the relevant questions and assigned a numerical value based on the evaluation of at least three components of the polygraph recording. Total points for all polygraph charts are compiled and compared against predetermined cutoff values. These cutoff values assist the examiner in his or her determination of the truthfulness of the polygraph subject.

Guilty-Knowledge (G-K) Test

Another technique that tends to show a great amount of accuracy is the guilty-knowledge (G-K) test. This approach requires that there are case facts or information that only the investigators and those involved in the event or crime would know. A naive subject would have no knowledge of this privileged information. In a criminal case the G-K testing process would start with an introductory statement followed by several possible choices. The choices are appropriately spaced, usually fifteen seconds apart, so that each item can be individually assessed for any physiological activity.

For example, a G-K polygraph technique might be used in a robbery case in which only the police and the actual offender would have information about such things as method of entry, articles stolen, or type of weapon used. A separate G-K test could be used for each of these areas. When constructing such a test it is important that the padding choices are similar in nature to the key choice. The key choice is the correct information, while the padding choices are incorrect.

In the above scenario, the questioning sequence might be as follows:

"If you were the person who robbed the EZ Food Store, you would know exactly what type of weapon was used."

"Was it a club?"

"Was it a revolver?"

"Was it a knife?"

"Was it a shotgun?"

"Was it a crowbar?"

"Was it an automatic weapon?"

"Was it a lead pipe?"

Recall that each of these questions is separated by an appropriate interval of time. An innocent subject would have no idea which type of weapon was used; however, the individuals with the guilty knowledge would possess this information, which they would be trying to conceal. This testing procedure might include other questions about other aspects of the crime. A sequence could be developed for the property stolen, comments made by the offender at the crime scene, or any other relevant facts that would lend themselves to this process. The theory suggests that with each additional questioning series, the probability of an error, particularly a false positive, declines.

The G-K technique involves a comparison of all choices presented in each test, excluding the first choice, which is omitted to compensate for the possible startle effect at the beginning of the test. After asking the G-K question series the first time, the examiner usually repeats the test sequence, after a brief pause, in order to produce a number of polygrams for comparison. Field polygraph results are usually separated into one of three classifications: deceptive, truthful, or inconclusive. The G-K question that is associated with the most consistent physiological reaction is compared with the physiological reaction to the key choice.

POLYGRAPH PROCEDURE

There are typically several phases to the usual polygraph examination. Initially, after brief introductions, the subject is asked to fill out a questionnaire that asks relevant information helpful in the construction of the testing series. The examiner uses the information provided by the subject, as well as information pertinent to the issue under investigation, to create the questions that will be asked during the polygraph examination. The examiner typically attempts to establish some level of rapport with the subject and provides answers to questions from the subject regarding the polygraph instrument, the process, or the testing sequence. Typically, each question that will be asked during the exam will be presented to the subject for comment or modification before the process begins. Polygraph examinations, by their very nature, are voluntary. If the subject so requests, the examination will be discontinued.

After all questions have been satisfactorily worded, the examiner explains the polygraph instrumentation and places the measuring components on the subject. Basic attachments include a blood pressure (BP) cuff, one or more pneumotubes (measuring respiration), and GSR electrodes are placed on the nonconsecutive fingertips of one hand (opposite the one attached to the pressure cuff). Once the attachments are in place, the examiner tells the subject to relax but remain still

during the recording process. The BP cuff is then inflated and the testing process can begin.

Often, the examiner may start the process with a demonstration sequence that is unrelated to the matter under review. For example, the examiner may have the subject write down a number, or select a symbol or card from a series. The examiner may then attempt to identify the selection based on the physiological responses. This can serve to bolster the confidence of the truthful subject while increasing the concerns of the deceptive individual. After this process, the polygraph examination begins, with the examiner asking the questions previously crafted in unique order. The question series may be repeated a number of times (with brief pauses between each session) in order to get a clear indication.

VALIDITY OF RESULTS

The validity and reliability of polygraph results has been the subject of much debate. Legal issues have curtailed the once-widespread use of polygraph for preemployment purposes; however, polygraph testing continues to be a part of the hiring process for many sensitive areas such as law enforcement, security couriers, national defense personnel, and many federal agencies. Today, most active polygraph examiners are licensed and employed by federal, state, or local governmental agencies. Research involving polygraph techniques varies in its construction, methodology, and conclusions. Many studies further caution against the comparison to actual field settings of results in experimental studies involving few measurements and contrived scenarios, because the laboratory cannot dispense punishment or provide the type of perceived rewards that might proceed from the involvement in an actual criminal offense. While no clear conclusions can be offered from the conflicting data, certain techniques, such as the G-K technique, would seem to offer both face validity and empirical support. Having protected case facts creates a unique opportunity for investigators to use polygraph testing.

—*R. L. Garner*

See also DETECTION OF DECEPTION

Further Reading

Garner, R. L. (1989). *Guilty Knowledge Polygraph: The Effects of Examiner Experience and Education on Interpretation Accuracy*. Houston, TX: University of Houston-Clear Lake.

Reid, John, and Fred Inbau. (1977). *Truth and Deception*. Baltimore: Williams & Wilkins.

▼ FORENSIC SCIENCE

The word *forensic* means "public" in Latin and "forum" in French. Commonly, forensic scientists define their field as the application of the methods of the natural and physical sciences to matters of civil and criminal law. Forensic science can be involved not only in investigation and prosecution of crimes such as rape, murder, and drug dealing but also in matters where a crime has not been committed but in which someone is charged with a civil wrong, such as willful pollution of air or water or causing industrial injuries. Because of popular television programs such as *Quincy, M.E.,* many people equate forensic science with forensic pathology or forensic medicine. Clearly, forensic medicine is an important branch of forensic science, but it is only one of many areas of this field.

BRANCHES OF FORENSIC SCIENCE

Almost any science can be a forensic science because almost any science can contribute to solving a crime or evaluating a civil harm. In fact, with few exceptions, forensic sciences are no different in what they study than traditional sciences. The only difference is that forensic scientists apply the methods and techniques of established sciences to legal matters. For example, modern forensic DNA typing uses methods commonly employed by molecular biologists and geneticists to study chromosomes, genes, and DNA. The only difference is that forensic DNA typing is done on evidence from crimes or other legally scrutinized areas, such as disputed paternity.

Although it seems that all sciences are potentially forensic sciences, certain sciences often play an important role in the courts. One useful list of branches of forensic science can be gleaned from the divisions of the American Academy of Forensic Sciences. They list the following as their main sections: anthropology, criminalistics, engineering, general, jurisprudence, odontology, pathology/biology, psychiatry/behavioral science, questioned documents, and toxicology. The "general" section of the American Academy of Forensic Sciences, is more or less a catchall for disciplines that are not covered in the other sections. A short description of each of the other main areas of forensic science follows.

Forensic Anthropology

There are a number of applications of anthropology to the forensic sciences. A large part of physical anthropology deals with skeletal biology, which includes bone and bone system structures and their relationships to characteristics such as gender, age, race, socioeconomic status, and so forth. This knowledge can be applied to the examination of characteristics of skeletal remains that are part of a crime scene. In such cases, the goal of the analysis may be to determine the identity of the remains and, perhaps, the cause of death. To these ends, forensic anthropologists make use of a number of unique techniques.

Two major types of human remains evidence confront the forensic anthropologist. First is the single bone or bone fragment or small group of bones. When this is the only type of evidence present, the forensic anthropologist seeks to determine if the bone is human and, if not, what type of animal the bone belongs to. If the sample is human bone, then the anthropologist will determine the part of the body from which it came. For example, if a single human arm bone is recovered from a field, there will most likely be other human bones belonging to the same individual around also.

The second major type of forensic anthropological evidence is the complete, or nearly so, skeleton. From this evidence, the accomplished forensic anthropologist may be able to determine gender, race, approximate age, stature, and approximate socioeconomic status. If there is damage to some of the bones, the anthropologist may be able to determine what type of trauma caused it. If the skull is present, it may be possible to prepare an approximate face on the skull using skull superimposition—building a face out of clay using average thickness measurements developed by anatomists, pathologists, and anthropologists. Investigators may then publish a picture of this face to see if it evokes a response from a relative of a missing person. If a possible match to the skeleton is found and there are antemortem pictures available, then a new video superimposition technique may be used. This technique utilizes two cameras to superimpose the skull over the picture of the actual face to determine if that skull could be the right one.

How does one become a forensic anthropologist? There is a certification process for forensic anthropology in the United States, which requires that an applicant meet minimum standards in education and training. Typically, a forensic anthropologist will have a Ph.D. in physical anthropology and will also have taken course work in anatomy and physiology. There are some university-based courses and graduate degrees in forensic anthropology, but most forensic anthropologists get their training on the job, often working with more experienced colleagues.

Criminalistics

Criminalistics has the largest membership in the American Academy of Forensic Sciences and the most people employed in the field. It can be defined as the application of scientific methods to the recognition, collection, identification, and comparison of physical evidence generated by criminal or illegal civil activity. It also involves the reconstruction of these events by evaluation of the physical evidence and the crime scene.

Criminalists, usually called "forensic scientists," analyze evidence such as body fluids, to determine if DNA in those fluids matches blood found at a crime scene. Other forensic scientists may help identify, collect and evaluate physical evidence at a crime scene.

Forensic Engineering

Forensic engineering uses the concepts of mechanical, chemical, civil, and electrical engineering as tools in the reconstruction of crimes and accidents and the determination of their cause. A major component of this work involves traffic incident reconstruction. Forensic engineers use evidence such as skid marks; damage to cars and their positions after an incident; road and environmental conditions; injuries to drivers, passengers, and pedestrians; and witness accounts to determine what may have caused an accident. In developing their explanations, engineers may work in consort with forensic pathologists, toxicologists, criminalists, and other engineers. Some forensic engineers specialize in marine incidents or aircraft crashes.

Another major area of forensic engineering is in failure analysis. Mechanical, chemical, civil, and structural engineers all bring their skills to bear on problems involving how and why buildings or other structures deteriorate or fail prematurely. An example of this is the collapse of a balcony high above the lobby of the Kansas City Hyatt Regency Hotel, which killed and injured many people. Forensic engineers were called in to determine why the balcony collapsed.

A somewhat unusual application of forensic engineering involves animals on farms where high voltage power lines or communication transmission lines pass overhead. For many years, there have been suggestions

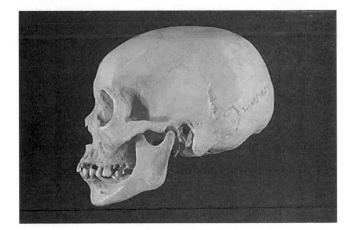

Human skull.

by farmers that transients from these power lines affect the health of their animals, including cows' ability to give milk. Many electrical engineers have studied this problem and cases have ended up in court.

Forensic engineers are usually educated engineers who have earned their Ph.D.s and who develop expertise in one or more of the forensically important disciplines. There are no university graduate programs in forensic engineering, so most of the expertise is developed on the job, perhaps working with more experienced practitioners.

Jurisprudence

Lawyers comprise most of the jurisprudence section of the American Academy of Forensic Sciences. They have a strong interest in the legal aspects of the status of scientific evidence in the courts. They study and comment on the admissibility of scientific evidence, especially new types of evidence. They are also concerned with the role of forensic science in general in the criminal justice system and about ethical issues as they apply to judges and lawyers. Some of these lawyers have a strong background themselves in scientific issues and are well positioned to work with other lawyers and scientists on these matters.

Forensic Odontology

Perhaps a more familiar term for this branch would be forensic dentistry. There are several important applications of dentistry to the forensic sciences. One of the longest standing and most important is the identification of a body from its dentition. This may be the only reliable way of identifying human remains in mass disasters, such as airplane crashes, fires, or wars. A body may be too badly damaged to have any fingerprints or useable DNA for typing, but dentition is very hardy and can survive crashes, fires, and even explosions. The forensic dentist can obtain an X-ray of the surviving teeth and compare it to antemortem dental X-rays. Of course, there must be some information about the possible identity of the body, and there must be some antemortem X-rays available for comparison. Almost anyone who has been to a dentist will have dental X-rays on file, so the main difficulty in this type of analysis is knowing whose X-rays to compare to the dental remains. A comparison of dental X-rays can lead to a definitive identification.

Forensic dentists also have an important role in the analysis of facial injuries received in a suspected battering. This is especially important in the case of children who may be brought to an emergency room at a hospital with facial injuries. A forensic dentist may be able to verify or refute a claim that the injuries were accidental, as a result of falling down a flight of stairs, for example. In this type of analysis, the forensic dentist will work closely with emergency room physicians and nurses and perhaps forensic pathologists.

A relatively recent application of forensic dentistry is in the area of bite mark analysis. In many sex crime and homicide situations, the perpetrator may bite the victim. Often these are deep bites that persist for a long time, especially if the victim is bitten after death. During the postmortem exam, the pathologist can take a cast of the bite mark using dental plaster or some other medium. This cast can be compared to a cast taken of the suspect's dentition. Everyone's teeth are believed to be unique in their bite surfaces (taken as a whole) and thus, this comparison can individualize the bite mark to a particular person.

This type of evidence can show up in a variety of crimes. During one reported case of burglary in England, the perpetrator evidently got hungry and bit off a piece of Swiss cheese, leaving a bite mark that was traced back to his mouth! A more serious and notorious case where bite mark evidence was important was the Theodore Bundy case. Bundy was believed to have killed more than forty people during his life, most of them young women. One of his habits was to bite his victims, often after they were dead. This was the case during his last killing in Florida. A forensic odontologist, Dr. Lowell Levine, was able to match a bite mark impression taken from the victim's flesh to Bundy's dentition. This was pivotal evidence in Bundy's conviction.

Forensic dentists are, of course, first and foremost dentists. They should have a particular interest and expertise in taking and interpreting dental X-rays or bite marks, or they should have some special training or expertise in the interpretation of facial injuries.

Forensic Pathology and Biology

This is a very large group in the forensic science field. The best known and largest subgroup is forensic pathology. In cases of suspicious death, a forensic pathologist is charged with determining the cause and manner of death. Each state has its own regulations that govern what constitutes a forensic case, and each state has a system set up to accomplish the tasks of forensic pathology. Many states have a medical examiner system, in which a city or county will have a chief medical examiner, who must be a physician. The chief medical examiner will, in turn, have a number of associate medical examiners who perform the actual duties of the forensic pathologist. Other states have a coroner system, in which the chief officer may not be a physician but employs forensic pathologists to carry out the necessary duties.

Forensic pathologists have three major duties to perform. They are called to crime scenes to make a preliminary examination of the body and perhaps an initial determination of the postmortem interval (the time since death). They will take charge of the body and direct the trained death scene investigators to carefully prepare and remove the body and transport it to the morgue for later analysis.

Forensic pathologists determine the cause and manner of death by use of the postmortem examination or autopsy. This involves a careful dissection of the body to search for injury patterns, disease, or poisoning that point to the ultimate cause of death. In this activity, the forensic pathologist will work closely with forensic toxicologists, who take tissue samples and determine what, if any, substances may be in the body that could have caused or contributed to death. Forensic pathologists also work closely with the criminal investigators so as to get a complete picture of the circumstances surrounding the death. At times, the forensic pathologist may consult with forensic anthropologists or entomologists in helping to reach relevant conclusions about the cause and manner of death.

When a person dies, a physician must fill out and

sign a death certificate. In all forensic cases, the certificate must list a manner of death. The possible manners of death are homicide, accident, suicide, and natural causes. In some states, one of these four must be listed. In other states, the pathologist is also permitted to enter "undetermined" or a variant. Although this determination may be straightforward in a normal case, it can be very problematic in a death of suspicious origin.

The final duty of the forensic pathologist is to render opinions in court as to the cause and manner of death. Medical examiners and coroners are called to court quite often and must be able to present their testimony without shocking the jury with gory photographs. Many times, judges will limit or not admit such photos for fear of prejudicing the jury.

Forensic pathologists are physicians who specialize in pathology through a residency that may take three to four years beyond medical school. An additional one-year residency in forensic pathology will enable a pathologist to become certified in forensic pathology. There is a shortage of qualified forensic pathologists in the United States today, and this is a critical need. In complicated death cases, it is easy for an untrained pathologist to make a mistake in determination of the cause and manner of death, which may lead to a miscarriage of justice. It is therefore important to encourage pathologists to become certified if they are going to be doing forensic work.

In addition to forensic pathology, there are other biological sciences that have important forensic applications, including forensic entomology. It has been said that the first visitors to a corpse, especially one left outdoors, are insects. Many different types of insects will seek out a corpse and inhabit it for a short time, to deposit their eggs or larvae and feed on the body. The role of the forensic entomologist is mainly to help determine the postmortem interval by examining which insect populations inhabit the body. Certain insects will attack the body right after death, whereas others will wait until some decay has taken place. Knowledge of this pattern of insect succession can give important information about when the person died. This takes a great deal of training and education because there are many environmental factors, such as temperature, humidity, moisture, burial conditions, type of clothing, that can affect the postmortem interval. There have been poisoning cases in which the only source of the poison after decay of a body was the insects who had ingested the poison. Strictly speaking, this is not part of forensic entomology, but it does involve insect behavior after death.

Most forensic entomologists are employed by universities full time and will lend their knowledge and skills to law enforcement agencies on an as-needed basis. Very few people practice forensic entomology as their only vocation.

Psychiatry and Behavioral Science

The general area of behavioral forensic science has expanded greatly in recent years. Forensic psychiatrists (and to some extent psychologists) have long been involved in determining if a person is mentally competent to stand trial and aid in his or her own defense. Although each state has its own standards for determining responsibility, the question usually boils down to whether a defendant had the mental capacity to form an intent to commit a crime. Intent is usually considered to be a prime factor in determining if a crime has been committed.

In addition to this role of the behavioral forensic scientist, there are several other emerging duties. One is in the area of psychological crime scene reconstruction and psychological profiling. Recent movies, TV shows, and books, as well as real cases, have elevated this important function in the mind of the public. People who repeat the same type of crime are known as serial criminals. Such people usually have particular motivations and reasons for committing this type of crime and will tend to form behavioral patterns that show up time after time. A trained behavioral scientist can uncover some of these patterns and help predict when, how, and against whom the serial criminal will strike next. This may enable the police to head off the next crime in the series. In addition, ritualistic behavior by serial criminals may result in crime scene clues that can enable a behavioral scientist to develop a physical and psychological profile of the perpetrator, which can help the police narrow down the search for an unknown criminal.

Behavioral scientists also engage in other activities that are less well known to the public. They may be called upon to develop a physical and behavioral profile of a likely airplane hijacker so that airport security personnel can look out for such people and pay extra attention to their movements in the airport.

A very important role of a behavioral forensic scientist is in interviewing and interrogating suspects and witnesses to crimes. These processes may involve the use of a polygraph to help determine the veracity of a statement being given by a witness or suspect. Scien-

---

On the Use of Science to Solve Crimes

The outline given by Nigel Morland shows how far science can go in the examination of inanimate clues. The extent to which this knowledge can be used in actual inquiries is well worth consideration. Does the knowledge, for instance, form an integral, if unadvertised, part of the detective's equipment, or is it used only in abnormal cases when all other methods have failed?

1. The Uses of Science

A general answer cannot be given to such a postulation, but the possibilities of scientific criminology have been sketched in such a manner that their value will become apparent: the use to which science is put depends to a remarkable extent on the national outlook.

Some countries, in crime investigation as in other spheres of human activity, seem eager to adopt every aid that science can supply; others use the scientific method more sparingly, and as an adjunct to routine inquiry rather than as a normal part of it.

It is an old principle in government that the resources of science should not be called upon until the rule-of-thumb method has shown its disadvantages. Science has always marched a long way ahead of the official outlook—indeed, of the average outlook—that is why science is frequently not used until too late.

Source: Morland, Nigel. (1950). *An Outline of Scientific Criminology.* New York: Philosophical Library, Inc., p. 241.

---

tists who engage in these activities must not only be well trained in the behavioral sciences but must also have an intimate knowledge of police procedures and criminology.

Behavioral scientists usually have advanced degrees in psychiatry or clinical psychology or criminology. They also usually have some type of law enforcement experience that enables them to understand the behavioral aspects of crime.

Questioned Documents

Questioned document analysis involves a number of areas of forensic inquiry. It is an apprenticeship field, requiring years of practice and work with an experienced examiner. The most familiar area of questioned document examination is handwriting comparison. Here the examiner is called upon to determine if a particular person was the author of a document. The examiner compares characteristics of the questioned document to those of a document either previously written by the suspect or purposely taken as a known handwriting sample, also called an exemplar. There are no universal standards for the number of characteristics that must be present in order for the document examiner to conclude that a particular person was the author of a document. It is up to the individual examiner to determine when there is sufficient evidence.

Forensic document examiners may also be called upon to determine if a particular instrument made a typewritten or printed document or if a particular copier made a copy of a document. Unless there are some unusual characteristics or defects in the instrument, it is generally not possible to determine this definitively.

Document examiners are also called upon to examine alterations in documents such as erasures, addition of material, obliterated writing, charred documents. This involves chemical analysis as well as physical and observational techniques. Examiners are frequently asked, as well, to determine the age of a document. Often this involves documents handwritten in ink. A document may consist of a number of entries made at different times, and questions may arise as to whether a particular entry was made when it was purported to have or it was entered at a much later time. In other cases, the age of an entire document may be called into question. The determination of the age of the ink on a document is accomplished by uncovering changes in the chemical composition of the ink that take place over time. A similar type of analysis may also be done on the paper, especially if ink was not used to write the document.

TOXICOLOGY

Toxicology is the analysis and interpretation of poisons and drugs in the body. Forensic toxicology applies this analytical science to cases where death or injury may be caused by the ingestion of drugs or poisons. By far, the most common application of toxicology to forensic science is in cases involving drunk or drugged driving. Such cases comprise more than half of all toxicology cases in the United States.

Every state has a set of laws that govern the use of alcohol while operating or driving a motor vehicle.

Each state sets limits for the permissible level of alcohol in a driver's bloodstream. Usually there are two categories of intoxication: impaired and under the influence. The latter requires a higher concentration of alcohol. In many states, merely having a blood-alcohol level greater than the limit constitutes an offense; in other states, there must also be a demonstration that the driver was actually impaired or under the influence of alcohol. This demonstration is accomplished by requiring the driver to undergo a series of motor coordination tests.

The role of the forensic toxicologist in such cases is to measure the quantity of alcohol in the body, usually by blood analysis, and then to be able to explain the effects of the quantity on the person's ability to drive. Toxicologists are often asked to "back calculate" what the alcohol concentration may have been at an earlier time, although this can be a difficult undertaking owing to the large number of variables.

In recent years, forensic toxicologists have also been called upon to interpret cases where a driver has been taking a drug, usually illicit, such as marijuana, and then driving. There are no established limits for the amount of a drug that can be present in order for a driver to be impaired or under the influence. Therefore, a forensic toxicologist must be intimately familiar with the effects of many types of drugs on motor coordination. In many states, the presence of any amount of a drug that can be reliably detected by a forensic toxicologist constitutes enough to affect the driver.

In addition to drunk or drugged driving cases, forensic toxicologists handle cases where there has been an overdose of an illicit drug, which may contribute to or cause death. The toxicologist must be able to determine blood levels of the drugs or their metabolites and to interpret these findings and ascertain the role that this drug played in the death. In many cases, more than one drug is taken or a drug may be taken in conjunction with alcohol, and the toxicologist must be able to interpret the interactions among these substances. In these cases, the toxicologist works closely with the forensic pathologist.

In recent years, many companies and public organizations such as police and fire departments have been concerned about the use of drugs by employees on the job. Many drug-testing programs have been set up to measure drug concentrations in workers on a routine or random basis. These laboratories virtually always employ one or more forensic toxicologists to maintain standards, offer training to technicians, and take overall responsibility for the laboratory. Mostly such labs test urine samples donated by employees. Some of the more progressive of the drug testing labs have gotten away from urine testing and now use head hair for drug testing. This is far superior to urine as a medium for drug testing in that it is less invasive to obtain and can give a drug history of many months duration, unlike urine testing, which provides only a "snapshot" of what drugs may be present. Also, hair testing is not subject to some of the manipulations that plague urine testing such as the use of diuretics to flush out the drugs from the urine.

SUMMARY

Forensic science is the part of the criminal investigation process that involves the use of scientific methods to evaluate evidence. Any scientific endeavor that has an application in the arena of justice can be a forensic science. Forensic scientists must not only be competent in the analysis and interpretation of evidence in their area of specialty, but they must also be effective witnesses in court.

—*Jay A. Siegel*

See also ANTHROPOLOGY, FORENSIC; COGNITIVE INTERVIEWING; CRIME LABORATORY; CRIMINALISTICS; DETECTION OF DECEPTION; DNA TESTING; EXPERT WITNESS; FIREARMS IDENTIFICATION; FORENSIC BEHAVIORAL SCIENCES; FORENSIC INTERROGATION; FORENSIC POLYGRAPH; MEDICAL EXAMINER; ODONTOLOGY; PSYCHIATRY, FORENSIC; PSYCHOLOGY, FORENSIC; SCIENTIFIC EVIDENCE; TOXICOLOGY; VOICE IDENTIFICATION

Further Reading

DeMaio, Vincent et al. (2001). *Forensic Pathology*, 2d ed. Boca Raton, FL: CRC Press.

Eckert, William (1996). *Introduction to Forensic Sciences*. Boca Raton, FL: CRC Press.

Fisher, Barry (2000). *Techniques in Crime Scene Investigation*, 6th ed. Boca Raton, FL: CRC Press.

Gerber, Samuel, and Richard Saferstein, eds. (1997). *More Chemistry and Crime*. Washington, DC: American Chemical Society

Houck, Max, ed. (2000). *Mute Witnesses*. San Diego, CA: Academic Press

Inman, Keith, and Nora Rudin. (2000). *Principles and Practice of Criminalistics: The Profession of Forensic Science*. Boca Raton, FL: CRC Press.

Ressler, Robert et al. (1994). *Whoever Fights Monsters*. New York: St. Martin's.

Saferstein, Richard (2001). *Criminalistics: An Introduction to Forensic Science,* 7th ed. Englewood Cliffs, NJ: Prentice Hall.

Swanson, Charles (1999). *Criminal Investigation*, 7th ed. New York: McGraw-Hill.

▼ FORGERY

When one thinks about the crime of forgery, the image of a skilled artist working delicately with tiny brushes on official documents such as a passport or driver license may come to mind. After altering the document, the forger's goal is to pass it off as genuine, thus fooling the person who accepts it. For example, in an effort to purchase alcohol illegally, a young person may change the date of birth on a driver license from eighteen to twenty-one. Alterations may be made using traditional tools, such as grease pencils and fine ink brushes, or by employing more technologically advanced equipment (e.g., optical scanners, inkjet printers, desktop publishing, and image enhancement software).

Although such activities may appear harmless, forgery is a serious crime. Title 18 of the United States Code (18 U.S.C.), Chapter 25, provides penalties of up to twenty years for producing fake or altered currency (commonly referred to as counterfeiting), or for changing the dollar amount or payee signature on government obligations such as savings bonds and treasury checks. In 1996, Section 514 was added to 18 U.S.C. This section allows the U.S. Department of Justice and the Department of the Treasury to actively investigate and prosecute persons who use forged documents to commit other forms of fraud.

A HISTORICAL PERSPECTIVE

The word *forgery* derives from the French *forger*, which means to make or fabricate. While the majority of modern day acts of forgery are perpetrated for financial gain, early forgeries were produced in order to expand power or prestige. Perhaps the most famous example is the Donation of Constantine (*Donatio Constantini*). Allegedly written by Emperor Constantine the Great and addressed to Pope Sylvester I, the document ceded authority for the western half of the former Roman Empire to the Roman Church. The document also describes Constantine's conversion to Christianity, including his baptism, profession of faith, and the subsequent miraculous end to his leprosy. In reality the document was produced sometime between 750 and 850 CE, most likely to aid Pope Stephen II in his negotiations with Pepin the Short, who was seeking to supplant the ruling Merovingian royal family. After Pope Stephen II anointed Pepin king in 754, the church was given a large tract of land in Italy, based at least in part

on the forged Donation, which provided a basis for papal territorial claims in Italy. The forgery was uncovered in the fifteenth century by Lorenzo Valla, who used a variety of historical analytical techniques to discredit the document. Similarly, chemical analysis of the Iron Crown of Charlemagne, the first Holy Roman Emperor, found that the beeswax used to hold several of the gemstones in place dated to between 700 and 780 CE, twenty years prior to Charlemagne's coronation on December 25, 800. More recently radiocarbon dating was successfully used to examine the authenticity a written account of the conquest of Peru by Francisco Pizarro (1474–1541).

Although the use of forgery to gain political influence or garner prestige is historically significant, the majority of forgeries alluded to in the criminal code pertain to acts committed for financial gain. Indeed, throughout history, people have attempted to produce copies or replicas of items with tangible value, such as deeds to property, money, or well-known works of art. Roman artists frequently copied Greek sculptures, and counterfeit coins have been found dating back to the reign of King Gyges of Lydia (c. 648 BCE). Often these copies were passed to unsuspecting merchants or buyers who assumed they were genuine. In the time of the Old Testament, representing something as legitimate that the merchant or seller knew was not authentic was a punishable offense. Exodus 20:16 states, "You shall not bear false witness against your neighbor." The Western legal tradition refers to such misrepresentation as fraud, or theft by deception. One of the most common forms of fraud is the forgery of financial instruments, such as currency, checks, bonds, and postage stamps.

Financial instrument forgery and currency counterfeiting are not new problems. Fraudulent coins dating back to the thirteenth and fourteenth centuries have been uncovered in the collections of French art patrons. Well-respected Italian artists, including Giovanni Cavino and Pirro Ligorio, were considered experts in the forging of counterfeit coins during the sixteenth century. In the United States, by the time of the Civil War in 1861, nearly one-third of currency and treasury obligations in general circulation were fake. Compounding this problem was the wide range of designs—more than 1,600—used by the states during the period 1793–1861. It was often difficult for merchants, customers, and even banks to determine if financial instruments were genuine, or simply the product of an artist with an active imagination. The passage of the Act of July 17, 1861, which authorized the U.S. Treasury Department to print and circulate demand notes ("greenbacks"), and the issuance of U.S. Notes in 1862 helped standardize U.S. paper money. Printing of national bank notes (1863–1929) and silver certificates (1878–1923), coupled with the passage of the Federal Reserve Act of 1913—which established the National Federal Reserve System and authorized issuance of the Federal Reserve bank note—further aided in defining U.S. national monetary instruments, and reducing opportunities for forgers and counterfeiters.

While counterfeiting and alteration of financial documents have been the most common forms of forgery, a variety of other documents have been produced, depending on various social and economic events. During the U.S. Civil War, for example, fake military orders frequently allowed spies to travel behind enemy lines to obtain secret tactical information. During the period that Adolph Hitler and the Nazis ruled Germany, Jews and others who were fortunate enough to obtain forged travel papers or counterfeit passports were able to escape death in the concentration camps located throughout Nazi-controlled areas of Europe.

In the United States and Western Europe, World War II required that citizens give up many common items such as sugar, rubber, tin, and gasoline. U.S. and British citizens were issued ration cards and coupon books that had to be presented to government officials in exchange for limited amounts of these good. These cards and coupons were frequently forged. After World War II, Dutch painter Hans van Meegeren (1884–1947) was arrested and convicted for producing a number of forged Vermeers and Pieter de Hoochs paintings. Van Meegeren's forgeries were so accurate that he was able to fool many of the most eminent art critics of his time. The artist argued that he had produced the forgeries in an effort to keep the originals out of the hands of the Third Reich. Based upon this argument Van Meegeren's sentence was reduced from treason to forgery. He spent about one year in prison.

During the 1980s through the early 1990s, a series of trade and tariff disputes between the United States and emerging markets in Asia resulted in limited amounts of goods being exported from the United States, and curtailed the import of products from the Pacific Rim. To make up for these shortages, both within the United States and abroad, a substantial amount of counterfeit merchandise—auto parts, baby formula, medical devices, cosmetics, and jewelry—found its way into U.S. and foreign markets. Such items were generally inferior in quality, and in some cases were actually unsafe.

Document forgery continues to prove problematic for scholars, historians, and serious collectors of artifacts. In 1997, the Jones Library in Amherst, Massachusetts, purchased an "original" Emily Dickinson poem at auction for $24,150. The item was subsequently determined to be a forgery, produced by skilled artisan Mark Hofmann. Hofmann, who admitted producing and selling copies of fictitious historical documents linked to the Church of Jesus Christ of Latter-day Saints, was sentenced to ten years imprisonment in the 1980s on two counts of second-degree murder in the deaths of Steven F. Christensen and Kathleen Webb Sheets. The murders occurred on the morning Hofmann and Christensen were scheduled to close a deal on the sale of the McLellin Collection, a fictitious series of documents that Hofmann claimed to have in his possession.

The late 1990s saw a rapid increase in the counterfeiting of software and information technology equipment. In 1999 alone, the U.S. firm Lucent Technologies uncovered more than 103 reels of counterfeit SYSTI-MAX Power Sum 1061 copper cable, and 130 cases of counterfeit SYSTIMAX products in various retail outlets within the Republic of China. On October 25, 2000, Adaptec Inc., an electronic information storage provider located in Milpitas, California, seized more than $1 million in counterfeit software and peripherals from six U.S. companies. Similarly, Microsoft Corporation, the largest provider of computer operating systems in the world, seized more than $1 million worth of counterfeit software from two Georgia businesses that were allegedly distributing unauthorized versions of Windows 98 and Office 2000. U.S. law allows for penalties of up to $2 million and ten years imprisonment for each incident of breach of trademark and copyright infringement.

More recently, law enforcement officials have begun to see an influx in altered and counterfeit source documents. Source documents, sometimes referred to as foundation records, are a means of establishing personal identity for the purpose of establishing credit, conducting financial transactions, or gaining access to areas or information not generally available to the public. Examples of source documents include birth certificates, social security cards, driver licenses, vehicle registrations and titles, high school and college transcripts, and tax records and business forms. Forged or counterfeit foundation records are used to obtain credit cards, secure mortgages, and purchase automobiles or other luxury items. In some cases the forger will surreptitiously obtain personal information from an unsuspecting victim, construct an altered or counterfeit source document, and use this information to purchase goods and services. This type of offense, known as identity fraud, is becoming increasingly common in the United States and other industrialized nations.

METHODS

Since the 1990s, the availability of inexpensive personal computers, and low-cost, high-quality image scanners and color printers has led to an increase in counterfeit currency, altered source documents, and false identification. Improved video graphics adapters (VGA) and audio drivers (MIDI) have greatly enhanced the quality of images that can be transmitted via the Internet. Despite the romanticized image of forgers such as Ivan Miassojedof and Sali Smolianoff, who painstakingly produced U.S. $100 federal reserve notes in post World War II Germany, using their own engraving plates, inks and papers, the majority of modern counterfeit currency is hastily produced using low-cost image scanners and color printers. Referred to by the U.S. Secret Service as "casual counterfeiters," these individuals use a variety of techniques. Some pass "raised notes" by gluing the corner of a higher denomination bill to the corner of a lower denomination bill and fanning several of these notes together—with just the corners exposed—at a bar, nightclub, or other location where currency is exchanged quickly and without thorough inspection. Others use black and white, monochromatic, or color copiers to produce high-quality reproductions of genuine U.S. currency. The higher the image quality, the more likelihood that the note will not be questioned. In some cases, black-and-white currency is hand-colored by the suspect or another party involved in the offense. High-quality counterfeit notes (called "*P-notes*") can be produced using an inkjet printer (i.e., a computer printer that employs water-soluble ink). Armed with an inexpensive graphic editing software program, the forger can further alter or enhance the counterfeit note, thus improving the odds that it will be successfully passed.

A variety of paper is used to simulate the unique feel and texture of genuine U.S. currency. Ivory-laid medium stock paper is frequently used. In some cases, a suspect may attempt to draw fibers of various colors on the paper prior to printing in an effort to replicate the fibers found in genuine U.S. notes. False watermarks and security threads can also be copied onto the counterfeit note either prior to, or after printing, thus creating the appearance that the note is genuine. Lastly, black and green glitter may be used to simulate the color-shifting ink found in authentic U.S. paper currency.

Many of the techniques employed by the casual counterfeiter are also employed for other types of forgeries. Scores of fictitious identification Web sites can be found on the Internet where, for a small fee, identity templates such as driver licenses, birth certificates, and college transcripts can be downloaded to a personal computer. Using inexpensive desktop publishing software the forger is able to construct an alternate identity that can be used to obtain genuine credit cards, cash counterfeit checks, and conduct other illicit transactions. Legitimate check printing programs can be used to produce authentic-looking checks for fictitious persons or business. Genuine checks from a business or an individual can be captured electronically using an optical scanner. Subsequently, the payee name, dollar amount, and authorized signature can be altered using desktop publishing software, and the document can be printed on commercial check stock, readily available at most office and stationary stores.

Counterfeit or altered credit cards can also be easily produced. Credit card number generating software programs such as Credit Master, Card Pro, and Credit Wizard are available via the Internet, and are not illegal to possess. These programs generate the same logarithmic tables used by major credit card companies to issue valid card numbers to new members. Used in concert with a high-quality color printer or silk-screening kit, and an embossing device, counterfeit credit cards ("white plastic") can be produced on plastic card stock. More experienced computer users can download a card number generated by these software programs to a magnetic stripe and affix it to the back of the counterfeit credit card. Working in partnership with a dishonest merchant, account information is entered on charge slips, or the magnetic stripe is swiped into a point of sale terminal, completing the transaction. As new forms of technology emerge, it is likely that the forger will be limited only by their imagination with respect to the range of possible unlawful activities.

CHARACTERISTICS OF THE FORGER

Today's casual counterfeiters and forgers are often motivated by the hope of immediate financial gain.

Between 1986 and 1995 the United States saw an increase in arrests for forgery and counterfeiting of 31 percent, from 64,005 to 84,068. During this same period arrests of juveniles for forgery and counterfeiting rose nationally from 5,968 to 6,103 (2.3 percent). By 1999, the U.S. Secret Service had determined that nearly 15 percent of all arrests for producing counterfeit currency created using an optical scanner, computer, and inkjet printer involved juveniles.

The rapid increase in youth involvement in forgery and fraud has led to the development of the theory of consumptive criminality. Consumptive criminality is defined as "the commission of a non-violent, non-drug related, illegal act, by a juvenile, exclusively for the purpose of immediate financial gain"(Brightman 2000: 1). Young offenders have also been apprehended for similar offenses such as forging college transcripts, counterfeiting audio CDs for sale or distribution, and creating fictitious Web sites used to trap credit card information used for purchasing luxury items such as stereos, televisions, and computers, jewelry, and designer clothing.

LAW ENFORCEMENT

Federal, state, and local law enforcement agencies play a crucial role in combating forgery and counterfeiting within the United States and abroad. Agencies such as the U.S. Secret Service (established in 1861 to curtail the circulation of counterfeit currency) and the U.S. Customs Service (created in 1789 for the purpose of collecting duties and tariffs on imported goods) have seen their roles expand in recent years to include the investigation of check forgery, credit card fraud, and the distribution of counterfeit merchandise. Other federal law enforcement entities such as the Federal Bureau of Investigation, the Department of State, and the U.S. Marshals Service also participate in the investigation and apprehension of individuals involved in the production of fictitious forms of identity, and the commission of other crimes through identity fraud.

State and local law enforcement agencies are the first line of defense in the battle against forgery and counterfeiting, and often serve as the point of initial contact for most victims. The majority of cases in this area tend to be brought to court at the state level. As forging capabilities become enhanced through technology, so do opportunities for detection and apprehension. Through radiocarbon dating, variable wavelength light source illumination, and ink analysis, law enforcement agencies are better able to identify forgeries. By developing ink and paper databases and the extensive cataloging of specimens, analysts are quickly able to determine the geographic region in which the counterfeit note or forgery was produced, and dispatch investigators to the scene.

With reported losses from forgery and counterfeiting estimated to be $200 billion in the United States alone, and international losses far higher, such incidents are a matter of great concern for law enforcement agencies and businesses throughout the world. Considering the increases in prices that result from product counterfeiting, and the possible safety issues associated with inferior, defective products, such crimes must also not be taken lightly by the general public.

SUMMARY

Although forgery can take many forms, from fictitious deeds and faux pieces of art to counterfeit currency and altered obligations, the motivation for nearly all such acts is financial. As technology continues to improve the production of high-quality copies of items with tangible value, and public access to personal information becomes commonplace, incidents of forgery are likely to increase.

—*Hank J. Brightman*

See also ART THEFT AND FRAUD; IDENTITY THEFT; QUESTIONED DOCUMENTS/INK DATING

Further Reading

Anonymous. (1998). *How to Create a New Identity.* Secaucus, NJ: Citadel Press.

Brightman, Heath Jordan. (2000). *The Four "C's" of Education: A Study of the Relationships Between New Jersey's Children, Curricula, Computers, and Consumptive-Criminality.* Ann Arbor, MI: University Microfilms International.

Clifton, E., and McLaughlin, J. (1904). *A New Dictionary of the French and English Languages.* New York: David McKay.

Geis, Gilbert, Robert F. Meier, and Lawrence M. Salinger. (1995). *White-Collar Crime: Classic and Contemporary Views.* New York: Free Press.

Rosoff, Stephen M., Henry, N. Pontell, and Robert Tillman. (1998). *Profit Without Honor: White-Collar Crime and the Looting of America.* Saddle River, NJ: Prentice Hall.

Schlegel, Kip and David Weisburd, eds. (1992). *White-Collar Crime Reconsidered.* Boston: Northeastern University Press.

Wang, Wallace. (1998). *Steal This Computer Book: What They Won't Tell You About the Internet.* San Francisco: No Starch Press.

Wells, Joseph T. (1992). *Fraud Examination: Investigative and Audit Procedures.* Westport, CT: Quorum Books.

▼ FRANCE

The French Republic is located in Western Europe and borders the nations of Belgium, Luxembourg, Switzerland, and Italy on the west and Spain on the south. It faces the English Channel to the north, the Atlantic Ocean to the west, and the Mediterranean Sea on the southeast. France covers 212,935 square miles and has a resident population of some 60 million, including 3.2 million foreigners. The population is 72 percent Catholic, 8 percent Muslim, 2 percent Protestants, 1 percent Jewish, 1 percent Buddhist, and 6 percent unaffiliated. The national language is French, although there are several regional languages as well (Basque, Breton, Catalan, Corsican, Dutch, German, and Provencal). Greater powers of self-government were granted to the overseas departments of Guyana, Guadeloupe, Martinique, and Reunion in 1982; these former colonies had enjoyed departmental status since 1946, and regional status since 1974. France also encompasses the "territorial collectivities" of Mayotte, St. Pierre, and Miquelon, and the overseas territories of French Polynesia, New Caledonia, Wallis and Futunas.

France is a republic. The legislative branch is bifurcated: The two-house Parliament consists of a Senate, indirectly elected by an electoral college, and the National Assembly, directly elected by popular vote. The government is headed by the prime minister (Lionel Jospin, since June 1997) who is nominated by the General Assembly, and appointed by the popularly elected president (Jacques Chirac, since May 1995) who is chief of state.

France operates under the civil law tradition (as distinguished from the common law tradition). The Code Napoléon, the French civil code, enacted in 1804, was the main influence on the civil codes of many nations of continental Europe and Latin America. Criminal justice is based on inquisitorial rather than adversarial principles. The *juge d'instruction* is arguably the most important figure, a magistrate who has considerable powers in examining witnesses and assessing evidence.

The unified French police forces are divided into the National Police, which is responsible for urban areas with more than 10,000 people, and the Gendarmerie (military police), which covers all other areas. The French Ministry of the Interior reports that the National Police and the Gendarmerie together solved less than one-third of all crimes reported in 1999. However, over three-fourths of all homicides and rapes were reported cleared. The courts, prisons, and juvenile institutions are also unified and centralized.

CRIME

France has a crime rate similar to those found in most industrialized countries; crime rates in France have remained remarkably stable over time. A total of 3,567,864 crimes and misdemeanors were recorded in France in 1999, a .07 percent increase from 1998. Assault and battery (95,235 incidents) increased by nearly 10 percent. Sexual assaults (12,732 incidents), homicides (953 incidents), and attempted homicides (1,044 incidents) all decreased. However, in 2000 the crime rate increased by nearly 6 percent, a significant increase comparable to the one in 1991, which was above 7 percent. The increase in crime, occurring mainly in major urban areas, is difficult to explain since France has been enjoying relatively high economic growth and low unemployment.

People living in social housing and other poverty-stricken areas experience a high level of crime. They blame the poor services they get from the state and the commercial sector. The local authorities, for example, are reluctant to repair broken windows and other acts of vandalism. This creates resentment, which in turn may generate further destructive acts. When workers do carry out repairs, however, they often become targets of assault by local youth. Fire brigades have been assaulted as well. Because of the pressure of the public opinion, the government is taking measures to address this state of affairs. The Interior Ministry has introduced a new policing scheme called "*police de proximite*" whereby incentives (e.g., free housing and public transportation, and rapid promotion) are offered to police officers who volunteer to work in such difficult environs. Officers are also encouraged to get involved in the life of the community they police. Citizens as well are encouraged to come forward with proposals that they feel may help deal with increasing crime, as well as to take preventive measures against crime. In addition, some local authorities have stopped the payment of benefits to families in which there is evidence of criminal activity.

Role models are being used as mentors for young people who seem to have lost any sense of purpose in life. These individuals, from the world of sport, media, business and entertainment, grew up in the same kind of social environment as the youth they mentor. The government encourages these efforts since it does not need to provide additional resources.

The increase in the crime rate cannot be accounted for by economic and social conditions because the French economy is not in crisis. Obviously, reasons are to be found elsewhere. Crime, of course, occurs for a variety of reasons: social, economic, cultural, and so on. Moreover, the situation is quite paradoxical: The more police officers there are in the field, the more crimes they record. Increasing crime rates, therefore, may not indicate a real increase in crime; rather, they may simply indicate stricter enforcement or more accurate measurement of the same amount of crime.

In any event, the crime rate is still a matter of public concern. In France, crime and criminal justice is a matter of much political debate, more so even than unemployment, which was for a very long time the preoccupation of the French public. For example, crime and punishment was at the center of the last municipal elections in March 2001.

THE NATURE OF OFFENSES AND OFFENDERS

White-collar crime increased dramatically, by more than 40 percent in 2000. This is the direct result of money laundering legislation at the European Union as well as the national level. Fraud and embezzlement are also very common, affecting mostly major insurance and financial companies. Because there is recognition that corporate crime represents a great danger to democratic institutions and should be dealt with severely, the government is planning to introduce new legislation to combat it. Furthermore, the judiciary is being provided training and equipment to enable it to more effectively tackle corporate crime.

Adults between the ages of twenty-four and fifty are responsible for one-third of all crime in France. A significant proportion of these are unemployed or facing other social problems. Until 1997, France had one of the highest unemployment rates in Europe, which is widely believed to have been a contributing factor to lawless behavior. Unemployed adults are unlikely to have family responsibilities, and unmarried men especially are more likely to be involved in violent crime such as assault, sexual assault, robbery, manslaughter, and murder.

The French prison population is estimated to be 350,000; this figure is increasing. Prisons are overcrowded and it is not uncommon for three inmates to share a small cell intended for one. This overcrowding may be due to the fact that new criminal legislation has

In France and many other European nations, immigrants from Africa are often blamed for rising crime rates in major cities. Here, North African immigrants arrested for illegally entering France from Italy wait to be returned to Italian authorities.
Source: © David and Peter Turnley/Corbis; used with permission.

been introduced (e.g., money laundering) or that existing laws are being more strictly enforced. There is an overrepresentation of minority groups, especially North and Sub-Saharan Africans, in penal institutions; since they are involved in less than half of recorded crimes, this may indicate a propensity to incarcerate minorities for minor offenses. (The French State has often been condemned by the European Court of Human Rights—based, ironically, in Strasbourg, France—for violations of human rights under the 1950 European Convention on Human Rights.) Community and noncustodial penalties are used less than custodial penalties, since the French public and politicians view such penalties as an incentive to commit further crimes

Although males commit the vast majority of crime in France, the number of female offenders is growing rapidly: Since 1970, the crime rate for women has increased by 14 percent. Prison conditions for female inmates are not much better than those for men, and very few facilities are offered to inmates who are also mothers. Fewer women are involved in violent crime than men, even though the rate of violent crime has increased. Women are predominantly involved in minor offenses (e.g., theft, shoplifting, welfare fraud) that do not carry custodial penalties in many countries.

Most offenders of both sexes recidivate—for example, once released the majority of women convicted of sex offenses return to the sex industry—because the system does not encourage prisoners to prepare themselves for life outside prison. Instead, for most inmates prison is a place where they develop the skills to outwit law enforcement agents when they are released. Prostitution, drug trafficking, illicit sexual activity, and dealing in contraband are widespread. Many prison officers turn a blind eye to these activities, for two reasons: fear of reprisal, and a lack of commitment to their jobs. The latter is the main reason French correctional officers are generally opposed to any proposed penal reform. The result is that instead of being a place where inmates learn to reintegrate into the community, prisons serve as a breeding ground for more efficient criminals and further criminal activity.

There was a 15 percent decrease in juvenile crime from 1998 from 1999. However, juveniles still account for approximately 20 percent of all criminal arrests. Police authorities estimate that minors are responsible for over one-third of all street crime, and over one-fourth of those cases involving assault and battery. Much of this activity has occurred in or has originated from the immigrant communities that are largely found in the suburbs of major metropolitan areas. A number of French sociologists have commented that the juveniles who commit these criminal acts tend to be unemployed, live in crowded low-income housing, see no hope for the future, and claim that they are victims of routine harassment and discrimination.

FUTURE CONCERNS

The increase in the crime rate is a source of constant concern for the government because the public is very sensitive about crime and punishment. Since crime, like unemployment, is a product of society, it is only society that can find ways to deal with it. Better training of law enforcement officers will have an important effect on reducing crime. This can be coupled with social measures aimed at marginalized groups, which are more likely to offend because of social and economic circumstances. Currently, such an investment in public services is either absent or ineffective. The government should open a public debate on crime and punishment. This debate, however, cannot take place if the French government continues its reluctance to publish statistics on crimes. These statistics are not government property. Without these figures it will be impossible to produce a long-term plan addressing the increasing crime rate.

—Jean-Pascal Obembo

See also CIVIL LAW LEGAL TRADITIONS

Further Reading
Engueleguele, S. (1998). *Les politiques penales (1958-1995)*. Paris: L'Harmattan.
Evans, P., Rueshmeyer, P., Stokpol, T. eds. (1985). *Bringing the State Back In*. Cambridge, UK: Cambridge University Press.
Foucault, M. *Surveiller et punir*. (1975). Paris: Gallimard.
Michaud, Y. (1978). *Violence et politique* Paris: Gallimard.
Olsen, J. *Organised Democracy: Political Institution in a Welfare State* (1983). Bergen, Norway: Universitatsverlag Bergen
Savelsberg, J.-J. "Knowledge Domination and Criminal Punishment." (1994). *AJS* 99, 4 (January): 911–943
———. "Rationalities and Experts in the Making of Criminal Law Against Economic." (1988). *Law and Society* 1: 2–3.
Statistiques officielles sur les crimes et delits en France, année 2000. Paris: Ministere de l'Interieur. http://www.interieur.gouv.fr/statistiques/stat00/interieur.htm

◢ FRAUD

Throughout the 1990s and into the twenty-first century, the incidence of "street crimes" such as robberies, burglaries, simple assaults, aggravated assaults, rapes, and homicides declined in the United States. During the same time period, however, the incidence of fraud increased. Fraud has not only emerged as a growing problem for individual citizens but also has become an increasing burden for private industry and state, local, and federal governments. All are potential victims of fraud. Unlike other crime victims, victims of fraud may not realize that they have been victimized until long after the criminal act is committed. Some victims lose substantial amounts of money to fraud, depleting savings and retirement accounts and, consequently, resulting in great emotional distress. For a variety of reasons, fraud remains one of the most underreported crimes, exacerbating the efforts of law enforcement authorities to effectively control fraud. Techniques for committing fraud are many, and the offenders often target potential victims based upon behavior patterns that may make one more susceptible to victimization. Advances in technology, particularly the arrival of the Internet, have permitted present-day "fraudsters" to conveniently reach enormous numbers of potential victims to ply their criminal trade.

Considering the amount of government funding allocated to the control of "street crime," there has been relatively little funding set aside for the control of fraud. This is due in part to a long-standing belief that the public is apathetic towards fraud. Groups like the

National Fraud Investigation Center have reported that government funding for the investigation and prosecution of fraud remained fairly flat from 1992 through 1998, despite a rise in financial costs and arrests associated with these crimes during the same time period. While it is difficult to precisely measure the sum of the financial losses attributed to fraud, criminologists generally agree that fraud exacts a cost that dwarfs that incurred from street crime. The Federal Bureau of Investigation's Uniform Crime Reports (UCR) national arrest statistics for the period from the beginning of 1979 through the end of 1999 show that while arrest rates for most crimes of violence and property crimes have declined, arrest rates for fraud have risen, peaking in 1996.

WHAT IS FRAUD?

Fraud is similar to other types of crimes in that it involves the illegal taking of property from another. It is the method used, however, that makes it different from a crime like robbery. With fraud, there is no threat or act of violence that forces the victim to turn over property. In fact, the goal of the fraudster is often to convince the victim to relinquish property willingly. The criminal tool that the fraudster uses is "deception." Fraudsters usually are adept at misrepresenting facts to somehow trick the potential victim. As a way of enticing the potential victim to pay, the fraudster can engage in any one of a variety of preplanned schemes in which he promises goods, services, or other financial benefits that will not be provided or may, in fact, not even exist. Other types of frauds occur with the victim having no personal contact with the offender, as in check fraud and credit card fraud. Individual credit card holders are protected against incurring the total cost of such frauds, but these costs are passed along to the credit card companies and banks supporting them.

Types of Fraud

Fraud can take many forms and are usually categorized by either the method used or the target of the fraud. Some common types of fraud include health care and insurance fraud, credit card fraud, pension and trust fund fraud, securities fraud, product-pricing fraud, and telemarketing fraud. One of the most serious types of fraud is "identity theft" in which the fraudster uses the victim's Social Security number or other personal information to apply for credit cards and loans. When

added up, the commission of these frauds takes a devastating toll on the economy. The economic costs of "street crime" pale beside the costs exacted from fraud every year. Estimates vary, but the annual costs of fraud in the United States range from $200 billion to $500 billion. Much of these costs are incurred by private businesses and financial institutions.

HOW FRAUD CAN AFFECT VICTIMS

With individual citizens who are victims of fraud, the initial economic loss is often only the first of a series of harms suffered. As an aftermath to the initial victimization, victims of fraud often experience feelings of embarrassment, guilt, blame, anger, and depression. In cases in which substantial sums are lost, victims report feeling a sense of being "raped" and feeling responsible for letting down family members who may have been depending upon the lost funds to reach future goals. In such cases, victim distress can lead to divorce and to attempts at suicide. While counseling and support group services are readily provided through government funding for victims of violent crimes, such services are scarce for victims of fraud. The serious nature of the emotional costs for individual victims of fraud, and the lack of services to address it, has led to the development of assertive groups of victims of "economic violence," primarily in California, who advocate the creation of fraud victim self-help groups and the participation of victims in the sentencing proceedings of convicted fraudsters.

CHECK FRAUD, HEALTH CARE FRAUD, AND INTERNET FRAUD

Some of the most serious types of fraud presently perpetuated in the United States are check fraud, health care fraud and Internet fraud. The following sections present some key insights into these types of fraud.

Check Fraud

Check fraud has become one of the most perplexing problems for financial institutions. Annual loss estimates for check fraud in the United States hover around $10 billion and continue to rise at a frightening rate. In its 1994 Check Fraud Survey, The American Bankers Association (ABA) indicated that 54 percent of community banks, 94 percent of mid-sized banks, and 88 percent of large banks sustained losses from check

Fraud Involving Weights and Measures

Fraud is considered a serious crime when it involves trade in economically valuable goods and services. In an agricultural society such as China, fraud in weights and measures is a serious offense because it affects the trade and sale of farm products such as grains, vegetables, and fruits.

Section (LU) 155.

Illegal manufacture of weights and measures.

Whoever manufactures weights, measures or scales contrary to the law, and uses them at the market, also whoever departs from the weights, measures and scales issued by the Government, either by augmentation or diminution, shall be punished with 60 blows (g.b.) [greater bamboo sticks].

The manufacturer incurs the same penalty.

A magistrate who issues weights, measures, scales, that do not correspond with the regulations, shall, as well as the manufacturer, receive 40 blows (l.b.) [lesser bamboo sticks] each.

The superintending officer, who fails to verify and examine, shall be liable to a punishment on degree less than that fixed for the magistrate and manufacturer. If, however, he was cognizant of the circumstances and connives at it he incurs the full penalty.

Anyone using weights, measures or scales on the market, which, though being accurate, have not been examined, verified and branded, shall be punished, as if it were illegal manufacture with 40 blows (l.b.).

If officers, employed at the granaries, illegally enlarge or diminish measures, weights, or scales issued by the Government, so that the amount of articles received or issued by the Government would be incorrect viz: the amount of received be increased and that of articles issued be diminished, they shall be punished with 100 blows (g.b.).

If the punishment, in proportion to the profit derived by that mode of increasing or diminishing, amounts to more than 100 blows (g.b.), the case shall be treated according to the law against "Obtaining unjust profit" (section 345).

Source: Rosenstein, S. S. (1887). *A Chapter of the Chinese Penal Code*. Leiden: E. J. Brill, pp. 65-67.

mates are that if commercial banks and other institutions combined their check fraud losses, the total would be $12 billion to $15 billion annually.

There are various ways to commit check fraud, including (1) drawing on closed accounts, (2) forging checks, (3) counterfeiting checks, (4) altering amounts, and (5) altering the name of the payee. Chemical alteration to checks is commonly referred to as "check washing." "Check washing" involves the use of chemicals to obliterate printing on the amount and payee without affecting the check's preprinted information. The amount on the washed check is then typically increased and made payable to the fraudster. Computer technology has also made it easier to commit check fraud. Laser scanners, personal computers, and laser printers are used to reproduce the check's image, make changes to the check and print out a fake check.

A popular form of check fraud involves checks written against closed checking accounts in which fraudsters take advantage of the interbank transaction "float time." These types of frauds depend on individuals failing to destroy checks from unused accounts and those not properly informing their banks about the status of their accounts. Check fraudsters are also known to open new bank accounts with the sole intention of defrauding the bank. In this situation, the fraudster opens a new account using false employment information and incorrect addresses and telephone numbers. The fraudster then deposits altered or counterfeited checks into the account and withdraws large proportions of the account balance before the bank realizes it has been victimized.

fraud in 1993. Between 1991 and 1993, the number of fraudulent checks submitted increased 136 percent, from 537,000 to 1,267,000. Over the same period, annual losses from those frauds increased to reach $815 million for 1993. That is twelve times the amount banks lose annually because of bank robberies. Also falling victim to check fraud are thrifts, savings banks, and other financial institutions, retail merchants, government agencies, and large corporations. FBI esti-

Health Care Fraud

Like check fraud, health care fraud exacts a heavy financial toll for the U.S. Some of the more prevalent forms of health care fraud are (1) fraudulent billing schemes in health care services rendered, (2) kickbacks or inducements with the intent to influence the sale of health care, and (3) self-referrals for the purpose of financial gain. Health care fraudsters can include patients, health care providers, and billing services. The national Medicare program is one of the primary targets for health care fraudsters. Part of the problem of controlling healthcare fraud is the vulnerability of the healthcare system itself. Four billion health insurance claims are generated annually by one million providers and are processed by fifteen hundred insurers and government programs. Medicare claims make up 20 percent of these, with payments processed by about seventy different contractors in a highly automated process that rarely has a claim being seen by an employee of the company. While the number of claims has consistently risen, the number of reviews of claims has decreased. Irregularities identified by contractors usually result in claims that are denied without further investigation.

Internet Fraud

The role of the advancement of technology in the proliferation of fraud is no more pronounced than it is in the case of the Internet. The original creators of the Internet (which began as a cooperative effort between computer scientists and the U.S. military) had not intended the Internet for public use, and so did not foresee the vast criminal opportunities it presented to fraudsters. From one perspective, the types of fraud committed on the Internet are no different than frauds committed prior to the Internet's arrival. But since so many individuals and businesses access the Internet, fraudsters have the luxury of being able to easily reach many more potential victims in a short time period than if they depended on personal or telephone contacts. Not only does the Internet provide perfect anonymity to fraudsters, tracing the offenses to the source is difficult for law enforcement authorities. The "borderless" nature of the Internet presents another serious problem for law enforcement. Situations in which the fraudster may be residing in a foreign country can become a difficult hurdle for law enforcement to surmount if the extradition treaty with the offender's country is weak. Some Internet fraudsters have been known to "jurisdiction shop" to help ensure that they are in a jurisdiction that will complicate their arrest and prosecution should they be detected.

The Internet not only furnishes fraudsters with the means to commit frauds that help hide detection but also allows them the ability to commit frauds that would not be worth the effort in the real world. For example, "salami attacks" involve using the Internet to instantaneously break into numerous interest-bearing accounts and steal fractions of pennies from the accounts, one "slice" at a time, resulting in huge profits that can go unnoticed. The most common Internet frauds take other forms. By far, the most frequent type of Internet fraud against individuals is "auction fraud," in which a buyer enters an Internet auction site, pays for merchandise, and either does not receive the merchandise or receives another item well below the original item's value. Another common type of Internet fraud occurs when the victim purchases used computer hardware or software through a private seller and the equipment is never delivered. While not as prevalent as auction fraud or "nondeliverable fraud," investment fraud on the Internet represents the highest economic cost to individuals. Other Internet fraud types include fraudulent prize/sweepstakes schemes, bogus business opportunities or franchises, and fraudulent toll transfers. Overall, the new criminal terrain made possible by the Internet dramatically expands the profit possibilities for fraudsters and translates into a rising economic cost to society as more enter the world of the Internet.

PUBLIC PERCEPTIONS OF AND EXPERIENCES WITH FRAUD

In the world of criminal justice research, there has been relatively little attention paid to the study of the characteristics of fraud and its victims. The number of research studies on fraud pales in comparison with the many studies on the commission and control of violent crimes and property crimes. Surveys on telemarketing fraud have been conducted by Harris and Associates and by the American Association of Retired Persons. A notable survey that examined fraud victimization was administered by Titus, Heinzelmann, and Boyle in 1991.

The National White Collar Crime Center Study

The most recent information provided on public perceptions of and experiences with fraud was generated through a national household survey report published by the National White Collar Crime Center in 2000. The results of the survey revealed that the general public in the United States is (1) often victimized by fraud, (2) rarely reports the offenses, (3) views fraud as being quite serious, (4) has misperceptions about the characteristics of the average fraud victim, and (5) is concerned about the criminal justice system's ability to control fraud.

Results demonstrated that many now believe that fraud is as serious as or more serious than certain types of street crimes. When asked to compare a street theft (stealing $100 on the street) with a fraud (a contractor defrauding someone of $100), slightly more respondents believed the fraud to be more serious—44 percent, compared to 38 percent who found the street theft to be more serious. The remaining respondents (18 percent) viewed the crimes as equally serious. Results from additional scenarios underscored the importance that the status or authority of the fraudster has in perceptions of seriousness. Findings on the perceived seriousness of health care fraud show that the criminal actions of health insurance companies and physicians are generally viewed as more serious than similar actions conducted by individual patients. Sixty-seven percent of those surveyed believed that a doctor lying on a claim to collect more money was more serious than a patient filing a false insurance claim, while only 12 percent believed the patient's false claim to be more serious.

On the basis of the National White Collar Crime study, the general public also seems to be concerned about the quality of control of fraud. This is based upon public perceptions of the likelihood of apprehension of persons committing frauds, how they are sanctioned if convicted, how they should be sanctioned, and the level of resources respondents are willing to support to ensure tighter control of white-collar crime. Respondents were presented with a scenario comparing the chances of apprehension of someone stealing one thousand dollars in a robbery with someone obtaining one thousand dollars through a fraudulent action. Less than one quarter (22 percent) of the sample believed the fraudster had a greater likelihood of apprehension. An even lower percentage (16 percent) believed that the convicted fraudster would be punished more severely by the criminal justice system. A comparison of these results with the beliefs of respondents as to who should be punished more severely revealed a marked difference. Only slightly more than 30 percent believe that the robber should be punished more severely, while higher percentages believe the fraudster deserved greater punishment (31 percent) and that both should be punished with equal severity (38 percent).

To determine the extent of fraud victimization survey respondents were asked if they or anyone in their household had been defrauded in the twelve months prior to the survey by financial planners/stockbrokers, auto repairmen, or merchants (i.e., product-pricing fraud). Respondents were also asked if they or others in their household had fallen victims to fraud through Internet transactions, unauthorized use of their credit cards, use of 800 or 900 telephone numbers, or unauthorized use of a personal identification number (PIN). Finally, respondents were asked if anyone in the household had responded to an offer for a free prize or vacation that turned out not to be free or a free product sample that turned out not to be free. Results indicated that more than one in three households (36 percent) in the study had been victimized by at least one of these types of frauds.

Victims were asked if they reported the crime to law enforcement agencies (i.e., police or related law enforcement, district attorney, state attorney general), consumer protection agencies (including Better Business Bureaus), or other entities (i.e., personal lawyer, credit card company, telephone company, the company or individual initiating the offense). Only 41 percent were found to have reported the crimes to one of the above. Of those crimes reported, few were reported to crime control agencies (13 percent) or consumer protection agencies (8 percent). In over eight in ten cases (82 percent) in which a fraud was reported, the entity receiving the report was something other than a crime control or consumer protection agency.

A final area of question on fraud victimization was devoted to the respondents' impressions of who they believed would be most likely to be victimized in terms of age and education level. The majority of respondents (60 percent) believed that those most likely to be victimized would be over sixty years of age. Nearly half (49 percent) also believed that those with less than a college education would be more likely to be victimized than those who had some college experience. These perceptions are inconsistent with findings of demographics of victims surveyed in earlier victimization surveys which found that younger adults (eighteen to thirty-four years of age) and those with some college or college degrees were more likely to be victimized.

Used properly, the responses to these questions on fraud can play an integral role in improving efforts to prevent and control fraud in the future. The results indicate that the American public (as its victims) is becoming well acquainted with theft by deception and tends to view the commission of such crime with an increasingly jaundiced eye. The incidence of fraud victimizations may be a reflection of a rise in criminal activity in this crime area, or might be a sign that the public may not be sufficiently aware of their vulnerability to being victimized. Reporting of the crimes remains low, possibly a result of confusion about to whom to report the crimes, embarrassment (i.e., at being "duped"), or pessimism regarding recovery of funds. Public perceptions of the demographics of average victims (i.e., older and less educated) are quite divorced from the actual demographics of victims drawn from victimization studies (i.e., younger, college educated). This misperception may cause some to become complacent, thinking that fraud victimization only happens to people unlike them. The single finding on crime control perceptions that stands out is the discovery of a serious confidence gap between public demands for "just desserts" for persons committing frauds and the perception of the criminal justice system's ability, or willingness, to administer adequate punishment.

This information should be of great value to those responsible for preventing and controlling fraud. The public's sensitivity to the threat of fraud crime and the call for strict sanctioning of offenders is strong empirical evidence for the support crime control professionals can expect to receive for effective programs. Such evidence can serve as support for fraud control programs and for the enhancement of such programs in the future as offenders' methods become more sophisticated. The results send a clear message that the hardening of public sentiment on the punishment of fraud criminals may require more stringent judicial scrutiny of those convicted of fraud. The results also represent a challenge to agents of fraud control, particularly with regard to crime prevention and reporting. By implementing organized programs, the criminal justice community can increase public recognition of the behavior that can precipitate victimization and advise the public on what measures can be followed to prevent their victimization.

THE FUTURE

Fraud promises to be as much of a problem in the future as it has been in the past. Fraudsters are criminal innovators who continue to sharpen their skills by experimenting with new methods to put other people's money in their own pockets. To escape detection and punishment, they often depend on the victim's reluctance to report. To effectively control fraud in the future, it will be a responsibility of fraud control agents to explore new avenues to raise the level of the reporting of frauds to the appropriate law enforcement agencies. This translates into identifying, developing, and testing innovative strategies for increasing public awareness of the fraud control responsibilities of the respective law enforcement agencies. Expanding awareness should not be seen as the only factor that can enhance the reporting of fraud. Fraud investigators and prosecutors must become aware of the need to build fraud control enforcement credibility by keeping the public informed of important fraud control initiatives and the extent to which they succeed. This can help build the credibility of these programs in the public's eyes.

There is every reason to believe that the nation's prior pattern of increasing frequency of crimes like fraud will continue in the twenty-first century. It is not hard to see that the rapid advances in technology designed to serve the general public and legitimate businesses have also created more tantalizing criminal opportunities for fraudsters. Some of these criminals have already taken advantage of the public's growing use of the Internet to repackage traditional scams on a whole new playing field, one on which the public may unwittingly have a false sense of security. Other criminals are transforming basic telemarketing fraud and securities fraud scams into finely tuned, sophisticated criminal operations. The target of these criminals remains the unsuspecting, average American citizen. Controlling the commission of these crimes in the future will be a formidable task. Much depends on how well the general public understands and reports the offenses. Successfully building an educated public in this area can only be achieved with comprehensive awareness/control programs that acknowledge the attitudes and behavior of the individual American citizen as the locus of effective fraud control efforts.

—*Donald J. Rebovich*

See also CYBERCRIME; IDENTITY THEFT; SECURITIES FRAUD

Further Reading
American Association of Retired Persons (AARP). (1999). *America Speaks Out on Health Care Fraud: A Consumer Survey.* Washington, DC: AARP.
———. (1996). *Findings from a Baseline Omnibus Survey on Telemarketing Solicitations.* Washington, DC: AARP.
———. (1996). *Telemarketing Fraud and Older Americans.* Washington, DC: AARP.
Bass, Ronald, and Lois Hoeffler. (1992). *Telephone Based Fraud: A Survey of the American Public.* New York: Louis Harris and Associates.

Evans, T. David, Francis T. Cullen, and Paula J. Dubeck. (1993). "Public Perceptions of Corporate Crime." In *Understanding Corporate Criminality,* edited by Michael B. Blankenship. New York: Garland, 85–114.

Federal Bureau of Investigation. (2000). *Crime in the United States 1998: Uniform Crime Reports.* Washington, DC: U.S. Department of Justice, Federal Bureau of Investigation.

Geis, Gilbert, Robert F. Meier, and Lawrence M. Salinger, eds. (1995). *White Collar Crime: Classics and Contemporary Views.* New York: Free Press.

Goff, Colin, and N. Nason-Clark. (1989). "The Seriousness of Crime in Fredrickton, New Brunswick: Perceptions Towards White Collar Crime." Canadian Journal of Criminology 31: 19–33.

National Fraud Investigation Center and Trans Union. (1995). *Fraud Assessment and Impact Study.* Horsham, PA: National Fraud Investigation Center.

President's Commission on Law Enforcement and Administration of Justice. (1968). *Challenge of Crime in a Free Society.* Washington, DC: Government Printing Office.

Rebovich, Donald, and Jenny Layne. (2000). *The National Public Survey on White Collar Crime.* Morgantown, WV: National White Collar Crime Center.

Rossi, Peter, J. Simpson, and J. Miller. (1985). "Beyond Crime Seriousness: Fitting the Punishment to the Crime." Journal of Quantitative Criminology 1: 59–90.

Rossi, Peter, Emily Waite, Christine E. Rose, and Richard E. Berk. (1974). "The Seriousness of Crimes: Normative Structure and Individual Differences." American Sociological Review 39: 224–37.

Sutherland, Edwin. (1940). "White Collar Criminality." American Sociological Review 5: 1–12.

Titus, Richard, Fred Heinzelmann, and John M. Boyle. (1995). "Victimizations of Persons by Fraud." *Crime and Delinquency* 41: 54–72.

Wolfgang, Marvin, Robert Figlio, Paul Tracy, and Simon Singer. (1985). *The National Survey of Crime Severity.* Washington, DC: Government Printing Office.

▼ FRYE RULE

See SCIENTIFIC EVIDENCE

▼ FURLOUGH PROGRAMS

The prison population in the United States has grown precipitously since the 1980s. According to the Bureau of Justice Statistics, the number of incarcerated Americans approached 2 million at the midpoint of the year 2000. Nearly 40 percent of former prison inmates are reimprisoned within three years of release. A wide range of correctional programs have been implemented to alleviate prison overcrowding and lower recidivism rates. Some were established as alternatives to incarceration. Intensive probation supervision and electronic monitoring, for example, are two popular community-based sentences that are imposed in lieu of incarceration for offenders who can be managed safely under strict conditions of supervision. Other programs were developed as early release mechanisms that involve community corrections facilities, such as halfway houses and prerelease centers, in which inmates can receive treatment and social services outside of prisons.

One major reason for the high rate of reincarcerations in the United States is the paucity of job training and employment opportunities available to former prison inmates. Work release or furlough programs, also known as work furlough, day parole, or work parole programs, are a form of partial incarceration designed to relieve prison overcrowding by permitting offenders to reside in community-based work release facilities. More important, these programs give selected inmates chances to learn and test new job skills, earn legitimate incomes, pay taxes, support their families, elevate their self-esteem, and improve their self-concepts. In short, furlough programs provide inmates with experiences and proficiencies that can facilitate their reintegration and readjustment into the community.

BRIEF HISTORY OF FURLOUGH PROGRAMS

Furlough programs were created mostly with rehabilitative or humanitarian intentions. The earliest programs, however, were developed to achieve more punitive goals and were based on the notion that inmates should work as hard as law-abiding citizens and should not be permitted to sit idly in their prison cells, wasting time and taxpayers' money. Ironically, the opponents of current furlough programs argue that inmates should be prohibited from working because they are taking jobs away from good citizens.

In 1913, Wisconsin became the first state to authorize work release programs by enacting the Huber Act. Wisconsin's first programs accepted only misdemeanants (i.e., less serious offenders). Other states soon passed similar laws. But it was not until 1957, with the implementation of an extensive work release initiative in North Carolina, that furlough programs began to gain nationwide attention and appear in numerous states throughout the country. In 1965, Congress enacted the Federal Prisoner Rehabilitation Act, establishing work release and community treatment centers for federal minimum-security prisoners. By 1975, all fifty states and the District of Columbia had laws permitting the establishment of furlough programs.

PROGRAM OPERATIONS

Furlough programs allow inmates, usually nearing the end of their prison terms, to leave prisons during the day in order to work or seek employment. Many furlough programs also allow inmates to leave prisons during the day for the purpose of completing their education in high schools, vocational schools, community colleges, or universities. After school or work hours, participants return to confinement in correctional institutions or community-based residential facilities. Inmates are paid directly by employers and must submit their wages to correctional administrators. Approximately 10 to 15 percent of the inmates' wages cover the costs of imprisonment or room and board in community-based facilities. In addition, offenders' incomes can be used to pay victim restitution, fines, or court costs. Inmates may also save a portion of their incomes for use when they are released from prisons. Small withdrawals during incarceration are permitted for the purchases of cigarettes, radios, and other personal items.

Furlough participants are restricted in their movements, while they are in the community, and they are considered prison escapees if they fail to return to confinement at the end of the workday. Furlough inmates are prohibited from working in skilled areas of employment in which there is a surplus of skilled workers. Furthermore, union leaders must approve the placement of furloughed inmates in unionized positions, and inmates are barred from employment during labor disputes or strikes. Furlough program employees must work under the same job conditions and in the same work environments as nonoffender employees, and they must meet the same job eligibility standards as their civilian counterparts. Program participants work with and are supervised by civilians. They also must work for the same wages as civilians receive for comparable jobs. Federal Public Law 89-176, which controls federal work release programs, prohibits inmates from earning lower than the prevailing wage for specific jobs. When furlough participants return to prisons or prerelease facilities at the end of the workday, they follow the same rules and regulations as all other inmates.

In some work furlough programs, inmates are solely responsible for finding their own jobs and arranging for their own transportation to and from work. In others, work release coordinators assist inmates in identifying employment and transportation options. Work release coordinators also negotiate formal or informal agreements with employers and schedule interviews for job candidates. Prison officials can establish long-term employer contracts that secure a fixed number of job positions for inmates. In such instances, employers automatically accept job candidates who are recommended by prison staff.

PARTICIPANT SELECTION

Participation in work furlough programs is voluntary. The success of these programs depends in part on the careful screening and selection of inmates who are most likely to work safely and securely in the community. There is no perfect formula for selecting the best program candidates (i.e., those who will be least likely to commit crimes or to attempt escapes). Prison administrators often apply general criteria in selecting inmates for furlough programs. Typically, violent offenders, inmates who are considered flight risks, and those serving life sentences are excluded from furlough programs. Other selection criteria include offenders' institutional records and their willingness to comply with searches, drug tests, and other conditions of program participation.

Candidates for work release furloughs usually spend time in orientation sessions to ensure that they thoroughly understand the conditions of program participation, and they must be assessed for their specific employment skills and readiness for work before they can be placed in jobs. In Washington State, for example, inmates can apply for work release only if they have been convicted of crimes other than first-degree murder or rape, and if they are on minimum security status and have fewer than two years remaining in their prison terms. Inmates who meet these criteria can still be denied admission to work release if they have been "assaultive" in prison, made threats to their victims while imprisoned, or failed two or more times in previous furlough programs.

PROGRAM EFFECTIVENESS

Research on the effectiveness of furlough programs has been largely inconclusive because of poorly designed studies. Investigations have found that work release participants are no different from non–work-release inmates with regard to recidivism, self-esteem, or motivation to achieve success through legitimate activities. Other investigations have reported that work release participants had fewer prison disciplinary problems, compared with nonparticipating inmates. A well-crafted study of work release participants in Washington State found that nearly two-thirds were successful while in the program (i.e., they committed no crimes and remained out of prison) and that the program was no more expensive than the cost of keeping releasees behind bars. Research in Massachusetts examined recidivism trends over eleven years and found that furlough participants in the state, compared with nonparticipants, were significantly less likely to relapse into criminal behavior.

CONTROVERSIES

Although furlough programs are authorized throughout the United States, only one-third of the prisons in America actually use them, and less than 3 percent of prisoners are enrolled in the programs. The use and expansion of work release programs have been greatly hampered by widely publicized and sensational stories concerning furlough escapees who commit subsequent crimes. Such cases are rare, but they have inordinately swayed public opinion about furlough programs. The best known and most notorious of such cases involved a Massachusetts prisoner named Willie Horton. Horton was serving a life-without-parole sentence for first-degree murder when he absconded from a work release program and brutally murdered a young Maryland couple.

In his successful 1988 presidential campaign, George H. W. Bush, at the time vice president, used the Horton case to portray his opponent Michael Dukakis, the governor of Massachusetts, as soft on crime. A nationally televised political advertisement for Bush featured Willie Horton, and a parade of persons wearing prisoner's uniforms and constantly moving through a revolving door, spinning in and out of prison. The advertisement was pulled from the airwaves amidst a barrage of criticisms for its racist overtones and unfair and misleading depiction of Governor Dukakis's crime control policies. The number of inmates enrolled in furlough programs in Massachusetts declined substantially in the aftermath of the Horton advertisement. In other states, furlough programs became more restrictive in their admissions and operational policies following the Horton tragedy. For example, some shortened the time that inmates are permitted to participate in the programs.

In conclusion, the risk of absconding and serious criminal behaviors among furlough participants is generally low. Furlough programs can play an important role in our correctional system and have many potential advantages: They help manage the inmate population by encouraging offenders to behave well during incarceration for the privilege of working in the community; they yield financial benefits to crime victims, the families of offenders, and the public coffers; and they are a useful tool for assisting inmates to successfully transition from prison to community life.

—*Arthur J. Lurigio*

See also DAY RELEASE; HALFWAY HOUSE; PAROLE

Further Reading
Allen, Harry, E. and Clifford E. Simonsen. (1995). *Corrections in America: An Introduction,* 7th ed. Englewood Cliffs, NJ: Prentice Hall.
Katz, Jonathon and Scott Decker. (1982). "An Analysis of Work Release: The Institutionalization of Unsubstantiated Reforms." *Criminal Justice and Behavior* 9: 229–250.
LeClair, Daniel, P. and Susan Guarino-Ghezzi. (1991). "Does Incapacitation Guarantee Public Safety? Lessons from the Massachusetts Furlough and Prerelease Program." *Justice Quarterly* 8: 9–36.
McCreary, Phyllis, and John McCreary. (1975). *Job Training and Placement for Offenders and Ex-Offenders.* Washington, DC: Government Printing Office.
Turner, Susan, and Joan Petersilia. (1996). *Work Release: Recidivism and Corrections Costs in Washington State.* Washington, DC: U.S. Department of Justice, National Institute of Justice.

G

▼ GAMBLING

Nevada, which legalized casino gambling in 1931, was the only state to allow this form of recreation until the first of the Atlantic City, New Jersey, casinos opened in 1978. Although on-track wagering on horse races was largely accepted across the United States, legalization of other forms of gambling proceeded at a slow pace, because the general public regarded most forms of gambling as an unacceptable or even quasi-criminal activity. A majority of citizens believed that proliferation of legal gambling sites would cause a nationwide crime wave. Even state lotteries, a form of wagering currently considered to be routine and harmless, did not exist until New Hampshire, seeking to improve its cash flow, initiated a lottery in 1964. Other states gradually followed suit, and eventually, took the next step in legalization of gambling by introducing off-track betting on horse races.

With this recent history, the rapid evolution of legalized gambling in the 1980s and 1990s into a nationwide, mainstream business, with $50 billion in annual gross revenues is somewhat surprising. Part of the explanation stems from the introduction of computerized technology into the gambling business. The advent of innovative software and computers facilitated government regulation and greatly reduced the possibility of fraud, suspicious bookkeeping methods, and other dishonest activities. In addition, entrepreneurs and state government officials who had foresight understood that legalized gambling could be extremely profitable to the private sector, which would in turn provide a steady source of tax revenues. Among the entrepreneurs was a group of Native Americans who brought gambling to their reservations in the 1980s. They intended to use this enterprise to offset federal funding reductions, but more important, they wanted to help their community raise itself out of its abject poverty. Their plan was to hire Native Americans to construct gambling venues and then hire Native American staff to run the completed gambling sites. Completed casinos would draw non-Native Americans and their discretionary capital onto the reservation.

The self-improvement efforts of the Native American community, however, are not the only results of legalized gambling. Where legal gambling is widely accessible and available, some of the patrons of gambling establishments will inevitably be individuals for whom gambling is a self-destructive obsession (National Opinion Research Center 1999: 1, 5).

AN ABUNDANCE OF GAMBLING OPPORTUNITIES

A recent National Gambling Impact Study Commission (NGISC) report showed that 86 percent of Americans report having gambled at least once during their lives, and 68 percent of Americans report having gambled at least once in the past year. In some states, gambling parlors are "as common as fast food outlets" (NGISC 1999). Currently, forty-eight of the fifty states have some form of legalized gambling. Advertising agencies have done an excellent job in helping their clients earn huge amounts of money. Clearly, gambling has significant economic and social impacts on individuals, communities, and on the United States as a whole.

TYPES OF GAMBLING

Lotteries, the most widespread form of gambling in the United States, have been established in thirty-seven states and the District of Columbia, and more states are poised to follow (NGISC 1999: 2, 3–4). All of the state lotteries fall into one of three basic categories:

1. *Instant games.* A paper ticket displays geometric shapes coated with a material that can be scratched off. The buyer scratches off a certain number of spaces to reveal whether it is a winning or losing ticket.

2. *Daily numbers games.* For both of the following types of daily numbers games, winning numbers are drawn frequently, up to several times each hour. (1) Lotto: On the game card, the player specifies the three- or four-digit number s/he has chosen; (2) Video keno: Each player chooses a few numbers out of a larger group of available numbers.

3. *Electronic gambling devices (EGDs).* This classification covers complex gaming apparatus, such as slot and video poker machines. The existence of individuals who become obsessed with playing with these machines justifies the labeling of EGDs as the "crack cocaine of gambling" (NGISC 1999: 2, 4–6).

In many states, EGDs are routinely found in convenience stores, bars, and truck stops. Although several states have legalized stand-alone EGDs, many bars and fraternal organizations use illegal and quasi-legal EGDs, known as "gray machines," that offer a gambling experience similar, if not identical, to legal EGDs. Quasi-legal EGDs exist because of unclear, or "gray," language in the law that should regulate the presence and operation of these EGDs. To circumvent questions regarding legality, gray machines are often labeled "For Amusement Only," to indicate that the machine does not actually pay winners with real currency. Instead, the establishment in which the machine is located pays the winners surreptitiously, in either monetary or nonmonetary forms (NGISC 1999).

LEGALIZATION OF GAMBLING IN THE UNITED STATES

Prior to 1990, casino gambling was legal only in the state of Nevada and in Atlantic City, New Jersey. However, by January 2000, an individual who wanted to participate in legal casino gambling could choose from approximately 500 casinos in twenty-eight states, or from approximately one hundred "riverboat" and "dockside" casinos that were afloat in six states (NGISC 1999).

In addition to this total of about 600 conventional and dockside casinos, approximately 260 casinos are located on Native American reservations throughout the United States (NGISC 1999). The Native Americans became involved in casino gambling after the U.S. Supreme Court's landmark 1987 decision in *California v. Cabazon Band of Mission Indians.* In *Cabazon,* the Supreme Court ruled that states are not empowered to regulate commercial gambling on Native American reservations. To offset cutbacks in federal funding in the 1980s, Native Americans brought bingo halls to their reservations. To prevent chaos from occurring in the wake of *Cabazon,* in 1988, Congress passed the Indian Gaming Regulatory Act, which provides a regulatory framework specific to gambling operations conducted on Native American reservations.

Over forty states offer pari-mutuel betting on horse racing, greyhound racing, and/or jai alai (NGISC 1999). Winnings are paid according to odds determined by comparing the total of the wagers placed on each contestant in an event. Horseracing is the most popular form of pari-mutuel gambling. Prior to the mid-1970s, a bettor could legally place a wager on a horse race only if he or she was physically present at the betting window at the race venue. Off-track betting was legalized only after advancements in computer software and satellite-broadcasting technology enabled "simulcasting," or displaying the race at an off-track betting venue while the race is actually occurring. Currently, the total of horseracing wagers placed off-site exceeds the total of wagers made at racetracks.

Although wagering on sporting events other than horse racing is legal only in Nevada and Oregon, it may be the most widespread and popular form of gambling in America (NGISC 1999). Wagering activities such as sports betting pools are common in both white- and blue-collar workplaces. The individuals who initiate or conduct sports betting schemes are rarely prosecuted, because management generally ignores or tacitly accepts this pervasive form of gambling as a normal, workplace activity.

Since the mid-1990s, an increasing number of creative Internet gambling enterprises have been founded, including online casinos, lotteries, bingo games, and sporting event betting sites. These Web sites have already gained a diverse audience and are particularly attractive to adolescents, who can legally gamble throughout the United States at age eighteen. Internet gambling has raised unprecedented issues that have yet to be addressed and has exacerbated concerns associated with traditional forms of gambling. Internet gamblers are remote from, and can be anonymous to, individuals operating gambling Web sites. When they are dealing with unidentified clients, it is virtually impossible for Web site operators to screen clients to determine their age or history of gambling problems. The accessibility of Internet gambling has renewed public interest in the relationship between gambling and crime, including money laundering.

PATHOLOGICAL AND PROBLEM GAMBLING

The vast majority of Americans choose either not to gamble or to gamble recreationally, experiencing no measurable, gambling-related side effects. Unfortunately, a small percentage of individuals become so involved in gambling that it has damaging impact on other aspects of their lives, their families, and their communities. Throughout the United States, the proliferation of sites at which one can legally gamble has stimulated participation in this activity, while simultaneously increasing the pool of people to whom gambling is available. Within this group of people, there are always individuals who are at risk for developing the mental disorder that Gamblers Anonymous and most laypeople call "compulsive gambling" and psychiatrists call "pathological gambling." This is an impulse control disorder, defined by The American Psychiatric Association as

> a failure to resist an impulse, drive, or temptation to perform some act that is harmful to the individual or others, an increasing sense of tension before committing the act, and an experience of either pleasure, gratification, or release at the time of committing the act. . . . The essential feature of pathological gambling is persistent and recurrent maladaptive gambling behavior that disrupts personal, family, or vocational pursuits." (American Psychiatric Association, *Diagnostic and Statistical Manual of Mental Disorders* 1994: 615)

Estimates of the prevalence of pathological and problem gambling in the United States vary. A recent estimate, based on research conducted by National Opinion Research Center (NORC) for the National Gambling Impact Study Commission, is that approximately 1.8 percent of the adult population (about 3.7 million people) are pathological gamblers. An additional 2.2 percent (approximately 4.4 million people)

A Gambling Poem from Stuart England

There is probably no human activity that someone, somewhere, sometime has not placed a wager on. The following description is of gambling in seventeenth-century England. Like gambling in the twenty-first century, it was condemned as sinful and seen as a cause of poverty and other social ills.

The most famous bowling ground in the capital was situated in Piccadilly, and thither the best company were wont at that time to resort. Adjacent to this bowling ground, which was divided into an upper and a lower green, was a gaming house, notorious for the case with which money changed hands within its walls. Numbers of people were ruined by their excesses at play at Piccadilly. Richard Flecknoe, in a poem, which bears the date of 1656, composed "on the occasion of his being left alone in the Mulberry Garden to wait on all the ladies of the times," complained that the London citizens carried their money to Piccadilly only for the sake of losing it.

But we behold
Them daily more bold
And their lands to coyn they disht ye,
And then with the money
You see how they run ye
To lose it in Piccadilly.

Source: Sydney, William C. (1892). *Social Life in England From the Restoration to the Revolution 1600-1690.* New York: Macmillan, p. 338.

---

are problem gamblers (NORC 1999:6). NORC also found that an additional 15 million Americans were "at-risk gamblers," a term for individuals who meet one or two of the *DSM-IV* criteria. Although people in this group have the potential to become problem gamblers, it is possible for some of them to gamble recreationally throughout their lives without any negative consequences (NORC 1999: 9).

Research has established that adolescent gamblers are more likely than adults to become problem or pathological gamblers. The National Research Council (NRC), in a review prepared for the National Gambling Impact Study Commission, estimates that as many as 1.1 million adolescents (ages twelve to eighteen) are pathological gamblers (NRC 1999: 9). Another study found the rate of problem gambling among adolescents to be twice that of adults (Shaffer et al. 1999: 1446). Research has also established that residents of lower-income communities are more likely to gamble than residents of wealthier areas. Minorities in general, and, in particular, Latinos and people with incomes below $10,000 per year, are at especially high risk for developing gambling problems (NGISC 1999: 4–9).

GAMBLING AND CRIME

Researchers have identified and studied several links between gambling and crime. Most studies that establish a relationship between pathological gambling and crime have found that pathological gamblers are predisposed to commit crimes, such as embezzlement, forgery, fraud, and theft, in order to pay for current wagers or to repay debts from previous gambling losses. However, other research shows that pathological gamblers are often involved in a wide range of illegal activities, including drug dealing, to obtain money to gamble and to pay debts. As involvement in gambling intensifies, options for funding gambling activities decrease and involvement in illegal activities may increase (Blaszczynski and McConaghy 1994; Spunt et al. 1998). The NORC study found that pathological gamblers had higher arrest and imprisonment rates than nonpathological gamblers (NORC 1999: 10). The National Gambling Impact Study Commission (NGISC 1999) questions the reliability of many of the studies that have explored the relationship between gambling and crime. For instance, some studies were limited to particular types of crime and/or particular locations. Generalizing results from such a limited study would be invalid.

Historically, a majority of the general public was biased against the introduction of legalized gambling, based on the fear that gambling would increase criminal activity. Contrary to this, some studies have noted that legalized gambling reduces crime because it eliminates incentives for illegal gambling. When a large sample of the available literature is examined, it shows that communities with casinos are just as safe as communities that do not have casinos (NGISC 1999). Particularly during the 1990s, rapid expansion of casino gaming venues has resulted in widespread concern that casino gambling is the inevitable precursor to increased incidence of white-collar crimes. To determine whether a pathological gambler, desperate to cover debts incurred in casinos, would be likely to steal from the nearest, easiest targets, such as employers, employees,

or other business contacts, Albanese (1999) examined trends in arrests for embezzlement, forgery, and fraud in nine of the largest casino gambling markets. Albanese found no consistent pattern of increase or decrease in white-collar crimes, except that more jurisdictions reported decreasing than increasing arrest rates. Clearly, these results do not support the theory that introduction of legalized gambling inevitably leads to higher crime rates.

Miller and Schwartz (1998) studied casino gambling and street crime, including robbery, burglary, assault, rape, theft, and murder, to determine if the introduction of casino gambling is indeed linked to an increase in street crime. They examined some studies that claimed to demonstrate a relationship between casino gambling and street crime. They discovered that most of these studies were reported in terms of per capita crime rates, based on the number of permanent residents of the area. Miller and Schwartz determined that per capita street crime statistics might not actually increase if tourists were included in the average daily population count. However, their study highlighted the fact that increasing the number of visitors in a certain area will inevitably increase the total number of crimes in that area, creating additional work for police, filling more jail cells, and requiring more court sessions.

Organized crime, one of Hollywood's favorite topics, has been subjected to intense press coverage throughout repeated federal and state investigations and prosecutions of casino owners and operators. This publicity linking casino gambling and organized crime has forever biased the general public against legalized casino gambling. According to NGISC, organized crime has been eliminated from the direct ownership and operation of casinos by enforcement of strict state regulatory codes, and by and large, public corporations that now own a majority of casinos (NGISC 1999). Although the U.S. General Accounting Office (2000) study of Atlantic City, New Jersey, found increased rates for some white-collar and property crimes after casinos began to operate there, the state has not had a major scandal nor discovered any organized crime influence in the casino industry. Does law enforcement's challenging yet low-priority effort to eradicate illegal and quasi-legal EGDs demonstrate existence of a link between gambling and crime? Some states report that the continued operation of illegal and quasi-legal EGDs is assured through bribery of law enforcement officers. Although confiscation of these machines is a law enforcement method that appears useful, sensible, and foolproof, confiscation has proven ineffective, as EGDs are relatively inexpensive and easily replaced. In addition, penalty fees for ownership and operation of EGDs are usually low in comparison to the profit generated when the machines are operational (NGISC 1999).

GAMBLING AND SUBSTANCE ABUSE

The apparent similarity between pathological gambling and addictive behaviors has been the topic of a significant amount of research. Most researchers agree that the pathological gambler is drawn to this activity because it provides (1) a means of escape from other problems, (2) a way to make a great deal of money, and (3) "action." This term refers to an aroused, euphoric state that gamblers typically compare with either sexual excitement or the high derived from cocaine. The desire to remain in action is so intense that it takes priority over all other concerns, with the result that some pathological gamblers deprive themselves of sleep, food, or even trips to the lavatory for several consecutive days, all for the sake of uninterrupted gambling (Lesieur et al. 1986).

Problem or pathological gamblers and substance abusers share several lifestyle characteristics, including the following:

1. the individuals did not intend to make gambling and drugs central to their existence;

2. the individual's perception of gambling, or of obtaining and using drugs, evolves from the category of "essential, daily activity" into an obsession;

3. gambling, or obtaining and using drugs, requires ever-increasing amounts of the individual's time, energy, material resources, and emotional reserves;

4. cessation of gambling or substance abuse results in withdrawal symptoms;

5. the lives of the individuals with gambling or drug problems display similar patterns of engagement and abstinence, and of abstinence and relapse; and

6. to achieve the desired state, the gambler or drug abuser must constantly increase the amount of gambling or the size and/or frequency of the dosage of the drug (Lesieur and Wallisch 1993: 3).

Researchers have long known that drug and/or alcohol abuse may occur concurrently with pathological gambling. Gamblers often use drugs to stay awake in order to prolong the action they crave, and they frequently need to deal drugs to finance their growing gambling and drug habits (NGISC 1999). Research has consistently found higher rates of gambling problems among substance abusers than in the general population. Most gambling research among substance abusers has focused on individuals in drug abuse treatment programs. For example, Spunt et al. (1995) found high rates of pathological gambling in a sample of methadone patients.

Studies of substance abusers who are not in treatment may include anecdotal accounts of gambling but typically do not focus on gambling. However, law enforcement acknowledges that individuals addicted to heroin may gamble on a regular basis, and may be capable of supporting their habit primarily through gambling or hustling at gambling games. Knowledgeable researchers currently estimate that 15 to 30 percent of adult substance abusers have gambling-related problems.

Teenagers who are problem or pathological gamblers tend also to be heavily involved with drugs. A Harvard Medical School Study (Shaffer et al. 1999: 93) revealed that over 75 percent of their sampling of teenagers had gambled by their senior year in high school. Fifteen percent of the gamblers in this study also used illegal drugs, showing that they were more than twice as likely as non-gamblers to use drugs. In addition, youths who gambled were three times more likely to have used cocaine, twice as likely to have used inhalants, and four times more likely to have taken steroids than youth who did not gamble According to the Massachusetts Council on Compulsive Gambling (2000), many young gamblers are so deeply indebted that they resort to selling drugs to make money.

RESEARCH DIRECTIONS

Millions of Americans regularly participate in various types of legal and/or illegal gambling. The costs and benefits of this activity, if any, have not been studied extensively and are little understood. There is a growing interest in the study of pathological and problem gambling. Although most people who gamble do so recreationally and with negligible consequences, for many Americans, gambling is like a disease in that it can cause a plethora of negative results, including major harm to themselves and to others.

The first recommendation of the newly created National Gambling Impact Study Commission focused on the "immediate need" to address pathological gambling. The Commission urged Congress to

Gambling—The Good and the Bad

In 1991, casinos opened in Florissant, Missouri. A study of the impact of casino gambling on the community conducted by the National Opinion Research Center in the late 1990s indicated many favorable comments but also some concern about problems with crime. Here are some community members' opinions.

We asked individuals what community changes they have seen over the last 10 years and whether they thought any of these changes was related to gaming. Everyone mentioned the population boom or some change that was related to the increased number of people moving to the area, such as the lack of housing or the traffic and demand for new roads. The thriving economy appears to be the main reason for this influx. People without jobs or many resources come to the Florissant area to start a new life.

Due to the casinos, according to one interviewee, "Investment into schools and public services has been greater. Also, there has been more investment in highways and sanitation services . . . . More people are working; there are more two-income families than ever before. The MSA now has more businesses that any other region . . ."

Gaming, according to the newspaper editor we interviewed, compromises one-quarter to one-half of the local economy, and all respondents except one indicated that they were pleased with the overall direction of the local economy (the exception abstained). The thread that connects most of these comments is the dramatic improvement in employment opportunities.

Respondents also mentioned what could be considered less desirable changes attributable to the casinos, including the rise in problem gambling. According to a respondent in law enforcement, "there are now Gamblers Anonymous meetings in [Florissant] every single night of the week, when there used to be none." An addiction counselor stated that problem gamblers were not known before the casinos. The detective stated, "We already had alcohol and drug addiction services. The casinos opened up . . . and we saw our first problem gamblers [within 18 months]. These people were often both alcoholics and problem gamblers. They have [access to] free booze in the casinos." Two respondents mentioned an increase in bankruptcies. But help is advertised—"They have help-lines now, and more people are aware that help is available." Another told us, "Casinos are proactive in combating gambling problems and are bringing money into the community."

An interviewee in social services mentioned seeing an increase in neglect, though not abuse, over the past several years: "We've seen children left unattended, people losing their money who can't afford to pay for their food and rent . . . ." Another reported that "[h]ousing prices have gone up. We have traffic congestion and crowded schools. There's been a strain on infrastructure, construction is up. Not a huge rise in crime. Some traditional neighborhoods have been stressed by growth—high-rise condos, shopping centers, hotels appearing. All of [this change was due to gambling], though some of it was indirect." One person indicated that chain restaurants were moving in and "chasing away the local restaurants."

We asked our informants whether they thought the nature or number of crimes in Florissant had changed. Everyone mentioned an increase in robberies. According to an officer in law enforcement, crime in general has increased. He added that burglaries account for the greatest proportion of crime in the city . . . .

On the other hand, according to a newspaper reporter, prostitution is now less visible than it was before the casinos, and it should be noted that we were unable to find any escort agencies in the Florissant Yellow Pages. The reporter also stated that "there have been some isolated, weird crimes, from people freaking out after losing their money. One woman faked her own kidnapping, then disappeared for a month."

Source: National Opinion Research Center at the University of Chicago. (1999). *Gambling Impact and Behavior Study. Report to the National Gambling Impact Study Commission*, April 1, 1999, pp. 80–82.

"encourage the appropriate institutes within the National Institutes of Health to convene a multidisciplinary advisory panel that will help to establish a broad framework for research on problem and pathological gambling issues within its range of expertise" (NGISC 1999: 8-3).

Research on the relationship between gambling and crime, if any, is still in its infancy. As noted by Miller and Schwartz (1998), research questions need to become more specific. Different types of legalized gambling need to be examined separately for their effects on specified crimes. Researchers must develop the theoretical specification of a causal relationship between gambling and crime.

The existence of an obvious connection between gambling and drug abuse, particularly among adolescents, highlights the necessity of an expedited research project that focuses on the relationship between gambling and drugs. To date, research has focused almost exclusively on the incidence and prevalence of gambling among individuals who abuse substances, especially those enrolled in drug treatment programs. As a result, little is known about the nature and scope of this relationship.

—*Barry Spunt*

Further Reading

Albanese, Jay. (1999). *Casino Gambling and White-Collar Crime.* Washington, DC: American Gaming Association.

American Psychiatric Association. (1994). *Diagnostic and Statistical Manual of Mental Disorders.* 4th ed. Washington, DC: American Psychiatric Association.

Blaszczynski, A., and N. McConaghy. (1994). "Criminal Offences in Gamblers Anonymous and Hospital Treated Pathological Gamblers." *Journal of Gambling Studies* 10, 2: 99–127.

Blume, S. B. (1992). Quoted in "As Addiction Medicine Gains, Experts Debate What it Should Cover." *New York Times* (31 March): C3.

Brown, R. I. F. (1987). "Pathological Gambling and Associated Patterns of Crime: Comparisons with Alcohol and Other Drug Addictions." *Journal of Gambling Behavior* 3, 2 (Summer): 98–114.

Custer, R. L. (1992). "Gambling and Addiction." In *Drug Dependent Patients: Treatment and Research,* edited by R. Craig and S. Baker. Springfield, IL: Charles C Thomas, 367–381.

Hall, G. W., N. J. Carriero, D. A. Gorelick, I. D. Montoya, K. L. Preston, and R. Y. Takushi. (2000). "Pathological Gambling Among Cocaine-Dependent Outpatients." *American Journal of Psychiatry* 157: 1127–1133.

Indian Gaming Regulatory Act (1987). 25 U.S.C. §§2701–2721.

Johnson, B. D., P. J. Goldstein, D. S. Lipton, T. Miller, E. Preble, J. Schmeidler, and B. J. Spunt. (1985). *Taking Care of Business: The Economics of Crime by Heroin Abusers.* Lexington, MA: Lexington Books.

Lesieur, Henry. (1987). "Gambling, Pathological Gambling, and Crime." In *The Handbook of Pathological Gambling,* edited by Thomas Galski. Springfield, IL: Charles C Thomas, 89–110.

Lesieur, Henry, and S. Blume. (1991). "Evaluation of Patients Treated for Pathological Gambling in a Combined Alcohol, Substance Abuse and Pathological Gambling Treatment Unit, Using the Addiction Severity Index." *British Journal of Addiction* 86: 1017–1028.

Lesieur, Henry, S. Blume, and R. Zoppa. (1986). "Alcoholism, Drug Abuse and Gambling." *Alcoholism: Clinical and Experimental Research* 10: 33–38.

Lesieur, Henry, and L. Wallisch. (1993). "Problematic Gambling and Problematic Drug Use: Their Interactions." Paper presented at the annual meeting of the Academy of Criminal Justice Sciences, Kansas City (March). http://www.masscompulsivegambling.org

Miller, W., and M. Schwartz. (1998). "Casino Gambling and Street Crime." *Annals of the American Academy of Political and Social Science* 556 (March): 124–137.

National Gambling Impact Study Commission (NGISC). (1999) *Final Report to the President, Congress, State Governors, and Tribal Leaders.* Washington, DC: National Gambling Impact Study Commission.

National Opinion Research Center at the University of Chicago (NORC). (1999). *Gambling Impact and Behavior Study.* Report to the National Gambling Impact Study Commission (April). Chicago, IL: National Opinion Research Center at the University of Chicago.

National Research Council (NRC). (1999). *Pathological Gambling: A Critical Review.* Report to the National Gambling Impact Study Commission (April). Chicago, IL: National Research Council.

Rupcich, N., G. R. Frisch, and R. Govoni. (1997). "Comorbidity of Pathological Gambling in Addiction Treatment Facilities." *Journal of Substance Abuse Treatment* 14, 6: 573–574.

Shaffer, H. J., T. Cummings, and E. M. George. (1999). "Strange Bedfellows: A Critical View of Pathological Gambling and Addiction." *Addiction* 94: 1445–1448.

Spunt, Barry, L. Cahill, Dana Hunt, and Henry Lesieur. (1995). "Gambling Among Methadone Patients." *International Journal of the Addictions* 30: 929–962.

Spunt, Barry, Dana Hunt, and Henry Lesieur. (1995). *Prevalence of Gambling Problems Among Methadone Patients.* Final Report to the National Institute on Drug Abuse. Bethesda, MD: National Institute on Drug Abuse.

Spunt, Barry, Dana Hunt, Henry Lesieur, and Hilary James Liberty. (1996). "Pathological Gamblers in Methadone Treatment: A Comparison Between Men and Women." *Journal of Gambling Studies* 12, 4: 431–449.

Spunt, Barry, I. Dupont, Dana Hunt, Henry Lesieur, and Hilary James Liberty. (1998). "Pathological Gambling and Substance Misuse: A Review of the Literature." *Substance Use and Misuse* 33, 13: 2535–2560.

U.S. General Accounting Office. (2000). "Impact of Gambling: Economic Effects More Measurable than Social Effects." Report to the Honorable Frank Wolf, House of Representatives (April). Washington, DC: U.S. General Accounting Office.

Court Case

California v. Cabazon Band of Mission Indians (1987). 480 U.S. 202.

▼ GANGS

As street gangs grow in number across the United States, greater attention is focused on both prevention of new gang membership and intervention with existing gang members.

DEFINITION OF A GANG

Although there is disagreement about the exact definition of a gang, every definition includes some mention of a group. Because most delinquent acts or crimes committed by juveniles are done in groups, distinguishing between groups and gangs is important, and more elements of a definition of gangs are needed. The use of symbols is a second element in defining gangs. Most gangs have some symbols of membership, which take a number of forms, including hand signs, clothes, and certain ways of wearing clothes. Gang definitions also include some level of permanence to the group, because many confederations of young people form over a single time-bounded issue, only to disband. Most gang definitions require that the gang be in existence over a prolonged period of time, generally a year or more. A number of definitions of gangs include turf or gang-identified territory as a requisite element. Many contemporary gangs do claim some territory as their own, because it is either where the gang began or where most of the members live. A final element, which is the key to distinguishing a gang from other groups, is involvement in crime.

It is not as difficult to define a gang member as it is to define a gang. The best indicator of who is in a gang comes from self-identification or self-reports of membership. Many police departments keep detailed records of the names of gang members as gang identification files. There can be shortcomings in these files, however, as information can be dated or based on misinformation, or can fail to reflect changes in gang affiliation by individuals.

THE EVOLUTION OF GANGS IN THE UNITED STATES

Gang development in the United States has been cyclical rather than linear—that is, gangs have tended to come and go rather than to be a constant feature of society. In the late 1800s, youth gangs emerged in the slums of New York, Philadelphia, Boston, Chicago, St. Louis, and Pittsburgh during periods of rapid immigration. Italians and Irish immigrants were overrepresented in the ranks of gang members. These gangs roamed the streets of their neighborhoods, engaging in petty forms of property crime and conflict with members of rival gangs.

Gang activity declined between the turn of the century and the 1920s. These youth gangs were very different organizationally from the adult gangs of the Prohibition Era, although many organized crime figures were members of delinquent youth gangs before moving on to organized crime. The major activity of these gangs was the search for thrills, excitement, and fighting. During the Depression and World War II,

gang activity declined. When gangs reemerged in the 1950s, they included large numbers of African American, Puerto Rican, and Mexican American youths. In addition, levels of violence were higher than in previous periods of gang activity. This can be attributed to the presence of guns and automobiles.

Gang activity increased in the 1980s. At the beginning of that decade, gang problems were recognized in only a few large cities, particularly Chicago, Detroit, and Los Angeles. But, by the end of the decade, gangs appeared in large and medium-sized cities as well as in many rural areas. The levels of violence were much higher than in any previous wave of gang problems, corresponding with even more widespread availability of automobiles and firearms. The spread of gangs at the end of the twentieth century has been attributed, on the one hand, to the emergence of an urban underclass and, on the other, to the effects of popular culture, which makes gang symbols, clothing, and language commodities available in large and small cities.

THE LINK BETWEEN GANGS AND CRIME

Gang members participate in a large number of serious delinquent and criminal acts. The distinction between gang-related crimes and other crimes committed by gang members is important. It is known that gang members are responsible for greater levels of crime and delinquency than their nongang counterparts. In addition, gang-related delinquency is more violent than nongang-related delinquency. Studies also demonstrate that involvement in crime increases while an individual is a member of a gang and declines once he or she leaves the gang.

Frederic Thrasher's pioneering study in 1927 found that gangs originated from the spontaneous group activity of adolescents and that patterns of association were strengthened by conflict over time. In its earliest stage, the gang was diffuse, little leadership existed, and the gang might have been short-lived. Conflict with other gangs played a notable role in helping to define group boundaries and strengthen the ties between members, uniting them in the face of threats from rivals. Working in Chicago in the 1960s, Jim Short and Fred Strodtbeck emphasized the community context, relationships among gang members, and the social characteristics of gang members that influence the degree to which gangs varied in their level of conflict orientation. Two concepts central to their perspective on gangs were threat and status, each of which contributed to gang crime.

Malcolm Klein found that delinquency increased among gang members who received the most group-oriented services and that solidarity among gang members seemed to increase as a result of the attention paid to the gang by street workers. Based on these results, he concluded that gang intervention programs might enhance the attractiveness of gangs, and increase their solidarity, thereby promoting violence. Most important, Klein found that criminal offending among gang members was cafeteria-style; that is, gang members rarely specialized in committing certain forms of crime, and generally committed a variety of offenses.

Joan Moore placed primary importance on the role of Chicano culture and the position of Mexican Americans in the cultural and institutional life of East Los Angeles to explain gang formation and activities in the 1970s. The detachment of Chicano culture from mainstream social and political life was the foundation of her explanation of gang life and criminal involvement. Like Moore, James Diego Vigil emphasized the role of Chicano culture in the formation of gangs, pointing to *choloization*, the process by which Chicano youth are marginalized from mainstream society. The street provides an alternative socialization path for these youths, leading to increased involvement in crime and delinquency.

John Hagedorn explained the origin of Milwaukee gangs by noting that most gangs in his city emerged on a more or less spontaneous basis from corner groups made up of young men who hung out together in their neighborhoods. Others emerged from dancing groups that experienced physical threats and fighting, strengthening their alliances and ultimately resulting in gang formation. The formation of these groups was affected by the presence of an underclass.

Scott Decker and Barrik Van Winkle conducted a field study of gang members in St. Louis in the early 1990s. Their work describing gang structures and processes combines local neighborhood dynamics and the national-level diffusion of gang cultures. St. Louis neighborhood rivalries that dated back for decades and contemporary friendship networks were transfigured into a system of conflict structures that bear the names and symbols of California's longstanding conflict between the Bloods and Crips, with occasional symbolic manifestations of Chicago gang culture. Their research underscored the cafeteria-style offending patterns of gang members, while emphasizing the ever-present violence in gang life.

When Cheryl Maxson, Margaret Gordon, and Mal-

colm Klein examined Los Angeles police and sheriff's department records, they found that gang homicides were more likely to involve minority males, involve automobiles, take place in public places, involve the use of firearms, and involve a greater number of participants. Gang homicide perpetrators and victims were significantly younger than their counterparts involved in nongang homicides, but they were older than the typical youth gang member. The Blocks used Chicago police department data to study patterns of lethal and nonlethal gang related violence over time. They found that (1) gang violence is more likely to be turf related than drug related, (2) patterns of violence of the four largest established street gangs and smaller less established gangs were different, and (3) guns were the lethal weapons in practically all Chicago gang-related homicides between 1987 and 1990.

Another source of information the gang-crime nexus has been surveys of populations of at-risk youth. Jeff Fagan and his research team interviewed high school students and dropouts in Chicago, Los Angeles, and San Diego. They found that gang members committed more delinquent acts, as well as more serious offenses, than did nongang members. In a longitudinal survey of an at-risk population of youth in Denver, Finn Esbensen and David Huizinga found that, while gang membership was rare among the Denver respondents, gang members reported two or three times as much delinquency as nongang members. When gang members in the Denver study were asked what kinds of activities their gang was involved in, fighting with other gangs was the most frequently reported behavior. From longitudinal survey results on a representative sample of Rochester youth, Terry Thornberry and his colleagues found that gang-involved youths were significantly more likely to report involvement in violence and other delinquency. Their analysis showed gang involvement to be a transitional process, with delinquent activity increasing during gang involvement and declining afterward. They concluded that gang members commit more delinquency than

---

Graffiti as a Political Statement

Gang members rarely write graffiti to "get back" at society or to claim something that is not theirs. They write graffiti to represent themselves and their own political system in the places where they live. One Chicano gang member reiterated this perspective:

> It's just a communication between us. We all communicate with each other. I mean like you wake up and the morning and you go to work: welcome to the neighborhood. That's just us. Not to say that we can't change our program, but that's just us. That is our life style. Change what? This is us. What are you going to do, go sit up in a café and have a cappuccino? The reality is that is not going to happen. This is reality here. Everyday no matter what happens we gotta go to work, working with my homeboys. And if I'm not here, the rest of my homeboys might come. All the stuff we been through together . . . How you gonna change your homeboys for something you got no part in? Why do they want to change us, you know what I mean? Why can't we be ourselves and it be alright?

Source: Phillips, Susan. (1999). *Wallbangin': Graffiti and Gangs in L.A.* Chicago: University of Chicago Press.

---

non-gang members, and that individuals commit more delinquency while gang members than before or after their gang membership.

GANG PROCESSES

A critical point about the gang experience is that it is a dynamic process, one that changes over time and across individuals. The experience includes joining the gang, initiation, getting rank in the gang, and leaving the gang. In addition, it is important to note the correlates of gang involvement, such as age, race, and socioeconomic status of gang members.

Joining the Gang

A key issue to understand in this context is whether individuals are pulled or pushed into gang membership. Young people who are pulled into membership join their gang because of the attractions it offers to them—for example, they are attracted to the gang with the promise or expectation of friendship, opportunities

to make money, or the ability to provide something for the neighborhood. Being pushed into the gang implies a very different motivation or coercion for joining the gang. Most of the available evidence supports the view that individuals are pulled toward their gang because of what they see as the positive features of gang involvement, such as friends or the need to affiliate. A number of observers report that the gang is a magnet for prospective members because of the prospect of making money, typically through drug sales but also often through other crimes such as robbery or burglary. Cultural pride or ethnic identification also may play a role in the decision to join a gang.

Initiation

Regardless of the motivation for joining the gang, becoming a member typically takes place over time, and the individual takes on a gang identity in a process with a number of steps. Most gangs have an initiation process, and there is variation in initiation rituals. Most have few formal aspects to them, and joining usually involves some form of violence, typically by current members of the gang directed against the initiate. The most common form of initiation reported is that of being beaten. In other circumstances, a recruit will be required to go on a "mission" against a rival gang. While this can take a variety of forms, it typically requires the recruit to fight or shoot a rival gang member, or to conduct a crime such as robbery in rival gang territory. Most observers of the female gang scene report that girls tend to be initiated in the same way as boys—through beating—often by both boys and girls. A number of highly publicized reports document rapes of prospective female gang members. There is not widespread support, however, for the claim that this is the typical method by which girls are initiated into their gangs.

Roles in the Gang

Most gangs are not very well organized; however, there are distinctions within the gang between the status and functions of members. While a few gangs in chronic gang cities such as Chicago have well-defined distinctions between roles, this is not generally the case in most cities. The process of acquiring rank is based primarily on length of time in the gang, blood relationships with current leaders, and level of criminal activity. In emerging gang cities, gangs tend to have fewer roles, and those roles are not very well defined.

Participating in Gang Violence

Understanding the role of violence in the gang is a key to learning more about the gang experience. There is considerable evidence to show that gang members are the victims and perpetrators of high levels of violence. In Chicago, the number of gang-motivated homicides between 1987 and 1992 increased fivefold, and, in Los Angeles County, the number doubled in that period of time. Some cities (Chicago and St. Louis) report that about one in four homicide victims are gang members; Los Angeles County reports that nearly half of its homicide deaths were gang members. Homicides committed by gang members are more likely than other crimes of violence to involve firearms, particularly handguns. The victims of gang homicide are likely to be of the same race, age, sex, and neighborhood of residence as the people who kill them. Surprisingly, most gang homicides lack a relationship to drug trafficking. Instead, gang homicides seem to be motivated by revenge or battles over turf. Violence helps to hold the gang together. Most studies of gangs conclude that the sources of gang solidarity are external to the gang and do not come from inside the gang. In practice, the threats posed by rival gangs, and sometimes police and other adult officials, help to increase cohesion among gang members.

Leaving the Gang

There is considerable mythology about whether it is possible to leave one's gang. Gang lore provides stories that gang members must kill one of their parents if they ever want to leave the gang. Most of the available evidence dispels these myths and documents a considerable number of ex-gang members. Few of the individuals who leave their gang report that they faced physical consequences for doing so, although some are threatened with violence. The obligations that come with growing older, such as a job, becoming a parent, or getting older, are the key reasons that help an individual end a relationship with his or her gang.

CORRELATES OF GANG INVOLVEMENT

Age is a primary correlate of gang membership. Gang members range across a wide variety of ages but typically are teenagers. It is not easy to pinpoint a single age as the average age of gang members, but a number of studies identify seventeen or eighteen as the average age of members in their sample.

There is considerable evidence that racial and ethnic minorities are overidentified as gang members, largely as a consequence of the use of police data to identify gang members. National surveys of police departments indicate that racial and ethnic minorities, particularly African Americans and Hispanics, are the primary members of gangs. School survey data reveal higher percentages of white gang members.

Socioeconomic status is another important correlate of gang membership. It is not surprising that the majority of gang members come from the lowest socioeconomic groups in American society. The current cycle of gangs began in cities and neighborhoods with large concentrations of urban poor, often the urban underclass. This observation seems a logical consequence of the historical characteristics of gangs, but the emergence of gangs in suburbs and rural areas presents a challenge to the view that gang members are drawn exclusively from the poorest members of society.

CHARACTERISTICS OF GANG ORGANIZATION

One view of gang organization is that it is a vertically organized entity with a formal structure that enforces rules and acts in the same ways that a business may act. An alternative view argues that most gangs are horizontal and lack the formal-rational character of organizations with established leadership structures and well-defined roles and missions. Most of the research supports the latter view.

Most gangs have leaders. Gang leaders in most cases, however, are less likely to resemble corporate executives than captains of sports teams, a role that can change from one circumstance or one day to another. Most organizations need rules, and gangs are no exception to this. A relatively small number of gangs have written sets of rules or constitutions; the great majority of gangs simply have a set of rules that are understood among the members.

Nearly all gangs distinguish between the roles members play in the gang. In the least organized case, this distinction is only between core and fringe members, with the former participating more fully in decisions about activities to pursue. A final aspect of gang organization is what happens to the money made in gang-involved crime. In some cases, all of the money is reinvested in the organization so that it can grow. In other cases, the money raised by individual members of an organization is kept for their own use. The first model is the corporate model, and the second is a model of individual entrepreneurship. With few exceptions, gang members function as individual entrepreneurs, selling drugs or committing crimes for their own benefit, rarely if ever reinvesting their profits into the larger gang.

National surveys of police departments were used to identify five distinct gang types that reflect the size, presence of subgroups, age range, duration, territoriality, and versatility of gangs. The five gang types identified were (1) traditional, (2) neotraditional, (3) compressed, (4) collective, and (5) specialty. Traditional and neotraditional gangs are large, with subgroups of territoriality and versatility, but neotraditional gangs are of more recent emergence, typically less than ten years old. Compressed gangs are small and recent, with a narrow age range and versatility in their offending. Collective gangs are medium in size, age range, and duration, and versatile in their offending. Specialty gangs are small, of recent vintage, and specialize in one particular form of offending.

SUMMARY

Gangs are diverse in nature, origin, and activity. They also are dynamic, changing in their structure, membership, and activities over time. Gang definitions include a common set of elements, such as involvement in crime, permanence of membership, a group context, and the use of symbols. In addition, gang membership has the impact of increasing involvement in crime and delinquency, as well as the seriousness of such involvement. When individuals leave their gangs, their levels of crime decrease significantly. Historically, gangs have been associated with cities, particularly ethnic minorities in economically disadvantaged positions. There is evidence, however, that this may be changing. Gang structure and organization are variable, although there is little evidence to suggest that other than in a small number of cities gangs are well organized.

—Scott H. Decker and G. David Curry

Further Reading

Block, Carolyn R., and Richard Block. (1993). *Street Gang Crime in Chicago*. National Institute of Justice Research in Brief. Washington, DC: U.S. Department of Justice.

Curry, G. David, and Irving A. Spergel.(1992). "Gang Involvement and Delinquency among Hispanic and African American Adolescent Males." *Journal of Research in Crime and Delinquency* 29: 273–291.

Curry, G. David, and Scott H. Decker. (1998). *Confronting Gangs: Crime and Community*. Los Angeles, CA: Roxbury.

Decker, Scott H., and Barrik Van Winkle. (1994). "'Slinging Dope': The Role of Gangs and Gang Members in Drug Sales." *Justice Quarterly* 11: 583–604.

Decker, Scott H., and Barrik Van Winkle. (1996). *Life in the Gang: Family, Friends, and Violence*. New York: Cambridge University Press.

Esbensen, Finn-Aage, and David Huizinga. (1993). "Gangs, Drugs, and Delinquency in a Survey of Urban Youth." *Criminology* 31, 4 (November): 565–587.

Fagan, Jeffrey. (1989). "The Social Organization of Drug Use and Drug Dealing among Urban Gangs." *Criminology* 27, 4: 633–669.

Hagedorn, John M. (1988). *People and Folks: Gangs, Crime, and the Underclass in a Rustbelt City*. Chicago: Lakeview Press.

———. (1994). "Homeboys, Dope Fiends, Legits, and New Jacks." *Criminology* 32: 197–219.

Huff, Ronald. (1996). *Gangs in America*. Newbury Park, CA: Sage Publications.

Klein, Malcolm W. (1971). *Street Gangs and Street Workers*. Englewood Cliffs, NJ: Prentice Hall.

———. (1995a). "Street Gang Cycles." In *Crime*, edited by J. Q. Wilson and J. Petersilia. San Francisco: Institute for Contemporary Studies.

———. (1995b). *The American Street Gang*. New York: Oxford University Press.

Maxson, Cheryl L., M. A. Gordon, and Malcolm W. Klein. (1985). "Differences between Gang and Nongang Homicides." *Criminology* 23: 209–222.

Maxson, Cheryl L., and Malcolm W. Klein. (1995). "Investigating Gang Structures." *Journal of Gang Research* 3: 33–40.

Moore, Joan W. (1978). *Homeboys: Gangs, Drugs, and Prison in the Barrios of Los Angeles*. Philadelphia: Temple University Press.

Padilla, Felix. (1992). *The Gang as an American Enterprise*. New Brunswick, NJ: Rutgers University Press.

Sanchez-Jankowski, Martin. (1991). *Islands in the Street: Gangs and American Urban Society*. Berkeley: University of California Press.

Short, James F., Jr., and Fred L. Strodtbeck. (1974). *Group Process and Gang Delinquency*. 2d ed. Chicago: University of Chicago Press.

Skolnick, Jerome. (1990). "The Social Structure of Street Drug Dealing." *American Journal of Police* 9: 1–41.

Thornberry, Terrence, Marvin D. Krohn, Alan J. Lizotte, and Deborah Chard-Wierschem. (1993). "The Role of Juvenile Gangs in Facilitating Delinquent Behavior." *Journal of Research in Crime and Delinquency* 30: 55–87.

Thrasher, Frederic. (1927). *The Gang: A Study of 1,313 Gangs in Chicago*. Chicago: University of Chicago Press.

Vigil, James Diego. (1988). *Barrio Gangs*. Austin: University of Texas Press.

▼ GATED COMMUNITIES

Gated communities are residential areas with restricted access that use a wall, fence, shrubs, or trees to close off the perimeter. To enter, nonresidents—visitors, employees, and tradespeople—must get past a physical barrier such as a guardhouse or an electronic gate. Residents must identify a visitor before the individual is allowed to enter. People who do not live in the gated community cannot use its enclosed streets, sidewalks, park, beach, playground, pool, clubhouse, and biking or hiking trails. What were formerly public spaces are private.

HISTORY OF GATED COMMUNITIES

Gated communities are not a new phenomenon. Defensive walls surrounded ancient cities such as Athens, Rome, London, and Paris. During the Middle Ages and Renaissance, cities were located around or in a fortress. Kings and noble families lived in castles with walls and moats. The trend toward gates continued during the nineteenth century as wealthy and famous individuals built exclusive, private communities. These private communities were separate from their surroundings. They were maintained and controlled by covenants, restrictions, and land deeds. Some early examples are Gramercy Park (1831) and Tuxedo Park (1866), both in New York City, and Louisberg Square in Boston (1844). Streets could also be privatized to restrict public access. St. Louis, Missouri, contained private streets where wealthy industrialists had their homes; for example, Benton Place (1866) had its own security guards and is one of the earliest private streets in the United States.

The idea of building common interest developments (CIDs) such as condominiums, cooperatives, and planned developments of single homes (e.g., gated communities) was derived from the Englishman Sir Ebenezer Howard (1850–1928), who advocated the garden city concept. His ideas were explained in his book *Tomorrow: A Peaceful Path to Real Reform* (1898), which was reissued in 1902 as *Garden Cities of Tomorrow*. A garden city was a new community that was planned from the bottom up (physical layout, number of inhabitants, economic means of support, and governing structure) and merged the best of country life and city life. The citizens in the garden community would collectively have permanent ownership and control of the land and the leasehold property (houses, businesses, and farms). The moderate rents paid by the leaseholders and any surplus derived from the prosperity of the town would take care of the debt used to buy the land for the community and pay for the town's services and improvements. Ebenezer Howard did not want private developers to take over the land and profit from

it. The renters would elect individuals with practical expertise to serve on the governing body.

During the 1920s, American private developers, architects, and planners took parts of the garden city concept (e.g., planned community, recreational space, and green belts) and constructed, for profit, the common interest development communities. The wealthy community of Radburn, New Jersey, begun in 1929, even had a homeowners association (HOA) to administer the restrictions imposed in the covenant. This served as a model for the governing structure of present-day homeowners associations and the common interest developments they govern.

Gated communities have increased since the 1970s. Real estate marketers and housing developers began promoting common interest development communities for the middle class in the 1960s. Planned communities were popular with senior citizens and others wishing to pursue certain types of recreation and sports. Later, communities were planned for upper- and middle-income citizens of all types. Land cost was high, and planned communities enabled more people to live on smaller land units. The homeowners would share in the common open spaces, security systems, and private security guards. They would also have common amenities, for example, park, playground, pool, golf course, and parking lot. Street lighting, sanitation, sidewalks, maintenance of streets, and pest control—services normally provided by city government—would be provided. The developments included a private government (the homeowners association) to run them. Homeowners were assessed fees to maintain the community and its security. Municipal governments faced shrinking budgets in the 1970s, and the common interest development community or "new town" had great economic appeal. The city would receive a new tax base but would not have to spend a great deal of money on supplying services to the planned community.

GROWTH OF GATED COMMUNITIES

Examining the growth of homeowners associations provides an estimate of the increase in planned private communities, gated and ungated. The *1999 Community Association Factbook* (Treece 1999: 19) noted that fewer than 500 homeowners associations existed in 1964. By 1970, there were 10,000—twenty times more than in 1964. The increase continued, and by 1985, there was a total of 55,000. As of 1990, there were 130,000 homeowners associations. Blakely and Snyder (1997: 3) estimated

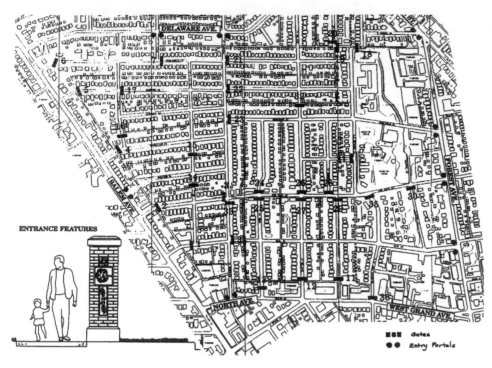

ENTRANCE FEATURES

■■■ Gates
●● Entry Portals

This plan shows the location of gates and entries for the neighborhood of Five Oaks in Dayton, Ohio. The plan is designed to control traffic flow into the neighborhood and thereby to reduce crime.
Source: Newman, Oscar (1996). *Creating Defensible Space*. Washington, D.C.: U.S. Department of Housing and Urban Development, p. 47.

home investment. Gated communities have grown in the United States because of fear of crime, fear of the randomness of crime, and the belief that the government cannot protect the citizen or provide quality, essential services.

Residents of gated communities believe that they are safer than the residents of nongated communities. Gates give residents a perception of security. However, crime can come from the residents, their guests, and teenagers who commit vandalism and let in friends from the outside. Criminals may target gated/walled communities. Residents may become careless about safety because of their perception that vulnerability is very low. Residents may also become less concerned about participating in community safety programs and Neighborhood Watch programs, both in their gated community and the outside community, because they have given the security responsibility to others whom they pay. The high costs may prevent some gated communities from having security officers present at all access points twenty-four hours a day. Vehicles that tailgate the car of an entering resident may penetrate the gates and bring in unauthorized visitors. A gated/walled community cannot prevent all crimes.

that 3 million households live in gated communities. This figure is derived from the results of a survey they conducted with the Community Association Institution (CAI). Most gated communities are in the Sunbelt states of Arizona, California, Florida, and Texas. For example, gated communities are to be found around Phoenix, Los Angeles, Miami, and Houston. The trend is growing, and gated communities are found in many states in the northeast, midwest, and northwest, for example, around New York City, Chicago, and Seattle, Washington, and in Massachusetts, Nevada, Michigan, and Pennsylvania. There are gated communities within the five boroughs of New York City. Two gated, beach-front communities are Breezy Point, Queens, and Sea Gate, Brooklyn. The Breezy Point Cooperative owns the land. Security officers monitor the central gate, and each side street has a gate accessible to residents with magnetic key cards. The Sea Gate Association employs private security personnel.

GATED COMMUNITIES AND CRIME

Gated community residents want to control their environment, have neighbors with a similar lifestyle and socioeconomic level, and increase the value of their

IMPACT OF THE GATED COMMUNITY

David Kennedy (1995) and Evan McKenzie (1994) have likened homeowner associations to a form of private government. Through the restrictive covenants, controls, and regulations (CCRs) that run with the land, the HOAs enforce restrictions on property and the use of property that homeowners and renters must abide by. For example, decorations and physical changes to the property, the amount of time a guest stays, and the physical age of residents may be restricted. Residents who do not abide by the CCRs may be fined or taken to court by the HOAs if they do not comply. Homeowners who do not pay their maintenance fees may find the HOA has put a lien on their property. The private developers draw up the covenants before the property is sold. This limits future homeowners' ability to participate in the governing process. It is also very hard to change the CCRs. Potential customers thoroughly read and understand the CCRs before buying into a CID, because the courts assume that homeowners have voluntarily accepted the covenants, controls, and restrictions of the common interest development. Evan McKenzie explains that, "Most significantly boards of directors [CIDs] operate outside constitutional restrictions because the law views them as business entities rather than as governments" (1994: 21). A new area of law has been opened up by lawsuits challenging the sometimes onerous rules of the private covenants, controls, and restrictions and the community's maintenance fees imposed by the developers and the homeowner associations.

In some jurisdictions, a private security officer has no greater arrest powers than a private citizen has. One must check the state law and state case law to see if private security officers have expanded arrest powers. In general, a private security officer is not empowered by any government body to act as a peace officer. Gated communities are increasing, and so is the use of private security officers. With increases in the number of private security officers, it is believed that they will increasingly perform duties similar to those of the public police and that more test court cases will appear. Hence, many citizens are beginning to question whether a private security officer should be bound by the same Fourth Amendment standards of conduct for search and seizure and arrest that bind a public police officer.

Another issue is the First Amendment and freedom of speech. Many homeowners associations have rules against canvassing, campaigning, circulating flyers, displaying signs, and bringing outside newspapers into the gated community. Girl Scouts selling cookies or individual canvassers must take their activities outside the wall. Gated communities and streets with barricades make it hard for individuals to exchange views or publicly support causes. City governments need to look ahead and set criteria and policies to determine whether a gated community is practical and feasible for the larger community, and evaluate the impact on contiguous neighborhoods and the balance of the region. City officials, planners, and citizens should assess and plan for mechanisms that will fall into place if the gated community goes bankrupt, does not have the resources for maintenance, or cannot provide the services and amenities promised by the developer. Residents outside a gated community need to understand how to organize themselves to protect the needs of the larger community if gated residents organize and vote en masse against taxes for needed services and programs for the larger community. City government needs to have a policy that will answer the demand of homeowners association lobbyists for tax rebates when gated residents do not wish to pay again for services they already have. City governments should also plan for crime prevention, traffic control, and better delivery of essential services for less economically fortunate, nongated neighbors.

—*Marvie Brooks*

See also ENVIRONMENTAL DESIGN

Further Reading

Atlas, Randall, and William G. LeBlanc. (1994). "The Impact on Crime of Street Closures and Barricades: A Florida Case Study." *Security Journal* 5: 141–145.

Barton, Stephen E., and Carol J. Silverman, eds. (1994). *Common Interest Communities: Private Governments and the Public Interest.* Berkeley, CA: Institute of Governmental Studies Press, University of California at Berkeley.

Bintliff, Russell L. (1992). *The Complete Manual of Corporate and Industrial Security.* Englewood Cliffs, NJ: Prentice Hall.

Blakely, Edward J., and Mary Gail Snyder. (1997). *Fortress America: Gated Communities in the United States.* Washington, DC: Brookings Institution Press.

Canin, Brian C. (1994). "Mastering Crime in Your Master Planned Community." Washington, DC: Urban Land Institute. http://www.canin.com/mastering_crime.html

Cohen, Mark Francis. (1996). "Neighborhood Report: Sea Gate." *New York Times* (24 November): 10.

Egan, Timothy. (1995). "The Serene Fortress: A Special Report." *New York Times* (3 September): 1.

Guterson, David. (1992). "No Place Like Home: On the Manicured Streets of a Master-Planned Community." *Harper's Magazine* (July): 55–64.

Helsley, Robert W., and William C. Strange. (1999). "Gated Communities and the Economic Geography of Crime." *Journal of Urban Economics* 46: 80–105.

Herman, Patricia. (1996). "Escapism in America: The Search for Utopia in Gated Communities." Master's thesis, Ball State University.

Herszenhorn, David M. (2001). "Breezy Point, Queens." *New York Times* (18 June): B5.

Howard, Ebenezer. (1965 [1898]). *Garden Cities of Tomorrow.* Cambridge, MA: MIT Press.

Johnston, Edwin. (2001). "On Growing Up in the Whitest Part of New York City." http://www.coup2k.com/edwinwhitenyc.html

Kennedy, David J. (1995). "Residential Associations as State Actors: Regulating the Impact of Gated Communities on Nonmembers." *Yale Law Journal* 105: 761–793.

Lang, Robert E., and Karen A. Danielsen. (1997). "Gated Communities in America: Walling Out the World." *Housing Policy Debate* 8: 867–899.

McKenzie, Evan. (1994). *Privatopia: Homeowner Associations and the Rise of Residential Private Government.* New Haven, CT: Yale University Press.

Newman, Oscar. (1972). *Defensible Space: Crime Prevention through Urban Design.* New York: Macmillan.

———. (1980). *Community of Interest.* New York: Anchor Press/ Doubleday.

Owens, John B. (1997). "Westec Story: Gated Communities and the Fourth Amendment." *American Criminal Law Review* 34: 1127–1160.

Stransky, Dennis W. (2000). "Gated Communities as Public Entities." Master's thesis, Greenspun College of Urban Affairs, University of Nevada. http://www.unlv.edu/Colleges/Urban/pubadmin/papers/dstransky.htm

Treece, Clifford J. (1999). *1999 Community Associations Factbook.* Alexandria, VA: Community Associations Institute.

Urban Research and Design Center, Washington University School of Architecture for the City of St. Louis CDA/SLDC. (1997). *St. Louis Historic Context: Community Planning.* St. Louis, MO: Urban Research and Design Center. http://stlouis.missouri.org/government/heritage/history/planning.htm

▼ GENDER

Although gender is likely the strongest predictor of criminal involvement, its influence on offending is not well understood. In fact, early theorizing about the causes of crime tended to focus on structural forces rather than gender. Recent work, however, particularly that conducted by feminists, highlights the disparity in male and female offending and victimization rates and explores why these differences persist over time and place.

THE SOCIAL CONSTRUCTION OF GENDER

Whereas *sex* is defined as the biological and physiological division between men and women, *gender* refers to the disparity between males and females that is socially constructed and reinforced by institutions, culture, and everyday interactions. Gender differences are most apparent when examining the social stereotypes that result in different attitudes, actions, and expectations of masculinity and femininity.

In fact, *sex* and *gender* are often used interchangeably by researchers, perhaps because of the difficulty in discerning whether differences between women and men can be attributed to biological or sociological forces. For example, whereas it may be argued that men are more aggressive than women because the former have higher levels of testosterone, it also is true that disparity in aggression and violence are influenced by differences in socialization processes. Parents, teachers, and friends often reward the aggressive behavior of boys and discourage them from appearing weak or sensitive, while encouraging girls to be "nice" and refrain from physical displays of anger. These examples illustrate the need for a closer examination of our beliefs about the innate natures of women and men and increased awareness of the ways in which society influences these perceptions.

GENDER DIFFERENCES IN OFFENDING

Likewise, gender disparities in offending have long been noted by criminologists, but traditional theorists assumed that the overrepresentation of men in the criminal justice system was a simple reflection of male biology and needed no further exploration. By contrast, recent theorizing about the causes of crime, particularly that produced by feminist theorists, emphasizes that a better understanding of the relationship between gender and crime will improve our ability to predict and prevent criminal involvement.

Despite their varying theoretical perspectives, criminologists agree that men commit the majority of crimes. Numerous sources, including arrest records, victimization reports, and self-report surveys, provide evidence for this claim. According to 1995 data from the Uniform Crime Reports (UCR), men accounted for approximately 81 percent of all arrests and were arrested more frequently than women for all crimes except prostitution (Steffensmeier 2001). Although self-report studies reflect somewhat smaller differences in male and female participation in crime, data from the National Youth Survey—a longitudinal study of adolescents living across the United States—reveal that women are underrepresented in every category of delinquency and crime (Canter 1982). Similarly, information from the 1994 National Crime Victimization Survey also reflects a gendered involvement in crime, with female perpetrators accounting for only 5 percent of all burglaries, 8 percent of all robberies, and 15 percent of all simple assaults (Steffensmeier 2001). The largest disparity between female and male crime rates is participation in violent offenses. UCR data demonstrate that women accounted for only 13.5 percent of all arrests for violent offenses in 1995 (versus 26 percent of all arrests for property offenses), including only 9 percent of all homicides.

Research reveals that gender differences in criminal offending have held steady over time, place, and culture. Although the media have proclaimed the emergence of a "new, violent female criminal," there has been little evidence to support this view. Arrest records reveal some convergence in male and female involvement in crime, with the proportion of female arrests increasing from 11 percent in 1960 to 19 percent in 1995. This trend can largely be explained, however, by increases in arrests for nonviolent crimes such as larceny, theft, and fraud. For the majority of other offenses, the female percentage of all arrests has increased only slightly (1 or 2 percent in each decade), and data reveal that the proportion of female homicides has decreased over time. Thus, convergence in female and male rates of offending is the result of women's increasing participation in nonviolent crimes, rather than acts of violence. Moreover, even though women's overall participation in crime has increased, female offenders still account for less than 20 percent of all criminal arrests (Steffensmeier 2001). The overrepresentation of males as violent offenders is not limited to the United States. Instead, cross-national data indicates that women represent a very small percentage of homicide offenders (the only crime for which detailed, comparable, and reliable records exist), and their homicide arrest rates have either remained steady or decreased over the past twenty years (Kruttschnitt 2000). In addition to gender differences in rates of offending, research demonstrates that women and men often engage in different types of offending, and the context of their crimes also differs. For example, UCR data reveal that minor property crimes such as larceny and fraud comprise a larger proportion of women's crime than of men's crimes, accounting for one-quarter of all female arrests, compared to only 12 percent of male arrests. Similarly, prostitution accounts for a larger percentage of female arrests, while a larger proportion of male arrests are for crimes against persons and major property crimes. Women differ from men not only in their propensity for committing violent offenses, but also in their motivations for engaging in such crimes. For example, homicide studies indicate that when women kill, they are more likely than males to target intimate partners and/or family members. In contrast, male homicides tend to be instrumental, committed during felonies or occurring during fights to "save face." Female homicide offenders also tend to be older than males, with involvement peaking in the twenties and continuing into the thirties, while male rates peak earlier and end earlier.

These trends suggest that patterns of offending reflect differences in gender roles, behaviors, and opportunities. For example, women's greater involvement in minor property crime such as shoplifting, check fraud, and credit card fraud can be viewed as an extension of the female consumer role and women's greater likelihood of shopping for their families. Similarly, female criminals often report that the items they stole were necessities for themselves or their children, which they could not afford to buy. In fact, there is mounting evidence of a "feminization of poverty," resulting from women's segregation into low-paying jobs and single-parent status, that may increase their involvement in crimes of economic gain, especially welfare fraud. Likewise, interviews with female prostitutes reveal that many began sex work as a means to support themselves and their children when faced with limited or no access to other resources or to legitimate means of earning money.

GENDER AND VICTIMIZATION

The relationship between gender and victimization follows a pattern similar to that between gender and offending, with men comprising the majority of victims but women overrepresented as victims of particular crimes. Most notably, women are much more likely to be victims of sexual assault and intimate partner violence than are men. In fact, 1998 statistics from the Bureau of Justice indicate that women are three times more likely to report domestic violence victimization and four times more likely to be victims of stalking than men, and women over the age of twelve accounted for 98 percent of all rape victims (Tjaden and Thoennes 2000). Not surprisingly, women are also more at risk for victimization in their homes and by someone they know, and they are more likely to be injured during such assaults than men. Similar evidence exists for juveniles, with boys slightly more likely than girls to be victims of crime (comprising 55 percent of victims), according to 1997 National Incident-Based Reporting System (NIBRS) data (Finkelhor and Omrod 2000). In addition, girls are more likely to be victims of sex offenses and kidnappings (representing 82 and 63 percent of all victims, respectively), and boys are more likely to be victims of robbery and larceny (comprising 91 and 69 percent of all victims). Again, it is likely that the disparity in victimization reflects differences in gender roles and opportunity. For example, societal mores dictate that girls be kept close to home, and, as a result, they are more likely to be victimized by family members. By contrast, boys, whose activities and peers are not as heavily monitored, are more likely to be victimized outside the home, by strangers in two-thirds of all victimization cases (compared to one-third for women).

DIFFERENTIAL PROCESSING BY THE CRIMINAL JUSTICE SYSTEM

Gender disparity occurs not only in rates of victimization and offending but also in processing by the criminal justice system. It is difficult, however, to determine the specific ways in which gender impacts sentencing and incarceration. For example, the "chivalry" hypothesis predicts that women receive more lenient sentences than men because they are viewed as either less threatening or more in need of protection from the harsh conditions of prison. There is little empirical support for this hypothesis, however, as evidence demonstrates that men and women who commit similar crimes tend to receive similar sentences.

Feminists propose a more complex relationship between gender and sentencing, positing that women and girls will receive lighter sentences if their crimes conform to traditional gender roles but harsher treatment when they oppose gender stereotypes. For example, a study of judicial sentencing revealed that judges were sympathetic toward women with children, asserting that imprisoning mothers resulted in a higher cost to society than setting them free. Moreover, judges deemed women's caregiving responsibilities as the most important factor in determining sentencing. By contrast, they did not feel that providing financial support to children was as critical; as a result, judges were not more likely to give fathers lighter sentences. As this example illustrates, society continues to expect mothers to provide emotional support and fathers to provide financial resources to children, and, in this case, social stereotypes work in favor of female offenders (as long as they conform to their ascribed gender role).

By contrast, women who cross gender boundaries may encounter less sympathy from the criminal justice system. For example, girls tend to be arrested more frequently than boys for crimes such as truancy and running away, which may be characterized as antifeminine rebellions that do not uphold the virtues of passivity, virginity, and obedience. Moreover, girls are subjected to a double standard by caregivers and criminal justice officials, who view them as more in need of

protection and control then boys. Because their actions are monitored more closely, their offenses are more likely to be discovered and punished. Girls' delinquency is viewed as especially dangerous and in need of reformation when it relates to their sexuality, and girls' offenses are often actively sexualized. In fact, as late as the mid-twentieth century, criminal justice officials systematically questioned female offenders about their sexual experiences, and tests of virginity were routinely performed. Girls who admitted to or were deemed "guilty" of engaging in consensual sex were more likely to receive additional charges.

Stiffer penalties for nontraditional female offenders also can be seen in the late twentieth and early twenty-first-century War on Drugs, which has resulted in disproportionate numbers of women being arrested and sentenced for drug-related crimes. In fact, over one-third of women in prison are currently incarcerated for drug offenses, compared to one-fifth of men. This differential treatment may reflect social stereotypes regarding appropriate masculine and feminine behavior. For example, female drug offenders may be viewed as more deviant than males, because society dictates that women should not engage in heavy drug use or in crime. Female addicts who are also mothers are viewed as especially evil, for their dependency often leaves them unable to adequately care for their children. Feminists assert that women's drug addiction must be understood in context and should not automatically result in lengthy sentences. There is considerable evidence that many female offenders have histories of physical and sexual victimization, and this abuse may lead victims to use drugs to self-medicate (i.e., to counter the low self-esteem and trauma caused by victimization). Feminists advocate treatment rather than incarceration for these women, but the criminal justice system (and society) has been reluctant to adopt this view.

The increase in women in prison has further implications. Many feminists note that although the female incarceration rate is rapidly increasing, adequate services for female offenders are severely lacking. This is especially true in facilities housing both sexes, in which services designed specifically for women are minimal or nonexistent. Thus, many feminists call for better programming for female offenders, including gender-specific services that will provide women with treatment for victimization and/or drug addiction, as well as vocational programs to bolster their ability to provide for themselves and their children.

EXPLANATIONS OF THE INFLUENCE OF GENDER ON CRIME

Despite the multitude of evidence demonstrating gender differences in offending and victimization, it is difficult to understand the specific ways in which gender affects crime. In fact, numerous studies reveal much similarity between male and female offending. For example, both female and male criminals are least likely to be involved in violent crimes and most likely to be arrested for nonviolent crimes. Similarly, cross-national data demonstrate that countries having high rates of male arrests also have high rates of female arrests, and countries with low rates of male offending have low rates of female offending. Likewise, trends in arrests are similar for men and women: when men's crime is on the rise, so is women's, and the same is true for declining or steady arrest rates. Offender characteristics also are similar, with both male and female violent criminals most likely to be younger than thirty; poor; unemployed; members of minority groups; residents of neighborhoods characterized by high rates of poverty, female-headed households, and residential instability; and dependent on drugs and alcohol.

These patterns suggest that the etiology of offending may be similar for men and women, especially when examining the structural correlates of crime. In fact, many scholars assert that the same theories can be used to explain male and female offending, and there is some evidence demonstrating that macro-level perspectives of crime, such as strain, differential association, and social control theories, are relevant for both sexes. Thus, many scholars assert that the same criminogenic forces influence women and men, but that the gender disparity in offending can be explained by differential exposure to these influences. For example, it may be that females commit fewer crimes than males because they do not face the same pressure for material success (strain theory), are less exposed to delinquent peers (differential association), and are subject to greater supervision and encouraged to form greater social bonds with others (social control theory).

By contrast, many feminists argue that this reasoning cannot adequately explain why women and men face different levels of exposure and reaction to criminogenic influences, and they emphasize that the ways in which gender impacts institutions, culture, and everyday interactions—and, ultimately, criminal involvement—must be examined in much more detail. Moreover, they assert that separate theories of offend-

ing are warranted not only because women's and men's lives are very different but also because traditional theories were specifically created to explain male offending and did not take women's experiences into account. In particular, feminists urge that theories of female offending that are women-centered and rely on detailed examinations of women's lives are especially needed. In the past, explanations of female criminality were based on chauvinistic and stereotypical views of women and depicted female offenders as "unnatural" and devious. Even more recent attempts to explain women's involvement in crime have been limited in their exploration of sex roles and stereotypes. For example, the "liberation hypothesis" espoused in the 1970s theorized that as women gained status and power in society (and became more masculine) their involvement in crime would increase (to mirror that of men's). This theory, however, was based on the assumption that women would be able to make great advances in society, occupy high-status jobs, and be viewed as equal to men in ability and intelligence. In fact, research indicates that such widespread emancipation has not been achieved, convergence in male and female crime rates has not occurred, and most female offenders hold traditional views of femininity and masculinity.

Feminists seek to replace these inadequate theories of female offending with more detailed examinations of women's lives and experiences. For example, many feminists conduct in-depth, qualitative interviews with female criminals to allow women to tell their own stories and better illuminate the forces that lead them to break the law. Although feminists recognize that there are many pathways to crime, one of the most widely accepted theories of female offending proposes that women's crimes are often directly related to their histories of victimization. In fact, studies reveal that a large percentage of female offenders have been victims of violent crime, including physical or sexual abuse as children, sexual assault, or intimate partner violence. Often, childhood maltreatment may cause girls to run away from home and commit property crimes (especially prostitution) to survive on the streets. Many of these women also report drug or alcohol dependency, with many using illicit substances to counteract the trauma of victimization. Dependency typically prolongs involvement in crime, as women commit more crimes to buy drugs. Intimate partner victimization also may lead to involvement in crime, as victims may be forced by their partners to break the law—hoping to reduce the amount of violence they endure—or engage in illegitimate money-making schemes (such as prostitution or shoplifting) to support their and their partners' drug addictions.

Although such theories contribute to our understanding of female offending, their failure to directly compare men's and women's experiences results in a limited ability to analyze gender differences in crime. Very few theories have been able to adequately address this complex issue. Recent work by Darrell Steffensmeier and Emilie Allen (1996) provides a better understanding of the ways in which gender impacts criminal involvement. Their theory utilizes a broad framework that explores social, cultural, historical, biological, and reproductive differences between men and women and illustrates how these differences influence criminality. More specifically, they identify the ways in which gender differences—including differences in norms, moral development, social control, physical strength/aggression, and sexuality—lead to disparity in men's and women's motivation, opportunity, and context of offending. For example, when women are rewarded for being nurturing and relationship-oriented, and males are taught to be aggressive and domineering, female offending is inhibited and male offending promoted. While some of these concepts are utilized in other gender-related theories of crime, Steffensmeier and Allen's work is notable for presenting a comprehensive understanding of the relationship between gender and crime, while maintaining a focus on the everyday interactions between men and women.

THE INTERSECTION OF RACE, CLASS, AND GENDER

Although this entry clearly implicates gender as a significant predictor of involvement in crime, scholars increasingly are recognizing that its influence is interrelated to other important social and demographic characteristics, particularly race/ethnicity and socioeconomic status. For example, criminals, especially violent offenders, tend to be not only male but also poor, unemployed, members of minority groups, residents of disorganized neighborhoods, and so on. Moreover, evidence suggests that involvement in crime is affected as much by race/ethnicity as gender, as evidenced in the similar arrest rates for violent crimes of African American females and white males. In addition, cross-national studies reveal that black women do not have high rates of criminal involvement in other countries, which suggests that the unique eco-

nomic conditions in the United States—including high concentrations of economic disparity—are important risk factors in leading to criminal involvement. Similarly, studies of the criminal justice processing of females have found that people of color and poor women are likely to receive more punitive sentences than white women and wealthier defendants. These examples illustrate that the impact of race, class, and gender on crime are interrelated, and the relationships between these forces need further theoretical and empirical specification.

FUTURE DIRECTIONS

As is evident, there is much debate regarding the differential involvement in crime of women and men. The growing interest in gender issues, however, is a needed and refreshing departure from earlier theorizing about crime, which either ignored gender as a motivating force or presented inadequate or distorted views of masculinity and femininity. As recent work suggests, gender differences are rooted in multiple levels of society, and only by examining how these forces interact can we understand what motivates women and men to commit crime. Although much more investigation is needed to illuminate the complex relationship between gender and crime, as well as the intersection between gender, race/ethnicity, class, and other factors, criminologists are beginning to recognize and explore these issues.

—*Abigail A. Fagan*

See also FEAR OF CRIME; FEMINIST THEORY; RAPE; RAPE, DATE AND MARITAL; SEXUAL VIOLENCE; WOMEN AND CRIME IN A GLOBAL PERSPECTIVE; WOMEN AND POLICING; WOMEN AS OFFENDERS, WOMEN AS VICTIMS; WOMEN IN PRISON, WOMEN WHO KILL

Further Reading

Belknap, Joanne. (1996). *The Invisible Woman: Gender, Crime, and Criminal Justice*. Cincinnati: Wadsworth Publishing Company.

Canter, Rachelle J. (1982). "Sex Differences in Self-Report Delinquency." *Criminology* 20, 3/4: 373–393.

Chesney-Lind, Meda. (1997). *The Female Offender: Girls, Women and Crime*. Thousand Oaks, CA: Sage Publications.

Chesney-Lind, Meda, and Randall G. Shelden. (1998). *Girls, Delinquency, and Juvenile Justice*, 2nd ed. Belmont, CA: Wadsworth.

Daly, Kathleen. (1995). *Gender, Crime, and Punishment*. New Haven, CT: Yale University Press.

Daly, Kathleen, and Meda Chesney-Lind. (1988). "Feminism and Criminology." *Justice Quarterly* 5: 497–538.

Finkelhor, David, and Richard Ormrod. (2000). "Characteristics of

Crimes Against Juveniles." Washington, DC: U.S. Department of Justice.

Kruttschnitt, Candace (2001). "Gender and Violence." In *Women, Crime, and the Criminal Justice System: Original Feminist Readings,* edited by Claire M. Renzetti and Lynne Goodstein. Los Angeles, CA: Roxbury Publishing Company, 77–92.

Lindsey, Linda L. (1997). *Gender Roles: A Sociological Perspective.* Upper Saddle River, NJ: Prentice-Hall, Inc.

Renzetti, Claire M., and Lynne Goodstein, eds.. (2001). *Women, Crime, and the Criminal Justice System: Original Feminist Readings.* Los Angeles, CA: Roxbury Publishing Company.

Smith, Douglas A., and Raymond Paternoster. (1987). "The Gender Gap in Theories of Deviance: Issues and Evidence." *Journal of Research in Crime and Delinquency* 24, 2: 140–172.

Steffensmeier, Darrell. (2001). "Female Crime Trends, 1960–1995." In *Women, Crime, and the Criminal Justice System: Original Feminist Readings,* edited by Claire M. Renzetti and Lynne Goodstein. Los Angeles, CA: Roxbury Publishing Company, 191–211.

Steffensmeier, Darrell, and Emilie Allen. (1996). "Gender and Crime: Toward a Gendered Theory of Female Offending." *Annual Review of Sociology* 22: 459–487.

Tjaden, Patricia and Nancy Thoennes. (2000). *Extent, Nature, and Consequences of Intimate Partner Violence.* Washington, DC: U.S. Department of Justice.

◤ GENOCIDE

Human massacres of various forms have been recurrent events in world history. In recent years, human massacre in the form of genocide has stunned and morally outraged the public, as has the apparent inability of nations to curb it or to bring its perpetrators to justice. The work of international human rights groups and the documentation of journalists have brought such stark attention to these crimes against humanity—such as those in Bosnia, Rwanda, Chechnya, East Timor, and Chiapas, Mexico— that the detection, prevention, and punishment of genocide and the obligations of individual nations have occupied the agenda of the international community. To this end, a perceptual, social, and legal distinction has been made between mass murder and genocide. This has led to the emergence of a new area of scholarship that attempts to understand and explain genocide in the hopes of preventing it.

SOCIAL CONFLICT AND MASS MURDER

In 477 BCE, the democratic polis of Athens put to death the entire male population of the island of Melos and sold all the women and children into slavery following a siege that took place because the citizens of Melos voted for neutrality in the Peloponnesian War between Sparta and Athens. From 149 to 146 BCE, the Romans laid siege to Carthage, killing 150,000 out of a population of 200,000. When the crusaders seized the Holy Land, the victors, it is said, waded to their ankles in the blood of Muslims. Massacres, the annihilation of towns and cities in war, the mass slaughter of combatants, and the liquidation of conquered populations are etched in the history of civilization (Chalk and Jonassohn 1990). It is noteworthy that these atrocities were collective acts sanctioned by religious and/or secular authorities, were typically acts of state policy, and were often carried out with a sense of righteousness. It is also noteworthy that these atrocities are not particular to antiquity. The worst atrocities in human history are living memories, primary among them the killing of 1.5 million Armenians by the Turks during World War I and 6 million European Jews by the Nazis during World War II.

THE LEGAL CONSTRUCTION OF GENOCIDE

The term *genocide* was coined by Raphael Lemkin in 1944 "to signify a coordinated plan of different actions aiming at the destruction of essential foundations of the life of national groups, with the aim of annihilating the groups themselves" (Gutman and Rieff 1999: 155). In Lemkin's view, groups can be annihilated physically or assimilated forcibly by expunging their distinctive attributes. Lemkin proposed in 1933 that an international treaty be drafted to identify attacks on national, religious, and ethnic groups as international crimes. The backdrop to his writing was the rise of the Nazis and their conceptualization and implementation of plans to murder the European Jews.

At the Nuremberg trials in 1945, the Allies prosecuted the surviving figures of the Nazi era for war crimes and for crimes against humanity (Bass 2000). These crimes included "deliberate and systematic genocide, viz., the extermination of racial and national groups" (Gutman and Rieff 1999: 155). In 1946, the United Nations affirmed for the first time in a General Assembly motion that genocide is a war crime under international law. This was further consolidated in 1948 with the U.N. Convention on the Prevention and Punishment of the Crime of Genocide (the Geneva Convention).

INTERNATIONAL HUMANITARIAN LAW

Recognition of the specific crime of genocide is part of the growing body of legal theory collectively called

▽

Selection from *Deportationsliste: Jüdischer Kleinkinder, Schülerinnen und Schüler sowie Jugendlicher aus Frankfurt/M Jahrgang 1921–1941.*

A small sample from a list of Jewish children born between 1921 and 1941 who wer deported from Frankfurt am Main, Germany to concentration camps by the Nazi government. The list was compiled from Nazi records by the Jewish Museum in Frankfurt and made available to the public. They estimate that about 9,400 Jews were deported to camps from Frankfurt from October 1941 to October 1943 and nearly all were killed.

Nachname	Vorname	Geburtsdatum	Alter 1942	Lager
Gruenewald	Bertha	05.04.25	17	unbekannt
Gruenewald	Erna	13.09.23	19	Minsk
Gruenewald	Ferdinand	07.09.22	20	Gross-Rosen
Gruenewald	Hanna	26.04.25	17	Minsk
Gruenewald	Otto	02.06.29	13	Minsk
Gruenewald	Rueben	29.05.39	3	Lodz
Gruenfeld	Alfred	22.03.34	8	Lodz
Gruenglueck	Lea	12.06.38	4	Minsk
Gruenspan	Leo	20.03.28	14	Lodz
Grunebaum	Alice	27.04.38	4	Auschwitz
Grynfogel	Meier F.	08.08.29	13	Minsk
Guggenheim	Hedwig	01.09.36	6	Minsk
Gurbitsch	Alex	22.04.23	19	Minsk
Gutenstein	Paul Heinz	31.03.28	14	Auschwitz
Gutmann	Ernst	21.11.27	15	Riga
Gutmann	Josua	01.05.38	4	Auschwitz
Gutmann	Ruth S.	04.02.23	19	Osten

international humanitarian law (IHL). IHL emerged in the context of nineteenth-century European military conflict; it attempted to clarify the responsibilities of states during the conduct of war. Jean-Henri Dunant, a Swiss businessman, established the International Committee of the Red Cross in 1863 after seeing the carnage of the clash between Austrian and Franco-Italian forces in 1859, in which tens of thousands of combatants died from untreated wounds. The Red Cross convened the Geneva Convention of 1864 "for the amelioration of the conditions of the wounded of armies in the field." Subsequent Geneva conventions prohibited the wartime use of poison gas and biological weapons (1925), established the rights of wounded and sick combatants on land and at sea, prohibited medical experiments on and mistreatment of prisoners of war, and protected the status of civilian noncombatants (1949). The most recent initiative under IHL has been an attempt to outlaw the worldwide use of land mines in armed conflict because of the devastating legacy left buried in the ground afterward.

These developments are part of the history of such international governing bodies as the League of Nations and its successor, the United Nations. Other key stakeholders, such as Amnesty International, Médecins Sans Frontières, and the Red Cross and Red Crescent, have expedited these developments. For the first time in world history, international bodies have developed a sophisticated legal framework to mitigate the effects of violence associated with war and other intergroup conflict. Of course, the documentation of violence and the vivid portrayal of human rights violations by news media have also influenced the development of IHL.

Besides genocide, IHL addresses crimes against humanity and war crimes—areas that are clearly related. Whereas crimes of war have been acknowledged by states since antiquity, more recently, the Hague Conventions of 1899 and 1907 established that breaches of the customary rules of war are international crimes. The 1945 Charter of the International Military Tribunal at Nuremberg defined war crimes as violations of the customs of war, such as murder, ill treatment of civilians in occupied territory, forcible deportation of civilians, mistreatment of POWs, killing of hostages, plundering of property, and the unnecessary destruction of municipalities. The four Geneva Conventions of 1949 laid out such crimes in further detail (Ball 1999).

The laws of war apply only to crimes that occur within armed interstate conflict. However, many of the crimes of this century occurred during times of civil war or instability within national borders. Examples include Stalin's liquidation of the Kulaks and the forced collectivization of Soviet agriculture; Pinochet's "disappearance" of progressives in post-Allende Chile;

and Guatemala's murder of thousands of Mayan peasants in the 1980s. In such cases, the provisions of IHL covering crimes against humanity may apply.

The International Criminal Tribunal for Rwanda extended IHL for the first time to civil wars. In Rwanda, the tribunal identified serious violations under Protocol II of the 1977 Geneva Convention, namely, violence to life and person, outrages to personal dignity, hostage taking, and summary execution. In addition, the tribunal identified twelve serious violations of the customs of war, including attacks on civilians, pillage, rape, and mutilation.

Anomalies and Limitations of IHL

The rise of IHL may be grounds for optimism, but its success is not assured. The creation of IHL after the rise of the Red Cross has been, in the words of Lawrence Weschler, a "maddeningly halting, vexed, and compromised effort to expand the territory of law itself" (Gutman and Rieff 1999: 19). The aim of IHL has been to create international procedures not only to punish war crimes but also, in the case of genocide, to prevent them. However, IHL has proved to be weak; most observers might assume, for example, that the Geneva Convention governing genocide would apply to such events as the killing fields of Cambodia, where 1.5 million of the country's 7 million citizens were butchered by the Khmer Rouge; or to the Iraqi government's lethal gassing of 50,000 Kurds at Anfal in 1988; or to the indiscriminate annihilation of towns in the self-declared independent state of Chechnya by Russian troops in the mid-1990s that resulted in 90,000 (mostly civilian) casualties; or to ethnic massacres in the former Yugoslavia in the past decade. Yet, international action has occurred only in the last case. The 1948 Geneva Convention has been marred by a nearly total failure to live up to its provisions. The international criminal tribunal envisaged by the 1948 convention was not created until 1991, when it was convened to investigate crimes of genocide in Yugoslavia. No state brought such a case before the World Court until 1993, when Bosnia-Herzegovina charged Yugoslavia with genocide. The international criminal tribunal was convened a second time, in 1995, to prosecute Hutu leaders responsible for fomenting the murder of between 500,000 and 1 million Tutsis in Rwanda.

Members of the U.N. Security Council, who exercise a veto over decisions of the General Assembly, have been reluctant to create an autonomous international criminal court for various reasons, primary among them being that such a court would necessarily place limits on the sovereignty of individual member states. Furthermore, the policies of Security Council members might themselves be subject to international scrutiny (e.g., the U.S. bombing of Cambodia and Laos is reported to have resulted in hundreds of thousands of civilian casualties, exposing Secretary of State Henry Kissinger to charges of war crimes [Hitchens 2001]). Strategic interests and the global balance of power play another major role. The maintenance of an international court of judges, prosecutors, and investigators creates a new level of institutional justice that U.N. states are required to fund but over which they have little political control.

In addition, the Geneva conventions are effective only if the U.N. member states sign international accords promising to comply. In fact, the United States did not sign the 1948 accords dealing with genocide until 1989. Further problems arise in the process by which U.N. member states actually recognize and label genocide. In the Rwanda case, Belgium and the United States actually resisted labeling the 1994 massacres that were documented by U.N. peacekeepers as "genocide" because this would have required the United Nations to prevent the genocide—a process that would have entailed a massive commitment of ground troops and logistical support, which member states were reluctant to commit (Power 2001).

In Rwanda, the Tutsis and Hutus were distinct ethnic groups whose differences were exploited by colonial rule (Mamdani 2001). In the case of the Khmer Rouge in Cambodia, perpetrators and victims were overwhelmingly from the same ethnic group. The vast majority of victims were killed for reasons of political differences, but this category was expressly excluded from the definition of genocide in the 1948 convention. In the case of the murder of the Iraqi Kurds, was this a campaign against ethnic Kurds as such or rather an opportunistic action against political opponents? In other words, was this "mere" murder really a massacre and therefore an issue of national jurisdiction? The world may recognize mass murder when it happens, but establishing the crime of genocide under international law is a more exacting problem.

THE STUDY OF GENOCIDE IN THE SOCIAL SCIENCES AND EXPLANATIONS OF GENOCIDE

Only in recent decades has serious attention been given to the study of genocide. Scholarship in the area

Convention on the Prevention and Punishment of the Crime of Genocide

Adopted by Resolution 260 (III) A of the United Nations General Assembly on December 9, 1948.

Article 1

The Contracting Parties confirm that genocide, whether committed in time of peace or in time of war, is a crime under international law which they undertake to prevent and to punish.

Article 2

In the present Convention, genocide means any of the following acts committed with intent to destroy, in whole or in part, a national, ethnical, racial or religious group, as such:

(a) Killing members of the group;
(b) Causing serious bodily or mental harm to members of the group;
(c) Deliberately inflicting on the group conditions of life calculated to bring about its physical destruction in whole or in part;
(d) Imposing measures intended to prevent births within the group;
(e) Forcibly transferring children of the group to another group.

Article 3

The following acts shall be punishable:

(a) Genocide;
(b) Conspiracy to commit genocide;
(c) Direct and public incitement to commit genocide;
(d) Attempt to commit genocide;
(e) Complicity in genocide.

Article 4

Persons committing genocide or any of the other acts enumerated in Article 3 shall be punished, whether they are constitutionally responsible rulers, public officials or private individuals.

Article 5

The Contracting Parties undertake to enact, in accordance with their respective Constitutions, the necessary legislation to give effect to the provisions of the present Convention and, in particular, to provide effective penalties for persons guilty of genocide or any of the other acts enumerated in Article 3.

Article 6

Persons charged with genocide or any of the other acts enumerated in Article 3 shall be tried by a competent tribunal of the State in the territory of which the act was committed, or by such international penal tribunal as may have jurisdiction with respect to those Contracting Parties which shall have accepted its jurisdiction.

Article 7

Genocide and the other acts enumerated in Article 3 shall not be considered as political crimes for the purpose of extradition.

The Contracting Parties pledge themselves in such cases to grant extradition in accordance with their laws and treaties in force.

Article 8

Any Contracting Party may call upon the competent organs of the United Nations to take such action under the Charter of the United Nations as they consider appropriate for the prevention and suppression of acts of genocide or any of the other acts enumerated in Article 3.

Article 9

Disputes between the Contracting Parties relating to the interpretation, application or fulfilment of the present Convention, including those relating to the responsibility of a State for genocide or any of the other acts enumerated in Article 3, shall be submitted to the International Court of Justice at the request of any of the parties to the dispute.

Article 10

The present Convention, of which the Chinese, English, French, Russian and Spanish texts are equally authentic, shall bear the date of 9 December 1948.

Article 11

The present Convention shall be open until 31 December 1949 for signature on behalf of any Member of the United Nations and of any non-member State to which an invitation to sign has been addressed by the General Assembly.

The present Convention shall be ratified, and the instruments of ratification shall be deposited with the Secretary-General of the United Nations.

After 1 January 1950, the present Convention may be acceded to on behalf of any Member of the United Nations and of any non-member State which has received an invitation as aforesaid.

Instruments of accession shall be deposited with the Secretary-General of the United Nations.

Article 12

Any Contracting Party may at any time, by notification addressed to the Secretary-General of the United Nations, extend the application of the present Convention to all or any of the territories for the conduct of whose foreign relations that Contracting Party is responsible.

Article 13

On the day when the first twenty instruments of ratification or accession have been deposited, the Secretary-General shall draw up a process-verbal and transmit a copy of it to each Member of the United

continued

Nations and to each of the non-member States contemplated in Article 11.

The present Convention shall come into force on the ninetieth day following the date of deposit of the twentieth instrument of ratification or accession.

Any ratification or accession effected subsequent to the latter date shall become effective on the ninetieth day following the deposit of the instrument of ratification or accession.

Article 14

The present Convention shall remain in effect for a period of ten years as from the date of its coming into force.

It shall thereafter remain in force for successive periods of five years for such Contracting Parties as have not denounced it at least six months before the expiration of the current period.

Denunciation shall be effected by a written notification addressed to the Secretary-General of the United Nations.

Article 15

The present Convention shall remain in effect for a period of ten years as from the date of its coming into force.

It shall thereafter remain in force for successive periods of five years for such Contracting Parties as have not denounced it at least six months before the expiration of the current period.

Denunciation shall be effected by a written notification addressed to the Secretary-General of the United Nations.

If, as a result of denunciations, the number of Parties to the present Convention should become less than sixteen, the Convention shall cease to be in force as from the date on which the last of these denunciations shall become effective.

Article 16

A request for the revision of the present Convention may be made at any time by any Contracting Party by means of a notification in writing addressed to the Secretary-General.

The General Assembly shall decide upon the steps, if any, to be taken in respect of such request.

Article 17

The Secretary-General of the United Nations shall notify all Members of the United Nations and the non-member States contemplated in Article 11 of the following:

(a) Signatures, ratifications and accessions received in accordance with Article 11;

(b) Notifications received in accordance with Article 12;

(c) The date upon which the present Convention comes into force in accordance with Article 13;

(d) Denunciations received in accordance with Article 14;

(e) The abrogation of the Convention in accordance with Article 15;

(f) Notifications received in accordance with Article 16.

Article 18

The original of the present Convention shall be deposited in the archives of the United Nations.

A certified copy of the Convention shall be transmitted to all Members of the United Nations and to the non-member States contemplated in Article 11.

Article 19

The present Convention shall be registered by the Secretary-General of the United Nations on the date of its coming into force.

---

includes discussions of how to define genocide and comparative analyses of the processes involved, including types and levels of genocide and the forces that contribute to its occurrence. Some literature—although very little—looks at how genocide affects the survivors of victim groups and how a society, in the aftermath of genocide, attempts to restore itself.

Among the debates that are relevant to the study of genocide is how to define the term. Of the many considerations in this area is the way a social science definition of *genocide* differs from a legal definition of the term, especially as it is expressed in the Geneva Convention. Chalk and Jonassohn (1990) have noted the deficiencies of relying on a legal definition, arguing that the Geneva Convention struggles with the distinction between killing and inflicting harm, between destroying a group whole or in part, and between physical and cultural annihilation. Social science literature confronts another tension that the Geneva Convention definition of genocide suffers, that is, the problem of including all types of victim groups. Some social scientists resolve the latter problem by defining a group of victims as one that has been identified and systemically targeted by a perpetrator as such.

Another area in the literature on genocide deals with comparative analyses. This area examines the conditions and sequences of events that are common to acts of genocide, comparing modern and premodern societies. This analysis offers insights on how genocide is used as a weapon to enact an ideology, ensure conformity, eliminate a perceived threat, or resolve a conflict. The events that are often identified as common to genocide include the dehumanization of the victim group, the existence of a centralized authority that commands the obedience of the majority of citizenry, the development of a methodological plan for murder, and the preparation of a means to identify the victims and carry out a plan of extermination.

These analyses have led to the development of various typologies of genocide. These typologies are often based on characterizing the type of society, perpetrator, victim group, and the outcome and/or on characterizing the intent of the perpetrator. With typologies that focus on intent, much of the work carefully considers whether these acts are politically, ideologically, economically, or culturally motivated. One of the important considerations in this debate is how to adequately consider the level of intent of the perpetrator—a distinction that is most easily described by the legal difference between manslaughter and murder. Overall, however, although this area of scholarship contributes important understandings, these typologies are heuristic. As such, the insights of social science literature that focuses on why acts of genocide occur and that examines the genocidal behavior and mentality of those who perpetrate such plans are critical to developing a clearer understanding of the most important contribution of research in this area: how to better predict and prevent genocide.

Within criminology, explanations of homicide focus on why individuals act criminally, but why communities attempt to annihilate other communities has received scant attention. The most famous attempt to make sense of such phenomena appeared in Stanley Milgram's studies of obedience to authority. Milgram's work was initiated at the time of Adolf Eichmann's trial for his role in the deportation of European Jews to the eastern death camps (Arendt 1994). Like so many other Nazis, he offered the defense of "just following orders." From this, Milgram hypothesized that individuals could be coerced to participate in genocide because of the pressure to obey placed on subordinates in bureaucratic organizations. According to Milgram, because of a defect in human nature, people are incapable of resisting the coercive force of "malevolent" authority (Milgram 1974: 189). From this perspective, genocide is made possible because low-level functionaries in war bureaucracies are incapable of resisting superiors' orders.

In Milgram's obedience studies, the unknowing subject, the "teacher," was asked to give the "learner" electric shocks increasing in power each time the learner missed a correct answer. (The learner, played by a student or an actor, was actually unharmed.) The teacher typically continued administering higher and higher doses of the shock therapy once assured that the experimenter would assume complete responsibility. Milgram's work, though extremely provocative, was deficient in terms of both internal and external validity. On the former count, evidence suggests that persons most prone to administer the supposedly lethal levels of electric shocks to an innocent learner, because of pressure from an authority figure, were those least likely to believe the learner actually was harmed. In other words, persons in psychological experiments tend to believe that, whatever the appearances, no one can actually be hurt.

In terms of external validity, the obedience paradigm seems ill equipped to explain the actual behavior of genocide perpetrators. The recent historiography of the Holocaust suggests that ordinary soldiers typically did not require coercion to obey orders to kill innocent civilians. Indeed, many of the most effective agents of genocide were middle-aged policemen in occupied Poland, persons with little of the fanatical zeal of the Nazi SS. Evidence suggests that they frequently found the work distasteful in its particulars but that they experienced little moral opposition to the extermination of Jews—although with respect to the execution of Polish patriots, they were often conflicted. Daniel Goldhagen draws a telling parallel between the agents of genocide in the Holocaust and the perpetrators of genocide in the last decade. "Who doubts that the Tutsis who slaughtered Hutus in Burundi or the Hutus who slaughtered Tutsis in Rwanda . . . that the Serbs who have killed Croats or Bosnian Muslims, did so out of conviction in the justice of their actions? Why do we not believe the same for the German perpetrators?" (Goldhagen 1997: 14–15).

Goldhagen's own explanation of the Holocaust, however, is as monocausal as that of Milgram, which Goldhagen seeks to challenge. He attributes the genocide to "eliminationist antisemitism" (Goldhagen 1997: 80ff). Given the Nazi racial antipathy to other groups—Slavs, Gypsies, and so forth—what is needed is a special mental orientation for each of the exterminated groups that is tautological and not parsimonious. Eliminationist anti-Semitism does not explain the Holocaust so much as it redescribes the mind-set of those who engaged in it.

ELIAS AND GENOCIDE

Norbert Elias has developed a theory that provides a framework for understanding more broadly the history of genocide and the legal and political responses to it. At the core of this theory is the observation that a "civilizing process" took root in Western society during the feudal period. This process was associated with the cultivation of norms of self-restraint and the inhibition of impulses. The civilizing process appeared simultaneously with the rise of nation-states that reserved the right to use violence to central authorities. As societies developed, the process of integration required the shaping of a subjectivity ("psychogenesis") that was appropriate for the changing forms of financial and cultural transaction in modern societies ("sociogenesis"). Commerce necessitated manners, and manners fostered codes of respectable, "civic" conduct.

Elias implies that the processes of civilization are inconsistent with such barbarian practices as genocide. He comments that the Holocaust was a "throwback to the barbarism and savagery of earlier times" (1996: 302). Despite this, Elias does suggest that "the continuous intertwining of human activities again and again acts as a lever which over the centuries produces changes in human conduct in the same direction—although, today as in the past, these trends can go at any time into reverse gear" (1994: 522). Because the acquisition of a monopoly of violence is a feature of modernizing states, a state itself can initiate aggression on a scale previously unprecedented. Such aggression can become a way of managing and achieving higher levels of integration (i.e., forced assimilation), especially because, in the early stages, state formation is a fierce, competitive process. In this process, conflicts arise because the states are becoming more interdependent through trade in material and cultural resources.

However, integration cannot be achieved solely by force, because doing so undermines the legitimacy of state power. Other processes of integration are social, political, and economic, exemplified by the development of central taxation systems, police forces, the creation of laws, and, more recently, central policies and codes of behavior, including constitutions, legal codes, and charters of rights. Although the codes of behavior may have acted initially to curb impulsiveness and cultivate a sense of civic obligation, states, in order to preserve their own legitimacy, have an obligation to ensure the personal security and dignity of their citizens.

Integration, therefore, has resulted in the invention of rights and the creation of institutions designed to identify and protect them.

The dark side of the civilizing process is the cultural superiority that more advanced states feel over less advanced states. The history of colonization and the genocidal massacres that have characterized the conquest of the Americas and the African nations in many ways illustrate this ironic tendency of state formation and civilization to prosper hand in hand with intergroup violence. Elias writes that "an essential phase of the civilizing process was concluded at exactly the time when the consciousness of civilization, the consciousness of the superiority of their own behavior . . . spread over the whole nations of the West" (1994: 41). The invidious cultivation of civilization provided a rationale for the subjugation of other groups. Also, the changing levels of integration tended to produce both a structural and an emotional disequilibrium. "If two groups become more, or more reciprocally, interdependent than they were before, each of them has reason to fear that it may be dominated, or even annihilated, by the other" (Elias 1972: 279). Integration creates vulnerability, particularly if the groups have radically different and exclusive codes of conduct based on their own standards of civilization, even if these codes are more apparent than real. Ironically, this suggests that the potential for genocide is greatest where the groups are internal to the domestic state, with outsiders already significantly integrated into the dominant culture (such as the European Jews and the Armenian Turks), and not foreigners.

RESPONDING TO GENOCIDE AND THE FUTURE OF IHL

Is the development of IHL consistent with Elias's theory of state formation and the civilizing process? Clearly, the international development of policies to define and condemn acts of genocide is a further step in the process of world integration. Elias writes, "one can see the first outline of a world-wide system of tensions composed of alliances and supra-state units of various kinds, the prelude of struggles embracing the whole globe, which are the precondition for a world-wide monopoly of physical force" (1994: 523). The long history of international agreements about the conduct of war serves as an example of this potential monopoly of force (as well as of the unstable consequences of its use). Nations have not necessarily eliminated the potential for mass violence, but they have created codes that reinvent the boundaries of war.

An important element of those codes is the attempt to "humanize war" through international humanitarian laws. Political progress on these matters has been motivated by public outcry. The outcry of international groups and the pictures that citizens around the world have witnessed in the daily news have stimulated a collective fear and shame. This fear and shame implicate people's deep moral senses and suggest that people are still "barbarians." Action by state leaders to develop policies and frameworks to prevent genocide and punish perpetrators of such crimes is a continuation of the civilizing process. As one reporter noted, "it is no exaggeration to say that these codes were intended to establish, even in war, a firebreak between civilization and barbarism" (Gutman and Rieff 1999: 8).

While the relationships between groups and states and between communities within states remain grossly unequal in political, economic, and social power, and while people live in a state of global economic interdependence, preventing genocide will require constant vigilance. Just as earlier mass murders resulted in U.N. action to outlaw genocide, the legacy of atrocities in Rwanda and Yugoslavia and other places and the feelings of shame evoked by these events are compelling a change in the landscape of conflict to prevent genocide. Most directly responsible for this change is the growing number of intergovernmental and nongovernmental organizations that, as the eyes and ears of the world, are the grim witnesses to genocide. In response, they transcend state agendas, forwarding policies and methods for the detection and prevention of genocide. To that end, such groups offer some hope that in the longer term this recurring crime will be abated.

—Augustine Brannigan and Viola R. Cassis

See also MASS MURDER; WAR CRIMES

Further Reading

Arendt, Hannah. (1994). *Trial in Jerusalem*. London: Penguin.

Ball, Howard. (1999). *Prosecuting War Crimes and Genocide: The Twentieth-Century Experience*. Lawrence: University Press of Kansas.

Bass, Gary J. (2000). *Stay the Hand of Vengeance: The Politics of War Crimes Tribunals*. Princeton, NJ: Princeton University Press.

Chalk, Frank, and Kurt Jonassohn. (1990). *The History and Sociology of Genocide*. New Haven, CT: Yale University Press.

Charny, Israel, ed. (1999). *Encyclopedia of Genocide*. Santa Barbara, CA: ABC-CLIO.

Elias, Norbert. (1972). "Process of State Formation and Nation Building." In *Transactions of the Seventh World Congress on Sociology, Varna, September 1970*, vol. 4. Sofia, Bulgaria: International Sociological Association, 274–284.

———. (1994). *The Civilizing Process*. Trans. by Edmund Jephcott. Oxford, UK: Blackwell.

———. (1996). *The Germans: Power Struggles and the Development of Habitus in the Nineteenth and Twentieth Centuries*. Translated by Eric Dunning and Stephen Mennell. Oxford, England: Polity Press.

Goldhagen, Daniel. (1997). *Hitler's Willing Executioners*. New York: Vintage Books.

Gutman, Roy, and David Rieff. (1999). *Crimes of War: What the Public Should Know*. New York: W. W. Norton.

Hitchens, Christopher. (2001). *The Trial of Henry Kissinger*. New York: Verso.

Mamdani, Mahmood. (2001). *When Victims Become Killers: Colonialism, Nativism and the Genocide in Rwanda*. Princeton, NJ: Princeton University Press.

Milgram, Stanley. (1974). *Obedience to Authority*. New York: Harper & Row.

Power, Samantha. (2001) "Bystanders to Genocide." *Atlantic Monthly* (September). http://www.theatlantic.com/issues/2001/09/power.htm

GEOGRAPHIC INFORMATION SYSTEMS

The general purpose of an information system is to process facts into useful information for guiding decision making and for ascertaining, describing, and analyzing problems. One of the products of the phenomenal advance of computer technology during the late twentieth century has been the introduction, dissemination, and development of geographic information systems (GISs). The main beneficiary of the GIS in the field of criminal justice has been policing. GISs have been applied to matters concerning crime analysis, community policing, problem solving, and strategic planning. The GIS has an integral role in geographical profiling, an evolving investigative tool for analyzing violent serial offenders. Currently, the GIS is becoming an important tool for both basic and applied research in criminal justice operational and academic settings.

GIS AND ITS COMPONENTS

A GIS is like other information systems in that it provides for data input, database management, data manipulation and analysis, and an output format. Yet, it is the way a GIS performs these functions that sets it apart from the other information systems. The essential core of a GIS is that the fundamental units of analysis are geographically based and defined by a coordinate system indicating their north-south, east-west positions. Therefore, the input data and all its attributes (its characteristics and features) are geographically referenced. These data can be features referenced with a single pair of coordinates (points); a series of coordinate pairs corresponding to linear features (lines); or a series of coordinates, with the first and last pairs being the same, forming a boundary around a specific space, thus forming an area (polygon). Thus, the database management component involves working with these different spatial databases.

Manipulating and analyzing the data, because they are geo-referenced, involves using graphic display devices (e.g., monitors) to view the spatial distribution of the data. The manipulation involves many procedures. One such procedure is overlaying different layers of information to form a single map. For example, a city boundary outline (polygon) is overlaid with a street map (lines) and then overlaid with the coordinates of armed robberies (points).

Spatial query and search is another procedure whereby the user can query the database to find and display all the data satisfying a certain criterion or surpassing a particular threshold (e.g., street intersections recording x amount of traffic accidents during a particular time period). A spatial join involves joining layers of information based on a spatial criterion. A point-in-polygon count makes it possible to count the number features in a point layer that are located in a polygon layer (e.g., number of domestic disputes in a particular neighborhood).

Buffering entails drawing a circle of a specific radius around a particular type of feature and then counting the number of a specific type of phenomenon that falls within or outside the buffer. This procedure has become popular for developing maps of the residences of registered sex offenders and assessing their spatial proximities to the activity places of children, such as schools, playgrounds, and day care centers). While there are other GIS data manipulation procedures, the one procedure that made GIS particularly useful for policing was geocoding or address matching.

Address matching entails taking the block number—street name of a crime or call for service location—and matching it with a reference file, which calculates the coordinates for the address. Generally, in the United States, the file containing the address coordinates emanates from a derivative of the topologically integrated geographic encoding and referencing files (Tiger Files) developed by the U.S. Census Bureau. The

absolute geographic location of an address is not calculated; rather the streets in the Tiger files are divided into sections bounded on both sides by unique intersections or "nodes." Assigned between the nodes is a specific block number range, therefore the block number coordinates assigned from the Tiger File are interpolated from the block ranges. There are other ways of geocoding or address matching depending upon the reference file. For example, if the addresses for a list of crimes contain the zip codes it is possible to match the address file with a reference file that has the geographic coordinates for each zip code area.

There are two types of GISs with different data structures that influence the analytical capabilities of the software: rastor and vector. A raster GIS has a simple data structure where the geographic features are stored and referenced in a grid or matrix. Each cell of the matrix receives a value or notation as to the type of feature that the cell represents. An analogy can be made with the TV screen where each cell or pixel emits a different color, tone, and brilliance to form a picture. The other type of GIS has a vector data structure whereby digitally stored coordinates represent geographic features. Each cell in the raster system represents a unique location, therefore efficiently allowing the overlaying of different layers of attributes using the same grid. Many forms of mathematical and other analyses are possible because of the raster data structure. But the raster data structure requires large amounts of computer storage space, and the resulting maps are not as aesthetically pleasing as vector maps, because the cells are plotted. The vector system has better storage efficiency, but from an analytical standpoint it is more limited; its only advantage pertains to network analyses. The maps emanating from a vector system are more aesthetically pleasing than raster maps, and in many instances are comparable to publication quality maps. Initially, GIS systems were either solely raster or vector. More recently, the systems have been equipped with add-on programs, modules, or extensions authored by GIS companies, third-party vendors, and users, therefore expanding and merging some of the raster-vector functionality.

The analytical software for GISs includes spatial statistical and geostatistical routines. The former routines are used for analyzing discrete distributions while the latter are concerned with continuous distributions. Continuous distributions are phenomena that are unbounded or ubiquitous and usually occur in nature, like temperature or elevation. Discrete distributions are

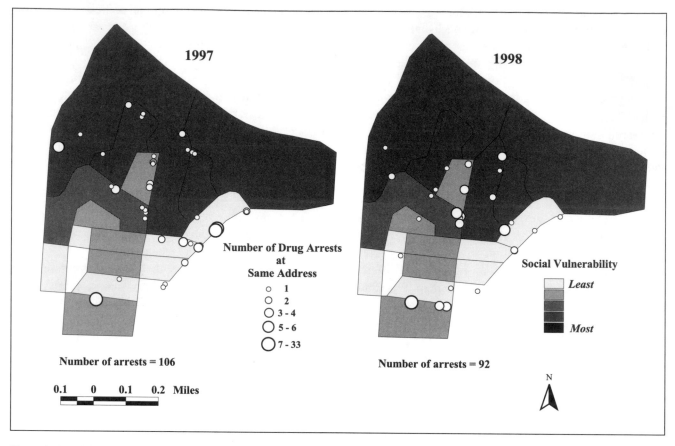

Figure 1. Area 27: Repeat Address Drug Arrests, 1997 and 1998

bounded and are not ubiquitous, like the locations of crimes across different neighborhoods or police precincts. Because a majority of the data pertinent to crime mapping are discrete, spatial statistics have been used more for police crime analysis.

Spatial statistics are concerned with assessing two spatial orders. The first is the intensity of a phenomenon across space. How is it distributed? What is its density? How does the intensity of a phenomenon increase or decrease with distance from some type of reference location? The second spatial order to be assessed is the spatial dependency or autocorrelation of a phenomenon. Spatial statisticians have long observed that things are not independently distributed in spaces and that, just like serial correlation with time series data, spatial autocorrelation is an important property of spatial data. Spatial autocorrelation is concerned with the proximity of locations and the degree to which the phenomena at those locations are similar or dissimilar. Positive spatial autocorrelation in regard to neighborhood crime rates implies that neighborhoods with similar crime rates tend to be closer to each other. Negative

spatial autocorrelation implies that the crime rates for surrounding neighborhoods tend to be dissimilar. The most popular spatial statistical routines used by police crime analysts pertain to examining the spatial distributions of crimes or problem locations for ascertaining and visualizing hot spots. Many of these routines emanate from Crimestat.

The most popular component of a GIS is its output, namely maps. Computer technology has made it possible to store maps digitally, thus making their retrieval, modification, editing, and production relatively fast, simple, easy, and inexpensive. Gone are the days of the pen-and-ink cartographer who labored for hours over the production of a single map. Also rendered nearly obsolete is the need for large amounts of space for the storage and cataloguing of physical maps. Computer technology and GISs have made map production faster and more efficient. Moreover, map-making has become more accessible to people with a broad range of cartography and spatial analysis skills. The downside is that in many instances people who have very little expertise in cartography, geography, spatial analysis, and graphic communication are now making maps.

AN EXAMPLE OF GIS

Figure 1 is an example of a simple exercise accomplished with a GIS. The maps depict a seventeen-block area in a police beat known as Area 27 in a city in the southeastern United States during 1997 and 1998. The GIS allows one to view the same area for two different years. Moreover, the GIS allows two different layers of data and two different mapping techniques to appear on a single map. The first layer appearing on both maps is the 1990 U.S. Census Blocks (the seventeen blocks). The blocks are shaded according to their intensity on the Social Vulnerability Index, which is a scale composed of four census variables (social, economic, demographic, and housing) with 4.0 indicating the most vulnerable to crime and 0 the least vulnerable. Maps depicting intensity across area units, like the blocks in Figure 1, are known as choropleth maps.

The second data layer appearing on the map is a graduated circle depicting the number of drug arrests at the same address. A graduated circle map depicts the frequency of a phenomenon at a place by changing or graduating the size of a circle. Acquiring the data for this layer involved matching the addresses of the drug arrests with a Tiger-based file in order to obtain a set of coordinates for each point. Counting the number of times that the same address was the site of a drug arrest was achieved through the use of the data base manager. (See Tables 1 and 2.) The end result is a graduated circle layer of repeat drug arrest locations overlaid on the choropleth map of Social Vulnerability.

An inspection of Figure 1 and Tables 1 and 2 reveals at least three important features about drug arrests in Area 27 during 1997 and 1998. First, drug arrests in this seventeen-block area are primarily a repeat address phenomenon. During 1997, 27 or 25.47 percent of the 106 arrests were made at single-occurrence addresses. The most arrests at one address was 29. During 1998, 15 arrests or 16.3 percent of the 92 arrests were made at single-occurrence addresses with 33 being the most arrests at one address. Second, from visually inspecting the maps it is apparent that during both years the majority of the arrests did not occur in the most socially vulnerable areas. Finally, reviewing the maps makes it very apparent that drug

Table 1. Repeat Address Drug Arrests, 1997

Number of Drug Arrests at Same Address	Number of Separate Addresses	Total Drug Arrests	Percent of Total Arrests
1	27	27	25.47
2	9	18	16.98
3	1	3	2.83
4	2	8	7.55
6	1	6	5.66
7	1	7	6.60
8	1	8	7.55
29	1	29	27.36
Total	**43**	**106**	

Table 2. Repeat Address Drug Arrests, 1998

Number of Drug Arrests at Same Address	Number of Separate Addresses	Total Drug Arrests	Percent of Total Arrests
1	15	15	16.30
2	7	14	15.22
3	5	15	16.30
4	1	4	4.35
5	1	5	5.43
6	1	6	6.52
33	1	33	35.87
Total	**31**	**92**	

arrests shifted or were displaced between the two years. During 1997, the high-frequency drug arrest addresses are on the east side of the area in a block of Least Social Vulnerability. During 1998, this same block has declined in drug arrests and the majority of the activity has shifted to the west central and southern portions of the area. The GIS makes it possible to assemble such a simple map in a short time. Not so long ago, the same task would have taken at least several days.

GIS AND CRIMINAL JUSTICE

GISs have been the basis for interaction and cooperation between multiple law enforcement agencies focusing on regional or interjurisdictional problems. GIS technology and the Internet are enabling the police to engage in an innovative form of communication with their constituents. Through Web-based mapping, citizens are able to review crime and in some cases construct crime maps of their cities and neighborhoods. Inroads are also being made in the use of GISs for corrections; studies have been conducted testing the use of GISs for monitoring probationers and parolees and designing service areas for community corrections personnel.

During 1997, the National Institute of Justice, the research and evaluation branch of the U.S Department of Justice, established the Crime Mapping Research Center (CMRC). The purpose of this innovative organization is to promote crime mapping research and evaluation in criminal justice and to serve criminal justice agencies as a clearinghouse for information regarding crime mapping and the GIS. The success of the CMRC has been phenomenal, and its importance is international in scope. Two works sponsored by the CMRC are enhancing the adoption, use, and efficacy of GISs by countless agencies and researchers across the world. The first is a monograph authored by Keith Harries (1999) titled *Mapping Crime: Principle and Practice.* The work is an in-depth guide to using a GIS for mapping and analyzing crime. The second work, *Crimestat,* by Ned Levine (1999), is a suite of spatial statistics routines that can be incorporated into a variety of GIS packages. Both *Mapping Crime* and *Crimestat* are available free to the public.

FUTURE DEVELOPMENTS

Geographic information systems are tools that will shortly become permanent fixtures in criminal justice operational and research settings. Improvements and advancements in the GIS and crime mapping will come from many areas, but the sources of some improvements will be developments in the complementing technologies of global positioning systems (GPSs) and remote sensing. The former is concerned with real-time identification and tracking of locations through an electronic device that interacts with a network of satellites. Thus, instead of writing down the address of a crime, a police officer will simply use a handheld GPS and will retrieve the coordinates for the location from the network of satellites. This technology will eliminate the need for address matching. Remote sensing is the technology pertaining to the acquisition, interpretation, and analysis of satellite images of the earth. In the future, the need for storing base map information will be reduced, for the police officer using the GPS will be able to instantaneously

plot the crime location on a base map that is a remote sensing image in real time.

—*James L. LeBeau*

See also GEOGRAPHIC PROFILING; POLICE INFORMATION SYSTEMS; POLICE STRATEGIES AND OPERATIONS; PROBLEM-ORIENTED POLICING

Further Reading

Aronoff, Stan. (1991). *Geographic Information Systems: A Management Perspective.* Ottawa, Canada: WDL Publications.

Bailey, Trevor C., and Anthony C. Gatrell. (1995). *Interactive Spatial Data Analysis.* Essex, UK: Addison Wesley Longman Limited.

Berry, Joseph K. (1995). *Spatial Reasoning for Effective GIS.* Fort Collins, CO: GIS World Books.

Fotheringham, Stewart, and Peter Rogerson, eds. (1995). *Spatial Analysis and GIS.* London, UK: Taylor & Francis.

Goodchild, Michael F. (1997). "Geographic Information Systems." In *10 Geographic Ideas That Changed The World,* edited by Susan Hanson. New Brunswick, NJ: Rutgers University Press, 60–83.

Harries, Keith D. (1999). *Mapping Crime: Principle and Practice.* Washington, DC: U.S Department of Justice.

Hirschfield, Alex, and Kate Bowers. (2001). *Mapping and Analysing Crime Data: Lessons From Research and Practice.* London, UK: Taylor & Francis.

Hutchinson, Scott, and Larry Daniel. (1997). *Inside ArcView GIS.* 2d ed. Santa Fe, NM: OnWord Press.

Levine, Ned (1999). *CrimeStat: A Spatial Statistics Program for the Analysis of Crime Incident Locations.* Washington, DC: U.S. Department of Justice.

Longley, Paul, and Michael Batty, eds. (1996). *Spatial Analysis: Modelling in a GIS Environment.* Cambridge, UK: GeoInformation International.

Monmonier, Mark. (1993). *Mapping It Out: Expository Cartography for the Humanities and Social Sciences.* Chicago, IL: The University of Chicago Press.

Rossmo, D. Kim. (2000). *Geographic Profiling.* Boca Raton, FL: CRC Press.

▼ GEOGRAPHIC PROFILING

During the investigation of many serial violent crimes, law enforcement officials are confronted with a large volume of information identifying several possible suspects. Several methods have been developed to increase efficiency and focus investigative inquiry in this situation. One such technique is that of geographic profiling, a method of identifying the area of probable residence of an unknown offender based on the location of and the spatial relationships among various crime sites. Once they have identified this area, police can then concentrate their efforts, and a variety of investigative strategies—suspect prioritization, patrol saturation, stakeouts, or neighborhood canvasses—can be employed to identify and apprehend the offender.

The model of geographic profiling (also referred to as "geoforensic analysis") was developed by D. Kim Rossmo and currently operates as an information management strategy performed by the Vancouver Police Department's Geographic Profiling Section. Upon request, this unit provides support to government agencies responsible for the investigation and prosecution of serial violent crime. The first report is now used by law enforcement agencies on every level throughout North America and Europe. While geographic profiling was designed to support investigative efforts in cases of serial murder, rape, and arson, its area of application has expanded to include serial bombings, bank robbery, and specialized forms of kidnapping.

THEORETICAL ASSUMPTIONS

The ability to determine where an offender is likely to be found, based on a series of crime site locations, depends on predictable behavior patterns among offenders as well as their victims. The model of geographic profiling and its validity thus rest upon several theoretical assumptions, among which three are primary.

Routine Activities Theory

Under the routine activity perspective, offered by Lawrence Cohen and Marcus Felson (1979), there are three essential elements that are required in order for a crime to occur: First, there must be the presence of a "motivated offender." Second, this motivated offender must come into contact with a suitable target. Third, both the motivated offender and suitable target must converge in time and space when there is no capable guardian present. Once these conditions are met, a crime is then able to occur.

In addition to these fundamental elements, routine activity theory provides a framework within which to understand the normal spatial patterns of offenders and victims in everyday life. According to this perspective, what are called "rhythms" are important in identifying and recognizing the normal or routine patterns individuals follow in their day-to-day activities. For example, one can assume that individuals follow, for the most part, a repetitive pattern when traveling to and from work, school, or recreation. Thus, where individuals

can be found forms a relatively predictable pattern, with distinct areas traveled between the fundamental anchor points of a person's employment, home, and places of leisure. Routine activities theory, then, provides a theoretical blueprint for understanding spatial mobility patterns of offenders and their victims.

Rational Choice Theory

While routine activities theory provides a framework for identifying patterns of time and space in victim and offender movement, rational choice theory offers insight into the decision-making processes of the offender. Explained by Derek Cornish and Ronald Clarke (1986), this view submits that criminal behavior is the product of a calculation by the offender that takes into consideration the effort, cost, and reward of engaging in any given illicit act. Therefore, if a crime can be committed with little effort, if the risk of apprehension is low, and if the benefit obtained is high, then it is more likely to occur. If, on the other hand, the potential offender perceives that too much effort is required in committing the crime or the risk of apprehension too high, therefore outweighing the anticipated benefit of the act, then it is less likely that the crime will occur.

In addition, rational choice theory suggests that offenders follow this reasoning process in determining when and where to commit a crime, as well as in target or victim selection. In short, the theory is that offenders select their targets or victims not at random times and places, but rather when and where there exists a suitably low level of risk and effort, and where the prospect of obtaining the reward or benefit is high.

This decision-making model of offenders provided by rational choice theory, coupled with routine activities theory, provides the basis for understanding predatory criminal behavior. These theories also supply the conceptual components of geographic profiling and offer direction in its application.

Crime Pattern Theory

Crime pattern theory, in turn, builds on both routine activity and rational choice theories in identifying more specifically the geographic composition of crime. Articulated by Paul and Patricia Brantingham (1993), crime pattern theory proposes that crimes are more likely to occur in places where suitable targets and an offender's "awareness space" overlap. An awareness space includes locations that an offender frequents and surroundings to which he or she is accustomed. Examples of this would be travel routes to and from work, home, or a friend's residence. The total spatial awareness of an offender makes up what is called his or her "mental map," or the mental picture that the offender carries in his or her head and that serves as a template dictating the offender's spatial mobility. The concept of pattern in this construct refers to the interconnectedness of these processes, ideas, and objects.

From the overlap locations of suitable targets and an offender's awareness space, search patterns are then extended outward. Thus, an offender is likely to begin in areas with the most familiarity and then move outward until a victim or target is found that affords a suitably low level of risk of being observed or apprehended. In addition, crime pattern theory holds that "Each element in the criminal event has some historical trajectory shaped by past experience and future intention, by the routine activities and rhythms of life, and by the constraints of the environment" (Brantingham and Brantingham 1993: 259).

In brief, the implication is that offenders do not choose crime sites randomly, but rather are more likely to commit crimes in areas with which they maintain some degree of familiarity. Where this is true, there is a pattern of offending that can be determined and used in the prediction and understanding of crime events. By tracing and identifying the spatial positioning of one crime site in relation to others, insight can be gathered into possible relationships between the offender, the victim, and their environment.

DEVELOPMENT OF A GEOGRAPHIC PROFILE

Through examination of information gleaned from crime site locations, their relationships to one another, and the demographics and characteristics of the surrounding neighborhoods, investigators use geographic profiling to identify the area where an offender most likely can be found. Geographic profiling, then, represents an application in reverse of the theoretical constructs just discussed. If, as these theories hold, there is a coherent and recognizable interconnection between an offender's spatial routines and his or her selection of crime site locations, it follows that by identification of crime sites, determinations can be made as to the likely areas an offender inhabits (i.e. resides, works, or frequently visits).

To develop a profile, investigators use both quantitative (objective) and qualitative (subjective) analytical techniques. The subjective component refers to the assessment of the offender's psychological composition and characteristics. Although it is not required, the geographic profile is often used in conjunction with a psychological profile, which provides insight into possible motives, behavior, and lifestyles of an offender. The two profiles provide investigators with an assessment of the person responsible for the series of crimes under inquiry.

The objective component, in turn, is composed of a series of spatial statistical techniques and other quantitative measures that make sense out of the pattern created by the location of the target sites. The primary quantitative technique employed in geographic profiling is a computational process identified by Rossmo as "criminal geographic targeting" or CGT. The CGT model follows a four-step process which, in short, consists of the following:

1. Connections (i.e., lines on paper) are made between the relevant crimes or other significant locations, and boundaries are identified.

2. Distances are computed from point to point measured along a street grid.

3. These distances are then used to weight all of the crime or relevant locations on the map in relation to every other point on the map, strengthening those located within the determined boundary and weakening those outside. The result is a series of numbers; the number of points on the map determines the number of numbers in the series. For example, if there are ten points on the map, each point will end up with a sequence of ten numbers.

4. Each point being assigned a series of numbers, these numbers are then multiplied to produce a single score for each map point. The higher the score, the greater the probability the point contains the location or residence of the offender.

The result of this process is a three-dimensional map, termed a "jeopardy surface," with the varying heights at each point indicating the probability that the offender either resides or works at that location. In other words, the higher the point on the map, the higher the likelihood the offender is located in that area. The lower the map point, the lower the possibility the offender is in that location. This three-dimensional surface is then placed over a street map of the area where the crimes have occurred. This map is called a "geoprofile." The heights on the map are identified by an accompanying scale of colors that correlate with the heights to indicate the probability of offender residence or occupancy.

To conduct a geographic profile, several crime locations are needed. The more crime points that can be used in the analysis, the better the predictive power of the profile. Given this dependence on more than one crime site and the assumption of interdependent crime events, geographic profiling is suitable only for serial crimes, or, rather, a succession of similar crimes that are known or believed to be committed by one offender. As such, this method is not suitable for investigations that seek to apprehend an offender who has committed only one known crime, such as an armed robbery or auto theft. There are cases, however, when a geoprofile can be conducted with locations other than crime sites: "Examples of such locations include credit or bank card use, mailings, telephone calls, vehicle rentals or drops, witness sightings, and found property or evidence sites. In these cases, it may be possible to geographically profile a single crime, depending upon the number and types of locations" (Rossmo 2000: 215).

When implemented, geographic profiling occupies a distinct phase of the investigative process. Once a series of crimes has been linked to one offender or the crimes have been connected to one another, and traditional investigative techniques have been unsuccessful, a geographic profile can then be devised as a tool and focal point for new investigative strategies. Rossmo offers the following sequence of operational tasks involved in the formulation of a geographic profile: (1) examination of the case file (which includes investigation reports, witness statements, autopsy report, and, if obtainable, the psychological profile); (2) inspection of the crime scenes and area photographs; (3) discussions with investigators and crime analysts; (4) visits to the crime sites when possible; (5) analysis of neighborhood crime statistics and demographic data; (6) study of street, zoning, and rapid transit maps; (7) analysis; and (8) report of findings.

In addition to offense locations, several other locations and factors must be considered while generating and discerning the results of a geographic profile. Rossmo identifies at least twelve for consideration. They include crime locations, offender typologies, roads and highways, bus and transit stops, physical and psychological boundaries of the offender, zoning and land use, neighborhood demographics, and victim routine activities.

Once these factors are considered and the geoprofile is complete, direction and priorities can then be given in future investigative efforts. For example, investigators may have identified a list of several possible suspects but lack the resources to adequately investigate all of them in a timely manner. With a geoprofile, they are able to focus their investigation on those suspects who are known to reside in or have some connection to the areas identified. Another example of how geoprofiles can be used is in making decisions to implement stakeouts or increase the level of patrol in the identified area.

ASSESSMENT

Since its first application in 1990, the geographic profiling model has grown in popularity and has increasingly been used in serial crime investigation spanning two continents. In many respects, its increased use and acceptance by law enforcement as a legitimate tool in crime investigation offers testament to its utility and validity. Although there has yet to be an independent assessment of the validity of geographic profiling, there have been scientific evaluations conducted by researchers at both Simon Fraser University and the Geographic Profiling Section at the Vancouver Police Department. In short, both analyses have found high levels of accuracy in predicting offender location. More specifically, one analysis found that using a geographic profile increased the chance of finding an offender in 12 percent of the time it would take if a random search were conducted (Rossmo 2000: 206).

Aside from this, however, there are two main instances when the use of a geoprofile is limited in its predictive ability. First, research has indicated that in order for there to be suitable accuracy in prediction, there must be anywhere from six to eleven crime sites used in the analysis. If there are fewer points than this available for computation, then the accuracy level of prediction decreases. Second, since the CGT model assumes that the offender lives somewhere inside the hunting location, it is limited in its ability to identify predatory offenders who reside outside this area and commute to the crime sites in search of suitable victims. However, benefit can still be derived in such cases, as it is likely that the geoprofile will identify points of significance other than the offender's residence, such as a friend or relative's house or place of employment.

Geographic profiling, then, is useful in a number of ways. The most obvious is its benefit in the identification and apprehension of those who tend to be responsible for the most heinous criminal assaults and who are able to remain elusive under the scrutiny of conventional investigative techniques. The other, less visible, contribution of geographic profiling is its representation of a practical application of criminological theory to the real world of criminal investigation. In this respect, geographic profiling has made a step toward bridging the gap that exists between research and its application in everyday life. The future utility of geographic profiling therefore rests as much with criminologists in refining its application and extending its relevance to other areas of crime investigation and prevention, as it does with police professionals in recognizing its value and implementing its use.

—Rob T. Guerette

See also CARTOGRAPHIC SCHOOL OF CRIMINOLOGY; GEOGRAPHIC INFORMATION SYSTEMS

Further Reading

Brantingham, Paul, and Patricia Brantingham. (1993). "Environment, Routine and Situation: Toward a Pattern Theory of Crime." In *Routine Activity and Rational Choice,* edited by Ronald V. Clarke and Marcus Felson. New Brunswick, NJ: Transaction, 259–294.

Clarke, Ronald V., and Marcus Felson, eds. (1993). *Routine Activity and Rational Choice.* New Brunswick, NJ: Transaction.

Cohen, Lawrence, and Marcus Felson. (1979). "Social Change and Crime Rate Trends: A Routine Activities Approach." *American Sociological Review* 44: 588–608.

Cornish, Derek B., and Ronald V. Clarke. (1986). "Introduction." In *The Reasoning Criminal: Rational Choice Perspectives on Offending,* edited by Derek B. Cornish and Ronald V. Clarke. New York: Springer-Verlag, 1–16.

Rossmo, D. Kim. (1993). "Target Patterns of Serial Murderers: A Methodological Model." *American Journal of Criminal Justice* 17: 1–21.

———. (1995). "Place, Space, and Police Investigations: Hunting Serial Violent Criminals." In *Crime and Place: Crime Prevention Studies,* vol. 4, edited by John Eck and David Weisburd. New York: Criminal Justice Press, 217–235.

———. (1995). "Targeting Victims: Serial Killers and the Urban Environment." In *Serial and Mass Murder: Theory, Research and Policy,* edited by Thomas O'Reilly-Fleming. Toronto, Canada: Canadian Scholars' Press, 133– 153.

———. (1997). "Geographic Profiling." In *Offender Profiling: Theory, Research and Practice,* edited by Janet Jackson and Debra Bekerian. New York: John Wiley & Sons Ltd., 159–175.

———. (2000) *Geographic Profiling.* Boca Raton, FL: CRC Press.

▼ GERMANY

For more than forty years, Germany was split in two. Following World War II, the territory was divided into East (the German Democratic Republic, or GDR) and West (the Federal Republic of Germany, or FRG). German unification took place at the beginning of the 1990s, after the collapse of the socialist-communist regime in the GDR toward the end of the 1980s, which followed the opening and democratization of Eastern Europe.

East and West Germany were under completely different governmental and economical regimes during the second half of the twentieth century. The FRG developed as a free, capitalist-oriented state within the western pact. The GDR, on the other hand, was locked into the Eastern Bloc under the state administration of the so-called real-existing socialism *(real existierender Sozialismus)*, which had an enormous effect on the lives of East Germans. Citizens had no proprietary rights to land and property (all land, farms, and real estate were state owned from 1949 onward), no freedom of the press and expression, and no freedom to travel. Formal and informal social controls touched on all aspects of life, including the criminal justice system.

While West Germany was oriented toward general freedom, those in the GDR lived under a number of imposed restrictions and limitations. During the communist regime, there was only one party, the Social Unionists *(Sozialistische Einheitspartei Deutschlands,* or SED), and crime statistics became a measure of success for the nation's socioeconomic advancement and the superiority of socialist rule (Kerner 1997). The GDR was neither democratic nor sovereign, for its dependence on Moscow was total. Travel between East and West Germany was subject to considerable restrictions, particularly after the erection of the Berlin Wall in 1961, which made it almost impossible for relatives to see each other.

Unauthorized crossing of the border, known as the "Iron Curtain" *(Eiserner Vorhang),* into West Germany was declared "escape from the republic" *(Republikflucht)* and was punished under GDR criminal law by long-term imprisonment. Those who were caught attempting to flee across the border were often shot by East German border guards.

The former FRG, which comprised 249,334 square kilometers, was made up of eleven federal states: Schleswig-Holstein, Niedersachsen (Lower Saxony), Nordrhein-Westfalen (Northrhine Westphalia), Hessen (Hesse), Rheinland-Pfalz, Saarland, Bayern (Bavaria), and Baden-Württemberg. In addition, there were three city-states *(Stadtstaaten)*: Hamburg, Bremen, and West Berlin. The city of Berlin itself was divided into East and West (East Berlin being the capital city of the

GDR at that time). Bonn was the administrative capital of West Germany until unification. Today Berlin is once again the governmental seat and capital of the united Germany.

The GDR incorporated five administrative regions, the "new states" of Mecklenburg-Vorpommern, Brandenburg, Sachsen-Anhalt, Sachsen (Saxony), and Thüringen (Thuringia). The total area of the GDR comprised 107,677 square kilometers at the time. Both parts of Germany (East and West) comprise 357,011 square kilometers.

After World War II, West Germany's population stood at 47 million. East Germany's was 18 million. Even before the opening of the border in 1989, there had been a considerable population shift from East to West, which continued even after unification. The population in 1999 was 67 million people in the former FRG and 15 million in the former GDR.

The deep impact and change brought about by unification were manifest particularly in the minds of citizens of the former GDR; after all, they had experienced a massive ideological change. After more than forty years of a socialist-communist regime, suddenly they were living under a Western capitalist one. The five new states had to adapt from a limited, state-run provider system to a capitalist free market economy. Toward the end of the 1980s, East Germany's unemployment rate rose by 10 percent and continued to rise. Even the current unemployment in former GDR states is higher than in the states of the former FRG. The GDR institutions had provided considerable social and medical support, many of which ceased to exist in unified Germany. The GDR citizens were given sudden and enormous freedom overnight, and some were not ready to meet the challenge of a new freethinking spirit and decision making that the West Germans demanded of them. East Germans found enforced responsibility a rather tall order, and their feelings of insecurity and existential fears (*Existenzangst*) rose during the early 1990s.

While economic and monetary union was completed by 1992, social union and integration of two very different peoples has taken much longer. Some would say that this has still not been completed. Social unrest increased among East and West German citizens. This was not helped by the fact that West Germans had to pay increased income tax to support their East German brothers and sisters. West Germans still pay a solidarity tax (*Solidaritätszuschlag*), an extra 5 percent on their income, to support the social health and welfare system of the new states. Germans' anxiety at unification has found one expression in an increased fear of crime.

Other repercussions of the collapse of the Eastern Bloc continue to affect Germans. Germany shares borders with Poland and the Czech Republic, two relatively impecunious former socialist states, where a considerable pressure to immigrate to the wealthier Germany exists. Similar pressure to emigrate from countries like the former USSR and other Eastern European countries from the former socialist-communist continues.

GERMAN CRIMINAL LAW

The main sources of law in Germany are the criminal code (*Strafgesetzbuch*), the Juvenile Courts Act (*Jugendgerichtsgesetz*), and the Administrative Offenses Act (*Ordnungswidrigkeitsgesetz*), which includes public order offenses. The *Strafvollstreckungsordnung* (initiation, execution and suspension of penalties and procedural provisions) and the Enforcement of Criminal Sentences Act (*Strafvollzugsgesetz*) deal with all aspects of imprisonment, education, and rehabilitation of offenders. Criminal law is divided into substantive law (*materielles Strafrecht*) and procedural or formal law (*Strafverfahrensrecht* or *formelles Strafrecht*). The criminal code also distinguishes between felonies (*Verbrechen*) and misdemeanors (*Vergehen*). Usually, felonies are codified as "unlawful acts" and are punishable with at least one year's imprisonment. Misdemeanors typically attract a fine. The categories of misdemeanors are quite extensive and include fraud and extortion. For felonies, the accused is allowed to plead guilty without a court appearance; the action is begun by the state prosecutor (*Staatsanwalt*), who then dispenses with the interim proceedings and presents the court with details of the proof of the offense and the desired sentence and punishment. The result is sent to the accused, who has two weeks in which to object and ask for an ordinary procedural hearing (Foster 1996: 201–228).

The fundamental difference between Anglo-American and German criminal procedure legislation is that the Anglo-American system is accusatorial, while the German system is inquisitorial. The inquisitorial principle grants independence to the investigation and prosecution and guarantees the division between the state prosecutor, the police, and the courts. Without the official accusation by the state prosecutor's office there can be no official criminal charge or "accusation." The offense in question must meet the physical and mental elements of a crime, unlawfulness (*Rechtswidrigkeit*) and guilt (*Schuld*). If one is missing from the case, no crime has been committed and, therefore, there will be no punishment. The concept of guilt incorporates social responsibility; an offender is punished for violating the legal order against better understanding. According to the code, guilt is the basis for punishment and is determined by the ability of the offender to choose between lawful and unlawful conduct. The offense must also meet the statutorily defined constituent elements of the particular offense. An offending act is defined as every deliberate physical behavior that fits the statutory description of the offense.

The preliminary investigation is conducted in private by the state prosecutor's office. The investigation ends with either the filing of an appropriate charge or the closing of the case due to the lack of evidence. The state prosecutor applies to the court for the main proceedings in interim proceedings; once the evidence has been found sound, the main proceedings can commence with the oral hearing in court. After judgment, there is an appeals process.

The European Convention on Human Rights and Fundamental Freedoms and the German Basic Constitution form the fundamental principles for the criminal code and all criminal proceedings. The code grants the police provisional powers of arrest, but in such a case, police must present the detainee to a judge before the next day. A defense attorney (*Verteidiger*) in criminal proceedings is allowed, and the code permits the accused to select an attorney of his or her choice.

The nature and seriousness of the offense determines the choice of court. Minor offenses for which the penalty is up to six months, private prosecutions, and prosecutions brought be the state prosecutor's office for which a punishment of up to twelve months duration only is requested are conducted before a single judge in the lower, local court (*Amtsgericht*). More serious first offenses are heard before the *Schöffengericht,* composed of one professional and two lay members. Serious crimes go immediately to a criminal chamber of the federal state court (*Landgericht*). Three professional judges sit in the *Große Strafkammer* with two lay members. This court also acts as an appeal court. For the most serious criminal offenses, such as homicide, assault causing grievous bodily harm, and sexual offenses, a *Schwurgericht*, which has a similar constituency to the *Schöffengericht*, is established. Exceptionally serious offenses are heard at the *Oberlandesgericht*, which is composed of five professional

judges. This court also acts as an appeal court, presided over by three professional judges. There is no jury as in the Anglo-American sense, and the judge's role is laid down to ensure that he constitutionally applies the criminal law. There are no legal rules compelling the judge to consider evidence in any particular way and stating what emphasis to put on any particular piece of evidence.

There is a special juvenile chamber presided over by a single professional youth judge. The age of criminal responsibility in Germany begins at fourteen; young persons under the age of fourteen are not prosecuted according to the criminal code. Rather, a separate youth criminal code (*Jugendgerichtsgesetz*) exists for young persons between the ages of fourteen to seventeen. This code is primarily educational and rehabilitative in character. The youth criminal code has largely been extended to criminal trials of eighteen- to twenty-one-year-olds, so-called young adults.

CRIME

Looking at crime statistics in the industrialized states since World War II, Germany has followed Western Europe in recording a general increase in crime and criminality. The average crime rate (number of criminal offenses per 100,000 population) at the beginning of the 1990s was five times higher than during the 1950s. The rate of increase slowed during the 1950s and 1980s. The growth in the total crime rate in Great Britain, France, West Germany, Italy, Sweden, and the Netherlands during the period from 1951 to 1960 amounted to 3.3 percent; from 1961 to 1970, it was 4.4 percent; from 1971 to 1980, it was 5.3 percent; and from 1981 to 1990, it was 3.3 percent (Eisner 1994).

Germany witnessed an increasing total crime rate from the mid-1960s into the 1990s; from the second half of the mid-1990s, however, there has been a steady decrease. (See Figure 1.) At the same time, crime suspect figures have steadily increased. This supports the assumption that a large number of crimes are committed on a "multiple" basis, by a relatively small number of the same offenders who commit multiple crimes on charges such as burglary, theft, and drug-related offenses. The majority of offenses (about two-thirds) are property offenses of relatively little damage. Insurance companies now require a theft or burglary to be reported to the police, which explains the increase in recorded crime to some extent. "Given that most recorded crimes are property crimes the development of overall crime rates may be assumed to be a good indicator of the development of property crimes. However, trends of violent crime rates do not seem to have differed much from the overall trend." (Eisner 1994: 15).

The number of violent offenses and imprisonment rates in Germany from 1961 to 2000 demonstrates a steady increase in these serious offenses. (See Figure 2.)

Beginning in the mid-1980s, however, there has been a slight downward trend in violent criminal offenses, as well as in the national imprisonment rate. (See Figure 3.) The 1980s witnessed a downward trend in sexual offenses, followed by a slight increase in the 1990s.

Statistics from the former GDR show a noticeably lower crime rate than West Germany recorded. However, crime rates of the GDR have to be viewed with some skepticism. In general, figures from the Eastern Bloc socialist-communist states showed a lower incidence of crime than in Western capitalist industrialized countries. At the same time, the imprisonment rate for Eastern Bloc countries was considerably higher than that in Western states. This points to a stricter and indeed harsher criminal justice and punishment policy in the Eastern Bloc. For example, the death penalty was abolished in West Germany in 1949 with the new German Basic Constitution, but the GDR constitution continued the use of capital punishment until 1987. However, the low crime rates in the former GDR cannot be attributed wholly to the harsh sanctions and seemingly tougher punitiveness of the socialist-communist regime; rather, an important cause is the rather unorthodox or means of registration and recording practices by the state authorities at the time.

The official GDR crime rate during

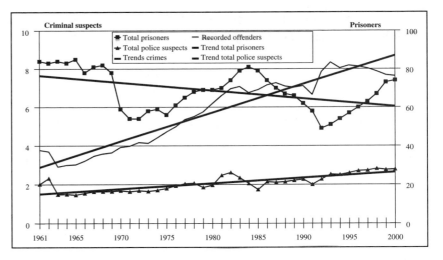

Figure 1. Crime Rates: Prison Population (Including Sicherungsverwahrte— *Special, Secure Units) and Suspected Criminals, Germany, 1961–2000*

Note: In Figures 1-4, graphs represent statistics for West Germany (FRG) only, from 1961 through 1992. Statistics from 1993 to 2000 represent statistics for the unified Germany.

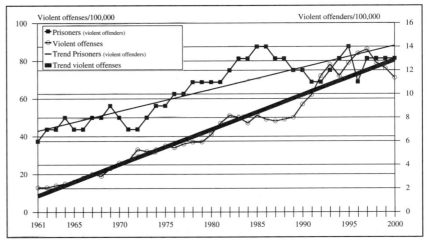

Figure 2. Violent Offenses, Germany, 1961–2000

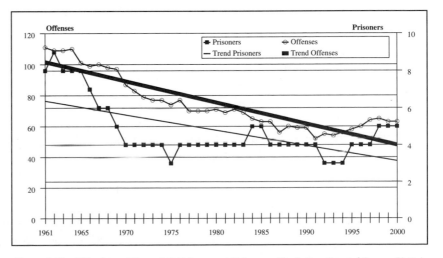

Figure 3. Total Number of Recorded Crimes and Prisoners (Including Special Secure Units), Germany, 1961–2000: Sexual Offenses

the 1980s was around 10 percent that of West Germany. In 1980, the East Germany registered 772 criminal offenses per 100,000 inhabitants, compared with 6,180 in the FRG. By the end of the GDR regime in 1989, there were a mere 601 crimes per 100,000 in the East, compared with 7,031 in West Germany. A sizable dark figure of unreported crime (about 90 percent) thus existed in the GDR. This must, however, not be seen as a phenomenon exclusive to East Germany, for dark crime figures equally exist in Western countries, where the dark figures are also estimated to lie between 80 and 90 percent (Kury 2001).

The enormous difference can partly be explained by reasons of higher social control, harsher state sanctions, and reduced opportunity structures. The East German Politburo, the Ministry of Justice, and the Secret Service Police continuously tried to show that, due to the political leadership in the East, crime and criminality in the GDR was on a downward trend compared with West Germany. At the same time, East German citizens did tend to adhere to traditional social values, attitudes, and beliefs, which led to a generally more placid population with reduced conflict potential. The GDR also maintained a lower unemployment rate, and the intensive social care system supported people adequately with social housing, a reasonably functioning national health system, and ample child support for working mothers.

Although all these social reasons no doubt influenced the East German crime rate, it is also certain that the state authorities massaged the official crime statistics. Recorded crimes in the GDR stood at 119,124 in the year 1988 (715 per 100,000). The painstaking recalculation and revision of GDR crime statistics after unification, however, presented a rather different picture (Von der Heide and Lautsch 1991). Using the West Germany statistical model to analyze the data from East Germany, researchers established that the crime rate there was three times higher than previously recorded (at 2,364 per 100,000), totaling 393,940 recorded crimes. Today, it can safely be assumed that the crime rate of the former GDR was about one-third to half that of West Germany (Kerner 1997). The rate of solved crimes in the GDR was about twice as high as those in the FRG, the rate of crimes solved in the GDR in 1985 standing at 84.5 percent compared to 47.2 percent in the FRG. These figures were based on "special" calculations. For instance, "mass crimes" such as bicycle theft, child or youthful offenses, or police-registered misdemeanors were partly taken out of the equations. Based on the recalculations, the GDR solved-crime rate comes down to 55.2 percent.

After unification, the former East German crime rate rose, a 50 percent increase during the early 1990s, quickly matching that of West Germany (Kury et al. 1996). During the second half of the 1990s, victim surveys showed that the crime rate in the new East German states had moderately risen above that of the old West German states (Kury and Obergfell-Fuchs 1996). The police crime statistics for 1999 show 7,682 crimes per 100,000 (for a total of 6.3 million recorded crimes), a slight decrease from previous years. This large increase in recorded crime led to an increased fear of crime, particularly in the former GDR. During SED rule, the East German media rarely reported on crime, but following unification, press and TV coverage of the crime increase abounded. Media attention focused party political thinking on law and order and shaped the political agenda and criminal justice policies toward "more punishment" of the 1990s.

In the former East German states, the unemployment rate, social unrest, and dissatisfaction all grew as a result of vast increases in living costs, a reduction in social and medical services and child care provision, and competition for jobs. In addition, hate crimes against foreigners in the new states, such as persecution of Turkish immigrant citizens and asylum seekers, have become more common. Long-term studies into the crime rate and criminality among the states German federal states have determined that the crime rate is generally higher in northern Germany (Niedersachsen and Schleswig-Holstein, for example), than in the south (Baden-Württemberg, Bayern). One main reason is that the northern states are less economically "blessed," having high unemployment and lower salaries. This means that the southern states are, on the whole, wealthier in their living conditions and social status (Kury et al. 1996).

PUNISHMENT

There were 217 prison establishments in Germany in 1998 with a total capacity of 73,980 places. At the same time, the prison population stood at 69,817, which represents 94.4 percent of total capacity. In 1995 to 1996, the total capacity stood at 91 percent. As in other Western European countries, in Germany the way in which the courts use and administer sanctions has changed enormously. About 120 years ago, the courts of the Deutsches Reich used imprisonment as their primary punitive measure (for about 80 percent of convictions); monetary fines were uncommon (20 percent). The picture has now changed dramatically: Fines are the most commonly used sanction, and only about 5 percent of convicted criminals receive custodial sentences (Kaiser 1996: 986). The fact that criminals have increasingly not been sentenced to a term of imprisonment, despite the general rise in the crime rate, means that there has been a general downward trend in the prison population from the mid-1990s onward. (See Figure 4.)

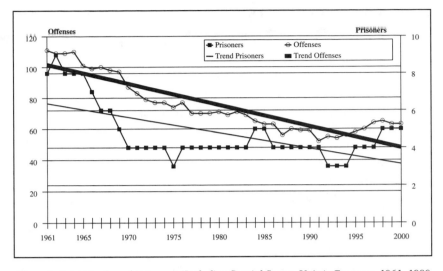

Figure 4. Total Number of Prisoners (Including Special Secure Units), Germany, 1961–1999

This trend can be attributed to a change in legislation and sentencing practices. Beginning in the mid-1980s, sentencers made increasing use of alternative forms of punishments, so-called sanction diversion measures that included alternative forms to youth custody, victim-offender mediation and restorative justice measures by the chief prosecutor's office, victim compensation schemes, and community sentences. For juvenile offenders, judges increasingly make use of these young offender sanctions. The highest punishment under the youth criminal code is ten years' imprisonment.

After the introduction of new legislation within the German Criminal Code of 1969, a number of sociotherapeutic prison units (*Sozialtherapeutische Anstalten*) were introduced. Trained social workers or psychologists conduct therapy sessions in these special units. Inmates spend the last years of their sentences at a sociotherapeutic unit, from which they will generally be released to the outside or at least to open prison conditions. In spite of this rehabilitative feature, less than 5 percent of the total prison population are currently receiving treatment in these specialist units. At present, there are 1,034 available places for adult males (plus 34 places for women) in the units (Rehn 2001: 73). The treatment concepts vary considerably among the different facilities. A number of empirical studies have demonstrated that some of the rehabilitative programs appear to be working, at least for certain categories of offenders (Lösel et al. 1987; Kury 1998).

As already stated, since unification, fear of crime among the population has risen, exacerbated by the media. Sex offenses have been the source of extensive media attention, and child molesters have been especially targeted by the German press. Popular fear of crime has led to an increased demand for "law and order" and for harsher criminal sanctions. This is in spite of a generally downward trend in the actual rate of sex offenses as recorded by the police. But one or two major cases involving rape and child molestation offenders have hit the headlines and have brought the discussion to a crescendo. This has resulted in a new Sex Offender Treatment Act, passed in 1998, which recommends special secure units for custody for sex offenders. The additional secure custody can be added to the custodial sentence by the courts. Even if a sentence has been completed by the prisoner, he or she can be kept in custody for an indefinite period beyond the sentence if the prison administration, consulting with an external expert psychologist, is of the opinion that the offender continues to represent a risk to the public. In addition to maximum and specially secure custody, every serious, violent offender or sex offender with a sentence of more than two years will now have to undergo treatment in a sociotherapy prison unit as part of the sentence.

Against this punitively political background, the numbers in custody and secure custody have swelled, which, in turn, has led to overcrowding in certain states' prison facilities. In 1995 the imprisonment rate stood at 75 per 100,000 inhabitants. By 1999, it had risen to 85. In 1995, there was not yet any visible overcrowding in prisons. One of the main reasons for recent prison overcrowding has been the increase in foreign prisoners; a second reason is the increase in drug offenses.

CONTINUING CONTROVERSIES

In line with criminal justice policies of the major Western industrial nations, the crime rate in Germany has gone down during the 1990s. However, imprisonment rates in Western Europe have gone up (with the exception of the Scandinavian countries). Crime and punishment, law and order feature particularly noticeably in the German media, particularly focusing on sex offenders and youth crime. Official crime figures and actually recorded crime rates do not support this focus. A much-hyped "increase" in youth crime is not backed by any long-term empirical research; youth crime in Germany is thus no different from any other Western European crime trend. Sex offenses have decreased over the past forty years, although there has been a slight recorded increase in sex offenses since the early 1990s. The media shaping popular opinion do not accurately report these actual trends. Popular opinion sees merely an increase in the crime rate and this, in addition to other reasons, has increased the fear of crime, particularly among the former East German population during the 1990s.

Since German unification in 1990, increased unease and fear of crime have shaped criminal justice policies of the last two governments. Current trends support an increased use of imprisonment with longer custodial sentences, particularly for serious, violent, and sex offenders. Legislation from 1998 supports this trend. There is talk that the juvenile code should no longer be applied to young adults aged eighteen to twenty-one and that their offenses should be dealt with under the adult criminal code. Also part of the ongoing law and order debate has been the proposed lowering of the age of criminal responsibility from fourteen to twelve.

Criminologists doubt that increased sanctions and longer sentences will, in fact, reduce criminality. Kury and Ferdinand (1999) advocate increased preventive measures that could more meaningfully assist education at home, in the family, and at school. The main aims of imprisonment are the rehabilitation of the offender and the security of the public: "The use of imprisonment of the offender is for him lead a law-abiding life without committing any further criminal offenses after release from custody. The use of custody is to protect the general public from future criminal offenses" (Kury and Ferdinand 1999: 381). Formerly, corrections targeted the reintegration of the offender into society. Today's criminal justice policies tend to favor the "secure custody" and "safeguarding of society" models. This means that custodial sentences are getting longer, which is adding to the already rising prison population and prison overcrowding. Recently, successive governments have been reluctant to reduce a prisoner's level of security or to grant early release from prison.

—Helmut Kury and Ursula Smartt

Further Reading

Eisner, Manuel. (1994). "The Effects of Economic Structures and Phases of Development on Crime. Council of Europe." Eleventh Criminological Colloquium: Crime and Economy, November 28–30. Strasbourg, Germany.

Foster, Nigel. (1996). *German Legal System and Laws*, 2d ed. London: Blackstone Press.

Heinz, Wolfgang, and Gerhard Spiess. (2001). "Kriminalitätsfurcht—Befunde aus neueren Repräsentativbefragungen." In *Raum und Kriminalität. Sicherheit der Stadt. Migrationsprobleme. Möchengladbach*, edited by Joerg-Martin Jehle. Bonn, Germany: Forum Verlag Godesberg, 147–191.

Kaiser, Guenter. (1996). *Kriminologie: Ein Lehrbuch*. Heidelberg, Germany: C.F. Müller.

Kerner, Hans-Juergen. (1997). "Kriminologische Forschung im Umbruch. Ein Zwischenresümee nach sechs Jahren deutsch-deutscher Kooperation." In *Sozialer Umbruch und Kriminalität in Deutschland*, edited by Klaus Boers, Guenter Gutsche, and Klaus Sessar. Opladen, Germany: Westdeutscher Verlag, 331–367.

Kury, Helmut. (1997). "Crime Development in the East and the West: A Comparison." In *Crime and Criminology at the End of the Century*, edited by Erat Raska and Jueri Saar. Tallinn, Estonia: University Press, 187–251.

———. (1998). "Zum Stand der Behandlungsforschung oder: Wie erfolgreich sind Behandlungsprogramme bei Straffälligen?" *Forensische Psychiatrie und Psychotherapie. Werkstattschriften* 5: 67–104.

———. (2001). "Das Dunkelfeld der Kriminalität. Oder: Selektionsmechanismen und andere Verfälschungsstrukturen." *Kriminalistik* 55: 74–84.

Kury, Helmut, Uwe Dörmann, Harald Richter, and Michael Würger. (1996). *Opfererfahrungen und Meinungen zur Inneren Sicherheit in Deutschland*. Wiesbaden, Germany: Bundeskriminalamt.

Kury, Helmut, and Theodore Ferdinand. (1999). "Public Opinion and Punitivity." *International Journal of Law and Psychiatry* 22: 373–392.

Kury, Helmut, and Joachim Obergfell-Fuchs. (1996). "Crime Development and Fear of Crime in Postcommunist Societies." In *Impact of Political, Economic and Social Change on Crime and Its Image in Society*, edited by Barbara Szamota-Saeki and Dobrochna Wojcik. Warsaw, Poland: Dom Wydawniczy, 117–146.

Kury, Helmut, Joachim Obergfell-Fuchs, and Michael Würger. (1996). "The Regional Distribution of Crime: Results from Different Countries." *Studies on Crime and Crime Prevention* 5: 5–29.

Lösel, Friedrich, Paul Köferl, and Florian Weber. (1987). *Meta-Evaluation der Sozialtherapie*. Stuttgart, Germany: Enke.

Rehn, Gerhard. (2001). " 'Wer A sagt...': Haftplätze und Haftplatzbedarfe in Sozialtherapeutischen Einrichtungen." In *Behandlung "gefährlicher Straftäter": Grundlagen, Konzepte, Ergebnisse,* edited by Gerhard Rehn, Bernd Wischka, Friedrich Lösel, and Michael Walter. Herbolzheim, Germany: Centaurus Verlag, 264–275.

Von der Heide, Franz, and Erwin Lautsch. (1991). "Entwicklung der Straftaten und der Aufklärungsquote in der DDR von 1985–1989." *Neue Justiz* 45: 11–15.

▼ GET-TOUGH INITIATIVES

Beginning in the late 1970s and early 1980s, legislators began to take a "get-tough" approach to crime control in the United States, a strategy that stresses harsh punishment for criminal offenses. Get-tough initiatives focus on deterrence, incapacitation, and retribution as primary goals of criminal sentencing. Their proponents assert that making the penalty especially severe not only will enhance public safety, by taking the criminal off the street, but also will deter other potential offenders from committing crimes, because they will desire to avoid such difficult sanctions. Philosophically, get-tough proponents suggest that harsh punishment is the appropriate and fitting response to crime.

HISTORY

Get-tough legislation grew out of a confluence of social factors in the 1960s and 1970s. The spiraling crime rate, the controversial decisions of the Warren Court, the perception that nothing worked in rehabilitating offenders, and general social unrest all contributed to the belief that the criminal justice system was failing. Specifically, the Supreme Court had issued a number of controversial decisions in favor of due process (for instance, *Miranda v. Arizona* and *Gideon v. Wainwright*), which changed some long-standing criminal justice methods, such as police interrogation practices and a person's constitutional right to an attorney. Many critics felt that the consequence of these decisions was to tie law enforcement's hands in controlling crime. In the years immediately following these landmark decisions, social scientific research evaluated the effectiveness of rehabilitative programming, concluding that rehabilitation was basically unsuccessful in controlling offenders' behavior. These factors led to growing disillusionment with the criminal justice system.

Throughout the 1960s and 1970s, the crime problem came to be increasingly defined by partisan politics in the national arena. Conservative Republicans argued that offenders were undeserving of government programming or treatment and that they should instead take responsibility for their actions through harsh punishment. These conservatives vehemently refuted the democratic ideal that the government had an obligation to ameliorate some of the root causes of crime, such as poverty and substandard education. The national mood shifted concern from social welfare to social control. Moreover, conservatives portrayed anyone in favor of rehabilitative philosophies as ineffective in protecting the public and as contributing to the moral decline of the nation by absolving criminals of their natural responsibility.

Several key incidents solidified the perception that rehabilitative goals were unnecessarily threatening public safety and that tough responses were warranted. Momentum for get-tough policies built during the 1980s, playing a decisive role in the 1988 presidential election in the example of Willie Horton, a convicted felon who committed rape and murder while out on a prison furlough. Horton was touted as the product of "soft on crime" programs in Massachusetts that placed the public at risk. George Bush's decisive victory ensured support for a get-tough approach to crime on a national level.

The second major incident that rallied support for get-tough measures was the abduction and murder of twelve-year-old Polly Klaas in 1993. The man responsible for the crime had been recently paroled after serving only half of his sixteen-year sentence for a prior kidnapping conviction. Such tragic and highly publicized events fueled the perception that the criminal justice system had unrestrained and irresponsibly managed discretion and that changes needed to be made to correct the system.

The result has been a sweeping political endorsement of get-tough initiatives. Although Democrats have traditionally been more inclined toward social remedies for crime, such as state financial assistance and improvements in education, both Democrats and Republicans have initiated such reforms. President Clinton signed the Crime Control Bill of 1994 to add 100,000 more police officers nationally. Similarly, the Democratic governor of Florida signed a bill in 1997 approving chemical castration for first-time sex offenders. The distinction between the two political parties over the last ten years has been less whether they support get-tough initiatives than to what degree they endorse such programs.

Over the past twenty years, get-tough initiatives have been brought up in nearly every state in the country. Examples of such initiatives include the explosion of mandatory minimum sentences (specifically, the "three strikes and you're out" sentencing), legislation that pushes for more juveniles to be tried as adults, the resurgence of chain gangs in Alabama and Florida, legislation authorizing the death penalty for dozens of crimes other than murder, the proliferation of maximum security prisons around the country, the national push for sentencing reforms and "truth in sentencing," the abolition of parole in many communities, the stripping of prison amenities such as weight rooms and television privileges, and the introduction of public shaming sentences (such as public notification laws for drunk driving or sex offenders). In each of these initiatives, the goal has been to make the correctional system focus on punishment and to make punishment hard.

CHANGES IN CRIMINAL PROCESSING

These measures have changed the role of several key criminal justice actors. First, several get-tough measures, such as determinate sentencing, mandatory minimums, and statutorily assigning juveniles to the adult court, restrain the level of judicial discretion in the criminal justice process. Because of these reforms, judges have fewer sentencing options. Often, mitigating circumstances involved in the crime are no longer considered, because the judge is required to follow the guidelines set by the state legislature.

While the tendency of these initiatives has been to circumscribe the role of the judge, the role of the prosecutor has expanded. The decision to charge defendants becomes even more consequential when mandatory minimums are concerned, because once the charge is made, the sentence becomes a foregone conclusion. Prior to such legislation, judges formed their own opinions, within varying guidelines, about what a just sentence would be. With get-tough sentencing laws, such as mandatory minimums or presumptive sentencing, however, judicial discretion is limited and the prosecutor becomes the most important player in the court arena. Critics point out that the prosecutor has traditionally been the figure with the most unbridled discretion within the justice system, and get-tough laws have essentially expanded this discretion beyond the reach of due process. As one author pointed out, such legislation is the equivalent of allowing the pitcher—instead of the umpire—the ability to call balls and strikes in baseball.

In terms of correctional processing, get-tough legislation removes discretion from the hands of correctional professionals as well. Many communities have abolished parole boards altogether, and other legislation has eliminated "good time" as a vehicle for offenders to earn their way out of prison before their sentence is up. Indeterminate sentences, which allowed parole boards to release offenders when they were "cured," are being replaced with fixed periods of incarceration, regardless of an inmate's behavior or progress. The goals for correctional professionals have shifted from reforming the offenders to warehousing them. Furthermore, get-tough initiatives tout the idea that offenders should go to prison *for* punishment and not simply *as* punishment.

CONSEQUENCES OF GET-TOUGH INITIATIVES

If these initiatives are meant to reduce crime and make the public safer, there is reason to believe that get-tough initiatives may not meet their goal. Although proponents of get-tough legislation credit these reforms with the declining crime rate over the 1990s, the evidence is far from conclusive. When people are incarcerated, they are less able to commit crimes in the community. From this perspective, get-tough measures do affect rates of crime.

However, most research indicates that the growing prison population has had only minimal effects on the reductions in crime in the last decade. Most criminologists acknowledge that the strong economy, demographics, changes in the gun market, and changing police practices have more to do with decreasing crime rates than does building more prisons. It is possible that the reduction in crime may not have been so swift or so large without the increase in prison population. However, there is no evidence to support the assertion that prison deters offenders from committing crimes once released. Even those offenders sent to prison for long periods of time will eventually return to society, and the question of whether these offenders will come out worse than they went in should be a serious consideration for legislators and the public.

Two separate, highly regarded studies examined the effect of trying juveniles in adult court in Florida and in New York and New Jersey, concluding that in many cases bringing juveniles to adult court actually increased juveniles' propensity to commit serious crimes. Such findings suggest that "getting tough" may be counterproductive. Some speculate that the reason the waiver laws had such detrimental effects on recidivism is that, once released from adult prison, these juveniles were labeled as hopeless cases by communities, making them more likely to continue criminal activity.

In general, get-tough initiatives are exceptionally expensive for both courts and correctional agencies. For the courts, fewer defendants choose to plea bargain in mandatory minimum cases because the stakes are so high, forcing the state to hold more trials than ever before—clogging the courts on matters that would have been settled by plea bargaining in the past. For correctional agencies, mandatory minimums and truth in sentencing laws ensure that convicted offenders serve the sentence assigned by the legislature, with little room for parole, accruement of good time, or other early release measures. The consequence has been skyrocketing costs of corrections. Funding for these measures must come from existing tax bases. For the first time in recent history, states now spend more money on corrections than on education. Several studies have chronicled the increase in correctional spending with the proportional decrease in spending for higher education. Furthermore, because states cannot keep pace with demand for prison space, other—sometimes serious—offenders are being released earlier to make room for those sentenced under minimum mandatory guidelines. In some cases, this means filling jail space with nonviolent drug offenders while releasing violent offenders. The question of long-term priorities remains important for communities to consider.

Many critics point out that the U.S. criminal justice system has had ongoing problems with systemic discrimination, and the brunt of severe criminal sanctions is being administered disproportionately on minority (largely African American and Hispanic) offenders. One of the unintended consequences of this legislation may be to heighten racial tensions in the country, widening the gap between races and promoting an adversarial, rather than cooperative, relationship. Other critics point out that in some legislators' haste to "get tough," poorly crafted statutes have been enacted, casting too wide a net and failing to stop serious, violent offenders. For instance, anecdotal evidence suggests that "three strikes and you're out" legislation has imprisoned offenders when their third strike was stealing a pizza or a pair of sneakers without using violence. Also, although shoplifting is an offense, many question whether the system's responses to it have been wildly disproportionate to the crime, and perhaps more

> **DID YOU KNOW...**
>
> Get-tough initiatives are based on the belief that harsh punishment will control crime. Across the United States, numerous get-tough initiatives have been started since the 1960s, including mandatory minimum sentencing, three strikes sentencing, juveniles tried as adults, chain gangs and boot camps, legislation authorizing the death penalty for dozens of crimes other than murder, more maximum security prisons, sentencing reforms, truth in sentencing, abolition of parole, stripping of prison amenities such as weight rooms and television privileges, public shaming sentences, placing more police officers on the street, and chemical castration of sex offenders.

important, whether this excessive response has used scarce resources that are needed to incarcerate violent offenders who commit more serious crimes.

WANING EFFECTS OF GET-TOUGH PROGRAMS

Get-tough initiatives started in the late 1970s and early 1980s, using classical criminologist Cesare Beccaria's often-cited prescription that punishment should be certain, swift, and proportional. However, the idea of proportionality has been largely forgotten, with get-tough reforms yielding to "get even tougher" initiatives. Proponents of the get-tough ideology, fueled by recent reductions in crime, feel confident that these initiatives are having the desired effect on crime and that more harsh punishments will have an even greater effect. Critics assert that the declining crime rate is largely unrelated to these policies and that the country cannot incarcerate its way out of the crime problem, using "bumper sticker solutions" on complex social issues. They point out that the short-term gains of incapacitation of offenders may lead to disastrous results in the long run. Given the cyclical nature of criminal justice trends over the centuries in America, it is possible that these "even tougher" policies will wane in popularity in the future.

—Jennifer M. Balboni

See also BOOT CAMPS; CAPITAL PUNISHMENT; DETERMINATE SENTENCES; DETERRENCE THEORY; MANDATORY SENTENCING; RETRIBUTIVE JUSTICE; SCARED STRAIGHT PROGRAMS; SHAME PENALTIES; SHOCK INCARCERATION; SUPERMAX PRISONS

Further Reading

Beckett, Katherine, and Theodore Sasson. (2000). *The Politics of Injustice*. Thousand Oaks, CA: Pine Forge Press.

Benekos, Peter, and Alida Merlo. (1995). "Three Strikes and You're Out: The Political Sentencing Game." *Federal Probation* 59, 1: 3–9.

Chambliss, William. (2000). *Power, Politics and Crime*. Boulder, CO: Westview Press.

Currie, Elliot. (1998). *Crime and Punishment in America*. New York: Metropolitan Books.

Reske, Henry J. (1994). "Throwing Away the Key." *ABA Journal* (April): 66–69.

Spelman, William. (2000). "The Limited Importance of Prison Expansion." In *The Crime Drop*, edited by Alfred Blumstein and Joel Wallman. Cambridge: Cambridge University Press.

Court Cases

Gideon v. Wainwright (1963). 372 U.S. 335.
Miranda v. Arizona (1996). 384 U.S. 436.

▼ GLOBAL ISSUES

See ART THEFT AND FRAUD; COMPARATIVE LAW AND JUSTICE; COMPARATIVE POLICING; CORPORATE CRIME; COUNTERTERRORISM; CYBERCRIME; DRUG COURIER PROFILES; DRUG TRAFFICKING; DRUGS; ENVIRONMENTAL CRIME; GENOCIDE; HUMAN RIGHTS; ILLICIT ANTIQUITIES; INTERNATIONAL CRIMINAL COURT; INTERNATIONAL IMPRISONMENTS; INTERPOL; MONEY LAUNDERING; ORGANIZED CRIME—GLOBAL; PIRACY, INTELLECTUAL PROPERTY; PIRACY, SEA; POLICING DEMOCRACY; POLITICAL CORRUPTION; SMUGGLING; TERRORISM; WAR CRIMES; WOMEN AND CRIME IN A GLOBAL PERSPECTIVE

▼ GRAFFITI

The word *graffiti* is derived from an Italian word meaning "little scribblings," generally those found on walls. The desire to write on walls is apparently an age-old one: Arguably, the first graffiti were Stone Age cave paintings. Archaeologists have found important clues to ancient cultures through analysis of graffiti found in the ruins of Pompeii (Reisner and Weschler 1974; Abel and Buckley 1977). In a criminal justice context, graffiti may refer to tag graffiti, gang graffiti, political graffiti, or to simpler acts of vandalism or desecration. Probably the most important graffiti are the elaborate, multicolored, calligraphy-like tag graffiti that have spread from New York City to engender an international youth subculture. Tag graffiti may be seen on walls, buses, and trains in virtually every major city in the world today, flourishing in cities as diverse as Tokyo, Amsterdam, and Rio de Janeiro.

TAG GRAFFITI

Tag graffiti originated in New York City and (to a lesser extent) Philadelphia in the late 1960s and early 1970s. Teenagers began writing their nicknames ("tags") on walls, often followed by their street number or other forms of geographic identification. For example, TAKI 183, a notorious early New York graffiti writer often cited as the inventor of this type of graffiti, lived on 183rd Street. Signatures grew more elaborate and stylized as youths competed for peer status in both audacious placement of their tags and in style and technique. Writers employed ink markers and spray paint, modifying the spray paint cans to produce a wider spray and thus larger tags.

Tag graffiti might have remained a fad in a few low-income neighborhoods but for the fact that a few graffiti writers began spray-painting subway trains. Suddenly, their tags were seen by people all over the city, not just by those who passed a particular wall. Teenagers began an ever more intense competition in the placement and stylization of their signatures. Graffiti "pieces" became more elaborate, eventually becoming large enough to cover the entire side of a subway car with a multicolored cartoon-like signature requiring several hours of clandestine spray-painting. From the early 1970s to the mid-1980s, nearly every subway car in New York City was covered, inside and out, with the calligraphy of teenage writers. This occurred against the backdrop of a city on the verge of bankruptcy, with municipal services, including policing, cut back drastically.

A graffiti-based subculture evolved, with its own vocabulary: "Bombing" (writing graffiti), "throw-ups" (quickly executed pieces involving only a background color and a contrasting outline), "racking" (shoplifting spray paint from hardware store paint racks), "burner" (an especially good piece), and "toy" (poorly executed graffiti) are some terms that have survived as the graffiti subculture spread. Ironically, one force that fostered a citywide subculture of graffiti in New York City was a crackdown on graffiti by the transit police and the courts.

Graffiti writers were sentenced to clean up graffiti in subway yards. There they met other writers from other areas whom they might not otherwise have encountered. Citywide alliances and rivalries were the result. As the popularity of subway graffiti increased, enforcement efforts also increased, with arrests and increased security at subway yards, eventually including razor-wire fences and attack dogs. Sales of spray paint and large ink markers to those under eighteen years of age were banned in New York City and many surrounding areas. The omnipresence of graffiti was seen as a sign of urban decay, of "vandals in control" (to borrow the name of a graffiti crew of the time).

But some people were not so sure that graffiti writers were simply vandals. In 1974, the celebrated American author Norman Mailer wrote "The Faith of Graffiti," which hailed graffiti writers as folk artists and was later published in a book of the same name that included color photographs of graffiti. A group of influential art critics and avant-garde art galleries continued to promote the idea of graffiti as urban folk art, with shows of graffiti-style paintings executed with spray paint on canvas and photographs of subway graffiti. Craig Castleman (1982) documents this period extensively. Interestingly, Castleman's sociological work is extremely popular among younger graffiti writers who seek to emulate the exploits of the New York City pioneers he discusses. *Style Wars,* a 1983 documentary by New York filmmakers Tony Silver and Henry Chalfont, chronicles the peak years of the subway graffiti phenomenon in New York City. A fictional film by Charlie Ahearn entitled *Wild Style* (1982) stars many real-life New York graffiti writers. (The term "wild style" refers to an extreme form of graffiti calligraphy in which the forms of the letters are extended and interlaced in such a way as to be completely unrecognizable as letters to noninitiates). Paintings on canvas by graffiti writers such as Lee Quinones ("Lee," perhaps the most respected tag graffiti artist of all time, both because of his innovative visual style and because legend has it that he was the first to execute a "whole-car piece"—one that covers the entire side of a subway car), "Futura 2000" (Lenny McGurr), and "Quik" (Linwood Felton) continue to sell in the international art market. Keith Haring (1958–1990) and Jean-Michel Basquiat (1960–1988), both generally considered to be major late-twentieth-century American artists, came out of the graffiti art movement of the 1980s. Works of tag graffiti art have appeared in art museums in the United States and Europe.

Tag graffiti were also intimately associated with another major cultural phenomenon that arose in the 1980s: hip-hop or rap music. Many early "MCs" (hip-hop vocalists) were graffiti writers, and graffiti were often prominently featured in hip-hop performances, videos, and films, as well as on the covers of recordings by hip-hop musicians. The connection between graffiti and hip hop spurred tag graffiti to international proportions, and today imitations of New York-style tag graffiti can be seen on public transportation and walls in every large city in the world. For example, Jeff Ferrell's (1996) ethnographic work documents a Denver, Colorado, tag graffiti crew.

As a result of crackdowns on subway graffiti by several mayors, subway graffiti are now rare in New York City, although graffiti on walls continue to flourish unabated. Several internationally circulated magazines cater to fans of graffiti, and Web sites devoted to graffiti proliferate on the Internet. One recent development in tag graffiti has been a shift from spray paint and ink markers to acidic glass-etching fluid to tag plate-glass surfaces.

GANG GRAFFITI

Gang graffiti usually consist of graffiti by gang members intended to mark the territory they consider "theirs," graffiti intended to provoke other gangs, and graffiti intended to memorialize those who have died in gang struggles. Gang graffiti may be intended to be understood by the general public, as in the proclamation, ubiquitous in the United Kingdom, that the local gang "Rules!" or the 1960s Chicago "Black P. Stone Nation" (referring to the long-time gang now known as El Rukn but originally known as the Blackstone Rangers). Or gang graffiti may be more cryptic, as in the 1950s New York "DTK" ("Down [willing] To Kill"). Susan Phillips (1999) distinguishes gang graffiti from tag graffiti, which she refers to as "hip-hop" graffiti, on the grounds that gang graffiti are intended for a much more limited public than are tag graffiti. She argues that, whereas tag graffiti writers seek fame for their creativity and audacity, gang graffiti writers speak only to the closed community of "gangbangers," affirming the ownership of "turf" and the solidarity of the group, as well as challenging rivals. Her work is based on ethnographic research among black and Hispanic gangs of Los Angeles and includes an extensive overview of the literature on graffiti.

Gang graffiti differ from tag graffiti in being generally less stylized (although there may be a locally

Cleaning Up Graffiti in San Francisco

"Muni spends approximately three million a year on graffiti. We have a Clean Fleet Program that concentrates on graffiti removal. We have a mobile crew of three vans with five–car Cleaning Personnel in each vehicle. When people see graffiti on the interior of the buses, they get uncomfortable and fear for their safety. That's our main concern, we want people to feel safe when they're riding our buses. Eighteen months ago, Phil Adams, Director of Muni, did a public survey on priorities to make Muni a better transit system, and out of fifteen concerns, graffiti was number five, which says a lot. We get gang graffiti, stuff from tagging crews who are not gang related, and we've caught vandals that go to some very prestigious private schools. One kid in the south that got popped for graffiti was the son of a prominent doctor."

—Anthony Tufo, Deputy Chief of Staff,
Municipal Railway, San Francisco

"Our program is definitely working, and the citizens are telling us how much they appreciate it. Women are especially happy because many of them told us how intimidating areas such as the area around "Psycho City" used to be for them. Is graffiti going to go away? Yeah, when people start paying their taxes and nobody kills anybody anymore."

—Scott Shaw, Assistant Superintendent,
Bureau of Street Environmental Services, San Francisco

Source: Walsh, Michael (1996). *Graffito*. Berkeley, CA: North Atlantic Books.

accepted style, as in the angular Old English-type lettering favored in California gang graffiti or the extremely cryptic runes employed by Brazilian *favela* (gangs) and in generally not displaying the multiple colors and visual inventiveness that characterize tag graffiti, although there is some overlap between tag graffiti and gang graffiti. Gang graffiti often involve iconography using gang symbols, ritualized formulations of boasts or threats, and, characteristically, local place names or nicknames ("Sacto" for Sacramento [California], for example) identifying the gang's "turf." One consequence of the high death rate among young men in the battles over crack cocaine distribution in many large cities in the United States in the 1980s was the institutionalization of "mourning walls" paying tribute to dead community members, which became common in poorer and gang-dominated neighborhoods.

POLITICAL GRAFFITI

Writing on walls is clearly an economical means of getting the attention of the public and also carries an implicit message of defiance of authority. Political graffiti have long been a propaganda method of those dissatisfied with the political order. The invention of spray paint greatly facilitated this form of graffiti (as it did all forms of graffiti), because it let writers paint slogans much more rapidly, an advantage particularly relevant to political graffitists, who may face harsher sanctions than others because of the political content of their work.

Little has been written about political graffiti. Jill Posener (1982) has brought together many examples of leftist and feminist graffiti in the United Kingdom, often involving ironic commentary added to commercial advertising. Much of the graffiti she compiles fits into the tradition of "*detournement*." This term was first used by the Situationists, a group of French leftist intellectuals of the 1960s who advocated using elements of popular culture to critique that culture by, for example, inserting discussions of the Vietnam War into the speech balloons of romance comics. In the 1990s, so-called ad-busters further extended this form of graffiti through technically proficient alterations of billboards to promote leftist and environmentalist causes by, for example, substituting the face of Cuban revolutionary Che Guevera for that of Albert Einstein in an Apple Computer campaign that exhorted consumers to "Think Different." The recent trend of computer hackers altering Web pages to reflect their political views represents an extension of this type of graffiti into cyberspace.

VANDALISM AND DESECRATION

Although most graffiti, no matter what their purpose, are probably legally classifiable as vandalism (unless executed with the permission of the owner of the property on which they appear), some graffiti are purely acts of vandalism. They are done with no other purpose than to deface or to desecrate the target. Swastikas painted on synagogues and satanic pentagrams painted on churches are two examples of this type of graffiti.

Other forms of graffiti are perhaps more benign in that they involve property damage but are not intended primarily for that purpose. Graffiti extolling the athletic prowess of local sports teams are common throughout much of the world, although sports fans in the United States seem less inclined to this activity than those in Europe and Latin America. Sexual graffiti and scatological graffiti, often referred to as *latrinalia* (a term coined by the ethnographer Alan Dundes [1966]), have been the subject of considerable attention by folklorists, psychologists, and social scientists. Robert Reisner and Lorraine Weschler (1974) and Ernest Abel and Barbara Buckley (1977) compile and analyze many examples of this type of graffiti.

—Travis Wendel

Further Reading

Abel, Ernest, and Barbara Buckley. (1977). *The Handwriting on the Wall: Toward a Sociology and Psychology of Graffiti.* Westport, CT: Greenwood Press.

Castleman, Craig. (1982). *Getting Up: Subway Graffiti in New York.* Cambridge, MA: MIT Press.

Dundes, Alan. (1966). "Here I Sit: A Study of American Latrinalia." *The Kroeber Society Anthropological Papers* 34: 91–105 (February).

Ferrell, Jeff. (1993). *Crimes of Style: Urban Graffiti and the Politics of Criminality.* New York: Garland Press.

Mailer, Norman. (1974). "The Faith of Graffiti." In *The Faith of Graffiti,* edited by Melvin Kurlansky. New York: Praeger.

Phillips, Susan. (1999). *Wallbangin': Graffiti and Gangs in L.A.* Chicago: University of Chicago Press.

Posener, Jill. (1982). *Spray It Loud.* London: Routledge & Kegan Paul.

Reisner, Robert, and Lorraine Weschler. (1974). *The Encyclopedia of Graffiti.* New York: Macmillan.

▼ GRAND JURY

The Fifth Amendment to the U.S. Constitution guarantees that no person shall be tried for a serious crime "unless upon a presentment or indictment of a Grand Jury." So named because it comprises a larger number of jurors than a trial or "petit" jury, a grand jury is "a jury of inquiry . . . whose duty it is to receive complaints and accusations in criminal cases, hear evidence adduced on the part of the state, and find bills of indictment in cases where they are satisfied a trial ought to be had" (Black 1983: 444). Because the grand jury can refuse to issue an indictment if it does not find probable cause to believe that a particular crime has been committed, it can be viewed as a "shield" that screens against unjust prosecutions. Because the grand jury can subpoena witnesses and documents, it can also be viewed as a "sword" that helps the prosecutor acquire evidence.

BACKGROUND

The grand jury functions both to assist the prosecutor and to limit the prosecutor's discretion to take cases to trial. In part because these roles are in tension, and in part because grand jury proceedings and records are not public, far less is known about grand juries than about any other institution in the criminal justice process. The existing information, however, leads some commentators to say that grand juries are too effective in compelling the production of evidence and that they should be abolished.

England, where the grand jury first developed some 800 years ago, abolished it by an act of Parliament in 1933. Grand juries have never played a role outside the Anglo-American legal world.

GRAND JURY FUNCTIONS

The screening function, the "shield" against unjust prosecutions, is formally performed in every case, because before the grand jury can issue an indictment, it must find probable cause to believe that the defendant has committed the crime with which he or she is charged. If the grand jury does not find probable cause, the case is dismissed, although federal prosecutors can refile the same case and seek to persuade a different grand jury that there is sufficient evidence of the defendant's guilt.

Grand juries are selected in much the same way as trial juries: The names of citizens are drawn from those who own property, register to vote, or hold a driver's license. But grand juries function quite differently from trial juries. The grand jury can stay in session for as long as two years, usually meeting only one day a week, and can screen hundreds of cases. Trial juries decide guilt or innocence in a single case and must find proof beyond a reasonable doubt—a much higher standard than probable cause—before it can rule against the defendant. Federal grand juries consist of twenty-three members and can return an indictment by majority vote, while the trial jury consists of twelve members and must reach a unanimous verdict.

The only participants in the process who are in the grand jury room are the grand jurors, the prosecutor, and the witness. There is no judge, and more important,

▼

Grand Jury Secrecy Rules: Rule 6(e) of the Federal Rules of Criminal Procedure

Recording and Disclosure of Proceedings.

(1) Recording of Proceedings. All proceedings, except when the grand jury is deliberating or voting, shall be recorded stenographically or by an electronic recording device. An unintentional failure of any recording to reproduce all or any portion of a proceeding shall not affect the validity of the prosecution. The recording or reporter's notes or any transcript prepared therefrom shall remain in the custody or control of the attorney for the government unless otherwise ordered by the court in a particular case.

(2) General Rule of Secrecy. A grand juror, an interpreter, a stenographer, an operator of a recording device, a typist who transcribes recorded testimony, an attorney for the government, or any person to whom disclosure is made under paragraph (3)(A)(ii) of this subdivision shall not disclose matters occurring before the grand jury, except as otherwise provided for in these rules. No obligation of secrecy may be imposed on any person except in accordance with this rule. A knowing violation of Rule 6 may be punished as a contempt of court.

(3) Exceptions.

(A) Disclosure otherwise prohibited by this rule of matters occurring before the grand jury, other than its deliberations and the vote of any grand juror, may be made to:
(i) an attorney for the government for use in the performance of such attorney's duty; and (ii) such government personnel (including personnel of a state or subdivision of a state) as are deemed necessary by an attorney for the government to assist an attorney for the government in the performance of such attorney's duty to enforce federal criminal law.

(B) Any person to whom matters are disclosed under subparagraph (A)(ii) of this paragraph shall not utilize that grand jury material for any purpose other than assisting the attorney for the government in the performance of such attorney's duty to enforce federal criminal law. An attorney for the government shall promptly provide the district court, before which was impaneled the grand jury whose material has been so disclosed, with the names of the persons to whom such disclosure has been made, and shall certify that the attorney has advised such persons of their obligation of secrecy under this rule.

(C) Disclosure otherwise prohibited by this rule of matters occurring before the grand jury may also be made:—
(i) when so directed by a court preliminarily to or in connection with a judicial proceeding; (ii) when permitted by a court at the request of the defendant, upon a showing that grounds may exist for a motion to dismiss the indictment because of matters occurring before the grand jury;

(iii) when the disclosure is made by an attorney for the government to another federal grand jury; or (iv) when permitted by a court at the request of an attorney for the government, upon a showing that such matters may disclose a violation of state criminal law, to an appropriate official of a state or subdivision of a state for the purpose of enforcing such law. If the court orders disclosure of matters occurring before the grand jury, the disclosure shall be made in such manner, at such time, and under such conditions as the court may direct.

(D) A petition for disclosure pursuant to subdivision (e)(3)(C)(i) shall be filed in the district where the grand jury convened. Unless the hearing is ex parte, which it may be when the petitioner is the government, the petitioner shall serve written notice of the petition upon (i) the attorney for the government, (ii) the parties to the judicial proceeding if disclosure is sought in connection with such a proceeding, and (iii) such other persons as the court may direct. The court shall afford those persons a reasonable opportunity to appear and be heard.

(E) If the judicial proceeding giving rise to the petition is in a federal district court in another district, the court shall transfer the matter to that court unless it can reasonably obtain sufficient knowledge of the proceeding to determine whether disclosure is proper. The court shall order transmitted to the court to which the matter is transferred the material sought to be disclosed, if feasible, and a written evaluation of the need for continued grand jury secrecy. The court to which the matter is transferred shall afford the aforementioned persons a reasonable opportunity to appear and be heard.

(4) Sealed Indictments. The federal magistrate judge to whom an indictment is returned may direct that the indictment be kept secret until the defendant is in custody or has been released pending trial. Thereupon the clerk shall seal the indictment and no person shall disclose the return of the indictment except when necessary for the issuance and execution of a warrant or summons.

(5) Closed Hearing. Subject to any right to an open hearing in contempt proceedings, the court shall order a hearing on matters affecting a grand jury proceeding to be closed to the extent necessary to prevent disclosure of matters occurring before a grand jury.

(6) Sealed Records. Records, orders and subpoenas relating to grand jury proceedings shall be kept under seal to the extent and for such time as is necessary to prevent disclosure of matters occurring before a grand jury.

no defendant or defense lawyer to argue the other side of the case. Grand jurors, but not trial jurors, are permitted to ask questions of the witnesses and to discuss the case with the prosecutor. The proceedings are secret, the records are sealed, and no official report is ever made as to why the grand jury chose to indict or not to indict—although in political cases "leaks" are frequent.

As described below, modern grand juries very rarely screen out cases; thus, their most important function today is that of the sword. The sword function is not utilized in every case because prosecutors usually have enough evidence from other sources, typically in the form of a confession, eyewitness testimony, or physical evidence linking the defendant to the crime. But when a grand jury performs the sword function, it can be very effective in compelling the production of evidence through its subpoena power. There are few objections that witnesses can make to keep from having to testify or produce documents to the grand jury, a rule that has existed for centuries. As the U.S. Supreme Court put this common law principle: "[T]he public [through the grand jury] has a right to every man's evidence" (*Kastigar v. United States*). The prosecutor directs this function and can use the grand jury to develop a case against a particular suspect or to determine who might be guilty of a particular crime.

The sword and shield functions of the grand jury exist in tension. This tension, combined with the secrecy of the proceedings, makes the grand jury one of the most unusual institutions in Anglo-American criminal justice.

Jesus Perez, a dishwasher at the Ambassador Hotel, outside the grand jury room after testifying about the murder of Senator Robert F. Kennedy in Los Angeles in 1968. Perez's testimony helped lead to the indictment and conviction of Sirhan Bishara Sirhan.
Source: © Bettmann/Corbis; used by permission.

HISTORY

Henry II of England (reigned 1154–1189) is credited with the development of a system of justice that included an early form of the grand jury. From 1154 to 1163, Henry II, great-grandson of William of Normandy (also known as William the Conqueror), consolidated his military power over the kingdom of England. By 1163, the kingdom was at peace.

With his enemies subdued, Henry II directed his intellect and energy to imposing his rule uniformly throughout the kingdom. Part of securing a uniform rule, Henry realized, was to have a uniform court system. He implemented a series of laws, beginning in 1164, that increased the jurisdiction and authority of the royal courts, which were staffed by judges he appointed. These new laws increased the penalties, which generally owed to the king, while diminishing the role of the individual court systems that each baron administered.

Crime was, then as now, a concern of both government and citizens. Then, however, there was no police force, and limited jurisdiction and resources made it difficult for local sheriffs to ferret out malfeasants. To fill this gap, one of Henry's innovations was a new law requiring that each village call together sixteen men whose function was to report whether "there be any man who is accused or generally suspected of being a robber or murderer or thief . . . since our lord the king was king" (Assize of Clarendon § 1: 1166). This 1166 law was the beginning of the grand jury. Its role in the twelfth century was limited to acting as a sword, identifying those who might be guilty of crimes.

The history of the grand jury functioning as a shield against unjust prosecutions is less clear. Two early instances in which a grand jury resisted the power of king and prosecutor were the treason cases brought by Charles II in 1687 against the Earl of Shaftesbury and Stephen Colledge. As Professor Andrew Leipold puts it, "Although there is some dispute over whether the charges were valid, there is no doubt that each grand jury withstood great pressure from the court, and indirectly from the Crown, and refused to indict" (Leipold 1995: 282). But the victory against the (possibly) unjust prosecution was short-lived: The king moved the Colledge case to a different part of England where he was viewed more favorably, and a new grand jury indicted Colledge, who was tried, convicted, and executed. Shaftesbury, realizing that the same fate probably awaited him, fled the country. This example does not inspire much confidence in the grand jury's shield function.

There was, however, one period when the grand jury did function effectively as a shield, and this period led to its inclusion in the U.S. Constitution. As American colonists grew weary of British rule, they increasingly challenged the laws imposed on them from England and the authority of the governors appointed by the king. In 1734, John Peter Zenger published a New York newspaper critical of New York Governor William Cosby. The governor charged him with the common-law crime of "seditious libel," that is publishing untrue material that might lead to revolution. Three grand juries heard the case of the king's prosecutors, but each refused to indict. The governor prosecuted Zenger without getting an indictment. Although this procedure was permitted at the time (and is permitted in many states today), the governor's avoidance of the grand jury in Zenger's case was "a controversial move that further eroded popular support for the Governor's actions" (Leipold 1995: 284). The trial jury acquitted Zenger.

As the Revolutionary War approached, colonists used the grand jury as "a potent weapon . . . to harass royal officials and protest against British authority" (Younger 1963: 27). While prosecutors and judges were appointed by the king, grand juries were selected in town meetings, and thus they included "the very people who have committed all these riots" against British authority (Younger 1963: 31). In 1765, for example, a Boston grand jury refused to indict the leaders of the Stamp Act riots, and three years later a Boston grand jury refused to indict the publisher of the *Boston Gazette* for libeling the governor of Massachusetts. Another role for the grand jury in this era was to protect colonists as they increasingly violated the laws imposing British customs and duties. The grand jury was thus an effective shield against the enforcement of oppressive laws that the British Parliament and monarch had forced on the colonists. Little wonder, then, that the framers included the grand jury right in the Fifth Amendment to the U.S. Constitution.

But it is far from clear today that the grand jury serves any function beyond that of the sword—permitting the prosecutor to compel evidence that the police cannot get by other means, or that the police cannot get as easily.

THE FUTURE OF THE GRAND JURY

The Fifth Amendment grand jury requirement applies only in federal court. The U.S. Supreme Court has never ruled that states must provide grand juries in criminal cases, and more than half of the U.S. states do not have a statutory grand jury requirement. In these states, prosecutors can file an "information," setting out the details of the crime and swearing that there is probable cause to believe the defendant guilty (which is what Governor Cosby did in the Zenger case). The next stage in these states is a preliminary hearing in which the state must persuade a judge that probable cause exists. Preliminary hearings also occur in some jurisdictions that require grand juries, typically when the case begins with an arrest. The role of the preliminary hearing in these cases is to make certain that grounds exist to refer the case to the grand jury.

In a preliminary hearing, the defendant is present, with his or her lawyer and has an opportunity to hear and refute the state's case. This hearing would thus be more likely than the grand jury to function as an effective screen to keep weak cases from going to trial. The preliminary hearing does not, of course, involve citizens in the screening of cases; what is lost is the voice of the people. Presumably, for example, a judge appointed by the king would have found probable cause in 1734 to believe that John Peter Zenger committed seditious libel.

But however effective the grand jury was in pre-Revolution days in protecting colonists from the overreaching of the British government, the modern grand jury does not seem to do much screening. Because no defense is presented, and because the grand jury need find only probable cause, and only by a majority vote, grand juries rarely reject the prosecution's view of the case. The cliché offered to describe this phenomenon is that an able prosecutor can get a grand jury to "indict a ham sandwich," and in fact, data from federal courts suggest that grand juries indict in 99 percent of cases (Leipold 1995: 274). The full significance of these data is open to question. It might be that prosecutors do such a good job screening cases that there is little work for grand juries to do. But the data clearly suggest that very little screening occurs at the grand jury stage.

Grand juries remain an effective sword—their original role in 1166 when created by England's Henry II. Grand jury subpoenas produce large amounts of evidence difficult to get in other ways, particularly in complex federal cases involving multiple defendants and large-scale crimes like conspiracy and racketeering. But there is no apparent reason to require a grand jury indictment in every case. Although we lack perfect data, it appears that the grand jury is a rubber stamp for the prosecutor, as its critics have maintained. Judges screening cases at a preliminary hearing surely could do no worse; also, defendants can probe the state's case at the preliminary hearing, which makes it less of a rubber stamp.

The Fifth Amendment grand jury requirement cannot, of course, be abolished without a constitutional amendment. The difficulty of amending the Constitution might be reason enough to leave the federal grand jury requirement in place, but it is not surprising that England and about half of U.S. states do not use grand juries at all.

SUMMARY

The grand jury was born as a "sword" to help the king's prosecutors. It functioned as an effective "shield" to protect against unjust accusations for only a brief time in our history—when the American colonists were resisting British rule. It continues today to function effectively as a sword, but its shield function is often performed by a preliminary hearing before a judge.

—*George C. Thomas III*

See also JURY SYSTEM; PROSECUTOR; PROSECUTORIAL DISCRETION

Further Reading

Beale, Sara Sun, et al. (1997). *Grand Jury Law & Practice*. St. Paul, MN: West Group.

Black, Henry C. (1983). Black's Law Dictionary. St Paul, MN: West Publishing

Blank, Blanche Davis. (1993). *The Not So Grand Jury: the Story of the Federal Grand Jury System*. Lanham, MD: University Press of America.

Bolstad, Max. (2000). "The Grand Jury: Eight Centuries of Myth and Reality." *Criminal Law Bulletin* 36, 4: 281–315.

Brenner, Susan W. (1995). "The Voice of the Community: A Case for Grand Jury Independence." *Virginia Journal of Social Policy & Law* 3: 67–131.

Brenner, Susan W. (1997). "Federal Grand Jury" Web site. http://www.udayton.edu/~grandjur

Brenner, Susan W., and Gregory G. Lockhart. (1996). *Federal Grand Jury Practice*. St. Paul, MN: West Group.

Clark, Leroy D. (1975). *The Grand Jury: the Use and Abuse of Political Power.* New York: Quadrangle/The New York Times Book Company.

Edwards, George J. (1973). *The Grand Jury.* New York: AMS Press.

Frankel, Marvin E., and Gary P. Naftalis. (1977). *The Grand Jury: An Institution on Trial.* New York: Hill & Wang.

"The Grand Jury as an Investigatory Body." (1961). *Harvard Law Review* 74: 590–605.

Kadish, Mark. (1996). "Behind the Locked Door of an American Grand Jury: Its History, Its Secrecy, and Its Process." *Florida State University Law Review* 24: 1–77.

Leipold, Andrew D. (1995). "Why Grand Juries Do Not (and Cannot) Protect the Accused." *Cornell Law Review* 80: 260–324.

Richman, Daniel. (1999). "Grand Jury Secrecy: Plugging the Leaks in An Empty Bucket." *American Criminal Law Review* 36: 339–356.

"Symposium on the Grand Jury." (1984). *Journal of Criminal Law & Criminology* 75: 1047–1196.

Whyte, James P. (1959). "Is the Grand Jury Necessary?" *Virginia Law Review* 45: 461–491.

Younger, Richard D. (1963). *The People's Panel: The Grand Jury in the United States, 1634–1941*. Providence, RI: Brown University Press.

Court Case

Kastigar v. United States (1972). 406 U.S. 441, 443.

▼ GREAT BRITAIN

Great Britain (GB) comprises England, Wales, and Scotland. The United Kingdom (UK) as a whole incorporates Northern Ireland and some dependencies (e.g., the Channel Islands, Gibraltar, the Falkland Islands, the British Overseas Caribbean Territories of the Commonwealth including the British Virgin Islands, Turks and Caicos, and the Cayman Islands; see Smartt, 1999a). All can be seen as distinct jurisdictions. Although many laws apply to just one of these jurisdictions, laws can be applied, by act of Parliament, to all or any combination of them, the UK as a whole, or GB. The United Kingdom is a constitutional monarchy; Elizabeth II became queen in 1952. The British Parliament is divided into two chambers: the elected House of Commons and the hereditary/appointed House of Lords.

BRITISH EMPIRE

BRITISH INSPECTOR
HONG KONG

NATIVE CONSTABLE
BURMA

NATIVE INSPECTOR
BURMA

MALAY CONSTABLE
STRAIT SETTLEMENTS

BRITISH SERGEANT
(WINTER BLUES)
HONG KONG

CHINESE CONSTABLE
HONG KONG

SIKH CONSTABLE
(WINTER BLUES)
HONG KONG

Uniforms worn by criminal justice officers at various locales in the British Empire.
Source: Blakeslee, Major F. Gilbert (1934). *Police Uniforms of the World.* Illustrations by Bert Offord. Norwood, MA: Plimpton Press, p. 83.

For a measure, or bill, to become law (by act of Parliament, or statute), it must be passed by both Houses and receive "royal assent." According to the doctrine of supremacy, Parliament is legislatively omnipotent, which means that law can be made and unmade with every newly elected Parliament. In this entry, factual information relating to crime figures and the criminal justice system refers to England and Wales (hereafter, "England"). England's population is projected to rise from the current 50 million to 51.8 million by 2008 (an increase of 3.8 percent). The greatest increase in population has been in the southeast of England and in London, the capital region and seat of government. Greater London covers about 620 square miles, with a population of 7.2 million in 2000. The county with the largest projected increase (from 1998 to 2008) is Cambridgeshire (11 percent). The population in northwestern and northeastern England declined from 1998, matching the highest unemployment and poverty trends. There has been a 1 percent decline in population in the metropolitan areas of Manchester, Liverpool, Leeds, and Birmingham (but not in London).

THE LEGAL SYSTEMS

The doctrine of Parliamentary supremacy was modified when Britain entered the European Economic Community (EEC) in 1972 (renamed the European Union [EU] after the Treaty of the European Union [TEU] 1992, also known as the Maastricht Treaty). Thereafter, the UK incorporated EU law, which takes precedence over all national legislations of the member states of Europe. The European Court of Justice (ECJ) in Luxembourg is the supreme court in the EU (for civil matters only), comprising fifteen judges from the member states of the EU. The ECJ can overrule all other courts on matters of Community law. On October 2, 2000, the European Convention on Human Rights and Fundamental Freedoms (the "Convention") was incorporated into UK law by means of the Human Rights Act 1998.

The highest civil appellate court is the House of Lords (HL), which sits in Westminster (London). The judges include the Lord Chancellor, the Lords of Appeal in Ordinary, and those peers (i.e., members of the House of Lords) who hold or have held high judicial office. The HL has an appellate jurisdiction from Scottish courts in civil matters only. It has no Scottish criminal jurisdiction. The Judicial Committee of the Privy Council is the ultimate court of appeal for the overseas territories except for those that independently have abolished the right of appeal. The Judicial Committee consists of all members of the Privy Council who hold or have held high judicial office under the Crown (mainly of Lords of Appeal in Ordinary), and, occasionally, privy councillors from overseas who have the necessary judicial qualifications. Territories from which an appeal lies to Her Majesty in Council include New Zealand, Jamaica, and other West Indies islands, and areas such as the sovereign base in Cyprus. The national courts (High Court, Court of Appeal, and House of Lords) are based in London; local courts of first instance (magistrates' courts and county courts) are based throughout the country, and the crown court has many locations.

Although there is now some governmental devolution to the Welsh Assembly, Wales has not since early medieval times had a legal system distinct from England. The Province of Northern Ireland has some unusual features in its system, centered in Belfast. Its legal system is based on the English one, especially since the imposition of direct rule under a British secretary of state since mid-1972. There was political instability and violence in the twentieth and twenty-first century, which was endemic in the province since the establishment of rules such as that of no jury in trials of terrorists.

Scotland has its own legal system, with law courts based in Edinburgh. Scots law is more akin to continental European (Roman) law-based systems. It does not, however, have its own legislature (i.e., a body that has the function of making new law), because of the union of parliaments of England and Scotland under the Acts of Union 1707. But there are some distinct differences, particularly in criminal law. The Scotland Act 1998 brought about devolution, establishing a distinct Scottish Parliament in 1999. The Westminster Parliament may make a statue that is applicable only to Scotland, signified by "Scotland" in the title (e.g., the Age of Legal Capacity [Scotland] Act 1991). The Scottish superior court is the Court of Session, the High Court of Justiciary, and the sheriff courts.

THE ADMINISTRATION OF THE ENGLISH LEGAL SYSTEMS

The Lord Chancellor's Department (LCD) is responsible for the justice system in England and Wales. It promotes the provision of legal services, wider access to justice, and the reform of the civil law. Through the Legal Services Commission and the courts, the LCD is responsible for funding legal services (formerly known as Legal Aid). It supports the Lord Chancellor in the appointment of judges, Queen's Counsel, magistrates, and tribunal chairmen, and, overseas, the administration of the magistrates' courts. In December 1999, the Lord Chancellor appointed Lord Justice Auld to conduct a wide and independent review of the criminal courts following the White Paper (CM 4181) in December 1998, *Public Services for the Future: Modernising, Reform, Accountability.*

Criminal cases usually start in the magistrates' courts (there are about 400 in England). Less serious criminal cases (summary offenses, that is, no committal or jury) are sent for speedy trial to the magistrates' court. More serious indictable offenses are tried at the

---

Poaching

In medieval England, poaching was a serious crime. Laws that protected game and prevented poaching were supported by the royalty and nobility (who were allowed to hunt) and despised by the peasants, as shown in this popular rhyme.

> He made great protection for the game
> And imposed laws for the same,
> So that who so slew hart or hind
> Should be made blind.
>
> He preserved the harts and boars
> And loved stags as much
> As if he were their father.
> Moreover, for the hares did he not decree that
>   they should go free.
> Powerful men complained of it and poor men
>   lamented it,
> But so fierce was he that he cared not for the
>   rancour of them all.

Source: Whitelock, Dorothy, ed. (1961). *The Anglo-Saxon Chronicle.* London: Eyre and Spottiswoode, pp. 164-165.

---

crown court in front of twelve jury members. The jury decides the facts of the case and applies the law to those facts; the jury reaches the verdict on the guilt or innocence of the defendant. The prosecution is on behalf of the Crown (the State); it has the burden of proof in this adversarial system that incorporates the not-guilty principle (i.e., innocent until proven guilty). The standard (level) of proof is heavy, and guilt must be proven beyond reasonable doubt. All criminal cases are referred to in the legal citation *Regina (R) v. The Defendant* (e.g., *R v. Woollin 2000*). In 1986, the name of the official prosecution agency was changed to the Crown Prosecution Service (CPS). The CPS takes the case over from the police, who have already investigated most of the evidence.

Civil courts range from about 250 county courts (mostly small claims of less than £3,000 [approximately U. S. $4,240), presided over by district judges. There are Divisions of the High Court (in London), such as the Family Division (dealing with divorce, child welfare, and the administration of wills), the Chancery Division (considers complex matters, for example, disputes over wills, settlements, trusts, bankruptcy, land law, intellectual property, and corporate laws), and the Queen's Bench Division (deals with remaining disputes, for example, contracts, torts, and land law). For the purpose of court hierarchy, the English courts are placed as follows: Up to Court of Appeal (CA) level, each judge follows the decision of all the higher courts above it but need not follow the views of other judges in the same or lower court. The CA is normally bound by its own previous decisions in civil cases as well as those of the HL. The CA can depart from its own decisions in civil cases in the circumstances laid down in *Young v. Bristol Aeroplane Co.* The Criminal Division of the CA is not bound by its previous decisions; it is considered to be more important to be just to the individual than to provide legal certainty. The HL is not bound by other courts (except the ECJ).

CRIME

The Home Office (department of the government headed by the Secretary of State for the Home Department, or Home Secretary) compiles data on crime, prison and probation populations, and commissions statistical and qualitative research in crime reduction, such as the *British Crime Survey* (BCS). The BCS is a large national survey that asks people about crimes they have experienced in the previous year and about various other crime-related topics; it also chronicles *unrecorded* crime.

The *BCS 2000* concentrated on people's contacts with the police and their views on police performance. There was a large victim survey about the service received from the police, including evaluation of response time, levels of interest and effort, and how well the police had kept the victim informed. The majority stated that their local police did a "fairly good job" (78 percent). Levels of confidence in the police had decreased since the *BCS 1998*, particularly among ethnic minority groups; under half of the respondents (48 percent) had at least one type of contact with the police. Seventy-one percent of Asian respondents and 74 percent of black respondents said their local police still did a "reasonably good job." The proportion of respondents stopped by the police while in a car or on a motorcycle (12 percent) or on foot (3 percent) remained constant throughout the 1990s. Young black and Asian males (aged sixteen to twenty-nine) are highly likely to be stopped while on foot or in a vehicle. The *BCS 2000* indicated that many victims of crime did not report the incident to the police (only 39 percent). Although property crimes have generally diminished, crimes of violence have increased. Of the total sentenced male prison population in 2000, 10,850 were jailed for "violent crimes against the person" (compared with 10,300 in 1999). Sexual offenses also have increased (from 4,960 to 5,020 of the sentenced male population in prison). Robbery committed by females is on the increase (from 160 to 200 incarcerated women), making violence against the person and drug-related offenses increasing crimes for females.

THE METROPOLITAN POLICE SERVICES AND OTHER POLICE FORCES

There are forty-three police forces in England and Wales. The London Metropolitan Police Force ("The Met"), founded by Sir Robert Peel in 1829, is possibly one of the most famous police forces in the world. The Met is the largest of the three police forces operating in Greater London (the others are City of London Police and British Transport Police). The Met employs about 26,000 officers plus about 11,000 civilians and about 850 traffic wardens. The Metropolitan Police Service (MPS) was established in July 2000, mainly as a result of the disturbances in Brixton, in south London (the Brixton Riots 1981) between the local, mainly black, communities and the police. The main aims of the MPS is to deliver a policing service within the community, to work with local partnerships and criminal justice agencies, to reduce illegal drug dealing, to divert young people from crime, and to strengthen local faith in the police force. Each MPS branch works in close partnership with the Drug Action Teams (DATs) and Youth Offending Teams (YOTs—established in 2000 under the Crime and Disorder Act 1998). YOTs exist in all areas of England and are made up of police and probation officers and local authority staff from education and health departments. The main aim of the YOTs is to break the cycle of crime through programs of early intervention, the construction of planned court orders, diversionary schemes, and reparation orders. Early indications from pilot schemes suggest that the combination of new fast tracking of youth offenders by the police and the subsequent interviews by YOTs have had a positive effect on reducing youth crime. Neighborhood Watch schemes (set up by local police forces) assist in tackling crime in the community by providing community and criminal intelligence by ordinary citizens and residents' associations.

THE CROWN PROSECUTION SERVICE (CPS)

The Royal Commission on Criminal Procedure, set up under Sir Cyril Philips in 1978, published a report in 1981 with three main criticisms:

The police should no longer investigate offenses or decide whether to prosecute, because the investigating police officer could often not be relied on to make a fair decision whether to prosecute;

the different police forces were using different standards to decide whether to prosecute; and

the police were allowing too many weak cases to come to court, which led to a high percentage of judge-directed acquittals.

The CPS was created by the Prosecution of Offences Act 1985, and became fully operational in October 1986. The CPS (completely independent of the police) prosecutes people in England who have been charged by the police with a criminal offense. It is headed by the Director of Public Prosecutions (DPP). The DPP is superintended by the Attorney General (AG), who is the minister responsible to Parliament for the conduct of most criminal prosecutions. There are two CPS headquarters: London and York. Because of initial vast understaffing and government expenditure curbs, only one in every nine police prosecutions resulted in a charge or summons (in 1996, nearly 5 million charges brought by the police and only 576,000 cases went from the CPS to court). In 1998, the CPS dealt with 1.4 million cases in the magistrates' courts and 128,064 in the crown courts. Following the Glidewell Report in 1998 (a critical review of the workings of the CPS by Sir Iain Glidewell), the CPS increased from fourteen to forty-two areas in April 1999, which line up with the existing police force boundaries. The CPS now employs 6,000 people. Special casework lawyers are used throughout the country, allocated to offices of the National Crime Squad and the judicial circuits, leaving the DPP free to deal with the more serious prosecution cases. Within each of the forty-two areas, one or more branch offices (ninety-three in total), handling all prosecutions, are headed by a branch crown prosecutor.

SENTENCING

The overall use of custody (prison sentence) continues to increase; at the crown court, it increased from 60.8 to 62.9 percent and at the magistrates' courts from 11.9 to 12.6 percent (1997 to 1998). Numbers sentenced by the magistrates' courts increased from 10.5 percent in 1997 to 11.5 percent in 1998, with the result that the numbers of people receiving a prison sentence increased one-fifth, from 25,200 to 30,200. There was a modest increase in the numbers sentenced to prison at the crown court (from 46,600 in 1997 to 47,100 in 1998). The total numbers sentenced to custody at all courts in England increased between 1997 and 1998 by 8 percent; but, in 1999, the total number sentenced by the courts was down by 2 and 4 percent respectively (magistrates' and crown courts).

There was a reduction in average sentence lengths between 1997 and 1998. Average sentence length for adult males (aged twenty-one and over) to prison at the crown court reduced from 24.2 months in 1997 to 23.6 months in 1998. Sentence lengths for young males (eighteen to twenty-one years old) also decreased. The overall reduction has been due to the introduction of "plea before venue" (Crime and Disorder Act 1998), meaning that a plea ("guilty" or "not guilty") has to be made at an earlier stage (plea and direction hearing) in the proceedings.

PROBATION

The main themes for the Probation Service (Probation) during the 1980s were: supervision of offenders at risk, bail supervision, young offenders' education, training, and "throughcare" after release from young offender institutions. The role of the English Probation Service changed immensely during the 1990s. The Criminal Justice Act (CJA) 1993 reduced bail and approved bail and probation hostels. From 1994 onwards, Probation's work experienced a vast shakeup, and its efficiency and effectiveness regarding fine and bail defaulters was questioned. The HM Inspectorate of Probation (HMIP) reports independently to ministers concerning performance. HMIP conducts "Thematic Reviews" every three years. Thematic inspections from the mid-1990s onward concentrated on "value for money and working within crime partnerships," leading eventually to the reorganization of the whole service. At the turn of the twenty-first century, Probation contributes to the Home Office aim of achieving the effective execution of the sentences of the court so as to reduce reoffending and protect the public. The National Probation Directorate comprises fifty-four probation services, each administered by a Probation Committee. It is

▼

The Disappearance of Lord Lucan (1974)

While virtually unknown in the United States, Richard John Bingham, the 7th Earl of Lucan, remains a symbol of the dissolute aristocracy and, in the public mind, Britain's most wanted criminal. Lord Lucan was accused of having murdered his children's nanny in November 1974. He is a celebrity on par with O. J. Simpson, and many believe that Lord Lucan is alive and well in Argentina or Canada. Although Veronica, Lady Lucan, claims that her husband is dead, a Scotland Yard spokesperson said in 1998, "The matter is never closed until we have a conviction. Strange as it may sound, we would still like to speak to Lord Lucan in connection with our inquiries into the death of Sandra Rivett."

The violence of the murder, which took place in the basement kitchen of Lucan's estranged wife's house on Eaton Square, in London, bears some similarity to the Simpson case. The murderer lay in wait in the dark kitchen and when a woman—whom police believe Lord Lucan mistook for his wife—came downstairs, she was battered to death with a lead pipe—a weapon popular in English whodunits. Her body was found folded into a canvas mailbag. Lady Lucan had gone down to look for the nanny, leaving her children upstairs watching television, and claims to have been attacked by her husband, who then escaped up the kitchen stairs to the street. She ran screaming down the street to the Plumber's Arm pub, where the police were called.

Lucan was a professional gambler with large debts. He had recently lost a custody battle with his wife. It is generally thought that his family and his powerful, wealthy friends helped him to escape, or try to escape, from Britain. Among those closely associated with Lucan were Sir James Goldsmith, the financier.

The inquest jury brought in a verdict of "Murder by Lord Lucan." As a result of this case, the right of an inquest jury to name a murderer was abolished by the Criminal Law Act of 1977. Lady Lucan agrees with the inquest jury that Sandra Rivett was murdered by Lord Lucan, though, she writes on her Web site, she was not surprised "that my late husband's rather uncivilized blood relations would make futile attempts to clear his name." She insists that he must have died in the English Channel, a claim supported in 2000 by his friend John Aspinall.

Lady Lucan has her own Web site on which she contradicts not only new press articles but the statements of her son and daughter. She shut a LordLucan.co.uk Web site (as an infringement of her son's intellectual property rights), but the operator moved the site to the United States. In addition to articles, scandal, conspiracy theories, and links, the Lord Lucan site includes a page where visitors can post "Lord Lucan sightings" (along with sightings of Elvis and Hitler).

In 2000, Muriel Spark, author of *The Prime of Miss Jean Brodie*, published *Aiding and Abetting*, a fictionalized account of the disappearance of Lord Lucan. Spark carefully avoided potential lawsuits for libel by focusing not on living members of the Lucan family but on Lucan himself, who is either dead or unlikely to bring the matter to court.

—Karen Christensen

Sources: Spark, Muriel. (2000). *Aiding and Abetting*. London: Viking. www.ladylucan.co.uk; www.lordlucan.com.

drugs in the community, electronic monitoring (home curfew), and family court welfare.

PRISONS

The main factors that determine the size of the prison population are the number of offenders sentenced, the proportion given custody, and the average length of sentences. There were 138 prisons in England in 2001, a number of which were privatized, that is, contracted out to the private sector. For example, the Young Offenders Institution of Her Majesty's Prison (HMP) in Doncaster and HMP Dovegate Prison in Staffordshire were contracted out to Premier Prisons in Wackenhut, U.K.; Wolds Prison in Hull and Fazakerley Prison in Liverpool were contracted out to Group 4 Securitas; and Park Prison in Bridgend, Wales, was contracted out to Securicor. Following a period of steady growth, which began in the early 1990s, the prison population peaked in July 1998 at 66,500. Police cells were not used by the Prison Service to allay overcrowding after June 1995. At the end of October 2000, the prison population in England stood at 64,218, making England one of the highest incarcerating countries per capita in western Europe (although this showed a decrease by 2.5 percent from 65,900 in October 1999). Young prisoners decreased by 5.7 percent (from 11,503 to 10,847) and remand (pretrial) prisoners decreased by 16 percent (from 12,818 to 10,722). The female prison population increased by 1 percent (from 3,396 to 3,433). The prison population was 1 percent higher (overcrowded) than the Certified Normal Accommodation (CNA is the capacity of the prisons with no overcrowding; operational capacity is

accountable to the Home Secretary for the strategic direction and performance of service, jointly funded by the Home Office and local authorities. Effective practice now includes a victim perspective, tackling the maximum number of prisoners that can be accommodated in the prisons, albeit some with overcrowding). The number of sentenced prisoners was up by 0.5 percent over the year 2000 (from 52,522 in 1999 to 52,814 in 2000). The number of prisoners aged fifteen to seventeen increased by 1 percent. There were forty-four persons sentenced to imprisonment (including two females) after failing to pay a fine imposed for an offense. They were held for about one week each. The prison population also included 682 civil prisoners, 92 percent of whom were held under the Immigration Act 1971. The prison population projection was expected to rise to about 68,000 by March 2002.

In 2000, among male British nationals in the prison population, 85.5 percent were white; 10.2 percent were black, 2.2 percent were South Asian (i.e., Indian, Pakistani, or Bangladeshi), and 2 percent belonged to Chinese or other ethnic groups. This compared with the general population of England (British nationals aged 15 to 64), of whom 94.8 percent were white, 1.4 percent black, 3 percent South Asian, and 0.8 percent belonged to other ethnic groups (Labour Force Survey 1999–2000). For female British nationals in the prison population, 85.3 percent were white, 11.3 percent were black, 0.8 percent South Asian, and 2.4 percent belonged to Chinese or other ethnic groups.

Her Majesty's Chief Inspector of Prisons is an independent body that was established in 1980 (May Report). The Inspectorate carries out its functions as an independent body, under section 5A (as amended by section 57 CJA 1982) of the Prison Act 1952. The statute specifies the duty of the Chief Inspector to inspect or arrange for the inspection of *all* prisons in England and to make recommendations to the Home Secretary, particularly the treatment of prisoners and their conditions inside. Fully announced and sudden unannounced prison inspections take place around the clock throughout the year. The Chief Inspector is accompanied by a team of specialists, for example, healthcare, education, building works, farms, and so on. His reports are published within six months of each inspection and are open to public access.

The Prisons Ombudsman is another independent body available to all prisoners within the prison system. The ombudsman investigates complaints regarding treatment in prison, including torture. Prisoners must have completed (and exhausted) the Prison Service's internal requests and complaints structure and abided by strict complaints procedures. Prison adjudications are the main source of complaint; these are internal hearings at each prison each day for breaches of the Prison Rules 1964 (as amended 2000). Adjudicators (prison governors [wardens]) can extend the effective length of a prisoner's sentence of imprisonment by up to forty-two days as a form of punishment, akin to a three-month sentence from a court. Lesser penalties include confinement to cells and forfeiture of prisoners' earnings or facilities (e.g., television; home leave; visits). Adjudications should be addressed immediately and fairly; each prison should keep an adequate record. Criteria for the conduct of adjudications were set out by the Division Court in *R. v. Secretary for the Home Department ex part Tarrant*; for example, adjudicators should ensure that an inmate's request for legal representation is upheld. This can be complied with by having the inmate accompanied by a friend (e.g., a cellmate) at the hearing.

Home detention curfew (HDC) was introduced at the end of January 1999, in the Crime and Disorder Act 1998. This allowed 2,000 prisoners to spend up to the last two months of the custodial part of their sentences on a curfew enforced by electronic monitoring (or "tagging"), by December 2000, subject to a risk assessment within the prison.

—Ursula Smartt

See also AUSTRALIA; CANADA; FOOT PATROL; SCOTLAND YARD

Further Reading

European Court of Human Rights Web site. http://www.echr.coe.int

HM Chief Inspector of Prisons Web site. http://www.homeoffice.gov.uk/hmipris

HM Inspectorate of Probation Web site. http://www.homeoffice.gov.uk/hmiprob

HM Prison Service Web site. http://www.hmprisonservice.gov.uk/news

Home Office. (1995). *Review of Prison Service Security in England and Wales and the Escape from Parkhurst Prison on Tuesday 3rd January, 1995* (the "Learmont Report"). Cm 3020. London: HMSO.

Home Office. (1997). *Prison Service Annual Report and Accounts April 1996–March 1997*. HC 274. London: HMSO.

Home Office Web site. http://www.homeoffice.gov.uk

House of Commons. (1998). *Library Research Papers: Northern Ireland—Political Developments Since 1972*, No. 98/57 (May).

London Metropolitan Police Force Web site. http://www.met.police.uk

Lord Chancellor's Department (LCD) Web site. http://www.open.gov.uk/lcd

MacQueen, Hector L. (1993). *Studying Scots Law*. Edinburgh: Butterworths.

The Office of National Statistics (ONS). (1999). *Database: Subnational Population Projections—England*, Series PP3. No. 10. London: HMSO.

The Office of National Statistics ONS. (1999). *Report: Mid-1998 Population Estimates. Population Trends, 1999,* 91–93. http://www.statistics.gov.uk/statbase

Reynolds, Jack, and Smartt, Ursula (1996). *Prison Policy and Practice.* Leyhill, Bristol: HM Prison Service.

Scots Law Web site. http://www.law.gla.ac.uk/scot

Scottish Courts Web site. http://www.lawscot.org.uk

Scottish Office. (2000). *Factsheet 9, The Scottish Courts.* Edinburgh: Information Directorate, HMSO.

Sims, Lorraine, and Andy Myhill. (2001). *Policing and the Public: Findings from the British Crime Survey 2000.* Research Findings Bulletin No. 136 (Home Office). http://www.crimereduction.gov.uk

Smartt, Ursula. (1999a). "Constitutionalism in the British Dependent Territories of the Caribbean." *European Journal of Crime, Criminal Law and Criminal Justice.* The Hague: Kluwer Law International, 300–313.

———. (1999b). "Her Majesty's Prisons of the Dependent Territories in the Caribbean. Part I." *Prison Service Journal* 126 (November): 20–26.

———. (2000). "Her Majesty's Prisons of the Dependent Territories in the Caribbean. Part II." *Prison Service Journal* 127 (January): 33–38.

———. (2000). "Her Majesty's Prisons of the Dependent Territories in the Caribbean. Part III." *Prison Service Journal* 128 (February): 28–35.

Court Cases

R. v. Secretary for the Home Department ex part Tarrant. (1984) 1 All ER 799.

Young v. Bristol Aeroplane Co. (1944). 1 KB 718.

▼ GUN CONTROL

Gun control is one of the most controversial issues in the United States. The controversy centers largely on interpretation of the Second Amendment to the U.S. Constitution, which states: "A well-regulated militia, being necessary to the security of a free state, the right of the people to keep and bear arms, shall not be infringed." Some argue that this can be interpreted as a clear declaration of the right of individuals to bear arms, whereas others argue that this individual right was in reference only to maintaining a state militia.

THE RIGHT TO BEAR ARMS

Many debates, discussions, and court cases have addressed this issue. A closer look at the views of the framers of the Constitution, including their personal notes and earlier drafts of the Second Amendment, indicates that the framers believed individuals do indeed have a "natural" right to bear arms (Dawlut 1997; Kopel and Little 1997; Dennis 1995).

Few Supreme Court cases have addressed the right to bear arms issue directly, and what they have stated has also been open to interpretation. *Presser v. Illinois (1886), Miller v. Texas* (1894), and *Robertson v. Baldwin* (1897), either directly or indirectly, support the individual right to bear arms (Kopel and Little 1997). However, in *Presser v. Illinois* and *Miller v. Texas* the Court upheld the view that regardless of the interpretation of the Bill of Rights, these rulings are meant to restrict the federal government and cannot be applied to various states.

The most notable (and most recent) case regarding the right to bear arms was *United States v. Miller* (1939). As in previous cases, interpretation of the Court's ruling has led only to more debates regarding gun control. In this case, the Supreme Court ruled that

> In the absence of any evidence tending to show the possession or use of a "shotgun having a barrel less than eighteen inches in length" at this time has some reasonable relationship to the preservation or efficiency of a well regulated militia, we cannot say that the Second Amendment guarantees the right to keep and bear such an instrument.

Gun control lobbyists argue that this ruling supports their view that the Second Amendment does not necessarily provide each individual with the right to bear arms. Gun lobbyists argue that, in the light of previous cases and the specifics of this case, people do have the right to bear arms.

FEDERAL AND STATE LAWS REGARDING GUN CONTROL

Controversy over the language of the Second Amendment and Supreme Court cases that have addressed the right to bear arms does not necessarily explain the current debates on gun control. Lobbyists for gun control argue that tougher restrictions on guns are needed to curb gun-related violence. Gun lobbyists argue that tougher gun restrictions will not make people's lives safer. Gun lobbyists also do not want gun control measures to infringe on an individual's rights.

The United States has about 20,000 gun control laws. However, these laws are mostly state or local laws. Such laws vary widely from state to state. In "Gun Control in the United States: A Comparative Survey of Firearms Laws" (Open Society Institute

2001), the Center on Crime, Communities, and Culture at the Open Society Institute reported that thirty-five states have neither registration nor licensing requirements for any type of gun, thirty-one states have no waiting periods for handguns, and only two states have banned private assault weapons.

Only six federal laws address gun control. The National Firearms Act of 1934 regulates the possession of submachine guns, silencers, and several other weapons. The Federal Arms Act of 1938 requires the licensing of firearm manufacturers and dealers. The 1968 Gun Control Act prohibits the interstate retailing of all firearms, restricts the type of people who can own a gun, requires serial numbers on all guns, requires licensed dealers to keep records, sets minimum ages to purchase a gun, and bans "Saturday night specials."

The Brady Handgun Violence Protection Act (Brady Law), which took seven years to pass in Congress, was signed into law on November 30, 1993, and went into effect in February 1994. In its original form, the Brady Law required a five-day waiting period and a background check before completion of the sale of a handgun. But the gun lobby was able to weaken the Brady Law, so that on November 30, 1998, the five-day waiting period for handgun sales expired. The waiting period was replaced by a mandatory, computerized National Instant Check System (NICS), which provides information for criminal background checks on people buying any firearm, not just handguns.

The Violent Crime Control and Law Enforcement Act of 1994 bans the manufacture, sale, and possession of nineteen types of semiautomatic weapons, makes it a crime to sell guns to those under the age of eighteen, and toughens the requirements for dealer licenses. Finally, the Domestic Violence Offender Gun Ban of 1996 prohibits anyone convicted of a misdemeanor domestic violence offense from owning a gun.

In 1986, the gun lobby countered some of these measures by being instrumental in passage of the Firearms Owner's Protection Act, which amends the Gun Control Act of 1968. The 1986 act permits the interstate sale of rifles and shotguns, provided that they are unloaded and not readily accessible.

Current Legislation and Debates

As of late 2001, Congress has before it a number of bills that, if passed, will affect gun control. Many of these bills increase gun control, including limiting access to firearms by children (H.R. 2221, S. 602,

S. 1355); closing the gun show loophole (H.R. 2377, S. 330); and closing the loophole in trafficking gun parts (S. 609). Also, the gun lobby has introduced bills such as H.R.1762, which restores the Second Amendment rights of all Americans, and S. 906, which protects ownership rights and the privacy of gun owners.

On September 13, 2001, the California Legislature passed one of the strongest safety licensing bills in the country. Luis Tolley, western director of the Brady Campaign (a gun control lobby), stated that "mandatory safety tests, thumbprinting, and enhanced background checks will set a responsible standard for handgun safety laws that we hope the rest of the country will soon follow" (Brady Campaign Web site, 14 September 2001 press release).

Statistics show that between 40 and 60 percent of small arms are illegal. At a United Nations conference on illegal small arms trafficking in 2001, more than 170 nations agreed to a watered-down plan to combat such trafficking. The United States, which produces more than half of all the small arms in the world, said it would not support the plan unless its call to governments to "seriously consider legal restrictions on unrestricted trade in and ownership of small arms and light weapons" is dropped (Associated Press 2001). The United States also said it would reject a measure that bans governments from supplying small arms to "non-state actors," such as rebel groups. Nonetheless, the U.N. plan is a first step in a global trend to curb the usage of guns. There will be a follow-up conference in 2006 .

Neither side of the gun control issue appears to be waning. The gun lobby does not want the so-called basic right of an individual to bear arms infringed upon. Those who argue that gun control is necessary because of the gun violence in this country want strict laws to ensure safety. They argue that loopholes in gun laws allow children to have access to guns, allow purchasers of guns at gun shows to avoid background checks, and allow persons to purchase guns on the Internet.

Loopholes

Although gun control legislation has helped limit illegal firearm purchases, decrease gun-related crimes, deter criminal gun trafficking, and reduce overall gun violence, loopholes allow guns to be accessible to children and criminals. These loopholes exist largely because of the intransigence of the gun lobby.

Prosecutors and other law enforcement officials nationwide have called for closing loopholes that allow guns to flow to children and criminals. The Brady Campaign supports legislation that would build upon the success of the Brady Law and strengthen existing laws to keep guns from juveniles, convicted felons, and other prohibited purchasers.

The Child Access Loophole

Adults are prohibited from transferring firearms to children, but because of the child access loophole, adults are not required to store guns so that children cannot get access to them. A child access prevention (CAP) proposal would require parents to keep loaded firearms out of the reach of children and would hold gunowners criminally responsible if children gain access to an unsecured firearm and use it to injure themselves or someone else. The National Rifle Association (NRA) opposes CAP laws.

The Gun Show Loophole

Private collectors can sell guns at gun shows and flea markets without performing background checks because the Brady Law requires only federally licensed gun dealers to conduct a background check. This is the so-called gun show loophole. Gun control advocates generally believe that no gun should be sold at a gun show without a background check and appropriate documentation. Those who support closing this loophole tend to claim that doing so would put gun shows out of business. But gun show advocates argue that gun shows are thriving in states such as California, which has closed the gun show loophole with a state law, and that the loophole needs to be closed on a federal level.

The Internet Loophole

Like the gun show loophole, the Internet loophole allows guns to be sold online, without a background check, to criminals and other prohibited purchasers. Advocates of closing this loophole argue that no one should be able to sell guns over the Internet without complying with background check requirements.

FIREARMS AND CRIME

According to the National Crime Victimization Survey (NCVS) in 2000, 533,470 victims (8 percent) of 6.3 million violent crimes (sexual assault, robbery, and aggravated assault) stated that they faced an offender with a firearm. The FBI's *Crime in the United States* (2000) estimated that 65 percent of the 15,533 murders in 1999 were committed with firearms.

Arrestees and Offenders

Weapons arrestees are predominantly male, age eighteen or over, and white. However, weapons arrest rates per 100,000 population are highest for teens and for African Americans. According to the 1991 Survey of State Prison Inmates, among those inmates who possessed a handgun during the commission of the crime for which they were incarcerated, 9 percent had acquired it through theft, 28 percent had acquired it through an illegal market such as a drug dealer or fence, 10 percent had stolen at least one gun, and 11 percent had sold or traded stolen guns.

Guns in the Home

Estimates of the number of guns in America range from 193 million to 250 million. This is almost one gun for every man, woman, and child in the United States. Guns are everywhere—cities, towns, suburbs, and farms. In fact, there is a gun in 43 percent of households with children in America. There is a loaded gun in one in every ten households with children, and there is a gun that is left unlocked and just "hidden away" in one in every eight homes. From 1990 to 1998, two-thirds of spouse and ex-spouse murder victims were killed by guns.

Guns are the weapon of choice for individuals who commit suicide. In 1998, guns were used in 17,424 suicide deaths in America. One youth aged ten to nineteen committed suicide with a gun every seven hours—over 1,2000 young people in a year. Having a gun in the home also increases the likelihood of an unintentional shooting, particularly among children. Unintentional shootings commonly occur when children find an adult's loaded handgun in a drawer or closet and shoot themselves, a sibling, or a friend while playing with it. The rate of deaths of children up to age fourteen by unintentional shootings is nine times higher in the United States than in twenty-five other industrialized nations combined (Centers for Disease Control and Prevention 1997).

Children and Guns

It should not take a school shooting or an inner-city neighborhood shooting to show that American children are more at risk from firearms than are the children of any other industrialized nation. In one year, firearms killed no children in Japan, 19 in Great Britain, 57 in

Germany, 109 in France, 153 in Canada, and 5,285 in the United States.

In the United States, children die or are badly injured when they find improperly stored firearms and use them unintentionally on themselves or other children. Older children are more at risk from horseplay with available guns, and teenagers use guns for impulse suicides and for crime. All are vulnerable to getting caught in the crossfire from guns used in domestic violence and in crime.

As the rate of gun violence dramatically increased during the 1980s and early 1990s, American children paid the price. From 1984 to 1994. the firearm death rate for youth aged fifteen to nineteen increased 222 percent, whereas the nonfirearm death rate decreased almost 13 percent. Although deaths from gunfire have been decreasing since 1994, firearms are still expected to overtake motor vehicle accidents as the leading cause of death among American children (Brady Campaign Web site).

According to the Centers for Disease Control (1997), the rate of firearms deaths of children up to age fourteen is nearly twelve times higher in the United States than in twenty-five other industrialized nations combined. The firearms-related homicide rate is nearly sixteen times higher for children in the United States than in those twenty-five other countries combined. The suicide rate of children up to age fourteen is twice as high in the United States as it is in those twenty-five other countries combined. Interestingly, there is no difference between the nonfirearms suicide rates in the United States and these other countries. Virtually all the difference is attributable to suicides committed with guns in the United States.

Over 3,500 students were expelled in the 1998–1999 school year for bringing guns to school. Of these, 43 percent were in elementary or junior high school. This means that, in a forty-week school year, an average of eighty-eight children per week nationwide are expelled for bringing a gun to school. These figures include only the children who get caught.

In 1999, 52 percent of all murder victims under age eighteen in the United States were killed by guns. In 1986, guns were used in 38 percent of such murders. In 1999, 82 percent of murder victims aged thirteen to nineteen were killed by a gun.

As noted above, in 1998, more than 1,200 children aged ten to nineteen committed suicide with firearms. Unlike suicide attempts using other methods, suicide attempts using guns are nearly always fatal, meaning that temporarily depressed teenagers who attempt suicide with guns will never get a second chance at life. Nearly two-thirds of all completed teenage suicides involve a firearm. In 1998, 3,792 American children (age nineteen and under) died by gunfire in murders, suicides, and unintentional shootings—more than ten young people a day.

Very few laws govern children's access to guns. The Brady Law made it illegal for children under age twenty-one to purchase handguns from licensed dealers, although a loophole permits persons eighteen to twenty-one years old to purchase handguns from private or unlicensed individuals. The shooters in the Columbine High School massacre used four guns purchased at gun shows, three of which were bought by an eighteen-year-old friend who did not have to undergo a background check.

Each state has different laws governing the transfer and possession of guns to and by juveniles. Most states permit teenagers to possess long guns, including assault weapons grandfathered by the 1994 assault weapon ban, without adult supervision. Eighteen states have passed child access prevention (CAP) laws, which hold gunowners criminally liable if children access their unsecured weapons and hurt themselves or someone else. In 1995, the *Journal of the American Medical Association* (Amnest 1995) published a study showing that accidental deaths of children from firearms decreased 23 percent in the two years after CAP laws went into effect.

SUMMARY

Strong controversies surrounding the interpretation of the Second Amendment remain among U.S. citizens and legislators. Both supporters and opponents of gun control have powerful organizations that vie for media attention and lobby for legislation promoting their diametrically opposed positions. Although the United States has some 20,000 gun control laws, significant loopholes and gaps dilute the effects of these laws.

—*Barry Spunt and Polly Sylvia*

See also ARMED ROBBERY; CAPITAL PUNISHMENT; DEADLY FORCE; HOMICIDE AND MURDER; POLICE, KILLING OF

Further Reading

Annest, J. L. (1995). "National Estimates of Non-Fatal Firearm-Related Injuries: Beyond the Tip of the Iceberg." *Journal of the American Medical Association* 273: 1749–1754.

Associated Press. (2001). "Nations Agree to Limit Sales of Illicit Arms." *New York Times* (22 July).

Brady Campaign Web site. http://www.bradycampaign.org/facts/issuebriefs

Bruce, John, and Clyde Wilcox, eds. (1998). *The Changing Politics of Gun Control*. Lanham, MD. Rowman and Littlefield.

Bureau of Justice Statistics. (2001). *Firearms and Crime Statistics*. http://www.ojp.usdoj.gov/bjs/guns.htm

Centers for Disease Control and Prevention. (1997). "Rates of Homicide, Suicide and Firearm-related Death Among Children—26 Industrialized Countries." *Morbidity, Mortality Weekly Report* 46, 5 (7 February): 101–105.

Dennis, Anthony. (1995). "Clearing The Smoke From The Right to Bear Arms and the Second Amendment." *Akron Law Review*: 57–92.

Dizard, Jan, Robert Muth, and Stephen Andrews, eds. (1999). *Guns in America: A Reader*. New York: New York University Press.

Dowlut, Robert. (1997). "The Right to Keep and Bear Arms: A Right to Self-Defense Against Criminals and Despots." *Stanford Law and Policy* Review 25–40.

Federal Bureau of Investigation. (2000). *Crime in the United States, 1999*. Washington, DC: U.S. Department of Justice.

Kopel, David, and Christopher Little. (1997). "Communitarians, Neorepublicans, and Guns: Assessing the Case for the Firearms Prohibition." *Maryland Law Review* 438–554.

Lott, John. (1998). *More Guns, Less Crime: Understanding Crime and Gun-Control Laws*. Chicago: University of Chicago Press.

Open Society Institute. (2001). "Gun Control in the United States: A Comparative Survey of Firearms Laws." http://www.soros.org/crime/Prguncontrol.htm

Pontonne, S. (1997). *Gun Control Issues*. Commack, NY: Nova Science Publishers.

Court Cases

Miller v. Texas (1894). 153 U.S. 535.

Presser v. Illinois (1886). 116 U.S. 252.

Robertson v. Baldwin (1897). 165 U.S. 275, 281–282.

United States v. Miller (1939). 307 U.S. 174.

HABITUAL FELONY LAWS

Habitual felony laws—commonly known as "three-strikes" laws—have been enacted since 1994 by lawmakers at the federal and state levels. These laws require that judges sentence offenders with three convictions to long prison terms. Aimed at repeat offenders, three-strikes laws are based on the premise that a three-time offender has demonstrated an inability to conform to the laws of society and should be incarcerated for an extended period, perhaps for life.

The logic behind three-strikes laws is simple. If the cost of a behavior greatly exceeds its benefits, the behavior is less likely to be chosen. If the behavior continues in spite of the cost, the cost must be increased. This view, which represents a simplified version of deterrence theory, typically does not examine the influence of social factors on behavior. Following the logic of this argument to the extreme, the imposition of the death penalty for jaywalking would result in its elimination. This, however, introduces a proportionality problem: The punishment does not fit the crime. Some have argued that three-strikes laws, when broadly applied, create problems regarding proportionality, due process, and fairness.

Three-strikes laws vary regarding what constitutes a strike, the number of strikes that trigger a sanction, and the penalties imposed in response to the final strike. These laws also vary in impact. Several states have experienced significant and often unintended consequences as the result of three-strikes laws. The variety of laws and the degree to which the laws have been applied make it difficult to clearly assess their impact. Although there is evidence of deterrent effects, the cost of deterring these crimes greatly exceeds the benefits to the state (Greenwood et al. 1994).

HABITUAL OFFENDER LAWS

Although three-strikes laws are a relatively recent development, the legal system has long recognized the need for stricter sentencing as a result of repeat offenses. As early as the seventeenth century, both England and the American colonies passed statutes that imposed strict penalties on repeat offenders. Habitual offender laws, however, have always been controversial, and in many cases, the laws were abandoned before being extensively applied. In spite of this controversy, habitual offender statutes remain popular; the public considers these laws a necessary remedy for offenders who have not been or cannot be rehabilitated. The call for tougher sentences for habitual offenders typically leads to legislative action, followed by evidence that these laws are ineffective in deterring criminal behavior and create additional problems for the justice system. The laws are then weakened or abandoned. Typically, this cycle repeats as segments of the public continue to call for efforts to "get tough on crime." Three-strikes laws are the most recent example of this cycle.

Judicial discretion is at the core of the controversy over habitual offender laws. These laws typically limit judicial discretion while widening prosecutorial discretion. During the first half of the twentieth century, habitual offender laws acknowledged the importance of judicial discretion and provided judges with a range of possible sanctions. In the United States, the foundation for contemporary habitual offender laws was established in 1926 when New York mandated a sentence of life imprisonment for third time offenders. Other states followed New York's lead, and by 1949, forty-eight states had enacted mandatory sentencing for repeat offenders. The majority of states, however, acknowledging that judicial discretion is necessary in criminal proceedings, did not require judges to impose mandatory sentences if circumstances compelled a different result.

Beginning in the 1980s, calls for tougher sentencing, coupled with the perception that judges were "soft" on criminals, resulted in legislation that limited judicial discretion. Judges were required to impose determinant sentences for repeat offenders, without regard to the circumstances surrounding the offense. "Get tough on crime" rhetoric, along with the cyclical public debate and subsequent policy reaction, resulted in increasingly harsh punishments and a greater reliance on incarceration.

The 1980s and 1990s were marked by a general impression that violent crime was on the increase, even though the overall crime rate was dropping. In addition to this commonly held misperception, the political focus was shifting to career criminals. The perception, supported by criminological research, was that a small percentage of criminals were responsible for a large percentage of total crime. The idea was that if this small percentage of chronic offenders could be identified and incarcerated, ideally for extended periods, the crime rate would decrease. In addition, there was a growing belief that rehabilitation was not possible: Recidivism rates indicated that a large percentage of those who spent time in prison would eventually return there. Again, this suggested that incarceration for longer periods of time would provide a solution to the crime problem.

CONTEMPORARY THREE-STRIKES LAWS

Between 1993 and 1995, three-strikes laws were enacted by twenty-two states, most of which already had habitual offender statutes, and by the federal government. While the state of Washington was the first to enact a modern three-strikes law, the California version of three-strikes legislation is the most controversial, and most heavily examined, of these laws. The California experience provides a clear example of the context in which three-strikes laws were enacted. Even as the law was being written, a RAND study suggested that although there would be a reduction in crime, the proposed law would lead to a 120 percent

increase in the prison budget and an overall implementation cost of $5.5 billion.

Several events precipitated the California three-strikes law. In 1992, Joe Davis, a paroled felon with a long criminal record, murdered Kimber Reynolds when she resisted his attempt to steal her purse. In response to his daughter's murder, Mike Reynolds began work on a draft of the original version of the California three-strikes law. Rejected by the California legislature, the three-strikes initiative, known as Proposition 184, was eventually approved by over 70 percent of California voters—many no doubt influenced at least in part by the highly publicized 1993 abduction and murder of twelve-year-old Polly Klaas by a state prison parolee.

Three-strikes laws were soon enacted in other states. Although generically referred to as "three-strikes," state laws differ greatly. While California's law includes a wide range of crimes, other states are typically less inclusive. In most cases, the three offenses must be felonies. In some states, all felony convictions count as strikes; in others, the felonies must be violent. States also differ in the sanctions imposed and the amount of judicial discretion allowed. While some states mandate life in prison as a minimum sentence, other states set a maximum penalty that extends sentences up to life imprisonment with no parole. Finally, the laws vary to the degree in which they limit judicial and prosecutorial discretion, at times offering the chance to redefine offenses to avoid the triggering of three-strikes provisions.

IMPACT OF THREE STRIKES

Despite political rhetoric surrounding three strikes, research indicates that these laws have not affected violent crime in the states where they have been enacted (Shichor and Sechrest 1996). There are many problems associated with efforts to quantify the impact of "three strikes." One problem is related to the underutilization of these laws. Although California has had over 40,000 second- or third-strike convictions, many states with three-strikes laws have had fewer than 100. Another difficulty is the fact that crime rates are affected by many factors. Unless these are controlled, any effort to statistically demonstrate the impact of three-strikes laws is likely to fail.

The unintended consequences of three-strikes laws, especially in relation to the California experience, are troubling to many criminologists. These laws compound an existing racial disparity, putting more members of minority groups in prison for longer periods of time. A National Institute of Justice (NIJ) study lists additional concerns. The first is related to the type of offender charged under three strikes: Although these laws were enacted to punish the most severe offenses and offenders, about 70 percent of defendants charged under three-strikes laws are nonviolent. The NIJ study also points out that three-strikes laws have had a major impact on plea bargaining, which has dropped from 90 percent of criminal cases prior to three strikes to 14 percent after three strikes. This in turn leads to an increased strain on already limited judicial resources. The reduction in plea bargains also impacts jail overcrowding. Crowded jails or prisons lead to civil liberties issues, expensive construction, and the release of other inmates to make room for those imprisoned under mandatory three-strikes provisions. Another impact of three strikes is that some actors in the justice system see inequalities that may result from mandatory sentences. As a result, prosecutors, judges, and juries who perceive injustice may find ways to circumvent the intent of three-strikes legislation. The full impact of three-strikes laws may not be felt for many years, especially as those sentenced to long prison sentences grow old in crowded prisons. States with three-strikes laws may have to spend billions on prison construction, diverting money from more effective programs. Unless taxes are increased, three-strikes laws will divert money from education, health and welfare, and other programs (Greenwood et al. 1994). Finally, researchers point out that although crime rates in California are dropping, they were dropping prior to "three strikes." There is no evidence that three-strikes laws result in decreased crime rates (Flynn et al. 1995).

Another concern is that three-strikes laws will increase crime rates, because offenders faced with a third conviction act in ways they may not have absent the threat of life in prison without parole. One study suggests that three-strikes laws may produce a 10 percent short-term increase in homicides that might not have occurred without the laws. The researchers project a 25 percent long-term increase, which implies that there could be an additional 3,300 homicides each year. This research projected a long-run social cost of $11 billion per year (Marvell and Moody 2001).

SUMMARY

When fully enacted, three-strikes law have resulted in a range of negative consequences. Many of these conse-

quences were unintended or unexpected. In some cases, the impact was so severe that state legislatures have been forced to reduce the scope of their laws. The recent experience with three strikes represents a short and controversial experiment. The three-strikes experiment is informative to those interested in the process of policy making. A critical evaluation of the content of a law, as well as the process through which an idea becomes a law, is instrumental in any effort to address social problems.

The issue of three-strikes laws and the habitual offender statutes they represent is clearly not closed. More study is needed to demonstrate the strengths and weaknesses of these policies. Further study may clarify issues regarding the political motivations behind policy choices and the context in which these choices are made. An examination of these laws also provides information on the cost and limitations of incarceration, the motivation for committing criminal acts, alternative sentencing policies, effective crime control strategies, and a full range of issues relevant to society.

—Kenneth W. Mentor

See also DETERMINATE SENTENCES; SENTENCING; SENTENCING GUIDELINES

Further Reading

Austin, James et al. (1999), "The Impact of Three Strikes and You're Out." *Punishment and Society* 1: 131–162.

Clark, John, James Austin, and D. Alan Henry. (1997). "Three Strikes and You're Out: A Review of State Legislation." Washington, DC: National Institute of Justice.

Flynn, Edith E. et al. (1995). "Three-Strikes Legislation: Prevalence and Definitions." *Critical Criminal Justice Issues.* NIJ 158837: 122–133. Washington, DC: National Institute of Justice.

Greenwood, Peter W. et al. (1994). *Three Strikes and You're Out: Estimated Benefits and Costs of California's New Mandatory-Sentencing Law.* Santa Monica, CA: RAND.

Marvell, Thomas B., and Carlisle E. Moody. (2001). "The Lethal Effects of Three-Strikes Laws." *Journal of Legal Studies* 30: 89.

Schichor, David. (1997). "Three Strikes as a Public Policy: The Convergence of the New Penology and the McDonaldization of Punishment." *Crime and Delinquency* 43: 470–492.

Schichor, David, and Dale K. Sechrest. (1996). *Three Strikes and You're Out: Vengeance as Public Policy.* Thousand Oaks, CA: Sage Publications.

Schmertmann, Carl P., Adansi A. Amankwaa, and Robert D. Long. (1998). "Three Strikes and You're Out: Demographic Analysis of Mandatory Prison Sentencing." *Demography* 35: 445–463.

Schultz, David. (2000). "No Joy in Mudville Tonight: The Impact of Three Strike Laws on State and Federal Corrections Policy, Resources, and Crime Control." *Cornell Journal of Law and Public Policy* 9: 557.

Stolzenberg, Lisa, and Stewart J. D'Alessio. (1997). "Three Strikes and You're Out: The Impact of California's New Mandatory

Sentencing Law on Serious Crime Rates." *Crime and Delinquency* 43: 457–469.

Turner, Michael G., et al. (1995). "Three Strikes and You're Out Legislation: A National Assessment." *Federal Probation* 59: 16–35.

Tyler, Tom R., and Robert J. Boeckmann. (1997). "Three Strikes and You Are Out, but Why? The Psychology of Public Support for Punishing Rule Breakers." *Law and Society Review* 31: 237–265.

Vitielos, Michael. (1997). "Three Strikes: Can We Return to Rationality?" *Journal of Criminal Law and Criminology* 87: 395–481.

Zimring, Franklin E. (1996). "Populism, Democratic Government, and the Decline of Expert Authority: Some Reflections on 'Three Strikes' in California." *Pacific Law Journal* 28: 243–256.

Zimring, Franklin E., Gordon Hawkins, and Sam Kamin. (2001). *Punishment and Democracy: Three Strikes and You're Out in California.* New York: Oxford University Press.

◤ HALFWAY HOUSE

Halfway houses are community-based facilities for those on the fringes of society; they provide access to community resources and offer transitional opportunities for individuals who are attempting to return to society as healthy, law-abiding, and productive members of the community. The concept of the halfway house is predicated upon the ideals of humanitarianism, rehabilitation, and reintegration.

More often referred to as "community treatment centers" in contemporary criminal justice and social services systems, halfway houses have been inextricably linked to the dominant punishment philosophy of their eras. According to Hugh Barlow (1990: 523), "no single description adequately conveys the myriad forms the nation's halfway houses have taken. . . . the facilities provide housing for psychiatric patients, delinquent children, alcoholics and other problem drug users, neglected children, homeless adults, [and] the mentally retarded, as well as criminal offenders."

HISTORY OF THE HALFWAY HOUSE

From the mid-eighteenth to the early part of the nineteenth century, correctional philosophy in Europe and the United States was dominated by the "classical" deterrence model as espoused by the Italian Cesare Beccaria in his book *Essays on Crime and Punishment* (1764) (Clear and Cole 2000: 30). This approach assumed that offenders were rational, thinking individuals who exercised free will, and whose punishment should fit their crime accordingly. Punishment applied with certainty, swiftness, and proportionate severity, it was believed, would deter offenders from further criminal activities.

By the beginning of the twentieth century, explanations regarding crime and criminals had shifted to the new paradigm of "positivism" (Curran and Renzetti 2001: Vold et al. 1998). According to Hagan (2002: 127), "criminological positivists emphasize a consensus world view, a focus on the criminal actor rather than the criminal act, a deterministic model (usually biological or psychological in nature), a strong faith in the scientific expert, and a belief in rehabilitation of 'sick' offenders rather than the punishment of 'rational' actors" (Hagan 2002: 127). This shift to positivism clearly focused penology on the philosophy of rehabilitation.

When the first halfway house was developed is subject to debate. Residential programs designed to provide transitional services and assistance have existed in the United States since the beginning of the nineteenth century. Originally housing the homeless and the poor, by 1845 these facilities, such as New York's Isaac T. Hopper House (Silverman 2001: 484), had become popular resources for convicted offenders, as they provided prerelease opportunities for individuals to return to society through a structured program with supportive staff members. Similar to parole in that both have been considered early release mechanisms, halfway houses differ in that they have often served as intermediate, transitional programs for inmates who leave prison due to overcrowding and who are paroled following the completion of their sentences in a community-based residential program.

"Residents," as they were called in order to distinguish them from inmates or ex-convicts, were granted provisional access to the community to pursue vocational, educational, or employment opportunities, as well as to attend specialized treatment programs such as Alcoholics Anonymous. These efforts were consistent with the belief, becoming popular at the time, that criminal behavior was determined by various biological, psychological, environmental, and social factors, and therefore was amenable to remediation through individualized treatment.

In the 1930s, these concepts were further enhanced by the "medical model" of corrections, with its reliance on classification, diagnosis, and treatment, and by the concurrent popularity of the new correctional ideas of probation, indeterminate sentencing, and parole. As they became further integrated with the formal correctional system, eventually becoming the primary prerelease opportunities for inmates, these programs were often characterized as "halfway-out of prison" (Latessa and Travis 1992: 167).

By 1950, these programs were further adapted to serve specialized populations, such as criminally involved drug and alcohol abusers. In the early 1960s, the mentally ill became residents as the state hospitals were deinstitutionalized by the federal government. During that turbulent decade, when virtually every governmental institution and traditional practice in America was being challenged, corrections turned to the philosophy of reintegration. One of the premises of this theory was that society in general, as well as its communities and individual members, participates in the creation of economic, social, and cultural situations that engender criminal behavior. Consequently, according to the theory, amelioration of crime and recidivism requires that the individual, neighborhood, community, and all of society be responsible for and involved in the reintegration of offenders.

The 1967 President's Commission on Crime and the Administration of Justice acknowledged the value of the reintegrative ideal; with this legitimization, and with unprecedented funding from the Law Enforcement Assistance Administration (LEAA), the rest of the 1960s and early 1970s became the golden era of the halfway house movement. However, this era was short-lived; rising crime rates, combined with conservative politics and a new punitive philosophy, led to a new era of crime control. In fact, the reported failure of the reintegrative model was bolstered by Robert Martinson's now-classic study, "What Works? Questions and Answers About Prison Reform" (1974), in which Martinson pointed out that "with few and isolated exceptions, the rehabilitative efforts that have been reported so far have had no appreciable effect on recidivism" (22) By the 1980s, independent of the early (pre-parole) release, or postrelease (parole) function of the halfway house, they remained community-based residential programs that provided structure and services to offenders. The majority were operated by private, nonprofit organizations with boards of directors made up of leaders from the criminal justice, educational, and religious communities, as well as other dedicated citizens. Board members often provided access to recreational, religious, medical, vocational, and transportation services, as well as assistance with obtaining gainful employment.

CONTEMPORARY HALFWAY HOUSES

Philosophically, halfway houses are designed to uphold the ideals of humanitarianism, rehabilitation, and integration. According to Ira Silverman (2001: 484), "the humanitarian ideal of halfway houses was based on the perception that removing offenders from the harsh prison environment was more beneficial than continued exposure to the criminogenic effects of incarceration." Moreover, as a punishment philosophy, rehabilitation has "the goal of restoring a convicted offender to a constructive place in society through some form of vocational or educational training or therapy" (Clear and Cole 2000: 59). Finally, reintegration of offenders into a lawful and productive place in the community continues to be the goal of most treatment-oriented community corrections professionals.

The shift to a more punitive punishment philosophy from the 1980s through the end of the twentieth century was manifested in determinate and mandatory minimum sentences. The three-strikes law in California, enacted in 1994 both by the legislature and citizen initiative, has already snared over 50,000 "strikers," each eligible for at least a doubling of their normal sentence, with 5,000 "third strikers" already sentenced to twenty-five years to life in prison (Meehan, 2000).

These developments might have been expected to be the death knell for the halfway house movement; however, with jails and prisons becoming increasingly crowded, halfway house programs demonstrated remarkable functional flexibility. They adapted to serve the role of alternatives to incarceration, and in this capacity they were known as "halfway-in houses" (Reichel 2001: 299). In the 1990s, the term *halfway house* was replaced by the more benign, descriptive, and inclusive *community residential treatment centers* (Allen and Simonson 2001: 222).

These adaptations, however, came with a cost, as the treatment orientation of the traditional halfway houses became secondary to concerns about supervision and control. In these new halfway houses, although there was still "counseling, substance abuse treatment, educational and vocational training, and a host of social services . . . the atmosphere is closer to that of a minimum-security prison than a rehabilitative community" (Latessa and Travis 1992: 169–170). Reichel (2001) has adapted material from Latessa and Travis to show graphically how traditional halfway houses differ from contemporary community residential treatment centers. (See Table 1). Residents at both types of facility must live there, but are generally allowed to leave without escort during specified hours and for approved purposes.

Table 1. Comparing Halfway Houses and Community Residential Treatment Centers

Traditional Halfway Houses	*Community Residential Treatment Centers*
A treatment-oriented atmosphere is provided.	A security-oriented atmosphere is provided.
Enforcement of rules and regulations shows tolerance.	Enforcement of rules and regulations is rigid.
Clients are either being diverted from or are recently released from prison.	Clients range from persons as yet not convicted, to prison inmates under prerelease status or on parole.
Full treatment services are provided at the facility or through community programs.	Treatment services range from full-service programs to situations where no direct services are available to residents.
Facility size tends to be small, with only ten to twenty residents	Facilities may house fewer than ten residents but may house those with resident populations numbering in the hundreds.

Source: Reichel (2001), adapted from information in Latessa and Travis (1992: 166–181).

IDEALISM VERSUS ECONOMICS

At the start of the twenty-first century, correctional populations reached record levels and were continuing to increase, and institutional overcrowding became epidemic in some jurisdictions. In many situations at the municipal, county, state, and federal levels, this led to successful litigation by prisoners' advocates, with various government agencies being ordered to reduce overcrowding and pay substantial fines and attorney's fees. For example, the sheriff and entire board of supervisors in Orange County, California, were held in contempt of court by U.S. District Court Judge William P. Gray "for intentionally violating his orders." The defendants received fines of $50,000 and $10 per day for each inmate found to have slept on the floor more than one night (Welsh and Pontell 1991: 82). Despite these developments, a continuing conservative "tough on crime" philosophy dominated the American political landscape; California, for example, attempted to build its way out of the dilemma by erecting over twenty new prisons in the last decades of the twentieth century.

As of the late 1990s, the estimated cost of constructing a new cell was approximately $100,000. Once occupied, a cell costs in the range of $20,000 to $25,000 annually to operate. Residential beds in the community, on the other hand, cost on average in the neighborhood of $12,000 annually. Thus, in a society where citizens are harshly punitive with respect to crime but frugal with their tax dollars when it comes to supporting correctional institutions, residential correctional programs are a popular option. When taxpayers are offered a choice—as occurred in 2001 with California's Proposi-

tion 36, which mandated drug treatment rather than incarceration for first or second offenses of possession or use of drugs—they often select the more economical, treatment-oriented option. The California law was to require a multitude of residential community correctional facilities, as part of a continuum of services for substance-abusing offenders. Thus, in the final analysis, cost more than philosophy may lead to a burgeoning population of residential community treatment centers and correctional programs as alternatives to incarceration and as the nuclei of community corrections.

—*Kevin E. Meehan*

See also EARLY RELEASE PROGRAMS; INDETERMINATE SENTENCES; INTERMEDIATE SANCTIONS

Further Reading

Allen, Harry, and Clifford Simonson. (2001). *Corrections in America: An Introduction*. 9th ed. Upper Saddle River, NJ: Prentice Hall.

Barlow, Hugh. (1990). *Introduction to Criminology*. 5th ed. Glenview, IL: Scott, Foresman and Company.

California Department of Corrections Data Analysis Unit. (2000). Sacramento, CA: State of California. http:/www.facts1.com/reasons/unjust.htm

Camp, Camille, and George Camp. (1998). *The Corrections Yearbook*. Middletown, CT: Criminal Justice Institute.

Clear, Todd, and George Cole. (2000). *American Corrections*. 5th ed. Belmont, CA: Wadsworth Publishing Company.

Curran, Daniel, and Claire Renzetti. (2001). *Theories of Crime*. 2nd ed. Needham Heights, MA: Allyn & Bacon.

Hagan, Frank. (2002). *Introduction to Criminology*. 5th ed. Belmont, CA: Wadsworth /Thompson Learning.

Latessa, Edward, and Lawrence Travis. (1992). "Residential Community Correctional Programs." In *Smart Sentencing: The Emergence of Intermediate Sanctions*, edited by James M. Byrne, Arthur Lurigio, and Joan Petersilia. Newbury Park, CA: Sage Publications, 166–181.

Little Hoover Commission. (1998). *Beyond Bars: Correctional Reforms to Lower Prison Costs and Reduce Crime.* Sacramento, CA: Little Hoover Commission.

Martinson, Robert. (1974). "What Works? Questions and Answers About Prison Reform. *The Public Interest* 42, 22–54.

Meehan, Kevin. (2000). "California's Three Strikes Law: The First Six Years." *Corrections Management Quarterly* 4, 4 (Fall): 22–33.

Reichel, Phillip. (2001). *Corrections: Philosophies, Practices, and Procedures.* 2nd ed. Needham Heights, MA: Allyn & Bacon.

Silverman, Ira. (2001). *Corrections: A Comprehensive View.* 2nd ed. Belmont, CA: Wadsworth Publishing Company.

Vold, George, Thomas Bernard, and Jeffrey Snipes. (1998). *Theoretical Criminology.* 4th ed. New York: Oxford University Press.

Welsh, Wayne, and Henry Pontell. (1991). "Counties in Court: Interorganizational Adaptations to Jail Litigation in California." *Law and Society Review* 25, 1: 73–102.

◪ HARM REDUCTION

Harm reduction focuses on reducing the adverse consequences of psychoactive drug use and drug control policies. It is usually thought of having its roots in Dutch drug policy, which takes a public health or sociomedical approach in recognizing and responding to drug use and its consequences. A simplistic conceptualization posits that if users are unable or unwilling to refrain from drug use, then they should be assisted in reducing the harm caused to themselves and others. Harm reduction is pragmatic. It tries to minimize the damage that drug users do to themselves, to other people, and to society at large. Inherent in the conceptual fuzziness of harm reduction is deciding what constitutes harm, who is harmed, and how harms should be prioritized.

Harm-reduction advocates view a "drug-free" society as unachievable, since drug use has been a part of human societies since the dawn of mankind. Therefore, they give greater priority to reducing the harms to the drug user and others, instead of focusing on decreasing drug use itself. Although the official U.S. view tends to equate harm reduction with legalization, most advocates of harm reduction do not support legalization, on the grounds that it would increase drug use. Still, they recognize that prohibition not only does not stop drug use but creates crime and marginalizes drug users. Harm reduction interventions focus on integrating or reintegrating drug users into the community, taking care not to further isolate, demonize, or ostracize them. Priority is placed on maximizing the number of drug users in contact with public health and social services.

Drug policies are evaluated in terms of their potential effects on minimizing the harms of drugs to the user and to the larger society.

Harm reduction advocates ask: How can we reduce the likelihood that drug users will engage in criminal and other undesirable activities? How can we reduce the overdoses and cases of HIV/AIDS and hepatitis B and C associated with the use of some drugs? How can we increase the chances that drug users will act responsibly toward others? How can we increase the likelihood of rehabilitation? And more generally, how do we ensure that drug control policies do not cause more harm to users and society than drug use itself?

THE EMERGENCE OF HARM REDUCTION

The Dutch instituted their first needle-exchange program in Amsterdam in 1984, in an attempt to stem the rising number of hepatitis cases related to injection drug use (IDU). They decided that hepatitis was a greater evil than IDU and therefore established programs to provide new needles and syringes to injection drug users (IDUs). These programs were in place not long after AIDS was first recognized in 1981, and the connection was made between the spread of HIV/AIDS and IDU. As a result, the AIDS epidemic among Dutch injection drug users has never reached the levels seen in most countries.

Several other European countries, including the United Kingdom and Switzerland, adopted harm-reduction policies in response to the AIDS epidemic, stating that AIDS represents a greater threat to public health than does drug use, and that AIDS prevention should take precedence over antidrug efforts. In 1986, the World Health Organization urged that policies aimed at reducing drug use not be allowed to compromise measures to prevent the spread of AIDS. The British Advisory Council on the Misuse of Drugs echoed that sentiment in 1988. In 1986, the Mersey Regional Drug Training and Information Center became one of the first syringe exchange programs in the U.K.—and presumably the world—to make sterile injecting equipment available to users as a way of preventing HIV/AIDS.

The Australian government officially implemented harm-reduction policies in 1985 with the introduction of its National Campaign Against Drug Use, also largely in response to the AIDS epidemic. By 1997, Australia reported a 5 percent HIV infection rate among IDUs, compared to 14 percent in the United

States. One estimate suggests that between 4,000 and 10,000 HIV infections could have been prevented in the United States, had needle-exchange programs followed the same pattern of growth as in Australia. Prevention of HIV/AIDS has therefore become a cornerstone in the harm-reduction paradigm.

THE THREE STAGES OF HARM REDUCTION

Canadian sociologist Patricia Erickson posits three stages in the development of the harm-reduction paradigm over the last third of the twentieth century. In the first, public health concerns arose about the legal drugs—alcohol and tobacco. Because it was unrealistic to ban these substances, interest turned to a variety of public health interventions. Also during this early phase, methadone was provided to heroin users, which permitted them to continue drug use, but in a form that was less risky to the user and society.

The second phase began with the coining of the term *harm reduction* and the convening of the first International Conference on the Reduction of Drug-Related Harm in the U.K. in 1990. It marked the recognition of an impeding HIV/AIDS epidemic and the realization that IDUs were at great risk due to the practice of sharing scarce injection equipment.

The third emerging stage was characterized by the shift towards an integrated public health perspective on the convergence of approaches to both licit and illicit drugs. The success of harm reduction depends on its ability to develop innovative strategies and interventions in both prohibitory and regulatory frameworks, for both illicit and licit drugs.

Countries that have more openly embraced the harm reduction paradigm in setting drug policy have often been concerned about alcohol and tobacco as well. This is especially evident in Australia, where the National Campaign has worked to educate the public about the

DID YOU KNOW...

Harm reduction is based on the belief that a drug-free society cannot be created and maintained. Therefore, advocates argue that the goal should be to reduce the harm caused by drug use to the user and others. The focus is on treatment and rehabilitation and on controlling harmful behaviors of drug users. Harm reduction is used in nations such as Australia and the Netherlands, but it is unpopular among officials in the United States, who prefer a punitive approach.

harms associated with tobacco and alcohol use. In the opening of the 1994 Commission on Narcotic Drugs, Giorgio Giacomelli, the head of the United Nation's Drug Control Program, noted that it was "increasingly difficult to justify the continued distinction among substances solely according to their legal status and social acceptability." At the same meeting, Hans Emblad, then the director of the World Health Organization Programme on Substance Abuse, said, "Current drug strategies are, to some extent, driven by a few industrialized countries. On the one hand, they are making strenuous efforts to exclude from their shores every conceivable kind of illegal substance. But on the other hand, these countries are also vigorously pushing their own substances, such as alcohol, tobacco, and pharmaceuticals onto the very same countries from which they are doing their best to exclude illegal drugs."

It is important to note that although harm reduction has been embraced in varying degrees by a number of European countries, Australia, and Canada, the amount and proportion of criminal justice resources devoted to drug law enforcement has increased dramatically, even in those countries, over the past decade or so. This also applies to the Netherlands, despite its relatively low level of drug use and emphasis on harm reduction in formulating drug policy. Although Dutch laws are very similar to those in most countries, including the United States, users are not typically arrested. Instead, the Netherlands practices selective nonenforcement. Many police stations also exchange syringes. Police in several European countries employ a strategy of cautioning, in which users are brought to the police station but are not actually arrested. There they are cautioned about their drug use, and perhaps given educational information or referrals to service providers.

THE FUTURE OF HARM REDUCTION

Because harm reduction is an emerging paradigm, and there is no clear consensus on its definition, its supporters can hold widely divergent opinions. This has tended to splinter rather than unify them. It is perhaps best conceived as a litmus test against which drug policies, strategies, and interventions can be judged to determine which are effective in reducing the amount of drug-related harm. Harm reduction requires a pragmatic process of identifying, measuring, and assessing drug problems and attendant harms, and the cost-benefit ratio of interventions. This exercise should be engaged in by a diverse group that includes members of the public health, criminal justice, scientific, and policy-making communities, as well as drug users themselves. The dilemma may always be how to balance possible harm reduction for some against perceived potential harm to others. Care must be taken to ensure that the harms to be reduced are not only those of society but also those of the individual or the community.

Another challenge looming in the twenty-first century is integrating approaches to the various legal and illegal drugs. Responses to problems related to the legal drugs present examples of harm-reduction strategies, such as restrictions on smoking in public places to reduce exposure to secondary smoke and the availability of nicotine gum and patches. With respect to alcohol, examples include campaigns to encourage the use of designated drivers and programs training bar and restaurant servers to identify and refuse service to patrons who are drunk. These policies or programs help to limit the problems associated with these drugs without requiring a reduction in use. Examples with respect to the illicit drugs include methadone maintenance, which essentially entails switching users to a long-lasting synthetic opiate that is provided free or at low cost. Research consistently demonstrates that providing methadone at low cost and fairly accessibly can greatly reduce the crime engaged in by heroin addicts in order to support their habit. Their health also improves, which decreases their use of health care services. The lessons from methadone are enormous, including that drug users can sometimes be switched to a different drug or to a less harmful method of administration. In the U.K. and Switzerland, methadone and other drugs may be prescribed by a physician. Other innovative approaches include the "tolerance areas" or "injection rooms" that have been implemented in some countries, some staffed by medical or public health professionals who provide information, referrals, or treatment. They are regarded as preferable to "shooting galleries," which are usually unhygienic and controlled by drug dealers. Education and outreach programs to maximize users' contact with helping agencies are also a form of harm reduction, as are the police practices of cautioning and selective enforcement.

It is increasingly apparent that a prohibitionist policy is limited in its ability to control drug problems. All drugs carry with them the potential for harm, and these harms can be quantified to a marked extent. This requires an epidemiological approach that recognizes that drug use and its attendant harms arise not solely from the drug but also from the interaction of the drug,

the user, and the setting. Harm reduction may well provide the unifying paradigm to create more rational drug policy in this century.

—Lana D. Harrison

See also DRUG COURTS; DRUG TREATMENT; DRUGS

Further Reading

Ball, John, Lawrence Rosen, John Flueck, and David Nurco. (1981). "The Criminality of Heroin Addicts When Addicted and When Off Opiates." In *The Drug Crime Connection*, edited by James Inciardi. Beverly Hills, CA: Sage Publications, 39–66.

Berridge, Virginia. (1999). "Histories of Harm Reduction: Illicit Drugs, Tobacco, and Nicotine." *Substance Use and Misuse* 34, 1: 35–47.

Brecher, Edward M. (1972). *Licit and Illicit Drugs*. Boston: Little, Brown.

Buning, Ernst, R. Coutinho, G. H. A. van Brussel, and A. W. van Zadelhoff. (1986). "Preventing AIDS in Drug Addicts in Amsterdam." *Lancet* ii, 8521: 1435, letter.

Drucker, Ernest. (2000). "From Morphine to Methadone: Maintenance Drugs in the Treatment of Opiate Addiction." In *Harm Reduction: National and International Perspectives*, edited by James Inciardi and Lana Harrison. Thousand Oaks, CA: Sage Publications, 27–46.

Erickson, Patricia. (1999). "A Special Issue on Harm Reduction." *Substance Use and Misuse* 34, 1.

———. (2000). "The Harm Minimization Option for Cannabis: History and Prospects in Canadian Drug Policy." In *Harm Reduction: National and International Perspectives,* edited by James Inciardi and Lana Harrison. Thousand Oaks, CA: Sage Publications, 27–46.

Grapendaal, Martin, Eddy Leuw, and Hans Nelen. (1992). "Drugs and Crime in an Accommodating Social Context: The Situation in Amsterdam." *Contemporary Drug Problems* 19, 2: 303–326.

Harrison, Lana. (1992). "The Drug Crime-Nexus in the USA." *Contemporary Drug Problems* 19, 2: 203–246.

———. (1992). "International Perspectives on the Interface of Drug Use and Criminal Behavior." *Contemporary Drug Problems* 19, 2: 181–202.

Harrison, Lana, and Stephen Mugford. (1994). "Cocaine Using Careers in Perspective." *Addiction Research* 2, 1.

Heather, Nicholas, Alexander Wodak, Ethan Nadelman, and Pat O'Hare. (1993). *Psychoactive Drugs and Harm Reduction: From Faith to Science*. London: Whurr.

Hunt, Dana, Douglas Lipton, and Barry Spunt. (1984). "Patterns of Criminal Activity among Methadone Clients and Current Narcotics Users Not in Treatment." *Journal of Drug Issues* (Fall): 687–701.

Inciardi, James, and Lana Harrison. (2000). *Harm Reduction: National and International Perspectives*. Thousand Oaks, CA: Sage Publications.

Korf, Dirk, and Ernst Buning. (2000). "Coffee Shops, Low-Threshold Methadone, and Needle Exchange: Controlling Illicit Drug Use in the Netherlands." In *Harm Reduction: National and International Perspectives*, edited by James Inciardi and Lana Harrison. Thousand Oaks, CA: Sage Publications, 27–46.

Kreek, Mary Jane. (1983). "Health Consequences Associated with the Use of Methadone." In *Research on the Treatment of Narcotic Addiction: State of the Art*, edited by J. R. Cooper. Rockville, MD: National Institute on Drug Abuse.

Lurie, Peter, and Ernest Drucker. (1997). "An Opportunity Lost: HIV Infections Associated with Lack of a National Needle-Exchange Programme in the USA." *The Lancet* 349: 604–608.

Makkai, Toni. (2000). "Harm Reduction in Australia: Politics, Policy, and Public Opinion." In *Harm Reduction: National and International Perspectives*, edited by James Inciardi and Lana Harrison. Thousand Oaks, CA: Sage Publications, 27–46.

Nadelmann, Ethan. (1998). "Commonsense Drug Policy." *Foreign Affairs* 77, 1: 111–126.

Nurco, David, Thomas Hanlon, Thomas Kinlock, and K. R. Duszynski. (1988). "Differential Criminal Patterns of Narcotic Addicts over an Addiction Career." *Criminology* 26, 3: 407–423.

Reinarman, Craig, Sheigla Murphy, and Daniel Waldorf. (1994). "Pharmacology is Not Destiny: The Contingent Character of Cocaine Abuse and Addiction." *Addiction Research* 2, 1: 21–36.

Reuband, Karl-Heinz. (1992). "Drug Addiction and Crime in West Germany: A Review of the Empirical Evidence." *Contemporary Drug Problems* 19, 2: 327–350.

Reuter, Peter, and Robert MacCoun. (1996). "Harm Reduction and Social Policy." *Drug and Alcohol Review* 15: 225–230.

Riley, Diane, and Pat O'Hare. (2000). "Harm Reduction: History, Definition, and Practice." *Harm Reduction: National and International Perspectives*, edited by James Inciardi and Lana Harrison. Thousand Oaks, CA: Sage Publications, 27–46.

Riley, Diane, Ed Sawka, Peter Conley, David Hewitt, Wayne Mitic, Christiane Poulin, Robin Roon, Eric Single, and John To. (1999). "Harm Reduction: Concepts and Practice. A Policy Discussion Paper." *Substance Use and Misuse* 34, 1: 9–24.

Speckart, George, and M. Douglas Anglin. (1985). "Narcotics and Crime: An Analysis of Existing Evidence for a Causal Relationship." *Behavioral Sciences and the Law* 3, 3: 259–282.

Stimson, Gerald. (1995). "AIDS and Injecting Drug Use in the UK, 1988–1993: The Policy Response and the Prevention of the Epidemic." *Social Science and Medicine* 41, 5: 599–716.

Trebach, Arnold, and James Inciardi. (1993). *Legalize It? Debating American Drug Policy*. Washington, DC: American University Press.

van Haastrecht, Harry. (1997). "HIV infection and Drug Use in the Netherlands: The Course of the Epidemic." *Journal of Drug Issues* 27, 1: 57–72.

Wodak, Alexander, and Peter Lurie. (1997). "A Tale of Two Countries: Attempts to Control HIV among Injecting Drug Users in Australia and the United States." *Journal of Drug Issues* 27, 1: 117–134.

▼ HATE CRIMES

Hate crimes are committed against individuals because they are perceived to be different in some socially significant way. The particular groups protected under hate crime statutes vary from state to state.

At present, more than forty states have some form of anti-hate crime legislation; most jurisdictions cover offenses against individuals who are targeted because of their race, religion, or ethnicity. However, only twenty states include sexual orientation and disability, with even fewer states covering gender and age. In some states, a separate statute prohibits hate crime behavior, while in other states the hate crime statute is a "penalty enhancement." This means that if an existing crime is committed and it is motivated by bias, the penalty for the existing crime may be increased (Levin and McDevitt 1993).

THE PREVALENCE OF HATE CRIMES

Prior to the 1990s, before the Federal Bureau of Investigation (FBI) began to gather hate crime data at a national level, a primary source of hate crime statistics consisted of reports issued by advocacy groups such as the Anti-Defamation League (ADL) and the Southern Poverty Law Center. Though valuable to researchers, such data were also regarded with suspicion by some legal scholars, who argued that the ADL and other advocacy organizations had a vested interest in reporting inflated numbers (Jacobs and Henry 1996; Jacobs and Potter 1997).

The FBI's effort to collect data on hate-motivated offenses has also had its detractors. Like other offenses covered by the Uniform Crime Reports, hate crimes are voluntarily reported by local jurisdictions to the FBI. Even as late as 1999, there were still many police jurisdictions that simply did not participate in the National Reporting System. For example, the state of Alabama failed to report any hate crimes for the year 1999. At the same time, the percentage of jurisdictions voluntarily reporting hate offenses has gradually increased since the early 1990s. Most of the population of the United States is now covered in nationally reported hate crime statistics. In comparison to the counts taken since 1990 by the FBI, the later hate crime figures have become more representative; however, there is still reason to believe that hate crimes are vastly underestimated. Whether from ignorance, fear of retaliation, or distrust of the police, many victims of hate attacks do not report their victimization to the police.

In 1999, there were only seventeen hate-motivated murders reported to the FBI (Federal Bureau of Investigation 2000). On the other hand, some 60 percent of the thousands of hate crimes reported annually were directed not against property but against persons, most of which took the form of intimidation and assaults. The location of hate crime incidents varied, but they seemed to be concentrated in homes, on the streets, and in schools and colleges. Racial bias was the most common basis for committing a hate offense, with anti-black attacks most likely to occur and anti-white attacks in second place. Anti-Jewish and anti-gay offenses were also quite prevalent, followed by anti-Latino and anti-Asian offenses. A wide range of groups were represented among the victims of hate crimes, including people with physical and mental disabilities, bisexuals, Islamics, Protestants, Catholics, and American Indians (Levin 2002).

TYPES OF HATE CRIMES

The term *hate crime* was first used during the mid-1980s by journalists and politicians, but it rather quickly became employed by scholarly researchers as well. In a sense, the term is somewhat misleading in its emphasis on "hate" as a defining basis for choosing and attacking a particular victim. The level of brutality in certain high-profile hate-motivated murders (e.g., the sadistic murder of Jasper, Texas resident James Byrd, a black man who was dragged behind a pickup truck for miles to his death) suggests the presence of intense hostility or anger—that is, hatred—in the motivation of the assailants. In the more typical hate crime, however, the perpetrators may be motivated more by a desire for belonging or profit than by hatred for a particular victim. They may go along simply because their friends do; or they may act out of a need to feel important or to protect their territory. In many crimes, hatred toward the victim may be present, but the motivation for the crime may not have been bias; these crimes can confound the ability of police to identify hate crimes.

In fact, in terms of their motivational bases, hate crimes can be treated as four major types: thrill, defensive, retaliatory, and mission. The majority seem to be "thrill hate crimes"—recreational offenses committed

---

Anti-Semitism in Eighteenth-Century London

Behaviors that were criminalized as hate crimes in the late twentieth century in the United States were often commonplace and accepted in other places and at other times in human history. Violence against religious, racial, and ethnic minorities is the most common form of such behavior, and the following account of violence against Jews in eighteenth-century London is typical of such behavior.

Every Jew was in public opinion implicated, and the prejudice, ill will and brutal conduct this brought upon the Jews, even after they had been detected and punished for it, did not cease for many years. "Go to Chelsea" was a common exclamation when a Jew was seen in the streets and it was often the signal of assault. I have seen many Jews hooted, hunted, cuffed, pulled by the beard, sit upon and so barbarously assaulted in the streets, without any protection for the passers-by or the police, as seems when compared with present times, almost impossible to have existed at any time. Dogs could not be used in the streets in the manner many Jews were treated. One circumstance among others put an end to the ill-usage of Jews. . . . About the year 1787 Daniel Mendoza, a Jew, became a celebrated boxer and set up a school to teach the art of boxing as a science, the art soon spread among the Jews and they became generally expert at it. The consequence was in a very few years seen and felt too. It was no longer safe to insult a Jew unless he was an old man and alone. . . . But even if the Jews were unable to defend themselves, the few who [now would] be disposed to insult them merely because they are Jews, would be in danger of chastisement from the passers-by and of punishment from the police.

Source: George, Mary D. (1965). *London Life in the 18th Century*. New York: Capricorn Books, p. 132.

---

by youngsters (usually teenaged boys or young men operating in groups) who seek excitement at someone else's expense. They are more than willing to travel to another neighborhood or some other part of town where they believe that the members of a targeted group congregate. From their attack on a victim, such young offenders get "bragging rights" with friends who regard hate as cool, and they achieve a sense of their own importance. For a teenager who isn't getting along at home, isn't successful at school, and has little hope for the future, the benefits of committing a hate crime—a sense of power and kinship—may seem considerable. Although many of the hate crimes directed against property—acts of desecration and vandalism—can be included in the thrill-seeking category, there are also numerous thrill hate offenses that involve intimidation, threats, and assaults.

A second type of hate crime, from the motivational standpoint of the perpetrator, is "defensive." That is, the attack is designed to protect an individual's neighborhood, workplace, school, or women from those who are

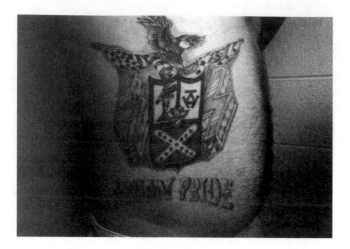

One of the tattoos worn by John William King, one of the three white men (the others being Shawn Berry and Lawrence Russell Brewer) convicted of capital murder in the dragging death of African American James Byrd, Jr., in Jasper County, Texas, on June 7, 1998.
Source: © AFP/Corbis; used by permission.

considered to be outsiders or intruders. Defensive hate crimes have often occurred when a family from a different racial group moves into a previously all-white neighborhood, dormitory, or school. Even the unexplained presence of "outsiders" who walk through "the wrong neighborhood" has, in the past, been enough reason to commit a hate offense.

Wherever it occurs, a defensive attack is often an act of domestic terrorism because it is designed to send a message to every member of the victim's group: that they had better watch their step or they could easily be next. It sends a loud and clear signal to those who come from the victim's group to back off, to get lost, to stay in their place. "Don't come to this school, don't move into this community, don't take this job."

Some hate crimes are motivated by an individual's need for revenge as a result of a hate attack directed against his or her own group members. Such "retaliatory" hate crimes seem defensive in their motivation, but they are actually precipitated by a need to get even for some previous attack rather than by the intrusion of "outsiders." In addition, the targets of a retaliatory crime are not necessarily the particular individuals who had perpetrated the initial offense. More typically, the retaliatory attack targets any members of the perpetrators' group, regardless of whether they had been involved in the original offense. More than any other type of hate crime, a series of retaliatory offenses may serve as the basis for escalating from individual criminal acts to large-scale group conflict. Hate crimes in a

particular area tend to increase after a well-publicized hate attack has occurred and the members of a victimized group seek justice. The potential for escalation indicates the importance of an effective police response in apprehending the perpetrators of a hate crime, so that individuals do not feel a need for vigilante justice.

A fourth and final type of hate crime is a "mission" offense, usually committed by the members of an organized hate group. Actually, no more than 5 percent of all hate crimes nationally are committed by the members of organizations like the Ku Klux Klan, Aryan Nations, or the White Aryan Resistance. But, behind the scenes, organized hate groups continue to inspire murder, assault, and vandalism. They encourage and support much larger numbers of violent offenses committed by nonmembers who may be totally unsophisticated with respect to the ideology of hate: racist skinheads, alienated teenagers, or hate-filled young men looking to have a good time at someone else's expense.

Organized hate groups are found not only in our communities but in our penitentiaries. Such identity groups, based on race or ethnicity, now exist in prisons around the country. While serving time behind bars for burglary convictions, two of the suspects in the Jasper attack apparently had links with the Aryan Brotherhood, a prison hate group whose members are often recruited by white supremacists after they have been released. Established in many states around the country, the Aryan Brotherhood introduces inmates to the theology of the Identity Church, according to which Jews are the children of Satan and blacks are subhuman "mud people." It has long been known that prison is a school for crime; now it appears that prison is a crash course in hatred.

According to the ADL, in 1995 there were some 3,500 racist skinheads in the United States, most of whom probably lacked connections to white supremacist groups. According to the Southern Poverty Law Center's Klanwatch project, there may be 20,000 but almost certainly no more than 50,000 members of white supremacist groups across the United States—a country whose residents number more than 265 million. Membership in citizens' militias has been estimated at between 15,000 and 100,000. (Karl 1995). According to Klanwatch, these militia groups number 370 and are only loosely connected to one another. (*Klanwatch Bulletin* 1997). It should also be pointed out that the militia movement in the United States is diverse. Some members are clearly racist in their beliefs, but there are also Jewish and black militia members; their uniting belief is a hardened distrust of the national government (Levin 1999).

Very rarely is any other type of hate crime committed by a single individual; and the few perpetrators of mission hate crimes who operate alone typically suffer from a profound mental illness that may cause hallucinations, impaired ability to reason, and withdrawal from contact with other people. The mission of such an individual is to get even for the horrific problems that he has suffered. In his paranoid and delusional way of thinking, he sees a conspiracy of some kind for which he seeks revenge. His mission is in part suicidal. Before taking his own life, however, he must attempt to eliminate the entire category of people he is absolutely convinced is responsible for his personal frustrations.

HATE CRIMES VERSUS OTHER OFFENSES

Because hate crimes by definition involve behavior that is already prohibited by state or federal statute (e.g. assault, threats, vandalism), a frequent question is, Why are additional penalties needed? Are these crimes truly different?

Important characteristics of hate incidents separate them from other types of offenses. First, hate crimes are directed at large groups of people. Offenders use a criminal event to put the members of an entire group on notice, for example, that they are not welcome in a community, in a workplace, on a college campus, or at school. Their intention is to send a message not just to that victim but to every member of his or her group—all blacks, all Latinos, all Asians, all whites, all gays—informing them that their presence will not be tolerated.

Second, the victim characteristic motivating the attack (e.g., race or ethnicity) is in most cases ascribed and immutable. A person cannot change her or his race,

▼

Survivor's Story, by William Edward Hassel

In their book Hate Crimes: Confronting Violence Against Lesbians and Gay Men, *Gregory M. Herek and Kevin T. Berrill report this account of a hate crime:*

I perceived these two to be lovers. I didn't suspect that there would be a problem. And, like a fool, I agreed to go with them to a party on American University's Campus.

Instead, they took me to Battery Kimball Park, which is over behind Georgetown University off Chain Bridge Road in the District. They forced me at knifepoint to strip. They beat me. One of them stood on my wrists leaning over my face holding a knife point at my throat so that any way I moved would dislodge him and he would fall on to me, forcing the knife through my throat, while the other one systematically kicked me in the groin, in the side.

They made me address them as "Sir." They made me beg to be made into a real woman. They threatened to castrate me. They threatened to emasulate me. They called me "Queer," "Faggot." One of them urinated on me. They threatened me with sodomy.

They kept me this way for about an hour. And there is an old southern expression called "playing possum." I kept trying, but they were hurting me so badly that I couldn't help but cry out in pain.

Finally, I think that I probably was close to passing out—I don't know—but I finally fooled them. They relaxed a little bit. They stopped kicking me around for a few moments while they talked.

One of them said to the other one, "Let's finish him off and get out of here." The one holding the knife raised the knife over his head and swung it at my throat. I reached up and grabbed the blade of the knife to avoid it going through my throat and managed to roll my body onto his legs. He fell across me. I managed to get out from under him, and I ran for my life.

The police arrested the one who had been following me on foot within minutes. The two young men were seniors at St. John's College high school here in Washington. It is a prestigious Catholic military prep school . . .

Source: Herek, Gregory M. and Kevin T. Berrill, eds. (1992). *Hate Crimes: Confronting Violence Against Lesbians and Gay Men*. Newbury Park, CA: Sage Publications, pp. 144-145.

ethnicity, age, gender, or disability status. Even a religious identity cannot be modified without causing an individual to make dramatic and difficult changes in lifestyle. There is absolutely no way for victims to escape the reason for their victimization.

Thus, the motivation for victimization in a hate attack is a perception of who an individual is rather than what he or she has done. The target is defined by the perpetrators as the "enemy"—as lacking in human qualities and therefore exempt from the rules governing civilized society. The feeling on the part of victims that they lack control over the characteristic that motivated their victimization causes most hate crime victims to feel extremely vulnerable to future bias-motivated attacks.

A third characteristic of hate crimes that differentiates them from many other offenses is that the individual victims typically did nothing to provoke the attack and is therefore interchangeable with other, similar people, at least from the perpetrator's standpoint. To a group of youths waiting outside a gay bar to attack someone whom they believe might be gay, it does not matter which individual comes through the door next. Whoever comes out is likely to become a victim, because all bar patrons are identical in the mind of the perpetrator.

Indeed, the interchangeability of victims also tends to apply across groups of victims. In general, youngsters who commit thrill hate crimes do not specialize with respect to their targets. For example, if they cannot locate someone to "bash" who is black, they might instead target a Latino or an Asian. If they cannot find someone gay, they might search out someone who is Jewish or Muslim. This aspect of hate crimes suggests that they are often motivated by an offender's psychological need to feel important at the expense of his or her victims.

Finally, hate-motivated attacks tend to be more damaging to victims than comparable non-hate crimes. Some research suggests that hate-motivated assaults against individuals can be incredibly violent. In Boston, for example, victims of hate-motivated assaults were three times more likely to need hospital treatment than other assault victims (Levin and McDevitt 1993). (For a contrasting view, see Jacobs and Potter 1997).

Moreover, recent research suggests that hate attacks result in greater emotional distress experienced by victims of these crimes compared to similar non-bias-motivated offenses (Craig 1999). Victims of bias crimes have been shown to manifest higher levels of prolonged depression, anxiety, anger, and symptoms of posttraumatic stress than victims of non-bias crimes. (Herek et al. 1997). Once the community becomes aware of the attack, the psychological trauma associated with the hate crime is thought to be transferred from the original victim to other members of the victim's group. This in turn may provoke further social discord between groups, potentially leading to a desire for retaliation by members of the victim's group (*Wisconsin v. Mitchell* 1993; Craig 1999; Levin 1999).

SUMMARY

The especially brutal nature of hate violence may be due to the depersonalization that many hate crime offenders employ in justifying their offenses. Hate-mongers frequently view members of targeted groups as less that human. They reason, therefore, that it is appropriate to treat their victims in the manner they might treat a wild animal or a demon rather than a human being.

—*Jack Levin and Jack McDevitt*

Further Reading

Anti-Defamation League. (1995). *The Skinhead International*. New York: ADL.

Craig, K. M. (1999). "Retaliation, Fear, or Rage: An Investigation of African American and White Reactions to Racist Hate Crimes." *Journal of Interpersonal Violence* 14: 138–151.

Federal Bureau of Investigation. (2001). *Hate Crime Reporting Statistics*. Washington, DC: U.S. Government Printing Office.

Fox, James, and Jack Levin. (1996). *Overkill: Mass Murder and Serial Killing Exposed*. New York: Dell.

Franklin, Karen. (2000). "Antigay Behaviors Among Young Adults: Prevalence, Patterns, and Motivators in a Noncriminal Population." *Journal of Interpersonal Violence* 15, 4 (April): 339–362.

Herek, G. M., Gillis. J. R., Cogan J. C., et al. (1997). "Hate Crime Victimization Among Lesbian, Gay, and Bisexual Adults: Prevalence, Psychological Correlates, and Methodological Issues." *Journal of Interpersonal Violence* 12, 2: 195–215.

Jacobs, James B., and Jessica S. Henry. (1996). "The Social Construction of a Hate Crime Epidemic." *The Journal of Criminal Law and Criminology* (Winter): 366–391.

Jacobs, James B., and Kimberly A. Potter. (1997). "Hate Crimes: A Critical Perspective." In *Crime and Justice: A Review of Research,* edited by Michael Tonry. Chicago: University of Chicago Press.

Karl, Jonathan. (1995). *The Right to Bear Arms*. New York: Harper.

Levin, Brian. (1999). "Hate Crimes; Worse by Definition." *Journal of Contemporary Criminal Justice* 15, 1: 6–21.

Levin, Jack. (1997). "Visit to a Patriot Potluck." *USA Today* (1 March): 6A.

———. (2002). *The Violence of Hate: Confronting Racism, Anti-Semitism, and Other Forms of Bigotry*. Boston: Allyn and Bacon.

Levin, Jack, and Jack McDevitt. (1993). *Hate Crimes: The Rising Tide of Bigotry and Bloodshed*. New York: Plenum.

Martin, Susan. (1995). "A Cross-Burning is Not Just an Arson: Police Social Construction of Hate Crimes in Baltimore County." *Criminology* 33, 3: 303–330.

McDevitt, Jack, Jack Levin, and Susan Bennett. (in press). "Hate Crime Offenders-An Expanded Typology." *Journal of Interpersonal Violence*.

"Two Years After: The Patriot Movement Since Oklahoma City." (1997). *Klanwatch Intelligence Report* (Spring): 18–20.

Court Case

Wisconsin v. Mitchell (1993). 508 U.S. 476.

◥ HINDUISM

Hinduism is the major religion of India and is a world religion, having been spread beyond India's borders by Indian Hindus who have settled elsewhere. There are about 800 million adherents of Hinduism around the world. Hinduism permeates all aspects of life in India and contains ritual, experiential, narrative, philosophical, ethical, legal, social, material, and artistic dimensions. Hinduism is a complex religion, and there is much variation in belief and practice across the villages of India. Compared to other world religions, the scholarly study of Hindu criminal law has been limited, largely because during and following British rule, criminal justice in India was strongly influenced by Thomas Macauley's secular Indian Penal Code, imposed by the British in 1860.

SIN AND PUNISHMENT IN VEDIC AND CLASSICAL HINDU TRADITION (1500–500 BCE)

Unlike Imperial China, ancient India was only rarely a unified empire. This absence of centralized political rule meant that the state did not rely on Hindu ideas about punishment. Hindu literary tradition developed into a complex system of texts, beginning with the hymn collections known as the four Vedas, which relate basic Hindu concepts. These texts reflect the gradual development of an increasingly sophisticated religious and social philosophy, but frequently the basic key elements are taken for granted and are not explained. They demonstrate the growth of assumptions about mankind and its role in the world, linked to claims about control of individual behavior in the interest of a larger whole—ultimately, the entire cosmos. Making the distinction between the great universal macrocosmic Order (*rita*) and the intricately connected microcosmic order (*dharma*) is central to an understanding of all Hindu concepts. An element of dynamism is introduced through the linking concept of *karma*, which implies that all actions inevitably have visible and invisible consequences within the framework of *rita* and *dharma*.

This complex underlying concept of Order/order is not the result of human effort, nor is any particular god primarily credited with its creation (though later theistic forms of Hinduism try to make such claims). The system simply exists, like the sun and the moon; all beings, including gods, are inescapably subject to it and ideally should be conscious of this existing linkage; all

human action becomes measured, in some form, against the criteria of this higher Order, which is viewed as a self-supporting equilibrium in a continuous process of readjustment, and not subject to the authority of one divine power. It may be seen as a kind of volatile ecosystem with infinite self-healing capacity. The Hindu gods Varuna and Mitra often are associated with *rita*, but these gods also serve the higher Order and do not govern it (Day 1982: 29), although they do serve as punishers of violations and have deterrent functions. Order is certain, ultimately regulated outside the human sphere, and at a level beyond human control but closely linked to human activity.

The ancient Vedic literature focuses on the ritualized connections between this higher Order and the human sphere. Performing rituals and sacrifices is seen as a major means of strengthening and upholding cosmic Order, as well as human order. While the Vedic literature is not concerned with guiding humans on how to maintain harmony and peace on earth, the later classical Hindu "religious" literature circumscribes all individual behavior as good or bad, always with an eye on universal concerns. The class of literature called *dharmasutra* or *dharmashastra*, in particular, focuses on all aspects of righteousness (*dharma*), the key term in Hindu culture. The essence of Hinduism, hardly ever explicitly verbalized in such texts, lies precisely in understanding the interlinked nature of an individual's *dharma* with all other beings or parties within such a cosmic framework of reference. Being Hindu, then, is not so much a matter of belief as of "right action" in the light of cosmic awareness. The actions of a good Hindu should be conducive to the stability of cosmic order and social harmony at the same time.

A Hindu's wrong action would be seen as anything not in accordance with order, not conducive to *rita/dharma*. But how would one ascertain what is good or bad? Because the regulatory mechanisms were invisible, the rules of the game were not known to mankind. Apart from intuition and pious endeavor, guidance might be sought from the ancient texts, but a major influence was certainly exerted by local customs. In the minds of individual Hindus, therefore, a combination of external customary forces and of internalized awareness of the *rita/dharma* complex and its expectations came together to achieve a largely invisible method of self-controlled ordering that worked on the individual conscience rather than visible adherence to codified formal rules. There could be no one rule for everyone.

Vedic and classical Hindu texts contain, therefore, a

confusing diversity of statements as to which actions may not be in line with *rita* and *dharma*. Because so much depends on facts and circumstances, however, it seems that any position could be proved from these texts, creating an atmosphere of total flexibility and fluidity. For example, a general statement that killing is bad would be accepted by Hindus as correct, but at the same time killing an individual is certainly justified in Hindu culture in various circumstances; thus, Hinduism as a whole does not uphold a total unqualified prohibition on the taking of human life. Because of *rita* consciousness, Hindus are aware of higher values than individual human survival, subordinating the individual's position to the concerns of higher levels of existence.

This has interesting political implications. As in ancient China, a bad ruler should be killed, in the higher interest of cosmic Order. Thus, the prominent Hindu divine figure of Lord Krishna is as a young hero first of all engaged in killing his evil maternal uncle, whose rule by terror caused misery to his people as well as cosmic disturbance.

Everywhere, thus, even outwardly secular Hindus perceive cosmic linkages. Life experience shows that destruction can hit anyone without warning. Sudden disasters (such as the Gujarat earthquake in January 2001) and inexplicable personal tragedies raise questions about punishment, which are partly answered by reference to the retributive dimensions of *rita* and *dharma*. Ignorant of the higher criteria for righteousness, humans can only try their best and hope to get it right.

The ancient literature offers ample guidance on what forms of human behavior are seen as unacceptable. Certain human deficiencies and acts are consistently portrayed as violating *rita* and *dharma*. While Hinduism and the religions that derive from it praise balance and detachment as superior values, excesses of passion, anger, lust, or greed are perceived as negative and sinful. Kane (1973: 10) refers to the prominent concept of the "seven limits" or seven sinful acts: (1) theft, (2) adultery with the teacher's wife, (3) murder of a Brahman, (4) murder of an embryo, (5) drinking of alcohol, (6) the repeated performance of the same sinful act, and (7) telling lies about sinful matters.

While this is an open list, the idea that certain human actions will result in definite retribution points to the emergence of more concrete understandings about norm violations among Hindus. Yet, there are no fixed assumptions, so murder as such is not seen as a crime, only the murder of a Brahman and of innocent unborn life. Nor is adultery treated as a serious matter in the ancient Vedic system, while classical Hinduism develops a new understanding of sexual morality in which women are treated as property of men and threatened with more serious punishments.

The Vedic idea that any transgression will have inescapable and invisible consequences remained strong, exemplified in Varuna as the divine guardian of *rita*, pursuing transgressors to the remotest places. Nothing could remain hidden in this cosmic system of automatic retribution. Because there was no published binding code of conduct, however, Hindus who wished to be safe from transgressions and sins would have to rely on intuition and their inner desire to comply with imagined ideal standards.

This idealized Vedic system did not survive, however, since manifestly bad people prospered, disasters did not spare the innocent, and doubts over theories of causal links and automatic retribution through divine agents became stronger. By the end of the classical Hindu period, *rita* had metamorphosed into an invisible concept overshadowed by the more tangible ordering system of *dharma*, and greater human control over retributive processes was seen as desirable.

CRIME AND PUNISHMENT IN POSTCLASSICAL HINDU LAW

The gradual evolution of the classical Hindu framework had focused on the key concept of *dharma*, which placed all individual Hindus under an inherent obligation to do the right thing at any time of their life, while maintaining the old system of relativity about what was right and wrong. Because self-controlled order manifestly did not work, however, the center of activity in maintaining order now shifted from the macrocosmic sphere down to earth during the postclassical period (500 BCE–200 CE). Thus, the Hindu ruler became a key figure in watching over punishment. The emergence of criminal law under more explicit state control goes hand in hand with a shift of emphasis from sin to crime.

The flexible criterion of *dharma* as the ultimate yardstick remains in place. Thus, killing never becomes bad in itself, and it may indeed be essential to protect *dharma*. For example, a lion who kills for food just follows his *dharma*, but were he to kill for pleasure, he would violate his *dharma*. Lingat (1973: 4) circumscribed *dharma* as follows: "In internal terms, *dharma* signifies the obligation, binding upon every man who desires that his actions should bear fruit, to submit himself to the laws which govern the universe and to direct his life in consequence. That obligation constitutes his duty, and that is a further sense of the word."

Such Hindu axioms of individual submission to a higher order are reinforced by the concept of *karma*, which contains in itself a retributive theory, "an autonomous principle or self-enacting law of moral operations independent of any divine will" (Day 1982: 71). Postclassical Hindu law, however, went beyond this, and brought in the figure of the ruler as a guardian of *dharma* to strengthen the earlier self-controlled order. Therefore, although one is tempted to see the Hindu ruler as the embodiment of the state, and, thus, the controller of criminal law, in reality the Hindu ruler presided over a system of continuing self-controlled order and let people get on with their lives as they saw fit.

Two important conceptual elements are added through the figure of the Hindu ruler. First, he is seen wielding the stick of punishment or punishing rod (*danda*). Second, the king developed, over time, the power to make rules for the people of his realm, thus coming closer to Western concepts of rule of law. A closer look shows, however, that the ruler remained mainly a tool of self-controlling *dharma*, not an authority above it; his authority to make laws for the people in his realm was limited. While the Hindu ruler may not have regulated the daily life of his people to a large extent, he watched over excesses of egoism and lawlessness. This can be linked to the ruler's role as an arbitrator in dispute settlement, always conscious of the basic rule that justice is in danger if uniform legal rules are applied in all situations, as several *smriti* texts clearly suggest.

Hindu law thus cultivates the principle that the facts and circumstances of any particular case determine what is good or bad. Hindu texts candidly admit that the first arbiter of appropriateness is the individual conscience itself (*atmanastushti*), that local norms (*sadacara*) are the key element of measuring what is good and bad, and that the texts are really only used as a last resort—and then not as binding statutes but as sources of guidance. (See Manusmriti 2.6 and 2.12, two verses of a major guidebook on *dharma*, both of which imply that the roots of *dharma* are the entire Veda, the traditions of those who know the Veda, the conduct of virtuous people, and satisfaction of one's conscience.)

Such cultural evidence has been misread by legalists, however, and the role of the texts often has been overstated. In postclassical Hindu culture, self-controlled order is more and more seen as inefficient, while the punishing rod (*danda*) and dispute settlement (*vyavahara*) become more prominent. Although self-controlled order does not disappear altogether, what one might call assisted self-control through the threat of punishment moves center stage. The *danda* as a symbol of this shift of emphasis has both a coercive and a deterrent aspect. Literary models of threatening punishment now portray gruesome images of harsh penalties. The critical question is whether such models are to be applied in reality or whether they are merely put up as dramatic threats. Many texts emphasize the deterrent factor. Thus, Manusmriti 7.18 reads, punishment [*danda*] alone governs all creatures, punishment alone protects them, punishment watches over them while they sleep; the wise declare punishment to be identical with *dharma*." Similarly, Manusmriti 7.22 states, "The whole world is kept in order by punishment, since it is hard to find a guiltless man. Through fear of punishment the whole world duly yields what it owes."

Dispute settlement is seen as a technique to remove the thorn of discontent between parties, and a clever judge would become adept at removing such thorns. Hindu criminal law and the punishment of crimes continued to coexist with assumptions about sins rather than crimes, preventing the state from claiming exclusive jurisdiction. As a result, there is no Hindu science of penology as a separate field; it remains interlinked with religious and cultural concerns (Banerjee 1980; Doongaji 1986; Lahiri 1986). In some literature, the impression is created that a Hindu science of crimes has developed and that there are fixed catalogues of punishments for certain crimes, but such images are deceptive. Conceptually as well as in reality, the ruler was still only a supervisory functionary. The Hindu sociocultural system continued to rely largely on informal, self-regulatory mechanisms rather than on external force, clearly under the wider concept of *dharma* as self-controlled order. Punishment also is perceived, however, as indispensable for social control (Day 1982: 121), and the duty of the state to suppress crimes and to punish the offender is highlighted.

In a system of differential statuses, penalties for one and the same offense committed by different kinds of people varied. Thus, high-caste Brahmans might be punished more severely than lower-cast people for some offenses and more leniently for others, and they are not subject to the death penalty (Day 1982: 180–182). Rulers are not exempt from punishment, either.

Generally speaking, the Hindu system relied heavily on self-regulatory processes and on the jurisdiction of local bodies and even families. The textual statements about penalties for certain crimes must be read as guidelines, not as statutory and fixed provisions, because taking account of the facts and circumstances of a case was always an overriding consideration. It is therefore impossible to give a comprehensive description of Hindu crime and resulting punishment, as too much depends on circumstances. This is well expressed in a statement from Brihaspatismriti 2.12: "No sentence shall be passed merely according to fixed textual rules. If a decision is arrived at without considering the circumstances of the case, violation of justice will be the result." This was even cited in a modern Indian court a few decades ago, when it was held in *P. V. Kunhikannan v. State of Kerala* (1968) that rigid adherence to legal technical detail might indeed go against justice

The idea that punishments should be proportionate and should "match the crime" is clearly inherent in the principle of cosmic balance underlying the *rita/dharma* complex. Thus, overly harsh punishments would violate *dharma*. Still, Hindu law reluctantly permitted the death penalty in certain circumstances, based on apprehensions about taking a life as well as awareness that the dead person was not thereby rendered nonexistent. Because concepts of sin coexisted with those of crime, punishment and expiation also ran concurrently.

Later developments in the postclassical periods (500 CE TO 1200 CE) indicate that the legal authority of the ruler as an administrator of criminal justice increased, but self-help and self-regulation remained an important element (Derrett 1968: 183), and criminal law retained a place within the customary legal system rather than being regulated by the state. The texts of the later periods reflect subject specialization, concentrating more explicitly on evidence law. Despite much attention to the subject, no key text on Hindu criminal law emerged during this period. After 1100, the Muslim (Mughal) rule of India meant that Islamic criminal law became the official law. Hindu criminal law, rather than being superseded altogether, retained its local importance and flexibility.

HINDU CRIME AND PUNISHMENT DURING BRITISH RULE

Hindu concepts of crime and punishment continued to exist in Indian society under British rule (in 1600, the British East India Company started trading; from 1765,

the Company acted as a local authority under Mughal rule; from 1858 until 1947 formal British sovereignty existed). Under Mughal rule, criminal law allegedly had deteriorated into an oppressive machinery for extortion, harassment of one's enemies, and cruel punishments; the British civilizing mission, however, included a program to regulate criminal law (Fisch 1983).

This was finally achieved in 1860 through the famous Indian Penal Code of Thomas Macauley, which became law on January 1, 1862. Contrary to popular assumptions, this was not English law transported into India but a new, purpose-built edifice of criminal law, which had taken elements from many different legal traditions—not least, Scottish law—with some influences from Islamic and Hindu criminal law. The new code replaced the indigenous concepts of status differentials and brought equality before the law. The formal nature of this law, however, made its practical application cumbersome, slow, and very costly. The formal legal emphasis on criminal law as a branch of public law reinforced the role of the state as the main punisher and maintainer of order in society. This had the practical effect that many crimes would never be reported to the state and that much of local criminal law went underground. This trend was increased by the cultural mismatch between Hindu norms and worldviews and the secular assumptions of the new code.

The change in the view of adultery illustrates this cultural mismatch. Under section 497 of the Indian Penal Code, adultery became a crime—not an offense against the woman but a crime of property against the woman's husband—while the woman herself remained unpunished. The range of punishments reflected the enlightened approach of nineteenth-century Europe, involving the death penalty, imprisonment for life, rigorous or simple imprisonment for certain periods, forfeiture of property, and monetary fines. One particular penalty, transportation beyond the seas (*kala pani,* "the black water"), which had been prominent under early British criminal law administration, was still part of the scheme but was later dropped. It turned out to be too expensive but, more interestingly, Hindus discovered that life beyond the supposedly terrifying black seas could be quite comfortable, and some asked for such punishment—which sometimes meant being sent to Mauritius!

There is a significant literature that suggests that despite the impressive formal application of the Indian Penal Code, its actual impact was severely undermined by local social norms, to the detriment of women, children, and members of the lower castes (see especially Dhagamwar 1992). The most significant official drawback was that the official letter of the criminal law often was not followed, because it was hoped that justice, including criminal justice, would be achieved locally in accordance with traditional Hindu norms rather than the modern secular law.

FUTURE TRENDS

Although no one would know how to revive the traditional Hindu criminal law, post-Independence public debates in India have focused on the continued presence of the death penalty on the statute book. At the same time, there has been much evidence that the provisions of the criminal law are selectively used against certain groups of people and lead to the criminalization of poor people, in particular. The late-twentieth-century phenomenon of Indian public interest litigation has brought to light many cases of illegal detentions and violations of legal rules in the application of criminal laws.

In modern Indian criminal law, there is therefore a sense of crisis and a feeling that the modern state's secular law may not be the sole mechanism to achieve an appropriate balance between the conflicting pulls of cosmic order (the *rita/dharma* complex and public interest) and of private interest and selfishness. The eternal dilemma of crime control and finding appropriate punishment—the need to control excesses of greed and selfishness to ensure harmonious human survival—remains unsolved also in the modern Indian sociolegal context.

—*Werner F. Menski*

See also INDIA

Further Reading
Banerjee, S. C. (1980). *Crime and Sex in Ancient India.* Calcutta, India: Riddhi.
Banerjee, Tapas Kumar. (1962). *History of Indian Criminal Law.* Calcutta, India: Riddhi.
DasGupta, Ramprashad. (1978). *Crime and Punishment in Ancient India*, vol. 1, no.1. Varanasi, India: Bhartiya Publishing House.
Day, Terence. (1982). *The Conception of Punishment in Early Indian literature.* Waterloo, Canada: Wilfred Laurier University Press.
Derrett, J. D. M. (1968). *Religion, Law, and the State in India.* London: Faber & Faber.
Dhagamwar, Vasudha. (1992). *Law, Power, and Justice: The Protection of Personal Rights in the Indian Penal Code.* New Delhi: Sage Publications.
Doongaji, Damayanti. (1986). *Crime and Punishment in Ancient Hindu Society.* New Delhi: Ajanta.
Fisch, Joerg. (1983). *Cheap Lives and Dear Limbs: The British Transformation of the Bengal Criminal Law 1769–1817.* Wiesbaden: Franz Steiner Verlag.
Jolly, Julius. (1975). *Hindu Law and Custom.* Varanasi: Bhartiya Publishing House.
Kane, P. V. (1973). *History of dharmashastra.* Poona: Bhandarkar Oriental Research Institute.
Lahiri, Tarapada. (1986). *Crime and Punishment in Ancient India.* New Delhi: Sangam.
Lingat, Robert. (1973). *The Classical Law of India.* Berkeley: University of California Press.

Court Case
P. V. Kunhikannan v. State of Kerala (1968). *Kerala Law Times* 19.

HIV/AIDS AND THE CRIMINAL JUSTICE SYSTEM

Many of the same people who encounter crime also come into contact with HIV, the virus that causes AIDS. For example, more than 750,000 persons have been diagnosed with AIDS in the United States since 1981; around one-third acquired HIV through unsafe injection practices or sex with an injecting drug user. At the end of 1999, prison inmates were five times more likely than the general population to have AIDS. By some estimates, at least half of all new HIV infections in the United States occur among people under age twenty-five, many of whom exchange sex for money, food, or shelter in order to survive on the streets. Every day, police officers and correctional officers encounter suspects, offenders, and colleagues who are HIV positive. Many rape victims fear that their assailant had HIV.

HIV is most commonly spread through sexual contact with someone who is infected with HIV. It is also spread through contact with HIV-infected blood, as may happen when an injecting drug user shares needles or other injection equipment with someone who is HIV-positive. Spitting, biting, or needlesticks, on the other hand, pose a low threat of HIV transmission (Flavin 1998). Needlesticks, which may occur as the result of accidental contact with a syringe or an assault, pose a lesser threat of transmission than injection drug use because they typically involve much smaller volumes of blood. According to the Centers for Disease Control and Prevention (CDC), 99.7 percent of needlestick exposures or exposures through a cut in one's skin and 99.9 percent of eye, nose, or mouth exposures do not lead to infection. Biting presents a greater risk of HIV transmission than does spitting, a lesser risk than a

▼

HIV: The Risk to Police Officers

The risk of HIV infection is an issue in police departments around the world, as indicated by this news report about Cambodia.

POLICE TO ARM AGAINST AIDS

Phnom Penh [Cambodia]— National police got a new order from the Government yesterday: wear a condom when you visit brothels.

Concerned at the high rate of HIV infection among police and military, the Ministry of Interior called more than 100 police chiefs from around the country to Phnom Penh to tell them that condom use was now mandatory for the country's 60,000-plus officers.

"The nature of humans when they have sex is not to use condoms, but in order to protect ourselves, we have to change our nature," Secretary of State Em Sam An said yesterday.

Cambodia has the highest HIV infection rate in Southeast Asia, with three per cent of the population infected with the deadly virus, according to the National AIDS Programme.

A survey in 1997 found that more than 11 per cent of military and police personnel were infected. The infection rate among prostitutes is a staggering 42 per cent.

Dr Tia Phalla, head of the National Aids Programme, said that extending the campaign to police would reinforce the prevention message.

Mr Em Sam An said: "The Cambodian national police have fought on the battlefield, been wounded, survived in the jungle and been infected with malaria. All these enemies the Cambodian police have defeated. If the police now die of AIDS, it would be a great shame."

Source Johnson, Kay (1999, September 17). *South China Morning Post.*

needlestick. Although the likelihood of HIV transmission by needlestick is extremely low, needlesticks are estimated to transmit, on average, twenty times more HIV-infected cells than a human bite (Richman and Rickman 1993). Typically, a biter is more likely to come into contact with the victim's blood than vice versa. Neither a small amount of blood being exposed to intact skin, nor exposure to sweat, tears, saliva, or airborne droplets (as in a sneeze) has ever been shown

to result in HIV transmission (CDC 1997; Richman and Rickman 1993). Lack of education about these basic facts can cause people to overreact to the threat of AIDS in crime-related situations.

SEXUAL ASSAULT AND HIV/AIDS

The risk of HIV transmission during a sexual assault is greater than during consensual sex, but it is still relatively small. The estimated likelihood of HIV transmission following unprotected and receptive anal or vaginal intercourse with a person who is HIV-positive is between one and three in a thousand. On the other hand, sexual violence that produces trauma or an inflammatory or ulcerative sexually transmitted disease is associated with a higher risk of transmission (Bamberger 2000; Gostin et al. 1994). Because sexual assaults pose a risk of transmission, the CDC (1998) recommends that people who have been sexually assaulted receive medical evaluations, including HIV-antibody tests at baseline (to determine HIV status at the time of the assault) and periodically for at least six months after the incident. In many states, funding is provided for immediate medical follow-up for victims who report their rape to the police. Funding may not be available for later medical follow-up or to victims who do not report the assault to police (Kilpatrick et al. 1992).

Rape victims have the option of taking antiretroviral drugs (which kill or suppress a retrovirus such as HIV) after the assault to reduce the likelihood of HIV infection. Since 1996, postexposure prophylaxis (PEP) has been standard practice for health care workers occupationally exposed to HIV and has been found to result in a 79 percent lower rate of seroconversion (the change in an antibody status from negative to positive) when compared to no treatment. However, it is not clear that PEP works as well for exposures to HIV through sexual contact or drug injection (CDC 1998; Mirken 1998). PEP involves taking multiple drugs several times a day for at least thirty days. The regimen is difficult, can have severe side effects, and costs $600 to $1,000. A study of New York City rape victims found that only 16 percent completed the regimen as prescribed (Mirken 1998). Among health care workers in the United States, just over 60 percent complete the regimen.

Medical experts recommend that victims be provided with the best available information regarding PEP, including the potential side effects, to help them make an informed decision. Victims should also undergo an assessment to determine the risk associated with the exposure. This assessment should consider available information on the assailant's HIV status, the type of exposure, the nature of the physical injuries, and the number of assaults. Should victims choose to undergo PEP, treatment should be initiated no later than seventy-two hours following the assault, and should be continued for twenty-eight days (Bamberger et al. 1999; Gostin et al. 1994).

Because a rape victim rarely knows whether the assailant was infected with HIV, some victims claim a right to have their assailants tested for HIV and to have access to the test results. Ideally, pieces of state legislation guaranteeing these rights are structured to balance the usefulness of the information to the survivor with the privacy interests of the accused. Federal law makes the receipt of certain Bureau of Justice Assistance grant funds contingent on a state's testing sex offenders after conviction. However, because few assailants are arrested, charged, and convicted in a timely fashion, and because PEP, if initiated, should be initiated early, some say that mandatory testing laws have limited value. At the same time, others argue that it is unfair for victims to shoulder all of the uncertainty and fear engendered by an HIV antibody test. For this reason, some legislators propose that rape victims be permitted to request preconviction testing of the accused. Under these proposals, if certain conditions are met (e.g., there is reason to believe that an assault was committed by the accused and that the assault could transmit HIV infection, and the privacy interests of the survivor and the accused are guaranteed), then preconviction testing would be authorized.

Sexual Abuse and HIV-Risk Behavior

Victimization and HIV are also linked by the relationship that exists between sexual abuse and HIV-risk behavior. Several studies have found that family violence, sexual abuse, and sexual assault are associated with injection drug use and sex work among adolescent and adult women (Miller 1999; Ryan and Futterman 1997). Women may initiate or rely on drug use as a means of coping with the sexual abuse experience, which in turn may lead to an increased risk of syringe-sharing and a lower likelihood of seeking drug treatment. Sexual abuse may create problems with sexual adjustment that may lead a woman to participate in sex work or exchange sex for drugs. Sexual abuse may also lead to depression and posttraumatic stress disorder,

which may contribute to women's participation in self-damaging sex or drug-use behaviors.

It has been estimated that at least half of all new HIV infections in the United States occur among people under twenty-five, many of whom are homeless and exchange sex for money, food, or shelter in order to survive. Many homeless youth have run away to escape family violence and sexual abuse, or were "thrown away" because of conflicts over their sexual identity or because their families were economically unable to continue to care for them. These teenagers may engage in "survival sex," which places them at increased risk of contracting HIV or other sexually transmitted diseases. Older street youth (aged twenty-two to twenty-three years) are significantly more likely than younger ones to report having had unprotected sex with one or more partners, to be currently involved in commercial sex work, to inject drugs, and to use crack cocaine. Although older street youths are at significantly greater risk for becoming infected with HIV and are more likely to evidence HIV-related illnesses, many youth-focused prevention and treatment services are not extended to older street youth (Clatts et al. 1998).

OFFENDERS AND HIV/AIDS

Many advocates of a "law and order" perspective suggest that the spread of HIV can be reduced by enacting tougher laws. This has led to calls for criminal penalties for HIV transmission that would punish those who intentionally expose others to HIV, and that would deter others from engaging in similar behavior. At least twenty-seven states provide criminal penalties for knowingly exposing others to HIV. Some legislative proposals favor harsher penalties for HIV-positive persons who commit a sex- or drug-related offense even if the offense has virtually no chance of transmitting HIV (Hansen 1998). People with HIV have been criminally convicted for various behaviors, not all of which have been scientifically found to pose a significant risk of transmission (Gostin 1996). One study found 101 cases in which individuals had been prosecuted for HIV-related offenses, including 22 involving spitting or biting (Whitehorn 2000).

Opponents of criminalizing intentional HIV transmission argue that it may be difficult to establish that a person knew he or she was HIV-positive prior to engaging in the proscribed activity, or that the person believed that the activity would lead to HIV transmission. They also argue that it may lead to increased stigmatization of and discrimination against already marginalized groups (e.g., gays and lesbians, injecting drug users, sex workers), and that it is less effective in changing sexual behavior or drug use than counseling, education, and harm reduction. Harm-reduction approaches emphasize measures, such as the distribution of condoms and injection equipment, intended to reduce the spread of HIV through sex and drug use. The underlying philosophy is that the health and well-being of people, including those who use drugs, is most important.

Inmates

In 1999, approximately 1.7 percent of jail inmates and 2.1 percent of state and federal prison inmates were HIV positive. The incidence of HIV in United States prisons parallels larger trends in the uneven racial/ethnic and geographic distribution of HIV in injection drug users. The prevalence of HIV and AIDS is higher among black and Hispanic inmates than among white inmates. In 1999, three states, New York, Florida, and Texas housed nearly half of all HIV-positive state prisoners. Women's greater social, economic, and anatomic vulnerability to getting HIV through injection drug use or sexual contact partly accounts for the greater percent of all women state inmates who are HIV-positive compared to men. At the end of 1999, 3.5 percent of all female state inmates and 2.2 percent of all male state inmates were HIV-positive. The rate of death due to AIDS is three times higher in the state prison population than it is in the general population (Maruschak 2001).

A government report, *1996–1997 Update: HIV/AIDS, STDs, and TB in Correctional Facilities* (Hammett, Harmon, and Maruschak 1999), documents the response to the presence of HIV in U.S. correctional facilities. The report found that inmate behaviors, such as consensual and coerced sexual activity, rape, drug use, and sharing of injection equipment, place some at risk for HIV infection. To date, however, condom distribution and other strategies designed to reduce the risk of HIV transmission among inmates have not been widely adopted in U.S. correctional facilities. Although HIV transmission does occur within prisons, the rates are low. For example, an Illinois Department of Corrections study identified 140 inmates who had been continuously incarcerated since 1977 and who were tested for HIV antibodies. Only one of these inmates was HIV-positive.

Most correctional systems provide HIV antibody testing on some basis. As of 1997, only seventeen state prison systems were conducting mandatory testing of all incoming inmates. Most jurisdictions test inmates upon inmate request or if the inmate exhibits HIV-related symptoms. Other testing policies include random testing, testing after involvement in an incident, testing inmates who belong to specific high-risk groups, or testing all inmates at time of release.

In terms of housing, the number of state and federal systems that segregate inmates with AIDS from the rest of the population has declined from thirty-eight in 1985 to three in 1997. In two of these states—Alabama and Mississippi—inmates infected with HIV, regardless of whether they have developed AIDS, are completely separated from the rest of the inmate population residentially and programmatically. In California, inmates with AIDS live separately from other inmates in most correctional facilities, but join the general population for work assignments and educational and vocational programs. Some systems exclude inmates with HIV from food service assignments, potentially feeding the mistaken impression that HIV can be transmitted through food.

The introduction in 1996 of protease inhibitors (a class of anti-HIV drug that prevents creation of an HIV-specific enzyme that breaks down proteins and is used in cell replication) and combination antiretroviral therapy ("cocktails") revolutionized the treatment of HIV/AIDS. These new HIV therapies have reduced morbidity and mortality in the general population, and are widely available in correctional systems. Still, there remain barriers to medical treatment of inmates, such as high medication costs, inmate reluctance to seek testing and treatment out of fear, denial, or mistrust, and uneven medical competence and treatment standards. The drug regimens are complicated, and many inmates have highly chaotic and stressful lives that make it difficult for them to adhere to the regimen. If an antiretroviral regimen is pursued, but fails, it may lead to resistance to other drugs of the same class, thus limiting future treatment options. To determine the best treatment for the HIV-positive inmate, a clinician must take into account what will work best bio-

HIV/AIDS and the Criminal Justice System

logically, what will be most tolerable to the inmate-patient, and what will gain maximum inmate-patient adherence. Inmates with HIV benefit most from a "continuum of care" encompassing early detection, effective medical and psychosocial support, hospice care and substance abuse treatment when appropriate, prerelease planning, and linkage to community-based services (Hammett, Harmon, and Maruschak 1999).

CRIMINAL JUSTICE WORKERS AND HIV/AIDS

Exposure of police officers and correctional officers to HIV is intermittent rather than routine. A Denver study found that the rate of police officers' exposure to HIV-infected blood was quite small, ranging from .09 to 1.52 per 10,000 person-days, or one exposure every forty years (Hoffman et al. 1994). Furthermore, the most common types of occupational exposure (contact with body fluids, needlesticks) present a very low risk of infection. To date, according to the CDC, no police officers or correctional officers have become infected with HIV as the result of workplace exposure.

Although officers' exposure to HIV while on the job is a relatively rare event, and the actual incidence of occupational transmission of HIV is extremely low to nonexistent, the fear of HIV among police officers is substantial (Burgess et al. 1992). Some criminal justice workers' response to people with HIV may be influenced by this fear, as well as by the unpredictable nature of police and correctional work, prejudice against persons who use drugs or are gay, and shortcomings in HIV/AIDS education (Flavin 1998).

According to the concept of universal precautions, to which criminal justice workers are subject, body fluids that are considered potentially infective (especially blood and semen) should be treated as if they contain HIV, hepatitis B virus, or other blood-borne pathogens, and personal protective equipment such as gloves or a mask should be used. In reality, officers may find themselves in unanticipated situations that do not provide sufficient time to take prescribed precautions. For example, a study of Denver police officers from 1989 to 1991

documented forty-two exposures to blood. Two-thirds of the exposures occurred in circumstances in which either the officer was restraining or being assaulted by a suspect and did not have time to put on protective gloves and clothing, or gloves would not have been protective because of penetration by needles (Hoffman et al. 1994). Although precautionary routines and procedures are helpful, they cannot address the full range of situations an officer may encounter. This, in turn, may contribute to officers' fear and subsequent overreaction to the threat of HIV exposure.

Social taboos against homosexuality and drug use also have made HIV a particularly sensitive issue among police officers and correctional workers. Criminal justice workers' treatment of people with HIV cannot be separated from their attitudes toward other marginalized groups, including gays, lesbians, and injection drug users. For example, the police and the lesbian and gay community have a long history of mutual distrust (though the existence of organizations such as the Gay Officer's Action League demonstrates that these groups' memberships are not mutually exclusive). Only 14 percent of the victims in bias crimes against gays and lesbians in Los Angeles and Santa Barbara, California, reported a courteous response from police. In 1998, a New York City Police Department chaplain was pressured to retire after using an antigay slur to refer to an assistant district attorney while presenting awards at a banquet (Cooper 1998).

People with AIDS are protected from discrimination

▼

HIV: The Risk to Corrections Officers

Dealing with the risks associated with HIV requires the balancing of medical and legal considerations, as indicated in this directive from the New York State Commission of Correction.

This case appears to suggest that absent a medical or behavioral justification, segregation of prisoners solely on the basis of their HIV status may not be supported in courts. Local correctional facilities should be aware that any such segregation will have to be based on legitimate penological goals or medical advice. Remember that his case found that a stigmatization occurred because officials involuntarily identified the prisoners as HIV positive through the transfer and use of special housing. This further underscores the need to maintain confidentiality of HIV-related information. The court was cognizant of the recent passage of Article 27-F and considered its purpose of preventing discrimination based on their HIV status in reaching its decision.

Source: *HIV/AIDS in Local Correctional Facilities: A Management Resource Manual.* (1990). Albany: New York State Commission of Correction, p. 32.

by Section 504 of the Rehabilitation Act of 1973 and the Americans with Disabilities Act (ADA) of 1990 (Goldfein and Hanssens 1996). The purpose of these acts is to assure civil rights protections to qualified people with disabilities. The ADA is modeled after the Rehabilitation Act, so the two acts are very similar in scope. The main difference between them is found in the sectors to which they apply. In very general terms, the ADA prohibits disability-based discrimination in the private sector and in state and local government, whereas the Rehabilitation Act applies to employers and organizations receiving federal assistance.

Harassment and discriminatory treatment of people with HIV occurs in the criminal justice system despite the protections provided by federal legislation. On occasion, police officers and correctional guards have reacted to the remote possibility of HIV infection with physical violence. In Pennsylvania, a man who bit a police officer was killed when another officer pressed down on his shoulders and neck with a collapsible metal club. The officer also stood and knelt briefly on his neck. The officer who was bitten recalled saying at the time of attack, "If I die, then I hope you die" (Associated Press 1995). In Florida, nine guards beat an HIV-positive prison inmate after the inmate bit another guard. The inmate later attempted suicide and bled to death while chained naked to his bed in the psychiatric ward (Dougherty 1998). Some criminal justice workers have claimed a "right to know" the names of all known HIV-positive suspects and offenders.

Experiences reported by gay police officers suggest that bias may be extended to colleagues as well. Some gay police officers have reported a reluctance to disclose that they are gay for fear that fellow officers will not help them if they are injured (Leinen 1993). A Miami police officer assumed to be HIV-positive was assigned to front desk duty when administrators became afraid for his safety. Three weeks later, he was teargassed in a restricted area of the police station. He eventually resigned from the police department and charged the Miami Beach Police Department with discrimination (Buhrke 1996). Officers' fears and prejudices have resulted in failure to administer first aid and people being forced to undergo unwarranted antibody testing.

Educational programs and departmental policies are one means of addressing criminal justice workers' fears and sometimes inappropriate responses. Most training programs and policies, however, are focused more on protecting officers against infection than promoting the humane treatment of people with HIV. Most agencies have developed educational programs and policies because of legal requirements (e.g., mandates from the Occupational Safety and Hazard Administration) and a desire to protect personnel (Edwards and Tewksbury 1996). A 1996 study found that only 10 percent of agencies, for example, cited a desire to treat citizens with HIV/AIDS fairly as a reason for developing an HIV/AIDS-related policy. Similarly, while twenty-nine agencies had policies addressing how to handle a person with HIV, only nine of these policies addressed the employment of people with HIV.

ASSESSING THE THREAT

Because AIDS is fatal and currently incurable, people are rightly concerned about it and should take all appropriate measures to avoid contracting it. It is also appropriate that the seriousness of the epidemic be publicly acknowledged so that it can be combated effectively. Proper public education about HIV and AIDS can do much to counteract hysteria and attendant discrimination against those who are infected—and help people develop a more realistic sense of their risk of contracting HIV.

HIV/AIDS poses a serious and complex set of challenges for the criminal justice system. Future policy-making and research efforts should consider harm reduction strategies, as the evidence is growing that zero tolerance approaches are less effective than public health approaches in reducing the spread of HIV among injection drug users, sex workers, and homeless and runaway youth (Tucker 1999). While many medical advances have been made in the treatment of HIV infection, room for improvement remains to ensure that people's privacy rights are protected and that the criminal justice system's response to HIV is based on the best available epidemiological information rather than prejudice and fear.

—*Jeanne Flavin*

Further Reading

Associated Press. (1995). "Officer Wished for Man's Death: Suspect Suffocated in Police Custody." *Houston Chronicle,* November 2.

Bamberger, Joshua D. (2000). "Issues in HIV Postexposure Prophylaxis." *Bulletin of Experimental Treatments for AIDS* (Summer).

Bamberger, Joshua D., C. R. Waldo, and J .L. Gerberding. (1999). "Postexposure Prophylaxis for Human Immunodeficiency Virus (HIV) Infection Following Sexual Assault." *American Journal of Medicine* 106, 3: 323–326.

Buhrke, Robin A. (1996). *A Matter of Justice: Lesbians and Gay*

Men in Law Enforcement. New York: Routledge.

Burgess, Ann W., Barbara S. Jacobsen, Timothy Baker, Joyce Thompson, and Christine Grant. (1992). "Workplace Fear of Acquired Immunodeficiency Syndrome." *Journal of Emergency Nursing* 18, 3: 233–238.

Centers for Disease Control and Prevention. (1997). "Transmission of HIV Possibly Associated with Exposure of Mucous Membrane to Contaminated Blood." *Morbidity and Mortality Weekly Report* 46, 27: 620

———. (1998). "Management of Possible Sexual, Injecting-Drug-Use, or Other Nonoccupational Exposure to HIV, Including Considerations Related to Antiretroviral Therapy." *Morbidity and Mortality Weekly Report* 47, RR17: 1–14.

Clatts, Michael C., W. Rees Davis, J. L. Sotheran, and Aylin Atillasoy. (1998). "Correlates and Distribution of HIV Risk Behaviors among Homeless Youths in New York City: Implications for Prevention and Policy." *Child Welfare* 77, 2: 195–207.

Cooper, Michael. (1998). "Report of an Anti-Gay Slur Prompts Chaplain to Retire." *New York Times*, May 6, sec. B.

Dougherty, L. (1998). "9 Guards Indicted in Beating." *St. Petersburg Times*, July 11.

Edwards, Terry D., and Richard Tewksbury. (1996). "HIV/AIDS: State Police Training Practices and Personnel Policies." *American Journal of Police* 15, 1: 45–62.

Flavin, Jeanne. (1998). "Police and HIV/AIDS: The Risk, the Reality, the Response." *American Journal of Criminal Justice* 23, 1: 33–58.

Goldfein, Ronda B., and Catherine Hanssens. (1996). "Protecting HIV-Positive Workers: Whose Act Is It Anyway?" *Trial* (February) 32, 2: 26–31.

Gostin, Lawrence O. (1996). *The AIDS Litigation Project II: A Look at HIV/AIDS in the Courts of the 1990s*. Washington, DC: Georgetown University Law Center.

Gostin, Lawrence O., Zita Lazzarini, Diane Alexander, Allan M. Brandt, Kenneth H. Mayer, and Daniel C. Silverman. (1994). "HIV Testing, Counseling, and Prophylaxis after Sexual Assault." *Journal of the American Medical Association* 27, 18: 136–144.

Hammett, Theodore M., Patricia Harmon, and Laura M. Maruschak. (1999). *1996–1997 Update: HIV/AIDS, STDs, and TB in Correctional Facilities*. NCJ 176344. Washington, DC: National Institute of Justice.

Hansen, Mark. (1998). "Can the Law Stop AIDS?" *ABA Journal* (May) 26: 28.

Hoffman, Richard E., Nancy Henderson, Kelly O'Keefe, and Rachel C. Wood. (1994). "Occupational Exposure to Human Immunodeficiency Virus (HIV)-Infected Blood in Denver, Colorado, Police Officers." *American Journal of Epidemiology* 139, 9: 910–917.

Kilpatrick, D.G., C. Edmunds, and A. Seymour. (1992). *Rape in America: A Report to the Nation*. Arlington, VA: National Center for Victims of Crime; Charleston, SC: Medical University of South Carolina, Crime Victims Research and Treatment Center.

Leinen, Stephen. (1993). *Gay Cops*. New Brunswick, NJ: Rutgers University Press.

Maruschak, Laura M. (2001). *HIV in Prisons, 1999*. NCJ 187456. Washington, DC: Bureau of Justice Statistics.

Miller, Maureen. (1999). "A Model to Explain the Relationship between Sexual Abuse and HIV Risk among Women." *AIDS Care* 11, 1: 3–20.

Mirken, Bruce. (1998). "Post-Exposure Prophylaxis: Still More Questions than Answers." *Bulletin of Experimental Treatments for AIDS* (October): 29–32.

Richman, Katherine M., and Leland S. Rickman. (1993). "The Potential for Transmission of Human Immunodeficiency Virus through Human Bites." *Journal of AIDS* 6, 4: 402–406.

Ryan, Caitlin, and Donna Futterman. (1997). *Lesbian and Gay Youths: Care and Counseling*. Philadelphia: Hanley and Belfus, Inc.

Tucker, Jalie. (1999). "From Zero Tolerance to Harm Reduction." *National Forum* 79, 4: 19–23.

Whitehorn, Laura. (2000). "America's Most Unwanted." *POZ* (September) 62: 44–49.

HOMELESS MEN AND CRIME

Homeless men are a diverse group. They include those whose economic resources or behaviors make it difficult to obtain housing, as well as those who choose to be homeless. Depending on the historical period, Americans have labeled these men as vagrants, hoboes, tramps, bums, migrants, skidrowers, urban nomads, and the displaced. At times, scholars, the general public, and the homeless themselves have emphasized differences between these men, debating the characteristics that distinguish, for example, a hobo from a migrant; at other times people have simply grouped these people together and called them the homeless.

VAGRANTS

One of the earliest conceptualizations of the homeless was that of the vagrant. Vagrants were typically defined as people who had no visible means of support and who traveled from area to area. They were a concern in England as early as 370 CE, but laws against vagrancy reached a pinnacle in the fourteenth through sixteenth centuries. In this period, the harsh penalties for vagrancy included whipping, branding, years of servitude, and death. Vagrancy laws and the punishments they inflicted reflected the respective interests of the crown, landowners, the church, towns and cities, and industry in restricting the movement of people. Although these groups described vagrants as being responsible for an array of crimes—from theft to highway robbery, assault, and murder—a lack of historical data makes it difficult to assess the veracity of these claims.

Vagrancy was also prohibited in the thirteen colonies, and this prohibition became state law in most of the country; in some states, these laws survived well into the twentieth century. For example, as late as the 1930s, Mississippi police were paid $2.50 for each vagrant arrested. Vagrants were then fined $75, and many were forced to work out their fine at 20 cents a day. Consistent with earlier perceptions, U.S. legislators typically claimed that vagrants were responsible for crimes other than vagrancy, although they also lacked systematic data to substantiate this charge.

HOBOES, TRAMPS, AND BUMS

The Civil War displaced an unprecedented number of Americans; waves of immigration and economic collapse in the 1860s through the 1900s added to these numbers. As a result, breadlines, soup kitchens, shelters, and other emergency services were commonplace throughout the northern United States after 1865. For example, Brooklyn and Boston each provided relief to almost fifty thousand people in the mid-1870s. Although most of these people were local residents, unemployment and poverty forced an increasing number of people to leave their homes in search of a better life. These people often slept in the woods near cities and towns or established more permanent encampments called jungles. In 1873, there were an estimated thirty-eight thousand homeless people in the United States; by 1890 the number had increased to forty-five thousand. The popular press, government, and concerned public offered opposing views of these people: At times the homeless were described as victims of larger economic forces in need of support; alternatively, they were labeled tramps and portrayed as criminals who threatened the well-being of towns and cities and their inhabitants. By 1900, more than twenty states passed tramp laws that restricted these people's movements and encampments.

In 1923, sociologist Nels Anderson published *The Hobo: The Sociology of the Homeless Man*. In this influential book, Anderson drew on his own experiences as a migrant worker and hobo, as well as interviews he conducted with homeless men in Chicago. He concluded that, although typologies create boundaries that do not always exist, homeless men could be divided into five types: (1) the seasonal worker, (2) the transient worker or hobo, (3) the tramp who travels and works only when convenient, (4) the bum who seldom works or travels, and (5) the home guard who does not migrate from and works sporadically where homeless men congregate (i.e., "Hobohemia"). Anderson argued that several conditions cause men to become homeless, ranging from unemployment and seasonal work to personal crises and wanderlust.

Anderson did not use his typology of homeless men in his discussion of crime, except to suggest that the seasonal worker is the least likely to offend. Instead, he described an array of legal and illegal activities that homeless men adopt to "get by." The most frequent crimes committed by the homeless involved alcohol (e.g., public intoxication or drinking during Prohibition). Some men also struggled with cocaine or morphine addictions, but the secrecy of drug use makes it difficult to ascertain the extent of drug addiction in this period. The paucity of data notwithstanding, Anderson suggested that drug addicts were more likely to become "criminals" than were hoboes, who, Anderson claimed, were "not clever enough to be first-class crooks nor daring enough to be classified as criminals" (1923: 51).

Other common offenses committed by the homeless included grafts, stealing, and "jack-rolling" (i.e., stealing from a drunk man or assaulting him in order to rob him). Popular grafts included soliciting for charities, then pilfering valuables from the donations; faking medical maladies (e.g., deafness) or membership in associations (e.g., unions, ex-serviceman) to obtain benefits; and making fraudulent claims about goods in order to inflate their prices (e.g., when selling jewelry). Some hoboes also stole. Anderson argued that most of this theft was minor (typically involving the theft of food or clothing) and often consisted of victimizing other homeless men. Although hoboes and tramps spoke heatedly against picking pockets and jack-rolling, Anderson concluded that, "there are few [tramps] who would overlook an opportunity to take a few dollars from a 'drunk' seeing that he was in the possession of money that someone else was bound to take sooner or later" (1923: 52). Finally, Anderson noted that some hoboes, albeit only a minority, sold themselves for sex. Consistent with the prevailing attitudes of his time, Anderson referred to these men as "perverts" and "homos" who engaged in sex acts prohibited in the 1920s (i.e., homosexual sex). He noted that many of these men preyed upon younger men, offering them protection, shelter, and other necessities (and comforts) in exchange for sex. He surmised that although coercion probably happened in some situations, it is unlikely that it occurred in all of them.

Moreover, Anderson argued that, to some extent, homosexual practices "arise almost inevitably" in single-sex groups.

MIGRANT WORKERS

The conceptualization of homelessness changed dramatically during the Great Depression. By 1933, the U.S. government estimated that there were between one and two million homeless Americans. Although some of these people resembled the hoboes and tramps of earlier periods, the majority took to the roads in search of work. In 1936, the celebrated criminologist Edwin Sutherland and his colleague Harvey Locke studied the lives of twenty thousand homeless men who lived in Chicago relief shelters. Sutherland and Locke provided few details of these men's involvement in crime; however, Sutherland later drew upon this research in his work on professional thieves. He argued that a crisis, particularly an economic one, was a key factor in the development of a career in theft. Although arrests decreased throughout the Depression, Joan Crouse's 1986 study of the "homeless transient" in New York State in the 1930s suggested that many of the homeless broke the law. Drawing on the small number of available testimonies of homeless men from this period, Crouse argued that an unknown number of men, made desperate by want, stole food and money, and exchanged sex for these necessities.

SKID ROWERS

Skid row refers to a distinct part of a city where businesses (e.g., bars, pawnshops, and dilapidated rooming houses and hotels) serve the homeless. These areas have existed in the United States at least since the end of the Civil War, and many migrant workers and people labeled hoboes, tramps, and bums have stayed on skid row at some point. In the years after World War II however, "skid rowers" were increasingly seen as a unique group of men. In this period, the term *homeless,* which once described the vagrant classes as a whole, was typically applied specifically to the unattached (i.e., single) and often alcoholic males who lived on skid row.

As with works on other homeless men, most scholarly studies of skid row do not discuss offending in any great detail; indeed, the more common approach has been to focus on arrest and imprisonment as a means of controlling the homeless. In an ethnography of the Minneapolis skid row, Samuel Wallace found that most men on skid row were arrested not for crimes but for behaviors that, if undertaken in private, would not lead to arrest. Thus, most homeless men were arrested for drinking, urinating, sleeping, asking for money, and loitering in public places. Wallace also noted that these men were frequently the victims of crime and faced increased risk of theft and assault, including victimization by the police. In order to assess the veracity of skid rowers' reports that the police rob them, Wallace pretended to be drunk and sleeping on the street. He was arrested and robbed by the police officers on duty, one of whom remarked, "They'll never know the difference, and nobody will believe 'em anyhow" (1965: 97). Wallace did not provide any information on offending by skid rowers. Indeed, he went as far as to claim that the skid rower "does not even steal" and that these men's lives "involve little violence" within their community (1965: 99, 144).

James Spradley's (1970) ethnography of skid rowers in the Seattle area offered further details of skid row men's victimization at the hands of the police. Spradley acknowledged that many skid rowers may exaggerate police victimization or deny their own violent behavior; thus he relied on reports of witnesses, as well as the testimonies of victims. He described assaults on street corners, in squad cars ("paddy wagons"), in police station elevators, and in holding cells. Spradley concluded that police often used excessive force when dealing with the men from skid row. Moreover, he reported that the police often arrested skid rowers without just cause, incarcerating them for being drunk, disorderly, or vagrant when they were not. In contrast to Wallace, Spradley provided some material on homeless men's offending; noting that many skid rowers assaulted each other, shoplifted, and engaged in other petty crimes. However, he suggested that these infractions were infrequent and rarely led to arrest. Instead, skid rowers were arrested because they were homeless "urban nomads," rather than for their behavior.

Jaqueline Wiseman's (1970) study of a California city provided the most detail on skid row crime. She argued that skid rowers' financial resources were often inadequate for obtaining food, shelter and other daily requirements, including alcohol. Thus, many men resorted to illegal means of obtaining the money they needed. According to Wiseman, skid rowers often stole, but typically attempted only petty theft. She argued that they had neither the equipment nor the organizational abilities to complete robberies or burglaries. Moreover, most of these men avoided felonies because they feared lengthy jail sentences that would interfere with their access to alcohol. Instead, skid rowers preferred stealing inexpensive, easily transportable, and sellable items from other skid row inhabitants, local stores and unlocked vehicles. These victims were unlikely to report their loss to the police, and, if they did, were unlikely to have their case investigated. Wiseman also noted that some men claimed that other skid rowers—not themselves—sold homosexual sex to young servicemen, gay men and other homeless males.

HOMELESS MEN AT THE END OF THE TWENTIETH CENTURY

In the 1980s, the United States witnessed a dramatic rise in the number of homeless people and a corresponding increase in academic interest in this population. Indeed, as Anne Shlay and Peter Rossi (1992) have noted, at least sixty local and national studies of homelessness in the United States were conducted between 1981 and 1988; however, the majority of these provided little detailed information on crime. An important exception is the study done by David Snow and Leon Anderson (1993) on homelessness in Austin, Texas. Snow and Anderson analyzed police records and found support for some of the conclusions by earlier, less systematic studies of the homeless. Consistent with earlier research, Snow and Anderson reported that about 80 percent of homeless adult male arrests were for substance use and public order offenses (e.g., trespassing). This rate was about six times higher than the rate for the non-homeless. They also found that only a small percentage of homeless men's arrests were for more serious crimes. Notwithstanding this low level of involvement, Snow and Anderson noted that the homeless' arrest rate for serious crimes exceeded the arrest rate of the non-homeless; the property crime arrest rate among homeless adult males was more than 35 percent higher than the rate for males with a permanent address, and their arrest rate for violent crime was about 24 percent higher.

RESEARCH DIRECTIONS

Studies of several historical periods indicate that homeless men have engaged in several types of crime more frequently and had considerably higher arrest rates than people who were housed. However, the majority of these arrests were for minor, public ordinance offenses involving substance use or behaviors (e.g., sleeping,

urinating) that would not warrant arrest if conducted in private. The homeless have also been charged more frequently with property and violent offenses; many of these offenses involve other homeless people or the businesses that cater to them, but other people and businesses were also victimized. John Hagan and Bill McCarthy's 1997 research on homeless youth indicated that many youth committed crimes before they left home; however, inadequate food, shelter, and income, as well as other indignities of homelessness, increased offending among these youth and encouraged others to begin offending. The same patterns likely occur for homeless men, but subsequent research will need to verify this.

—Bill McCarthy and John Hagan

See also HOMELESS WOMEN AND CRIME; POVERTY; VAGRANCY

Further Reading

Anderson, Nels. (1923). *The Hobo: The Sociology of the Homeless Man*. Chicago: University of Chicago Press.

———. (1940). *Men on the Move*. Chicago: University of Chicago Press.

Crouse, Joan M. (1986). *The Homeless Transient in the Great Depression: New York State, 1929–1941*. Albany: State University of New York Press.

Hagan, John, and Bill McCarthy. (1997). *Mean Streets: Youth Crime and Homelessness*. New York: Cambridge University Press.

Shlay, Anne B., and Peter H. Rossi. (1992). "Social Science Research and Contemporary Studies of Homelessness." *Annual Review of Sociology* 18: 129–160.

Snow, David A., and Leon Anderson. (1993). *Down on Their Luck: A Study of Homeless People*. Berkeley: University of California Press.

Spradley, James P. (1970). *You Owe Yourself a Drunk: An Ethnography of Urban Nomads*. Boston: Little, Brown.

Sutherland, Edwin H., and Harvey J. Locke. (1936). *Twenty Thousand Homeless Men: A Study of Unemployed Men in the Chicago Shelters*. Chicago and Philadelphia: J. B. Lippincott Company.

Wallace, Samuel E. (1965). *Skid Row as a Way of Life*. Totowa, NJ: The Bedminister Press.

Wiseman, Jaqueline P. (1970). *Stations of the Lost: The Treatment of Skid Row Alcoholics*. Englewood Cliffs, NJ: Prentice-Hall.

▼ HOMELESS WOMEN AND CRIME

"Homeless women," "shopping-bag ladies," or "urban transient females" are labels used for women who have no established residence, wander idly from place to place without visible means of support, and are living on the streets due to a situational housing problem. As with homeless men, these women are considered to be members of the penniless segment of society, with local variations in lifestyle and in relative numbers; they are found in all major cities in the United States and other nations in both the developed and developing world.

There is no way to determine the true number of these types of homeless women in the United States; an accurate measure does not exist, and all figures are estimates. Estimates from the 1990 U.S. Census indicate that there are 282,372 homeless people in the United States, and approximately 25 percent are female. Coston (1989) believes that there are fewer homeless women because the U.S. social system is used more by females than by males. The majority (71 percent) of recorded homeless females live in major cities, 21 percent are in the suburbs and the urban fringe, and 9 percent occupy rural areas. Compared with all U.S. adults, the female homeless are disproportionately black non-Hispanics (U.S. Housing and Urban Development 1996). The racial or ethnic makeup of homeless people does not differ according to family status. Thirty-eight percent of single homeless females have dropped out of high school, and although 34 percent of them have a high school diploma, fewer than 25 percent have any education beyond high school (U.S. Housing and Urban Development 1996). Homeless females are less educated than the mainstream adult population of females in the United States, based on the finding that "only 25% of American adults have less than a high school education, 34% have a high school diploma, and 45% have some education beyond high school" (U.S. Housing and Urban Development 1996: 2).

Literature regarding homeless women is scarce and runs the gamut from newspaper articles and essays to dramatized pictorials of these women. The few ethnographic and scientific survey research articles have focused on their lifestyle characteristics, including, but not limited to, their modes of survival, reasons for living on the streets, interactions with the police, worries, criminal victimization experiences, use of protective behaviors, and fear of crime.

FACTORS LEADING TO HOMELESSNESS

Homelessness has been recognized as a significant social problem in the United States for many years. In the early 1980s, when homelessness gained promi-

nence as a social phenomenon, the views of the issues it posed were relatively simple. Some researchers believed that the problem was temporary, due to the recession from 1981 to 1982, and that the problem would go away when the economy recovered; others believed that homelessness arose from a shortage of decent, low-cost housing and that the homeless represented a cross-section of poor Americans. Over the past twenty years, however, researchers and practitioners have suggested more complex explanations for homelessness among women (Martin 1983; Coston 1989; Wright 1989).

Based on the limited research, it appears that homelessness results from an accumulation of difficulties, and while there appears to be an array of significant contributing factors, there is no common route to homelessness beyond extreme poverty and the absence of stable housing (Blau 1993). The route to homelessness appears to be a gradual process rather than an abrupt occurrence (Coston 1989; Barak 1992). The reasons for homelessness are "rooted in the political economy of the nation; at another level, it is a consequence of various personal pathologies and failings" (Wright 1989: 76).

Within this constellation of factors, analysts have discovered three widespread conditions that appear to be universal identifiers along the road to homelessness: extreme poverty, high levels of disabilities of all sorts, and an excessive degree of social isolation (Coston 1993; Barak 1992). Rossi (1989) and Coston (1989) make a distinction between the "literal homeless," or those who have no home to go to, and the precariously housed—those who have a tenuous hold on housing of the lowest quality. They also report that some of the homeless suffer homelessness in episodes over the years, while others suffer homelessness for long periods of time.

People become homeless because they are extremely poor and cannot find or cannot compete for the limited supply of low-cost decent housing. When housing costs absorb anywhere from 70 to 80 percent or more of the average income, and the person or family is below, at, or slightly above the poverty line, there may not be an alternative to homelessness. Analysts appear to agree that some women can avoid homelessness by relying on family and friends, or the volunteer sector, to provide them with the essentials that their incomes alone cannot. The constant increase in rates for rental apartments and single-occupancy hotel rooms can result in eviction for eventual nonpayment, forcing people into homeless-

Abuse and Homelessness

In the following extract, Maria, a homeless woman, recounts how violence and abuse drove her out of her home, a common scenario for many homeless women.

When I was thirteen, my stepfather raped me. I ran away, but each time my mother would find me and bring me back. I ran away nine or ten times, and each time my mother would find me and punish me. So I went to stay with my father when I was fifteen, only he beat me. My mother was an alcoholic but she didn't beat me. I stayed with my father for a while, but he was beating me. Then I ran away again. From the time I was sixteen or seventeen, I have boyfriends, and they hit me. I was introduced to crack by a boyfriend when I was twenty, and I got hooked real bad. I have been prostituting since I was twenty-three, selling myself on the Avenue. My boyfriend was killed in my arms, a bullet grazed my face. I don't want to live like that. I was in [the city jail], in the OPTIONS program, for drugs and alcohol. They had all different kinds of classes—about being raped in the street, about being raped in your family. I needed both of those classes. It's a real good unit—help you out a lot.

Source: Hirsch, Amy E. (1999). *"Some Days Are Harder Than Hard": Welfare Reform and Women with Drug Convictions in Pennsylvania.* Washington, DC: Center for Law and Social Policy, p. 14.

ness. Those who do not have networks such as those mentioned above on which to rely will likely become homeless, particularly given that over the past twenty years, the United States has witnessed a disintegration of the nuclear family and its networks.

Alcohol and drug abuse, a general inability to manage one's finances, chronic mental illness, and chronically poor physical health have also been implicated in the process of becoming a homeless woman (Wertlieb et al. 1987; Coston 1989). Cumulatively, it appears that a combination of personal and structural problems is responsible for homelessness among women.

MODES OF SURVIVAL

Homeless women rely upon a combination of strategies for surviving on the streets (Martin 1983; Coston 1989). Homeless women rely most often on shelters and soup kitchens for food. However, some homeless women report buying their own food after receiving monthly welfare checks via general delivery at the post office, while others panhandle for food money from passersby. There are reports of women who rely primarily on the kindness of passersby for food, as well as of those who sift through refuse or receive leftover food from fast food restaurants at closing time.

Strategies for sleeping include using abandoned buildings or sleeping on the streets. Other sleeping locations include cheap hotel rooms or shelters provided by the government or charitable organizations. Some homeless women sleep on moving buses, trains, or subway cars, in transit stations, or on park benches. Another place to bed down is the steam tunnels located under subway systems. No matter which sleeping place is used, homeless women have very restless nights. Lack of rest is one of the reasons, along with lack of proper nutrition, for the swollen, ulcerated feet and legs that plague homeless women.

Homeless women normally do not have health insurance. When they are in need of medical attention, they can go to a shelter or treat themselves in local public restrooms. For emergency situations, homeless women can be treated at the emergency rooms in public hospitals. Some homeless women maintain cleanliness by relying on shelters for showers and clean clothes, while others bathe in the bathrooms of department stores or in various transportation depots. Paradoxically, some homeless women might not want to bathe regularly, or rid themselves of afflictions like lice, because being dirty or unattractive provides some protection from being preyed upon by thieves and other would-be tormentors. Based upon available research, some homeless women are lonely, but the fear of being criminally victimized or ignored keeps them from reaching out to others (Martin 1983).

There appears to be an immense communication network of homeless women assisting other homeless women with their knowledge of available resources. These women readily supply other homeless women with knowledge, based on their own experiences, of methods of survival (Coston 1989). Although they rely upon networks of information, beyond this point there is no real sense of camaraderie. These women appear to be true isolates.

TYPES OF HOMELESS WOMEN

Coston (1989) identifies four basic types of homeless women, but allows that the list might not be exhaustive. What all these women have in common is an inability to deal adequately (by society's standards, not their own) with severe personal problems.

1. The *full-time homeless woman* is the type of homeless woman whom people most often think of as being a "bag lady." She has lived on the streets for a long period of time and is usually seen carrying shopping bags or pushing a shopping cart piled high with her possessions. Her swollen, ulcerated legs and feet are often prominent, as well as her clothing of various textures and designs. For the full-time homeless woman, this is a permanent state of existence, perhaps for all of her life.

2. The *part-time homeless woman* lives a precarious existence, with housing but perhaps no money for food. She relies on shelters for food or for bathroom facilities, which she might not have in her dwelling.

3. The *situational homeless woman* is only on the streets temporarily. She could be going through a divorce or receiving treatment for substance abuse. These women often go unnoticed by the public; they have been known to curl their hair at night and wear makeup.

4. The *mentally troubled homeless woman* is someone who has become mentally ill while living on the streets, or has been deinstitutionalized from a mental hospital without the appropriate resources to help her gradually reintegrate into society.

CRIMINAL VICTIMIZATION, VULNERABILITY, FEAR OF CRIME, AND USE OF PROTECTIVE DEVICES

Living on the streets is very dangerous. Homeless women are a subgroup within the United States who are at high risk for criminal victimization. Research indicates that homeless women who have not been victims of crime perceive their vulnerability to crime to be less than those who have been victimized (Weinstein 1980; Weinstein 1984; Perloff 1983; Coston 1993). This lower perception of vulnerability by nonvictims may be harmful to the women themselves, as they may be less able to cope if they are victimized (Perloff 1983). Compared to the general population's perception of victimization risk, homeless women's self-estimates of risk are 75 percent higher (Ennis 1967; Miethe 1984; Coston and Fickenauer 1993). The great majority of homeless women (95 percent) have reported being the victims of several types of criminal acts (Coston and Finckenauer 1993). These women are often robbed, frequently in combination with being raped or assaulted; some have even been burglarized in the makeshift boxes that they call home.

Fear of crime, one of the daily concerns faced by these women, is shared by many urban dwellers; but in the case of homeless women, this fear could be amplified by their greater exposure to risk. Researchers have found that, overall, homeless women consider their victimization risk high; however, when asked how much they worry about becoming victims, they report that they are generally not worried (Coston and Finckenauer 1993). There are several reasons for this paradox. First, perceiving vulnerability is different from fearing vulnerability; arriving at a self-perception of vulnerability requires rational thought or logic, not fear, which is an emotion. Second, research shows that perhaps homeless women have other concerns that are more important: finding food and a safe place to sleep (Hanrahan 1990). Coston's (1993) research reports that homeless women's worries about being criminally victimized ranked third in their order of worries.

Homeless women may avoid certain places and may carry weapons while living on the streets (Martin 1983; Coston and Finckenauer 1993). Ironically, the places you might most expect to find them are those avoided due to the threat of victimization: places where drugs are used, bought, or sold; unfamiliar places; abandoned buildings; places where prostitutes hang out; overcrowded places; deserted area, and parks. Types of weapons carried for self-defense include chemicals such as lye, ammonia, rubbing alcohol, or hair spray, as well as knives, scissors, cloth bags with rocks in them, lead pipes, and even guns. In some instances, homeless women rely on previous training in martial arts as their weapon, or they rely on faith in God to protect them.

Many cities that have a substantial number of homeless are located in the northern United States, where during the harsh winter months, local government policies require that the police forcibly remove the homeless from the streets and place them in a shelter (Blau 1993). Police treatment can be uneven in quality. Occasionally, the police will harass these women because they seek refuge in transportation centers or on the vehicles themselves. At times, the police will allow them to use the restroom facilities late at night, but they do not like them to sleep or rest (whether in plain sight or not) in any public place, particularly at times when there are crowds in public places, as during elections or parades. If by chance they do fall asleep in one of these places, it is not unusual, according to many of these women, for a police officer to wake them up and throw them out. This act often results in a variety of altercations between the police and homeless women, which can range from a simple verbal exchange to vulgarity or even a physical fight. Police officers have also been known to check on homeless women while walking their beat, since the women are easy prey for criminals.

POLICY RECOMMENDATIONS

Budgetary cutbacks in both the public and private sectors have left the problems of homelessness inadequately addressed. This problem is made worse by jurisdictional disputes between city and state agencies. Cities claim to need monetary assistance from the state, and states often believe that paying for solutions to homelessness are the responsibility of local government.

To improve the situation of homeless women and to reduce their high level of victimization, several major changes are required. First, if one accepts that shelter is a basic human right, it is then the responsibility of cities to provide separate, quality, public shelters for both men and women. Smaller shelters should also be provided in order for mental health and social workers to expand their services. The specific roles of states should be to supplement funding for those projects, such as shelters and mobile food canteens, that only cities can adequately carry out.

Second, mental health professionals need to be more careful in making decisions about releasing people from institutions. They should make sure that every patient who is released has a secure residence. In addition, the mental health profession should make sure it has qualified professionals available for service in facilities that cater to homeless women.

Third, social service agencies need to provide special assistance to homeless women. This special assistance involves helping them apply for benefits, gather lost or stolen documents, complete necessary forms, and solve problems that may arise. A major problem to be dealt with is the delayed, discontinued, or reduced welfare check. For the mentally disabled on the streets, therapeutic and survival imperatives are linked; they cannot learn basic life skills without addressing their mental challenges.

Fourth, assistance, whenever possible, should also come from individual citizens and the volunteer sector. Homeless women, although they elicit a more sympathetic response than homeless men, still face public attitudes that are laced with fear and suspicion.

If physical assistance cannot be given, then at least the general public needs to develop an overall understanding of the state of homelessness and become conscious of it as a problem.

Generally, the criminal justice system cannot provide adequate service for homeless women; it is barely equipped to efficiently handle the subculture of serious criminal offenders. However, law enforcement can best aid homeless women by becoming aware of their plight, so they can protect them from victimization and maintain a safe environment for them. Finally, the overall approach to dealing with homelessness should be one that views it as a temporary problem and provides services only to a level that does not make it an attractive lifestyle. Shelters should be opened and more services offered, but these acts should be to alleviate suffering; the ultimate goal should be to help homeless women resolve their situation.

—Charisse T. M. Coston

See also POVERTY; PROSTITUTION; WOMEN AS VICTIMS

Further Reading

Barak, Gregory. (1992). *Gimme Shelter: A Social History of Homelessness in Contemporary America.* New York: Praeger Publishers.

Blau, Joel. (1993). *The Visible Poor: Homelessness in the U.S.* New York: Oxford University Press.

Coston, Charisse. (1982). *The Original Designer Label: Prototypes of New York City's Shopping Bag Ladies.* Master's thesis. Newark, NJ: Rutgers University, School of Criminal Justice.

———. (1989). "The Original Designer Label: Prototypes of New York City's Shopping-bag Ladies." *Deviant Behavior* 10: 157–172.

———. (1993). "Worries about Crime: Rank-Ordering Survival Concerns among Urban Transient Females." *Deviant Behavior* 2, 2.

Coston, Charisse T. M., and James Finckenauer. (1993). "Fear of Crime among Vulnerable Populations: Homeless Women." *Journal of Social Distress* 2: 1–19.

Ennis, P.H. (1967). *Criminal Victimization in the United States: A Report of a National Survey.* Washington, DC: U.S. Government Printing Office.

Gordon, M. T., and S. Riger. (1989). *The Female Fear.* New York: The Free Press.

Hanrahan, K. J. (1990). "Exploring Fear of Crime among Elderly Urban Females." Ph.D. diss. Newark: State University of New Jersey at Rutgers.

Martin, M. (1983). *Strategies of Adaptation: Coping Strategies of the Urban Transient Female.* Ann Arbor, MI: Dissertation Abstracts.

Miethe, T. (1984). "Fear of Crime among Older People: A Reassessment of the Predictive Power of Crime-Related Factors." *Sociological Quarterly* 16: 397–414.

Perloff, L .D. (1983). "Perceptions of Vulnerability to Victimization." *Journal of Social Issues* 39: 41–61.

———. (1986). "Self-Other Judgements and Perceived Vulnerability to Victimization." *Journal of Personality and Social Psychology* 50: 502–510.

Riger, S., M. Gordon, and R. LeBailley. (1982). "Coping with Urban Crime: Women's Use of Precautionary Behaviors." *American Journal of Community Psychology* 3, 1: 17–29.

Rossi, P. H. (1989). *Down and Out in America: The Origins of Homelessness.* Chicago: University of Chicago Press.

U.S. Census Bureau. (1980). *Summary Characteristics of Social Economic and Housing.* Washington, DC: Government Printing Office.

———. (1990). *Characteristics of the Population.* Washington, DC: Government Printing Office.

U.S. Housing and Urban Development. (1996). *Annual Report.* Washington, DC: Government Printing Office.

Weinstein, N. D. (1980). "Unrealistic Optimism about Future Life Events." *Journal of Personality and Social Psychology* 39, 2: 806–820.

———. (1984). "Why It Won't Happen to Me: Perceptions of Risk Factors and Susceptibility." *Health Psychology* 3, 1: 431–457.

Wertlieb, D., C. Weigel, T. Springer, and M. Feldstein. (1987). "Locus of Control." *American Journal of Orthopsychiatry* 57, 2: 234–245.

Wright, J.D. (1989). *Address Unknown: The Homeless in America.* New York: de Gruyter.

▼ HOMICIDE AND MURDER

Murder and *homicide* are among the first terms to come to mind when Americans think about violent crime. Although both murder and homicide refer to instances in which one human being is killed by another, these terms are defined differently and evoke different responses from the legal system and society in general.

DEFINITIONS OF HOMICIDE AND MURDER

Both murder and homicide refer to instances in which one human being is killed by another. Murder and homicide are distinct, however, in that *murder* refers to incidents in which a killing is defined as criminal and wrongful by the legal system, whereas *homicide* is broader and more encompassing. It includes incidents in which a killing is criminal and also incidents in which a killing is defined as justifiable by the legal system. According to the Federal Bureau of Investigation (FBI), a homicide is justifiable if a person is killed by a private citizen or by a law enforcement officer in the line of duty while that person is in the course of committing a felony offense. Homicides can be distinguished in terms of whether they are criminal or noncriminal, with murder referring to instances of criminal

homicide, which are defined as unlawful or wrongful and *not* justifiable by the legal system.

An important point here is that not all incidents in which one person kills another are viewed as wrongful. Instead, through the voice of the state, society has said that, in certain circumstances, killing a human being is acceptable. As noted, a killing is justifiable if it involves self-defense or the killing of a person committing a felony. Killing another human being also is defined as acceptable if it occurs in the context of war and the victim is not an innocent civilian, but instead poses a threat, such as is likely the case if the victim is an armed enemy. Finally, killing is also deemed acceptable in the case of the death penalty and executions.

CRIMINAL HOMICIDE AND DEGREES OF MURDER

Although specific definitions of criminal homicide vary across jurisdictions, there are basically three types of unlawful killings. The most serious form of criminal homicide is *first-degree murder,* which has the defining characteristics of premeditation and malice aforethought. Premeditation refers to the offender having an intent to kill the victim prior to the occurrence of the incident, and typically implies that the offender engaged in some degree of planning the murder. Malice aforethought refers to the deliberate intention to kill another person (and not merely harm or injure them). In addition to incidents involving premeditation and malice aforethought, first-degree murders also include killings that fall under the felony-murder rule (FMR). According to the FMR, if a person (other than the offender) is killed during the course of, or as a result of, the offender committing a felony, the offender and his or her accomplices can be charged with first-degree murder even if the killing is accidental or unintentional. Courts generally agree that the FMR should only apply to "inherently dangerous" felonies; however, there are differences in how the term *dangerous* is defined, as some courts make a determination by examining the facts of the particular case, while others use a more abstract definition and note that certain felonies are "dangerous" (e.g., rape, robbery, burglary, arson, and assault), but others that are theft-related (e.g., larceny) are not.

The second type of unlawful killing is *second-degree murder,* which involve malice aforethought—the intent to kill—but not premeditation. The classic example of a second-degree murder is if a man or woman were to come home unexpectedly and find his or her spouse with a lover, and then, in a fit of rage, were to grab a gun and kill both the spouse and the lover. As another example, if a fight broke out in a bar between two people who had been drinking heavily and one pulled a knife and fatally stabbed the other, this would constitute second-degree murder. In both cases, the intent to kill may have been present due to raging emotions, but the incident lacked premeditation.

The third type of unlawful killing is *manslaughter,* which lacks both premeditation and malice aforethought, and typically involves incidents where the death of the victim can be traced to the actions or negligence of the offender. An example of manslaughter is the accidental shooting of one hunter by another, who mistakes the victim for an animal at least in part because of the victim's failure to wear hunter's orange. Another example would be a person dying during or as a result of injuries sustained during an automobile accident caused by another person's reckless or drunk driving. Such a situation could be treated as murder, however, if the drunk driver had been on probation or banned from driving because of a prior drunk driving history.

INSTRUMENTAL VERSUS EXPRESSIVE LETHAL VIOLENCE

Related to the distinction between first- and second-degree murder is the idea that there are two types of murder. *Instrumental murders* are those committed as a means to an end or as a way of accomplishing some other goal, which means that they often involve prior planning or premeditation. For example, a person kills his or her spouse but plans the incident so that it looks like an accident in order to collect on a life insurance policy. In another example, the leader of a rival gang is targeted in order to send a message in a gangland turf war. By contrast, *expressive murders* are typically rooted in conflict and committed as an end in themselves with no other goal or purpose than hurting and/or killing the victim. Individuals commit these

murders largely during periods of extreme emotional duress, such as in a fit of anger or a jealous rage, which is why they frequently are called crimes of passion. The majority of these murders are expressive in nature and may involve an argument between intimate partners; a fight between friends, acquaintances, or neighbors; or even an altercation with a stranger in a bar or a parking lot.

SOURCES OF HOMICIDE DATA

There are two primary sources of data that researchers analyze in an attempt to gain a better understanding of the nature and extent of lethal violence in the United States. First, there are the *Uniform Crime Reports* (UCR), which are compiled by the FBI from reports that law enforcement agencies submit on homicides in their jurisdictions. The second source, commonly known as vital statistics data, is compiled by the National Center for Health Statistics from coroner and medical examiner reports. Although both police and vital statistics data began to be collected in the late 1800s and early 1900s for various cities and states, neither source of data became fully national until the early 1930s. Consequently, researchers studying historical trends in levels of violence in the United States, such as Roger Lane, Eric Monkonnen, and Ted Robert Gurr, have had to estimate historical violence rates based on areas where records were kept and by studying other types of historical documents (e.g., executions, newspaper accounts, and court records).

HISTORICAL TRENDS IN HOMICIDE RATES

According to UCR data, in 1997 there were an estimated 18,210 murders and nonnegligent manslaughters known to police, resulting in a murder rate of 6.8 per 100,000 persons. Vital statistics data are comparable, indicating that there were 19,846 homicides in 1997 and a homicide rate of 7.4 per 100,000. The numbers from the two sources are not exactly the same, because of the broader definition of homicide used in the compilation of vital statistics data. While vital statistics figures are always slightly higher than UCR numbers, the temporal trends exhibited by each are highly correlated with one another, meaning that they trend over time in the same direction.

Many people believe that contemporary levels of lethal violence far exceed levels of violence in the past. Although lethal violence rates did increase sharply

---

DID YOU KNOW...

In the United States, three types of unlawful killing are recognized by the federal government and the states: (1) first-degree murder, which involves premeditation and malice aforethought; (2) second-degree murder, which involves only malice aforethought; and (3) manslaughter, which involves neither.

from the mid-1960s to the early 1990s, they actually have receded in recent years. Furthermore, other periods in the history of the United States have been characterized by high violence rates. Historical studies have found evidence of a long downward trend in violence rates, at least since the 1700s, with the exception of surges beginning in the mid-1800s and the early 1900s. For example, in the early twentieth century, homicide rates increased from around 6.4 per 100,000 in 1900 to a high of 9.8 in 1933, with the sharpest increases coinciding with nationwide Prohibition (1920–1933). Although Prohibition diminished violence stemming from drunkenness, it spawned a new type associated with bootlegging and the rise of organized crime. The end of Prohibition marked the beginning of a decline in homicide rates, which reached a low of 4.5 per 100,000 in the mid-1950s. In the early 1960s, homicide rates began to climb steadily, reaching a peak of 10.7 per 100,000 in 1980, followed by a short lull, and then another increase peaking at 10.5 in 1991. Since then, homicide rates actually declined, and, by 1997, had reached a low of 6.8 per 100,000 persons.

In their research on homicide rates, researchers (e.g., Ted Robert Gurr, Roger Lane) have found that a variety of macrolevel factors are associated with trends in nineteenth- and twentieth-century homicide rates, including economic deprivation, immigration, alcohol consumption, prohibitionist legislation, divorce rates, involvement in wars, the age structure of the population, and the availability of medical and health care. It is important to remember, however, that the impact of these factors on violence rates is not unchanging over time. Instead, the effect each has on homicide rates is historically contextual, meaning that it varies over time and is shaped by the larger social and cultural context of society.

Less is known about violence rates of the more distant past, because few sources of information have been preserved over time. Using coroner and court records that have survived, however, Ted Robert Gurr has found evidence that violent death was not uncommon, especially during medieval times. In fact, homicide and murder rates may have been ten to twenty times higher than those at the end of the twentieth century. Gurr and other historical researchers, such as Roger Lane, have theorized that declining violence rates, especially during the nineteenth and early twentieth century, were a function of modernizing and civilizing influences that accompanied the Industrial Revolution. Cross-national comparisons are generally supportive of this view, in that homicide rates tend to be higher in less developed and economically deprived nations than in the more affluent, industrialized countries. However, the United States is a major exception, as homicide rates are consistently much higher in the United States than rates in other industrialized nations and often are higher even than those in underprivileged nations.

CORRELATES OF HOMICIDE OFFENDING AND VICTIMIZATION

Research on the demographic correlates of homicide indicate that members of certain social groups exhibit higher rates of homicide victimization and offending.

The Gender Gap

One of the most salient and persistent findings of homicide research is the gender gap, which refers to the disproportionate representation of males in both the victim and offender categories. More specifically, around three-quarters of homicide victims are males, while only about one-quarter are females, which is a pattern that has persisted over several decades. Although male and female rates of homicide victimization adhere to a similar pattern in terms of times when they are relatively high or low, victimization rates for males are consistently three to four times higher than those for females. For example, since the mid-1970s, the rate of victimization per 100,000 has ranged between 10.8 in 1997 and 16.3 in 1980 for males and between 3.0 in 1997 and 4.5 in 1980 for females.

The gender gap is present to an even greater degree in data on homicide offending. Arrest statistics indicate that, typically, 85 to 90 percent of homicide offenders are male. In 1997, 89.7 percent of the 12,764 persons arrested and charged with murder or nonnegligent manslaughter were male, while 10.3 percent were female. It is estimated that, in 1997, the rate of homicide offending was 14.1 per 100,000 for males and 1.5 for females. Rates of offending for males have consistently been five to ten times those for females since the mid-1970s. More specifically, estimated rates of offending for males increased from 16.3 in 1976 to 20.6 in 1980, declined to 15.2 in 1984–1985, began climbing and reached a high of 20.7 per 100,000 in 1991, and since then have decreased to current rates. The estimated rates for females exhibit fewer fluctuations and are characterized by a steady decline; they were 3.1 per 100,000 in 1976, 2.3 in 1986, and 1.7 in 1996. Regardless of changes in the status of women in society, homicide victimization and offending remain predominantly male spheres.

Disproportionate Minority Representation

Studies of racial/ethnic differences in homicide indicate that members of minority groups, African Americans in particular, are disproportionately represented in homicide statistics. According to UCR data for 1997, whites (including Hispanics) and African Americans each comprised slightly less than half (48 percent) of homicide victims. The remaining 4 percent of victims consisted of members of other racial/ethnic groups and cases in which the victim's race was unknown. The disproportionate representation of minorities among homicide victims is not new in that over the last thirty-five years, the proportion of African American homicide victims has ranged from a low of 41 percent in 1984 to a high of 55 percent in 1969–1971. Only figures since the mid-1960s are discussed, because information on the race of the victim from earlier decades has been questioned.

Looking at racial/ethnic differences in rates of victimization, the increased risk of victimization for minorities is even more apparent in that, since the mid-1970s, victimization rates for African Americans have been six to seven times those of whites. For example, in 1976, victimization rates per 100,000 were 5.2 for whites and 37.3 for African Americans. Ten years later in 1986, they were 5.4 and 31.5, respectively. Twenty years later in 1996, they had declined some to 4.4 for whites and 28.6 for African Americans.

Racial/ethnic minorities also are overrepresented in murder arrest statistics. In 1997, approximately 56 percent of the 12,759 persons arrested and charged with murder or nonnegligent manslaughter were African American, while around 42 percent were white (including Hispanics). The remaining 2 percent were members of other racial/ethnic groups. The disparity between African Americans and whites is even more apparent when rates of offending are examined. In 1997, the estimated rate of homicide offending for African Americans was 32.3 per 100,000, compared to 4.0 for whites. This represents a decrease from 1991, when the rates were 50.4 and 5.7, respectively. Although homicide offending had increased some for both African Americans and whites from 1976 to 1980, rates subsided for both groups in the mid-1980s before climbing to the high 1991 levels. Estimated

rates of homicide offending are currently lower for both whites and African Americans than they have been at any time since 1976.

Age Differences

In addition to sex and racial/ethnic differences, age differences also exist in rates of homicide victimization and offending. Risk of victimization increases during childhood and early adolescence and peaks in the late teen years and early adulthood. From there, victimization rates decline steadily throughout the remainder of the life cycle. This pattern is illustrated in the figures for 1997, which indicate victimization rates per 100,000 were 1.7 for persons thirteen and under, 7.5 for fourteen- to seventeen-year-olds, 19.7 for eighteen- to twenty-four-year-olds, 11.6 for twenty-five- to thirty-four-year-olds, 6.9 for thirty-five- to forty-nine-year-olds, and 3.2 for persons over fifty. This general pattern of age differences in the risk of victimization has persisted at least over the last several decades.

Similar to the risk of victimization, the likelihood of homicide offending is low during childhood, rises during adolescence, peaks during late adolescence and early adulthood, remains somewhat high in the late twenties and early thirties, and then declines throughout the remainder of the life span. For example, the following are estimates of homicide offending rates per 100,000 in 1997 for members of different age groups: .2 for persons thirteen and under, 16.5 for fourteen- to seventeen-year-olds, 33.2 for eighteen- to twenty-four-year-olds, 12.4 for twenty-five- to thirty-four-year-olds, 5.5 for thirty-five- to forty-nine-year-olds, and 1.7 for persons fifty and over.

Over the last several years, Americans have become increasingly concerned about rising youth violence rates. Although the proportion of persons under the age of eighteen arrested and charged with murder or nonnegligent manslaughter increased 10 percent from 1988 to 1997, the majority of persons charged with homicide are actually over the age of eighteen: 81 percent in 1997. In recent decades, the estimated levels of offending indicate that, for fourteen- to seventeen- and eighteen- to twenty-four-year-olds, rates had increased some from the mid-1970s to about 1980 when they were 12.9 and 29.5, respectively. They then declined until around 1984, at which point they began to rise, reaching their highest point since 1976 in 1993 at 30.2 and 41.3 per 100,000, respectively. In recent years, the rates for these two groups have declined significantly. There also have been more minor decreases in rates of offending for other age groups.

Victimization Rates

When we look at the demographic correlates of homicide victims and offenders, we see that, to a large extent, victims and offenders resemble each other in terms of sex, race/ethnicity, and age. More specifically, young males—especially young males who are members of minority groups—are disproportionately represented in data on both homicide victims and offenders. For example, in 1997, the homicide victimization rate for eighteen- to twenty-four-year-old African American males was 143.4 per 100,000. This figure is much higher than the comparable figures for eighteen- to twenty-four-year-old African American females (15.9), white males (15.1), and white females (3.5). A similar pattern exists for homicide offenders, according to estimates based on the characteristics of known offenders. For eighteen- to twenty-four-year-olds, the estimated rates for 1997 are 246.4 and 18.1 for African American males and females, respectively and 28.3 and 2.8 for white males and females, respectively. The disproportionate involvement of young, minority males in homicides is the subject of a significant amount of scholarly research. Although researchers disagree on their relative importance, explanations tend to focus on economic deprivation and barriers to social mobility, the presence of a subculture condoning the use of violence and aggression in certain social situations, and/or the lifestyles and routine activities of various social groups and how they are related to the risk of victimization.

WEAPONS

Since the mid-1960s, firearms have topped the list of weapons used in homicides, followed distantly by knives and other sharp/cutting instruments, personal weapons (e.g., hands, feet, fists), blunt objects (e.g., club, hammer), and other weapons. In every year since 1964, firearms have been the weapon used in more than half of all homicides, ranging from a low of 55 percent in 1964 to a high of 70 percent in 1993 and 1994. The increase in the use of firearms is mirrored in a decrease in the use of knives and cutting instruments, from around 24 percent in the mid-1960s to 13 percent in 1997. The use of both personal weapons and blunt objects has been fairly consistent over this time, with the former used in 7 to 10 percent and the latter in 4 to 6 percent of homicides each year.

VICTIM-OFFENDER RELATIONSHIP AND CIRCUMSTANCES

The circumstances surrounding homicides can be distinguished in terms of whether they are felony-related. In 1997, approximately 19 percent of homicides were felony-related, meaning that they occurred in conjunction with the commission of another felony. Of these, about 50 percent involved a robbery, and 27 percent involved narcotic drug laws. Nearly half (48.6 percent) of homicides in 1997 involved circumstances other than felonies. The vast majority of nonfelony homicides are conflict-based and involve some form of argument or fight between intimates, family members, friends, acquaintances, or strangers. Finally, the nature of the circumstances in a significant proportion of homicides is undetermined. In 1997, 31.3 percent of homicides known to police involved undetermined circumstances.

The relationship between the victim and the offender tends to be more socially distant in felony-related homicides. For example, in 1997, 26.9 percent of felony-related homicides involved strangers, 32.1 percent involved friends, acquaintances, or neighbors, and the relationship was unknown in 35.9 percent of incidents. By contrast, nonfelony homicides are more likely to involve social intimates. While less than 5 percent of felony-related homicides involved familial relationships, 15.8 percent of nonfelony homicides involved intimate partners (including girlfriends and boyfriends) and 12.3 percent involved other family members. Additionally, 43.8 percent of nonfelony incidents involved friends, acquaintances, or neighbors, and only 13.2 percent involved strangers. The nature of the relationship was unknown in 14.8 percent of these incidents. Finally, and perhaps not surprisingly, little is known about the victim-offender relationship in incidents with unknown circumstances. While 5.7 percent of these incidents involved strangers and 13 percent involved friends, acquaintances, or neighbors, the vast majority (75.5 percent) were characterized by undetermined relationships.

Gender differences also exist in terms of the nature of the victim-offender relationship and the surrounding circumstances. In comparison to males, females are disproportionately likely to be involved in intimate partner homicides and homicides arising out of domestic conflicts. For example, from 1976 to 1997, 29.6 percent of female victims were killed by their spouse, ex-spouse, or boyfriend, in comparison to 5.6 percent of male victims. The disproportionate involvement of females in domestic and intimate partner homicides also extends to offending. More specifically, although females comprise only 10 to 15 percent of homicide offenders, many incidents perpetrated by females (45.1 percent from 1976 to 1997) have been against a spouse, boyfriend, or lover, in comparison to 11.5 percent of male-perpetrated homicides.

TEMPORAL AND SPATIAL DISTRIBUTION OF HOMICIDES

With regard to the temporal and spatial distribution of homicides, there are a variety of important factors. First, and smallest in scope, are the timing and setting of homicidal incidents. In other words, when and where are homicides most likely to occur? They are most likely to occur in the evening hours and on weekend nights. This is largely due to the greater levels of interaction that occur in public places during these times. In terms of the setting of the incident, the majority of homicides occur in or near the victim's home. The setting of the homicide is affected by the nature of the victim-offender relationship and the circumstances surrounding the incident, in that incidents involving intimates and family members are more likely to occur in or near the victim's home, while those involving friends or acquaintances are more likely to occur in public settings, such as in bars or taverns. Lawrence Cohen and Marcus Felson's (1979) routine activities perspective posits a high risk of violent victimization when the routine activities of suitable targets intersect in time and space with those of potential offenders, and there is a simultaneous absence of capable guardians to stop the crime.

The second issue of interest in terms of the spatial distribution of homicides is the effect of urbanization. At one time, homicide rates were higher in rural areas than urban areas, at least in part because of the inability of victims to obtain prompt medical care and attention. In the modern era, however, homicide rates are higher in urban than in rural areas. In 1997, metropolitan areas were characterized by 7.4 murders per 100,000 persons. In contrast, rural areas had 4.6 per 100,000. Homicide rates also tend to be higher in large urban areas than small ones, especially in the inner-city regions of large metropolitan areas.

Researchers are also interested in regional differences in homicide rates. For decades, higher violence rates have been detected in the South than in other regions of the United States. For example, in 1997, five of the ten states with the highest murder rates were southern states: Louisiana (15.7), Mississippi (13.1), Arkansas (9.9), Alabama (9.9), and Tennessee (9.5). High Southern homicide rates are mirrored in arrest rates as well, which indicate that, since the mid-1960s, arrest rates have generally been higher in the South than in other regions, with the exception of a few years around 1987. Prior to this time, the murder arrest rates in the South were followed by those of the West. In the 1990s, however, murder arrest rates in the South were followed by those in the Midwest, with the West coming in third. Compared to those in other regions, murder arrest rates in the Northeast have been relatively low.

Explanations of regional differences in homicide rates have been the subject of a significant amount of scholarly research. One theory suggests that the South is characterized by a distinct subculture in which violence and aggression are defined as appropriate modes of behavior in various social situations, such as those involving a challenge to one's honor or an insult to one's reputation. The essence of this perspective can be found in the landmark works of Marvin Wolfgang and Franco Ferracutti, Sheldon Hackney, and Raymond Gastil. In the 1970s, Colin Loftin and Robert Hill advanced a second line of thought emphasizing the social structural conditions associated with severe poverty and their role in high violence rates. Although the level of support for each of these explanations is disputed, researchers do agree that there is little support for a third notion suggesting that high Southern violence rates are a product of the South's legacy of slavery.

FUTURE TRENDS

After nearly thirty years of rising levels of lethal violence in the United States, homicide rates began to fall in the early 1990s. Regardless of a decline, between 15,000 and 20,000 Americans still fall victim to homicide each year. Homicide victims and offenders come from all walks of life and represent members of every social group in their numbers. Young males, especially racial/ethnic minorities, are disproportionately represented, however, in both homicide victim and offender statistics.

Because homicides often are rooted in strong emotions and in the individual's perceptions or definition of the social situation at hand, it is difficult to theorize about the circumstances in which murders are likely to occur. Still, researchers have found that, at an aggregate level, homicide rates are associated with a number of structural and cultural factors, such as economic deprivation, urbanization, social integration, and a subculture of violence. In the light of these findings, no dominant theoretical perspective about homicide or homicide rates has been developed. Instead, theories tend to be more eclectic, focusing on specific types of homicide defined by the victim-offender relationship (e.g., intimate partner, friend/acquaintance, stranger) or the surrounding circumstances (e.g., conflict, felony-related, drug-related).

Whether the downward trend in lethal violence from the 1990s will continue remains to be seen. Although many have made predictions about a coming wave of youth violence, no one can accurately predict what violence rates will look like in the mid-twenty-first century, because the structural and cultural conditions that give rise to violence have not yet occurred. One thing that many researchers do agree on, however, is that a comprehensive, preventative approach is necessary for a long-term reduction in lethal violence rates. Consequently, researchers will continue studying the causes and correlates of lethal violence in the United States in an effort to enhance our understanding of lethal violence and to identify means of combating it.

—Candice Batton

See also ASSASSINATION; CAPITAL CRIMES; EUTHANASIA; FEUDING; GENOCIDE; HOMICIDE INVESITGATION; INFANTICIDE; POLICE, KILLING OF; SPREE MURDER; WOMEN WHO KILL

Further Reading

Cohen, Lawrence, and Marcus Felson. (1979). "Social Change and Crime Rate Trends: A Routine Activity Approach." *American Sociological Review* 44: 588–608.

Eckberg, Doug. (1995). "Estimates of Early Twentieth-Century U.S. Homicide Rates: An Econometric Forecasting Approach." *Demography* 32, 1: 1–16.

Gastil, Raymond. (1971). "Homicide and a Regional Culture of Violence." *American Sociological Review* 36: 412–427.

Gurr, Ted Robert. (1989). *Violence in America: The History of Crime.* Newbury Park, CA: Sage Publications.

Hackney, Sheldon. (1969). "Southern Violence." *American Historical Review* 74: 906–925.

Jensen, Gary. (2000). "Prohibition, Alcohol, and Murder: Untangling Countervailing Mechanisms." *Homicide Studies* 4, 1: 18–36.

Land, Kenneth, Patricia McCall, and Lawrence Cohen. (1990). "Structural Covariates of Homicide Rates: Are There any Invariates Across Time and Social Space?" *American Journal of Sociology* 95, 4: 922–963.

Lane, Roger. (1999). *Violent Death in the City: Suicide, Accident, and Murder in Nineteenth Century Philadelphia.* Cambridge, MA: Harvard University Press.

Loftin, Colin, and Robert Hill. (1974). "Regional Subculture and Homicide: An Examination of the Gastil-Hackney Thesis." *American Sociological Review* 39: 714–724.

Maguire, Kathleen, and Ann Pastore. (1999). *Sourcebook of Criminal Justice Statistics 1998.* Washington, DC: U.S. Department of Justice, Bureau of Justice Statistics, U.S. Government Printing Office.

Messner, Steven, and Richard Rosenfeld. (1997). "Political Restraint of the Market and Levels of Criminal Homicide: A Cross-National Application of Institutional-Anomie Theory." *Social Forces* 75, 4: 1393–1416.

———. (1999). "Social Structure and Homicide: Theory and Research." In *Homicide: A Sourcebook of Social Research*, edited by Dwayne Smith and Margaret Zahn. Thousand Oaks, CA: Sage Publications, 27–41.

Monkonnen, Eric. (1995). "New York City Homicides." *Social Science History* 19, 2: 201–214.

Nisbett, Richard, and Dov Cohen. (1996). *Culture of Honor: The Psychology of Violence in the South.* Boulder, CO: Westview Press.

Parker, Robert Nash, and Kathleen Auerhahn. (1999). "Drugs, Alcohol, and Homicide: Issues in Theory and Research." In *Homicide: A Sourcebook of Social Research*, edited by Dwayne Smith and Margaret Zahn. Thousand Oaks, CA: Sage Publications, 176–191.

Riedel, Marc. (1999). "Sources of Homicide Data: A Review and Comparison." In *Homicide: A Sourcebook of Social Research.*, edited by Dwayne Smith and Margaret Zahn. Thousand Oaks, CA: Sage Publications, 75–95.

Smith, Dwayne, and Victoria Brewer. (1992). "A Sex-Specific Analysis of Correlates of Homicide Victimization in United States Cities." *Violence and Victims* 7, 4: 279–286.

Websdale, Neil. (1999). *Understanding Domestic Homicide.* Boston, MA: Northeastern University Press.

Wolfgang, Marvin, and Franco Ferracuti. (1967).. *The Subculture of Violence.* London: Tavistock Publications.

Zahn, Margaret, and Patricia McCall. (1999). "Trends and Patterns of Homicide in the 20th-Century United States." In *Homicide: A Sourcebook of Social Research*, edited by Dwayne Smith and Margaret Zahn. Thousand Oaks, CA: Sage Publications, 9–23.

Zimring, Franklin. (1998). *American Youth Violence.* New York: Oxford University Press.

Zimring, Franklin, and Gordon Hawkins. (1997). *Crime is Not the Problem: Lethal Violence in America.* New York: Oxford University Press.

▼ HOMICIDE INVESTIGATION

A general overview of homicide investigation requires consideration of three basic concepts: coordination, technical services, and investigation. Coordination refers to the need to have one person assigned to coordinate all of the activities. That person directs the activities of all the services applied to the investigation and makes all of the final decisions.

Those decisions may include when to close the crime scene, what additional technical services are required, how far a neighborhood canvass should extend, or when witness interviews are complete. The coordinator is the liaison between the medical examiner, pathologist, media and prosecutor. The coordinator also directs the focus of the ongoing investigation, and is the person who pulls the case together for presentation to the prosecutor.

Technical services refers to the use of crime laboratory personnel for crime scene searches, the location and identification of evidence, and the proper marking, collection, transportation of evidence for later laboratory examination and analysis. Typically, technical services would also include crime scene sketching, photography, measurements, and latent print activities.

The investigation includes locating and interviewing witnesses, conducting area canvassing, and interrogation of suspects. Investigation activities also include the coordination and investigatory follow-up on all leads.

IMPORTANCE OF THOROUGH HOMICIDE INVESTIGATION

It is patently unethical for the police to conduct a homicide investigation that is less than thorough. Police investigators are required by law and ethics to search for and report exculpatory as well as inculpatory evidence. In states that utilize capital punishment, persons wrongly convicted of murder are particularly vulnerable because executions cannot be recalled.

Contemporary advances in DNA technology indicate that some people have been wrongfully convicted. Some anti-capital punishment interest groups in the United States have formed organizations to assist convicted murderers in obtaining new trials based on potential DNA evidence. The number of cases of miscarriage of justice involving wrongful convictions for homicide is not known with any certainty. The reasons for such wrongful convictions are equally as elusive. One case revealed that the prosecuting attorney withheld exculpatory fingerprint evidence that would have provided reasonable doubt for a jury. Other cases reveal that eyewitness testimony has frequently been shown to be erroneous and sometimes self-serving. Other reasons include perjured testimony, or testimony from forensic specialists who have testified beyond the scope of what the evidence

scientifically indicated. For example, one person with an I.Q. of 64 admitted to a murder because the police said they would turn him over to the mob outside the jail. Errors like these are not common occurrences in the justice system, but poor investigations, poor procedures, fear of looking like a fool, and a host of other reasons have resulted in the convictions of persons who were in fact innocent. A thorough homicide investigation is absolutely necessary not only for convicting the guilty but also for proving the innocence of persons arrested for crimes.

For example, in 1950, Robert Bailey Ballard was convicted of first-degree murder in West Virginia and sentenced to death. His alibi witnesses were two Charleston police officers who, at the time of the murder, were in the process of arresting him for drunk driving. Two witnesses wrongly identified him as the killer. In spite of the overwhelming evidence of his innocence, the U.S. Supreme Court refused to hear his case. Forty-eight hours before he was to be executed, he obtained a reprieve after the warden called the famous crime author Erle Stanley Gardner. In 1951, the governor commuted his sentence to life in prison, and in 1960 he was awarded a pardon. In a 1913 case, made famous by a movie and a novel, Leo M. Frank of Georgia was convicted of a murder he did not commit. In 1915 his sentence was commuted to life in prison. Two months later, he was lynched by fellow inmates. In 1982, a witness admitted having seen the chief witness against Frank carrying the body. The chief witness was the real culprit. Mr. Frank was pardoned posthumously.

SOURCES OF INFORMATION

Quite simply, people and things are sources of information. They differ dramatically from each other, and the investigations dealing with them differ as well. Particular skills and abilities are needed to competently interview people, and other skills are needed to locate and examine trace evidence. Investigators deal almost exclusively with people in emotionally charged situations. They must deal with the problems of human weakness, such as perception and communication issues. A lab examiner, on the other hand, deals with things that cannot lie, fight, or flee. Although the investigator deals primarily with people as sources of information, he or she must also be well-informed and talented in matters dealing with the recognition, collection, and preservation of physical evidence. The skills needed by investigators can be learned with experience, education, and professional mentoring.

VALUE OF EVIDENCE

Evidence found at a homicide scene is used to establish the elements of the crime, to assist in the identification of the person who committed the murder, and to determine how the crime was committed. The evidentiary value of information obtained from things as compared to information obtained from persons has been firmly established by trial and appellate courts. Physical evidence cannot lie, it is not affected by emotion, and it cannot be impeached. Every homicide investigator would be wise to consider "the theory of transfer" at a crime scene. That theory posits that when two objects meet, some effect of that meeting can generally be established and verified at a later time. For example, when two automobiles collide, there is a transfer of paint and other vehicle matter. When a vehicle hits a person, some relationships between the vehicle and the person may be established by glass that may be fracture-matched or by vehicle materials embedded in a person's clothing. (A fracture-match is the joining of two separate pieces of glass—from a common source—that fit together like two pieces of a puzzle. If one piece of the fractured glass remains on the vehicle, and the matched piece is found on the victim, such evidence indicates that the victim was struck by the suspect vehicle.) Impressions of a person's body are often left on vehicles that collide with people. Similarly, in homicides fingerprints are often left at a scene, body fluids containing DNA are left behind, and tool marks are left that can be compared to the tool that originally made the mark. Likewise, shoe and tire impressions are left behind, as well as hairs and fibers. The potential list of possible trace evidence is very long.

THE INVESTIGATION PROCESS

The process begins with the initial notification of the crime and it continues until the final testimony is presented in a court. For purposes of maintaining control of evidence, this process continues until the last appeal of a conviction has expired. In those cases that do not result in an arrest, the evidence should be maintained indefinitely. The original officer at the scene must determine if a homicide has been committed, or,

if a person is still alive, he or she must summon medical assistance.

Arrival and Preliminary Investigation

The first responders to homicide scenes are usually patrol officers. While en route, they should observe and note any vehicles or persons that could be coming from the scene. On arrival, the first priority is to render assistance to injured parties. The second priority is to protect physical evidence from contamination by use of "scene tapes," ropes, or other means after determining the size of the crime scene. A good rule of thumb is to make the scene larger. It may also be possible to effect an arrest. Once the scene is properly protected, patrol officers should seek out and identify possible witnesses. If preliminary information is obtained as to a possible suspect or suspect vehicle, that information should be broadcast to other units. An adage of a good investigation is, "If you didn't write it down, you didn't do it"; therefore, all conditions, events, actions and remarks should be fully and accurately documented.

There is a relationship between arrival time and preservation of evidence. The longer it takes to protect the scene, the greater the opportunity there is for bystanders or well-meaning people to unknowingly contaminate evidence. An excess of time may also affect the availability and reliability of witnesses. Scene protection also includes keeping unassigned police from walking about a crime scene. In investigations by larger police agencies, crime scene specialists and other technicians may be assigned. In smaller agencies, the complete investigation may be the responsibility of just a few officers. If a small department does not have trained officers or the proper equipment and expertise, it is well advised to protect the scene and call a larger agency for investigative and forensic support.

Documentation of the Crime Scene

The crime scene in homicides is proof that a crime was committed. It often contains the elements of the corpus delicti and provides physical evidence that may connect a suspect to the crime. A crime scene may be defined as the location where a suspect changed intent into action, and it continues through the escape route.

A crime scene should be photographed and documented prior to any search for evidence. It is best to start with the approach and then narrow down to the actual scene. The rule of thumb is to photograph from the general to the specific. No item should be moved in any way prior to photographing the scene. In order to be admissible as evidence. a photograph must be a true graphic representation of the scene as it actually was. Therefore, chalk or rulers should not be used to enhance photos, because they add something to the scene. Color film is best, and many specialists use color and black and white. Videotaping a crime scene is also employed and provides a clear perspective of the scene and its detail. Video recording a scene does not replace the still photographic process.

If the scene is a building, the entry and exit should be photographed. The location of the body should be photographed at a distance to show its general relationship to the scene. Then, close-up photos of the body and its wounds should be taken. The nature of the scene dictates the method of photography. If it is an inside location, most prefer to use a clockwise method of taking photographs, but still from the general view to the specific. Outside scenes can be photographed from compass points (north, east, south, and west) and are best shot at eye level to portray what the investigator saw. What is important is that the photograph represents the view seen by the investigator at the scene. Therefore, police equipment and officers should be removed from the "photo field" prior to any photographs being taken. Posed pictures of officers are useless and only indicate incompetence. As with any other process in a homicide investigation, each and every step of the photographic process must be documented. A photographic notebook should include details such as the type of camera used, type of film, film speed, and aperture used, and each photograph should be chronologically accounted for and numbered. To reduce the chain of custody on photographic evidence, it is best to have the photographer maintain custody of the film and personally deliver it to the photo lab for processing. There is no set rule on how many pictures to take, but it is always better to take more than less. A view of a photograph later may reveal something the investigators missed when viewing the scene.

After all the photographs are taken, unless the scene is being processed by crime scene specialists, the investigator should prepare a crime scene sketch. The sketch does not have to be drawn to scale at the time, but all the measurements taken must be accurate. At least two persons are needed to take proper measurements. Items of possible evidentiary value, such as the body, weapons, overturned furniture, blood spots, or tire tracks, must be located on the preliminary sketch. Measurements are then taken so as to be able to relocate the specific item in a crime scene reconstruction. Measurement to at least two fixed objects is helpful in this regard. For example, measurements to locate a revolver found lying on the ground can be triangulated by measuring the distances from two or more permanent objects such as a tree, boundary marker, the corner of a building, or a road edge. Like photographs, all such sketches should be an accurate representation of the scene and its important aspects. Once the crime scene sketch is finished, it can later be drawn to scale using the measurements taken. Only after the scene is documented by photography and measured crime scene sketches have been completed should the search for evidence be conducted.

Physical Evidence and the Crime Scene

Essentially, physical evidence is any tangible article, large or small, that tends to prove or disprove a point in question. To be of value, such evidence must be obtained using legal methods; must be properly photographed, collected, and preserved; and must have appropriate tests conducted upon it by competent personnel.

Physical evidence may be found anywhere. It may be nearest to where a critical act took place, at a point of entry or exit, on the approach or escape route, or on a victim's or suspect's body and clothing. It may also be found on a weapon or at the weapon's location, in a vehicle if one was used, at a suspect's residence, or at a location where an initial assault took place if there is a secondary crime scene. For example, a person may be killed in one location and the body may be moved to a secondary location. In these cases, there are multiple crime scenes.

Once an item of evidence is moved or altered in any way, it is impossible to restore it to its original position or condition. If an investigator must move or secure something at the scene, its location should be documented and reasons provided for why it was moved. Transport of a dying person from the scene is an example of such a reason.

Crime Scene Protection

A crime scene should be held secure until after an initial canvass is complete and reviewed, until all known witnesses are interviewed, and their statements reviewed; it should not be unsecured until a final check is made by the coordinator. In those cases when a suspect is in custody, the scene should be preserved until the suspect is processed and his or her statements are verified.

The method used to protect a scene is often determined by the nature of the scene. If it is a room in a building, then keeping others away will suffice. However, if the scene is an open field or a yard adjacent to a home, other complications arise. Crime scene tape is a common supply in police agencies. If the scene is outdoors, ropes or even a car can be used to block access until additional help arrives to further secure the scene. The idea is to maintain the primary scene in a pristine manner so that it factually reflects the scene as it was when the offender left.

Examples of Possible Physical Evidence

Physical evidence will vary according to how the crime was committed, how long the suspect stayed at the scene, the nature of the crime, and a host of other variables. A few examples of physical evidence include body fluids, blood spots, tracks, displaced furniture, prints, firearms, impressions, fibers, glasses and cups, spittle, bullet holes, tissue, papers, vehicles, exposed food, cigarette or cigar butts, dishes, dents, automobile brakes, and a host of other items.

Classification of Evidence

Evidence is classified as either class evidence or individual evidence. Class evidence exists when a characteristic of physical evidence is common to a group of objects or persons. Such evidence can only be placed in a broad category, as there may be more than one source of the evidence. Examples include hair, soil, glass fragments, and DNA. DNA may appear to be individual, but because it uses probability to establish its probative value it is still a class characteristic.

Individual characteristics originate from a particular source. Examples include fingerprints, palm prints, and footprints. Shoe prints may be class evidence if from new shoes, but if unique individual markings exist in the sole or heel of a shoe, the evidence may approach individual. Though generally glass fragments are a class characteristic, a particular fracture may match an originating source, and it then would be classified as individual. Similarly, paint marks are usually class characteristics, but a specific paint chip may be a perfect fracture match to its source and become individual.

The medical examiner and homicide detectives examine a body pulled from the East River in New York City on July 12, 1963. Bullet holes in the man's head suggest that he was the victim of a homicide.
Source: © Betttmann/Corbis; used by permission.

The Canvass

A canvass consists of seeking out people who may have seen or heard something, or who are in a position to know something about the victim or suspect. The canvass of the surrounding area is a critical aspect of a homicide investigation. The goal of a canvass is to identify eyewitnesses, information about circumstances and relationships, approximate times of occurrences, and information about a victim's habits, friends, and possible motives. At a minimum, the scope of the canvass should include any place from which the scene could be seen or heard and possible routes taken to or from the scene by a suspect. Most investigators use a canvass form as a guide. A canvass form is a preprinted list of questions to ask potential witnesses, such as the time and date of their observations or their general knowledge of the victim. The form assists the investigator in obtaining a broad base of information in a chronological and documented manner.

Media Releases

Several news services monitor police radio calls. It is therefore common for reporters and photographers to arrive at the crime scene shortly after the police. The crime scene coordinator, in conjunction with the prosecutor, should determine the content of media release information. Critical information that only the perpetrator would know should not be released. Likewise, the type of wounds, the specific weapon used, and other detailed and relevant information that could tie a suspect to the crime should not be revealed. It is best to set up a media briefing location away from the scene.

Post-Scene Activities

Once the crime scene has been cleared, the primary investigators begin the work of investigating to identify, locate, and arrest a suspect. Statements of witnesses are compared and evaluated. This process may indicate a need to reinterview certain witnesses. Additional relevant witnesses may be located and interviewed. Once a suspect has been identified, the process of linking him or her to the homicide takes place. At the right time, as determined by the lead investigator, a suspect will be picked up and interrogated. As with any interrogation, an exhaustive personal background investigation should be conducted prior to actually sitting down with the suspect. All legal requirements relating to interrogation must be followed to the letter. When indicated, search warrant affidavits should be drawn to conduct searches for additional evidence, especially with respect to the suspect. All Fourth Amendment search-and-seizure safeguards must be followed explicitly.

When there are no suspects, a "tip line" system should be developed to receive tips from citizens. Each and every tip must be carefully investigated and records made of such interviews. In the more complicated cases, it may be advisable to set up an investigative task force. This is particularly important in multiple murders that cross jurisdictional boundaries. In such cases, the volume of incoming tips will require computer support.

SUMMARY

The thoroughness of an initial homicide investigation is crucial, because without the appropriate safeguards, crucial evidence may be compromised, lost, or overlooked. Proper protection of the crime scene is paramount. The best efforts of an investigator or a crime scene specialist could be nullified by an improperly conducted interrogation of a suspect or the improper handling of evidence. Likewise, a professional, ethical, and scientifically sound approach to such an investigation is required to avoid a miscarriage of justice and to insure that all of the activities taken by investigators meet legal and constitutional standards.

—*Dennis M. Payne*

See also CRIME SCENE ASSESSMENT; DETECTIVE WORK; EYEWITNESS TESTIMONY; FORENSIC SCIENCE; MEDICAL EXAMINER; WRONGFUL CONVICTIONS

Further Reading

Becker, Ronald F. (2000). *Criminal Investigation.* Gaithersburg, MD: Aspen Publishers.

Bedau, Hugo Adam, and Michael L. Radelet. (1987). "Miscarriages of Justice in Potentially Capital Cases." *Stanford Law Review* 40,1 (November): 91–120.

Fisher, Barry A.J. (2000). *Techniques of Crime Scene Investigation.* 6th ed. Boca Raton, FL: CRC Press.

Geberth, Vernon J. (1996). *Practical Homicide Investigation: Tactics, Procedures and Forensic Techniques.* 3d ed. Boca Raton, FL: CRC Press.

Gilbert, James N. (1993). *Criminal Investigation.* 3d ed. New York: Macmillan.

Lyman, Michael D. (1993). *Criminal Investigation: The Art and the Science.* Englewood Cliffs, NJ: Regents/Prentice Hall.

Swanson, Charles R., Neil C. Chamelin, and Leonard Territo. (2000). *Criminal Investigation.* 7th ed. New York: McGraw-Hill.

Wilson, John B. (1993). *Criminal Investigations: A Behavioral Approach.* Prospect Heights, IL: Waveland Press, Inc.

▼ HOT SPOT POLICING

Crime prediction is not limited to predicting what individuals in which situations will turn to delinquency or criminality. In recent years, researchers have employed new technologies and data sources to identify the "where" and "when" of offending. Knowing that certain locations and times are prone to criminal activity has led to the concepts of "hot spots" and "burning times." Hot spots are clusters of crimes in space; burning times are concentrations of crime at specific repeated moments (Brantingham and Brantingham 1999).

Although the observation that criminal activity is concentrated at some locations and not others is not new, past research focused on criminals' residences as a catalyst for the occurrence of crime (Brantingham and Brantingham 1999)—this despite the fact that crime is often concentrated in other areas. By the mid 1980s, with the computerization of police records and the development of computerbased mapping systems, the geographic mapping of the distribution of reported crimes led to the discovery of concentrations of criminal activity in discrete areas—hot spots.

According to routine activity theory, crime does not occur randomly but, rather, is produced by the convergence in time and space of motivated offenders, suitable targets, and the absence of capable guardians (Koper 1995). This convergence in turn is affected by daily activity, traffic patterns, community organization, and other factors. Sherman et al. (1989) tested the basic premise of routine activity theory—that crime is not randomly distributed—by providing a more complete description of the variation of crime across places. Their assessment of police data in Minneapolis revealed a substantial concentration of all police calls in relatively few hot spots. Over a one-year period, 50.4 percent of all calls to the police came from 3.3 percent of places; all robbery calls were located at 2.2 percent of places, all rape calls at 1.2 percent of places, and all auto theft calls at 2.7 percent of places. Conversely, 95 percent of the city was free from any of these crimes. The concentration of calls in these hot spots was significantly greater than would occur by chance. Moreover, hot spots were not limited to crime in public places; comparable patterns were found for many domestic calls as well. Sherman et al. report that all domestic disturbances were recorded at 9 percent of places.

IDENTIFICATION

There are three ways to identify criminal hot spots. Visual inspection involves the detection of high crime addresses through police calls and mapping; statistical identification uses mathematical tools to identify small areas with disproportionately high crime rates; and theoretical prediction draws on what is known about how environment and routine shape the probability that crime will occur in some locations and not others. Brantingham and Brantingham (1995) suggest that the formation of hot spots can sometimes be predicted by relying on concepts from environmental criminology, where crime is seen as the result of multistaged decisions. That is, the potential that criminal activity will occur at a given location depends on the convergence of several factors, poverty and heavy traffic among them. This information makes it possible to identify crime generators (sites to which large numbers of people are attracted, e.g., shopping malls, housing estates, and parking lots) and crime attractors (sites that create criminal opportunities to which motivated offenders are drawn, e.g., ATMs) and predict the formation of crime hot spots.

POLICE PATROLS

Taking the Minneapolis data on the distribution of crime into account, it would make sense to concentrate policing in those areas where crime is most prevalent.

An experiment with the Minneapolis Police Department showed that an increase in patrol dosage at 55 of 110 crime hot spots effected a reduction in total crime ranging from 6 to 13 percent; in addition, observed disorder was only half as prevalent in experimental as in control hot spots. These results demonstrate that a substantial increase in police presence can have a place-specific, if not general, deterrent effect (Sherman and Weisburd 1995).

Using the same data, Koper (1995) investigated the residual deterrent effect of police presence to determine whether there is an optimum length of time for police to remain at high crime locations. His results showed that patrols must reach a threshold dosage (as measured by duration of police presence) of about ten minutes in order to generate significantly longer periods without disorder than those generated by routine patrol. According to Koper, the optimum duration is between eleven and fifteen minutes. The implication is that optimizing patrol duration at troublesome locations can help to reduce crime.

DRUGS

In response to the drug epidemic of the 1980s, many U.S. cities increased their efforts to address narcotic problems by implementing strategies that specifically targeted drug hot spots. For example, the 1995 Drug Market Analysis experiment in Jersey City focused on street-level drug hot spots. Using computer mapping techniques, Weisburd and Green identified 56 locations that were the site of a substantial proportion of the arrests and calls for service in the city. A police crackdown ensued. In comparing the seven-month pre- and post-intervention periods, the authors found consistent, strong effects on disorder-related emergency calls. However, the experiment did not influence calls for violent or property crimes. More surprisingly, no con-

> **DID YOU KNOW...**
> Hot spot policing is the assignment of police resources to control clusters of crimes that regularly occur in particular places. The wisdom of this approach was suggested by a study in Minneapolis which showed that over a one-year period, 50.4 percent of all calls to the police came from 3.3 percent of places, all robbery calls were located at 2.2 percent of places, all rape calls at 1.2 percent of places, and all auto theft calls at 2.7 percent of places. Conversely, 95 percent of the city was free from any of these crimes.

sistent effects were found on narcotic calls. Despite improvement in the experimental areas, "the effect of treatment is evident primarily in very large changes in a few of the most active hot spots" (Weisburd and Green 1995: 727). The authors also found no evidence of displacement (movement to another location) of drug activity to surrounding areas. On the contrary, there was a diffusion of benefits.

A diffusion of benefits could also be seen in the Specialized Multi-Agency Response Team (SMART) approach, a program that used municipal codes and drug nuisance abatement laws to control drug and disorder problems (Green 1995). A study analyzed the changes within the area surrounding SMART locations and identified the spatial movements of individuals arrested or contacted in areas surrounding SMART intervention sites. The results suggest that fewer people were contacted in the surrounding areas after the SMART program than before. In addition, there was "a small net diffusion of benefits" in the areas surrounding the hot spots (Green 1995: 749).

GUN VIOLENCE

Because gun crimes are highly concentrated in certain areas, hot spot identification has become a crucial factor in gun crime prevention. Data from an Indianapolis experiment showed that gun crimes were reported at only 3 percent of all addresses. At such gun crime hot spots, the percentage of persons carrying a weapon may be far higher than elsewhere in the city (Sherman and Rogan 1995). The Kansas City Gun Experiment tested the hypothesis that stricter enforcement of weapons laws in these hot spots can reduce gun crime overall. Hot spot patrol officers found twenty-nine guns in addition to the forty-seven seized by regular police units, and there were eighty-three fewer gun crimes in the target area, a 49 percent decline (Sherman and Rogan 1995). Hot spot patrols also led to a decline in drive-by shootings and homicides. No displacement effect was found; in fact, "some evidence suggests that the program's benefits were diffused to two of the adjoining beats" (Sherman and Rogan 1995: 686). Although it may seem unlikely that the seizure of only 29 guns could result in a significant reduction in gun crime, it is possible that because some offenders are far more frequent gun users than others, their capture may prevent a large number of gun crimes (Sherman and Rogan 1995). Deterrence due to increased police visibility, traffic stops and arrests may also be a factor.

SUMMARY

The formation of crime hot spots is influenced by a myriad of factors—fiscal policy, land use, transportation and activity patterns, marketing, and social and economic conditions—and their identification is essential to crime prevention efforts. At the primary prevention level, government policies with respect to housing, land use, zoning, and transportation can shape an infrastructure that minimizes hot spot formation. At the secondary level, hot spot prevention requires cooperation between citizens, community leaders, and local government. At the tertiary level, focused law enforcement and situational intervention are necessary to address established hot spots. Research should continue to develop better methods for analyzing hot spots so that adequate preventative measures can be taken.

—*Don Hummer and Akemi Hoshi*

See also FOOT PATROL; GEOGRAPHIC PROFILING

Further Reading

Brantingham, P. L., and P. J. Brantingham. (1999). "A Theoretical Model of Crime and Hot Spot Generation." *Studies on Crime and Crime Prevention* 8, 1: 7–26.

Green, Lorraine. (1995). "Cleaning Up Drug Hot Spots in Oakland, California: The Displacement and Diffusion Effects." *Justice Quarterly* 12, 4: 737–754.

Koper, Christopher S. (1995). "Just Enough Police Presence: Reducing Crime and Disorderly Behavior by Optimizing Patrol Time in Crime Hot Spots." *Justice Quarterly* 12, 4: 649–671.

Sherman, L. W., P. R. Gartin, and M. E. Buerger. (1989). "Hot spots of Predatory Crime: Routine Activities and the Criminology of Place." *Criminology* 27, 1: 27–55.

Sherman, L. W., and D. P. Rogan. (1995). "Effects of Gun Seizures on Gun Violence: 'Hot Spots' Patrol in Kansas City." *Justice Quarterly*.12, 4: 673–693.

Sherman, L. W., and D. Weisburd. (1995). "General Deterrent Effects of Police Patrol in Crime 'Hot Spots': A Randomized, Controlled Trial." *Justice Quarterly* 12, 4: 625–648.

Weisburd, D., and L. Green. (1995). "Policing Drug Hot Spots: The Jersey City Drug Market Analysis Experiment." *Justice Quarterly*. 12, 4: 711–735.

▼ HOUSE ARREST

To many, the term *house arrest* may invoke images of repressive political control and manipulation. However, within the criminal justice system the term refers to court-ordered confinement in one's own home and is viewed as an important alternative to standard incarceration at various stages of the criminal justice process. The order of house arrest comes from various parts of the criminal justice system, is employed by local, state, and federal agencies, and often entails very different requirements; thus, the term is somewhat ambiguous. There are several forms of house arrest, depending on where in the criminal justice system the house arrest is applied and the severity of the requirements of the court order; examples include curfew, home confinement or home detention, and home incarceration.

Curfew generally refers to restricting an offender to his or her home during specified times, usually during the evening and nighttime hours. *Home confinement* or *home detention* usually refers confinement of the offender to the home for most hours, with stated exceptions like school or work, religious services, medical or drug treatment, or food shopping. These exceptions are generally specified in advance and are relatively strictly enforced. Finally, *home incarceration,* perhaps the most severe form of house arrest, generally refers to cases in which the offender is required to remain in the home constantly, with relatively rare exceptions such as medical or court-ordered correctional treatment (e.g., drug abuse counseling). The latter two forms of house arrest are often accompanied by electronic surveillance via an electronic device placed on the offender's ankle, thus enabling his or her presence or absence from the home to be monitored very closely (see Electronic Monitoring). Each of these forms of house arrest can be used at almost any stage of the criminal justice system and are used for various purposes.

APPLICATIONS

House arrest can be useful as a form of pretrial confinement for defendants who appear inappropriate candidates for being released on their own recognizance or who are unable to post bond. The primary goals of pretrial house arrest are to guarantee that the defendant shows up at trial, to insure public safety, to reduce jail overcrowding, and to reserve jail space for the most dangerous or untrustworthy defendants. One major advantage of the use of home confinement at this stage is that people not yet found guilty are not subjected to a serious form of punishment: incarceration with other possibly more serious offenders. Alternatively, house arrest can be described as a form of punishment, but one less punitive than incarceration in jail or prison. Because of this premise, house arrest should be used only for offenders who would normally not be let out on bail, or

in cases where a very high bail is set but is reduced on the condition of house arrest. House arrest at this stage is also particularly useful for juveniles, who are often detained for relatively long periods of time prior to adjudication for relatively minor offenses, only to be released following adjudication and sentencing.

House arrest is also used as criminal sanction meted out by judges at sentencing. The purposes of house arrest at sentencing are to administer a reasonable punishment, protect public safety, reserve jail space for more serious offenders, reduce the potential criminogenic effects of incarceration, and help rehabilitate the offender. The basic goal in this case is to provide a cost-effective alternative to incarceration. House arrest may cover the entire length of incarceration, or only a part of a sentence. For instance, in some jurisdictions a sentence is broken down into three parts: an offender is incarcerated for a period of time, then allowed to participate in a work release program (see Work Release), and then graduated to home confinement. In general, there is agreement among both criminal justice professionals and the general public that house arrest is a reasonable sanction for certain low-risk offenders who seem likely to profit from not being exposed to other criminals and from maintaining employment and family ties. Research also suggests that offenders experience the sanction as a punishment, although less punitive than incarceration in jail or prison (Gainey and Payne 2000).

An interesting debate has recently emerged over the application of "good time"—a reduced period of incarceration for offenders who behave themselves—to offenders serving their sentence in their homes. Some argue that offenders on house arrest are already getting a break and should not receive good time, while others argue that they are in fact being punished, and they should be rewarded for obeying the often stringent rules of house arrest (Payne and Gainey 2000).

House arrest is also used at the tail end of the criminal justice system, as a form of early release and community reintegration. Again, the goals are to reduce jail and prison crowding, but also to act as a mechanism to help the offender readjust to life "on the outside," with all the attendant pressures and enticements to reoffend. In an age of "truth in sentencing" legislation (e.g., legislation that limits or eliminates various forms of early release), the use of house arrest for early release may be met with heavy criticism by politicians and the general public unless they are educated as to the punitive nature of house arrest. In addition, the dramatic increases in rates of incarceration in state and federal prisons during the 1980s and 1990s, and the costs associated with such massive incarceration, suggest that alternatives to standard incarceration, such as house arrest, are sorely needed.

COST-EFFECTIVENESS

A major concern about house arrest is whether it is cost-effective. The cost-effectiveness of house arrest is dependent on a number of conditions, including where in the system it is being used, how it is implemented, what types of offenders are deemed eligible, and whether they recidivate or not. The cost-effectiveness of house arrest programs is a controversial issue and one that is often researched. Given the high costs of incarceration, however, evidence would appear to weigh in favor of house arrest.

At the front end of the system, for pretrial defendants, a limited use of house arrest is likely to be cost-effective as long as it is used for people who normally would not be released on their own recognizance or who cannot make bail. Likewise, at the sentencing stage, house arrest is likely to be cost-effective if used on lesser offenders who would normally be detained, or on those who may have gotten probation but who need the extra formal controls to resist criminal temptations. At the tail end of the criminal justice system, house arrest is almost certainly cost-effective, because the costs of housing offenders and building new prisons is immense in comparison to the costs of monitoring their home confinement or curfew. Furthermore, the fact that offenders often are allowed to work enables them to support families, pay restitution, and even help pay for the equipment costs used to monitor them. Finally, offenders often have to do without the medical services provided to them in jail or prison, which can also reduce costs. (Note, however, that this raises ethical problems concerning offenders with serious ailments who cannot afford to pay for medical treatment.) Of course, one must also consider rates of recidivism and the safety of the public when considering cost-effectiveness. Unfortunately, quality recidivism studies have been rare, and most of these have focused more specifically on house arrest with electronic monitoring.

ELIGIBILITY

An important aspect of house arrest is deciding who should be eligible. In general, violent offenders are not considered eligible for house arrest, and it is inappropriate to use house arrest for offenders such as drug dealers convicted for selling drugs out of their homes. With the exception of habitual traffic offenders and convictions for driving under the influence of alcohol, extensive prior records generally preclude the use of house arrest, at least at the sentencing stage. Other factors that are often taken into consideration are employability, history of substance abuse, and unstable living arrangements. The health status of the offender might also be taken into account; house arrest is sometimes used for people with terminal illnesses who pose minimal risks to the community and wish to die with dignity in their homes or with their families. House arrest is not a good option, however, if there are known offenders residing in or near the home, or if the victim resides in the home. Careful screening and follow-up is necessary for the effective use of house arrest.

SUMMARY

House arrest provides a useful alternative to incarceration for certain defendants and convicted offenders at various stages of the criminal justice process. There remain unresolved issues, however, surrounding unmeasured costs of monitoring offenders, rates of recidivism, and the eligibility criteria for determining who gets the sanction. House arrest is no panacea; however, it does offer a potentially useful tool for detaining some defendants prior to trial, for punishing some offenders without or in addition to standard incarceration, and for early release and reintegration into the community.

—*Randy R. Gainey*

See also ELECTRONIC MONITORING

Further Reading

Gainey, Randy R., and Brian K. Payne. (2000). "Understanding the Experience of House Arrest with Electronic Monitoring: An Analysis of Quantitative and Qualitative Data." *International Journal of Offender Therapy and Comparative Criminology* 44: 84–96.

Gainey, Randy R., Brian K. Payne, and Michael O'Toole. (2000). "The Relationship between Time in Jail, Time on Electronic Monitoring and Recidivism: An Event History Analysis of a Jail-Based Program." *Justice Quarterly* 17: 733–752.

Latessa, Edward J., and Harry E. Allen. (1999). *Corrections in the Community*. Cincinnati, OH: Anderson.

Maxfield, Michael G., and Terry L. Baumer. (1990). "Home Detention with Electronic Monitoring: Comparing Pretrial and Postconviction Programs." *Crime and Delinquency* 36: 521–536.

Payne, Brian K., and Randy R. Gainey. (2000). "Is Good Time

Appropriate for Offenders on Electronic Monitoring: Attitudes of Monitoring Directors." *Journal of Criminal Justice* 28: 1–10.

Rackmill, Stephen. (1994). "An Analysis of Home Confinement as a Sanction." *Federal Probation* 58: 45–52.

▼ HUMAN RIGHTS

Human rights are those rights that belong to all human beings simply as a consequence of being human, regardless of citizenship in a particular nation or membership in a particular religious, ethnic, racial, gender, or class-based group. Because groups with power have often tried to deny these rights to those without power, a movement has emerged to enshrine human rights in law and to protect them with national and international legal processes.

DEVELOPMENT OF THE CONCEPT

Judaism, Christianity, Islam, and Buddhism have all produced writings suggesting that divine order imposes certain duties on believers in their treatment of other people. Many human rights scholars, however, find the origin of the concept in Greek stoicism, particularly the work of Epictectus, who held that a divine force pervades all creation and that human conduct should therefore be judged by the extent to which it was in harmony with this force. From this it was a short step to the idea of a "law of nature" or "natural law," which is a system of justice derived from nature that transcends the laws of any one nation and that applies to all human beings. Through the Middle Ages, the concept of natural law informed the thinking of political and religious writers who tried to discover its essence so that secular law could be crafted in a way that reflected this natural law. The resulting secular laws often concerned the duties of various socially unequal parties toward each other (e.g., ruler and subject, lord and peasant); they also accepted the institutions of serfdom and slavery. Nevertheless, laws that set limits to governmental exercise of power over the governed set valuable precedents. The most famous example is England's Magna Carta (1215) which, among other things, forced King John to acknowledge the right of every freeman to own property, to leave and return to the kingdom, and not to be " arrested or detained in prison, or deprived of his freehold, or outlawed, or banished, or in any way molested . . . unless by the lawful judgment of his peers and by the law of the land." The "liberties, rights, and conces-

sions" listed in the Magna Carta were considered fundamental enough to be cited by other and later documents declaring human rights, such as England's Petition of Right (1628) and the Habeas Corpus Act (1679), as well as the national and several state constitutions of the United States.

It was during the Renaissance that the gradual decline of feudalism and the surge of new ideas provided the context for a concept of human rights that rested on the notions of equality and liberty. Humanism, with its central emphasis on the individual, supported the shift from natural law as specifying duties to natural law as identifying rights. It encouraged a view of each person as being created with certain "inalienable" rights that were not diminished by membership in a particular class or group and that could not be weakened by the power of a ruler. This view was put to the test by fifteenth- and sixteenth-century discoveries of people who differed greatly from Europeans in their appearance, living conditions, and religion. The desire to exploit or convert these peoples made it tempting to define them as less than human and therefore not endowed with the rights of humans. A vocal minority, however, courageously asserted the universality of the human ability to reason and therefore to be possessed of the right to freedom and equality. Foremost among these was Bartolomé de Las Casas, a Spanish Dominican missionary in the Americas. In his *In Defense of the Indians* (c.1548), he called upon the emperor Charles V to recognize that God had endowed the inhabitants of the New World with "the natural light that is common to all peoples" and therefore to protect them against the depredations of the conquering Spanish soldiers and priests.

This growing confidence in human reason as the foundation for human rights flourished in the eighteenth century, the so-called Age of Enlightenment. The discoveries of scientists such as Sir Isaac Newton and Galileo inspired Enlightenment thinkers in the belief that there was order and law in the universe and that human reason could discover them. Dutch scholar Hugo Grotius (1625), in a plea for the universal nature of natural law, suggested that just as rulers must recognize the rights of their subjects, nations must recognize the rights of other nations. In England, philosopher John Locke argued (1690) that man had possessed certain rights in the state of nature and that when individuals formed a "social contract" to live together in civil society, they did not surrender these rights to the state but, on the contrary, gave the state the power to enforce

Demonstrators in London support the extradition of General Augusto Pinochet, former ruler of Chile, for a trial on human rights violations against the people of Chile.
Source: Photo courtesy of Karen Christensen.

them. Chief among the rights recognized by Locke were life, liberty, and property. Locke's ideas were taken up by the French philosophes Montesquieu, Voltaire, and Rousseau, who used their faith in reason and science to attack bigotry, dogmatism, censorship, and discrimination based on socioeconomic class. They based their political theories on the recognition of the basic "rights of man," a phrase that would echo through the following centuries.

SUBJECTS OF THE STATE OR PARTIES TO A CONTRACT

The theory that the social contract gave the state the duty to enforce the rights of its citizens produced the logical conclusion that those citizens had the right to revolt when the state failed in its duties. This was the philosophy behind the American Revolution. Thomas Jefferson asserted that the colonists held their rights by the "laws of nature" and in 1776 summed up the ideas he had gathered from his study of the natural law philosophers in the Declaration of Independence: "We hold these truths to be self-evident, that all men are created equal, that they are endowed by their Creator with certain inalienable Rights, that among these are Life, Liberty and the pursuit of Happiness." These words and the philosophy behind them appear again in the French Declaration of the Rights of Man and of the Citizen (1789), which

asserts that the French Revolution was justified by the statement that "ignorance, forgetfulness, or contempt of the rights of man are the sole causes of public misfortunes and of the corruption of governments."

Although the idea of natural law and natural rights gained currency through the early nineteenth century, it was never without its detractors. It became clear that observers could interpret natural law in different ways; slavery, religious discrimination, the oppression of women, and wars of colonialism were all seen as "natural" at one time or another. Conservatives were afraid that the doctrine of natural rights would bring about social turmoil, while liberals felt that simple declarations of natural rights would lead to the belief that the labor of enacting rights through the laws of society was unnecessary. Students of comparative law noted that rights seemed to be a product of the culture that proclaimed them. Legal realists insisted that the only meaningful law was that supported by the powerful while philosophical empiricists held that natural law could not be discovered by logic, because the only real truth was that which could be verified by experience.

INTERNATIONAL HUMAN RIGHTS

During the late nineteenth and early twentieth centuries, the gradual abolition of slavery, the extension of the suffrage, worker protection legislation, and other movements established that the idea of individual rights was still powerful, even if it was not supported by the concept of natural law. Several nations undertook diplomatic and military operations on behalf of persecuted ethnic and religious minorities in the Ottoman Empire, Eastern Europe, and the Middle East. Such "humanitarian intervention" reflected a doctrine of customary international law and asserted that people had intrinsic rights independent of those bestowed by a government. Nevertheless, it took the shock of Nazi atrocities in World War II to force the world to recognize and articulate the fundamental rights of each individual, rights that insured dignity and human worth. The Charter of the United Nations (1945) established some important human rights provisions, such as "promoting and encouraging respect for human rights and for fundamental freedoms for all without distinction as to race, sex, language or religion." The charter is actually international law because it is a treaty and legally binding upon those nations that signed it; however, although it declared universal respect for human rights, the charter never spelled out exactly what those rights were. Realizing the need to give content to its proclamation, the United Nations created a Commission on Human Rights, and in 1948, member nations without dissent adopted the Universal Declaration of Human Rights. The Universal Declaration is not a treaty and does not have the force of law; it merely sets forth a "common standard of achievement for all peoples and all nations." Since its adoption, however, member states have used it, both domestically and internationally, as a standard for judging compliance with the human rights obligations of the UN Charter and it is often considered part of international common law.

Two international covenants guarantee most of the rights enumerated in the Universal Declaration of Human Rights. The International Covenant on Economic, Social and Cultural Rights describes the basic social, economic, and cultural rights of individuals and nations, including the right to work; to reasonable standards of living, education, health, social security, and family life; and to freedom of cultural and scientific practice. The International Covenant on Civil and Political Rights, which went into force in 1976, includes freedoms of thought, conscience, expression, opinion, and religion; the right to free association and peaceable assembly; the right to own and dispose of property; the right to seek asylum from persecution; and a number of rights pertaining to the criminal justice system. The latter include protection from arbitrary arrest or detention, equality before the law, the right to a fair trial, freedom from torture and slavery, and freedom from ex post facto laws.

The covenants are treaties and are thus legally binding upon the countries that sign them. Signatories to the second covenant undertake to respect the listed rights of all people "within its territory and subject to its jurisdiction . . . without distinction of any kind, such as race, color, sex, language, religion, political or other opinion, national or social origin, property, birth, or other status." The covenant departs from the Universal Declaration of Human Rights in not including the right to own property and the right to asylum, but adds the right of self-determination and the right of minorities to enjoy their own cultures, religions, and languages. It also establishes an elected Human Rights Committee to study signatories' reports on what they have done to guarantee the enumerated rights. An Optional Protocol accompanied the covenant; signing the protocol gives the Human Rights Committee the right to investigate and act upon individual's claims to be victims of human rights abuse.

RIGHTS, CRIME, AND PUNISHMENT

The concept of human rights developed as a way to limit the power of the state against its citizens, but, as Locke pointed out, the state also has the duty to protect its citizens against the transgressions of other citizens—and it must do so without abusing the rights of any of the parties involved. There are three ways in which the criminal justice system may become involved in the abuse of human rights. The first is when it enforces laws that are themselves abusive, such as laws of apartheid or racial segregation. The second is when it does not protect some of its constituents against abusive acts by others. The third is when employees of the criminal justice system carry out their mission using tactics that violate human rights.

Among the first to address directly the delicate balance demanded was the Italian criminologist Cesare Beccaria, author of *Treatise on Crimes and Punishments* (1766). Acknowledging his debt to Montesquieu ("Every punishment which is not derived from absolute necessity is tyrannous"), Beccaria maintained that punishments should be related in degree to the severity of the crime, be no harsher than what was minimally necessary to promote social order, and imposed only when the defendant's guilt was certain; he thus rejected the common practice of using torture to gain a confession. Beccaria was among the first to advocate the abolition of the death penalty, arguing that capital punishment "is not a matter of right . . . but an act of war of society against the citizen."

The French Declaration of the Rights of Man also recognized the criminal justice needs of a society that respected individual rights. It did so by concentrating on what would come to be referred to as "due process." It stated, "no man may be accused, arrested, or detained except in the cases determined by law, and according to the forms prescribed thereby. Whoever solicit, expedite, or execute arbitrary orders, or have them executed, must

Citizenship and Human Rights

One of the most significant human rights issues is the denial of citizenship, as people without citizenship in the nation where they live often have far fewer rights, including the right to vote, than do citizens. The Constitution of the Orange Free State in South Africa in the late nineteenth century afforded citizenship only to whites, not to indigenous Africans.

Constitution of the Orange Free State

CHAPTER I. – CITIZENSHIP

Section I. – How Citizenship Is Obtained.

1. Burghers of the Orange Free State are
   a. White persons born from inhabitants of the State both before and after 23 February, 1854.
   b. White Persons who have obtained burgher-right under the regulations of the Constitution of 1854 or the altered Constitution of 1866.
   c. White persons who have lived a year in the State and have fixed property registered under their own names to at least the value of £150.
   d. White persons who have lived three successive years in the State and have made a written promise of allegiance to the State and obedience to the laws, whereupon a certificate of citizenship (burghership) shall be granted by the Landrost of the district where they have settled.
   e. Civil and judicial officials who, before accepting their offices, have taken an oath of allegiance to the State and its laws.

Source: MacFadyen, W. A., trans. (1896). *The Political Laws of South Africa.* Cape Town: J. C. Juta and Co., p. 73.

be punished." It followed Beccaria by establishing proportional penalties and it forbade ex post facto laws. Since, it affirmed, everyone was presumed innocent until proven guilty, arrest and detention must be carried out with only that severity deemed necessary. Some of these provisions evoke the Magna Carta and many would be adopted in the first ten amendments (Bill of Rights) to the Constitution of the United States.

Aware that criminal justice systems were uniquely prone to civil rights violations, the United Nations has issued a number of documents specifically addressing such violations. Relying on the moral authority of the Universal Declaration of Human Rights and the treaty status of the International Covenant on Civil and Political Rights, various U.N. bodies have concerned themselves with the duties and limitations of the agencies that comprise such systems. Among the earliest (1979) is the Code of Conduct for Law Enforcement Officials, adopted by the General Assembly with the recommendation that governments use it as a framework for national legislation. The code calls upon law enforcement officials to protect the human dignity and uphold the human rights of all persons; to limit the use of force; to maintain confidentiality; to prohibit the use of torture or other cruel and degrading treatment; to protect the health of those in their custody; to combat corruption; and to respect the law and the code.

In 1988, the General Assembly adopted a more detailed document addressed to corrections officials, called The Body of Principles for the Protection of All Persons Under Any Form of Detention and Imprisonment. This document contains 39 principles, most of which can be seen as elaborations of Principle 1, "All persons under any form of detention or imprisonment shall be treated in a humane manner and with respect for the inherent dignity of the human person." Other principles specifically call for all arrests, detentions or imprisonments to be carried out in strict accordance with the law and under proper authority; without discrimination; with special status given to the needs of women, children, the elderly, and the handicapped; without torture or cruel, inhuman, or degrading treatment, or punishment under any circumstances; the accused to be informed of the charges and for relatives or others to be informed of the arrest and place of detention; communication with legal counsel; the prohibition of forced confession or self-incrimination; a presumption of innocence for detainees; and entitlement to trial within a reasonable length of time or pending trial. The World War II origin of the contemporary human rights concept can be gleaned from Principle 22, which states, "No detained or imprisoned person shall, even with his consent, be subjected to any medical or scientific experimentation which may be detrimental to his health."

These principles, which enjoined governments not to interfere with a prisoner's rights, were supplemented in 1990 when the General Assembly adopted the Basic

Principles for the Treatment of Prisoners. These latter principles ask prison officials to take positive actions for the well-being of prisoners and begin with the observation that the "function of the criminal justice system is to contribute to safeguarding the basic values and norms of society." After restating that all prisoners should be treated with respect due to their inherent human dignity and value, the document asks member states to recognize prisoners' religious beliefs and cultural precepts; to acknowledge their right to take part in cultural activities and education aimed at "full development of the human personality"; to encourage the abolition of solitary confinement as punishment; to enable prisoners to undertake meaningful remunerated employment that will facilitate their reintegration into the labor market; and to work with the community to create conditions for the reintegration of former prisoners into society. Other U.N. documents bearing directly on criminal justice issues are the Declaration of Protection of All Persons from Enforced Disappearances (1992), the Principles on the Effective Prevention and Investigation of Extra-legal, Arbitrary and Summary Executions (1989), the Convention Against Torture and Other Forms of Cruel, Inhuman or Degrading Treatment or Punishment (1987), and the United Nations Standard Minimum Rules for the Administration of Juvenile Justice (Beijing Rules; 1985). Especially pertinent is the U.N. Declaration on Human Rights Defenders (1988), which calls on states not to harass those who criticize governments for their shortcomings in dealing with human rights abuses. These declarations, principles, and rules do not have the force of international law; they rely on moral suasion and the pressure of public opinion within signatory states.

Although the courts of individual nations handle most human rights abuses, the 43 member states of the Council of Europe have established machinery for "the collective enforcement of certain of the rights stated in the Universal Declaration" (Preamble to the European Convention on Human Rights, 1953). The council has promulgated its own specific and detailed Declaration on the Police and Minimum Standards for the Treatment of Prisoners. Individuals claiming mistreatment under the council's standards may petition the European Commission of Human Rights, which, after investigation, may refer the petition to the European Court on Human Rights. In 1998, the United Nations completed the Rome Statute of the International Criminal Court, another tool for international enforcement of human rights. In it the United Nations laid the ground-

work for an international criminal court for trying and punishing individuals accused of genocide and other crimes against humanity. Once this statute is ratified by 60 signatories, the court will have the power to investigate and bring to justice those accused of such crimes in cases where a state is unable or unwilling to try its own nationals.

ARE HUMAN RIGHTS UNIVERSAL?

Although the concept of human rights tends to elicit general approval, the enumeration of particular rights does not. There has been and continues to be debate over whether rights actually are universal or whether they are culturally based and, therefore, vary with time and place. One approach to this debate is the model of "generations of human rights," advanced by the French jurist Karel Vasak. The first generation of rights was meant to set limits to the power of the state vis-à-vis its citizens. These political and civil rights of individuals clearly reflect secular Western values such as liberal individualism and laissez-faire economics. They are phrased largely—although not entirely—in terms of what the government must *not* do. The assumptions and concepts of the socialist and welfare states added a second generation of socioeconomic and cultural rights. These include rights to employment and fair working conditions, a standard of living that guarantees health as well as social security and education, and special rights for women and children. Most—again, not all—second generation rights favor affirmative duties of the state, requiring that the state implement certain rights for its citizens rather than simply refrain from interfering in their lives. A third generation is sometimes referred to as solidarity or development rights and these are eloquently captured in the African Charter on Human and People's Rights (adopted in 1981), which asserts that the state has an obligation to pursue goals of human betterment and public good above and beyond the protection of the individual. Some of these rights are based on the manifestation of Third World nationalism; these include the right to political, social, cultural, and economic self-determination; the right to economic and social development; and the right to participate in and benefit from "the common heritage of mankind," including scientific and technical information. Other third generation rights suggest that if state power sometimes needs restraint, there are other times when the power of one state is insufficient; included here are the right to peace, to a healthy environment, and to humanitarian relief in times of disaster. The charter specifically recognizes the virtues of Africa's historical tradition and the values of African civilization and it lists duties as well as rights, including duty to family, community, national solidarity, African cultural values, and African unity. Indigenous peoples in many parts of the world may be adding a fourth generation of rights—that of indigenous rights. These are to protect their right to political self-determination and control over socioeconomic development, rights that may be threatened by the state or multinational economic interests. These rights are expressed as belonging to indigenous groups, not to individuals, and explicitly reject the "orientation of earlier standards." Although it is possible to look upon these succeeding generations of rights as simply expanding the concept of human rights, it is impossible to ignore that they shift the locus of rights among the individual, the community, and the state; that they challenge the notion of universality; and that they are at times mutually exclusive.

Although there may be occasional disagreement over the priority or the judicablity of specific rights, there is wide international agreement on their moral status. The concept of human rights has provided a language in which all the peoples of the planet can express their highest aspirations for a better world.

—*Dorothy H. Bracey*

See also GENOCIDE; INTERNATIONAL CRIMINAL COURT; PRISONER RIGHTS; VICTIM RIGHTS AND RESTITUTION; WAR CRIMES

Further Reading

Crawshaw, Ralph, Barry Devlin, and Tom Williamson. (1998). *Human Rights and Policing: Standards for Good Behavior and a Strategy for Change.* The Hague, The Netherlands: Kluwer Law.

International Human Rights Standards for Law Enforcement: A Pocket Book on Human Rights for the Policy. (1966). New York and Geneva: United Nations.

Ishay, Micheline, ed. (1997). *The Human Rights Reader.* New York: Routledge.

Lauren, Paul Gordon. (1998). *The Evolution of International Human Rights.* Philadelphia: University of Pennsylvania Press.

Little, David, et al., eds. *Human Rights and the Conflict of Cultures.* Columbia: University of South Carolina Press.

Mayer, Elizabeth. (1995). *Islam and Human Rights: Tradition and Politics.* San Francisco and Boulder, CO: Westview/Harper-Collins.

Vasak, Karel, and Philip Alston. (1982). *The International Dimensions of Human Rights.* Westport, CT: Greenwood Press.

Welch, Claude, and Virginia Leary, eds. (1990). *Asian Perspectives on Human Rights.* Boulder, CO: Westview.

▼ HYPNOSIS

Hypnosis may be best described as an altered state of consciousness in which a person is more prone to accept appropriate suggestions. A person in a state of hypnosis can sometimes be induced to recall events or details of events that he or she may not be able, for a variety of reasons, to call up while fully conscious. Because of this ability, hypnosis has been found to be occasionally useful in criminal investigations to help victims or witnesses recall details of alleged crimes. When employed in a criminal investigatory setting, this approach is called forensic hypnosis. Many types of cases have benefited from the application of forensic hypnosis techniques: investigations of numerous robberies, assaults, and kidnappings have been aided with the information gleaned from an investigative hypnosis session.

While the use of hypnosis for criminal investigations is a relatively recent phenomenon, the practice of what is now called hypnosis has a history that dates back more than three thousand years. Evidence of hypnotic events is found in nearly every culture and is intertwined with many rituals and religious ceremonies. In contemporary Western history, there are descriptions of induced states that were believed to have a great impact on an individual's well-being.

HYPNOSIS: MYTH AND REALITY

In 1843, James Braid, a Scottish physician who has been called the father of modern hypnotism, coined the term *hypnosis* from the Greek word *hypnos*, meaning to sleep. This was later determined to be an unfortunate term, as the state now described as hypnosis does not involve sleep. In fact, Braid later tried to change the term to "neurynology" or "monoideism"; however, the original term had already taken root. Braid first became involved with the practice of mesmerism, named for Franz Anton Mesmer, a German physician of the late eighteenth and early nineteenth century. Mesmer claimed the ability to cure or control many biological and psychological disorders. By most accounts, however, he was more charlatan than scientist, and was reported to have based much of his work on ideas that were plagiarized from an English physician, Dr. Richard Mead. Interestingly, Mead's writings were derived from the research of one of his patients—none other than Sir Isaac Newton.

Through the years, much has been written about

hypnosis, primarily as it relates to the work of physicians and psychologists; however, the extravagant and often frivolous claims offered by early practitioners continue to cloud the credibility of this practice. Misconceptions about hypnosis abound, and the continuing exploits of stage hypnotists and other entertainers have done little to clear the waters. As a result, the adoption of hypnosis techniques in the criminal forensic arena met with some difficulty. There were cases using hypnosis in criminal investigations going back hundreds of years, but the investigative use of hypnosis became more popular in the United States in the early 1970s.

The actual hypnotic experience can be somewhat different for each individual, making a strict definition of it elusive. Hypnosis is not sleep; this is probably one of the most common myths regarding hypnosis. Stage hypnotists' use of statements such as, "You are getting sleepy," and their repetition of the word "sleep," are carryovers from the nineteenth century. Actually, the hypnotized subject is not asleep, as that would clearly preclude asking questions. The depth or level of this state can be quite different for each person. A deep state of hypnosis has been described by some as similar to the twilight time either right before one falls asleep or right before one fully awakes in the morning. Many people have experienced what has been termed "highway hypnosis": a person may occasionally arrive at a point in traveling down a highway where the person suddenly realizes that he or she does not recall recent events in the drive. Clearly, the person was operating a vehicle and was not asleep, but the person's attentive state was altered. It is most likely the case that the person was processing some event or thought that took conscious precedence over the routine of driving.

The definition above also indicates that appropriate suggestions are important. Another popular myth about hypnosis implies that people may lose control while hypnotized and do things that would go against their nature. The reality is much less sinister: in many ways, all hypnosis is self-hypnosis. If a person does not wish to be hypnotized, or does not wish to cooperate in the process, it will not work; there is little that anyone can do to create a state of hypnosis in an unwilling subject. Other people are sometimes concerned that they will not "come out" of hypnosis, resulting in some form of continuing altered state. However, the subject is always aware of all events surrounding the hypnosis session; any event or circumstance that might elicit psychological discomfort can result in the hypnotized individual's willfully returning to full consciousness.

Stage hypnotists would have people believe that they possess unusual powers to command the consciousness of their participants. However, a more careful review of what a stage hypnotist actually does reveals that the suggestibility of most individuals is related to the art of performance. To be willing to go up on stage in the first place, one must be willing to expose a part of oneself to others. Further, as the stage hypnotist continues the routine, if a person on the stage does not comply or go along, they are usually dismissed from the platform. As a result, the stage hypnotist is left with individuals who have "contracted" to follow the directions of the entertainer. There are a whole host of other psychological issues involved in this compliance process, but they are too involved to elaborate here.

Another myth regarding hypnosis involves the notion that those who are of below-average intelligence make ideal hypnotic subjects, because they are weak-minded. Actually, it appears that just the opposite is the case. Because hypnosis requires one's consent and acquiescence, and because the induction process often involves following particular visualization and other instructions, the best subjects are also often the brightest.

THE FORENSIC HYPNOSIS SESSION

There are a number of types of people who are not appropriate subjects for a forensic hypnosis session. Offenders are not hypnotized, as they would be less likely to be sincere and may simply create new fictions in this hypersuggestible state. Additionally, the legal implications for employing this technique are prohibitive. Others who are typically not good hypnosis subjects are those who are very old or very young, or those with below-average intelligence; these individuals lack the ability to fully concentrate and follow the careful directions of the hypnotist. Those who may express an outward willingness to be hypnotized, but are inwardly reluctant (possibly because the associated myths have not been fully dispelled) will also not make good subjects.

The main value of forensic hypnosis for the investigator is in refreshing or enhancing the recollections of victims and witnesses. A forensic hypnotist who wishes to be successful in doing this must remove any of a subject's concerns regarding the misconceptions elaborated above. Without rapport and trust between the hypnotist and the subject, no effective session can be achieved.

The typical hypnosis session usually begins with a brief questionnaire to provide the hypnotist with important information used in the induction process, such as whether a subject is more likely to be a visualizer (seeing things in the mind's eye) or a sensor (e.g., responding to warmth). This is followed by a period of rapport-building and an explanation of the process. After all the subject's questions have been answered and he or she seems comfortable, the hypnotist may employ one or more "suggestibility tests" to develop a hypnotic induction profile (HIP). This helps the hypnotist determine what induction approach might be best and roughly what level of hypnosis depth might be expected. Typically, there are three to six levels of depth of hypnosis, ranging from light hypnosis to somnambulism, a very deep state of consciousness.

The induction process itself often follows a relaxation and visualization pattern that is tailored to the subject based on his or her responses in the questionnaire. This process is critical if the subject is to achieve a sufficient state of hypnosis to provide the investigator with useful information. After an appropriate depth level is achieved, the forensic hypnotist may then proceed with certain questions in an attempt to elicit key information.

There are numerous techniques that can be employed in this process. The "documentary technique" involves suggesting to the subject that he or she is viewing the events in question as though they were a documentary film, and the subject has complete control over the film, including the ability to reverse, pause, and fast-forward the events. The detached nature of the documentary suggestion helps to remove overwhelming emotions that might be present, and the control feature allows the subject to direct the internal images.

Another approach involves the "covered chalkboard." Here the subject is asked to visualize a chalkboard with a velvet (for example) cover over it so that the writing on the board is not presently visible. This process best serves cases in which the subject is trying to recall some particular information, such as a license plate. At the appropriate time, the subject is told to mentally remove the cover and read the information on the chalkboard.

Once the hypnotist concludes that all useful information has been obtained, or that further attempts during the session would not be productive, the subject is slowly directed to realign his or her conscious state. (After being in a relatively relaxed condition for some time, the subject often needs a few minutes to adjust his or her mindset.) Of course, the subject is fully aware of all discussions and events that occurred during the session. The subject may ask any questions that he or she may have and, depending on the results of the process, there may be some suggestions for further attempts at recollection or future hypnosis sessions.

Despite the many misconceptions that linger regarding the hypnosis process, forensic hypnosis remains one of many valuable tools available to the criminal investigator. If a subject is unwilling to be hypnotized, or is convinced that hypnotism does not work, then the procedure will be ineffective. However, with a cooperative and competent subject, it is sometimes possible through hypnosis to glean crucial bits of information that may lead to the resolution of a criminal case.

—*Randall L. Garner*

Further Reading

Arons, Harry. (1977). *Hypnosis in Criminal Investigation*. New Jersey: Power Publishers, Inc.

Garner, R. L. (1994). *Forensic and Therapeutic Hypnosis*. Houston: University of Houston.

Kroger, William. (1977). *Clinical and Experimental Hypnosis*. Philadelphia: Lippincott.

▼ IDENTITY THEFT

Identity theft is one of the fastest growing crimes of the new millennium. It occurs when, for fraudulent purposes, someone uses bits and pieces of information about an individual—usually a Social Security number—to represent him- or herself as that person.

There are numerous varieties of identity theft. Examples of application fraud, also called "true name fraud," include obtaining credit cards and loans in someone else's name and then not paying the bills, opening utility accounts, renting an apartment, getting a cellular phone, and purchasing a car or home. Another variety, account takeover, occurs when the thief obtains the account number of the victim's existing credit card or bank account by wallet theft, or perhaps by fishing transaction slips out of the trash. The perpetrator usually makes many purchases in a short period of time, often by mail order or over the Internet. Account takeover is often detected and halted early when the victim notices the fraudulent charges on his or her monthly account statement and reports them to the creditor.

One of the most serious types of identity fraud is criminal identity theft. This occurs when the perpetrator is arrested for crimes and provides the victim's name to law enforcement, thus giving that person a criminal record. Criminal identity theft and application fraud are often not detected by the victim for many months or even years.

Under federal law, victims are not liable for the bills accumulated by the thieves. But they do have the anxiety and frustration of spending months—sometimes years—restoring their credit history.

CRIME STATISTICS

There are no sources of accurate statistics on identity theft. However, based on credit industry figures, the Privacy Rights Clearinghouse (PRC) estimates there were 500,000 to 700,000 thousand victims in 2000. A 1998 report by the U.S. General Accounting Office (GAO) tracked identity theft statistics from 1992 to 1997, based on figures provided by the Trans Union credit reporting agency (CRA). A graph in the report shows a dramatic sixteen-fold increase in the volume of telephone calls to Trans Union's fraud department during that six-year period (U.S. General Accounting Office 1998: 40). Other CRAs, such as Equifax and Experian, also maintain records on identity theft.

REASONS FOR THE GROWTH OF IDENTITY THEFT

There are three reasons why identity theft is rampant. First, it is easy for criminals to obtain the information needed, in particular, Social Security numbers (SSNs). Second, not all credit issuers use stringent application verification procedures, making it easy to obtain credit. Finally, because of law enforcement resource shortages and light sentences, the crime is low risk for the perpetrators.

Use of SSNs by the private sector has not to date been prohibited by law. As a result, SSNs are used as identification and account numbers by many entities, including insurance companies, universities, cable television companies, the military, banks, and brokerage firms. In about a dozen states, the SSN is used as the driver's license number.

Identity thieves obtain Social Security numbers by stealing mail, seeking documents that contain account numbers and Social Security numbers. They sift through the trash outside of businesses and residences to find unshredded documents containing identifying information. Dishonest employees can obtain the numbers in the workplace by obtaining access to personnel files or using credit reporting databases, commonly available in auto dealerships, realtors' offices, banks, and other businesses that approve loans.

A significant percent of identity theft cases—one in eight, according to Federal Trade Commission (FTC) statistics—are perpetrated by family members, relatives, friends, roommates, home health-care providers, and others who have easy access to their victims' SSNs. Wallet theft is another common source of identifying information. Increasingly, thieves obtain SSNs from the Web sites of information brokers who sell "credit headers." The headers, sold by credit bureaus to information brokers, include the identification portion of the credit report: name, current and past addresses, phone number, year and month of birth, and SSN. At this writing, Congress has not been able to pass legislation to prohibit the commercial sale of SSNs, primarily because of opposition from those who sell and use credit headers—information brokers, the credit industry, and private investigators.

Credit issuer practices also facilitate identity theft. In this highly competitive industry, zeal to attract new customers often contributes to lax application verification procedures, especially in instant credit situations. Another reason identity theft is skyrocketing is that most law enforcement agencies do not have adequate staff and resources to investigate the crime and apprehend the criminals. Not only is the investigation of such crimes highly labor-intensive and time-consuming, but most cases involve multiple jurisdictions. Many violent criminals and organized crime rings have begun to commit identity theft because they know that law enforcement resources are not sufficient to investigate the majority of such crimes. As a result, identity thieves are rarely apprehended and sentenced. If they are, penalties are minimal and may include only brief jail sentences. Typical sentences are community service and probation.

IMPACT ON VICTIMS

Even though each identity fraud case is different, what happens to victims is, unfortunately, all too similar.

Because of society-wide institutional failures, the majority of victims find they must shoulder the burden themselves. As explained above, law enforcement agencies are unable to investigate many such crimes because of a shortage of resources. Some police and sheriff's departments do not issue police reports to the victims, claiming that banks and credit card companies are the real victims because they suffer the financial losses. Yet many victims find they need the police report to prove their innocence to credit card companies and check-guarantee services. Staffing and budget shortfalls also prevent the agencies that issue the most common forms of identification—the various state Departments of Motor Vehicles (DMVs) and the Social Security Administration (SSA)—from adequately assisting victims.

Many victims report they do not get effective help from financial institutions. They describe difficulty in reaching the credit reporting agencies, and they say that some creditors do not believe their reports of identity theft. Victims also report that flagging their credit report for fraud does not always stop the imposter from obtaining more credit. Victims must also deal with abusive collection agencies; they are threatened with lawsuits, garnished wages, and having their homes taken away from them.

Victims must spend a great deal of time to regain their financial health. Many have to take time off from work to make the necessary phone calls, write letters, and get affidavits notarized. A study by CALPIRG and the Privacy Rights Clearinghouse (2000) found the average amount of time spent by victims to regain their financial health was 175 hours, or about four working weeks. On average, it takes two years before victims' credit reports are back to normal.

Victims are often scarred emotionally. They feel violated, helpless, angry, and frustrated. Little wonder. They may be unable to rent an apartment, get a job, qualify for a mortgage, or buy a car, all because, due to no fault of their own, someone else's bad credit history is recorded on their credit report.

The worst-case scenario is when the thief is arrested or cited for crimes in the victim's name. Victims can be arrested and detained unexpectedly, for example, when stopped for a minor traffic violation. When the officer runs a criminal check and finds an outstanding warrant for the arrest of the imposter—for, say, DUI or shoplifting and failure to appear in court—the victim is likely to be arrested on the spot and jailed, despite his or her most ardent protestations.

Such victims find it virtually impossible to erase the wrongful criminal record, and they can be saddled with it for life. Because background checks are increasingly being conducted by employers, such individuals can find it virtually impossible to find work. Another worst-case scenario is when the imposter works under the victim's name and/or SSN, and the earnings are reported on the victim's SSA record. Victims of employment fraud often must deal with the Internal Revenue Service because tax records show they are underreporting their wages.

Finally, in order for victims to recover from the crime of identity theft, they must be fairly savvy and possess good communication skills. They must be assertive with financial industry representatives, as well as law enforcement officers and officials of the DMV and SSA. Those who do not speak English well or have limited literacy are unable to write the necessary letters and to communicate verbally with those who have the power to clear their wrongful records. Unfortunately, there are not enough consumer assistance offices to help such victims.

LEGISLATIVE, INDUSTRY, AND LAW ENFORCEMENT SOLUTIONS

The awareness of identity theft among consumers has skyrocketed in recent years, primarily because of media coverage. Outcries by consumers have resulted in legislative activity at both the federal and state levels. In 1998, Congress passed the Identity Theft and Assumption Deterrence Act (18 USC § 1028). It makes identity theft, when someone knowingly uses the identification of another person with the intention to commit any unlawful activity, a felony under federal law. This law also establishes an identity theft clearinghouse within the Federal Trade Commission. The FTC offers a toll-free number for consumers to call (877-IDTHEFT), as well as a Web site. In recent years, many states have criminalized identity theft.

However, criminalizing identity theft has not decreased the incidence of this crime. Prevention and victim assistance are the key policy solutions now facing legislators and industry. In recent years, several legislative measures have been introduced, at both the state level and in Congress, although few at this writing have been passed into law. These provisions include address discrepancy notification, credit grantor penalties for ignoring fraud alerts, a ban on the commercial sale of SSNs, limitations on uses and display of SSNs,

> ### Protecting Your Social Security Number
>
> Your employer and financial institution will likely need your SSN for wages and tax reporting purposes. Other private businesses may ask you for your SSN to do a credit check, such as when you apply for a car loan. Sometimes, however, they simply want your SSN for general record keeping. You don't have to give a business your SSN just because they ask for it. If someone requests your SSN, ask the following questions:
>
> Why do you need my SSN?
>
> How will my SSN be used?
>
> What law requires me to give you my SSN?
>
> What will happen if I don't give you my SSN?
>
> Sometimes a business may not provide you with the service or benefit you're seeking if you don't provide your SSN. Getting answers to these questions will help you decide whether you want to share your SSN with the business. Remember, though, that the decision is yours.
>
> Source: *ID Theft: When Bad Things Happen to Your Good Name.* (2001). Washington, DC: Federal Trade Commission.

expedited removal of fraudulent accounts from credit reports, development of uniform reporting requirements for victims, funding for DMV biometrics systems, and development of mechanisms for criminal identity theft victims to clear their wrongful criminal records.

Legislation is not the entire answer to the vexing problem of identity theft. The credit granting and reporting industries must step up their efforts to prevent fraud altogether and to help victims recover from identity theft. The crime of identity theft also calls for new approaches by law enforcement. One approach that is being explored in California, pioneered by the Los Angeles Sheriff's Department, is the development of a single unit within the police department that specializes in identity theft. Another promising approach—one that addresses the multi-jurisdictional aspect of identity theft—is the development of multi-agency task forces comprised of area law enforcement agencies; the Department of Motor Vehicles in the various states; federal agencies such as the Secret Service, FBI, Postal Inspection Services, and SSA; and county and federal prosecutors and court systems. One such task force has been established in Santa Clara County, California.

IMPLICATIONS

A multitude of institutional failures in both the private and public sectors have contributed to the epidemic of identity theft in the United States. Reforms in credit industry practices are essential to preventing this crime. Law enforcement agencies must develop new multi-jurisdictional approaches to investigating identity theft and bringing the perpetrators to justice. The court system must reexamine its lenient approach to sentencing. The debilitating impact of identity theft on victims calls for streamlined reporting mechanisms, swift repair of credit histories, and, in the worst-case scenario of criminal identity theft, mechanisms to enable individuals to clear their wrongful criminal records.

—Beth Givens

See also CYBERCRIME; DIGITAL CRIME

Further Reading

CALPIRG and Privacy Rights Clearinghouse. (2000). "Nowhere to Turn: Victims Speak Out on Identity Theft." http://www.calpirg.org. http://www.privacyrights.org

Federal Trade Commission. http: www.consumer.gov/idtheft

Frank, Mari. (1998). *From Victim to Victor*. Laguna Niguel, CA: Porpoise Press.

Frank, Mari, and Beth Givens. (2001). *Privacy Piracy: A Guide to Protecting Yourself from Identity Theft*. Laguna Niguel, CA: Porpoise Press.

Identity Theft Resource Center. http://www.idtheftcenter.org

Privacy Rights Clearinghouse. (2000). "Organizing Your Identity Theft Case." http://www.privacyrights.org/fs/fs17b-org.htm

———. (2001). "Identity Theft: What to Do If It Happens To You." http://www.privacyrights.org/fs/fs17a.htm

U.S. General Accounting Office. (1998). "Identity Fraud." Report No. GGD-98-100BR. http://www.gao.gov

▼ ILLICIT ANTIQUITIES

Most nations have placed some kind of sovereign claim on their archaeological heritage. In nations with strong patrimony laws, it is illegal for an unauthorized individual to excavate or own antiquities (which are in effect taken into state ownership); in those with less stringent legislation, it is legal to own antiquities but not to export them.

Illicit antiquities are archaeological objects—whether artifacts from below ground or pieces forcibly removed from standing monuments—that have been illegally excavated and/or exported from their country of origin. There is a thriving trade in such material, whether it be Paracas textiles from Peru, stone Khmer sculpture from Cambodia, ceramic vases from Italy, coins from England, terra-cotta statuettes from West Africa, or bronze Natarajas from India. Trade in illicit antiquities is thought to rank third in illegal trade value, after arms and narcotics. Every antiquity, it seems, can command a price, and every country has a supply.

The demand for illicit antiquities is created by museums and private collectors in Europe, North America, and, increasingly, Japan. Historically, antiquities have been collected as "works of art"; however, when compared to mainstream art (Old Masters, Picasso, etc.), they are thought to be undervalued, so they are increasingly being collected for their investment potential. They also are popular as designer ornaments, and they appear on television studio sets and in the salons of the stylish.

CONCERNED PARTIES

Archaeologists are concerned about the trade in illicit antiquities because the method of their acquisition entails destruction of archaeological context and a loss of archaeological provenance. In other words, if it is not known with what other objects an antiquity was found, or even where it was found, its potential as an object of historical study is sharply diminished. For example, the monetary value of a small Roman pot can be readily established, but the historical interest of such a pot found in India far outweighs that of an identical specimen found in Italy. When details of the find spot are lost, so is the historical interest. Furthermore, archaeologists rely on meticulous recovery and examination of all available evidence, the microscopic and everyday as much as the beautiful and valuable; yet fragile material or material thought to be of no value is routinely destroyed during illicit excavation. Again, archaeologists view this as a loss of historical knowledge.

Collectors and dealers disagree; they argue that their actions are not harmful because they are "rescuing" material that would otherwise be destroyed during agricultural, urban, or industrial development projects. They also suggest that the aesthetic merit of a piece—its beauty—may outweigh its historical interest, and that its destructive or clandestine excavation can therefore be justified. Better to be seen than left in the ground, they claim.

Governments are concerned about the trade in illicit antiquities, because it is a challenge to the sovereignty of the state and an attack on the national heritage. This heritage increasingly is seen to have an economic potential, because intact archaeological sites and monuments can provide a base for the development of cultural tourism. Gaping holes in the ground and mutilated temples make poor tourist attractions.

Law enforcement agencies are concerned not only because the trade in illicit antiquities is itself criminal, but also because it has links with other criminal enterprises. For example, in some areas of South Asia and Central and South America, local drug barons are active in the looting and smuggling of antiquities. The Italian police suspect that antiquities from southern Italy may be used in money-laundering operations by the Mafia, while U.S. Customs officials suggest that Miami has become a crossroads for the trade in illicit antiquities because of the large amounts of "dirty money" in circulation there.

THE TRADE IN ILLICIT ANTIQUITIES

From a criminological perspective, the trade in illicit antiquities is unique for two reasons. First, it has a widely dispersed—indeed, global—pattern of supply but relatively focused areas of demand. Thus, most countries of the world have an archaeological heritage that can be plundered, but the ultimate demand lies mainly in the West, with a small (albeit growing) group of private and institutional collectors. Second, the trade is neither totally licit nor totally illicit. In Europe and North America, antiquities are sold openly at public auctions and reputable galleries, and bought by law-abiding citizens. Thus, an antiquity that was originally obtained through illegal means must, at

▼

Illicit Antiquities: The Red List

The Red List (www.icom.org/redlist) is a Web site maintained by the International Council of Museums to list archaeological objects at risk for looting in Africa. The following listing is for Ife terra-cotta and bronzes in Nigeria.

Provenance
The regions of Ife and Owo, southwest Nigeria.

Characteristics
Ife, as the capital and religious center of southwest Nigeria, was one of the first cities to emerge at this latitude at the end of the first millennium AD. Substantial numbers of anthropomorphic and zoomorphic sculptures (elephants, rams, etc.), mainly in terra-cotta but also in brass, were produced in the region between the eleventh and the fifteenth centuries. Human and animal representations with the same characteristics were also added in high relief on spherical pottery. All these items are known on the market as "Ife art," although they may come from other cities such as Owo. These brass objects (commonly known as "bronze") are strikingly realistic, although they are almost certainly idealised portraits of dead kings or Oni. In most cases, they are isolated life-sized heads, sometimes broken off busts, and exceptional full-length figurines around 50 centimeters high, crowned and wearing heavy necklaces. Some heads are circled with a diadem, whereas others exhibit perforations around the skull and on occasions on the neck, on the chin, and around the mouth. The terra-cotta heads are far more numerous and varied. Their height ranges from 25 centimeters to close to life-size. Effigies of bodies, whole or fragmented, have also been found elsewhere. The heads from Owo generally carry headgear in the place of diadems, and many of them are gagged. Some of the faces, whether made of brass or terra-cotta, carry vertical parallel incisions. Alongside these naturalistic figures, some highly abstract human heads were produced. On a cone, a mouth has been gouged out, and eyes are represented in the form of round holes. A number of horn-like excrescences emerge from the top of the skull.

The Urgency of the Situation
The policy of keeping the local population informed, adopted by the Nigerian authorities from 1945 onward, has led to the setting up of public collections of Ife works found during excavations or given by the king or local inhabitants if the objects were discovered during construction work. But the scarcity value of items now available on the market, combined with rising demand over the last few years, has been an incentive to violence and robbery on a massive scale from Nigerian museums. Between April 1993 and November 1994, some forty items were stolen from the Ife museum. Between May 1993 and May 1997, security staff in the Owo museum were savagely attacked, one killed and others seriously wounded. In the last ten years, dozens of objects of this kind have appeared on the art market in Europe and North America. However, three terra-cotta heads stolen from the Ile-Ife National Museum were recovered in Paris and restituted to Nigeria in 1996.

some point in its trading history, enter the legitimate market so that its purchase will not contravene the law and its ownership will not attract public censure. In effect, it must be laundered. During this laundering process, a respectable ownership history is substituted for an originally illicit one. Usually it is claimed that the antiquity is from an old family collection that dates back several generations, so that original, documentary proof of legal acquisition has long been lost, and furthermore, the vendor or previous owner wishes to remain anonymous so that inquiries into its history are blocked. Thus, it is not possible for a discerning buyer to carry out a rigorous check on the pedigree of a potential purchase, and the licit cannot be distinguished from the illicit.

There are two circumstances that conspire to facilitate antiquities laundering. First, most illicit antiquities, particularly those that have been illegally and thus clandestinely excavated, were not registered on any inventory of museum acquisitions or stolen property before they entered circulation. They cannot be securely identified as stolen property. Even when it can be recognized that an antiquity is from a country that claims state ownership (a vase from southern Italy, for instance), it will not be treated as stolen property unless the country in question can prove that the piece was exported after the date of the relevant patrimony statute—which in most cases was in the twentieth century. Obviously, if the antiquity has been secretly excavated and smuggled, the date of export is unlikely to be revealed.

Second, many antiquities are sold in civil law countries of continental Europe, whose property law differs from that of the United Kingdom and United States in that title to a stolen object can be obtained by means of a good-faith purchase and may subsequently become a legitimate object of commerce. So, even if it can be demonstrated unequivocally that an antiquity was taken illegally from its country of origin, it will no longer be regarded in law as stolen if it was subsequently bought in good faith in a country such as Switzerland—which is a major center of the antiquities trade. This loophole has led to the development of the concept of due diligence: the level of diligence that a prospective purchaser must exercise when investigating the history of a piece, in order to establish a claim to have acted in good faith.

Thus, although quantitative studies of market trends, together with evidence of on-the-ground destruction, can demonstrate which categories of antiquities are likely to be largely illicit, it is generally not possible to determine definitively in any particular instance that an antiquity was originally obtained illicitly.

INTERNATIONAL RESPONSE

The trade in illicit antiquities, and indeed in other types of cultural material, was recognized as a threat to the world's archaeological heritage in the late 1960s. Two international conventions have been drafted as a result.

The first was the 1970 United Nations Educational, Scientific and Cultural Organization (UNESCO) Convention on the Means of Prohibiting and Preventing the Illicit Import, Export, and Transfer of Ownership of Cultural Property. As of December 1999, this Convention had been ratified by 91 countries, including the United States (but not the United Kingdom or Switzerland, although both were considering ratification).

The relevant U.S. legislation is the 1983 Convention on Cultural Property Implementation Act (CCPIA), which allows the U.S. government to respond to requests from other states party to the UNESCO convention to impose import restrictions on certain classes of archaeological or ethnographic material. Import restrictions apply even if material is exported to the United States from a country other than that of its origin. The CCPIA is not retrospective; therefore, its emphasis is on the protection of material with a still undisturbed context rather than on the return of material whose context is already lost. As of December 2000, the United States had agreements with nine countries and was considering requests from several more. To help customs officers recognize restricted material, a Web site is maintained by the U.S. State Department, which carries images of typical restricted objects so that they can be quickly and easily identified at border checkpoints.

In 1995, the International Institute for the Unification of Private Law (UNIDROIT) Convention on Stolen and Illegally Exported Cultural Objects was created. It was intended to remedy some of the deficiencies of the UNESCO Convention. As of April 2000, it had been ratified by twelve countries, but not the United States or the United Kingdom.

OTHER SOLUTIONS

Several solutions to the trade in illicit antiquities have been suggested, but none have gained the assent or even the acquiescence of all interested parties. A supply-side strategy is favored by collectors and dealers. First, they ask that the so-called source countries make greater efforts to protect their own heritage. Second, they suggest that if these countries made a greater number of licit objects available on the open market, then the incentive to buy or trade in illicit material would diminish. Opponents argue that collectors would not want to buy the poorer quality material that would probably be released onto the market—both collectors and governments would want to own unique pieces, not the mundane ones.

Demand-side strategies tend to be favored by archaeologists and international organizations such as UNESCO and ICOM (International Council of Museums). First, campaigns of public education should be carried out to convince potential collectors that the trade and collection of illicit antiquities are economically as well as culturally destructive enterprises. Second, there should be greater regulation of the international market to render it more transparent and make it more difficult to launder antiquities. Advocates of deregulation oppose this solution, arguing that increased regulation might serve only to drive the trade further underground and lead to greater criminalization.

—*Neil Brodie*

See also ART THEFT AND FRAUD; SMUGGLING

Further Reading

Briat, Martine, and Judith A. Freedberg, eds. (1996). *Legal Aspects of International Trade in Art*. The Hague, The Netherlands: Kluwer Law International.

Culture Without Context (Newsletter of the Illicit Antiquities Research Centre, Cambridge, United Kingdom). http://www-mcdonald.arch.cam.ac.uk/IARC/CWOC/contents.htm

Messenger, Phyllis M., ed. (1999). *The Ethics of Collecting Cultural Property*. Albuquerque: University of New Mexico.

O'Keefe, Patrick J. (1997). *Trade in Antiquities: Reducing Destruction and Theft*. London: Archetype/UNESCO.

Renfrew, Colin. (2000). *Loot, Legitimacy, and Ownership*. London: Duckworth.

Tubb, Kathryn W., ed. (1995). *Antiquities: Trade or Betrayed*. London: Archetype/UKIC.

U.S. State Department: International Cultural Property Protection. http://exchanges.state.gov/education/culprop

▼ INCAPACITATION

See REHABILITATION MODEL; SELECTIVE INCAPACITATION

▼ INDETERMINATE SENTENCES

An indeterminate sentence is a term of imprisonment with no definite duration, only a specified maximum and minimum number of years. The philosophy behind indeterminate sentences is that sentencing should be based on individual circumstances and on the offender's rehabilitation efforts while incarcerated. In some states, a trial judge choosing a sentence is limited by law to a narrow range of options, called determinate sentences; for example, burglary might be punishable by three, five, or seven years in prison. In states with indeterminate sentences, however, a crime such as first-degree murder may be punishable with a sentence of "twenty years to life." In such a case, the state's parole board decides when, if ever, the defendant should be paroled after he or she has served the twenty-year minimum; eligibility for parole is determined on the basis of the characteristics and behavior of the convicted individual. Statutes for determinate sentences usually provide for parole eligibility after a specified fraction of the full term—in most instances, from one-half to two-thirds of the original sentence.

DETERMINATE VERSUS INDETERMINATE SENTENCING

A defendant sentenced to "thirty days in county jail" or "five years in state prison" has received a determinate sentence. Defendants who receive determinate sentences know the maximum period of incarceration as soon as they are sentenced, and in most cases even before sentencing, because the crime determines the sentence. They may get out earlier, however, because of parole, because they have earned "good time" credits, or because the jail or prison is overcrowded and their beds are needed for new inmates.

In states that require judges to give indeterminate sentences, the defendant has no idea, even after sentencing, how long his or her sentence will actually be. The punishment is not known because it depends on future decisions by a parole board. For example, a defendant sentenced to serve "not less than two nor more than twenty years in the state penitentiary" has received an indeterminate sentence. As a general rule, indeterminate sentences are imposed only on people who are sentenced to state prison after being convicted of a felony.

In current practice, release on parole from an indeterminate sentence is initiated by the recommendation of prison staff personnel, field parole officers, and the parole authorities. Evaluation of the offender's conduct in prison, life history, prospects in the community, general personality, and attitude, together with the nature of the original offense, determines his or her suitability for parole. With indeterminate sentencing, two individuals convicted of identical crimes may be treated differently depending on their character, their life histories, or their motives and intentions. Determinate sentencing, on the other hand, is supposed to treat identical crimes in an identical fashion. There is little or no discretion in determinate sentencing; there is considerable discretion in indeterminate sentencing.

HISTORY OF INDETERMINATE SENTENCING

The word *parole* means "word" in French, and its use in connection with the release of prisoners was derived from the idea that prisoners (usually prisoners of war) could be released on their word of honor. A captured knight in the Hundred Years' War between England and France (1338–1453), for instance, could be released in return for a promise not to run away and rejoin his own side; or, he could promise to return by a certain date or pay a ransom.

The practice of allowing prisoners to be released from prison before serving the sentence of imprisonment pronounced by the court became more commonplace in eighteenth-century England. At that time, almost all serious crimes were punishable by death, but only a small proportion of those who were convicted of felonies were actually executed. The majority of those who were sentenced to death were pardoned by the king on the condition that they consent to be transported to one of the penal colonies where labor was required. During the seventeenth and eighteenth centuries, this was America; following American independence, Australia. Convicts were sent to these settlements as a way to reduce the number of felons in the British Isles. The hope was that these settlements would be places where the convicts could be rehabilitated.

Eventually, the courts were given power to pass these "sentences of transportation," as they were called, usually for a specified period; however, most sentences of transportation were modified by executive action. In particular, there developed the system of "ticket-of-leave," under which a convict detained in a sentence of transportation was allowed a measure of freedom or the right to return to England, in return for good behavior.

When the sentence of transportation was abolished in the mid-nineteenth century, the sentence that replaced it in English law—penal servitude (imprisonment with hard labor)—incorporated the same procedure under a different name, "release on license." Prisoners who had been sentenced to penal servitude could earn their release from the penitentiary, but not from the shadow of the sentence, by their good behavior while in custody. Whether they were released was decided by the executive government and was conditional on good behavior once the prisoner was outside of prison; if another offense was committed, the prisoner could be returned to prison to serve out the rest of the sentence (known as the "remanet"). However, the system of release from sentences of penal servitude became almost inflexible toward the end of the nineteenth century, with the result that all prisoners serving the sentence were released after serving a fixed and determinate sentence. In the United States at this time, however, the principle of the indeterminate sentence became widely accepted and eventually formed the basis of the sentencing laws of many states. New York put the first significant indeterminate sentence law into effect in 1877 for offenders sentenced to Elmira Reformatory.

In states where the indeterminate sentence was adopted, the law required that a judge sentencing an offender to a term of imprisonment fix maximum and minimum limits of confinement; the actual date and the conditions of the offender's release were then decided by an executive body usually known as the parole board, which also had the power to revoke the offender's parole and return him or her to prison if the board deemed it necessary. The indeterminate sentence was seen to have a number of advantages over the more rigid sentence in which the prisoner could work out the exact date of release from the moment he or she was sentenced. For one thing, the indeterminate sentence allowed the authorities to observe the behavior and attitudes of offenders while they were serving the sentences, and, in particular, to determine whether they had changed for the better. It also provided an incentive to the prisoner to improve, in order to convince the authorities that he or she was ready for release.

In addition to contributing to the rehabilitation of the offender, the indeterminate sentence had a number of administrative advantages for the prison authorities. It provided a powerful sanction against misbehavior; a prisoner who was violent or disruptive in prison knew that he risked losing or delaying the chance of release. The indeterminate sentence also allowed the authorities to compensate for disparities in the sentences imposed by judges (believed to be a source of friction and discontent among prisoners). Furthermore, it provided a means by which the population of the prisons could be kept within reasonable limits.

SENTENCING CHALLENGES

In countries following the Anglo-American legal tradition, sentencing is a separate procedure from that of determining guilt or innocence, and it is normally the responsibility of the judge rather than of the jury (although in some parts of the United States the jury is empowered to determine the sentence). Most such systems of law traditionally give the judge wide discretion in determining both the kind of penalty to be imposed (imprisonment, fine, probation) and its extent.

As modern sentencing systems provide an increasingly wide range of forms of sentence, choosing a sentence becomes a more complex task. The extensive discretion involved in sentencing and the wide variety of forms of sentence available to judges means that, in many cases, there are complaints of disparity in sentences passed on different offenders, as well as complaints of arbitrariness and idiosyncrasy in the decisions of individual judges. It is sometimes said that the sentence imposed may depend more on the judge or parole board members and on the offender's values, beliefs, and personality, than on the gravity of the offense or the offender's record. Proponents of indeterminate sentencing might respond that while it is wrong for different sentences to be determined on the basis of caprice or idiosyncrasy, there is nothing inherently wrong with offenders convicted of the same crimes receiving different sentences when justified by the unique character and circumstances of the offenders.

It has long been recognized that the quality of the decisions made by judges in sentencing depends on the information available to them. In a case in which there has been a contested trial, the judge will have heard all the evidence related to the immediate background of the offense, but he or she will not necessarily know much about the background of the offender. In order to hand down an appropriate sentence based on the theory that every offender is unique, this knowledge gap is filled in for judges in many jurisdictions by a report (a "presentence report" or "social-inquiry report") prepared by a probation officer and submitted to the court after the offender has been convicted or has pled guilty.

THE DECLINE OF INDETERMINATE SENTENCING

The Model Penal Code, which was developed in the 1950s, was intended to provide a coherent, principled, unified approach to defining various crimes and defenses to crimes. A number of state legislatures have enacted criminal codes taken in large part from the Model Penal Code. At the high point of indeterminate sentencing, prosecutors, psychiatrists, mental health specialists, and leading corrections professionals wrote this code for the American Law Institute. By today's standards, the code gave an unusual amount of attention to the treatment needs and prospects of the offenders and very little attention to public opinion or justice for the victim.

From the 1930s to the 1970s, indeterminate sentencing existed in every American jurisdiction. By the mid-1970s, however, indeterminate sentencing began to be questioned and challenged. California, the first state to formally adopt indeterminate sentencing, was also the first state to return to the use of determinate sentencing when it adopted the Determinate Sentencing Law (Penal Code Section 1170), which became effective on July 1, 1977. California and Maine became the first states to reject core features of indeterminate sentencing, such as parole release and the idea that probation ought to be available in nearly every case.

Questions were raised about many aspects of indeterminate sentencing. Civil rights and prisoners' rights activists claimed that broad discretion in sentencing resulted in arbitrary and inconsistent sentencing, because of racial and other biases that influenced officials. Research began to suggest that rehabilitative treatments were not as effective as once believed. Proceduralists—those who value the judicial process and who question how cases should be represented—argued that broad, standardless discretion denied constitutionally mandated due process. Meanwhile, conservatives argued that broad discretion permitted undue leniency and undermined the deterrent effects of sanctions. Lastly, some argued that not tailoring the punishment to fit the crime was unjust. According to Michael Tonry (1999), determinate sentencing, restorative justice, community justice, three-strikes laws, and other methods of punishing the criminal developed and implemented since the 1970s have led to a hodgepodge of laws that do not reflect any broad agreement about the purpose of the criminal justice system.

FUTURE DIRECTIONS

The criminal justice system will continue to deal with the question of indeterminate versus determinate sentencing and how best to make the offender "pay" for his or her crimes, as it explores new and different options and public opinion changes with the times. Whatever future trends may develop, rehabilitation and individualized decisions about offenders that take into consideration such factors as their personal histories, level of remorse, and behavior during incarceration will probably continue to be considered in some fashion by most corrections officials and judges. Opponents of indeterminate sentencing are likely to continue to monitor disparities in sentencing, bias against and stereotyping of offenders by officials, and inadequate implementation of rehabilitative and vocational training, and they will attempt to ensure that victims' rights are not disregarded at the time of sentencing

—Amy J. Benavides

See also DETERMINATE SENTENCES; REHABILITATION MODEL

Further Reading

American Friends Service Committee. (1971). *Struggle for Justice: A Report on Crime and Punishment in America*. New York: Hill and Wang.

Davis, Kenneth Culp. (1969). *Discretionary Justice: A Preliminary Inquiry*. Baton Rouge, LA: Louisiana State University Press.

Ebbesen, E. B. (2001). "Dr. Ebbesen's Home Page." http://psy. ucsd.edu/~eebbesen/psych16298/162Week5_Issues.html

Frankel, Marvin. (1972). *Criminal Sentences: Law Without Order*. New York: Hill and Wang.

Freecaselaw. http://freecaselaw.com/ca/F026945.htm

Martinson, Robert. (1974). "What Works?—Questions and Answers About Prison Reform." *Public Interest* 35, 2: 22–54.

Skruba, Angela. (2001). "The History of the Australian Penal Colonies." http://www.umd.umich.edu/casl/hum/eng/classes/434/geweb/AUSTRALI.htm

Tonry, Michael. (1999). *Sentencing and Corrections: Issues for the 21st Century*, no. 2. Washington, DC: U.S. Department of Justice.

Wanker, William. (1983). *Indeterminate and Determinate Sentencing*. Salem, OR: Legislative Research.

Wilson, James Q. (1975). *Thinking About Crime*. New York: Basic Books.

Van den Haag, Ernest. (1975). *Punishing Criminals: Concerning a Very Old and Painful Question*. New York: Basic Books.

▼ INDIA

India is a federal republic with a total land area of 2.97 million square kilometers and 1.03 billion inhabitants as of 2001. About 72 percent of the Indian population lives in rural areas (*Census of India* 2001), primarily in farming villages where traditional ways of life still prevail. Indian beliefs and practices about crime, justice, and punishment have been influenced by Hinduism, Islam, and Western traditions. Modern criminal law has existed in codified form following Western patterns since British colonization, beginning in the eighteenth century. Criminal jurisdiction rests with the national government and the state governments. The Indian Penal Code of 1862 (IPC), as amended after independence in 1948, and the Criminal Procedure Code of 1973 (CPC) apply, with some exceptions, to the entire territory of India (cf. PC sec. 1, and CPC ss. 1, 4, and 5) and take precedence over any state legislation. However, it is always important to remember that Indian criminal law is one component of a complex and multilayered legal system whose uniqueness has been described as "unity in diversity" (Derrett 1979; Menski 1991: 295–296). In contemporary India, ancient customs and principles of justice and Western institutions often coexist in an uneasy balance of power.

PRINCIPLES OF CRIMINAL LAW IN ANCIENT TIMES (1500 BCE TO 1100 CE)

In ancient times, *dharma,* whose Sanskrit roots signify the actions of maintaining and sustaining, was the sacrificial act that preserves the cosmic order (Lingat 1998: 3–4). Later, the concept of *dharma* came to mean norms of conduct. The Hindu literature on *dharma*, however, should not be considered a source of law, as it has never been a collection of positive precepts observed by society and applied by law courts. The earliest Hindu sacred writings are the Vedas, which are the basic textual source of *dharma.* They do not set forth any positive rule of conduct, nor do they provide a model for the administration of justice (Lingat 1998: 7–8). The classical literature of *dharmasutra* and *dharmashastra* (treatises on *dharma*) focus more systematically on the teaching of rules of conduct. However, these texts are neither an accurate description of life of that time nor a direct source of law (Lingat 1998: 135–142). Rather, they are efforts to preserve and favor the knowledge of the Brahman, a literate group who sought to control and influence Indian society (Menski 1992: 323).

Ancient Hindu texts list seven acts as the gravest sins: theft, adultery with the teacher's wife, murder of a Brahman (member of the highest caste in India), killing of an unborn child, consumption of alcohol, the repeated performance of the same sinful act, and telling lies about sinful matters (Kane 1930-1962, vol. 4: 10). This list, dating back to the Vedas and mentioned later in the *dharma* treatises, has been interpreted as proof of the legal nature of Hindu texts, as have systematic lists of

Police officers at the funeral procession for Indira Gandhi, Prime Minister of India from 1966-1977 and 1980-1984, who was assassinated by her Sikh bodyguards in 1984.
Source: © David and Peter Turnley/Corbis; used by permission.

crimes compiled by more recent scholarship (Doongaji 1986; Kaul 1993). However, the underlying concept of *dharma* as cosmic order concerns the preeminent concept of sin as against a divine order rather than against society. The societal order as set forth in the *dharmashastra* is to be interpreted in a cosmic dimension where the punishment can be inflicted by divine, semidivine, human, or even anonymous agents (Menski 1991: 309).

The king, whose duty did not include any legislative power, was supposed to merely apply the *dharma* as it is defined by the Hindu tradition. The king seemed to lack any personal prerogative for the maintenance of order in his kingdom, where daily life was presumably regulated by local systems of justice. Nevertheless, the *dharma* treatises emphasized the king's duty to suppress crimes and to punish offenders. Therefore, the king's nonintervention in the preconstituted system of *dharma* signified two things. First, in practice, customary systems of justice were recognized (Menski 1991: 304, 306). Second,

as dramas frequently attest, the king used his own means to achieve order and to administer justice beyond the *dharma* precepts (Bonnan 1986).

Punishment varied according to the status of both the offender and the victim and in accord with the facts and circumstances of the case. Brahman and women offenders were accorded a privileged position as a general rule, but for certain crimes, such as theft, Brahmans were punished more harshly than lower castes (Menski 1991: 314). The treatises of *dharma* provide indications about a wide range of penalties (fines; banishment; expiations, including expiational suicide; corporal punishment including mutilations, death sentences, and jail). The trial procedure described in the treatises attests to the existence of a highly sophisticated tradition regarding burden of proof, testimony, and the rules of evidence (Kane 1930-1962, vol. 4; Kaul 1993: 79–147). Ordeals were provided for as a last resort to settle disputes (Jolly 1928: 312–316; Kane, vol. 4: chap. 14; Kaul 1993: 119–137; Larivière 1981). However,

From *Thag* to *Thug*

The English word *thug* comes from the Hindu word *thag*. *Thags* were highwaymen in India who made their living robbing and often killing travelers, including traders, pilgrims, and the wealthy. The first written reference to *thags* was in the late thirteenth century; organized bands of such robbers operated in India into the early twentieth century, although their activities were severely curtailed by the Thugee and Dacoity Department during the period of British rule. The term *thug* was introduced by British colonial official William Sleeman (1788–1856), who published a dictionary of the argot used by *thags* and *dacoits* (bandits) in nineteenth-century India in his *Ramaseena* in 1863.

In India, *thugs* were a socially recognized group and *thugee* an accepted profession. The gangs numbered anywhere from 10 to 200 men, and they operated in both Hindu and Muslim regions across most of India. They wore distinctive garb, strangled their victims with scarves, and used a pickax to dig a hole in which to hide the body. *Thugs* were followers of Kali, the Hindu goddess of destruction. They acted upon omens that communicated Kali's wishes and made monetary offerings to her. *Thugs* also paid taxes from their earnings to Hindu and Muslim rulers. Their religious clothing, payment of taxes, and devotion to Kali made them socially acceptable. This, along with their secrecy and formal social structure, allowed them to survive for centuries. The British finally ended *thugee*, although late in the twentieth century it still occurred occasionally in remote parts of India.

From the viewpoint of criminal justice, *thugee* was a complex social institution with elements similar to those found in modern gangs, in vigilante and bandit groups, and in organized crime families.

Further Reading
Sleeman, William (1936). *Ramaseena; or a Vocabulary of the Peculiar Language Used by the Thugs.* Calcutta: G. H. Hultmann, Military Orphan Press.

ing the differences between the rules set forth in the Hindu texts and the actual application of law.

ISLAMIC LAW (FROM 1100 CE)

Beginning in the twelfth century, the Mughals, the Muslim conquerors of India, introduced Islamic law to India as the official law of the empire. However, despite their strong preference for a centralized system of rules, the Mughals did not interfere in the local administration of justice, provided that the local chiefs paid regular tribute to the emperor. In the cities inhabited by Muslims, justice was administered by the emperor and his agents, whereas in rural areas, Hindu customary systems continued to be enforced by local councils (Menski 1991: 322; Sangar 1967: 10).

Mughal law courts took as their authority the Hanafi school of jurisprudence of the Sunni branch of Islam. However, both the procedure in trials and the concepts of crime and punishment reflected a merging of Muslim and Hindu principles of justice. The emperor and his agents dealt mostly with criminal matters such as theft, robbery, and rebellion that threatened order and the peace. The *quazi* (a judge in Muslim law) settled disputes concerning family relations, religious crimes, and moral offenses such as alcohol consumption, gambling, prostitution, blasphemy, forbidden Hindu practices, fornication, adultery, sodomy, and incest. Accounts of oath-taking and trials by ordeal are common in travelers' descriptions, as is the application of the *lex talionis,* or law of retaliation—according to which the punishment ideally mirrors the crime (Thévenot 1696: 136). Hanging, beheading, and impaling were the more frequent methods of inflicting capital punishment. Imprisonment was common in Mughal India, but expiations such as pilgrimages to Mecca or to other sacred places were used as well. Both the deterrent function of the punishment and its expiatory features are similar to Hindu principles of justice administration (Menski 1991: 322).

CRIMINAL LAW IN BRITISH INDIA

The system of administration of justice introduced by the British in the eighteenth century was basically driven by the need to assist the revenue authorities in collecting taxes. In 1772, Warren Hastings was appointed to the position of governor-general of the Bengal territories in eastern India. His crucial intervention was to designate in each district a British officer

since the actual penalties were determined locally, the texts should be seen as general guidelines rather than as descriptions of the actual procedures (Menski 1991: 314). Here again, the Hindu treatises provide evidence of the imposition of a religious and elitist system of knowledge on a customary system. Traces of the existence of that customary system can be found in contextual sources, such as dramatic works or novels, show-

(the "collector") who, following the preexisting Mughal system of revenue, had both executive and judicial powers. The British collector not only directed the collection of land revenues but also oversaw the proceedings of the provincial criminal courts (*Faujdari Adalat*) that derived their authority from the Mughal government. Two parallel systems of courts existed in British India until 1861: the Crown courts, in the presidency towns, and the East India Company courts, which derived their power from local governments. The first followed English law; the second followed Hindu and Muslim law and did not have jurisdiction over Europeans. From the beginning of the nineteenth century, steps were taken to remove this dual system. The Code of Criminal Procedure, enacted in 1861 and repealed in 1872, provided British India with four grades of criminal courts; however, the control of the judiciary by the executive remained one of the principal features of the system.

The difficulty in managing the overwhelming variety of local practices affected the territories under British control so severely that trade itself was disrupted (Cohn 1997: 57–76). Hastings's initial plan, to maintain Mughal criminal law but ensure its application under the general control of the East India Company, did not work as well as anticipated. Major concerns about the establishment of law and order, along with a distrust of local systems of justice and the rejection of cruel punishments, led to important transformations. The aim of the British colonizers was to enforce their sovereignty, and by doing so they also promoted a policy of social engineering through law that had links to evangelical Christianity (Dhavan 2000: 267).

Mughal criminal law continued to be the principal source of law until the adoption of the Indian Penal Code in 1860, the first draft of which had been submitted to the British Governor General by Lord Macaulay and his colleagues in 1837. Under the new code, indigenous systems of justice were rejected, on the grounds that Hindu law had been superseded by Islamic law and that what survived of it had changed markedly from its original principles (Dhavan 2000: 269). The code focused on the equality of citizens before the law (except for some exceptions which favored Europeans) and on the deterrent role of punishment.

The state gradually took over the administration of criminal law, and Islamic legal principles were repressed. For example, the intention of the murderer came to be determined not from the nature of the murder weapon, but from circumstances and positive evidence. In 1790, the rule by which a murderer avoided criminal prosecution if he or she obtained a pardon from the victim's next of kin was suppressed. Capital punishment was extended to all forms of homicide that had been justifiable under Islamic law. All forms of mutilation were superseded by corporal punishment, imprisonment, and fines (Menski 1991: 324–325). The belief that it was the fear of punishment, rather than the actual pain caused by punishment, that deterred criminal behavior was the basis for criminal law and led the British to retain practices such as exile to the Andaman Islands (Dhavan 2000: 273, 276). Other forms of punishments were forfeiture of property, fines, imprisonment, imprisonment for life, and the death penalty (ss. 53–75). Finally, nonpayment of fines could also lead to imprisonment (ss. 63–69).

The pressures for the humanization of native practices and for social reforms favoring the protection of women and the sanctity of marriage did not lead to radical innovations (Dhavan 2000: 275). Crimes and torts were not clearly differentiated, and, surprisingly, some indigenous concepts remained untouched; adultery was still an offense committed by the man against the husband of the woman with whom he had an adulterous relationship, and the punishment for bigamy was left to later regulations. The code's definitive draft, however, was revised in order to include more rigorous measures dealing with public order and the security of the British administration. Furthermore, sati (or suttee, the burning of the widow on the funeral pyre of her dead husband) and child marriage were made illegal. Despite generating criticism from both Hindus and Muslims, the use of criminal law as an instrument of social change was considered by the British to be one of the most significant accomplishments of the Macaulay Code, the Indian penal code imposed by the British (Dhavan 2000: 276–277). Yet the British regulations did not succeed in preventing crime, as the new rulers lacked the religious and moral authority of the Hindu and Muslim lawgivers (Menski 1991: 328).

MODERN INDIAN CRIMINAL LAW (FROM 1947)

The principles informing the Penal Code of 1860, read together with the Criminal Procedure Code, repealed and replaced in 1973, constitute the legacy on which independent India has based further social reform. These reforms deal with women and children, untouchables and tribal peoples (in traditional Hindu society, any group outside the caste system), conditions of employment, and socioeconomic offenses (Dhavan 2000: 278–288).

Amendments to the Indian Penal Code, along with a great number of new statutes, provide enhanced punishments in relation to family law. Bigamy, which is a crime according to the Hindu Marriage Act of 1955, is punishable with a maximum of seven years' imprisonment (IPC s. 494). The action of giving or taking dowry is punishable by five years' imprisonment (Dowry Prohibition Act, 1961). Traffic in women for prostitution is punishable with imprisonment for three to seven years (Suppression of Immoral Traffic in Women and Girls Act, 1956). Death or life imprisonment is provided for abetting the commission of sati (The Commission of Sati Prevention Act, 1987).

Independent India has also implemented strict penal measures to eradicate untouchability and other forms of discrimination. The Scheduled Castes and Scheduled Tribes (Prevention of Atrocities) Act of 1989 provides for life imprisonment for giving false evidence against a scheduled caste or tribe, or death if an innocent scheduled caste or tribe is convicted and executed. (Scheduled castes and tribes are ethnic subgroups that have faced discrimination and economic privations.) The same statute provides imprisonment for life and a fine for any of the mentioned offenses punishable by a term of ten years according to the Indian Penal Code.

Penal legislation punishing economic offenses has also been enacted in order to protect workers and increase consumer safety. Among the most important statutes are the Apprenticeship Act (1961), the Contract Labour (Regulation and Abolition) Act (1970), the Bonded Labour System (Abolition) Act (1976), the Equal Remuneration Act (1976), the Industrial Disputes Act (1947), the Minimum Wages Act (1948), the Prevention of Food Adulteration Act (1954), the Maternity Benefit Act (1961), the Foreign Exchange Regulation Act (1973), the Foreign Contribution (Regulation) Act (1976), and the Prevention of Corruption Act (1988).

The principal punishments are provided for by the Penal Code, section 53: death, imprisonment for life, rigorous (with hard labor) or simple imprisonment, forfeiture of property, and fines. The death penalty can be applied only in the "rarest of the rare" cases. Yet, on average, a dozen executions per year are carried out (Amnesty International 1999). The death penalty can also be commuted to a life sentence. Fines are another alternative to prison sentences, but law courts are empowered to impose sentences in default of payment of fines.

The Indian Constitution contains provisions with regard to the judiciary. Unlike other federal systems, India does not have separate hierarchies of federal and state courts. The Supreme Court is the highest court of the land and a court of record. It has original, appellate, and advisory jurisdiction. Each Indian state has its own high court, which supervises all courts throughout the state. A court of session is established for every sessions division and is presided over by a judge appointed by the high court. The districts are provided with courts of a judicial magistrate of the first class and second class. Finally, in accord with state laws, minor criminal cases are settled by *panchayat* (local self-governing councils with judicial authority).

The Criminal Procedure Code of 1974 provides a uniform criminal procedure applicable throughout India, but a state legislature may modify its provisions to accomodate local needs. For the purpose of the administration of justice, the territory of India is divided into session divisions, districts, and subdivisions. All offenses are divided into bailable and nonbailable offenses and cognizable and noncognizable offenses (CPC s. 2), and all criminal cases are classified as summons cases or warrant cases (CPC s. 204). The basis for this categorization is the first schedule of the code. However, further legislation blurred these distinctions by allowing a great degree of discretion in the registration of complaints.

The Criminal Procedure Code confers specific powers to investigate and to make arrests to the police as established under the Police Act of 1861. The present police system remains heavily influenced by British colonial policy, under which its first task was to assist the revenue authorities in collecting taxes. The unofficial but widespread practice of torture therefore seems to constitute one of the principal British legacies to Indian police culture. On the other hand, during the 1990s, more than a thousand policemen per year lost their lives in the line of duty. Low pay, together with poor access to facilities, may increase the likelihood that police officers will become involved in corruption (Karan 2000).

Cases are tried under procedures based on the adversarial system of justice, which requires the defendant to prove his or her case beyond reasonable doubt, giving him or her fair and adequate opportunity before the court. However, the system departs from the pure adversarial model in that the prosecutor cannot withdraw from the case without the consent of the court, and the charge against the defendant is framed by the court after considering the circumstances of the case.

The CPC provides legal relief to the poor and dispositions to prevent abuses and expedite the judicial process. The Children's Act of 1960 requires that juvenile offenders be considered a separate category from other offenders. However, the current situation in India does not favor indigent defendants and other disadvantaged groups such as children, women, and tribal peoples (Dhagamwar 1992, 1997). The trial procedure is often so slow that many spend more time in jail than the punishment of their crimes would provide, should they be convicted. Sixteen years after the *Hussainara Khatoon* case (1980)—the historic Supreme Court decision that released 40,000 prisoners whose trial had not commenced within four months of the filing of the first petition—India still had 163,000 prisoners awaiting trial, 72 percent of all prisoners in the nation (Malik and Chakravarty 1998). Virtually none of the 1,200 prisons in India is able to ensure the protection of human rights to which prisoners are entitled; overcrowding, lack of educational and rehabilitation programs, and the absence of basic facilities are the prison system's defining characteristics (Singh 2000).

Statistics of the National Crime Records Bureau (1998) report an overall crime rate in India of 183.2 per 100,000 inhabitants per year. Between 1951 and 1991, a reasonable growth of 9.8 percent in the overall crime rate under the Penal Code was recorded. Among the crimes listed were murder, robbery, burglary, theft, kidnapping and abduction, rape, cheating, riots,

▼

Crime and National Integration in India

After India became an independent nation in 1947, a major task facing the government was to create a unified nation that integrated peoples who spoke many different languages, were members of many different ethnic groups, and followed different religions. Part of the strategy recommended by the Indian National Congress called for the creation of a secure society.

III. Maintenance of Security of Person and Property

It is obvious that in our democracy every citizen whether of the majority of the community or any of the minority communities is entitled to full protection of person and property. The existing provisions of the normal law have been declared sufficient for dealing with the dissemination of communal hatred and incitement to communal violence. But in view of recent events some slight amendments may be necessary. It is up to the State Governments to enforce the law promptly, efficiently and impartially.

The Committee, in the light of the reports received and discussions held, has came to the following conclusions:

1. Where the administration is efficient, rioting, loot and arson do not take place; where there is a breach of peace, the responsibility for it should be fixed and appropriate action taken.
2. In recruitment, adequate care should be taken to see that people of the right outlook are chosen. Inculcation of right outlook should be part of all training.
3. Constant vigilance should be exercised by higher officials to see that communal and sectarian tendencies do not develop in the lower staff.
4. It should be possible to apply the provisions of the Detention Act when communal situation deteriorates in any area or there is apprehension of breach of peace.
5. Section 133 (a) of the Indian Penal Code should be suitably amended and effectively enforced. Collective fines should be imposed against the community which has committed aggression.
6. It would be worthwhile to examine the desirability and feasibility of Federal Police Force.
7. Insistent complaints by Members of Parliament and the Press that firing was resorted to without discrimination is partly responsible for hesitancy on the part of the police to take strong action. While it is necessary to make it clear that discretion of Police Administration in all grave and difficult situations remains untouched, it should be emphasized that there would be no need to resort to firing or the like if the Administration is vigilant and precautionary measures are taken in all cases of apprehended trouble.
8. Members of the minority community in any particular situation should have facility to approach officers and seek adequate action.
9. People should not immediately do so in all such cases.
10. While the administration should be strong and effective, the need for public cooperation should be fully recognized.
11. There should be Standing Vigilance Committees in areas where trouble is apprehended.

Source: Sharma, Jagdish Saran, ed. (1965). *India's Struggle for Freedom: Select Documents and Sources*. Volume 11. New Delhi: S. Chand & Co., pp. 431-32.

criminal breach of trust, counterfeiting, arson, molestation, sexual harassment, cruelty by husband and relatives, and "dowry death"—the death of a married woman following physical or mental cruelty by her husband or in-laws in connection with a demand for a dowry. Surprisingly, from that year onward, stability was reported, except for a slight increase (1.8 percent) between 1996 and 1998.

The examination of specific figures discloses some patterns, such as the relative stability of violent crimes (around 14 percent between 1996 and 1998), with a decrease in violent crimes affecting women (down 2 percent between 1997 and 1998). Similarly, the incidence of rape cases showed a decline of 2 percent. However, dowry death cases, as well as torture cases (cruelty by husband and relatives), increased from 12.9 percent in 1997 to 15.2 percent in 1998. The most spectacular rise was recorded in the number of sexual harassment cases, which rose by 40.1 percent from 1997 to 1998. Child rape incidence decreased by 8 percent in 1998 over 1997, and cases reported under the Child Marriage Restraint Act showed a substantial decrease of 28.2 percent. Data on crimes against scheduled castes and tribes show a continuous declining trend.

Notwithstanding these statistics, the present system of criminal law does not seem to ensure compliance with the welfare agenda of modern India. Social activists and legal scholars lament the failure of law courts to rigorously implement penal measures in domains such as human rights and socioeconomic offenses (Dhagamwar 1992; Dhavan 2000: 294–295; Menski 1991, 2000). Consequently, the punitive aspect of Indian criminal law has been strengthened without achieving all its original objectives of progressive social change.

CONCLUSION

On the one hand, the process of codification, undertaken by the British almost two centuries ago and carried further by independent India, docs not seem to have had substantial effects in terms of humanistic and public interest goals. On the other hand, the overall crime rate in India remains quite low in comparison with high-crime nations such as the United States. This can be partly explained by the reluctance of both the police and the victims, for different reasons, to report crimes. However, studies provide evidence of the use of local, customary control and justice systems that are not reported in official crime statistics (Hayden 1999;

Herrenschmidt 1989: 212–213; Moore 1985; Srinivas 1987). Indian law courts themselves have rediscovered the positive economic implications of the recognition of customs that ensure the settlement of disputes without weighing on the state budget (Menski 2000). Thus, the courts' reluctance to apply criminal law in matters relating to the demands of a welfare state model can be understood in the light of a reinterpretation of the relevance of local traditions.

—*Livia S. Holden*

See also HINDUISM

Further Reading

Amnesty International Online. (1999). http://www.amnesty.org

Annual Report of Crime in India. (1998) New Delhi: National Crime Records Bureau.

Baxi, Upendra. (1982). *The Crisis of the Indian Legal System.* New Delhi: Vikas Publications.

Bhatnagar, R. (1990). *Crimes in India.* New Delhi: Ashish Publishing House.

Bonnan, Jean-Claude. (1986). "Le roi souverain du chatiment dans l'Inde ancienne." *Droit et Cultures* 11. Nanterre, France: Université de Paris X, 123–127.

Census of India. (2001). http://www.censusindia.net/results/rudist.html

Chiba, Masajii, ed. (1986). *Asian Indigenous Law in Interaction with Received Law.* London: KPI.

Cohn, Bernard. (1987). *An Anthropologist Among the Historians and Other Essays.* Delhi: Oxford University Press.

———. (1997). *Colonialism and Its Forms of Knowledge.* New Delhi: Oxford University Press.

Derrett, John D. (1979). "Unity in Diversity: The Hindu Experience." *Bharata Manisha* 5, 1: 21–36.

Dhagamwar, Vasudha. (1992). *Law, Power and Justice.* New Delhi: Sage Publications.

———. (1997). *Criminal Justice or Chaos.* New Delhi: Har-Anand Publications.

Dhavan, Rajeev. (2000). "Kill Them for Their Bad Verses: On Criminal Law and Punishment in India." In *Punishment and the Prison*, edited by Rani Dhavan Shankardass. New Delhi: Sage Publications, 261–343.

Doongaji, Damayanti. (1986). *Crime and Punishment in Ancient Hindu Society.* New Delhi: Ajanta Publications.

Hayden, Robert. (1999). *Disputes and Arguments Amongst Nomads.* New Delhi: Oxford University Press.

Herrenschmidt, Olivier. (1989). *Les meilleurs dieux sont hindous.* Lausanne, Switzerland: L'Age d'Homme.

Jolly, Julius. (1928). *Hindu Law and Custom.* Calcutta: Greater India Society.

Kane, Panduranga V. (1930–1962). *History of Dharmashastra.* Poona, India: Bhandarkar Oriental Research Institute.

Karan, Vijay. (2000). "India's Police: The Dilemmas of an Aberrated System." In *Punishment and the Prison*, edited by Rani Dhavan Shankardass. New Delhi: Sage Publications, 211–232.

Kaul, Anjali. (1993). *Administration of Law and Justice in Ancient India.* New Delhi: Sarup and Sons.

Larivière, Richard. (1981). *The Divyatattva of Raghunandana Bhattacarya: Ordeals in Classical Hindu Law.* New Delhi: Manohar Publications.

———. (1991). "The Last Resort for Dispute Settlement in Classical India." *Droit et Cultures* 22. Nanterre, France: Université de Paris X, 25–32.

Lingat, Robert. (1998). *The Classical Law of India.* New Delhi: Oxford University Press.

Malik, Ashok, and Sayantan Chakravarty. (1998). "Hell's Prisoners." *India Today* (August 17). http://www.india-today.com/itoday/17081998/invest.html

Menski, Werner F. (1991). "Crime and Punishment in Hindu Law and Under Modern Indian Law." *Récueils de la Société Jean Bodin* 58, 4. Brussels, Belgium: De Boeck Université, 295–334.

———. (1992). "The Role of Custom in Hindu Law." *Récueils de la Société Jean Bodin* 52, 3. Brussels, Belgium: De Boeck Université, 311–347.

———. (2000). *Comparative Law in a Global Context: The Legal Systems of Asia and Africa.* London: Platinum.

———. (2000). *Modern Indian Family Law.* Richmond, UK: Curzon Press.

Moore, Erin P. (1985). *Conflict and Compromise: Justice in an Indian Village.* Lanham, MD: University Press of America.

Rao, Venugopal. (1981). *Dynamics of Crime.* New Delhi: Indian Institute of Public Administration.

Sangar, Satya P. (1967). *Crime and Punishment in Mughal India.* New Delhi: Sterling Publisher.

Shah, Giriraj. (1999). *Encyclopaedia of Crime, Police and Judicial System.* New Delhi: Anmol Publications.

Singh, Hira. (2000). "Prison Administration in India: Contemporary Issues." In *Punishment and the Prison*, edited by Rani Dhavan Shankardass. New Delhi: Sage Publications.

Srinivas, Mysore N. (1987). *The Dominant Caste and Other Essays.* Bombay: Oxford University Press.

Thévenot, Melchisédec. (1696). *Relations de divers voyages curieux.* Paris: Thomas Moette.

Yang, Anand A., ed. (1985). *Crime and Criminality in British India.* Tucson, AZ: University of Arizona Press.

Court Case

Hussainara Khatoon v. Secretary (1980). State of Bihar ([1] SCC 81).

▼ INDONESIA

The Republic of Indonesia's 17,000 islands form a 5,120-kilometer archipelago bordering India's Nicobar Islands to the west and Papua New Guinea to the east. Its ethnically diverse population of 210 million has a long history of interaction with maritime powers, generating a rich legacy of Indian, Chinese, Portuguese, and Dutch cultural and religious influences. Indonesia inherited its current boundaries and administrative structures from the Netherlands East Indies, the colonial empire that lasted until the Japanese occupation (1942–1945).

After four years of revolution, Indonesia won its independence in 1949, establishing first a federal, then a unitary republic with a parliamentary system. In 1959, President Sukarno brought the parliamentary system to an end when he revived the illiberal "1945 Constitution," ushering in a presidential system that survives today. Sukarno was deposed in 1966 by General Soeharto, whose military-backed "New Order" regime ruled until May 1998. Soeharto's fall precipitated an outpouring of reform sentiment that led to election of a democratic government in 1999 and a comprehensive review of the legal and institutional legacies of the past. The breakdown of authoritarian rule has also been accompanied by an upsurge in ethnic violence and separatism. Conflicts in Aceh, Kalimantan, the Moluccas, East Timor, and West Papua have generated 1.3 million internal refugees since 1998.

Following recent subdivisions and the U.N.-assisted birth of an independent East Timor in 1999, Indonesia has thirty provinces. A decentralization law that came into force in January 2001 gave provincial governments considerable autonomy, including limited police powers.

CRIME

Since colonial times, the state in Indonesia has been preoccupied with internal security. Its criminal code, written in 1918 and adopted with minimal amendments by the post-independence state, includes provisions that specify a range of political activities—criticism of the government for example—as criminal acts. With the addition of the "exorbitant rights" enjoyed by the Dutch governor general—and adapted by the independent state—the definition of crime further expands. This tradition of unlimited executive discretion helps explain how over 500,000 alleged Communists could be arrested and held without trial after Soeharto took power in 1966.

Official statistics indicate that Indonesia has low rates of crime. According to a mid-1970s study by INTERPOL, the reported crime rate for Indonesia was only 87.15 per 100,000 people. This figure had risen to 713 per 100,000 in 1991, 931 in 1994, and 1,112 in 1997, the most recent aggregated figure available from Indonesia's Central Bureau of Statistics.

Burglary routinely tops the list of nationally reported crimes, followed by assault and aggravated assault. There are between 1,500 and 2,000 murders reported each year, a rate of only 1.0 to 1.4 per 100,000.

Cities have a higher crime rate than do the rural towns and villages where most people still live. In 1997, 46.5 percent of victims of crime lived in cities, up sharply from 1991, when the figure was 38.5 percent. This growth is commonly attributed to the large numbers of rural migrants drawn to industrial centers such as Jakarta, Surabaya, and Medan in search of work. It also appears to be linked to the existence of organized "youth" groups that recruit unemployed youths and ex-prisoners to work as "standover men" (enforcers), drug dealers, prostitutes, and petty thieves. The largest of these groups enjoy the protection of elements within the political elite and the military. In 1997, 74 percent of victims of crime were male, a proportion that has gradually decreased over the decade. Statistics on domestic violence are difficult to obtain in Indonesia, because domestic violence is not recorded separately from other crimes and rape within marriage is not formally recognized.

Several categories of offenses fall outside the criminal code and are regulated by separate laws. These so-called special cases include offenses relating to narcotics, weapons, smuggling, and other economic crimes, including corruption. In the fiscal year 1997–1998, the courts settled only 185 such cases. Despite evidence of spectacular levels of official corruption (a 1998 survey of eighty-five countries by Transparency International rated Indonesia the sixth most corrupt), it is rare for large corruption cases to be heard in court, let alone be successfully prosecuted. According to *Indonesia: An Official Handbook,* published in 2000, in "special cases" trials, the state has recouped just over 1 percent of its estimated losses due to economic crimes.

The 1997 Asian economic crisis hit Indonesia harder than any other nation, plunging approximately 10 million people into poverty. Panic over the sudden loss of value of the rupiah led to food shortages and looting of urban food stores. According to statistics from Jakarta and other parts of the country, total crime, along with crimes such as robbery with violence and bank fraud, has risen dramatically (15 to 20 percent). Internet crime is also growing rapidly. According to the Bank of Central Asia, one of Indonesia's largest banks, more than 70 percent of Internet credit card transactions attempted in Indonesia are fraudulent.

Crime figures in Indonesia must be treated with caution. Many crimes go unreported because of a lack of faith in the police and the legal system. A 1989 survey in East Java conducted over five years found that only 18 percent of crimes were reported. More recently, although dozens of women of Chinese descent were widely believed to have been raped during the devastating riots of May 13 and 14, 1998, in Jakarta, not a single case was reported to the police, apparently for fear of humiliation or further victimization. Likewise, many people do not report routine thefts, believing that, in the words of a popular saying, "If you report your goat missing, you are liable to lose your chicken as well."

Many people prefer to bypass the state justice system and deal with problems informally. This can take the form of mediation by local figures of authority such as religious elders, government administrators, or customary law specialists. It can also involve on-the-spot retribution by large groups. There was a steep rise in vigilantism after 1998, largely in response to the increased level of violent crime. In the eighteen-month period to May 2000, the press reported that fifty-six suspected criminals were bashed to death in greater Jakarta alone.

POLICE

The Indonesian National Police, known as Polri, consists of about 250,000 personnel—one officer for every 840 people. It comprises 22,000 detectives and the 40,000 strong Mobile Brigades that are used to quell serious or large-scale disturbances. The police are assisted by a number of volunteer parapolice organizations, including Hansip (about 5 million strong) and neighborhood-watch type committees. The official aim is to increase the size of the main police force to 300,000 by 2004.

The current police force grew out of the colonial force, a powerful organization that had the dual function of fighting crime and protecting the government's authority from all perceived threats. This political and surveillance role of the police was reinforced during the Japanese occupation and is still evident today, albeit in less overt forms. In 1962, the police were formally militarized and placed under the authority of the armed forces. Though formally charged for maintaining order, the police in reality played second fiddle to the army, both in terms of status and funding.

On April 1, 1999, following the fall of Soeharto, the police were separated from the armed forces and given exclusive responsibility for law enforcement and for maintaining domestic security. As a result, their capacities have been severely stretched, especially in conflict zones such as Aceh, the Moluccas, and West Papua.

Now under the control of the president, the national

police have reverted to a system of civilian ranks. Despite new legislation allowing for the creation of civilian police units (Polisi Pamong Praja) as part of the local government apparatus, administration and training of the police remains centralized.

Public trust in the police is low, due to endemic corruption and perceived inefficiency. Police violence is also routine, especially during interrogation. The promulgation of a new code of criminal procedure in 1981 (replacing the 1848 code) attempted to improve the rights of detainees by imposing time limits to detention and forbidding the use of torture to extract confessions. The absence of sanctions for violating the code, however, has seen breaches continue. Police claimed to have an overall clearance rate of 55 percent in 1998, but this figure is difficult to interpret since it varies widely from province to province and from year to year.

COURTS

The Netherlands East Indies operated a dual justice system with separate courts and codes of procedure for Europeans and natives. In some regions, courts dispensed justice on the basis of local customary law. In 1951, the government abolished the customary law courts and adopted a uniform system of courts for the whole nation.

Article 24 of the 1945 Constitution implies a separation of powers. Sukarno, however, rejected this principle and treated judges as public servants. The Basic Law on the Judiciary (Law No. 14 1970) confirmed Justice Department control over judges' appointments, pay, and promotions, effectively ensuring their loyalty to the minister. Domination of the legal bureaucracy by military aides of the president during the three decades of the Soeharto era further undermined judicial independence.

Indonesia has four kinds of courts: general, military, religious, and administrative. All civilian criminal cases are handled in the three-tier general court system consisting of courts of first instance (Pengadilan Negeri), appellate courts (Pengadilan Tinggi), and a Supreme Court (Mahkamah Agung). Criminal cases take place before three judges, one of whom acts as the chair of the panel. Because Indonesia follows the continental European legal tradition, no jury is involved. A prosecutor responsible to the office of the attorney general (Kejaksaan Agung) puts the state's case, while the accused is defended by an advocate provided by the court or engaged privately. Judges take an active role in proceedings, questioning witnesses and deciding on the guilt of the defendant as well as determining the sentence.

General courts also handle juvenile crime. A Juvenile Justice Law was passed by Parliament in 1996 and was signed by President Soeharto in 1997. It defines juveniles as children between the ages of eight and eighteen and establishes a special court system and criminal code for them. As of 2000, neither had been implemented.

Weak supervision over the past four decades has seen corruption become deeply entrenched at all levels of the Indonesian criminal justice system. There is also regular collusion between judges and prosecutors (and sometimes advocates) to arrange outcomes in advance, a system referred to as the "court mafia." This is not to suggest that all judges are corrupt or that the guilty are never punished, but it does help explain a pervasive cynicism in Indonesia about the ability of the courts to deliver justice.

Democratic change since 1998 has brought domestic and international pressures for legal reform. A separate system of Human Rights Courts is in the process of being established, where it will be possible—potentially—to prosecute those responsible for major abuses of human rights, including crimes against humanity committed by the military in the past.

PUNISHMENT

Many, if not most, offenders in Indonesia are dealt with in summary fashion by their local communities, often with the tacit agreement of the police. Imprisonment rates are very low. The total prison population in 1999 was 55,026, an increase of about 15,000 over the 1989 figure. The 1999 total gives Indonesia a rate of 26 per 100,000, far below most nations in Asia (the rate for Malaysia in the same year was 123 per 100,000).

Of those incarcerated in 1997, 6.8 percent were children (under sixteen), 22 percent were juveniles (sixteen to eighteen), and 71.2 percent were adults. Ninety-seven percent of the new prisoners were male, a proportion that had risen from 94 percent in 1991.

In 1990, Indonesia had 441 prisons. Most of them dated from colonial times, some of them from the first half of the nineteenth century. This figure includes special prisons for women, high-security prisons, and juvenile prisons (although juveniles continue to be locked up with adult offenders in many cases). All of the correctional facilities are run by the directorate of corrections under the Department of Justice. There are also military-run prisons where torture is common and where detainees do not enjoy the limited protection offered by the code of criminal procedure. The best known of these was the penal colony on the island of Buru, where thousands of political prisoners were incarcerated without trial for more than a decade in the early years of the Soeharto regime.

Prison conditions are generally harsh, but treatment of individual prisoners depends largely on their ability to provide services in cash or in kind to underpaid prison guards. According to the U.S. State Department's report on human rights in Indonesia (2001), "criminal prisoners in some facilities are beaten routinely and systematically as punishment for infractions of prison discipline and to extract information about developments within the prison. Punishments include use of electric shock batons and stapling of the ears, nose, and lips."

Indonesian law retains the death penalty for serious offenses relating to narcotics, murder, and military desertion, but in past decades, it has been applied more often to political prisoners than to criminals. Amnesty International estimated in 1999 that there were at least thirty-three people on death row.

Far more common are extrajudicial executions. Hundreds of thousands of alleged Communists were executed without process in 1965–1966. In the period between 1982 and 1984, several thousand suspected criminals were shot dead in a military intelligence operation and left, in many cases, in public places. Though the killings were officially blamed on "gang warfare, President Soeharto admitted in his 1989 autobiography that they were implemented as a form of "shock therapy." Killings of suspected criminals "while trying to escape" continued to be reported in the Indonesian media throughout the 1980s and 1990s.

A revised criminal code intended to replace the spirit of retribution embodied in the existing code with a more humanitarian approach has been under consideration by jurists for more than a decade. Attempts to promulgate a new code have repeatedly stalled, however, over issues including the death penalty, rape within marriage, and adultery. The democratic revival since 1998 has, if anything, made reaching agreement over a new code more difficult than ever.

—*David Bourchier*

Further Reading

Asia Watch. (1990). *Prison Conditions in Indonesia: An Asia Watch Report.* New York: Human Rights Watch.

Himawan, Charles. (1997). "Indonesia." In *Asian Legal Systems:* *Law, Society and Pluralism in East Asia,* edited by Poh-Ling Tan. Sydney, Australia: Butterworths, 196–262.

Indonesia: An Official Handbook 2000. (2000). Jakarta, Indonesia: Department of Information/National Communication and Information Board.

International Crisis Group. (2001). *Indonesia: National Police Reform,* ICG Asia Report Number 13. Brussels, Belgium: ICG. http://www.crisisweb.org/projects/asia/indonesia/reports/A400 239_20022001.pdf

Kitada, Mikinao. (2001). "Prison Population In Asian Countries: Facts, Trends And Solutions." U.N. Programme Network Institutes Technical Assistance Workshop, Vienna, Austria (May 10). http://www.ojp.usdoj.gov/search97cgi97_cgi

Reksodiputro, Mardjono. (1992). "The State of Crime in Indonesia: A Preliminary Overview." In *International Trends in Crime: East Meets West,* edited by Heather Strang and Julia Vernono. Canberra, Australia: Australian Institute of Criminology, 5–14.

Statistics Indonesia. (2000). "Social Welfare Statistics." Jakarta, Indonesia: Statistics Indonesia. http://www.bps.go.id/statbysector/socwel/table6.shtml

Thoolen, Hans, ed. (1997). *Indonesia and the Rule of Law: Twenty Years of 'New Order' Government.* London: Frances Pinter, 1987.

Transparency International. (2001). "Annual Corruption Perception Indices." http://www.transparency.org/documents/cpi/index.html

U.S. State Department, Bureau of Democracy, Human Rights, and Labor. (2001). *Indonesia: Country Reports on Human Rights Practices, 2000.* Washington, DC: GPO. http://www.state.gov/g/drl/rls/hrrpt/2000/eap/index.cfm?docid 707

van Dijk, Jan J. M., Pat Mayhew, and Martin Killias. (1990). *Experiences of Crime Across the World: Key Findings from the 1989 International Crime Survey.* Boston: Kluwer.

Wagstaff, Jeremy. (2001). "Web Gives Credit-Card Fraudsters Ideal Set For Schemes." *Asian Wall Street Journal* (June 24).

▼ INFANTICIDE

Infanticide has a lengthy history that reaches back to ancient societies. In some instances, it took place as part of socially sanctioned religious sacrifice, was a means to dispose of physically defective infants, was a way to dispose of female infants when males were preferred, or was a form of population control. Although condemned for more than 2,000 years in societies that adhered to the Judeo-Christian tradition, infanticide was accepted in ancient Greece, Rome, China, India, Western Europe, and early German society.

INFANTICIDE IN PRELITERATE SOCIETIES

Although the study of crime in general has been relatively neglected with respect to preliterate societies, infanticide has been reasonably well-documented. Perhaps this is because infanticide was especially abhorrent to the missionaries, travelers, and ethnographers who studied these societies, and therefore, they made note of it. Several surveys suggest that infanticide, although rare in nearly all societies, was practiced in more than half and perhaps in as many as 75 percent of preliterate societies. Because members of these societies lacked modern forms of birth control, infanticide served that purpose in many societies. Infanticide was used most often to dispose of infants who were the product of illegitimate conception (as a result of adultery or, rape or to an unwed mother) or who could not be supported by the family because the infant was one of a multiple birth, the infant was ill or handicapped, or there were simply too many children already in the family. In general, girls were more likely to be disposed of than boys, although the sex of the infant alone was justification for disposal in only a minority of societies. The infant was usually disposed of before any formal birth or naming ceremony (that is, before he or she was recognized as a member of the community), and the mother usually carried out the infanticide of her child.

TYPES OF INFANTICIDE

There are two types of infanticide in modern, industrialized nations. Medical infanticide occurs when an imminent, painful death is medically expedited for a malformed or terminally ill infant (aged twelve months and younger). Criminal infanticide occurs when an infant dies as the result of action or inaction by another person. The difference between medical infanticide (a form of euthanasia) and criminal infanticide is a complex issue, one that continues to challenge legal and medical scholars as well as religious and political leaders.

A BRIEF HISTORY OF INFANTICIDE LAW

Until the late twentieth century, prosecution of infanticide fell under the rubric of homicide laws—such as manslaughter, first-degree murder, and murder by omission. Since 1990, most countries have adopted various "injury to child" laws, which drops the requirement that the prosecution prove intent to harm. In effect, these laws stipulate that causing injury to a child under a certain age, such as fourteen, is the fault of the caretaker, regardless of the parent or caretaker's intention. This means that labeling the injurious event an accident is not always an effective legal defense. Along with easing the prosecution's burden in obtaining convictions for infanticide, this law also increases pressure

on parents and caretakers to better supervise children. In cases in which the injury to child laws do not apply, homicide laws are still utilized.

Infanticide in China has been attributed to gender discrimination, famine, poverty, rebellion, filial piety, and birth control. The extent of the practice is evidenced by "baby towers"—designated places of abandonment or burial of unwanted infants. The earliest infanticide law appears to have been written in 1138 CE, when the court in Hangzhou prohibited infanticide and ordered the establishment of foundling hospitals. Population statistics from the early twentieth century, however, are suspiciously low for female births, and the Marriage Law of 1950 includes a prohibition against infanticide, suggesting that infanticide was still taking place at that time.

India has a history of female infanticide due to a preference for boys. The complex caste system in India dictated intense control of children to ensure that marriage and lineage would be maintained or to increase caste standing. A daughter was viewed as a liability, as she might become pregnant through relations with a man from a lower caste, thereby damaging her family's standing. This fear was fueled by the belief that girls were prone to undesirable feminine exuberance during their youth.

In England, the historical record suggests that infanticide occurred for economic reasons as well as to dispose of infants who were born to unmarried women. It is also clear that poor, unmarried women were the ones most likely to be prosecuted. In 1624, England passed its first infanticide law, which rendered the concealment of the death of a newborn bastard presumptive of murder. In 1922, England passed a new "felony of infanticide" law, which reduced the fatal assault of a newborn to manslaughter. In 1929, England passed the Infant Life Preservation Act, which carries a maximum penalty of life imprisonment for the murder of a child over the age of one.

INFANTICIDE IN THE UNITED STATES

An examination of the Uniform Crime Reports reveals that homicides of persons under the age of four increased from 2.4 percent of the total homicides in 1979 to 3.9 percent in 1998. In a study of eighteen developed countries, the United States ranked fifth in homicides of infants under one year of age, with a rate of 5.4 per every 100,000 live births. The U.S. Advisory Board on Child Abuse and Neglect (1995) report

Why Quick Disposal of the Infant?

When an infanticide takes place, the newborn is commonly disposed of before he or she is recognized as a member of the community. Immediate disposal is used because it makes the death emotionally less painful for the parents, keeps the infanticide secret or hidden, and allows the infant to be defined as less than fully human. An example of quick disposal is set forth in the following description of infanticide as practiced by the Dogon people of West Africa.

Infanticide is also practiced, this time openly, on malformed children, whose birth would be due, according to a very general belief, to the union, perhaps involuntary, of the woman with a spirit of the bush, Yeban or Gyinou.

Fetus and stillborn child, in case of infanticide, are put in a new pottery vessel and carried to ayene bodi, "the hole for the still born"; a depression in the ground is reserved for this purpose outside the village. The child that comes into the world without having lived is supposed to be interred in the very earth of the room, in order, it is said that the breath which should have animated the child return to be reincarnated in the mother and she conceives anew. Finally, the child that dies two or three days after the birth is carried to the ossuary reserved for the dead of its paternal family; the body of the baby is not wrapped in the shroud that envelops the body of the adults; no one is obliged to weep; no gunshot is fired in honor of the dead tot.

Source: Paulme, Denise. (1940). *Organization Sociale des Dogon (Soudan Francais)*. Paris: Editions Domat-Montchrestien, F. Lovitan et Cie, p. 410. Translated from the French for the Human Relations Area Files by Frieda Schutze.

the physiological vulnerability of infants. This syndrome involves the severe shaking of an infant, resulting in cerebral swelling and hemorrhage. Infants are especially susceptible, as most adults do not have the strength to lift older toddlers and children and shake them severely enough to cause the brain to swell and hemorrhage. Although toddlers and older children are just as likely to be injured by aggressive parental action, injuries sustained by infants are more likely to have fatal consequences.

As the age of victims increases, child fatalities due to homicide decrease. Additionally, the largest percentage of homicide victims aged twelve months or younger occur in the newborn-to-six-months age range. Research on victim gender is mixed, with some studies concluding that boys are at greater risk, other studies concluding that girls are at greater risk, and still others holding that girls and boys are equally at risk.

CAUSES OF INFANTICIDE

Recent research on the causes of infanticide emphasizes stress experienced by the offender, who is typically a parent or caretaker. This stress is often attributed to emotionally damaging life experiences of the offender as both a child and an adult. As children, many offenders experienced physical and emotional abuse. As adults, many offenders experience adverse or poor living conditions and abuse by spouses or intimate partners. Another significant cause of stress is the intense demands placed on women in the role of mothers. During the last decades of the twentieth century, the cultural expectations of working mothers increased tremendously, becoming increasingly unrealistic. Certain highly publicized infanticide cases have also used postpartum depression as an insanity-based defense.

PREVENTION AND CONTROL

Prevention and control efforts within the criminal justice system have focused on detection and criminalization, and both of these efforts have been intensified across the United States since the early 1980s. Medical examiners and other death certifiers now conduct more intensive analyses of child deaths than in the past. In addition, many states now require that child fatality review teams investigate child deaths.

In terms of long-term prevention at the societal level, many experts believe that it is important to pro-

estimates that there are approximately 2,000 deaths annually due to abuse or neglect by parents or caretakers. Many authors agree that child murder is most often perpetrated by the parents and that more mothers than fathers kill their infant children.

A wider range of objects—such as adult hands and belts—can be used for infanticide than for adult homicide. Moreover, unlike in adult homicide, head trauma and asphyxiation are the most frequent causes of death, and the most commonly used weapons for inflicting these injuries are "personal" weapons such as adult hands or feet. Another common form of infant homicide is "shaken baby syndrome," which attests to vide economic support for working families and parents, and social/mental health support for parents who themselves experienced physical abuse. In addition, programs designed to teach parenting skills and to reduce stress associated with parenting are believed to be effective in reducing the stress experienced by the most likely offenders.

—*Martha Smithey*

See also CHILD HOMICIDE; CHILD MALTREATMENT; CHILD NEGLECT; CHILD PHYSICAL ABUSE

Further Reading

Adler, Christine, and June Baker. (1997). "More Than One Story to Be Told." *Women and Criminal Justice* 9: 15–39.

Alexander, Randall, D. P. Schor, and W. L. Smith. (1990). "Incidence of Impact Trauma With Cranial Injuries Ascribed to Shaking." *American Journal of Diseases of Children* 144: 723–726.

Bourget, Daniel, and Bradford, J. M. W. (1990). "Homicidal Parents." *Canadian Journal of Psychiatry* 35: 233–237.

Cherland, E., and P. C. Matthews. (1989). "Attempted Murder of a Newborn: A Case History." *Canadian Journal of Psychiatry* 34: 337–339.

Crimmins, Susan, H. H. Brownstein, and B. Spunt. (1994). *Convicted Women Who Kill Children: A Self Psychology Perspective.* Paper presentation at the annual meeting of the American Psychological Association, Los Angeles, CA.

DeMausse, Lloyd. (1988). "The Evolution of Childhood." In *Centuries of Childhood*, edited by L. DeMausse. New York: Peter Bedrick, 8–36.

DiMaio, Dominick J., and Vincent J. M. DiMaio. (1989). *Forensic Pathology.* New York: Elsevier.

Gartner, Rosemary. (1990). "The Victims of Homicide: A Temporal and Cross-National Comparison." *American Sociological Review* 55: 92–106.

Guisso, Richard W., and Stanley Johannesen. (1981). *Women in China: Current Directions in Historical Scholarship.* Lewiston, NY: Philo Press.

Hays, Sharon. (1996). *The Cultural Contradictions of Motherhood.* New Haven, CT: Yale University Press.

Husain, A., and D. Annasseril. (1984). "A Comparative Study of Filicidal and Abusive Mothers." *Canadian Journal of Psychiatry.* 29: 596–598.

Knight, Bernard. (1991). *Forensic Pathology.* New York: Oxford University Press.

Levinson, David. (1989). *Family Violence in Cross-Cultural Perspective.* Newbury Park: Sage Publications.

Margolin, Leslie. (1990). "Fatal Child Neglect." *Child Welfare* LXIX: 309–319.

Minturn, Leigh, and Jerry Stashak. (1982). "Infanticide as a Terminal Abortion Procedure." *Behavior Science Research* 17: 70–90.

Pakrasi, K. B. (1970). *Female Infanticide in India.* Calcutta: Calcutta Press.

Resnick, Phillip J. (1969). "Child Murder by Parents: A Psychiatric Review of Filicide." *American Journal of Psychiatry* 126: 325–334.

Rodenberg, M. (1971). "Child Murder by Depressed Parents." *Canadian Psychological Association Journal* 16, 1: 41–49.

Saxena, R. K. (1975). *Social Reforms: Infanticide and Sati.* New Delhi: Trimurti Publications.

Smithey, Martha. (1997). "Infant Homicide at the Hands of Mothers: Toward a Sociological Perspective." *Deviant Behavior* 18: 255–272.

———. (1998). "Infant Homicide: Victim/Offender Relationship and Causes of Death." *Journal of Family Violence* 13, 3: 219–232.

———. (Forthcoming). "Maternal Infanticide and Modern Motherhood." In *Women and Criminal Justice.*

Somander, Lis K. H., and Lennart M. Rammer. (1991). "Intra- and Extrafamilial Child Homicide in Sweden 1971–1980." *Child Abuse and Neglect* 15: 45–55.

Spaide, Richard F., Richard M. Swengel, and Calvin E. Meine. (1990). "Shaken Baby Syndrome." *American Family Physician* (April): 1145–1152.

Turner, J. W. C., ed. (1966). *Kenny's Outlines of Criminal Law,* 19th ed. Cambridge, UK: Cambridge University Press.

U.S. Advisory Board on Child Abuse and Neglect. (1995). *A Nation's Shame: Fatal Child Abuse and Neglect in the United States.* Washington, DC: Government Printing Office.

INFORMANTS

Criminal investigation is a very complex process that requires gathering an enormous amount of information. A significant portion of this information is acquired by law enforcement personnel through the development and management of informants. Both academics and law enforcement professionals suggest that 90 to 95 percent of criminal cases are brought to a successful conclusion through the development and use of informants. The term *informant* may be defined as a person, directed by law enforcement and usually compensated, who furnishes information regarding unlawful activity or performs tasks as specified by law enforcement investigators.

ACTIVITIES OF INFORMANTS

Informants may also be referred to as "cooperating individuals" (CIs), "confidential sources," or simply "sources." They may be street-level criminals, including members of street gangs, or professionals who may or may not have involved themselves in some type of criminal activity—airline employees, bankers, and even attorneys or law enforcement personnel can be recruited as informants. The value of informants is in their "insider" knowledge of the criminal activity of individuals or organizations. It would take law

Mafia informant Joseph Valachi at the Queens County District Attorney's Office in New York City on October 16, 1963. Valachi played a major role in describing to law enforcement officials the structure and function of organized crime in the United States. However, some experts believe that some of his testimony was exaggerated or false.
Source: © Bettmann/Corbis; used by permission.

enforcement a long time to develop the information on criminal activity that informants possess by virtue of their personal involvement in or proximity to criminal activity. Law enforcement personnel develop informants in various areas of their community to ensure that they have knowledge of who is involved in what type of criminal activity. This requires the development of informants knowledgeable about both street-level crime and white-collar crimes such as fraud, Internet crime, and various types of economic or organized crime.

Informants can improve the efficiency and effectiveness of law enforcement in several ways. They can introduce undercover agents into criminal organizations to gather evidence. They can provide testimony or background information on the criminal activity of individuals or organizations, or they can conduct surveillance ("covert observation") on them. They can also identify the assets of criminals for seizure and forfeiture or identify potential targets for investigations. Informants are highly valuable because they can supply information on criminal activity that no one else can provide. This information allows law enforcement to

discover what type of criminal activity is occurring in their community and who is conducting it.

METHODS OF ACQUISITION

Informants are most commonly people who have been arrested or charged with criminal activity by law enforcement and who want to cooperate in exchange for leniency during sentencing. (The prosecutor, however, must be involved in any agreements concerning sentencing recommendations.) Informants may be acquired through various methods, including "walk-ins" or referrals from other agencies. A walk-in is an individual who simply walks into the law enforcement office and explains that he or she has information or can provide some service to the police. Often, an enforcement agency will develop an informant who can provide information or services about an area outside their jurisdiction. The agency will then contact the department that works the area where the informant can provide assistance. Both agencies cooperate by sharing the information, thus solving more crimes.

MOTIVES FOR COOPERATION

Law enforcement must know why an individual has decided to work as an informant. By understanding the informant's motivation, investigators can better control the informant and create an environment that maximizes the informant's potential. A successful investigation will provide incentives that meet the identified needs of the informant. The most common motives for people to become informants usually fall into one of four categories: money, ideology, competition, or ego. Other, more specific, motives for cooperation include the following:

- *Self-interest:* Money or some other personal gain is one of the more common motives for cooperation. Informants have been and will continue to be paid for their services and information; some have been paid in excess of $1 million. More frequently, informants are paid on a per-case basis, depending on the outcome of the investigation, evidence seized, assets forfeiture, and seriousness of the crime.

- *Revenge:* "An eye for an eye" best describes this motivation. Ex-spouses, former lovers, family members, or friends of a criminal may inform on him or her because they feel that their trust has been betrayed by the person. They use law enforcement to punish this breach of trust.

- *Altruism:* The welfare of others is another motive for cooperation. These informants are often referred to as "good citizens." Often, a criminal organization will employ a noncriminal person (an accountant, banker, attorney, or other type of professional or business person) to conduct part of its activity. Once the good citizen discovers that he or she has information concerning criminal activity, the person cooperates with law enforcement.

- *Vanity:* Informants motivated in this way seek favors or approval of law enforcement. Ego is the key to working these informants. Referred to as "police buffs," they like being around police and like to "play police."

- *Fear of punishment:* A common motive for cooperation, fear of punishment for criminal activity is used by law enforcement to force the informant to work or provide information. The desire to avoid jail or loss of freedom is what motivates this informant.

- *Perversity:* The perverse informant is one who hides his or her real motive for cooperation. This informant seeks some advantage through his or her cooperation. The purpose of cooperation might be to learn the identity of undercover agents or identify techniques used by law enforcement to apprehend criminal violators, thus allowing the informant or his or her criminal organization to become more efficient and effective in its criminal activities.

There are many other motives for cooperation. Investigators need to identify their informants' motives and work the informants with these motives in mind.

INFORMANT CONTROL, EVALUATION, AND PROTECTION

The investigator must be effective in developing informants and knowledgeable regarding control, evaluation, and protection of them. Informants must be debriefed, and any information they provide about criminals or criminal activity must be recorded. Because many informants are from the criminal element of society, investigators must be aware of the informant's activity while the informant is employed by law enforcement. Informants are trained by law enforcement with regard to obtaining admissible evidence and understanding legal issues such as entrapment. Informants are cautioned not to disclose information or techniques used during investigations.

Investigators must remember that today's informant may be tomorrow's defendant. To help ensure that the informant is not involved in criminal activity, investigators must covertly monitor their informants and develop other informants who can report on the activity of the informant being monitored. Informants must be evaluated with regard to their reliability and productivity. Any information produced by an informant must be corroborated through independent sources before any action is taken as a result of informant debriefings. Surveillance is often used to corroborate informant information. Informant information may also be tested or verified by interrogation techniques used on the informant or by requiring the informant to submit to a polygraph examination. The evaluation process requires that documentation be generated to ensure that informants are productive and reliable. This documentation is very sensitive and is stored in high-security areas with access on a need-to-know basis.

Control and protection go hand in hand regarding the investigator's role in handling informants. The informant must be willing to be educated on legal and procedural requirements of investigations and be willing to follow instructions. Informants who do not follow procedures as outlined by investigators become very dangerous to law enforcement agencies and their personnel; undercover agents can be exposed and killed or injured as a result of informants' failure to follow instructions, and evidence can be lost in court if informants do not follow procedure. Protection involves keeping the identity of informants confidential during and after the operation. Informants are exposed during court proceedings only if the case requires this exposure and the case is of major importance to the law enforcement agency. Once a case has concluded, protection of the informant continues and may involve relocation of the informant or placement of the informant in the federal witness-protection program.

SUMMARY

Informant development and management are complex processes that can result in loss of life or damage to the reputation of a law enforcement agency if not handled properly. Informants are a critical part of law enforcement and will continue to play a major role in criminal investigations in the future. Professional and progressive police agencies develop written guidelines addressing such topics as employment and termination of informants; their control, evaluation, and protection; and legal aspects of informant management. These policies are constantly reviewed for compliance with court decisions concerning informant use by law enforcement.

Although informants supply massive amounts of

information to law enforcement, investigators must corroborate this information to ensure its reliability. If informants provide false information, place investigators in danger, or involve themselves in actions that embarrass the agency, they must be terminated. Payments to informants must be well documented and monitored for accuracy. The acquisition, development, and management of informants involve the investigator, his or her supervisor, and often other administrators. This ensures that the complex task of informant development and management gets the resources needed to prevent the informant from becoming a problem for the agency. Informants are often referred to as the "bread and butter" of investigations, but they also function as "double-edged swords" that can destroy an individual officer or department by their criminal or unethical acts. Investigators must know what motivates their informants, monitor their activity, and ensure that they follow instructions.

—*Stephen L. Mallory*

See also DETECTIVE WORK

Further Reading

Fitzgerald, Dennis G. (1996). *Informant Law Deskbook*. New York: Clark Boardrman and Callaghan.

Katel, Peter. (1995). "Justice: The Trouble with Informants." *Newsweek* (January 30): 48–52.

Mallory, Stephen L. (2000). *Informants: Development and Management*. Incline Village, NV: Copperhouse Publishing Co.

Nugent, Hugh, Frank J. Leahy, and Edward F. Connors. (1991). "Managing Confidential Informants." Monograph, Bureau of Justice Assistance. Washington, DC: Government Printing Office.

Court Cases

Aguilar v. Texas (1964). 387 U.S. 108: 83, 93, 95.

Illinois v. Gates (1957). 353 U.S. 59–62.

Illinois v. Gates (1983). 462 U.S. 213, 238: 62, 83, 93, 100.

Jacobson v. U.S. (1992). 503 U.S. 540: 101, 102.

Liuzzo v. U.S. (1983). 565 F. Supp. 640: 107.

Middlebrook v. Mississippi (1990). 555 So.2d. 1009: 92.

Roviaro v U.S. (1957). 353 U.S. 53: 84, 86, 93.

Slage v. U.S. (1980). 612 F. 2d. 1157: 107.

Spinelli v. U.S. (1969). 393 U.S. 410: 83, 93.

U.S. v. Mahler (1961). 196 F. supp. 418: 100.

U.S. v. Medina-Reyes (1998). 854 F, 2d, 1319: 100.

U.S. v. Price (1986). 783 F. 2d. 1132: 92.

U.S. v. Wilson (1990). 904 F. 2d. 656: 99.

▼ INFORMATION SYSTEMS

Law enforcement has always been a data-intensive industry. Investigating criminal activity, implementing problem-oriented policing, processing court cases, and managing correctional facilities are all heavily dependent on information for their successful operation. Until recently, however, implementing integrated information systems to better manage available data has typically been beyond the technical and fiscal reach of most organizations within the criminal justice system. Not surprisingly, the technical and fiscal constraints experienced by the criminal justice system are similar for many other organizations in the public sector.

In the early twenty-first century, however, the technical, fiscal, and management barriers to implementing integrated information systems are falling dramatically. Both hardware and application software are becoming less expensive and easier to manage, and they provide greater performance. Equally important, de facto standards have emerged over the last decade that have significantly reduced the fiscal and technical management costs of data communications (e.g., TCP/IP, HTML), operating systems (e.g., UNIX, Windows) and applications software (U.S. Department of Commerce 2000). All these factors are converging to offer new opportunities for systems development and integration for public sector organizations.

In addition to technological change, however, the structure and geographic organization of criminal justice have had profound effects on the development of information systems. The American criminal justice system comprises local, county, metropolitan, state, and federal governments. At each level of government, criminal justice agencies are typically divided along functional lines, such as police, courts, prosecution and defense, corrections, probation, and parole. The juvenile justice system, which is a separate entity, has many of the same components as the adult criminal justice system and is not discussed here. Finally, each state jurisdiction and many local ones enforce different laws and operate under different legal infrastructures. Thus, the organizational disjunctures that exist within the criminal justice system by level of government, agency function, geography, and legal structure represent not only significant potential barriers to developing integrated information systems but also a major reason to promote the development of such systems.

The Colorado Integrated Criminal Justice Information System (CICJIS) is a good example of an information system approach that provides integrated support for the criminal justice system. The system allows for information to be instantaneously moved across criminal justice agencies and departments within the state and greatly reduces the need for multiple entries of the same data (e.g., offender name and address) across different agencies (Holmes, Usery, and Roper 2000/2001).

LAW ENFORCEMENT

At the local level, the majority of police forces in America have implemented 911 systems, the most basic of all law enforcement information systems. These systems provide both an easy-access point of contact for citizens to request public safety services and a means for law enforcement agencies, emergency medical services, and fire departments to quickly dispatch assistance. In addition, these systems provide the infrastructure needed to identify on an ongoing basis the broad range of problems relating to public safety that citizens face. More recently, some cities such as Baltimore, have implemented 311 systems for non-emergency requests for assistance. These systems help make 911 operations more manageable by off-loading less time-sensitive calls, while maintaining a mechanism for citizens to request assistance.

Along with 911 systems, many local police departments have implemented Computer-Aided Dispatch (CAD) systems. CAD information systems are used to record incidents for all call-related data as well as to support the dispatch of officers (Sparrow 1991). CAD systems also can be directly networked to patrol cars with Mobile Digital Communications devices (MDC). According to Huettl, "Officers are better protected as the screen provides a listing of any past incidents at an address each time a 911 call is received. Dispatchers can ascertain if the address is a domestic-violence location, houses elderly or disabled individuals, or is used to store hazardous chemicals. The responding officers know if there is a warrant issued for a resident of the premises" (2001: 36).

Local police departments have also begun implementing Automated Fingerprint Identification Systems (AFISs). An AFIS can function as a stand-alone database used for querying fingerprint images contained in the system. Fingerprints are collected at crime scenes and entered into a database. An AFIS allows for fingerprints recovered from crime scenes to be searched against the entire database, which increases the probability of identification. When a fingerprint is entered into the AFIS, points of identification are compared against the existing files, and a list of possible matches is generated. Other information systems currently implemented by local law enforcement agencies include records management, online booking, jail management, and local warrants systems.

Local Geographic Information Systems

Local law enforcement departments have begun to integrate analytic information systems capabilities into their operations. Thus, some cities as well as some state and federal agencies have begun to implement a Geographic Information System (GIS) into their routine activities. A GIS has been used for crime analysis by identifying crime "hot spots" in order to forecast possible crime areas. GIS capabilities have been influential in identifying and predicting areas of burglary and drug use. A fifteen-month survey of 2,000 law enforcement agencies conducted by the National Institute of Justice (NIJ) Crime Mapping Research Center found that only 261 used computerized crime mapping, although such mapping has been proven effective. Larger departments with more than 100 sworn officers were much more likely to use the computerized crime mapping technology (36 percent) than smaller departments (3 percent) (Mamalian and La Vigne 1999). According to Hickman, "Sixteen percent of all local police agencies in 1999 reported using computers for the purpose of crime mapping" (2001: 55).

Local law enforcement departments implementing a GIS into their existing systems have encountered some unforeseen problems. When independent agencies implement a GIS, local agencies need to buy hardware and software and pay for updating the actual digital base maps of their cities/communities. As geographic areas change over time, there is a need for new digital base maps. Therefore, in order for police to stay current, new maps need to be purchased, often at unexpectedly high prices (Rogers and Craig 1996). Another unforeseen problem with GISs is the need to train or hire experienced new staff so that departments can effectively use the capabilities of these systems. For example, Overland Park, Kansas, uses a GIS; however, many officers do not use the GIS, because they are not proficient on the computer and find even the most basic of applications intimidating (Institute for Law and Justice 2001).

State and Regional Systems

At the next level of government, individual states maintain information systems that manage criminal history records, stolen and wanted systems, and warrants. Each state collects information from local police departments and from the state police. For example, the state of Massachusetts maintains the Crime Reporting Unit (CRU). The CRU is the contact point between state, local and campus police departments and the Federal Bureau of Investigation (FBI). The CRU has the responsibility of collecting, maintaining, analyzing, and reporting crime data for Massachusetts. State police have additional duties, including maintaining crime labs for the state, the sex offender registry, and links with the Department of Motor Vehicles. The state police have the same duties as the local police departments, albeit on a larger scale. The state police also have CAD systems; however, since their jurisdiction is not primarily in neighborhoods and local principalities, they do not generally use a GIS.

The third level of law enforcement is regional or multistate. Several states pool their resources to apprehend criminals—for example, the western states have a consortium, Western Identification Network (WIN) whose primary purpose is to use a linked AFIS. Nearly a dozen western states comprise the Southwest Border States Anti-Drug Information System (SWBSADIS), which is used to combat drug trafficking.

Federal Systems

Finally, at the federal level of government, major law enforcement agencies include the FBI; Bureau of Alcohol, Tobacco and Firearms (BATF); and Drug Enforcement Administration (DEA). Each of these agencies maintains separate information systems. The FBI's Violent Criminal Apprehension Program (VICAP) is a nationwide data information center designed to collect, collate, and analyze crimes of violence—specifically murder. VICAP's mission is to facilitate cooperation, communication, and coordination between law enforcement agencies and provide support in their efforts to investigate, identify, track, apprehend, and prosecute violent serial offenders. Another national system being developed by the FBI is the Integrated Automated Fingerprint Identification System (IAFIS). The purpose of the IAFIS is to sustain the FBI's mission to provide identification services to the nation's law enforcement community and to organizations where criminal background histories are a critical factor in employment consideration. According to the section of the FBI Web site on IAFIS (para. 2):

> The IAFIS will provide ten-print, latent print, subject search, and criminal history request services, document

submission, and image request services to FBI Service Providers, along with federal, state, and local law enforcement users. IAFIS is being procured as three segments: the Automated Fingerprint Identification System (AFIS) segment, the Interstate Identification Index (III) segment, and the Identification, Tasking, and Networking (ITN) segment, each of which is being delivered incrementally. Each segment provides discrete capabilities and works in conjunction with the other segments to support FBI Service Providers and external users in their law enforcement capacities.

The FBI also manages the Uniform Crime Reporting (UCR) and the National Incident Based Reporting System (NIBRS) programs, which are the primary systems for collecting and analyzing reported crime statistics in the United States. The UCR program collects primarily aggregate information on the number of violent and property crimes reported in the United States by law enforcement agencies. The NIBRS program is an "incident-based" system that collects detailed information on individual crimes, including data on location, property, weapons, victims, offenders, arrestees, and law enforcement officers injured or killed. In the future, NIBRS is intended to replace the UCR. By 2001, however, the transition of NIBRS had been not fully implemented. Not all states are certified to submit data, and those that are not do not receive funding for their state level programs. In addition, some agencies do not have the resources to train officers/staff to code crime reports for NIBRS reporting systems (Dunworth 2000). Finally, NIBRS seeks total information about one incident; one crime incident report can contain information on several different criminal offenses. As a result, the UCR system records only the most serious offense from a citizen crime report, while the NIBRS system documents each criminal offense contained in a crime report. The NIBRS approach to crime reporting will produce a more comprehensive assessment of crime, but it also will produce more reported criminal offenses (from a given set of citizen crime reports) than the UCR system. The higher level of reported offenses derived from citizen crime reports by NIBRS could make the transition to NIBRS sometimes difficult for local police agencies.

Other FBI-managed information systems include the Combined Offender DNA Index System (CODIS) and the National Instant Criminal Background Check System (NICS). CODIS contains DNA profiles of individuals convicted of felony sex crimes and other violent crimes. It also contains DNA profiles from evidence left at crime scenes. The NICS contains information on whether a person has been "disqualified from possessing a firearm under federal or state law." Finally, the National Integrated Ballistic Information Network is a collaborative effort between the ATF and FBI to coordinate ballistics imaging to trace guns. The Bureau of Alcohol, Tobacco and Firearms also operates and maintains the National Tracing Center Division (NTC). The NTC works with law enforcement and the firearms industry to trace the origin and initial sale history of a firearm recovered by an enforcement agency (BATF 2000). The National Law Enforcement Telecommunications System, which "is a sophisticated computer-controlled message switching network linking local, state, and federal agencies together for the purpose of information exchange," links many criminal justice information resources together (www.nlets.org/history.htm).

COURTS AND PROSECUTION

State court systems show significant variation in their jurisdictional and geographic organization. Such organizational variation makes it difficult to develop automation and information systems solutions that can be easily implemented across states and to create national court data/information standards that are relevant and applicable from state to state. The significant variability in state court systems means that, before automation and integration solutions are developed to address the more general needs of many courts, it is important to identify the differing needs and capabilities of individual courts (Bureau of Justice Assistance 1999b: 7).

Many court systems have attempted to automate court records and implement information systems for the purpose of improved record keeping. As a result, such systems typically were not designed to support the overall operations of the court systems or support the broader law enforcement objectives of courts. According to Polansky (1996, cited in Brown), "By the early 1970s, many major urban courts had begun building court information systems. But there was little systems analysis and planning, and systems—designed and programmed by people who knew little about courts—never showed the results to justify the high costs. Despite these difficulties, the first court-operated, computer-aided transcript system was installed in Allegheny County, PA, in 1973" (Brown 2000: 231). As of 1996, Polansky had found that no court system had initiated an information technology project with a specific objective of improving services or reducing costs (Brown 2000).

Beyond the judicial functions of courts, prosecutorial and public defense departments also play very important roles in the court system. Few of these types of departments, however, use information technology to do more than check the docket status of court cases or use software to help automate forms processing. These types of systems can help court personnel by reducing paperwork and allowing them to manage some of their case workload without being physically present in a court (Brown 2000).

Currently, some courts use data management software to help process dockets and allow for electronic filing, but such systems are still rare. Likewise, some prosecutor departments use software, similar to an electronic organizer, for office and case management (Brown 2000). One of the most advanced current approaches to statewide court system automation has been undertaken by the state of Wisconsin. Wisconsin has developed and implemented an information system called the Circuit Court Automation Program (CCAP), which is used to improve day-to-day operations of courts, such as managing case records, calendaring, jury selection, and financial management.

States are beginning to develop court system automation plans and have begun some actual implementation. A study conducted in 1996 of prosecutors in state courts found that "23 percent of offices indicated being part of an integrated systems with the courts, 16 percent with law enforcement, and 9 percent with district attorney offices statewide" (DeFrances and Steadman 1998: 7). Moreover, "[i]n 1996 about a third of all offices reported being part of an integrated computerized system with other criminal justice agencies" (DeFrances and Steadman 1998: 7). In the not-too-distant future, intra- and intersystem information integration will become a major objective of judicial information systems. The goal of integrated court systems is to collect information on warrants, pretrial services, presentencing reports, protection and restraining orders, and background of defendants, as well as to provide links to human service agencies outside the judicial system (International Association of Chiefs of Police 2000). This type of integration will greatly reduce the number of victims, defendants, and offenders who fall through the cracks of the judicial and human service systems. For example, a defendant may need substance abuse counseling as opposed to incarceration; with direct links to outside health agencies, it should be easier to develop and monitor a treatment plan for such clients.

Two other federal court systems allow for electronic

access to record keeping. One is the U.S. Supreme Court's Electronic Bulletin Board System, which provides online access to the docket, argument calendar, slip opinions, and so on. The other, the Public Access to Court Electronic Records (PACER), allows "any user with a personal computer to dial in to a district or bankruptcy court computer and retrieve official electronic case information and court dockets" (Administrative Office of the U.S. Courts 1996: 1).

CORRECTIONS, PROBATION, AND PAROLE

The corrections system can be viewed as including jails, prisons, probation, parole, and substance abuse treatment brokers. Typically, corrections systems from local and county jails to the state and federal prisons have implemented some type of information systems. These systems can vary from the highly sophisticated system with network links that integrate jail or prison systems with their partner probation and parole departments, to limited, stand-alone information systems. The most basic corrections information systems collect data on booking and release status, housing assignments, case management status, criminal charges and sentencing, and time served (Kichen, Murphy, and Levinson 1993). Some institutions maintain the same information in paper form.

A 1998 U.S. Department of Justice survey found that state and federal corrections information systems provide an overview of the type of data collected and managed by correction information systems. Perhaps the most striking finding of the survey was that no correctional system in the country collected and automated all the data element requirements of the Association of State Correctional Administrators. Some states (Alabama, Colorado, Florida, Georgia, Missouri, North Carolina, Washington, Oregon, and South Carolina) maintained information systems that collected data elements pertaining to sentencing information (U.S. Department of Justice 1998). Some of these same states, however, do not maintain a complete range of information about inmates in treatment programs. Some states with sophisticated corrections information systems collect a broader range of information and also provide some decision support capability for administrators and staff, such as jail or prison inmate management systems, historical record tracking, and basic reporting systems.

It is important to note that not all correctional facilities were built at the same time. Some facilities that were built in the 1940s are having a more difficult time upgrading than are the more high-tech facilities that are currently being built. Some of the newer prisons maintain information much more efficiently because the technological infrastructure was implemented at the time of construction. Some examples of high-tech prisons allow for live-scan fingerprint, barcoded armbands, electronic mug shots, and tracking of visitors.

BARRIERS TO INFORMATION SYSTEMS DEVELOPMENT AND INTEGRATION

Today, technical developments in computing, communications, and software make it possible to make significant progress in the development and integration of criminal justice systems. In many criminal justice agencies, however, there are still a variety of structural and administrative barriers to the development of integrated criminal justice systems at almost all levels within criminal justice.

Organizational decentralization may represent the single greatest barrier to systems integration and development in the American criminal justice system. As a result of this organizational structure, there are different standards of collecting information across states as well as across agencies. For example, the original crime information center in the state of Florida became outdated very quickly because it could not handle different types of data. Data accuracy is another major integration barrier to information systems integration. Examples of common types of data inaccuracies include misspellings of clients' names or street addresses and the transposing of dates.

Inadequate funding is also a major barrier to the development and integration of criminal justice information systems. Few agencies have the means to fully cover the cost of upgrading their information systems; as a result, agencies often seek federal funding for information system development. Federal grants, however, come with conditions and limitations that can reduce the flexibility agencies may need. A grant submission may allow funding for one specific element of a systems integration project or allow funding only for a stand-alone project. The Department of Justice recognizes this as an issue and allows agencies to coordinate grants to support the development of integrated information system projects (Bureau of Justice Assistance 1999a).

Inconsistent funding is another barrier to systems

development. Often, agencies may receive will initial funding but not follow-up funding for an information system. This is a problem, because few information systems meet all of an agency's intended objectives when they are first implemented. Without ongoing funding, information systems that are implemented cannot be adequately tested and modified. Equally important, long-term planning is required to ensure that funds are available to properly maintain the information systems once they have been implemented. Failure to properly test and maintain information systems can significantly reduce their value to agencies and also increase their long-term costs (International Association of Chiefs of Police 2000). Finally, along with the lack of funding for equipment and systems maintenance, agencies may implement systems and then have no funding for training.

Issues such as the politics associated with the separation of powers across departments and regions can impact the development of integrated information systems (International Association of Chiefs of Police 2000). Some agencies are resistant to change and see their way of conducting procedures as the most efficient. Moreover, different departments and jurisdictions conduct activities under different policies, procedures, and laws.

Issues and policies concerning citizen privacy can present barriers to criminal justice systems integration. Citizens, criminal or not, value their privacy. Privacy is a major policy and operational issue for any integrated criminal justice system. Privacy must be thought about at every level of information systems design, and the impact of privacy policies will vary across regions because privacy laws differ from state to state (*Privacy Design Principles* 2000)."The law in more than a dozen states restricts criminal history record information from being integrated or combined with intelligence and investigative information" (Bureau of Justice Assistance 1999a: 68). Moreover, beyond the impact of specific privacy laws, there is a more general concern regarding the linking of criminal justice databases, because some observers and citizens feel that this would allow for "citizen tracking" (Abell 1988: 58).

BENEFITS OF SYSTEMS INTEGRATION

The development of integrated criminal justice information systems can significantly reduce the transaction costs associated with maintenance of multiple of records systems, the work associated with repeated entry of data, and the substantial (but largely undocu-

mented) costs associated with the inefficient operation of criminal justice agencies due to lack of timely and/or comprehensive information on problems, clients, victims, and/or offenders. Comprehensive and timely information provided by integrated systems can promote the development of proactive strategies in criminal justice and reduce incidents in which clients within criminal justice fall through service delivery gaps.

Policing has changed over the years to a more community-based approach. Community policing focuses more on proactive measures to stopping crime than on active measures of responding to crimes only after they occur. For community policing to be successful, more open information systems are necessary (Sparrow 1991). This approach becomes even more information-intensive as new services are implemented and/or coordinated by police departments. For example, in a traditional policing context, an officer may be able to learn how chronic problems have been handled in the past only by reviewing individual cases. Historically, there has been little or no systematic effort to develop and share institutional knowledge across officers about what works in solving problems. In community policing, however, this type of information is crucial for effective problem solving (Abt Associates 2000: 6). Although it is imperative to have information from many sectors of the law enforcement agency, it is also necessary to have information from other public agencies for analysis. Problems arise because not all of the wanted information is in electronic format, or, if it has been captured electronically, it may not be compatible across systems (Boba 2000).

Another benefit to integration is efficiency. Often, with complex systems, information gets lost—for example, when a warrant is lost or never issued. Less mundane instances of information loss (such as people "falling through the cracks") can be detrimental to public safety. For example, in domestic violence cases, information about a victim can be taken during a 911 call, and a police officer will be sent to the disturbance. However, if information on repeat 911 domestic violence calls is not recorded and tracked, victims may be left in potentially harmful situations where intervention could prevent further violence.

Finally, enhanced strategic planning can be achieved with information provided via integrated systems. This policing allows for problems to be anticipated and intervention to occur before much larger problems ensue. This will increase public safety more intelligently by allowing for better decision making and ensuring that resources are not wasted on repeated efforts (Bureau of Justice Assistance 1999b).

AVENUES TO INTEGRATION

Technical advances continue to facilitate information systems development and integration. The recent emergence of XML (eXtensible Markup Language) provides a new approach to help realign different data standards. XML is designed specifically for Web-based documents. XML allows for links that point to multiple documents, which HTML (HyperText Markup Language) does not do, and XML allows for easier communication between systems because it can see images, sound, video, and text. In addition, XML supports several data formats and can cover all existing data structures. Because the Web has become a major avenue by which criminal justice agencies communicate with one another, XML can help to encourage the communication and sharing of information.

Comprehensive and inclusive planning processes are critical strategies for the successful development of integrated criminal justice systems. Personnel from various agencies (such as funding, legislative, and community representatives) are necessary for the endeavor (Bureau of Justice Assistance 1999a). An inclusive planning approach helps ensure that comprehensive mission statements and long-term plans can be developed for information systems projects and that plans will not be discarded over time because of politics or disinterest. Inclusive planning strategies also can help minimize political turf battles and allow organizations to see the "big picture" and the value that integrated systems can provide (Bureau of Justice Assistance 1999a).

Key stakeholders need to be brought together to develop governance structures, decision-making processes, goals, and project scope; to complete needs assessments, assess costs, and secure funding; to inform and educate the community; and to set standards and maintain and evaluate the system over time (International Association of Chiefs of Police 2000). For example, a nationwide committee could be instituted to design and implement data standards. These committee members could meet regularly via the Internet, which would minimize interference with their routine activities.

The lack of funding for systems has been partially overcome in some states by "piggybacking" on other state information systems initiatives, and this helps the local agencies to defray costs (Institute for Law and Justice 2001). Even with the lack of funding, the decrease in the price of information technology has made new and better software and hardware more readily available to all agencies. A department can get more memory and faster processing power at a fraction of the cost of even a couple of years ago, creating opportunities for information technology to play an ever larger role in all aspects of criminal justice.

—*Glenn L. Pierce and Roberta E. Griffith*

See also GEOGRAPHIC INFORMATION SYSTEMS; INTERPOL; UNIFORM CRIME REPORTS

Further Reading

Abell, R. B. (1988). "Effective Systems for Regional Intelligence Sharing." *The Police Chief* (November): 58.

Abt Associates. (2000). *Police Department Information Systems Technology Enhancement Project (ISTEP)*. Washington, DC: Department of Justice, Office of Community Oriented Policing Forces.

Administrative Office of the U.S. Courts. (1996). *Summary on Current Electronic Public Access Programs in the Federal Judiciary, July 24, 1996.* http://www.uscourts.gov/press_releases/summ.htm

Boba, Rachel. (2000). "Guidelines to Implement and Evaluate Crime Analysis and Mapping in Law Enforcement Agencies." *Report to the Office of Community Oriented Policing Services.* (October).

Brown, Maureen. (2000). "Criminal Justice Discovers Information Technology." *Criminal Justice* 1: 220, 229, 231.

Bureau of Alcohol, Tobacco and Firearms. (2000*). Crime Gun Trace Reports (1999)—National Report* (November). Washington, DC: Bureau of Alcohol, Tobacco and Firearms.

Bureau of Justice Assistance. (1999a). *Keynote Presentations: 1999 Symposium on Integrated Justice Information Systems* (August). NCJ 178231. Washington, DC: Bureau of Justice Assistance.

Bureau of Justice Assistance. (1999b). *Report of the National Task Force on Court Automation and Integration* (7 July). Washington, DC: Bureau of Justice Assistance.

DeFrances, Carol J., and Greg W. Steadman. (1998). "Prosecutors in State Courts, 1996." *1996 Bulletin of Justice Statistics.* USDOJ (July): 7.

Dunworth, Terence. (2000). "Criminal Justice and The IT Revolution." *Criminal Justice* 3: 373, 379.

Federal Bureau of Investigation. (2001). "IAFIS Incremental Builds." http://www.fbi.gov/hq/cjisd/iafis/iafis.htm

Hickman, Matthew J. (2001). "Computers and Information Systems in Local Police Departments, 1990–1999." *The Police Chief* (January): 55.

Holmes, Amir, David Usery, and Dr. Robert Roper (2000/2001). "Colorado Integrated Criminal Justice Information System: Project Overview and Recommendations." *Case Study Series, A Report of the National Task Force on Court Automation and Integration* (Fall/Winter). http://www.search.org/integration/default.asp

Huettl, Jerry. (2001). "Public Safety Partnership Debuts CAD, Records, and Jail System Serving 24 Agencies." *The Police*

Chief (January): 36.

Institute for Law and Justice. (2001). *Technology Acquisition Project Case Study (Overland Park, Kansas).* http://www.ilj.org

International Association of Chiefs of Police. (2000). *An Information Integration Planning Model.* http://www.theiacp.org/pubinfo/research/infintplanmodel.pdf

Kichen, Carol Cole, James Murphy, and Robert B. Levinson. (1993). *Correctional Technology: A User's Guide.* Washington, DC: National Institute of Corrections, U.S. Department of Justice.

Mamalian, Cynthia A., and Nancy G. La Vigne. (1999). *The Use of Computerized Mapping by Law Enforcement: Survey Results.* U.S. Department of Justice, National Institute of Justice. http://www.ncjrs.org/pdffiles1/fs000237.pdf

Polansky, Larry. (1996). "The Long and Winding Road." *Court Technology Bulletin* 8: 2.

Privacy Design Principles for an Integrated Justice System (Working Paper). (2000). Office of the Ontario Information and Privacy Commissioner and the U.S. Department of Justice, Office of Justice Programs. http://ojp.usdoj.gov/integratedjustice/pcpapril.htm

Rogers, Robert, and Delores E. Craig. (1996). "Geographic Information Systems: Computers in Law Enforcement." *Journal of Crime and Justice* 19, 1: 61–74.

Sparrow, Malcolm K. (1991). "Information Systems: A Help or Hindrance in The Evolution of Policing?" *The Police Chief* (April).

U.S Department of Commerce. (2000). *Digital Economy 2000.* Washington, DC: U.S Department of Commerce, Economics and Statistics Administration, Office of Policy Development.

U.S. Department of Justice, Association of State Correctional Administrators, Corrections Program Office, Bureau of Justice Statistics, and National Institute of Justice. (1998). *State and Federal Corrections Information Systems: An Inventory of Data Elements and An Assessment of Reporting Capabilities.* http://www.ojp.usdoj.gov/bjs/pub/pdf/sfcis.pdf

▼ INQUISITORIAL JUSTICE

Early in the twelfth century, the Fourth Lateran Council led by Pope Innocent III (1198–1216) took a step that drastically altered church law and criminal procedure in continental Europe, particularly in France. By the council's action, a new inquisitorial system of justice was developed and implemented to replace such earlier forms of justice as vengeance, the oath, and the ordeal.

Inquisitorial justice is a system of criminal justice in which the judge is also the prosecutor, proceedings are typically secret, and the accused must answer questioning. The Catholic Church adopted it in the belief that it was the best means to combat its biggest fear—heresy, or the rejection of mainstream Catholic doctrine.

The Church used inquisitorial justice both to destroy individual heretical beliefs and to keep individuals from spreading such beliefs to others. It believed that its pursuit of truth would be better served by inquisition than by the adversarial system of justice used in England. Both the adversarial and inquisitional systems of justice sought truth, but they did so in very different ways.

EARLY INQUISITORIAL JUSTICE

The rise of the inquisition in the twelfth century as an alternative to the adversarial system of justice was the Church's direct response to fears that heretics were weakening its bond with and control over its parishioners. Initially, it was used by clerics to help identify individuals they believed to be heretics. Ultimately, the Church adapted the inquisition to include the use of torture as a means to determine the guilt or innocence of suspected heretics.

In an effort to preserve the rights of the accused and lessen the chance that an innocent person would be found guilty, a very high standard of proof was instituted for inquisitions. Church law required complete proof of heresy in order for the accused to be judged guilty and punished. This meant that there had to be testimony from two witnesses in good standing in the community who had seen the accused commit the crime and whose testimony was credible and completely accurate as to the same facts.

Not surprisingly, this standard of proof was extremely difficult, if not impossible, to obtain with regard to crimes of thought such as heresy. After all, how can two witnesses know what a person is thinking? The impracticability of this legal proof, coupled with clerics' growing fear of the spread of heresy, resulted in an inquisition in which a confession by the accused became necessary not only for corroboration of witnesses' evidence but also for conviction. By the mid-thirteenth century, increasing fears of the spread of heresy, real or imagined, drove the Church to use new and innovative techniques to stop it. Interrogations and interviews with accused heretics became more confrontational, ultimately resulting in the use of torture as a means to gain confession.

In the interest of defending the faith against nonbelievers, torture of the accused was fully sanctioned by the Church. In fact, Innocent IV (Pope 1243–1254) oversaw the creation of machinery specifically designed for the torture of prisoners. But torture was not only physical; psychological methods of torture and imprisonment in dungeons were used as well. Regardless of method, torture was implemented for the sole purpose of gaining confession—a confession that had to be given freely and willingly after the accused had been tortured.

The Church justified the use of torture in several ways. It argued that the clergy who were a part of the inquisition were on a mission to save the faith by purifying it and ridding it of the sin of heresy. If torture was required to meet this end, it was a necessary evil. Moreover, the Church defended its practice of torture by suggesting that the confessions that the clergy extracted as a result of torture might actually save the souls of the accused, rescuing them from eternal damnation.

While early inquisitorial justice was used to adjudicate cases of heresy and therefore fell under the jurisdiction of the Church, exclusive use of this method of justice did not remain with the Church for long. As more common offenses became subject to inquisition and torture, secular authorities took over the implementation and administration of inquisitorial justice.

SECULAR INQUISITORIAL JUSTICE

The perceived success of the Church's methods in obtaining guilty pleas from heretics encouraged officials to adapt ecclesiastical methods to the secular world. If torture and the inquisition worked to rid the Church of heresy, it would certainly work when trying to assess guilt for all but the most petty of crimes.

Over time, only the actors changed—not the basic elements of the inquisition. Both ecclesiastical and secular judges allowed trials, the purpose of which was to confront the accused with the rumors and charges against them and to demand their confessions. The judges generally received evidence about the accused from an official investigator, but they often did more research if necessary, including interviewing witnesses, secret informers, and victims. These interviews were suspect, however, because they were conducted without the accused present, and because the motives of the individuals who provided evidence about the accused were often questionable. In many instances, they gave testimony to save themselves from inquisition, or they said what the judge wanted to hear simply because they were afraid of being detained and charged for something they did not do.

After reviewing the evidence, judges decided whether there were grounds for an inquisition to take place. Initially, the accusations against a person were established on the basis of reputation or rumor. By the thirteenth century, however, reputation played little or no part in a judge's decision of whether to go ahead with an inquisition. By this time, the power of the judge had grown tremendously. Essentially, judges assessed and determined the reputation of the accused. Their suspicions alone, regardless of merit, were enough to imprison a suspect and begin an inquisition. Consequently, as judges' control and power over the inquisition grew, the rights of the accused were substantially diminished. As more and more offenses came under the scope of what judges called "extraordinary procedure," those accused lost the right to know the allegations against them, and testimony was kept secret from them and the public.

For secular judges, the base requirement for guilt or innocence of a suspect was truth, and they believed that every effort must be directed at determining it. Only with overwhelming evidence would the accused be declared innocent or guilty. As in ecclesiastical courts, secular judges' emphasis on the conclusive nature of proof led to a reliance on confessions. However, for these judges, the confession served several purposes. It demonstrated that the accused accepted the conclusiveness of proof against them, it exonerated judges and courts from having to decide innocence or guilt based upon conflicting evidence, and it reassured the public.

As the inquisitorial system of justice became more elaborate, judges established levels of proof adequate for the conviction of certain crimes. Consequently, it became virtually impossible to obtain a conviction for major crimes without a confession by the accused. Not surprisingly, as confessions became a more significant part of the state's case against the accused, inquisitors perfected methods of obtaining confessions. Torture was expanded to all those accused, regardless of status, and it was used to obtain evidence from witnesses and accomplices.

HALLMARKS OF INQUISITORIAL JUSTICE

To better understand the uniqueness of inquisitorial justice, it is useful to highlight several aspects of this system that differentiate it from adversarial justice. First and foremost, in the inquisitorial system of justice, there is no definite accuser or victim. Charges are made and assessed by an inquisitor or judge, who does not necessarily specify or reveal to the accused the charges against them. In contrast, the fundamental basis of the adversarial system is that there is a definite accuser or victim who brings charges against a suspect. Furthermore, a grand jury system screens charges and produces an indictment against the accused.

Under the inquisitorial system, the accused are presumed guilty and must attempt to prove themselves innocent. In an effort to try to prove do so, those accused must often resort to self-incrimination, because they are not allowed to interview or call witnesses on their behalf. The judge, not the accused, assesses the veracity of witnesses and decides on guilt or innocence. The adversarial system, on the other hand, presumes that the accused is innocent until proven guilty, and it is confrontational in that attorneys for the prosecution and the defense present evidence and question witnesses. The judge's role is to moderate discussions between the prosecution and defense before and during the trial. The jury, not the judge, controls the verdict. In a trial conducted under the adversarial system of justice, a judge alone cannot determine the guilt or innocence of the accused.

THE MODIFICATION OF INQUISITIONS

By the sixteenth century, inquisitorial justice was the rule of law in France, but opposition to some of its methods led to changes in its practice. The Ordinance of 1539 provided for several modifications, including a two-stage inquisition process whereby an examination of evidence took place before one judge and was followed by a formal trial before a panel of judges. Other changes included the rule that defendants could not argue in their own defense. Evidence and defenses such as self-defense and insanity were permitted only if the court granted a motion and the accused was able to prove these defenses by means of witnesses.

By the eighteenth century, further modifications to the inquisitorial system were made. The Enlightenment had sparked a fundamental shift in the way many aspects of life were viewed, including crime and justice. Philosophers promoted the idea that those accused were innocent until proven guilty beyond a reasonable doubt, and they argued that society should be more concerned with the moral injustice of a wrongful conviction than with the need for an effective police force or control of the public. Not surprisingly, reforms to the inquisitorial system of justice during this century were drastic. They included a call to make all criminal trials public and to allow the accused to confront witnesses testifying against them. Another change was that the accused were no longer forced to self-incriminate. Most important, a full-scale attack on the use of torture was waged.

While the French system of criminal procedure has evolved since the thirteenth century, vestiges of the

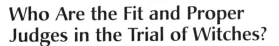

Who Are the Fit and Proper Judges in the Trial of Witches?

The question is whether witches, together with their patrons and protestors and defenders, are so entirely subject to the jurisdiction of the Diocesan Ecclesiastical Court and the Civil Court so that the Inquisitors of the crime of heresy can be altogether relieved from the duty of sitting in judgment upon them. And it is argued that this is so. For the Canon (c. *accusatus, sane,* lib. VI) says: Certainly those whose high privilege it is to judge concerning matters of the faith ought not to be distracted by other business: and Inquisitors deputed by the Apostolic See to inquire into the pest of heresy should manifestly not have to concern themselves with diviners and soothsayers, unless these are also heretics, nor should it be their business to punish such, but they may leave them to be punished by their own judges.

Source: *The Malleus Maleficarum of Heinrich Kramer and James Spenger* ([1486]). Translated with introductions, bibliography and notes by Rev. Montague Summers. (1971). New York: Dover Books, p. 194.

inquisitorial system still exist today. The current system of justice in France is actually a hybrid of both the accusatory and inquisitorial systems, as modified by the Enlightenment and codified in the Code of Criminal Instruction of 1808 and the Penal Code of 1810. In this revised system of justice, certain aspects of the inquisitorial system remain, such as the ability of the police to arrest and hold suspects without their knowledge of the charges against them.

—Melinda D. Schlager

See also ADVERSARIAL JUSTICE; RELIGIOUS DEVIANCE; TORTURE

Further Reading
The French Code of Criminal Procedure. (1988). Littleton, CO: Fred B. Rothman.
Johnson, Herbert A., and Nancy Travis Wolfe. (1996). *History of Criminal Justice.* 2d ed. Cincinnati, OH: Anderson Publishing.
Levy, Leonard W., (1999). *The Palladium of Justice: Origins of Trial By Jury.* Chicago: Ivan R. Dee.
Mueller, Gerhard O. W. (1960). *French Penal Code.* South Hackensack, NJ: Fred B. Rothman.
Mueller, Gerhard, O. W. and Fré Le Poole-Griffiths. (1969). *Comparative Criminal Procedure.* New York: New York University Press.
Von Bar, Carl Ludwig. (1916). *History of Continental Criminal Law.* Boston: Little, Brown.

▼ INTEGRATIVE THEORIES

Since the 1970s, theories of crime and punishment have blossomed in their diversity. Not only has the study of crime and punishment broadened throughout the behavioral and social sciences, but also criminologists have increasingly adopted perspectives that are no longer grounded in classical versus positivist views of human nature and social interaction. In the world of post-structuralism, post-Marxism, post-affirmative action, and post-feminism, criminologists from a variety of schools of thought, including the critical, constitutive, positivist, and integrative, have come to appreciate the numerous limitations of simple or "non-integrative" theories. In short, the traditional, one-dimensional models of crime that have tended to divide human beings and society into biological, cultural, psychological, or sociological entities are partially correct at best. At worst, these analyses ignore more factors than they consider.

In response to the limited range and application of most non-integrative theories, more criminologists, theorists and non-theorists alike, are embracing integrative and interdisciplinary frameworks for examining their field. Integrative theories, like theories in general, have become diversified in kind and approach. What makes these theories especially appealing is the diversity of models, which allows for a creative plurality of knowledge-based frameworks. Some integrative theories focus on criminal behavior and criminal activity; others focus on punishment and crime control; still others focus on crime, justice, and social control. Some are formalistic and consist of propositional statements derived from two or more theories, usually within the same discipline. Others are less formalistic and focus on conceptualizing the reciprocal or interactive relations between various levels of human motivation, social organization, and structural relationships. Integrative theories cover a wide range of interdisciplinary knowledge and methods of interpretation.

WAYS OF SEEING INTEGRATION

Most criminologists agree that integration involves synthesizing the relations and fragments of other models and theories into formulations that are more comprehensive than the traditional explanations of crime and crime control. Actual approaches to integration, however, vary significantly in both theory and practice. As a consequence, the development of inte-

grative theories and practices has, thus far, "proceeded in a somewhat anomic fashion with no [one] viable framework for synthetic work" having emerged (Tittle 1995: 115). Nevertheless, much of the impetus for integration, at least early on, was grounded in the disciplines of psychology, sociology, and occasionally social psychology.

The criminological literature on theoretical integration reveals a strong reliance on learning and control theories and a weaker reliance on strain theory, followed closely by subcultural, conflict, and Marxist theories. These sociological biases have traditionally marginalized theories deriving from studies of biology, evolution, history, gender, communication, economics, and law. In contrast to the more sociologically and psychologically based positivist and modern stances toward integration are the eclectically based constructivist and postmodern stances.

Both modernist and postmodernist approaches can be broken down further into a variety of explanations of crime and punishment. Moreover, integrative theories may be specific or general. Whereas the specific integrated theories have focused on a single form of criminality, such as rape or battering, the general integrated theories have attempted to make sense out of a broad range of harmful activities, including interpersonal, organizational, and structural forms. Some theorists have confined themselves to criminality, while others have focused more broadly on deviance and nonconformity. Finally, modernist forms of integration emphasize the centrality of theory both in scientific endeavors and in the construction of causal models for predicting transgression. Postmodernist forms of integration emphasize the ever-changing voices of plurality that provide meaning for the local sites of crime, justice, law, and community. These integrations are derived from harmful personal and social relationships (Barak 1998; Henry and Milovanovic 1996).

INTEGRATING BODIES OF THEORY

Approaches to integration have engaged in three basic types of positivist integration: structural, conceptual, and assimilative. Structural integration links existing theories, or at least their main components, in some kind of sequence, either by conceiving of the causal variables in some theories as outcome variables in other theories or by theorizing that under certain conditions, the causal processes of one theory interlock with those of other theories. The structural integrations can be either "end-to-end" or "side-by-side." End-to-end conceptualizations, such as those of mainline delinquency integration, tend to give no preference to the various components involved and assume a linear effect. Different theorists might therefore order the elements in different sequences. By contrast, side-by-side integrations provide a firmer basis for the sequencing of theoretical ingredients, in that later outcomes are conditional on earlier outcomes.

Conceptual and assimilative integrations assume one of two kinds of abstract causal processes. Conceptual types of "up-and-down" integration blend related theories, or they bring together preexisting theories that say the same types of things at different levels of analysis. By contrast, the assimilative type of "kitchen sink" integrations employ abstract causal processes that do not consume other theories one way or the other. Rather, they allow different theories to be united into larger conceptual frameworks without respect to the interactive relationships and conditional effects that these theories may have on each other. Modernist constructions of integrative theories may also be divided into three explanations of crime and punishment. They are social process micro models—those that emphasize kinds of people; social structure macro models—those that focus on kinds of organization; and micro-macro models—those that consider kinds of culture.

In *Crime and Human Nature,* Wilson and Herrnstein (1985: 195) provided a specific, social process micro theory of interpersonal, "aggressive, violent, or larcenous behavior" that focuses exclusively on predatory street behavior while ignoring white-collar, corporate, and governmental misbehavior. Their theory is an eclectic, social learning-behavioral choice formulation that relies on both positivist determinism and classical free will, claiming linkages between criminality and hereditary factors, impulsivity, low intelligence, family practices, school experiences, and the effects of mass media on the individual. Krohn (1986) bridged theoretical propositions from the delinquency-enhancing effects of differential association and the delinquency-constraining effects of social bonds, as these interact with social learning and social control. His network theory maintains that the lower the network density in relationship to population density, the weaker the constraints against nonconformity, and the higher the rates of delinquency.

In *Class, State and Crime*, Quinney (1977) provided a general and integrative theory expressed through the contradictions and development of capitalism. His political economy of crime and crime control articulates a class-structural analysis with two interconnected sets of criminality: the crimes of domination and repression, which are committed by capitalists and agents of control, and the crimes of accommodation and resistance, which are committed by workers and ordinary people. This social structure macro model argues that both the differential opportunities and the accompanying motivations for crime are class specific. Stark (1987) introduced an integrated set of thirty propositions as an approximation of a theory of deviant places. His ecological theory, or "kinds-of-place" explanation, analyzed the traits of places and groups rather than the traits of individuals. It contends that the deviant behavior of the poor varies in relation to the population density, poverty, mixed land use, transience, and dilapidation of where they live.

In *Power, Crime, and Mystification*, Box (1983) provided a conceptual integration of how corporate crime overcomes environmental uncertainties by illegally reducing or eliminating competition through fraud, bribery, manipulation, price-fixing, and so on. Box identified anomie and strain as the motivational sources behind corporate crime. He argues that "motivational strain" is translated into illegal acts through differential associations and corporate subcultures where elites learn to rationalize and neutralize their infractions with social and moral contracts. Pearson and Weiner's (1985) model of integration identifies concepts that are common to particular theories and structures them within a general framework. Their model searches for common vocabulary in which terms from one theoretical formulation have analogs in others. The central organizing concept of their model employs a social learning theory of crime and incorporates micro-social factors, macro-social structural factors, and behavioral consequences or feedback factors.

Two recent integrative theories that can also be described as providing micro-social process and macro-social structural analyses are Tittle's *Control Balance* (1995) and Colvin's *Crime and Coercion* (2000). Tittle's "synthetic approach" is a carefully articulated blending of structural, conceptual, and assimilative methods of integration. His control balance theory contends that the "amount of control to which people are subject relative to the amount of control they can exercise affects their general probability of committing some deviant acts as well as the probability that they will commit specific types of deviance" (Tittle 1995:

142). It also argues that people's control ratios, or the control balancing process is subject to a host of internal and external contingencies that can vary over time.

Colvin's (2000) differential coercion theory combines elements from Robert Agnew's general strain theory, Michael R. Gottfredson and Travis Hirschi's self-control theory, Ron Akers's social learning theory, Francis T. Cullen's social support theory, and Tittle's control balance theory. This theory is relevant to both the production and the reduction of crime and punishment, as it focuses on four dimensions of control that have had profoundly different effects on criminal and non-criminal outcomes, whether applied to chronic street criminals, exploratory offenders, or white-collar rule breakers. His integration at both the interpersonal and macro-social levels reveals how "differential levels of coercion and consistency appear in micro processes of social control and at the macro level involving larger economic and cultural forces in society" (Colvin 2000: 141). Colvin's theoretically driven responses to crime reduction and his policies toward a "non-coercive society" are aimed at preventing and altering the erratic coercive dynamics of criminality, especially in its more chronic or habitual forms.

INTEGRATING BODIES OF KNOWLEDGE

Postmodern integrationists are concerned less about theories per se than they are about knowledge. Rather than pursuing the cause-and-effect predictions of theoretical integration within several disciplines, these criminologists are creating explanatory models of crime and crime control that make connections across the entire range of interdisciplinary knowledge (Barak, 1998). Vila's (1994) evolutionary ecological theory, presented in "A General Paradigm for Understanding Criminal Behavior," incorporates a multiplicity of disciplinary causal factors and bases of knowledge. At one level of analysis, Vila integrates theories derived primarily from the disciplines of social psychology, such as strain, control, labeling, and learning. At another level, he examines the changes that are derived in the resource-acquisition and resource-retention behaviors of social actors, from the prenatal period through early adulthood. This model of synthesis not only "has its roots in the 'interdiscipline' of evolutionary ecology, but uses a problem-oriented, rather than a discipline-oriented approach to understanding criminal behavior" (Vila 1994: 315).

Whereas modernist integrations focus on linear and multiple causality, postmodernist integrations focus on interactive or reciprocal causality and on dialectical or codetermination causality. The latter forms of causality not only raise questions about whether modernist theorists have correctly ordered their causal variables, but, more fundamentally, also question whether there is a correct ordering of causal variables in the first place. Certain things may happen simultaneously, while other things may not, and these things or relations may not be constant over time. Some of the synthetic models of integrated knowledge can be classified as transdisciplinary integrations that strive to combine principles, facts, and values from both modern empiricism and postmodern reconstructionism. In these models, "cause" may refer to the influences and variations that are possible in the context of the multiple interrelations of discourse, ideology, imagination, unconsciousness, history, and political economy, all of which are never fully separated from each other (Henry and Milovanovic 1996). These models represent a hybrid of the methods of both modernism and postmodernism, or a third way of seeing integration.

A developing means of integrating knowledge across modernist and postmodernist divides is through the use of texts and narratives. As sociologist Richard Harvey Brown has maintained, "the conflict that exists in our culture between the vocabularies of scientific discourse and of narrative discourse, between positivism and romanticism, objectivism and subjectivism, and between system and lifeworld can be synthesized through a poetics of truth that views social science and society as texts" (1989: 1). According to this view, language is a reflection neither of the world nor of the mind. It is, instead, a social historical practice in which the meanings of words are not taken from things or intentions but arise from the socially coordinated actions of people.

For example, the source for the life course criminology of Sampson and Laub in *Crime in the Making* and their developmental or "stepping-stone" approach to delinquency is the narrative data of life histories and the social construction of crime. Sampson and Laub's explanation of crime emphasizes "the role of informal social controls that emerge from the role of reciprocities and structure of interpersonal bonds linking members of society to one another and to wider social institutions such as work, family, and school" (1993: 18).

Our strategy also included a new way of portraying life histories of individuals in context. Namely, our quantitative findings were systemically challenged through an intensive examination of qualitative data drawn from the Gluecks' original case files. Integrating divergent sources of information on life histories, the qualitative analysis supported the central idea of our theoretical model that there are both stability and change in behavior over the life course, and that these changes are systematically linked to the institutions of work and family relations in adulthood. (Sampson and Laub 1993, 248)

Arrigo has argued that the key to postmodernist integration is in the production of "nontotalizing" analyses and "nonglobalizing" assessments. His form of integration does not "presume to understand the conditions or the causes of criminal or legal controversies by offering either a homeostatically based integrative model or a rigidly specialized theory" (1995: 465). Rather, postmodernist integrations like Arrigo's prefer to think of synthesis as referring to the "relational, positional, and provisional function to interpret, reinterpret, validate, and repudiate *multiple discourses* and their expressions of reality construction in divergent social arrangements" (Arrigo 1995: 465). Accordingly, he is able to synthesize a conceptually rich narrative that incorporates psychoanalysis, semiotics, poststructuralism, deconstructionism, human agency, role formation, social change, and more.

Messerschmidt, in *Crime as Structured Action* (1997), engages in a grounded social constructionism that evolves not only through discourses but also through the ways in which people actively construct their own identities in relationship to crime and particular social contexts as these are differentiated through time and situation as well as through class, race, and gender. These types of integrative analyses that go beyond postmodernism argue that crimes are recursive productions, routinized activities that are part and parcel of historically and culturally specific discourses and structures that have attained a relative stability over time and place. Materialistically rooted, these discourses of structured inequality, for example, "become coordinates of social action whereby 'criminals' are no less than 'excessive investors' in the accumulation and expression of power and control" (Henry and Milovanovic 1996: x).

Barak and Henry (1999), in "An Integrative-Constitutive Theory of Crime, Law, and Social Justice," examine the co-production of crime and consumption. Their theory "links the study of culture with the study of crime. It is a theory that maintains the diversity of vocabularies through which different people experience violence and different criminal justice organizations exercise their power. It is a theory that integrates each of these points of view into a more complete, more robust regard for law, crime, and deviance" (Barak and Henry 1999: 151). In the end, this kind of synthesis attempts to bring the intersections of class, race, and gender together with the dynamics of social identity formation and mass communications.

SUMMARY

Integrating criminological perspectives is not a particularly new endeavor. It dates at least as far back as Merton (1938), Sutherland (1947), and Cohen (1955). However, it was not until the 1970s and 1980s that integrative models began to challenge the one-dimensional theories of crime and punishment. Throughout this developing period of integration, many criminologists remained skeptical about the merits and potentials of integrative models. Some turned to the "vertical" elaboration of older one-dimensional theories; others abandoned theory altogether in preference for the "horizontal" bits and pieces of knowledge that come from multiple disciplines that study crime and punishment. Nevertheless, by the turn of the twenty-first century, the integrative paradigm had become the newly emerging paradigm in criminology and penology. As for the future, this integrative paradigm looks strong and holds out the promise that the study of crime and punishment will soon become the truly interdisciplinary enterprise that most criminologists have always claimed it to be.

—Gregg Barak

See also ATTACHMENT THEORY; CONTROL THEORIES; CRITICAL CRIMINOLOGY; CULTURE CONFLICT AND CRIME; ECONOMIC THEORIES OF CRIME; FEMINIST THEORY; RADICAL CRIMINOLOGY; SOCIAL CONTROL THEORY; SOCIAL LEARNING THEORIES; SOCIAL PSYCHOLOGY; SOCIOLOGICAL THEORIES; STRAIN THEORY

Further Reading

Akers, Ronald L. (1985). *Deviant Behavior: A Social Learning Approach*. 3d ed. Belmont, CA: Wadsworth.

Arrigo, Bruce. A. (1995). "The Peripheral Core of Law and Criminology: On Postmodern Social Theory and Conceptual Integration." *Justice Quarterly* 12, 30: 447–472.

Barak, Gregg. (1998). *Integrating Criminologies*. Boston: Allyn and Bacon.

Barak, Gregg, Jeanne Flavin, and Paul Leighton. (2001). *Class, Race, Gender, and Crime: Social Realities of Justice in America*. Los Angeles: Roxbury.

Barak, Gregg, and Stuart Henry. (1999). "An Integrative-Constitutive Theory of Crime, Law, and Social Justice." In *Social Jus-*

tice/Criminal Justice: The Maturation of Critical Theory in Law, Crime, and Deviance edited by Bruce Arrigo. Belmont, CA: West/Wadsworth, 152–175.

Box, Steven. (1983). *Power, Crime, and Mystification*. London: Tavistock.

Braithwaite, John. (1989). *Crime, Shame, and Reintegration*. Cambridge, UK: Cambridge University Press.

Brown, Richard Harvey. (1989). "Textuality, Social Science, and Society." *Issues in Integrative Studies* 7: 1–19.

Cloward, Richard A., and Lloyd E. Ohlin. (1960). *Delinquency and Opportunity: A Theory of Delinquent Gangs*. New York: Free Press.

Cohen, Albert K. (1955). *Delinquent Boys: The Culture of the Gang*. Glencoe, IL: Free Press.

Colvin, Mark. (2000). *Crime and Coercion: An Integrated Theory of Chronic Criminality*. New York: St. Martin's Press.

Colvin, Mark, and John Pauly. (1983). "A Critique of Criminology: Toward an Integrated Structural-Marxist Theory of Delinquency Production." *American Journal of Sociology* 89: 513–551.

Glaser, Daniel. (1978). *Crime in Our Changing Society*. New York: Holt, Rinehart, and Winston.

Elliott, Delbert, Susan Ageton, and Rachelle Cantor. (1979). "An Integrated Theoretical Perspective on Delinquent Behavior." *Journal of Research in Crime and Delinquency* 16: 3–27.

Elliott, Delbert, David Huizinga, and Susan Ageton. (1985). *Explaining Delinquency and Drug Use*. Beverly Hills, CA: Sage.

Elliott, Delbert, David Huizinga, and Scott Menard. (1989). *Multiple Problem Youth*. New York: Springer Verlag.

Hagan, John. (1988). "Feminist Scholarship, Relational and Instrumental Control, and a Power-Control Theory of Gender and Delinquency." *British Journal of Sociology* 39, 3: 301–336.

Henry, Stuart, and Dragan Milovanovic. (1996). *Constitutive Criminology: Beyond Postmodernism*. London: Sage.

Johnson, Richard E. (1979). *Juvenile Delinquency and Its Origins*. Cambridge, UK: Cambridge University Press.

Kaplan, John B. (1975). *Self-Attitudes and Deviant Behavior*. Pacific Palisades, CA: Goodyear.

Krohn, Marvin D. (1986). "The Web of Conformity: A Network Approach to the Explanation of Delinquent Behavior." *Social Problems* 33: 81–93.

Merton, Robert K. (1938). "Social Structure and Anomie." *American Sociological Review* 3: 672–682.

Messerschmidt, James W. (1997). *Crime as Structured Action: Gender, Race, Class and Crime in the Making*. Thousand Oaks, CA: Sage.

Pearson, Frank S., and Neil A. Weiner. (1985). "Toward an Integration of Criminological Theories." *Journal of Criminal Law and Criminology* 76: 116–150.

Quinney, Richard. (1977). *Class, State and Crime*. New York: David McKay.

Sampson, Robert J., and John H. Laub. (1993). *Crime in the Making: Pathways and Turning Points Through Life*. Cambridge, MA: Harvard University Press.

Stark, Rodney. (1987). "Deviant Places: A Theory of the Ecology of Crime." *Criminology* 25: 893–909.

Sutherland, Edwin H. (1947). *Criminology*, 4th ed. Philadelphia, PA: Lippincott.

Tatum, Becky. (1996). "The Colonial Model as a Theoretical Explanation of Crime and Delinquency." In *African-American Perspectives on Crime Causation, Criminal Justice Administration and Crime Prevention,* edited by Anne T. Sulton. Boston: Butterworth-Heinemann, 35–52.

Tittle, Charles R. (1995). *Control Balance: Toward a General Theory of Deviance*. Boulder, CO: Westview Press.

Vila, Bryan. (1994). "A General Paradigm for Understanding Criminal Behavior: Extending Evolutionary Ecological Theory." *Criminology* 32: 311–360.

Wilson, James Q., and Richard J. Herrnstein. (1985). *Crime and Human Nature*. New York: Simon and Schuster.

▼ INTENSIVE PROBATION SUPERVISION

First becoming popular in the 1980s, intensive probation supervision (IPS)—also known as intensive supervision program (ISP)—is one of the most widely administered intermediate sanctions in the United States. Prior to that time, offenders were either incarcerated or given ordinary probation. This correctional dichotomy often resulted in sentencing that was too harsh or too lenient. Offenders whose crimes and criminality did not warrant prison were placed behind bars, while offenders whose crimes and criminality deserved stronger punishment were given probation. Compared to other criminal penalties, IPS is harsher and more restrictive than regular probation but less so than prison.

The first IPS programs were developed in the 1960s as experimental projects designed to determine the number of clients most optimally supervised in a single caseload. The first IPSs were actually smaller, experimental caseloads (15–35 offenders) that were compared to larger, standard-sized caseloads (75–150 offenders). The experiment examined whether a smaller caseload would allow for more intensive supervision of any one case and whether this enhanced supervision would increase the chances of successful outcomes. However, these early projects showed that client supervision levels did not differ greatly from those of larger caseloads, nor did close contact guarantee greater success (Clear and Hardyman 1990).

Current IPS programs were created in response to crowding in U.S. prisons and jails. As the correctional population grew, institutional crowding forced the courts to place more felons on probation or to give them early release from prison. IPS programs were designed to reduce prison crowding, to save money, and to protect public safety, while providing a punishment more punitive and intrusive than ordinary probation. As identified by Byrne, Lurigo, and Petersilia (1992), there are four primary goals of IPS and other intermediate sanctions:

1. to save taxpayers money by providing cost-effective alternatives to incarceration for prison- and jail-bound offenders;

2. to deter offenders (specifically) and the public (generally) from crime;

3. to protect the community by exerting more control (than does traditional probation) over offender behavior; and

4. to rehabilitate offenders by using mandatory treatment requirements, which are then reinforced by mandatory substance abuse testing and the swift revocation of violators' privileges.

CURRENT IPS MODELS

Although the general objectives of IPS are similar across programs, key features can vary considerably from one program to the next and may involve any combination of the following: curfew with house arrest (without electronic monitoring); curfew with house arrest (with electronic monitoring); special conditions established by the judge (such as employment, counseling); team supervision; drug and/or alcohol monitoring; community service; probation fees; split sentences or shock incarceration; community sponsors; restitution; and objective risk and need assessment (Byrne 1990).

In general, three types of IPS programs have been identified; they are differentiated based on selection processes. The first type represents efforts to manage caseloads of felony offenders already sentenced to regular probation. Probationers are assigned to IPS on the basis of scores on a risk scale that is used to predict potential for future crime. Created and controlled by probation managers, these programs serve neither as alternatives to prison nor as a direct means to reduce prison crowding or save public monies.

The other two types of IPS projects have been described as "front-end" and "back-end" programs. Front-end programs divert prison-bound offenders from incarceration. These cases are reviewed for eligibility after sentencing but prior to imprisonment. Based on program criteria, officers may ask judges to rescind prison orders and sentence an offender to IPS as an alternative. They prevent offenders from entering the prison's front door. Back-end programs offer early release from prison to IPS, thereby acting as an early-release mechanism for persons already in jail. The goal of these programs is to relieve institutional crowding and conserve scarce prison resources. After serving a minimum time of incarceration, offenders can leave prison before their anticipated dates of release if they are deemed eligible according to program criteria. (See Byrne 1986 for a review of additional theoretical and conceptual distinctions between programs.)

IPS programs also differ in the way in which they define intensive supervision. Types of contact can vary from face-to-face visits with probation officers and curfew checks, to periodic imprisonment, to collateral visits with employers and family members. The programs differ not only in type of contact but also in frequency of contact. The average number of contacts with intensive supervision is about four per month, compared to about one per month under standard probation. In the beginning of supervision, the frequency of contacts may be as much as once or twice daily. Although many IPS programs are conducted by specially selected and trained officers, there are also programs run by traditional probation officers. Some officers are given a great deal of discretion in planning and conducting supervision, while other officers' decisions are tightly controlled by elaborate program requirements. Caseload sizes can vary from twelve to forty cases or more per officer.

The other main difference between programs is in the decision of who will be placed on intensive probation supervision. On the whole, IPS programs accept a broad range of clients, including violent and nonviolent offenders, high- and low-risk offenders, probation and parole violators, and drug offenders. While many IPS programs justify the use of intensive methods by targeting "serious," "dangerous," or "high-risk" offenders, most programs establish certain bases for exclusion that result in IPS clients who are not a considerably higher risk than the regular probationer in the same jurisdiction (Clear and Hardyman 1990). For example, offenders with a violent current offense (and sometimes those with any prior history of violence) are often excluded. Other common exclusionary criteria include a long criminal record or an otherwise unusual risk to the community. Overall, offenders sentenced to prison in back-door IPS programs have committed more serious offenses and have lengthier criminal histories than those sentenced directly to IPS in front-end programs or those drawn from existing probation case-

Testimonials From Intensive Supervision Program Graduates in New Jersey

"I love the ISP Program because it has been a chance for me to see myself for what I am. It has given me the chance to restrict myself, to discipline myself, to say no to myself. For that reason, I think the program will succeed."

"If it wasn't for this program, I know my life would have continued the way it was before, useless."

"ISP has helped me to regain my self-respect, my dignity, and my love for myself. With the help of my ISP Officer, I have a new life. I am a responsible person, out in the free world."

"ISP is not for everyone; it is only for those of you who want a chance to change and for those who could follow some basic rules."

Source: *New Jersey Intensive Supervision Program: Progress Report.* (1992). Administrative Office of the Courts, State of New Jersey.

---

loads in probation-enhancement programs (Lurigio and Petersilia 1992).

Another common programmatic difference is organizational context. Some programs are located within the judiciary branch; others are housed with the county executive; still others are run by the state executive. Some projects are small in scale, run almost like experiments, while others are large, seemingly long-term program initiatives. Finally, programs that appear to be similar may emphasize different aspects of practice, such as emphasizing surveillance rather than treatment or responding differently to offender noncompliance (Byrne 1990).

THE GEORGIA IPS MODEL

Beginning in 1982, the state of Georgia implemented an IPS that would come to be widely regarded as a success. As a result of media and professional interest, many states subsequently moved to create programs modeled after Georgia's IPS, in an effort to combat prison crowding. Just five years after the inception of Georgia's program, IPS was the most frequently implemented probationary program. Forty states had created similar programs, and half of them were modeled after the Georgia IPS program.

Georgia's IPS program was targeted toward serious but nonviolent offenders who would have gone to prison in the jurisdiction in which they were sentenced were it not for the IPS option. Early statistics suggest that the offenders who were sentenced to IPS were pre-dominantly white men who had been convicted of property (43 percent) or drug- and alcohol-related (41 percent) offenses (Petersilia 1987).

Probation caseloads in the Georgia model are restricted to twenty-five offenders, managed by a supervision team consisting of a surveillance officer and a probation officer. The surveillance officer monitors the offender closely, ensuring compliance with IPS conditions, while the probation officer provides counseling and access to social services based on the client's particular needs. The surveillance officer usually visits the client in the home, while the probation officer ultimately has legal authority over the case, enforcing IPS conditions by revoking probation if necessary. During the first weeks of supervision, the offender is seen up to twice daily, and then five times a week by either member of the team. Probationers will usually spend six to twelve months under this level of supervision, followed by a year on basic probation. Offenders are required to perform 132 hours of community service and to be employed full-time in an educational/vocational program. Probationers are also required to pay a probation supervision fee of up to $50 per month, in addition to fines and restitution previously ordered by the court. Restrictions such as curfews and frequent, random drug or alcohol testing may also be imposed.

Evaluation of Georgia's IPS programs suggests that it is a cost-effective, low-risk alternative to prison. Recidivism rates were lower in IPS than in either regular probation or incarcerated comparison groups; most revocations were for minor rule infractions, with almost no new violent crime; and the majority of new crimes were property offenses. Given these results, Georgia's IPS is commonly credited with an 80 to 90 percent success rate (Petersilia 1987). However, these results cannot be generalized to all IPS programs, nor should they be used to suggest that similar programs would work as well in other locations. In addition, much of the outcome research has been suspect. Several critical issues concerning the effectiveness of any IPS program need to be considered.

EFFECTIVENESS OF IPS PROGRAMS

Initial claims of diversion and cost-effectiveness espoused by IPS program developers and evaluators have recently been critiqued by a number of experts. Some argue that the offenders who are placed in these programs would not otherwise be prison-bound and neither deserve the punishment nor need the control these programs provide. Even considering offenders appropriately placed in IPS, the consensus among experts is that IPS programs do not significantly reduce prison crowding, nor do they save money. Depending on the proportion of clients in an IPS who that are truly diverted from prison and the proportion imprisoned after revocation, it is possible that some front-door IPS programs actually increase prison populations. It is not necessarily the case that IPS clients would have otherwise gone to prison. Secondly, the intensity of these programs results in high revocation rates. Closer scrutiny and heightened surveillance uncover otherwise unobserved violations of probation conditions and new crimes, which, in turn, send more people to prison. It is estimated that 40 to 50 percent of IPS offenders will be returned to prison (Tonry 1990).

Similarly, the claims of recidivism reduction are not supported by either a critical review of evaluation results or the initial findings of a randomized field experiment (Petersilia and Turner 1990). For one thing, the notion that released prisoners will not recidivate is unfounded. "Diverting offenders from prison or releasing them earlier results in crimes and victims in the community that would not exist if those offenders had not been diverted or released" (Tonry 1990: 183). Furthermore, most reliable research studies fail to show any consistent crime reduction effects. Partly because programs place too much emphasis on surveillance and not enough emphasis on treatment, the goal of rehabilitation is often unmet as well. Although many probationers are identified as needing drug treatment, for example, very few actually receive such treatment. Not surprisingly, a significant percent of new arrests involve drugs.

The problem of high recidivism is compounded by aggressive control mechanisms and programmatic emphasis on being tough on crime and misconduct. When a person fails under the terms of intensive probation, for example, there is a tendency to respond with an even harsher term than was originally intended. An offender who fails is thus likely to receive a far more severe sentence than the original one from which he or she was diverted (Clear, Flynn, and Shapiro 1987).

FUTURE GOALS

Despite IPS's failure to achieve its stated goals of diversion from prison, cost savings, and crime prevention, there remain several positive results of these programs. The rebirth of probation in particular, and community supervision programs in general, can be credited to the IPS movement. A number of latent organizational, professional, and political goals have also been identified. First, because it is more punitive than traditional probation, IPS provides probation administrators and legislators with an effective response to the more punitive orientation of the public. Whereas standard probation was viewed as a token punishment, IPS programs increase the credibility of probation by enabling probation administration to be "tough on crime." Second, the increased institutional and political credibility of probation has allowed probation and parole to reclaim limited correctional resources, resulting in more staff, more money, new programs, and increased responsibility. Third, by attracting new popularity and new resources, IPS programs serve professional and psychological aims by enhancing both the esteem accorded probation and the professional and personal self-esteem of probation officers (Tonry 1990).

Future programs should recognize the limits of formal control strategies and be more creative in developing techniques to strengthen informal restraints (Byrne 1990). Rather than increasing surveillance and control, probation officers should return to traditional interventions that utilize diagnostic skills, brokerage skills, and advocacy skills. Changing offenders' behavior will not be successful without addressing their (usually long-standing) problems in the broader context of lifestyles and communities. Byrne suggests a four-part strategy for reintegrating the concept of community into community-based corrections. First, community resources that assist offenders with problems in the areas of substance abuse, employment/education, and marital/family problems must be coordinated and developed. Second, support must be generated for the deescalation of both community-based and institution-based sanctions. Third, in addition to those of the offender, the problems and needs of communities must be addressed. Fourth, probation officer teams must be placed directly in neighborhoods, charged with the responsibility of resource development (as well as offender control) within a specific geographic area.

SUMMARY

Although intensive probation programs appear to have good "face validity," in that they look good on the surface, research shows that they have not been effective in reducing correctional costs or preventing crime. IPS does hold the potential to provide the impetus for the creation of other novel approaches. For this reason and because of the latent benefits of IPS, there is still promise for IPS and other similar programs in the future.

—Laura Richardson

Further Reading

Byrne, James M. (1986). "The Control Controversy: A Preliminary Examination of Intensive Probation Supervision Programs in the United States." *Federal Probation* 50, 2: 4–16.

———. (1990). "The Future of Intensive Probation Supervision and the New Intermediate Sanctions." In *Intensive Probation Supervision: An Alternative to Prison in the 1980s*, edited by Arthur J. Lurigio; a special issue of *Crime & Delinquency* 36, 1, 6–41.

Byrne, James M., Arthur J. Lurigio, and Joan Petersilia, eds. (1992). *Smart Sentencing: The Emergence of Intermediate Sanctions.* Newbury Park, CA: Sage.

Clear, Todd R., Suzanne Flynn, and Carol Shapiro. (1987). "Intensive Supervision in Probation: A Comparison of Three Projects." In *Intermediate Punishments: Intensive Supervision, Home Confinement, and Electronic Surveillance*, edited by Belinda R. McCarthy. Monsey, NY: Criminal Justice Press, 31–51.

Clear, Todd R., and Hardyman, P. L. (1990). *Intensive Probation Supervision: An Alternative to Prison in the 1980s*, edited by Arthur J. Lurigio; a special issue of *Crime & Delinquency* 36, 1, 42–60.

Lurigio, Arthur J., and Joan Petersilia. (1992). "The Emergence of Intensive Probation Supervision Programs in the United States." In *Smart Sentencing: The Emergence of Intermediate Sanctions*, edited by James M. Byrne, Arthur J. Lurigio, and Joan Petersilia. Newbury Park, CA: Sage, 3–17

Petersilia, Joan. (1987). "Georgia's Intensive Probation: Will the Model Work Elsewhere?" In *Intermediate Punishments: Intensive Supervision, Home Confinement, and Electronic Surveillance*, edited by Belinda R. McCarthy. Monsey, NY: Criminal Justice Press, 15–30.

Petersilia, Joan, and Susan Turner. (1990). "Comparing Intensive and Regular Supervision for High-Risk Probationers: Early Results From an Experiment in California." In *Intensive Probation Supervision: An Alternative to Prison in the 1980s*, edited by Arthur J. Lurigio; a special issue of *Crime & Delinquency* 36, 1: 87–111.

Tonry, Michael. (1990). "Stated and Latent Features of ISP." In *Intensive Probation Supervision: An Alternative to Prison in the 1980s*, edited by Arthur J. Lurigio; a special issue of *Crime & Delinquency* 36, 1: 174–191.

◤ INTERMEDIATE SANCTIONS

Intermediate sanctions, also known as intermediate punishments (IPs), are those sanctions that exist along a continuum of criminal penalties somewhere between incarceration and probation. As an offender proceeds along the continuum, he or she is subjected to increased custody, control, and surveillance. Standard probation supervision is often ineffective, because the sanction is void of punishment and offender accountability. Indeed, for some offenders, regular supervision seems an inappropriate sanction. Surveillance-oriented community corrections programs grew in the last two decades of the twentieth century, responding both to crowded institutions and to the perceived need for increased control over offenders who are supervised in the community.

DIFFERENT TYPES OF IPs

Some of the more common types of IPs are the following:

1. *Day Fines.* Fines based on an offender's daily earnings. Offense categories are broken down into punishment units, and the value of each unit is then set at a percentage of the offender's daily income. Day fines are unlike regular fines, which are based on the offense and not on the offender's ability to pay.

2. *Restitution.* A cash payment by the offender to the victim to offset the loss incurred by the victim (insurance deductibles, medical expenses, etc.).

3. *Community Service.* Court-ordered nonpaid work for a specified number of hours that offenders must perform, usually for some charitable or public service organization. Unlike restitution, this sanction is concerned with paying back the community, not the victim per se.

4. *Day Reporting Centers.* Community centers to which offenders report in lieu of incarceration or as a condition of probation. A variety of community and in-house programs are usually offered, such as job readiness training and drug abuse education.

5. *Intensive Probation Supervision.* A court-ordered program of community supervision by probation officers working with very small caseloads to provide intensive supervision. This sanction is usually viewed as an alternative to incarceration.

6. *House Arrest.* A special condition of probation that requires an offender to remain within the confines of his or her home except for work, shopping, community service, and other court-sanctioned activities.

7. *Electronic Monitoring.* A telecommunications device designed to verify that an offender is at a specified location during specified times. This sanction is ordinarily combined with house arrest.

8. *Community Residential Centers* (formerly known as halfway houses). These are nonconfining residential facilities and are often intended for offenders who are failing on probation (front-door sanction) or who need a period of readjustment after being released from incarceration (a back-door sanction).

9. *Split Sentences.* A brief (perhaps six-month) period of jail incarceration followed by a term of probation. Variations include shock probation and intermittent incarceration.

10. *Boot Camps.* A physically rigorous, disciplined, and demanding regimen emphasizing conditioning, education and treatment, and job training. Typically designed for young, nonviolent felony offenders. Stays are usually short (90–120 days).

THE NEED FOR INTERMEDIATE PUNISHMENTS

Although some enhancement IPs have been around for some time (e.g., restitution and community service), many IPs—such as intensive supervision, electronic monitoring, and boot camps—began in earnest in the mid-1980s and grew substantially in the following decades. Their genesis and growth can be attributed to the following factors:

1. *Overcrowding crisis.* During the mid-1980s, correctional populations were soaring, forcing policy makers to search for alternative ways to sanction and control criminal offenders. Also, the effectiveness of jail and prison in controlling crime started to be seriously questioned.

2. *Standard probation's ineffectiveness.* A landmark study by Petersilia and colleagues (1985) forced policymakers and the public to rethink probation eligibility criteria and public safety, finding public safety risks in placing on routine probation felons who were ineffectively supervised. Two-thirds of the nearly 2,000 probationers tracked during this study were rearrested within three years, and more than half were reconvicted of serious offenses.

3. *Cost-savings potential.* Comparatively, jail and prison are very expensive sanctions, usually around $50 per day or $20,000 per year (a conservative estimate). Even the most expensive kind of community supervision—house arrest with electronic monitoring, using satellite technology—is around $15 to $20 per day, and, in many jurisdictions, offenders pay this fee themselves.

4. *Versatility.* IPs add more versatility to the sentencing and revocation process. Every offender is unique; for some, prison is too harsh; for others, probation is too

lenient. Many judges like the idea of having a number of sanctions available to them so they can more appropriately tailor the sentence to the specific offender's needs. Similarly, more versatility and options are available in the revocation process. Instead of sending offenders to jail or prison for noncompliance with supervision rules, judges can use IPs to tighten or increase the conditions of probation to encourage compliance with supervision. With "tourniquet sentencing" of this sort, a judge may order that an offender on regular probation who is not doing well be placed on house arrest with electronic monitoring, to "turn up the heat," so to speak. Adding to their versatility is the fact that many IPs can be used at different points within the criminal justice system. For instance, some IPs (such as electronic monitoring and house arrest) can be used on a pretrial basis (before guilt or innocence has been determined) in lieu of incarceration. Many of these sanctions also can be used on recently convicted offenders as a condition of probation, to help supervise offenders who require more control and/or surveillance than ordinary probation would provide. Finally, some IPs can be used as a condition of parole to require offenders who are being released from jail or prison to serve the remainder of their sentences within the community. IPs can and have been used on juveniles and adults alike.

5. *Meeting the public's need for punishment.* Many believe that, if nothing else, many of these relatively new sanctions are punitive or punishment oriented. The 1980s ushered in a new era of conservatism in which offenders were given increased doses of punishment, and rehabilitation and treatment were downplayed. This period witnessed the reinstatement of dormant death penalties, the advent and spread of "three-strikes" legislation, the abolition of parole in some states, the reinstitution of chain gangs, and the dispensing of military drill and discipline (through boot camps) to criminal offenders. There was nothing new about the use of many of these sanctions; for instance, even boot camp prisons had their beginnings in the late 1800s, when Zebulon Brockway was running the Elmira Reformatory in New York. These sanctions were simply brought back or modified somewhat to fit contemporary needs. Many researchers believe that these new sanctions had at least to appear punitive in order to be sold to the public and ultimately to the politicians and policy makers. Without a punitive component, it would have been difficult to promote sanctions that were giving many offenders an

opportunity to live in the community rather than in jail or prison.

When educated about different sanctions, what they realistically involve, and what their costs and effectiveness are, the public generally supports the use of IPs for appropriate offenders and believes them to be sufficiently punitive for many types of offenses and offenders. Also, according to many studies, the public has *not* given up on treatment and rehabilitation for the majority of criminal offenders, suggesting that the public may not be as punitive as criminal justice policy makers originally thought them to be. More important, what do offenders themselves think about IPs and where they fall on the punishment continuum? How punitive do offenders consider IPs to be? Spelman (1995) asked 128 convicted offenders to rate the severity of twenty-six felony punishments, ranging from six months' regular or standard probation to five years in prison. Seventy-five percent of offenders rated one or more IPs as more severe than an incarcerative sanction.

Spelman found that the average offender rated several punishments as about equally severe as a one-year jail term: six months' boot camp, one year in a drug treatment facility, one year on electronic monitoring, and two years on intensive probation supervision. This suggests that offenders themselves perceive at least some IPs to be equally or more punitive than a traditional incarcerative sanction. Many offenders believed that probation was a "trap" and that short jail terms were not very difficult: "It's the amount of supervision that gets you down," one offender responded. "When you're an addict, it's just impossible. You feel as though you're under watch all the time. In prison, you may never talk to somebody until you're leaving. That's why I prefer the joint to probation" (Spelman 1995: 125). Another offender had this to say: "Probation has too many conditions. If you can't meet them, you end up in jail anyway. I'd rather just do the time and pay off my debt to society that way" (126). Research examining public perception of IPs and their severity has found similar results, supporting the contention that IPs are indeed punitive.

SELECTED IPs

Three of the more popular IPs that embody the goals and philosophies of the IP movement are discussed below in more detail.

Intensive Supervision

After its start in Georgia in 1983, intensive supervision flourished, and today it is the most widely used IP. All states, as well as the federal government, have some kind of intensive supervision program in place. This kind of probation supervision stresses improved surveillance and control of the offender, as supervision ratios are normally 20 to 1, enabling probation officers to watch their clients much more carefully. Normally, probation officers oversee a much larger caseload. Although the average caseload for officers was 27 in 1997 (Champion 1999: 384), many caseloads are much larger (anywhere from 50 to 900), depending on the size of the jurisdiction. Most of these programs also stress mandated activities for offenders, such as drug and alcohol counseling, employment and vocational training, urine testing, and so on. Although not always the case in reality, these programs are typically viewed as an alternative to incarceration, meaning that offenders would be in jail had the program not existed. Many studies have questioned the effectiveness of these programs as recidivism reducers; however, other goals may be realized, such as greater protection of the community because offenders are under increased surveillance. Similarly, many studies have found that the technical violation rate (for rules infractions such as failing a urine screen, not obeying a curfew, etc.) is higher for those on intensive supervision programs than for those on regular probation, with the result that offenders who receive intensive supervision are returned to jail at a higher rate than are those on regular probation supervision. This higher return rate may simply be the result of these offenders being watched more closely and/or having to abide by more rules (conditions) of their probation—not necessarily because these offenders violate their conditions at a higher rate than do those placed on regular probation.

House Arrest With Electronic Monitoring

Offenders placed under this sanction must abide by prearranged schedules of activities; they are allowed to leave for "authorized" purposes, such as employment, religious worship, treatment, physician visits, and so on, but they must do so only at certain times of the day (these opportunities for authorized departures are called "windows"). The electronic component of house arrest merely determines whether the offenders' comings and goings are authorized and reports this information to a central computer and, ultimately, to criminal justice personnel. Today, offenders are monitored by various forms of technology, some using telemetry, others using satellites. Whichever method or type of technology is used, the goal is the same—to keep track of offenders' whereabouts.

There is nothing new about the use of house arrest (or "home confinement" as some refer to it) as a form of punishment. Galileo (1564–1642) was placed under this sanction by church authorities for his belief that the earth revolved around the sun. Home detention was used in the United States in St. Louis as early as 1971, and, by 1977, home detention programs for youth were put into practice in a number of states. What is relatively new, however, is the advent of the electronic technology that now commonly accompanies the sanction. The development of electronic monitoring can be traced back to experiments conducted at Harvard University in 1964, experiments using a two-pound transceiver that was worn on the belt, a network of repeater stations throughout the Boston and Cambridge areas, and a central monitoring station. The system was used to monitor the location of mental patients, parolees, and volunteers.

Many have written about the potential rehabilitative effect of house arrest with electronic monitoring by way of keeping the family intact, allowing the offender to continue working, avoiding the negative effects of confinement, and perhaps forcing the offender to adopt a lifestyle and routine he or she may not have had before. Unfortunately, the research literature has yet to clearly demonstrate the rehabilitative efficacy of electronic monitoring. Like intensive supervision, house arrest with electronic monitoring is often used as an alternative to incarceration and has the potential to increase the number of offenders who return to jail/prison for rules violations.

Boot Camp Prisons: "Shock Incarceration"

Boot camps combine military basic training with rehabilitation. Although programs vary, the typical boot camp is targeted toward young, nonviolent offenders. More specifically, the boot camp experience involves military drill and discipline, physical exercise, hard physical labor, specialized education and training, and substance abuse counseling and treatment (Latessa and Allen 1999). Shock incarceration programs first appeared in Georgia in 1983 and then in Oklahoma in 1984. The concept spread quickly; since 1983, fifty

boot camp prisons have opened in forty-one state correctional jurisdictions. Technically, shock incarceration is an institutional correctional program; however, it is considered by many to be an IP. Different states operate their programs differently, although all are targeted at young, nonviolent offenders. Some states allow the judge to sentence an offender directly to the sanction and then be placed on probation (e.g., Georgia), whereas others use this sanction for offenders who have already been sentenced to prison (e.g., New York). Participating offenders in the latter case agree to participate in order to shorten the length of their incarcerative stay. Many participants remain on active parole supervision after successfully completing the shock component of their sentence. Those not successful may be returned to the institution and placed in the general population, with the time spent in the shock incarceration component not counting as time served. This can provide tremendous incentive to finish once program participation is begun.

Recidivism reports on boot camp prisons have not been positive. Many states (such as New York) have found no significant recidivism reduction, but they have noticed substantial cost savings as a result of housing offenders for shorter periods of time; shock incarceration programs typically last only 90 to 120 days. Because these programs have been "sold" to the public as punitive, many are surprised to learn that, in addition to military drill and discipline, shock programs often incorporate mandated treatment components (such as drug and alcohol counseling and GED training). This militaristic and discipline-oriented punishment has gained wide support from the public and from state legislators. Shock incarceration programs are based on the premise that young offenders lack discipline and respect for authority. Whether this is a trait that can be transferred to an offender in a short period of time is the larger question.

CAUTIONS AND CONCERNS

Many researchers have argued that IPs are no more effective than jail or prison when it comes to rehabilitating offenders; in fact, some studies have found higher recidivism (failure) rates for those offenders participating in IP programs. When this is the case, issues of cost savings will usually reign supreme; IPs have the potential to save money, particularly if prison- or jail-bound offenders are selected for program participation. These sanctions cost substantially less than incarceration, but more than regular probation. Studies that find tremendously high recidivism rates (higher than 50 to 60 percent) suggest that if curbing offender recidivism is our *main* goal, then many IP programs have been failures. Success depends on the specific goals of the program in question and what the program is trying to achieve. Indeed, many of these programs seem to operate under multiple goals: stated goals (e.g., reductions in recidivism), latent goals (e.g., giving probation officers more law enforcement duties, thereby increasing their morale); and conflicting goals (e.g., punishment and rehabilitation).

There is the danger that new IP programs will emphasize surveillance over treatment. Almost a decade ago, Whitehead (1992: 167) expressed such a concern when he noted, "It is undeniable that many offenders in these programs have needs that are related to their criminal behavior. To focus only on punishment and incapacitation and to ignore such [treatment] needs is like keeping a persistent problem student after school and not dealing with that pupil's learning difficulties."

One of the more recent and consistent findings of IP evaluations is that programs combining surveillance with treatment are more effective than programs focusing on increased surveillance alone. Many researchers have found that more supervision without a substantive treatment component has very little effect on offenders' underlying criminal behavior, which, of course, manifests itself in criminal behavior and subsequently affects recidivism rates.

In addition, some evaluations have clearly found that IPs widen the net of social control. "Net widening" is said to occur when a treatment program brings more people under some form of social control than previously was the case. Sometimes, a new method (for instance, intensive probation supervison) brings increasing numbers of individuals into the corrections domain; offering a broader menu of correctional techniques also increases costs. The guidelines for many IP programs were initially developed to serve prison-bound offenders; however, many well-intentioned judges and prosecutors filled these programs with high-risk probationers. "The ISP [IP] experiment," according to Petersilia, "was definitely 'net widening,' but given the laxity of current supervision of serious felons on probation, it is more accurate to characterize it as 'net repairing'" (1998: 6).

Petersilia (1998: 3) finds that "in terms of sheer numbers and investments, the overall ISP experiment was more symbolic in its achievements than substantive." Although these sanctions have grown in popular-

ity and use, very few offenders, relatively speaking, participate in IP programs, the vast majority remaining on regular or standard probation. Indeed, "fewer than 6 percent of the 2.7 million adult probationers and parolees in the United States are estimated to be participating in [IP programs]" (Petersilia, 1998: 5). Perhaps even more important, very few dollars are spent on implementing and evaluating IP programs; community corrections in general has never fared well when funding allocations are set and money awarded. In addressing this point, Petersilia (1998: 5) writes that "as best as can be calculated, less than $10 million was invested by the federal government in ISP [IP] research and demonstration projects between 1985 and 1995. This can be compared to the $10 million the federal government invests in evaluations of community-oriented policing each year." Clearly, IPs have not flourished to the degree that some would have liked or had expected, perhaps due to inadequate funding of these programs.

In addition to these net-widening concerns, there is the very real possibility that offenders on an IP may not decrease their criminal behavior; many studies have questioned the deterrent effect of increased surveillance. In fact, overall justice system costs can *increase* because IP offenders are more likely to be returned for technical (rules) violations than are offenders undergoing regular probation supervision. Adding to this problem is the fact that many IP programs have "zero tolerance" policies that mandate a quick return to jail for violating program rules, such as failing a urine screen.

FUTURE TRENDS

Intermediate sanctions have become a vital component of contemporary community corrections, representing versatile sanctions that fill the vast void between prison and probation. Particularly when compared to standard probation, they can be punitive yet allow for offender rehabilitation and reintegration, largely by way of keeping an offender out of jail or prison and away from the potentially negative effects of incarceration. Combined with this versatility is the very real possibility of cost savings or "cost avoidance," providing net widening does not occur.

The past decade or so of experimenting with intermediate sanctions has shown that these punishments are not panaceas or cure-alls. They cannot solve all of the problems within community corrections; the community and other agencies must be involved if corrections, and particularly community corrections, is to be successful. Petersilia (1998: 9) sums this point up very well: "Crime is a complex, multifaceted problem that will not be overcome by simplistic, singularly focused solutions—whether they be boot camps, electronic monitoring, or intensive probation. Workable, long-term solutions must come from the community and be embraced and actively supported by the community."

Some called the 1990s the decade of the intermediate punishment and, indeed, much was learned about these sanctions during that decade. Given our steadily increasing incarceration rate, it is likely that intermediate punishments will continue to flourish in this decade, particularly if funding for both practice and evaluation of these sanctions is increased.

—*Kevin E. Courtright*

See also BOOT CAMPS; COMMUNITY SERVICE; DAY RELEASE; ELECTRONIC MONITORING; HOUSE ARREST; INTENSIVE PROBATION SUPERVISION; SPLIT SENTENCE

Further Reading

Byrne, James. (1990). "The Future of Intensive Probation Supervision and the New Intermediate Sanctions." *Crime & Delinquency* 36, 1: 6–41.

Byrne, James, Arthur Lurigio, and Christopher Baird. (1989). "The Effectiveness of the New Intensive Supervision Programs [Monograph]." *Research in Corrections* 2, 2.

Byrne, James, Arthur Lurigio, and Joan Petersilia, eds. (1992). *Smart Sentencing: The Emergence of Intermediate Sanctions.* Newbury Park, CA: Sage.

Camp, Camille, and George Camp. (1997). *The Corrections Yearbook 1997.* South Salem, NY: Criminal Justice Institute.

Champion, Dean. (1999). *Probation, Parole, and Community Corrections.* 3d ed. Upper Saddle River, NJ: Prentice Hall.

Clear, Todd, and James Byrne. (1992). "The Future of Intermediate Sanctions: Questions to Consider." In *Smart Sentencing: The Emergence of Intermediate Sanctions,* edited by James Byrne, Arthur Lurigio, and Joan Petersilia. Newbury Park, CA: Sage, 319–331.

Courtright, Kevin, Bruce Berg, and Robert Mutchnick. (2000). "Rehabilitation in the New Machine? Exploring Drug and Alcohol Use and Variables Related to Success Among DUI Offenders Under Electronic Monitoring—Some Preliminary Outcome Results." *International Journal of Offender Therapy and Comparative Criminology* 44, 3: 293–311.

Latessa, Edward, and Harry Allen. (1999). *Corrections in the Community.* 2d ed. Cincinnati, OH: Anderson Publishing Company.

Morris, Norval, and Michael Tonry. (1990). *Between Prison and Probation: Intermediate Punishments in a Rational Sentencing System.* New York: Oxford University Press.

Petersilia, Joan. (1998). "A Decade of Experimenting with Intermediate Sanctions: What Have We Learned?" *Federal Probation* 62, 2: 3–9.

Petersilia, Joan, Susan Turner, James Kahan, and Joyce Peterson. (1985). *Granting Felons Probation: Public Risks and Alternatives.* Santa Monica, CA: RAND.

Spelman, William. (1995). "The Severity of Intermediate Sanctions." *Journal of Research in Crime and Delinquency* 32, 2: 107–136.

St. Petersburg [FL] *Times.* (1997). "Orbiting Warden Watches Offenders." January 7, 1E and 2E.

Whitehead, John. (1992). "Control and the Use of Technology in Community Supervision." In *Corrections: Dilemmas and Directions,* edited by Peter Benekos and Alida Merlo. Cincinnati, OH: Anderson Publishing Company, 155–172.

▼ INTERNATIONAL CRIMINAL COURT

In 1998, more than 120 members of the United Nations approved the creation of an International Criminal Court (ICC), to be located in The Hague. Before the court could hear its first case, however, at least sixty nations had to ratify the enabling statute. Ratification in most countries has been a lengthy legislative process, and as of June 2001, only thirty-four countries had done so. Once convened, the court will have jurisdiction over four categories of crimes: genocide, crimes against humanity, serious war crimes, and aggression (after the member nations agree on a definition of aggression).

Although plans for laws and courts to govern wartime conduct had been on the international political agenda for centuries, it took the atrocities of World War II to galvanize the international community to action. As a result, the Nuremberg and Tokyo war crime tribunals were convened. Shortly after the war, in 1948, the United Nations adopted the Genocide Convention, making it an international crime to commit acts intended to destroy a national, ethnic, religious, or racial group. This was followed in 1949 by the Geneva Conventions, which codified the laws of war and created a legal obligation for the nations ratifying them to try people accused of "grave breaches" in their own countries.

During the Cold War years, international war crimes issues languished until incidents in the former Yugoslavia propelled the international community to action once again. In 1993, the U.N. Security Council established an ad hoc tribunal for the former Yugoslavia to try crimes committed from 1992 onward, and in 1994 a similar tribunal was established in Rwanda. However, the need still existed for a permanent court that was neither dependent on a Security Council vote for its existence nor limited in its scope. After considerable debate among U.N. committees, the Rome Treaty was signed. It focused on "the most serious crimes of concern to the international community

▼

The International Criminal Court Treaty

On December 31, 2000, President Bill Clinton issued this statement on the signature of the International Criminal Court Treaty by the United States, in Washington, DC.

The United States is today signing the 1998 Rome Treaty on the International Criminal Court. In taking this action, we join more than 130 other countries that have signed by the December 31, 2000 deadline established in the Treaty. We do so to reaffirm our strong support for international accountability and for bringing to justice perpetrators of genocide, war crimes, and crimes against humanity. We do so as well because we wish to remain engaged in making the ICC an instrument of impartial and effective justice in the years to come.

The United States has a long history of commitment to the principle of accountability, from our involvement in the Nuremberg tribunals that brought Nazi war criminals to justice, to our leadership in the effort to establish the International Criminal Tribunals for the Former Yugoslavia and Rwanda. Our action today sustains that tradition of moral leadership. . . .

In signing, however, we are not abandoning our concerns about significant flaws in the Treaty. In particular, we are concerned that when the Court comes into existence, it will not only exercise authority over personnel of states that have ratified the Treaty, but also claim jurisdiction over personnel of states that have not. With signature, however, we will be in a position to influence the evolution of the Court.. Without signature, we will not.

Signature will enhance our ability to further protect U.S. officials from unfounded charges and to achieve the human rights and accountability objectives of the ICC. In fact, in negotiations following the Rome Conference, we have worked effectively to develop procedures that limit the likelihood of politicized prosecutions. For example, U.S. civilian and military negotiators helped to ensure greater precision in the definitions of crimes within the Court's jurisdiction.

But more must be done. Court jurisdiction over U.S. personnel should come only with U.S. ratification of the Treaty. The United States should have the chance to observe and assess the functioning of the Court, over time, before choosing to become subject to its jurisdiction. Given these concerns, I will not, and do not recommend that my successor, submit the Treaty to the Senate for advice and consent until our fundamental concerns are satisfied.

Nonetheless, signature is the right action to take at this point. I believe that a properly constituted and structured International Criminal Court would make a profound contribution in deterring egregious human rights abuses worldwide, and that signature increases the chances for productive discussions with other governments to advance these goals in the months and years ahead.

Source: Office of the Ambassador-at-Large For War Crimes Issues, Department of State home page (http://usinfo.state.gov/topical/pol/usandum/00123101.htm).

---

as a whole": genocide, crimes against humanity, war crimes, and aggression.

The definition of *genocide* was taken from the 1948 Genocide Convention and protects national, ethnic, religious, and racial groups from a variety of crimes directed toward them as an entity. Crimes against humanity include widespread or systematic attacks against any civilian population that further a state or organizational policy. Because such crimes are limited to acts in furtherance of a state or organizational policy, the jurisdiction of the court will be restricted to only the most serious and systemic crimes.

The court will also have jurisdiction over serious crimes committed during armed conflict. Crimes committed during internal conflicts however, can be heard only when there is "protracted" armed conflict involving governmental and organized groups, or between organized groups. Since 1945, more than 80 percent of all armed conflict has been within rather than between nations. A fourth major category of crime, aggression,

was recognized; the United Nations has yet to define it, however, and the court will not have jurisdiction until it has done so.

—*Suzanne E. Carlton*

See also GENOCIDE; WAR CRIMES

Further Reading

Coalition for an International Criminal Court. http://www.iccnow.org

U.N. Web site for the Rome Statute. http://www.un.org/law/icc/index.html

▼ INTERNATIONAL IMPRISONMENTS

Increasing prison populations and particularly prison overcrowding are important concerns in all democratic countries. The undesirable effects of overcrowding are legion, including increases in correction costs, longer delays before imprisonment, and deterioration in living and working conditions for inmates and correction officers. Comparison of different countries' prison statistics is not an easy task. The prison population and changes in it result from complex processes that are affected by the frequency and seriousness of offenses, police efficiency, the strictness of the law, the way judges carry out the law, and by the modes of carrying out sentences (stay of sentence, amnesty, release on parole, mandatory minimum sentences, etc.). The main indicator used to measure the number of inmates is the prisoner rate (also called "detention rate" or even "incarceration rate"). It is obtained by relating the number of prisoners on a specific date or as an annual average to the number of inhabitants in a certain country or state. The prisoner rate is generally expressed by the number of inmates per 100,000 inhabitants; it varies from about 22 in Indonesia to 694 in Russia (see Table 1). In western Europe, the 2000 prisoner rates vary between 29 (Iceland) and 124 (England and Wales).

Whereas the prisoner rate is a "stock" statistic that relates to the size and the structure of prison populations and gives a picture of the number of people who are in prison at a given time, it is often confused with the incarceration rate, which is a "flow" statistic and relates to entries into prison. To understand the difference between them, one has to include the length of the detention into the equation. Indeed, stock statistics are a composition of the flow and the length. Only the prisoner rate is used here because it is the expression of the prison situation at a given moment and includes the length as well as the flow.

The following sections examine the rates from many countries. The choice of countries examined depended on the availability of the needed data and on their interest and ability to point to factors explaining the trends in prison populations. This overview will give us some indication of the reasons for the enormous differences between countries in this respect.

EUROPE

This section reviews data from large nations, such as Germany and Italy, as well as data from smaller countries, such as Portugal and Finland.

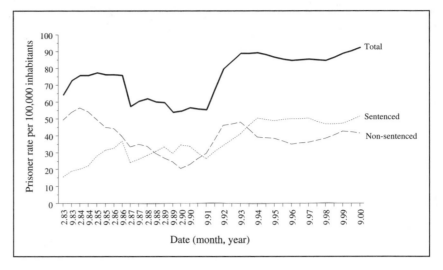

Figure 1. Prisoner Rate per 100,000 Inhabitants in Italy

Italy

In Italy, the overall prisoner rate dropped from 76.3 to 57.4 prisoners per 100,000 inhabitants between September 1, 1986, and February 1, 1987 (Figure 1), mainly because of a December 1986 amnesty.

The example of Italy shows that an amnesty can significantly reduce the prisoner rate in the short term. The question, though, is whether it is an appropriate way to solve the prison overcrowding problem in the middle and long terms. The Italian data suggest that an amnesty is incapable of reducing the prison population for any length of time, as the sentenced prisoner rate quickly returned to the pre-amnesty level. The overall prisoner rate did not rise for a while after the amnesty because of a decreasing pretrial detainee rate. This decrease was partly due to a change in pretrial detention law, which abolished compulsory arrest and introduced stricter conditions for pretrial detention. Therefore, the drop in corrections' populations resulting from amnesties was only temporary.

Since 1991, the overall prisoner rate has increased significantly. This seems to be an effect of illegal Albanian immigration, enlargement of the anti-Mafia fight after the murder of judges, and the anti-corruption operations led by Italian magistrates.

France

From January 1, 1968, to January 1, 1975, France showed a decrease of its prisoner rate of approximately 25 percent, which was due to a combination of several statutes. Later, the number of prisoners increased

Table 1. Prisoner Rates Across the World

Nation	Year	Prisoner Rate per 100,000	Nation	Year	Prisoner Rate per 100,000
Albania[1]	1997	37	Macao[2]	1995	107
Australia[2]	1994	89	Macedonia[1]	1997	49
Austria[1]	1997	86	Malaysia[2]	1995	104
Bangladesh[2]	1995	37	Malta[1]	1996	62
Belgium[1]	1997	82	Mexico[3]	1993	97
Brazil[3]	1993	84	Moldova[1]	1996	263
Brunei Darussalam[2]	1995	110	Nepal[2]	1994	33
Bulgaria[1]	1997	142	Netherlands[1]	1997	74
Cambodia[2]	1995	26	New Zealand[2]	1995	127
Canada[3]	1994	114	Northern Ireland[1]	1997	95
China[2]	1995	103	Norway[1]	1997	53
Cook Islands[2]	1995	225	Papua New Guinea[2]	1994	107
Croatia[1]	1997	47	Peru[3]	1993	91
Cyprus[1]	1997	40	Philippines[2]	1995	26
Czech Rep.[1]	1997	209	Poland[1]	1997	148
Denmark[1]	1997	62	Portugal[1]	1997	145
Egypt[3]	1993	62	Romania[1]	1997	197
England and Wales[1]	1997	120	Russia[1]	1997	713
Estonia[1]	1997	300	Scotland[1]	1997	119
Fiji[2]	1995	123	Singapore[2]	1995	287
Finland[1]	1997	56	Slovakia[1]	1997	138
France[1]	1997	90	Slovenia[1]	1997	39
Germany[1]	1997	90	Solomon Islands[2]	1995	45
Greece[1]	1997	54	South Korea[2]	1995	137
Hong Kong[2]	1995	207	South Africa[3]	1993	368
Hungary[1]	1997	136	Spain[1]	1997	113
Iceland[1]	1997	43	Sri Lanka[2]	1994	68
India[2]	1995	23	Sweden[1]	1997	59
Indonesia[2]	1993	22	Switzerland[4]	1997	88
Ireland[1]	1997	68	Thailand[2]	1995	180
Italy[1]	1997	86	Tonga[2]	1994	87
Japan[2]	1995	37	Turkey[1]	1997	94
Kiribati[2]	1995	130	U.S.A.[4]	1998	668
Latvia[1]	1997	407	Ukraine[1]	1997	415
Lithuania[1]	1997	356	Vanuatu[2]	1994	73
Luxembourg[1]	1996	104	Western Samoa[2]	1994	146

Sources: [1] Council of Europe PACE data 2000; [2] Biles 1995; [3] Normandeau 1995; [4] National statistic agency data or other official data.

continuously from 1975 to 1981.

A July 1981 presidential pardon and an August 1981 amnesty law temporarily stopped that "correctional inflation." But the numbers increased even more from 1982 until 1988. Following the presidential election of 1988, general pardons and an additional amnesty were pronounced. A general pardon was also granted on the occasion of the French Revolution bicentennial in 1989. But despite all those measures, prison populations increased between 1990 and 1996. Since 1997, efforts to avoid pretrial detention seem to have decreased the incarceration rate.

The French experience suggests that amnesties and other pardons temporarily mask upward structural trends in prison populations. They certainly do not solve the problem of prison overcrowding.

Greece

Since 1911, the Greek penal code has allowed judges to replace some prison sentences by fines. If an offender is found guilty, the judge first has to determine an appropriate prison term. If that sentence is not higher than a certain limit, it is automatically converted into a fine, and if the prison sentence is not higher than another limit, the judge may convert it into a fine. In 1911, the compulsory conversion limit was set at six months (every prison sentence of less than six months had to be converted into a fine, except where special deterrence did not allow the conversion), and the facultative conversion limit was set at twelve months (every six to twelve month sentence could be converted under some conditions). In 1984, the facultative conversion limit became eighteen months, and in 1991, the compulsory conversion limit was extended to twelve months and the facultative one to twenty-four months.

Figure 3 shows that, despite the 1984 and 1991 changes, there was an increase in prisoner rates from 37.0 to 71.0 between 1984 and 1994. Therefore, the Greek experience shows that the replacement of short terms of imprisonment by fines did not decrease the prison populations but pushed them upwards.

Germany

In Germany, following the reform of criminal law in 1969, the use of short terms of imprisonment was limited. This restriction temporarily reduced the prisoner rate. However, the prison

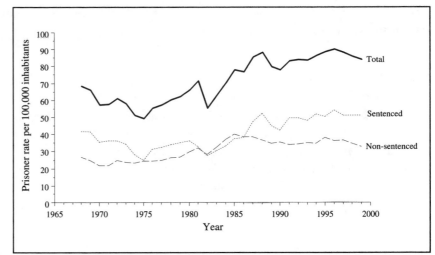

Figure 2. Prisoner Rate per 100,000 Inhabitants in France

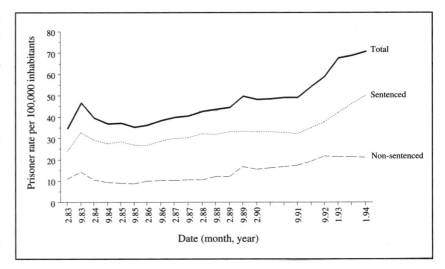

Figure 3. Prisoner Rate per 100,000 Inhabitants in Greece

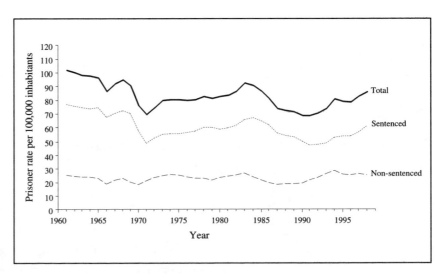

Figure 4. Prisoner Rate per 100,000 Inhabitants in Germany

population grew quickly because of an increase in the length of some sentences. Judges seem to have replaced some of the short sentences they could no longer impose with longer ones.

Between 1983 and 1991, the German prisoner rate per 100,000 inhabitants significantly decreased from 93.3 to 69.2 (see Figure 4). This phenomenon has not been fully explained by criminal policy specialists, although it may be imputed, in part, to changes in the attitudes of judges and prosecutors. Nevertheless, the German prisoner rate has been increasing since 1990.

Austria

In Austria, the use of sentences of less than six months was limited in 1975. As in Germany, this measure does

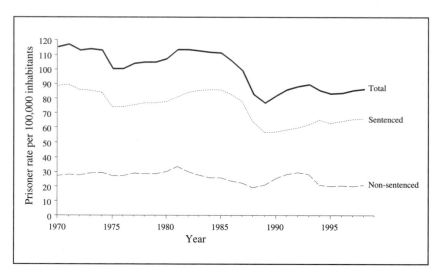

Figure 5. Prisoner Rate per 100,000 Inhabitants in Austria

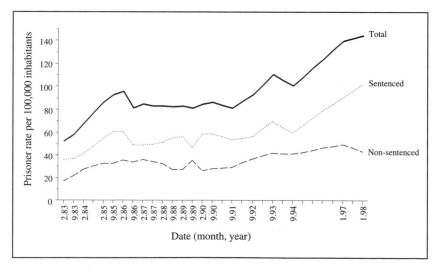

Figure 6. Prisoner Rate per 100,000 Inhabitants in Portugal

not seem to have been a long-term solution to lowering the prisoner rate. The decrease in 1975 was quickly offset.

The main interest of the Austrian figure lies in the second decrease, which is essentially due to the establishment of partly suspended sentences and the reduction of the eligibility date for parole release from two-thirds of the sentence to half of it.

The total prisoner rate was relatively stable until it fell from 96 per 100,000 inhabitants in February 1988, to 77 in September of the same year. This is mainly because the law reducing the Parole eligibility date came into force on March 1, 1988. Nearly 1,500 prisoners were released (those who had served more than half but less than two-thirds of their sentence). But the extension of parole release seems also to have had a perverse effect: Parole use has become more restrictive. Thus, the reduction of the parole eligibility date was offset by decreased use of parole. Therefore the relative stability (despite some fluctuations) in the prisoner rate following its drop in 1988 seems mainly to be due to the introduction of the partly suspended sentence.

Portugal

In Portugal, a new penal code came into force on January 1, 1983. The new legislation—largely inspired by the German law—limited the use of short-term imprisonment and was supposed to replace most short-term sentences with other sanctions. However, these amendments generated an increase in the prisoner rate per 100,000 inhabitants from 53 to 96 between 1983 and 1986.

Here again, limiting the use of short terms of imprisonment did not reduce the prison population. The 1986 reduction occurred mainly because of an amnesty.

The stability of the overall prisoner rate between 1986 and 1990 involved an offset between the increasing rate of sentenced offenders and a decreasing rate of pretrial detainees. The latter resulted from a new procedure act, which limited use of pretrial detention. In 1991, a further amnesty reduced the prisoner rate, but it resumed growing after 1992. In 1994, once more, an amnesty was enacted and the prisoner rate decreased. Finally, after a new penal code came into force in 1995, Portugal's prisoner rate became definitively one of the highest in Western Europe.

Finland

In contrast to the European countries previously mentioned, Finland has had a long-term decreasing prisoner rate. Thus, prisoner rates are not inevitably fated to increase.

Twenty-five years ago, the Finnish prisoner rate was one of the highest in Europe. Today, with about 52 inmates per 100,000 population, Finland is—with Albania, Croatia, and Iceland—one of the European countries with the lowest prison population (Council of Europe 2000).

At the end of World War II, Finland moved gradually toward a criminal justice system holding that it is important that criminals are caught and punished, but in which the severity of the sanction is, in comparison, a minor issue. Therefore, the Finnish criminal justice system emphasizes the certainty of the sanction rather than its severity. That philosophy has had a significant effect on Finland's prisoner rate.

Another important element is that the authorities and experts in charge of reform planning shared an almost unanimous conviction that Finland's internationally high prisoner rate was a disgrace and, therefore, they decided to "normalize" it. As a result, the average length of prison terms for some offenses diminished, release on parole was facilitated, an increase was achieved in the proportion of fines and suspended sentences, and the average length of prison sentences actually served steadily declined. All these changes to the criminal justice system were introduced without any major or abnormal development in the crime rate or recidivism.

Therefore, the case of Finland shows that if a government really wants to decrease its prison population and takes steps towards that end, there is no reason why the

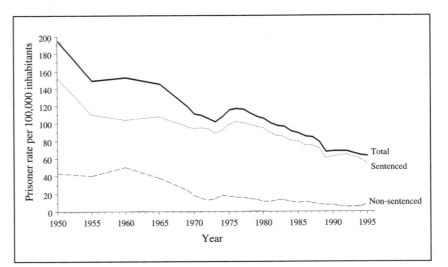

Figure 7. Prisoner Rate per 100,000 Inhabitants in Finland

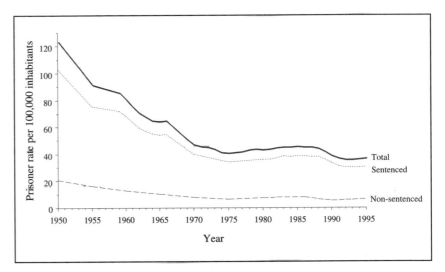

Figure 8. Prisoner Rate per 100,000 Inhabitants in Japan

prisoner rate should not decrease. The problem is to know which measures have to be taken. In most European countries, it is believed that abolishing short terms of imprisonment and/or replacing them by alternative sanctions are very important measures, but Finland's experience demonstrates the contrary. The minimum sentence is fourteen days, and the system is built on only three basic sentencing alternatives: unconditional imprisonment, conditional (suspended) imprisonment, and fines (set on the basis of the day-fine system). Community service was introduced nationwide only in 1996.

JAPAN

Like Finland, Japan has experienced a decreasing trend in its prison population and is today one of the industrialized countries with the lowest prisoner rate. A simplistic way to explain both the Finnish and the Japanese situations would be that both are homogeneous countries with very few foreigners. Nevertheless, as we have shown for Finland, the real reasons for a decreasing prison population are more complicated and do not depend on a single factor.

After Japan's defeat in World War II, the Japanese prisoner rate peaked briefly in 1950 but dropped precipitously thereafter as a consequence of a tremendous decrease in the crime rate, especially in the numbers of reported homicides and robberies. In addition, the sentencing policy in the courts changed to emphasize more noncustodial sentences, decreasing the number of sentences of deprivation of liberty since the 1950s, especially for thefts.

> The feudal principle of a hierarchical social order lingers in the Japanese social psychology today: knowing one's place in the societal scheme, fulfilling the Confucian obligations that the ruler be benevolent and the ruled be obedient, and holding the respect of others by maintaining social harmony, even at the expense of self-interest. Within that normative system, the lawbreaker is expected to be repentant and to undertake self-correction. (Johnson 1996: 5)

It is therefore understandable that criminal justice is "lenient" to those offenders expressing repentance and showing a willingness and capacity for self-correction. Legal standards and procedures extensively permit diversion of defendants from trials and suspended prison sentences. That partly explains the low prisoner rate, which is much lower than would be expected given the incidence of crime in Japan. Moreover, the offender who does go to prison is given a relatively short sentence. Furthermore, the very low pretrial detention rate seems to be related to the high speed at which the Japanese criminal justice system operates.

AUSTRALIA

Like most prison populations in the world, the Australian prisoner rate has increased, especially since 1984. Nevertheless, Figure 9 shows an uncommon feature: The Australian nonsentenced prisoner rate is low when compared to that of most of the other countries.

The Australian trend is mainly due to the evolution of the New South Wales prison population, which accounts for almost 40 percent of the total prison population in Australia and showed a strong increase between 1988 and 1996, pulling the national trend upwards. Also in 1988, a new conservative state government was elected and introduced "truth in sentencing" legislation, so that the sentences carried out by offenders correspond to the sentences imposed by the judges.

The new legislation had a huge impact on the length of the sentences, which increased dramatically. As politicians from all around the country note that "get tough on crime" campaigns win elections, and as "three strikes and you're in" legislation took effect in 1995 in New South Wales, the Australian prison population is not expected to decrease in the near future.

THE UNITED STATES

It is common knowledge that the U.S. prisoner rate is one of the highest (with that of Russia) in the world. But that was not true thirty years ago. The prisoner rate was much lower and relatively stable until the 1970s.

Later, the U.S. prisoner rate started to rise sharply (see Figure 10). The number of inmates in the nation's jails and prisons quadrupled between 1978 and 2000, even though crime rates have tended to decrease slightly. According to the experts, the increase in the U.S. prisoner rate is not expected to stop in the next few years.

The biggest problem for analysts is to know how the rate of growth will be affected by recent or future state and federal legislation, generally aimed at increasing the amount of actual time

Figure 9. Prisoner Rate per 100,000 Inhabitants in Australia

served, often referred to as "truth in sentencing." Other relevant legistlation includes such widely adopted measures as parole abolition coupled with increased law enforcement.

IMPLICATIONS

Increases in crime are often invoked to explain increasing prison populations. In recent years, however, many criminologists have concluded that imprisonment rates are to a great degree a function of criminal justice and social policies that either encourage or discourage the use of incarceration. For example, a survey of whether prisoner rates in six industrialized nations could be explained by national crime rates concluded that "only a small measure of the differences in prison populations between one jurisdiction and another or the changes in prison populations within particular jurisdictions seem to be related to crime rates" (Young and Brown 1993: 33). Furthermore, inside the United States, no violent crime wave could explain the huge increase in prisoner rates since the 1970s. Moreover, the crime rate cannot explain the Finnish or the Japanese decrease in prison populations. Therefore, "crime rates rise and fall according to laws and dynamics of their own and sanction policies develop and change according dynamics of their own: these two systems have not very much to do with each other" (Tonry 1996: 32).

There is no doubt that the American criminal justice system is much more punitive than the European systems. Even allowing for differences in crime rates, sentencing severity (use of prison as a sentence and length of prison sentences) is much higher in the United States than in Europe. But according to Young and Brown (1993: 39), the view that variation in prison populations is explainable in terms of criminal justice policies is "simplistic and largely unhelpful." They argue that policies adopted to reduce the prison population often do not have the intended effect, and that the pressures within the criminal justice system itself or within the wider socioeconomic and political structures are much more important in the explanation of prison trends. According to them, attitudes toward punishment are driven by a range of cultural factors that are deeply rooted in a society's history, values, and socioeconomic structure. The greater the differentials of income and

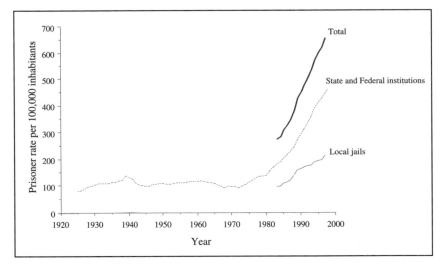

Figure 10. Prisoner Rate per 100,000 Inhabitants in the United States

other rewards, and the greater the gaps between rich and poor in society, the more extreme the scale of punishment will be. "Ultimately, effecting very substantial shifts in the use of imprisonment . . . involves changing a range of socio-cultural attitudes and values that go well beyond the technical penological agenda" (Young and Brown 1993: 45).

This point of view is very interesting. It is effectively true that attitudes towards punishment are related to the cultural background. But if deep social changes are the only way to work toward a general evolution of attitudes and, thus, to diminish prison populations, one would have to change public opinion first; then, the criminal justice system would follow. But the existing correlation between public opinion and severity of sanctions could also be reversed. In other words, the severity of sanctions may influence public opinion; the latter may adapt itself to the delivered sanctions. That is why the author thinks that one can really shorten the prison terms (and change public opinion) through changes in criminal justice policies. The Finnish case is an example of a voluntary decrease in prison populations and of the adaptability of the criminal justice system.

Unfortunately, as in Australia, American politicians know that "get tough on crime" campaigns win elections. As their main focus is to be elected, many of them are not interested in the long-term health of American society, and they have only short-term views of the future. Even worse, most American prosecutors and judges have the same kind of short-term views and compete for votes by promising to increase satisfaction of public opinion's demand. Having an independent judiciary is one of the fundamental rules of a healthy democracy. Unfortunately, the American judiciary has to play the game of politics and therefore loses part of its independence and its role as "moral guide of the nation."

If, in fact, sentence length is a key variable in understanding rates of prisoners, and if the goal is to reduce the prisoner rate, ways must be found to reduce long-term imprisonment. One means that could be tried is an extension of parole release and the introduction of partly suspended sentences (as in Austria). Such a reduction could also be achieved by a change in attitudes and punitiveness of judges (as in Germany, Finland, and Japan); or it could be accomplished by a general reduction in the terms of imprisonment imposed. Sentences would become shorter and would weigh less on prison populations, which would consequently be reduced.

—André Kuhn

See also COMPARATIVE LAW AND JUSTICE; PENAL COLONIES

Further Reading

Aho, Timo. (1997). *Land of Decreasing Prison Population.* Helsinki, Finland: Ministry of Justice, Department of Prison Administration.

Ashworth, Andrew. (1983). *Sentencing and Penal Policy.* London: Weidenfeld and Nicolson.

Australian Law Reform Commission. (1988). *Sentencing.* Canberra: Australian Government Publishing Service.

Beckett, Katherine. (1997). *Making Crime Pay: Law and Order in Contemporary American Politics.* New York: Oxford University Press.

Biles, David. (1995). "Prisoners in Asia and Pacific." *Overcrowded Times* 6, 6: 5–6.

Edna McConnell Clark Foundation. (1995). *Seeking Justice: Crime and Punishment in America.* New York: Edna McConnell Clark Foundation.

Council of Europe. (2000). *Prison Overcrowding and Prison Population Inflation: Recommendation No R (99) 22 and Report.* Strasbourg, France: Council of Europe.

HEUNI (European Institute for Crime Prevention and Control). (1995). *Profiles of Criminal Justice Systems in Europe and North America.* Publication Series No. 26, edited by Kristiina Kangaspunta. Helsinki, Finland: HEUNI.

Kuhn, André. (2000). *Détenus: Combien? Pourquoi? Que faire?* Bern, Switzerland: Haupt.

Japan Ministry of Justice (1965–1995). *Summary of the White Paper on Crime.* Tokyo: Japan Ministry of Justice.

Johnson, Elmer H. (1996). *Japanese Corrections: Managing Convicted Offenders in an Orderly Society.* Carbondale, IL: Southern Illinois University Press.

Maguire, Kathleen, and Ann L. Pastore. (1994–1999). *Sourcebook of Criminal Justice Statistics.* Washington, DC: U.S. Department of Justice, Bureau of Justice Statistics.

Mauer, Mark. (1997). *Americans Behind Bars: U.S. and International Use of Incarceration, 1995.* Washington, DC: Sentencing Project.

Normandeau, Andre. (1995). "La nouvelle pénologie des États-Unis d'Amérique." *Revue Internationale de Criminologie et de Police Technique,* 48, 3: 350–365.

Tonry, Michael H. (1996). "Controlling Prison Population Size." *European Journal on Criminal Policy and Research* 4, 3: 26–45.

Törnudd, Patrick. (1993). *Fifteen Years of Decreasing Prisoner Rates in Finland.* Helsinki, Finland: National Research Institute of Legal Policy.

Walmsley Roy. (2000). *World Prison Population List.* 2d ed. Research Findings No. 116. London: Home Office Research, Development and Statistics Directorate.

———. (1995). *Developments in the Prison System of Central and Eastern Europe.* Paper No. 4. Helsinki, Finland: HEUNI.

Young, Warren, and Mark Brown. (1993). "Cross-National Comparisons of Imprisonment." In *Crime and Justice: A Review of Research*, vol. 17, edited by Michael Tonry. Chicago: University of Chicago Press, 1–9

▼ INTERPOL

The International Criminal Police Organization (INTERPOL) assists law enforcement agencies worldwide as an information clearinghouse. Information provided to member nations helps law enforcement agencies prevent and detect crimes. Although the concept for such an organization first emerged in 1914, INTERPOL was not established until 1923. Originally headquartered in Vienna, INTERPOL was disbanded during World War II. Its operations resumed in 1946, with a new headquarters in Paris. "Interpol," once the telegraphic address for the organization, was officially incorporated into the new name adopted in 1956: International Criminal Police Organization (abbreviated to ICPO-Interpol or simply INTERPOL).

Contrary to popular belief, INTERPOL is not a police agency. It does not apprehend suspects or criminals, nor does it have any police powers. Rather, it provides law enforcement agencies with information they can use to combat international crime. These services are primarily information exchanges. To facilitate communications between personnel associated with the various agencies in its member nations, INTERPOL uses Arabic, French, English, and Spanish as its official languages. Data collected by INTERPOL were originally stored in files and collated manually in response to requests. The system was cumbersome, and responses might take days to complete. Communications between nations were typically transmitted via telex, Morse code, and/or high-frequency radio broadcasts. The broadcasts had their own coded language to ensure the security of the information. In 1994, INTER-POL began conversion to computer-based technology, with transmission over a secure network.

INTERPOL does not intervene in religious, political, military, or racial disagreements in any member countries. This policy ensures that the agency can continue to access information about crime and criminals in member nations even during international conflicts and internal political instability.

In an interview with *CIO Magazine* (Dragoon 2000), Peter J. Nevitt, director of INTERPOL's information services, said information shared among agencies has created huge databases with detailed descriptions of missing persons, organized crime groups, and stolen artwork, to give a few examples. Because of issues raised by international politics and police work, any information provided by a nation can be selectively blocked by INTER-POL at the request of that nation. Similarly, access might be denied to law enforcement in a particular nation for diplomatic reasons or to maintain the security of ongoing investigations. In addition to the database, law enforcement agents in one nation can send e-mail about a specific need for cooperation to those in another nation. An estimated 2.4 million such messages were transmitted through INTERPOL's secure network in 1998.

Nevitt said in that same interview that the organization is commonly "seen as a semimythical organization of super-sleuths. We want to get rid of the myth; we're not interested in it. Well, we like it a little, of course, but the reality is better" (Dragoon 2000: para. 5). INTER-POL is most concerned with "ordinary law crimes" and assists in tracking criminals, such as thieves and terrorists. Among the crimes with which the organization has been most concerned are counterfeiting, forgery, smuggling, and narcotics trafficking. INTERPOL has also pledged to assist its members with tracking computer-related crimes. As of 2001, INTERPOL had almost 180 member nations. It has U.N. Observer Status and works with various other international agencies such as the International Telecommunications Union, World Customs Organization, and World Health Organization.

—Linda Dailey Paulson

Further Reading

Anderson, Malcolm. (1989). *Policing the World: Interpol and the Politics of International Police Co-operation.* New York: Oxford University Press.

Bresler, Fenton S. (1993). *Interpol.* London: Sinclair-Stevenson.

Dragoon, Alice. (2000). "The Man from Interpol." *CIO Magazine* (June 15). http://www.cio.com/archive/061500_interpol.html

---

An Example of INTERPOL's Role in International Crime

An American-born, naturalized Australian citizen was charged with murder in Sydney, Australia. The victim had been shot seven times with a shotgun. The defendant admitted firing the fatal bullets but claimed it had been a reflexive act of self-defense resulting from his specialized training with the U.S. Armed Forces in Vietnam. He said that his role in the Vietnam War had been so secret that the U.S. government would deny any knowledge of him or his special training. Through the Australian NCB, the Sydney police asked U.S. authorities to check out the man's claims. The FBI representative at the Washington NCB, after contacting three Federal agencies, four FBI field offices, and more than twenty witnesses, proved the man was talking nonsense: He had received no special training, and there was nothing in his wartime career to supply any possible excuse for the murder.

After four trials, three of which ended in hung juries, he was convicted and sentenced to life imprisonment.

Source: Bresler, Fenton. (1992). *INTERPOL*. London: Sinclair-Stevenson, pp. 195-196.

Fooner, Michael. (1985). *A Guide to INTERPOL: The International Criminal Police Organization in the United States.* Washington, DC: U.S. Dept. of Justice, National Institute of Justice.

———. (1989). *INTERPOL: Issues in World Crime and International Criminal Justice.* New York: Plenum Press.

"Interpol to Target Web Crime." (2000). *London Globe and Mail* (November 9).

U.S. General Accounting Office. (1987). *Counterterrorism: Role of Interpol and the U.S. National Central Bureau.* Washington, DC: U.S. General Accounting Office.

▼ INTERROGATION

Interrogation is an essential investigative activity in all police work, yet it has always been a controversial one in many democratic societies. Historically, America police have sometimes relied on fear and violence to elicit station-house confessions; more recently, they have relied primarily on psychological manipulation, persuasion, and deception. Even though confessions are necessary to solve crimes, there is sometimes skepticism about the means by which they are elicited, about whether police have abided by existing laws, and about whether the confessions are trustworthy.

THE DEVELOPMENT OF METHODS OF INTERROGATION

The modern institution of policing emerged in England in the early part of the nineteenth century and in the United States in the mid- to late-nineteenth century. Police interrogation at the station house is therefore a relatively recent practice. In the early years of modern policing, there were no established interrogation techniques. Instead, officers might interrogate by intuition, learn how to question suspects as part of their job, or not interrogate at all. In America, the "third degree"—the infliction of physical pain and/or psychological distress to extract confessions of guilt—was common (Leo 1992). Through at least the early 1930s, American police routinely beat, tortured, and threatened criminal suspects during interrogation (especially for more serious crimes), sometimes employing methods that left external signs of abuse, but more commonly using physical force in ways that did not (Hopkins 1931). Not only was the third degree common inside the interrogation room but the confessions police elicited were often admitted into court.

As a result of the influential Wickersham Commission Report in 1931, a number of Supreme Court cases beginning with *Brown v. Mississippi* (1936), and the movement toward police professionalization, use of the third degree began to decline in the 1930s and, less than three decades later, appeared to be rare in America (Leo 1992).

In its place, American police developed increasingly subtle and sophisticated psychological methods of interrogation that they and others came to believe were more effective at eliciting confessions than the old "third degree." In 1940, W. R. Kidd published *Police Interrogation*, the first American police interrogation manual, exhorting American police in the new science of modern interrogation. In 1942, Fred Inbau published the first edition of his seminal interrogation manual, *Lie Detection and Criminal Interrogation.* With John Reid, Inbau published successive versions of this training manual in 1948 and 1953. In 1962, Inbau and Reid reorganized and expanded their teachings on police interrogation and confessions into the first edition of *Criminal Interrogation and Confessions.* Inbau's *Criminal Interrogation and Confessions*—now in its fourth edition (Inbau et al. 2001)—is the bible of modern police interrogation training; it has virtually defined the teaching and practice of interrogation in America. The social science research literature confirms that many of the techniques developed by Inbau and Reid are commonly used by detectives in America (Leo 1996; Simon 1991; Wald et al. 1967).

MODERN INTERROGATION TECHNIQUES

Social scientists and psychologists have researched the interrogation process and proffered empirically supported theoretical models to explain how and why contemporary psychological techniques lead to the decision to confess (Gudjonsson 1992; Kassin 1997; Ofshe and Leo 1997). Modern interrogation techniques and strategies are designed to break the resistance of rational people who know they are guilty, manipulate them to stop denying their culpability, and persuade them, instead, to confess (Ofshe and Leo 1997). Police interrogators elicit the decision to confess by influencing suspects' perception of (1) the nature and gravity of their immediate situation, (2) their available choices or alternatives given their situation, and (3) the consequences of each of these choices. By continuously manipulating the suspects' perception of their situation and their available alternatives, the interrogators labor to persuade the suspects that they have few options but to confess and that the act of admitting culpability is the most sensible course of action.

American police interrogation is essentially a two-step process (Ofshe and Leo 1997). The goal of the first step of modern interrogation is to break suspects' resistance by causing them to perceive that they are caught and that their situation is hopeless. The interrogators seek to accomplish this by leading suspects to believe that their guilt can be objectively demonstrated to the satisfaction of any reasonable person; that this fact is indisputable and cannot be changed; that there is no way out of their predicament; and that, as a result, the suspects are trapped and their fate is determined. Detectives often strive to create the perception that suspects are dependent on the interrogators' help and can be released from the pressures of interrogation only through confession.

Presuming that the suspect is guilty, the interrogator is likely to rely on several well-known interrogation techniques and strategies to communicate the message that the suspect is caught and to persuade the suspect that his or her situation is hopeless. The interrogators are likely to repeatedly accuse suspects of having committed the crime. Interrogators will express unwavering confidence in these repeated assertions of guilt, ignoring or rolling past all the suspects' objections.

This is likely to cause unknowing suspects to believe that they bear the burden of proving their innocence. Yet the interrogators may seek to prevent suspects from issuing denials or asserting their innocence. If a suspect offers an alibi, the interrogators may attack it as inconsistent, implausible, contradicted by all the case evidence, or simply impossible—even if none of these characterizations is true. Perhaps the most important and effective technique police use to convince suspects that their situation is hopeless is to confront them with objective and irrefutable evidence of their guilt—whether or not any actually exists. American law permits interrogators to pretend they have evidence when they do not, and American police often confront suspects with fabricated evidence such as nonexistent eyewitnesses, false fingerprints, make-believe videotapes, or false polygraph results (Leo 1992, 1996).

In the second phase of interrogation, detectives seek to influence suspects to perceive that the only way to improve their otherwise hopeless situation is to admit their guilt. The interrogators' general strategy is to persuade suspects that the benefits of admitting guilt clearly outweigh the costs of continuing to assert innocence. To accomplish this goal, the interrogators present suspects with inducements that are intended to communicate that they will receive some personal, moral, communal, procedural, material, legal, or other benefit if they confess to the offense. These inducements, which can be arrayed along a continuum ranging from offers of legally permissible benefits to explicitly coercive threats of harm, convey to suspects that—given their immediate situation and limited choices—it is in their self-interest to confess.

Effective psychological interrogation is a gradual yet cumulative process. As they progress through the two steps of interrogation, the detectives work to structure suspects' perceptions about the nature of their immediate situation, the limited choices available to them, and what follows from these choices. Through techniques that rely on deception, manipulation, and sometimes coercion, the interrogators seek to transform the psychological context within which the suspects come to perceive their situation and make the decision about whether or not to confess. At the beginning of the interrogation—when their subjective confidence of leaving the interrogation without incriminating themselves is high—suspects may have thought that they would never agree to make an admission. At that point, the suspects would have had nothing to gain and everything to lose by making an admission, and they may not

Homicide detectives in San Francisco with a 19-year-old youth who was arrested for killing two other youths in a gang fight over a girl and confessed to doing so.
Source: © Bettmann/Corbis; used with permission.

even have thought it possible that they would be made to confess. However, once suspects have been convinced that they will almost certainly be arrested, convicted, and punished, their evaluation of their immediate situation and their decision-making calculus are likely to change. Once suspects have been persuaded that they are caught and that their situation is hopeless, the act of confessing—given how they now view their circumstances and limited alternatives—may now appear to be in their rational self-interest (Ofshe and Leo 1997).

THE *MIRANDA* DECISION AND SUSPECTS' RIGHTS

The interrogation process typically begins after the police have arrested the suspect but before he or she is booked. If suspects are in custody or are not free to leave at the time of questioning, then American police are required to issue the well-known Miranda warnings, informing suspects that they have the right to remain silent, that they have the right to appointed counsel, and that anything they say can be used against them in court. American police are also required to elicit a "knowing, voluntary, and intelligent" waiver of rights from their suspects. If a suspect invokes one of his or her rights and the detective follows the law, the detective is required to terminate the interrogation. If interrogators fail to inform suspects properly of their Miranda rights or fail to obtain a proper waiver from

Interrogation Techniques, Pre-*Miranda*

Guidelines for police interrogation include this instruction with regard to suspects who insist on presence of counsel, as presented in a New York police journal.

Police are frequently confronted by the suspect who immediately starts clamoring for his attorney. Some suggestions which may prove helpful are set out below.

You might argue:

"Why should this very confidential matter get into the hands of a third person? Maybe this lawyer is your friend, but maybe he will use the information against you at some later time. You have nothing to fear if innocent."

In the case of the suspect who declines to talk and reiterates his demands for an attorney, it is sometimes effective to make a verbatim record of the questions and the suspect's answers, no matter what they may be. The interrogation can be continued with an explanation that the interrogation intends to show in court that the suspect was not denied an opportunity to freely state his own version of the case.

Source: Kidd, W. R. (1954). "Police Interrogation." Brooklyn, NY: *The Police Journal*, pp. 169–170.

them, then, in theory, the court is legally required to exclude any admissions or confessions from subsequent court proceedings against the accused.

In practice, however, American police have devised numerous strategies to maximize the likelihood that they will elicit a waiver to the Miranda warnings. These include reading the Miranda warnings in a quick, confusing, or perfunctory manner; de-emphasizing or playing down the significance of the Miranda warnings; obscuring the adversarial nature of the police-suspect interaction; telling suspects that the interrogator can help them only if they first waive their Miranda rights; or using techniques of interrogation to persuade them to waive their Miranda rights (Leo and White 1999). Perhaps it is not surprising that, in the United States, 80 to 90 percent of suspects waive their Miranda rights and thus appear to consent to interrogation (Leo and Thomas 1998). As a result, the Miranda warnings have not had an adverse effect on the ability of police to

obtain confessions and convictions (Leo 2001). In those rare cases in which American suspects request counsel, police typically either terminate the interrogation altogether or continue to question the suspect in violation of *Miranda* (a practice that is sometimes referred to as questioning "outside *Miranda*"). Police virtually never interrogate a suspect in the presence of the suspect's lawyer because they know that most lawyers would never permit their clients to be interrogated in the first place. Even if a defense attorney alleges that detectives failed to issue Miranda warnings properly or failed to properly obtain the suspect's waiver, it is rare for an American trial judge to exclude a suspect's confessions from evidence in subsequent trial proceedings.

The most promising reform in America involves electronically recording (either by audio- or videotape) the entirety of the suspect's interrogation. Police in Great Britain have been required to contemporaneously record interrogations since 1986; two states in America (Alaska since 1985 and Minnesota since 1994) require that police electronically record interrogations. Approximately 20 to 30 percent of American police departments voluntarily record the interrogation or confession (Geller 1993).

The benefits of electronic recording should be clear. It creates an objective, comprehensive, and reviewable record of what occurred in the interrogation room, forgoing the need for triers of fact to guess who is telling the truth about a disputed interrogation based on which witness or which side appears more credible (the so-called swearing contest). Electronic recording of the entire interrogation should also deter both police misconduct inside the interrogation room and any false allegations of police impropriety. Also, the electronic recording requirement should increase public confidence in the criminal justice system by allowing jurors to view the techniques interrogators actually use or do not use ("good cop–bad cop," for example, appears more common in popular folklore and American cinema than in actual practice). This allows jurors to determine for themselves whether contemporary police interrogation techniques are acceptable.

In a democratic society that values fair procedures and just outcomes, police interrogation is a necessary and important investigative activity. At the same time, it is also one that requires proper supervision and regulation if the people are to trust the voluntariness and reliability of the statements, admissions, or confessions that it produces.

—Richard A. Leo

See also ARREST PRACTICES; CONFESSION; DETECTION OF DECEPTION; FORENSIC INTERROGATION; FORENSIC POLYGRAPH; MIRANDA RIGHTS

Further Reading

Geller, William. (1993). "Videotaping Interrogations and Confessions." *National Institute of Justice Research in Brief* (NCJ 139962): 1–11.

Gudjonsson, Gisli. (1992). *The Psychology of Interrogations, Confessions and Testimony.* West Sussex, UK: John Wiley and Sons.

Hopkins, Ernest Jerome. (1931). *Our Lawless Police: A Study of the Unlawful Enforcement of the Law.* New York: Viking.

Inbau, Fred, John Reid, Joseph Buckley, and Brian Jayne. (2001). *Criminal Interrogation and Confessions.* 4th ed. Gaithersburg, MD: Aspen.

Kassin, Saul. (1997). "The Psychology of Confession Evidence." *American Psychologist* 52, 3: 221–233.

Leo, Richard A. (1992). "From Coercion to Deception: The Changing Nature of Police Interrogation in America." *Crime, Law and Social Change: An International Journal* 18, 1–2: 35–59.

———. (1996). "Inside the Interrogation Room." *Journal of Criminal Law and Criminology* 86, 2: 266–303.

———. (2001). "Questioning the Relevance of *Miranda* in the Twenty-First Century." *Michigan Law Review* 99, 5: 1000–1029.

Leo, Richard A., and George Thomas. (1998). *The Miranda Debate: Law, Justice, and Policing.* Boston: Northeastern University Press.

Leo, Richard A., and Welsh White. (1999). "Adapting to *Miranda*: Modern Interrogators' Strategies for Dealing with the Obstacles Posed by *Miranda*." *Minnesota Law Review* 84, 2: 397–472.

National Commission on Law Observance and Enforcement. (1931). *Report on Lawlessness in Law Enforcement.* Vol. 11. Washington, DC: Government Printing Office.

Ofshe, Richard J., and Richard A. Leo (1997). "The Social Psychology of Police Interrogation: The Theory and Classification of True and False Confessions." *Studies in Law, Politics, and Society* 16: 189–251.

Simon, David. (1991). *Homicide: A Year on the Killing Streets.* Boston: Houghton Mifflin.

Wald, Michael, R. Ayres, D. W. Hess, M. Schantz, and C. H. Whitebread. (1967). "Interrogations in New Haven: The Impact of *Miranda*." *Yale Law Review* 76, 8: 1519–1648.

Court Cases

Brown v. Mississippi (1936). 297 U.S. 278.

Miranda v. Arizona (1996). 384 U.S. 436.

▼ ISLAM

Islamic law is a significant element in crime, justice, and punishment in the twenty-first century. The discussion of Islamic law is complicated because, contrary to popular belief, Islam is not a monolithic religion with a uniform legal code that applies everywhere to all Muslims. There are at least three major religious divisions within Islam—Sunni, Shi'ite, and Sufi—that utilize different legal/punitive codes. Within these three divisions, there are various schools of legal thought, including four Sunni, two Shi'ite, and multiple Sufi paths. Thus, any discussion of Islamic crime and punishment must specify the legal code being examined and consider its applicability to the other schools of thought.

Although most Muslim nations have codified modern laws, many also use some form of Islamic (Shari'a) law in formal civil, criminal and/or administrative matters. This reliance on both secular and Islamic law suggests a key feature of Islamic law—it is an intricate system of social control that did not simply "pop out of the head of the Prophet" in one day and remain unchanged for fourteen centuries. Rather, although Islamic law is derived from Muslim religious texts, the system has been socially constructed to serve communities in specific historical circumstances. The Islamic legal system, like all other legal systems, is challenged with the tidal waves of social change in contemporary societies. Sometimes the change is swift and dynamic; at other times, it is resisted by those with power or in power.

DEFINING ISLAMIC LAW

At the most dogmatic or theoretical level, Islamic law is God given in the Qur'an, but "between the original divine proposition and the eventual human disposition is interposed an extensive field of intellectual activity and decision" (Coulson 1969: 2). Qur'anic verses in many cases provided general rules. Sometimes these rules were "absolute" and clear, while the meanings of other rules were complex and hidden, leading to different interpretations. During the years of the Qur'anic revelation, the Prophet Muhammad provided the interpretation. After the completion of the revelation and the Prophet's death, however, the caliphs (as the Prophet's successors) disagreed on the interpretation, and, as a result, Muslim legal theory was required to explain divine revelation. The human interpreters of divine revelation in Islam developed the science of jurisprudence, *Ilm al-Fiqh*. The Arabic word *fiqh* is used to denote both the basis of law and the means of understanding the reason or cause of the speaker's words.

In the tenth century CE (fourth century Hijri), the doors of interpretation (*ijtihad*) closed for Sunni Muslims. The disagreement among jurists led them to agree that "all principles had been completely settled" (Khoja

The Application of Islamic Law

This extract of text from a 1992 Federal Shariat Court 44 decision in Pakistan shows how Islamic principles are applied to legal issues.

JUDGMENT

TANZIL-UR-RAHMAN, C.J. – This Shariat Petition challenges section 34 of the Pakistan Penal code on the ground of its being repugnant to the Injunctions of Islam as laid down in the Holy Qur'an and Sunnah of the Holy Prophet (p.b.u.h.). The said section is reproduced as below:

"S.34 When a criminal act is done by several persons, in furtherance of the common intention of all, each of such persons is liable for that act in the same manner as if it were done by him alone."

According to section 34, when a criminal act is done by several persons in furtherance of the common intention of all, each of such persons is liable for that act in the same manner as if it were done by him alone.

2. The contention of the petitioner is that in Islam there is no punishment for intention. Reliance has been placed on the following verse:

"No bearer of the burden can bear the burden of others." (Al-Qur'an, 165:6).

It however, seems relevant to also quote the following verses of the Holy Qur'an:

"Every soul will be held in pledge for its deeds." (Al-Qur'an, 79:38).

"In his favour shall be whatever good he does, and against him whatever evil he does." (Al-Qur'an, 16:126).

"If you have to respond to an attack (in argument) respond only to the extent of the attack leveled against you." (Al-Quaian, 16: 126).

"And whatever (wrong) any human being commits rest upon himself alone." (Al-Qur'an, 6:164).

3. According to the above verses of the Holy Qur'an the basic principle of Islamic criminal justice seems to be that the person who commits a crime, he alone would be liable to punishment for the commission of the crime and no other person would be liable in his place.

4. As regards the contention of the petitioner that here is no punishment for mere intentions, the following Ahadith seem to be relevant and are thus quoted below:

(i.) It is reported from the Holy Prophet (p.b.u.h.) to have said that –

"Allah Almighty has exempted their followers from any penalty for what is in their hearts unless it is translated into action."

(ii.) It is also reported from the Holy Prophet (p.b.u.h.) to have said that—

"The person who intends to do any virtuous act but does not perform it, a reward shall be written in his account and the person who intends to commit a crime, but for some reason, does not act upon it in such circumstance, nothing shall be recorded against him."

5. Abu Zahra, a renowned jurist of Egypt in his Al-Jarima wal Uquba fil Shari'ah Al-Islamia

Page 350 writes that—

"Mere intention is not subject to punishment (unless it is done practically)."

6. On account of this principal mere intention not coupled with any preparation of attempt to translate the intention into action is not liable for any punishment. Thus even after having an intention to commit a crime followed by preparation to commit it, if a crime is not committed for some reason the mere intention or preparation is not liable to punishment specified for the crime itself, unless the preparation by itself is a crime.

7. The petitioner also submitted that the actions (liable to reward) go with intentions. This phrase is, in fact, a part of a long Hadith of the Holy Prophet (p.b.u.h.) narrated from him by Hazrat Umar. This hadith is narrated by Imam Bukhari in his Sahih as first Hadith under Kitab al-Wahhi and is also mentioned in Al-Mishkat as the first Hadith under Kitab al-Imam after the above part of the Hadith the Holy Prophet (p.b.u.h.) said

i.e. a human being will get (in result) what he intends for.

It was then stated by the Holy Prophet in the said Hadith that:

"i.e. who migrates with the intention to seek pleasure of Allah and his Apostle, his migration from Makka to Madina will be for the sake of Allah and His Apostle and who migrates (from Makka to Madina) for wordly gain or marrying with certain woman, his migration will be relatable to that intention with which he migrated."

24. It may thus be stated that an individual involved in a criminal act may not be sufficiently motivated to execute his criminal design but aided, abetted and encouraged by the presence and participation of others may provide him the sufficient tools to complete the offence. The culpability of all the accused in such cases is co-extensive and embraces the principal actor and his accessories to the act. All participants with common intention deserve like treatment to be meted out to them in law.

25. We are, therefore, of the considered view that the above section 34, P.P.C. does not offend any Injunction of Islam, laid down in the Holy Qur'an and Sunnah of the Holy Prophet (p.b.u.h.).

26. The petition is, therefore, dismissed being without merit.

Source: Saeed, Malik Muhammad, chief editor. (1993). The All Pakistan Legal Decisions. Lahore, Pakistan: P.L.D. Publishers, vol. *XLV*: 45–47, 53.

1978: 52). At the turn of the twenty-first century, in Sunni Islam there are four schools of jurisprudence (*Mathahib*) on which the Islamic legal codes are based: *Hanafi'i, Shafi'i, Maliki'i,* and *Hanbali.*

In Shi'a Islam, the issue of interpretation of the divine revelation and the sources of the law are different. Whereas Sunnis assign literal and explicit meaning to the text, Shi'as and Sufis look to the internal and hidden symbolism. This difference for Shi'a Muslims lies in the concept of "Imam's judgment." According to Shi'a Muslims, "The Imam is not there by the suffrage of people, but by divine right. And He is the final interpreter of the Qur'an" (Khoja 1978: 54–58). For the Shi'a, the Prophet's sayings are a source of law. Shi'a, however, accept only hadiths related by the Imams descended from the Prophet, whereas the Sunnis have developed a science *(Ilm al-hadith),* to ascertain genuine from fabricated hadiths (Khoja 1978: 59).

The focus in this entry is on crime and punishment from a Sunni perspective because 80 percent of Muslims are Sunni, and because of the Sunni parameter of legal codes. These are codes derived from a sacred source, products of fallible humans who strove to understand God's sacred words, although the codes themselves are not.

THE THEOLOGICAL COSMOLOGY OF CRIME AND PUNISHMENT

In Islam, the concept of unity *(Tawhid)* places the individual in direct obligation toward serving the one God, and in a unified/solidarity relationship with the community *(Ummah).* The individual is "part and parcel of society . . . society is not a system, but the highest form of integral and integrated collectivity" (Bassiouni 1982: 14). Within this integral collectivity, however, each individual is God's vice-regent *(Khalifa),* and, therefore, is obligated to preserve His creation (Bassiouni 1982). This by no means suggests, however, that the individual becomes unthinking or unreasoning. Within this view of the intimate relationship between community and individual, crime is seen as an abrogation of the individual's responsibility toward God as well as the harmony/solidarity of the community both in public and private spheres. This concept of crime leads to the classification of crime and punishment in three categories: *Hudud, Quisas,* and *Ta'zir.* These categories indicate different bases of infringed rights and obligations, God's right (is the individual's obligation toward God's creation for public and communal good) or indi-

vidual right (individual's obligation to God's creation for personal enjoyment); various levels of judicial discretion in implementing punishments; the harshness of penalties imposed; and different evidentiary/fact-finding standards. The final objective in this classification of crime and punishment, all jurists agree, is to achieve a just society. "When they are angry, even then forgive" (*Holy Qur'an,* al-Shura: 37); "The recompense for an injury is an injury equal thereto (in degree); but if a person forgives and makes reconciliation, his reward is due from Allah" (*Holy Qur'an,* al-Shura: 40).

ISLAMIC CLASSIFICATIONS OF CRIME AND PUNISHMENT

Hudud crimes include (1) theft, (2) adultery, (3) slander, (4) drinking alcohol, (5) highway robbery, (6) rebellion, and (7) apostasy (Bahnasi 1988). *Had* (the singular of *Hudud*) refers to the crime and the penalty. According to jurists, the penalties of *Hudud* crimes are mandated in the Qur'an and not by a judge. *Had* punishments include cutting off hands for theft and highway robbery; 100 whips for adultery for the unmarried, and stoning to death for those who are married; 80 whips for drinking; 100 whips for slander; range of forgiveness to killing for rebellion; range of other punishment includes imprisonment for three days until return to Islam or immediate return to Islam to immediate killing for apostasy (jurists disagree).

Hudud crimes are the most serious of crimes, and their punishments are the harshest. This is because the individual has violated God's right *(Haq Allah)* by injuring the harmony of the community. Offenders of God's right (the public right) are perceived as people who have strayed from the straight path and require a hand to lead them back to it. The Prophet recommended respect toward the person being punished. In a hadith, the Prophet brought a drunk in front of the community and said: "Beat him, 40 slaps for a drunk is the penalty." Some slapped him, some beat him with their garments and others with their sandals. When he was leaving some of the people present said: "May God shame you." The Prophet in response said: "Don't say this, never demonize him for his crime" (Khan 1996: 339).

In *Hudud* crimes, the condition for incriminating an offender is based on committing the act under no coercion, being an adult, being in full possession of his or her mental faculties, not being ignorant of the law and having no doubt in the evidence of guilt. There are seven types of evidentiary processes in Islamic Criminal *Fiqh*: (1) lay witnesses, (2) self-incrimination, (3) presumption, (4) expert witnesses, (5) personal knowledge of the judge, (6) written evidence left by a deceased, and (7) written evidence accepted by the offender as belonging to him/her. In all cases, the judge has to follow very precise procedures to ensure the accuracy of the evidence against the offender. Historically, this rule has often made the *Had* crime and punishment difficult to prove and execute; instead, the crime was reclassified to the lower categories of *Quisas* and *Ta'zir*, a process known as "the nullification of *Had*." In numerous cases where adultery was a consequence of rape, or where apostasy was extracted for certain benefits, the charges were nullified against the accused. In cases of adultery, if four witnesses to the actual act don't testify, or if there is no repeated self-incrimination, the *Had* crime charges are dropped. *Hudud* crimes apply only in a just society. During the reign of the second caliph after the death of the Prophet, *Umar*, the crime of cutting off hands for stealing, was universally dropped because there was a famine.

The victim in *Hudud* crimes is a more silent participant than in the other categories of crime. The state commences the criminal procedure and the victim has no right to intervene at any stage of the process, except as a witness, and then only according to certain schools of jurisprudence (Salama 1982: 141). The witness and offender should encounter each other in the trial. But if the witness is also the victim, only the *Hanafi'i* school permits his or her encounter with the offender in the case of *Hudud* crimes. The *Maliki'i* school allows their encounter only in highway robbery *Hudud* crimes. *Shafi'i* and *Hanbali* schools disallow the victim's testimony, because it is viewed as the testimony of "enemies against each other." Neither the arbitrator nor the victim have much freedom in their participation in the *Hudud* criminal process. The punishment is predetermined and, hence, the arbitrator's function is to determine the accuracy of the testimonies and evidence.

Quisas is the second category of crime in Islamic criminal *fiqh*. These crimes include all types of murder—voluntary and involuntary—and crimes against persons, including assault, battery, mayhem, and other bodily harm that result in injury or death (Bahnasi 1984; Bassiouni 1982: 24). The kinds of rights that are violated in *Quisas* are subject to debate; however, modern Islamic jurists agree that this category combines both public and private rights in the case of intentional homicide. It is public, because

humans are God's creation, and private, because the victim's family has lost a loved one. The penalties for *Quisas* are not strictly mandated in the Qur'an, but retaliation, compensation, and reconciliation are prescribed. It was within the pre-Islamic context of retaliating against the murder of one person by annihilating entire clans that the Qur'an stated the range of possible punitive measures: "O ye who believe the law of equality is prescribed to you in cases of murder: the free for the free, the slave for the slave, the woman for the woman. But if any forgiveness is made by the brother of the slain, then grant any reasonable demand, and compensate him with handsome gratitude. This is a concession and a mercy from God" (*Holy Qur'an*, al-Baqarah: 178).

The Qur'an cautions against vengeful retaliation: "We ordained there in for them life for life, eye for an eye, nose for nose, ear for ear, tooth for tooth, and wounds for equal. Anyone remits the retaliation by way of charity, it is an act of atonement" (*Holy Qur'an* al-Maidah: 45).

To guarantee the equitable application of punishment in *Quisas* crimes, the administration of justice should be in the hands of an "appointed guardian" (*wali amr*), a mediator who can be a judge or local administrator. The procedural rules of executing a *Quisas* crime have been a subject of disagreement among the various schools of Sunni jurisprudence. Some argue that retaliation by death is prescribed; others note equitable methods of retaliation, and still others argue that although retaliation is the maximum penalty, it is not the recommended one. Judicial opinion notes that the legislative rule of dismissing any crime that has inadequate evidence, and the strict evidentiary procedures required to prove guilt, encourage remorse and forgiveness. More specifically, retaliation is categorically not recommended in the Qur'an, and particularly not in crimes of murder: "If you stretch your hand against me, to slay me, it is not for me to stretch my hand against thee: for I do fear Allah, God of the universe" (*Holy Qur'an,* al-Maidah: 28). Forgiveness, notes Houidi (1982: 75) "is desirable in *Quisas* crimes, particularly the verse 178 of surat al-Baqarah that follows the mention of *Quisas,* which states: 'but if any forgiveness is made by the brother of the slain, then grant any reasonable demand and compensate him with handsome gratitude.'" All the Prophet's sayings related to *Quisas* include indications that forgiveness is desirable in order to strengthen solidarity and mercifulness. Bahnasi (1988: 75–79) notes

Islamic Law in Saudi Arabia

Saudi Arabia is an Islamic nation, and its laws are those of Islamic law, as indicated by the following extracts from its constitution, adopted in March 1992 by decree of King Fahd.

Chapter 1: General Principles
Article 1
The Kingdom of Saudi Arabia is a sovereign Arab Islamic state with Islam as its religion; God's Book and the Sunnah of His Prophet, God's prayers and peace be upon him, are its constitution, Arabic is its language and Riyadh is its capital.

Chapter 2: Monarchy
Article 6
Citizens are to pay allegiance to the King in accordance with the holy Koran and the tradition of the Prophet, in submission and obedience, in times of ease and difficulty, fortune and adversity.

Article 7
Government in Saudi Arabia derives power from the Holy Koran and the Prophet's tradition.

Article 8 [Government Principles]
Government in the Kingdom of Saudi Arabia is based on the premise of justice, consultation, and equality in accordance with the Islamic Shari'ah.

Chapter 5: Rights and Duties
Article 23 [Islam]
The state protects Islam; it implements its Shari'ah; it orders people to do right and shun evil; it fulfills the duty regarding God's call.

Article 24 [Holy Places]
The state works to construct and serve the Holy Places; it provides security and care for those who come to perform the pilgrimage and minor pilgrimage in them through the provision of facilities and peace.

Article 26 [Human Rights]
The state protects human rights in accordance with the Islamic Shari'ah.

Article 36 [Arrest]
The state provides security for all its citizens and all residents within its territory and no one shall be arrested, imprisoned, or have their actions restricted except in cases specified by statutes.

Article 37 [Home]
The home is sacrosanct and shall not be entered without the permission of the owner or be searched except in cases specified by statutes.

Article 38 [Punishment, nulla poena]
Penalties shall be personal and there shall be no crime or penalty except in accordance with the Shari'ah or organizational law. There shall be no punishment except for acts committed subsequent to the coming into force of the organizational law.

Chapter 6: The Authorities of the State
Article 44
The authorities of the state consist of the following: the judicial authority; the executive authority; the regulatory authority. These authorities cooperate with each other in the performance of their duties, in accordance with this and other laws. The King shall be the point of reference for all these authorities.

Article 45
The source of the deliverance of fatwa in the Kingdom of Saudi Arabia are God's Book and the Sunnah of His Messenger. The law will define the composition of the senior ulema body, the administration of scientific research, deliverance of fatwa and its (the body of senior ulema's) functions.

Article 46
The judiciary is an independent authority. There is no control over judges in the dispensation of their judgments except in the case of the Islamic Shari'ah.

Article 47
The right to litigation is guaranteed to citizens and residents of the Kingdom on an equal basis. The law defines the required procedures for this.

Article 48
The courts will apply the rules of the Islamic Shari'ah in the cases that are brought before them, in accordance with what Is indicated in the Book and the Sunnah, and statutes decreed by the Ruler which do not contradict the Book or the Sunnah.

Article 49
Observing what is stated in Article 53, the courts shall arbitrate in all disputes and crimes.

Article 55
The King carries out the policy of the nation, a legitimate policy in accordance with the provisions of Islam; the King oversees the implementation of the Islamic Shari'ah, the system of government, the state's general policies; and the protection and defence of the country.

Article 67
The regulatory authority lays down regulations and motions to meet the interests of the state or remove what is bad in its affairs, in accordance with the Islamic Shari'ah. This authority exercises its functions in accordance with this law and the laws pertaining to the Council of Ministers and the Consultative Council.

The Complexities of Islamic Law

Although all Islamic Law is based on the Qur'an and the teachings of the Prophet Muhammad, there is variation in time, place, and social circumstance in the interpretation and application of Islamic law. This extract of text from a Muslim legal text in nineteenth-century India shows how legal scholars had to balance the different interpretations and applications from two different schools of Islamic law (Hanafi and Maliki) and two Muslim sects (Shiah and Shafei).

Under the old Hanafi Law, missing persons were supposed to be alive for 90 years. But the more reasonable principle of the Maliki Law is now in force among the Hanafis, viz., that if a person be unheard of for four years he is to be presumed dead.

The same principal is in force among the Shiahs. Among the Shafeis the recognized period is seven years.

Among the Hanafis, a missing person or Mafkud-ul-khabar is "considered alive during this period so far as regards his own property, but dead as regards the property of others." On the expiration of this period, "he is to be accounted dead with respect to his own property and with respect to the property of others, as if he had died on the day of his being missing."

A captive is subject to the same rules as other Moslems in respect of inheritance unless he renounces his religion, and if he renounces it, he is subject to the same rules as missing persons.

Source: Ali, Syed Ameer. (1894). *Mahommedan Law. Compiled from Authorities in the Original Arabic.* Calcutta: Thacker, Spink and Co. vol. 2: 73.

that forgiveness from the victim's family in intentional homicide does not abrogate the state's right to punish less punitively by imprisonment or compensation.

An offender in cases of *Quisas* crimes is granted the same respect and rights as in those of *Hudud*. Here, however, alternatives to retributive punishment can be given, including a *Diyya* (victim's compensation) or reconciliation. *Wali amr* (appointed guardian), the victim, or the victim's family can order the forgiveness and consider the alternatives. Complete forgiveness in *Quisas* crimes can only be granted by a victim who forgives and then dies. In all other cases, forgiveness is conditional. Such cases have been documented by many sociologists and anthropologists. *Diyya* (compensation) in *Quisas* crimes can be procedurally complex, and should be accepted as an option by the offender; otherwise, the *Quisas* punishment applies. Compensation is paid by the offender according to a predetermined amount and over a prescribed period of time. In cases in which the offender has neither the funds nor the resources to pay, the immediate blood relatives are responsible. If, however, the offender is a female or a juvenile offender, then the offender's immediate relatives are exempt from repayment. If the

offender has no immediate blood relatives, then the state is responsible for compensation. *Diyya* can be revoked in cases in which the guilty is found innocent, or else (according to the *Maliki* school), if the victim requires the cessation of payment and then dies. Some argue that after a period of fifteen years without legal inheritors, *Diyya* payment should stop (Bahnasi 1988: 160).

The amount of *Diyya* payment is not mentioned in the Qur'an, but jurists have agreed that an amount equivalent to 100 camels to be the minimum. Some have added gold to the camels (communities in Syria, Egypt, and the Maghreb), and others have added legal tender (communities in Iraq and Iran). There also is a system of compensation, called *Errish*, which is calculated in terms of the value of loss. This applies to cases where there is injury but not loss of life, including the loss of a pregnancy due to beatings and broken bones. The *Diyya* system is not equivalent to victims' monetary compensation as in civil lawsuits in Western criminal justice systems; rather, it carries an element of punitive damage. The money, however, goes to the victim or his or her inheritors and not to the state (Bassiouni 1982: 206).

Solh (reconciliation) is not an alternative to compensation or *Diyya* but rather an additional step in the process. It is highly recommended in cases in which injuries have not led to death. *Solh* takes the place of forgiveness and requires negotiations in the presence of a *wali amr*. *Solh* does not have to occur between all injured parties and offenders but can be partial, that is, between the offender and one of the injured.

Quisas crimes are mostly initiated by the victim or the victim's family. Since forgiveness that leads to *Diyya* and *Solh* can only be initiated with the agreement of the victim, the offender also has an important role in transforming *Quisas* punishment into restorative justice, by accepting to pay the *Diyya* and be forgiven. In *Quisas* crimes, the community's role of appointing a *wali amr*, through the authority of the democratically elected ruler, is essential, because this person guarantees equitable punishment to the crime. More important is the role this person plays in transforming the process of justice. The encounter between the offender and the victim or his or her family is arranged by a *wali amr*, and it is up to the person appointed to mediate the conflict to a peaceful resolve or a punitive one.

The participation of the victim, the offender, and the community is very clear in this process. The victim has full participation in either granting the forgiveness or not. The offender also participates in accepting the ruling on compensation or rejecting it. Finally, the community plays the role of the arbitrator in the choosing of the *wali amr*. The harshness of punishment obligates the public (represented by the arbitrator) to be careful in deciding guilt or innocence. This often results in suspending judgment for this particular crime and considering less punitive options.

Ta'zir is the third category of crime in Islam. This category includes all crimes for which the Qur'an or *Sunna* do not prescribe a penalty or in which there was doubt on the evidence for *Hudud* or *Quisas* crimes. *Ta'zir* literally means "chastisement for bad behavior." The aim of this chastisement is the public good. *Ta'zir* crimes and punishment have been defined by the *Hanafi* school of jurisprudence as the "politics of punishment," rather than the "science of punishment" whose aim is the rehabilitation of the criminal. It is the discretionary power of the judge, the contextual setting of the society, and the status and personality of the offender that contribute to the definition of a crime and the implementation of a penalty. *Ta'zir* crimes have not been codified by all countries where Islamic law is practiced, and even in those where the laws have been codified, they are manmade and can be changed. It is, therefore, in this category of crimes that the practice of restorative justice in all its programs—including mediation, offender-victim conferences, victim's compensation programs, and so on—can be implemented with little resistance. In *Ta'zir* crimes and punishment, forgiveness and minimum punitive measures are central features of punishment. Penal sanctions can be set aside under four conditions: (1) the death of the convict; (2) the granting of grace, *'aft* (initially by the victim and then by the judge or arbitrator); (3) the victim and the offender forgive each other prior to the matter appearing before the judge or sovereign; or (4) the offender has repented.

PRISONS

There are nine references to prison as an institution in the Qur'an, and all are in Surat Yusuf (Joseph), relating to pre-Islamic times. The Prophet and his first caliph had no specific imprisonment space, but placed people in custody in homes, mosques, or placed a guard over them while they were at home (house arrest without its military symbols). It was not until Islam had expanded beyond the bounds of Arabia that the second caliph, Umar, bought a home in Mecca and transformed it to a prison. Jurists agree that in Islamic prisons inmates should not be chained so that they can pray, with the exception of murderers, who should be chained (but only at night). Prisoners should be given ample food and drink. They also should be given clothing suitable for winter and summer. Prisoners who die in prison are buried at the expense of the state.

THE FUTURE

Although the traditional crime rates in many countries with a Muslim majority are not as high as those in Western countries, the increased call for more punitive measures against "the criminal" is similar to those in the West. Some even argue that the "few true Islamic" punitive measures that some Muslim societies apply contribute to the lower crime rates. Ayatollah Khomeini of Iran pushed this argument furthest by stating:

> If the punitive laws of Islam were applied for only one year, all the devastating injustices would be uprooted. Misdeeds must be punished by the law of retaliation: cut off the hands of the thief; kill the murderer; flog the adulterous woman and man. Your concerns, your humanitarian scruples are more childish than reasonable. (quoted in Mackey 1983: 36)

In the last quarter of the twentieth century, Islamic criminal law was reduced to its most punitive methods. The world witnessed the murder of a "princess" for adultery in the late 1970s, the hunting of Salman Rushdie and Nasr Abu Zeid on charges of apostasy, the cold-blooded murder of the famous Egyptian thinker Farg Fouda, and the attempted killing for apostasy of the winner of the Nobel Prize for Literature, Naguib Mahfouz. All these were so-called executions of Islamic justice. This extreme miscarriage of justice must be understood within the socioeconomic and political contexts of inequity, the increase in poverty and marginality, lack of genuine democratic dialogue, deteriorating educational systems, shrinking employment opportunities, and the disparity between the oil-rich countries and other Muslim nations. According to Houidi (1982: 73), "The Qur'an in general is not 'obsessed' with crime and punishment. This is evidenced by the fact that only 30 Ayah (unit of revelation) out of 6,236 address crime and punishment."

—*Nawal Ammar*

See also INDIA; INDONESIA

Further Reading

Bahnasi, A. F. (1983). *al-uqubah fi al-fiqh al-Islami* (*Punishment in Islamic Law*). Cairo: Dar al-shorouq.

———. (1984). *al-qasas fi al-fiqh al-Islami* (*Quisas in Islamic Law*). Cairo: Dar al-shorouq.

———. (1988). *Tatbiq al-hudud fi al-tashriat al-jinaiah al-haditha* (*The Application of* Hudud *in Modern Criminal Law*). Cairo: Mu'sasit al-Khalij al-Arabi.

Bassiouni, M. Cherif. (1982). "Sources of Islamic Law and the Protection of Human rights in the Islamic Criminal Justice System." In *The Islamic Criminal Justice System*, edited by M. Cherif Bassiouni. New York: Oceana Publications, 3–54.

Coulson, N. J. (1969). *Conflicts and Tensions in Islamic Jurisprudence*. Chicago: Chicago University Press.

The Holy Qur'an. (1989). Trans. by Abdullah Ysaf Ali. Brentwood, MD: Amana Coporation.

Houidi, F. (1982). *al-Quran wa al-sultan: humum Islamiah muasirah* (*The Qur'an and the Sultan: Contemporary Islamic Problems*). Cairo: Dar al-shourouk.

Khan, Muhammed M., trans. (1996). *Summarized Sahih Al-Kukhari*. Riyadh, Saudi Arabia: Maktaba Dar-es-Salam.

Khoja, A. M. (1978). *Elements of Islamic Jurisprudence*. Karachi, Pakistan: The Mirror Press.

Mackey, Virginia. (1983). "Punishment in the Scripture and Tradition of Judaism, Christianity and Islam." National Interreligious Task Force on Criminal Justice. Paper presented to the National Religious Leaders Consultation in Criminal Justice, Claremont, CA.

Salama, M. M. (1982). "General Principles of Criminal Evidence in Islamic Jurisprudence." In *The Islamic Criminal Justice System*, edited by C. M. Bassiouni. New York: Oceana Publications, 109–126.

▼ ITALIAN MAFIA

The Italian Mafia has been regarded as the prototype of organized crime in the United States since the days of Prohibition. In its native country, however, there has never been such a consensus, and many different phenomena have been labeled as a "mafia" ever since the term became popular immediately following Italy's unification in 1861. In the late nineteenth century, some members of the Sicilian political and cultural elites even tried to rehabilitate the term. The Mafia was defined as "the awareness of one's own being, an exaggerated concept of individual strength," and a mafioso was presented as "a courageous and skilful man, who does not bear a fly on his nose" (Pitrè [1889] 1993: 292). Until the early 1980s, the predominant view in the scientific debate considered the Mafia a cultural attitude and a form of power, denying it a corporate dimension. According to supporters of this approach, there were mafiosi, that is, individuals who behaved according to specific subcultural codes, but the Mafia—as a formal organization—did not exist (Hess [1970] 1973; Blok [1974] 1988; Schneider and Schneider 1976; Arlacchi [1983, 1986] 1988; Catanzaro [1988] 1992).

The judicial investigations conducted in the last two decades of the twentieth century, however, left no doubt about the existence of formalized and lasting Mafia groups in southern Italy. The Sicilian Cosa Nostra and the Calabrian 'Ndrangheta are the largest and most stable Mafia coalitions. Each is composed of about a hundred groups, or "families," as the adherents call them.

THE CORE OF THE MAFIA PHENOMENON: THE SICILIAN COSA NOSTRA AND THE CALABRIA 'NDRANGHETA

At the turn of the twenty-first century, there are more than 500 witnesses who can confirm the existence of either the Cosa Nostra or the 'Ndrangheta, because they themselves were members. Thanks to their statements, it also is clear that the two Mafia consortia possess the distinguishing trait of the organization (Weber [1922] 1978: 48): independent government bodies that regulate the internal life of each associated family and that clearly are different from the authority structure of their members' biological families. Moreover, starting from the 1950s, superordinate bodies of coordination were set up—first in the Cosa Nostra, then in the 'Ndrangheta as well. Composed of the most important family chiefs, they are known as "commissions." Although the powers of these collegial bodies are rather limited, the unity of the two confederations cannot be doubted. In fact, it is guaranteed by the sharing of common cultural codes and a single organizational formula. According to a model very frequent in premodern societies, in fact, the Cosa Nostra and the 'Ndrangheta are segmentary societies; that is, their collective identity derives from the replication of homologous corporate and cultural forms.

Neither the Cosa Nostra nor the 'Ndrangheta can be fully understood as a form of Weber's ideal type of legal-rational bureaucracy, as was suggested by Donald Cressey (1969) with reference to the American La Cosa Nostra. Far from recruiting their staff and organizing the latter's work according to the criteria and procedures of modern bureaucracies, Mafia groups impose a veritable "status contract" on their members (Weber [1922] 1978: 672). With the ritual initiation into a Mafia brotherhood, the novice is required to assume a new identity permanently—to become a "man of honor"—and to subordinate all his previous allegiances to the Mafia membership. If necessary, he must be ready to sacrifice even his life for the Mafia family.

Maintaining secrecy about the group composition, action, and strategies represents one of the most important duties associated with the role of "man of honor," both in Sicily and in Calabria. In the Cosa Nostra, in particular, the duty of silence is absolute; from the nineteenth century, this silence has included not divulging the existence of the Mafia association itself. Mafia groups have never given up the use of violence to pursue their goals; from the time of Italy's unification, they conflicted with state institutions and thus needed to resort to secrecy in order to protect themselves from state repression.

The ceremony of affiliation also creates ritual brotherhood ties among the members of a Mafia family: The status contract is at the same time a "contract of fraternization." New recruits are bound to become brothers of the other adherents and to show altruistic attitudes and behaviors without expecting any short-term reward. As the most acute observers noted, ever since the late nineteenth century, Mafia groups have constituted brotherhoods whose "essential character" lies in "mutual aid without limits and without measure, and even in crimes" (Lestingi 1884: 453). Only thanks to the trust and solidarity created by fraternization contracts does it become possible to achieve specific goals and thus satisfy the instrumental needs of individual members.

Both the strength and the weakness of the two Mafia confederations lie in status and fraternization contracts. Thanks to this contractual instrument, the Cosa Nostra and the 'Ndrangheta families are able to obtain absolute faithfulness and subordination from their affiliates, who are expected to execute any order given by their chiefs. This grants the *cosche* (gangs) of the two coalitions an extraordinary elasticity and flexibility. In the short term, the Mafia leaders can dispose of the members' workforce—and even their lives—to reach whatever goal suits them.

Limits and contradictions are, however, also rooted in the reliance on this type of contract. In order to be effective, status and fraternization contracts can be imposed only on persons who are already socialized to some specific values. Those who know nothing about honor and have not grown up within a specific subculture may eventually undergo a ceremony of Mafia initiation, but only with great difficulty will they accomplish the process of alternation that the ceremony symbolizes, assuming a new identity and subordinating all their previous ties to the Mafia group. Aware of this constraint, the families belonging to the Cosa Nostra and the 'Ndrangheta almost exclusively accept the sons and relatives of "men of honor" or, at the very least, individuals who have grown up in their own town or neighborhood. The acquisition of the resources necessary to successfully compete in international illegal markets is thus considerably more difficult. For example, the Sicilian and Calabrian Mafia associations have never succeeded in inserting themselves in the oligopolistic sector of the illegal arms market and often have had problems laundering their "dirty money."

An element of serious weakness also lies in the ever deeper hiatus between the value system transferred by status and fraternization contracts, and the concrete action of most "men of honor" and, particularly, the Mafia chiefs. Although this tension has always existed, it grew sharply during the last thirty years of the twentieth century, as a result of modernization processes in southern Italy that made the traditional concept of honor and its related lifestyle seem obsolete. The "entrepreneurial transformation" of Mafia groups, undertaken in order to adapt to macrosocial transformations, has further sharpened this tension. As a result, the entire apparatus of Mafia legitimation is in a deep crisis, as shown by the rapid increase in the number of Mafia witnesses coming from the ranks of Cosa Nostra and, to a lesser extent, the 'Ndrangheta from 1992 onwards (Paoli 2000).

Although economic activities acquired a growing relevance in the last thirty years of the twentieth century, the members of Sicilian and Calabrian Mafia sodalities have always relied on strong Mafia bonds to pursue different ends. It is therefore hardly possible to single out an encompassing function or goal that characterizes the Mafia phenomenon, as has been suggested by the supporters of the "economistic" paradigm (Catanzaro [1988] 1992; Santino and La Fiura, 1990), and, more recently, by Diego Gambetta, who categorizes the Mafia as "an industry of private protection" (1993).

Indeed, the official goal of the two Mafia consortia

The American View of the Italian Mafia

The Mafia has been portrayed in various ways by the media, in film, in fiction, and by scholars. The following extract is one view that was not uncommon in the United States in the 1930s, the heyday of organized crime activity.

The *Mafia* and the Camorra are not associations. The *Mafia* is a Sicilian attribute, born in the blood of the people. In general a *Mafioso* is not a criminal, very often he is a gentleman. He is a man of courage, high temper, not blood and one whom it is dangerous to insult. He will resent any injustice. He never forgets a wrong regardless of how long he may live. All classes are of the *Mafia*, low class, middle class and high class. Thus we find different bands of *Mafiosos*, each having their own leader. In each village or city of Sicily we find a different band. The work of a *Mafioso* gang is a campaign of intimidation, forcing their will or the wishes of those who have hired them, upon others.

Wrongs and injustices in Italy are handed down from father to son through many generations the same as a feud handed down in this country. The family on each side of this feud will secure the services of the *Mafioso* gang on which they rely, to deal with the other side, they in turn doing likewise. Thus the trouble is not actively handled by the immediate parties concerned, but by intermediaries, the different gangs of *Mafiosos*, who settle the matter for their principals.

Source: Ferrucci, Giovanni. (1932). *Bootlegger.* New York: Independent Publishing Company, pp. 116–117.

has been obvious ever since the nineteenth century: It is mutual aid, as the statement of the Procuratore del Re Lestingi in 1884 proves. Such an aim is confirmed by contemporary Mafia witnesses. Tommaso Buscetta, for example, affirms the central roles of "the protection and safeguard of one's business, the reciprocal support in the defense of economic and power interests was the cement of the whole [Cosa Nostra] building" (Arlacchi 1994: 22). But, if the enhancement of the members' interests through mutual aid seems to have been the major "official goal" of Mafia associations ever since their founding, this general aim has been a mix of "operative goals" (Perrow 1961), depending on the priorities set by the chiefs of each family.

Far from being reduced to illegal enterprises, the

Cosa Nostra and 'Ndrangheta constitute functionally diffused associations. As early as 1877, Leopoldo Franchetti highlighted the "extraordinary elasticity" of the Sicilian associations: "[T]he goals multiply, the field of action widens, without the need to multiply the statutes; the association divides for certain goals, remains united for others" ([1877] 1993: 100).

Within this wide range of functions, there is one that usually was neglected by late twentieth-century observers: the exercise of a political dominion. The ruling bodies of the Cosa Nostra and the 'Ndrangheta claim, above all, an absolute power over their members, so as to cover every aspect of their life. They also impose the key principles of their legal order on nonaffiliates and, in particular, on those who collaborate in various ways with Mafia members. Through a generalized system of extortion, they tax—as a nation would do—the main productive activities carried out within their territory (Paoli 2000).

SUMMARY

Although the term *Mafia* has been variously defined over the past 150 years, there is no doubt that the hard core of the Mafia phenomenon is made up of two lasting and structured coalitions—the Sicilian Cosa Nostra and the Calabrian 'Ndrangheta—each composed by about 100 Mafia groups. The groups are called families by their adherents, but they are clearly distinct from the blood families of their members, so much so that they have their own ruling bodies. Through rites and symbols, ritual brotherhood ties are established among their affiliates. The two Mafia associations systematically resort to violence and secrecy to defend themselves from state repression and to pursue their aims, and historically have performed many functions within their social environments.

—*Letizia Paoli*

See also ITALY; ORGANIZED CRIME—GLOBAL

Further Reading
Arlacchi, Pino. ([1983, 1986] 1988). *Mafia Business. The Mafia Ethic and the Spirit of Capitalism.* Oxford, UK: Oxford University Press.
———. ([1992] 1993). *Men of Dishonor. Inside the Sicilian Mafia: An Account of Antonino Calderone.* New York: William Morrow.
———. (1994). *Addio Cosa Nostra. La vita di Tommaso Buscetta.* Milano: Rizzoli.
Blok, Anton. ([1974] 1988). *The Mafia of a Sicilian Village, 1860–1960: A Study of Violent Peasant Entrepreneurs.* New

York and Oxford, UK: Polity Press.

Catanzaro, Raimondo. ([1988] 1992). *Men of Respect. A Social History of the Sicilian Mafia.* New York: The Free Press.

Cressey, Donald. (1969). *Theft of the Nation.* New York: Harper and Row.

Franchetti, Leopoldo. ([1877] 1993). *Condizioni politiche ed amministrative della Sicilia.* Rome: Donzelli.

Gambetta, Diego. (1993). *The Sicilian Mafia. The Business of Private Protection.* Cambridge, MA and London: Harvard University Press.

Hess, Henner. ([1970] 1973). *Mafia and Mafiosi. The Structure of Power.* Westmead: Saxon House.

Lestingi, F. (1884). "L'associazione della Fratellanza nella provincia di Girgenti." *Archivio di Psichiatria, Antropologia Criminale e Scienze Penali.* V: 452–463.

Paoli, Letizia. (2000). *Fratelli di Mafia. Cosa Nostra e 'Ndrangheta.* Bologna, Italy: Il Mulino.

Perrow, Charles. (1961). "The Analysis of Goals in Complex Organizations." *American Sociological Review* 26: 854–866.

Pitrè, Giuseppe. ([1889] 1993). *Usi e costumi, credenze e pregiudizi del popolo siciliano.* Catania: Clio.

Santino, Umberto, and Giovanni La Fiura. (1990). *L'impresa mafiosa. Dall'Italia agli Stati Uniti.* Milano, Italy: Franco Angeli.

Schneider, Jane, and Peter Schneider. (1976). *Culture and Political Economy in Western Sicily.* New York: Academic Press.

Weber, Max. ([1922] 1978). *Economy and Society*, edited by G. Roth and C. Wittich. Berkeley and Los Angeles: University of California Press.

ITALY

Italy is a nation in southern Europe with a population of about 60 million, about 69 percent of whom live in around major cities. Italy's modern criminal justice system has never enjoyed a good reputation, and the main problems of the Italian criminal system—a huge backlog of civil cases and seemingly endless criminal trials, as well as an enormous number of disputes that are delayed—are well known. From 1996 to 2000, various laws were enacted to reform the system. The challenge for the new millennium is to allocate the resources that will be needed to make these reforms operational and to implement the new legislation.

CRIME

According to the current Italian criminal code, crimes can be divided into offenses and contraventions. This distinction is based merely on the type of punishment that these crimes entail. Offenses are punishable by life sentence, detention, or fine, whereas contraventions are punishable by amend (a monetary punishment that is less than a standard fine) and arrest. In addition, although offenses require the mens rea (*dolo*), contraventions only require fault (*colpa*). Offenses can be further subdivided into offenses with mens rea, fault, and preterintentions (*preterintenzione*). Offenses can be classified in various categories, such as offenses against the state, the public administration, the administration of justice, public order, and so on.

Criminal proceedings begin with the registration of the crime report (*notizia di reato*) with the office of the public prosecutor. This report leads to a preliminary investigation that can result in either a request for archivation (not to prosecute) or a request for prosecution. Prosecution is characterized by the indictment (*imputazione*), which contains the objective and subjective details of the accusation and may be exercised either by starting ordinary legal proceedings or by triggering one of the special, or fast-track, proceedings. In ordinary proceedings, a preliminary hearing takes place before a judge, who may issue either a decree for the continuation of the proceedings or a sentence not to proceed (*sentenza di non luogo a procedere*). If the proceedings go on, various public hearings may follow. These hearings are mainly oral ones, and the judge may either acquit or convict the individual. Prosecution also may be exercised through several special and fast-track proceedings that allow for the preliminary hearing to be missed—for example, the direct and immediate proceedings (*giudizio direttissimo* and *giudizio immediato*). At the completion of the trial, those who are not satisfied with its outcome may appeal on both legal and factual grounds. In any case, all sentences may be appealed to the Supreme Court of Cassation (*Corte di Cassazione*) on legal grounds only. After pursuing all instances, the sentence will become final (*res judicata*) and will carry power of execution—that is, enforcement by the relevant agencies.

One of the main problems that the Italian justice system has faced is the length of trials and the huge number of pending and outstanding cases. It has been reported, however, that the number of pending cases decreased 4.22 percent in 1999–2000 (Ministero della Giustizia 2001).

A decrease in the total numbers of types of offense has also been reported. In particular, in the year 1999–2000, the following cases were reported:

- Homicides, including attempts: 2,476 (– 28 percent)
- Robberies: 50,301 (– 21.26 percent)
- Exortions: 6,661 (– 29.40 percent)
- Sexual violence: 3,797 (– 9.55 percent)

- Kidnappings with the purpose of robbery or extortion 264 (+ 68.15 percent)

- Ill treatment in the family or toward minors: 2,020 (– 31.60 percent)

- Drug-related offenses: 34,948 (+ 14.37 percent)

- Thefts: 1,670,092 (– 9.12 percent)

An alarming trend is the increased involvement of children and young people in criminal events either as victims of violence or as perpetrators, often as members of organized criminal groups (Ministero della Giustizia 2001).

The need to fight organized crime by more effective means and procedures has become important in Italy in the twenty-first century. As a result, urgent changes were introduced in the code of criminal procedure, and specific measures were taken to combat organized crime. Italian organized criminal groups changed during the latter part of the twentieth century: First, there was a widespread penetration into Italy by foreign criminal groups; second, there was an expansion abroad, into Europe, Africa, and North America, by the main Italian criminal groups.

Beginning in 1996, the legislature introduced various new laws in order to bring about changes in the justice system and redress its current pitfalls and shortcomings One of these changes was the introduction of the "single judge" (*giudice unico*), a change that has been in effect since January 2, 2000. This has unified in a single office the ordinary jurisdiction of first instance (the initial judicial proceedings), thus facilitating the access of individuals to justice and rationalizing the structure of the judiciary. The idea underpinning the establishment of the single judge is to avoid detention sentences, instead inflicting monetary sentences or alternative measures such as community work, house arrest, and similar punishments. From a procedural point of view, the main novelty is simplification of the proceedings.

Another major reform can be seen in an amendment to Article 111 of the Italian Constitution. Traditionally, the public prosecutor has had more power in investigations than the defense counsel. This amendment aims to balance the defense counsel powers with the powers of the public prosecutor and of the judiciary police, although it is difficult to foresee complete equality.

PUNISHMENT

The work of Cesare Beccaria (1738–1794) has been instrumental in the reform of Italian and European criminal justice systems. Beccaria relied on two key philosophical concepts: social contract and utility. Beccaria argues that punishment is justified only to defend the social contract and to ensure that everyone will be motivated to abide by it. Beccaria also argues that the method of punishment selected should be that which serves the greatest public good. For Beccaria, the purpose of punishment is to create a better society, not to gain revenge. Punishment serves to deter others from committing crimes and to prevent the criminal from repeating his or her crime. In addition, Beccaria argues that punishment should be swift, becase then it has the greatest deterrence value. For Beccaria, when a punishment quickly follows a crime, the two ideas of "crime" and "punishment" will be more easily associated in a person's mind. Also, the link between a crime and a punishment is stronger if the punishment is somehow related to the crime. Given that the swiftness of punishment, not its severity, has the greatest impact on deterring others, Beccaria argues that there is no justification for severe punishments. In time, people will naturally grow accustomed to increases in severity of punishment and, thus, the initial increase in severity will lose its effect. The best ways to prevent crime, according to Beccaria, are to enact clear and simple laws, reward virtue, and improve education. In his seminal work, *On Crimes and Punishments* (1764), Beccaria presents one of the first sustained critiques of the use of capital punishment. His position is that capital punishment is not necessarily a deterrent, and long-term imprisonment is a more powerful deterrent, as execution is transient.

The Italian criminal justice system has adhered to Beccaria's ideas since the eighteenth century. The Italian Constitution stipulates that criminal responsibility is personal. It also states that punishment must not be contrary to the principle of humanity and must aim at the reintegration of the convicted person. Therefore, in addition to a retribution function, punishment has a rehabilitative role. The death penalty is forbidden under all circumstances. Law No. 589 of October 13, 1994, abolished capital punishment for the offenses provided by the Wartime Military Penal Code and Wartime Military Laws. It also repealed article 241 of the Wartime Military Penal Code, dating back to 1941, which provided that in the event of flagrant crimes, such as those of disobedience, insubordination, mutiny, or revolt, or crimes perpetrated by enemy prisoners of war on board a military vessel or aircraft that place the safety of the ship or aircraft or their war-preparedness in imminent jeopardy, the captain was empowered to order the execution of the culprits who were manifestly guilty, with an obligation to submit a report to his superiors.

After the eighteenth-century Enlightenment, the influence of liberal disciplines tended to remove punishment from the area of administrative law and to extend the area of criminal law, but the current historical moment has seen the opposite trend. The punishment established for the protection of public interests through a public proceeding can now take the form of administrative sanction and criminal punishment. In addition, there is the increasing need for minor punishments to be applied in the context of administrative law.

This is even more compelling in the case of overcrowding in Italian prisons. Compared to a capacity of 42,785 units, with room for up to 48,362 units, at the end of June 2000, 53,537 inmates were being detained.

The types of punishment provided for by the Italian criminal system can be divided into primary and accessory punishments. The judge inflicts the former. Primary sentences, in turn, can be divided into detention (such as life sentences and others) and fines. Unlike primary sentences, which have to be inflicted by the judge, accessory sentences automatically follow convictions for certain kinds of offenses. Accessory sentences include prohibition of holding public offices; prohibition or suspension of exercising a profession or an art; diminished rights; prohibition or suspension of holding managing positions in certain undertakings and companies; incapability of contracting with the public administration; removal or suspension of exercising parents' powers; and publication of the sentence. If the law does not expressly determine the duration of accessory sentences, then these sentences will be imposed for the same duration as the main sentences. In determining the main sentence, the judge has discretion as to the minimum and maximum threshold established by the relevant provision. In exercising such discretion, the judge takes into account a series of factors, including the seriousness of the offense and the personality of the individual. The minimum and maximum thresholds can be extended, according to explicitly defined limits, on the basis of mitigating or aggravating circumstances. Limits may also be extended for the main sentence on the grounds of two or more interrelated offenses (*concorso di reato*). At the same time, fast-track proceedings allow for some reduction of the sentence. The judge also may replace short detention sentences with the sanction of probation or "controlled freedom" (*libertà controllata*), semi-detention, or a fine.

The Italian system of crime and punishment also has been influenced by a mix of theories that (1) remove form the individual full criminal responsibility, (2) link criminal activity to social and psychophysical factors, and (3) emphasize the function of punishment as a means for the defense of both the concerned individual and the society. According to this line of reasoning, an individual who has broken the law is ill and incapable of assuming responsibility for his or her actions; therefore, he or she cannot be punished but, rather, should be rendered incapable of harming others and rehabilitated to whatever degree possible. The influence of such theories has been considerable and has resulted in the establishment—alongside sentences—of security measures (*misure di sicurezza*) aimed at combating the threat posed by individuals.

—Federica Donati

See also ITALIAN MAFIA

Further Reading

Ministero della Giustizia (Ministry of Justice). (2000a). Audizione del Ministro alla Commissione Giustizia della Camera dei Deputati." http://www.giustizia.it

———. (2000b)."Relazione sull'amministrazione della giustizia nell'anno 2000, Dott. Francesco Favara, Procuratore Generale della Repubblica presso la Suprema Corte di Cassazione." http://www.giustizia.it

———. (2001)."Inaugurazione dell'anno giudiziario, Relazione del Ministro sull'amministrazione della giustizia." http://www.giustizia.it

Treccani, Giovanni. (1995). *La piccola Treccani, Enciclopedia*, Vol. VIII. Rome: Istitutio della Enciclopedia Italiana.

Luigi, Alibrandi, and Corso Pier Maria, eds. (1993). *Il nuovo codice penale e di procedura penale*. Piacenza, Italy: La Tribuna.

Chronology

1795 BCE–1750 BCE — Hammurabi reigns as the king of Babylonia, setting down a code of laws known as the Code of Hammurabi—the earliest written code that specifies prohibited behaviors. The Code of Hammurabi of Babylon recognizes over two dozen capital crimes, creates punishments for offenders, and introduces the law of retaliation, as in "an eye for an eye, a tooth for a tooth."

1650–1300 BCE — The Hebrews, or the Israelites, migrate into Egypt and develop the Mosaic Law or the Law of Moses, considered to be a covenant between humans and God.

1000 BCE — The ancient Hindu concept of *dharma* (generally, the belief that certain eternal truths maintain the world) and principles of law become the foundation of classical Indian law.

624 BCE — The law of Draco is commissioned by the ancient Greeks to codify the oral law and customs of the land.

451–450 BCE — The Twelve Tables are drawn up in the first attempt by the Romans to codify their laws.

4th century BCE — Chinese author Sun Tzu, in his *The Art of War*, surveys the customs of sparing the wounded and elderly and develops a concept of command responsibility for violations.

4th century BCE — In Athens, magistrates begin criminal trials by reading the charge and asking the defendant if he admits his guilt. Confessions relieve the defendant of the need to submit a formal statement of denial and typically result in less than the maximum penalty.

270 BCE — Asoka comes to the Indian throne and promulgates thirty or forty edicts, which represent the earliest extant law records of Buddhism.

2nd century BCE — Roman tribunes (magistrates) preside over public trials conducted before crowds of spectators. If a defendant denies a crime three times, the tribune proceeds to a hearing that takes place before a formal assembly of the people. The assembly decides by majority vote whether guilt has been established and what punishment is to be imposed.

200 BCE — The concept of war crimes is mentioned in the Hindu Code of Manu.

44 BCE — Julius Caesar is assassinated, an event that later becomes famous as a model of political betrayal.

28 BCE — During the reign of Augustus, the Roman army is used as a police force.

Compiled by Robin O'Sullivan.

14 BCE — in Rome, Augustus develops the *Vigiles* or night watchers, the first recorded civilian public law enforcement unit largely responsible for public safety and social control.

1st century CE — Pliny the Elder warns of improper mixing and measurement of medicines, and he denounces the common practice of including additives such as wood, sulphur, and ashes in consumer-grade honey.

14–41 CE — Ancient Roman emperors such as Tiberius (14-37 CE) and Caligula (37-41 CE) rely on banishment and executions to eliminate political opponents.

66–70 CE — The Sicarii, a religious sect whose members are active within zealot struggles in Palestine, use terrorist tactics that are also directed against Jewish moderates.

5th century — The Ordinances of Manu, part of classical Indian law, warns sinners of the necessity of expiating their misdeeds and attaches a purifying effect to confession and repentance.

518–618 — During the Sui dynasty, codified Chinese law provides for more lenient penalties for those who confess truthfully and voluntarily.

6th century — Boethius writes the *Consolation of Philosophy* while awaiting execution under Theordoric the Ostrogoth.

604 — Laws written by King Æthelberht set payment for crimes according to culpability; more serious injuries require paying a higher wergild.

618–907 — During the Tang Dynasty in China, a comprehensive legal code is established, the fundamental elements of which are retained by subsequent dynasties. Confessions of guilt are extracted through an inquisitorial process that includes a closely monitored system of torture.

701 — The first *ritsu*, the ancient penal code of the Shinto religion in Japan, is compiled in six volumes, together with the *Taihôryô*, the collection of laws, in eleven volumes.

c. 890 — Alfred the Great sets forth an early theory of justice with his decree: "Judge very evenly; do not judge one judgment to the rich, another to the poor; nor judge one to your friend, another to your foe."

c. 950 — In England, the King appoints a "shire-reeve" to sustain his interests in the shire (equivalent to a county) through maintaining the peace, collecting taxes, checking on the local militia, and crime control. The shire-reeve is a precursor to the office of the sheriff.

c. 1000 — During the Middle Ages, dishonest vendors place kittens in burlap sacks (referred to as *pokes*) that are supposed to contain piglets; thus the customer is charged for expensive livestock only to receive an item of little value (this is also the origin of the phrases "pig in a poke" and "don't let the cat out of the bag").

1066 — King Alfred establishes the Frankpledge system in England, a method of law enforcement that relies on self-help and mutual aid of extended families living in close proximity.

1100s — The Fourth Lateran Council led by Pope Innocent III convenes and develops a new inquisitorial system of justice.

1100 — The Muslim (Moghul) rulers of India establish Islamic criminal law as the official law.

1100 — In Burma, Buddhist law becomes dominant.

1116 — King Henry I of England pens his *Leges Henrici,* which redefines offenses as crimes against the king or government, thus refocusing justice away from concern for the victim.

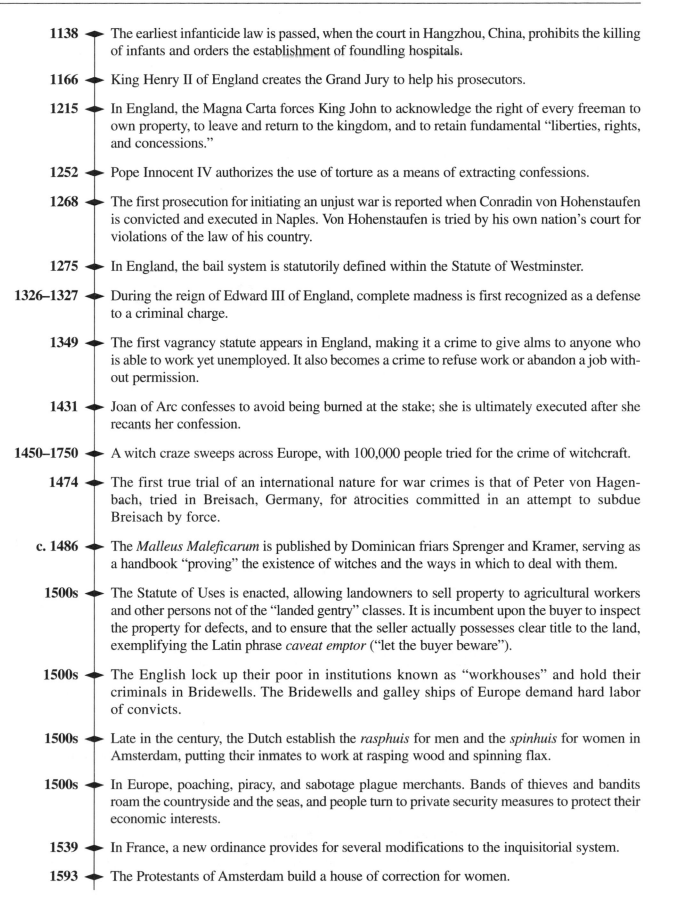

1138 — The earliest infanticide law is passed, when the court in Hangzhou, China, prohibits the killing of infants and orders the establishment of foundling hospitals.

1166 — King Henry II of England creates the Grand Jury to help his prosecutors.

1215 — In England, the Magna Carta forces King John to acknowledge the right of every freeman to own property, to leave and return to the kingdom, and to retain fundamental "liberties, rights, and concessions."

1252 — Pope Innocent IV authorizes the use of torture as a means of extracting confessions.

1268 — The first prosecution for initiating an unjust war is reported when Conradin von Hohenstaufen is convicted and executed in Naples. Von Hohenstaufen is tried by his own nation's court for violations of the law of his country.

1275 — In England, the bail system is statutorily defined within the Statute of Westminster.

1326–1327 — During the reign of Edward III of England, complete madness is first recognized as a defense to a criminal charge.

1349 — The first vagrancy statute appears in England, making it a crime to give alms to anyone who is able to work yet unemployed. It also becomes a crime to refuse work or abandon a job without permission.

1431 — Joan of Arc confesses to avoid being burned at the stake; she is ultimately executed after she recants her confession.

1450–1750 — A witch craze sweeps across Europe, with 100,000 people tried for the crime of witchcraft.

1474 — The first true trial of an international nature for war crimes is that of Peter von Hagenbach, tried in Breisach, Germany, for atrocities committed in an attempt to subdue Breisach by force.

c. 1486 — The *Malleus Maleficarum* is published by Dominican friars Sprenger and Kramer, serving as a handbook "proving" the existence of witches and the ways in which to deal with them.

1500s — The Statute of Uses is enacted, allowing landowners to sell property to agricultural workers and other persons not of the "landed gentry" classes. It is incumbent upon the buyer to inspect the property for defects, and to ensure that the seller actually possesses clear title to the land, exemplifying the Latin phrase *caveat emptor* ("let the buyer beware").

1500s — The English lock up their poor in institutions known as "workhouses" and hold their criminals in Bridewells. The Bridewells and galley ships of Europe demand hard labor of convicts.

1500s — Late in the century, the Dutch establish the *rasphuis* for men and the *spinhuis* for women in Amsterdam, putting their inmates to work at rasping wood and spinning flax.

1500s — In Europe, poaching, piracy, and sabotage plague merchants. Bands of thieves and bandits roam the countryside and the seas, and people turn to private security measures to protect their economic interests.

1539 — In France, a new ordinance provides for several modifications to the inquisitorial system.

1593 — The Protestants of Amsterdam build a house of correction for women.

1558–1603 — During the rule of Queen Elizabeth of England, roughly a dozen common law crimes, including murder, treason, larceny, robbery, burglary, rape, arson, and thirty additional statutory crimes, are punishable by execution.

1600s — English colonists in the United States adapt English criminal justice practices to the New World. In need of a policing body for crime control and order maintenance, colonists import the office of the sheriff into America.

1600s — Both England and colonial America pass criminal offender statutes that impose strict penalties on repeat offenders.

1600s — France establishes a centralized police force.

1603 — The Protestants of Amsterdam build a house of correction for men.

1624 — England passes its first infanticide law, which renders the concealment of the death of a newborn bastard presumptive of murder.

1625 — The Dutch legal scholar Hugo Grotius, considered to be the founder of modern international law, is able to collect various historical writings on the customs and usages of warfare in a treatise, *The Law of War and Peace*.

1641 — The "Capital Laws" of Massachusetts, strongly influenced by the Puritans, proscribe idolatry, witchcraft, blasphemy, murder, manslaughter, poisoning, bestiality, sodomy, adultery, "man-stealing" (i.e., kidnapping), bearing false witness in capital cases, conspiracy, and rebellion.

1642 — The Plymouth colonists order that anyone who lacks a means of support has to leave town.

1647–1691 — Community vigilantes conduct eighty-three witchcraft trials in colonial New England.

1656 — The French create the largest and most complex web of carceral institutions when Louis XIVth establishes the *Hôpital Général* hospital-prison complex.

1661 — The term *smugglers* (also written as "smuckellors") is used to describe those who have begun to defy trade regulations and "to steal and defraud His Majesty of His Customs."

1670 — In England, the argument that juries have a right to nullify laws begins when *Bushell's Case* is decided.

1681 — English Quaker William Penn is granted land in America and founds Pennsylvania. A political and religious reformer, his *Great Act* or *Law* makes hard labor at a house of correction the principal punishment for most crimes and restricts the death penalty to the crimes of treason and murder. He also grants considerable religious freedom to all Christians in the colony.

1682 — France passes the first nationwide law restricting the possession of arsenic to certain trades and professions.

1692 — During the witch trials in Salem, Massachusetts, alleged witches are arrested, tried, and found guilty. Accused witches are told they will live if they confess but will be executed if they do not.

1693 — Philosopher John Locke, writing on the subject of cruelty (in *Some Thoughts Concerning Education*), warns that children who delight in torturing animals may be predisposed to engage in interpersonal violence later in life. Research over 250 years later confirms his prediction.

1700s — Prisoners in the British Empire are given a chance to earn their release from prison, and inmates in the United States are allowed to work to pay for their incarceration.

1700s — Smuggling is the most popular method of importing a variety of commodities (tea, silks, spices, tobacco, alcohol) into England.

1703 — In Rome, Pope Clement XI builds the famous Michel Prison as a house of correction for younger offenders with separation, silence, work, and prayer emphasized.

1713 — In a sign of revolts to come later in the century, a crowd of citizens from Boston begins rioting, angry because some of the local merchants are exporting corn and increasing prices during a time of food shortages.

1718 — In a new approach to crime prevention, England begins transporting all felons serving sentences of three years or more to New South Wales (Australia).

1733 — The British Parliament authorizes magistrates to appoint chaplains to all prisons.

1740s — Laws are passed by states in the American south authorizing slave patrols to quell insurrections, protect people from fleeing slaves, search "Negro" residences for firearms, and flog runaway slaves.

1750 — In response to the proliferation of crime in London, magistrate Henry Fielding and his brother, Sir John Fielding, organize a group called the Bow Street Runners, who, acting as constables, run to the scene of crimes to investigate and apprehend criminals.

1760s — Vigilantism first appears in the South Carolina backcountry in communities without formal law enforcement.

1762 — In his *Contrat social*, French philosopher Jean-Jacques Rousseau singles out the Corsicans in Europe as the one people fit to produce just laws.

1764 — *Dei delitti e delle pene (Treatise on Crimes and Punishments)* by Cesare Beccaria is published. It initiates a spirit of criminal law reform in America and is also the origin of the classical theory of crime, which suggests that people choose to commit crime after weighing the benefits and costs of their actions.

1774 — The Declaration of Rights of the First Continental Congress includes trial by peers as a "great and inestimable privilege." The colonists were influenced by the concept of the jury trial, which came to the colonies from England.

1774 — The first prison riot reportedly takes place in Simsbury, Connecticut.

1787 — Philadelphia emerges as the center of criminal and penal reform in the United States when Quakers and other philanthropists found the first prison reform organization—the Philadelphia Society for Alleviating the Miseries of Public Prisons. In the same year, physician Benjamin Rush publishes "Enquiry into the Effects of Public Punishments Upon Criminals and Upon Society," which advocates rehabilitation rather than punishment.

1789 — The Judiciary Act sets the original size of the U.S. Supreme Court as a chief justice and five associate justices. It establishes the nature and jurisdiction of the appellate and trial courts and creates the offices of United States attorney, attorney general, and marshal. The act also creates a three-tiered federal judicial structure (district courts, circuit appellate courts, and the Supreme Court).

1789 — The United States Congress creates the office of federal marshal to provide support to the federal courts, execute orders handed down by the judges, and enforce many judiciary acts.

1789 ◆ *An Introduction to the Principles of Morals and Legislation* and *Moral Calculus*, by Jeremy Bentham, are published in England. Bentham, along with Beccaria, is a founder of the classical theory of crime.

1790 ◆ The Walnut Street Jail opens in Philadelphia, the first jail to model itself on the beliefs of Early Quaker reformers. A four-tier classification of prisoners is instituted: those sentenced to confinement only, the misdemeanor class, the probationary class, and the repeat offender class. Offenders are given an opportunity to reflect on their guilt and repent by being placed in isolation with a Bible and receiving regular visits from the warden and a minister.

1791 ◆ Several amendments to the U.S. Constitution pertain to crime and punishment. The First Amendment protects the freedom of Americans to speak, assemble, associate freely, and practice their religion without undue restrictions from the government. The Second Amendment protects "the right of the people to keep and bear arms." The Fourth Amendment protects the right of citizens to be free from "unreasonable searches and seizures" by governmental officials. The Fifth Amendment commands that no person "shall be compelled in any criminal case to be a witness against himself." The Sixth Amendment provides that each criminal defendant "shall enjoy the right . . . to have the assistance of counsel for his defense." The Eighth Amendment expressly bars "cruel and unusual punishments."

1791 ◆ In France, the French Code tries to implement Beccaria's theory of equality and proportionality in judicial proceedings.

1793 ◆ The terms *terrorism* and *terrorist* are coined during the French Revolution and used to describe the actions of the revolutionary government that ruled the people through a Reign of Terror.

1794 ◆ To protest an excise tax on domestically produced whiskey, 100 men attack a U.S. marshal serving delinquent taxpayers with court summonses. President Washington leads a militia of 15,000 soldiers to quell the Whisky Rebellion. The event marks the beginning of a continuing conflict between the U.S. government and individuals over taxes on items such as alcoholic beverages and cigarettes.

1794 ◆ The Pennsylvania legislature passes a law that abolishes the death penalty for all crimes except the newly created offense of first-degree murder. Pennsylvania is the first jurisdiction in the United States to distinguish between different degrees of murder.

1795 ◆ President George Washington pardons the only two individuals convicted in the so-called Whiskey Rebellion of 1794.

1797 ◆ New York State opens Newgate Prison, the first of its kind to pattern itself after the Pennsylvania model.

1798 ◆ The United States Congress passes the Alien and Sedition Acts to control espionage in the face of foreign threats.

1800s ◆ The watch system is developed to patrol at night and protect property in larger cities of England.

1803 ◆ The Supreme Court issues its famous decision of *Marbury v. Madison*, the seminal case concerning judicial review that drew direct inspiration from Alexander Hamilton's exposition of that power in *The Federalist* No. 78.

1804 ◆ The French *Code Napoléon* is set forth and is especially influential in continental Europe and Latin America. It is meant to be an easily read and understood handbook that will allow citizens to figure out for themselves their legal rights and obligations.

1819 ◆ Auburn Prison opens in New York State as a maximum security prison for men. It is renamed the Auburn Correctional Facility in 1970.

1819 ◆ The U.S. Supreme Court decision of *McCulloch v. Maryland* reveals the true positive power of judicial review through the Constitution's "necessary and proper" clause.

1817 ◆ The nation's first good time law is created in New York, allowing prisoners who behave well to receive a reduction in sentence.

1825 ◆ Prison labor from Auburn State Prison is used to build Sing Sing Prison, which opens in Ossining, New York.

1827 ◆ France publishes its first national report on criminal statistics—the *Compte*. It is this work that is used by the early researchers of the cartographic school of criminology.

1828 ◆ The first modern police department in London provides mechanisms for both internal and external review of citizens' complaints about police misconduct.

1829 ◆ Sir Robert Peel, credited as the founder of modern policing, develops the London Metropolitan Police Force.

1829 ◆ New York State becomes the first state to collect court statistics.

1829 ◆ Eastern State Penitentiary opens outside Philadelphia.

1830s ◆ The concept of conditional liberty is developed in France as an intermediary step between prison confinement and complete freedom.

1830s ◆ The theory of indeterminate sentencing starts to take form during the progressive era, when education of inmates begins to be more widespread.

1830s ◆ Charles Dickens's early works (the so-called Newgate Novels), including *Oliver Twist*, focus on London crime and criminals.

1831 ◆ *Recherches sur le penchant au crime aux différents ages* by Belgian mathematician Adolphe Quételet is published in France. The book marks the beginning of the use of statistics to study crime.

1832 ◆ The enactment of the Anatomy Laws in Britain makes the taking of corpses from graves illegal.

1832 ◆ Plea bargains become common in Boston, Massachusetts, when public ordinance violators can expect less severe sentences if they plead guilty.

1833 ◆ After an Irishman kills a man in Charleston, Massachusetts, enraged citizens smash and burn the Irish section of town while troops stand by and do nothing.

1834 ◆ Massachusetts is the first state to collect police data, although they are data only about crimes where the criminal is caught and convicted.

1835 ◆ New York is the first state to end public executions.

1835 ◆ Samuel Colt receives a patent in Britain and France for his multiple-chamber, rotating cylinder that is the basis of the six-shooter. He receives a patent in the United States in 1936. Versions of the revolver and his rifle are adopted by the U.S. Army, and the revolver becomes the weapon of choice in the West.

1836 ◆ The first reliable method for detecting arsenic in human remains is developed.

1839 ◆ Great Britain publishes its first official crime data.

1839 ◆ The first women's prison in America, Mt. Pleasant, opens at Sing Sing in New York State.

1840s ◆ The term *terrorism* begins to refer to the actions of revolutionaries opposed to governments.

1840 ◆ England suspends transportation of convicts to New South Wales, Australia, and all transported convicts are now sent to Van Diemen's Land or Norfolk Island.

1841 ◆ Edgar Allan Poe, known for his tales of horror and his poetry and inventor of the "mystery," publishes "The Murders in the Rue Morgue," the first of his "tales of ratiocination" featuring the amateur sleuth, Monsieur C. Auguste Dupin.

1843 ◆ The M'Naghten case formally establishes an insanity defense for those with cognitive impairment. English and American courts embrace the M'Naghten Rule as a test for insanity until the middle of the twentieth century.

1844 ◆ The first metropolitan police department in the United States is established in New York City, to deal with rioting, the growth of the slums, immigration, and rising crime. It is modeled after the police reforms that had taken place in England.

1844 ◆ The New York Prison Association (NYPA) is founded, laying a foundation for the parole systems and prison treatment programs of the latter nineteenth century.

1844 ◆ The Association of Medical Superintendents of American Institutions for the Insane (AMSAII), a precursor of the American Psychiatric Association, is formed to further moral treatment for the insane and to fight the view that criminality and insanity are directly related.

1846 ◆ The first prison library in New York State is established at Sing Sing.

1848 ◆ The Marxist/conflict theory of crime emerges with the publication of Karl Marx's *Communist Manifesto*, stating that crime is a function of class struggle.

1850 ◆ A private detective agency, Pinkerton's, provides private watchmen, railroad security, and intelligence gathering for the Union Army.

1850 ◆ As part of the 1850 U.S. Census, citizens are asked if they were convicts or if any family members were in prison.

1852 ◆ The French Devil's Island prison complex begins operation in French Guiana.

1852 ◆ The state of California purchases over 400 acres of land on Quentin Point in Marin County to build San Quentin Prison.

1853 ◆ The British Parliament passes the Penal Servitude Act, which ends the practice of sending criminals to the American colonies and Australia and enables prison inmates to be released on a ticket of leave.

1856 ◆ Many seafaring nations sign the Declaration of Paris, making the use of privateers illegal. Notable exceptions who do not sign the treaty are Spain and the United States.

1858 ◆ The Joliet Correctional Center, the oldest maximum security prison in Illinois, opens.

1860s ◆ The unique nature of each individual's fingerprints is accidentally discovered by British civil servant William James Herschel in India when he collects and compares prints of Indians applied to official documents. When his findings are later confirmed, the use of fingerprints to identify criminals becomes standard police practice.

1860 ◆ Under British influence, the secular Indian Penal Code becomes the official law of India.

c. 1861 ◆ The term *Mafia* is first used in Italy to refer to organized crime groups in Sicily.

1863 ◆ Cesare Lombroso publishes a pamphlet on his theory of crime (known as biological positivist theory), stating that some people have biological and mental traits that make them prone to crime. His initial study is expanded into *L'uomo delinquente (The Criminal Man).*

1863 ◆ Jean Henri Dunant establishes the International Committee of the Red Cross.

1864 ◆ The Geneva Convention ("Convention for the Amelioration of the Condition of the Wounded in Armies in the Field") is the first in a series of multinational legal instruments with potentially worldwide application for the protection of war victims.

1865 ◆ Congress recognizes the need for special measures to suppress counterfeiting by creating the Secret Service under the Secretary of the Treasury.

1865 ◆ The Ku Klux Klan (KKK) begins carrying out some of the worst acts of bloodshed and terrorism in American history.

1865 ◆ U.S. President Abraham Lincoln is shot on April 14 by John Wilkes Booth in Washington, D.C., and dies the next day.

1866 ◆ *Crime and Punishment*, the classic novel by Russian author Fyodor Dostoyevsky, is published. It focuses on the student Raskolnikov's act of murder and the aftermath of his crime, including his imprisonment.

1867 ◆ Canada's Constitution Act gives the federal government exclusive rights and powers to legislate criminal law. It defines and establishes the division of power and authority between the federal and provincial levels of government.

1868 ◆ The United States Supreme Court decision in *Regina v. Hicklin* becomes the foundation of early American obscenity law and establishes the guidelines for determining whether a work in question may be legally restricted.

1868 ◆ The due process clause of the Fourteenth Amendment is ratified and provides, in part, that "[no] state shall deprive any person of life, liberty, or property without due process of law."

1870s ◆ Vagrancy statutes, often called "tramp acts," are aimed at those who use the railroads to cross the country without paying for their rides.

1870 ◆ The American Prison Association is founded in the United States. In 1954, its name is changed to the American Correctional Association.

1870 ◆ The U.S. Congress mandates that the U.S. attorney general collect crime statistics.

1870 ◆ Prison reformers convene in Cincinnati, Ohio, at the National Congress on Penitentiary and Reformatory Discipline.

1871 ◆ The Virginia Supreme Court states in *Ruffin v. Commonwealth* that the inmate is a "slave of the state" with only those rights that the state chooses to give him.

1873 ◆ The first penal institution for female offenders opens in Indiana.

1873 ◆ Canada's first Prime Minister, Sir John A. MacDonald, founds the North-West Mounted Police (NWMP) force to control growing lawlessness in Saskatchewan and Alberta.

1876 ◆ The first reformatory opens in Elmira, New York. By 1913, almost twenty states have built correctional facilities based on this model.

1877 ◆ New York institutes the first indeterminate sentencing law and other states quickly follow suit.

1881 ◆ U. S. President James Garfield is shot on July 2 by Charles Guiteau in Washington, D.C., and dies on September 19.

1882 ◆ On April 3, Jesse James is shot and killed by Robert Ford, who claims the $10,000 reward on James's head. James and his James-Younger gang were legendary outlaws, robbing stage-coaches, trains, and banks in the American West.

1882 ◆ Roy Bean (c. 1825–1902), a saloon keeper in Vinegarroon, Texas, is appointed justice of the peace and begins a career in which he promotes himself as "The Law West of Pecos." In fact, he had no legal training and dispensed justice in an arbitrary and capricious manner.

1884 ◆ The United States Supreme Court in *Hopt v. People of Territory of Utah* rules that the federal courts must enforce strictly the common law rule prohibiting the use of confessions extracted by physical force or threats of violence.

1885 ◆ Raffaele Garofalo first uses the term *criminology* to refer to the scientific study of crime and criminals.

1886 ◆ *Professional Criminal of America* by New York City Chief of Detectives Thomas F. Byrnes (1842–1910) is published. It is a catalogue of photographs and descriptions of all arrested criminals in New York City to be used by law enforcement agencies and banks to prevent crime.

1887 ◆ Sir Arthur Conan Doyle introduces the detective Sherlock Holmes in the short story "A Study in Scarlet," published in *Beeton's Christmas Annual*.

1888 ◆ Between August and December, five prostitutes are murdered and their bodies mutilated by "Jack the Ripper" in London. The crime is never solved, and various suspects have been "convicted" in print over the years. A crude and early use of what later is called criminal profiling is used in the case when the chief police surgeon, Dr. Phillips, tries to guide investigators by inferring personality characteristics of Jack the Ripper from the wounds that had been inflicted on the victim.

1888 ◆ New York's Elmira Reformatory is the first correctional program to incorporate the idea of shock incarceration programs.

1890 ◆ The first execution by electric chair takes place on August 6 at Auburn Prison in New York. The model used at Auburn is designed by Harold P. Brown—an inventor working at Thomas Edison's research laboratory.

1890 ◆ The New York City Police Department begins using crime maps.

1890 ◆ The United States federal government passes the Sherman Antitrust Act, intended to prevent price fixing and the formation of monopolies.

1891 — The Office of the Pardon Attorney in the U.S. Department of Justice is established to administer the pardon process.

1892 — The Canadian Criminal Code becomes the first example of a merging of common and statute criminal law by a self-governing jurisdiction of the British Empire.

1892 — The *Police and Prison Cyclopedia* by Lawrence, Massachusetts, police officer George Hale is published. Based on survey research of police departments around the world, it provides a wealth of information on law enforcement rules and procedures, police personnel, and criminology. It is the first police science encyclopedia.

1892 — On August 4, in Fall River, Massachusetts, Andrew and Abby Borden are killed. Andrew's daughter Lizzie is charged with the murders but is acquitted in June. Despite the acquittal, Lizzie Borden is generally believed to have killed her father and stepmother.

1893 — Publication of Hans Gross's *Criminal Investigation* helps to establish the science of forensics, especially in terms of a cross-transfer of evidence.

1893 — The International Association of Chiefs of Police is founded.

1895 — The United States Supreme Court in *Sparf and Hansen v. United States* decides that juries "have the physical power to disregard the law," but they do *not* have the "right to decide the law according to their own notions or pleasure."

1896 — The United States Supreme Court rules in *Plessy v. Ferguson* that desegregation ("separate but equal") does not violate the U.S. Constitution.

1896 — The Canadian Bar Association is formed. In 1921, it will be incorporated by a special act of Parliament.

1897 — Interest develops in sociological explanations for crime with the publication of Emile Durkheim's work on social order and suicide in France.

1899 — The first juvenile court is created in Illinois with passage of the Juvenile Court Act.

1900s — The early part of the century is dubbed the "Golden Age" of crime and detective fiction. In the novels of writers such as Agatha Christie, Dorothy Sayers, and Ellery Queen, clues are provided to the reader, who is challenged to solve the mystery before the fictional detective does so.

1900 — The German Civil Code of 1896, a historically oriented, scientific, and professional document that assumes that lawyers will be needed to interpret and apply the law, takes effect.

1900 — August Vollmer, Chief of Police of Berkeley, California, introduces the English technique of the systematic classification of known offender motives in the United States.

1901 — U.S. President William McKinley is shot in Buffalo, New York on September 6 by anarchist Leon Czolgosz. He dies on September 14.

1903 — The first inmates are transferred to Leavenworth Federal Penitentiary in Kansas.

1903 — *The Great Train Robbery* is the first blockbuster in the cine-crime genre, depicting the criminal justice system as hypocritical and all-accepting of the criminal underworld. It features the first scene in which a cowboy points his gun barrel straight at the camera and pulls the trigger.

1904 ◆ Upton Sinclair, an author and social activist, writes *The Jungle*, about abuses and health hazards in the meat processing industry.

1904 ◆ The British Government introduces the first Criminal Code of Nigeria. One of the customary practices defined as criminal in the Criminal Code of 1904 is polygamy (bigamy), a normative behavior in Nigeria.

1905 ◆ The efforts of moral progressives and industrialists leads to the creation of the Pennsylvania State Police, the first state police force.

1906 ◆ The U.S. Congress passes the Pure Food and Drug Act. It establishes an agency to evaluate the health and safety of foodstuffs and medical products. The act outlaws the interstate sale of substances that are adulterated or whose contents are mislabeled, and it requires that addictive drugs must be labeled as "habit-forming."

1906 ◆ China launches an anti-opium campaign. To ensure trade with that country, the U.S. government bans the importation of all opium into the United States.

1907 ◆ The National Council on Crime and Delinquency is founded.

1907 ◆ The Children's Aid Society brings suits against various New York City cinemas for "imperiling the morals of young boys." Supreme Court Justice O'Gorman enforces an 1860 "blue law" and forces the closure of cinemas on Sundays.

1908 ◆ In the Oregon Supreme Court case *Muller v. Oregon*, Louis Brandeis's legal brief on women's health plays a key role in limiting excessively long workdays.

1908 ◆ The Bureau of Investigation is created to conduct Department of Justice investigations and later becomes the FBI.

1908 ◆ The Penal Code is adopted as the basic source of criminal law in Japan.

1909 ◆ The United States Supreme Court in *Weems v. United States* holds that a sentence of twelve to twenty years at hard labor, with ankle and wrist chains to be worn during the entire service of the sentence and perpetual loss of civil rights, is too harsh a punishment for being an accessory to falsification of a government document.

1910 ◆ The White Slave Traffic Act (Mann Act) criminalizes prostitution, making it a federal crime to transport women across state lines for immoral purposes.

1910 ◆ Alice Stebbins Wells becomes the first full-time paid policewoman in America.

1912 ◆ Twelve countries, including the United States, sign the Hague Convention, which agrees to restrict opium and cocaine production.

1912 ◆ The first public defender office in the United States that gives legal assistance to the poor in the criminal field is established in Oklahoma.

1913 ◆ The Huber Law passes in Wisconsin, the first state to authorize work release programs.

1914 ◆ The United States Supreme Court holds in *Weeks v. United States* that evidence illegally obtained by federal law enforcement officers is not admissible in a federal criminal trial.

1914 ◆ Congress passes the Harrison Act, the model for all subsequent drug legislation. This law requires persons who produce, sell, or distribute opium and its derivatives (which includes morphine and heroin), as well as cocaine, to register with the Treasury Department and pay taxes on the transactions.

1915–1918 ◆ In the first major genocide of the twentieth century, Muslim Turks kill about 1.5 million Armenian Christians in Turkey. The killings are directed by the Young Turks who seized power from the Ottoman Sultan in 1913. The killings take place through mass marches, starvation, mass executions, and rapes. Some Armenians are forced to work as slaves and some children are taken from their families and forcibly converted to Islam.

1915 ◆ Alice Stebbins Wells establishes the International Association of Policewomen (IAP). The organization is later incorporated and becomes the International Association of Women Police (IAWP).

1916 ◆ Dutch Marxist Willem Bonger argues that, by its nature, capitalism created a strong desire for material accumulation, and that this is the cause of much crime.

1917 ◆ The Illinois Supreme Court, in *People v. Munday,* calls for an outright ban on still and newsreel photography in the state courts.

1918 ◆ The first criminology textbook in the United States, *Criminology,* by Maurice Parmelee, is published.

1918 ◆ The Criminal Code is written and adopted in Indonesia with minimal amendments by the independent state. It includes a range of provisions criminalizing criticism of the government and other activities usually categorized as political.

1919 ◆ In one of the greatest sports scandals in history, the Chicago White Sox throw the World Series when eight players are bribed by New York organized crime figure Arnold Rothstein, who hoped to make a fortune by betting on the series. The scandal damaged the careers of the players and the reputation of baseball, but Rothstein escaped prosecution.

1920s ◆ Widespread use of the patrol car changes the mode of policing from foot to motor patrol, thereby reducing face-to-face contact between police and the citizenry.

1920s ◆ The "tough guy" genre of detective fiction emerges in the form of detectives created by writers such as Raymond Chandler and Dashiell Hammett.

1920 ◆ Passage of the Eighteenth Amendment and the onset of Prohibition criminalizes the sale and consumption of alcohol in the United States and gives a major boost to organized crime, which imports "bootlegged" liquor.

1920 ◆ The Royal Canadian Mounted Police (RCMP) assumes federal policing duties across the entire country of Canada.

1920 ◆ The Criminal Justice Section of the American Bar Association is founded.

1922 ◆ England passes a new "felony of infanticide" law, which reduces fatal assault of a newborn to manslaughter.

1922 ◆ The advent of talking motion pictures results in a quasi-governmental entity, "Motion Picture Producers and Distributors Association (MPPDA), created to establish a list of sex- and crime-scene "do's," "don'ts," and "be carefuls" for movie-makers.

1923 ◆ The International Criminal Police Organization is established to provide law enforcement agencies with information they can use to prevent international crime.

1923 ◆ The new Russian government takes control of the Solovetsky monastery in the Gulag Archipelago and converts it into a prison camp.

1923 ◆ The *Frye* standard is first articulated in an appellate case, *Frye v. United States*. It requires that scientific testimony be based on a method or technique that is "generally accepted" by the "relevant scientific community."

1924 ◆ Edwin Sutherland, the leading criminologist of the first half of the twentieth century, writes *Criminology*, one of the earliest and most prominent textbooks published in the field. Now in its eleventh edition, the book, with later coauthors added, is still in print.

1924 ◆ J. (John) Edgar Hoover is appointed as the head the Federal Bureau of Investigation. He remains director until his death in 1972, and the FBI remains the leading law enforcement agency in the United States.

1924 ◆ Mary Hamilton is appointed head of the new Women's Police Bureau of the New York City Police Department. She is the first female police officer to head a field unit. In 1918, Ellen O'Grady had been appointed deputy police commissioner.

1925 ◆ The United States Congress passes [the Federal Probation Act], authorizing the use of probation in the federal courts.

1925 ◆ Theodore Dreiser publishes *An American Tragedy*, a novel based on the true story of the Chester Gillette-Grace Brown murder case in 1906.

1926 ◆ The state of New York mandates a sentence of life imprisonment for third-time offenders. Other states follow this lead and enact mandatory sentencing for repeat offenders.

1927 ◆ *The Hobo: The Sociology of the Homeless Man* by Nels Anderson is published. It provides a firsthand account of hobo life in the United States.

1928 ◆ Illinois develops a risk assessment instrument for predicting future crime to determine parole eligibility for inmates.

1928 ◆ *A Panorama of the World's Legal Systems* by John Henry Wigmore is published. The book provides a framework for classifying and comparing legal systems across nations and eras.

1928 ◆ The International Protocol for the Prohibition of the Use in War of Asphyxiating, Poisonous or Other Gases, and of Bacteriological Methods of Warfare is enacted.

1929 ◆ Leaders of several major crime organizations in the United States meet in Atlantic City. The meeting marks the emergence of national organized crime in the United States, with the leaders dividing the nation into territories and agreeing to cooperate with one another.

1929 ◆ President Herbert Hoover appoints George W. Wickersham, the attorney general, to chair the National Commission on Law Observance and Enforcement (NCLOE). The Wickersham Commission begins a critical examination of the U.S. criminal justice system. By the early 1930s, reports by the commission lead the way to broad reforms.

1929 ◆ Congress passes legislation creating the first federally funded drug treatment programs, called "narcotic farms," which are mandatory residential treatment facilities.

1930 ◆ The Federal Bureau of Investigation's Uniform Crime Reporting Program is established as the first system in the United States for recording crimes known to the police.

1931 ◆ Al Capone, the Chicago organized crime leader and a worldwide symbol of organized crime in America, is prosecuted by the Internal Revenue Service for tax evasion, convicted, and sentenced to eleven years in prison. He is released in 1939 suffering the effects of tertiary syphilis and dies at home in 1947.

1931 ◆ Attica is built as a correctional facility in upstate New York, at a cost of $9 million, making it the most expensive facility of its day. It is one of the last so-called big house prisons built in the United States.

1932 ◆ The United States Supreme Court decision in *Sorrells v. United States* first recognizes the federal entrapment defense.

1932 ◆ The United States Supreme Court creates a narrow rule in *Powell v. Alabama* to require a state to provide counsel for defendants in death penalty cases when the defendants are unable to afford counsel and unable to represent themselves.

1932 ◆ Charles Lindbergh, Jr., the son of American aviation pioneer Charles Lindbergh and his wife Anne, is kidnapped and found dead in the woods near their home in New Jersey. In 1935, Bruno Richard Hauptmann is tried and convicted of the kidnapping and murder. The federal government enacts the Lindbergh Act, making kidnapping punishable by life imprisonment.

1933 ◆ The Arkansas penal facility is moved to Tucker State Farm, which later gains notoriety for its harsh treatment of prisoners.

1933 ◆ The United States Army officially transfers ownership of Alcatraz to the U.S. Department of Justice for use as a federal penitentiary. Notorious inmates include Al Capone, George "Machine Gun" Kelly, and Robert Stroud, also known as "The Birdman of Alcatraz."

1933 ◆ England, the country that developed the grand jury, abolishes it by Act of Parliament.

1934 ◆ In an effort to control organized crime and widespread bank robberies, the National Firearms Act regulates the possession of submachine guns, silencers, and several other weapons.

1934 ◆ On July 22, FBI agents shoot and kill John Dillinger, the bank robber and jail escapee, dubbed "Public Enemy Number One" by FBI Director J. Edgar Hoover. The FBI's failure to capture and hold him earlier had damaged the agency's reputation, which was rehabilitated to some degree by his killing.

1936 ◆ The United States Supreme Court in *Brown v. Mississippi* rules that the confessions of three farmhands who were coerced and tortured by police to confess to the murder of a white farmer are unconstitutional.

1937 ◆ The Law and Society Association is founded.

1937 ◆ The worst single atrocity of World War II takes place when the Japanese military executes about 300,000 Chinese in Nanking, the capital of China. The event becomes notorious as the Rape of Nanking.

1937 ◆ The Housing Act of 1937 establishes public housing in the United States, and local governments are given the responsibility for providing public housing residents with the full gamut of municipal services, including police protection.

1937 ◆ The American Bar Association passes Canon 35, recommending the prohibition of all motion picture and still cameras in the courtroom. Later, they broaden the recommendation to include television.

1937 ◆ The American Criminal Justice Association, Lambda Alpha Epsilon, is founded.

1937 ◆ *The Professional Thief*, by Edwin H. Sutherland, is published.

1938 ◆ The United States Supreme Court in *Johnson v. Zerbst* holds that indigent federal defendants prosecuted for federal crimes involving incarceration are entitled to appointed counsel under the Sixth Amendment.

1938 ◆ The Federal Arms Act requires the licensing of firearm manufacturers and dealers.

1938 ◆ Robert K. Merton's influential article "Social Structure and Anomie" first appears in the *American Sociological Review*, explaining that some people are at greater risk for involvement in deviance than others. His writings become the roots of strain theory and anomie theory.

1938–1945 ◆ The Nazi Holocaust takes place in Europe. About 6 million people are killed, many in Nazi concentration camps. Most of those killed are Jews as part of Adolf Hitler's "Final Solution," but Gypsies, homosexuals, and the disabled are also executed.

1939 ◆ Indiana becomes the first state in the United States to follow the Scandinavian model by prohibiting the driving of a motor vehicle with a blood-alcohol level above a specific concentration, although this concentration is set at the extremely high level of .15 percent.

1939 ◆ The concept of white-collar crime is first introduced in the social sciences by Edwin Sutherland, in a presidential address to the American Sociological Association. He later publishes a pioneering book on the subject, *White Collar Crime* (1949). Sutherland also makes his first formal statement of differential association theory, in which he posits that crime is learned in the same way that any other behavior is learned.

1939 ◆ Missouri becomes the first state to adopt a merit selection process (often referred to as the "Missouri Plan") for selecting judges.

1939 ◆ Kidd publishes *Police Interrogation*, the first American police interrogation manual, exhorting American police in the new science of modern interrogation.

1940s ◆ Las Vegas emerges as a gambling center when organized crime figures Meyer Lansky and Bugsy Siegel invest in casinos. Siegel is killed by the mob in 1947 for skimming profits from the casinos.

1940s ◆ Motorized patrols become increasing popular in the United States, replacing foot patrols in many cities.

1940 ◆ The National Sheriffs' Association is founded.

1940 ◆ The United States Supreme Court in *Chambers v. Florida* holds that the use of mental torture, accompanied by threats of violence, is enough to justify the suppression of a confession.

1941 ◆ National Association of College Police Officials is founded. The organization later changes its name to Society for the Advancement of Criminology. In 1958, it becomes the American Society of Criminology.

1941 ◆ Hervey Cleckley's *The Mask of Sanity* is published, offering one of the earliest and most extensive clinical descriptions of the antisocial personality and psychopath syndrome. It remains in print through five subsequent editions.

1942 ◆ The United States Supreme Court decides in *Betts v. Brady* that it is not necessary for a state to select a court-appointed attorney for a poor person who is charged with a state felony.

1942 ◆ Fred Inbau publishes the first edition of his seminal interrogation manual, *Lie Detection and Criminal Interrogation*.

1942 ◆ *Juvenile Delinquency and Urban Areas*, by Clifford R. Shaw and Henry D. McKay, is published.

1943 ◆ The United States Supreme Court in *Mallory v. United States* rules that confessions obtained after "unreasonable delay" in taking suspects to court for arraignment cannot be used as evidence in a federal court.

1944 ◆ The United States Supreme Court in *Korematsu v. United States* upholds against a constitutional challenge the detention of Japanese Americans on grounds no more substantial than their race.

1944 ◆ Congress enacts Rule 53 of the Federal Rules of Criminal Procedure, banning radio broadcasting and taking photographs in any criminal trial in federal courts. In 1962, Rule 53 is amended to include television under the prohibition.

1944 ◆ C. Gray and G. Kopp develop a device capable of displaying speech visually, a sound spectrograph.

1944 ◆ In *Ashcroft v. Tennessee*, a case in which a suspect confessed after thirty-six hours of continuous interrogation under the glare of bright lights, the United States Supreme Court rules that intense psychological pressure, even in the absence of physical brutality, can render a confession inadmissible.

1945 ◆ Allied leaders meet in London and agree upon an ad hoc tribunal for prosecution of German war criminals. The statute agreed upon becomes the Charter of the International Military Tribunal (IMT) sitting at Nuremberg. About 200 Nazi doctors, lawyers, SS leaders, generals, and diplomats are tried.

1946 ◆ The "Blast Out" riot takes place at the federal prison of Alcatraz. It requires military intervention and forty-eight hours to subdue the uprising and regain control of the institution.

1946 ◆ The United Nations affirms for the first time in a General Assembly motion that genocide is a war crime under international law.

1946 ◆ The National Association of Claimants' Compensation Attorneys is founded. In 1972, it will become the Association of Trial Lawyers of America.

1947 ◆ Edwin Sutherland, who developed differential association theory, publishes his classic *Principles of Criminology* textbook, in which he advances nine formal propositions to explain crime.

1947 ◆ Congress enacts the Federal Insecticide, Fungicide, and Rodenticide Act (FIFRA) to ensure that pesticides are being used in a manner consistent with their labeling.

1948 ◆ The United Nations Convention on the Prevention and Punishment of the Crime of Genocide is adopted by the General Assembly. It is entered into force in 1951.

1948 ◆ The Universal Declaration of Human Rights is proclaimed by the U.N. General Assembly. It specifies in Article 5 that "no one shall be subjected to torture or to cruel, inhuman, or degrading treatment or punishment."

1948 ◆ Mohandas Gandhi, the leader of India's independence movement and an advocate of civil disobedience, is assassinated by Nathuram Godse, a Hindu nationalist who opposes Gandhi's policy of religious toleration.

1949 ◆ The United Nations Geneva Convention for the Amelioration of the Condition of Wounded, Sick and Shipwrecked Members of Armed Forces at Sea, Geneva Convention relative to the Treatment of Prisoners of War, and the Geneva Convention relative to the Protection of Civilian Persons in Time of War are adopted. They are entered into force in 1950.

1949 ◆ The death penalty is abolished in West Germany with the new German Basic Constitution.

1949 ◆ The United States Supreme Court in *Wolf v. Colorado* applies the Fourth Amendment to the states, incorporating it into the Due Process Clause of the Fourteenth Amendment.

1949 ◆ *White Collar Crime*, by Edwin Sutherland, is published and makes the study on nonviolent crimes part of the criminological enterprise.

1949 ◆ The United Nations Convention for the Suppression of the Traffic in Persons and of the Exploitation of the Prostitution of Others is adopted by the General Assembly. It is entered into force in 1951.

1950s ◆ Early television crime dramas such as *Dragnet* depict law enforcement officials as honest, clean-cut, and always successful.

1950s ◆ The "police procedural" phase of crime fiction emerges with an emphasis on how police officers and detectives solve crimes.

1950 ◆ *Unraveling Juvenile Delinquency*, by Sheldon Glueck and Eleanor Glueck, is published.

1951 ◆ American Academy of Forensic Sciences is founded in Chicago, Illinois, and begins publication of the *Journal of Forensic Science (JFS)*.

1951 ◆ Congress enacts the Uniform Code of Military Justice (UCMJ), a common criminal code for all military services.

1951 ◆ The independent government of Indonesia abolishes the customary law courts and adopts a uniform system of courts for the whole country.

1952 ◆ The Alcohol and Tobacco Tax Division of the Internal Revenue Service is formed. It is later renamed the Bureau of Alcohol, Tobacco and Firearms and becomes a bureau of the Treasury Department in 1972.

1953 ◆ The French penal colony known as Devil's Island off the coast of northern South America closes.

1953 ◆ Namibia passes a law that allows community service to replace prison sentences of up to five years.

1953 ◆ The work of James D. Watson and Francis H. C. Crick results in discovery of the content, structure, and function of the DNA molecule. DNA analysis is subsequently used to identify perpetrators of crimes.

1953–1969 ◆ During the so-called Warren Court era, named after Chief Justice Earl Warren, the Supreme Court publishes a number of opinions that expand the civil rights of several groups of people, including students, the mentally ill, racial minorities, criminal defendants, and prisoners.

1954 ◆ The United States Supreme Court in *Durham v. United States* holds "that an accused is not criminally responsible if his unlawful act was the product of mental disease or mental defect."

1954 ◆ The United States Supreme Court in *Brown v. Board of Education* declares that separate but equal classroom instruction amounts to racial discrimination and is, therefore, unconstitutional.

1955 ◆ *Delinquent Boys: The Culture of the Gang,* by Albert Cohen, is published. It relies heavily on Robert K. Merton's writings but also expands strain theory.

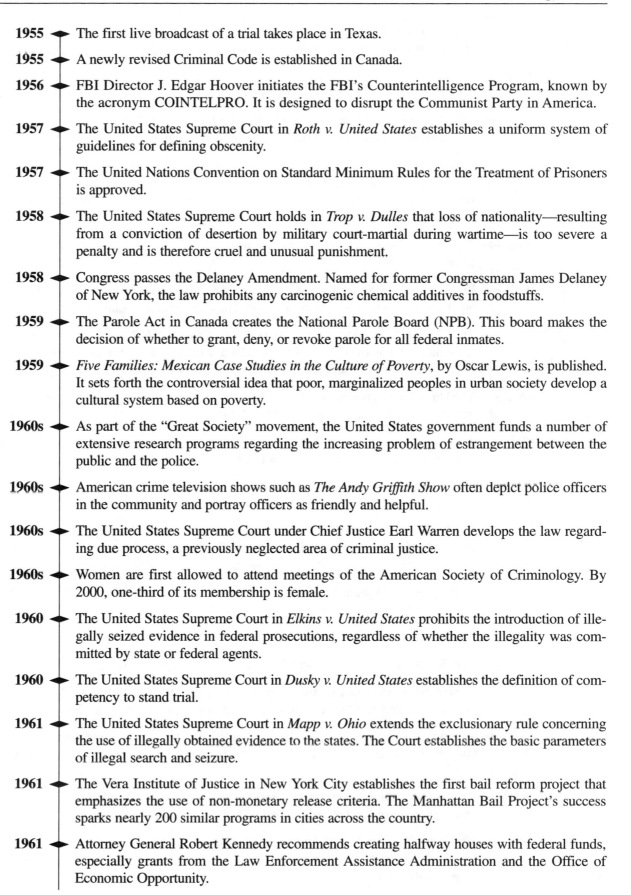

1955 The first live broadcast of a trial takes place in Texas.

1955 A newly revised Criminal Code is established in Canada.

1956 FBI Director J. Edgar Hoover initiates the FBI's Counterintelligence Program, known by the acronym COINTELPRO. It is designed to disrupt the Communist Party in America.

1957 The United States Supreme Court in *Roth v. United States* establishes a uniform system of guidelines for defining obscenity.

1957 The United Nations Convention on Standard Minimum Rules for the Treatment of Prisoners is approved.

1958 The United States Supreme Court holds in *Trop v. Dulles* that loss of nationality—resulting from a conviction of desertion by military court-martial during wartime—is too severe a penalty and is therefore cruel and unusual punishment.

1958 Congress passes the Delaney Amendment. Named for former Congressman James Delaney of New York, the law prohibits any carcinogenic chemical additives in foodstuffs.

1959 The Parole Act in Canada creates the National Parole Board (NPB). This board makes the decision of whether to grant, deny, or revoke parole for all federal inmates.

1959 *Five Families: Mexican Case Studies in the Culture of Poverty*, by Oscar Lewis, is published. It sets forth the controversial idea that poor, marginalized peoples in urban society develop a cultural system based on poverty.

1960s As part of the "Great Society" movement, the United States government funds a number of extensive research programs regarding the increasing problem of estrangement between the public and the police.

1960s American crime television shows such as *The Andy Griffith Show* often depict police officers in the community and portray officers as friendly and helpful.

1960s The United States Supreme Court under Chief Justice Earl Warren develops the law regarding due process, a previously neglected area of criminal justice.

1960s Women are first allowed to attend meetings of the American Society of Criminology. By 2000, one-third of its membership is female.

1960 The United States Supreme Court in *Elkins v. United States* prohibits the introduction of illegally seized evidence in federal prosecutions, regardless of whether the illegality was committed by state or federal agents.

1960 The United States Supreme Court in *Dusky v. United States* establishes the definition of competency to stand trial.

1961 The United States Supreme Court in *Mapp v. Ohio* extends the exclusionary rule concerning the use of illegally obtained evidence to the states. The Court establishes the basic parameters of illegal search and seizure.

1961 The Vera Institute of Justice in New York City establishes the first bail reform project that emphasizes the use of non-monetary release criteria. The Manhattan Bail Project's success sparks nearly 200 similar programs in cities across the country.

1961 Attorney General Robert Kennedy recommends creating halfway houses with federal funds, especially grants from the Law Enforcement Assistance Administration and the Office of Economic Opportunity.

1961 ◆ The United States Supreme Court in *Culombe v. Connecticut* uses a "totality of circumstances" test to insure a voluntary confession.

1961 ◆ The first U.S. aircraft is hijacked on May 1 when Puerto Rican–born Antuilo Ramierez Ortiz forces a National Airlines plane to fly to Havana, Cuba, where he is granted asylum.

1962 ◆ The United States Supreme Court in *Manual Enterprises v. Day* decides that the new obscenity standard requires sexual material to be both "patently offensive" and absent any significant value.

1962 ◆ The American Law Institute adopts the Model Penal Code, which permits a substantial impairment of a person's mental faculties as sufficient to meet the test of insanity rather than a showing of total incapacity.

1962 ◆ The Indonesian police are formally militarized and placed under the authority of the armed forces.

1962 ◆ Frank Morris, John Anglin, and Clarence Anglin engineer one of the most famous escape attempts in prison history from Alcatraz. The three men are believed to have drowned.

1962 ◆ The U.S. District Court for the District of Columbia in *Fulwood v. Clemmer* rules that correctional officials must recognize the Muslim faith as a legitimate religion and not restrict those inmates who wish to hold services.

1962 ◆ The United States Supreme Court in *Baker v. Carr* announces the "one person, one vote" doctrine to mandate reapportioning electoral districts.

1963 ◆ The Academy of Criminal Justice Sciences is founded. Originally designed for police educators, by 2001 it is the largest criminal justice association in the United States.

1963 ◆ Alcatraz is closed as a federal maximum security facility and is replaced by a new facility in Marion, Illinois.

1963 ◆ The United States Supreme Court, in the landmark case of *Gideon v. Wainwright*, decides that indigent defendants are constitutionally entitled to free legal counsel.

1963 ◆ U.S. President John F. Kennedy is assassinated on November 22 by Lee Harvey Oswald in Dallas, Texas. Oswald is shot and killed two days later by Jack Ruby while being taken from prison.

1963 ◆ The Academy of Criminal Justice Sciences is founded.

1963 ◆ The Equal Pay Act makes wage discrimination based on sex illegal.

1963 ◆ *Outsiders: Studies in the Sociology of Deviance,* by Howard S. Becker, is published. It becomes an important statement on the definitions and meanings of deviance.

1964 ◆ American legal scholar Herbert L. Packer publishes his discussion of the crime control model and the due process model as two interrelated value systems that drive the operation of the criminal process.

1964 ◆ The Civil Rights Act is passed to protect individual employees from discrimination based on race, sex, religion, and ethnicity. Title VII of the Act prohibits "disparate treatment."

1964 ◆ Under the Criminal Justice Act in the federal court system, indigent representation is provided by federal defender organizations or by panel attorneys, who are private attorneys appointed on a case-by-case basis.

1964 ◆ The first electronic monitoring system is used to monitor the location of mental patients, parolees, and volunteers in Boston, Massachusetts.

1964 ◆ The United States Supreme Court in *Malloy v. Hogan* establishes that the Fifth Amendment's self-incrimination clause applies to the states as well as to the federal government.

1964 ◆ The American Law Institute (ALI) develops the new Model Penal Code that offers a tempered view on insanity.

1964 ◆ *Report of the President's Commission on the Assassination of President Kennedy*, by the Warren Commission, is published. It fails to resolve questions about a conspiracy to kill Kennedy, and, in fact, leads to even more conspiracy theories about his assassination.

1965 ◆ The formalized practice of diversion as an acceptable activity of the justice system originates in Genesee County, Michigan.

1965 ◆ The United States Supreme Court holds in *Estes v. Texas* that the right to a public trial belongs to the defendant alone and not to the media.

1965 ◆ Tucker State Farm officials are restricted from using corporal punishment in *Talley v. Stephens* when Federal Judge J. Smith Henley requires that adequate safeguards be established for the convicts.

1965 ◆ Congress passes the Federal Prisoner Rehabilitation Act, which provides work release, furloughs, and community treatment centers for federal minimum-security prisoners.

1965 ◆ The Watts Riot in Los Angeles reveals that citizens of the Watts area are suffering from unemployment, poor housing, inadequate transportation, and poor medical and social services. By the end of the riot, 4,000 people are arrested, 34 killed, and hundreds injured.

1965 ◆ While in prison, Malcolm X writes *The Autobiography of Malcolm X* (with Alex Haley). It becomes the best-known example of prisoner literature of the 1960s and 1970s in which African American prisoners react to oppression while in prison.

1966 ◆ Arkansas Governor Orval Faubus orders an investigation into allegations of extortion, misuse of state property, and inmate drunkenness at penal institutions.

1966 ◆ The United States Supreme Court in *Pate v. Robinson* holds that where there exists a "bona fide doubt" as to the defendant's present sanity, a hearing must be held to prevent infringement upon the defendant's constitutional right to comprehend and assist in his or her own defense.

1966 ◆ Robert Burgess and Ronald Akers propose integrating principles of behavioral learning theory into differential association theory; the result is what they call "differential association-reinforcement theory."

1966 ◆ The United States Supreme Court decision in *Miranda v. Arizona* establishes specific procedural guidelines for the police to follow when informing criminal suspects of their Constitutional rights, after taking individuals into custody and before interrogating them. The procedures have come to simply be called Miranda warnings.

1966 ◆ The United States Supreme Court in *Kent v. U.S.* extends limited due process guarantees to juveniles.

1966 ◆ In Canada's House of Commons, the government introduces and passes Bill C-168, which limits capital murder to the killing of on-duty police officers and prison guards.

1966 — In New York City, the Civilian Complaint Review Board is established. It survives only four months but receives 422 complaints in that period.

1966 — *In Cold Blood: A True Account of a Multiple Murder and Its Consequences*, by Truman Capote, is published. The first true-crime book that is acclaimed as a literary genre, it uses narrative techniques to tell the story of a murder case in Kansas.

1966 — The United Nations International Covenant on Civil and Political Rights is adopted by the General Assembly. It is entered into force in 1976.

1967 — The U.S. Department of Labor begins to fund pretrial diversion programs for offenders.

1967 — *The Subculture of Violence: Towards an Integrated Theory in Criminology*, by Marvin E. Wolfgang and Franco Ferracuti, is published. The subculture of violence theory becomes both influential and controversial in criminology.

1967 — An influential report by the President's Commission on Law Enforcement and Administration of Justice documents the widespread use of plea bargaining and recommends formal recognition of its use.

1967 — Congress passes the Wholesome Meat Act, effectively ensuring that all meat and associated products meet federal regulatory standards for safety.

1967 — In the Road Safety Act, the United Kingdom prohibits driving with a blood-alcohol level of .08 percent.

1967 — Detroit experiences a massive race riot when police raid five drinking and gambling establishments. Eighty-two African Americans are arrested during the raids. Angry citizens attack police cars with rocks, smash windows, and loot businesses.

1968 — The Omnibus Crime Control and Safe Streets Act and the Gun Control Act are passed, overhauling federal firearms legislation. These laws also give federal jurisdiction for criminal use of explosives to the Bureau of Alcohol, Tobacco and Firearms.

1968 — The Law Enforcement Assistance Administration (LEAA) is created as the division of the United States Department of Justice responsible for providing funding assistance to law enforcement agencies.

1968 — The National Institute of Justice is created as the research and development branch of the United States Department of Justice.

1968 — The United States Supreme Court in *Duncan v. Louisiana* rules that the right to a trial by jury is a fundamental right that is also binding on state court systems.

1968 — The American Psychology–Law Society (AP–LS) is founded to humanize the law through the values and insights of psychology.

1968 — The Indianapolis Police Department becomes the first police force in the United States to assign women to full-time field patrol.

1968 — Civil rights leader Martin Luther King, Jr. is assassinated in Memphis, Tennessee, by James Earl Ray.

1969 — The United States Supreme Court in *Chimel v. California* establishes a guiding definition for allowing the police to search the area immediately within the suspect's control, once an arrest has been made.

1969 ◆ Harvard students riot at University Hall, protesting the presence of the Reserve Officers Training Corps (ROTC) on campus.

1969 ◆ The German Criminal Code introduces a number of sociotherapeutic prisons or prison units (*Sozialtherapeutische Anstalten*) into the prison systems.

1969 ◆ John Bowlby publishes the first of his attachment trilogy, *Attachment*, followed in 1973 by *Separation*, and in 1980 by *Loss*. In these books, he rejects the psychoanalytic notion that children's emotional problems are the result of their internal conflicts.

1969 ◆ The United States Supreme Court in *Boykin v. Alabama* reverses the conviction of a man who had received five death sentences after pleading guilty to five counts of robbery because the trial judge had not ensured that the guilty pleas were voluntary.

1969 ◆ The American Academy of Psychiatry and the Law (AAPL) is established for psychiatrists who dedicate a significant portion of their professional activities to forensic psychiatry.

1969 ◆ The Security Industry Association is founded.

1969 ◆ In August, seven people are brutally slain in the Tate-LaBianca killings in southern California. Charles Manson, the leader of a local cult, and several Manson "family" members are charged, convicted, and sentenced to life in prison. Mason remains a cult figure while in prison and is routinely denied parole.

1970s ◆ Community-based mediation initiatives give rise to alternative dispute resolution, designed to find better, more efficient, and less expensive alternatives to traditional litigation.

1970s ◆ American television crime shows emphasize law and order, perhaps reflecting a public desire for stability in a time of social change. The law and order emphasis continues in the 1980s.

1970s ◆ Following the civil rights and feminist movements, female and African American detectives appear more often in crime fiction.

1970 ◆ The Police Foundation is founded (as the Police Development Fund).

1970 ◆ The Bank Secrecy Act, the first piece of American legislation to identify cash movements, is enacted.

1970 ◆ The Narcotic Control Act in Canada is designed to control the flow of narcotics by making narcotic offenses a federal crime.

1970 ◆ The United States Supreme Court in *Brady v. United States* rules that is acceptable to reward with reduced penalties those defendants who plead guilty.

1970 ◆ The United States Supreme Court in *Carolina v. Alford* rules that defendants may plead guilty without admitting culpability, meaning they can plea bargain even when they feel they are factually innocent.

1970 ◆ Congress, with strong support from the Justice Department, enacts the District of Columbia Court Reform Act, which contains the nation's first preventive detention statute.

1970 ◆ The United States Marshals Service begins operating a federal witness-protection program.

1971 ◆ Howard Teten, who had developed a technique that would eventually evolve into criminal profiling, completed the first profile by the FBI to be provided to a local law enforcement agency.

1971 ◆ The Bail Reform Act in Canada is enacted to prevent unnecessary detention of accused persons.

1971 ◆ The first recognized modern-day women's shelter, Chiswick's Women's Aid, opens in England.

1971 ◆ A prisoner uprising at the Attica Correctional Facility in New York claims the lives of eleven prison employees and twenty-nine inmates.

1971 ◆ The American War on Drugs is officially declared during President Nixon's term to communicate the government's zero tolerance for illegal drugs.

1971 ◆ In the United Kingdom, the Misuse of Drugs Act distinguishes between the possession and trafficking of illegal drugs and establishes a range of penalties for the offenses proscribed.

1971 ◆ The United States Supreme Court in *Santobello v. New York* rules that defendants are entitled to legal remedy if prosecutors break conditions specified in plea bargains.

1972 ◆ The new FBI Academy in Quantico opens, and a new division of the FBI is created and headquartered at Quantico. Jack Kirsch heads this new department, the Behavioral Sciences Unit.

1972 ◆ Title IX of the Education Amendments prohibits discrimination in education benefits based on race, religion, sex, or ethnicity.

1972 ◆ The first hotline for battered women is started by Women's Advocates in St. Paul, Minnesota.

1972 ◆ The National Crime Victimization Survey (NCVS) begins the official collection of detailed information about certain criminal offenses, both attempted and completed, that concern the general public and law enforcement. The NCVS is administered by the Bureau of Justice Statistics, an agency of the U.S. Department of Justice.

1972 ◆ The United States Supreme Court in *Morrissey v. Brewer* sets parole violation procedures.

1972 ◆ The United States Supreme Court in *Furman v. Georgia* declares that the arbitrary way the death penalty is being used violates the Eighth Amendment and constitutes cruel and unusual punishment.

1972 ◆ Alcatraz is turned over to the National Park Service as part of the Golden Gate National Recreation Area. It opens to the public the following year and becomes a popular tourist destination.

1972 ◆ British criminologist Stanley Cohen publishes his book *Folk Devils and Moral Panics.*

1972 ◆ The United States Supreme Court in *Papachristou v. City of Jacksonville* voids that city's vagrancy ordinance.

1972 ◆ Oscar Newman, an architect and university professor, publishes a seminal study of crime in New York City's high-rise public housing, titled *Defensible Space.*

1972 ◆ The United States Supreme Court in *Cruz v. Beto* rules that it is discriminatory and a violation of the Constitution to deny a Buddhist prisoner the right to practice his or her faith in a comparable way to members of the major religious denominations.

1972 ◆ The United States Supreme Court in *Barker v. Wingo* adopts a balancing test in determining whether the defendant's speedy trial rights have been violated.

1972 ◆ The Criminal Justice Act of 1972 and the Powers of Criminal Courts Act establish the legal origins of community service in the United States. Both make it possible for judges to invoke creative individualized penalties mandating labor performed in the community.

1972 ◆ "Bloody Friday" occurs in Northern Ireland on July 21 when an Irish Republican Army (IRA) bomb attack kill eleven people and injures 130 in Belfast.

1972 ◆ On September 5, eight Palestinian "Black September" terrorists seize eleven Israeli athletes in the Olympic Village in Munich, West Germany. Nine of the hostages and five terrorists are killed when German troops storm the plane.

1972 ◆ The Convention on the Prohibition of the Development, Production and Stockpiling of Bacteriological (Biological) and Toxin Weapons and on Their Destruction is signed by the United States, Russia, and Great Britain.

1972 ◆ The content of American television crime dramas becomes more violent, a trend that continues for the next three decades.

1973 ◆ The Knapp Commission Report on Police Corruption is published and reveals widespread corruption in the New York City police department.

1973 ◆ The United States Supreme Court in *Miller v. California* decides that obscenity is now to be defined not using a national standard but on the basis of local community standards.

1973 ◆ Ronald Akers introduces the social learning theory of deviance in his book *Deviant Behavior: A Social Learning Approach.*

1973 ◆ *The Gulag Archipelago,* by Aleksandr Solzhenitsyn, formerly a political prisoner on Solovetsky Island in Siberian Russia, is published.

1973 ◆ The United States Supreme Court in *United States v. Robinson* establishes the right of police to automatically search an arrested person regardless of the offense, immediately following a lawful arrest.

1973 ◆ The United States Supreme Court in *Roe v. Wade* rules that the state cannot interfere with a woman's decision to have an abortion unless it has a compelling reason to do so.

1973 ◆ The first *Sourcebook of Criminal Justice Statistics* is published, a reference tool that provides comprehensive data on crime and criminal justice-related issues in the United States.

1973 ◆ The American Society of Crime Laboratory Directors begins to form when thirty crime laboratory directors from across the United States are brought together by FBI director Clarence Kelly. The society is incorporated in 1976 with Briggs White, the director of the FBI Laboratory, as the first chairman.

1973 ◆ The Rehabilitation Act, later amended in 1980, prohibits discrimination against handicapped individuals by the federal government, federal contractors, and recipients of federal aid.

1973 ◆ Governor Nelson Rockefeller of New York ushers in mandatory minimum sentences, presenting them as vital tools in the war against drugs. These statutes specify a certain amount of time, usually of considerable length, that an offender must serve.

1973 ◆ The lockdown, a disciplinary and protective measure taken by the prison administration in which all the inmates are confined to their cells twenty-four hours a day and leave only for meals, is first used at San Quentin.

1974 ◆ *Obedience to Authority,* by Stanley Milgram, is published. It reports the results of psychological research suggesting that individuals will cause serious harm to others under authoritarian conditions.

1974 ◆ The U.S. Congress passes the Juvenile Justice and Delinquency Prevention Act (JJDPA).

1974 ◆ The American Society of Crime Laboratory Directors is founded.

1974 ◆ Congress enacts the Federal Speedy Trial Act, imposing time limits for criminal prosecutions in federal courts.

1974 ◆ On August 8, Richard M. Nixon resigns as president of the United States rather than face impeachment for his role in the cover-up in the Watergate scandal. He is replaced by Gerald Ford, who had been appointed vice president to replace Spiro Agnew. Agnew had resigned in the face of corruption charges dating to when he was governor of Maryland. Nixon escapes criminal prosecution when Ford issues him a blanket pardon.

1974 ◆ The United States Supreme Court in *Wolff v. McDonnell* decides that before a prisoner can be deprived of good time (time taken off the end of a sentence for good behavior) because of alleged rule violations, there must be some due process.

1975 ◆ The National Organization for Victim Assistance (NOVA) is founded to help unify the diverse energies of what had become the victim movement.

1975 ◆ Former U.S. Attorney General John Newton Mitchell is convicted of perjury, obstruction of justice, and conspiracy for his role in the Watergate scandal. He serves nineteen months in prison and is the only attorney general in U.S. history to serve time in prison.

1975 ◆ Metropolitan Correctional Centers, based on the new generation jail model, are opened in New York City, Chicago, and San Diego.

1975 ◆ Robert Heck develops the Patrol Emphasis Program, which encourages agencies to use crime analysis information, together with other strategies, to manage calls-for-service and increase the quality of the preliminary investigation process.

1975–1979 ◆ An estimated two million people die in Cambodia from starvation, overwork, and executions at the direction of Khmer Rouge leader Pol Pot, who seeks to create a Communist farming society.

1976 ◆ The federal Resource Conservation and Recovery Act (RCRA) makes it a crime to indiscriminately dispose of wastes that pose significant risks for human health and for the general environment.

1976 ◆ The first major judicial decision concerning passive euthanasia in the United States is decided in the case of Karen Quinlan, who is diagnosed as brain dead following an overdose of drugs. Quinlan is taken off artificial life support but lives for some time, confounding both supporters and critics of euthanasia.

1976 ◆ The House of Commons in Canada passes Bill C-84 on a free vote, abolishing capital punishment from the Canadian Criminal Code and replacing it with a mandatory life sentence without possibility of parole for twenty-five years for all first-degree murders.

1976 ◆ The Juvenile Awareness Project, which later evolves into Scared Straight Programs, begins at New Jersey's Rahway State Prison to make juveniles aware of what being in prison is like.

1976 ◆ The U.S. Supreme Court in *Meachum v. Fano* holds that a prisoner has no due process rights before being transferred to a harsher prison.

1977 ◆ U.S. Congress passes the Foreign Corrupt Practices Act, which prohibits the payment of bribes in order to obtain business contracts.

1977 ◆ The Parole Act is amended to allow Canadian provinces to establish their own parole boards for provincial inmates.

1977 ◆ Oklahoma adopts the first statute authorizing execution by lethal injection in 1977, and the first such execution takes place in Texas in 1982. At the start of the twenty-first century, lethal injection is the primary or exclusive method of execution in almost all of the states and under federal law.

1977 ◆ Oregon becomes the first state to pass a law mandating arrest when a law officer has probable cause to believe that a misdemeanor domestic violence crime has been committed.

1977 ◆ A federal court rules in *Theriault v. Carlson* that the First Amendment does not protect so-called religions that are obvious shams, that tend to mock established institutions, and whose members lack religious sincerity. This is one of the first cases to shift the tide away from decisions in favor of inmates' religious rights.

1977 ◆ The U.S. government emulates German and British examples by developing the Delta Force as a division capable of operating as a counterterrorist component.

1977 ◆ Florida begins a yearlong experiment, allowing cameras in the courtroom without the consent of the parties if the judge agreed to allow them.

1977 ◆ California is the first state to return to the use of determinate sentencing with passage of the Determinate Sentencing Law.

1978 ◆ The American Correctional Association begins offering a national accreditation program for adult and juvenile corrections, through the Commission on Accreditation for Corrections.

1978 ◆ In New York, Remove Intoxicated Drivers (RID) is founded as a large-scale nationwide non-profit organization actively campaigning against drunk driving.

1978 ◆ The United States Supreme Court in *Woodson v. North Carolina* rejects a mandatory death sentence law for convictions of first-degree murder.

1978 ◆ The National Coalition Against Domestic Violence (NCADV) is founded with the goal of becoming the voice of the battered women's movement in America.

1978 ◆ The Pregnancy Discrimination Act forbids discrimination in employment based on the basis of pregnancy, childbirth, and related conditions.

1978 ◆ The Royal Commission on Criminal Procedure is set up under Sir Cyril Philips in Great Britain.

1978 ◆ The United States Supreme Court in *Bellew v. Georgia* rules that six is the lower limit for a jury.

1978 ◆ Reverend Jim Jones and his 900 followers commit mass suicide in Guyana. The event brings much media and public attention to religious cults around the world.

1978 ◆ The United States Supreme Court rules in *Bordenkircher v. Hayes* that prosccutors may threaten to bring additional charges against defendants who refuse to bargain as long as those charges are valid.

1978 ◆ The United Kingdom outlaws terrorism.

1978 ◆ The Foreign Intelligence Surveillance Act is passed to control suspected terrorist activity in the United States. The act enlarges the surveillance authority of the government and is further expanded in 1994.

1979 ◆ In China, the National People's Congress (NPC) enacts the first Criminal Code and Criminal Procedure Code in the nation's history. Most of the laws and decrees promulgated since 1949 remain in force. In 1997, the Criminal Code is amended.

1979 ◆ Dan White murders San Francisco Mayor George Moscone and councilman and gay activist Harvey Milk. His defense, later labeled the "Twinkie defense," is that he stopped eating normally and went on a junk food diet that included Coca-Cola, chocolate candy, and Twinkies.

1979 ◆ The United States Supreme Court in *Gannett Co. v. DePasquale* affirms the proposition that the Sixth Amendment right to a public trial belongs to the criminal defendant alone and not to the press or the public.

1979 ◆ Sweden becomes the first country to prohibit corporal punishment in all sectors of society, including in the home and in schools.

1979 ◆ The United States Supreme Court in *Bell v. Wolfish* rules that pretrial detainees held in jails, who are still legally "innocent," have no more rights than those convicted and that only those rights "consistent with their confinement" will be recognized.

1980s ◆ In the biggest series of white-collar crimes in American history, the "Great Savings and Loan Scandal" reflects increased criminal opportunity resulting from an economic crises and deregulation.

1980s ◆ Foot patrols return to favor in American cities under the label of community policing.

1980 ◆ The U.S. Supreme Court in *U.S. v. Mendenhall* establishes the "free to leave" test for determining if a person has been arrested.

1980 ◆ Wisconsin becomes the first state to enact a "crime victims' bill of rights."

1980 ◆ A race riot occurs in Miami, Florida, in response to the acquittal by an all-white jury of four white police officers charged with beating a black businessman to death.

1980 ◆ Mothers Against Drunk Driving (MADD) is founded by the mother of a young woman killed by a repeat drunk driver who received lenient treatment in the court system.

1981 ◆ A new Code of Criminal Procedure in Indonesia (replacing the colonial code of 1848) attempts to improve the rights of detainees by imposing time limits to detention and forbidding the use of torture to extract confessions.

1981 ◆ John Hinckley shoots President Ronald Reagan in a scenario attributed to his twenty-six viewings of the 1976 movie *Taxi Driver*. Hinckley successfully uses the substantial capacity test as his defense at his trial for the attempted assassination. Hinckley is found not guilty by reason of insanity.

1981 ◆ The United States Supreme Court in *Chandler v. Florida* holds that there is no absolute ban on cameras in the courtroom and that the defendant must show actual adverse impact on the trial in order to win.

1981 ◆ The American Jail Association is founded.

1981 ◆ Peter Barnett, Ed Blake, and Robert Ogle, Jr. each present papers at the American Academy of Forensic Sciences annual meeting that criticize the FBI crime lab's practices. They are charged with misrepresenting the lab and its practices but are subsequently cleared.

1981 ◆ President Anwar Sadat of Egypt is assassinated on October 6 by soldiers who are secretly members of the Takfir Wal-Hajira sect.

1982 ◆ The Missing Children's Act authorizes the FBI's National Crime Information Center to take missing children reports.

1982 ◆ The Canadian Charter of Rights and Freedoms becomes Part I of the Constitution Act. For the first time in Canada, the Constitution includes guarantees of certain rights and freedoms, which, except with certain limitations, have to be observed by all who make or administer the law.

1982 ◆ James Q. Wilson and George L. Kelling popularize the broken windows theory of crime control in an article in the *Atlantic Monthly*.

1982 ◆ Congress enacts the Pretrial Service Act mandating the establishment of pretrial services programs in each federal judicial district.

1982 ◆ Congress passes the Federal Victim and Witness Protection Act in order to provide model legislation for the states to improve and safeguard the victims' role in the criminal justice system without encroaching upon the constitutional rights of the defendant.

1982 ◆ California voters approve Proposition Eight, which includes a "victims' bill of rights."

1982 ◆ The Barbados-based Regional Security System (RSS) is formed as a Caribbean regional alliance to combat drug trafficking.

1982 ◆ President Ronald Reagan appoints a Presidential Commission on Drunk Driving to systematically survey state laws and local programs addressing the problem of drinking and driving.

1983 ◆ The first boot camp programs for adults are implemented in Georgia and Oklahoma. Boot camp programs for juveniles do not become popular until the 1990s.

1983 ◆ The Convention on Cultural Property Implementation Act passes, allowing the U.S. government to impose import restrictions on certain classes of archaeological or ethnographic material.

1983 ◆ The stabbing deaths of officers at a federal penitentiary in Marion, Illinois, compels administrators and critics to argue the need for a facility specifically designed to hold violent, disruptive inmates. This moment is widely regarded as the birth of supermax prisons.

1984 ◆ The federal Bail Reform Act, designed to reduce pretrial crime, allows bailees to be detained and presented to federal marshals who ensure that they appear in court.

1984 ◆ The United States Supreme Court holds in *Massachusetts v. Sheppard* that evidence obtained by the police acting in good faith on a search warrant issued by a neutral and detached magistrate, which is ultimately found to be invalid, may nonetheless be admitted at trial.

1984 ◆ The United States Supreme Court in *Strickland v. Washington* holds that a defendant's right to counsel is violated if the trial attorney's performance is deficient and that deficiency prejudices the defendant.

1984 ◆ The United States Supreme Court in *Nix v. Williams* creates an "inevitable discovery" exception to the *Miranda* requirements. Under *Nix*, a confession obtained in violation of *Miranda* is still admissible in a criminal prosecution if it appears that evidence from the confession would ultimately have been discovered as police continued to investigate the case.

1984 ◆ Congress passes the Insanity Defense Reform Act, which requires defendants to plead insanity as an affirmative defense and to prove the defense with a standard of clear and convincing evidence.

1984 ◆ The Federal Uniform Drinking Act provides federal highway funds only to states that raise their drinking age to twenty-one.

1984 ◆ The Missing Children's Assistance Act leads to establishment of the federally supported National Center for Missing and Exploited Children (NCMEC).

1984 ◆ President Ronald Reagan announces the formation of the National Center for the Analysis of Violent Crime (NCAVC). Reagan identifies the primary mission of this new center as the identification and tracking of serial killers.

1984 ◆ The Netherlands institutes the first needle exchange program in Amsterdam in an attempt to stem the rising number of hepatitis cases related to injection drug use.

1984 ◆ The Sentencing Reform Act creates the United States Sentencing Commission, abolishes federal parole, and narrows judicial discretion at sentencing through the use of standardized sentencing ranges.

1984 ◆ Washington State enacts the first truth-in-sentencing law, and the federal government passes the Comprehensive Crime Control Act. These drastically restrict or eliminate parole and good-time credits.

1984 ◆ The federal Family Violence Prevention and Services Act sets aside significant resources for shelters.

1984 ◆ The Victim of Crimes Act (VOCA) secures federal commitment to victim assistance programs by establishing the first national Crime Victims Fund for state and local victim service programs.

1984 ◆ The Cable Communications Policy Act regulates various aspects of the cable television industry and includes provisions that protect the privacy of individual cable subscribers' records.

1984 ◆ The Computer Fraud and Abuse Act is passed, protecting a broad range of computers that facilitate interstate and international commerce and communications.

1984 ◆ On June 5, Sikh separatists in India seize the Golden Temple in Amritsar, India. One hundred people die when Indian security forces retake the Sikh holy shrine. On October 31, Indian Prime Minister Indira Gandhi is assassinated by bodyguards.

1984 ◆ The United Nations Convention against Torture and Other Cruel, Inhuman or Degrading Treatment or Punishment is adopted by the General Assembly. It is entered into force in 1987.

1985 ◆ The Australian government officially implements harm reduction policies with the introduction of its National Campaign against Drug Use, largely in response to the AIDS epidemic.

1985 ◆ The United States Supreme Court in *Tennessee v. Garner* establishes the minimum legal standard that deadly force cannot be used against a non-dangerous fleeing felon.

1985 ◆ The Young Offenders Act passes in Canada, raising the age of minimum criminal responsibility to twelve years old for all provinces and territories. It also sets the age of adult criminal culpability at eighteen years old across the country.

1985 ◆ The Controlled Drugs (Penalties Act) in the United Kingdom increases the maximum sentence for trafficking to life imprisonment.

1985 ◆ In Portland, Oregon, Penny E. Harrington becomes the first woman chief of police of a major city in the United States.

1986 ◆ President Ronald Reagan declares a "War on Drugs," proposing huge increases in federal expenditures devoted to the drug problem.

1986 ◆ The Immigration Reform and Control Act prohibits discrimination against qualified aliens as well as discrimination based on national origin.

1986 ◆ The Money Laundering Control Act, part of the Anti-Drug Abuse Act, makes money laundering a federal crime.

1986 ◆ The Firearms Owner's Protection Act amends the Gun Control Act of 1968 to permit the interstate sale of rifles and shotguns provided they are unloaded and not readily accessible.

1986 ◆ The United States Supreme Court in *Batson v. Kentucky* rules that prosecutors can no longer exclude blacks from juries simply because of the color of their skin.

1986 ◆ Congress enacts the Electronic Communications Privacy Act in an effort to strike a workable balance among the privacy interests of telecommunications users, the business interests of service providers, and the legitimate needs of government investigators.

1986 ◆ Jeanne Clery is murdered while she sleeps in her dormitory room at Lehigh University. Her death sparks a grassroots effort by her parents, eventually resulting in federal legislation forcing colleges and universities to publicly report criminal incidents occurring on their campuses.

1986 ◆ William Rehnquist becomes chief justice of the U.S. Supreme Court when Warren Burger retires. President Reagan's crime control agenda is supported by the Court's commitment to strengthening the criminal justice system.

1986 ◆ The Career Criminals Amendment Act amends the federal criminal code to provide increased criminal penalties for any person who transports firearms or ammunition in interstate or foreign commerce if such person has multiple convictions for serious drug offenses and/or violent felonies.

1987 ◆ British Society of Criminology meets for the first time in the United Kingdom.

1987 ◆ East Germany (German Democratic Republic–GDR) abolishes the death penalty.

1987 ◆ The United Nations Convention against Torture and Other Cruel, Inhuman or Degrading Treatment or Punishment (CAT) is entered into force on June 27.

1987 ◆ The United States Supreme Court in *McCleskey v. Kemp* considers statistical data that indicates that the race of the defendant and the race of the victim are factors that influence whether the death sentence is given.

1987 ◆ The National Institute of Justice (NIJ) establishes the Drug Use Forecasting (DUF) program to measure trends in illicit drug use in ten geographically diverse, predominantly large American cities (or counties).

1987 ◆ The United States Supreme Court in *Turner v. Safley* establishes a "balancing test" to decide between the legitimate interests of inmates and the correctional facility.

1987 ◆ The United States Supreme Court in *O'Lone v. Estate of Shabazz* rules that depriving an inmate of attending a religious service for "legitimate penological interests" is not in violation of the First Amendment.

1987 ◆ The first DNA dragnet, chronicled in Joseph Wambaugh's book *The Blooding*, helps police solve two murders in Leicester, England.

1988 ◆ A documentary by Errol Morris titled *The Thin Blue Line* elicits additional information by real players in the case of *Adams v. Texas,* resulting in a virtual confession by the person actually responsible for the murder for which Randall Adams was convicted. The film becomes the basis for Adams's appeal from death row and eventually results in his complete exoneration.

1989 ◆ The United States Supreme Court in *Stanford v. Kentucky* holds that the Eighth Amendment is not violated when the death sentence is given to individuals who were sixteen or older when they committed their offense.

1989 ◆ The United States Supreme Court in *Penry v. Lynaugh* declines to hold that the execution of a mentally retarded individual is a violation of the Eighth Amendment to the United States Constitution.

1989 ◆ The United States Supreme Court in *Duckworth v. Eagan* asserts that it is not necessary for police to read Miranda warnings in the same words used in the *Miranda* decision itself.

1990s ◆ American television crime dramas focus heavily on the day-to-day nature of police and legal work and on the lives of police officers. Shows such as *Law & Order* are touted as being more realistic than early television crime genres.

1990 ◆ Congress passes the Student Right to Know and Campus Security Act. The legislation forces colleges and universities receiving federal financial aid to publicly report criminal incidents that occur on their campuses. It is later amended and renamed the Jeanne Clery Disclosure of Campus Security Policy and Campus Crime Statistics Act (1998).

1990 ◆ The Hate Crime Statistics Act is passed by Congress, mandating that a database of crimes motivated by religion, ethnic, racial, or sexual orientation be collected.

1990 ◆ Famous works by Vermeer and Rembrandt are stolen from the Isabella Stewart Gardiner Museum in Boston.

1990 ◆ California passes the nation's first antistalking law, and other states quickly follow suit.

1990 ◆ The Victims' Rights and Restitution Act incorporates a bill of rights for federal crime victims and codifies services that Congress determined should be available to victims of crime.

1990 ◆ The Americans with Disabilities Act prohibits discrimination against handicapped individuals by all state and local governments.

1990 ◆ The United Nations convention on Basic Principles for the Treatment of Prisoners is approved by the General Assembly.

1991 ◆ Four white Los Angeles police offices are videotaped beating Rodney King, a black motorist. The incident sets off a national outcry about police brutality toward blacks and other minorities.

1991 ◆ The United States Supreme Court rules in *Wilson v. Seiter* that an individual inmate's conditions should meet "standards of decency."

1991 ◆ The United States Supreme Court rules in *Groves v. U.S.* that a police officer cannot be allowed to risk the lives of innocent people when pursuing an offender for a minor infraction.

1991 ◆ The American Psychology–Law Society Committee on Specialty Guidelines for Forensic Psychologists votes to approve a broad definition of forensic psychology, encompassing expertise in both civil and criminal domains of professional practice and research.

1991 ◆ The United States Supreme Court in *Payne v. Tennessee* achieves a measure of headway in the promotion of victims' rights by permitting the use of "victim impact" evidence.

1992 ◆ The acquittal of the Los Angeles police officers accused of beating Rodney King leads to prolonged rioting in the city. Nearly sixty people are killed, more than 2,300 injured, more than 6,000 arrested, and more than a half billion dollars worth of destruction occurs before the National Guard and police take back control of the streets after days of looting and destruction.

1992 ◆ On a remote ridge in northern Idaho, a weeklong standoff between white supremacist Randy Weaver and federal agents ends in a shootout in which an FBI sniper shoots and kills Weaver's wife, Vicky. The Ruby Ridge confrontation began a week earlier when federal marshals tried to arrest Weaver for failing to appear in court on weapons charges. At that time, a gun battle erupted between marshals and Weaver's fourteen-year-old son, resulting in the deaths of Weaver's son and a marshal.

1992 ◆ The United Nations Security Council establishes an ad hoc tribunal, which becomes the International Criminal Tribunal for the Former Yugoslavia (ICTFY). It has jurisdiction over crimes that are unquestionably violations of customary international law.

1992 ◆ Canada's Corrections and Conditional Release Act sparks new interest in the operations and outcome of day parole, by redefining its purpose to be "preparation of offenders for full parole or statutory release."

1992 ◆ The Anti-Car Theft Act makes armed carjacking a federal offense under certain conditions such as causing the victim serious bodily harm or death, and taking a motor vehicle that has been transported, shipped, or received in interstate or foreign commerce from the person by force, violence, or intimidation.

1992 ◆ The United Nations adopts the Rome Convention as an international standard relating to piracy, in the wake of an attack on the *Achille Lauro*.

1992 ◆ Attorneys Barry Scheck and Peter Neufeld found the Innocence Project at the Benjamin N. Cardozo Law School at Yeshiva University in New York City. Relying on postconviction DNA testing and other evidence, the project works to reverse wrongful convictions of death row inmates and to pass legislation toward the same end.

1992 ◆ On April 10, former Panama leader Manuel Noriega is convicted in a U.S. court of drug trafficking, money laundering, and other crimes and sentenced to forty years in prison. He had been captured by U.S. troops in Panama and brought to the United States for trial. He is the only foreign head of state brought by U.S. forces to the United States and the only one tried in a U.S. court.

1993 ◆ The United States Supreme Court ruling in *Daubert v. Merrell Dow Pharmaceuticals* becomes the new precedent for admissibility of scientific evidence.

1993 ◆ The Family and Medical Leave Act protects employees of both genders by allowing twelve weeks of unpaid leave during a twelve-month employment period for the birth or placement of a child, the care of an immediate family member with a serious health condition, and/or the employee's own medical care for a serious health condition.

1993 ◆ ATF and FBI agents are involved in a fifty-one-day standoff with a group of Branch Davidians led by David Koresh at a compound in Waco, Texas. After tear gas is injected into the compound, over seventy occupants die from fires and self-inflicted gunshot wounds.

1993 ◆ The Criminal Justice Act (CJA) in Great Britain reduces bail and approves bail and probation hostels.

1993 ◆ The World Trade Center in New York City is damaged on February 26 by a car bomb planted by Islamic terrorists in an underground garage. The bomb kills six people and injures 1,000.

1994 ◆ A "three-strikes law" is enacted in California. This law provides that a repeat violent offender will served a minimum of twenty-five years and up to life after he or she has been convicted three times for a violent offense.

1994 ◆ The Brady Handgun Violence Protection Act (Brady Law) passes, requiring a mandatory five-day waiting period for handgun purchases.

1994 ◆ Congress passes the Violence Against Women Act, which is signed into law by President Clinton. The bill provides more than $1 billion in funding to assist shelters, train law enforcement personnel and judges, and support programs addressing crimes against women.

1994 ◆ Capital punishment is abolished in Italy under all circumstances.

1994 ◆ A convicted pedophile who rapes and kills seven-year-old Megan Kanka inspires "Megan's Law," which requires that communities be notified of sex offenders living in the neighborhood.

1994 ◆ Passage of the Violent Crime Control and Law Enforcement Act adds 100,000 new police officers to police departments across the United States over a six-year period and expands the number of federal capital offenses from two to fifty-eight. The crime bill also adopts a "three strikes and you're out" provision that imposes lengthy sentences for repeat offenders. In addition, the act also sets aside $4 billion in federal prison construction funds. To be eligible for these monies, called Truth in Sentencing Incentive Funds, states must guarantee that certain violent offenders will serve 85% of their sentences.

1994 ◆ The Administrative Maximum Security Penitentiary (ADX) in Florence, Colorado, becomes the first supermaximum security federal facility built solely for the consolidation of disruptive inmates in the Federal Bureau of Prisons.

1994 ◆ The Telemarketing Fraud Act passes, designed to shut down dishonest telemarketing schemes.

1994 ◆ In mass political violence in Rwanda, some 800,000 Tutsis are killed by Hutu soldiers.

1995 ◆ Timothy McVeigh kills 168 people and wounds hundreds more in the Oklahoma City bombing of the Alfred P. Murrah Federal Building.

1995 ◆ The 1994 film *Natural Born Killers* (based partially on the real-life crime spree of Charles Starkweather and Caril Fugate) is cited as the inspiration for two Oklahoma teens who embark on a deadly crime spree, traveling through two states, robbing and shooting innocent victims along the way.

1995 ◆ The televised trial of former football star O.J. Simpson is viewed by people around the world. Simpson is found not guilty of killing his former wife and her friend. The trial raises various issues about criminal justice in the United States, including the role of racism and public opinion, as well as jury competence. The case also demonstrates how crucial it is that a crime scene investigation be careful, accurate, and thorough (particularly in terms of forensic serology). Although blood found at the site of the two murders contained Simpson's DNA, the issues of contamination, mishandling, and reliability concerning genetic evidence resulted in a "not guilty" verdict in the criminal trial, but not in the following civil trial.

1995 ◆ The National Center for Women and Policing (NCWP) is established by the Feminist Majority Foundation.

1995 ◆ Nelson Mandela, the first president of the new South Africa, appoints the Truth and Reconciliation Commission (TRC) to investigate the crimes of apartheid.

1995 ◆ Several Caribbean countries sign a treaty commonly known as the Shiprider Agreement in which they agree to six counternarcotic measures: shipboarding, shiprider, pursuit, entry-to-investigate, overflight, and order-to-land.

1995 ◆ In Japan, the Aum Shinri Kyo cult launches a nerve gas attack in a Tokyo subway station, killing twelve people and wounding several thousand. Cult leader Shoko Asahara is arrested, convicted, and sentenced to life imprisonment.

1996 ◆ The Anti-Terrorist and Effective Death Penalty Act sharply limits prisoners' ability to file more than one habeas corpus petition, thereby streamlining the conviction and execution process. The act adds penalties for arson and other explosives violations. It gives the secretary of state the authority to designate foreign terrorist organizations and prohibit U.S. citizens and institutions from conducting business and providing funds to such organizations.

1996 ◆ Congress votes to stop funding the postconviction defender organizations that have played a vital role in representing death row inmates; similarly, lawmakers enact the Prison Litigation Reform Act that significantly curtails prisoners' rights.

1996 ◆ Theodore Kaczynski, the notorious "Unabomber," is arrested, ending the nation's longest, most expensive hunt for a serial killer. Kaczynski orchestrated sixteen Unabomber attacks between 1978 and 1995. In a plea bargain, he is sentenced to life imprisonment without the possibility of parole.

1996 ◆ The Church Arson Prevention Act further bolsters existing laws regarding church burning and desecration. It is enacted following a series of dozens of fires at rural black churches in the South.

1996 ◆ The National Institute of Justice establishes the Crime Mapping Resource Center and funds several research projects intended to advance the usefulness of computer-based crime analysis.

1996 ◆ The federal government passes the Interstate Stalking Punishment and Prevention Act.

1996 ◆ The United States Supreme Court in *Whren v. U.S.* validates the long-standing police practice commonly referred to as pretextual stops.

1996 ◆ Congress passes the Prisoner Litigation Reform Act, making it more difficult for prisoners to file suits challenging conditions in prison and limiting the ability of lower federal court judges to intervene in the management of prisons through injunctive relief.

1996 ◆ The Domestic Violence Offender Gun Ban prohibits anyone convicted of a misdemeanor domestic violence offense from owning a gun.

1996 ◆ The Antiterrorism and Effective Death Penalty Act is passed and gives the government increased authority to restrict entry to the United States and also increases the government's surveillance power.

1996 — The Special Rapporteur on Prisons and Conditions of Detention in Africa is appointed, after criminal justice reform became a focus of activity in several countries in sub-Saharan Africa.

1996 — At a seminar in Kampala, Uganda, representatives from forty African nations produce the Kampala Declaration, which sets out a broad reform agenda covering both prison conditions and the use of prison in Africa.

1997 — A Juvenile Justice Law is passed by Parliament in Indonesia and signed by President Soeharto.

1997 — The American Bar Association calls for a temporary halt to executions while states put in place policies to ensure fairness and to minimize the risk of executing the innocent.

1997 — The Drug Use Forecasting program evolves into the Arrestee Drug Abuse Monitoring (ADAM) program.

1997 — The National Institute of Justice establishes the Crime Mapping Research Center to promote the use of crime mapping in local police departments.

1997 — The Crime Sentences Act in Great Britain introduces for the first time, mandatory sentences for drug offending.

1997 — The FBI identifies thirteen STR (short tandem repeat) DNA loci that it deems appropriate for forensic testing.

1998 — Congress passes the Identity Theft and Assumption Deterrence Act, making identity theft a federal felony.

1997 — The FBI and ATF join together to form the formation of a National Integrated Ballistic Information Network, known as NIBIN.

1997 — The international terrorist and assassin Carlos (Ilich Ramirez Sanchez, known as "Carlos the Jackal") is convicted in France of murdering two French law enforcement agents in 1975 and sentenced to life in prison. His best-known achievement was kidnapping eighty-one OPEC oil ministers in Vienna in 1975 and extorting at least $5 million from Arab governments for their release.

1998 — The Digital Millennium Copyright Act protects video and computer game manufacturers against Web sites and Internet service providers that host sales of pirated software.

1998 — In order to guarantee safe access to the Internet by minors, the Children's Online Privacy Protection Act is passed. It bars Internet sites from collecting personally identifiable information from children under thirteen without parental consent.

1998 — The death penalty in Canada is abolished with the passage of legislation removing all references to capital punishment from the National Defence Act.

1998 — There are significant moves towards the creation of an International Criminal Court (ICC) at The Rome Conference, which ends with 122 countries voting for establishing the ICC, to be situated at The Hague.

1998 — Under the new Sex Offender Treatment Act in Germany, secure custody for sex offenders (Special Secure Units) is increased.

1999 — Two students, Dylan Klebold and Eric Harris, open fire on other students and staff at Columbine High School in Littleton, Colorado, killing thirteen and wounding twenty-six.

1999 ◆ Criticism of aggressive crime control measures increases when Amadou Diallo, an African immigrant, is killed in a barrage of forty-one bullets fired by New York City police who mistake him for a suspected armed rapist.

1999 ◆ In near-simultaneous attacks on U.S. embassies in Nairobi, Kenya, and Dar es Salaam, Tanzania, 224 people are killed. The terrorist network of Osama bin Laden is accused by the United States of masterminding the bombings.

1999 ◆ In Seattle, Washington, a meeting of the World Trade Organization is disrupted by political protests and riots.

2000 ◆ Barry Scheck, Peter Neufeld, and Jim Dwyer publish *Actual Innocence*, a study of sixty-five cases in which DNA testing proved that a person convicted of a felony was innocent. Fifteen of the sixty-five wrongful convictions resulted, in whole or in part, from a false confession.

2000 ◆ Congress sets a .08 percent BAC level as the national standard for alcohol-impaired driving.

2000 ◆ A class action lawsuit brought by surviving inmates and their families of the Attica uprising in 1971 against New York is settled with an award of $8 million to those who had been hostages and $4 million to cover legal fees.

2000 ◆ The Religious Land Use and Institutionalized Persons Act (RLUIPA) is signed into law, assuring that those confined in government institutions such as prisons will be protected in the practice of their faith.

2000 ◆ Sponsors of the Victims' Bill of Rights Amendment to the Constitution withdraw it from consideration when it becomes apparent the amendment will not receive the requisite two-thirds majority vote for approval.

2000 ◆ A trial judge in New York issues a watershed ruling recognizing a presumptive free speech right under the First Amendment to televise court proceedings. New York joins the forty-seven other states permitting television cameras in the courtroom and the thirty-seven other states permitting televised trials, when it allows television coverage of the trial of four New York City police officers accused of murdering Amadou Diallo, an unarmed African.

2000 ◆ Nintendo, Sega of America, and Electronic Arts sue Yahoo! in federal court for running a "cyber flea market" for counterfeit video games.

2000 ◆ Michael McDermott, a forty-two-year-old employee of Edgewater Technology in Wakefield, Massachusetts, opens fire on his coworkers, killing seven.

2000 ◆ British physician Harold Shipman is convicted of murdering 15 female patients and forging the will of one. In Britain's largest serial killing, police believe that Shipman killed as many as 150 patients. Nearly all were elderly women living alone, whom Shipman visited at home and injected with morphine.

2001 ◆ The Association of Caribbean Commissioners of Police (ACCP) collectively adopts community policing as a "modernized" policing mission.

2001 ◆ A religious riot occurs in Nigeria between Christians and Muslims. The riot begins when Muslims attack Christians protesting the adoption of Islamic law in Nigeria. After a week of hostility, the riots spread to the eastern part of the country, leaving 300 dead and several buildings destroyed by fire.

2001 In June, Timothy McVeigh, who had been convicted of the 1995 Oklahoma terrorist bombing that killed 167 people, is executed by lethal injection at the federal facility in Terre Haute, Indiana. He is the first person executed for a federal crime in thirty-eight years.

2001 On September 11, planes are hijacked by Muslim terrorists in the United States and crashed into the two towers of the World Trade Center in New York City and the Pentagon in Washington, D.C. A fourth plane, thought to be headed for the U.S. Capitol building, crashes in rural Pennsylvania. The dead on the planes and in the two collapsed World Trade Center towers and the Pentagon are estimated at about 3,500. The attack leads to a worldwide antiterrorism effort led by the United States, the military aspect of which begins on October 7 with a missile and air attack on Afghanistan military and communications centers by American and British forces.

2001 On November 13, Attorney General John Ashcroft issues an order that physicians are to be punished for participating in assisted suicides. The order is meant to end euthanasia in Oregon.

2002 Investigations begin into the bankruptcy of Enron, the seventh-largest company in the United States. The Justice Department and four congressional committees look into whether Enron and Arthur Anderson LLP, its auditing firm, defrauded investors and employees who held stock in the company. It remains to be seen how Enron's ties to both Repbulican and Democratic politicians will affect the political landscape.